GO FAR...WITHOUT GOING FAR FROM HOME.
Nearby colleges want to hear from you!

Peterson's Regional College Survey lets you show colleges in your geographic area what makes you a great applicant. Complete the survey online at www.petersons.com/studentnetworks or return this completed form by mail, indicating which colleges interest you.

FAST   Mail your completed form back to Peterson's

FASTER   Fill out your form online at www.petersons.com/studentnetworks

Enter Peterson's $5000 scholarship giveaway!
No purchase necessary to win.
Review the official rules at www.petersons.com/promo/code/scholarship_rules.asp.

*❏ **I have read and agree to the 2007 $5000 Peterson's Scholarship Rules.**
(Box must be checked to be eligible to participate in the Regional College Survey Program and the $5000 scholarship drawing)

*All fields marked with an asterisk are required.

Midwest

*Name: _____

*Address: _____

*City: _____ *State: _____ *Zip: _____

Student Home Phone: _____

Student Mobile Phone: _____

Student E-mail: _____

Parent/Guardian E-mail: _____

Preferred method of contact: ❏ E-mail ❏ Home Ph. ❏ Mobile Ph. ❏ US Mail

*DOB (mm/dd/yyyy): _____ Gender: ❏ Male ❏ Female

Race/ethnic background—U.S. citizens and permanent residents only (optional):

❏ American Indian or Aleut   ❏ Asian or Pacific Islander
❏ Black or African American   ❏ Caucasian
❏ Latin American or Hispanic   ❏ Mexican American or Chicano
❏ Puerto Rican   ❏ Other

School & Scores
Name and location of your high school:

High School Name: _____

City: _____ State: _____

*Expected year of high school graduation: _____

Estimated Current GPA: (4.0 = A) _____

PSAT Scores: Critical Reading _____ Math _____ Writing _____

SAT Scores: Critical Reading _____ Math _____ Writing _____

PLAN Score: _____ ACT Score: _____

Please indicate your top choice for field of study (Mark only one choice):

❏ Architecture   ❏ Dance   ❏ Music
❏ Art   ❏ Education   ❏ Physical Sciences
❏ Biology   ❏ Engineering   ❏ Prelaw Studies
❏ Business   ❏ Health Science   ❏ Premedical Studies
❏ Communications   ❏ Humanities/ Humanistic Studies   ❏ Social Sciences
❏ Computer and Information Sciences   ❏ Mathematics   ❏ Undecided

---

For each item, mark an "X" on the appropriate line if you participate in this activity in high school or expect to participate in it in college.

	HIGH SCHOOL	COLLEGE
Academic interest groups	____	____
Arts	____	____
Community service	____	____
Debate	____	____
Drama and theatrical productions	____	____
Intramural sports	____	____
Junior varsity and varsity athletics	____	____
Music, including chorus, band, and orchestra	____	____
National Honor Society	____	____
Political/social issues group	____	____
Religious groups	____	____
School spirit organization	____	____
Student government	____	____
Student publications (newspaper, yearbook)	____	____

❏ **Check here to receive information about relevant products and services from Peterson's and its partners.**

*Please mark below the colleges you find most appealing and from which you would like to receive catalogs, viewbooks, and other admission/financial aid material.

ILLINOIS
❏ Aurora University
❏ Columbia College Chicago

INDIANA
❏ Ball State University

IOWA
❏ Mount Mercy College
❏ Simpson College

MICHIGAN
❏ Aquinas College

MINNESOTA
❏ Bethel University
❏ Crown College

MISSOURI
❏ Columbia College

OHIO
❏ Ohio Northern University
❏ Otterbein College
❏ University of Dayton

These out-of-area schools also want to hear from you. Check those that interest you!

NEW YORK
❏ Clarkson University

PENNSYLVANIA
❏ Gannon University

*All fields marked with an asterisk are required.

PETERSON'S
A **nelnet** COMPANY

BUSINESS REPLY MAIL
FIRST-CLASS MAIL   PERMIT NO. 4764   TRENTON, NJ

POSTAGE WILL BE PAID BY ADDRESSEE

REGIONAL COLLEGES CONSORTIUM
PETERSON'S
PRINCETON PIKE CORPORATE CENTER
2000 LENOX DRIVE
LAWRENCEVILLE, NJ 08648-9913

▲   Fold here to return (do not detach)   ▲

Please tape closed to mail
▼

PETERSON'S
COLLEGES IN
THE MIDWEST

2008

PETERSON'S

A **nelnet** COMPANY

PETERSON'S
A nelnet COMPANY

About Peterson's, a Nelnet company

Peterson's (www.petersons.com) is a leading provider of education information and advice, with books and online resources focusing on education search, test preparation, and financial aid. Its Web site offers searchable databases and interactive tools for contacting educational institutions, online practice tests and instruction, and planning tools for securing financial aid. Peterson's serves 110 million education consumers annually.

For more information, contact Peterson's, 2000 Lenox Drive, Lawrenceville, NJ 08648; 800-338-3282; or find us on the World Wide Web at www.petersons.com/about.

Editor: Fern A. Oram; Production Editor: Mark D. Snider; Copy Editors: Bret Bollmann, Michael Haines, Brooke James, Sally Ross, Pam Sullivan, Valerie Bolus Vaughan; Research Project Manager: Daniel Margolin; Research Associate: Mary Penniston; Programmer: Phyllis Johnson; Manufacturing Manager: Ray Golaszewski; Composition Manager: Linda M. Williams; Client Relations Representatives: Janet Garwo, Mimi Kaufman, Karen D. Mount, Danielle Vreeland

ISSN Pending
ISBN-13: 978-0-7689-2417-6
ISBN-10: 0-7689-2417-0

Printed in the United States of America

10 9 8 7 6 5 4 3 2 1   09 08 07

Twenty-second Edition

CONTENTS

A Note from the Peterson's Editors   v

THE COLLEGE ADMISSIONS PROCESS
Surviving Standardized Tests   3
The Whys and Whats of College Visits   6
Applying 101   10
Successful Transfer   13
Who's Paying for This? Financial Aid Basics   15
Financial Aid Programs for Schools in the Midwest   20
Searching for Four-Year Colleges Online   33
How to Use This Guide   37

PROFILES OF COLLEGES IN THE MIDWEST
Map of the Midwest   44
State-by-State Listings of Schools in the Midwest   45

CLOSE-UPS OF COLLEGES IN THE MIDWEST
Featured Schools   230

PROFILES AND CLOSE-UPS OF OTHER COLLEGES TO CONSIDER
Profiles   309
Featured Schools   314

INDEXES
Majors and Degrees   336
Athletic Programs and Scholarships   432
ROTC Programs   451
Alphabetical Listing of Colleges and Universities   453

A Note from the Peterson's Editors

Welcome to the world of college decision making. You are probably considering at least one college that is relatively near your home. It may surprise you to learn that the majority of all students go to college within a 300-mile radius of where they live. Because of that factor, we publish this series of college guides that focuses on the colleges in each of six regions of the country so that students can easily compare the colleges in their own area. (Two-year public and proprietary colleges are not included because their admission patterns are significantly different from other colleges.)

For advice and guidance in the college search and selection process, just turn the page. "Surviving Standardized Tests" describes the most frequently used tests and lists test dates for 2007–08. Of course, part of the college selection process involves visiting the schools themselves and "The Whys and Whats of College Visits" is just the planner you need to make those trips well worth your while. Next, "Applying 101" provides advice on how best to approach the application phase of the process. If you've got questions about transferring, "Successful Transfer" has got the answers you need. "Who's Paying for This? Financial Aid Basics" and the "Financial Aid Programs for Schools in the Midwest" articles provide you with the essential information on how to meet your education expenses. "Searching for Four-Year Colleges Online" gives you all the tips you'll need to integrate the Web into your college search. Lastly, you'll want to read through "How to Use This Guide" and learn how to use all the information presented in this volume.

Following these articles are the **Profiles of Colleges** sections. The **Profiles** are easy to read and should give you a good sense of whether a college meets your basic needs and should be considered further. This consistently formatted collection of data can provide a balance to the individual mailings you are likely to receive from colleges. The **Profiles** appear in geographical order by state.

In a number of the **Profiles** (those marked with a *Sponsor* icon), you will find helpful information about social life, academic life, campus visits, and interviews. These **Special Messages to Students** are written in each case by a college admissions office staff member. You will find valuable insights into what each writer considers special about his or her institution (both socially and academically), what is expected of you during your interview at that college, and how important the interview is there. You will also be alerted to outstanding attractions on campus or nearby so you can plan a productive visit. In many cases, travel information (nearest commercial airport and nearest interstate highway) that will be of help on your campus visit is included.

And if you still thirst for even more information, look for the two-page narrative descriptions appearing in the **Close-Ups of Colleges** sections of the book. These descriptions are written by admissions deans and provide great detail about each college. They are edited to provide a consistent format across entries for your ease of comparison.

The **Indexes** at the back of the book ("Majors and Degrees," "Athletic Programs and Scholarships," and "ROTC Programs") enable you to pinpoint colleges listed in the **Profiles** according to their specific offerings. In addition, there is an "Alphabetical Listing of Colleges and Universities" to enable you to quickly find a school that you may have already determined meets your criteria.

We hope you will find this information helpful. Our advice is to relax, enjoy high school, and do as well as you can in your courses. Give yourself enough time during the early stages of your search to think about what kind of person you are and what you want to become so you can choose colleges for the right reasons. Read all college materials with an open mind, and visit as many campuses as you can. Plan ahead so you do not rush through your applications. Try to remember that admission directors are as interested in you and the possibility of your attending their college as you are in the possibility of applying. They spend most of their time reaching out to students, explaining their colleges' programs and policies, and simplifying the application process whenever they can. If you think of them as people who like students and if you can picture them taking the time to carefully provide the information in this book for you, it might help to lessen any anxiety you are feeling about applying. In fact, the admission people whose names you will find in this book hope to hear from you.

We welcome any comments or suggestions you may have about this publication and invite you to complete our online survey at **www.petersons.com/booksurvey**. Or you can fill out the survey at the back of this book, tear it out, and mail it to us at:

Publishing Department
Peterson's, a Nelnet company
2000 Lenox Drive
Lawrenceville, NJ 08648

Your feedback will help us make your education dreams possible.

The editors at Peterson's wish you success and happiness wherever you enroll.

The College Admissions Process

Surviving Standardized Tests

WHAT ARE STANDARDIZED TESTS?

Colleges and universities in the United States use tests to help evaluate applicants' readiness for admission or to place them in appropriate courses. The tests that are most frequently used by colleges are the ACT of American College Testing, Inc., and the College Board's SAT. In addition, the Educational Testing Service (ETS) offers the TOEFL test, which evaluates the English-language proficiency of nonnative speakers. The tests are offered at designated testing centers located at high schools and colleges throughout the United States and U.S. territories and at testing centers in various countries throughout the world. The ACT and SAT are each taken by more than a million students each year. The TOEFL test is taken by more than 800,000 students each year.

Upon request, special accommodations for students with documented visual, hearing, physical, or learning disabilities are available. Examples of special accommodations include tests in Braille or large print and such aids as a reader, recorder, magnifying glass, or sign language interpreter. Additional testing time may be allowed in some instances. Contact the appropriate testing program or your guidance counselor for details on how to request special accommodations.

College Board SAT Program

Currently, the SAT Program consists of the SAT and the SAT Subject Tests. The SAT is a 3-hour 45-minute test made up of ten sections, primarily multiple-choice, that focuses on college success skills of writing, critical reading, and mathematics. The writing component measures grammar and usage and includes a short, student-written essay. The critical reading sections test verbal reasoning and critical reading skills. Emphasis is placed on reading passages, which are 400–850 words in length. Some reading passages are paired; the second opposes, supports, or in some way complements the point of view expressed in the first. The three mathematics sections test a student's ability to solve problems involving arithmetic, Algebra I and II, and geometry. They include questions that require students to produce their own responses, in addition to questions with four or five answer choices from which students can choose. Calculators may be used on the SAT mathematics sections.

The SAT Subject Tests are 1-hour tests, primarily multiple-choice, in specific subjects that measure students' knowledge of these subjects and their ability to apply that knowledge. Some colleges may require or recommend these tests for placement, or even admission. The Subject Tests measure a student's academic achievement in high school and may indicate readiness for certain college programs. Tests offered include Literature, U.S. History, World History, Mathematics Level 1, Mathematics Level 2, Biology E/M (Ecological/Molecular), Chemistry, Physics, French, German, Modern Hebrew, Italian, Latin, and Spanish, as well as Foreign Language Tests with Listening in Chinese, French, German, Japanese, Korean, and Spanish. The Mathematics Level 1 and 2 tests require the use of a scientific calculator.

SAT scores are automatically sent to each student who has taken the test. On average, they are mailed about three weeks after the test. Students may request that the scores be reported to their high schools or to the colleges to which they are applying.

DON'T FORGET TO . . .

- Take the SAT or ACT before application deadlines.
- Note that test registration deadlines precede test dates by about six weeks.
- Register to take the TOEFL test if English is not your native language and you are planning on studying at a North American college.
- Practice your test-taking skills with **Peterson's Master the SAT, Peterson's Ultimate ACT Tool Kit, The Real ACT Prep Guide** (published by Peterson's), and **Peterson's Master TOEFL Reading Skills, Peterson's Master TOEFL Vocabulary,** and **Peterson's Master TOEFL Writing Skills.**
- Contact the College Board or American College Testing, Inc., in advance if you need special accommodations when taking tests.

ACT Program

The ACT Program is a comprehensive data collection, processing, and reporting service designed to assist in educational and career planning. The ACT instrument consists of four academic tests, taken under timed conditions, and a Student Profile Section and Interest Inventory, completed when students register for the ACT.

The academic tests cover four areas—English, mathematics, reading, and science reasoning. The ACT consists of 215 multiple-choice questions and takes approximately 3 hours and 30 minutes to complete with breaks (testing time is actually 2 hours and 55 minutes). They are designed to assess the student's educational development and readiness to handle college-level work. The minimum standard score is 1, the maximum is 36, and the national average is 21. Students should note that an optional writing test is also offered.

The Student Profile Section requests information about each student's admission and enrollment plans, academic and out-of-class high school achievements and aspirations, and high school course work. The student is also asked to supply biographical data and self-reported high school grades in the four subject-matter areas covered by the academic tests.

The ACT has a number of career planning services, including the ACT Interest Inventory, which is designed to measure six major dimensions of student interests–business contact, business operations, technical, science, arts, and social service. Results are used to compare the student's interests with those of college-bound students who later majored in each of a wide variety of areas. Inventory results are also used to help students compare their work-activity preferences with work activities that characterize twenty-three "job families."

Because the information resulting from the ACT Program is used in a variety of educational settings, American College Testing, Inc., prepares three reports for each student: the Student Report, the High School Report, and the College Report. The Student Report normally is sent to the student's high school, except after the June test date, when it is sent directly to the student's home address. The College Report is sent to the colleges the student designates.

Early in the school year, American College Testing, Inc., sends registration packets to high schools across the country that contain all the information a student needs to register for the ACT. High school guidance offices also receive a supply of *Preparing for the ACT*, a booklet that contains a complete practice test, an answer key, and general information about preparing for the test.

Test of English as a Foreign Language (TOEFL)

The TOEFL is used by various organizations, such as colleges and universities, to determine English proficiency.

2007–08 ACT AND SAT TEST DATES

ACT
September 15, 2007*
October 27, 2007
December 8, 2007
February 9, 2008**
April 12, 2008
June 14, 2008

All test dates fall on a Saturday. Tests are also given on the Sundays following the Saturday test dates for students who cannot take the test on Saturday because of religious reasons. The basic ACT registration fee for 2006–07 was $29 ($49 outside of the U.S.). The optional writing test is $14 and is refundable for students who are absent on test day.

*The September test is available only in Arizona, California, Florida, Georgia, Illinois, Indiana, Maryland, Nevada, North Carolina, Pennsylvania, South Carolina, Texas, and Washington.

**The February test date is not available in New York.

SAT
October 16, 2007 (SAT and SAT Subject Tests)
November 3, 2007 (SAT, SAT Subject Tests, and Language Tests with Listening*)
December 1, 2007 (SAT and SAT Subject Tests)
January 26, 2008 (SAT, SAT Subject Tests, and ELPT)
March 1, 2008 (SAT only)**
May 3, 2008 (SAT and SAT Subject Tests)
June 7, 2008 (SAT and SAT Subject Tests)

For the 2006–07 academic year, the basic fee for the SAT was $41.50. The basic fee for the SAT Subject Tests was $18, $19 for the Language Tests with Listening, and $8 each for all other Subject Tests. Students can take up to three SAT Subject Tests on a single date, and an $18 basic registration and reporting fee should be added for each test date. Tests are also given on the Sundays following the Saturday test dates for students who cannot take the test on Saturday because of religious reasons. Fee waivers are available to juniors and seniors who cannot afford test fees.

*Language Tests with Listening are only offered in November. See the Registration Bulletin for details.

**The March test date is only available in the U.S. and its territories.

The test is offered in different formats depending on the test taker's location. The TOEFL iBT tests students in the areas of speaking, listening, reading, and writing in an Internet-based format.

The TOEFL PBT (paper-based test) tests students in the areas of listening, structure, reading comprehension, and writing. Score requirements are set by individual institutions. For more information on TOEFL, and to obtain a copy of the Information Bulletin, contact the Educational Testing Service.

The Whys and Whats of College Visits

Dawn B. Sova, Ph.D.

The campus visit should not be a passive activity for you and your parents. Take the initiative and gather information beyond that provided in the official tour. You will see many important indicators during your visit that will tell you more about the true character of a college and its students than the tour guide will reveal. Know what to look for and how to assess the importance of such indicators.

WHAT SHOULD YOU ASK AND WHAT SHOULD YOU LOOK FOR?

Your first stop on a campus visit is the visitor center or admissions office, where you will probably have to wait to meet with a counselor. Colleges usually plan to greet visitors later than the appointed time in order to give them the opportunity to review some of the campus information that is liberally scattered throughout the visitor waiting room. Take advantage of the time to become even more familiar with the college by arriving 15 to 30 minutes before your appointment to observe the behavior of staff members and to browse through the yearbooks and student newspapers that will be available.

If you prepare in advance, you will have already reviewed the college catalog and map of the campus. These materials familiarize you with the academic offerings and the physical layout of the campus, but the true character of the college and its students emerges in other ways.

Begin your investigation with the visitor center staff members. As a student's first official contact with the college, they should make every effort to welcome prospective students and project a friendly image.

- How do they treat you and other prospective students who are waiting? Are they friendly and willing to speak with you, or do they try their hardest to avoid eye contact and conversation?
- Are they friendly with each other and with students who enter the office, or are they curt and unwilling to help?
- Does the waiting room have a friendly feeling or is it cold and sterile?

If the visitor center staff members seem indifferent to *prospective* students, there is little reason to believe that they will be warm and welcoming to current students. View such behavior as a warning to watch very carefully the interaction of others with you during the tour. An indifferent or unfriendly reception in the admissions office may be simply the first of many signs that attending this college will not be a pleasant experience.

Look through several yearbooks and see the types of activities that are actually photographed, as opposed to the activities that colleges promise in their promotional literature. Some questions are impossible to answer if the college is very large, but for small and moderately sized colleges the yearbook is a good indicator of campus activity.

- Has the number of clubs and organizations increased or decreased in the past five years?
- Do the same students appear repeatedly in activities?
- Do sororities and fraternities dominate campus activities?
- Are participants limited to one sex or one ethnic group, or is there diversity?
- Are all activities limited to the campus, or are students involved in activities in the community?

Use what you observe in the yearbooks as a means of forming a more complete understanding of the college, but don't base your entire impression on just one facet. If time permits, look through several copies of the school newspaper, which should reflect the major concerns and interests of the students. The paper is also a good way to learn about the campus social life.

- Does the paper contain a mix of national and local news?
- What products or services are advertised?
- How assertive are the editorials?
- With what topics are the columnists concerned?
- Are movies and concerts that meet your tastes advertised or reviewed?
- What types of ads appear in the classified section?

The newspaper should be a public forum for students, and, as such, should reflect the character of the campus and of the student body. A paper that deals only with seemingly safe and well-edited topics on the editorial page and in regular feature columns might indicate administrative censorship. A lack of ads for restaurants might indicate either a lack of good places to eat or that area restaurants do not welcome student business. A limited mention of movies, concerts, or other entertainment might reveal a severely limited campus social life. Even if ads and reviews are included, you should still balance how such activities reflect your tastes.

You will have only a limited amount of time to ask questions during your initial meeting with the admissions counselor, for very few schools include a formal interview in the initial campus visit or tour. Instead, this brief meeting is often just a nicety that allows the admissions office to begin a file for the student and to record some initial impressions. Save your questions for the tour guide and for students on campus you meet along the way.

HOW CAN YOU ASSESS THE TRUE CHARACTER OF A COLLEGE AND ITS STUDENTS?

Colleges do not train their tour guides to deceive prospective students, but they do caution guides to avoid unflattering topics and campus sites. Does this mean that you are consigned to see only a sugarcoated version of life on a particular college campus? Not at all, especially not if you are observant.

Most organized campus visits include such campus facilities as dormitories, dining halls, libraries, student activity and recreation centers, and the health and student services centers. Some may only be pointed out, while you will walk through others. Either way, you will find that many signs of the true character of the college emerge if you keep your eyes open.

Bulletin boards in dormitories and student centers contain a wealth of information about campus activities, student concerns, and campus groups. Read the posters, notices, and messages to learn what *really* interests students. Unlike ads in the school newspaper, posters put up by students advertise both on- and off-campus events, so they will give you an idea of what is also available in the surrounding community.

Review the notices, which may cover either campuswide events or events that concern only small groups of students. The catalog may not mention a performance group, but an individual dormitory with its own small theater may offer regular productions. Poetry readings, jam sessions, writers' groups, and other activities may be announced and show diversity of student interests.

Even the brief bulletin board messages offering objects for sale and noting objects that people want to purchase reveal a lot about a campus. Are most of the items computer related? Or do the messages specify CDs, audio equipment, or musical instruments? Are offers to trade goods or services posted? Don't ignore the "ride wanted" messages. Students who want to share rides home during a break may specify widely diverse geographical locations. If so, then you know that the student body is not limited to only the immediate area or one locale. Other messages can also enhance your knowledge of the true character of the campus and its students.

As you walk through various buildings, examine their condition carefully.

- Is the paint peeling, and do the exteriors look worn?
- Are the exteriors and interiors of the building clean?
- Is the equipment in the classrooms up-to-date or outdated?

Pay particular attention to the dormitories, especially to factors that might affect your safety. Observe the appearance of the structure, and ask about the security measures in and around the dormitories.

- Are the dormitories noisy or quiet?
- Do they seem crowded?
- How good is the lighting around each dormitory?
- Are the dormitories spread throughout the campus or are they clustered in one main area?
- Who has access to the dormitories in addition to students?
- How secure are the means by which students enter and leave the dormitory?

While you are on the subject of dormitory safety, you should also ask about campus safety. Don't expect that the guide will rattle off a list of crimes that have been committed in the past year. To obtain that information, access the recent year of issues of *The Chronicle of Higher Education* and locate its yearly report on campus crime. Also ask the guide about safety measures that the campus police take and those that students have initiated.

- Can students request escorts to their residences late at night?
- Do campus shuttle buses run at frequent intervals all night?
- Are "blue-light" telephones liberally placed throughout the campus for students to use to call for help?
- Do the campus police patrol the campus regularly?

If the guide does not answer your questions satisfactorily, wait until after the tour to contact the campus police or traffic office for answers.

Campus tours usually just point out the health services center without taking the time to walk through. Even if you don't see the inside of the building, you should take a close look at the location of the health services center and ask the guide questions about services.

- How far is the health center from the dormitories?
- Is a doctor always on call?
- Does the campus transport sick students from their dormitories or must they walk?
- What are the operating hours of the health center?
- Does the health center refer students to a nearby hospital?

If the guide can't answer your questions, visit the health center later and ask someone there.

Most campus tours take pride in showing students their activities centers, which may contain snack bars, game rooms, workout facilities, and other means of entertainment. Should you scrutinize this building as carefully as the rest? Of course. Outdated and poorly maintained activity equipment contributes to your total impression of the college. You should also ask about the hours, availability, and cost (no, the activities are usually *not* free) of using the bowling alleys, pool tables, air hockey tables, and other ammenities.

As you walk through campus with the tour, also look carefully at the appearance of the students who pass. The way in which both men and women groom themselves, the way they dress, and even their physical bearing communicate a lot more than any guidebook can. If everyone seems to conform to the same look, you might feel that you would be uncomfortable at the college, however nonconformist that look might be. On the other hand, you might not feel comfortable on a campus that stresses diversity of dress and behavior, and your observations now can save you discomfort later.

- Does every student seem to wear a sorority or fraternity t-shirt or jacket?
- Is everyone of your sex sporting the latest fad haircut?
- Do all of the men or the women seem to be wearing expensive name-brand clothes?
- Do most of the students seem to be working hard to look outrageous with regards to clothing, hair color, and body art?
- Would you feel uncomfortable in a room full of these students?

Is appearance important to you? If it is, then you should consider very seriously if you answer *yes* to any of the above questions. You don't have to be the same as everyone else on campus, but standing out too much may make you unhappy.

As you observe the physical appearance of the students, also listen to their conversations as you pass them? What are they talking about? How are they speaking? Are their voices and accents all the same, or do you hear diversity in their speech? Are you offended by their language? Think how you will feel if surrounded by the same speech habits and patterns for four years.

WHERE SHOULD YOU VISIT ON YOUR OWN?

Your campus visit is not over when the tour ends because you will probably have many questions yet to be answered and many places to still be seen. Where you go depends upon the extent to which the organized tour covers the campus. Your tour should take you to view residential halls, health and student services centers, the gymnasium or field house, dining halls, the library, and recreational centers. If any of the facilities on this list have been omitted, visit them on your own and ask questions of the students and staff members you meet. In addition, you should step off campus and gain an impression of the surrounding community. You will probably become bored with life on campus and spend at least some time off campus. Make certain that you know what the surrounding area is like.

The campus tour leaves little time to ask impromptu questions of current students, but you can do so after the tour. Eat lunch in one of the dining halls. Most will allow visitors to pay cash to experience a typical student meal. Food may not be important to you now while you are living at home and can simply take anything you want from the refrigerator at any time, but it will be when you are away at college with only a meal ticket to feed you.

- How clean is the dining hall? Consider serving tables, floors, and seating.
- What is the quality of the food?
- How big are the portions?
- How much variety do students have at each meal?
- How healthy are the food choices?

While you are eating, try to strike up a conversation with students and tell them that you are considering attending their college. Their reactions and advice can be eye-opening. Ask them questions about the academic atmosphere and the professors.

- Are the classes large or small?
- Do the majority of the professors only lecture or are tutorials and seminars common?
- Is the emphasis of the faculty career-oriented or abstract?
- Are the teaching methods innovative and stimulating or boring and dull?
- Is the academic atmosphere pressured, lax, or somewhere in between?
- Which are the strong majors? The weak majors?

- Is the emphasis on grades or social life or a mix of both at the college?
- How hard do students have to work to receive high grades?

Current students can also give you the inside line on the true nature of the college social life. You may gain some idea through looking in the yearbook, in the newspaper, and on the bulletin boards, but students will reveal the true highs and lows of campus life. Ask them about drug use, partying, dating, drinking, and anything else that may affect your life as a student.

- Which are the most popular club activities?
- What do students do on weekends? Do most go home?
- How frequently do concerts occur on campus? Who has recently performed?
- How can you become involved in specific activities (name them)?
- How strictly are campus rules enforced and how severe are penalties?
- What counseling services are available?
- Are academic tutoring services available?
- Do they feel that the faculty really cares about students, especially freshmen?

You will receive the most valuable information from current students, but you will only be able to speak with them after the tour is over. And you might have to risk rejection as you try to initiate conversations with students who might not want to reveal how they feel about the campus. Still, the value of this information is worth the chance.

If you have the time, you should also visit the library to see just how accessible research materials are and to observe the physical layout. The catalog usually specifies the days and hours of operation, as well as the number of volumes contained in the library and the number of periodicals to which it subscribes. A library also requires accessibility, good lighting, an adequate number of study carrels, and lounge areas for students. Many colleges have created 24-hour study lounges for students who find the residence halls too noisy for studying, although most colleges claim that they designate areas of the residences as "quiet study" areas. You may not be interested in any of this information, but when you are a student you will have to make frequent

use of the campus library so you should know what is available. You should at least ask how extensive their holdings are in your proposed major area. If they have virtually nothing, you will have to spend a lot of time ordering items via interlibrary loan or making copies, which can become expensive. The ready answer of students that they will obtain their information from the Internet is unpleasantly countered by professors who demand journal articles with documentation.

Make a point of at least driving through the community surrounding the college because you will be spending time there shopping, dining, working in a part-time job, or attending events. Even the largest and best-stocked campus will not meet all of your social and personal needs. If you can spare the time, stop in several stores to see if they welcome college students.

- Is the surrounding community suburban, urban, or rural?
- Does the community offer stores of interest, such as bookstores, craft shops, and boutiques?
- Do the businesses employ college students?
- Does the community have a movie or stage theater?
- Are there several types of interesting restaurants?
- Do there seem to be any clubs that court a college clientele?
- Is the center of activity easy to walk to, or do you need other transportation?

You might feel that a day is not enough to answer all of your questions, but even answering some questions will provide you with a stronger basis for choosing a college. Many students visit a college campus several times before making their decision. Keep in mind that for the rest of your life you will be associated with the college that you attend. You will spend four years of your life at this college. The effort of spending several days to obtain the information to make your decision is worthwhile.

Dawn B. Sova, Ph.D., is a former newspaper reporter and columnist, as well as the author of more than eight books and numerous magazine articles. She teaches creative and research writing, as well as scientific and technical writing, newswriting, and journalism.

Applying 101

The words "applying yourself" have several important meanings in the college application process. One meaning refers to the fact that you need to keep focused during this important time in your life, keep your priorities straight, and know the dates that your applications are due so you can apply on time. The phrase might also refer to the person who is really responsible for your application—you.

You are the only person who should compile your college application. You need to take ownership of this process. The guidance counselor is not responsible for completing your applications, and neither are your parents. College applications must be completed in addition to your normal workload at school, college visits, and SAT, ACT, or TOEFL testing.

THE APPLICATION

The application is your way of introducing yourself to a college admissions office. As with any introduction, you want to make a good first impression. The first thing you should do in presenting your application is to find out what the college or university needs from you. Read the application carefully to find out the application fee and deadline, required standardized tests, number of essays, interview requirements, and anything else you can do or submit to help improve your chances for acceptance.

Completing college applications yourself helps you learn more about the schools to which you are applying. The information a college asks for in its application can tell you much about the school. State university applications often tell you how they are going to view their applicants. Usually, they select students based on GPAs and test scores. Colleges that request an interview, ask you to respond to a few open-ended questions, or require an essay are interested in a more personal approach to the application process and may be looking for different types of students than those sought by a state school.

In addition to submitting the actual application, there are several other items that are commonly required. You will be responsible for ensuring that your standardized test scores and your high school transcript arrive at the colleges to which you apply. Most colleges will ask that you submit teacher recommendations as well. Select teachers who know you and your abilities well and allow them plenty of time to complete the recommendations. When all portions of the application have been completed and sent in, whether

> ## FOLLOW THESE TIPS WHEN FILLING OUT YOUR APPLICATION
>
> - **Follow the directions to the letter.** You don't want to be in a position to ask an admissions officer for exceptions due to your inattentiveness.
> - **Proofread all parts of your application,** including your essay. Again, the final product indicates to the admissions staff how meticulous and careful you are in your work.
> - **Submit your application as early as possible,** provided all of the pieces are available. If there is a problem with your application, this will allow you to work through it with the admissions staff in plenty of time. If you wait until the last minute, it not only takes away that cushion but also reflects poorly on your sense of priorities.
> - **Keep a copy** of the completed application, whether it is a photocopy or a copy saved on your computer.

electronically or by mail, make sure you follow up with the college to ensure their receipt.

THE APPLICATION ESSAY

Whereas the other portions of your application—your transcript, test scores, and involvement in extracurricular activities—are a reflection of what you've accomplished up to this point, your application essay is an opportunity to present yourself in the here and now. The essay shows your originality and verbal skills and is very important. Test scores and grades may represent your academic results, but your essay shows how you approach a topic or problem and express your opinion.

Some colleges may request one essay or a combination of essays and short-answer topics to learn more about who you are and how well you can communicate your thoughts. Common essay topics cover such simple themes as writing about yourself and your experiences or why you want to attend that particular school. Other colleges will ask that you show your imaginative or creative side by writing about a favorite author, for instance, or commenting on a hypothetical situation. In such cases, they will be looking at your thought processes and level of creativity.

Admissions officers, particularly those at small or mid-size colleges, use the essay to determine how you, as a student, will fit into life at that college. The essay, therefore, is a critical component of the application process. Here are some tips for writing a winning essay:

- Colleges are looking for an honest representation of who you are and what you think. Make sure that the tone of the essay reflects enthusiasm, maturity, creativity, the ability to communicate, talent, and your leadership skills.
- Be sure you set aside enough time to write the essay, revise it, and revise it *again*. Running "spell check" will only detect a fraction of the errors you probably made on your first pass at writing it. Take a break and then come back to it and reread it. You will probably notice other style, content, and grammar problems—and ways that you can improve the essay overall.
- Always answer the question that is being asked, making sure that you are specific, clear, and true to your personality.
- Enlist the help of reviewers who know you well—friends, parents, teachers—since they are likely to be the most honest and will keep you on track in the presentation of your true self.

THE PERSONAL INTERVIEW

Although it is relatively rare that a personal interview is required, many colleges recommend that you take this opportunity for a face-to-face discussion with a member of the admissions staff. Read through the application materials to determine whether or not a college places great emphasis on the interview. If they strongly recommend that you have one, it may work against you to forego it.

In contrast to a group interview and some alumni interviews, which are intended to provide information about a college, the personal interview is viewed both as an information session and as further evaluation of your skills and strengths. You will meet with a member of the admissions staff who will be assessing your personal qualities, high school preparation, and your capacity to contribute to undergraduate life at the institution. On average, these meetings last about 45 minutes—a relatively short amount of time in which to gather information and leave the desired impression—so here are some suggestions on how to make the most of it.

Scheduling Your Visit

Generally, students choose to visit campuses in the summer or fall of their senior year. Both times have their advantages. A summer visit, when the campus is not in session, generally allows for a less hectic visit and interview. Visiting in the fall, on the other hand, provides the opportunity to see what campus life is like in full swing. If you choose the fall, consider arranging an overnight trip so that you can stay in one of the college dormitories. At the very least, you should make your way around campus to take part in classes, athletic events, and social activities. Always make an appointment and avoid scheduling more than two college interviews on any given day. Multiple interviews in a single day hinder your chances of making a good impression, and your impressions of the colleges will blur into each other as you hurriedly make your way from place to place.

Preparation

Know the basics about the college before going for your interview. Read the college viewbook or catalog in addition to this guide. You will be better prepared to ask questions that are not answered in the literature and that will give you a better understanding of what the college has to offer. You should also spend some time thinking about your strengths and weaknesses and, in particular, what you are looking for in a college education. You will find that as you get a few interviews under your belt, they will get easier. You might consider starting with a college that is not a top contender on your list, so that the stakes are not as high.

Asking Questions

Inevitably, your interviewer will ask you, "Do you have any questions?" Not having one may suggest that you're unprepared or, even worse, not interested. When you do ask questions, make sure that they are ones that matter to you and that have a bearing on your decision about whether or not to attend that college. The questions that you ask will give the interviewer some insight into your personality and priorities. Avoid asking questions that are answered in the college literature—again, a sign of unpreparedness. Although the interviewer will undoubtedly pose questions to you, the interview should not be viewed merely as a question-and-answer session. If a conversation evolves out of a particular question, so much the better. Your interviewer can learn a great deal about you from how you sustain a conversation. Similarly, you will be able to learn a great deal about the college in a conversational format.

Separate the Interview from the Interviewer

Many students base their feelings about a college solely on their impressions of the interviewer. Try not to characterize a college based only on your personal reaction, however, since your impressions can be skewed by whether you and your interviewer hit it off. Pay lots of attention to everything else that you see, hear, and learn about a college. Once on campus, you may never see your interviewer again.

In the end, remember to relax and be yourself. Your interviewer will expect you to be somewhat nervous, which will relieve some of the pressure. Don't drink jitters-producing caffeinated beverages prior to the interview, and suppress nervous fidgets like leg-wagging, finger-drumming, or bracelet-jangling. Consider your interview an opportunity to put forth your best effort and to enhance everything that the college knows about you up to this point.

THE FINAL DECISION

Once you have received your acceptance letters, it is time to go back and look at the whole picture. Provided you received more than one acceptance, you are now in a position to compare your options. The best way to do this is to compare your original list of important college-ranking criteria with what you've discovered about each college along the way. In addition, you and your family will need to factor in the financial aid component. You will need to look beyond these cost issues and the quantifiable pros and cons of each college, however, and know that you have a good feeling about your final choice. Before sending off your acceptance letter, you need to feel confident that the college will feel like home for the next four years. Once the choice is made, the only hard part will be waiting for an entire summer before heading off to college!

Successful Transfer

Adrienne Aaron Rulnick

Transfer students need and deserve detailed and accurate information but often lack direction as to where it can be obtained. Few general college guides offer information about transfer deadlines and required minimum grade point averages for transfer admission. College catalogs are not always clear about the specific requirements and procedures for transfer students who may be confused about whether they need to present high school records, SAT or ACT scores, or a guidance counselor's recommendation, particularly if they have been out of high school for several years. Transfer advisers are not available to those enrolled at a baccalaureate institution; at community and junior colleges, the transfer advising function may be performed by a designated transfer counselor or by a variety of college advisers who are less clearly identified.

The challenge for transfer students is to determine what they need to know in order to make good, informed decisions and identify the individuals and resources that can provide that information. An organized research process is very much at the heart of a successful transfer.

HOW TO BEGIN

Perhaps the most important first step in this process is one of self-analysis. Adopting a consumer approach is appropriate—higher education is a formidable purchase, no matter how it is financed. The reputation of the college from which you obtain your degree may open doors to future jobs and careers; friendships and contacts you make at college can provide a significant network for lifelong social and professional relationships. The environment of a transfer school may be the perfect opportunity for you to test out urban living or the joys of country life, explore a different area of the country, experience college residential living for the first time, or move out of the family nest into your first apartment. Like any major purchase in your life, there are costs and benefits to be weighed. Trade-offs include cost, distance, rigor of academic work, extra time in school required by a cooperative education program, and specific requirements, such as foreign language competence at a liberal arts institution or courses in religion at an institution with a denominational affiliation.

USE EXPERIENCE AS A GUIDE

The wise consumer reflects on his or her own experience with a product (i.e., your initial college or colleges) and then seeks out people who have firsthand experience with the new product being considered. Talk to friends and family members who have attended the colleges you are considering; ask college faculty members you know to tell you about the colleges they attended and how they view these schools. Talk to people engaged in the careers you are considering: What are their impressions of the best programs and schools in their field? Make sure you sample a variety of opinions, but beware of dated experiences. An engineering department considered top-notch when Uncle Joe attended college twenty years ago might be very different today!

THE NITTY-GRITTY

Once your list is reduced to a manageable number of schools, it is important to identify academic requirements, requisite grade point averages for admission, and deadline dates. Most schools admit for both the fall and spring semesters; those on a trimester system may have winter and summer admissions as well. Some schools have rolling admission policies and will process applications as they are received; others, particularly the more selective colleges, have firm deadlines because their admission process involves a committee review, and decisions are made on a competitive basis. It is helpful to know how many transfer students are typically accepted for the semester you wish to begin, whether the minimum grade point average is indicative of the actual average of accepted students (this can vary widely), and whether the major you are seeking has special prerequisites and admission procedures. For example, fine arts programs admission procedures usually require portfolios or auditions. For engineering, computer science, and some business majors, there are specific requirements in mathematics that must be met before a student is considered for admission. Many specialized health-care programs, including nursing, may only admit once a year. Some schools have different standards for sophomore and junior transfers or for in-state and out-of-state students.

Other criteria that you should identify include whether college housing and financial aid are available for transfer students. Some colleges have special transfer scholarships that require separate applications and references, while others simply award aid based on applications that indicate a high grade point average or membership in a nationally recognized junior and community college honor society, such as Phi Theta Kappa. There are also scholarships for transfer students who demonstrate accomplishment in specified academic and performance areas; the latter may be based on talent competitions or accomplishment evidenced in a portfolio or audition.

NONTRADITIONAL STUDENTS

For the nontraditional student, usually defined as anyone beyond the traditional college age range of 18 to 23, there may be additional aspects to investigate. Some colleges award credit based on demonstrated life experience; many colleges grant credit for qualifying scores on the CLEP exams or for participation in the DANTES program. Experience in industry may yield college credit as well. If you are ready and able to pursue further college work but are not in a position to attend regular classes, there are a variety of distance learning options at fully accredited colleges. Other colleges provide specialized support services for nontraditional students and may allow students the opportunity to attend part-time if they have family and work responsibilities. In some cases, usually at large universities, there may be married student housing or family housing available. More and more schools have established day-care facilities, although the waiting lists are often very long.

APPLYING

Once you have identified the schools that meet the needs you have established as priorities, it is time to begin the application process. Make sure you observe all the indicated deadlines. It never hurts to have everything in early, as there can be consequences, such as closed-out majors and the loss of housing and financial aid, if you submit your application late. Make appointments with faculty members and others who are providing references; make sure they understand what is required of them and when and where their references must be sent. It is your responsibility to follow through to make sure all of your credentials are received, including transcripts from all colleges previously attended, even if you only took one summer course or

attended for less than a semester. If you have not yet had the opportunity to visit the schools to which you are applying, now is the time to do so. Arrange interviews wherever possible, and make sure to include a tour of the campus and visits to the department and career offices to gain a picture of the facilities and future opportunities. If you have questions about financial aid, schedule an appointment in the financial aid office, and make sure you are aware of all the deadlines and requirements and any scholarship opportunities for which you are eligible.

MAKING YOUR CHOICE

Congratulations! You have been accepted at the colleges of your choice. Now what? Carefully review the acceptance of your previous college credit and how it has been applied. You are entitled to know how many transfer credits you have received and your expected date of graduation. Compare financial aid packages and housing options. The best choice should emerge from this review process. Then, send a note to the schools you will not be attending. Acknowledge your acceptance, but indicate that you have chosen to attend elsewhere. Carefully read everything you have received from the college of your choice. Return required deposits within the deadline, reserve time to attend transfer orientation, arrange to have your final transcript sent from the college you currently attend, and review the financial picture. This is the time to finalize college loan applications and make sure you are in a position to meet all the costs entailed at this college. Don't forget to include the costs of travel and housing.

You've done it! While many transfer students reflect on how much work was involved in the transfer admission process, those who took the time to follow all of the steps outlined report a sense of satisfaction with their choices and increased confidence in themselves.

Adrienne Aaron Rulnick was formerly a Transfer Counselor at Berkshire Community College.

Who's Paying for This? Financial Aid Basics

A college education can be expensive—costing more than $150,000 for four years at some of the higher priced private colleges and universities. Even at the lower cost state colleges and universities, the cost of a four-year education can approach $60,000. Determining how you and your family will come up with the necessary funds to pay for your education requires planning, perseverance, and learning as much as you can about the options that are available to you. But before you get discouraged, recent College Board statistics show that 42 percent of full-time students attend four-year public and private colleges with tuition and fees less than $6000, while 13 percent attend colleges that have tuition and fees more than $24,000. College costs tend to be less in the western states and higher in New England.

Paying for college should not be looked at as a four-year financial commitment. For many families, paying the total cost of a student's college education out of current income and savings is usually not realistic. For families that have planned ahead and have financial savings established for higher education, the burden is a lot easier. But for most, meeting the cost of college requires the pooling of current income and assets and investing in longer-term loan options. These family resources, together with financial assistance from state, federal, and institutional sources, enable millions of students each year to attend the institution of their choice.

FINANCIAL AID PROGRAMS

There are three types of financial aid:

1. Gift-aid—Scholarships and grants are funds that do not have to be repaid.
2. Loans—Loans must be repaid, usually after graduation; the amount you have to pay back is the total you've borrowed plus any accrued interest. This is considered a source of self-help aid.
3. Student employment—Student employment is a job arranged for you by the financial aid office. This is another source of self-help aid.

The federal government has four major grant programs—the Federal Pell Grant, the Federal Supplemental Educational Opportunity Grant, Academic Competitiveness Grants (ACG), and SMART grants. ACG and SMART grants are limited to students who qualify for a Pell grant and are awarded to a select group of students. Overall, these grants are targeted to low-to-moderate income families with significant financial need. The federal government also sponsors a student employment program called the Federal Work-Study Program, which offers jobs both on and off campus; and several loan programs, including those for students and for parents of undergraduate students.

There are two types of student loan programs: subsidized and unsubsidized. The subsidized Federal Stafford Student Loan and the Federal Perkins Loan are need-based, government-subsidized loans. Students who borrow through these programs do not have to pay interest on the loan until after they graduate or leave school. The unsubsidized Federal Stafford Student Loan and the Parent Loan Program are not based on need, and borrowers are responsible for the interest while the student is in school. There are different methods on how these loans are administered. Once you choose your college, the financial aid office will guide you through this process.

After you've submitted your financial aid application and you've been accepted for admission, each college will send you a letter describing your financial aid award. Most award letters show estimated college costs, how much you and your family are expected to contribute, and the amount and types of aid you have been awarded. Most students are awarded aid from a combination of sources and programs. Hence, your award is often called a financial aid "package."

SOURCES OF FINANCIAL AID

More than 12 million students and family apply for financial aid each year. Financial aid from all sources exceeds $152 billion per year. The largest single source of aid is the federal government, which awarded more than $94 billion during 2005–06.

The next largest source of financial aid is found in the college and university community. Institutions award an estimated $24.4 billion to students each year. Most of this aid is awarded to students who have a demonstrated need based on the Federal Methodology. Some institutions use a different formula, the Institutional Methodology (IM), to award their own funds in conjunction with other forms of aid. Institutional aid may be either need-based or non-need based. Aid that is not based on need is usually awarded for a student's academic performance (merit awards), specific talents or abilities, or to attract the type of students a college seeks to enroll.

Another source of financial aid is from state government, awarding more than $6.8 billion per year. All states offer grant and/or scholarship aid, most of which is need-based. However, more and more states are offering substantial merit-based aid programs. Most state programs award aid only to students attending college in their home state.

Other sources of financial aid include:

- Private agencies
- Foundations
- Corporations
- Clubs
- Fraternal and service organizations
- Civic associations
- Unions
- Religious groups that award grants, scholarships, and low-interest loans
- Employers that provide tuition reimbursement benefits for employees and their children

More information about these different sources of aid is available from high school guidance offices, public libraries, college financial aid offices, directly from the sponsoring organizations, and on the Web at www.petersons.com and www.finaid.org.

HOW NEED-BASED FINANCIAL AID IS AWARDED

When you apply for aid, your family's financial situation is analyzed using a government-approved formula called the Federal Methodology. This formula looks at five items:

1. Demographic information of the family
2. Income of the parents
3. Assets of the parents
4. Income of the student
5. Assets of the student

This analysis determines the amount you and your family are expected to contribute toward your college expenses, called your Expected Family Contribution or EFC. If the EFC is equal to or more than the cost of attendance at a particular college, then you do not demonstrate financial need. However, even if you don't have financial need, you may still qualify for aid, as there are grants, scholarships, and loan programs that are not need-based.

If the cost of your education is greater than your EFC, then you do demonstrate financial need and qualify for assistance. The amount of your financial need that can be met varies from school to school. Some are able to meet your full need, while others can only cover a certain percentage of need. Here's the formula:

$$\begin{aligned} &\text{Cost of Attendance}\\ -\ &\underline{\text{Expected Family Contribution}}\\ =\ &\text{Financial Need} \end{aligned}$$

The EFC remains constant, but your need will vary according to the costs of attendance at a particular college. In general, the higher the tuition and fees at a particular college, the higher the cost of attendance will be. Expenses for books and supplies, room and board, transportation, and other miscellaneous items are included in the overall cost of attendance. It is important to remember that you do not have to be "needy" to qualify for financial aid. Many middle and upper-middle income families qualify for need-based financial aid.

APPLYING FOR FINANCIAL AID

Every student must complete the Free Application for Federal Student Aid (FAFSA) to be considered for financial aid. The FAFSA is available from your high school guidance office, many public libraries, colleges in your area, or directly from the U.S. Department of Education.

Students are encouraged to apply for federal student aid on the Web. The electronic version of the FAFSA can be accessed at http://www.fafsa.ed.gov. Both the student and at least one parent must apply for a federal pin number at http://www.pin.ed.gov. The pin number serves as your electronic signature when applying for aid on the Web.

To award their own funds, some colleges require an additional application, the Financial Aid PROFILE® form. The PROFILE asks supplemental questions that some colleges and awarding agencies feel provide a more accurate assessment of the family's ability to pay for college. It is up to the college to decide whether it will use only the FAFSA or both the FAFSA and the PROFILE. PROFILE applications are available from the high school guidance office and on the Web. Both the paper application and the Web site list those colleges and programs that require the PROFILE application.

If Every College You're Applying to for Fall 2008 Requires the FAFSA

. . . then it's pretty simple: Complete the FAFSA after January 1, 2008, being certain to send it in before any college-imposed deadlines. (You are not permitted to send in the 2008–09 FAFSA before January 1, 2008.) Most college FAFSA application deadlines are in February or early March. It is easier if you have all your financial records for the previous year available, but if that is not possible, you are strongly encouraged to use estimated figures.

After you send in your FAFSA, either with the paper application or electronically, you'll receive a Student Aid Report (SAR) that includes all of the information you reported and shows your EFC. If you provided an e-mail address, the SAR is sent to you electronically; otherwise, you will receive a paper copy in the mail. Be sure to review the SAR, checking to see if the information you reported is accurately represented. If you used estimated numbers to complete the FAFSA, you may have to resubmit the SAR with any corrections to the data. The college(s) you have designated on the FAFSA will receive the information you reported and will use that data to make their decision. In many instances, the colleges you've applied to will ask you to send copies of your and your parents' federal income tax returns for 2007, plus any other documents needed to verify the information you reported.

If a College Requires the PROFILE

Step 1: Register for the Financial Aid PROFILE in the fall of your senior year in high school.

You can apply for the PROFILE online at http://profileonline.collegeboard.com/index.jsp. Registration information with a list of the colleges that require the PROFILE are available in most high school guidance offices. There is a fee for using the Financial Aid PROFILE application ($23 for the first college and $18 for each additional college). You must pay for the service by credit card when you register. If you do not have a credit card, you will be billed. A limited number of fee waivers are automatically granted to first-time applicants based on the financial information provided on the PROFILE.

Step 2: Fill out your customized Financial Aid PROFILE.

Once you register, your application will be immediately available online and will have questions which all students must complete, questions which must be completed by the student's parents (unless the student is independent and the colleges or programs selected do not require parental information), and *may* have supplemental questions needed by one or more of your schools or programs. If required, those will be found in Section Q of the application.

In addition to the PROFILE Application you complete online, you may also be required to complete a Business/Farm Supplement via traditional paper format. Completion of this form is not a part of the online process. If this form is required, instructions on how to download and print the supplemental form are provided. If your biological or adoptive parents are separated or divorced and your colleges and programs require it, your noncustodial parent may be asked to complete the Noncustodial PROFILE.

Once you complete and submit your PROFILE Application, it will be processed and sent directly to your requested colleges and programs.

IF YOU DON'T QUALIFY FOR NEED-BASED AID

If you are not eligible for need-based aid, you can still find ways to lessen the burden on your parents.

Here are some suggestions:

- Search for merit scholarships. You can start at the initial stages of your application process. College merit awards are becoming increasingly important as more and more colleges award these grants to students they especially want to attract. As a result, applying to a college at which your qualifications put you at the top of the entering class may give you a larger merit award. Another source of aid to look for is private scholarships that are given for special skills and talents. Additional information can be found at www.petersons.com and at www.finaid.org.

- Seek employment during the summer and the academic year. The student employment office at your college can help you locate a school-year job. Many colleges and local businesses have vacancies remaining after they have hired students who are receiving Federal Work-Study Program financial aid.

- Borrow through the unsubsidized Federal Stafford Student Loan programs. These are generally available to all students. The terms and conditions are similar to the subsidized loans. The biggest difference is that the borrower is responsible for the interest while still in college, although most lenders permit students to delay paying the interest right away and add the accrued interest to the total amount owed. You must file the FAFSA to be considered.

- After you've secured what you can through scholarships, working, and borrowing, your parents will be expected to meet their share of the college bill (the Expected Family Contribution). Many colleges offer monthly payment plans that spread the cost over the academic year. If the monthly payments are too high, parents can borrow through the Federal Parent Loan for Undergraduate Students (Federal PLUS Program), through one of the many private education loan programs available, or through home equity loans and lines of credit. Families seeking assistance in financing college expenses should inquire at the financial aid office about what programs are available at the college. Some families seek the advice of professional financial advisers and tax consultants.

HOW IS YOUR EXPECTED FAMILY CONTRIBUTION CALCULATED?

The chart on the next page makes the following assumptions:

- two parent family where age of older parent is 45
- lower income families (under $30,000) will file the 1040A or 1040EZ tax form

- student income is less than $2300
- there are no student assets
- there is only one family member attending college

All figures are estimates and may vary when the complete FAFSA or PROFILE application is submitted.

Approximate Expected Family Contribution

ASSETS	INCOME BEFORE TAXES								
FAMILY SIZE	$20,000	30,000	40,000	50,000	60,000	70,000	80,000	90,000	100,000
$ 20,000									
3	$ 0	160	1,800	3,500	5,800	9,100	12,600	14,100	17,400
4	0	0	850	2,500	4,400	7,100	10,600	12,000	15,300
5	0	0	0	1,600	3,300	5,500	8,600	10,100	13,400
6	0	0	0	600	2,200	4,100	6,600	7,900	11,200
$ 30,000									
3	$ 0	160	1,800	3,500	5,800	9,100	12,600	14,100	17,400
4	0	0	850	2,500	4,400	7,100	10,600	12,000	15,300
5	0	0	0	1,600	3,300	5,500	8,600	10,100	13,400
6	0	0	0	600	2,200	4,100	6,600	7,900	11,200
$ 40,000									
3	$ 0	160	1,800	3,500	5,800	9,100	12,600	14,100	17,400
4	0	0	850	2,500	4,400	7,100	10,600	12,000	15,300
5	0	0	0	1,600	3,300	5,500	8,600	10,100	13,400
6	0	0	0	600	2,200	4,100	6,600	7,900	11,200
$ 50,000									
3	$ 0	340	2,000	3,800	6,200	9,500	13,000	14,500	17,800
4	0	0	1,100	2,700	4,700	7,400	11,000	12,400	15,700
5	0	0	0	1,800	3,500	5,800	9,000	10,400	13,750
6	0	0	0	800	2,400	4,300	6,900	8,300	11,600
$ 60,000									
3	$ 0	600	2,300	4,100	6,600	10,000	13,600	15,000	18,300
4	0	0	1,300	3,000	5,000	8,000	11,500	13,000	16,300
5	0	0	400	2,050	3,800	6,200	9,600	11,000	14,300
6	0	0	0	1,000	2,700	4,600	7,400	8,800	12,150
$ 80,000									
3	$ 0	1,130	2,800	4,800	7,600	11,200	14,700	16,150	19,500
4	0	170	1,800	3,600	5,900	9,100	9,600	14,100	17,400
5	0	0	900	2,600	4,500	7,200	10,700	12,100	15,450
6	0	0	0	1,600	3,200	5,400	8,500	10,000	13,300
$ 100,000									
3	$ 0	1,660	3,400	5,600	8,800	12,300	15,900	17,300	20,600
4	0	700	2,400	4,200	6,800	10,250	13,800	15,200	18,500
5	0	0	1,400	3,100	5,300	8,300	11,800	13,300	16,600
6	0	0	400	2,100	3,900	6,300	9,700	11,100	14,400
$ 120,000									
3	$ 0	2,190	4,000	6,500	9,900	13,400	17,000	18,400	21,700
4	0	1,220	3,000	4,900	7,800	11,400	14,900	16,350	19,650
5	0	310	2,000	3,700	6,100	9,500	13,000	14,400	17,700
6	0	0	1,000	2,600	4,600	7,300	10,800	12,200	15,550
$ 140,000									
3	$ 0	2,700	4,700	7,500	11,000	13,400	18,100	19,500	22,850
4	0	1,750	3,500	5,700	9,000	12,500	16,000	17,750	20,800
5	0	850	2,500	4,400	7,100	10,500	14,100	15,500	18,850
6	0	0	1,500	3,200	5,300	8,400	11,900	13,350	16,650

Financial Aid Programs for Schools in the Midwest

Each state government has established one or more state-administered financial aid programs for qualified students. The state programs may be restricted to legal residents of the state, or they also may be available to out-of-state students who are attending public or private colleges or universities within the state. In addition, other qualifications may apply.

The program descriptions are arranged by state in alphabetical order, along with information about how to determine eligibility and apply. The information refers to awards for 2006–07, unless otherwise stated. Students should write to the address given for each program to request award details for 2007–08 be sent to them as soon as they are available.

ILLINOIS

Golden Apple Scholars of Illinois. 100 scholars are selected annually. Scholars receive $7000 a year for four years. Applicants must be between 17 and 21 and maintain a GPA of 2.5. Eligible applicants must be residents of Illinois studying in Illinois. Deadline: December 1. Recipients must agree to teach in high-need Illinois schools. *Academic Fields/Career Goals:* Education. *Award:* Scholarship for use in freshman, sophomore, junior, or senior year; not renewable. Award amount: $4500. Number of awards: 100. *Eligibility Requirements:* Applicant must be age 17-21; enrolled or expecting to enroll full-time at a four-year institution or university; resident of Illinois and studying in Illinois. Applicant must have 2.5 GPA or higher. Available to U.S. citizens. *Application Requirements:* Application, autobiography, essay, interview, photo, references, test scores, transcript. *Deadline:* December 1. **Contact:** Pat Kilduff, Director of Recruitment and Placement, Golden Apple Foundation, 8 South Michigan Avenue, Suite 700, Chicago, IL 60603-3318. E-mail: kilduff@goldenapple.org. Phone: 312-407-0006. Fax: 312-407-0344. Web site: www.goldenapple.org.

Grant Program for Dependents of Police, Fire, or Correctional Officers. Awards dependents of police, fire, and correctional officers killed or disabled in line of duty. Provides for tuition and fees at approved Illinois institutions. Must be resident of Illinois. The number of grants made through this program and the individual dollar amount awarded are subject to sufficient annual appropriations by the Illinois General Assembly and the governor. Deadline varies. *Award:* Grant for use in freshman, sophomore, junior, senior, graduate, or postgraduate years; renewable. Award amount: varies. Number of awards: varies. *Eligibility Requirements:* Applicant must be enrolled or expecting to enroll full- or part-time at a two-year, four-year, or technical institution or university; resident of Illinois and studying in Illinois. Available to U.S. citizens. *Application Requirements:* Application, proof of status. *Deadline:* varies. **Contact:** College Zone Counselor, Illinois Student Assistance Commission (ISAC), 1755 Lake Cook Road, Deerfield, IL 60015-5209. E-mail: collegezone@isac.org. Phone: 800-899-4722. Web site: www.collegezone.org.

Higher Education License Plate Program-HELP. Need-based grants for students who attend Illinois institutions. Funds for the program are raised by the sale of special license plates commemorating the institutions. Must be Illinois resident. May be eligible to receive the grant for the equivalent of 10 semesters of full-time enrollment. The number of grants made through this program and the individual dollar amount awarded varies. *Award:* Grant for use in freshman, sophomore, junior, or senior year; not renewable. Award amount: varies. Number of awards: varies. *Eligibility Requirements:* Applicant must be enrolled or expecting to enroll full- or part-time at a two-year or four-year institution or university; resident of Illinois and studying in Illinois. Available to U.S. citizens. *Application Requirements:* Application, financial need analysis, FAFSA. *Deadline:* varies. **Contact:** College Zone Counselor, Illinois Student Assistance Commission (ISAC), 1755 Lake Cook Road, Deerfield, IL 60015-5209. E-mail: collegezone@isac.org. Phone: 800-899-4722. Web site: www.collegezone.org.

Illinois College Savings Bond Bonus Incentive Grant Program. Program offers Illinois college savings bond holders a grant for each year of bond maturity payable upon bond redemption if at least 70 percent of proceeds are used to attend college in Illinois. The amount of grant will depend on the amount of the bond, ranging from a $40 to $440 grant per $5000 of the bond. Applications are accepted between August 1 and May 30 of the academic year in which the bonds matured, or in the academic year immediately following maturity. *Award:* Grant for use in freshman, sophomore, junior, senior, graduate, or postgraduate years; not renewable. Award amount: $40–$440. Number of awards: varies. *Eligibility Requirements:* Applicant must be enrolled or expecting to enroll full- or part-time at a two-year, four-year, or technical institution or university and studying in Illinois. Available to U.S. citizens. *Application Requirements:* Application. *Deadline:* May 30. **Contact:** College Zone Counselor, Illinois Student Assistance Commission (ISAC), 1755 Lake Cook Road, Deerfield, IL 60015-5209. E-mail: collegezone@isac.org. Phone: 800-899-4722. Web site: www.collegezone.org.

Illinois Department of Public Health Center for Rural Health Allied Health Care Professional Scholarship Program. Scholarship for Illinois student who wants to be a nurse practitioner, physician assistant, or certified nurse midwife. Funding available for up to two years. Must fulfill an obligation to practice full-time in a designated shortage area as an allied healthcare professional in Illinois for one year for each year of scholarship funding. *Academic Fields/Career Goals:* Health and Medical Sciences; Nursing. *Award:* Scholarship for use in freshman, sophomore, junior, or senior year; renewable. Award amount: up to $7500. Number of awards: varies. *Eligibility Requirements:* Applicant must be enrolled or expecting to enroll full- or part-time at a two-year or four-year institution or university; resident of Illinois and studying in Illinois. Available to U.S. citizens. *Application Requirements:* Application, financial need analysis. *Deadline:* May 15. **Contact:** Marcia Franklin, Department of Public Health, Illinois

Student Assistance Commission (ISAC), 535 West Jefferson Street, Springfield, IL 62761. Phone: 217-782-1624. Web site: www.collegezone.org.

Illinois Department of Public Health Center for Rural Health Nursing Education Scholarship Program. Scholarship for Illinois students pursuing a certificate, diploma, or degree in nursing. Must demonstrate financial need. Provides up to four years of financial aid in return for full- or part-time employment as a licensed practical or registered nurse in Illinois upon graduation. Must remain employed in Illinois for a period equivalent to the educational time that was supported by the scholarship. Deadline: May 31. *Academic Fields/Career Goals:* Health and Medical Sciences; Nursing. *Award:* Scholarship for use in freshman, sophomore, junior, or senior year; renewable. Award amount: $1500–$6000. Number of awards: varies. *Eligibility Requirements:* Applicant must be enrolled or expecting to enroll full- or part-time at a two-year or four-year institution or university; resident of Illinois and studying in Illinois. Available to U.S. citizens. *Application Requirements:* Application, financial need analysis, transcript. *Deadline:* May 31. **Contact:** Illinois Department of Public Health, Illinois Student Assistance Commission (ISAC), 535 West Jefferson Street, Springfield, IL 62761-0001. Phone: 212-782-1624. Web site: www.collegezone.org.

Illinois Future Teachers Corps Program. Scholarships are available for students planning to become teachers in Illinois. Students must be Illinois residents, enrolled or accepted as a junior or above in a Teacher Education Program at an Illinois college or university. By receiving the award, students agree to teach for five years at either a public, private, or parochial Illinois preschool, or at a public elementary or secondary school. *Academic Fields/Career Goals:* Education. *Award:* Forgivable loan for use in junior, senior, or graduate year; renewable. Award amount: up to $15,000. Number of awards: 1150. *Eligibility Requirements:* Applicant must be enrolled or expecting to enroll full- or part-time at a four-year institution or university; resident of Illinois and studying in Illinois. Applicant must have 2.5 GPA or higher. Available to U.S. citizens. *Application Requirements:* Application, financial need analysis, FAFSA. *Deadline:* March 1. **Contact:** College Zone Counselor, Illinois Student Assistance Commission (ISAC), 1755 Lake Cook Road, Deerfield, IL 60015-5209. E-mail: collegezone@isac.org. Phone: 800-899-4722. Web site: www.collegezone.org.

Illinois General Assembly Scholarship. Scholarships available for Illinois students enrolled at an Illinois four-year state-supported college. Must contact the general assembly member for eligibility criteria. Deadline varies. *Award:* Scholarship for use in freshman, sophomore, junior, or senior year; not renewable. Award amount: varies. Number of awards: varies. *Eligibility Requirements:* Applicant must be enrolled or expecting to enroll full- or part-time at a four-year institution or university; resident of Illinois and studying in Illinois. Available to U.S. citizens. *Application Requirements:* Application. *Deadline:* varies. **Contact:** College Zone Counselor, Illinois Student Assistance Commission (ISAC), 1755 Lake Cook Road, Deerfield, IL 60015-5209. E-mail: collegezone@isac.org. Phone: 800-899-4722. Web site: www.collegezone.org.

Illinois Monetary Award Program. The program provides grants, which do not need to be repaid. Awards to Illinois residents who demonstrate financial need, based on the information provided on the Free Application for Federal Student Aid. The number of grants made through this program, and the individual dollar amount awarded, are subject to sufficient annual appropriations by the Illinois General Assembly. Deadlines: August 15 and September 30. *Award:* Grant for use in freshman, sophomore, junior, or senior year; renewable. Award amount: $2365. Number of awards: 146,853. *Eligibility Requirements:* Applicant must be enrolled or expecting to enroll full- or part-time at a two-year, four-year, or technical institution or university; resident of Illinois and studying in Illinois. Available to U.S. citizens. *Application Requirements:* Financial need analysis, FAFSA online. *Deadline:* varies. **Contact:** College Zone Counselor, Illinois Student Assistance Com-

mission (ISAC), 1755 Lake Cook Road, Deerfield, IL 60015-5209. E-mail: collegezone@isac.org. Phone: 800-899-4722. Web site: www.collegezone.org.

Illinois National Guard Grant Program. Members of the Illinois National Guard are eligible to receive the grant. The grant can pay for eligible tuition and certain fees for undergraduate or graduate study at Illinois two- or four-year public colleges. It can be used for a maximum of the equivalent of four academic years of full-time enrollment. Deadlines: October 1 of the academic year for full year, March 1 for second/third term, or June 15 for the summer term. *Award:* Grant for use in freshman, sophomore, junior, senior, or graduate year; renewable. Award amount: varies. Number of awards: varies. *Eligibility Requirements:* Applicant must be enrolled or expecting to enroll full- or part-time at a two-year or four-year institution or university; resident of Illinois and studying in Illinois. Available to U.S. citizens. Applicant must have served in the Air Force National Guard or Army National Guard. *Application Requirements:* Application, documentation of service. *Deadline:* varies. **Contact:** College Zone Counselor, Illinois Student Assistance Commission (ISAC), 1755 Lake Cook Road, Deerfield, IL 60015-5209. E-mail: collegezone@isac.org. Phone: 800-899-4722. Web site: www.collegezone.org.

Illinois Special Education Teacher Tuition Waiver. Teachers or students who are pursuing a career in special education as public, private or parochial preschool, elementary or secondary school teachers in Illinois may be eligible for this program. This program will exempt such individuals from paying tuition and mandatory fees at an eligible institution, for up to four years. The number of scholarships and the individual dollar amount awarded are subject to sufficient annual appropriations by the Illinois General Assembly. Deadline: March 1. *Academic Fields/Career Goals:* Special Education. *Award:* Forgivable loan for use in freshman, sophomore, junior, senior, or graduate year; renewable. Award amount: varies. Number of awards: up to 250. *Eligibility Requirements:* Applicant must be enrolled or expecting to enroll full- or part-time at a four-year institution or university; resident of Illinois and studying in Illinois. Available to U.S. citizens. *Application Requirements:* Application. *Deadline:* March 1. **Contact:** College Zone Counselor, Illinois Student Assistance Commission (ISAC), 1755 Lake Cook Road, Deerfield, IL 60015-5209. E-mail: collegezone@isac.org. Phone: 800-899-4722. Web site: www.collegezone.org.

Illinois Student-to-Student Program of Matching Grants. Grant is available to undergraduates at participating state-supported colleges through voluntary contributions from students and matching grants from the state. The number of grants made through this program, and the individual dollar amount awarded, are subject to sufficient annual appropriations by the Illinois General Assembly. Contact financial aid office at the institution. *Award:* Grant for use in freshman, sophomore, junior, or senior year; not renewable. Award amount: varies. Number of awards: varies. *Eligibility Requirements:* Applicant must be enrolled or expecting to enroll full- or part-time at a two-year or four-year institution or university; resident of Illinois and studying in Illinois. Available to U.S. citizens. *Application Requirements:* Application, financial need analysis. *Deadline:* varies. **Contact:** College Zone Counselor, Illinois Student Assistance Commission (ISAC), 1755 Lake Cook Road, Deerfield, IL 60015-5209. E-mail: collegezone@isac.org. Phone: 800-899-4722. Web site: www.collegezone.org.

Illinois Veteran Grant Program-IVG. Awards qualified veterans and pays eligible tuition and fees for study in Illinois public universities or community colleges. Program eligibility units are based on the enrolled hours for a particular term, not the dollar amount of the benefits paid. Applications are available at college financial aid office and can be submitted any time during the academic year for which assistance is being requested. *Award:* Grant for use in freshman, sophomore, junior, senior, or graduate year; renewable. Award amount: $1400–$1600. Number of awards: 11,000–13,000. *Eligibility Requirements:* Applicant must be enrolled or expecting to enroll full- or part-time at a two-year or four-year institution or university; resident of Illinois and studying in Illinois. Available to U.S. citizens. Applicant must have general military experience. *Application Requirements:* Application. *Deadline:* continuous. **Contact:** College Zone Counselor, Illinois Student Assistance Commission (ISAC), 1755 Lake Cook Road, Deerfield, IL 60015-5209. E-mail: collegezone@isac.org. Phone: 800-899-4722. Web site: www.collegezone.org.

Merit Recognition Scholarship (MRS) Program. Awards students who were ranked in the top 5 percent of their high school class or scored among the top 5 percent of scores in the ACT, SAT or Prairie state achievement exam. May be eligible to receive an one-time, nonrenewable scholarship of $1000. The number of scholarships granted varies. *Award:* Scholarship for use in freshman year; not renewable. Award amount: up to $1000. Number of awards: varies. *Eligibility Requirements:* Applicant must be high school student; planning to enroll or expecting to enroll full- or part-time at a two-year or four-year institution or university; resident of Illinois and studying in Illinois. Applicant must have 3.5 GPA or higher. Available to U.S. citizens. *Application Requirements:* Application. *Deadline:* varies. **Contact:** College Zone Counselor, Illinois Student Assistance Commission (ISAC), 1755 Lake Cook Road, Deerfield, IL 60015-5209. E-mail: collegezone@isac.org. Phone: 800-899-4722. Web site: www.collegezone.org.

MIA/POW Scholarships. One-time award for spouse, child, or stepchild of veterans who are missing in action or were a prisoner of war. Must be enrolled at a state-supported school in Illinois. Candidate must be U.S. citizen. Must apply and be accepted before beginning of school. Also for children and spouses of veterans who are determined to be 100 percent disabled as established by the Veterans Administration. Scholarship value and the number of awards granted varies. Deadline: continuous. *Award:* Scholarship for use in freshman, sophomore, junior, senior, or graduate year; renewable. Award amount: varies. Number of awards: varies. *Eligibility Requirements:* Applicant must be enrolled or expecting to enroll full- or part-time at a two-year or four-year institution or university; resident of Illinois and studying in Illinois. Available to U.S. citizens. Applicant or parent must meet one or more of the following requirements: general military experience; retired from active duty; disabled or killed as a result of military service; prisoner of war; or missing in action. *Application Requirements:* Application. *Deadline:* continuous. **Contact:** Ms. Tracy Mahan, Grants Section, Illinois Department of Veterans Affairs, 833 South Spring Street, Springfield, IL 62794-9432. Phone: 217-782-3564. Fax: 217-782-4161. Web site: www.state.il.us/agency/dva.

Minority Teachers of Illinois Scholarship Program. The program awards students who are planning to become school teachers and are of African American/Black, Hispanic American, Asian American or Native American origin. May qualify for up to $5000 per year. The number of scholarships and the individual dollar amount awarded are subject to sufficient annual appropriations by the Illinois General Assembly and the governor. Deadline: March 1. *Academic Fields/Career Goals:* Education; Special Education. *Award:* Forgivable loan for use in freshman, sophomore, junior, senior, graduate, or postgraduate years; renewable. Award amount: up to $5000. Number of awards: 450–550. *Eligibility Requirements:* Applicant must be American Indian/Alaska Native, Asian/Pacific Islander, Black (non-Hispanic), or Hispanic; enrolled or expecting to enroll full- or part-time at a two-year or four-year institution or university; resident of Illinois and studying in Illinois. Applicant must have 2.5 GPA or higher. Available to U.S. citizens. *Application Requirements:* Application. *Deadline:* March 1. **Contact:** College Zone Counselor, Illinois Student Assistance Commission (ISAC), 1755 Lake Cook Road, Deerfield, IL 60015-5209. E-mail: collegezone@isac.org. Phone: 800-899-4722. Web site: www.collegezone.org.

Paul Douglas Teacher Scholarship (PDTS) Program. Program enables and encourages outstanding high school graduates to pursue teaching careers at the preschool, elementary or secondary school level by providing financial assistance. Deadline: August 1. *Academic Fields/Career Goals:* Education. *Award:* Scholarship for use in freshman year; not renewable. Award amount: varies. Number of awards: varies. *Eligibility Requirements:* Applicant must be enrolled or expecting to enroll full-time at a four-year institution or university; resident of

Illinois and studying in Illinois. Available to U.S. citizens. *Application Requirements:* Application, financial need analysis. *Deadline:* August 1. **Contact:** College Zone Counselor, Illinois Student Assistance Commission (ISAC), 1755 Lake Cook Road, Deerfield, IL 60015-5209. E-mail: collegezone@isac.org. Phone: 800-899-4722. Web site: www.collegezone.org.

Silas Purnell Illinois Incentive for Access Program. Students whose information provided on the FAFSA results in a calculated zero expected family contribution when they are college freshmen may be eligible to receive the grant of up to $500. To apply, the student must complete the FAFSA as soon as possible after January 1, prior to the academic year that starts on or after July 1. *Award:* Grant for use in freshman year; not renewable. Award amount: up to $500. Number of awards: varies. *Eligibility Requirements:* Applicant must be enrolled or expecting to enroll full- or part-time at a two-year, four-year, or technical institution or university; resident of Illinois and studying in Illinois. Available to U.S. citizens. *Application Requirements:* Financial need analysis, FAFSA. *Deadline:* July 1. **Contact:** College Zone Counselor, Illinois Student Assistance Commission (ISAC), 1755 Lake Cook Road, Deerfield, IL 60015-5209. E-mail: collegezone@isac.org. Phone: 800-899-4722. Web site: www.collegezone.org.

Veterans' Children Educational Opportunities. Award for each child of age 18 or younger of a veteran who died or became totally disabled as a result of service during World War I, World War II, Korean, or Vietnam War. Must be studying in Illinois. Death must be service-connected. Disability must be rated 100 percent for two or more years. Grant value is $250. Deadline: June 30. *Award:* Grant for use in freshman year; not renewable. Award amount: $250. Number of awards: varies. *Eligibility Requirements:* Applicant must be age 10-18; enrolled or expecting to enroll full- or part-time at a two-year or four-year institution or university; resident of Illinois and studying in Illinois. Available to U.S. citizens. Applicant or parent must meet one or more of the following requirements: general military experience; retired from active duty; disabled or killed as a result of military service; prisoner of war; or missing in action. *Application Requirements:* Application. *Deadline:* June 30. **Contact:** Tracy Mahan, Grants Section, Illinois Department of Veterans Affairs, 833 South Spring Street, Springfield, IL 62794-9432. Phone: 217-782-3564. Fax: 217-782-4161. Web site: www.state.il.us/agency/dva.

INDIANA

Child of Disabled Veteran Grant or Purple Heart Recipient Grant. Free tuition at Indiana state-supported colleges or universities for children of disabled veterans or Purple Heart recipients. Must submit Form DD214 or service record. Dollar amount and number of awards varies. *Award:* Grant for use in freshman, sophomore, junior, senior, graduate, or postgraduate years; renewable. Award amount: varies. Number of awards: varies. *Eligibility Requirements:* Applicant must be enrolled or expecting to enroll full- or part-time at a two-year or four-year institution or university; resident of Indiana and studying in Indiana. Available to U.S. citizens. Applicant or parent must meet one or more of the following requirements: general military experience; retired from active duty; disabled or killed as a result of military service; prisoner of war; or missing in action. *Application Requirements:* Application. *Deadline:* continuous. **Contact:** Jon Brinkley, State Service Officer, Indiana Department of Veterans Affairs, 302 West Washington Street, Room E-120, Indianapolis, IN 46204-2738. E-mail: jbrinkley@dva.state.in.us. Phone: 317-232-3910. Fax: 317-232-7721. Web site: www.ai.org/veteran.

Department of Veterans Affairs Free Tuition for Children of POW/MIA's in Vietnam. Renewable award for residents of Indiana who are the children of veterans declared missing in action or prisoner-of-war after January 1, 1960. Provides tuition at Indiana state-supported institutions for undergraduate study. *Award:* Grant for use in freshman, sophomore, junior, senior, graduate, or postgraduate years; renewable. Award amount: varies. Number of awards: varies. *Eligibility Requirements:* Applicant must be age 24 or under; enrolled or expecting to enroll full- or part-time at a two-year or four-year institution or university; resident of Indiana and studying in Indiana. Available to U.S. citizens. Applicant or parent must meet one or more of the following requirements: general military experience; retired from active duty; disabled or killed as a result of military service; prisoner of war; or missing in action. *Application Requirements:* Application. *Deadline:* March 10. **Contact:** Jon Brinkley, State Service Officer, Indiana Department of Veterans Affairs, 302 West Washington Street, Room E-120, Indianapolis, IN 46204-2738. E-mail: jbrinkley@dva.state.in.us. Phone: 317-232-3910. Fax: 317-232-7721. Web site: www.ai.org/veteran.

Frank O'Bannon Grant Program. The Higher Education Award (Frank O'Bannon) is a need-based, tuition-restricted program for students attending Indiana public, private, or proprietary institutions seeking a first undergraduate degree. Students (and parents of dependent students) who are U.S. citizens and Indiana residents must file the FAFSA yearly by the March 10 deadline. *Award:* Grant for use in freshman, sophomore, junior, or senior year; not renewable. Award amount: $200–$5172. Number of awards: 38,000–70,239. *Eligibility Requirements:* Applicant must be enrolled or expecting to enroll full-time at a two-year, four-year, or technical institution or university; resident of Indiana and studying in Indiana. Available to U.S. citizens. *Application Requirements:* Application, financial need analysis, FAFSA. *Deadline:* March 10. **Contact:** Grants Counselor, State Student Assistance Commission of Indiana (SSACI), 150 West Market Street, Suite 500, Indianapolis, IN 46204-2805. E-mail: grants@ssaci.state.in.us. Phone: 317-232-2350. Fax: 317-232-3260. Web site: www.in.gov/ssaci.

Hoosier Scholar Award. The Hoosier Scholar Award is a $500 nonrenewable award. Based on the size of the senior class, one to three scholars are selected by the guidance counselor(s) of each accredited high school in Indiana. The award is based on academic merit and may be used for any educational expense at an eligible Indiana institution of higher education. *Award:* Scholarship for use in freshman year; not renewable. Award amount: $500. Number of awards: 689–840. *Eligibility Requirements:* Applicant must be high school student; planning to enroll or expecting to enroll full-time at a two-year or four-year institution or university; resident of Indiana and studying in Indiana. Applicant must have 3.5 GPA or higher. Available to U.S. citizens. *Application Requirements:* Application, references. *Deadline:* March 10. **Contact:** Ada Sparkman, Program Coordinator, State Student Assistance Commission of Indiana (SSACI), 150 West Market Street, Suite 500, Indianapolis, IN 46204-2805. Phone: 317-232-2350. Fax: 317-232-3260. Web site: www.in.gov/ssaci.

Indiana National Guard Supplemental Grant. The award is a supplement to the Indiana Higher Education Grant program. Applicants must be members of the Indiana National Guard. All Guard paperwork must be completed prior to the start of each semester. The FAFSA must be received by March 10. Award covers certain tuition and fees at select public colleges. *Award:* Grant for use in freshman, sophomore, junior, or senior year; not renewable. Award amount: $200–$7110. Number of awards: 503–925. *Eligibility Requirements:* Applicant must be enrolled or expecting to enroll full- or part-time at a two-year or four-year institution or university; resident of Indiana and studying in Indiana. Available to U.S. citizens. Applicant must have served in the Air Force National Guard or Army National Guard. *Application Requirements:* Application. *Deadline:* March 10. **Contact:** Kathryn Moore, Grants Counselor, State Student Assistance Commission of Indiana (SSACI), 150 West Market Street, Suite 500, Indianapolis, IN 46204-2805. E-mail: grants@ssaci.state.in.us. Phone: 317-232-2350. Fax: 317-232-2360. Web site: www.in.gov/ssaci.

Indiana Nursing Scholarship Fund. Need-based tuition funding for nursing students enrolled full- or part-time at an eligible Indiana institution. Must be a U.S. citizen and an Indiana resident and have a minimum 2.0 GPA or meet the minimum requirements for the nursing program. Upon graduation, recipients must practice as a nurse in an Indiana health care setting for two years. *Academic Fields/Career Goals:* Nursing. *Award:* Scholarship for use in freshman, sophomore, junior, or senior year; not renewable. Award amount: $200–$5000. Number of awards: 490–690. *Eligibility Requirements:* Applicant must

be enrolled or expecting to enroll full- or part-time at a two-year or four-year institution or university; resident of Indiana and studying in Indiana. Available to U.S. citizens. *Application Requirements:* Application, financial need analysis, FAFSA. *Deadline:* continuous. **Contact:** Yvonne Heflin, Director, Special Programs, State Student Assistance Commission of Indiana (SSACI), 150 West Market Street, Suite 500, Indianapolis, IN 46204-2805. Phone: 317-232-2350. Fax: 317-232-3260. Web site: www.in.gov/ssaci.

Part-time Grant Program. Program is designed to encourage part-time undergraduates to start and complete their associate or baccalaureate degrees or certificates by subsidizing part-time tuition costs. It is a term-based award that is based on need. State residency requirements must be met and a FAFSA must be filed. Eligibility is determined at the institutional level subject to approval by SSACI. *Award:* Grant for use in freshman, sophomore, junior, or senior year; not renewable. Award amount: $50–$4000. Number of awards: 4680–6700. *Eligibility Requirements:* Applicant must be enrolled or expecting to enroll part-time at a two-year, four-year, or technical institution or university; resident of Indiana and studying in Indiana. Available to U.S. citizens. *Application Requirements:* Application, financial need analysis. *Deadline:* continuous. **Contact:** Grants Counselor, State Student Assistance Commission of Indiana (SSACI), 150 West Market Street, Suite 500, Indianapolis, IN 46204-2805. E-mail: grants@ssaci.state.in.us. Phone: 317-232-2350. Fax: 317-232-3260. Web site: www.in.gov/ssaci.

Twenty-first Century Scholars Gear Up Summer Scholarship. Grant of up to $3000 that pays for summer school tuition and regularly assessed course fees (does not cover other costs such as textbooks or room and board). *Award:* Scholarship for use in freshman, sophomore, junior, or senior year; not renewable. Award amount: up to $3000. Number of awards: 1. *Eligibility Requirements:* Applicant must be enrolled or expecting to enroll full-time at a two-year or four-year institution or university; resident of Indiana and studying in Indiana. Available to U.S. citizens. *Application Requirements:* Application, must be in twenty-first century scholars program, have high school diploma. *Deadline:* varies. **Contact:** GEAR UP Coordinator, Office of Twenty-first Century Scholars, State Student Assistance Commission of Indiana (SSACI), 150 West Market Street, Suite 500, Indianapolis, IN 46204. E-mail: 21stscholars@ssaci.in.gov. Phone: 317-234-1394. Web site: www.in.gov/ssaci.

IOWA

Governor Terry E. Branstad Iowa State Fair Scholarship. Awards up to four scholarships ranging from $500 to $1000 to students graduating from an Iowa high school. Must actively participate at the Iowa State fair. For more details see Web site: http://www.iowacollegeaid.org. *Award:* Scholarship for use in freshman year; not renewable. Award amount: $500–$1000. Number of awards: up to 4. *Eligibility Requirements:* Applicant must be high school student; planning to enroll or expecting to enroll full- or part-time at a four-year institution or university; resident of Iowa and studying in Iowa. Available to U.S. citizens. *Application Requirements:* Application, essay, financial need analysis, references, transcript. *Deadline:* May 1. **Contact:** Misty Thompson, Program Planner, Iowa College Student Aid Commission, 200 Tenth Street, Fourth Floor, Des Moines, IA 50309-3609. E-mail: misty.thompson@iowa.gov. Phone: 515-725-3424. Web site: www.iowacollegeaid.gov.

Iowa Grants. Statewide need-based program to assist high-need Iowa residents. Recipients must demonstrate a high level of financial need to receive awards ranging from $100 to $1000. Awards are prorated for students enrolled for less than full-time. Awards must be used at Iowa postsecondary institutions. *Award:* Grant for use in freshman, sophomore, junior, or senior year; not renewable. Award amount: $100–$1000. Number of awards: varies. *Eligibility Requirements:* Applicant must be enrolled or expecting to enroll full- or part-time at a two-year, four-year, or technical institution or university; resident of Iowa and studying in Iowa. Available to U.S. citizens. *Application Requirements:* Application, financial need analysis. *Deadline:* continuous. **Contact:** Julie Leeper, Director, Program Administration, Iowa

College Student Aid Commission, 200 Tenth Street, Fourth Floor, Des Moines, IA 50309-3609. E-mail: icsac@max.state.ia.us. Phone: 515-725-3420. Web site: www.iowacollegeaid.gov.

Iowa National Guard Education Assistance Program. Program provides postsecondary tuition assistance to members of Iowa National Guard Units. Must study at a postsecondary institution in Iowa. Contact the office for additional information. *Award:* Grant for use in freshman, sophomore, junior, or senior year; not renewable. Award amount: up to $1200. Number of awards: varies. *Eligibility Requirements:* Applicant must be enrolled or expecting to enroll full- or part-time at a two-year, four-year, or technical institution or university; resident of Iowa and studying in Iowa. Available to U.S. citizens. Applicant must have served in the Air Force National Guard or Army National Guard. *Application Requirements:* Application. *Deadline:* continuous. **Contact:** Julie Leeper, Director, Program Administration, Iowa College Student Aid Commission, 200 Tenth Street, Fourth Floor, Des Moines, IA 50309-3609. E-mail: icsac@max.state.ia.us. Phone: 515-242-3370. Web site: www.iowacollegeaid.gov.

Iowa Teacher Shortage Forgivable Loan Program. Forgivable loan assists students who will teach in Iowa secondary schools. Must be an Iowa resident attending an Iowa postsecondary institution. Contact the office for additional information. *Academic Fields/Career Goals:* Education. *Award:* Forgivable loan for use in freshman, sophomore, junior, or senior year; not renewable. Award amount: $2686. Number of awards: varies. *Eligibility Requirements:* Applicant must be enrolled or expecting to enroll full- or part-time at a four-year institution or university; resident of Iowa and studying in Iowa. Applicant or parent of applicant must have employment or volunteer experience in teaching. Available to U.S. citizens. *Application Requirements:* Application, financial need analysis. *Deadline:* continuous. **Contact:** Julie Leeper, Director, Program Administration, Iowa College Student Aid Commission, 200 Tenth Street, Fourth Floor, Des Moines, IA 50309-3609. E-mail: icsac@max.state.ia.us. Phone: 515-725-3420. Web site: www.iowacollegeaid.gov.

Iowa Tuition Grant Program. Program assists students who attend independent postsecondary institutions in Iowa. Iowa residents currently enrolled, or planning to enroll, for at least 3 semester hours at one of the eligible Iowa postsecondary institutions may apply. Awards currently range from $100 to $4000. Grants may not exceed the difference between independent college and university tuition and fees and the average tuition and fees at the three public Regent universities. *Award:* Grant for use in freshman, sophomore, junior, or senior year; not renewable. Award amount: $100–$4000. Number of awards: varies. *Eligibility Requirements:* Applicant must be enrolled or expecting to enroll full- or part-time at a two-year or four-year institution or university; resident of Iowa and studying in Iowa. Available to U.S. citizens. *Application Requirements:* Application, financial need analysis. *Deadline:* July 1. **Contact:** Julie Leeper, Director, Program Administration, Iowa College Student Aid Commission, 200 Tenth Street, Fourth Floor, Des Moines, IA 50309-3609. E-mail: icsac@max.state.ia.us. Phone: 515-725-3420. Web site: www.iowacollegeaid.gov.

Iowa Vocational Rehabilitation. Provides vocational rehabilitation services to individuals with disabilities who need these services in order to maintain, retain, or obtain employment compatible with their disabilities. Must be Iowa resident. *Award:* Grant for use in freshman, sophomore, junior, senior, graduate, or postgraduate years; renewable. Award amount: $4000. Number of awards: 4000. *Eligibility Requirements:* Applicant must be enrolled or expecting to enroll full- or part-time at a two-year, four-year, or technical institution or university and resident of Iowa. Applicant must be hearing impaired, learning disabled, physically disabled, or visually impaired. Available to U.S. and non-U.S. citizens. *Application Requirements:* Application, interview. *Deadline:* varies. **Contact:** Ralph Childers, Policy and Workforce Initiatives Coordinator, Iowa Division of Vocational Rehabilitation Services, Division of Vocational Rehabilitation Services, 510 East 12th Street, Des Moines, IA 50319. E-mail: ralph.childers@iowa.gov. Phone: 515-281-4151. Fax: 515-281-4703. Web site: www.ivrs.iowa.gov.

Iowa Vocational-Technical Tuition Grant Program. Program provides need-based financial assistance to Iowa residents enrolled in career education (vocational-technical), and career option programs at Iowa area community colleges. Grants range from $150 to $1250, depending on the length of the program, financial need, and available funds. *Award:* Grant for use in freshman or sophomore year; not renewable. Award amount: $150–$1200. Number of awards: varies. *Eligibility Requirements:* Applicant must be enrolled or expecting to enroll full- or part-time at a technical institution; resident of Iowa and studying in Iowa. Available to U.S. citizens. *Application Requirements:* Application, financial need analysis. *Deadline:* July 1. **Contact:** Julie Leeper, Director, Program Administration, Iowa College Student Aid Commission, 200 Tenth Street, Fourth Floor, Des Moines, IA 50309-3609. E-mail: julie.leeper@iowa.gov. Phone: 515-725-3420. Web site: www.iowacollegeaid.gov.

State of Iowa Scholarship Program. Program provides recognition and financial honorarium to Iowa's academically talented high school seniors. Honorary scholarships are presented to all qualified candidates. Approximately 1700 top-ranking candidates are designated as State of Iowa scholars every March, from an applicant pool of nearly 5000 high school seniors. Must be used at an Iowa postsecondary institution. Minimum 3.5 GPA required. *Award:* Scholarship for use in freshman year; not renewable. Award amount: varies. Number of awards: up to 1700. *Eligibility Requirements:* Applicant must be high school student; planning to enroll or expecting to enroll full-time at a two-year, four-year, or technical institution or university; resident of Iowa and studying in Iowa. Applicant must have 3.5 GPA or higher. Available to U.S. citizens. *Application Requirements:* Application, test scores. *Deadline:* November 1. **Contact:** Misty Thompson, Program Planner, Iowa College Student Aid Commission, 200 Tenth Street, Fourth Floor, Des Moines, IA 50309-3609. E-mail: misty.thompson@iowa.gov. Phone: 515-725-3424. Web site: www.iowacollegeaid.gov.

KANSAS

Kansas Educational Benefits for Children of MIA, POW, and Deceased Veterans of the Vietnam War. Scholarship awarded to students who are children of veterans. Must show proof of parent's status as missing in action, prisoner of war, or killed in action in the Vietnam War. Kansas residence required of veteran at time of entry to service. Must attend a state-supported postsecondary school. *Award:* Scholarship for use in freshman, sophomore, junior, or senior year; not renewable. Award amount: varies. Number of awards: 1. *Eligibility Requirements:* Applicant must be enrolled or expecting to enroll full- or part-time at a two-year, four-year, or technical institution or university and studying in Kansas. Available to U.S. citizens. Applicant or parent must meet one or more of the following requirements: general military experience; retired from active duty; disabled or killed as a result of military service; prisoner of war; or missing in action. *Application Requirements:* Application, report of casualty, birth certificate, school acceptance letter, military discharge of veteran. *Deadline:* varies. **Contact:** Wayne Bollig, Program Director, Kansas Commission on Veterans Affairs, 700 Jackson, SW, Suite 701, Topeka, KS 66603-3743. E-mail: bhayes@kcva.org. Phone: 785-296-3976. Fax: 785-296-1462. Web site: www.kcva.org.

Ted and Nora Anderson Scholarships. Scholarship of $250 for each semester (one year only) given to the children of American Legion members or Auxiliary members who are holding membership for the past three consecutive years. Children of a deceased member can also apply. Parent of the applicant must be a veteran. Must be high school seniors or college freshmen or sophomores in a Kansas institution. Scholarship for use at an approved college, university, or trade school in Kansas. Must maintain a C average in college. *Award:* Scholarship for use in freshman or sophomore year; not renewable. Award amount: $250–$500. Number of awards: 4. *Eligibility Requirements:* Applicant must be enrolled or expecting to enroll full-time at a two-year, four-year, or technical institution or university; resident of Kansas and studying in Kansas. Applicant or parent of applicant must be member of American Legion or Auxiliary. Available to U.S. citizens. Applicant or parent must meet one or more of the following requirements: general military experience; retired from active duty; disabled or killed as a result of military service; prisoner of war; or missing in action. *Application Requirements:* Application, essay, financial need analysis, photo, references, transcript. *Deadline:* February 15. **Contact:** Jim Gravenstein, Chairman of the Scholarship Committee, American Legion, Department of Kansas, 1314 Topeka Boulevard, SW, Topeka, KS 66612. Phone: 785-232-9315. Fax: 785-232-1399. Web site: www.ksamlegion.org.

MICHIGAN

Children of Veterans Tuition Grant. Awards available for students who are children of a disabled or deceased Michigan veteran. Must be enrolled at least half-time in a degree-granting Michigan public or private nonprofit institution. Must be a U.S. citizen or permanent resident and must be residing in Michigan. *Award:* Grant for use in freshman, sophomore, junior, or senior year; renewable. Award amount: up to $2800. Number of awards: varies. *Eligibility Requirements:* Applicant must be age 17-25; enrolled or expecting to enroll part-time at a two-year or four-year institution or university; resident of Michigan and studying in Michigan. Available to U.S. citizens. Applicant or parent must meet one or more of the following requirements: general military experience; retired from active duty; disabled or killed as a result of military service; prisoner of war; or missing in action. *Application Requirements:* Application. *Deadline:* varies. **Contact:** Program Director, Michigan Bureau of Student Financial Assistance, PO Box 30462, Lansing, MI 48909-7962. E-mail: osg@michigan.gov. Phone: 888-447-2687. Web site: www.michigan.gov/studentaid.

Michigan Adult Part-Time Grant. Grant is intended for financially needy, independent undergraduates who have been out of high school for at least two years. Must be Michigan resident. Deadlines determined by college. *Award:* Grant for use in freshman, sophomore, junior, or senior year; renewable. Award amount: up to $600. Number of awards: varies. *Eligibility Requirements:* Applicant must be enrolled or expecting to enroll part-time at a two-year or four-year institution or university; resident of Michigan and studying in Michigan. Available to U.S. citizens. *Application Requirements:* Financial need analysis. *Deadline:* varies. **Contact:** Program Director, Michigan Bureau of Student Financial Assistance, PO Box 30462, Lansing, MI 48909-7962. E-mail: osg@michigan.gov. Phone: 888-447-2687. Web site: www.michigan.gov/studentaid.

Michigan Competitive Scholarship. Renewable award of $1300 for undergraduate study at a Michigan institution. Awards limited to tuition. Must maintain a C average and meet the college's academic progress requirements. Must file Free Application for Federal Student Aid. Deadline: March 1. Must be Michigan resident. *Award:* Scholarship for use in freshman, sophomore, junior, or senior year; renewable. Award amount: $100–$1300. Number of awards: varies. *Eligibility Requirements:* Applicant must be enrolled or expecting to enroll full- or part-time at a two-year or four-year institution or university; resident of Michigan and studying in Michigan. Available to U.S. citizens. *Application Requirements:* Application, financial need analysis, test scores, FAFSA. *Deadline:* March 1. **Contact:** Scholarship and Grant Director, Michigan Bureau of Student Financial Assistance, PO Box 30466, Lansing, MI 48909-7962. E-mail: osg@michigan.gov. Phone: 888-447-2687. Web site: www.michigan.gov/studentaid.

Michigan Educational Opportunity Grant. Need-based program for Michigan residents who are at least half-time undergraduates attending public Michigan colleges. Must maintain good academic standing. Deadline determined by college. Award of up to $1000. *Award:* Grant for use in freshman, sophomore, junior, or senior year; renewable. Award amount: up to $1000. Number of awards: varies. *Eligibility Requirements:* Applicant must be enrolled or expecting to enroll full- or part-time at an institution or university; resident of Michigan and studying in Michigan. Available to U.S. citizens. *Application Requirements:* Financial need analysis. *Deadline:* varies. **Contact:** Program Director, Michigan Bureau of Student Financial Assistance,

PO Box 30462, Lansing, MI 48909-7962. E-mail: osg@michigan.gov. Phone: 888-447-2687. Web site: www.michigan.gov/studentaid.

Michigan Indian Tuition Waiver. Renewable award provides free tuition for Native-American of 1/4 or more blood degree who attend a Michigan public college or university. Must be a Michigan resident for at least one year. The tuition waiver program covers full-time, part-time or summer school student attending a public, state, community, junior college, public college, or public university. Deadline: continuous. *Award:* Scholarship for use in freshman, sophomore, junior, senior, graduate, or postgraduate years; renewable. Award amount: varies. Number of awards: varies. *Eligibility Requirements:* Applicant must be American Indian/Alaska Native; enrolled or expecting to enroll full- or part-time at a two-year, four-year, or technical institution or university; resident of Michigan and studying in Michigan. Available to U.S. citizens. *Application Requirements:* Application, driver's license, transcript, tribal certification, proof of residency. *Deadline:* continuous. **Contact:** Christin McKerchie, Executive Assistant to Programs, Inter-Tribal Council of Michigan Inc., 2956 Ashmun Street, Suite A, Sault Ste. Marie, MI 49783. Phone: 906-632-6896 Ext. 136. Fax: 906-632-6878. Web site: www.itcmi.org.

Michigan Merit Award. Scholarship for students scoring well on state's standardized assessment tests. Students will have four years from high school graduation to use the award. *Award:* Scholarship for use in freshman, sophomore, junior, or senior year; not renewable. Award amount: $1000–$2500. Number of awards: varies. *Eligibility Requirements:* Applicant must be enrolled or expecting to enroll full- or part-time at a two-year, four-year, or technical institution or university and resident of Michigan. Available to U.S. citizens. *Application Requirements:* Test scores. *Deadline:* varies. **Contact:** Program Director, Michigan Bureau of Student Financial Assistance, PO Box 30466, Lansing, MI 48909-7962. E-mail: osg@michigan.gov. Phone: 888-447-2687. Web site: www.michigan.gov/studentaid.

Michigan Nursing Scholarship. Scholarship for students enrolled in an LPN, associate degree in nursing, bachelor of science in nursing, or master of science in nursing programs. Colleges determine application procedure and select recipients. Recipients must fulfill in-state work commitment or repay scholarship. *Academic Fields/Career Goals:* Nursing. *Award:* Scholarship for use in freshman, sophomore, junior, senior, or graduate year; renewable. Award amount: up to $4000. Number of awards: varies. *Eligibility Requirements:* Applicant must be enrolled or expecting to enroll full- or part-time at a two-year or four-year institution or university; resident of Michigan and studying in Michigan. Available to U.S. citizens. *Application Requirements:* *Deadline:* varies. **Contact:** Program Director, Michigan Bureau of Student Financial Assistance, PO Box 30462, Lansing, MI 48909-7962. E-mail: osg@michigan.gov. Phone: 888-447-2687. Web site: www.michigan.gov/studentaid.

Michigan Promise Scholarship. Scholarship available for students who have taken the state's assessment test. Students who meet or exceed state assessment test may receive $1000 during each of their first two years of college and another $2000 after completing two years with at least a 2.5 GPA. Students who do not meet or exceed state assessment test may receive $4000 after completing two years of postsecondary study with at least a 2.5 GPA. Must be a Michigan resident enrolled at an approved Michigan postsecondary institution. *Award:* Scholarship for use in freshman, sophomore, or junior year; not renewable. Award amount: up to $4000. Number of awards: varies. *Eligibility Requirements:* Applicant must be enrolled or expecting to enroll full- or part-time at a two-year, four-year, or technical institution or university; resident of Michigan and studying in Michigan. Available to U.S. citizens. *Application Requirements:* Test scores. *Deadline:* varies. **Contact:** Program Director, Michigan Bureau of Student Financial Assistance, PO Box 30462, Lansing, MI 48909-7962. E-mail: osg@michigan.gov. Phone: 888-447-2687. Web site: www.michigan.gov/ studentaid.

Michigan Tuition Grant. Need-based program. Students must attend a Michigan private, nonprofit, degree-granting college. Must file the

Free Application for Federal Student Aid and meet the college's academic progress requirements. Deadline: March 1. Must be Michigan resident. Renewable award of $2100. *Award:* Grant for use in freshman, sophomore, junior, senior, or graduate year; renewable. Award amount: $100–$2100. Number of awards: varies. *Eligibility Requirements:* Applicant must be enrolled or expecting to enroll full- or part-time at a two-year or four-year institution or university; resident of Michigan and studying in Michigan. Available to U.S. citizens. *Application Requirements:* Financial need analysis, FAFSA. *Deadline:* March 1. **Contact:** Scholarship and Grant Director, Michigan Bureau of Student Financial Assistance, PO Box 30462, Lansing, MI 48909-7962. E-mail: osg@michigan.gov. Phone: 888-447-2687. Web site: www.michigan.gov/studentaid.

Michigan Veterans Trust Fund Tuition Grant Program. Provides grants for the emergency needs of veterans, tuition grants to dependents of disabled and deceased veterans, and emergency education loans to veterans and their children. Tuition grants are available to sons and daughters of totally disabled or deceased service-connected veterans attending Michigan institutions of higher education. Refer to Web Site: http://www.michigan.gov/textonly/0,2964,7-153-10366_10871-44121—,00.html for details. *Award:* Grant for use in freshman, sophomore, junior, or senior year; renewable. Award amount: up to $2800. Number of awards: varies. *Eligibility Requirements:* Applicant must be age 17-25; enrolled or expecting to enroll full-time at a two-year, four-year, or technical institution or university; resident of Michigan and studying in Michigan. Available to U.S. citizens. Applicant or parent must meet one or more of the following requirements: general military experience; retired from active duty; disabled or killed as a result of military service; prisoner of war; or missing in action. *Application Requirements:* Application. *Deadline:* continuous. **Contact:** Mary Kay Bitten, Scholarship Committee, Michigan Veterans Trust Fund, 3423 North, Martin Luther King Jr. Boulevard, Lansing, MI 48909-7962. Phone: 517-335-1636. Fax: 517-335-1631. Web site: www.michigan.gov/dmva.

Tuition Incentive Program (TIP). Award for Michigan residents who receive or have received Medicaid for required period of time through the Department of Human Services. Scholarship provides two years tuition towards an associate degree at a Michigan college or university and $2000 total assistance for third and fourth years. Must apply before graduating from high school or earning a general education development diploma. *Award:* Grant for use in freshman, sophomore, junior, or senior year; renewable. Award amount: varies. Number of awards: varies. *Eligibility Requirements:* Applicant must be enrolled or expecting to enroll full- or part-time at a two-year or four-year institution or university; resident of Michigan and studying in Michigan. Available to U.S. citizens. *Application Requirements:* Application, Medicaid eligibility for specified period of time. *Deadline:* continuous. **Contact:** Program Director, Michigan Bureau of Student Financial Assistance, PO Box 30462, Lansing, MI 48909-7962. E-mail: osg@michigan.gov. Phone: 888-447-2687. Web site: www.michigan.gov/studentaid.

MINNESOTA

Leadership, Excellence and Dedicated Service Scholarship. Scholarship will award a maximum of thirty $1000 to selected high school seniors who become a member of the Minnesota National Guard and complete the application process. The award recognizes demonstrated leadership, community services and potential for success in the Minnesota National Guard. Deadline: March 15. *Award:* Scholarship for use in freshman year; not renewable. Award amount: $1000. Number of awards: 30. *Eligibility Requirements:* Applicant must be high school student; planning to enroll or expecting to enroll full- or part-time at a two-year, four-year, or technical institution or university and must have an interest in leadership. Applicant or parent of applicant must have employment or volunteer experience in community service. Available to U.S. citizens. Applicant must have served in the Air Force National Guard or Army National Guard. *Application Requirements:* Essay, resume, references, transcript. *Deadline:* March 15. **Contact:**

Barbara O'Reilly, Education Services Officer, Minnesota Department of Military Affairs, 20 West 12th Street, Veterans Services Building, St. Paul, MN 55155-2098. E-mail: barbara.oreilly@mn.ngb.army.mil. Phone: 651-282-4508. Web site: www.minnesotanationalguard.org.

Minnesota Indian Scholarship Program. Applicant must be one quarter Native-American and a resident of Minnesota. Must re-apply for scholarship annually. *Award:* Scholarship for use in freshman, sophomore, junior, senior, or graduate year; renewable. Award amount: $3300–$4000. Number of awards: 6–700. *Eligibility Requirements:* Applicant must be American Indian/Alaska Native; enrolled or expecting to enroll full-time at a two-year, four-year, or technical institution or university; resident of Minnesota and studying in Minnesota. Available to U.S. citizens. *Application Requirements:* Application, financial need analysis. *Deadline:* July 1. **Contact:** Yvonne Novack, Director, Minnesota Indian Scholarship Office, 1500 Highway 36W, Roseville, MN 55113-4266. E-mail: cfl.indianeducation@state.mn.us. Phone: 800-657-3927. Web site: www.mheso.state.mn.us.

Minnesota Reciprocal Agreement. Renewable tuition waiver for Minnesota residents. Waives all or part of non-resident tuition surcharge at public institutions in Iowa, Kansas, Michigan, Missouri, Nebraska, North Dakota, South Dakota, and Wisconsin. Deadline: last day of academic term. *Award:* Scholarship for use in freshman, sophomore, junior, senior, graduate, or postgraduate years; renewable. Award amount: varies. Number of awards: varies. *Eligibility Requirements:* Applicant must be enrolled or expecting to enroll full- or part-time at a two-year, four-year, or technical institution or university; resident of Minnesota and studying in Iowa, Kansas, Michigan, Missouri, Nebraska, North Dakota, South Dakota, or Wisconsin. Available to U.S. citizens. *Application Requirements:* Application. *Deadline:* varies. **Contact:** Ginny Dodds, Manager, Minnesota Higher Education Services Office, 1450 Energy Park Drive, Suite 350, St. Paul, MN 55108-5227. Phone: 651-642-0567 Ext. 1. Web site: www.getreadyforcollege.org.

Minnesota State Grant Program. Need-based grant program available for Minnesota residents attending Minnesota colleges. Student covers 46% of cost with remainder covered by Pell Grant, parent contribution and state grant. Students apply with FAFSA and college administers the program on campus. *Award:* Grant for use in freshman, sophomore, junior, or senior year; not renewable. Award amount: $100–$8372. Number of awards: 71,000–75,000. *Eligibility Requirements:* Applicant must be age 17 and over; enrolled or expecting to enroll full- or part-time at a two-year, four-year, or technical institution or university; resident of Minnesota and studying in Minnesota. Available to U.S. citizens. *Application Requirements:* Application, financial need analysis. *Deadline:* varies. **Contact:** Scholarship Committee, Minnesota Higher Education Services Office, 1450 Energy Park Drive, Suite 350, St. Paul, MN 55108. Phone: 651-642-0567. Web site: www.getreadyforcollege.org.

Minnesota State Veterans' Dependents Assistance Program. Tuition assistance to dependents of persons considered to be prisoner-of-war or missing in action after August 1, 1958. Must be Minnesota resident attending Minnesota two- or four-year school. *Award:* Scholarship for use in freshman, sophomore, junior, or senior year; renewable. Award amount: varies. Number of awards: varies. *Eligibility Requirements:* Applicant must be enrolled or expecting to enroll full- or part-time at a two-year or four-year institution; resident of Minnesota and studying in Minnesota. Available to U.S. citizens. Applicant or parent must meet one or more of the following requirements: general military experience; retired from active duty; disabled or killed as a result of military service; prisoner of war; or missing in action. *Application Requirements:* Application. *Deadline:* continuous. **Contact:** Ginny Dodds, Manager, Minnesota Higher Education Services Office, 1450 Energy Park Drive, Suite 350, Saint Paul, MN 55108-5227. E-mail: ginny.dodds@state.mn.us. Phone: 651-642-0567 Ext. 3410. Fax: 651-642-0675. Web site: www.getreadyforcollege.org.

Postsecondary Child Care Grant Program-Minnesota. Grant available for students not receiving MFIP. Based on financial need. Cannot exceed actual child care costs or maximum award chart (based on income). Must be Minnesota resident. For use at Minnesota two- or four-year school, including public technical colleges. *Award:* Grant for use in freshman, sophomore, junior, or senior year; renewable. Award amount: $100–$2300. Number of awards: varies. *Eligibility Requirements:* Applicant must be enrolled or expecting to enroll full- or part-time at a two-year, four-year, or technical institution or university; resident of Minnesota and studying in Minnesota. Available to U.S. citizens. *Application Requirements:* Application, financial need analysis. *Deadline:* continuous. **Contact:** Ginny Dodds, Manager, Minnesota Higher Education Services Office, 1450 Energy Park Drive, Suite 350, St. Paul, MN 55108-5227. Phone: 651-642-0567 Ext. 3410. Fax: 651-642-0675. Web site: www.getreadyforcollege.org.

Safety Officers' Survivor Grant Program. Grant for eligible survivors of Minnesota public safety officers killed in the line of duty. Safety officers who have been permanently or totally disabled in the line of duty are also eligible. Must be used at a Minnesota institution participating in State Grant Program. Write for details. Must submit proof of death or disability and Public Safety Officers Benefit Fund Certificate. Must apply each year. Can be renewed for four years. *Award:* Grant for use in freshman, sophomore, junior, or senior year; renewable. Award amount: up to $9438. Number of awards: 1. *Eligibility Requirements:* Applicant must be age 23 or under; enrolled or expecting to enroll full- or part-time at a two-year, four-year, or technical institution or university; resident of Minnesota and studying in Minnesota. Applicant or parent of applicant must have employment or volunteer experience in police/firefighting. Available to U.S. citizens. *Application Requirements:* Application, proof of death/disability. *Deadline:* continuous. **Contact:** Ginny Dodds, Manager, Minnesota Higher Education Services Office, 1450 Energy Park Drive, Suite 350, St. Paul, MN 55108-5227. Phone: 651-642-0567 Ext. 1. Web site: www.getreadyforcollege.org.

MISSOURI

ACES/PRIMO Program. Program of the Missouri Area Health Education Centers (MAHEC) And the Primary Care Resource Initiative for Missouri students interested in Primary Care. Applicant should have a minimum GPA of 3.0. *Academic Fields/Career Goals:* Health and Medical Sciences. *Award:* Forgivable loan for use in freshman, sophomore, junior, senior, graduate, or postgraduate years; not renewable. Award amount: $3000–$5000. Number of awards: 100. *Eligibility Requirements:* Applicant must be enrolled or expecting to enroll full- or part-time at a four-year institution or university. Applicant must have 3.0 GPA or higher. Available to U.S. and non-U.S. citizens. *Application Requirements:* Application, driver's license, proof of Missouri residency. *Deadline:* June 30. **Contact:** Jan Shipley, Programs Director, Missouri Department of Health and Senior Services, 1101 Yuane Avenue, Rolla, MO 65401. Phone: 573-364-4797. Fax: 573-364-8972. Web site: www.dhss.mo.gov.

Charles Gallagher Student Assistance Program. Program was the first state grant program to provide need-based grants for Missouri citizens to access Missouri postsecondary education. Must be a full-time undergraduate student at a participating Missouri postsecondary school, working toward a first baccalaureate degree. Must be a Missouri resident and a U.S. citizen. Must maintain satisfactory academic progress as defined by the school. *Award:* Grant for use in freshman, sophomore, junior, or senior year; not renewable. Award amount: $1500. Number of awards: varies. *Eligibility Requirements:* Applicant must be enrolled or expecting to enroll full-time at a two-year, four-year, or technical institution or university; resident of Missouri and studying in Missouri. Available to U.S. citizens. *Application Requirements:* Financial need analysis, FAFSA. *Deadline:* April 1. **Contact:** MDHE Information Center, Missouri Department of Higher Education, 3515 Amazonas Drive, Jefferson City, MO 65109-5717. E-mail: info@dhe.mo.gov. Phone: 800-473-6757 Ext. 1. Fax: 573-751-6635. Web site: www.dhe.mo.gov.

Environmental Education Scholarship Program (EESP). Scholarship to minority and other underrepresented students pursuing a bachelor's or master's degree in an environmental course of study.

Must be a Missouri resident having a cumulative high school GPA of 3.0 or if enrolled in college, must have cumulative GPA of 2.5. Deadline: June 1. *Academic Fields/Career Goals:* Environmental Science. *Award:* Scholarship for use in freshman, sophomore, junior, senior, or graduate year; not renewable. Award amount: varies. Number of awards: varies. *Eligibility Requirements:* Applicant must be American Indian/Alaska Native, Asian/Pacific Islander, Black (non-Hispanic), or Hispanic; enrolled or expecting to enroll full-time at a four-year institution or university and resident of Missouri. Applicant must have 3.0 GPA or higher. Available to U.S. citizens. *Application Requirements:* Application, essay, references, transcript. *Deadline:* June 1. **Contact:** Toni Clark, Office Support, Missouri Department of Natural Resources, Environmental Educational Scholarship Program, PO Box 176, Jefferson City, MO 65102. Phone: 800-361-4827. Web site: www.dnr.mo.gov.

Lillie Lois Ford Scholarship Fund. Two awards of $1000 each are given each year to one boy and one girl. Applicant must have attended a full session of Missouri Boys/Girls State or Missouri Cadet Patrol Academy. Must be a Missouri resident of age below 21, attending an accredited college/university as a full-time student. Must be an unmarried descendant of a veteran having served at least 90 days on active duty in the Army, Air Force, Navy, Marine Corps or Coast Guard of the United States. Deadline: April 20. *Award:* Scholarship for use in freshman year; not renewable. Award amount: $1000. Number of awards: 2. *Eligibility Requirements:* Applicant must be high school student; age 21 or under; planning to enroll or expecting to enroll full-time at a four-year institution or university; single and resident of Missouri. Available to U.S. citizens. Applicant or parent must meet one or more of the following requirements: general military experience; retired from active duty; disabled or killed as a result of military service; prisoner of war; or missing in action. *Application Requirements:* Application, financial need analysis, test scores, copy of the veteran's discharge certificate. *Deadline:* April 20. **Contact:** John Doane, Chairman, Education and Scholarship Committee, American Legion, Department of Missouri, PO Box 179, Jefferson City, MO 65102-0179. Phone: 417-924-8186. Web site: www.missourilegion.org.

Marguerite Ross Barnett Memorial Scholarship. Scholarship was established for students who are employed while attending school part-time. Must be enrolled at least half-time but less than full-time at a participating Missouri postsecondary school, be employed and compensated for at least 20 hours per week, be 18 years of age, be a Missouri resident and a U.S. citizen or an eligible non-citizen. *Award:* Scholarship for use in freshman, sophomore, junior, or senior year; renewable. Award amount: varies. Number of awards: varies. *Eligibility Requirements:* Applicant must be age 18 and over; enrolled or expecting to enroll part-time at a two-year, four-year, or technical institution or university; resident of Missouri and studying in Missouri. Available to U.S. and non-U.S. citizens. *Application Requirements:* Application, financial need analysis. *Deadline:* varies. **Contact:** MDHE Information Center, Missouri Department of Higher Education, 3515 Amazonas Drive, Jefferson City, MO 65109-5717. E-mail: info@dhe.mo.gov. Phone: 800-473-6757 Ext. 1. Fax: 573-751-6635. Web site: www.dhe.mo.gov.

Missouri College Guarantee Program. Grant is based on demonstrated financial need, as well as high school and college academic achievement. Must have a high school GPA of 2.5 or higher, be enrolled full-time at a participating Missouri postsecondary school, be a Missouri resident and a U.S. citizen. Must have participated in high school extracurricular activities. *Award:* Scholarship for use in freshman, sophomore, junior, or senior year; not renewable. Award amount: varies. Number of awards: varies. *Eligibility Requirements:* Applicant must be enrolled or expecting to enroll full-time at a two-year or four-year institution or university; resident of Missouri and studying in Missouri. Applicant must have 2.5 GPA or higher. Available to U.S. citizens. *Application Requirements:* Financial need analysis, test scores, FAFSA. *Deadline:* varies. **Contact:** MDHE Information Center, Missouri Department of Higher Education, 3515 Amazonas Drive,

Jefferson City, MO 65109-5717. E-mail: info@dhe.mo.gov. Phone: 800-473-6757 Ext. 1. Fax: 573-751-6635. Web site: www.dhe.mo.gov.

Missouri Higher Education Academic Scholarship (Bright Flight). Program encourages top-ranked high school seniors to attend approved Missouri postsecondary schools. Must be a Missouri resident and a U.S. citizen. Must have a composite score on the ACT or the SAT in the top three percent of all Missouri students taking those tests. Annual scholarship of $2000 is awarded in two payments of $1000 each semester. *Award:* Scholarship for use in freshman, sophomore, junior, or senior year; renewable. Award amount: $2000. Number of awards: varies. *Eligibility Requirements:* Applicant must be high school student; planning to enroll or expecting to enroll full-time at a two-year, four-year, or technical institution or university; resident of Missouri and studying in Missouri. Available to U.S. citizens. *Application Requirements:* Test scores. *Deadline:* varies. **Contact:** MDHE Information Center, Missouri Department of Higher Education, 3515 Amazonas Drive, Jefferson City, MO 65109-5717. E-mail: info@dhe.mo.gov. Phone: 800-473-6757 Ext. 1. Fax: 573-751-6635. Web site: www.dhe.mo.gov.

Missouri Minority Teaching Scholarship. Scholarship is competitive and is a renewable award of $3000 for up to four years. Must be a Missouri resident, be African American, Asian American, Hispanic American, or Native American, be a high school senior, college student or returning adult. For details refer to Web Site: http://www.dese.mo.gov/divteachqual/scholarships/mmts_cover.pdf. *Academic Fields/Career Goals:* Education. *Award:* Scholarship for use in freshman, sophomore, junior, or senior year; renewable. Award amount: $3000. Number of awards: varies. *Eligibility Requirements:* Applicant must be American Indian/Alaska Native, Asian/Pacific Islander, Black (non-Hispanic), or Hispanic; enrolled or expecting to enroll full-time at a four-year institution or university; resident of Missouri and studying in Missouri. Applicant must have 3.0 GPA or higher. Available to U.S. citizens. *Application Requirements:* Application, essay, financial need analysis, resume, references, test scores, transcript. *Deadline:* February 15. **Contact:** Laura Harrison, Administrative Assistant, Missouri Department of Elementary and Secondary Education, PO Box 480, Jefferson City, MO 65102-0480. E-mail: laura.harrison@dese.mo.gov. Phone: 573-751-1668. Fax: 573-526-3580. Web site: www.dese.mo.gov.

Missouri Teacher Education Scholarship (General). Nonrenewable award for Missouri high school seniors or Missouri resident college students. Must attend approved teacher training program at a participating Missouri institution. Must rank in top 15 percent of high school class on ACT/SAT. Merit-based award. Recipients must commit to teach in Missouri for five years at a public elementary or secondary school or award must be repaid. *Academic Fields/Career Goals:* Education. *Award:* Scholarship for use in freshman, sophomore, junior, or senior year; not renewable. Award amount: up to $2000. Number of awards: 200–240. *Eligibility Requirements:* Applicant must be enrolled or expecting to enroll full-time at a two-year or four-year institution or university; resident of Missouri and studying in Missouri. Applicant must have 3.5 GPA or higher. Available to U.S. citizens. *Application Requirements:* Application, essay, resume, references, test scores, transcript. *Deadline:* February 15. **Contact:** Laura Harrison, Administrative Assistant II, Missouri Department of Elementary and Secondary Education, PO Box 480, Jefferson City, MO 65102-0480. E-mail: laura.harrison@dese.mo.gov. Phone: 573-751-1668. Fax: 573-526-3580. Web site: www.dese.mo.gov.

Primary Care Resource Initiative for Missouri Loan Program. Forgivable loans for Missouri residents attending Missouri institutions pursuing a degree as a primary care physician or dentist, studying for a bachelors degree as a dental hygienist, or a master of science degree in nursing leading to certification as an Advanced Practice Nurse. To be forgiven participant must work in a Missouri health professional shortage area. *Academic Fields/Career Goals:* Dental Health/Services; Health and Medical Sciences; Nursing. *Award:* Forgivable loan for use in freshman, sophomore, junior, senior, graduate, or postgraduate years; not renewable. Award amount: $3000–$25,000. Number of awards: 100. *Eligibility Requirements:* Applicant must be

enrolled or expecting to enroll full- or part-time at a four-year institution or university; resident of Missouri and studying in Missouri. Applicant must have 3.0 GPA or higher. Available to U.S. and non-U.S. citizens. *Application Requirements:* Application, driver's license, proof of Missouri residency. *Deadline:* June 30. **Contact:** Kristie Frank, Health Program Representative, Missouri Department of Health and Senior Services, PO Box 570, Jefferson City, MO 65102-0570. E-mail: frank@dhss.mo.gov. Phone: 800-891-7415. Fax: 573-522-8146. Web site: www.dhss.mo.gov.

Robert C. Byrd Honors Scholarship-Missouri. Award for Missouri high school seniors who are residents of Missouri. The amount of the award per student each year depends on the amount the state is allotted by the U.S. Department of Education. The highest amount of award per student is $1500. Students must rank in top 10 percent of high school class and score in top 10 percent of ACT test. *Award:* Scholarship for use in freshman year; renewable. Award amount: $1100–$1500. Number of awards: 100–150. *Eligibility Requirements:* Applicant must be high school student; planning to enroll or expecting to enroll full-time at a two-year, four-year, or technical institution or university and resident of Missouri. Applicant must have 3.5 GPA or higher. Available to U.S. citizens. *Application Requirements:* Application, test scores, transcript. *Deadline:* April 15. **Contact:** Laura Harrison, Administrative Assistant II, Missouri Department of Elementary and Secondary Education, PO Box 480, Jefferson City, MO 65102-0480. E-mail: laura.harrison@dese.mo.gov. Phone: 573-751-1668. Fax: 573-526-3580. Web site: www.dese.mo.gov.

Teacher Education Scholarship. The scholarship is a competitive, one-time, nonrenewable award of $2000 to be used in one academic year. Applicants must be a Missouri resident and a high school senior or student enrolled fulltime at a community or four-year college or university in Missouri. Deadline: February 15. *Award:* Scholarship for use in freshman, sophomore, junior, or senior year; not renewable. Award amount: $2000. Number of awards: varies. *Eligibility Requirements:* Applicant must be enrolled or expecting to enroll full- or part-time at a four-year institution or university; resident of Missouri and studying in Missouri. Available to U.S. citizens. *Application Requirements:* Application, essay, references, test scores, transcript. *Deadline:* February 15. **Contact:** Laura Harrison, Administrative Assistant, Missouri State Department of Elementary/Secondary Education, 205 Jefferson Street, Seventh Floor, PO Box 480, Jefferson City, MO 65102. E-mail: Laura.Harrison@dese.mo.gov. Phone: 573-751-1668. Fax: 573-526-3580. Web site: www.dese.mo.gov.

NEBRASKA

Nebraska State Grant. Available to undergraduates attending a participating postsecondary institution in Nebraska. Available to Pell Grant recipients only. Nebraska residency required. Awards determined by each participating institution. Contact financial aid office at institution for application and additional information. *Award:* Grant for use in freshman, sophomore, junior, or senior year; not renewable. Award amount: $100–$1032. Number of awards: varies. *Eligibility Requirements:* Applicant must be enrolled or expecting to enroll full- or part-time at a two-year, four-year, or technical institution or university; resident of Nebraska and studying in Nebraska. Available to U.S. citizens. *Application Requirements:* Application, financial need analysis. *Deadline:* continuous. **Contact:** J. Ritchie Morrow, Financial Aid Coordinator, State of Nebraska Coordinating Commission for Postsecondary Education, 140 North Eighth Street, Suite 300, PO Box 95005, Lincoln, NE 68509-5005. E-mail: rmorrow@ccpe.st.ne.us. Phone: 402-471-0032. Fax: 402-471-2886. Web site: www.ccpe.state.ne.us.

NORTH DAKOTA

North Dakota Indian Scholarship Program. The scholarship assists American Indian students in obtaining a college education by providing scholarships ranging in amount from $500 to $2000 per year. The scholarship is based upon scholastic ability and unmet financial need. Must be a resident of North Dakota, must be enrolled full-time, and may not have a GPA below 2.0. *Award:* Scholarship for use in fresh-man, sophomore, junior, senior, or graduate year; renewable. Award amount: $500–$2000. Number of awards: 150–175. *Eligibility Requirements:* Applicant must be American Indian/Alaska Native; enrolled or expecting to enroll full-time at a two-year or four-year institution or university; resident of North Dakota and studying in North Dakota. Applicant must have 3.5 GPA or higher. Available to U.S. citizens. *Application Requirements:* Application, financial need analysis, transcript, proof of tribal enrollment, budget completed by a financial aid officer at the institution being attended. *Deadline:* July 15. **Contact:** Rhonda Schauer, Coordinator of American Indian Higher Education, State of North Dakota, 919 South Seventh Street, Suite 300, Bismarck, ND 58504-5881. E-mail: rhonda.schauer@ndus.nodak.edu. Phone: 701-328-9661. Web site: www.ndus.nodak.edu.

North Dakota Scholars Program. Provides scholarships equal to cost of tuition at the public colleges in North Dakota for North Dakota residents. Must score at or above the 95th percentile on ACT and rank in top twenty percent of high school graduation class. Must take ACT in fall. For high school seniors with a minimum 3.5 GPA. Deadline: October or June ACT test date. *Award:* Scholarship for use in freshman year; renewable. Award amount: varies. Number of awards: 15–20. *Eligibility Requirements:* Applicant must be high school student; planning to enroll or expecting to enroll full-time at a two-year or four-year institution or university; resident of North Dakota and studying in North Dakota. Applicant must have 3.5 GPA or higher. Available to U.S. citizens. *Application Requirements:* Application, references, test scores, transcript. *Deadline:* varies. **Contact:** Peggy Wipf, Director of Financial Aid, State of North Dakota, 600 East Boulevard Avenue, Department 215, Bismarck, ND 58505-0230. E-mail: peggy.wipf@ndus.nodak.edu. Phone: 701-328-4114. Web site: www.ndus.nodak.edu.

North Dakota State Student Incentive Grant Program. Aids North Dakota residents attending an approved college or university in North Dakota. Must be enrolled in a program of at least nine months in length. Must be a U.S. citizen. Deadline: March 15. *Award:* Grant for use in freshman, sophomore, junior, or senior year; renewable. Award amount: up to $600. Number of awards: 2500–2600. *Eligibility Requirements:* Applicant must be enrolled or expecting to enroll full-time at a two-year or four-year institution or university; resident of North Dakota and studying in North Dakota. Available to U.S. citizens. *Application Requirements:* Application, financial need analysis. *Deadline:* March 15. **Contact:** Peggy Wipf, Director of Financial Aid, State of North Dakota, 600 East Boulevard Avenue, Department 215, Bismarck, ND 58505-0230. Phone: 701-328-4114. Web site: www.ndus.nodak.edu.

OHIO

Accountancy Board of Ohio Educational Assistance Program. Program intended for minority students or students with financial need. Applicant must be enrolled as accounting major at an accredited Ohio college or university in a five-year degree program. Applicant must be an Ohio resident. Please refer to Web site for further details: http://acc.ohio.gov/educasst.html. *Academic Fields/Career Goals:* Accounting. *Award:* Scholarship for use in sophomore, junior, or senior year; not renewable. Award amount: $7700. Number of awards: varies. *Eligibility Requirements:* Applicant must be enrolled or expecting to enroll full- or part-time at a four-year institution or university; resident of Ohio and studying in Ohio. Available to U.S. citizens. *Application Requirements:* Application, financial need analysis, transcript, FAFSA. *Deadline:* November 15. **Contact:** Kay Sedgmer, Scholarship Secretary, Accountancy Board of Ohio, Accountancy Board of Ohio, 77 South High Street, 18th Floor, Columbus, OH 43215-6128. E-mail: kay.sedgmer@acc.state.oh.us. Phone: 614-466-4135. Fax: 614-466-2628. Web site: acc.ohio.gov.

Ohio Academic Scholarship Program. Award for academically outstanding Ohio residents planning to attend an approved Ohio college. Must be a high school senior intending to enroll full-time. Award is renewable for up to four years. Must rank in upper quarter of class or have a minimum GPA of 3.5. *Award:* Scholarship for use in freshman, sophomore, junior, or senior year; renewable. Award amount: $2205. Number of awards: 1000. *Eligibility Requirements:* Applicant must be high school student; planning to enroll or expecting to enroll full-time at a two-year or four-year institution; resident of Ohio and studying in Ohio. Applicant must have 3.5 GPA or higher. Available to U.S. citizens. *Application Requirements:* Application, test scores, transcript. *Deadline:* February 23. **Contact:** Jathiya Abdullah, Program Administrator, Ohio Board of Regents, 30 East Broad Street, 36th Floor, Columbus, OH 43215-3414. E-mail: jabdullah@regents.state.oh.us. Phone: 614-752-9528. Fax: 614-752-5903. Web site: www.regents.ohio.gov.

Ohio Environmental Science & Engineering Scholarships. Merit-based, non-renewable, tuition-only scholarships given to undergraduate students admitted to Ohio state or private colleges and universities who can demonstrate their knowledge and commitment to careers in environmental sciences or environmental engineering. Deadline: June 1. *Academic Fields/Career Goals:* Environmental Science. *Award:* Scholarship for use in senior year; not renewable. Award amount: $1250–$2500. Number of awards: 18. *Eligibility Requirements:* Applicant must be enrolled or expecting to enroll full- or part-time at a two-year or four-year institution or university; resident of Ohio and studying in Ohio. Applicant must have 3.0 GPA or higher. Available to U.S. citizens. *Application Requirements:* Application, essay, resume, references, self-addressed stamped envelope, transcript. *Deadline:* June 1. **Contact:** Mr. Lynn E. Elfner, Chief Executive Officer, Ohio Academy of Science/Ohio Environmental Education Fund, 1500 West Third Avenue, Suite 228, Columbus, OH 43212-2817. E-mail: oas@iwaynet.net. Phone: 614-488-2228. Fax: 614-488-7629. Web site: www.ohiosci.org.

Ohio Instructional Grant. Award for low- and middle-income Ohio residents attending an approved college or school in Ohio or Pennsylvania. Must be enrolled full-time and have financial need. May be used for any course of study except theology. *Award:* Grant for use in freshman, sophomore, junior, or senior year; renewable. Award amount: $78–$5466. Number of awards: varies. *Eligibility Requirements:* Applicant must be enrolled or expecting to enroll full-time at a two-year or four-year institution or university; resident of Ohio and studying in Ohio or Pennsylvania. Available to U.S. citizens. *Application Requirements:* Application, financial need analysis. *Deadline:* October 1. **Contact:** Lamar Burch, Program Administrator, Ohio Board of Regents, 30 East Broad Street, 36th Floor, Columbus, OH 43215-3414. E-mail: lburch@regents.state.oh.us. Phone: 614-752-9489. Fax: 614-752-5903. Web site: www.regents.ohio.gov.

Ohio Missing in Action and Prisoners of War Orphans Scholarship. Renewable award aids children of Vietnam conflict servicemen who have been classified as missing in action or prisoner of war. Applicants must be under the age of 25 and be enrolled full-time at an Ohio college. Full tuition awards. Dollar value of each award varies. *Award:* Scholarship for use in freshman, sophomore, junior, or senior year; renewable. Award amount: varies. Number of awards: 1–5. *Eligibility Requirements:* Applicant must be age 25 or under; enrolled or expecting to enroll full-time at a four-year institution or university; resident of Ohio and studying in Ohio. Available to U.S. citizens. Applicant or parent must meet one or more of the following requirements: general military experience; retired from active duty; disabled or killed as a result of military service; prisoner of war; or missing in action. *Application Requirements:* Application. *Deadline:* July 1. **Contact:** Jathiya Abdullah, Program Administrator, Ohio Board of Regents, 30 East Broad Street, 36th Floor, Columbus, OH 43215-3414. E-mail: jabdullah@regents.state.oh.us. Phone: 614-752-9528. Fax: 614-752-5903. Web site: www.regents.ohio.gov.

Ohio National Guard Scholarship Program. Scholarships are for undergraduate studies at an approved Ohio postsecondary institution. Applicants must enlist for six years of Selective Service Reserve Duty in the Ohio National Guard. Scholarship pays 100% instructional and general fees for public institutions and an average of cost of public schools is available for private schools. Must be 18 years of age or older. Award is renewable. Deadlines: July 1, November 1, February

1, April 1. *Award:* Scholarship for use in freshman, sophomore, junior, or senior year; renewable. Award amount: up to $3000. Number of awards: 3500–8000. *Eligibility Requirements:* Applicant must be age 18 and over; enrolled or expecting to enroll full- or part-time at a two-year, four-year, or technical institution or university and studying in Ohio. Available to U.S. citizens. Applicant must have served in the Air Force National Guard or Army National Guard. *Application Requirements:* Application. *Deadline:* varies. **Contact:** Toni Davis, Grants Administrator, Ohio National Guard, 2825 West Dublin Granville Road, Columbus, OH 43235-2789. E-mail: toni.davis@tagoh.gov. Phone: 614-336-7032. Fax: 614-336-7318. Web site: www.ongsp.org.

Ohio Safety Officers College Memorial Fund. Renewable award covering up to full tuition is available to children and surviving spouses of peace officers and fire fighters killed in the line of duty in any state. Children must be under 26 years of age. Dollar value of each award varies. Must be an Ohio resident and enroll full-time or part-time at an Ohio college or university. *Award:* Scholarship for use in freshman, sophomore, junior, or senior year; renewable. Award amount: varies. Number of awards: 50–65. *Eligibility Requirements:* Applicant must be age 25 or under; enrolled or expecting to enroll full- or part-time at a two-year or four-year institution or university; resident of Ohio and studying in Ohio. Applicant or parent of applicant must have employment or volunteer experience in police/firefighting. Available to U.S. citizens. *Application Requirements: Deadline:* continuous. **Contact:** Barbara Thoma, Program Administrator, Ohio Board of Regents, 30 East Broad Street, 36th Floor, Columbus, OH 43215-3414. E-mail: bthoma@regents.state.oh.us. Phone: 614-752-9535. Fax: 614-752-5903. Web site: www.regents.ohio.gov.

Ohio Student Choice Grant Program. Renewable award available to Ohio residents attending private colleges within the state. Must be enrolled full-time in a bachelor's degree program. Do not apply to state. Dollar value of each award varies. Check with financial aid office of college. *Award:* Grant for use in freshman, sophomore, junior, or senior year; renewable. Award amount: up to $900. Number of awards: varies. *Eligibility Requirements:* Applicant must be enrolled or expecting to enroll full-time at a four-year institution or university; resident of Ohio and studying in Ohio. Available to U.S. citizens. *Application Requirements: Deadline:* continuous. **Contact:** Barbara Thoma, Program Administrator, Ohio Board of Regents, 30 East Broad Street, 36th Floor, Columbus, OH 43215-3414. E-mail: bthoma@regents.state.oh.us. Phone: 614-752-9535. Fax: 614-752-5903. Web site: www.regents.ohio.gov.

Ohio War Orphans Scholarship. Aids Ohio residents attending an eligible college in Ohio. Must be between the ages of 16-25, the child of a disabled or deceased veteran, and enrolled full-time. Renewable up to five years. Amount of award varies. Must include Form DD214. *Award:* Scholarship for use in freshman, sophomore, junior, or senior year; renewable. Award amount: varies. Number of awards: 300–450. *Eligibility Requirements:* Applicant must be age 16-25; enrolled or expecting to enroll full-time at a two-year or four-year institution or university; resident of Ohio and studying in Ohio. Available to U.S. citizens. Applicant or parent must meet one or more of the following requirements: general military experience; retired from active duty; disabled or killed as a result of military service; prisoner of war; or missing in action. *Application Requirements:* Application. *Deadline:* July 1. **Contact:** Jathiya Abdullah, Program Administrator, Ohio Board of Regents, 30 East Broad Street, 36th Floor, Columbus, OH 43215-3414. E-mail: jabdullah@regents.state.oh.us. Phone: 614-752-9528. Fax: 614-752-5903. Web site: www.regents.ohio.gov.

Part-time Student Instructional Grant. Renewable grants for part-time undergraduates who are Ohio residents. Award amounts vary. Must attend an Ohio institution. *Award:* Grant for use in freshman, sophomore, junior, or senior year; renewable. Award amount: varies. Number of awards: varies. *Eligibility Requirements:* Applicant must be enrolled or expecting to enroll part-time at a two-year or four-year institution or university; resident of Ohio and studying in Ohio. Available to U.S. citizens. *Application Requirements:* Application, financial need analysis. *Deadline:* continuous. **Contact:** Barbara Thoma, Program

Administrator, Ohio Board of Regents, 30 East Broad Street, 36th Floor, Columbus, OH 43215-3414. E-mail: bmethene@regents.state.oh.us. Phone: 614-752-9535. Fax: 614-752-5903. Web site: www.regents.ohio.gov.

Robert C. Byrd Honors Scholarship-Ohio. Renewable award for graduating high school seniors who demonstrate outstanding academic achievement. Each Ohio high school receives applications by January of each year. School can submit one application for every 200 students in the senior class. Deadline: second Friday in March. *Award:* Scholarship for use in freshman, sophomore, junior, or senior year; renewable. Award amount: up to $1500. Number of awards: varies. *Eligibility Requirements:* Applicant must be high school student; planning to enroll or expecting to enroll full-time at a two-year or four-year institution or university; resident of Ohio and studying in Ohio. Applicant must have 3.5 GPA or higher. Available to U.S. citizens. *Application Requirements:* Application, test scores. *Deadline:* varies. **Contact:** Mr. Mark Lynskey, Program Administrator, Ohio Department of Education, 25 South Front Street, 2nd Floor, Columbus, OH 43215. Phone: 614-466-2650. Web site: www.ode.state.oh.us.

Student Workforce Development Grant Program. Provides tuition assistance to Ohio students. Students must be pursuing an associate or bachelor's degree and must not have been enrolled full-time in a private career school prior to July 1, 2000. *Award:* Grant for use in freshman, sophomore, junior, or senior year; renewable. Award amount: $300. Number of awards: 1. *Eligibility Requirements:* Applicant must be enrolled or expecting to enroll full-time at a four-year institution or university; resident of Ohio and studying in Ohio. Available to U.S. citizens. *Application Requirements: Deadline:* varies. **Contact:** Barbara Thoma, Program Administrator, Ohio Board of Regents, 30 East Broad Street, 36th Floor, Columbus, OH 43215-3414. E-mail: bthoma@regents.state.oh.us. Phone: 614-752-9535. Fax: 614-752-5903. Web site: www.regents.ohio.gov.

OKLAHOMA

Academic Scholars Program. The program encourages students of high academic ability to attend institutions in Oklahoma. Renewable up to four years. ACT or SAT scores must fall between 99.5 and 100th percentiles, or applicant must be designated as a National Merit scholar or finalist. Oklahoma public institutions can also select institutional nominees. *Award:* Scholarship for use in freshman, sophomore, junior, or senior year; renewable. Award amount: $1800–$5500. Number of awards: varies. *Eligibility Requirements:* Applicant must be high school student; planning to enroll or expecting to enroll full-time at a two-year or four-year institution or university and studying in Oklahoma. Available to U.S. citizens. *Application Requirements:* Application, test scores, transcript. *Deadline:* continuous. **Contact:** Scholarship Programs Coordinator, Oklahoma State Regents for Higher Education, PO Box 108850, Oklahoma City, OK 73101-8850. E-mail: studentinfo@osrhe.edu. Phone: 800-858-1840. Fax: 405-225-9230. Web site: www.okhighered.org.

Future Teacher Scholarship-Oklahoma. Open to outstanding Oklahoma high school graduates who agree to teach in shortage areas. Must rank in top 15 percent of graduating class or score above 85th percentile on ACT or similar test, or be accepted in an educational program. Students nominated by institution. Reapply to renew. Must attend college/university in Oklahoma. Deadline varies. *Academic Fields/Career Goals:* Education. *Award:* Scholarship for use in freshman, sophomore, junior, senior, or graduate year; renewable. Award amount: $500–$1500. Number of awards: varies. *Eligibility Requirements:* Applicant must be enrolled or expecting to enroll full- or part-time at a two-year or four-year institution or university; resident of Oklahoma and studying in Oklahoma. Available to U.S. and non-U.S. citizens. *Application Requirements:* Application, essay, test scores, transcript. *Deadline:* varies. **Contact:** Scholarship Programs Coordinator, Oklahoma State Regents for Higher Education, PO Box 108850, Oklahoma City, OK 73101-8850. E-mail: studentinfo@osrhe.edu. Phone: 800-858-1840. Fax: 405-225-9230. Web site: www.okhighered.org.

Oklahoma Tuition Aid Grant. Award for Oklahoma residents enrolled at an Oklahoma institution at least part time each semester in a degree program. May be enrolled in two- or four-year or approved vocational-technical institution. Award of up to $1000 per year. Application is made through FAFSA. *Award:* Grant for use in freshman, sophomore, junior, or senior year; renewable. Award amount: $200–$1000. Number of awards: 23,000. *Eligibility Requirements:* Applicant must be enrolled or expecting to enroll full- or part-time at a two-year, four-year, or technical institution or university; resident of Oklahoma and studying in Oklahoma. Available to U.S. citizens. *Application Requirements:* Application, financial need analysis, FAFSA. *Deadline:* varies. **Contact:** Alicia Harris, Scholarship Programs Coordinator, Oklahoma State Regents for Higher Education, PO Box 3020, Oklahoma City, OK 73101-3020. E-mail: aharris@osrhe.edu. Phone: 405-225-9131. Fax: 405-225-9230. Web site: www.okhighered.org.

Regional University Baccalaureate Scholarship. Renewable award for Oklahoma residents attending one of 11 participating Oklahoma public universities. Must have an ACT composite score of at least 30 or be a National Merit semifinalist or commended student. In addition to the award amount, each recipient will receive a resident tuition waiver from the institution. Must maintain a 3.25 GPA. Deadlines vary depending upon the institution attended. *Award:* Scholarship for use in freshman, sophomore, junior, or senior year; renewable. Award amount: $3000. Number of awards: varies. *Eligibility Requirements:* Applicant must be enrolled or expecting to enroll full-time at an institution or university; resident of Oklahoma and studying in Oklahoma. Available to U.S. citizens. *Application Requirements:* Application. *Deadline:* varies. **Contact:** Alicia Harris, Scholarship Programs Coordinator, Oklahoma State Regents for Higher Education, PO Box 108850, Oklahoma City, OK 73101-8850. E-mail: aharris@osrhe.edu. Phone: 405-225-9131. Fax: 405-225-9230. Web site: www.okhighered.org.

Robert C. Byrd Honors Scholarship-Oklahoma. Scholarships available to high school seniors. Applicants must be U.S. citizens or national, or be permanent residents of the United States. Must be legal residents of Oklahoma. Must have a minimum ACT composite score of 32 and/or a minimum SAT combined score of 1420 and/or 2130 or a minimum GED score of 700. Deadline: March 16. Application URL: http://www.sde.state.ok.us/pro/Byrd/application.pdf. *Award:* Scholarship for use in freshman year; not renewable. Award amount: $1500. Number of awards: 10. *Eligibility Requirements:* Applicant must be high school student; planning to enroll or expecting to enroll full-time at a four-year institution or university and resident of Oklahoma. Available to U.S. citizens. *Application Requirements:* Application, essay, references, transcript. *Deadline:* March 9. **Contact:** Certification Specialist, Oklahoma State Department of Education, 2500 North Lincoln Boulevard, Suite 212, Oklahoma City, OK 73105-4599. Phone: 405-521-2808. Web site: www.sde.state.ok.us.

SOUTH DAKOTA

Haines Memorial Scholarship. One-time scholarship for South Dakota public university students who are sophomores, juniors, or seniors having at least a 2.5 GPA and majoring in a teacher education program. Must include resume with application. Must be South Dakota resident. *Academic Fields/Career Goals:* Education. *Award:* Scholarship for use in sophomore, junior, or senior year; not renewable. Award amount: $2150. Number of awards: 1. *Eligibility Requirements:* Applicant must be enrolled or expecting to enroll full-time at an institution or university; resident of South Dakota and studying in South Dakota. Applicant must have 2.5 GPA or higher. Available to U.S. citizens. *Application Requirements:* Application, autobiography, essay, resume. *Deadline:* February 9. **Contact:** Janelle Toman, Director of Institutional Research, South Dakota Board of Regents, 306 East Capitol Avenue, Suite 200, Pierre, SD 57501-2545. E-mail: info@sdbor.edu. Phone: 605-773-3455. Fax: 605-773-2422. Web site: www.sdbor.edu.

South Dakota Opportunity Scholarship. The scholarship is worth up to $5000 over four years to students who take a rigorous college-prep curriculum while in high school and stay in the state for their postsecondary education. *Award:* Scholarship for use in freshman,

sophomore, junior, or senior year; renewable. Award amount: up to $1000. Number of awards: 1000. *Eligibility Requirements:* Applicant must be enrolled or expecting to enroll full-time at a two-year, four-year, or technical institution or university; resident of South Dakota and studying in South Dakota. Applicant must have 3.0 GPA or higher. Available to U.S. citizens. *Application Requirements:* Application, test scores, transcript. *Deadline:* September 1. **Contact:** Janelle Toman, Director of Institutional Research, South Dakota Board of Regents, 306 East Capitol Avenue, Suite 200, Pierre, SD 57501-2545. E-mail: info@sdbor.edu. Phone: 605-773-3455. Fax: 605-773-2422. Web site: www.sdbor.edu.

WISCONSIN

Handicapped Student Grant-Wisconsin. One-time award available to residents of Wisconsin who have severe or profound hearing or visual impairment. Must be enrolled at least half-time at a nonprofit institution. If the handicap prevents the student from attending a Wisconsin school, the award may be used out-of-state in a specialized college. Refer to Web site for further details: http://www.heab.state.wi.us. *Award:* Grant for use in freshman, sophomore, junior, or senior year; not renewable. Award amount: $250–$1800. Number of awards: varies. *Eligibility Requirements:* Applicant must be enrolled or expecting to enroll full- or part-time at a four-year institution or university and resident of Wisconsin. Applicant must be hearing impaired or visually impaired. Available to U.S. citizens. *Application Requirements:* Application, financial need analysis. *Deadline:* continuous. **Contact:** Sandy Thomas, Program Coordinator, Wisconsin Higher Educational Aids Board, PO Box 7885, Madison, WI 53707-7885. E-mail: sandy.thomas@heab.state.wi.us. Phone: 608-266-0888. Fax: 608-267-2808. Web site: www.heab.state.wi.us.

Minority Undergraduate Retention Grant-Wisconsin. The grant provides financial assistance to African-American, Native-American, Hispanic, and former citizens of Laos, Vietnam, and Cambodia, for study in Wisconsin. Must be Wisconsin resident, enrolled at least half-time in Wisconsin Technical College System schools, non-profit independent colleges and universities, and tribal colleges. Refer to Web site for further details: http://www.heab.state.wi.us. *Award:* Grant for use in sophomore, junior, senior, or graduate year; not renewable. Award amount: $250–$2500. Number of awards: varies. *Eligibility Requirements:* Applicant must be American Indian/Alaska Native, Asian/Pacific Islander, Black (non-Hispanic), or Hispanic; enrolled or expecting to enroll full- or part-time at a two-year, four-year, or technical institution or university; resident of Wisconsin and studying in Wisconsin. Available to U.S. and non-U.S. citizens. *Application Requirements:* Application, financial need analysis. *Deadline:* continuous. **Contact:** Mary Lou Kuzdas, Program Coordinator, Wisconsin Higher Educational Aids Board, PO Box 7885, Madison, WI 53707-7885. E-mail: mary.kuzdas@heab.state.wi.us. Phone: 608-267-2212. Fax: 608-267-2808. Web site: www.heab.state.wi.us.

Nursing Student Loan Program. The program provides forgivable loans to students enrolled in a nursing program. Must be Wisconsin residents studying in Wisconsin. Deadline is last day on which the student is enrolled. Refer to Web site for further details: http://www.heab.state.wi.us. *Academic Fields/Career Goals:* Nursing. *Award:* Forgivable loan for use in freshman, sophomore, junior, or senior year; renewable. Award amount: $250–$3000. Number of awards: 150–1800. *Eligibility Requirements:* Applicant must be enrolled or expecting to enroll full- or part-time at a two-year, four-year, or technical institution or university; resident of Wisconsin and studying in Wisconsin. Available to U.S. citizens. *Application Requirements:* Application, financial need analysis. *Deadline:* varies. **Contact:** Cindy Lehrman, Program Coordinator, Wisconsin Higher Educational Aids Board, PO Box 7885, Madison, WI 53707-7885. E-mail: cindy.lehrman@heab.state.wi.us. Phone: 608-267-2209. Fax: 608-267-2808. Web site: www.heab.state.wi.us.

Talent Incentive Program Grant. Grant assists residents of Wisconsin who are attending a nonprofit institution in Wisconsin, and who have substantial financial need. Must meet income criteria, be considered economically and educationally disadvantaged, and be enrolled at least half-time. Refer to Web site for further details: http://www.heab.state.wi.us. *Award:* Grant for use in freshman, sophomore, junior, or senior year; renewable. Award amount: $250–$1800. Number of awards: varies. *Eligibility Requirements:* Applicant must be enrolled or expecting to enroll full- or part-time at a two-year or four-year institution or university; resident of Wisconsin and studying in Wisconsin. Available to U.S. citizens. *Application Requirements:* Application, financial need analysis, nomination. *Deadline:* continuous. **Contact:** John Whitt, Program Coordinator, Wisconsin Higher Educational Aids Board, PO Box 7885, Madison, WI 53707-7885. E-mail: john.whitt@heab.state.wi.us. Phone: 608-266-1665. Fax: 608-267-2808. Web site: www.heab.state.wi.us.

Teacher of the Visually Impaired Loan Program. Forgivable loans to students who enroll in programs that lead to certification as a teacher of the visually impaired or an orientation and mobility instructor. Must be a Wisconsin resident. For study in Wisconsin, Illinois, Iowa, Michigan, and Minnesota. Refer to Web site for further details: http://www.heab.state.wi.us. *Academic Fields/Career Goals:* Special Education. *Award:* Forgivable loan for use in freshman, sophomore, junior, senior, or graduate year; not renewable. Award amount: $250–$10,000. Number of awards: varies. *Eligibility Requirements:* Applicant must be enrolled or expecting to enroll full- or part-time at a two-year, four-year, or technical institution or university; resident of Wisconsin and studying in Illinois, Iowa, Michigan, Minnesota, or Wisconsin. Available to U.S. citizens. *Application Requirements:* Application, financial need analysis. *Deadline:* continuous. **Contact:** John Whitt, Program Coordinator, Wisconsin Higher Educational Aids Board, PO Box 7885, Madison, WI 53707-7885. E-mail: john.whitt@heab.state.wi.us. Phone: 608-266-1665. Fax: 608-267-2808. Web site: www.heab.state.wi.us.

Veterans Education (VetEd) Reimbursement Grant. Open only to Wisconsin veterans enrolled at approved schools for undergraduate study. Benefit is based on length of time serving on active duty in the armed forces (active duty for training does not apply). Pre-application due no later than 30 days after the start of semester. Application deadline no later than 60 days after the course completion. Veterans may be reimbursed up to 100 percent of tuition and fees. *Award:* Grant for use in freshman, sophomore, junior, or senior year; renewable. Award amount: up to $3365. Number of awards: varies. *Eligibility Requirements:* Applicant must be enrolled or expecting to enroll full- or part-time at a two-year, four-year, or technical institution or university and resident of Wisconsin. Available to U.S. citizens. Applicant must have served in the Air Force, Army, Coast Guard, Marine Corps, or Navy. *Application Requirements:* Application. *Deadline:* varies. **Contact:** Mr. Joe Bertalan, Supervisor, Wisconsin Department of Veterans Affairs, PO Box 7843, Madison, WI 53707-7843. Phone: 800-947-8387. Web site: www.dva.state.wi.us.

Wisconsin Academic Excellence Scholarship. Renewable award for high school seniors with the highest GPA in graduating class. Must be a Wisconsin resident. Award covers tuition for up to four years. Must maintain 3.0 GPA for renewal. Scholarships value is $2250 each. Must attend a nonprofit Wisconsin institution full-time. Refer to Web site for further details: http://www.heab.state.wi.us. *Award:* Scholarship for use in freshman, sophomore, junior, or senior year; renewable. Award amount: up to $2250. Number of awards: varies. *Eligibility Requirements:* Applicant must be enrolled or expecting to enroll full-time at a two-year, four-year, or technical institution or university; resident of Wisconsin and studying in Wisconsin. Applicant must have 3.5 GPA or higher. Available to U.S. citizens. *Application Requirements:* Transcript. *Deadline:* continuous. **Contact:** Alice Winters, Program Coordinator, Wisconsin Higher Educational Aids Board, PO Box 7885, Madison, WI 53707-7885. E-mail: alice.winters@heab.state.wi.us. Phone: 608-267-2213. Fax: 608-267-2808. Web site: www.heab.state.wi.us.

Wisconsin Higher Education Grants (WHEG). Grants for residents of Wisconsin enrolled at least half-time in degree or certificate programs at University of Wisconsin or Wisconsin Technical College. Must show financial need. Refer to Web site for further details: http://www.heab.state.wi.us. *Award:* Grant for use in freshman, sophomore, junior, or senior year; not renewable. Award amount: $250–$3000. Number of awards: varies. *Eligibility Requirements:* Applicant must be enrolled or expecting to enroll full- or part-time at a two-year, four-year, or technical institution or university; resident of Wisconsin and studying in Wisconsin. Available to U.S. citizens. *Application Requirements:* Application, financial need analysis. *Deadline:* continuous. **Contact:** Sandra Thomas, Program Coordinator, Wisconsin Higher Educational Aids Board, PO Box 7885, Madison, WI 53707-7885. E-mail: sandy.thomas@heab.state.wi.us. Phone: 608-266-0888. Fax: 608-267-2808. Web site: www.heab.state.wi.us.

Wisconsin Native American/Indian Student Assistance Grant. Grants for Wisconsin residents who are at least one-quarter American Indian. Must be attending a college or university within the state. Refer to Web site for further details: http://www.heab.state.wi.us. *Award:* Grant for use in freshman, sophomore, junior, senior, graduate, or postgraduate years; not renewable. Award amount: $250–$1100. Number of awards: varies. *Eligibility Requirements:* Applicant must be American Indian/Alaska Native; enrolled or expecting to enroll full- or part-time at a two-year, four-year, or technical institution or university; resident of Wisconsin and studying in Wisconsin. Available to U.S. citizens. *Application Requirements:* Application, financial need analysis. *Deadline:* continuous. **Contact:** Sandra Thomas, Program Coordinator, Wisconsin Higher Educational Aids Board, PO Box 7885, Madison, WI 53707-7885. E-mail: sandy.thomas@heab.state.wi.us. Phone: 608-266-0888. Fax: 608-267-2808. Web site: www.heab.state.wi.us.

Searching for Four-Year Colleges Online

The Internet can be a great tool for gathering information about four-year colleges and universities. There are many worthwhile sites that are ready to help guide you through the various aspects of the selection process, including Peterson's College Search at www.petersons.com.

HOW PETERSON'S COLLEGE SEARCH CAN HELP

Peterson's College Search is a comprehensive information resource that will help you make sense of the college admissions process and is a great place to start your college search-and-selection journey—it's as easy as these three steps:

1. Decide what's important
2. Define your criteria
3. Get results

Decide What's Important

There's no such thing as a best college—there's only the best college *for you*! Peterson's College Search site is organized into various sections and offers you enhanced search criteria—and it's easy to use! You can find colleges by name or keyword for starters, or do a detailed search based on the following:

- The Basics (location, setting, size, cost, type, religious and ethnic affiliation)
- Student Body (male-female ratio, diversity, in-state vs. out-of-state)
- Getting In (selectivity, GPA)
- Academics (degree type, majors, special programs and services)
- Campus Life (sports, clubs, fraternities and sororities, housing)

Define Your Criteria

Now it's time to take to define your criteria by taking a closer look at some more specific details. Here you are able to answer questions about what is important to you, skip questions that aren't important, and click for instant results. You'll be prompted to think about criteria such as:

- Where do you want to study?
- What range of tuition are you willing to consider?
- How many people do you want to go to school with?
- What kinds of clubs and activities are you looking for?

Get Results

Once you have gotten your results, simply click on any school to get information about the institution, including school type, setting, degrees offered, comprehensive cost, entrance difficulty, application deadline, undergraduate student population, minority breakdown, international population, housing info, freshman, faculty, majors, academic programs, student life, athletics, facilities/endowment, costs, financial aid, and applying. Keep reading but take a peek at all the great info you'll see on Petersons.com on the next page!

Get Free Info

If, after looking at the information provided on Peterson's College Search, you still have questions, you can send an e-mail directly to the admissions department of the school. Just click on the "Get Free Info" button and send your message!

Visit School Site

For institutions that have provided information about their Web sites, simply click on the "Visit School Site" button and you will be taken directly to that institution's Web page. Once you arrive at the school's Web site, look around and get a feel for the place. Often, schools offer virtual tours of the campus, complete with photos and commentary.

Close-Up

If the schools you are interested in have provided Peterson's with a **Close-Up,** you can do a keyword search on that description. Here, schools are given the opportunity to communicate unique features of their programs to prospective students.

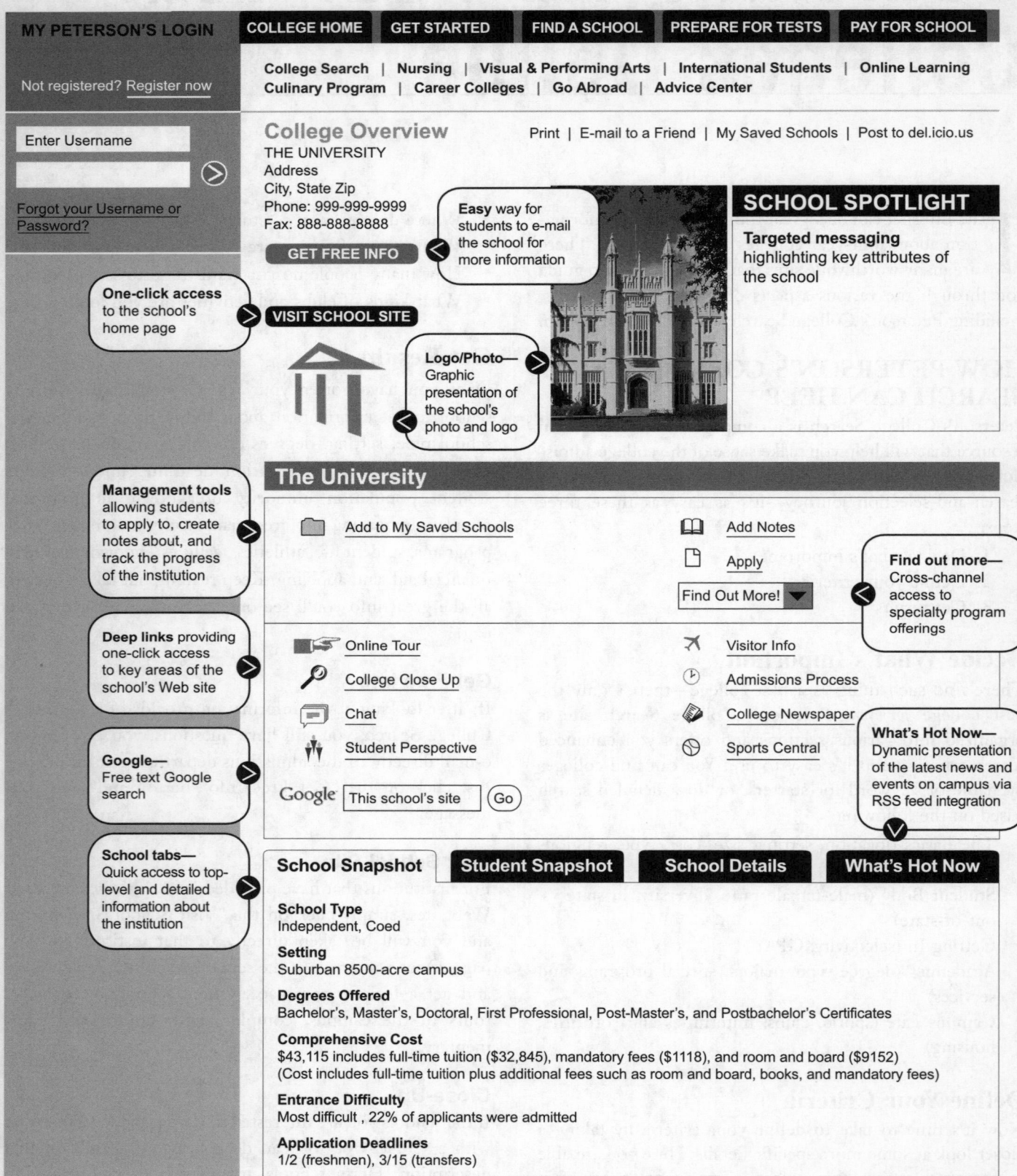

MY PETERSON'S LOGIN

COLLEGE HOME | GET STARTED | FIND A SCHOOL | PREPARE FOR TESTS | PAY FOR SCHOOL

College Search | Nursing | Visual & Performing Arts | International Students | Online Learning
Culinary Program | Career Colleges | Go Abroad | Advice Center

Not registered? Register now

Enter Username

Forgot your Username or Password?

College Overview

Print | E-mail to a Friend | My Saved Schools | Post to del.icio.us

THE UNIVERSITY
Address
City, State Zip
Phone: 999-999-9999
Fax: 888-888-8888

GET FREE INFO

SCHOOL SPOTLIGHT

Targeted messaging highlighting key attributes of the school

Easy way for students to e-mail the school for more information

One-click access to the school's home page

VISIT SCHOOL SITE

Logo/Photo— Graphic presentation of the school's photo and logo

The University

Management tools allowing students to apply to, create notes about, and track the progress of the institution

Add to My Saved Schools

Add Notes

Apply

Find Out More! ▼

Find out more— Cross-channel access to specialty program offerings

Deep links providing one-click access to key areas of the school's Web site

Online Tour

College Close Up

Chat

Student Perspective

Visitor Info

Admissions Process

College Newspaper

Sports Central

Google— Free text Google search

Google | This school's site | Go

What's Hot Now— Dynamic presentation of the latest news and events on campus via RSS feed integration

School tabs— Quick access to top-level and detailed information about the institution

| School Snapshot | Student Snapshot | School Details | What's Hot Now |

School Type
Independent, Coed

Setting
Suburban 8500-acre campus

Degrees Offered
Bachelor's, Master's, Doctoral, First Professional, Post-Master's, and Postbachelor's Certificates

Comprehensive Cost
$43,115 includes full-time tuition ($32,845), mandatory fees ($1118), and room and board ($9152)
(Cost includes full-time tuition plus additional fees such as room and board, books, and mandatory fees)

Entrance Difficulty
Most difficult , 22% of applicants were admitted

Application Deadlines
1/2 (freshmen), 3/15 (transfers)

Add to My Saved Schools/Add Notes/Apply

The "Add to My Saved Schools" features are designed to help you with your college planning with management tools to create notes about and track the school. The Apply link gives you the ability to directly apply to the school online.

WRITE ADMISSIONS ESSAYS

This year, 500,000 college applicants will write 500,000 different admissions essays. Half will be rejected by their first-choice school, while only 11 percent will gain admission to the nation's most selective colleges. With acceptance rates at all-time lows, setting yourself apart requires more than just blockbuster SAT scores and impeccable transcripts—it requires the perfect application essay. Named "the world's premier application essay editing service" by the *New York Times* Learning Network and "one of the best essay services on the Internet" by the *Washington Post*, EssayEdge (www.essayedge.com) has helped more applicants write successful personal statements than any other company in the world. Learn more about EssayEdge and how it can give you an edge over hundreds of applicants with comparable academic credentials.

PRACTICE FOR YOUR TEST

At Peterson's, we understand that the college admissions process can be very stressful. With the stakes so high and the competition getting tighter every year, it's easy to feel like the process is out of your control. Fortunately, preparing for college admissions tests, like the PSAT/NMSQT, SAT, and ACT, helps you exert some control over the options you will have available to you. You can visit Peterson's Prep Central to learn more about how Peterson's can help you maximize your scores—and your options.

USE THE TOOLS TO YOUR ADVANTAGE

Choosing a college is an involved and complicated process. The tools available to you on www.petersons.com can help you to be more productive in this process. So, what are you waiting for? Fire up your computer; your future alma mater may be just a click away!

How to Use This Guide

This article provides an outline of the **Profile** format, describing the items covered. All college information presented was supplied to Peterson's by the colleges themselves. Any item that does not apply to a particular college or for which no current information was supplied may be omitted from that college's **Profile**. Colleges that were unable to supply usable data in time for publication are listed by name and, if available, Web address.

PROFILES OF COLLEGES IN THE MIDWEST

This section presents pertinent factual and statistical data for each college in a standard format for easy comparison.

General Information

The first paragraph gives a brief introduction to the college, covering the following elements.

Type of student body: The categories are *men's* (100 percent of the student body), *primarily men's*, *women's* (100 percent of the student body), *primarily women's*, and *coed*. A few schools are designated as *undergraduate: women only; graduate: coed* or *undergraduate: men only; graduate: coed*. A college may also be designated as coordinate with another institution, indicating that there are separate colleges or campuses for men and women, but facilities, courses, and institutional governance are shared.

Institutional control: A *public* college receives its funding wholly or primarily from the federal, state, and/or local government. The term *private* indicates an independent, nonprofit institution, that is, one whose funding comes primarily from private sources and tuition. This category includes independent, religious colleges, which may also specify a particular religious denomination or church affiliation. Profit-making institutions are designated as *proprietary*.

Institutional type: A *two-year college* awards associate degrees and/or offers the first two years of a bachelor's degree program. A *primarily two-year college* awards bachelor's degrees, but the vast majority of students are enrolled in two-year programs. A *four-year college* awards bachelor's degrees and may also award associate degrees, but it does not offer graduate (postbachelor's) degree programs. A *five-year college* offers a five-year bachelor's program in a professional field such as architecture or pharmacy but does not award graduate degrees. An *upper-level institution* awards bachelor's degrees, but entering students must have at least two years of previous college-level credit; it may also offer graduate degree programs. A *comprehensive institution* awards bachelor's degrees and may also award associate degrees; graduate degree programs are offered primarily at the master's, specialist's, or professional level, although one or two doctoral programs may also be offered. A *university* offers four years of undergraduate work plus graduate degrees through the doctorate in more than two academic and/or professional fields.

Founding date: This is the year the college came into existence or was chartered, reflecting the period during which it has existed as an educational institution, regardless of subsequent mergers or other organizational changes.

Degree levels: An *associate* degree program may consist of either a college-transfer program, equivalent to the first two years of a bachelor's degree, or a one- to three-year terminal program that provides training for a specific occupation. A *bachelor's* degree program represents a three- to five-year liberal arts, science, professional, or preprofessional program. A *master's* degree is the first graduate degree in the liberal arts and sciences and certain professional fields and usually requires one to two years of full-time study. A *doctoral* degree is the highest degree awarded in research-oriented academic disciplines and usually requires from three to six years of full-time graduate study; the *first professional* degrees in such fields as law and medicine are also at the doctoral level. For colleges that award degrees in one field only, such as art or music, the field of specialization is indicated.

Campus setting: This indicates the size of the campus in acres or hectares and its location.

Academic Information

This paragraph contains information on the following items.

Faculty: The number of full-time and part-time faculty members is given, followed by the percentage of the full-time faculty members who hold doctoral, first professional, or terminal degrees, and then the student-faculty ratio. (Not all colleges calculate the student-faculty ratio in the same way; Peterson's prints the ratio provided by the college.)

Library holdings: The numbers of books, serials, and audiovisual materials in the college's collections are listed.

Special programs: *Academic remediation for entering students* consists of instructional courses designed for students deficient in the general competencies necessary for a regular postsecondary curriculum and educational setting. *Services for LD students* include special help for learning-disabled students with resolvable difficulties, such as dyslexia. *Honors programs* are any special programs for very able students, offering the opportunity for educational enrichment, independent study, acceleration, or some combination of these. *Cooperative (co-op) education programs* are formal arrangements with off-campus employers, allowing students to combine work and study in order to gain degree-related experience, usually extending the time required to complete a degree. *Study abroad* is an arrangement by which a student completes part of the academic program studying in another country. A college may operate a campus abroad or it may have a cooperative agreement with other U.S. institutions or institutions in other countries. *Advanced placement* gives credit toward a degree awarded for acceptable scores on College Board Advanced Placement tests. *Accelerated degree programs* allow students to earn a bachelor's degree in three academic years. *Freshmen honors college* is a separate academic program for talented freshmen. *English as a second language (ESL)* is a course of study designed specifically for students whose native language is not English. *Double major* consists of a program of study in which a student concurrently completes the requirements of two majors. *Independent study* consists of academic work, usually undertaken outside the regular classroom structure, chosen or designed by the student with departmental approval and instructor supervision. *Distance learning* consists of credit courses that can be accessed off campus via cable television, the Internet, satellite, videotapes, correspondence courses, or other media. *Self-designed major* is a program of study based on individual interests, designed by the student with the assistance of an adviser. *Summer session for credit* includes summer courses through which students may make up degree work or accelerate their program. *Part-time degree programs* offer students the ability to earn a degree through part-time enrollment in regular session (daytime) classes or evening, weekend, or summer classes. *External degree programs* are programs of study in which students earn credits toward a degree through a combination of independent study, college courses, proficiency examinations, and personal experience. External degree programs require minimal or no classroom attendance. *Adult/continuing education programs* are courses offered for nontraditional students who are currently working or are returning to formal education. *Internships* are any short-term, supervised work experience, usually related to a student's major field, for which the student earns academic credit. The work can be full- or part-time, on or off campus, paid or unpaid. *Off-campus study* is a formal arrangement with one or more domestic institutions under which students may take courses at the other institution(s) for credit.

Most popular majors: The most popular field or fields of study at the college, in terms of the number of undergraduate degrees conferred in 2006, are listed.

Student Body Statistics

Enrollment: The total number of students, undergraduates, and freshmen (or entering students for an upper-level institution) enrolled in degree programs as of fall 2006 are given.

With reference to the undergraduate enrollment for fall 2006, the percentages of women and men and the number of states and countries from which students hail are listed. The following percentages are also provided: in-state students, international students, and the percentage of last year's graduating class who went on to graduate and professional schools.

Expenses

Costs are given in each profile according to the most up-to-date figures available from each college for the 2006–07 or 2007–08 academic year.

Annual expenses may be expressed as a comprehensive fee (includes full-time tuition, mandatory fees, and college room and board) or as separate figures for full-time tuition, fees, room and board, and/or room only. For public institutions where tuition differs according to residence, separate figures are given for area and/or state residents and for nonresidents. Part-time tuition and fees are expressed in terms of a per-unit rate (per credit, per semester hour, etc.) as specified by the college.

The tuition structure at some institutions is complex in that freshmen and sophomores may be charged a different rate from that for juniors and seniors; a professional or vocational division may have a different fee structure from the liberal arts division of the same institution; or part-time tuition may be prorated on a sliding scale according to the number of credit hours taken. In all of these cases, the average figures are given along with an explanation of the basis for the variable rate. For colleges that report that room and board costs vary according to the type of accommodation and meal plan, the average costs are given. The phrase *no college housing* indicates that the college does not own or operate any housing facilities for its undergraduate students.

Financial Aid

This paragraph contains information on the following items.

Forms of financial aid: The categories of college-administered aid available to undergraduates are listed. College-administered means that the college itself determines the recipient and amount of each award. The types of aid covered are *non-need scholarships*, *need-based scholarships*, *athletic grants*, and *part-time jobs*.

Financial aid: This item pertains to undergraduates who enrolled full-time in a four-year college in 2005 or 2006. The figures given are the dollar amount of the average financial aid package, including scholarships, grants, loans, and part-time jobs, received by such undergraduates.

Financial aid application deadline: This deadline may be given as a specific date, as continuous processing up to a specific date or until all available aid has been awarded, or as a priority date rather than a strict deadline, meaning that students are encouraged to apply by that date in order to have the best chance of obtaining aid.

Freshman Admission

The supporting data that a student must submit when applying for freshman admission are grouped into three categories: *required for all*, *recommended*, and *required for some*. They may include an essay, a high school transcript, letters of recommendation, an interview on campus or with local alumni, standardized test scores, and, for certain types of schools or programs, special requirements such as a musical audition or an art portfolio.

The most commonly required standardized tests are the ACT and the College Board's SAT and SAT Subject Tests. TOEFL (Test of English as a Foreign Language) is for international students whose native language is not English.

The application deadline for admission is given as either a specific date or *rolling*. Rolling means that applications are processed as they are received, and qualified students are accepted as long as there are openings. The application deadline for out-of-state students is indicated if it differs from the date for state residents. *Early decision* and *early action* deadlines are also given when applicable. Early decision is a program whereby students may apply early, are notified of acceptance or rejection well in advance of the usual notification date, and agree to accept an offer of admission, the assumption being that only one early application has been made. Early action is the same as early decision except that applicants are not obligated to accept an offer of admission.

Transfer Admission

This paragraph gives the application requirements and application deadline for a student applying for admission as a transfer from another institution. In addition to the requirements previously listed for freshman applicants, requirements for transfers may also include a college transcript and a minimum college grade point average (expressed as a number on a scale of 0 to 4.0, where 4.0 equals A, 3.0 equals B, etc.). The name of the person to contact for additional transfer information is also given if it is different from the person listed in **For Further Information**.

Entrance Difficulty

This paragraph contains the college's own assessment of its *entrance difficulty* level, including notation of an *open admission policy* where applicable. Open admission means that virtually all applicants are accepted without regard to standardized test scores, grade average, or class rank. A college may indicate that open admission is limited to a certain category of applicants, such as state residents, or does not apply to certain selective programs, often those in the health professions.

The five levels of entrance difficulty are *most difficult*, *very difficult*, *moderately difficult*, *minimally difficult*, and *noncompetitive*.

The final item in this paragraph is the percentage of applicants accepted for the fall 2006 freshman (or entering) class.

For Further Information

The name, title, and mailing address of the person to contact for more information on application and admission procedures are given at the end of the **Profile**. A telephone number, fax number, e-mail address, and Web site are also included in this paragraph for **Profiles** that do not contain this information in the paragraph on interviews and campus visits.

SPECIAL MESSAGE TO STUDENTS

In addition, a number of college admissions office staff members, as part of a major information-dissemination effort, have supplemented their **Profile** with special descriptive information on four topics of particular interest to students.

Social Life: This paragraph conveys a feeling for life on campus by addressing such questions as: What are the most popular activities? Are there active fraternities and sororities? What is the role of student government? Do most students live on campus or commute? Does the college have a religious orientation?

Academic Highlights: This paragraph describes some of the special features and characteristics of the college's academic program, such as special degree programs and opportunities for study abroad or internships.

Interviews and Campus Visits: Colleges that conduct on-campus admission interviews describe the importance of an interview in their admission process and what they try to learn about a student through the interview. For those colleges that do not interview applicants individually, there is information on how a student interested in the college can visit the campus to meet administrators, faculty members, and currently enrolled students as well as on what the prospective applicant should try to accomplish through such a visit. This paragraph may also include a list of the most noteworthy places or things to see during a campus visit and the location, telephone number (including toll-free numbers if available), and business hours of the office to contact for information about appointments and campus visits. Also included, when available, is travel information, specifically the nearest commercial airport and the nearest interstate highway, with the appropriate exit.

For Further Information: The name and mailing address of the person and/or office to contact for more information on the school are included in this paragraph. A telephone number, fax number, e-mail address, and Web site may also be included.

CLOSE-UPS OF COLLEGES IN THE MIDWEST

Two-page narrative descriptions appear in this section, providing an inside look at colleges and universities, shifting the focus to a variety of other factors, some of them intangible, that should also be considered. The descriptions presented in this section provide a wealth of statistics that are crucial components in the college decision-making equation—components such as tuition, financial aid, and major fields of study. Prepared exclusively by college officials, the descriptions are designed to help give students a better sense of the individuality of each institution, in terms that include campus environment, student activities, and lifestyle. Such quality-of-life intangibles can be the deciding factors in the college selection process.

The absence from this section of any college or university does not constitute an editorial decision on the part of Peterson's. In essence, this section is an open forum for colleges and universities, on a voluntary basis, to communicate their particular message to prospective college students. The colleges included have paid a fee to Peterson's to provide this information. The descriptions are edited to provide a consistent format across entries for your ease of comparison and are presented alphabetically by the official name of the institution.

PROFILES AND CLOSE-UPS OF OTHER COLLEGES TO CONSIDER

Do you know that schools sometimes target specific areas of the country for student recruitment, even if those states are not part of a specific region? In this section, you'll find **Profiles** and **Close-Ups** of schools outside the region of this guide looking to recruit students like you. The format

of both the **Profiles** and the **Close-Ups** in this section matches the format in the previous sections.

INDEXES

Majors and Degrees

This index lists hundreds of undergraduate major fields of study that are currently offered most widely. The majors appear in alphabetical order, each followed by an alphabetical list of the colleges that report offering a program in that field and the degree levels (*A* for associate, *B* for bachelor's) available. The majors represented here are based on the National Center for Education Statistics (NCES) 2000 Classification of Instructional Programs (CIP). The CIP is a taxonomic coding scheme that contains titles and descriptions of instructional programs, primarily at the postsecondary level. CIP was originally developed to facilitate NCES's collection and reporting of postsecondary degree completions, by major field of study, using standard classifications that capture the majority of program activity. The CIP is the accepted federal government reporting standard for classifying instructional programs. However, although the term "major" is used in this guide, some colleges may use other terms, such as "concentration," "program of study," or "field."

Athletic Programs and Scholarships

This index lists the colleges that report offering intercollegiate athletic programs, listed alphabetically. An *M* or *W* following the college name indicates that the sport is offered for men or women, respectively. An *s* in parentheses following an *M* or *W* indicates that athletic scholarships (or grants-in-aid) are offered by the college for men or women, respectively, in that sport.

ROTC Programs

This index lists the colleges that report offering Reserve Officers' Training Corps programs in one or more branches of the armed services, as indicated by letter codes following the college name: *A* for Army, *N* for Navy, and *AF* for Air Force. A *c* in parentheses following the branch letter code indicates that the program is offered through a cooperative arrangement on another college's campus.

Alphabetical Listing of Colleges and Universities

This index gives the page locations of various entries for all the colleges and universities in this book. The page numbers for the **Profiles** are printed in regular type, those for **Profiles** with **Special Messages** in *italic* type, and those for **Close-Ups** in **boldface** type. When there is more than one number in **boldface** type, it indicates that the institution has more than one **Close-Up**.

DATA COLLECTION PROCEDURES

The data contained in the **Profiles** and **Indexes** were researched between fall 2006 and spring 2007 through *Peterson's Annual Survey of Undergraduate Institutions* and *Peterson's Annual Survey of Undergraduate Financial Aid*. Questionnaires were sent to the more than 2,100 colleges and universities that met the outlined inclusion criteria. All data included in this edition have been submitted by officials (usually admissions and financial aid officers, registrars, or institutional research personnel) at the colleges. In addition, many of the institutions that submitted data were contacted directly by the Peterson's research staff to verify unusual figures, resolve discrepancies, or obtain additional data. All usable information received in time for publication has been included. The omission of any particular item from an index or profile listing signifies that the information is either not applicable to that institution or not available. Because of Peterson's comprehensive editorial review and because all material comes directly from college officials, we believe that the information presented in this guide is accurate. You should check with a specific college or university at the time of application to verify such figures as tuition and fees, which may have changed since the publication of this volume.

CRITERIA FOR INCLUSION IN THIS BOOK

The term "four-year college" is the commonly used designation for institutions that grant the baccalaureate degree. Four years is the expected amount of time required to earn this degree, although some bachelor's degree programs may be completed in three years, others require five years, and part-time programs may take considerably longer. Upper-level institutions offer only the junior and senior years and accept only students with two years of college-level credit. Therefore, "four-year college" is a conventional term that accurately describes most of the institutions included in this guide, but it should not be taken literally in all cases.

To be included in this guide, an institution must have full accreditation or be a candidate for accreditation (preaccreditation) status by an institutional or specialized accrediting body recognized by the U.S. Department of Education or the Council for Higher Education Accreditation (CHEA). Institutional accrediting bodies, which review each institution as a whole, include the six regional associations of schools and colleges (Middle States, New England, North Central, Northwest, Southern, and Western), each of which is responsible for a specified portion of the United States and its territories. Other institutional accrediting bodies are national in scope and accredit specific kinds of institutions (e.g., Bible colleges, independent colleges, and rabbinical and Talmudic schools). Program registration by the New York State Board of Regents is considered to be the equivalent of institutional accreditation, since the board requires that all programs offered by an institution meet its standards before recognition is granted. There are recognized specialized or professional accrediting bodies in more than forty different fields, each of which is authorized to accredit institutions or specific programs in its particular field. For specialized institutions that offer programs in one field only, we designate this to be the equivalent of institutional accreditation. A full explanation of the accrediting process and complete information on recognized, institutional (regional and national) and specialized accrediting bodies can be found online at www.chea.org or at www.ed.gov/admins/finaid/accred/index.html.

Profiles of Colleges
in the Midwest

Map of the Midwest

This map provides a general perspective on the Midwest and shows the major metropolitan areas and capital of each state.

Illinois

AMERICAN ACADEMY OF ART
Chicago, Illinois

American Academy of Art is a coed, proprietary, comprehensive institution, founded in 1923, offering degrees at the bachelor's and master's levels.

Expenses for 2006–07 *Application fee:* $25. *Tuition:* $20,680 full-time. *Mandatory fees:* $250 full-time.
For Further Information Contact Mr. Stuart Rosenbloom, Director of Admissions, American Academy of Art, 332 South Michigan Avenue, Suite 300, Chicago, IL 60604-4302. *Telephone:* 312-461-0600 Ext. 159. *E-mail:* srosenbloom@aaart.edu. *Web site:* http://www.aaart.edu/.

AMERICAN INTERCONTINENTAL UNIVERSITY ONLINE
Hoffman Estates, Illinois

http://www.aiuonline.edu/

ARGOSY UNIVERSITY, CHICAGO
Chicago, Illinois

http://www.argosyu.edu/

ARGOSY UNIVERSITY, SCHAUMBURG
Schaumburg, Illinois

http://www.argosyu.edu/

AUGUSTANA COLLEGE
Rock Island, Illinois

Augustana College is a coed, private, four-year college, founded in 1860, affiliated with the Evangelical Lutheran Church in America, offering degrees at the bachelor's level. It has a 115-acre campus in Rock Island.

Academic Information The faculty has 235 members (63% full-time), 69% with terminal degrees. The student-faculty ratio is 12:1. The library holds 190,641 titles, 1,705 serial subscriptions, and 2,019 audiovisual materials. Special programs include services for learning-disabled students, an honors program, study abroad, advanced placement credit, accelerated degree programs, double majors, independent study, summer session for credit, part-time degree programs (daytime, evenings), and internships. The most frequently chosen baccalaureate fields are biological/life sciences, business/marketing, social sciences.
Student Body Statistics The student body is made up of 2,463 undergraduates (691 freshmen). 57 percent are women and 43 percent are men. Students come from 31 states and territories and 23 other countries. 89 percent are from Illinois. 1.1 percent are international students. 42 percent of the 2006 graduating class went on to graduate and professional schools.
Expenses for 2006–07 *Application fee:* $25. *Comprehensive fee:* $31,731 includes full-time tuition ($24,408), mandatory fees ($516), and college room and board ($6807). *College room only:* $3447. Full-time tuition and fees vary according to course load. Room and board charges vary according to board plan and housing facility. *Part-time tuition:* $1020 per credit hour.

Financial Aid Forms of aid include need-based and non-need-based scholarships and part-time jobs. The average aided 2006–07 undergraduate received an aid package worth an estimated $17,924. The priority application deadline for financial aid is March 15.
Freshman Admission Augustana College requires a high school transcript, SAT or ACT scores, and TOEFL scores for international students. An essay and an interview are required for some. The application deadline for regular admission is rolling.
Transfer Admission The application deadline for admission is rolling.
Entrance Difficulty Augustana College assesses its entrance difficulty level as moderately difficult. For the fall 2006 freshman class, 84 percent of the applicants were accepted.
For Further Information Contact Megan Cooley, Director of Admissions, Augustana College, 639 38th Street, Rock Island, IL 61201-2296. *Telephone:* 309-794-7341 or 800-798-8100 (toll-free). *Fax:* 309-794-7422. *E-mail:* admissions@augustana.edu. *Web site:* http://www.augustana.edu/.

AURORA UNIVERSITY
Aurora, Illinois

SPONSOR
See Front Insert for Details!

Aurora University is a coed, private, comprehensive institution, founded in 1893, offering degrees at the bachelor's, master's, and doctoral levels and post-master's and postbachelor's certificates. It has a 30-acre campus in Aurora near Chicago.

Academic Information The faculty has 293 members (35% full-time), 51% with terminal degrees. The undergraduate student-faculty ratio is 16:1. The library holds 92,025 titles, 210 serial subscriptions, and 7,621 audiovisual materials. Special programs include academic remediation, services for learning-disabled students, an honors program, study abroad, advanced placement credit, accelerated degree programs, double majors, independent study, self-designed majors, summer session for credit, part-time degree programs (daytime, evenings, weekends, summer), adult/continuing education programs, internships, and arrangement for off-campus study with 3 members of the Council of West Suburban Colleges. The most frequently chosen baccalaureate fields are business/marketing, education, health professions and related sciences.
Student Body Statistics The student body totals 3,791, of whom 1,974 are undergraduates (375 freshmen). 67 percent are women and 33 percent are men. Students come from 24 states and territories and 2 other countries. 93 percent are from Illinois. 0.1 percent are international students.
Expenses for 2007–08 *Application fee:* $25. *Comprehensive fee:* $23,884 includes full-time tuition ($16,750), mandatory fees ($100), and college room and board ($7034). *College room only:* $3080. *Part-time tuition:* $510 per semester hour.
Financial Aid Forms of aid include need-based and non-need-based scholarships and part-time jobs. The average aided 2006–07 undergraduate received an aid package worth an estimated $17,515. The priority application deadline for financial aid is April 15.
Freshman Admission Aurora University requires a high school transcript, a minimum 2.0 high school GPA, SAT or ACT scores, and TOEFL scores for international students. An essay and an interview are recommended. 2 recommendations and an interview are required for some. The application deadline for regular admission is May 1 and for nonresidents it is May 1.
Transfer Admission The application deadline for admission is rolling.
Entrance Difficulty Aurora University assesses its entrance difficulty level as moderately difficult. For the fall 2006 freshman class, 71 percent of the applicants were accepted.

SPECIAL MESSAGE TO STUDENTS

Social Life Aurora University is a great place to get involved. Students may choose to participate in social clubs, theater, student government, service activities, Campus Ministries, the University Chorale, and intramural sports. Students may also take advantage of the various social

Aurora University (continued)

activities that are offered in and near Aurora—the second-largest city in Illinois—and Chicago, 40 miles to the east. Aurora University combines a residential and commuter population.

Academic Highlights The curriculum ranges from traditional academic programs in arts, sciences, and business to the "helping" disciplines of athletic training, criminal justice, education, nursing, and social work. There are three colleges: the College of Arts and Sciences, the College of Professional Studies, and the College of Education.

Interviews and Campus Visits Aurora University encourages campus visits. Fall, winter, and spring open houses are held. Individual visits are always welcome. Students can meet with an admission counselor, faculty members, a financial aid counselor, and coaches as well as take a tour of campus and visit with current students. Campus tours include academic buildings such as Dunham and Stephens Halls, the Institute for Collaboration (AU's newest classroom building), and four residence halls. Housed in Dunham Hall is the Schingoethe Museum of Native American Culture, which is open to the public. The University is accessible by train and local bus lines. For more information about appointments and campus visits, students should call the Office of Admission and Financial Aid at 630-844-5533 or 800-742-5281 (toll-free). The nearest commercial airport is O'Hare International.

For Further Information Write to the Office of Admission and Financial Aid, Aurora University, Aurora, IL 60506. *Web site:* http://www.aurora.edu.

See page 234 for the College Close-Up.

BARAT COLLEGE

See DePaul University.

BENEDICTINE UNIVERSITY
Lisle, Illinois

Benedictine University is a coed, private, Roman Catholic, comprehensive institution, founded in 1887, offering degrees at the associate, bachelor's, master's, and doctoral levels and postbachelor's certificates. It has a 108-acre campus in Lisle near Chicago.

Academic Information The faculty has 353 members (25% full-time). The undergraduate student-faculty ratio is 13:1. The library holds 201,190 titles, 14,177 serial subscriptions, and 2,500 audiovisual materials. Special programs include academic remediation, services for learning-disabled students, an honors program, study abroad, advanced placement credit, accelerated degree programs, double majors, independent study, distance learning, summer session for credit, part-time degree programs (evenings, weekends, summer), adult/continuing education programs, internships, and arrangement for off-campus study with 3 members of the Council of West Suburban Colleges. The most frequently chosen baccalaureate fields are business/marketing, health professions and related sciences, psychology.

Student Body Statistics The student body totals 3,900, of whom 2,657 are undergraduates (379 freshmen). 57 percent are women and 43 percent are men. Students come from 41 states and territories and 9 other countries. 97 percent are from Illinois. 0.8 percent are international students.

Expenses for 2006–07 *Application fee:* $40. *Comprehensive fee:* $27,010 includes full-time tuition ($19,800), mandatory fees ($510), and college room and board ($6700). Full-time tuition and fees vary according to class time, degree level, and location. Room and board charges vary according to board plan and housing facility. *Part-time tuition:* $660 per credit hour. *Part-time mandatory fees:* $15 per credit hour. Part-time tuition and fees vary according to class time and degree level.

Financial Aid Forms of aid include need-based and non-need-based scholarships and part-time jobs. The average aided 2005–06 undergraduate received an aid package worth $11,980. The application deadline for financial aid is continuous.

Freshman Admission Benedictine University requires an essay, a high school transcript, recommendations, ACT scores, and TOEFL scores for international students. Rank in upper 50% of high school class, minimum ACT score of 21 is recommended. An interview is required for some. The application deadline for regular admission is rolling.

Transfer Admission The application deadline for admission is rolling.

Entrance Difficulty Benedictine University assesses its entrance difficulty level as moderately difficult. For the fall 2006 freshman class, 81 percent of the applicants were accepted.

For Further Information Contact Ms. Kari Gibbons, Dean of Enrollment, Benedictine University, 5700 College Road, Lisle, IL 60532-0900. *Telephone:* 630-829-6300 or 888-829-6363 (toll-free out-of-state). *Fax:* 630-829-6301. *E-mail:* admissions@ben.edu. *Web site:* http://www.ben.edu/.

See page 240 for the College Close-Up.

BLACKBURN COLLEGE
Carlinville, Illinois

Blackburn College is a coed, private, Presbyterian, four-year college, founded in 1837, offering degrees at the bachelor's level. It has an 80-acre campus in Carlinville near St. Louis.

Academic Information The faculty has 68 members (51% full-time), 62% with terminal degrees. The student-faculty ratio is 13:1. The library holds 61,586 titles and 79 serial subscriptions. Special programs include an honors program, cooperative (work-study) education, study abroad, advanced placement credit, double majors, independent study, self-designed majors, summer session for credit, internships, and arrangement for off-campus study with American University.

Student Body Statistics The student body is made up of 605 undergraduates (176 freshmen). 57 percent are women and 43 percent are men. Students come from 1 state or territory and 4 other countries. 87 percent are from Illinois. 0.7 percent are international students. 16 percent of the 2006 graduating class went on to graduate and professional schools.

Expenses for 2007–08 *Application fee:* $0. *Comprehensive fee:* $17,525 includes full-time tuition ($13,370) and college room and board ($4155). *College room only:* $2100. *Part-time tuition:* $526 per semester hour.

Financial Aid Forms of aid include need-based and non-need-based scholarships and part-time jobs. The priority application deadline for financial aid is April 1.

Freshman Admission Blackburn College requires an essay, a high school transcript, a minimum 2.0 high school GPA, SAT or ACT scores, and TOEFL scores for international students. 1 recommendation and an interview are required for some. The application deadline for regular admission is rolling.

Transfer Admission The application deadline for admission is rolling.

Entrance Difficulty Blackburn College assesses its entrance difficulty level as moderately difficult. For the fall 2006 freshman class, 59 percent of the applicants were accepted.

For Further Information Contact Ron Bryan, Director of Admission, Blackburn College, 700 College Avenue, Carlinville, IL 62626-1498. *Telephone:* 217-854-3231 Ext. 4293 or 800-233-3550 (toll-free). *Fax:* 217-854-3713. *E-mail:* admit@mail.blackburn.edu. *Web site:* http://www.blackburn.edu/.

BLESSING-RIEMAN COLLEGE OF NURSING
Quincy, Illinois

Blessing-Rieman College of Nursing is a coed, primarily women's, private, four-year college, founded in 1985, offering degrees at the bachelor's level. It has a 1-acre campus in Quincy.

Academic Information The faculty has 18 members (83% full-time), 22% with terminal degrees. The student-faculty ratio is 15:1. The library holds 3,767 titles and 125 serial subscriptions. Special programs include academic remediation, an honors program, advanced placement credit, double majors, distance learning, summer session for credit, part-time degree programs (daytime, evenings), adult/continuing education programs, and internships. The most frequently chosen baccalaureate field is health professions and related sciences.

Student Body Statistics The student body is made up of 214 undergraduates (23 freshmen). 93 percent are women and 7 percent are men. Students come from 8 states and territories. 53 percent are from Illinois.

Expenses for 2006–07 *Application fee:* $0. *Comprehensive fee:* $23,850 includes full-time tuition ($16,800), mandatory fees ($500), and college room and board ($6550). *College room only:* $3500. Full-time tuition and fees vary according to course load, location, and student level. Room and board charges vary according to board plan, location, and student level. *Part-time tuition:* $319 per credit hour. Part-time tuition varies according to course load, location, and student level.

Financial Aid Forms of aid include need-based scholarships. The application deadline for financial aid is continuous.

Freshman Admission Blessing-Rieman College of Nursing requires a high school transcript, a minimum 3.0 high school GPA, SAT or ACT scores, and TOEFL scores for international students. An essay and an interview are recommended. The application deadline for regular admission is rolling.

Transfer Admission The application deadline for admission is rolling.

Entrance Difficulty Blessing-Rieman College of Nursing assesses its entrance difficulty level as moderately difficult. For the fall 2006 freshman class, 72 percent of the applicants were accepted.

For Further Information Contact Ms. Heather Mutter or Ms. Kate Boster, Admissions Counselors, Blessing-Rieman College of Nursing, PO Box 7005, Quincy, IL 62305-7005. *Telephone:* 800-897-9140 or 800-877-9140 Ext. 6964 (toll-free). *Fax:* 217-223-4661. *E-mail:* admissions@brcn.edu. *Web site:* http://www.brcn.edu/.

BRADLEY UNIVERSITY
Peoria, Illinois

Bradley University is a coed, private, comprehensive institution, founded in 1897, offering degrees at the bachelor's, master's, and first professional levels. It has an 85-acre campus in Peoria near Chicago and St. Louis.

Academic Information The faculty has 547 members (61% full-time), 50% with terminal degrees. The undergraduate student-faculty ratio is 14:1. The library holds 518,000 titles and 3,529 serial subscriptions. Special programs include academic remediation, an honors program, cooperative (work-study) education, study abroad, advanced placement credit, accelerated degree programs, double majors, independent study, distance learning, self-designed majors, summer session for credit, part-time degree programs (daytime, evenings, summer), adult/continuing education programs, internships, and arrangement for off-campus study with Georgetown University. The most frequently chosen baccalaureate fields are business/marketing, communications/journalism, engineering.

Student Body Statistics The student body totals 6,126, of whom 5,315 are undergraduates (1,075 freshmen). 55 percent are women and 45 percent are men. Students come from 43 states and territories and 26 other countries. 89 percent are from Illinois. 0.9 percent are international students. 17 percent of the 2006 graduating class went on to graduate and professional schools.

Expenses for 2006–07 *Application fee:* $35. *Comprehensive fee:* $26,810 includes full-time tuition ($19,900), mandatory fees ($160), and college room and board ($6750). *College room only:* $3900. Full-time tuition and fees vary according to program and student level. Room and board charges vary according to board plan. *Part-time tuition:* $550 per credit. Part-time tuition varies according to course load.

Financial Aid Forms of aid include need-based and non-need-based scholarships, athletic grants, and part-time jobs. The average aided 2005–06 undergraduate received an aid package worth $13,037. The priority application deadline for financial aid is March 1.

Freshman Admission Bradley University requires an essay, a high school transcript, recommendations, SAT or ACT scores, and TOEFL scores for international students. A minimum 3.0 high school GPA and an interview are recommended. The application deadline for regular admission is rolling.

Entrance Difficulty Bradley University assesses its entrance difficulty level as moderately difficult. For the fall 2006 freshman class, 83 percent of the applicants were accepted.

For Further Information Contact Mr. Rodney San Jose, Director of Admissions, Bradley University, 1501 West Bradley Avenue, 100 Swords Hall, Peoria, IL 61625-0002. *Telephone:* 309-677-1000 or 800-447-6460 (toll-free). *Fax:* 309-677-2797. *E-mail:* admissions@bradley.edu. *Web site:* http://www.bradley.edu/.

CHICAGO STATE UNIVERSITY
Chicago, Illinois

Chicago State University is a coed, public, comprehensive institution, founded in 1867, offering degrees at the bachelor's, master's, and doctoral levels. It has a 161-acre campus in Chicago.

Academic Information The faculty has 453 members (67% full-time), 59% with terminal degrees. The undergraduate student-faculty ratio is 13:1. The library holds 426,691 titles, 1,654 serial subscriptions, and 1,688 audiovisual materials. Special programs include academic remediation, services for learning-disabled students, an honors program, cooperative (work-study) education, study abroad, advanced placement credit, accelerated degree programs, Freshman Honors College, double majors, independent study, distance learning, self-designed majors, summer session for credit, part-time degree programs (daytime, evenings, weekends, summer), external degree programs, adult/continuing education programs, internships, and arrangement for off-campus study. The most frequently chosen baccalaureate fields are business/marketing, liberal arts/general studies, psychology.

Student Body Statistics The student body totals 7,035, of whom 5,167 are undergraduates (423 freshmen). 73 percent are women and 27 percent are men. Students come from 25 states and territories and 13 other countries. 98 percent are from Illinois. 0.5 percent are international students.

Expenses for 2006–07 *Application fee:* $25. *State resident tuition:* $5670 full-time, $189 per credit hour part-time. *Nonresident tuition:* $11,280 full-time, $376 per credit hour part-time. *Mandatory fees:* $1468 full-time, $227 per term part-time. *College room and board:* $6492.

Financial Aid Forms of aid include need-based and non-need-based scholarships and part-time jobs. The priority application deadline for financial aid is March 30.

Freshman Admission Chicago State University requires a high school transcript, a minimum 2.5 high school GPA, SAT or ACT scores, and TOEFL scores for international students. An essay and an interview are required for some.

Transfer Admission Chicago State University requires a minimum 2.0 college GPA.

Entrance Difficulty Chicago State University assesses its entrance difficulty level as minimally difficult. For the fall 2006 freshman class, 56 percent of the applicants were accepted.

For Further Information Contact Ms. Addie Epps, Director of Admissions, Chicago State University, 95th Street at King Drive, ADM 200, Chicago, IL 60628. *Telephone:* 773-995-2513. *Fax:* 773-995-3820. *E-mail:* ug-admissions@csu.edu. *Web site:* http://www.csu.edu/.

CHRISTIAN LIFE COLLEGE
Mount Prospect, Illinois
http://www.christianlifecollege.edu/

COLLEGE OF ST. FRANCIS
See University of St. Francis.

COLUMBIA COLLEGE CHICAGO
Chicago, Illinois

SPONSOR See Front Insert for Details!

Columbia College Chicago is a coed, private, comprehensive institution, founded in 1890, offering degrees at the bachelor's and master's levels and postbachelor's certificates.

Academic Information The faculty has 1,477 members (22% full-time). The undergraduate student-faculty ratio is 14:1. The library holds 258,883 titles, 1,232 serial subscriptions, and 21,257 audiovisual materials. Special programs include academic remediation, services for learning-disabled students, cooperative (work-study) education, study abroad, advanced placement credit, ESL programs, independent study, self-designed majors, summer session for credit, part-time degree programs (daytime, evenings, weekends, summer), internships, and arrangement for off-campus study with Adler Planetarium. The most frequently chosen baccalaureate fields are liberal arts/general studies, communications/journalism, visual and performing arts.

Student Body Statistics The student body totals 11,499, of whom 10,771 are undergraduates (1,986 freshmen). 50 percent are women and 50 percent are men. Students come from 52 states and territories and 36 other countries. 70 percent are from Illinois. 1.2 percent are international students. 10 percent of the 2006 graduating class went on to graduate and professional schools.

Expenses for 2006–07 *Application fee:* $35. *Comprehensive fee:* $26,553 includes full-time tuition ($16,328), mandatory fees ($460), and college room and board ($9765). *College room only:* $8265. *Part-time tuition:* $565 per credit hour.

Financial Aid Forms of aid include need-based and non-need-based scholarships and part-time jobs. The priority application deadline for financial aid is August 15.

Freshman Admission Columbia College Chicago requires an essay, a high school transcript, and recommendations. A minimum 2.0 high school GPA, an interview, and SAT or ACT scores are recommended.

Entrance Difficulty Columbia College Chicago has an open admission policy.

SPECIAL MESSAGE TO STUDENTS

Social Life When Columbia students are not showing at campus galleries, publishing in award-winning magazines, or freestyling at poetry slams, they are actively participating in the life of Chicago's arts community. Columbia's young talent can be felt in theaters, bookstores, and radio stations throughout the city, and every spring, students return the favor by inviting Chicago to their doorstep for Manifest, the city's largest student arts exhibition.

Academic Highlights Columbia College takes a "hands-on, minds-on" approach to learning that encourages students to fully explore their chosen field of interest in the arts and communications. Intimate class settings facilitate personal attention and practical mentoring with a faculty of working professionals. Columbia's faculty and student body comprise a widely diverse mix of cultures and backgrounds, creating a stimulating environment ideally suited to the pursuit of creative innovation. A required core series of liberal arts classes provides a broad and enriching academic foundation.

Interviews and Campus Visits Columbia College Chicago encourages all prospective students to visit, get a feel for the urban campus life, and see up close whether or not Columbia is the right college for them. Campus tours are offered Monday through Friday at 10 and 2 and Saturday at 11. The nearest commercial airport is O'Hare International.

For Further Information Write to Murphy Monroe, Executive Director of Admissions, Columbia College Chicago, 600 South Michigan Avenue, Chicago, Illinois 60647.Phone: 312-344-7130 *E-mail:* admissions@colum.edu. *Web site:* http:www.colum.edu.

See page 244 for the College Close-Up.

CONCORDIA UNIVERSITY
River Forest, Illinois

Concordia University is a coed, private, comprehensive unit of Concordia University System, founded in 1864, affiliated with the Lutheran Church–Missouri Synod, offering degrees at the bachelor's, master's, and doctoral levels and post-master's and postbachelor's certificates. It has a 40-acre campus in River Forest near Chicago.

Academic Information The faculty has 349 members (28% full-time). The undergraduate student-faculty ratio is 17:1. The library holds 140,000 titles, 235 serial subscriptions, and 2,250 audiovisual materials. Special programs include academic remediation, services for learning-disabled students, an honors program, study abroad, advanced placement credit, accelerated degree programs, double majors, independent study, distance learning, summer session for credit, part-time degree programs (daytime, evenings, summer), adult/continuing education programs, internships, and arrangement for off-campus study with Chicago Consortium of Colleges and Universities, Dominican University. The most frequently chosen baccalaureate fields are business/marketing, education, theology and religious vocations.

Student Body Statistics The student body totals 3,710, of whom 1,074 are undergraduates (206 freshmen). 61 percent are women and 39 percent are men. Students come from 22 states and territories and 1 other country. 65 percent are from Illinois. 23 percent of the 2006 graduating class went on to graduate and professional schools.

Expenses for 2007–08 *Comprehensive fee:* $28,312 includes full-time tuition ($20,900), mandatory fees ($420), and college room and board ($6992). *Part-time tuition:* $650 per semester hour.

Financial Aid Forms of aid include need-based and non-need-based scholarships. The average aided 2005–06 undergraduate received an aid package worth $13,580. The application deadline for financial aid is April 1 with a priority deadline of April 1.

Freshman Admission Concordia University requires a high school transcript, a minimum 2.0 high school GPA, 1 recommendation, minimum ACT score of 20 or SAT score of 930, SAT or ACT scores, and TOEFL scores for international students. An essay and an interview are required for some. The application deadline for regular admission is rolling.

Transfer Admission The application deadline for admission is rolling.

Entrance Difficulty Concordia University assesses its entrance difficulty level as moderately difficult. For the fall 2006 freshman class, 65 percent of the applicants were accepted.

For Further Information Contact Dr. Evelyn Burdick, Vice President for Enrollment Services, Concordia University, 7400 Augusta Street, River Forest, IL 60305. *Telephone:* 708-209-3100 or 800-285-2668 (toll-free). *Fax:* 708-209-3473. *E-mail:* crfadmis@cuchicago.edu. *Web site:* http://www.curf.edu/.

DePAUL UNIVERSITY
Chicago, Illinois

DePaul University is a coed, private, Roman Catholic university, founded in 1898, offering degrees at the bachelor's, master's, doctoral, and first professional levels and post-master's and postbachelor's certificates. It has a 36-acre campus in Chicago.

Academic Information The faculty has 1,697 members (50% full-time), 52% with terminal degrees. The undergraduate student-faculty ratio is 16:1. The library holds 897,564 titles, 28,514 serial subscriptions, and 27,242 audiovisual materials. Special programs include academic remediation, services for learning-disabled students, an honors program, cooperative (work-study) education, study abroad, advanced placement credit, accelerated degree programs, Freshman Honors College, ESL programs, double majors, independent study, distance learning, self-designed majors, summer session for credit, part-time degree programs, adult/continuing education programs, and internships. The most frequently chosen baccalaureate fields are business/marketing, computer and information sciences, liberal arts/general studies.

Student Body Statistics The student body totals 23,149, of whom 14,893 are undergraduates (2,537 freshmen). 56 percent are women and 44 percent are men. Students come from 50 states and territories and 74 other countries. 84 percent are from Illinois. 1.4 percent are international students. 14 percent of the 2006 graduating class went on to graduate and professional schools.

Expenses for 2006–07 *Application fee:* $40. *Comprehensive fee:* $32,967 includes full-time tuition ($22,365), mandatory fees ($210), and college room and board ($10,392). *College room only:* $6771. Full-time tuition and fees vary according to program. Room and board charges vary according to board plan, housing facility, and location. *Part-time tuition:* $405 per quarter hour. *Part-time mandatory fees:* $50 per term. Part-time tuition and fees vary according to program.

Financial Aid Forms of aid include need-based and non-need-based scholarships, athletic grants, and part-time jobs. The average aided 2005–06 undergraduate received an aid package worth $16,309. The application deadline for financial aid is April 1 with a priority deadline of March 1.

Freshman Admission DePaul University requires a high school transcript, a minimum 2.0 high school GPA, 1 recommendation, SAT or ACT scores, and TOEFL scores for international students. A minimum 3.0 high school GPA is recommended. A minimum 3.0 high school GPA, an interview, and audition are required for some. The application deadline for regular admission is rolling and for early action it is November 15.

Transfer Admission The application deadline for admission is rolling.

Entrance Difficulty DePaul University assesses its entrance difficulty level as moderately difficult. For the fall 2006 freshman class, 70 percent of the applicants were accepted.

For Further Information Contact Carlene Klaas, Undergraduate Admissions, DePaul University, 1 East Jackson Boulevard, Suite 9100, Chicago, IL 60604. *Telephone:* 312-362-8300. *E-mail:* admitdpu@depaul.edu. *Web site:* http://www.depaul.edu/.

DeVRY UNIVERSITY
Addison, Illinois

DeVry University is a coed, proprietary, four-year college of DeVry University, founded in 1982, offering degrees at the associate and bachelor's levels. It has a 14-acre campus in Addison near Chicago.

Academic Information The faculty has 106 members (48% full-time). The student-faculty ratio is 15:1. The library holds 18,500 titles and 4,000 serial subscriptions. Special programs include academic remediation, advanced placement credit, accelerated degree programs, distance learning, summer session for credit, part-time degree programs (daytime, evenings, weekends, summer), and adult/continuing education programs. The most frequently chosen baccalaureate fields are business/marketing, computer and information sciences, engineering technologies.

Student Body Statistics The student body is made up of 1,440 undergraduates (177 freshmen). 29 percent are women and 71 percent are men. 99 percent are from Illinois. 4.5 percent are international students.

Expenses for 2007–08 *Application fee:* $50. *Tuition:* $12,900 full-time, $490 per credit part-time. *Mandatory fees:* $320 full-time.

Financial Aid Forms of aid include need-based and non-need-based scholarships and part-time jobs. The application deadline for financial aid is continuous.

Freshman Admission DeVry University requires a high school transcript, an interview, and TOEFL scores for international students. The application deadline for regular admission is rolling.

Transfer Admission The application deadline for admission is rolling.

Entrance Difficulty DeVry University assesses its entrance difficulty level as minimally difficult; moderately difficult for electronics engineering technology program.

For Further Information Contact Admissions Office, DeVry University, 1221 North Swift Road, Addison, IL 60101. *Telephone:* 630-953-1300 or 800-346-5420 (toll-free). *Web site:* http://www.devry.edu/.

DeVRY UNIVERSITY
Chicago, Illinois

DeVry University is a coed, proprietary, comprehensive unit of DeVry University, founded in 1931, offering degrees at the associate and bachelor's levels. It has a 17-acre campus in Chicago.

Academic Information The faculty has 103 members (49% full-time). The student-faculty ratio is 22:1. The library holds 16,573 titles and 79 serial subscriptions. Special programs include academic remediation, services for learning-disabled students, advanced placement credit, accelerated degree programs, distance learning, summer session for credit, part-time degree programs (daytime, evenings, weekends, summer), and adult/continuing education programs. The most frequently chosen baccalaureate fields are business/marketing, computer and information sciences, engineering technologies.

Student Body Statistics The student body is made up of 2,055 undergraduates (282 freshmen). 39 percent are women and 61 percent are men. 99 percent are from Illinois. 7.4 percent are international students.

Expenses for 2007–08 *Application fee:* $50. *Tuition:* $12,900 full-time, $490 per credit part-time. *Mandatory fees:* $320 full-time.

Financial Aid Forms of aid include need-based and non-need-based scholarships and part-time jobs. The application deadline for financial aid is continuous.

Freshman Admission DeVry University requires a high school transcript, an interview, and TOEFL scores for international students. The application deadline for regular admission is rolling.

Transfer Admission The application deadline for admission is rolling.

Entrance Difficulty DeVry University assesses its entrance difficulty level as minimally difficult; moderately difficult for electronics engineering technology program.

For Further Information Contact Admissions Office, DeVry University, 3300 North Campbell Avenue, Chicago, IL 60618-5994. *Telephone:* 773-929-8500. *Web site:* http://www.devry.edu/.

DeVRY UNIVERSITY
Elgin, Illinois
http://www.devry.edu/

DeVRY UNIVERSITY
Gurnee, Illinois
http://www.devry.edu/

DeVRY UNIVERSITY
Naperville, Illinois

DeVry University is a coed, proprietary, comprehensive institution, offering degrees at the associate, bachelor's, and master's levels and postbachelor's certificates.

Academic Information The faculty has 2,248 members. The undergraduate student-faculty ratio is 6:1. Special programs include accelerated degree programs and distance learning.

Student Body Statistics The student body totals 8,828, of whom 6,083 are undergraduates (856 freshmen). 48 percent are women and 52 percent are men. 11 percent are from Illinois.

Expenses for 2007–08 *Application fee:* $50. *Tuition:* $14,320 full-time, $525 per credit part-time. *Mandatory fees:* $120 full-time.

Freshman Admission The application deadline for regular admission is rolling.

Transfer Admission The application deadline for admission is rolling.

For Further Information Contact Admissions Office, DeVry University, 1200 East Diehl Road, Naperville, IL 60563. *Telephone:* 630-428-9086 or 877-496-9050 (toll-free). *Web site:* http://www.devry.edu/.

DeVRY UNIVERSITY
Oakbrook Terrace, Illinois
http://www.devry.edu/

DeVRY UNIVERSITY

Tinley Park, Illinois

DeVry University is a coed, proprietary, comprehensive unit of DeVry University, founded in 2000, offering degrees at the associate, bachelor's, and master's levels and postbachelor's certificates. It has a 12-acre campus in Tinley Park.

Academic Information The faculty has 120 members (30% full-time). The undergraduate student-faculty ratio is 13:1. The library holds 17,500 titles and 82 serial subscriptions. Special programs include academic remediation, services for learning-disabled students, advanced placement credit, accelerated degree programs, distance learning, summer session for credit, part-time degree programs (daytime, evenings, weekends, summer), and adult/continuing education programs. The most frequently chosen baccalaureate fields are business/marketing, computer and information sciences, engineering technologies.

Student Body Statistics The student body totals 1,261, of whom 1,023 are undergraduates (235 freshmen). 29 percent are women and 71 percent are men. 92 percent are from Illinois. 0.9 percent are international students.

Expenses for 2007–08 *Application fee:* $50. *Tuition:* $12,900 full-time, $490 per credit part-time. *Mandatory fees:* $320 full-time.

Financial Aid Forms of aid include need-based and non-need-based scholarships and part-time jobs. The application deadline for financial aid is continuous.

Freshman Admission DeVry University requires a high school transcript, an interview, and TOEFL scores for international students. The application deadline for regular admission is rolling.

Transfer Admission The application deadline for admission is rolling.

Entrance Difficulty DeVry University assesses its entrance difficulty level as minimally difficult; moderately difficult for electronics engineering technology program.

For Further Information Contact Admissions Office, DeVry University, 18624 West Creek Drive, Tinley Park, IL 60477-6243. *Telephone:* 708-342-3300. *Web site:* http://www.devry.edu/.

DeVRY UNIVERSITY ONLINE

Oakbrook Terrace, Illinois

DeVry University Online is a coed, proprietary, comprehensive institution, founded in 2000, offering degrees at the associate, bachelor's, and master's levels and postbachelor's certificates.

Expenses for 2006–07 *Application fee:* $50. *Comprehensive fee:* $22,248 includes full-time tuition ($12,340), mandatory fees ($310), and college room and board ($9598). *College room only:* $7310. Full-time tuition and fees vary according to course load. *Part-time tuition:* $465 per credit. *Part-time mandatory fees:* $200 per year. Part-time tuition and fees vary according to course load.

For Further Information Contact Admissions Office, DeVry University Online, One Tower Lane, Suite 1000, Oakbrook Terrace, IL 60181. *Telephone:* 630-574-1960 or 866-338-7934 (toll-free). *Web site:* http://online.devry.edu/.

DOMINICAN UNIVERSITY

River Forest, Illinois

Dominican University is a coed, private, Roman Catholic, comprehensive institution, founded in 1901, offering degrees at the bachelor's and master's levels and post-master's certificates. It has a 30-acre campus in River Forest near Chicago.

Academic Information The faculty has 315 members (36% full-time), 45% with terminal degrees. The undergraduate student-faculty ratio is 12:1. The library holds 255,840 titles, 14,089 serial subscriptions, and 4,635 audiovisual materials. Special programs include services for learning-disabled students, an honors program, study abroad, advanced placement credit, accelerated degree programs, ESL programs, double majors, independent study, distance learning, self-designed majors, summer session

for credit, part-time degree programs (daytime, evenings, weekends, summer), adult/continuing education programs, internships, and arrangement for off-campus study with Concordia University (IL), Illinois Institute of Technology. The most frequently chosen baccalaureate fields are business/marketing, psychology, social sciences.

Student Body Statistics The student body totals 3,292, of whom 1,462 are undergraduates (362 freshmen). 71 percent are women and 29 percent are men. Students come from 28 states and territories and 18 other countries. 89 percent are from Illinois. 1.2 percent are international students. 15 percent of the 2006 graduating class went on to graduate and professional schools.

Expenses for 2006–07 *Application fee:* $25. *Comprehensive fee:* $27,870 includes full-time tuition ($21,150), mandatory fees ($100), and college room and board ($6620). Full-time tuition and fees vary according to program. Room and board charges vary according to board plan and housing facility. *Part-time tuition:* $705 per semester hour. *Part-time mandatory fees:* $10 per course. Part-time tuition and fees vary according to location and program.

Financial Aid Forms of aid include need-based and non-need-based scholarships and part-time jobs. The average aided 2006–07 undergraduate received an aid package worth an estimated $16,344. The priority application deadline for financial aid is June 1.

Freshman Admission Dominican University requires an essay, a high school transcript, a minimum 2.75 high school GPA, SAT or ACT scores, and TOEFL scores for international students. Recommendations and an interview are recommended. 2 recommendations and an interview are required for some. The application deadline for regular admission is rolling.

Transfer Admission The application deadline for admission is rolling.

Entrance Difficulty Dominican University assesses its entrance difficulty level as moderately difficult. For the fall 2006 freshman class, 84 percent of the applicants were accepted.

For Further Information Contact Mr. Glenn Hamilton, Director of Freshman Admission, Dominican University, 7900 West Division Street, River Forest, IL 60305. *Telephone:* 708-524-6800 or 800-828-8475 (toll-free). *Fax:* 708-524-6864. *E-mail:* domadmis@dom.edu. *Web site:* http://www.dom.edu/.

EASTERN ILLINOIS UNIVERSITY

Charleston, Illinois

Eastern Illinois University is a coed, public, comprehensive institution, founded in 1895, offering degrees at the bachelor's and master's levels and post-master's and postbachelor's certificates. It has a 320-acre campus in Charleston.

Academic Information The faculty has 770 members (80% full-time), 57% with terminal degrees. The undergraduate student-faculty ratio is 16:1. The library holds 1 million titles, 14,714 serial subscriptions, and 14,129 audiovisual materials. Special programs include academic remediation, services for learning-disabled students, an honors program, study abroad, advanced placement credit, double majors, independent study, distance learning, summer session for credit, part-time degree programs (daytime, evenings, weekends, summer), external degree programs, adult/continuing education programs, internships, and arrangement for off-campus study with Olney Central College, Kaskaskia College, Parkland College, Danville Aea Community College, Richland Community College, Lakeland College. The most frequently chosen baccalaureate fields are business/marketing, education, English.

Student Body Statistics The student body totals 12,349, of whom 10,592 are undergraduates (1,773 freshmen). 58 percent are women and 42 percent are men. Students come from 29 states and territories and 22 other countries. 99 percent are from Illinois. 0.5 percent are international students. 28 percent of the 2006 graduating class went on to graduate and professional schools.

Expenses for 2006–07 *Application fee:* $30. *State resident tuition:* $5207 full-time, $174 per credit hour part-time. *Nonresident tuition:* $15,620 full-time, $521 per credit hour part-time. *Mandatory fees:* $1862 full-time, $66 per credit hour part-time. Both full-time and part-time tuition and fees vary according to course load. *College room and board:* $6660. Room and board charges vary according to board plan and housing facility.

Financial Aid Forms of aid include need-based scholarships, athletic grants, and part-time jobs. The average aided 2006–07 undergraduate received an aid package worth an estimated $10,902. The priority application deadline for financial aid is March 1.

Freshman Admission Eastern Illinois University requires an essay, a high school transcript, a minimum 2.25 high school GPA, audition for music program, SAT or ACT scores, and TOEFL scores for international students. The application deadline for regular admission is rolling.

Transfer Admission The application deadline for admission is rolling.

Entrance Difficulty For the fall 2006 freshman class, 73 percent of the applicants were accepted.

For Further Information Contact Brenda Major, Director of Admissions, Eastern Illinois University, 600 Lincoln Avenue, Charleston, IL 61920-3099. *Telephone:* 217-581-2223 or 800-252-5711 (toll-free). *Fax:* 217-581-7060. *E-mail:* admissions@eiu.edu. *Web site:* http://www.eiu.edu/.

EAST-WEST UNIVERSITY
Chicago, Illinois

East-West University is a coed, private, four-year college, founded in 1978, offering degrees at the associate and bachelor's levels.

Academic Information The faculty has 70 members (21% full-time), 24% with terminal degrees. The student-faculty ratio is 15:1. The library holds 32,000 titles and 3,450 serial subscriptions. Special programs include academic remediation, double majors, independent study, summer session for credit, part-time degree programs (daytime, evenings, summer), and internships.

Student Body Statistics The student body is made up of 1,040 undergraduates. 65 percent are women and 35 percent are men. Students come from 5 states and territories and 12 other countries. 94 percent are from Illinois. 6.5 percent are international students.

Expenses for 2006–07 *Application fee:* $30. *Tuition:* $12,120 full-time, $385 per credit hour part-time. *Mandatory fees:* $525 full-time. Full-time tuition and fees vary according to course level.

Financial Aid Forms of aid include need-based and non-need-based scholarships and part-time jobs. The priority application deadline for financial aid is June 30.

Freshman Admission East-West University requires an essay, a high school transcript, a minimum 2.0 high school GPA, an interview, and ACT scores. TOEFL scores for international students are recommended. 1 recommendation is required for some. The application deadline for regular admission is rolling and for early decision it is July 1.

Transfer Admission The application deadline for admission is rolling.

Entrance Difficulty East-West University assesses its entrance difficulty level as minimally difficult. For the fall 2006 freshman class, 91 percent of the applicants were accepted.

For Further Information Contact Mr. William Link, Director of Admissions, East-West University, 819 South Wabash Avenue, Chicago, IL 60605-2103. *Telephone:* 312-939-0111. *Fax:* 312-939-0083. *E-mail:* seeyou@eastwest.edu. *Web site:* http://www.eastwest.edu/.

ELMHURST COLLEGE
Elmhurst, Illinois

Elmhurst College is a coed, private, comprehensive institution, founded in 1871, affiliated with the United Church of Christ, offering degrees at the bachelor's and master's levels. It has a 38-acre campus in Elmhurst near Chicago.

Academic Information The faculty has 313 members (39% full-time), 47% with terminal degrees. The undergraduate student-faculty ratio is 14:1. The library holds 222,441 titles and 2,010 serial subscriptions. Special programs include academic remediation, services for learning-disabled students, an honors program, cooperative (work-study) education, study abroad, advanced placement credit, accelerated degree programs, double majors, independent study, summer session for credit, part-time degree programs (daytime, evenings, weekends, summer), adult/continuing education programs, internships, and arrangement for off-campus study.

Student Body Statistics The student body totals 3,107, of whom 2,841 are undergraduates (485 freshmen). 65 percent are women and 35 percent are men. Students come from 26 states and territories and 21 other countries. 92 percent are from Illinois. 1.1 percent are international students. 17 percent of the 2006 graduating class went on to graduate and professional schools.

Expenses for 2007–08 *Application fee:* $0. *Comprehensive fee:* $31,824 includes full-time tuition ($24,600), mandatory fees ($60), and college room and board ($7164). *College room only:* $4200. *Part-time tuition:* $700 per semester hour. *Part-time mandatory fees:* $30 per term.

Financial Aid Forms of aid include need-based and non-need-based scholarships and part-time jobs. The average aided 2006–07 undergraduate received an aid package worth an estimated $15,692. The priority application deadline for financial aid is April 15.

Freshman Admission Elmhurst College requires a high school transcript, SAT or ACT scores, and TOEFL scores for international students. An essay and an interview are recommended. An essay, recommendations, and an interview are required for some. The application deadline for regular admission is July 15.

Entrance Difficulty Elmhurst College assesses its entrance difficulty level as moderately difficult. For the fall 2006 freshman class, 72 percent of the applicants were accepted.

For Further Information Contact Mrs. Stephanie Levenson, Director of Admission, Elmhurst College, Elmhurst College Admission Office, 190 South Prospect Avenue, Elmhurst, IL 60126-3296. *Telephone:* 630-617-3400 or 800-697-1871 (toll-free out-of-state). *Fax:* 630-617-5501. *E-mail:* admit@elmhurst.edu. *Web site:* http://www.elmhurst.edu/.

EUREKA COLLEGE
Eureka, Illinois

http://www.eureka.edu/

GOVERNORS STATE UNIVERSITY
University Park, Illinois

Governors State University is a coed, public, upper-level institution, founded in 1969, offering degrees at the bachelor's and master's levels. It has a 750-acre campus in University Park near Chicago.

Expenses for 2006–07 *Application fee:* $0. *State resident tuition:* $3912 full-time, $163 per credit part-time. *Nonresident tuition:* $11,736 full-time, $489 per credit part-time. *Mandatory fees:* $580 full-time, $11 per credit part-time, $170 per term part-time. Both full-time and part-time tuition and fees vary according to course load and location.

For Further Information Contact Mr. Randall Tumblin, Director of Admissions, Governors State University, One University Parkway, University Park, IL 60466. *Telephone:* 708-534-4490. *Fax:* 708-534-1640. *E-mail:* gsunow@govst.edu. *Web site:* http://www.govst.edu/.

GREENVILLE COLLEGE
Greenville, Illinois

Greenville College is a coed, private, Free Methodist, comprehensive institution, founded in 1892, offering degrees at the bachelor's and master's levels. It has a 12-acre campus in Greenville near St. Louis.

Academic Information The faculty has 152 members (36% full-time), 37% with terminal degrees. The undergraduate student-faculty ratio is 16:1. The library holds 134,569 titles, 490 serial subscriptions, and 3,711 audiovisual materials. Special programs include academic remediation, an honors program, cooperative (work-study) education, study abroad, advanced placement credit, accelerated degree programs, double majors, independent study, self-designed majors, summer session for credit, part-time degree programs (daytime, evenings, summer), adult/continuing education programs, internships, and arrangement for off-campus study with 13 members of the Christian College Consortium; 100 members of

Greenville College (continued)

the Council for Christian Colleges and Universities. The most frequently chosen baccalaureate fields are business/marketing, education, visual and performing arts.

Student Body Statistics The student body totals 1,451, of whom 1,322 are undergraduates (299 freshmen). 55 percent are women and 45 percent are men. Students come from 40 states and territories and 15 other countries. 71 percent are from Illinois. 1.3 percent are international students.

Expenses for 2006–07 *Application fee:* $25. *Comprehensive fee:* $24,068 includes full-time tuition ($17,812), mandatory fees ($120), and college room and board ($6136). *College room only:* $2904. Room and board charges vary according to housing facility. *Part-time tuition:* $375 per credit hour. Part-time tuition varies according to course load.

Financial Aid Forms of aid include need-based and non-need-based scholarships and part-time jobs. The average aided 2005–06 undergraduate received an aid package worth $14,307. The application deadline for financial aid is continuous.

Freshman Admission Greenville College requires an essay, a high school transcript, a minimum 2.5 high school GPA, 2 recommendations, agreement to code of conduct, and SAT or ACT scores. An interview is required for some. The application deadline for regular admission is August 1.

Transfer Admission The application deadline for admission is August 1.

Entrance Difficulty Greenville College assesses its entrance difficulty level as moderately difficult. For the fall 2006 freshman class, 82 percent of the applicants were accepted.

For Further Information Contact Mr. Michael Ritter, Director of Admissions, Greenville College, 315 East College Avenue, Greenville, IL 62246. *Telephone:* 618-664-7100 or 800-345-4440 (toll-free). *Fax:* 618-664-9841. *E-mail:* admissions@greenville.edu. *Web site:* http://www.greenville.edu/.

HARRINGTON COLLEGE OF DESIGN
Chicago, Illinois

Harrington College of Design is a coed, primarily women's, proprietary, four-year college of Career Education Corporation, founded in 1931, offering degrees at the associate and bachelor's levels.

Academic Information The faculty has 142 members (12% full-time). The student-faculty ratio is 12:1. The library holds 22,000 titles, 149 serial subscriptions, and 450 audiovisual materials. Special programs include study abroad, part-time degree programs, and internships. The most frequently chosen baccalaureate field is visual and performing arts.

Student Body Statistics The student body is made up of 1,563 undergraduates (423 freshmen). 87 percent are women and 13 percent are men. Students come from 19 states and territories. 94 percent are from Illinois.

Expenses for 2007–08 *Application fee:* $60. *Tuition:* $18,000 full-time, $600 per credit part-time. *Mandatory fees:* $2520 full-time, $1260 per term part-time. *College room only:* $2600.

Financial Aid Forms of aid include need-based and non-need-based scholarships. The application deadline for financial aid is continuous.

Freshman Admission Harrington College of Design requires a high school transcript, an interview, and TOEFL scores for international students. An essay and 1 recommendation are recommended. The application deadline for regular admission is rolling.

Entrance Difficulty Harrington College of Design assesses its entrance difficulty level as noncompetitive.

For Further Information Contact Ms. Melissa Laurentius, Director of Admissions, Harrington College of Design, 200 West Madison, Chicago, IL 60606. *Telephone:* 312-939-4975 or 877-939-4975 (toll-free). *Fax:* 312-939-8032. *E-mail:* barrington@interiordesign.edu. *Web site:* http://www.interiordesign.edu/.

HEBREW THEOLOGICAL COLLEGE
Skokie, Illinois
http://www.htcnet.edu/

ILLINOIS COLLEGE
Jacksonville, Illinois

Illinois College is a coed, private, interdenominational, four-year college, founded in 1829, offering degrees at the bachelor's level. It has a 62-acre campus in Jacksonville near St. Louis.

Academic Information The faculty has 90 members (81% full-time), 73% with terminal degrees. The student-faculty ratio is 12:1. The library holds 163,810 titles and 10,234 serial subscriptions. Special programs include study abroad, advanced placement credit, accelerated degree programs, double majors, independent study, summer session for credit, and internships. The most frequently chosen baccalaureate fields are biological/life sciences, business/marketing, social sciences.

Student Body Statistics The student body is made up of 1,023 undergraduates (293 freshmen). 53 percent are women and 47 percent are men. Students come from 20 states and territories and 14 other countries. 92 percent are from Illinois. 1.7 percent are international students. 27 percent of the 2006 graduating class went on to graduate and professional schools.

Expenses for 2006–07 *Application fee:* $0. *Comprehensive fee:* $23,830 includes full-time tuition ($17,100) and college room and board ($6730). *College room only:* $2800. *Part-time tuition:* $715 per credit hour.

Financial Aid Forms of aid include need-based and non-need-based scholarships and part-time jobs. The average aided 2006–07 undergraduate received an aid package worth an estimated $13,570. The priority application deadline for financial aid is March 1.

Freshman Admission Illinois College requires a high school transcript, 1 recommendation, SAT or ACT scores, and TOEFL scores for international students. An essay, a minimum 2.5 high school GPA, and an interview are recommended. An essay is required for some. The application deadline for regular admission is July 1.

Transfer Admission The application deadline for admission is July 1.

Entrance Difficulty Illinois College assesses its entrance difficulty level as moderately difficult. For the fall 2006 freshman class, 73 percent of the applicants were accepted.

For Further Information Contact Mr. Rick Bystry, Associate Director of Admission, Illinois College, 1101 West College, Jacksonville, IL 62650. *Telephone:* 217-245-3030 or 866-464-5265 (toll-free). *Fax:* 217-245-3034. *E-mail:* admissions@ic.edu. *Web site:* http://www.ic.edu/.

THE ILLINOIS INSTITUTE OF ART–CHICAGO
Chicago, Illinois

The Illinois Institute of Art–Chicago is a coed, proprietary, four-year college of Education Management Corporation, founded in 1916, offering degrees at the associate and bachelor's levels. It has a 2-acre campus in Chicago.

Academic Information The faculty has 175 members (42% full-time). The student-faculty ratio is 24:1. The library holds 11,324 titles and 264 serial subscriptions. Special programs include academic remediation, services for learning-disabled students, cooperative (work-study) education, study abroad, advanced placement credit, accelerated degree programs, independent study, distance learning, summer session for credit, part-time degree programs (daytime, evenings, weekends, summer), adult/continuing education programs, internships, and arrangement for off-campus study with members of the International Council of Design Schools. The most frequently chosen baccalaureate fields are communication technologies, communications/journalism, visual and performing arts.

Student Body Statistics The student body is made up of 2,680 undergraduates (1,004 freshmen). 61 percent are women and 39 percent are men. Students come from 38 states and territories and 24 other countries. 65 percent are from Illinois. 3 percent of the 2006 graduating class went on to graduate and professional schools.

Expenses for 2007–08 *Application fee:* $50. *Tuition:* $19,968 full-time, $416 per credit part-time. *Mandatory fees:* $316 full-time. *College room only:* $11,512.

Financial Aid Forms of aid include need-based and non-need-based scholarships and part-time jobs. The application deadline for financial aid is continuous.

Freshman Admission The Illinois Institute of Art–Chicago requires an essay, a high school transcript, and an interview. A minimum 2.0 high school GPA and ACT scores are recommended. Recommendations, a portfolio, and ACT ASSET are required for some. The application deadline for regular admission is rolling.

Transfer Admission The application deadline for admission is rolling.

Entrance Difficulty The Illinois Institute of Art–Chicago assesses its entrance difficulty level as minimally difficult. For the fall 2006 freshman class, 48 percent of the applicants were accepted.

For Further Information Contact Ms. Janis Anton, Vice President, Director of Admissions, The Illinois Institute of Art–Chicago, 350 North Orleans Street, Chicago, IL 60654. *Telephone:* 800-351-3450 or 800-351-3450 (toll-free). *Fax:* 312-280-8562. *E-mail:* janton@aii.edu. *Web site:* http://www.ilic.artinstitutes.edu/.

See page 254 for the College Close-Up.

THE ILLINOIS INSTITUTE OF ART–SCHAUMBURG
Schaumburg, Illinois

The Illinois Institute of Art–Schaumburg is a coed, proprietary, four-year college of Education Management Corporation, offering degrees at the associate and bachelor's levels.

Academic Information The faculty has 72 members (50% full-time), 92% with terminal degrees. The student-faculty ratio is 19:1. Special programs include services for learning-disabled students, advanced placement credit, accelerated degree programs, double majors, independent study, self-designed majors, summer session for credit, part-time degree programs (daytime, evenings, weekends, summer), internships, and arrangement for off-campus study.

Student Body Statistics The student body is made up of 1,213 undergraduates (205 freshmen). 49 percent are women and 51 percent are men. Students come from 19 states and territories and 2 other countries. 87 percent are from Illinois. 0.2 percent are international students.

Expenses for 2006–07 *Application fee:* $0. *Tuition:* $18,675 full-time, $416 per credit hour part-time.

Financial Aid Forms of aid include need-based and non-need-based scholarships and part-time jobs. The priority application deadline for financial aid is May 1.

Freshman Admission The Illinois Institute of Art–Schaumburg requires an essay, a high school transcript, a minimum 2.0 high school GPA, and TOEFL scores for international students. Recommendations and an interview are required for some. The application deadline for regular admission is rolling.

Transfer Admission The application deadline for admission is rolling.

Entrance Difficulty The Illinois Institute of Art–Schaumburg assesses its entrance difficulty level as minimally difficult. For the fall 2006 freshman class, 83 percent of the applicants were accepted.

For Further Information Contact Mr. Brian Cicero, Interim Director of Admissions, The Illinois Institute of Art–Schaumburg, 1000 Plaza Drive, Suite 100, Schaumburg, IL 60173. *Telephone:* 847-619-3450 or 800-314-3450 (toll-free). *Fax:* 847-619-3064. *Web site:* http://www.ilis.artinstitutes.edu/.

ILLINOIS INSTITUTE OF TECHNOLOGY
Chicago, Illinois

Illinois Institute of Technology is a coed, private university, founded in 1890, offering degrees at the bachelor's, master's, doctoral, and first professional levels and postbachelor's certificates. It has a 120-acre campus in Chicago.

Academic Information The faculty has 631 members (58% full-time), 49% with terminal degrees. The undergraduate student-faculty ratio is 7:1. The library holds 1 million titles, 21,498 serial subscriptions, and 3,266 audiovisual materials. Special programs include services for learning-disabled students, cooperative (work-study) education, study abroad, advanced placement credit, ESL programs, double majors, independent study, distance learning, summer session for credit, part-time degree programs (daytime, evenings, summer), and internships.

Student Body Statistics The student body totals 6,795, of whom 2,353 are undergraduates (484 freshmen). 25 percent are women and 75 percent are men. Students come from 48 states and territories and 74 other countries. 57 percent are from Illinois. 14.3 percent are international students. 77 percent of the 2006 graduating class went on to graduate and professional schools.

Expenses for 2006–07 *Application fee:* $30. *Comprehensive fee:* $32,162 includes full-time tuition ($23,329), mandatory fees ($784), and college room and board ($8049). *College room only:* $4212. Room and board charges vary according to board plan and housing facility. *Part-time tuition:* $727 per credit hour. *Part-time mandatory fees:* $7 per credit hour, $250 per term. Part-time tuition and fees vary according to course load.

Financial Aid Forms of aid include need-based and non-need-based scholarships, athletic grants, and part-time jobs. The average aided 2005–06 undergraduate received an aid package worth $21,490.

Freshman Admission Illinois Institute of Technology requires a high school transcript, a minimum 3.0 high school GPA, 1 recommendation, minimum ACT score of 24 or SAT score of 1150, SAT or ACT scores, and TOEFL scores for international students. An essay is recommended. An interview is required for some. The application deadline for regular admission is August 1 and for nonresidents it is August 1.

Transfer Admission The application deadline for admission is rolling.

Entrance Difficulty Illinois Institute of Technology assesses its entrance difficulty level as very difficult. For the fall 2006 freshman class, 54 percent of the applicants were accepted.

For Further Information Contact Mr. Gerald Doyle, Associate Vice President, Undergraduate Admissions, Illinois Institute of Technology, 10 West 33rd Street, Perlestein Hall Room 101, Chicago, IL 60616-3793. *Telephone:* 312-567-3025 or 800-448-2329 (toll-free out-of-state). *Fax:* 312-567-6939. *E-mail:* admission@iit.edu. *Web site:* http://www.iit.edu/.

See page 256 for the College Close-Up.

ILLINOIS STATE UNIVERSITY
Normal, Illinois

Illinois State University is a coed, public university, founded in 1857, offering degrees at the bachelor's, master's, and doctoral levels and post-master's and postbachelor's certificates. It has an 850-acre campus in Normal.

Academic Information The faculty has 1,113 members (77% full-time), 70% with terminal degrees. The undergraduate student-faculty ratio is 19:1. The library holds 2 million titles and 14,166 serial subscriptions. Special programs include academic remediation, services for learning-disabled students, an honors program, cooperative (work-study) education, study abroad, advanced placement credit, accelerated degree programs, ESL programs, double majors, independent study, distance learning, self-designed majors, summer session for credit, part-time degree programs (daytime, evenings, summer), adult/continuing education programs, internships, and arrangement for off-campus study with National Student Exchange. The most frequently chosen baccalaureate fields are business/marketing, education, social sciences.

Student Body Statistics The student body totals 20,521, of whom 17,885 are undergraduates (3,200 freshmen). 57 percent are women and 43 percent are men. Students come from 48 states and territories and 38 other countries. 98 percent are from Illinois. 0.7 percent are international students.

Expenses for 2006–07 *Application fee:* $40. *State resident tuition:* $6150 full-time, $205 per credit hour part-time. *Nonresident tuition:* $12,840 full-time, $428 per credit hour part-time. *Mandatory fees:* $1,890 full-time, $52.45 per credit hour part-time, $786.75 per term part-time. Both full-time and part-time tuition and fees vary according to course load. *College room and board:* $6148. *College room only:* $3200. Room and board charges vary according to board plan.

Financial Aid Forms of aid include need-based and non-need-based scholarships, athletic grants, and part-time jobs. The average aided

Illinois

Illinois State University (continued)

2006–07 undergraduate received an aid package worth an estimated $9515. The priority application deadline for financial aid is March 1.
Freshman Admission Illinois State University requires an essay, a high school transcript, SAT or ACT scores, and TOEFL scores for international students. The application deadline for regular admission is March 1.
Transfer Admission The application deadline for admission is rolling.
Entrance Difficulty Illinois State University assesses its entrance difficulty level as moderately difficult. For the fall 2006 freshman class, 68 percent of the applicants were accepted.
For Further Information Contact Ms. Molly Arnold, Director of Admissions, Illinois State University, Campus Box 2200, Normal, IL 61790-2200. *Telephone:* 309-438-2181 or 800-366-2478 (toll-free in-state). *Fax:* 309-438-3932. *E-mail:* admissions@ilstu.edu. *Web site:* http://www.ilstu.edu/.

ILLINOIS WESLEYAN UNIVERSITY
Bloomington, Illinois

Illinois Wesleyan University is a coed, private, four-year college, founded in 1850, offering degrees at the bachelor's level. It has a 79-acre campus in Bloomington.

Academic Information The faculty has 224 members (72% full-time), 80% with terminal degrees. The student-faculty ratio is 12:1. The library holds 313,495 titles, 12,238 serial subscriptions, and 13,084 audiovisual materials. Special programs include services for learning-disabled students, an honors program, study abroad, advanced placement credit, double majors, independent study, self-designed majors, internships, and arrangement for off-campus study with Midwest College Arts program, Colleges of the Midwest Urban Education program, Washington semester, United Nations semester. The most frequently chosen baccalaureate fields are business/marketing, social sciences, visual and performing arts.
Student Body Statistics The student body is made up of 2,144 undergraduates (552 freshmen). 58 percent are women and 42 percent are men. Students come from 39 states and territories and 19 other countries. 86 percent are from Illinois. 2.1 percent are international students. 32 percent of the 2006 graduating class went on to graduate and professional schools.
Expenses for 2007–08 *Application fee:* $0. *Comprehensive fee:* $37,780 includes full-time tuition ($30,580), mandatory fees ($170), and college room and board ($7030). *College room only:* $4330. *Part-time tuition:* $3823 per course.
Financial Aid Forms of aid include need-based and non-need-based scholarships and part-time jobs. The average aided 2006–07 undergraduate received an aid package worth an estimated $21,417. The application deadline for financial aid is March 1 with a priority deadline of March 1.
Freshman Admission Illinois Wesleyan University requires an essay, a high school transcript, a minimum 2.0 high school GPA, 1 recommendation, SAT or ACT scores, and TOEFL scores for international students. A minimum 3.0 high school GPA, 2 recommendations, and an interview are recommended.
Entrance Difficulty Illinois Wesleyan University assesses its entrance difficulty level as very difficult. For the fall 2006 freshman class, 52 percent of the applicants were accepted.
For Further Information Contact Mr. Tony Bankston, Dean of Admissions, Illinois Wesleyan University, PO Box 2900, Bloomington, IL 61702-2900. *Telephone:* 309-556-3031 or 800-332-2498 (toll-free). *Fax:* 309-556-3820. *E-mail:* iwuadmit@iwu.edu. *Web site:* http://www.iwu.edu/.

INTERNATIONAL ACADEMY OF DESIGN & TECHNOLOGY
Chicago, Illinois

International Academy of Design & Technology is a coed, proprietary, four-year college of Career Education Corporation, founded in 1977, offering degrees at the associate and bachelor's levels. It has a 1-acre campus in Chicago.

Academic Information The faculty has 166 members (16% full-time), 2% with terminal degrees. The student-faculty ratio is 14:1. The library holds 6,500 titles and 80 serial subscriptions. Special programs include academic remediation, services for learning-disabled students, study abroad, advanced placement credit, independent study, summer session for credit, part-time degree programs (daytime, evenings, weekends, summer), adult/continuing education programs, and internships. The most frequently chosen baccalaureate fields are business/marketing, computer and information sciences, visual and performing arts.
Student Body Statistics The student body is made up of 2,341 undergraduates (564 freshmen). 69 percent are women and 31 percent are men. Students come from 19 states and territories. 95 percent are from Illinois. 2.8 percent are international students.
Expenses for 2006–07 *Application fee:* $50. *Tuition:* $22,400 full-time, $2200 per course part-time. *Mandatory fees:* $600 full-time, $150 per term part-time. Both full-time and part-time tuition and fees vary according to course load and program.
Financial Aid Forms of aid include need-based scholarships and part-time jobs. The application deadline for financial aid is continuous.
Freshman Admission International Academy of Design & Technology requires a high school transcript and an interview. An essay and a minimum 2.0 high school GPA are recommended. GED is required for some. The application deadline for regular admission is rolling.
Transfer Admission The application deadline for admission is rolling.
Entrance Difficulty International Academy of Design & Technology assesses its entrance difficulty level as minimally difficult. For the fall 2006 freshman class, 52 percent of the applicants were accepted.
For Further Information Contact Suzanne Reichart, Director of Student Management, International Academy of Design & Technology, One North State Street, Suite 400, Chicago, IL 60602. *Telephone:* 312-980-9200 or 877-ACADEMY (toll-free out-of-state). *Fax:* 312-541-3929. *E-mail:* sreichart@iadtchicago.com. *Web site:* http://www.iadtchicago.edu/.

See page 258 for the College Close-Up.

ITT TECHNICAL INSTITUTE
Burr Ridge, Illinois

ITT Technical Institute is a coed, proprietary, primarily two-year college of ITT Educational Services, Inc, founded in 1998, offering degrees at the associate and bachelor's levels.

Expenses for 2006–07 *Application fee:* $100. Contact school for program costs.
Financial Aid Forms of aid include need-based scholarships and part-time jobs. The application deadline for financial aid is continuous.
Freshman Admission ITT Technical Institute requires a high school transcript, an interview, and Wonderlic aptitude test. Recommendations are recommended. The application deadline for regular admission is rolling.
Transfer Admission The application deadline for admission is rolling.
Entrance Difficulty ITT Technical Institute assesses its entrance difficulty level as minimally difficult.
For Further Information Contact Mr. Andrew Mical, Director of Recruitment, ITT Technical Institute, 7040 High Grove Boulevard, Burr Ridge, IL 60527. *Telephone:* 630-455-6470 or 877-488-0001 (toll-free in-state). *Fax:* 630-455-6476. *Web site:* http://www.itt-tech.edu/.

ITT TECHNICAL INSTITUTE
Mount Prospect, Illinois

ITT Technical Institute is a coed, proprietary, primarily two-year college of ITT Educational Services, Inc, founded in 1986, offering degrees at the associate, bachelor's, and master's levels. It has a 1-acre campus in Mount Prospect near Chicago.

Expenses for 2006–07 *Application fee:* $100. Contact school for program costs.
Financial Aid Forms of aid include need-based scholarships and part-time jobs. The application deadline for financial aid is continuous.

54 *www.petersons.com*

Peterson's Colleges in the Midwest 2008

Freshman Admission ITT Technical Institute requires a high school transcript, an interview, and Wonderlic aptitude test. Recommendations and TOEFL scores for international students are recommended. The application deadline for regular admission is rolling.
Transfer Admission The application deadline for admission is rolling.
Entrance Difficulty ITT Technical Institute assesses its entrance difficulty level as minimally difficult.
For Further Information Contact Mr. Cesar Rodriguez Jr., Director of Recruitment, ITT Technical Institute, 1401 Feehanville Drive, Mount Prospect, IL 60056. *Telephone:* 847-375-8800. *Fax:* 847-375-9022. *Web site:* http://www.itt-tech.edu/.

ITT TECHNICAL INSTITUTE
Orland Park, Illinois

ITT Technical Institute is a coed, proprietary, primarily two-year college of ITT Educational Services, Inc, founded in 1993, offering degrees at the associate and bachelor's levels. It is located in Orland Park near Chicago.

Expenses for 2006–07 *Application fee:* $100. Contact school for program costs.
Financial Aid Forms of aid include need-based scholarships and part-time jobs. The application deadline for financial aid is continuous.
Freshman Admission ITT Technical Institute requires a high school transcript, an interview, and Wonderlic aptitude test. Recommendations are recommended. The application deadline for regular admission is rolling.
Transfer Admission The application deadline for admission is rolling.
Entrance Difficulty ITT Technical Institute assesses its entrance difficulty level as minimally difficult.
For Further Information Contact Mr. James Tannheimer, ITT Technical Institute, 11551 184th Place, Orland Park, IL 60467. *Telephone:* 708-326-3200. *Fax:* 708-747-0023. *Web site:* http://www.itt-tech.edu/.

JUDSON COLLEGE
Elgin, Illinois

Judson College is a coed, private, Baptist, comprehensive institution, founded in 1963, offering degrees at the bachelor's and master's levels. It has an 80-acre campus in Elgin near Chicago.

Academic Information The faculty has 133 members (43% full-time), 32% with terminal degrees. The undergraduate student-faculty ratio is 14:1. The library holds 104,331 titles, 450 serial subscriptions, and 12,500 audiovisual materials. Special programs include academic remediation, an honors program, study abroad, advanced placement credit, accelerated degree programs, double majors, independent study, distance learning, part-time degree programs (evenings, weekends), external degree programs, adult/continuing education programs, internships, and arrangement for off-campus study with Christian College Coalition.
Student Body Statistics The student body totals 1,243, of whom 1,180 are undergraduates (160 freshmen). 59 percent are women and 41 percent are men. Students come from 18 states and territories and 28 other countries. 76 percent are from Illinois. 3.7 percent are international students.
Expenses for 2007–08 *Application fee:* $35. *Comprehensive fee:* $27,620 includes full-time tuition ($20,100), mandatory fees ($320), and college room and board ($7200). *Part-time tuition:* $670 per credit hour.
Financial Aid Forms of aid include need-based and non-need-based scholarships, athletic grants, and part-time jobs. The average aided 2005–06 undergraduate received an aid package worth $12,036. The application deadline for financial aid is continuous.
Freshman Admission Judson College requires a high school transcript, a minimum 2.0 high school GPA, lifestyle statement, SAT and SAT Subject Test or ACT scores, and TOEFL scores for international students. An essay, 3 recommendations, and an interview are required for some. The application deadline for regular admission is rolling.
Transfer Admission The application deadline for admission is rolling.

Entrance Difficulty Judson College assesses its entrance difficulty level as moderately difficult. For the fall 2006 freshman class, 53 percent of the applicants were accepted.
For Further Information Contact Mr. Billy Dean, Director of Admissions, Judson College, 1151 North State Street, Elgin, IL 60123-1498. *Telephone:* 847-695-2500 or 800-879-5376 (toll-free). *Fax:* 847-628-2526. *E-mail:* bdean@judsoncollege.edu. *Web site:* http://www.judsoncollege.edu/.

KENDALL COLLEGE
Chicago, Illinois

Kendall College is a coed, private, United Methodist, four-year college, founded in 1934, offering degrees at the associate and bachelor's levels. It has a 4-acre campus in Chicago.

Academic Information The faculty has 80 members (46% full-time). The student-faculty ratio is 19:1. The library holds 37,000 titles and 215 serial subscriptions. Special programs include academic remediation, cooperative (work-study) education, study abroad, advanced placement credit, accelerated degree programs, ESL programs, independent study, self-designed majors, summer session for credit, part-time degree programs (daytime, evenings, weekends, summer), adult/continuing education programs, and internships.
Student Body Statistics The student body is made up of 950 undergraduates. 66 percent are women and 34 percent are men. Students come from 20 states and territories and 19 other countries. 87 percent are from Illinois.
Expenses for 2006–07 *Application fee:* $50. *Comprehensive fee:* $27,600 includes full-time tuition ($16,950), mandatory fees ($450), and college room and board ($10,200).
Financial Aid Forms of aid include need-based and non-need-based scholarships, athletic grants, and part-time jobs. The priority application deadline for financial aid is May 1.
Freshman Admission Kendall College requires an essay, a high school transcript, minimum ACT score of 18, SAT or ACT scores, and TOEFL scores for international students. A minimum 2.0 high school GPA is recommended. Recommendations and an interview are required for some. The application deadline for regular admission is rolling.
Transfer Admission The application deadline for admission is rolling.
Entrance Difficulty Kendall College assesses its entrance difficulty level as moderately difficult. For the fall 2006 freshman class, 44 percent of the applicants were accepted.
For Further Information Contact Susanne Noel, Vice President of Admissions, Kendall College, 900 N North Branch Street, Chicago, IL 60622. *Telephone:* 312-752-2020, 866-667-3344 (toll-free in-state), or 877-588-8860 (toll-free out-of-state). *Fax:* 312-752-2021. *E-mail:* admissions@kendall.edu. *Web site:* http://www.kendall.edu/.

KNOX COLLEGE
Galesburg, Illinois

Knox College is a coed, private, four-year college, founded in 1837, offering degrees at the bachelor's level. It has an 82-acre campus in Galesburg near Peoria.

Academic Information The faculty has 127 members (76% full-time), 86% with terminal degrees. The student-faculty ratio is 13:1. The library holds 316,886 titles, 519 serial subscriptions, and 7,461 audiovisual materials. Special programs include academic remediation, services for learning-disabled students, an honors program, study abroad, advanced placement credit, double majors, independent study, self-designed majors, part-time degree programs (daytime), internships, and arrangement for off-campus study with Associated Colleges of the Midwest, Great Lakes College Association. The most frequently chosen baccalaureate fields are English, social sciences, visual and performing arts.
Student Body Statistics The student body is made up of 1,351 undergraduates (407 freshmen). 56 percent are women and 44 percent are men. Students come from 45 states and territories and 44 other countries.

Knox College (continued)

51 percent are from Illinois. 6.9 percent are international students. 35 percent of the 2006 graduating class went on to graduate and professional schools.

Expenses for 2006–07 *Application fee:* $40. *Comprehensive fee:* $33,825 includes full-time tuition ($27,606), mandatory fees ($294), and college room and board ($5925). *College room only:* $2865. Room and board charges vary according to board plan. *Part-time tuition:* $921 per credit. Part-time tuition varies according to course load.

Financial Aid Forms of aid include need-based and non-need-based scholarships and part-time jobs. The average aided 2006–07 undergraduate received an aid package worth an estimated $22,477. The priority application deadline for financial aid is February 1.

Freshman Admission Knox College requires an essay, a high school transcript, 2 recommendations, and TOEFL scores for international students. An interview and SAT or ACT scores are recommended. The application deadline for regular admission is February 1 and for early action it is December 1.

Transfer Admission The application deadline for admission is April 1.

Entrance Difficulty Knox College assesses its entrance difficulty level as very difficult. For the fall 2006 freshman class, 74 percent of the applicants were accepted.

For Further Information Contact Mr. Paul Steenis, Director of Admissions, Knox College, Box K-148, Galesburg, IL 61401. *Telephone:* 309-341-7100 or 800-678-KNOX (toll-free). *Fax:* 309-341-7070. *E-mail:* admission@knox.edu. *Web site:* http://www.knox.edu/.

LAKE FOREST COLLEGE
Lake Forest, Illinois

Lake Forest College is a coed, private, comprehensive institution, founded in 1857, offering degrees at the bachelor's and master's levels. It has a 110-acre campus in Lake Forest near Chicago.

Academic Information The faculty has 155 members (57% full-time), 77% with terminal degrees. The undergraduate student-faculty ratio is 13:1. The library holds 263,918 titles, 1,798 serial subscriptions, and 5,800 audiovisual materials. Special programs include services for learning-disabled students, an honors program, study abroad, advanced placement credit, accelerated degree programs, Freshman Honors College, double majors, independent study, self-designed majors, summer session for credit, part-time degree programs, adult/continuing education programs, internships, and arrangement for off-campus study with 14 members of the Associated Colleges of the Midwest. The most frequently chosen baccalaureate fields are communications/journalism, business/marketing, social sciences.

Student Body Statistics The student body totals 1,448, of whom 1,422 are undergraduates (386 freshmen). 58 percent are women and 42 percent are men. Students come from 48 states and territories and 54 other countries. 36 percent are from Illinois. 7.3 percent are international students. 40 percent of the 2006 graduating class went on to graduate and professional schools.

Expenses for 2006–07 *Application fee:* $40. *One-time mandatory fee:* $200. *Comprehensive fee:* $36,124 includes full-time tuition ($28,700), mandatory fees ($464), and college room and board ($6960). *College room only:* $3500. Full-time tuition and fees vary according to course load. Room and board charges vary according to housing facility. *Part-time tuition:* $3590 per course. Part-time tuition varies according to course load.

Financial Aid Forms of aid include need-based and non-need-based scholarships and part-time jobs. The average aided 2006–07 undergraduate received an aid package worth an estimated $23,024. The priority application deadline for financial aid is March 1.

Freshman Admission Lake Forest College requires an essay, a high school transcript, 2 recommendations, graded paper, and TOEFL scores for international students. An interview is recommended. SAT or ACT scores are required for some. The application deadline for regular admission is February 15; for early decision it is December 1; and for early action it is December 1.

Transfer Admission The application deadline for admission is rolling.

Entrance Difficulty Lake Forest College assesses its entrance difficulty level as very difficult. For the fall 2006 freshman class, 63 percent of the applicants were accepted.

For Further Information Contact Mr. William Motzer, Vice President for Admissions and Career Services, Lake Forest College, 555 North Sheridan Road, Lake Forest, IL 60045-2399. *Telephone:* 847-735-5000 or 800-828-4751 (toll-free). *Fax:* 847-735-6271. *E-mail:* admissions@lakeforest.edu. *Web site:* http://www.lakeforest.edu/.

LAKEVIEW COLLEGE OF NURSING
Danville, Illinois

http://www.lakeviewcol.edu/

LEWIS UNIVERSITY
Romeoville, Illinois

Lewis University is a coed, private, comprehensive institution, founded in 1932, affiliated with the Roman Catholic Church, offering degrees at the associate, bachelor's, master's, and doctoral levels and postbachelor's certificates. It has a 375-acre campus in Romeoville near Chicago.

Academic Information The faculty has 499 members (40% full-time), 27% with terminal degrees. The undergraduate student-faculty ratio is 12:1. The library holds 149,870 titles and 1,990 serial subscriptions. Special programs include academic remediation, services for learning-disabled students, an honors program, study abroad, advanced placement credit, accelerated degree programs, ESL programs, double majors, independent study, distance learning, self-designed majors, summer session for credit, part-time degree programs (daytime, evenings, weekends, summer), adult/continuing education programs, internships, and arrangement for off-campus study. The most frequently chosen baccalaureate fields are business/marketing, health professions and related sciences, security and protective services.

Student Body Statistics The student body totals 5,289, of whom 3,850 are undergraduates (569 freshmen). 60 percent are women and 40 percent are men. Students come from 24 states and territories and 26 other countries. 97 percent are from Illinois. 3.2 percent are international students. 15 percent of the 2006 graduating class went on to graduate and professional schools.

Expenses for 2007–08 *Application fee:* $40. *Comprehensive fee:* $28,250 includes full-time tuition ($20,450) and college room and board ($7800). *College room only:* $5200. *Part-time tuition:* $660 per credit hour.

Financial Aid Forms of aid include need-based and non-need-based scholarships, athletic grants, and part-time jobs. The priority application deadline for financial aid is May 1.

Freshman Admission Lewis University requires a high school transcript, a minimum 2.0 high school GPA, SAT or ACT scores, and TOEFL scores for international students. An interview is required for some. The application deadline for regular admission is August 1.

Transfer Admission The application deadline for admission is rolling.

Entrance Difficulty Lewis University assesses its entrance difficulty level as moderately difficult; minimally difficult for applicants 24 or over. For the fall 2006 freshman class, 68 percent of the applicants were accepted.

For Further Information Contact Mr. Ryan Cockerill, Associate Director, Lewis University, Box 297, One University Parkway, Romeoville, IL 60446. *Telephone:* 815-838-0500 or 800-897-9000 (toll-free). *Fax:* 815-836-5002. *E-mail:* admissions@lewisu.edu. *Web site:* http://www.lewisu.edu/.

LEXINGTON COLLEGE
Chicago, Illinois

Lexington College is a women's, private, four-year college, founded in 1977, offering degrees at the associate and bachelor's levels.

Academic Information The faculty has 17 members (24% full-time), 100% with terminal degrees. The student-faculty ratio is 6:1. The library

holds 3,000 titles and 40 serial subscriptions. Special programs include academic remediation, cooperative (work-study) education, study abroad, advanced placement credit, independent study, part-time degree programs (daytime, evenings, weekends), adult/continuing education programs, and internships.

Student Body Statistics The student body is made up of 57 undergraduates (17 freshmen). Students come from 5 states and territories and 3 other countries. 82 percent are from Illinois. 5.3 percent are international students.

Expenses for 2006–07 *Application fee:* $30. *Tuition:* $17,000 full-time, $566 per credit hour part-time. *Mandatory fees:* $810 full-time, $300 per term part-time.

Financial Aid Forms of aid include need-based scholarships and part-time jobs. The average aided 2006–07 undergraduate received an aid package worth an estimated $9200. The application deadline for financial aid is October 1 with a priority deadline of May 15.

Freshman Admission Lexington College requires an essay, a high school transcript, a minimum 2.0 high school GPA, and minimum ACT score of 18 or minimum SAT score of 1000. An interview is recommended. 2 recommendations and SAT or ACT scores are required for some. The application deadline for regular admission is rolling.

Entrance Difficulty Lexington College has an open admission policy. It assesses its entrance difficulty as minimally difficult for out-of-state applicants; minimally difficult for transfers.

For Further Information Contact Ms. Tammy Schofield, Director of Enrollment and Communication, Lexington College, 310 South Peoria Street, Chicago, IL 60607-3534. *Telephone:* 312-226-6294 Ext. 228. *Fax:* 312-226-6405. *E-mail:* pr@lexingtoncollege.edu. *Web site:* http://lexingtoncollege.edu/general-education.htm.

LINCOLN CHRISTIAN COLLEGE
Lincoln, Illinois

Lincoln Christian College is a coed, private, four-year college, founded in 1944, affiliated with the Christian Churches and Churches of Christ, offering degrees at the associate and bachelor's levels. It has a 227-acre campus in Lincoln.

Expenses for 2006–07 *Application fee:* $20. *Comprehensive fee:* $15,680 includes full-time tuition ($11,100) and college room and board ($4580). *Part-time tuition:* $370 per semester hour.

For Further Information Contact Mrs. Mary K. Davis, Assistant Director of Admissions, Lincoln Christian College, 100 Campus View Drive, Lincoln, IL 62656. *Telephone:* 217-732-3168 or 888-522-5228 (toll-free). *Fax:* 217-732-4199. *E-mail:* coladmis@lccs.edu. *Web site:* http://www.lccs.edu/.

LINCOLN COLLEGE
Lincoln, Illinois

Lincoln College is a coed, private, two-year college, founded in 1865, offering degrees at the associate level. It has a 42-acre campus in Lincoln.

Expenses for 2006–07 *Application fee:* $25. *Comprehensive fee:* $21,370 includes full-time tuition ($15,000), mandatory fees ($570), and college room and board ($5800). *College room only:* $2200. *Part-time tuition:* $500 per credit. *Part-time mandatory fees:* $19 per credit.

For Further Information Contact Mr. Tony Schilling, Director of Admissions, Lincoln College, 300 Keokuk Street, Lincoln, IL 62656-1699. *Telephone:* 217-732-3155 or 800-569-0556 (toll-free). *Fax:* 217-732-7715. *E-mail:* information@lincolncollege.com. *Web site:* http://www.lincolncollege.edu/.

LINCOLN COLLEGE–NORMAL
Normal, Illinois

Lincoln College–Normal is a coed, private, primarily two-year college, founded in 1865, offering degrees at the associate and bachelor's levels. It has a 10-acre campus in Normal.

Expenses for 2006–07 *Application fee:* $25. *Tuition:* $15,000 full-time. *Mandatory fees:* $810 full-time. *College room only:* $3200.

For Further Information Contact Mr. Joe Hendrix, Dean of Student Affairs, Lincoln College–Normal, 715 West Raab Road, Normal, IL 61761. *Telephone:* 309-454-0500 or 800-569-0558 (toll-free). *Fax:* 309-454-5652. *E-mail:* ncadmissionsinfo@lincolncollege.edu. *Web site:* http://www.lincolncollege.edu/normal/.

LOYOLA UNIVERSITY CHICAGO
Chicago, Illinois

Loyola University Chicago is a coed, private, Roman Catholic (Jesuit) university, founded in 1870, offering degrees at the bachelor's, master's, doctoral, and first professional levels and post-master's and postbachelor's certificates (also offers adult part-time program with significant enrollment not reflected in profile). It has a 105-acre campus in Chicago.

Academic Information The faculty has 1,143 members (48% full-time). The undergraduate student-faculty ratio is 13:1. The library holds 1 million titles, 136,663 serial subscriptions, and 16,486 audiovisual materials. Special programs include academic remediation, services for learning-disabled students, an honors program, study abroad, advanced placement credit, accelerated degree programs, ESL programs, double majors, independent study, summer session for credit, part-time degree programs (evenings), adult/continuing education programs, internships, and arrangement for off-campus study with School of the Art Institute of Chicago. The most frequently chosen baccalaureate fields are business/marketing, biological/life sciences, psychology.

Student Body Statistics The student body totals 15,194, of whom 9,725 are undergraduates (2,134 freshmen). 65 percent are women and 35 percent are men. Students come from 50 states and territories and 60 other countries. 67 percent are from Illinois. 1.4 percent are international students.

Expenses for 2007–08 *Application fee:* $25. *Comprehensive fee:* $37,896 includes full-time tuition ($27,200), mandatory fees ($766), and college room and board ($9930). *College room only:* $6680. *Part-time tuition:* $550 per semester hour. *Part-time mandatory fees:* $80 per semester hour.

Financial Aid Forms of aid include need-based and non-need-based scholarships, athletic grants, and part-time jobs. The average aided 2006–07 undergraduate received an aid package worth an estimated $21,689. The application deadline for financial aid is continuous.

Freshman Admission Loyola University Chicago requires an essay, a high school transcript, SAT or ACT scores, and TOEFL scores for international students. An interview is recommended. The application deadline for regular admission is April 1.

Transfer Admission The application deadline for admission is July 1.

Entrance Difficulty Loyola University Chicago assesses its entrance difficulty level as moderately difficult. For the fall 2006 freshman class, 77 percent of the applicants were accepted.

For Further Information Contact Ms. April Hansen, Director of Admission, Loyola University Chicago, 820 North Michigan Avenue, Suite 613, Chicago, IL 60611-9810. *Telephone:* 773-508-3080 or 800-262-2373 (toll-free). *Fax:* 312-915-7216. *E-mail:* admission@luc.edu. *Web site:* http://www.luc.edu/.

See page 264 for the College Close-Up.

MacCORMAC COLLEGE
Chicago, Illinois

http://www.maccormac.edu/

MacMURRAY COLLEGE

Jacksonville, Illinois

MacMurray College is a coed, private, United Methodist, four-year college, founded in 1846, offering degrees at the associate and bachelor's levels. It has a 60-acre campus in Jacksonville.

Academic Information The faculty has 79 members (56% full-time), 29% with terminal degrees. The student-faculty ratio is 12:1. The library holds 2 million titles and 185 serial subscriptions. Special programs include academic remediation, services for learning-disabled students, an honors program, advanced placement credit, double majors, independent study, summer session for credit, part-time degree programs (daytime, evenings, summer), internships, and arrangement for off-campus study with 5 members of the Western Illinois Foreign Language Consortium. The most frequently chosen baccalaureate fields are personal and culinary services, psychology, social sciences.

Student Body Statistics The student body is made up of 699 undergraduates (163 freshmen). 64 percent are women and 36 percent are men. Students come from 21 states and territories and 1 other country. 88 percent are from Illinois. 0.1 percent are international students. 10 percent of the 2006 graduating class went on to graduate and professional schools.

Expenses for 2007–08 *Application fee:* $0. *Comprehensive fee:* $22,896 includes full-time tuition ($16,400), mandatory fees ($330), and college room and board ($6166). *College room only:* $2900. *Part-time tuition:* $400 per credit. *Part-time mandatory fees:* $111 per term.

Financial Aid Forms of aid include need-based and non-need-based scholarships and part-time jobs. The average aided 2005–06 undergraduate received an aid package worth $12,981. The priority application deadline for financial aid is May 31.

Freshman Admission MacMurray College requires a high school transcript, SAT or ACT scores, and TOEFL scores for international students. An essay, a minimum 2.5 high school GPA, recommendations, and an interview are required for some. The application deadline for regular admission is rolling.

Transfer Admission The application deadline for admission is rolling.

Entrance Difficulty MacMurray College assesses its entrance difficulty level as moderately difficult. For the fall 2006 freshman class, 56 percent of the applicants were accepted.

For Further Information Contact Ms. Rhonda Cors, Vice President for Enrollment, MacMurray College, 447 East College Avenue, Jacksonville, IL 62650. *Telephone:* 217-479-7056 or 800-252-7485 (toll-free in-state). *Fax:* 217-291-0702. *E-mail:* admiss@mac.edu. *Web site:* http://www.mac.edu/.

McKENDREE COLLEGE

Lebanon, Illinois

McKendree College is a coed, private, comprehensive institution, founded in 1828, affiliated with the United Methodist Church, offering degrees at the bachelor's and master's levels. It has an 80-acre campus in Lebanon near St. Louis.

Academic Information The faculty has 215 members (40% full-time), 48% with terminal degrees. The undergraduate student-faculty ratio is 15:1. The library holds 109,000 titles, 450 serial subscriptions, and 6,637 audiovisual materials. Special programs include academic remediation, services for learning-disabled students, an honors program, study abroad, advanced placement credit, accelerated degree programs, double majors, independent study, self-designed majors, summer session for credit, part-time degree programs (daytime, evenings, summer), internships, and arrangement for off-campus study with University of Evansville.

Student Body Statistics The student body totals 3,212, of whom 2,399 are undergraduates (344 freshmen). 56 percent are women and 44 percent are men. Students come from 24 states and territories and 24 other countries. 68 percent are from Illinois. 2.6 percent are international students. 22 percent of the 2006 graduating class went on to graduate and professional schools.

Expenses for 2006–07 *Application fee:* $40. *Comprehensive fee:* $26,280 includes full-time tuition ($18,300), mandatory fees ($600), and college room and board ($7380). *College room only:* $3900. *Part-time tuition:* $615 per hour.

Financial Aid Forms of aid include need-based and non-need-based scholarships, athletic grants, and part-time jobs. The average aided 2006–07 undergraduate received an aid package worth an estimated $15,361. The priority application deadline for financial aid is May 31.

Freshman Admission McKendree College requires an essay, a high school transcript, a minimum 2.5 high school GPA, 1 recommendation, rank in upper 50% of high school class, minimum ACT score of 20, SAT or ACT scores, and TOEFL scores for international students. An interview is required for some. The application deadline for regular admission is rolling.

Transfer Admission The application deadline for admission is rolling.

Entrance Difficulty McKendree College assesses its entrance difficulty level as moderately difficult. For the fall 2006 freshman class, 75 percent of the applicants were accepted.

For Further Information Contact Chris Hall, Vice President for Admissions and Financial Aid, McKendree College, 701 College Road, Lebanon, IL 62254. *Telephone:* 618-537-6833 or 800-232-7228 Ext. 6831 (toll-free). *Fax:* 618-537-6496. *E-mail:* inquiry@mckendree.edu. *Web site:* http://www.mckendree.edu/.

MENNONITE COLLEGE OF NURSING

See Illinois State University.

MIDSTATE COLLEGE

Peoria, Illinois

http://www.midstate.edu/

MILLIKIN UNIVERSITY

Decatur, Illinois

Millikin University is a coed, private, comprehensive institution, founded in 1901, affiliated with the Presbyterian Church (U.S.A.), offering degrees at the bachelor's and master's levels. It has a 70-acre campus in Decatur.

Academic Information The faculty has 267 members (54% full-time), 51% with terminal degrees. The undergraduate student-faculty ratio is 13:1. The library holds 215,096 titles, 478 serial subscriptions, and 2,632 audiovisual materials. Special programs include services for learning-disabled students, an honors program, study abroad, advanced placement credit, accelerated degree programs, double majors, independent study, self-designed majors, summer session for credit, part-time degree programs (daytime, evenings, summer), adult/continuing education programs, internships, and arrangement for off-campus study with Drew University, American University, Urban Life Center. The most frequently chosen baccalaureate fields are business/marketing, education, visual and performing arts.

Student Body Statistics The student body totals 2,488, of whom 2,453 are undergraduates (476 freshmen). 59 percent are women and 41 percent are men. Students come from 31 states and territories and 9 other countries. 88 percent are from Illinois. 0.4 percent are international students. 22 percent of the 2006 graduating class went on to graduate and professional schools.

Expenses for 2007–08 *Application fee:* $0. *Comprehensive fee:* $31,055 includes full-time tuition ($23,250), mandatory fees ($595), and college room and board ($7210). *College room only:* $4010. *Part-time tuition:* $775 per credit hour.

Financial Aid Forms of aid include need-based and non-need-based scholarships and part-time jobs. The application deadline for financial aid is June 1 with a priority deadline of April 15.

Freshman Admission Millikin University requires a high school transcript, a minimum 2.0 high school GPA, 2 recommendations, audition for school of music; portfolio review for art program; audition for theatre and musical/theatre program, SAT or ACT scores, and TOEFL scores for international students. An interview is recommended. Audition for school of music; portfolio review for art program; audition for theatre and musical/theatre program is required for some. The application deadline for regular admission is rolling.

Transfer Admission The application deadline for admission is rolling.

Entrance Difficulty Millikin University assesses its entrance difficulty level as moderately difficult; most difficult for James Millikin Scholars, Presidential Scholars programs. For the fall 2006 freshman class, 72 percent of the applicants were accepted.

For Further Information Contact Ms. Stacey M. LaFeber, Associate Dean of Admission, Millikin University, 1184 West Main Street, Decatur, IL 62522-2084. *Telephone:* 217-424-6210 or 800-373-7733 (toll-free). *Fax:* 217-425-4669. *E-mail:* admis@millikin.edu. *Web site:* http://www.millikin.edu/.

MONMOUTH COLLEGE
Monmouth, Illinois

Monmouth College is a coed, private, four-year college, founded in 1853, affiliated with the Presbyterian Church, offering degrees at the bachelor's level. It has an 80-acre campus in Monmouth near Peoria.

Expenses for 2006–07 *Application fee:* $0. *Comprehensive fee:* $25,950 includes full-time tuition ($20,200) and college room and board ($5750). *College room only:* $3240.

For Further Information Contact Ms. Christine Johnston, Associate Dean of Enrollment, Monmouth College, 700 East Broadway, Monmouth, IL 61462-1988. *Telephone:* 309-457-2136 or 800-747-2687 (toll-free). *Fax:* 309-457-2141. *E-mail:* admit@monm.edu. *Web site:* http://www.monm.edu/.

MOODY BIBLE INSTITUTE
Chicago, Illinois
http://www.moody.edu/

MORRISON INSTITUTE OF TECHNOLOGY
Morrison, Illinois

Morrison Institute of Technology is a coed, primarily men's, private, two-year college, founded in 1973, offering degrees at the associate level. It has a 17-acre campus in Morrison.

Academic Information The faculty has 11 members (91% full-time). The student-faculty ratio is 13:1. The library holds 7,946 titles and 39 serial subscriptions. Special programs include academic remediation, double majors, part-time degree programs (daytime), and internships.

Student Body Statistics The student body is made up of 144 undergraduates (71 freshmen). 9 percent are women and 91 percent are men. Students come from 3 states and territories and 1 other country. 95 percent are from Illinois. 0.7 percent are international students. 20 percent of the 2006 graduating class went on to four-year colleges.

Expenses for 2007–08 *Application fee:* $100. *Tuition:* $12,700 full-time, $529 per credit part-time. *Mandatory fees:* $620 full-time. *College room only:* $2600.

Financial Aid Forms of aid include need-based scholarships and part-time jobs. The priority application deadline for financial aid is June 1.

Freshman Admission Morrison Institute of Technology requires a high school transcript and proof of immunization. SAT or ACT scores are recommended. The application deadline for regular admission is rolling.

Entrance Difficulty Morrison Institute of Technology has an open admission policy.

For Further Information Contact Mrs. Tammy Pruis, Admission Secretary, Morrison Institute of Technology, 701 Portland Avenue, Morrison, IL 61270. *Telephone:* 815-772-7218. *Fax:* 815-772-7584. *E-mail:* admissions@morrison.tec.il.us. *Web site:* http://www.morrison.tec.il.us/.

NATIONAL-LOUIS UNIVERSITY
Chicago, Illinois

National-Louis University is a coed, private university, founded in 1886, offering degrees at the bachelor's, master's, and doctoral levels and post-master's and postbachelor's certificates. It has a 12-acre campus in Chicago.

Expenses for 2006–07 *Application fee:* $25. *Tuition:* $17,640 full-time, $393 per quarter hour part-time. *Mandatory fees:* $120 full-time, $20 per term part-time, $40 per term part-time.

For Further Information Contact Ms. Pat Petillo, Director of Admissions, National-Louis University, 1000 Capitol Drive, Wheeling, IL 60090. *Telephone:* 888-NLU-TODAY, 888-NLU-TODAY (toll-free in-state), or 800-443-5522 (toll-free out-of-state). *Web site:* http://www.nl.edu/.

NORTH CENTRAL COLLEGE
Naperville, Illinois

North Central College is a coed, private, United Methodist, comprehensive institution, founded in 1861, offering degrees at the bachelor's and master's levels and postbachelor's certificates. It has a 56-acre campus in Naperville near Chicago.

Academic Information The faculty has 225 members (49% full-time), 59% with terminal degrees. The undergraduate student-faculty ratio is 15:1. The library holds 145,918 titles, 2,243 serial subscriptions, and 3,578 audiovisual materials. Special programs include academic remediation, services for learning-disabled students, an honors program, study abroad, advanced placement credit, accelerated degree programs, ESL programs, double majors, independent study, self-designed majors, summer session for credit, part-time degree programs, adult/continuing education programs, internships, and arrangement for off-campus study with Aurora University, Benedictine University. The most frequently chosen baccalaureate fields are business/marketing, education, social sciences.

Student Body Statistics The student body totals 2,556, of whom 2,236 are undergraduates (470 freshmen). 58 percent are women and 42 percent are men. Students come from 29 states and territories and 33 other countries. 92 percent are from Illinois. 1.3 percent are international students. 11 percent of the 2006 graduating class went on to graduate and professional schools.

Expenses for 2006–07 *Application fee:* $25. *Comprehensive fee:* $30,555 includes full-time tuition ($22,710), mandatory fees ($405), and college room and board ($7440). Room and board charges vary according to housing facility. *Part-time tuition:* $570 per semester hour. *Part-time mandatory fees:* $20 per term. Part-time tuition and fees vary according to course load.

Financial Aid Forms of aid include need-based and non-need-based scholarships and part-time jobs. The average aided 2006–07 undergraduate received an aid package worth an estimated $17,034. The application deadline for financial aid is continuous.

Freshman Admission North Central College requires a high school transcript, a minimum 2.0 high school GPA, SAT or ACT scores, and TOEFL scores for international students. An essay, 1 recommendation, and ACT scores are recommended. An interview is required for some. The application deadline for regular admission is rolling.

Transfer Admission The application deadline for admission is rolling.

Entrance Difficulty North Central College assesses its entrance difficulty level as moderately difficult. For the fall 2006 freshman class, 69 percent of the applicants were accepted.

For Further Information Contact Ms. Martha Stolze, Director of Freshman Admission, North Central College, 30 North Brainard Street, PO Box 3063, Naperville, IL 60566-7063. *Telephone:* 630-637-5800 or 800-411-1861 (toll-free). *Fax:* 630-637-5819. *E-mail:* admissions@noctrl.edu. *Web site:* http://www.noctrl.edu/.

See page 276 for the College Close-Up.

...LINOIS UNIVERSITY

...is a coed, public, comprehensive
...fering degrees at the bachelor's and
...e campus in Chicago.

Academic Information The faculty has 701 members (59% full-time),
50% with terminal degrees. The undergraduate student-faculty ratio is
15:1. The library holds 718,536 titles, 2,919 serial subscriptions, and 8,222
audiovisual materials. Special programs include academic remediation,
services for learning-disabled students, an honors program, cooperative
(work-study) education, study abroad, advanced placement credit, ESL
programs, double majors, independent study, distance learning, summer
session for credit, part-time degree programs (daytime, evenings, summer),
external degree programs, adult/continuing education programs,
internships, and arrangement for off-campus study with National Student
Exchange. The most frequently chosen baccalaureate fields are education,
business/marketing, liberal arts/general studies.
Student Body Statistics The student body totals 12,056, of whom 9,257
are undergraduates (1,114 freshmen). 61 percent are women and 39
percent are men. Students come from 18 states and territories and 45 other
countries. 99 percent are from Illinois. 1.4 percent are international
students. 32 percent of the 2006 graduating class went on to graduate and
professional schools.
Expenses for 2006–07 *Application fee:* $25. *State resident tuition:* $5250
full-time, $175 per credit hour part-time. *Nonresident tuition:* $10,500
full-time, $350 per credit hour part-time. *Mandatory fees:* $1011 full-time,
$34 per credit hour part-time. Full-time tuition and fees vary according to
student level.
Financial Aid Forms of aid include need-based and non-need-based
scholarships and part-time jobs. The average aided 2006–07 undergraduate
received an aid package worth an estimated $7231. The priority application
deadline for financial aid is March 1.
Freshman Admission Northeastern Illinois University requires a high
school transcript, ACT scores, and TOEFL scores for international
students. SAT or ACT scores are required for some. The application
deadline for regular admission is July 1.
Transfer Admission The application deadline for admission is July 1.
Entrance Difficulty Northeastern Illinois University assesses its entrance
difficulty level as minimally difficult; moderately difficult for transfers. For
the fall 2006 freshman class, 72 percent of the applicants were accepted.
For Further Information Contact Ms. Zarrin Kerwell, Admissions
Counselor, Northeastern Illinois University, 5500 North St. Louis Avenue,
Chicago, IL 60625. *Telephone:* 773-442-4026. *Fax:* 773-794-6243. *E-mail:*
admrec@neiu.edu. *Web site:* http://www.neiu.edu/.

NORTHERN ILLINOIS UNIVERSITY

De Kalb, Illinois

Northern Illinois University is a coed, public university, founded in
1895, offering degrees at the bachelor's, master's, doctoral, and first
professional levels. It has a 589-acre campus in De Kalb near
Chicago.

Academic Information The faculty has 1,193 members (75% full-time),
71% with terminal degrees. The undergraduate student-faculty ratio is
17:1. The library holds 3 million titles and 24,696 serial subscriptions.
Special programs include services for learning-disabled students, an honors
program, cooperative (work-study) education, study abroad, advanced
placement credit, accelerated degree programs, double majors, independent
study, self-designed majors, summer session for credit, part-time degree
programs, adult/continuing education programs, internships, and
arrangement for off-campus study with Rockford Regional Academic
Center, Quad-Cities Graduate Study Center, Hoffman Estate.
Student Body Statistics The student body totals 25,313, of whom
18,816 are undergraduates (3,282 freshmen). 52 percent are women and 48
percent are men. Students come from 50 states and territories and 105
other countries. 97 percent are from Illinois. 0.7 percent are international
students. 10 percent of the 2006 graduating class went on to graduate and
professional schools.

Expenses for 2006–07 *State resident tuition:* $5670 full-time, $189 per
credit hour part-time. *Nonresident tuition:* $11,100 full-time, $370 per credit
hour part-time. *Mandatory fees:* $1455 full-time, $60.63 per credit hour
part-time. Part-time tuition and fees vary according to course load. *College
room and board:* $6848. Room and board charges vary according to board
plan and housing facility.
Financial Aid Forms of aid include need-based and non-need-based
scholarships, athletic grants, and part-time jobs. The average aided
2005–06 undergraduate received an aid package worth $10,337.
Freshman Admission Northern Illinois University requires a high school
transcript, high school rank, SAT or ACT scores, and TOEFL scores for
international students. The application deadline for regular admission is
August 1.
Transfer Admission The application deadline for admission is August 1.
Entrance Difficulty Northern Illinois University assesses its entrance
difficulty level as moderately difficult. For the fall 2006 freshman class, 64
percent of the applicants were accepted.
For Further Information Contact Dr. Robert Burk, Director of Admissions, Northern Illinois University, Office of Admissions, DeKalb, IL
60445-257. *Telephone:* 815-753-0446 or 800-892-3050 (toll-free in-state).
E-mail: admission-info@niu.edu. *Web site:* http://www.niu.edu/.

NORTH PARK UNIVERSITY

Chicago, Illinois

http://www.northpark.edu/

NORTHWESTERN UNIVERSITY

Evanston, Illinois

Northwestern University is a coed, private university, founded in 1851,
offering degrees at the bachelor's, master's, doctoral, and first
professional levels and post-master's certificates. It has a 250-acre
campus in Evanston near Chicago.

Academic Information The faculty has 1,192 members (84% full-time),
100% with terminal degrees. The undergraduate student-faculty ratio is
7:1. The library holds 5 million titles and 45,259 serial subscriptions.
Special programs include services for learning-disabled students, an honors
program, cooperative (work-study) education, study abroad, advanced
placement credit, accelerated degree programs, double majors, independent
study, self-designed majors, summer session for credit, part-time degree
programs (daytime, evenings, summer), adult/continuing education
programs, and internships. The most frequently chosen baccalaureate fields
are communications/journalism, engineering, social sciences.
Student Body Statistics The student body totals 17,460, of whom 8,153
are undergraduates (2,062 freshmen). 53 percent are women and 47
percent are men. Students come from 51 states and territories and 48 other
countries. 25 percent are from Illinois. 5.1 percent are international
students. 23.9 percent of the 2006 graduating class went on to graduate
and professional schools.
Expenses for 2006–07 *Application fee:* $65. *Comprehensive fee:* $43,825
includes full-time tuition ($33,408), mandatory fees ($151), and college
room and board ($10,266). *College room only:* $5838. *Part-time tuition:*
$3963 per course.
Financial Aid Forms of aid include need-based and non-need-based
scholarships, athletic grants, and part-time jobs. The average aided
2006–07 undergraduate received an aid package worth an estimated
$26,573. The application deadline for financial aid is February 1.
Freshman Admission Northwestern University requires an essay, a high
school transcript, 1 recommendation, SAT or ACT scores, and TOEFL
scores for international students. SAT Subject Test scores are
recommended. Audition for music program and SAT Subject Test scores
are required for some. The application deadline for regular admission is
January 1 and for early decision it is November 1.
Transfer Admission The application deadline for admission is May 1.

Entrance Difficulty Northwestern University assesses its entrance difficulty level as most difficult; very difficult for transfers. For the fall 2006 freshman class, 30 percent of the applicants were accepted.
For Further Information Contact Ms. Carol Lunkenheimer, Dean of Undergraduate Admission, Northwestern University, PO Box 3060, Evanston, IL 60204-3060. *Telephone:* 847-491-7271. *E-mail:* ug-admission@northwestern.edu. *Web site:* http://www.northwestern.edu/.

OLIVET NAZARENE UNIVERSITY
Bourbonnais, Illinois
http://www.olivet.edu/

See page 280 for the College Close-Up.

PRINCIPIA COLLEGE
Elsah, Illinois

Principia College is a coed, private, Christian Science, four-year college, founded in 1910, offering degrees at the bachelor's level. It has a 2,600-acre campus in Elsah near St. Louis.

Expenses for 2006–07 *Application fee:* $0. *Comprehensive fee:* $29,346 includes full-time tuition ($21,150), mandatory fees ($300), and college room and board ($7896). *College room only:* $3831. *Part-time tuition:* $470 per quarter hour.
For Further Information Contact Mrs. Martha Quirk, Dean of Admissions, Principia College, One Maybeck Place, Elsah, IL 62028. *Telephone:* 618-374-5180 or 800-277-4648 Ext. 2802 (toll-free). *Fax:* 618-374-4000. *E-mail:* collegeadmissions@prin.edu. *Web site:* http://www.prin.edu/college/.

QUINCY UNIVERSITY
Quincy, Illinois

Quincy University is a coed, private, Roman Catholic, comprehensive institution, founded in 1860, offering degrees at the associate, bachelor's, and master's levels. It has a 75-acre campus in Quincy.

Academic Information The faculty has 130 members (40% full-time), 49% with terminal degrees. The undergraduate student-faculty ratio is 13:1. The library holds 204,557 titles, 365 serial subscriptions, and 9,293 audiovisual materials. Special programs include academic remediation, an honors program, study abroad, advanced placement credit, accelerated degree programs, ESL programs, double majors, independent study, distance learning, self-designed majors, summer session for credit, part-time degree programs (daytime, evenings, summer), adult/continuing education programs, and internships. The most frequently chosen baccalaureate fields are business/marketing, education, health professions and related sciences.
Student Body Statistics The student body totals 1,250, of whom 1,005 are undergraduates (162 freshmen). 58 percent are women and 42 percent are men. Students come from 27 states and territories and 9 other countries. 72 percent are from Illinois. 1.1 percent are international students. 29 percent of the 2006 graduating class went on to graduate and professional schools.
Expenses for 2007–08 *Application fee:* $25. *Comprehensive fee:* $26,990 includes full-time tuition ($18,950), mandatory fees ($650), and college room and board ($7390). *College room only:* $3990. *Part-time tuition:* $460 per credit hour. *Part-time mandatory fees:* $15 per credit hour.
Financial Aid Forms of aid include need-based and non-need-based scholarships, athletic grants, and part-time jobs. The priority application deadline for financial aid is March 15.
Freshman Admission Quincy University requires an essay, a high school transcript, a minimum 2.0 high school GPA, SAT or ACT scores, and TOEFL scores for international students. An interview is recommended. The application deadline for regular admission is rolling.
Transfer Admission The application deadline for admission is rolling.

Entrance Difficulty Quincy University assesses its entrance difficulty level as moderately difficult. For the fall 2006 freshman class, 62 percent of the applicants were accepted.
For Further Information Contact Mr. Mark P. Clynes, Vice President for Enrollment Management, Quincy University, Quincy University, Admissions Office, Quincy, IL 62301. *Telephone:* 217-228-5210 or 800-688-4295 (toll-free). *E-mail:* admissions@quincy.edu. *Web site:* http://www.quincy.edu/.

See page 282 for the College Close-Up.

ROBERT MORRIS COLLEGE
Chicago, Illinois

Robert Morris College is a coed, private, four-year college, founded in 1913, offering degrees at the associate, bachelor's, and master's levels.

Academic Information The faculty has 343 members (47% full-time), 16% with terminal degrees. The undergraduate student-faculty ratio is 26:1. The library holds 135,537 titles and 30,925 audiovisual materials. Special programs include academic remediation, services for learning-disabled students, an honors program, cooperative (work-study) education, study abroad, advanced placement credit, accelerated degree programs, Freshman Honors College, distance learning, summer session for credit, part-time degree programs (evenings), adult/continuing education programs, and internships. The most frequently chosen baccalaureate fields are business/marketing, computer and information sciences, visual and performing arts.
Student Body Statistics The student body totals 4,701, of whom 4,512 are undergraduates (1,008 freshmen). 64 percent are women and 36 percent are men. Students come from 33 states and territories and 14 other countries. 95 percent are from Illinois. 0.6 percent are international students.
Expenses for 2007–08 *Application fee:* $30. *Tuition:* $16,800 full-time.
Financial Aid Forms of aid include need-based and non-need-based scholarships, athletic grants, and part-time jobs. The average aided 2005–06 undergraduate received an aid package worth $11,059. The application deadline for financial aid is continuous.
Freshman Admission Robert Morris College requires a high school transcript and TOEFL scores for international students. A minimum 2.0 high school GPA and an interview are recommended. The application deadline for regular admission is rolling.
Transfer Admission The application deadline for admission is rolling.
Entrance Difficulty Robert Morris College assesses its entrance difficulty level as minimally difficult. For the fall 2006 freshman class, 77 percent of the applicants were accepted.
For Further Information Contact Ms. Connie Esparza, Vice President for Marketing, Robert Morris College, 401 South State Street, Chicago, IL 60605. *Telephone:* 312-935-4141 or 800-RMC-5960 (toll-free). *Fax:* 312-935-4440. *E-mail:* cesparza@robertmorris.edu. *Web site:* http://www.robertmorris.edu/.

See page 284 for the College Close-Up.

ROCKFORD BUSINESS COLLEGE
Rockford, Illinois

Rockford Business College is a coed, primarily women's, private, two-year college, founded in 1862, offering degrees at the associate level. It is located in Rockford near Chicago.

Academic Information The faculty has 26 members (31% full-time). The student-faculty ratio is 15:1. The library holds 1,823 titles, 161 serial subscriptions, and 50 audiovisual materials. Special programs include academic remediation, services for learning-disabled students, an honors program, cooperative (work-study) education, advanced placement credit, independent study, summer session for credit, part-time degree programs (daytime, evenings, weekends, summer), adult/continuing education programs, and internships.

Rockford Business College (continued)

Student Body Statistics The student body is made up of 428 undergraduates (90 freshmen). 89 percent are women and 11 percent are men. Students come from 2 states and territories. 99 percent are from Illinois.

Expenses for 2006–07 *Application fee:* $50. *Tuition:* $10,131 full-time.

Financial Aid Forms of aid include need-based scholarships and part-time jobs. The application deadline for financial aid is continuous.

Freshman Admission Rockford Business College requires a high school transcript, an interview, and TOEFL scores for international students. An essay is required for some. The application deadline for regular admission is September 4.

Transfer Admission The application deadline for admission is September 4.

Entrance Difficulty Rockford Business College has an open admission policy. It assesses its entrance difficulty as noncompetitive for out-of-state applicants; noncompetitive for transfers.

For Further Information Contact Ms. Barbara Holliman, Director of Admissions, Rockford Business College, 730 North Church Street, Rockford, IL 61103. *Telephone:* 815-965-8616. *Fax:* 815-965-0360. *Web site:* http://www.rbcsuccess.com/.

ROCKFORD COLLEGE
Rockford, Illinois

Rockford College is a coed, private, comprehensive institution, founded in 1847, offering degrees at the bachelor's and master's levels. It has a 130-acre campus in Rockford near Chicago.

Academic Information The faculty has 152 members (41% full-time). The undergraduate student-faculty ratio is 11:1. The library holds 140,000 titles and 831 serial subscriptions. Special programs include academic remediation, services for learning-disabled students, an honors program, study abroad, advanced placement credit, accelerated degree programs, ESL programs, double majors, independent study, summer session for credit, part-time degree programs (daytime, evenings, summer), adult/continuing education programs, internships, and arrangement for off-campus study with American University, Central College (IA), Drew University. The most frequently chosen baccalaureate fields are business/marketing, education, social sciences.

Student Body Statistics The student body totals 1,426, of whom 880 are undergraduates (100 freshmen). 65 percent are women and 35 percent are men. Students come from 16 states and territories and 5 other countries. 93 percent are from Illinois. 0.9 percent are international students.

Expenses for 2007–08 *Application fee:* $35. *Comprehensive fee:* $29,700 includes full-time tuition ($22,950) and college room and board ($6750). *College room only:* $3850. *Part-time tuition:* $610 per credit. *Part-time mandatory fees:* $30 per term.

Financial Aid Forms of aid include need-based and non-need-based scholarships and part-time jobs. The priority application deadline for financial aid is March 15.

Freshman Admission Rockford College requires a high school transcript, SAT or ACT scores, and TOEFL scores for international students. A minimum 2.65 high school GPA, an interview, and campus visit are recommended. An essay, a minimum 2.65 high school GPA, and 2 recommendations are required for some. The application deadline for regular admission is August 1.

Transfer Admission The application deadline for admission is August 1.

Entrance Difficulty Rockford College assesses its entrance difficulty level as moderately difficult. For the fall 2006 freshman class, 47 percent of the applicants were accepted.

For Further Information Contact Ms. Cassie Swanson, Assistant Director of Admission, Rockford College, Nelson Hall, Rockford, IL 61108-2393. *Telephone:* 815-226-4050 or 800-892-2984 (toll-free). *Fax:* 815-226-2822. *E-mail:* rcadmissions@rockford.edu. *Web site:* http://www.rockford.edu/.

ROOSEVELT UNIVERSITY
Chicago, Illinois

Roosevelt University is a coed, private, comprehensive institution, founded in 1945, offering degrees at the bachelor's, master's, and doctoral levels and post-master's and postbachelor's certificates.

Academic Information The faculty has 621 members (34% full-time). The undergraduate student-faculty ratio is 13:1. The library holds 186,944 titles and 1,195 serial subscriptions. Special programs include academic remediation, services for learning-disabled students, an honors program, study abroad, advanced placement credit, accelerated degree programs, ESL programs, double majors, independent study, distance learning, self-designed majors, summer session for credit, part-time degree programs (daytime, evenings, weekends, summer), external degree programs, adult/continuing education programs, internships, and arrangement for off-campus study with School of the Art Institute of Chicago. The most frequently chosen baccalaureate fields are business/marketing, computer and information sciences, psychology.

Student Body Statistics The student body totals 7,186, of whom 3,975 are undergraduates (337 freshmen). 66 percent are women and 34 percent are men. Students come from 41 states and territories and 44 other countries. 90 percent are from Illinois. 2.4 percent are international students. 65 percent of the 2006 graduating class went on to graduate and professional schools.

Expenses for 2007–08 *Application fee:* $25. *Comprehensive fee:* $25,730 includes full-time tuition ($16,680), mandatory fees ($300), and college room and board ($8750). *College room only:* $6100. *Part-time tuition:* $600 per semester hour. *Part-time mandatory fees:* $125 per term.

Financial Aid Forms of aid include need-based and non-need-based scholarships and part-time jobs. The priority application deadline for financial aid is April 1.

Freshman Admission Roosevelt University requires an essay, a high school transcript, a minimum 2.5 high school GPA, audition for music and theater programs, and SAT or ACT scores. TOEFL scores for international students are recommended. Recommendations and an interview are required for some. The application deadline for regular admission is August 15.

Entrance Difficulty Roosevelt University assesses its entrance difficulty level as moderately difficult; very difficult for performing arts. For the fall 2006 freshman class, 49 percent of the applicants were accepted.

For Further Information Contact Ms. Gwen Kanelos, Assistant Vice President for Enrollment Services, Roosevelt University, 430 South Michigan Avenue, Room 104, Chicago, IL 60605-1394. *Telephone:* 847-619-8620 or 877-APPLYRU (toll-free). *Fax:* 847-619-8636. *E-mail:* applyru@roosevelt.edu. *Web site:* http://www.roosevelt.edu/.

RUSH UNIVERSITY
Chicago, Illinois

http://www.rushu.rush.edu/

SAINT ANTHONY COLLEGE OF NURSING
Rockford, Illinois

Saint Anthony College of Nursing is a coed, primarily women's, private, Roman Catholic, upper-level institution, founded in 1915, offering degrees at the bachelor's level. It has a 17-acre campus in Rockford near Chicago.

Academic Information The faculty has 15 members (80% full-time), 13% with terminal degrees. The student-faculty ratio is 9:1. The library holds 1,258 titles, 3,136 serial subscriptions, and 321 audiovisual materials. Special programs include services for learning-disabled students, advanced placement credit, accelerated degree programs, independent study, summer session for credit, part-time degree programs (daytime, evenings, summer), internships, and arrangement for off-campus study. The most frequently chosen baccalaureate field is health professions and related sciences.

Student Body Statistics The student body totals 161, of whom 146 are undergraduates. 90 percent are women and 10 percent are men. Students

come from 2 states and territories. 96 percent are from Illinois. 2 percent of the 2006 graduating class went on to graduate and professional schools.
Expenses for 2007–08 *Application fee:* $50. *Tuition:* $17,220 full-time, $539 per credit part-time. *Mandatory fees:* $116 full-time.
Financial Aid Forms of aid include need-based scholarships. The average aided 2006–07 undergraduate received an aid package worth an estimated $14,518. The priority application deadline for financial aid is May 1.
Transfer Admission Saint Anthony College of Nursing requires a college transcript. A minimum 2.5 college GPA is recommended. The application deadline for admission is August 15.
Entrance Difficulty Saint Anthony College of Nursing assesses its entrance difficulty level as moderately difficult.
For Further Information Contact Ms. Nancy Sanders, Assistant Dean for Admissions and Student Affairs, Saint Anthony College of Nursing, 5658 East State Street, Rockford, IL 61108-2468. *Telephone:* 815-395-5100. *Fax:* 815-395-2275. *E-mail:* info@sacn.edu. *Web site:* http://www.sacn.edu/.

ST. AUGUSTINE COLLEGE
Chicago, Illinois

St. Augustine College is a coed, private, four-year college, founded in 1980, offering degrees at the associate and bachelor's levels (offers bilingual Spanish/English degree programs). It has a 4-acre campus in Chicago.

Academic Information The faculty has 132 members (20% full-time). The student-faculty ratio is 13:1. The library holds 21,000 titles and 48 serial subscriptions. Special programs include academic remediation, cooperative (work-study) education, ESL programs, independent study, summer session for credit, part-time degree programs (daytime, evenings, summer), and internships.
Student Body Statistics The student body is made up of 1,279 undergraduates (349 freshmen). 77 percent are women and 23 percent are men. Students come from 2 states and territories. 9 percent of the 2006 graduating class went on to graduate and professional schools.
Expenses for 2007–08 *Application fee:* $0. *Tuition:* $7128 full-time.
Financial Aid Forms of aid include need-based and non-need-based scholarships and part-time jobs. The application deadline for financial aid is continuous.
Freshman Admission St. Augustine College requires Ability-To-Benefit Admissions Test. The application deadline for regular admission is rolling.
Transfer Admission The application deadline for admission is rolling.
Entrance Difficulty St. Augustine College has an open admission policy.
For Further Information Contact Ms. Gloria Quiroz, Director of Recruitment, St. Augustine College, 1345 West Argyle Street, Chicago, IL 60604-3501. *Telephone:* 773-878-3256. *Fax:* 773-728-7067. *E-mail:* info@staugustine.edu. *Web site:* http://www.staugustinecollege.edu/.

SAINT FRANCIS MEDICAL CENTER COLLEGE OF NURSING
Peoria, Illinois

Saint Francis Medical Center College of Nursing is a coed, primarily women's, private, Roman Catholic, upper-level institution, founded in 1986, offering degrees at the bachelor's and master's levels.

Academic Information The faculty has 19 members (100% full-time). The undergraduate student-faculty ratio is 8:1. The library holds 6,215 titles and 125 serial subscriptions. Special programs include advanced placement credit, independent study, distance learning, and summer session for credit.
Student Body Statistics The student body totals 347, of whom 270 are undergraduates. 87 percent are women and 13 percent are men. Students come from 1 state or territory.
Expenses for 2006–07 *Application fee:* $50. *Tuition:* $13,200 full-time, $440 per semester hour part-time. *Mandatory fees:* $520 full-time, $250 per term part-time. Both full-time and part-time tuition and fees vary according to course load. *College room only:* $1880.

Financial Aid Forms of aid include need-based and non-need-based scholarships. The average aided 2006–07 undergraduate received an aid package worth an estimated $12,953. The priority application deadline for financial aid is March 1.
Transfer Admission Saint Francis Medical Center College of Nursing requires a college transcript and a minimum 2.5 college GPA.
Entrance Difficulty Saint Francis Medical Center College of Nursing assesses its entrance difficulty level as moderately difficult for transfers. For the fall 2006 entering class, 63 percent of the applicants were accepted.
For Further Information Contact Mrs. Janice Farquharson, Director of Admissions and Registrar, Saint Francis Medical Center College of Nursing, 511 Greenleaf Street, Peoria, IL 61603-3783. *Telephone:* 309-624-8980. *Fax:* 309-624-8973. *E-mail:* janice.farquharson@osfhealthcare.org. *Web site:* http://www.sfmccon.edu/.

ST. JOHN'S COLLEGE
Springfield, Illinois
http://www.st-johns.org/education/schools/nursing/

SAINT JOSEPH COLLEGE OF NURSING
See University of St. Francis.

SAINT XAVIER UNIVERSITY
Chicago, Illinois

Saint Xavier University is a coed, private, Roman Catholic, comprehensive institution, founded in 1847, offering degrees at the bachelor's and master's levels and post-master's and postbachelor's certificates. It has a 70-acre campus in Chicago.

Academic Information The faculty has 405 members (47% full-time), 58% with terminal degrees. The undergraduate student-faculty ratio is 15:1. The library holds 170,753 titles and 717 serial subscriptions. Special programs include academic remediation, services for learning-disabled students, an honors program, cooperative (work-study) education, study abroad, advanced placement credit, accelerated degree programs, ESL programs, double majors, independent study, self-designed majors, summer session for credit, part-time degree programs (daytime, evenings, weekends, summer), adult/continuing education programs, and internships. The most frequently chosen baccalaureate fields are business/marketing, education, health professions and related sciences.
Student Body Statistics The student body totals 5,657, of whom 3,316 are undergraduates (532 freshmen). 72 percent are women and 28 percent are men. Students come from 21 states and territories and 2 other countries. 96 percent are from Illinois. 0.4 percent are international students. 11 percent of the 2006 graduating class went on to graduate and professional schools.
Expenses for 2006–07 *Application fee:* $25. *Comprehensive fee:* $27,274 includes full-time tuition ($19,640), mandatory fees ($220), and college room and board ($7414). *College room only:* $4230. Full-time tuition and fees vary according to course load. Room and board charges vary according to board plan and housing facility. *Part-time tuition:* $658 per credit hour. *Part-time mandatory fees:* $130 per year. Part-time tuition and fees vary according to course load.
Financial Aid Forms of aid include need-based and non-need-based scholarships, athletic grants, and part-time jobs. The average aided 2006–07 undergraduate received an aid package worth an estimated $16,795. The priority application deadline for financial aid is March 1.
Freshman Admission Saint Xavier University requires a high school transcript, SAT or ACT scores, and TOEFL scores for international students. An essay, a minimum 2.5 high school GPA, and an interview are recommended. An interview is required for some. The application deadline for regular admission is rolling.
Transfer Admission The application deadline for admission is rolling.

Saint Xavier University (continued)

Entrance Difficulty Saint Xavier University assesses its entrance difficulty level as moderately difficult. For the fall 2006 freshman class, 73 percent of the applicants were accepted.

For Further Information Contact Ms. Elizabeth A. Gierach, Assistant Vice President, Saint Xavier University, 3700 West 103rd Street, Chicago, IL 60655-3105. *Telephone:* 773-298-3063 or 800-462-9288 (toll-free). *Fax:* 773-298-3076. *E-mail:* admissions@sxu.edu. *Web site:* http://www.sxu.edu/.

SCHOOL OF THE ART INSTITUTE OF CHICAGO
Chicago, Illinois

School of the Art Institute of Chicago is a coed, private, comprehensive institution, founded in 1866, offering degrees at the bachelor's and master's levels. It has a 1-acre campus in Chicago.

Academic Information The faculty has 468 members (26% full-time). The undergraduate student-faculty ratio is 11:1. The library holds 72,490 titles, 334 serial subscriptions, and 4,067 audiovisual materials. Special programs include academic remediation, services for learning-disabled students, cooperative (work-study) education, study abroad, advanced placement credit, ESL programs, double majors, independent study, self-designed majors, summer session for credit, part-time degree programs (daytime, evenings, weekends, summer), internships, and arrangement for off-campus study with Association of Independent Colleges of Art and Design. The most frequently chosen baccalaureate field is visual and performing arts.

Student Body Statistics The student body totals 2,873, of whom 2,274 are undergraduates (448 freshmen). 65 percent are women and 35 percent are men. Students come from 50 states and territories and 27 other countries. 23 percent are from Illinois. 17 percent are international students.

Expenses for 2007–08 *Application fee:* $65. *One-time mandatory fee:* $2,174.55. *Tuition:* $30,750 full-time. *Mandatory fees:* $270 full-time. *College room only:* $8900.

Financial Aid Forms of aid include need-based and non-need-based scholarships and part-time jobs. The priority application deadline for financial aid is March 15.

Freshman Admission School of the Art Institute of Chicago requires an essay, a high school transcript, 1 recommendation, a portfolio, SAT or ACT scores, and TOEFL scores for international students. An interview is recommended. The application deadline for regular admission is rolling and for early action it is January 2.

Transfer Admission The application deadline for admission is rolling.

Entrance Difficulty School of the Art Institute of Chicago assesses its entrance difficulty level as moderately difficult. For the fall 2006 freshman class, 84 percent of the applicants were accepted.

For Further Information Contact Mr. Scott Ramon, Director, Undergraduate Admissions, School of the Art Institute of Chicago, 37 South Wabash, Chicago, IL 60603. *Telephone:* 312-899-5219 or 800-232-SAIC (toll-free). *Fax:* 312-899-1840. *E-mail:* admiss@artic.edu. *Web site:* http://www.artic.edu/saic/.

SHIMER COLLEGE
Chicago, Illinois

Shimer College is a coed, private, four-year college, founded in 1853, offering degrees at the bachelor's level and postbachelor's certificates. It has a 3-acre campus in Chicago near Chicago and Milwaukee.

Academic Information The faculty has 15 members (87% full-time), 93% with terminal degrees. The student-faculty ratio is 8:1. The library holds 200,000 titles and 200 serial subscriptions. Special programs include cooperative (work-study) education, study abroad, double majors, independent study, distance learning, self-designed majors, summer session for credit, part-time degree programs (daytime, weekends, summer), adult/continuing education programs, internships, and arrangement for off-campus study with Barat College, Northwestern University.

Student Body Statistics The student body totals 138, of whom 126 are undergraduates (26 freshmen). 33 percent are women and 67 percent are men. Students come from 20 states and territories and 4 other countries. 58 percent are from Illinois. 4 percent are international students. 24 percent of the 2006 graduating class went on to graduate and professional schools.

Expenses for 2006–07 *Application fee:* $25. *Comprehensive fee:* $29,049 includes full-time tuition ($21,000) and college room and board ($8049).

Financial Aid Forms of aid include need-based and non-need-based scholarships and part-time jobs. The average aided 2005–06 undergraduate received an aid package worth $11,652.

Freshman Admission Shimer College requires an essay, a high school transcript, 1 recommendation, an interview, and TOEFL scores for international students. SAT or ACT scores are recommended. SAT or ACT scores are required for some. The application deadline for regular admission is August 30.

Transfer Admission The application deadline for admission is August 30.

Entrance Difficulty Shimer College has an open admission policy.

For Further Information Contact Ms. Elaine Vincent, Director of Admission, Shimer College, 3424 South State Street, Chicago, IL 60616. *Telephone:* 312-235-3504 or 800-215-7173 (toll-free). *Fax:* 847-249-8798. *E-mail:* e.vincent@shimer.edu. *Web site:* http://www.shimer.edu/.

SOUTHERN ILLINOIS UNIVERSITY CARBONDALE
Carbondale, Illinois

Southern Illinois University Carbondale is a coed, public unit of Southern Illinois University, founded in 1869, offering degrees at the associate, bachelor's, master's, doctoral, and first professional levels and first professional and postbachelor's certificates. It has a 1,133-acre campus in Carbondale near St. Louis.

Academic Information The faculty has 1,097 members (82% full-time), 80% with terminal degrees. The undergraduate student-faculty ratio is 17:1. The library holds 4 million titles, 18,271 serial subscriptions, and 371,180 audiovisual materials. Special programs include academic remediation, services for learning-disabled students, an honors program, cooperative (work-study) education, study abroad, advanced placement credit, ESL programs, double majors, independent study, distance learning, summer session for credit, part-time degree programs, adult/continuing education programs, internships, and arrangement for off-campus study with Southern Illinois University School of Medicine; off campus courses offered at 34 Military bases across the U.S. The most frequently chosen baccalaureate fields are education, business/marketing, engineering technologies.

Student Body Statistics The student body totals 21,003, of whom 16,294 are undergraduates (2,380 freshmen). 43 percent are women and 57 percent are men. Students come from 51 states and territories and 107 other countries. 86 percent are from Illinois. 1.7 percent are international students.

Expenses for 2007–08 *Application fee:* $30. *State resident tuition:* $5808 full-time, $211.60 per semester hour part-time. *Nonresident tuition:* $14,520 full-time, $529 per semester hour part-time. *Mandatory fees:* $2263 full-time. *College room and board:* $6666. *College room only:* $3650.

Financial Aid Forms of aid include need-based and non-need-based scholarships, athletic grants, and part-time jobs. The average aided 2006–07 undergraduate received an aid package worth an estimated $10,570. The priority application deadline for financial aid is April 1.

Freshman Admission Southern Illinois University Carbondale requires a high school transcript, SAT or ACT scores, and TOEFL scores for international students. The application deadline for regular admission is rolling.

Transfer Admission The application deadline for admission is rolling.

Entrance Difficulty Southern Illinois University Carbondale assesses its entrance difficulty level as moderately difficult. For the fall 2006 freshman class, 71 percent of the applicants were accepted.
For Further Information Contact Tina Collins, Assistant Vice Chancellor for Enrollment Management and Director of Records and Registration, Southern Illinois University Carbondale, Mail Code 4710, Southern Illinois University Carbondale, Carbondale, IL 62901-4710. *Telephone:* 618-536-4405. *Fax:* 618-453-4609. *E-mail:* joinsiuc@siu.edu. *Web site:* http://www.siu.edu/siuc/.

See page 290 for the College Close-Up.

SOUTHERN ILLINOIS UNIVERSITY EDWARDSVILLE
Edwardsville, Illinois

Southern Illinois University Edwardsville is a coed, public, comprehensive unit of Southern Illinois University, founded in 1957, offering degrees at the bachelor's, master's, and first professional levels and post-master's, first professional, and postbachelor's certificates. It has a 2,660-acre campus in Edwardsville near St. Louis.

Academic Information The faculty has 815 members (71% full-time). The undergraduate student-faculty ratio is 17:1. The library holds 847,631 titles, 24,530 serial subscriptions, and 30,078 audiovisual materials. Special programs include academic remediation, services for learning-disabled students, an honors program, cooperative (work-study) education, study abroad, advanced placement credit, accelerated degree programs, ESL programs, double majors, independent study, distance learning, self-designed majors, summer session for credit, part-time degree programs (daytime, evenings, weekends, summer), adult/continuing education programs, internships, and arrangement for off-campus study with University of Missouri–St. Louis, International Student Exchange Program, MBA program at southwestern Illinois College. The most frequently chosen baccalaureate fields are business/marketing, education, psychology.
Student Body Statistics The student body totals 13,449, of whom 10,960 are undergraduates (1,794 freshmen). 55 percent are women and 45 percent are men. Students come from 46 states and territories and 48 other countries. 92 percent are from Illinois. 1 percent are international students. 29 percent of the 2006 graduating class went on to graduate and professional schools.
Expenses for 2007–08 *Application fee:* $30. *State resident tuition:* $5938 full-time. *Nonresident tuition:* $13,075 full-time. *Mandatory fees:* $1180 full-time. *College room and board:* $6500. *College room only:* $3970.
Financial Aid Forms of aid include need-based and non-need-based scholarships, athletic grants, and part-time jobs. The average aided 2005–06 undergraduate received an aid package worth $9077. The priority application deadline for financial aid is March 1.
Freshman Admission Southern Illinois University Edwardsville requires a high school transcript, SAT or ACT scores, and TOEFL scores for international students. A minimum 2.5 high school GPA is recommended. The application deadline for regular admission is May 1.
Transfer Admission The application deadline for admission is July 21.
Entrance Difficulty Southern Illinois University Edwardsville assesses its entrance difficulty level as moderately difficult. For the fall 2006 freshman class, 75 percent of the applicants were accepted.
For Further Information Contact Mr. Todd Burrell, Director of Admissions, Southern Illinois University Edwardsville, Campus Box 1600, Rendleman Hall, Edwardsville, IL 62026-1600. *Telephone:* 618-650-3705 or 800-447-SIUE (toll-free). *Fax:* 618-650-5013. *E-mail:* admissions@siue.edu. *Web site:* http://www.siue.edu/.

SPRINGFIELD COLLEGE IN ILLINOIS
Springfield, Illinois

Springfield College in Illinois is a coed, private, two-year college, founded in 1929, affiliated with the Roman Catholic Church, offering degrees at the associate level (the college partners with Benedictine University, offering baccalaureate and master degree programs at Springfield College's campus). It has an 8-acre campus in Springfield.

Expenses for 2006–07 *Application fee:* $20. *Comprehensive fee:* $15,400 includes full-time tuition ($7490), mandatory fees ($1990), and college room and board ($5920). *Part-time tuition:* $312 per hour.
For Further Information Contact Ms. Kim Fontana, Director of Admissions, Springfield College in Illinois, 1500 North Fifth Street, Springfield, IL 62702-2694. *Telephone:* 217-525-1420 Ext. 241 or 800-635-7289 (toll-free). *Fax:* 217-525-1497. *Web site:* http://www.sci.edu/.

TELSHE YESHIVA–CHICAGO
Chicago, Illinois
For Information Write to Telshe Yeshiva–Chicago, Chicago, IL 60625-5598.

TRINITY CHRISTIAN COLLEGE
Palos Heights, Illinois

Trinity Christian College is a coed, private, Christian Reformed, four-year college, founded in 1959, offering degrees at the bachelor's level. It has a 53-acre campus in Palos Heights near Chicago.

Academic Information The faculty has 148 members (50% full-time), 36% with terminal degrees. The student-faculty ratio is 12:1. The library holds 81,714 titles and 435 serial subscriptions. Special programs include academic remediation, services for learning-disabled students, an honors program, cooperative (work-study) education, study abroad, advanced placement credit, double majors, independent study, part-time degree programs (evenings), adult/continuing education programs, internships, and arrangement for off-campus study with Saint Xavier College, Moraine Valley Community College. The most frequently chosen baccalaureate fields are business/marketing, education, theology and religious vocations.
Student Body Statistics The student body is made up of 1,310 undergraduates (227 freshmen). 67 percent are women and 33 percent are men. Students come from 35 states and territories and 6 other countries. 58 percent are from Illinois. 1.4 percent are international students. 13 percent of the 2006 graduating class went on to graduate and professional schools.
Expenses for 2006–07 *Application fee:* $20. *Comprehensive fee:* $25,125 includes full-time tuition ($17,920), mandatory fees ($195), and college room and board ($7010). *College room only:* $3650. Room and board charges vary according to board plan. *Part-time tuition:* $600 per semester hour. Part-time tuition varies according to course load.
Financial Aid Forms of aid include need-based and non-need-based scholarships, athletic grants, and part-time jobs. The priority application deadline for financial aid is February 15.
Freshman Admission Trinity Christian College requires an essay, a high school transcript, a minimum 2.0 high school GPA, an interview, SAT or ACT scores, and TOEFL scores for international students. ACT scores are recommended. 1 recommendation is required for some. The application deadline for regular admission is rolling.
Entrance Difficulty Trinity Christian College assesses its entrance difficulty level as moderately difficult. For the fall 2006 freshman class, 92 percent of the applicants were accepted.
For Further Information Contact Mr. Jeremy Klyn, Director of Admissions, Trinity Christian College, 6601 West College Drive, Palos Heights, IL 60463. *Telephone:* 708-239-4708 or 800-748-0085 (toll-free). *Fax:* 708-239-4826. *E-mail:* admissions@trnty.edu. *Web site:* http://www.trnty.edu/.

TRINITY COLLEGE OF NURSING AND HEALTH SCIENCES
Rock Island, Illinois

Trinity College of Nursing and Health Sciences is a coed, private, four-year college, founded in 1994, offering degrees at the associate

Trinity College of Nursing and Health Sciences (continued)

and bachelor's levels (general education requirements are taken off campus, usually at Black Hawk College, Eastern Iowa Community College District and Western Illinois University). It has a 2-acre campus in Rock Island.

Academic Information The faculty has 18 members (72% full-time), 17% with terminal degrees. The student-faculty ratio is 10:1. The library holds 8,500 titles and 791 serial subscriptions. Special programs include academic remediation, services for learning-disabled students, an honors program, cooperative (work-study) education, advanced placement credit, independent study, distance learning, summer session for credit, part-time degree programs (daytime, evenings), adult/continuing education programs, and arrangement for off-campus study with Black Hawk College, Western Illinois University.

Student Body Statistics The student body is made up of 211 undergraduates (3 freshmen). 82 percent are women and 18 percent are men. 67 percent are from Illinois.

Expenses for 2007–08 *Application fee:* $50. *Tuition:* $7848 full-time, $426 per semester hour part-time. *Mandatory fees:* $714 full-time.

Financial Aid Forms of aid include need-based scholarships and part-time jobs. The application deadline for financial aid is continuous.

Freshman Admission Trinity College of Nursing and Health Sciences requires a high school transcript, a minimum 2.5 high school GPA, SAT or ACT scores, and TOEFL scores for international students. A minimum 2.75 high school GPA and minimum ACT score of 21 are required for some. The application deadline for regular admission is rolling.

Entrance Difficulty Trinity College of Nursing and Health Sciences assesses its entrance difficulty level as moderately difficult. For the fall 2006 freshman class, 33 percent of the applicants were accepted.

For Further Information Contact Ms. Barbara Kimpe, Admissions Representative, Trinity College of Nursing and Health Sciences, 2122 25th Avenue, Rock Island, IL 61201. *Telephone:* 309-779-7812. *Fax:* 309-779-7748. *E-mail:* con@trinityqc.com. *Web site:* http://www.trinitycollegeqc.edu/.

TRINITY INTERNATIONAL UNIVERSITY
Deerfield, Illinois

Trinity International University is a coed, private university, founded in 1897, affiliated with the Evangelical Free Church of America, offering degrees at the bachelor's, master's, doctoral, and first professional levels and postbachelor's certificates. It has a 108-acre campus in Deerfield near Chicago.

Academic Information The faculty has 381 members (24% full-time), 61% with terminal degrees. The undergraduate student-faculty ratio is 13:1. The library holds 245,320 titles and 1,176 serial subscriptions. Special programs include academic remediation, an honors program, study abroad, advanced placement credit, double majors, independent study, part-time degree programs (daytime, evenings), adult/continuing education programs, internships, and arrangement for off-campus study with 13 members of the Christian College Consortium. The most frequently chosen baccalaureate fields are education, business/marketing, theology and religious vocations.

Student Body Statistics The student body totals 2,855, of whom 1,247 are undergraduates (166 freshmen). 59 percent are women and 41 percent are men. Students come from 33 states and territories. 64 percent are from Illinois. 0.2 percent are international students.

Expenses for 2006–07 *Application fee:* $25. *Comprehensive fee:* $26,656 includes full-time tuition ($19,800), mandatory fees ($306), and college room and board ($6550). *College room only:* $3620. Full-time tuition and fees vary according to location. Room and board charges vary according to board plan and housing facility. *Part-time tuition:* $820 per hour. *Part-time mandatory fees:* $153 per year. Part-time tuition and fees vary according to location.

Financial Aid Forms of aid include need-based and non-need-based scholarships, athletic grants, and part-time jobs. The average aided 2006–07 undergraduate received an aid package worth an estimated $17,823. The priority application deadline for financial aid is April 1.

Freshman Admission Trinity International University requires an essay, a high school transcript, a minimum 2.5 high school GPA, 1 recommendation, SAT or ACT scores, and TOEFL scores for

international students. A minimum 3.0 high school GPA is recommended. An interview is required for some. The application deadline for regular admission is rolling.

Transfer Admission The application deadline for admission is rolling.

Entrance Difficulty Trinity International University assesses its entrance difficulty level as moderately difficult. For the fall 2006 freshman class, 80 percent of the applicants were accepted.

For Further Information Contact Mr. Chris Welch, Interim Director of Undergraduate Admissions, Trinity International University, 2065 Half Day Road, Deerfield, IL 60015-1284. *Telephone:* 847-317-7000 or 800-822-3225 (toll-free out-of-state). *Fax:* 847-317-8097. *E-mail:* tcadmissions@tiu.edu. *Web site:* http://www.tiu.edu/.

UNIVERSITY OF CHICAGO
Chicago, Illinois

University of Chicago is a coed, private university, founded in 1891, offering degrees at the bachelor's, master's, doctoral, and first professional levels. It has a 211-acre campus in Chicago.

Academic Information The faculty has 1,630 members (65% full-time), 88% with terminal degrees. The undergraduate student-faculty ratio is 6:1. The library holds 7 million titles and 47,000 serial subscriptions. Special programs include study abroad, advanced placement credit, accelerated degree programs, double majors, independent study, self-designed majors, summer session for credit, adult/continuing education programs, internships, and arrangement for off-campus study with Committee on Institutional Cooperation, Associated Colleges of the Midwest. The most frequently chosen baccalaureate fields are biological/life sciences, mathematics, social sciences.

Student Body Statistics The student body totals 11,730, of whom 4,807 are undergraduates (1,259 freshmen). 50 percent are women and 50 percent are men. 22 percent are from Illinois. 7.4 percent are international students.

Expenses for 2006–07 *Application fee:* $60. *Comprehensive fee:* $44,613 includes full-time tuition ($33,336), mandatory fees ($669), and college room and board ($10,608). Room and board charges vary according to board plan and housing facility. *Part-time tuition:* varies with course load.

Financial Aid Forms of aid include need-based and non-need-based scholarships and part-time jobs. The priority application deadline for financial aid is February 1.

Freshman Admission University of Chicago requires an essay, a high school transcript, 3 recommendations, SAT or ACT scores, and TOEFL scores for international students. An interview is recommended. The application deadline for regular admission is January 2 and for early action it is November 1.

Transfer Admission The application deadline for admission is April 1.

Entrance Difficulty University of Chicago assesses its entrance difficulty level as most difficult. For the fall 2006 freshman class, 38 percent of the applicants were accepted.

For Further Information Contact Mr. Theodore O'Neill, Dean of Admissions, University of Chicago, Rosenwald Hall, 1101 East 58th Street, Suite 105, Chicago, IL 60637-1513. *Telephone:* 773-702-8650. *Fax:* 773-702-4199. *E-mail:* questions@phoenix.uchicago.edu. *Web site:* http://www.uchicago.edu/.

UNIVERSITY OF ILLINOIS AT CHICAGO
Chicago, Illinois

University of Illinois at Chicago is a coed, public unit of University of Illinois System, founded in 1946, offering degrees at the bachelor's, master's, doctoral, and first professional levels and first professional certificates. It has a 240-acre campus in Chicago.

Academic Information The faculty has 1,519 members (76% full-time), 77% with terminal degrees. The undergraduate student-faculty ratio is 15:1. The library holds 3 million titles, 38,392 serial subscriptions, and 28,670 audiovisual materials. Special programs include academic remediation, services for learning-disabled students, an honors program, cooperative (work-study) education, study abroad, advanced placement credit, accelerated degree programs, ESL programs, double majors, independent study, distance learning, self-designed majors, summer session for credit, part-time degree programs (daytime, summer), internships, and arrangement for off-campus study with University Center of Lake County. The most frequently chosen baccalaureate fields are biological/life sciences, business/marketing, engineering.

Student Body Statistics The student body totals 24,654, of whom 15,006 are undergraduates (2,852 freshmen). 54 percent are women and 46 percent are men. Students come from 42 states and territories and 49 other countries. 97 percent are from Illinois. 1.5 percent are international students. 23 percent of the 2006 graduating class went on to graduate and professional schools.

Expenses for 2006–07 *Application fee:* $40. *State resident tuition:* $6780 full-time. *Nonresident tuition:* $19,170 full-time. *Mandatory fees:* $2962 full-time. Full-time tuition and fees vary according to program. *College room and board:* $7446. Room and board charges vary according to board plan and housing facility.

Financial Aid Forms of aid include need-based and non-need-based scholarships, athletic grants, and part-time jobs. The average aided 2006–07 undergraduate received an aid package worth an estimated $11,482. The priority application deadline for financial aid is March 1.

Freshman Admission University of Illinois at Chicago requires a high school transcript, SAT or ACT scores, and TOEFL scores for international students. An essay is recommended. An interview is required for some. The application deadline for regular admission is January 15.

Transfer Admission The application deadline for admission is March 1.

Entrance Difficulty University of Illinois at Chicago assesses its entrance difficulty level as moderately difficult; very difficult for honors program, Guaranteed Professional Program. For the fall 2006 freshman class, 58 percent of the applicants were accepted.

For Further Information Contact Mr. Thomas E. Glenn, Executive Director of Admissions, University of Illinois at Chicago, Box 5220, Chicago, IL 60680-5220. *Telephone:* 312-996-4350. *Fax:* 312-413-7628. *E-mail:* uic.admit@uic.edu. *Web site:* http://www.uic.edu/.

UNIVERSITY OF ILLINOIS AT SPRINGFIELD
Springfield, Illinois

University of Illinois at Springfield is a coed, public, comprehensive unit of University of Illinois System, founded in 1969, offering degrees at the bachelor's, master's, and doctoral levels and post-master's and postbachelor's certificates. It has a 746-acre campus in Springfield.

Academic Information The faculty has 334 members (60% full-time), 67% with terminal degrees. The undergraduate student-faculty ratio is 12:1. The library holds 550,249 titles, 39,357 serial subscriptions, and 41,839 audiovisual materials. Special programs include services for learning-disabled students, an honors program, cooperative (work-study) education, study abroad, advanced placement credit, independent study, distance learning, self-designed majors, summer session for credit, part-time degree programs (daytime, evenings, weekends, summer), and internships. The most frequently chosen baccalaureate fields are business/ marketing, liberal arts/general studies, psychology.

Student Body Statistics The student body totals 4,761, of whom 2,758 are undergraduates (243 freshmen). 59 percent are women and 41 percent are men. Students come from 41 states and territories and 15 other countries. 90 percent are from Illinois. 0.8 percent are international students.

Expenses for 2006–07 *Application fee:* $40. *State resident tuition:* $5580 full-time, $186 per credit hour part-time. *Nonresident tuition:* $14,730 full-time, $491 per credit hour part-time. *Mandatory fees:* $1664 full-time, $597 per term part-time. *College room and board:* $7495. *College room only:* $3400. Room and board charges vary according to board plan and housing facility. Tuition for 2006-07 reflects the new Guaranteed tuition rate.

Financial Aid Forms of aid include need-based and non-need-based scholarships, athletic grants, and part-time jobs. The average aided 2005–06 undergraduate received an aid package worth $8233. The application deadline for financial aid is November 15 with a priority deadline of April 1.

Freshman Admission University of Illinois at Springfield requires an essay, a high school transcript, 3 recommendations, SAT or ACT scores, and TOEFL scores for international students. A minimum X high school GPA and class rank are recommended. An interview is required for some. The application deadline for regular admission is rolling.

Transfer Admission The application deadline for admission is rolling.

Entrance Difficulty University of Illinois at Springfield assesses its entrance difficulty level as moderately difficult. For the fall 2006 freshman class, 62 percent of the applicants were accepted.

For Further Information Contact Dr. Marya Leatherwood, Associate Vice Chancellor and Director of Enrollment Management, University of Illinois at Springfield, One University Plaza, Room 1015, Springfield, IL 62703. *Telephone:* 217-206-6581 or 888-977-4847 (toll-free). *Fax:* 217-206-6048. *E-mail:* admissions@uis.edu. *Web site:* http://www.uis.edu/.

UNIVERSITY OF ILLINOIS AT URBANA–CHAMPAIGN
Champaign, Illinois

University of Illinois at Urbana–Champaign is a coed, public unit of University of Illinois System, founded in 1867, offering degrees at the bachelor's, master's, doctoral, and first professional levels and post-master's certificates. It has a 1,470-acre campus in Champaign.

Academic Information The faculty has 2,051 members (97% full-time), 92% with terminal degrees. The undergraduate student-faculty ratio is 17:1. The library holds 10 million titles, 63,413 serial subscriptions, and 4,245 audiovisual materials. Special programs include academic remediation, services for learning-disabled students, an honors program, cooperative (work-study) education, study abroad, advanced placement credit, accelerated degree programs, ESL programs, double majors, independent study, distance learning, self-designed majors, summer session for credit, internships, and arrangement for off-campus study with members of the Committee on Institutional Cooperation, Midwest Universities Consortium for International Activities. The most frequently chosen baccalaureate fields are business/marketing, engineering, social sciences.

Student Body Statistics The student body totals 42,728, of whom 31,472 are undergraduates (7,172 freshmen). 47 percent are women and 53 percent are men. Students come from 52 states and territories and 62 other countries. 93 percent are from Illinois. 5.2 percent are international students. 26.4 percent of the 2006 graduating class went on to graduate and professional schools.

Expenses for 2007–08 *Application fee:* $40. *State resident tuition:* $8440 full-time. *Nonresident tuition:* $22,526 full-time. *Mandatory fees:* $2690 full-time. *College room and board:* $8196. Entering degree-seeking students are guaranteed the same tuition rates for 4 years.

Financial Aid Forms of aid include need-based and non-need-based scholarships, athletic grants, and part-time jobs. The average aided 2005–06 undergraduate received an aid package worth $10,180.

Freshman Admission University of Illinois at Urbana–Champaign requires an essay, a high school transcript, SAT or ACT scores, TOEFL scores for international students, and ACT Writing Component. Recommendations, an interview, and audition, statement of professional interest are required for some. The application deadline for regular admission is January 2.

Transfer Admission The application deadline for admission is March 1.

Entrance Difficulty University of Illinois at Urbana–Champaign assesses its entrance difficulty level as very difficult. For the fall 2006 freshman class, 65 percent of the applicants were accepted.

For Further Information Contact Mr. Abel Montoya, Acting Associate Director, University of Illinois at Urbana–Champaign, 901 West Illinois, Urbana, IL 61801. *Telephone:* 217-333-0302. *Fax:* 217-244-0903. *E-mail:* ugradadmissions@uiuc.edu. *Web site:* http://www.uiuc.edu/.

UNIVERSITY OF PHOENIX–CHICAGO CAMPUS

Schaumburg, Illinois

University of Phoenix–Chicago Campus is a coed, proprietary, comprehensive institution, founded in 2002, offering degrees at the bachelor's and master's levels.

Academic Information The faculty has 437 members (8% full-time), 24% with terminal degrees. The undergraduate student-faculty ratio is 8:1. The library holds 1,756 titles and 692 serial subscriptions. Special programs include services for learning-disabled students, advanced placement credit, accelerated degree programs, independent study, distance learning, external degree programs, and adult/continuing education programs. The most frequently chosen baccalaureate fields are business/marketing, computer and information sciences.
Student Body Statistics The student body totals 1,590, of whom 1,320 are undergraduates (69 freshmen). 60 percent are women and 40 percent are men. 7.3 percent are international students.
Expenses for 2006–07 *Application fee:* $45. *Tuition:* $11,190 full-time, $373 per credit part-time.
Financial Aid Forms of aid include need-based and non-need-based scholarships. The average aided 2005–06 undergraduate received an aid package worth $3787. The application deadline for financial aid is continuous.
Freshman Admission University of Phoenix–Chicago Campus requires 1 recommendation and TOEFL scores for international students. A high school transcript is required for some. The application deadline for regular admission is rolling.
Transfer Admission The application deadline for admission is rolling.
Entrance Difficulty University of Phoenix–Chicago Campus has an open admission policy.
For Further Information Contact Ms. Beth Barilla, Associate Vice President, Student Admissions and Services, University of Phoenix–Chicago Campus, 4615 East Elwood Street, Mail Stop AA-K101, Phoenix, AZ 85040-1958. *Telephone:* 480-317-6000, 800-776-4867 (toll-free in-state), or 800-228-7240 (toll-free out-of-state). *Fax:* 480-894-1758. *E-mail:* beth.barilla@phoenix.edu. *Web site:* http://www.phoenix.edu/.

UNIVERSITY OF ST. FRANCIS

Joliet, Illinois

University of St. Francis is a coed, private, Roman Catholic, comprehensive institution, founded in 1920, offering degrees at the bachelor's and master's levels. It has a 22-acre campus in Joliet near Chicago.

Academic Information The faculty has 206 members (36% full-time), 40% with terminal degrees. The undergraduate student-faculty ratio is 13:1. The library holds 111,546 titles, 24,985 serial subscriptions, and 3,214 audiovisual materials. Special programs include academic remediation, services for learning-disabled students, an honors program, study abroad, advanced placement credit, accelerated degree programs, double majors, independent study, distance learning, self-designed majors, summer session for credit, part-time degree programs (daytime, evenings, weekends, summer), external degree programs, adult/continuing education programs, internships, and arrangement for off-campus study. The most frequently chosen baccalaureate fields are business/marketing, education, health professions and related sciences.
Student Body Statistics The student body totals 2,060, of whom 1,289 are undergraduates (182 freshmen). 68 percent are women and 32 percent are men. Students come from 11 states and territories. 97 percent are from Illinois. 2.6 percent are international students. 23 percent of the 2006 graduating class went on to graduate and professional schools.
Expenses for 2006–07 *Application fee:* $30. *Comprehensive fee:* $26,820 includes full-time tuition ($19,150), mandatory fees ($390), and college room and board ($7280). *Part-time tuition:* $625 per credit hour.
Financial Aid Forms of aid include need-based and non-need-based scholarships, athletic grants, and part-time jobs. The average aided 2006–07 undergraduate received an aid package worth an estimated $16,063. The priority application deadline for financial aid is April 1.

Freshman Admission University of St. Francis requires a high school transcript, a minimum 2.0 high school GPA, SAT or ACT scores, and TOEFL scores for international students. An essay, 2 recommendations, and an interview are required for some. The application deadline for regular admission is August 1.
Entrance Difficulty University of St. Francis assesses its entrance difficulty level as moderately difficult. For the fall 2006 freshman class, 71 percent of the applicants were accepted.
For Further Information Contact Ms. Meghan Connolly, Director of Undergraduate Admissions, University of St. Francis, 500 North Wilcox Street, Joliet, IL 60435-6188. *Telephone:* 800-735-7500 or 800-735-3500 (toll-free). *Fax:* 815-740-5032. *E-mail:* mconnolly1@stfrancis.edu. *Web site:* http://www.stfrancis.edu/.

See page 300 for the College Close-Up.

VANDERCOOK COLLEGE OF MUSIC

Chicago, Illinois

VanderCook College of Music is a coed, private, comprehensive institution, founded in 1909, offering degrees at the bachelor's and master's levels. It has a 1-acre campus in Chicago.

Expenses for 2006–07 *Application fee:* $35. *Comprehensive fee:* $25,940 includes full-time tuition ($17,120), mandatory fees ($770), and college room and board ($8050). *Part-time tuition:* $590 per credit hour.
For Further Information Contact Mr. James Malley, Director of Undergraduate Admissions, VanderCook College of Music, 3140 South Federal Street, Chicago, IL 60616. *Telephone:* 312-225-6288 Ext. 230 or 800-448-2655 (toll-free). *Fax:* 312-225-5211. *E-mail:* admissions@vandercook.edu. *Web site:* http://www.vandercook.edu/.

WESTERN ILLINOIS UNIVERSITY

Macomb, Illinois

Western Illinois University is a coed, public, comprehensive institution, founded in 1899, offering degrees at the bachelor's, master's, and doctoral levels and post-master's and postbachelor's certificates. It has a 1,050-acre campus in Macomb.

Academic Information The faculty has 731 members (89% full-time), 65% with terminal degrees. The undergraduate student-faculty ratio is 17:1. The library holds 998,041 titles and 3,200 serial subscriptions. Special programs include academic remediation, services for learning-disabled students, an honors program, study abroad, advanced placement credit, Freshman Honors College, ESL programs, double majors, independent study, distance learning, self-designed majors, summer session for credit, part-time degree programs (daytime, evenings, weekends, summer), external degree programs, adult/continuing education programs, internships, and arrangement for off-campus study with Western Illinois Education Consortium. The most frequently chosen baccalaureate fields are education, liberal arts/general studies, security and protective services.
Student Body Statistics The student body totals 13,602, of whom 11,334 are undergraduates (1,922 freshmen). 48 percent are women and 52 percent are men. Students come from 41 states and territories and 50 other countries. 95 percent are from Illinois. 1.2 percent are international students. 25 percent of the 2006 graduating class went on to graduate and professional schools.
Expenses for 2006–07 *Application fee:* $30. *State resident tuition:* $5439 full-time, $181.30 per semester hour part-time. *Nonresident tuition:* $8158 full-time, $271.95 per semester hour part-time. *Mandatory fees:* $1972 full-time, $49.47 per semester hour part-time. Both full-time and part-time tuition and fees vary according to course load, location, and student level. *College room and board:* $6446. *College room only:* $3876. Room and board charges vary according to board plan, housing facility, and student level.
Financial Aid Forms of aid include need-based and non-need-based scholarships, athletic grants, and part-time jobs. The average aided 2006–07 undergraduate received an aid package worth an estimated $8525.
Freshman Admission Western Illinois University requires a high school transcript, GPA greater than or equal to 2.5 on a 4.0 scale and ACT/SAT

composite score of greater than or equal to 20/920, SAT or ACT scores, and TOEFL scores for international students. The application deadline for regular admission is May 15.

Transfer Admission The application deadline for admission is rolling.

Entrance Difficulty Western Illinois University assesses its entrance difficulty level as moderately difficult. For the fall 2006 freshman class, 70 percent of the applicants were accepted.

For Further Information Contact Mr. Eric Campbell, Director of Admissions, Western Illinois University, 1 University Circle, 115 Sherman Hall, Macomb, IL 61455-1390. *Telephone:* 309-298-3157 or 877-742-5948 (toll-free). *Fax:* 309-298-3111. *E-mail:* admissions@wiu.edu. *Web site:* http://www.wiu.edu/.

WEST SUBURBAN COLLEGE OF NURSING
Oak Park, Illinois
http://www.wscn.edu/

WESTWOOD COLLEGE–CHICAGO DU PAGE
Woodridge, Illinois
http://www.westwood.edu/

WESTWOOD COLLEGE–CHICAGO LOOP CAMPUS
Chicago, Illinois
http://www.westwood.edu/

WESTWOOD COLLEGE–CHICAGO O'HARE AIRPORT
Schiller Park, Illinois
http://www.westwood.edu/

WESTWOOD COLLEGE–CHICAGO RIVER OAKS
Calumet City, Illinois
http://www.westwood.edu/

WHEATON COLLEGE
Wheaton, Illinois

Wheaton College is a coed, private, nondenominational, comprehensive institution, founded in 1860, offering degrees at the bachelor's, master's, and doctoral levels and postbachelor's certificates. It has an 80-acre campus in Wheaton near Chicago.

Academic Information The faculty has 295 members (65% full-time), 74% with terminal degrees. The undergraduate student-faculty ratio is 12:1. The library holds 461,249 titles, 4,012 serial subscriptions, and 30,142 audiovisual materials. Special programs include services for learning-disabled students, study abroad, advanced placement credit, double majors, independent study, self-designed majors, summer session for credit, internships, and arrangement for off-campus study with members of the Christian College Consortium, Council for Christian Colleges and Universities. The most frequently chosen baccalaureate fields are education, social sciences, theology and religious vocations.

Student Body Statistics The student body totals 2,924, of whom 2,365 are undergraduates (572 freshmen). 51 percent are women and 49 percent are men. Students come from 51 states and territories and 18 other countries. 21 percent are from Illinois. 1.2 percent are international students. 27.5 percent of the 2006 graduating class went on to graduate and professional schools.

Expenses for 2006–07 *Application fee:* $50. *Comprehensive fee:* $29,490 includes full-time tuition ($22,450) and college room and board ($7040). *College room only:* $4160. Room and board charges vary according to board plan and housing facility. *Part-time tuition:* $623 per credit hour. Part-time tuition varies according to course load.

Financial Aid Forms of aid include need-based and non-need-based scholarships and part-time jobs. The average aided 2006–07 undergraduate received an aid package worth an estimated $19,307. The priority application deadline for financial aid is February 15.

Freshman Admission Wheaton College requires an essay, a high school transcript, 2 recommendations, SAT or ACT scores, and TOEFL scores for international students. An interview is recommended. The application deadline for regular admission is January 10 and for early action it is November 1.

Transfer Admission The application deadline for admission is March 1.

Entrance Difficulty Wheaton College assesses its entrance difficulty level as very difficult. For the fall 2006 freshman class, 56 percent of the applicants were accepted.

For Further Information Contact Ms. Shawn Leftwich, Director of Admissions, Wheaton College, 501 College Avenue, Wheaton, IL 60187. *Telephone:* 630-752-5011 or 800-222-2419 (toll-free out-of-state). *Fax:* 630-752-5285. *E-mail:* admissions@wheaton.edu. *Web site:* http://www.wheaton.edu/.

WORSHAM COLLEGE OF MORTUARY SCIENCE
Wheeling, Illinois
http://www.worshamcollege.com/

Indiana

ANCILLA COLLEGE
Donaldson, Indiana

Ancilla College is a coed, private, Roman Catholic, two-year college, founded in 1937, offering degrees at the associate level. It has a 63-acre campus in Donaldson near Chicago.

Expenses for 2006–07 *Application fee:* $25. *Tuition:* $10,800 full-time, $360 per credit hour part-time. *Mandatory fees:* $230 full-time, $55 per term part-time. Both full-time and part-time tuition and fees vary according to course load and program.

For Further Information Contact Erin Wittmeyer, Director of Admissions, Ancilla College, 9601 Union Road, Donaldson, IN 46513. *Telephone:* 574-936-8898 Ext. 350 or 866-262-4552 Ext. 350 (toll-free in-state). *Fax:* 574-935-1773. *E-mail:* admissions@ancilla.edu. *Web site:* http://www.ancilla.edu/.

ANDERSON UNIVERSITY
Anderson, Indiana

Anderson University is a coed, private, comprehensive institution, founded in 1917, affiliated with the Church of God, offering degrees at the associate, bachelor's, master's, doctoral, and first professional levels. It has a 100-acre campus in Anderson near Indianapolis.

Anderson University (continued)

Academic Information The faculty has 250 members (56% full-time), 41% with terminal degrees. The undergraduate student-faculty ratio is 14:1. The library holds 247,966 titles, 728 serial subscriptions, and 5,867 audiovisual materials. Special programs include academic remediation, services for learning-disabled students, an honors program, study abroad, advanced placement credit, accelerated degree programs, double majors, independent study, self-designed majors, summer session for credit, part-time degree programs, adult/continuing education programs, internships, and arrangement for off-campus study. The most frequently chosen baccalaureate fields are business/marketing, education, health professions and related sciences.

Student Body Statistics The student body totals 2,730, of whom 2,199 are undergraduates (457 freshmen). 58 percent are women and 42 percent are men. Students come from 41 states and territories and 23 other countries. 66 percent are from Indiana. 2 percent are international students. 21 percent of the 2006 graduating class went on to graduate and professional schools.

Expenses for 2006–07 *Application fee:* $25. *Comprehensive fee:* $26,450 includes full-time tuition ($19,990) and college room and board ($6460). *College room only:* $3940. *Part-time tuition:* $850 per semester hour.

Financial Aid Forms of aid include need-based and non-need-based scholarships and part-time jobs. The average aided 2006–07 undergraduate received an aid package worth an estimated $16,181. The priority application deadline for financial aid is March 1.

Freshman Admission Anderson University requires a high school transcript, a minimum 2.0 high school GPA, 2 recommendations, lifestyle statement, and SAT or ACT scores. An essay and TOEFL scores for international students are recommended. An interview is required for some. The application deadline for regular admission is July 1.

Transfer Admission The application deadline for admission is rolling.

Entrance Difficulty Anderson University assesses its entrance difficulty level as moderately difficult. For the fall 2006 freshman class, 91 percent of the applicants were accepted.

For Further Information Contact Mr. Jim King, Director of Admissions, Anderson University, 1100 East 5th Street, Anderson, IN 46012-3495. *Telephone:* 765-641-4080, 800-421-3014 (toll-free in-state), or 800-428-6414 (toll-free out-of-state). *Fax:* 765-641-3851. *E-mail:* info@anderson.edu. *Web site:* http://www.anderson.edu/.

THE ART INSTITUTE OF INDIANAPOLIS

Indianapolis, Indiana

The Art Institute of Indianapolis is a coed, proprietary, four-year college of Education Management Corporation, offering degrees at the associate and bachelor's levels.

Academic Information The student-faculty ratio is 15:1. Special programs include academic remediation, services for learning-disabled students, cooperative (work-study) education, study abroad, advanced placement credit, independent study, distance learning, summer session for credit, adult/continuing education programs, and internships.

Student Body Statistics The student body is made up of 392 undergraduates.

Expenses for 2007–08 *Application fee:* $150. *Tuition:* $19,872 full-time, $414 per quarter hour part-time. *College room only:* $4495.

Freshman Admission The Art Institute of Indianapolis requires an essay, a high school transcript, and an interview. The application deadline for regular admission is rolling and for nonresidents it is rolling.

Transfer Admission The application deadline for admission is rolling.

Entrance Difficulty The Art Institute of Indianapolis assesses its entrance difficulty level as noncompetitive. For the fall 2006 freshman class, 62 percent of the applicants were accepted.

For Further Information Contact Mr. Christopher Mesecar, The Art Institute of Indianapolis, 3500 Depauw Boulevard, Indianapolis, IN 46268. *Telephone:* 317-613-4800. *Fax:* 317-613-4808. *E-mail:* cjmesecar@aii.edu. *Web site:* http://www.artinstitutes.edu/indianapolis/.

BALL STATE UNIVERSITY

Muncie, Indiana

SPONSOR See Front Insert for Details!

Ball State University is a coed, public university, founded in 1918, offering degrees at the associate, bachelor's, master's, and doctoral levels and post-master's and postbachelor's certificates. It has a 955-acre campus in Muncie near Indianapolis.

Academic Information The faculty has 1,148 members (80% full-time), 65% with terminal degrees. The undergraduate student-faculty ratio is 16:1. The library holds 1 million titles, 2,937 serial subscriptions, and 516,000 audiovisual materials. Special programs include academic remediation, an honors program, cooperative (work-study) education, study abroad, advanced placement credit, accelerated degree programs, Freshman Honors College, ESL programs, double majors, independent study, distance learning, summer session for credit, part-time degree programs, adult/continuing education programs, and internships. The most frequently chosen baccalaureate fields are business/marketing, education, liberal arts/general studies.

Student Body Statistics The student body is made up of 17,082 undergraduates (3,995 freshmen). 52 percent are women and 48 percent are men. Students come from 49 states and territories and 47 other countries. 90 percent are from Indiana. 0.1 percent are international students. 29 percent of the 2006 graduating class went on to graduate and professional schools.

Expenses for 2006–07 *Application fee:* $25. *State resident tuition:* $6360 full-time, $231 per credit hour part-time. *Nonresident tuition:* $16,736 full-time, $593 per credit hour part-time. *Mandatory fees:* $450 full-time. Part-time tuition varies according to course load. *College room and board:* $6898. Room and board charges vary according to board plan and housing facility.

Financial Aid Forms of aid include need-based and non-need-based scholarships, athletic grants, and part-time jobs. The average aided 2005–06 undergraduate received an aid package worth $7663. The priority application deadline for financial aid is March 1.

Freshman Admission Ball State University requires a high school transcript, SAT or ACT scores, and TOEFL scores for international students. An essay, recommendations, and an interview are required for some. The application deadline for regular admission is rolling.

Transfer Admission The application deadline for admission is rolling.

Entrance Difficulty Ball State University assesses its entrance difficulty level as moderately difficult; very difficult for architecture program. For the fall 2006 freshman class, 79 percent of the applicants were accepted.

SPECIAL MESSAGE TO STUDENTS

Social Life At Ball State, the life lived outside the classroom is important, too. That is why Ball State offers more than 300 student organizations to help students get involved. Ball State University provides housing on campus for more than 6,300 students in nine complexes (thirty-one residence halls plus two apartment complexes), and they are safe, affordable, and convenient. When students arrive for the fall 2007 semester, some of them will move into a new residence hall that incorporates features suggested by current students. Among the proposed features are a focus on double-occupancy rooms clustered around semiprivate bathrooms, a limited number of single-occupancy rooms with private baths, as well as community space, including seminar and activity rooms to facilitate living and learning for students. Residence halls offer a wide range of visitation policies, and there are fitness and aerobic areas and special programs that emphasize positive lifestyle choices. Ball State has everything from chicken parmesan to vegetarian entrees at its seven dining hall locations.

Academic Highlights Ball State is a coed public university that offers degrees at the associate, bachelor's, master's, and doctoral levels. Founded in 1918, the 750-acre residential campus includes more than sixty major buildings, with an additional 285 acres of research property. Ball State was ranked as the nation's top wireless campuses in a 2005 survey conducted by Intel Corporation and published in *U.S. News &*

World Report. The University operates more than 200 computer labs and touts a completely wireless campus. Categorized as a doctoral professional-dominant institution by the Carnegie Foundation, the University has nine academic colleges—seven that house majors, an Honors College, and University College—and a graduate school. Ball State awards approximately 4,000 degrees each year. There are 910 full-time faculty members; 91 percent of the tenure-track faculty members hold terminal degrees. Ball State is featured in the 2007 edition of the book *America's Best Value Colleges*. The book profiles 150 public and private schools with excellent academics, generous financial aid packages, and relatively low cost.

Interviews and Campus Visits Students can experience Ball State during a Cardinal Preview Day, Football Saturday, or by scheduling an individual visit. An individual visit provides opportunities for students and their families to tour the campus, attend an admissions information session, and enjoy a free meal in a dining facility. To arrange a campus visit, students should call 866-770-3163 (toll-free) or 800-482-4BSU (toll-free) or visit http://www.bsu.edu/admissions/visit. The fax number is 765-285-1632. The nearest commercial airport is Indianapolis International.

For Further Information Write to Office of Admissions, Ball State University, Muncie, IN 47306-1099. *Web site:* http://www.bsu.edu/admissions.

See page 238 for the College Close-Up.

BETHEL COLLEGE
Mishawaka, Indiana

Bethel College is a coed, private, comprehensive institution, founded in 1947, affiliated with the Missionary Church, offering degrees at the associate, bachelor's, and master's levels. It has a 70-acre campus in Mishawaka.

Expenses for 2006–07 *Application fee:* $25. *One-time mandatory fee:* $600. *Comprehensive fee:* $22,830 includes full-time tuition ($17,450) and college room and board ($5380). *Part-time tuition:* $350 per hour.
For Further Information Contact Randy Beachy, Assistant Vice President for Enrollment/Marketing, Bethel College, 1001 West McKinley Avenue, Mishawaka, IN 46545-5591. *Telephone:* 574-257-3339 or 800-422-4101 (toll-free). *Fax:* 574-257-3335. *E-mail:* admissions@bethelcollege.edu. *Web site:* http://www.bethelcollege.edu.

BUTLER UNIVERSITY
Indianapolis, Indiana

Butler University is a coed, private, comprehensive institution, founded in 1855, offering degrees at the bachelor's, master's, and first professional levels. It has a 290-acre campus in Indianapolis.

Academic Information The faculty has 454 members (64% full-time), 63% with terminal degrees. The undergraduate student-faculty ratio is 12:1. The library holds 346,805 titles, 13,441 serial subscriptions, and 15,268 audiovisual materials. Special programs include services for learning-disabled students, an honors program, cooperative (work-study) education, study abroad, advanced placement credit, double majors, independent study, self-designed majors, summer session for credit, part-time degree programs (daytime, evenings, summer), adult/continuing education programs, internships, and arrangement for off-campus study with 6 members of the Consortium for Urban Education. The most frequently chosen baccalaureate fields are business/marketing, communications/journalism, health professions and related sciences.
Student Body Statistics The student body totals 4,437, of whom 3,652 are undergraduates (965 freshmen). 62 percent are women and 38 percent are men. Students come from 50 states and territories and 53 other countries. 60 percent are from Indiana. 3 percent are international students. 25 percent of the 2006 graduating class went on to graduate and professional schools.

Expenses for 2006–07 *Application fee:* $35. *Comprehensive fee:* $33,944 includes full-time tuition ($24,710), mandatory fees ($704), and college room and board ($8530). *College room only:* $4180. Full-time tuition and fees vary according to program. Room and board charges vary according to housing facility. *Part-time tuition:* $1030 per credit. Part-time tuition varies according to program.
Financial Aid Forms of aid include need-based and non-need-based scholarships, athletic grants, and part-time jobs. The average aided 2006–07 undergraduate received an aid package worth an estimated $18,743. The priority application deadline for financial aid is March 1.
Freshman Admission Butler University requires an essay, a high school transcript, SAT or ACT scores, and TOEFL scores for international students. An interview and audition are required for some. The application deadline for regular admission is rolling and for early action it is December 1.
Transfer Admission The application deadline for admission is August 15.
Entrance Difficulty Butler University assesses its entrance difficulty level as moderately difficult. For the fall 2006 freshman class, 74 percent of the applicants were accepted.
For Further Information Contact Mr. Scott McIntyre, Director of Admissions, Butler University, 4600 Sunset Avenue, Indianapolis, IN 46208-3485. *Telephone:* 317-940-8100 or 888-940-8100 (toll-free). *Fax:* 317-940-8150. *E-mail:* admission@butler.edu. *Web site:* http://www.butler.edu/.

CALUMET COLLEGE OF SAINT JOSEPH
Whiting, Indiana

Calumet College of Saint Joseph is a coed, private, Roman Catholic, comprehensive institution, founded in 1951, offering degrees at the associate, bachelor's, and master's levels and postbachelor's certificates. It has a 25-acre campus in Whiting near Chicago.

Academic Information The faculty has 142 members (21% full-time), 34% with terminal degrees. The undergraduate student-faculty ratio is 22:1. The library holds 106,000 titles, 21,850 serial subscriptions, and 1,000 audiovisual materials. Special programs include academic remediation, cooperative (work-study) education, advanced placement credit, accelerated degree programs, double majors, independent study, summer session for credit, part-time degree programs (daytime, evenings, weekends), external degree programs, adult/continuing education programs, and internships. The most frequently chosen baccalaureate fields are business/marketing, education, security and protective services.
Student Body Statistics The student body totals 1,252, of whom 1,091 are undergraduates (100 freshmen). 55 percent are women and 45 percent are men. Students come from 2 states and territories. 0.2 percent are international students.
Expenses for 2006–07 *Application fee:* $0. *Tuition:* $10,500 full-time, $350 per credit hour part-time. *Mandatory fees:* $150 full-time.
Financial Aid Forms of aid include need-based scholarships, athletic grants, and part-time jobs. The priority application deadline for financial aid is March 1.
Freshman Admission Calumet College of Saint Joseph requires a high school transcript and TOEFL scores for international students. A minimum 2.0 high school GPA, an interview, and SAT or ACT scores are recommended. An essay, an interview, and ACT COMPASS are required for some. The application deadline for regular admission is rolling.
Transfer Admission The application deadline for admission is rolling.
Entrance Difficulty Calumet College of Saint Joseph assesses its entrance difficulty level as noncompetitive. For the fall 2006 freshman class, 57 percent of the applicants were accepted.
For Further Information Contact Mr. Chuck Walz, Director of Admissions, Calumet College of Saint Joseph, 2400 New York Avenue, Whiting, IN 46394. *Telephone:* 219-473-4215 Ext. 379 or 877-700-9100 (toll-free). *Fax:* 219-473-4259. *E-mail:* admissions@ccsj.edu. *Web site:* http://www.ccsj.edu/.

CROSSROADS BIBLE COLLEGE

Indianapolis, Indiana

http://www.crossroads.edu/

DAVENPORT UNIVERSITY

Granger, Indiana

http://www.davenport.edu/

DAVENPORT UNIVERSITY

Hammond, Indiana

http://www.davenport.edu/

DAVENPORT UNIVERSITY

Merrillville, Indiana

http://www.davenport.edu/

DePAUW UNIVERSITY

Greencastle, Indiana

DePauw University is a coed, private, four-year college, founded in 1837, affiliated with the United Methodist Church, offering degrees at the bachelor's level. It has a 655-acre campus in Greencastle near Indianapolis.

Academic Information The faculty has 265 members (80% full-time), 87% with terminal degrees. The student-faculty ratio is 10:1. The library holds 333,346 titles, 2,030 serial subscriptions, and 22,491 audiovisual materials. Special programs include services for learning-disabled students, an honors program, study abroad, advanced placement credit, double majors, independent study, self-designed majors, part-time degree programs (daytime, evenings), internships, and arrangement for off-campus study with Great Lakes Colleges Association. The most frequently chosen baccalaureate fields are English, foreign languages and literature, social sciences.

Student Body Statistics The student body is made up of 2,326 undergraduates (596 freshmen). 56 percent are women and 44 percent are men. Students come from 43 states and territories and 32 other countries. 54 percent are from Indiana. 1.6 percent are international students. 23.1 percent of the 2006 graduating class went on to graduate and professional schools.

Expenses for 2006–07 *Application fee:* $40. *Comprehensive fee:* $35,580 includes full-time tuition ($27,400), mandatory fees ($380), and college room and board ($7800). *College room only:* $4100. Room and board charges vary according to board plan. *Part-time tuition:* $856.25 per semester hour.

Financial Aid Forms of aid include need-based and non-need-based scholarships and part-time jobs. The average aided 2005–06 undergraduate received an aid package worth $24,873. The application deadline for financial aid is February 15.

Freshman Admission DePauw University requires an essay, a high school transcript, 1 recommendation, and SAT or ACT scores. An interview and TOEFL scores for international students are recommended. The application deadline for regular admission is February 1; for early decision it is November 1; and for early action it is December 1.

Transfer Admission The application deadline for admission is March 1.

Entrance Difficulty DePauw University assesses its entrance difficulty level as moderately difficult. For the fall 2006 freshman class, 68 percent of the applicants were accepted.

For Further Information Contact Brett Kennedy, Senior Associate Director of Admission, DePauw University, 101 East Seminary Street, Greencastle, IN 46135-0037. *Telephone:* 765-658-4006 or 800-447-2495 (toll-free). *Fax:* 765-658-4007. *E-mail:* admission@depauw.edu. *Web site:* http://www.depauw.edu/.

DeVRY UNIVERSITY

Indianapolis, Indiana

DeVry University is a coed, proprietary, comprehensive unit of DeVry University, offering degrees at the associate, bachelor's, and master's levels and postbachelor's certificates.

Academic Information The faculty has 14 members. The undergraduate student-faculty ratio is 15:1. Special programs include academic remediation, services for learning-disabled students, advanced placement credit, accelerated degree programs, ESL programs, distance learning, summer session for credit, part-time degree programs (daytime, evenings, weekends, summer), and adult/continuing education programs.

Student Body Statistics The student body totals 246, of whom 143 are undergraduates (21 freshmen). 52 percent are women and 48 percent are men. 97 percent are from Indiana. 0.7 percent are international students.

Expenses for 2007–08 *Application fee:* $50. *Tuition:* $12,900 full-time, $490 per credit part-time. *Mandatory fees:* $120 full-time.

Freshman Admission DeVry University requires a high school transcript and an interview. The application deadline for regular admission is rolling.

Transfer Admission The application deadline for admission is rolling.

Entrance Difficulty DeVry University assesses its entrance difficulty level as minimally difficult; moderately difficult for Electronics Engineering Technology Program.

For Further Information Contact Admissions Office, DeVry University, 9100 Keystone Crossing, Suite 350, Indianapolis, IN 46240-2158. *Telephone:* 317-581-8854. *Web site:* http://www.devry.edu/.

DeVRY UNIVERSITY

Merrillville, Indiana

http://www.devry.edu/

EARLHAM COLLEGE

Richmond, Indiana

Earlham College is a coed, private, comprehensive institution, founded in 1847, affiliated with the Society of Friends, offering degrees at the bachelor's, master's, and first professional levels. It has an 800-acre campus in Richmond near Cincinnati, Indianapolis, and Dayton.

Academic Information The faculty has 111 members (86% full-time), 87% with terminal degrees. The undergraduate student-faculty ratio is 12:1. The library holds 406,699 titles, 22,571 serial subscriptions, and 6,855 audiovisual materials. Special programs include services for learning-disabled students, study abroad, advanced placement credit, accelerated degree programs, double majors, independent study, self-designed majors, internships, and arrangement for off-campus study with members of the Great Lakes Colleges Association. The most frequently chosen baccalaureate fields are biological/life sciences, social sciences, visual and performing arts.

Student Body Statistics The student body totals 1,410, of whom 1,248 are undergraduates (300 freshmen). 57 percent are women and 43 percent are men. Students come from 49 states and territories and 61 other countries. 31 percent are from Indiana. 8.4 percent are international students. 21 percent of the 2006 graduating class went on to graduate and professional schools.

Expenses for 2006–07 *Application fee:* $30. *Comprehensive fee:* $35,520 includes full-time tuition ($28,600), mandatory fees ($720), and college room and board ($6200). *College room only:* $3060. Room and board charges vary according to board plan. *Part-time tuition:* $953 per credit.

Financial Aid Forms of aid include need-based and non-need-based scholarships and part-time jobs. The priority application deadline for financial aid is March 1.

Freshman Admission Earlham College requires an essay, a high school transcript, a minimum 3.0 high school GPA, 2 recommendations, SAT or ACT scores, and TOEFL scores for international students. An interview is recommended. The application deadline for regular admission is February 15; for early decision it is December 1; and for early action it is January 1.

Transfer Admission The application deadline for admission is April 1.

Entrance Difficulty Earlham College assesses its entrance difficulty level as very difficult. For the fall 2006 freshman class, 70 percent of the applicants were accepted.

For Further Information Contact Mr. Jeff Rickey, Dean of Admissions and Financial Aid, Earlham College, 801 National Road West, Richmond, IN 47374. *Telephone:* 765-983-1600 or 800-327-5426 (toll-free). *Fax:* 765-983-1560. *E-mail:* admission@earlham.edu. *Web site:* http://www.earlham.edu/.

FRANKLIN COLLEGE
Franklin, Indiana

Franklin College is a coed, private, four-year college, founded in 1834, affiliated with the American Baptist Churches in the U.S.A., offering degrees at the bachelor's level. It has a 74-acre campus in Franklin near Indianapolis.

Academic Information The faculty has 115 members (56% full-time), 54% with terminal degrees. The student-faculty ratio is 16:1. The library holds 129,709 titles and 292 serial subscriptions. Special programs include academic remediation, services for learning-disabled students, cooperative (work-study) education, study abroad, advanced placement credit, double majors, independent study, summer session for credit, part-time degree programs (daytime, summer), internships, and arrangement for off-campus study with Marian College, University of Indianapolis, Indiana University-Purdue University at Indianapolis, Butler University, Martin University, Ivy Tech State College. The most frequently chosen baccalaureate fields are communications/journalism, education, social sciences.

Student Body Statistics The student body is made up of 1,013 undergraduates (277 freshmen). 49 percent are women and 51 percent are men. Students come from 16 states and territories and 4 other countries. 96 percent are from Indiana. 0.5 percent are international students. 12.7 percent of the 2006 graduating class went on to graduate and professional schools.

Expenses for 2006–07 *Application fee:* $30. *Comprehensive fee:* $26,295 includes full-time tuition ($20,150), mandatory fees ($175), and college room and board ($5970). *College room only:* $3480. Room and board charges vary according to board plan and housing facility. *Part-time tuition:* $280 per credit hour. Part-time tuition varies according to course load.

Financial Aid Forms of aid include need-based and non-need-based scholarships and part-time jobs. The average aided 2006–07 undergraduate received an aid package worth an estimated $16,712. The application deadline for financial aid is March 1.

Freshman Admission Franklin College requires an essay, a high school transcript, TOEFL for international students, SAT or ACT scores, and TOEFL scores for international students. A minimum X high school GPA and recommendations are recommended. An interview is required for some. The application deadline for regular admission is rolling.

Entrance Difficulty Franklin College assesses its entrance difficulty level as moderately difficult. For the fall 2006 freshman class, 74 percent of the applicants were accepted.

For Further Information Contact Ms. Jacqueline Acosta, Director of Admissions, Franklin College, 101 Branigin Boulevard, Franklin, IN 46131-2623. *Telephone:* 317-738-8062 or 800-852-0232 (toll-free). *Fax:* 317-738-8274. *E-mail:* jacosta@franklincollege.edu. *Web site:* http://www.franklincollege.edu/.

GOSHEN COLLEGE
Goshen, Indiana

Goshen College is a coed, private, Mennonite, four-year college, founded in 1894, offering degrees at the bachelor's level. It has a 135-acre campus in Goshen.

Academic Information The faculty has 110 members (66% full-time), 46% with terminal degrees. The student-faculty ratio is 10:1. The library holds 136,550 titles and 496 serial subscriptions. Special programs include academic remediation, services for learning-disabled students, an honors program, study abroad, advanced placement credit, accelerated degree programs, Freshman Honors College, double majors, independent study, self-designed majors, summer session for credit, part-time degree programs, adult/continuing education programs, internships, and arrangement for off-campus study with Northern Indiana Consortium for Education. The most frequently chosen baccalaureate fields are business/marketing, computer and information sciences, health professions and related sciences.

Student Body Statistics The student body is made up of 951 undergraduates (209 freshmen). 60 percent are women and 40 percent are men. Students come from 32 states and territories and 28 other countries. 45 percent are from Indiana. 7.5 percent are international students. 36 percent of the 2006 graduating class went on to graduate and professional schools.

Expenses for 2007–08 *Application fee:* $25. *Comprehensive fee:* $28,300 includes full-time tuition ($21,300) and college room and board ($7000). *College room only:* $3750. *Part-time tuition:* $850 per credit hour.

Financial Aid Forms of aid include need-based and non-need-based scholarships, athletic grants, and part-time jobs. The average aided 2005–06 undergraduate received an aid package worth $16,555. The priority application deadline for financial aid is February 15.

Freshman Admission Goshen College requires an essay, a high school transcript, a minimum 2.5 high school GPA, 2 recommendations, rank in upper 50% of high school class, minimum SAT score of 1000 or ACT score of 22, SAT or ACT scores, and TOEFL scores for international students. An interview is recommended. The application deadline for regular admission is August 15 and for early action it is December 1.

Transfer Admission The application deadline for admission is August 15.

Entrance Difficulty Goshen College assesses its entrance difficulty level as moderately difficult. For the fall 2006 freshman class, 76 percent of the applicants were accepted.

For Further Information Contact Lynn Jackson, Director of Enrollment, Goshen College, 1700 South Main Street, Goshen, IN 46526-4794. *Telephone:* 574-535-7535 or 800-348-7422 (toll-free). *Fax:* 574-535-7609. *E-mail:* lynnj@goshen.edu. *Web site:* http://www.goshen.edu/.

GRACE COLLEGE
Winona Lake, Indiana

Grace College is a coed, private, comprehensive institution, founded in 1948, affiliated with the Fellowship of Grace Brethren Churches, offering degrees at the associate, bachelor's, master's, doctoral, and first professional levels. It has a 160-acre campus in Winona Lake.

Academic Information The faculty has 53 members (89% full-time), 66% with terminal degrees. The undergraduate student-faculty ratio is 22:1. The library holds 156,637 titles, 23,972 serial subscriptions, and 3,806 audiovisual materials. Special programs include academic remediation, services for learning-disabled students, an honors program, cooperative (work-study) education, study abroad, advanced placement credit, accelerated degree programs, double majors, independent study, distance learning, summer session for credit, part-time degree programs (daytime, evenings, summer), adult/continuing education programs, internships, and arrangement for off-campus study with Coalition for Christian Colleges and Universities. The most frequently chosen baccalaureate fields are business/marketing, education, psychology.

Student Body Statistics The student body totals 1,291, of whom 1,179 are undergraduates (276 freshmen). 46 percent are women and 54 percent are men. Students come from 44 states and territories and 6 other countries. 53 percent are from Indiana. 0.6 percent are international students.

Grace College (continued)

Expenses for 2006–07 *Application fee:* $30. *Comprehensive fee:* $23,710 includes full-time tuition ($16,950), mandatory fees ($400), and college room and board ($6360). *College room only:* $3280. Room and board charges vary according to board plan and housing facility. *Part-time tuition:* $320 per credit. *Part-time mandatory fees:* $280 per year. Part-time tuition and fees vary according to course load.

Financial Aid Forms of aid include need-based and non-need-based scholarships and athletic grants. The average aided 2006–07 undergraduate received an aid package worth an estimated $14,540. The priority application deadline for financial aid is March 10.

Freshman Admission Grace College requires an essay, a high school transcript, a minimum 2.3 high school GPA, 2 recommendations, personal statement of faith, SAT or ACT scores, and TOEFL scores for international students. An interview is required for some. The application deadline for regular admission is August 1 and for early action it is December 1.

Transfer Admission The application deadline for admission is August 1.

Entrance Difficulty Grace College assesses its entrance difficulty level as moderately difficult. For the fall 2006 freshman class, 66 percent of the applicants were accepted.

For Further Information Contact Mr. Ken Moyer, Dean of Enrollment, Grace College, Admissions Office, 200 Seminary Drive, Winona Lake, IN 46590. *Telephone:* 574-372-5100 Ext. 6008, 800-54-GRACE Ext. 6412 (toll-free in-state), or 800-54 GRACE Ext. 6412 (toll-free out-of-state). *Fax:* 574-372-5120. *E-mail:* enroll@grace.edu. *Web site:* http://www.grace.edu/.

HANOVER COLLEGE
Hanover, Indiana

Hanover College is a coed, private, Presbyterian, four-year college, founded in 1827, offering degrees at the bachelor's level. It has a 630-acre campus in Hanover near Louisville.

Academic Information The faculty has 102 members (94% full-time), 99% with terminal degrees. The student-faculty ratio is 10:1. The library holds 224,478 titles, 1,035 serial subscriptions, and 5,080 audiovisual materials. Special programs include study abroad, advanced placement credit, double majors, independent study, self-designed majors, internships, and arrangement for off-campus study with 8 members of the Spring Term Consortium. The most frequently chosen baccalaureate fields are business/marketing, psychology, social sciences.

Student Body Statistics The student body is made up of 975 undergraduates (230 freshmen). 54 percent are women and 46 percent are men. Students come from 27 states and territories and 13 other countries. 63 percent are from Indiana. 4.1 percent are international students. 26 percent of the 2006 graduating class went on to graduate and professional schools.

Expenses for 2006–07 *Application fee:* $35. *Comprehensive fee:* $29,500 includes full-time tuition ($22,200), mandatory fees ($500), and college room and board ($6800). *College room only:* $3250. Full-time tuition and fees vary according to reciprocity agreements. Room and board charges vary according to housing facility and location. *Part-time tuition:* $2468 per unit. Part-time tuition varies according to course load and reciprocity agreements.

Financial Aid Forms of aid include need-based and non-need-based scholarships. The average aided 2005–06 undergraduate received an aid package worth $17,526.

Freshman Admission Hanover College requires an essay, a high school transcript, 1 recommendation, SAT or ACT scores, and TOEFL scores for international students. An interview is recommended. The application deadline for regular admission is March 1 and for early action it is December 1.

Transfer Admission The application deadline for admission is rolling.

Entrance Difficulty Hanover College assesses its entrance difficulty level as moderately difficult. For the fall 2006 freshman class, 64 percent of the applicants were accepted.

For Further Information Contact Mr. Bill Preble, Dean of Admission and Financial Assistance, Hanover College, PO Box 108, Hanover, IN 47243-0108. *Telephone:* 812-866-7021 or 800-213-2178 (toll-free). *Fax:* 812-866-7098. *E-mail:* admission@hanover.edu. *Web site:* http://www.hanover.edu/.

HOLY CROSS COLLEGE
Notre Dame, Indiana

Holy Cross College is a coed, private, Roman Catholic, primarily two-year college, founded in 1966, offering degrees at the associate and bachelor's levels. It has a 150-acre campus in Notre Dame.

Academic Information The faculty has 38 members (68% full-time), 32% with terminal degrees. The student-faculty ratio is 12:1. The library holds 15,000 titles and 160 serial subscriptions. Special programs include academic remediation, an honors program, study abroad, advanced placement credit, accelerated degree programs, Freshman Honors College, ESL programs, double majors, independent study, self-designed majors, summer session for credit, internships, and arrangement for off-campus study with members of the Northern Indiana Consortium for Education. The most frequently chosen baccalaureate field is liberal arts/general studies.

Student Body Statistics The student body is made up of 430 undergraduates (202 freshmen). 36 percent are women and 64 percent are men. Students come from 31 states and territories and 7 other countries. 36 percent are from Indiana. 1.6 percent are international students. 85 percent of the 2006 graduating class went on to four-year colleges.

Expenses for 2007–08 *Application fee:* $50. *Comprehensive fee:* $24,660 includes full-time tuition ($15,660), mandatory fees ($1000), and college room and board ($8000). *Part-time tuition:* $520 per credit hour. *Part-time mandatory fees:* $565 per year.

Financial Aid Forms of aid include need-based scholarships and part-time jobs. The priority application deadline for financial aid is March 1.

Freshman Admission Holy Cross College requires an essay, a high school transcript, a minimum 2.5 high school GPA, College Success Program (2.0), SAT or ACT scores, and TOEFL scores for international students. An interview is recommended. Recommendations are required for some. The application deadline for regular admission is rolling.

Transfer Admission The application deadline for admission is rolling.

Entrance Difficulty Holy Cross College assesses its entrance difficulty level as moderately difficult; minimally difficult for transfers. For the fall 2006 freshman class, 97 percent of the applicants were accepted.

For Further Information Contact Office of Admissions, Holy Cross College, PO Box 308, Notre Dame, IN 46556. *Telephone:* 574-239-8400. *Fax:* 574-239-8323. *E-mail:* vduke@hcc-nd.edu. *Web site:* http://www.hcc-nd.edu/.

HUNTINGTON UNIVERSITY
Huntington, Indiana

Huntington University is a coed, private, comprehensive institution, founded in 1897, affiliated with the Church of the United Brethren in Christ, offering degrees at the associate, bachelor's, and master's levels. It has a 170-acre campus in Huntington near Fort Wayne.

Academic Information The faculty has 84 members (69% full-time), 63% with terminal degrees. The undergraduate student-faculty ratio is 12:1. The library holds 166,122 titles. Special programs include academic remediation, services for learning-disabled students, study abroad, advanced placement credit, double majors, independent study, summer session for credit, part-time degree programs, adult/continuing education programs, internships, and arrangement for off-campus study with Saint Francis College (IN). The most frequently chosen baccalaureate fields are business/marketing, education, theology and religious vocations.

Student Body Statistics The student body totals 1,084, of whom 997 are undergraduates (252 freshmen). 55 percent are women and 45 percent are men. Students come from 32 states and territories and 15 other countries. 63 percent are from Indiana. 3.6 percent are international students. 10 percent of the 2006 graduating class went on to graduate and professional schools.

Expenses for 2007–08 *Application fee:* $20. *Comprehensive fee:* $26,160 includes full-time tuition ($18,980), mandatory fees ($450), and college room and board ($6730). *Part-time tuition:* $570 per semester hour. *Part-time mandatory fees:* $22 per semester hour.

Financial Aid Forms of aid include need-based and non-need-based scholarships, athletic grants, and part-time jobs. The average aided

2006–07 undergraduate received an aid package worth an estimated $13,300. The priority application deadline for financial aid is March 1.

Freshman Admission Huntington University requires an essay, a high school transcript, a minimum 2.3 high school GPA, SAT or ACT scores, and TOEFL scores for international students. An interview is recommended. The application deadline for regular admission is August 1.

Transfer Admission The application deadline for admission is rolling.

Entrance Difficulty Huntington University assesses its entrance difficulty level as moderately difficult. For the fall 2006 freshman class, 91 percent of the applicants were accepted.

For Further Information Contact Mr. Jeff Berggren, Vice President of Enrollment Management and Marketing, Huntington University, 2303 College Avenue, Huntington, IN 46750-1299. *Telephone:* 260-356-6000 Ext. 4016 or 800-642-6493 (toll-free). *Fax:* 260-356-9448. *E-mail:* admissions@huntington.edu. *Web site:* http://www.huntington.edu/.

INDIANA STATE UNIVERSITY
Terre Haute, Indiana

Indiana State University is a coed, public university, founded in 1865, offering degrees at the associate, bachelor's, master's, and doctoral levels and post-master's and postbachelor's certificates. It has a 91-acre campus in Terre Haute near Indianapolis.

Academic Information The faculty has 641 members (70% full-time), 63% with terminal degrees. The undergraduate student-faculty ratio is 17:1. The library holds 1 million titles, 43,464 serial subscriptions, and 32,843 audiovisual materials. Special programs include academic remediation, services for learning-disabled students, an honors program, cooperative (work-study) education, study abroad, advanced placement credit, accelerated degree programs, ESL programs, double majors, independent study, distance learning, summer session for credit, part-time degree programs (daytime, evenings, summer), adult/continuing education programs, internships, and arrangement for off-campus study with Saint Mary-of-the-Woods College, Rose-Hulman Institute of Technology. The most frequently chosen baccalaureate fields are business/marketing, education, social sciences.

Student Body Statistics The student body totals 10,568, of whom 8,537 are undergraduates (1,703 freshmen). 51 percent are women and 49 percent are men. Students come from 46 states and territories and 47 other countries. 89 percent are from Indiana. 1.4 percent are international students.

Expenses for 2006–07 *Application fee:* $25. *State resident tuition:* $6102 full-time, $220 per credit hour part-time. *Nonresident tuition:* $13,518 full-time, $476 per credit hour part-time. *Mandatory fees:* $334 full-time, $167 per term part-time. Full-time tuition and fees vary according to course load. *College room and board:* $6294. *College room only:* $3339. Room and board charges vary according to board plan, housing facility, and student level.

Financial Aid Forms of aid include need-based and non-need-based scholarships, athletic grants, and part-time jobs. The average aided 2005–06 undergraduate received an aid package worth $7410. The application deadline for financial aid is March 1 with a priority deadline of March 1.

Freshman Admission Indiana State University requires a high school transcript, SAT or ACT scores, and TOEFL scores for international students. Recommendations and an interview are required for some. The application deadline for regular admission is August 15.

Entrance Difficulty Indiana State University assesses its entrance difficulty level as moderately difficult. For the fall 2006 freshman class, 80 percent of the applicants were accepted.

For Further Information Contact Mr. Richard Toomey, Director of Admissions, Indiana State University, 218 North Sixth Street, Erickson Hall, Terre Haute, IN 47809-9989. *Telephone:* 812-237-2121 or 800-742-0891 (toll-free). *Fax:* 812-237-8023. *E-mail:* ADMISU@isugw.indstate.edu. *Web site:* http://web.indstate.edu/.

INDIANA TECH
Fort Wayne, Indiana

Indiana Tech is a coed, private, comprehensive institution, founded in 1930, offering degrees at the associate, bachelor's, and master's levels. It has a 25-acre campus in Fort Wayne.

Academic Information The faculty has 251 members (15% full-time), 6% with terminal degrees. The undergraduate student-faculty ratio is 21:1. The library holds 20,000 titles, 80 serial subscriptions, and 102 audiovisual materials. Special programs include academic remediation, services for learning-disabled students, advanced placement credit, accelerated degree programs, double majors, independent study, distance learning, self-designed majors, summer session for credit, part-time degree programs (daytime, evenings, weekends, summer), external degree programs, adult/continuing education programs, and internships. The most frequently chosen baccalaureate fields are business/marketing, computer and information sciences, engineering.

Student Body Statistics The student body totals 3,405, of whom 3,035 are undergraduates (355 freshmen). 53 percent are women and 47 percent are men. Students come from 38 states and territories and 3 other countries. 87 percent are from Indiana. 0.3 percent are international students. 5 percent of the 2006 graduating class went on to graduate and professional schools.

Expenses for 2007–08 *Application fee:* $50. *Comprehensive fee:* $26,760 includes full-time tuition ($19,200), mandatory fees ($260), and college room and board ($7300). *Part-time tuition:* $640 per credit hour.

Financial Aid Forms of aid include need-based and non-need-based scholarships and part-time jobs. The priority application deadline for financial aid is March 1.

Freshman Admission Indiana Tech requires a high school transcript, SAT or ACT scores, and TOEFL scores for international students. A minimum 3.0 high school GPA, an interview, and 2 references are recommended.

Entrance Difficulty Indiana Tech assesses its entrance difficulty level as moderately difficult. For the fall 2006 freshman class, 60 percent of the applicants were accepted.

For Further Information Contact Ms. Monica Ladig, Director of Admissions for Day Division, Indiana Tech, 1600 East Washington Boulevard, Fort Wayne, IN 46803. *Telephone:* 260-422-5561, 800-937-2448 (toll-free in-state), or 888-666-TECH (toll-free out-of-state). *Fax:* 260-422-7696. *E-mail:* admissions@indianatech.edu. *Web site:* http://www.indianatech.edu.

INDIANA UNIVERSITY BLOOMINGTON
Bloomington, Indiana

Indiana University Bloomington is a coed, public unit of Indiana University System, founded in 1820, offering degrees at the associate, bachelor's, master's, doctoral, and first professional levels and post-master's and postbachelor's certificates. It has a 1,933-acre campus in Bloomington near Indianapolis.

Academic Information The faculty has 2,233 members (85% full-time), 70% with terminal degrees. The undergraduate student-faculty ratio is 18:1. The library holds 7 million titles and 60,019 serial subscriptions. Special programs include academic remediation, services for learning-disabled students, an honors program, cooperative (work-study) education, study abroad, advanced placement credit, accelerated degree programs, Freshman Honors College, ESL programs, double majors, independent study, distance learning, self-designed majors, summer session for credit, part-time degree programs (daytime, evenings, summer), external degree programs, adult/continuing education programs, internships, and arrangement for off-campus study. The most frequently chosen baccalaureate fields are business/marketing, communications/journalism, education.

Student Body Statistics The student body totals 38,247, of whom 29,828 are undergraduates (7,259 freshmen). 52 percent are women and 48 percent are men. Students come from 56 states and territories and 135 other countries. 66 percent are from Indiana. 4.2 percent are international students.

Expenses for 2006–07 *Application fee:* $50. *State resident tuition:* $6657 full-time, $207.83 per credit hour part-time. *Nonresident tuition:* $19,669

Indiana University Bloomington (continued)

full-time, $614.75 per credit hour part-time. *Mandatory fees:* $803 full-time. Full-time tuition and fees vary according to location and program. Part-time tuition varies according to course load, location, and program. *College room and board:* $6352. *College room only:* $3872. Room and board charges vary according to board plan and housing facility.

Financial Aid Forms of aid include need-based and non-need-based scholarships, athletic grants, and part-time jobs. The average aided 2006–07 undergraduate received an aid package worth an estimated $7463.

Freshman Admission Indiana University Bloomington requires a high school transcript and SAT or ACT scores. An interview, SAT Subject Test scores, and TOEFL scores for international students are recommended. The application deadline for regular admission is rolling.

Transfer Admission The application deadline for admission is rolling.

Entrance Difficulty Indiana University Bloomington assesses its entrance difficulty level as moderately difficult. For the fall 2006 freshman class, 80 percent of the applicants were accepted.

For Further Information Contact Ms. Mary Ellen Anderson, Director of Admissions, Indiana University Bloomington, 300 North Jordan Avenue, Bloomington, IN 47405-1106. *Telephone:* 812-855-0661. *Fax:* 812-855-5102. *E-mail:* iuadmit@indiana.edu. *Web site:* http://www.iub.edu/.

INDIANA UNIVERSITY EAST
Richmond, Indiana

Indiana University East is a coed, public, four-year college of Indiana University System, founded in 1971, offering degrees at the associate and bachelor's levels and postbachelor's certificates. It has a 174-acre campus in Richmond near Indianapolis.

Academic Information The faculty has 186 members (44% full-time), 30% with terminal degrees. The student-faculty ratio is 13:1. The library holds 67,036 titles and 435 serial subscriptions. Special programs include academic remediation, services for learning-disabled students, cooperative (work-study) education, advanced placement credit, double majors, independent study, distance learning, summer session for credit, part-time degree programs, external degree programs, adult/continuing education programs, internships, and arrangement for off-campus study with Earlham College. The most frequently chosen baccalaureate fields are education, health professions and related sciences, liberal arts/general studies.

Student Body Statistics The student body totals 2,246, of whom 2,194 are undergraduates (281 freshmen). 68 percent are women and 32 percent are men. Students come from 7 states and territories. 87 percent are from Indiana. 0.1 percent are international students.

Expenses for 2006–07 *Application fee:* $25. *State resident tuition:* $4697 full-time, $156.55 per credit hour part-time. *Nonresident tuition:* $11,655 full-time, $388.50 per credit hour part-time. *Mandatory fees:* $343 full-time. Full-time tuition and fees vary according to course load, program, and reciprocity agreements. Part-time tuition varies according to course load, program, and reciprocity agreements.

Financial Aid Forms of aid include need-based and non-need-based scholarships and part-time jobs. The average aided 2006–07 undergraduate received an aid package worth an estimated $6467. The priority application deadline for financial aid is March 1.

Freshman Admission Indiana University East requires a high school transcript. A minimum 2.0 high school GPA and SAT or ACT scores are recommended. The application deadline for regular admission is rolling.

Transfer Admission The application deadline for admission is rolling.

Entrance Difficulty Indiana University East assesses its entrance difficulty level as moderately difficult. For the fall 2006 freshman class, 84 percent of the applicants were accepted.

For Further Information Contact Ms. Susanna Tanner, Admissions Counselor, Indiana University East, 2325 Chester Boulevard, WZ 116, Richmond, IN 47374-1289. *Telephone:* 765-973-8415 or 800-959-EAST (toll-free). *Fax:* 765-973-8288. *E-mail:* eaadmit@indiana.edu. *Web site:* http://www.iu.edu/.

INDIANA UNIVERSITY KOKOMO
Kokomo, Indiana

Indiana University Kokomo is a coed, public, comprehensive unit of Indiana University System, founded in 1945, offering degrees at the associate, bachelor's, and master's levels and postbachelor's certificates. It has a 51-acre campus in Kokomo near Indianapolis.

Academic Information The faculty has 174 members (55% full-time), 40% with terminal degrees. The undergraduate student-faculty ratio is 15:1. The library holds 132,424 titles and 1,513 serial subscriptions. Special programs include academic remediation, services for learning-disabled students, an honors program, study abroad, advanced placement credit, accelerated degree programs, Freshman Honors College, double majors, independent study, distance learning, summer session for credit, part-time degree programs, external degree programs, adult/continuing education programs, and internships. The most frequently chosen baccalaureate fields are education, health professions and related sciences, liberal arts/general studies.

Student Body Statistics The student body totals 2,734, of whom 2,604 are undergraduates (385 freshmen). 70 percent are women and 30 percent are men. Students come from 3 states and territories. 99 percent are from Indiana. 0.4 percent are international students.

Expenses for 2006–07 *Application fee:* $30. *State resident tuition:* $4694 full-time, $156.45 per credit hour part-time. *Nonresident tuition:* $11,648 full-time, $388.25 per credit hour part-time. *Mandatory fees:* $378 full-time. Full-time tuition and fees vary according to course load and program. Part-time tuition varies according to course load and program.

Financial Aid Forms of aid include need-based and non-need-based scholarships and part-time jobs. The average aided 2006–07 undergraduate received an aid package worth an estimated $5508. The application deadline for financial aid is March 1.

Freshman Admission Indiana University Kokomo requires a high school transcript and SAT or ACT scores. The application deadline for regular admission is rolling.

Entrance Difficulty Indiana University Kokomo assesses its entrance difficulty level as minimally difficult. For the fall 2006 freshman class, 81 percent of the applicants were accepted.

For Further Information Contact Ms. Jackie Kennedy-Fletcher, Admissions Director, Indiana University Kokomo, PO Box 9003, Kelley Student Center 230A, Kokomo, IN 46904-9003. *Telephone:* 765-455-9217 or 888-875-4485 (toll-free). *Fax:* 765-455-9537. *E-mail:* iuadmis@iuk.edu. *Web site:* http://www.iuk.edu/.

INDIANA UNIVERSITY NORTHWEST
Gary, Indiana

Indiana University Northwest is a coed, public, comprehensive unit of Indiana University System, founded in 1959, offering degrees at the associate, bachelor's, and master's levels and postbachelor's certificates. It has a 38-acre campus in Gary near Chicago.

Academic Information The faculty has 367 members (50% full-time), 47% with terminal degrees. The undergraduate student-faculty ratio is 14:1. The library holds 251,508 titles and 1,541 serial subscriptions. Special programs include academic remediation, services for learning-disabled students, an honors program, cooperative (work-study) education, study abroad, advanced placement credit, accelerated degree programs, double majors, independent study, distance learning, self-designed majors, summer session for credit, part-time degree programs, external degree programs, adult/continuing education programs, internships, and arrangement for off-campus study. The most frequently chosen baccalaureate fields are business/marketing, education, health professions and related sciences.

Student Body Statistics The student body totals 4,819, of whom 4,229 are undergraduates (680 freshmen). 70 percent are women and 30 percent are men. Students come from 6 states and territories. 99 percent are from Indiana. 0.2 percent are international students.

Expenses for 2006–07 *Application fee:* $25. *State resident tuition:* $4710 full-time, $157 per credit hour part-time. *Nonresident tuition:* $11,654 full-time, $388.45 per credit hour part-time. *Mandatory fees:* $432 full-time. Full-time tuition and fees vary according to course load and program. Part-time tuition varies according to course load and program.

Financial Aid Forms of aid include need-based and non-need-based scholarships, athletic grants, and part-time jobs. The average aided 2006–07 undergraduate received an aid package worth an estimated $7259.

Freshman Admission Indiana University Northwest requires a high school transcript, a minimum 2.0 high school GPA, and SAT or ACT scores. TOEFL scores for international students are recommended. The application deadline for regular admission is rolling.

Transfer Admission The application deadline for admission is rolling.

Entrance Difficulty Indiana University Northwest assesses its entrance difficulty level as minimally difficult; moderately difficult for out-of-state applicants. For the fall 2006 freshman class, 76 percent of the applicants were accepted.

For Further Information Contact Dr. Linda B. Templeton, Director of Admissions, Indiana University Northwest, Hawthorne 100, 3400 Broadway, Gary, IN 46408-1197. *Telephone:* 219-980-6767 or 800-968-7486 (toll-free). *Fax:* 219-981-4219. *E-mail:* admit@iun.edu. *Web site:* http://www.iun.edu/.

INDIANA UNIVERSITY–PURDUE UNIVERSITY FORT WAYNE

Fort Wayne, Indiana

Indiana University–Purdue University Fort Wayne is a coed, public, comprehensive unit of Indiana University System and Purdue University System, founded in 1917, offering degrees at the associate, bachelor's, and master's levels and postbachelor's certificates. It has a 643-acre campus in Fort Wayne.

Academic Information The faculty has 798 members (48% full-time), 48% with terminal degrees. The undergraduate student-faculty ratio is 15:1. The library holds 478,091 titles, 24,872 serial subscriptions, and 6,527 audiovisual materials. Special programs include academic remediation, services for learning-disabled students, an honors program, cooperative (work-study) education, study abroad, advanced placement credit, accelerated degree programs, ESL programs, double majors, independent study, distance learning, self-designed majors, summer session for credit, part-time degree programs (daytime, evenings, weekends, summer), adult/continuing education programs, internships, and arrangement for off-campus study with National Student Exchange. The most frequently chosen baccalaureate fields are business/marketing, education, liberal arts/general studies.

Student Body Statistics The student body totals 11,672, of whom 10,890 are undergraduates (1,882 freshmen). 56 percent are women and 44 percent are men. Students come from 46 states and territories and 67 other countries. 96 percent are from Indiana. 1.3 percent are international students. 15 percent of the 2006 graduating class went on to graduate and professional schools.

Expenses for 2006–07 *Application fee:* $30. *State resident tuition:* $4793 full-time, $178 per credit hour part-time. *Nonresident tuition:* $11,808 full-time, $437 per credit hour part-time. *Mandatory fees:* $644 full-time, $24 per credit hour part-time. Both full-time and part-time tuition and fees vary according to course load and student level. *College room only:* $4940. Room charges vary according to housing facility.

Financial Aid Forms of aid include need-based and non-need-based scholarships, athletic grants, and part-time jobs. The priority application deadline for financial aid is March 10.

Freshman Admission Indiana University–Purdue University Fort Wayne requires a high school transcript, SAT or ACT scores, and TOEFL scores for international students. Rank in upper 50% of high school class is recommended. The application deadline for regular admission is August 1.

Entrance Difficulty Indiana University–Purdue University Fort Wayne assesses its entrance difficulty level as minimally difficult; moderately difficult for out-of-state applicants; noncompetitive for students graduating high school over 2 years ago. For the fall 2006 freshman class, 97 percent of the applicants were accepted.

For Further Information Contact Ms. Carol Isaacs, Director of Admissions, Indiana University–Purdue University Fort Wayne, 2101 East Coliseum Boulevard, Fort Wayne, IN 46805-1499. *Telephone:* 260-481-6812 or 800-324-4739 (toll-free in-state). *Fax:* 260-481-6880. *E-mail:* Ask@ipfw.edu. *Web site:* http://www.ipfw.edu/.

INDIANA UNIVERSITY–PURDUE UNIVERSITY INDIANAPOLIS

Indianapolis, Indiana

Indiana University–Purdue University Indianapolis is a coed, public unit of Indiana University System, founded in 1969, offering degrees at the associate, bachelor's, master's, doctoral, and first professional levels and postbachelor's certificates. It has a 509-acre campus in Indianapolis.

Academic Information The faculty has 3,091 members (70% full-time), 66% with terminal degrees. The undergraduate student-faculty ratio is 16:1. The library holds 1 million titles and 14,673 serial subscriptions. Special programs include academic remediation, services for learning-disabled students, an honors program, cooperative (work-study) education, study abroad, advanced placement credit, accelerated degree programs, ESL programs, double majors, independent study, distance learning, summer session for credit, part-time degree programs, external degree programs, adult/continuing education programs, internships, and arrangement for off-campus study with 5 members of the Consortium for Urban Education. The most frequently chosen baccalaureate fields are business/marketing, health professions and related sciences, liberal arts/general studies.

Student Body Statistics The student body totals 29,764, of whom 21,193 are undergraduates (2,792 freshmen). 59 percent are women and 41 percent are men. Students come from 49 states and territories and 122 other countries. 97 percent are from Indiana. 1.7 percent are international students.

Expenses for 2006–07 *Application fee:* $50. *State resident tuition:* $5924 full-time, $197.46 per credit hour part-time. *Nonresident tuition:* $16,766 full-time, $558.86 per credit hour part-time. *Mandatory fees:* $600 full-time. Full-time tuition and fees vary according to course load and program. Part-time tuition varies according to course load and program. *College room and board:* $4834. *College room only:* $2434. Room and board charges vary according to board plan and housing facility.

Financial Aid Forms of aid include need-based and non-need-based scholarships, athletic grants, and part-time jobs. The average aided 2006–07 undergraduate received an aid package worth an estimated $7246. The priority application deadline for financial aid is March 1.

Freshman Admission Indiana University–Purdue University Indianapolis requires a high school transcript, SAT or ACT scores, and TOEFL scores for international students. Portfolio for art program is recommended. An interview is required for some. The application deadline for regular admission is June 1.

Transfer Admission The application deadline for admission is rolling.

Entrance Difficulty Indiana University–Purdue University Indianapolis assesses its entrance difficulty level as moderately difficult. For the fall 2006 freshman class, 71 percent of the applicants were accepted.

For Further Information Contact Mr. Michael Donahue, Director of Admissions, Indiana University–Purdue University Indianapolis, Cavanaugh Hall 129, 425 University Boulevard, Indianapolis, IN 46202-5143. *Telephone:* 317-274-4591. *Fax:* 317-278-1862. *E-mail:* apply@iupui.edu. *Web site:* http://www.iupui.edu/.

INDIANA UNIVERSITY SOUTH BEND

South Bend, Indiana

Indiana University South Bend is a coed, public, comprehensive unit of Indiana University System, founded in 1922, offering degrees at the associate, bachelor's, and master's levels and postbachelor's certificates. It has an 80-acre campus in South Bend near Chicago.

Academic Information The faculty has 523 members (53% full-time), 44% with terminal degrees. The undergraduate student-faculty ratio is 14:1. The library holds 300,202 titles and 1,937 serial subscriptions. Special programs include an honors program, study abroad, accelerated degree programs, ESL programs, double majors, distance learning, summer session for credit, part-time degree programs, external degree programs, adult/continuing education programs, internships, and arrangement for off-campus study with Bethel College, Saint Mary's College (IN), Holy

Indiana University South Bend (continued)

Cross College, Goshen College. The most frequently chosen baccalaureate fields are business/marketing, education, liberal arts/general studies.

Student Body Statistics The student body totals 7,420, of whom 6,371 are undergraduates (994 freshmen). 61 percent are women and 39 percent are men. Students come from 13 states and territories. 96 percent are from Indiana. 1.8 percent are international students.

Expenses for 2006–07 *Application fee:* $45. *State resident tuition:* $4826 full-time, $160.85 per credit hour part-time. *Nonresident tuition:* $12,612 full-time, $420.40 per credit hour part-time. *Mandatory fees:* $406 full-time. Full-time tuition and fees vary according to course load and program. Part-time tuition varies according to course load and program.

Financial Aid Forms of aid include need-based and non-need-based scholarships, athletic grants, and part-time jobs. The average aided 2006–07 undergraduate received an aid package worth an estimated $6198. The application deadline for financial aid is March 1.

Freshman Admission Indiana University South Bend requires a high school transcript, a minimum 2.0 high school GPA, SAT or ACT scores, and TOEFL scores for international students. An interview is required for some. The application deadline for regular admission is rolling.

Transfer Admission The application deadline for admission is rolling.

Entrance Difficulty Indiana University South Bend assesses its entrance difficulty level as moderately difficult. For the fall 2006 freshman class, 89 percent of the applicants were accepted.

For Further Information Contact Jeff Johnston, Director of Recruitment/ Admissions, Indiana University South Bend, 1700 Mishawaka Avenue, Administration Building, Room 169, PO Box 7111, South Bend, IN 46634-7111. *Telephone:* 574-237-4480 or 877-GO-2-IUSB (toll-free). *Fax:* 574-237-4834. *E-mail:* admissio@iusb.edu. *Web site:* http://www.iusb.edu/.

INDIANA UNIVERSITY SOUTHEAST

New Albany, Indiana

Indiana University Southeast is a coed, public, comprehensive unit of Indiana University System, founded in 1941, offering degrees at the associate, bachelor's, and master's levels and postbachelor's certificates. It has a 177-acre campus in New Albany near Louisville.

Academic Information The faculty has 425 members (45% full-time), 42% with terminal degrees. The undergraduate student-faculty ratio is 16:1. The library holds 215,429 titles and 962 serial subscriptions. Special programs include academic remediation, services for learning-disabled students, study abroad, advanced placement credit, accelerated degree programs, double majors, independent study, self-designed majors, summer session for credit, part-time degree programs, external degree programs, adult/continuing education programs, internships, and arrangement for off-campus study with 7 members of the Kentuckiana Metroversity. The most frequently chosen baccalaureate fields are business/marketing, education, liberal arts/general studies.

Student Body Statistics The student body totals 6,183, of whom 5,365 are undergraduates (838 freshmen). 63 percent are women and 37 percent are men. Students come from 3 states and territories. 77 percent are from Indiana. 0.3 percent are international students.

Expenses for 2006–07 *Application fee:* $30. *State resident tuition:* $4698 full-time, $157 per credit hour part-time. *Nonresident tuition:* $11,655 full-time, $388.50 per credit hour part-time. *Mandatory fees:* $420 full-time. Full-time tuition and fees vary according to course load, program, and reciprocity agreements. Part-time tuition varies according to course load, program, and reciprocity agreements.

Financial Aid Forms of aid include need-based and non-need-based scholarships, athletic grants, and part-time jobs. The average aided 2006–07 undergraduate received an aid package worth an estimated $5624. The priority application deadline for financial aid is March 1.

Freshman Admission Indiana University Southeast requires a high school transcript, SAT or ACT scores, and TOEFL scores for international students. An interview is required for some. The application deadline for regular admission is rolling.

Transfer Admission The application deadline for admission is rolling.

Entrance Difficulty Indiana University Southeast assesses its entrance difficulty level as minimally difficult; moderately difficult for out-of-state applicants; moderately difficult for transfers. For the fall 2006 freshman class, 88 percent of the applicants were accepted.

For Further Information Contact Ms. Anne Skuce, Director of Admissions, Indiana University Southeast, University Center Building, Room 100, 4201 Grant Line Road, New Albany, IN 47150. *Telephone:* 812-941-2212 or 800-852-8835 (toll-free in-state). *Fax:* 812-941-2595. *E-mail:* admissions@ius.edu. *Web site:* http://www.ius.edu/.

INDIANA WESLEYAN UNIVERSITY

Marion, Indiana

Indiana Wesleyan University is a coed, private, Wesleyan, comprehensive institution, founded in 1920, offering degrees at the associate, bachelor's, master's, and doctoral levels and post-master's and postbachelor's certificates (also offers adult program with significant enrollment not reflected in profile). It has a 132-acre campus in Marion near Indianapolis.

Academic Information The faculty has 265 members (53% full-time), 33% with terminal degrees. The undergraduate student-faculty ratio is 15:1. The library holds 141,236 titles, 76,011 serial subscriptions, and 11,321 audiovisual materials. Special programs include academic remediation, services for learning-disabled students, an honors program, study abroad, advanced placement credit, accelerated degree programs, Freshman Honors College, double majors, independent study, distance learning, self-designed majors, summer session for credit, part-time degree programs (daytime, evenings, weekends, summer), adult/continuing education programs, internships, and arrangement for off-campus study with Taylor University, Council for Christian Colleges and Universities.

Student Body Statistics The student body is made up of 2,935 undergraduates (727 freshmen). 62 percent are women and 38 percent are men. Students come from 48 states and territories and 14 other countries. 52 percent are from Indiana. 0.5 percent are international students.

Expenses for 2007–08 *Application fee:* $25. *Comprehensive fee:* $24,652 includes full-time tuition ($18,284) and college room and board ($6368). *College room only:* $3072. *Part-time tuition:* $653 per credit hour.

Financial Aid Forms of aid include need-based and non-need-based scholarships and part-time jobs. The priority application deadline for financial aid is March 1.

Freshman Admission Indiana Wesleyan University requires an essay, a high school transcript, a minimum 2.0 high school GPA, 1 recommendation, SAT or ACT scores, and TOEFL scores for international students. An interview is required for some. The application deadline for regular admission is rolling.

Transfer Admission The application deadline for admission is rolling.

Entrance Difficulty Indiana Wesleyan University assesses its entrance difficulty level as moderately difficult. For the fall 2006 freshman class, 77 percent of the applicants were accepted.

For Further Information Contact Mr. Daniel Solms, Director of Admissions, Indiana Wesleyan University, 4201 South Washington Street, Marion, IN 46953. *Telephone:* 866-GO TO IWU Ext. 2138 or 800-332-6901 (toll-free). *Fax:* 765-677-2333. *E-mail:* admissions@indwes.edu. *Web site:* http://www.indwes.edu/.

INTERNATIONAL BUSINESS COLLEGE

Fort Wayne, Indiana

International Business College is a coed, primarily women's, proprietary, primarily two-year college of Bradford Schools, Inc, founded in 1889, offering degrees at the associate and bachelor's levels. It has a 2-acre campus in Fort Wayne.

Academic Information The faculty has 68 members (18% full-time). The student-faculty ratio is 22:1. The library holds 2,100 titles and 100 serial subscriptions. Special programs include independent study, part-time degree programs (evenings), adult/continuing education programs, and internships.

Student Body Statistics The student body is made up of 758 undergraduates (443 freshmen). 78 percent are women and 22 percent are men. 86 percent are from Indiana.

Expenses for 2007–08 *Application fee:* $50. *Tuition:* $12,240 full-time.
Financial Aid Forms of aid include need-based scholarships. The priority application deadline for financial aid is March 1.
Freshman Admission International Business College requires a high school transcript. The application deadline for regular admission is September 4.
Entrance Difficulty International Business College assesses its entrance difficulty level as minimally difficult; moderately difficult for accounting, paralegal programs. For the fall 2006 freshman class, 94 percent of the applicants were accepted.
For Further Information Contact Mr. Steve Kinzer, School Director, International Business College, 5699 Coventry Lane, Fort Wayne, IN 46804. *Telephone:* 219-459-4513 or 800-589-6363 (toll-free). *Fax:* 219-436-1896. *Web site:* http://www.ibcfortwayne.edu/.

ITT TECHNICAL INSTITUTE
Fort Wayne, Indiana

ITT Technical Institute is a coed, proprietary, primarily two-year college of ITT Educational Services, Inc, founded in 1967, offering degrees at the associate and bachelor's levels.

Expenses for 2006–07 *Application fee:* $100. Contact school for program costs.
Financial Aid Forms of aid include need-based scholarships and part-time jobs. The application deadline for financial aid is continuous.
Freshman Admission ITT Technical Institute requires a high school transcript, an interview, TOEFL scores for international students, and Wonderlic aptitude test. Recommendations are recommended. The application deadline for regular admission is rolling.
Transfer Admission The application deadline for admission is rolling.
Entrance Difficulty ITT Technical Institute assesses its entrance difficulty level as minimally difficult.
For Further Information Contact Mr. Mike Cavins, Director of Recruitment, ITT Technical Institute, 2810 Dupont Conference Court, fort Wayne, IN 46825. *Telephone:* 260-497-6200 or 800-866-4488 (toll-free). *Fax:* 260-497-6299. *Web site:* http://www.itt-tech.edu/.

ITT TECHNICAL INSTITUTE
Indianapolis, Indiana

ITT Technical Institute is a coed, proprietary, primarily two-year college of ITT Educational Services, Inc, founded in 1966, offering degrees at the associate and bachelor's levels. It has a 10-acre campus in Indianapolis.

Academic Information Special programs include distance learning.
Expenses for 2006–07 *Application fee:* $100. Contact school for program costs.
Financial Aid Forms of aid include need-based scholarships and part-time jobs. The application deadline for financial aid is continuous.
Freshman Admission ITT Technical Institute requires a high school transcript, an interview, and Wonderlic aptitude test. Recommendations are recommended. The application deadline for regular admission is rolling.
Transfer Admission The application deadline for admission is rolling.
Entrance Difficulty ITT Technical Institute assesses its entrance difficulty level as minimally difficult.
For Further Information Contact Mr. James Mills, Director of Recruitment, ITT Technical Institute, 9511 Angola Court, Indianapolis, IN 46268. *Telephone:* 317-875-8640 or 800-937-4488 (toll-free). *Fax:* 317-875-8641. *Web site:* http://www.itt-tech.edu/.

ITT TECHNICAL INSTITUTE
Newburgh, Indiana

ITT Technical Institute is a coed, proprietary, primarily two-year college of ITT Educational Services, Inc, founded in 1966, offering degrees at the associate and bachelor's levels.

Expenses for 2006–07 *Application fee:* $100. Contact school for program costs.
Financial Aid Forms of aid include need-based scholarships and part-time jobs. The application deadline for financial aid is continuous.
Freshman Admission ITT Technical Institute requires a high school transcript, an interview, and Wonderlic aptitude test. Recommendations and TOEFL scores for international students are recommended. The application deadline for regular admission is rolling.
Transfer Admission The application deadline for admission is rolling.
Entrance Difficulty ITT Technical Institute assesses its entrance difficulty level as minimally difficult.
For Further Information Contact Mr. Thomas Montgomery, Director of Recruitment, ITT Technical Institute, 10999 Stahl Road, Newburgh, IN 47630. *Telephone:* 812-858-1600 or 800-832-4488 (toll-free in-state). *Fax:* 812-858-0646. *Web site:* http://www.itt-tech.edu/.

IVY TECH COMMUNITY COLLEGE–NORTHWEST
Gary, Indiana

Ivy Tech Community College–Northwest is a coed, public, primarily two-year college of Ivy Tech State College System, founded in 1963, offering degrees at the associate and bachelor's levels. It has a 13-acre campus in Gary near Chicago.

Expenses for 2006–07 *Application fee:* $0. *State resident tuition:* $2633 full-time, $87.75 per credit part-time. *Nonresident tuition:* $5355 full-time, $178.50 per credit part-time. *Mandatory fees:* $80 full-time.
For Further Information Contact Ms. Twilla Lewis, Associate Dean of Student Affairs, Ivy Tech Community College–Northwest, 1440 East 35th Avenue, Gary, IN 46409-499. *Telephone:* 219-981-1111 Ext. 2273 or 800-843-4882 (toll-free in-state). *Fax:* 219-981-4415. *E-mail:* tlewis@ivytech.edu. *Web site:* http://www.ivytech.edu/.

KAPLAN COLLEGE–INDIANAPOLIS
Indianapolis, Indiana

Kaplan College–Indianapolis is a coed, primarily women's, private, two-year college, offering degrees at the associate level.

Academic Information The faculty has 39 members (74% full-time). The student-faculty ratio is 12:1. Special programs include part-time degree programs (evenings) and internships.
Student Body Statistics The student body is made up of 469 undergraduates.
Financial Aid Forms of aid include need-based scholarships. The application deadline for financial aid is continuous.
Freshman Admission Kaplan College–Indianapolis requires an essay, a high school transcript, a minimum 1.7 high school GPA, and 2 recommendations. An interview and CPAt, health exam, keyboard test are required for some.
Entrance Difficulty Kaplan College–Indianapolis assesses its entrance difficulty level as minimally difficult. For the fall 2006 freshman class, 66 percent of the applicants were accepted.
For Further Information Contact Ms. Paulette M. Clay, Director of Admissions, Kaplan College–Indianapolis, 7302 Woodland Drive, Indianapolis, IN 46217. *Telephone:* 317-298-6342 or 800-849-4995 (toll-free). *E-mail:* lilgeneral9@hotmail.com. *Web site:* http://getinfo.kaplancollege.com/KaplanCollegePortal/KaplanCollegeCampuses/Indiana/Indianapolis/.

LUTHERAN COLLEGE OF HEALTH PROFESSIONS

See University of Saint Francis.

MANCHESTER COLLEGE
North Manchester, Indiana

Manchester College is a coed, private, four-year college, founded in 1889, affiliated with the Church of the Brethren, offering degrees at the associate, bachelor's, and master's levels. It has a 125-acre campus in North Manchester.

Academic Information The faculty has 90 members (80% full-time), 78% with terminal degrees. The undergraduate student-faculty ratio is 14:1. Special programs include services for learning-disabled students, an honors program, study abroad, advanced placement credit, double majors, independent study, self-designed majors, summer session for credit, part-time degree programs, adult/continuing education programs, internships, and arrangement for off-campus study. The most frequently chosen baccalaureate fields are business/marketing, education, psychology.
Student Body Statistics The student body is made up of 1,056 undergraduates (311 freshmen). 51 percent are women and 49 percent are men. Students come from 28 states and territories and 26 other countries. 89 percent are from Indiana. 4.4 percent are international students. 24 percent of the 2006 graduating class went on to graduate and professional schools.
Expenses for 2007–08 *Application fee:* $25. *Comprehensive fee:* $29,150 includes full-time tuition ($21,000), mandatory fees ($700), and college room and board ($7450). *College room only:* $4500. *Part-time tuition:* $670 per credit hour.
Financial Aid Forms of aid include need-based and non-need-based scholarships and part-time jobs. The average aided 2006–07 undergraduate received an aid package worth an estimated $18,984.
Freshman Admission Manchester College requires a high school transcript, 1 recommendation, rank in upper 50% of high school class, SAT or ACT scores, and TOEFL scores for international students. A minimum 2.3 high school GPA and an interview are recommended. An essay, a minimum 3.0 high school GPA, and an interview are required for some. The application deadline for regular admission is rolling.
Transfer Admission The application deadline for admission is rolling.
Entrance Difficulty Manchester College assesses its entrance difficulty level as moderately difficult. For the fall 2006 freshman class, 66 percent of the applicants were accepted.
For Further Information Contact Mr. Adam Hohman, Assistant Director of Admissions, Manchester College, 604 East College Avenue, North Manchester, IN 46962. *Telephone:* 260-982-5055 or 800-852-3648 (toll-free). *Fax:* 260-982-5239. *E-mail:* admitinfo@manchester.edu. *Web site:* http://www.manchester.edu/.

See page 266 for the College Close-Up.

MARIAN COLLEGE
Indianapolis, Indiana

Marian College is a coed, private, Roman Catholic, comprehensive institution, founded in 1851, offering degrees at the associate, bachelor's, and master's levels. It has a 114-acre campus in Indianapolis.

Academic Information The faculty has 138 members (51% full-time). The undergraduate student-faculty ratio is 15:1. The library holds 110,541 titles, 221 serial subscriptions, and 2,167 audiovisual materials. Special programs include academic remediation, services for learning-disabled students, an honors program, cooperative (work-study) education, study abroad, advanced placement credit, accelerated degree programs, ESL programs, double majors, independent study, summer session for credit, part-time degree programs (daytime, evenings, weekends, summer), adult/continuing education programs, internships, and arrangement for off-campus study with Franklin College of Indiana, Indiana University–Purdue University at Indianapolis, University of Indianapolis, Christian Theological Seminary, Butler University.
Student Body Statistics The student body totals 1,796, of whom 1,779 are undergraduates (280 freshmen). 70 percent are women and 30 percent are men. Students come from 20 states and territories and 9 other countries. 91 percent are from Indiana. 0.1 percent are international students. 6 percent of the 2006 graduating class went on to graduate and professional schools.
Expenses for 2007–08 *Application fee:* $20. *Comprehensive fee:* $27,900 includes full-time tuition ($20,800) and college room and board ($7100). *Part-time tuition:* $870 per credit hour.
Financial Aid Forms of aid include need-based and non-need-based scholarships, athletic grants, and part-time jobs. The average aided 2005–06 undergraduate received an aid package worth $15,345. The priority application deadline for financial aid is March 1.
Freshman Admission Marian College requires a high school transcript, a minimum 2.30 high school GPA, SAT or ACT scores, and TOEFL scores for international students. An essay, recommendations, and an interview are required for some. The application deadline for regular admission is August 1.
Transfer Admission The application deadline for admission is August 1.
Entrance Difficulty Marian College assesses its entrance difficulty level as moderately difficult. For the fall 2006 freshman class, 65 percent of the applicants were accepted.
For Further Information Contact Ms. Luann Brames, Marian College, 3200 Cold Spring Road, Indianapolis, IN 46222-1997. *Telephone:* 317-955-6300 or 800-772-7264 (toll-free in-state). *Web site:* http://www.marian.edu/.

MARTIN UNIVERSITY
Indianapolis, Indiana

http://www.martin.edu/

MID-AMERICA COLLEGE OF FUNERAL SERVICE
Jeffersonville, Indiana

Mid-America College of Funeral Service is a coed, primarily men's, private, primarily two-year college, founded in 1905, offering degrees at the associate and bachelor's levels. It has a 3-acre campus in Jeffersonville near Louisville.

Academic Information The faculty has 7 members (86% full-time). The student-faculty ratio is 13:1. The library holds 1,500 titles and 20 serial subscriptions. Special programs include academic remediation.
Student Body Statistics The student body is made up of 120 undergraduates. 45 percent are women and 55 percent are men. Students come from 6 states and territories.
Expenses for 2006–07 *Application fee:* $25. *Tuition:* $11,400 full-time, $200 per credit hour part-time. Full-time tuition varies according to course load and program.
Financial Aid Forms of aid include need-based scholarships. The application deadline for financial aid is continuous.
Freshman Admission Mid-America College of Funeral Service requires a high school transcript. The application deadline for regular admission is rolling.
Entrance Difficulty Mid-America College of Funeral Service has an open admission policy. It assesses its entrance difficulty as noncompetitive for transfers.
For Further Information Contact Mr. Richard Nelson, Dean of Students, Mid-America College of Funeral Service, 3111 Hamburg Pike, Jeffersonville, IN 47130-9630. *Telephone:* 812-288-8878 or 800-221-6158 (toll-free). *Fax:* 812-288-5942. *E-mail:* macfs@mindspring.com. *Web site:* http://www.mid-america.edu/.

OAKLAND CITY UNIVERSITY
Oakland City, Indiana

Oakland City University is a coed, private, General Baptist, comprehensive institution, founded in 1885, offering degrees at the associate, bachelor's, master's, doctoral, and first professional levels. It has a 20-acre campus in Oakland City.

Expenses for 2006–07 *Application fee:* $35. *Comprehensive fee:* $19,620 includes full-time tuition ($13,860), mandatory fees ($360), and college room and board ($5400). *College room only:* $1760. *Part-time tuition:* $462 per hour. *Part-time mandatory fees:* $15 per hour.

For Further Information Contact Mr. Brian Baker, Director of Admissions, Oakland City University, 138 North Lucretia Street, Oakland City, IN 47660. *Telephone:* 812-749-1222 or 800-737-5125 (toll-free). *Web site:* http://www.oak.edu/.

PROFESSIONAL CAREERS INSTITUTE

See Kaplan College–Indianapolis.

PURDUE UNIVERSITY

West Lafayette, Indiana

Purdue University is a coed, public unit of Purdue University System, founded in 1869, offering degrees at the associate, bachelor's, master's, doctoral, and first professional levels. It has a 2,307-acre campus in West Lafayette near Indianapolis.

Academic Information The faculty has 2,347 members (86% full-time), 96% with terminal degrees. The undergraduate student-faculty ratio is 14:1. The library holds 2 million titles and 20,829 serial subscriptions. Special programs include services for learning-disabled students, an honors program, cooperative (work-study) education, study abroad, advanced placement credit, accelerated degree programs, Freshman Honors College, ESL programs, double majors, independent study, distance learning, summer session for credit, part-time degree programs, adult/continuing education programs, and internships. The most frequently chosen baccalaureate fields are business/marketing, engineering, engineering technologies.

Student Body Statistics The student body totals 39,228, of whom 31,290 are undergraduates (7,389 freshmen). 41 percent are women and 59 percent are men. 73 percent are from Indiana. 5.9 percent are international students.

Expenses for 2006–07 *Application fee:* $30. *State resident tuition:* $7096 full-time, $254.15 per credit part-time. *Nonresident tuition:* $21,266 full-time, $706.25 per credit part-time. *College room and board:* $7546.

Financial Aid Forms of aid include need-based and non-need-based scholarships, athletic grants, and part-time jobs. The average aided 2006–07 undergraduate received an aid package worth an estimated $12,131. The priority application deadline for financial aid is March 1.

Freshman Admission Purdue University requires a high school transcript, SAT or ACT scores, and TOEFL scores for international students. The application deadline for regular admission is March 1.

Transfer Admission The application deadline for admission is rolling.

Entrance Difficulty Purdue University assesses its entrance difficulty level as moderately difficult; most difficult for engineering, aviation flight, nursing, veterinary technology, computer related, health related programs, hospitality and tourism management. For the fall 2006 freshman class, 85 percent of the applicants were accepted.

For Further Information Contact Ms. Pamela T. Horne, Assistant Vice President for Enrollment Management and Dean of Admissions, Purdue University, 475 Stadium Mall Drive, Schleman Hall, West Lafayette, IN 47907-2050. *Telephone:* 765-494-1776. *Fax:* 765-494-0544. *E-mail:* admissions@purdue.edu. *Web site:* http://www.purdue.edu/.

PURDUE UNIVERSITY CALUMET

Hammond, Indiana

Purdue University Calumet is a coed, public, comprehensive unit of Purdue University System, founded in 1951, offering degrees at the associate, bachelor's, and master's levels and postbachelor's certificates. It has a 167-acre campus in Hammond near Chicago.

Academic Information The faculty has 499 members (58% full-time), 36% with terminal degrees. The undergraduate student-faculty ratio is 18:1. The library holds 269,648 titles and 1,228 serial subscriptions. Special programs include academic remediation, services for learning-disabled students, an honors program, cooperative (work-study) education, advanced placement credit, accelerated degree programs, Freshman Honors College, ESL programs, double majors, independent study, distance learning, summer session for credit, part-time degree programs (daytime, evenings, weekends, summer), adult/continuing education programs, and internships. The most frequently chosen baccalaureate fields are engineering technologies, computer and information sciences, social sciences.

Student Body Statistics The student body totals 9,303, of whom 8,387 are undergraduates (1,290 freshmen). 57 percent are women and 43 percent are men. Students come from 27 states and territories and 30 other countries. 89 percent are from Indiana. 1.2 percent are international students.

Expenses for 2006–07 *Application fee:* $0. *State resident tuition:* $4961 full-time, $168 per credit hour part-time. *Nonresident tuition:* $11,654 full-time, $391 per credit hour part-time. *Mandatory fees:* $506 full-time, $18.40 per credit hour part-time. Full-time tuition and fees vary according to program. Part-time tuition and fees vary according to course load and program. *College room only:* $4150. Room charges vary according to housing facility.

Financial Aid Forms of aid include need-based and non-need-based scholarships, athletic grants, and part-time jobs. The average aided 2005–06 undergraduate received an aid package worth $5926. The priority application deadline for financial aid is March 10.

Freshman Admission Purdue University Calumet requires a high school transcript, a minimum 2.0 high school GPA, and SAT or ACT scores. The application deadline for regular admission is rolling.

Transfer Admission A minimum 2.0 college GPA is recommended. Standardized test scores and a college transcript are required for some. The application deadline for admission is rolling.

Entrance Difficulty Purdue University Calumet assesses its entrance difficulty level as moderately difficult. For the fall 2006 freshman class, 81 percent of the applicants were accepted.

For Further Information Contact Mr. Paul McGuinness, Director of Admissions, Purdue University Calumet, 2200-169th Street, Hammond, IN 46323-2094. *Telephone:* 219-989-2213 or 800-447-8738 (toll-free in-state). *E-mail:* adms@calumet.purdue.edu. *Web site:* http://www.calumet.purdue.edu/.

PURDUE UNIVERSITY NORTH CENTRAL

Westville, Indiana

Purdue University North Central is a coed, public, comprehensive unit of Purdue University System, founded in 1967, offering degrees at the associate, bachelor's, and master's levels. It has a 305-acre campus in Westville near Chicago.

Academic Information The faculty has 260 members (40% full-time), 32% with terminal degrees. The undergraduate student-faculty ratio is 18:1. The library holds 87,675 titles and 403 serial subscriptions. Special programs include academic remediation, services for learning-disabled students, an honors program, cooperative (work-study) education, study abroad, advanced placement credit, double majors, distance learning, self-designed majors, summer session for credit, part-time degree programs (daytime, evenings, summer), adult/continuing education programs, and internships. The most frequently chosen baccalaureate fields are business/marketing, engineering technologies, liberal arts/general studies.

Student Body Statistics The student body totals 3,724, of whom 3,635 are undergraduates (732 freshmen). 58 percent are women and 42 percent are men. Students come from 15 states and territories and 6 other countries. 99 percent are from Indiana. 0.2 percent are international students.

Expenses for 2006–07 *State resident tuition:* $4491 full-time, $186 per credit hour part-time. *Nonresident tuition:* $11,124 full-time, $434 per credit hour part-time. *Mandatory fees:* $471 full-time.

Financial Aid Forms of aid include need-based and non-need-based scholarships and part-time jobs. The priority application deadline for financial aid is March 1.

Freshman Admission Purdue University North Central requires a high school transcript and TOEFL scores for international students. SAT scores and ACT scores are recommended. An essay, a minimum 2.0 high school

Purdue University North Central (continued)
GPA, an interview, and SAT or ACT scores are required for some. The application deadline for regular admission is August 6.

Transfer Admission The application deadline for admission is August 1.

Entrance Difficulty Purdue University North Central assesses its entrance difficulty level as minimally difficult; moderately difficult for engineering, nursing programs. For the fall 2006 freshman class, 86 percent of the applicants were accepted.

For Further Information Contact Mr. Anthony Cardenas, Director of Admissions, Purdue University North Central, 1401 South U.S. Highway 421, Westville, IN 46391. *Telephone:* 219-785-5283 or 800-872-1231 (toll-free in-state). *E-mail:* cbuckman@pnc.edu. *Web site:* http://www.pnc.edu/.

ROSE-HULMAN INSTITUTE OF TECHNOLOGY
Terre Haute, Indiana

Rose-Hulman Institute of Technology is a coed, primarily men's, private, comprehensive institution, founded in 1874, offering degrees at the bachelor's and master's levels. It has a 200-acre campus in Terre Haute near Indianapolis.

Academic Information The faculty has 161 members (96% full-time), 99% with terminal degrees. The undergraduate student-faculty ratio is 12:1. The library holds 80,094 titles, 20,934 serial subscriptions, and 429 audiovisual materials. Special programs include services for learning-disabled students, cooperative (work-study) education, study abroad, advanced placement credit, accelerated degree programs, double majors, independent study, summer session for credit, adult/continuing education programs, and arrangement for off-campus study with Indiana State University, St. Mary-of-the-Woods College. The most frequently chosen baccalaureate fields are computer and information sciences, engineering, mathematics.

Student Body Statistics The student body totals 1,963, of whom 1,862 are undergraduates (525 freshmen). 19 percent are women and 81 percent are men. Students come from 51 states and territories and 21 other countries. 43 percent are from Indiana. 1.5 percent are international students. 18 percent of the 2006 graduating class went on to graduate and professional schools.

Expenses for 2006–07 *Application fee:* $40. *Comprehensive fee:* $36,864 includes full-time tuition ($28,530), mandatory fees ($465), and college room and board ($7869). *College room only:* $4491. Full-time tuition and fees vary according to course load. Room and board charges vary according to board plan. *Part-time tuition:* $831 per credit. Part-time tuition varies according to course load.

Financial Aid Forms of aid include need-based scholarships and part-time jobs. The average aided 2006–07 undergraduate received an aid package worth an estimated $22,011. The priority application deadline for financial aid is March 1.

Freshman Admission Rose-Hulman Institute of Technology requires a high school transcript, 1 recommendation, curricular, SAT or ACT scores, and TOEFL scores for international students. An essay and an interview are recommended. The application deadline for regular admission is March 1.

Entrance Difficulty Rose-Hulman Institute of Technology assesses its entrance difficulty level as very difficult. For the fall 2006 freshman class, 72 percent of the applicants were accepted.

For Further Information Contact Mr. James Goecker, Dean of Admissions and Financial Aid, Rose-Hulman Institute of Technology, 5500 Wabash Avenue, CM 1, Terre Haute, IN 47803-3920. *Telephone:* 812-877-8213 or 800-248-7448 (toll-free). *Fax:* 812-877-8941. *E-mail:* admis.ofc@rose-hulman.edu. *Web site:* http://www.rose-hulman.edu/.

SAINT FRANCIS COLLEGE
See University of Saint Francis.

SAINT JOSEPH'S COLLEGE
Rensselaer, Indiana

Saint Joseph's College is a coed, private, Roman Catholic, comprehensive institution, founded in 1889, offering degrees at the associate, bachelor's, and master's levels. It has a 180-acre campus in Rensselaer near Chicago.

Academic Information The faculty has 89 members (66% full-time), 56% with terminal degrees. The undergraduate student-faculty ratio is 15:1. The library holds 256,705 titles, 399 serial subscriptions, and 23,637 audiovisual materials. Special programs include academic remediation, services for learning-disabled students, an honors program, study abroad, advanced placement credit, accelerated degree programs, double majors, independent study, self-designed majors, summer session for credit, part-time degree programs (daytime), and internships. The most frequently chosen baccalaureate fields are business/marketing, education, security and protective services.

Student Body Statistics The student body totals 1,031, of whom 1,030 are undergraduates (237 freshmen). 59 percent are women and 41 percent are men. Students come from 19 states and territories and 6 other countries. 73 percent are from Indiana. 1.1 percent are international students. 13 percent of the 2006 graduating class went on to graduate and professional schools.

Expenses for 2006–07 *Application fee:* $25. *Comprehensive fee:* $27,680 includes full-time tuition ($20,800), mandatory fees ($160), and college room and board ($6720). Full-time tuition and fees vary according to reciprocity agreements. Room and board charges vary according to housing facility. *Part-time tuition:* $700 per credit. Part-time tuition varies according to course load and reciprocity agreements.

Financial Aid Forms of aid include need-based and non-need-based scholarships, athletic grants, and part-time jobs. The average aided 2005–06 undergraduate received an aid package worth $18,976. The priority application deadline for financial aid is March 1.

Freshman Admission Saint Joseph's College requires a high school transcript, a minimum 2.0 high school GPA, SAT or ACT scores, and TOEFL scores for international students. An essay and an interview are required for some. The application deadline for regular admission is rolling.

Transfer Admission The application deadline for admission is rolling.

Entrance Difficulty Saint Joseph's College assesses its entrance difficulty level as moderately difficult. For the fall 2006 freshman class, 74 percent of the applicants were accepted.

For Further Information Contact Ms. Karen Raftus, Director of Admissions, Saint Joseph's College, PO Box 815, Rensselaer, IN 47978-0850. *Telephone:* 219-866-6170 or 800-447-8781 (toll-free out-of-state). *Fax:* 219-866-6122. *E-mail:* admissions@saintjoe.edu. *Web site:* http://www.saintjoe.edu/.

SAINT MARY-OF-THE-WOODS COLLEGE
Saint Mary-of-the-Woods, Indiana

Saint Mary-of-the-Woods College is an undergraduate: women only; graduate: coed, private, Roman Catholic, comprehensive institution, founded in 1840, offering degrees at the associate, bachelor's, and master's levels and post-master's and postbachelor's certificates (also offers external degree program with significant enrollment not reflected in profile). It has a 67-acre campus in Saint Mary-of-the-Woods near Indianapolis.

Academic Information The faculty has 67 members (96% full-time), 57% with terminal degrees. The undergraduate student-faculty ratio is 14:1. The library holds 155,771 titles and 150 serial subscriptions. Special programs include academic remediation, study abroad, advanced placement credit, accelerated degree programs, double majors, independent study, distance learning, self-designed majors, summer session for credit, part-time degree programs (evenings, weekends, summer), external degree programs, adult/continuing education programs, internships, and arrangement for off-campus study with Indiana State University, Rose-Hulman Institute of Technology, DePauw University, Wabash College. The most frequently chosen baccalaureate fields are business/marketing, education, visual and performing arts.

Student Body Statistics The student body totals 1,668, of whom 1,540 are undergraduates (118 freshmen). 97 percent are women and 3 percent are men. Students come from 28 states and territories and 3 other countries. 81 percent are from Indiana. 0.4 percent are international students. 25 percent of the 2006 graduating class went on to graduate and professional schools.

Expenses for 2007–08 *Application fee:* $30. *Comprehensive fee:* $27,560 includes full-time tuition ($19,530), mandatory fees ($650), and college room and board ($7380). *College room only:* $2880. *Part-time tuition:* $370 per hour. *Part-time mandatory fees:* $120 per year.

Financial Aid Forms of aid include need-based and non-need-based scholarships and part-time jobs. The average aided 2005–06 undergraduate received an aid package worth $17,140. The application deadline for financial aid is continuous.

Freshman Admission Saint Mary-of-the-Woods College requires a minimum 2.5 high school GPA, 1 recommendation, SAT or ACT scores, and TOEFL scores for international students. An essay, a high school transcript, and an interview are required for some. The application deadline for regular admission is August 15.

Transfer Admission The application deadline for admission is August 15.

Entrance Difficulty Saint Mary-of-the-Woods College assesses its entrance difficulty level as moderately difficult.

For Further Information Contact Mr. Bryan Michel, Associate Director of Admission, Saint Mary-of-the-Woods College, Guerin Hall, Saint Mary-of-the-Woods, IN 47876. *Telephone:* 812-535-5106 or 800-926-SMWC (toll-free). *Fax:* 812-535-5010. *E-mail:* smwcadms@smwc.edu. *Web site:* http://www.smwc.edu/.

SAINT MARY'S COLLEGE
Notre Dame, Indiana

Saint Mary's College is a women's, private, Roman Catholic, four-year college, founded in 1844, offering degrees at the bachelor's level. It has a 275-acre campus in Notre Dame.

Academic Information The faculty has 205 members (63% full-time), 57% with terminal degrees. The student-faculty ratio is 10:1. The library holds 231,713 titles and 679 serial subscriptions. Special programs include academic remediation, services for learning-disabled students, cooperative (work-study) education, study abroad, advanced placement credit, accelerated degree programs, double majors, independent study, self-designed majors, summer session for credit, part-time degree programs (daytime), internships, and arrangement for off-campus study with University of Notre Dame, members of the Northern Indiana Consortium for Education. The most frequently chosen baccalaureate fields are business/marketing, communications/journalism, education.

Student Body Statistics The student body is made up of 1,527 undergraduates (426 freshmen). Students come from 44 states and territories and 7 other countries. 20 percent are from Indiana. 0.6 percent are international students. 22 percent of the 2006 graduating class went on to graduate and professional schools.

Expenses for 2007–08 *Application fee:* $30. *Comprehensive fee:* $35,550 includes full-time tuition ($26,282), mandatory fees ($590), and college room and board ($8678). *College room only:* $5346. *Part-time tuition:* $1039 per semester hour.

Financial Aid Forms of aid include need-based and non-need-based scholarships and part-time jobs. The average aided 2005–06 undergraduate received an aid package worth $20,191. The priority application deadline for financial aid is March 1.

Freshman Admission Saint Mary's College requires an essay, a high school transcript, 1 recommendation, SAT or ACT scores, and TOEFL scores for international students. An interview is recommended. The application deadline for regular admission is March 1 and for early decision it is November 15.

Transfer Admission The application deadline for admission is rolling.

Entrance Difficulty Saint Mary's College assesses its entrance difficulty level as moderately difficult. For the fall 2006 freshman class, 80 percent of the applicants were accepted.

For Further Information Contact Mona Bowe, Director of Admissions, Saint Mary's College, Notre Dame, IN 46556. *Telephone:* 574-284-4587 or 800-551-7621 (toll-free). *Fax:* 574-284-4841. *E-mail:* admission@saintmarys.edu. *Web site:* http://www.saintmarys.edu/.

See page 286 for the College Close-Up.

TAYLOR UNIVERSITY
Upland, Indiana

Taylor University is a coed, private, interdenominational, comprehensive institution, founded in 1846, offering degrees at the associate, bachelor's, and master's levels. It has a 950-acre campus in Upland near Indianapolis.

Academic Information The faculty has 192 members (66% full-time), 56% with terminal degrees. The undergraduate student-faculty ratio is 12:1. The library holds 189,007 titles and 12,625 serial subscriptions. Special programs include academic remediation, services for learning-disabled students, an honors program, cooperative (work-study) education, study abroad, advanced placement credit, ESL programs, double majors, independent study, distance learning, self-designed majors, summer session for credit, part-time degree programs, internships, and arrangement for off-campus study with members of the Christian College Coalition and the Christian College Consortium, Bowling Green University, Trinity Christian College. The most frequently chosen baccalaureate fields are business/marketing, education, psychology.

Student Body Statistics The student body is made up of 1,854 undergraduates (493 freshmen). 55 percent are women and 45 percent are men. Students come from 46 states and territories and 23 other countries. 33 percent are from Indiana. 1.5 percent are international students. 13 percent of the 2006 graduating class went on to graduate and professional schools.

Expenses for 2006–07 *Application fee:* $25. *Comprehensive fee:* $27,895 includes full-time tuition ($21,800), mandatory fees ($228), and college room and board ($5867). *College room only:* $2868. Full-time tuition and fees vary according to course load. Room and board charges vary according to board plan and housing facility. *Part-time tuition:* $780 per credit. *Part-time mandatory fees:* $68 per year. Part-time tuition and fees vary according to course load.

Financial Aid Forms of aid include need-based and non-need-based scholarships, athletic grants, and part-time jobs. The average aided 2006–07 undergraduate received an aid package worth an estimated $14,752. The application deadline for financial aid is March 10.

Freshman Admission Taylor University requires an essay, a high school transcript, 2 recommendations, an interview, SAT or ACT scores, and TOEFL scores for international students. A minimum 2.8 high school GPA is recommended. The application deadline for regular admission is rolling and for early action it is December 1.

Transfer Admission The application deadline for admission is rolling.

Entrance Difficulty Taylor University assesses its entrance difficulty level as very difficult. For the fall 2006 freshman class, 86 percent of the applicants were accepted.

For Further Information Contact Mrs. Kathy Thornburgh, Visit Coordinator, Taylor University, 236 West Reade Avenue, Upland, IN 46989-1001. *Telephone:* 765-998-5134 or 800-882-3456 (toll-free). *Fax:* 765-998-4925. *E-mail:* admissions_u@tayloru.edu. *Web site:* http://www.taylor.edu/.

TAYLOR UNIVERSITY FORT WAYNE
Fort Wayne, Indiana

Taylor University Fort Wayne is a coed, private, interdenominational, comprehensive unit of Taylor University, founded in 1992, offering degrees at the associate, bachelor's, and master's levels and postbachelor's certificates. It has a 32-acre campus in Fort Wayne.

Taylor University Fort Wayne (continued)

Academic Information The faculty has 45 members (51% full-time), 53% with terminal degrees. The undergraduate student-faculty ratio is 12:1. The library holds 88,100 titles and 487 serial subscriptions. Special programs include academic remediation, services for learning-disabled students, cooperative (work-study) education, study abroad, advanced placement credit, accelerated degree programs, double majors, independent study, distance learning, self-designed majors, summer session for credit, part-time degree programs (daytime, evenings, weekends, summer), external degree programs, adult/continuing education programs, internships, and arrangement for off-campus study with Council for Christian Colleges and Universities, Christian College Consortium, Christian Center for Urban Studies. The most frequently chosen baccalaureate fields are education, business/marketing, theology and religious vocations.

Student Body Statistics The student body is made up of 975 undergraduates (91 freshmen). 61 percent are women and 39 percent are men. Students come from 22 states and territories and 4 other countries. 70 percent are from Indiana. 9.8 percent of the 2006 graduating class went on to graduate and professional schools.

Expenses for 2006–07 *Application fee:* $20. *Comprehensive fee:* $24,236 includes full-time tuition ($18,940), mandatory fees ($116), and college room and board ($5180). *College room only:* $2300. Room and board charges vary according to board plan. *Part-time tuition:* $269 per credit hour. *Part-time mandatory fees:* $52 per year. Part-time tuition and fees vary according to course load.

Financial Aid Forms of aid include need-based and non-need-based scholarships, athletic grants, and part-time jobs. The average aided 2006–07 undergraduate received an aid package worth an estimated $16,287. The priority application deadline for financial aid is March 1.

Freshman Admission Taylor University Fort Wayne requires an essay, a high school transcript, 2 recommendations, SAT or ACT scores, and TOEFL scores for international students. A minimum 3.0 high school GPA and an interview are recommended. The application deadline for regular admission is rolling.

Transfer Admission The application deadline for admission is rolling.

Entrance Difficulty Taylor University Fort Wayne assesses its entrance difficulty level as moderately difficult. For the fall 2006 freshman class, 69 percent of the applicants were accepted.

For Further Information Contact Mr. Leo Gonot, Associate Vice President for Enrollment Management, Taylor University Fort Wayne, 1025 West Rudisill Boulevard, Fort Wayne, IN 46807-2197. *Telephone:* 260-744-8689 or 800-233-3922 (toll-free). *Fax:* 260-744-8850. *E-mail:* admissions@fw.taylor.edu. *Web site:* http://www.tayloru.edu/.

TRI-STATE UNIVERSITY

Angola, Indiana

Tri-State University is a coed, private, comprehensive institution, founded in 1884, offering degrees at the associate, bachelor's, and master's levels. It has a 400-acre campus in Angola.

Academic Information The faculty has 99 members (70% full-time), 51% with terminal degrees. The undergraduate student-faculty ratio is 13:1. The library holds 73,859 titles and 359 serial subscriptions. Special programs include academic remediation, an honors program, cooperative (work-study) education, study abroad, advanced placement credit, double majors, distance learning, summer session for credit, part-time degree programs (daytime, evenings, summer), adult/continuing education programs, and internships. The most frequently chosen baccalaureate fields are education, business/marketing, engineering technologies.

Student Body Statistics The student body totals 1,210, of whom 1,203 are undergraduates (319 freshmen). 32 percent are women and 68 percent are men. Students come from 21 states and territories and 12 other countries. 60 percent are from Indiana. 1.1 percent are international students. 30 percent of the 2006 graduating class went on to graduate and professional schools.

Expenses for 2006–07 *Application fee:* $0. *Comprehensive fee:* $27,450 includes full-time tuition ($21,210) and college room and board ($6240). *Part-time tuition:* $663 per credit hour.

Financial Aid Forms of aid include need-based and non-need-based scholarships and part-time jobs. The average aided 2006–07 undergraduate

received an aid package worth an estimated $15,450. The priority application deadline for financial aid is March 10.

Freshman Admission Tri-State University requires a high school transcript, a minimum 2.0 high school GPA, and SAT or ACT scores. Recommendations, an interview, and TOEFL scores for international students are recommended. The application deadline for regular admission is August 1.

Transfer Admission The application deadline for admission is August 1.

Entrance Difficulty Tri-State University assesses its entrance difficulty level as moderately difficult. For the fall 2006 freshman class, 76 percent of the applicants were accepted.

For Further Information Contact Mr. Scott Goplin, Dean of Admission, Tri-State University, 1 University Avenue, Angola, IN 46703. *Telephone:* 260-665-4365 or 800-347-4TSU (toll-free). *Fax:* 260-665-4578. *E-mail:* admit@tristate.edu. *Web site:* http://www.tristate.edu/.

See page 294 for the College Close-Up.

UNIVERSITY OF EVANSVILLE

Evansville, Indiana

University of Evansville is a coed, private, comprehensive institution, founded in 1854, affiliated with the United Methodist Church, offering degrees at the associate, bachelor's, and master's levels. It has a 75-acre campus in Evansville.

Academic Information The faculty has 239 members (75% full-time), 72% with terminal degrees. The undergraduate student-faculty ratio is 13:1. The library holds 289,593 titles, 970 serial subscriptions, and 11,534 audiovisual materials. Special programs include an honors program, cooperative (work-study) education, study abroad, advanced placement credit, accelerated degree programs, ESL programs, double majors, independent study, self-designed majors, summer session for credit, part-time degree programs (daytime, evenings, summer), external degree programs, adult/continuing education programs, and internships. The most frequently chosen baccalaureate fields are health professions and related sciences, business/marketing, visual and performing arts.

Student Body Statistics The student body totals 2,879, of whom 2,813 are undergraduates (644 freshmen). 60 percent are women and 40 percent are men. Students come from 39 states and territories and 46 other countries. 61 percent are from Indiana. 5.5 percent are international students. 21 percent of the 2006 graduating class went on to graduate and professional schools.

Expenses for 2006–07 *Application fee:* $35. *Comprehensive fee:* $30,100 includes full-time tuition ($22,370), mandatory fees ($610), and college room and board ($7120). *College room only:* $3540. Room and board charges vary according to board plan and housing facility. *Part-time tuition:* $615 per hour. *Part-time mandatory fees:* $35 per term. Part-time tuition and fees vary according to course load.

Financial Aid Forms of aid include need-based and non-need-based scholarships, athletic grants, and part-time jobs. The average aided 2006–07 undergraduate received an aid package worth an estimated $21,129. The priority application deadline for financial aid is March 10.

Freshman Admission University of Evansville requires a high school transcript, 1 recommendation, SAT or ACT scores, and TOEFL scores for international students. A minimum 3.0 high school GPA and an interview are recommended. An essay and an interview are required for some. The application deadline for regular admission is February 1; for nonresidents it is February 1; and for early action it is December 1.

Transfer Admission The application deadline for admission is rolling.

Entrance Difficulty University of Evansville assesses its entrance difficulty level as moderately difficult; very difficult for engineering, physical therapy. For the fall 2006 freshman class, 90 percent of the applicants were accepted.

For Further Information Contact Don Vos, Dean of Admission, University of Evansville, 1800 Lincoln Avenue, Evansville, IN 47722. *Telephone:* 812-488-2468 or 800-423-8633 Ext. 2468 (toll-free). *Fax:* 812-488-4076. *E-mail:* admission@evansville.edu. *Web site:* http://www. evansville.edu/.

UNIVERSITY OF INDIANAPOLIS

Indianapolis, Indiana

University of Indianapolis is a coed, private, comprehensive institution, founded in 1902, affiliated with the United Methodist Church, offering degrees at the associate, bachelor's, master's, and doctoral levels. It has a 65-acre campus in Indianapolis.

Academic Information The faculty has 447 members (40% full-time), 55% with terminal degrees. The undergraduate student-faculty ratio is 12:1. The library holds 173,363 titles and 1,015 serial subscriptions. Special programs include academic remediation, services for learning-disabled students, an honors program, cooperative (work-study) education, study abroad, advanced placement credit, accelerated degree programs, Freshman Honors College, ESL programs, double majors, independent study, self-designed majors, summer session for credit, part-time degree programs (evenings), adult/continuing education programs, internships, and arrangement for off-campus study with 7 members of the Consortium for Urban Education, 10 members of the May Term Consortium. The most frequently chosen baccalaureate fields are business/marketing, education, psychology.

Student Body Statistics The student body totals 4,389, of whom 3,352 are undergraduates (751 freshmen). 68 percent are women and 32 percent are men. Students come from 34 states and territories and 30 other countries. 75 percent are from Indiana. 3 percent are international students.

Expenses for 2006–07 *Application fee:* $20. *Comprehensive fee:* $26,230 includes full-time tuition ($18,700), mandatory fees ($150), and college room and board ($7380). *College room only:* $3490. Full-time tuition and fees vary according to program. Room and board charges vary according to board plan and housing facility. *Part-time tuition:* $780 per hour. Part-time tuition varies according to class time.

Financial Aid Forms of aid include need-based and non-need-based scholarships, athletic grants, and part-time jobs. The priority application deadline for financial aid is March 1.

Freshman Admission University of Indianapolis requires a high school transcript, a minimum 2.0 high school GPA, SAT or ACT scores, and TOEFL scores for international students. An interview is required for some. The application deadline for regular admission is rolling.

Transfer Admission The application deadline for admission is rolling.

Entrance Difficulty University of Indianapolis assesses its entrance difficulty level as moderately difficult. For the fall 2006 freshman class, 78 percent of the applicants were accepted.

For Further Information Contact Mr. Ronald Wilks, Director of Admissions, University of Indianapolis, 1400 East Hanna Avenue, Indianapolis, IN 46227-3697. *Telephone:* 317-788-3216 or 800-232-8634 Ext. 3216 (toll-free). *Fax:* 317-788-3300. *E-mail:* admissions@uindy.edu. *Web site:* http://www.uindy.edu/.

UNIVERSITY OF NOTRE DAME

Notre Dame, Indiana

University of Notre Dame is a coed, private, Roman Catholic university, founded in 1842, offering degrees at the bachelor's, master's, doctoral, and first professional levels. It has a 1,250-acre campus in Notre Dame.

Academic Information The faculty has 1,273 members (69% full-time), 83% with terminal degrees. The undergraduate student-faculty ratio is 11:1. The library holds 3 million titles, 10,553 serial subscriptions, and 21,095 audiovisual materials. Special programs include services for learning-disabled students, an honors program, study abroad, advanced placement credit, accelerated degree programs, double majors, independent study, distance learning, self-designed majors, summer session for credit, internships, and arrangement for off-campus study with Saint Mary's College (IN), Xavier University of Louisiana, Clark Atlanta University, St. Mary's University of San Antonio. The most frequently chosen baccalaureate fields are business/marketing, engineering, social sciences.

Student Body Statistics The student body totals 11,603, of whom 8,352 are undergraduates (2,039 freshmen). 47 percent are women and 53 percent are men. Students come from 53 states and territories and 48 other

countries. 8 percent are from Indiana. 3.2 percent are international students. 32 percent of the 2006 graduating class went on to graduate and professional schools.

Expenses for 2007–08 *Application fee:* $50. *Comprehensive fee:* $44,477 includes full-time tuition ($34,680), mandatory fees ($507), and college room and board ($9290). *Part-time tuition:* $1445 per credit.

Financial Aid Forms of aid include need-based and non-need-based scholarships, athletic grants, and part-time jobs. The average aided 2006–07 undergraduate received an aid package worth an estimated $28,373. The application deadline for financial aid is February 15.

Freshman Admission University of Notre Dame requires an essay, a high school transcript, 1 recommendation, SAT or ACT scores, and TOEFL scores for international students. SAT Subject Test scores are required for some. The application deadline for regular admission is December 31 and for early action it is November 1.

Transfer Admission The application deadline for admission is April 15.

Entrance Difficulty University of Notre Dame assesses its entrance difficulty level as most difficult. For the fall 2006 freshman class, 27 percent of the applicants were accepted.

For Further Information Contact Office of Undergraduate Admissions, University of Notre Dame, 220 Main Building, Notre Dame, IN 46556-5612. *Telephone:* 574-631-7505. *Fax:* 574-631-8865. *E-mail:* admissions@nd.edu. *Web site:* http://www.nd.edu/.

UNIVERSITY OF PHOENIX–INDIANAPOLIS CAMPUS

Indianapolis, Indiana

University of Phoenix–Indianapolis Campus is a coed, proprietary, comprehensive institution, founded in 2003, offering degrees at the bachelor's and master's levels.

Academic Information The faculty has 193 members (5% full-time), 7% with terminal degrees. The undergraduate student-faculty ratio is 7:1. The library holds 1,756 titles and 692 serial subscriptions. Special programs include services for learning-disabled students, advanced placement credit, accelerated degree programs, independent study, distance learning, external degree programs, and adult/continuing education programs. The most frequently chosen baccalaureate field is business/marketing.

Student Body Statistics The student body totals 602, of whom 497 are undergraduates (41 freshmen). 65 percent are women and 35 percent are men. 3.2 percent are international students.

Expenses for 2006–07 *Application fee:* $45. *Tuition:* $10,320 full-time, $336 per credit part-time.

Financial Aid Forms of aid include need-based and non-need-based scholarships. The average aided 2005–06 undergraduate received an aid package worth $4196. The application deadline for financial aid is continuous.

Freshman Admission University of Phoenix–Indianapolis Campus requires 1 recommendation. A high school transcript is required for some. The application deadline for regular admission is rolling.

Transfer Admission The application deadline for admission is rolling.

Entrance Difficulty University of Phoenix–Indianapolis Campus has an open admission policy.

For Further Information Contact Ms. Beth Barilla, Associate Vice President, Student Admissions and Services, University of Phoenix–Indianapolis Campus, 4615 East Elwood Street, Mail Stop AA-K101, Phoenix, AZ 85040-1958. *Telephone:* 480-317-6000, 800-776-4867 (toll-free in-state), or 800-228-7240 (toll-free out-of-state). *Fax:* 480-894-1758. *E-mail:* beth.barilla@phoenix.edu. *Web site:* http://www.phoenix.edu/.

UNIVERSITY OF SAINT FRANCIS

Fort Wayne, Indiana

University of Saint Francis is a coed, private, Roman Catholic, comprehensive institution, founded in 1890, offering degrees at the associate, bachelor's, and master's levels and postbachelor's certificates. It has a 74-acre campus in Fort Wayne.

University of Saint Francis (continued)

Academic Information The faculty has 223 members (45% full-time), 29% with terminal degrees. The undergraduate student-faculty ratio is 11:1. The library holds 50,186 titles and 549 serial subscriptions. Special programs include academic remediation, services for learning-disabled students, an honors program, cooperative (work-study) education, study abroad, advanced placement credit, Freshman Honors College, double majors, independent study, distance learning, summer session for credit, part-time degree programs (daytime, evenings, weekends, summer), adult/continuing education programs, internships, and arrangement for off-campus study. The most frequently chosen baccalaureate fields are business/marketing, education, health professions and related sciences.
Student Body Statistics The student body totals 2,039, of whom 1,784 are undergraduates (362 freshmen). 70 percent are women and 30 percent are men. Students come from 13 states and territories. 90 percent are from Indiana. 14 percent of the 2006 graduating class went on to graduate and professional schools.
Expenses for 2006–07 *Application fee:* $20. *Comprehensive fee:* $24,312 includes full-time tuition ($17,760), mandatory fees ($718), and college room and board ($5834). Full-time tuition and fees vary according to course load. Room and board charges vary according to housing facility. *Part-time tuition:* $560 per hour. *Part-time mandatory fees:* $17 per hour. Part-time tuition and fees vary according to course load.
Financial Aid Forms of aid include need-based and non-need-based scholarships, athletic grants, and part-time jobs. The average aided 2005–06 undergraduate received an aid package worth $13,008. The application deadline for financial aid is June 30 with a priority deadline of March 10.
Freshman Admission University of Saint Francis requires a high school transcript, a minimum 2.3 high school GPA, SAT or ACT scores, and TOEFL scores for international students. An essay is recommended. Recommendations and an interview are required for some. The application deadline for regular admission is rolling.
Transfer Admission The application deadline for admission is rolling.
Entrance Difficulty University of Saint Francis assesses its entrance difficulty level as moderately difficult. For the fall 2006 freshman class, 59 percent of the applicants were accepted.
For Further Information Contact Mr. Ron Schumacher, Vice President for Enrollment Management, University of Saint Francis, 2701 Spring Street, Fort Wayne, IN 46808. *Telephone:* 260-434-3279 or 800-729-4732 (toll-free). *Fax:* 260-434-7590. *E-mail:* admiss@sfc.edu. *Web site:* http://www.sf.edu/.

UNIVERSITY OF SOUTHERN INDIANA
Evansville, Indiana

University of Southern Indiana is a coed, public, comprehensive unit of Indiana Commission for Higher Education, founded in 1965, offering degrees at the associate, bachelor's, and master's levels and postbachelor's certificates. It has a 330-acre campus in Evansville.

Academic Information The faculty has 629 members (48% full-time), 34% with terminal degrees. The undergraduate student-faculty ratio is 20:1. The library holds 328,734 titles, 15,153 serial subscriptions, and 5,587 audiovisual materials. Special programs include academic remediation, services for learning-disabled students, an honors program, cooperative (work-study) education, study abroad, advanced placement credit, ESL programs, double majors, independent study, distance learning, summer session for credit, part-time degree programs (daytime, evenings, weekends, summer), adult/continuing education programs, and internships. The most frequently chosen baccalaureate fields are business/marketing, education, health professions and related sciences.
Student Body Statistics The student body totals 10,021, of whom 9,298 are undergraduates (2,105 freshmen). 60 percent are women and 40 percent are men. Students come from 26 states and territories and 26 other countries. 94 percent are from Indiana. 0.9 percent are international students.
Expenses for 2006–07 *Application fee:* $25. *State resident tuition:* $4460 full-time, $148.65 per credit hour part-time. *Nonresident tuition:* $10,631 full-time, $354.35 per credit hour part-time. *Mandatory fees:* $60 full-time, $22.75 per term part-time. *College room and board:* $6492. *College room only:* $3234.

Financial Aid Forms of aid include need-based and non-need-based scholarships, athletic grants, and part-time jobs. The average aided 2006–07 undergraduate received an aid package worth an estimated $8561. The application deadline for financial aid is March 1.
Freshman Admission University of Southern Indiana requires a high school transcript, SAT or ACT scores, and TOEFL scores for international students. An essay and a minimum 2.0 high school GPA are recommended. An interview is required for some. The application deadline for regular admission is August 15.
Entrance Difficulty University of Southern Indiana assesses its entrance difficulty level as noncompetitive; minimally difficult for transfers; moderately difficult for allied health, social work programs. For the fall 2006 freshman class, 83 percent of the applicants were accepted.
For Further Information Contact Mr. Eric Otto, Director of Admission, University of Southern Indiana, 8600 University Boulevard, Evansville, IN 47712-3590. *Telephone:* 812-464-1765 or 800-467-1965 (toll-free). *Fax:* 812-465-7154. *E-mail:* enroll@usi.edu. *Web site:* http://www.usi.edu/.

VALPARAISO UNIVERSITY
Valparaiso, Indiana

Valparaiso University is a coed, private, comprehensive institution, founded in 1859, affiliated with the Lutheran Church, offering degrees at the associate, bachelor's, master's, and first professional levels and post-master's and postbachelor's certificates. It has a 310-acre campus in Valparaiso near Chicago.

Academic Information The faculty has 378 members (67% full-time), 78% with terminal degrees. The undergraduate student-faculty ratio is 12:1. The library holds 471,645 titles, 41,649 serial subscriptions, and 5,770 audiovisual materials. Special programs include services for learning-disabled students, an honors program, cooperative (work-study) education, study abroad, advanced placement credit, accelerated degree programs, Freshman Honors College, ESL programs, double majors, independent study, distance learning, self-designed majors, summer session for credit, part-time degree programs (daytime, evenings, summer), adult/continuing education programs, internships, and arrangement for off-campus study with Associated Colleges of the Midwest, American University, Lutheran College Washington Consortium, Drew University. The most frequently chosen baccalaureate fields are business/marketing, education, social sciences.
Student Body Statistics The student body totals 3,868, of whom 2,960 are undergraduates (762 freshmen). 52 percent are women and 48 percent are men. Students come from 47 states and territories and 31 other countries. 36 percent are from Indiana. 2.1 percent are international students. 27 percent of the 2006 graduating class went on to graduate and professional schools.
Expenses for 2006–07 *Application fee:* $30. *Comprehensive fee:* $30,640 includes full-time tuition ($23,200), mandatory fees ($800), and college room and board ($6640). *College room only:* $4140. Room and board charges vary according to housing facility and student level. *Part-time tuition:* $1100 per credit hour. *Part-time mandatory fees:* $20 per credit hour. Part-time tuition and fees vary according to course load.
Financial Aid Forms of aid include need-based and non-need-based scholarships, athletic grants, and part-time jobs. The average aided 2006–07 undergraduate received an aid package worth an estimated $18,608. The priority application deadline for financial aid is March 1.
Freshman Admission Valparaiso University requires an essay, a high school transcript, and SAT or ACT scores. 2 recommendations, an interview, and TOEFL scores for international students are recommended. An interview is required for some. The application deadline for regular admission is August 15 and for early action it is November 1.
Entrance Difficulty Valparaiso University assesses its entrance difficulty level as moderately difficult. For the fall 2006 freshman class, 89 percent of the applicants were accepted.
For Further Information Contact Office of Admission, Valparaiso University, Kretzmann Hall, 1700 Chapel Drive, Valparaiso, IN 46383-6493. *Telephone:* 219-464-5011 or 888-GO-VALPO (toll-free). *Fax:* 219-464-6898. *E-mail:* undergrad_admissions@valpo.edu. *Web site:* http://www.valpo.edu/.

See page 302 for the College Close-Up.

WABASH COLLEGE
Crawfordsville, Indiana

Wabash College is a men's, private, four-year college, founded in 1832, offering degrees at the bachelor's level. It has a 50-acre campus in Crawfordsville near Indianapolis.

Academic Information The faculty has 88 members (97% full-time), 97% with terminal degrees. The student-faculty ratio is 10:1. The library holds 434,460 titles and 5,530 serial subscriptions. Special programs include services for learning-disabled students, study abroad, advanced placement credit, double majors, independent study, internships, and arrangement for off-campus study with members of the Great Lakes Colleges Association. The most frequently chosen baccalaureate fields are English, history, social sciences.

Student Body Statistics The student body is made up of 874 undergraduates (268 freshmen). Students come from 35 states and territories and 19 other countries. 74 percent are from Indiana. 4.6 percent are international students. 37 percent of the 2006 graduating class went on to graduate and professional schools.

Expenses for 2006–07 *Application fee:* $30. *Comprehensive fee:* $31,856 includes full-time tuition ($24,342), mandatory fees ($450), and college room and board ($7064). *College room only:* $2877. Room and board charges vary according to board plan and housing facility. *Part-time tuition:* $4057 per course. Part-time tuition varies according to course load.

Financial Aid Forms of aid include need-based and non-need-based scholarships and part-time jobs. The average aided 2006–07 undergraduate received an aid package worth an estimated $20,607. The application deadline for financial aid is March 1 with a priority deadline of February 15.

Freshman Admission Wabash College requires a high school transcript, SAT or ACT scores, and TOEFL scores for international students. An essay, recommendations, and an interview are recommended. The application deadline for regular admission is rolling; for early decision it is November 15; and for early action it is December 15.

Transfer Admission The application deadline for admission is March 15.

Entrance Difficulty Wabash College assesses its entrance difficulty level as moderately difficult. For the fall 2006 freshman class, 51 percent of the applicants were accepted.

For Further Information Contact Mr. Steve Klein, Dean of Admissions, Wabash College, PO Box 362, Crawfordsville, IN 47933-0352. *Telephone:* 765-361-6225 or 800-345-5385 (toll-free). *Fax:* 765-361-6437. *E-mail:* admissions@wabash.edu. *Web site:* http://www.wabash.edu/.

Iowa

AIB COLLEGE OF BUSINESS
Des Moines, Iowa

AIB College of Business is a coed, private, two-year college, founded in 1921, offering degrees at the associate level. It has a 20-acre campus in Des Moines.

Academic Information The faculty has 67 members (42% full-time), 7% with terminal degrees. The student-faculty ratio is 17:1. The library holds 5,400 titles and 185 serial subscriptions. Special programs include academic remediation, double majors, distance learning, summer session for credit, part-time degree programs (daytime, evenings, summer), adult/continuing education programs, and internships.

Student Body Statistics The student body is made up of 909 undergraduates. 71 percent are women and 29 percent are men. Students come from 5 states and territories. 99 percent are from Iowa.

Expenses for 2006–07 *Application fee:* $25. *Comprehensive fee:* $15,837 includes full-time tuition ($11,880) and college room and board ($3957). *College room only:* $2895. *Part-time tuition:* $330 per credit hour.

Financial Aid Forms of aid include need-based scholarships and part-time jobs. The priority application deadline for financial aid is April 1.

Freshman Admission AIB College of Business requires a high school transcript and TOEFL scores for international students. An interview and ACT scores are recommended. The application deadline for regular admission is rolling.

Transfer Admission The application deadline for admission is rolling.

Entrance Difficulty AIB College of Business assesses its entrance difficulty level as minimally difficult; moderately difficult for Real-time Reporting program. For the fall 2006 freshman class, 74 percent of the applicants were accepted.

For Further Information Contact Mr. Tim Hauber, Dean of Enrollment, AIB College of Business, Keith Fenton Administration Building, 2500 Fleur Drive, Des Moines, IA 50321-1799. *Telephone:* 515-244-4221 or 800-444-1921 (toll-free). *Fax:* 515-244-6773. *E-mail:* haubert@aib.edu. *Web site:* http://www.aib.edu/.

ALLEN COLLEGE
Waterloo, Iowa

Allen College is a coed, primarily women's, private, comprehensive institution, founded in 1989, offering degrees at the associate, bachelor's, and master's levels (liberal arts and general education courses offered at either University of North Iowa or Wartburg College). It has a 20-acre campus in Waterloo.

Academic Information The faculty has 31 members (61% full-time), 10% with terminal degrees. The undergraduate student-faculty ratio is 14:1. The library holds 2,797 titles and 199 serial subscriptions. Special programs include advanced placement credit, independent study, distance learning, part-time degree programs (daytime, evenings), internships, and arrangement for off-campus study. The most frequently chosen baccalaureate field is health professions and related sciences.

Student Body Statistics The student body totals 426, of whom 359 are undergraduates (31 freshmen). 94 percent are women and 6 percent are men. Students come from 6 states and territories. 95 percent are from Iowa.

Expenses for 2006–07 *Application fee:* $50. *Comprehensive fee:* $19,184 includes full-time tuition ($11,958), mandatory fees ($1514), and college room and board ($5712). *College room only:* $2666. *Part-time tuition:* $415 per credit hour. *Part-time mandatory fees:* $37 per credit hour, $170 per term.

Financial Aid Forms of aid include need-based and non-need-based scholarships and part-time jobs. The average aided 2005–06 undergraduate received an aid package worth $14,428. The application deadline for financial aid is continuous.

Freshman Admission Allen College requires an essay, a high school transcript, 1 recommendation, ACT scores, and TOEFL scores for international students. A minimum 2.3 high school GPA and rank in upper 50% of high school class, minimum ACT score of 18 are recommended. An interview is required for some. The application deadline for regular admission is July 1 and for early decision it is March 1.

Transfer Admission The application deadline for admission is July 1.

Entrance Difficulty Allen College assesses its entrance difficulty level as moderately difficult. For the fall 2006 freshman class, 66 percent of the applicants were accepted.

For Further Information Contact Dina Dowden, Education Secretary-Student Services, Allen College, Barrett Forum, 1825 Logan Avenue, Waterloo, IA 50703. *Telephone:* 319-226-2000. *Fax:* 319-226-2051. *E-mail:* allencollegeadmissions@ihs.org. *Web site:* http://www.allencollege.edu/.

ASHFORD UNIVERSITY
Clinton, Iowa

Ashford University is a coed, proprietary, four-year college, founded in 1918, offering degrees at the bachelor's and master's levels. It has a 24-acre campus in Clinton near Chicago.

Academic Information The faculty has 268 members (13% full-time). The undergraduate student-faculty ratio is 14:1. The library holds 98,974 titles and 639 serial subscriptions. Special programs include academic remediation, an honors program, advanced placement credit, Freshman

Ashford University (continued)

Honors College, double majors, independent study, distance learning, summer session for credit, part-time degree programs (daytime, evenings, summer), external degree programs, and internships.

Student Body Statistics The student body totals 3,836, of whom 3,485 are undergraduates (288 freshmen). 77 percent are women and 23 percent are men. Students come from 9 states and territories. 0.3 percent are international students. 28 percent of the 2006 graduating class went on to graduate and professional schools.

Expenses for 2006–07 *Application fee:* $20. *Comprehensive fee:* $21,140 includes full-time tuition ($15,340) and college room and board ($5800). *College room only:* $2500. *Part-time tuition:* $448 per credit.

Financial Aid Forms of aid include need-based and non-need-based scholarships and part-time jobs. The application deadline for financial aid is continuous.

Freshman Admission Ashford University requires a high school transcript and TOEFL scores for international students. A minimum 2.0 high school GPA and an interview are recommended. Recommendations, an interview, and SAT or ACT scores are required for some. The application deadline for regular admission is rolling.

Transfer Admission The application deadline for admission is rolling.

Entrance Difficulty Ashford University assesses its entrance difficulty level as minimally difficult; moderately difficult for transfers. For the fall 2006 freshman class, 60 percent of the applicants were accepted.

For Further Information Contact Ms. Waunita M. Sullivan, Director of Enrollment, Ashford University, 400 North Bluff Boulevard, PO Box 2967, Clinton, IA 52733-2967. *Telephone:* 563-242-4153 or 800-242-4153 (toll-free). *Fax:* 563-243-6102. *E-mail:* admissions@ashford.edu. *Web site:* http://www.ashford.edu/.

BRIAR CLIFF UNIVERSITY
Sioux City, Iowa

Briar Cliff University is a coed, private, Roman Catholic, comprehensive institution, founded in 1930, offering degrees at the associate, bachelor's, and master's levels. It has a 75-acre campus in Sioux City.

Academic Information The faculty has 64 members (88% full-time), 56% with terminal degrees. The undergraduate student-faculty ratio is 14:1. The library holds 84,540 titles, 10,409 serial subscriptions, and 1,583 audiovisual materials. Special programs include academic remediation, services for learning-disabled students, an honors program, study abroad, advanced placement credit, accelerated degree programs, double majors, independent study, distance learning, self-designed majors, summer session for credit, part-time degree programs (daytime, evenings, weekends, summer), adult/continuing education programs, internships, and arrangement for off-campus study with Colleges of Mid-America. The most frequently chosen baccalaureate fields are business/marketing, education, health professions and related sciences.

Student Body Statistics The student body totals 1,146, of whom 1,095 are undergraduates (260 freshmen). 58 percent are women and 42 percent are men. Students come from 25 states and territories and 2 other countries. 64 percent are from Iowa. 0.2 percent are international students. 5.6 percent of the 2006 graduating class went on to graduate and professional schools.

Expenses for 2006–07 *Application fee:* $20. *Comprehensive fee:* $24,948 includes full-time tuition ($18,714), mandatory fees ($525), and college room and board ($5709). *College room only:* $2835. Room and board charges vary according to board plan and housing facility. *Part-time tuition:* $624 per hour. *Part-time mandatory fees:* $17.50 per hour. Part-time tuition and fees vary according to class time and course load.

Financial Aid Forms of aid include need-based and non-need-based scholarships and part-time jobs. The application deadline for financial aid is March 15.

Freshman Admission Briar Cliff University requires a high school transcript, a minimum 2.0 high school GPA, minimum ACT score of 18, and SAT or ACT scores. TOEFL scores for international students are recommended. An essay, 3 recommendations, and an interview are required for some. The application deadline for regular admission is rolling and for nonresidents it is rolling.

Transfer Admission The application deadline for admission is rolling.

Entrance Difficulty Briar Cliff University assesses its entrance difficulty level as moderately difficult. For the fall 2006 freshman class, 71 percent of the applicants were accepted.

For Further Information Contact Briar Cliff Admissions, Briar Cliff University, 3303 Rebecca Street, Sioux City, IA 51104. *Telephone:* 712-279-5200 or 800-662-3303 Ext. 5200 (toll-free). *Fax:* 712-279-1632. *E-mail:* admissino@briarcliff.edu. *Web site:* http://www.briarcliff.edu/.

BUENA VISTA UNIVERSITY
Storm Lake, Iowa

Buena Vista University is a coed, private, comprehensive institution, founded in 1891, affiliated with the Presbyterian Church (U.S.A.), offering degrees at the bachelor's and master's levels. It has a 60-acre campus in Storm Lake.

Academic Information The faculty has 114 members (73% full-time), 54% with terminal degrees. The undergraduate student-faculty ratio is 12:1. The library holds 144,000 titles, 632 serial subscriptions, and 5,648 audiovisual materials. Special programs include academic remediation, services for learning-disabled students, an honors program, study abroad, advanced placement credit, ESL programs, double majors, independent study, distance learning, self-designed majors, summer session for credit, part-time degree programs, external degree programs, adult/continuing education programs, internships, and arrangement for off-campus study with Washington University in St. Louis. The most frequently chosen baccalaureate fields are business/marketing, education, interdisciplinary studies.

Student Body Statistics The student body totals 1,229, of whom 1,149 are undergraduates (266 freshmen). 51 percent are women and 49 percent are men. Students come from 21 states and territories and 2 other countries. 79 percent are from Iowa. 0.7 percent are international students. 17 percent of the 2006 graduating class went on to graduate and professional schools.

Expenses for 2006–07 *Application fee:* $25. *Comprehensive fee:* $28,852 includes full-time tuition ($22,556) and college room and board ($6296). Room and board charges vary according to board plan. *Part-time tuition:* $758 per semester hour.

Financial Aid Forms of aid include need-based and non-need-based scholarships and part-time jobs. The average aided 2006–07 undergraduate received an aid package worth an estimated $22,457. The priority application deadline for financial aid is June 1.

Freshman Admission Buena Vista University requires a high school transcript, recommendations, SAT or ACT scores, and TOEFL scores for international students. A minimum 3.0 high school GPA is recommended. An essay and an interview are required for some.

Entrance Difficulty Buena Vista University assesses its entrance difficulty level as moderately difficult. For the fall 2006 freshman class, 79 percent of the applicants were accepted.

For Further Information Contact Carol Williams, Dean of Admissions, Buena Vista University, 610 West Fourth Street, Storm Lake, IA 50588. *Telephone:* 712-749-2235 or 800-383-9600 (toll-free). *E-mail:* admissions@bvu.edu. *Web site:* http://www.bvu.edu/.

CENTRAL COLLEGE
Pella, Iowa

Central College is a coed, private, four-year college, founded in 1853, affiliated with the Reformed Church in America, offering degrees at the bachelor's level. It has a 133-acre campus in Pella near Des Moines.

Academic Information The faculty has 141 members (67% full-time), 76% with terminal degrees. The student-faculty ratio is 13:1. The library holds 220,526 titles and 1,161 serial subscriptions. Special programs include services for learning-disabled students, an honors program, study abroad, ESL programs, double majors, independent study, self-designed majors, summer session for credit, part-time degree programs (daytime, evenings), internships, and arrangement for off-campus study. The most frequently chosen baccalaureate fields are business/marketing, education, parks and recreation.

Student Body Statistics The student body is made up of 1,606 undergraduates (413 freshmen). 55 percent are women and 45 percent are men. Students come from 39 states and territories and 18 other countries. 80 percent are from Iowa. 1.6 percent are international students. 15 percent of the 2006 graduating class went on to graduate and professional schools.

Expenses for 2006–07 *Application fee:* $25. *Comprehensive fee:* $28,446 includes full-time tuition ($20,972), mandatory fees ($250), and college room and board ($7224). *College room only:* $3542. Room and board charges vary according to board plan. *Part-time tuition:* $728 per semester hour. Part-time tuition varies according to course load.

Financial Aid Forms of aid include need-based and non-need-based scholarships and part-time jobs. The average aided 2006–07 undergraduate received an aid package worth an estimated $18,016. The priority application deadline for financial aid is March 15.

Freshman Admission Central College requires a high school transcript, SAT or ACT scores, and TOEFL scores for international students. A minimum 2.5 high school GPA and an interview are recommended. An essay, 3 recommendations, and an interview are required for some. The application deadline for regular admission is rolling.

Transfer Admission The application deadline for admission is rolling.

Entrance Difficulty Central College assesses its entrance difficulty level as moderately difficult. For the fall 2006 freshman class, 80 percent of the applicants were accepted.

For Further Information Contact Ms. Carol Williamson, Dean of Admission and Student Enrollment Services, Central College, 812 University Street, Pella, IA 50219-1999. *Telephone:* 641-628-7600, 877-462-3687 (toll-free in-state), or 877-462-3689 (toll-free out-of-state). *Fax:* 641-628-5316. *E-mail:* admissions@central.edu. *Web site:* http://www.central.edu/.

CLARKE COLLEGE
Dubuque, Iowa

Clarke College is a coed, private, Roman Catholic, comprehensive institution, founded in 1843, offering degrees at the associate, bachelor's, and master's levels. It has a 55-acre campus in Dubuque.

Academic Information The faculty has 135 members (57% full-time), 37% with terminal degrees. The undergraduate student-faculty ratio is 11:1. The library holds 182,649 titles, 508 serial subscriptions, and 1,262 audiovisual materials. Special programs include an honors program, cooperative (work-study) education, study abroad, advanced placement credit, accelerated degree programs, ESL programs, double majors, independent study, distance learning, self-designed majors, summer session for credit, part-time degree programs (evenings), adult/continuing education programs, internships, and arrangement for off-campus study with Tri-College Cooperative Effort. The most frequently chosen baccalaureate fields are business/marketing, education, health professions and related sciences.

Student Body Statistics The student body totals 1,201, of whom 1,006 are undergraduates (164 freshmen). 71 percent are women and 29 percent are men. Students come from 23 states and territories and 8 other countries. 63 percent are from Iowa. 0.7 percent are international students. 14 percent of the 2006 graduating class went on to graduate and professional schools.

Expenses for 2006–07 *Application fee:* $25. *Comprehensive fee:* $26,871 includes full-time tuition ($19,682), mandatory fees ($615), and college room and board ($6574). *College room only:* $3198. Room and board charges vary according to board plan and housing facility. *Part-time tuition:* $498 per credit hour.

Financial Aid Forms of aid include need-based and non-need-based scholarships and part-time jobs. The average aided 2006–07 undergraduate received an aid package worth an estimated $17,276. The priority application deadline for financial aid is April 15.

Freshman Admission Clarke College requires a high school transcript, a minimum 2.0 high school GPA, rank in upper 50% of high school class, minimum ACT score of 21 or SAT score of 1000, SAT or ACT scores, and TOEFL scores for international students. An interview is required for some. The application deadline for regular admission is rolling.

Transfer Admission The application deadline for admission is rolling.

Entrance Difficulty Clarke College assesses its entrance difficulty level as moderately difficult; very difficult for physical therapy program. For the fall 2006 freshman class, 66 percent of the applicants were accepted.

For Further Information Contact Mr. Andy Shroeder, Director of Admissions, Clarke College, 1550 Clarke Drive, Dubuque, IA 52001-3198. *Telephone:* 563-588-6316 or 800-383-2345 (toll-free). *Fax:* 563-588-6789. *E-mail:* admissions@clarke.edu. *Web site:* http://www.clarke.edu/.

COE COLLEGE
Cedar Rapids, Iowa

Coe College is a coed, private, comprehensive institution, founded in 1851, affiliated with the Presbyterian Church, offering degrees at the bachelor's and master's levels. It has a 53-acre campus in Cedar Rapids.

Academic Information The faculty has 142 members (54% full-time), 54% with terminal degrees. The undergraduate student-faculty ratio is 10:1. The library holds 218,881 titles and 1,576 serial subscriptions. Special programs include services for learning-disabled students, an honors program, study abroad, advanced placement credit, accelerated degree programs, ESL programs, double majors, independent study, self-designed majors, summer session for credit, part-time degree programs (daytime, evenings, summer), internships, and arrangement for off-campus study with University of Iowa, Mount Mercy College, Associated Colleges of the Midwest, Washington University in St. Louis. The most frequently chosen baccalaureate fields are business/marketing, psychology, social sciences.

Student Body Statistics The student body totals 1,300, of whom 1,275 are undergraduates (276 freshmen). 54 percent are women and 46 percent are men. Students come from 43 states and territories and 18 other countries. 64 percent are from Iowa. 4.4 percent are international students. 26 percent of the 2006 graduating class went on to graduate and professional schools.

Expenses for 2007–08 *Application fee:* $30. *Comprehensive fee:* $32,990 includes full-time tuition ($26,100), mandatory fees ($290), and college room and board ($6600). *College room only:* $2990. *Part-time tuition:* $3300 per course.

Financial Aid Forms of aid include need-based and non-need-based scholarships and part-time jobs. The average aided 2006–07 undergraduate received an aid package worth an estimated $21,859. The priority application deadline for financial aid is March 1.

Freshman Admission Coe College requires an essay, a high school transcript, 1 recommendation, SAT or ACT scores, and TOEFL scores for international students. A minimum 3.0 high school GPA and an interview are recommended. The application deadline for regular admission is March 1 and for early action it is December 10.

Transfer Admission The application deadline for admission is rolling.

Entrance Difficulty Coe College assesses its entrance difficulty level as moderately difficult. For the fall 2006 freshman class, 68 percent of the applicants were accepted.

For Further Information Contact Mr. John Grundig, Dean of Admission, Coe College, 1220 1st Avenue, NE, Cedar Rapids, IA 52402-5070. *Telephone:* 319-399-8500 or 877-225-5263 (toll-free). *Fax:* 319-399-8816. *E-mail:* admission@coe.edu. *Web site:* http://www.coe.edu/.

CORNELL COLLEGE
Mount Vernon, Iowa

Cornell College is a coed, private, Methodist, four-year college, founded in 1853, offering degrees at the bachelor's level. It has a 129-acre campus in Mount Vernon.

Academic Information The faculty has 100 members (86% full-time), 86% with terminal degrees. The student-faculty ratio is 11:1. The library holds 194,131 titles, 490 serial subscriptions, and 3,559 audiovisual materials. Special programs include services for learning-disabled students, study abroad, advanced placement credit, ESL programs, double majors, independent study, self-designed majors, internships, and arrangement for off-campus study with Associated Colleges of the Midwest, Fisk University,

Cornell College (continued)

School for International Training. The most frequently chosen baccalaureate fields are education, psychology, social sciences.

Student Body Statistics The student body is made up of 1,121 undergraduates (248 freshmen). 53 percent are women and 47 percent are men. Students come from 47 states and territories and 21 other countries. 31 percent are from Iowa. 3 percent are international students.

Expenses for 2006–07 *Application fee:* $30. *Comprehensive fee:* $31,460 includes full-time tuition ($24,620), mandatory fees ($180), and college room and board ($6660). *College room only:* $3100. Full-time tuition and fees vary according to reciprocity agreements. Room and board charges vary according to board plan. *Part-time tuition:* $769 per credit hour. *Part-time mandatory fees:* $180 per year. Part-time tuition and fees vary according to course load.

Financial Aid Forms of aid include need-based and non-need-based scholarships and part-time jobs. The average aided 2006–07 undergraduate received an aid package worth an estimated $21,500. The application deadline for financial aid is March 1.

Freshman Admission Cornell College requires an essay, a high school transcript, 1 recommendation, SAT or ACT scores, and TOEFL scores for international students. A minimum 2.80 high school GPA, an interview, and SAT Subject Test scores are recommended. The application deadline for regular admission is March 1; for early decision it is November 1; and for early action it is December 1.

Transfer Admission The application deadline for admission is March 1.

Entrance Difficulty Cornell College assesses its entrance difficulty level as moderately difficult. For the fall 2006 freshman class, 62 percent of the applicants were accepted.

For Further Information Contact Todd White, Director of Admissions, Cornell College, 600 First Street West, Mount Vernon, IA 52314-1098. *Telephone:* 319-895-4167 or 800-747-1112 (toll-free). *Fax:* 319-895-4451. *E-mail:* twhite@cornellcollege.edu. *Web site:* http://www.cornellcollege.edu/.

DIVINE WORD COLLEGE

Epworth, Iowa

http://www.dwci.edu/

DORDT COLLEGE

Sioux Center, Iowa

Dordt College is a coed, private, Christian Reformed, comprehensive institution, founded in 1955, offering degrees at the associate, bachelor's, and master's levels. It has a 100-acre campus in Sioux Center.

Academic Information The faculty has 98 members (71% full-time), 77% with terminal degrees. The undergraduate student-faculty ratio is 14:1. The library holds 160,000 titles and 6,597 serial subscriptions. Special programs include academic remediation, services for learning-disabled students, an honors program, study abroad, advanced placement credit, ESL programs, double majors, independent study, distance learning, self-designed majors, part-time degree programs (daytime, evenings), internships, and arrangement for off-campus study with Christian College Coalition, Chicago Metro Program, American Studies Program, Los Angeles Film Studies Program. The most frequently chosen baccalaureate fields are business/marketing, education, English.

Student Body Statistics The student body totals 1,261, of whom 1,259 are undergraduates (337 freshmen). 53 percent are women and 47 percent are men. Students come from 38 states and territories and 14 other countries. 38 percent are from Iowa. 15.3 percent are international students. 15 percent of the 2006 graduating class went on to graduate and professional schools.

Expenses for 2006–07 *Application fee:* $25. *Comprehensive fee:* $23,820 includes full-time tuition ($18,400), mandatory fees ($260), and college room and board ($5160). *College room only:* $2720. Full-time tuition and fees vary according to course load. Room and board charges vary according to board plan and housing facility. *Part-time tuition:* $770 per credit hour. *Part-time mandatory fees:* $120 per term.

Financial Aid Forms of aid include need-based and non-need-based scholarships, athletic grants, and part-time jobs. The average aided

2006–07 undergraduate received an aid package worth an estimated $16,350. The priority application deadline for financial aid is April 1.

Freshman Admission Dordt College requires a high school transcript, a minimum 2.25 high school GPA, minimum ACT composite score of 19 or SAT Reasoning score of 920, SAT or ACT scores, and TOEFL scores for international students. An essay and an interview are required for some.

Transfer Admission The application deadline for admission is August 1.

Entrance Difficulty Dordt College assesses its entrance difficulty level as moderately difficult. For the fall 2006 freshman class, 89 percent of the applicants were accepted.

For Further Information Contact Mr. Quentin Van Essen, Executive Director of Admissions, Dordt College, 498 4th Avenue, NE, Sioux Center, IA 51250-1697. *Telephone:* 712-722-6080 or 800-343-6738 (toll-free). *Fax:* 712-722-1967. *E-mail:* admissions@dordt.edu. *Web site:* http://www.dordt.edu/.

DRAKE UNIVERSITY

Des Moines, Iowa

Drake University is a coed, private university, founded in 1881, offering degrees at the bachelor's, master's, doctoral, and first professional levels and post-master's certificates. It has a 120-acre campus in Des Moines.

Academic Information The faculty has 391 members (63% full-time). The undergraduate student-faculty ratio is 14:1. The library holds 511,168 titles, 31,500 serial subscriptions, and 2,163 audiovisual materials. Special programs include services for learning-disabled students, an honors program, cooperative (work-study) education, study abroad, advanced placement credit, accelerated degree programs, ESL programs, double majors, independent study, distance learning, self-designed majors, summer session for credit, internships, and arrangement for off-campus study with Des Moines Consortium. The most frequently chosen baccalaureate fields are business/marketing, communications/journalism, social sciences.

Student Body Statistics The student body totals 5,366, of whom 3,255 are undergraduates (781 freshmen). 56 percent are women and 44 percent are men. 39 percent are from Iowa. 6.1 percent are international students. 25 percent of the 2006 graduating class went on to graduate and professional schools.

Expenses for 2006–07 *Application fee:* $25. *Comprehensive fee:* $29,182 includes full-time tuition ($22,270), mandatory fees ($412), and college room and board ($6500). *College room only:* $3190. Full-time tuition and fees vary according to class time, course load, and student level. Room and board charges vary according to board plan. *Part-time tuition:* $430 per hour. *Part-time mandatory fees:* $40 per semester hour. Part-time tuition and fees vary according to class time.

Financial Aid Forms of aid include need-based and non-need-based scholarships, athletic grants, and part-time jobs. The average aided 2006–07 undergraduate received an aid package worth an estimated $18,450. The priority application deadline for financial aid is March 1.

Freshman Admission Drake University requires a high school transcript, SAT or ACT scores, TOEFL scores for international students, and PCAT for pharmacy transfers. An essay and an interview are recommended. The application deadline for regular admission is March 1.

Transfer Admission The application deadline for admission is rolling.

Entrance Difficulty Drake University assesses its entrance difficulty level as moderately difficult; most difficult for transfer students to the College of Pharmacy. For the fall 2006 freshman class, 80 percent of the applicants were accepted.

For Further Information Contact Ms. Laura Linn, Director of Admission, Drake University, 2507 University Avenue, Des Moines, IA 50311. *Telephone:* 515-271-3181 Ext. 3182 or 800-44DRAKE Ext. 3181 (toll-free). *Fax:* 515-271-2831. *E-mail:* admission@drake.edu. *Web site:* http://www.drake.edu/.

EMMAUS BIBLE COLLEGE

Dubuque, Iowa

http://www.emmaus.edu/

FAITH BAPTIST BIBLE COLLEGE AND THEOLOGICAL SEMINARY

Ankeny, Iowa

Faith Baptist Bible College and Theological Seminary is a coed, private, comprehensive institution, founded in 1921, affiliated with the General Association of Regular Baptist Churches, offering degrees at the associate, bachelor's, master's, and first professional levels. It has a 52-acre campus in Ankeny.

Academic Information The faculty has 27 members (63% full-time), 52% with terminal degrees. The undergraduate student-faculty ratio is 10:1. The library holds 63,840 titles, 395 serial subscriptions, and 6,563 audiovisual materials. Special programs include academic remediation, advanced placement credit, double majors, independent study, summer session for credit, part-time degree programs (daytime, summer), adult/continuing education programs, and internships. The most frequently chosen baccalaureate fields are education, theology and religious vocations, visual and performing arts.
Student Body Statistics The student body totals 404, of whom 319 are undergraduates (87 freshmen). 50 percent are women and 50 percent are men. Students come from 26 states and territories and 8 other countries. 55 percent are from Iowa. 0.3 percent are international students. 29 percent of the 2006 graduating class went on to graduate and professional schools.
Expenses for 2006–07 *Application fee:* $25. *Comprehensive fee:* $16,970 includes full-time tuition ($11,776), mandatory fees ($400), and college room and board ($4794). *College room only:* $2190. Full-time tuition and fees vary according to course load. Room and board charges vary according to board plan. *Part-time tuition:* $430 per semester hour. *Part-time mandatory fees:* $95 per term.
Financial Aid Forms of aid include need-based and non-need-based scholarships. The priority application deadline for financial aid is March 1.
Freshman Admission Faith Baptist Bible College and Theological Seminary requires an essay, a high school transcript, 2 recommendations, SAT or ACT scores, and TOEFL scores for international students. A minimum 2.0 high school GPA is recommended. An interview is required for some. The application deadline for regular admission is August 1.
Transfer Admission The application deadline for admission is August 1.
Entrance Difficulty Faith Baptist Bible College and Theological Seminary assesses its entrance difficulty level as minimally difficult; moderately difficult for International Students. For the fall 2006 freshman class, 81 percent of the applicants were accepted.
For Further Information Contact Mrs. Lindsey Messmer, Admissions Secretary, Faith Baptist Bible College and Theological Seminary, 1900 NW 4th Street, Ankeny, IA 50023. *Telephone:* 515-964-0601 or 888-FAITH 4U (toll-free). *Fax:* 515-964-1638. *E-mail:* admissions@faith.edu. *Web site:* http://www.faith.edu/.

GRACELAND UNIVERSITY

Lamoni, Iowa

Graceland University is a coed, private, Community of Christ, comprehensive institution, founded in 1895, offering degrees at the bachelor's and master's levels and post-master's certificates. It has a 169-acre campus in Lamoni near Des Moines.

Academic Information The faculty has 111 members (83% full-time), 51% with terminal degrees. The undergraduate student-faculty ratio is 15:1. The library holds 193,172 titles, 780 serial subscriptions, and 3,428 audiovisual materials. Special programs include academic remediation, services for learning-disabled students, an honors program, cooperative (work-study) education, study abroad, advanced placement credit, accelerated degree programs, ESL programs, double majors, independent study, distance learning, self-designed majors, summer session for credit, part-time degree programs (daytime), external degree programs, adult/continuing education programs, internships, and arrangement for off-campus study with Indian Hills Community College, North Central Missouri College.
Student Body Statistics The student body totals 2,116, of whom 1,820 are undergraduates (250 freshmen). 62 percent are women and 38 percent

are men. Students come from 43 states and territories and 40 other countries. 39 percent are from Iowa. 9.5 percent are international students.
Expenses for 2007–08 *Application fee:* $50. *Comprehensive fee:* $23,900 includes full-time tuition ($17,700), mandatory fees ($200), and college room and board ($6000). *College room only:* $2400. *Part-time tuition:* $560 per semester hour.
Financial Aid Forms of aid include need-based and non-need-based scholarships, athletic grants, and part-time jobs. The average aided 2006–07 undergraduate received an aid package worth an estimated $15,976. The application deadline for financial aid is continuous.
Freshman Admission Graceland University requires a high school transcript, a minimum 2.5 high school GPA, minimum SAT score of 960 or ACT score of 21, SAT or ACT scores, and TOEFL scores for international students. An essay, 2 recommendations, and an interview are required for some. The application deadline for regular admission is rolling.
Transfer Admission The application deadline for admission is rolling.
Entrance Difficulty Graceland University assesses its entrance difficulty level as moderately difficult. For the fall 2006 freshman class, 55 percent of the applicants were accepted.
For Further Information Contact Mr. Greg Sutherland, Interim Vice President for Enrollment, and Dean of Admission, Graceland University, 1 University Place, Lamoni, IA 50140. *Telephone:* 641-784-5110 or 866-GRACELAND (toll-free). *Fax:* 641-784-5480. *E-mail:* sutherla@graceland.edu. *Web site:* http://www.graceland.edu/.

See page 250 for the College Close-Up.

GRAND VIEW COLLEGE

Des Moines, Iowa

Grand View College is a coed, private, four-year college, founded in 1896, affiliated with the Evangelical Lutheran Church in America, offering degrees at the associate and bachelor's levels and postbachelor's certificates. It has a 25-acre campus in Des Moines.

Academic Information The faculty has 174 members (51% full-time), 44% with terminal degrees. The student-faculty ratio is 13:1. The library holds 106,432 titles, 13,068 serial subscriptions, and 4,686 audiovisual materials. Special programs include academic remediation, services for learning-disabled students, an honors program, cooperative (work-study) education, study abroad, advanced placement credit, accelerated degree programs, Freshman Honors College, double majors, independent study, distance learning, self-designed majors, summer session for credit, part-time degree programs (daytime, evenings, weekends, summer), adult/continuing education programs, internships, and arrangement for off-campus study with Drake University, Des Moines Area Community College. The most frequently chosen baccalaureate fields are business/marketing, health professions and related sciences, liberal arts/general studies.
Student Body Statistics The student body is made up of 1,707 undergraduates (200 freshmen). 68 percent are women and 32 percent are men. Students come from 32 states and territories and 8 other countries. 94 percent are from Iowa. 1 percent are international students.
Expenses for 2006–07 *Application fee:* $35. *Comprehensive fee:* $22,536 includes full-time tuition ($16,570), mandatory fees ($370), and college room and board ($5596). Full-time tuition and fees vary according to class time. Room and board charges vary according to board plan and housing facility. *Part-time tuition:* $450 per hour. Part-time tuition varies according to class time.
Financial Aid Forms of aid include need-based and non-need-based scholarships, athletic grants, and part-time jobs. The average aided 2005–06 undergraduate received an aid package worth $11,398. The priority application deadline for financial aid is March 1.
Freshman Admission Grand View College requires a high school transcript, SAT or ACT scores, and TOEFL scores for international students. A minimum 2.0 high school GPA is recommended. The application deadline for regular admission is August 15.
Transfer Admission The application deadline for admission is August 15.

Grand View College (continued)

Entrance Difficulty Grand View College assesses its entrance difficulty level as minimally difficult; very difficult for honors program. For the fall 2006 freshman class, 99 percent of the applicants were accepted.

For Further Information Contact Ms. Diane Schaefer, Director of Admissions, Grand View College, 1200 Grandview Avenue, Des Moines, IA 50316-1599. *Telephone:* 515-263-2810 or 800-444-6083 Ext. 2810 (toll-free). *Fax:* 515-263-2974. *E-mail:* admissions@gvc.edu. *Web site:* http://www.gvc.edu/.

GRINNELL COLLEGE
Grinnell, Iowa

Grinnell College is a coed, private, four-year college, founded in 1846, offering degrees at the bachelor's level. It has a 120-acre campus in Grinnell.

Academic Information The faculty has 201 members (81% full-time), 86% with terminal degrees. The student-faculty ratio is 8:1. The library holds 1 million titles, 20,186 serial subscriptions, and 31,183 audiovisual materials. Special programs include services for learning-disabled students, study abroad, advanced placement credit, accelerated degree programs, double majors, independent study, self-designed majors, internships, and arrangement for off-campus study. The most frequently chosen baccalaureate fields are foreign languages and literature, biological/life sciences, social sciences.

Student Body Statistics The student body is made up of 1,589 undergraduates (405 freshmen). 54 percent are women and 46 percent are men. Students come from 48 states and territories and 46 other countries. 22 percent are from Iowa. 10.1 percent are international students. 30 percent of the 2006 graduating class went on to graduate and professional schools.

Expenses for 2006–07 *Application fee:* $30. *Comprehensive fee:* $36,730 includes full-time tuition ($28,566), mandatory fees ($464), and college room and board ($7700). *College room only:* $3600. Room and board charges vary according to board plan and housing facility. *Part-time tuition:* $893 per credit hour.

Financial Aid Forms of aid include need-based and non-need-based scholarships and part-time jobs. The average aided 2006–07 undergraduate received an aid package worth an estimated $25,972. The application deadline for financial aid is February 1.

Freshman Admission Grinnell College requires an essay, a high school transcript, 3 recommendations, SAT or ACT scores, and TOEFL scores for international students. An interview is recommended. The application deadline for regular admission is January 20 and for early decision it is November 20.

Transfer Admission The application deadline for admission is May 1.

Entrance Difficulty Grinnell College assesses its entrance difficulty level as very difficult. For the fall 2006 freshman class, 45 percent of the applicants were accepted.

For Further Information Contact Mr. James Sumner, Dean for Admission and Financial Aid, Grinnell College, 1103 Park Street, Grinnell, IA 50112. *Telephone:* 641-269-3600 or 800-247-0113 (toll-free). *Fax:* 641-269-4800. *E-mail:* askgrin@grinnell.edu. *Web site:* http://www.grinnell.edu/.

HAMILTON COLLEGE
Cedar Falls, Iowa

Hamilton College is a coed, proprietary, primarily two-year college, founded in 2000, offering degrees at the associate and bachelor's levels.

Expenses for 2006–07 *Application fee:* $20. Contact school as costs vary with program selected. Tuition includes books.

For Further Information Contact Ms. Jill Lines, Director of Admissions, Hamilton College, 7009 Nordic Drive, Cedar Falls, IA 50613. *Telephone:* 319-277-0220 or 800-728-1220 (toll-free out-of-state). *Fax:* 319-268-0978. *E-mail:* jilines@hamiltoncf.com. *Web site:* http://www.hamiltoncf.com/.

HAMILTON COLLEGE
Cedar Rapids, Iowa

Hamilton College is a coed, proprietary, primarily two-year college, founded in 1900, offering degrees at the associate and bachelor's levels (branch locations in Des Moines, Mason City, and Cedar Falls with significant enrollment not reflected in profile). It has a 4-acre campus in Cedar Rapids.

Expenses for 2006–07 *Application fee:* $50. *Tuition:* $17,040 full-time, $355 per credit hour part-time.

For Further Information Contact Ms. Niki Donahue, Director of Admissions, Hamilton College, 3165 Edgewood Parkway SW, Cedar Rapids, IA 52404. *Telephone:* 319-363-0481 or 800-728-0481 (toll-free out-of-state). *Fax:* 319-363-3812. *Web site:* http://www.hamiltonia.edu/.

HAMILTON TECHNICAL COLLEGE
Davenport, Iowa

http://www.hamiltontechcollege.com/

IOWA STATE UNIVERSITY OF SCIENCE AND TECHNOLOGY
Ames, Iowa

Iowa State University of Science and Technology is a coed, public university, founded in 1858, offering degrees at the bachelor's, master's, doctoral, and first professional levels and post-master's certificates. It has a 1,788-acre campus in Ames.

Academic Information The faculty has 1,622 members (85% full-time), 88% with terminal degrees. The undergraduate student-faculty ratio is 15:1. The library holds 2 million titles and 52,533 serial subscriptions. Special programs include academic remediation, services for learning-disabled students, an honors program, cooperative (work-study) education, study abroad, advanced placement credit, accelerated degree programs, Freshman Honors College, ESL programs, double majors, independent study, distance learning, self-designed majors, summer session for credit, part-time degree programs (daytime, evenings, weekends, summer), external degree programs, adult/continuing education programs, internships, and arrangement for off-campus study with Iowa Regents' Universities Student Exchange, National Student Exchange. The most frequently chosen baccalaureate fields are business/marketing, agriculture, engineering.

Student Body Statistics The student body totals 25,462, of whom 20,440 are undergraduates (3,987 freshmen). 44 percent are women and 56 percent are men. Students come from 57 states and territories and 104 other countries. 74 percent are from Iowa. 3.1 percent are international students. 19 percent of the 2006 graduating class went on to graduate and professional schools.

Expenses for 2007–08 *Application fee:* $30. *State resident tuition:* $5352 full-time, $223 per semester hour part-time. *Nonresident tuition:* $16,110 full-time, $672 per semester hour part-time. *Mandatory fees:* $809 full-time.

Financial Aid Forms of aid include need-based and non-need-based scholarships, athletic grants, and part-time jobs. The priority application deadline for financial aid is March 1.

Freshman Admission Iowa State University of Science and Technology requires a high school transcript, rank in upper 50% of high school class, and SAT or ACT scores. TOEFL scores for international students are recommended. The application deadline for regular admission is July 1.

Transfer Admission The application deadline for admission is July 1.

Entrance Difficulty Iowa State University of Science and Technology assesses its entrance difficulty level as moderately difficult. For the fall 2006 freshman class, 90 percent of the applicants were accepted.

For Further Information Contact Mr. Phil Caffrey, Associate Director for Freshman Admissions, Iowa State University of Science and Technology, 100 Alumni Hall, Ames, IA 50011-2010. *Telephone:* 515-294-5836 or 800-262-3810 (toll-free). *Fax:* 515-294-2592. *E-mail:* admissions@iastate.edu. *Web site:* http://www.iastate.edu/.

IOWA WESLEYAN COLLEGE
Mount Pleasant, Iowa

Iowa Wesleyan College is a coed, private, United Methodist, four-year college, founded in 1842, offering degrees at the bachelor's level. It has a 60-acre campus in Mount Pleasant.

Academic Information The faculty has 94 members (57% full-time). The student-faculty ratio is 14:1. The library holds 107,227 titles and 431 serial subscriptions. Special programs include academic remediation, services for learning-disabled students, study abroad, advanced placement credit, ESL programs, double majors, independent study, distance learning, self-designed majors, summer session for credit, part-time degree programs (daytime, evenings, summer), adult/continuing education programs, internships, and arrangement for off-campus study with Southeastern Community College, Muscatine Community College.
Student Body Statistics The student body is made up of 849 undergraduates (118 freshmen). 58 percent are women and 42 percent are men. Students come from 22 states and territories and 14 other countries. 54 percent are from Iowa. 6 percent are international students. 2 percent of the 2006 graduating class went on to graduate and professional schools.
Expenses for 2007–08 *Application fee:* $0. *Comprehensive fee:* $24,750 includes full-time tuition ($18,870) and college room and board ($5880). *College room only:* $2430. *Part-time tuition:* $465 per credit hour.
Financial Aid Forms of aid include need-based and non-need-based scholarships, athletic grants, and part-time jobs. The average aided 2006–07 undergraduate received an aid package worth an estimated $12,513. The priority application deadline for financial aid is April 1.
Freshman Admission Iowa Wesleyan College requires a high school transcript, a minimum 2.0 high school GPA, SAT or ACT scores, and TOEFL scores for international students. An interview is recommended. An essay, 2 recommendations, and an interview are required for some. The application deadline for regular admission is August 15.
Transfer Admission The application deadline for admission is August 15.
Entrance Difficulty Iowa Wesleyan College assesses its entrance difficulty level as moderately difficult. For the fall 2006 freshman class, 64 percent of the applicants were accepted.
For Further Information Contact Mr. Mark T. Petty, Dean of Admissions, Iowa Wesleyan College, 601 North Main Street, Mount Pleasant, IA 52641-1398. *Telephone:* 319-385-6230 or 800-582-2383 Ext. 6231 (toll-free). *Fax:* 319-385-6240. *E-mail:* mpetty@iwc.edu. *Web site:* http://www.iwc.edu/.

KAPLAN UNIVERSITY
Davenport, Iowa

Kaplan University is a coed, proprietary, primarily two-year college of Kaplan Higher Education, founded in 1937, offering degrees at the associate and bachelor's levels (profile includes both traditional and on-line students).

Academic Information The faculty has 1,692 members (6% full-time), 6% with terminal degrees. The student-faculty ratio is 11:1. The library holds 7,000 titles and 120 serial subscriptions. Special programs include academic remediation, cooperative (work-study) education, double majors, independent study, distance learning, summer session for credit, part-time degree programs (daytime, evenings), adult/continuing education programs, and internships.
Student Body Statistics The student body totals 23,369, of whom 22,529 are undergraduates (4,211 freshmen). 74 percent are women and 26 percent are men. Students come from 54 states and territories. 4 percent are from Iowa.
Expenses for 2007–08 *Application fee:* $25. *Tuition:* $13,680 full-time, $380 per credit hour part-time.
Financial Aid Forms of aid include need-based scholarships and part-time jobs. The application deadline for financial aid is continuous.
Freshman Admission Kaplan University requires a high school transcript, an interview, and TOEFL scores for international students. The application deadline for regular admission is rolling.
Transfer Admission The application deadline for admission is rolling.

Entrance Difficulty Kaplan University assesses its entrance difficulty level as minimally difficult. For the fall 2006 freshman class, 87 percent of the applicants were accepted.
For Further Information Contact Ms. Carla Batchelor, Director of Admissions, Kaplan University, 1801 East Kimberly Road, Suite 1, Davenport, IA 52807. *Telephone:* 563-441-2496 or 800-747-1035 (toll-free in-state). *Fax:* 563-355-1320. *E-mail:* cbatchelor@kucampus.edu. *Web site:* http://www.kaplancollegeia.com/.

LORAS COLLEGE
Dubuque, Iowa

Loras College is a coed, private, Roman Catholic, comprehensive institution, founded in 1839, offering degrees at the associate, bachelor's, and master's levels. It has a 60-acre campus in Dubuque.

Academic Information The faculty has 162 members (72% full-time). The undergraduate student-faculty ratio is 12:1. The library holds 351,550 titles and 554 serial subscriptions. Special programs include academic remediation, services for learning-disabled students, an honors program, cooperative (work-study) education, study abroad, advanced placement credit, ESL programs, double majors, independent study, self-designed majors, summer session for credit, part-time degree programs (daytime, evenings, summer), adult/continuing education programs, internships, and arrangement for off-campus study. The most frequently chosen baccalaureate fields are business/marketing, education, security and protective services.
Student Body Statistics The student body totals 1,673, of whom 1,591 are undergraduates (403 freshmen). 48 percent are women and 52 percent are men. Students come from 23 states and territories and 9 other countries. 56 percent are from Iowa. 2.3 percent are international students. 16 percent of the 2006 graduating class went on to graduate and professional schools.
Expenses for 2006–07 *Application fee:* $25. *Comprehensive fee:* $28,358 includes full-time tuition ($20,890), mandatory fees ($1163), and college room and board ($6305). *College room only:* $3220. Full-time tuition and fees vary according to course load and degree level. Room and board charges vary according to board plan and housing facility. *Part-time tuition:* $425 per credit.
Financial Aid Forms of aid include need-based and non-need-based scholarships and part-time jobs. The average aided 2006–07 undergraduate received an aid package worth an estimated $19,655. The priority application deadline for financial aid is April 15.
Freshman Admission Loras College requires a high school transcript, a minimum 2.5 high school GPA, SAT or ACT scores, and TOEFL scores for international students. An essay and 1 recommendation are recommended. An interview is required for some. The application deadline for regular admission is rolling.
Transfer Admission The application deadline for admission is rolling.
Entrance Difficulty Loras College assesses its entrance difficulty level as moderately difficult. For the fall 2006 freshman class, 81 percent of the applicants were accepted.
For Further Information Contact Ms. Sharon Lyons, Director of Admissions, Loras College, 1450 Alta Vista, Dubuque, IA 52004-0178. *Telephone:* 563-588-7829 or 800-245-6727 (toll-free). *Fax:* 563-588-7119. *E-mail:* adms@loras.edu. *Web site:* http://www.loras.edu/.

LUTHER COLLEGE
Decorah, Iowa

Luther College is a coed, private, four-year college, founded in 1861, affiliated with the Evangelical Lutheran Church in America, offering degrees at the bachelor's level. It has a 200-acre campus in Decorah.

Academic Information The faculty has 246 members (74% full-time), 72% with terminal degrees. The student-faculty ratio is 12:1. The library holds 334,814 titles, 831 serial subscriptions, and 1,866 audiovisual materials. Special programs include academic remediation, services for learning-disabled students, an honors program, study abroad, advanced placement credit, double majors, independent study, self-designed majors,

Luther College (continued)

summer session for credit, part-time degree programs, internships, and arrangement for off-campus study. The most frequently chosen baccalaureate fields are business/marketing, biological/life sciences, visual and performing arts.

Student Body Statistics The student body is made up of 2,504 undergraduates (612 freshmen). 59 percent are women and 41 percent are men. Students come from 39 states and territories and 33 other countries. 34 percent are from Iowa. 3 percent are international students. 23 percent of the 2006 graduating class went on to graduate and professional schools.

Expenses for 2006–07 *Application fee:* $25. *Comprehensive fee:* $30,670 includes full-time tuition ($26,380) and college room and board ($4290). *College room only:* $2100. Full-time tuition varies according to course load. Room and board charges vary according to board plan and housing facility. *Part-time tuition:* $924 per semester hour. Part-time tuition varies according to course load.

Financial Aid Forms of aid include need-based and non-need-based scholarships and part-time jobs. The average aided 2006–07 undergraduate received an aid package worth an estimated $20,916. The priority application deadline for financial aid is March 1.

Freshman Admission Luther College requires an essay, a high school transcript, 1 recommendation, SAT or ACT scores, and TOEFL scores for international students. An interview is recommended.

Entrance Difficulty Luther College assesses its entrance difficulty level as moderately difficult. For the fall 2006 freshman class, 81 percent of the applicants were accepted.

For Further Information Contact Kirk Neubauer, Director of Recruiting Services, Luther College, 700 College Drive, Decorah, IA 52101. *Telephone:* 563-387-1287 or 800-458-8437 (toll-free). *Fax:* 563-387-2159. *E-mail:* admissions@luther.edu. *Web site:* http://www.luther.edu/.

MAHARISHI UNIVERSITY OF MANAGEMENT

Fairfield, Iowa

Maharishi University of Management is a coed, private university, founded in 1971, offering degrees at the bachelor's, master's, and doctoral levels and postbachelor's certificates. It has a 272-acre campus in Fairfield.

Academic Information The faculty has 57 members (82% full-time). The undergraduate student-faculty ratio is 16:1. The library holds 137,775 titles and 11,146 serial subscriptions. Special programs include academic remediation, services for learning-disabled students, an honors program, cooperative (work-study) education, study abroad, advanced placement credit, double majors, independent study, distance learning, self-designed majors, adult/continuing education programs, and internships. The most frequently chosen baccalaureate fields are biological/life sciences, business/marketing, visual and performing arts.

Student Body Statistics The student body totals 931, of whom 284 are undergraduates (32 freshmen). 51 percent are women and 49 percent are men. Students come from 32 states and territories and 16 other countries. 56 percent are from Iowa. 42.1 percent are international students.

Expenses for 2006–07 *Application fee:* $15. *Comprehensive fee:* $30,430 includes full-time tuition ($24,000), mandatory fees ($430), and college room and board ($6000). *Part-time tuition:* $350 per credit hour.

Financial Aid Forms of aid include need-based and non-need-based scholarships and part-time jobs. The average aided 2006–07 undergraduate received an aid package worth an estimated $23,963. The application deadline for financial aid is continuous.

Freshman Admission Maharishi University of Management requires an essay, a high school transcript, a minimum 2.5 high school GPA, 2 recommendations, minimum SAT score of 950 or ACT score of 19, and TOEFL scores for international students. An interview and SAT or ACT scores are recommended. The application deadline for regular admission is August 1.

Transfer Admission The application deadline for admission is August 1.

Entrance Difficulty Maharishi University of Management assesses its entrance difficulty level as moderately difficult. For the fall 2006 freshman class, 43 percent of the applicants were accepted.

For Further Information Contact Barbara Rainbow, Associate Dean of Admissions, Maharishi University of Management, Office of Admissions, Fairfield, IA 52557. *Telephone:* 641-472-1110 or 800-369-6480 (toll-free). *Fax:* 641-472-1179. *E-mail:* admissions@mum.edu. *Web site:* http://www.mum.edu/.

MERCY COLLEGE OF HEALTH SCIENCES

Des Moines, Iowa

Mercy College of Health Sciences is a coed, primarily women's, private, four-year college, founded in 1995, affiliated with the Roman Catholic Church, offering degrees at the associate and bachelor's levels. It has a 5-acre campus in Des Moines.

Academic Information The faculty has 66 members (52% full-time), 14% with terminal degrees. The student-faculty ratio is 11:1. The library holds 17,919 titles, 4,698 serial subscriptions, and 1,150 audiovisual materials. Special programs include academic remediation, services for learning-disabled students, advanced placement credit, accelerated degree programs, summer session for credit, and part-time degree programs.

Student Body Statistics The student body is made up of 655 undergraduates (48 freshmen). 92 percent are women and 8 percent are men.

Expenses for 2007–08 *Application fee:* $25. *Tuition:* $6300 full-time, $425 per credit hour part-time.

Financial Aid Forms of aid include need-based and non-need-based scholarships and part-time jobs. The application deadline for financial aid is July 1.

Freshman Admission Mercy College of Health Sciences requires a high school transcript, a minimum 2.25 high school GPA, and TOEFL scores for international students. An interview and ACT scores are required for some. The application deadline for regular admission is rolling.

Entrance Difficulty Mercy College of Health Sciences has an open admission policy.

For Further Information Contact Susan Hill/Sandi Nagel, Admissions Representative, Mercy College of Health Sciences, 928 Sixth Avenue, Des Moines, IA 50309-1239. *Telephone:* 515-643-3180 or 800-637-2994 (toll-free). *Fax:* 515-643-6698. *E-mail:* shill@mercydesmoines.org or snagel@mercydesmoines.org. *Web site:* http://www.mchs.edu/.

MORNINGSIDE COLLEGE

Sioux City, Iowa

Morningside College is a coed, private, comprehensive institution, founded in 1894, affiliated with the United Methodist Church, offering degrees at the bachelor's and master's levels. It has a 68-acre campus in Sioux City.

Academic Information The faculty has 152 members (45% full-time), 34% with terminal degrees. The undergraduate student-faculty ratio is 17:1. The library holds 98,912 titles, 485 serial subscriptions, and 2,701 audiovisual materials. Special programs include academic remediation, services for learning-disabled students, an honors program, study abroad, advanced placement credit, ESL programs, double majors, independent study, self-designed majors, summer session for credit, part-time degree programs (daytime, evenings, summer), adult/continuing education programs, internships, and arrangement for off-campus study with American University, Drew University. The most frequently chosen baccalaureate fields are business/marketing, education, health professions and related sciences.

Student Body Statistics The student body totals 1,722, of whom 1,232 are undergraduates (332 freshmen). 54 percent are women and 46 percent are men. Students come from 22 states and territories and 7 other countries. 68 percent are from Iowa. 1.5 percent are international students. 12 percent of the 2006 graduating class went on to graduate and professional schools.

Expenses for 2006–07 *Application fee:* $25. *Comprehensive fee:* $26,129 includes full-time tuition ($18,932), mandatory fees ($970), and college room and board ($6227). *College room only:* $3213. Full-time tuition and fees vary according to program. Room and board charges vary according to housing facility. *Part-time tuition:* $580 per semester hour. Part-time tuition varies according to course load.

Financial Aid Forms of aid include need-based and non-need-based scholarships, athletic grants, and part-time jobs. The average aided 2005–06 undergraduate received an aid package worth $16,302. The priority application deadline for financial aid is March 1.

Freshman Admission Morningside College requires a high school transcript, minimum SAT score of 930 or ACT score of 20 and rank in top 50% of high school class or achieved GPA of 2.5 or better, SAT or ACT scores, and TOEFL scores for international students. An interview is recommended. 2 recommendations are required for some. The application deadline for regular admission is rolling.

Transfer Admission The application deadline for admission is rolling.

Entrance Difficulty Morningside College assesses its entrance difficulty level as moderately difficult. For the fall 2006 freshman class, 90 percent of the applicants were accepted.

For Further Information Contact Mr. Joel Weyand, Director of Admissions, Morningside College, 1501 Morningside Avenue, Sioux City, IA 51106. *Telephone:* 712-274-5111 or 800-831-0806 Ext. 5111 (toll-free). *Fax:* 712-274-5101. *E-mail:* mscadm@morningside.edu. *Web site:* http://www.morningside.edu/.

See page 270 for the College Close-Up.

MOUNT MERCY COLLEGE

Cedar Rapids, Iowa

SPONSOR
See Front Insert
for Details!

Mount Mercy College is a coed, private, Roman Catholic, four-year college, founded in 1928, offering degrees at the bachelor's level. It has a 40-acre campus in Cedar Rapids.

Academic Information The faculty has 153 members (48% full-time). The student-faculty ratio is 12:1. The library holds 125,000 titles, 10,900 serial subscriptions, and 5,437 audiovisual materials. Special programs include academic remediation, services for learning-disabled students, an honors program, study abroad, advanced placement credit, accelerated degree programs, double majors, independent study, summer session for credit, part-time degree programs (daytime, evenings, weekends, summer), adult/continuing education programs, internships, and arrangement for off-campus study with Coe College. The most frequently chosen baccalaureate fields are business/marketing, computer and information sciences, education.

Student Body Statistics The student body is made up of 1,482 undergraduates (181 freshmen). 73 percent are women and 27 percent are men. Students come from 20 states and territories and 6 other countries. 94 percent are from Iowa. 0.4 percent are international students. 10 percent of the 2006 graduating class went on to graduate and professional schools.

Expenses for 2006–07 *Application fee:* $20. *Comprehensive fee:* $24,900 includes full-time tuition ($18,930) and college room and board ($5970). Full-time tuition varies according to course load. Room and board charges vary according to board plan and housing facility. *Part-time tuition:* $525 per credit hour. Part-time tuition varies according to course load.

Financial Aid Forms of aid include need-based and non-need-based scholarships and part-time jobs. The average aided 2006–07 undergraduate received an aid package worth an estimated $15,214. The priority application deadline for financial aid is March 1.

Freshman Admission Mount Mercy College requires an essay, a high school transcript, a minimum 2.5 high school GPA, recommendations, SAT or ACT scores, and TOEFL scores for international students. A minimum 3.0 high school GPA is recommended. The application deadline for regular admission is August 15.

Transfer Admission The application deadline for admission is August 15.

Entrance Difficulty Mount Mercy College assesses its entrance difficulty level as moderately difficult. For the fall 2006 freshman class, 71 percent of the applicants were accepted.

SPECIAL MESSAGE TO STUDENTS

Social Life Shows on campus by musicians and comedians on weekend nights, regular "Club Friday" at Lundy Commons, and the activities of more than thirty clubs and organizations, plus an active student government and newspaper, spark the social life on the Mount Mercy campus. When students are in the mood to expand their entertainment horizons, they are also in the right place, just 2 miles in either direction from downtown or a major mall. With city bus stops at the edge of campus, students have easy access to everything the thriving Midwestern city of Cedar Rapids has to offer—a noted symphony, Theater Cedar Rapids, the Paramount Theater, the Cedar Rapids Museum of Art, minor league baseball and hockey, a downtown arena that hosts popular concerts and shows, and the Science Station with an IMAX theater.

Academic Highlights With high academic quality, moderate cost, and generous scholarships, Mount Mercy College offers outstanding educational value. At Mount Mercy students prepare themselves for life and work in the twenty-first century, with a unique blend of career preparation and liberal arts strengthened by a strong emphasis on leadership and service. The Freshman Partnership program helps first-time freshmen make a smooth transition to college life; the Honors Program offers accomplished students unique classes that encourage exploration beyond traditional academic boundaries; and the Academic Achievement Center provides academic counseling and assistance to all students. Classes are small and the faculty members are focused on teaching. At Mount Mercy College, an active learning environment helps students gain confidence in discussing their views and opinions—an environment that well prepares students for a job or graduate school.

Interviews and Campus Visits The best way to learn about the College is to visit, sit in on a class, meet with students and faculty members, and learn about scholarships and other forms of financial assistance. Mount Mercy welcomes students on special visit days throughout the year, and the staff members are happy to arrange individual weekday or weekend appointments. For more information about campus visits, students should either call the Mount Mercy College Office of Admission at 319-368-6460 or 800-248-4504 (toll-free) Monday through Thursday 8 to 5 (CST) and Friday 8 to 4:30 or e-mail the College at http://admission@mtmercy.edu. The nearest commercial airport is Eastern Iowa (Cedar Rapids).

For Further Information Write to Admission Office, Mount Mercy College, 1330 Elmhurst Drive, NE, Cedar Rapids, IA 52402. *E-mail:* admission@mtmercy.edu. *Web site:* http://www.mtmercy.edu.

See page 274 for the College Close-Up.

MOUNT ST. CLARE COLLEGE

See Ashford University.

NORTHWESTERN COLLEGE

Orange City, Iowa

Northwestern College is a coed, private, four-year college, founded in 1882, affiliated with the Reformed Church in America, offering degrees at the bachelor's level. It has a 45-acre campus in Orange City.

Academic Information The faculty has 130 members (59% full-time), 49% with terminal degrees. The student-faculty ratio is 15:1. The library holds 125,000 titles and 615 serial subscriptions. Special programs include academic remediation, services for learning-disabled students, an honors program, cooperative (work-study) education, study abroad, advanced placement credit, ESL programs, double majors, independent study, self-designed majors, summer session for credit, part-time degree programs, internships, and arrangement for off-campus study with 5

Northwestern College (continued)

members of the Mid-America States Universities Association, Council for Christian Colleges and Universities. The most frequently chosen baccalaureate fields are business/marketing, biological/life sciences, education.

Student Body Statistics The student body is made up of 1,342 undergraduates (363 freshmen). 61 percent are women and 39 percent are men. Students come from 31 states and territories and 22 other countries. 57 percent are from Iowa. 2.7 percent are international students. 22 percent of the 2006 graduating class went on to graduate and professional schools.

Expenses for 2006–07 *Application fee:* $25. *Comprehensive fee:* $23,506 includes full-time tuition ($18,296) and college room and board ($5210). *College room only:* $2386. Room and board charges vary according to housing facility. *Part-time tuition:* varies with course load.

Financial Aid Forms of aid include need-based and non-need-based scholarships, athletic grants, and part-time jobs. The average aided 2006–07 undergraduate received an aid package worth an estimated $15,040. The priority application deadline for financial aid is April 1.

Freshman Admission Northwestern College requires an essay, a high school transcript, a minimum 2.0 high school GPA, 1 recommendation, SAT or ACT scores, and TOEFL scores for international students. A minimum 2.5 high school GPA and an interview are recommended. The application deadline for regular admission is rolling.

Transfer Admission The application deadline for admission is rolling.

Entrance Difficulty Northwestern College assesses its entrance difficulty level as moderately difficult. For the fall 2006 freshman class, 85 percent of the applicants were accepted.

For Further Information Contact Mr. Mark Bloemendaal, Director of Admissions, Northwestern College, 101 7th Street SW, Orange City, IA 51041-1996. *Telephone:* 712-737-7130 or 800-747-4757 (toll-free). *Fax:* 712-707-7164. *E-mail:* admissions@nwciowa.edu. *Web site:* http://www.nwciowa.edu/.

PALMER COLLEGE OF CHIROPRACTIC

Davenport, Iowa

Palmer College of Chiropractic is a coed, private, comprehensive institution, founded in 1897, offering degrees at the associate, incidental bachelor's, master's, and first professional levels.

Academic Information The faculty has 136 members (100% full-time). The undergraduate student-faculty ratio is 16:1. The library holds 55,278 titles and 525 serial subscriptions. Special programs include academic remediation, services for learning-disabled students, summer session for credit, and internships.

Student Body Statistics The student body totals 1,505, of whom 92 are undergraduates (24 freshmen). 48 percent are women and 52 percent are men.

Expenses for 2006–07 *Application fee:* $50. *Tuition:* $6060 full-time, $152 per credit part-time. *Mandatory fees:* $356 full-time, $100 per term part-time.

Financial Aid Forms of aid include need-based and non-need-based scholarships and part-time jobs. The application deadline for financial aid is continuous.

Freshman Admission Palmer College of Chiropractic requires a high school transcript, a minimum 2.0 high school GPA, minimum 2.0 in math, science, and English courses, and TOEFL scores for international students. An essay and an interview are required for some. The application deadline for regular admission is rolling.

Entrance Difficulty Palmer College of Chiropractic assesses its entrance difficulty level as moderately difficult.

For Further Information Contact Ms. Karen Eden, Director of Admissions, Palmer College of Chiropractic, 1000 Brady Street, Davenport, IA 52803-5287. *Telephone:* 563-884-5656 or 800-722-3648 (toll-free). *Fax:* 563-884-5414. *E-mail:* pcadmit@palmer.edu. *Web site:* http://www.palmer.edu/.

QUEST COLLEGE

See Kaplan University.

ST. AMBROSE UNIVERSITY

Davenport, Iowa

St. Ambrose University is a coed, private, Roman Catholic, comprehensive institution, founded in 1882, offering degrees at the bachelor's, master's, and doctoral levels and post-master's and postbachelor's certificates. It has a 50-acre campus in Davenport.

Academic Information The faculty has 310 members (52% full-time), 41% with terminal degrees. The undergraduate student-faculty ratio is 12:1. The library holds 150,328 titles, 738 serial subscriptions, and 3,687 audiovisual materials. Special programs include academic remediation, services for learning-disabled students, cooperative (work-study) education, study abroad, advanced placement credit, accelerated degree programs, double majors, independent study, distance learning, self-designed majors, summer session for credit, part-time degree programs (daytime, evenings, weekends, summer), external degree programs, adult/continuing education programs, internships, and arrangement for off-campus study with Black Hawk College, Eastern Iowa Community Colleges. The most frequently chosen baccalaureate fields are business/marketing, education, psychology.

Student Body Statistics The student body totals 3,780, of whom 2,829 are undergraduates (510 freshmen). 62 percent are women and 38 percent are men. Students come from 28 states and territories and 13 other countries. 54 percent are from Iowa. 1.2 percent are international students. 25 percent of the 2006 graduating class went on to graduate and professional schools.

Expenses for 2007–08 *Application fee:* $25. *Tuition:* $640 per semester hour part-time.

Financial Aid Forms of aid include need-based and non-need-based scholarships, athletic grants, and part-time jobs. The average aided 2006–07 undergraduate received an aid package worth an estimated $17,638. The priority application deadline for financial aid is March 15.

Freshman Admission St. Ambrose University requires a high school transcript, a minimum 2.5 high school GPA, minimum ACT score of 20 or rank in top 50% of high school class, SAT or ACT scores, and TOEFL scores for international students. An interview and ACT scores are recommended. Recommendations and an interview are required for some. The application deadline for regular admission is rolling.

Transfer Admission The application deadline for admission is rolling.

Entrance Difficulty St. Ambrose University assesses its entrance difficulty level as moderately difficult. For the fall 2006 freshman class, 84 percent of the applicants were accepted.

For Further Information Contact Ms. Meg Halligan, Director of Admissions, St. Ambrose University, 518 West Locust Street, Davenport, IA 52803-2898. *Telephone:* 563-333-6300 Ext. 6311 or 800-383-2627 (toll-free). *Fax:* 563-333-6297. *E-mail:* halliganmegf@sau.edu. *Web site:* http://www.sau.edu/.

ST. LUKE'S COLLEGE

Sioux City, Iowa

St. Luke's College is a coed, private, two-year college of St. Luke's Regional Medical Center, founded in 1967, offering degrees at the associate level. It has a 3-acre campus in Sioux City.

Academic Information The faculty has 19 members (68% full-time), 26% with terminal degrees. The student-faculty ratio is 12:1. The library holds 2,713 titles, 108 serial subscriptions, and 45 audiovisual materials. Special programs include cooperative (work-study) education, advanced placement credit, summer session for credit, and part-time degree programs (daytime, evenings, summer).

Student Body Statistics The student body is made up of 179 undergraduates (7 freshmen). 91 percent are women and 9 percent are men. Students come from 10 states and territories. 73 percent are from Iowa. 65 percent of the 2006 graduating class went on to four-year colleges.

Expenses for 2007–08 *Application fee:* $25. *Tuition:* $12,852 full-time, $357 per credit part-time. *Mandatory fees:* $600 full-time.

Financial Aid Forms of aid include need-based scholarships and part-time jobs. The priority application deadline for financial aid is March 1.

Freshman Admission St. Luke's College requires an essay, a high school transcript, a minimum 2.50 high school GPA, an interview, minimum ACT score of 19, and ACT scores. The application deadline for regular admission is August 1.

Entrance Difficulty St. Luke's College assesses its entrance difficulty level as minimally difficult. For the fall 2006 freshman class, 54 percent of the applicants were accepted.

For Further Information Contact Ms. Sherry McCarthy, Admissions Coordinator, St. Luke's College, 2720 Stone Park Boulevard, Sioux City, IA 51104. *Telephone:* 712-279-3149 or 800-352-4660 Ext. 3149 (toll-free). *Fax:* 712-233-8017. *E-mail:* mccartsj@stlukes.org. *Web site:* http://stlukescollege.edu/.

SIMPSON COLLEGE

Indianola, Iowa

SPONSOR
See Front Insert
for Details!

Simpson College is a coed, private, United Methodist, four-year college, founded in 1860, offering degrees at the bachelor's level. It has a 75-acre campus in Indianola.

Academic Information The faculty has 181 members (49% full-time), 62% with terminal degrees. The student-faculty ratio is 14:1. The library holds 157,713 titles and 558 serial subscriptions. Special programs include services for learning-disabled students, an honors program, cooperative (work-study) education, study abroad, advanced placement credit, double majors, independent study, summer session for credit, part-time degree programs (daytime, evenings, weekends, summer), external degree programs, adult/continuing education programs, internships, and arrangement for off-campus study with Drew University, American University, Washington Center Internships and Symposia, George Washington Carver Teacher Initiative Consortium agreement with Iowa State University and Des Moines Area Community College. The most frequently chosen baccalaureate fields are business/marketing, education, social sciences.

Student Body Statistics The student body totals 2,060, of whom 2,031 are undergraduates (412 freshmen). 59 percent are women and 41 percent are men. Students come from 21 states and territories and 16 other countries. 89 percent are from Iowa. 0.9 percent are international students. 11 percent of the 2006 graduating class went on to graduate and professional schools.

Expenses for 2007–08 *Application fee:* $0. *Comprehensive fee:* $30,251 includes full-time tuition ($23,251), mandatory fees ($345), and college room and board ($6655). *College room only:* $3194. *Part-time tuition:* $265 per credit hour.

Financial Aid Forms of aid include need-based and non-need-based scholarships and part-time jobs. The average aided 2006–07 undergraduate received an aid package worth an estimated $19,902. The application deadline for financial aid is continuous.

Freshman Admission Simpson College requires a high school transcript, 1 recommendation, SAT or ACT scores, and TOEFL scores for international students. Rank in upper 50% of high school class is recommended. The application deadline for regular admission is August 15.

Transfer Admission The application deadline for admission is August 15.

Entrance Difficulty Simpson College assesses its entrance difficulty level as moderately difficult. For the fall 2006 freshman class, 88 percent of the applicants were accepted.

SPECIAL MESSAGE TO STUDENTS

Social Life One of the characteristics of Simpson is the number of opportunities available on campus. Activities include vocal and instrumental music groups, Theatre Simpson, honor and professional societies, and religious life council. Simpson competes in Division III of the NCAA and offers eighteen intercollegiate teams for men and women. Students annually elect a president and vice president of the Student Government. Each housing unit elects representatives to Student Senate, and the senate appoints student members to

appropriate College committees. Simpson is a residential campus with five traditional residence halls, eight apartment-style residences, eight theme houses, three national fraternities, one local fraternity, and four national sororities.

Academic Highlights Simpson's academic program is based on the best traditions of the liberal arts, enhanced by a genuine respect for the career requirements of today. Simpson's professors are dedicated to teaching. With a student-faculty ratio of 16:1, professors get to know students personally. More than forty different majors and career programs are available. Simpson is on a 4-4-1 calendar, with two 4-month semesters and one 3-week term of concentrated study in May. The May-Term course offerings provide an in-depth exploration of a subject and include internships, study abroad, and career observations. Simpson has exchange programs with international and domestic universities and offers study-abroad programs on a regular basis.

Interviews and Campus Visits Simpson College strongly encourages all prospective students to visit the campus. An interview is not required but is considered an excellent opportunity for prospective students and their parents to discuss academic programs, financial assistance, and scholarship opportunities. During the visit, prospective students tour the campus with a Student Ambassador, perhaps meet with a professor or attend a class, and interview with an admissions counselor. Students can take advantage of music or theater productions, athletic events, or other activities during their visit. Simpson blends tradition with practicality, and this is reflected in the architecture on campus. Buildings of interest include the historic College Hall, built in 1869; Carver Science Center, named after George Washington Carver, who attended Simpson College; McNeill Hall for Business, housing a seminar room, conference center, computer labs, and classrooms; Dunn Library; the Amy Robertson Music Center, housing a 250-seat recital hall, studios, and practice rooms; and Cowles Athletic Center, in which a 25-meter swimming pool, physical education facilities, a weight room, racquetball courts, and a field house are located. For information about appointments and campus visits, students should call the Office of Admissions at 515-961-1624 or 800-362-2454 (toll-free), Monday through Friday, 8 to 4:30, or on designated Saturdays, 9 to noon. Students may also schedule visits online at http://www.simpson.edu. The fax number is 515-961-1870. The Office of Admissions is located on the first floor of College Hall. The nearest commercial airport is Des Moines International.

For Further Information Write to Office of Admissions, Simpson College, 701 North C Street, Indianola, IA 50125. *E-mail:* admiss@simpson.edu. *Web site:* http://www.simpson.edu.

See page 288 for the College Close-Up.

UNIVERSITY OF DUBUQUE

Dubuque, Iowa

University of Dubuque is a coed, private, Presbyterian, comprehensive institution, founded in 1852, offering degrees at the associate, bachelor's, master's, doctoral, and first professional levels. It has a 56-acre campus in Dubuque.

Expenses for 2006–07 *Application fee:* $25. *Comprehensive fee:* $23,420 includes full-time tuition ($17,250), mandatory fees ($220), and college room and board ($5950). *College room only:* $3100. *Part-time tuition:* $390 per credit.

For Further Information Contact Mr. Jesse James, Director of Admissions, University of Dubuque, 2000 University Avenue, Dubuque, IA 52001-5099. *Telephone:* 563-589-3214 or 800-722-5583 (toll-free in-state). *Fax:* 563-589-3690. *E-mail:* admissns@dbq.edu. *Web site:* http://www.dbq.edu/.

THE UNIVERSITY OF IOWA

Iowa City, Iowa

The University of Iowa is a coed, public university, founded in 1847, offering degrees at the bachelor's, master's, doctoral, and first professional levels and post-master's and first professional certificates. It has a 1,900-acre campus in Iowa City.

Academic Information The faculty has 1,673 members (95% full-time), 96% with terminal degrees. The undergraduate student-faculty ratio is 15:1. The library holds 4 million titles and 44,644 serial subscriptions. Special programs include academic remediation, services for learning-disabled students, an honors program, cooperative (work-study) education, study abroad, advanced placement credit, accelerated degree programs, ESL programs, double majors, independent study, distance learning, self-designed majors, summer session for credit, part-time degree programs (daytime, evenings, weekends, summer), external degree programs, adult/continuing education programs, internships, and arrangement for off-campus study with Iowa State University of Science and Technology, University of Northern Iowa, Committee on Institutional Cooperation. The most frequently chosen baccalaureate fields are business/marketing, communications/journalism, social sciences.

Student Body Statistics The student body totals 28,816, of whom 20,738 are undergraduates (4,289 freshmen). 53 percent are women and 47 percent are men. Students come from 52 states and territories and 57 other countries. 68 percent are from Iowa. 2 percent are international students.

Expenses for 2007–08 *Application fee:* $40. *State resident tuition:* $5376 full-time, $224 per semester hour part-time. *Nonresident tuition:* $18,548 full-time, $773 per semester hour part-time. *Mandatory fees:* $917 full-time.

Financial Aid Forms of aid include need-based and non-need-based scholarships, athletic grants, and part-time jobs. The average aided 2006–07 undergraduate received an aid package worth an estimated $7480. The application deadline for financial aid is continuous.

Freshman Admission The University of Iowa requires a high school transcript, rank in upper 50% for residents, rank in top 30% for nonresidents, SAT or ACT scores, and TOEFL scores for international students. The application deadline for regular admission is April 1.

Transfer Admission The application deadline for admission is April 1.

Entrance Difficulty The University of Iowa assesses its entrance difficulty level as moderately difficult; very difficult for engineering programs. For the fall 2006 freshman class, 83 percent of the applicants were accepted.

For Further Information Contact Mr. Michael Barron, Assistant Provost for Enrollment Services and Director of Admissions, The University of Iowa, 107 Calvin Hall, Iowa City, IA 52242. *Telephone:* 319-335-3847 or 800-553-4692 (toll-free). *Fax:* 319-335-1535. *E-mail:* admissions@uiowa. edu. *Web site:* http://www.uiowa.edu/.

UNIVERSITY OF NORTHERN IOWA

Cedar Falls, Iowa

University of Northern Iowa is a coed, public, comprehensive unit of Board of Regents, State of Iowa, founded in 1876, offering degrees at the bachelor's, master's, and doctoral levels. It has a 916-acre campus in Cedar Falls.

Academic Information The faculty has 810 members (78% full-time), 70% with terminal degrees. The undergraduate student-faculty ratio is 16:1. The library holds 1 million titles, 6,839 serial subscriptions, and 28,408 audiovisual materials. Special programs include academic remediation, services for learning-disabled students, an honors program, cooperative (work-study) education, study abroad, advanced placement credit, accelerated degree programs, ESL programs, double majors, independent study, distance learning, self-designed majors, summer session for credit, part-time degree programs (daytime, evenings, summer), external degree programs, adult/continuing education programs, internships, and arrangement for off-campus study with Iowa Regents' Universities Student Exchange, National Student Exchange. The most frequently chosen baccalaureate fields are business/marketing, education, social sciences.

Student Body Statistics The student body totals 12,327, of whom 10,727 are undergraduates (1,768 freshmen). 57 percent are women and 43 percent are men. Students come from 40 states and territories and 74 other countries. 95 percent are from Iowa. 2.4 percent are international students. 11 percent of the 2006 graduating class went on to graduate and professional schools.

Expenses for 2006–07 *Application fee:* $30. *State resident tuition:* $5086 full-time, $212 per hour part-time. *Nonresident tuition:* $13,002 full-time, $542 per hour part-time. *Mandatory fees:* $1026 full-time, $461 per term part-time. Both full-time and part-time tuition and fees vary according to course load. *College room and board:* $5740. *College room only:* $2695. Room and board charges vary according to board plan and housing facility.

Financial Aid Forms of aid include need-based and non-need-based scholarships, athletic grants, and part-time jobs. The average aided 2006–07 undergraduate received an aid package worth an estimated $6992. The application deadline for financial aid is continuous.

Freshman Admission University of Northern Iowa requires a high school transcript, rank in upper 50% of high school class, SAT or ACT scores, and TOEFL scores for international students. Recommendations and an interview are required for some. The application deadline for regular admission is August 15.

Transfer Admission The application deadline for admission is August 15.

Entrance Difficulty University of Northern Iowa assesses its entrance difficulty level as moderately difficult. For the fall 2006 freshman class, 78 percent of the applicants were accepted.

For Further Information Contact Mr. Roland Carrillo, Executive Director of Enrollment Management, University of Northern Iowa, 120 Gilchrist Hall, Cedar Falls, IA 50614-0018. *Telephone:* 319-273-2701 or 800-772-2037 (toll-free). *Fax:* 319-273-2885. *E-mail:* admissions@uni.edu. *Web site:* http://www.uni.edu/.

UPPER IOWA UNIVERSITY

Fayette, Iowa

Upper Iowa University is a coed, private, comprehensive institution, founded in 1857, offering degrees at the associate, bachelor's, and master's levels (also offers continuing education program with significant enrollment not reflected in profile). It has an 80-acre campus in Fayette.

Academic Information The faculty has 65 members (88% full-time), 62% with terminal degrees. The undergraduate student-faculty ratio is 14:1. The library holds 64,043 titles and 3,241 serial subscriptions. Special programs include academic remediation, study abroad, advanced placement credit, accelerated degree programs, double majors, independent study, distance learning, self-designed majors, summer session for credit, part-time degree programs (daytime, evenings, summer), external degree programs, adult/continuing education programs, and internships.

Student Body Statistics The student body totals 696, of whom 665 are undergraduates (224 freshmen). 40 percent are women and 60 percent are men. Students come from 25 states and territories. 58 percent are from Iowa.

Expenses for 2007–08 *Application fee:* $15. *Comprehensive fee:* $25,700 includes full-time tuition ($19,625) and college room and board ($6075). *College room only:* $2525.

Financial Aid Forms of aid include need-based and non-need-based scholarships and part-time jobs. The priority application deadline for financial aid is June 1.

Freshman Admission Upper Iowa University requires a high school transcript, a minimum 2.0 high school GPA, SAT or ACT scores, and TOEFL scores for international students. An essay, recommendations, and an interview are required for some. The application deadline for regular admission is rolling.

Transfer Admission The application deadline for admission is rolling.

Entrance Difficulty Upper Iowa University assesses its entrance difficulty level as moderately difficult. For the fall 2006 freshman class, 55 percent of the applicants were accepted.

For Further Information Contact Dr. Linda Hoopes, Director of Admissions, Upper Iowa University, Box 1859, 605 Washington Street, Fayette, IA 52142-1857. *Telephone:* 563-425-5279 or 800-553-4150 Ext. 2 (toll-free). *Fax:* 563-425-5323. *E-mail:* admission@uiu.edu. *Web site:* http://www.uiu.edu/.

VATTEROTT COLLEGE

Des Moines, Iowa

Vatterott College is a coed, proprietary, primarily two-year college, offering degrees at the associate and bachelor's levels. It has a 25-acre campus in Des Moines.

For Further Information Contact Mr. Henry Franken, Co-Director, Vatterott College, 6100 Thornton Avenue, Suite 290, Des Moines, IA 50321. *Telephone:* 515-309-9000 or 800-353-7264 (toll-free). *Fax:* 515-309-0366. *Web site:* http://www.vatterott-college.edu/.

VENNARD COLLEGE

University Park, Iowa

Vennard College is a coed, private, interdenominational, four-year college, founded in 1996, offering degrees at the associate and bachelor's levels. It has a 70-acre campus in University Park near Des Moines.

Academic Information The faculty has 14 members (29% full-time), 14% with terminal degrees. The student-faculty ratio is 9:1. The library holds 19,619 titles and 5,975 serial subscriptions. Special programs include academic remediation, cooperative (work-study) education, advanced placement credit, double majors, independent study, distance learning, self-designed majors, summer session for credit, part-time degree programs (daytime, evenings), internships, and arrangement for off-campus study with William Penn University.
Student Body Statistics The student body is made up of 78 undergraduates (17 freshmen). 53 percent are women and 47 percent are men. Students come from 17 states and territories and 1 other country. 35 percent are from Iowa. 1.3 percent are international students.
Expenses for 2007–08 *Application fee:* $20. *Comprehensive fee:* $13,800 includes full-time tuition ($8250), mandatory fees ($950), and college room and board ($4600). *Part-time tuition:* $275 per credit hour. *Part-time mandatory fees:* $900 per term.
Financial Aid Forms of aid include need-based scholarships and part-time jobs. The priority application deadline for financial aid is April 1.
Freshman Admission Vennard College requires an essay, a high school transcript, a minimum 2.2 high school GPA, and 3 recommendations. An interview and SAT or ACT scores are required for some.
Entrance Difficulty Vennard College assesses its entrance difficulty level as moderately difficult. For the fall 2006 freshman class, 35 percent of the applicants were accepted.
For Further Information Contact Mr. Larry Olson, Interim Director of Admissions, Vennard College, PO Box 29, University Park, IA 52595. *Telephone:* 641-673-8391 Ext. 110 or 800-686-8391 (toll-free). *Fax:* 641-673-8365. *E-mail:* larry.olson@vennard.edu. *Web site:* http://www.vennard.edu/.

WALDORF COLLEGE

Forest City, Iowa

Waldorf College is a coed, private, Lutheran, four-year college, founded in 1903, offering degrees at the bachelor's level. It has a 29-acre campus in Forest City.

Academic Information The faculty has 70 members (57% full-time), 34% with terminal degrees. The student-faculty ratio is 14:1. The library holds 33,422 titles and 55,989 serial subscriptions. Special programs include academic remediation, services for learning-disabled students, an honors program, cooperative (work-study) education, study abroad, advanced placement credit, accelerated degree programs, Freshman Honors College, ESL programs, double majors, summer session for credit, part-time degree programs, adult/continuing education programs, and internships.
Student Body Statistics The student body is made up of 670 undergraduates (172 freshmen). 50 percent are women and 50 percent are men. Students come from 24 states and territories and 14 other countries. 62 percent are from Iowa. 4.9 percent are international students.

Expenses for 2006–07 *Application fee:* $0. *Comprehensive fee:* $21,940 includes full-time tuition ($15,885), mandatory fees ($785), and college room and board ($5270). Full-time tuition and fees vary according to class time, course load, and program. Room and board charges vary according to board plan and housing facility. *Part-time tuition:* $205 per credit.
Financial Aid Forms of aid include need-based and non-need-based scholarships, athletic grants, and part-time jobs. The priority application deadline for financial aid is March 1.
Freshman Admission Waldorf College requires a high school transcript, 1 recommendation, SAT or ACT scores, and TOEFL scores for international students. A minimum 2.0 high school GPA is recommended. An interview is required for some. The application deadline for regular admission is rolling.
Transfer Admission The application deadline for admission is rolling.
Entrance Difficulty Waldorf College assesses its entrance difficulty level as moderately difficult. For the fall 2006 freshman class, 67 percent of the applicants were accepted.
For Further Information Contact Mr. Steve Hall, Assistant Dean of Admission, Waldorf College, 106 South 6th Street, Forest City, IA 50436. *Telephone:* 641-585-8119 or 800-292-1903 (toll-free). *Fax:* 641-585-8125. *E-mail:* admissions@waldorf.edu. *Web site:* http://www.waldorf.edu/.

WARTBURG COLLEGE

Waverly, Iowa

Wartburg College is a coed, private, Lutheran, four-year college, founded in 1852, offering degrees at the bachelor's level. It has a 118-acre campus in Waverly.

Academic Information The faculty has 164 members (65% full-time), 55% with terminal degrees. The student-faculty ratio is 12:1. Special programs include academic remediation, an honors program, study abroad, advanced placement credit, accelerated degree programs, double majors, independent study, self-designed majors, summer session for credit, part-time degree programs, internships, and arrangement for off-campus study with members of the May Term Consortium. The most frequently chosen baccalaureate fields are business/marketing, communications/journalism, education.
Student Body Statistics The student body is made up of 1,769 undergraduates (505 freshmen). 53 percent are women and 47 percent are men. Students come from 23 states and territories and 36 other countries. 77 percent are from Iowa. 4.5 percent are international students. 20 percent of the 2006 graduating class went on to graduate and professional schools.
Expenses for 2006–07 *Application fee:* $20. *Comprehensive fee:* $29,125 includes full-time tuition ($21,980), mandatory fees ($430), and college room and board ($6715). *College room only:* $3205. Room and board charges vary according to board plan and housing facility. *Part-time tuition:* $810 per credit. *Part-time mandatory fees:* $50 per term. Part-time tuition and fees vary according to course load.
Financial Aid Forms of aid include need-based and non-need-based scholarships and part-time jobs. The average aided 2005–06 undergraduate received an aid package worth $17,098. The priority application deadline for financial aid is March 1.
Freshman Admission Wartburg College requires a high school transcript, a minimum 2.0 high school GPA, SAT or ACT scores, and TOEFL scores for international students. Recommendations and secondary school report are recommended. An interview is required for some. The application deadline for regular admission is rolling and for early action it is December 1.
Transfer Admission The application deadline for admission is rolling.
Entrance Difficulty Wartburg College assesses its entrance difficulty level as moderately difficult. For the fall 2006 freshman class, 85 percent of the applicants were accepted.
For Further Information Contact Mr. Brent Matthias, Assistant Vice President for Admissions, Wartburg College, 100 Wartburg Boulevard, PO Box 1003, Waverly, IA 50677-0903. *Telephone:* 319-352-8264 or 800-772-2085 (toll-free). *Fax:* 319-352-8579. *E-mail:* admissions@wartburg.edu. *Web site:* http://www.wartburg.edu/.

WILLIAM PENN UNIVERSITY
Oskaloosa, Iowa

William Penn University is a coed, private, four-year college, founded in 1873, affiliated with the Society of Friends, offering degrees at the associate and bachelor's levels. It has a 60-acre campus in Oskaloosa near Des Moines.

Academic Information The faculty has 52 members (67% full-time), 37% with terminal degrees. The student-faculty ratio is 15:1. The library holds 72,907 titles, 354 serial subscriptions, and 738 audiovisual materials. Special programs include academic remediation, services for learning-disabled students, cooperative (work-study) education, study abroad, advanced placement credit, ESL programs, double majors, independent study, self-designed majors, summer session for credit, part-time degree programs (daytime, evenings, summer), adult/continuing education programs, and internships. The most frequently chosen baccalaureate fields are business/marketing, education, social sciences.

Student Body Statistics The student body is made up of 1,861 undergraduates (433 freshmen). 53 percent are women and 47 percent are men. Students come from 43 states and territories and 13 other countries. 72 percent are from Iowa. 0.6 percent are international students. 25 percent of the 2006 graduating class went on to graduate and professional schools.

Expenses for 2007–08 *Application fee:* $20. *Comprehensive fee:* $21,922 includes full-time tuition ($16,510), mandatory fees ($370), and college room and board ($5042). *Part-time tuition:* $215 per hour. *Part-time mandatory fees:* $7 per hour.

Financial Aid Forms of aid include need-based and non-need-based scholarships, athletic grants, and part-time jobs. The average aided 2005–06 undergraduate received an aid package worth $17,782. The priority application deadline for financial aid is April 15.

Freshman Admission William Penn University requires a high school transcript, a minimum 2.0 high school GPA, SAT or ACT scores, and TOEFL scores for international students. An essay, recommendations, and an interview are required for some.

Entrance Difficulty William Penn University assesses its entrance difficulty level as moderately difficult.

For Further Information Contact John Ottosson, Vice President for Enrollment Management, William Penn University, 201 Trueblood Avenue, Oskaloosa, IA 52577-1799. *Telephone:* 641-673-1012 or 800-779-7366 (toll-free). *Fax:* 641-673-2113. *E-mail:* admissions@wmpenn.edu. *Web site:* http://www.wmpenn.edu/.

Kansas

BAKER UNIVERSITY
Baldwin City, Kansas

Baker University is a coed, private, United Methodist, comprehensive institution, founded in 1858, offering degrees at the bachelor's level. It has a 26-acre campus in Baldwin City near Kansas City.

Academic Information The faculty has 115 members (58% full-time), 55% with terminal degrees. The student-faculty ratio is 11:1. The library holds 132,325 titles, 678 serial subscriptions, and 4,992 audiovisual materials. Special programs include services for learning-disabled students, an honors program, study abroad, advanced placement credit, double majors, independent study, self-designed majors, summer session for credit, and internships. The most frequently chosen baccalaureate fields are business/marketing, education, library science.

Student Body Statistics The student body is made up of 923 undergraduates (236 freshmen). 52 percent are women and 48 percent are men. Students come from 20 states and territories and 8 other countries. 73 percent are from Kansas. 0.3 percent are international students. 30 percent of the 2006 graduating class went on to graduate and professional schools.

Expenses for 2006–07 *Application fee:* $0. *Comprehensive fee:* $23,430 includes full-time tuition ($17,200), mandatory fees ($380), and college room and board ($5850). *College room only:* $2660. Full-time tuition and fees vary according to location and program. Room and board charges vary according to board plan and housing facility. *Part-time tuition:* $515 per credit hour. *Part-time mandatory fees:* $45 per term. Part-time tuition and fees vary according to course load.

Financial Aid Forms of aid include need-based and non-need-based scholarships, athletic grants, and part-time jobs. The average aided 2006–07 undergraduate received an aid package worth an estimated $14,231. The priority application deadline for financial aid is March 1.

Freshman Admission Baker University requires a high school transcript, 1 recommendation, SAT or ACT scores, and TOEFL scores for international students. A minimum 3.0 high school GPA and minimum ACT score of 21 are recommended. An essay and an interview are required for some. The application deadline for regular admission is rolling.

Transfer Admission The application deadline for admission is rolling.

Entrance Difficulty Baker University assesses its entrance difficulty level as moderately difficult. For the fall 2006 freshman class, 62 percent of the applicants were accepted.

For Further Information Contact Mr. Daniel McKinney, Director of Admissions, Baker University, PO Box 65, Baldwin City, KS 66006-0065. *Telephone:* 800-873-4282 or 800-873-4282 (toll-free). *Fax:* 785-594-8372. *E-mail:* admissions@bakeru.edu. *Web site:* http://www.bakeru.edu/.

BARCLAY COLLEGE
Haviland, Kansas

Barclay College is a coed, private, four-year college, founded in 1917, affiliated with the Society of Friends, offering degrees at the associate and bachelor's levels. It has a 13-acre campus in Haviland.

Academic Information The faculty has 19 members (32% full-time), 16% with terminal degrees. The student-faculty ratio is 8:1. The library holds 63,759 titles, 22,194 serial subscriptions, and 705 audiovisual materials. Special programs include academic remediation, advanced placement credit, accelerated degree programs, double majors, independent study, distance learning, self-designed majors, part-time degree programs (daytime, evenings), external degree programs, adult/continuing education programs, and internships. The most frequently chosen baccalaureate fields are psychology, business/marketing, theology and religious vocations.

Student Body Statistics The student body is made up of 89 undergraduates (17 freshmen). 51 percent are women and 49 percent are men. Students come from 13 states and territories. 58 percent are from Kansas. 18 percent of the 2006 graduating class went on to graduate and professional schools.

Expenses for 2006–07 *Application fee:* $15. *Comprehensive fee:* $17,830 includes full-time tuition ($12,730) and college room and board ($5100). *College room only:* $2000. Room and board charges vary according to board plan and housing facility. *Part-time tuition:* $390 per hour. Part-time tuition varies according to course load.

Financial Aid Forms of aid include need-based and non-need-based scholarships and part-time jobs. The priority application deadline for financial aid is March 15.

Freshman Admission Barclay College requires an essay, a high school transcript, a minimum 2.3 high school GPA, 2 recommendations, an interview, SAT or ACT scores, and TOEFL scores for international students. The application deadline for regular admission is September 1.

Transfer Admission The application deadline for admission is September 1.

Entrance Difficulty Barclay College assesses its entrance difficulty level as minimally difficult. For the fall 2006 freshman class, 74 percent of the applicants were accepted.

For Further Information Contact Mr. Justin Kendall, Admissions Recruiter, Barclay College, 607 North Kingman, Haviland, KS 67059. *Telephone:* 620-862-5252 Ext. 21 or 800-862-0226 (toll-free). *Fax:* 620-862-5242. *E-mail:* jkendall@barclaycollege.edu. *Web site:* http://www.barclaycollege.edu/.

BENEDICTINE COLLEGE
Atchison, Kansas

Benedictine College is a coed, private, Roman Catholic, comprehensive institution, founded in 1859, offering degrees at the associate, bachelor's, and master's levels. It has a 225-acre campus in Atchison near Kansas City.

Academic Information The faculty has 112 members (58% full-time), 60% with terminal degrees. The undergraduate student-faculty ratio is 15:1. The library holds 368,558 titles and 504 serial subscriptions. Special programs include academic remediation, cooperative (work-study) education, study abroad, advanced placement credit, ESL programs, double majors, independent study, self-designed majors, summer session for credit, part-time degree programs (daytime, evenings, summer), internships, and arrangement for off-campus study with 16 members of the Kansas City Regional Council for Higher Education, Kansas State University. The most frequently chosen baccalaureate fields are business/marketing, philosophy and religious studies, social sciences.

Student Body Statistics The student body totals 1,553, of whom 1,468 are undergraduates (360 freshmen). 53 percent are women and 47 percent are men. Students come from 43 states and territories and 21 other countries. 45 percent are from Kansas. 3 percent are international students. 28 percent of the 2006 graduating class went on to graduate and professional schools.

Expenses for 2006–07 *Application fee:* $25. *Comprehensive fee:* $22,918 includes full-time tuition ($16,060), mandatory fees ($650), and college room and board ($6208). *College room only:* $2730. Full-time tuition and fees vary according to course load and degree level. Room and board charges vary according to board plan and housing facility. *Part-time tuition:* $450 per credit hour. Part-time tuition varies according to course load and degree level.

Financial Aid Forms of aid include need-based and non-need-based scholarships and part-time jobs. The average aided 2005–06 undergraduate received an aid package worth $13,973. The priority application deadline for financial aid is March 15.

Freshman Admission Benedictine College requires a high school transcript, a minimum 2.0 high school GPA, SAT or ACT scores, and TOEFL scores for international students. An interview is required for some.

Entrance Difficulty Benedictine College assesses its entrance difficulty level as moderately difficult. For the fall 2006 freshman class, 34 percent of the applicants were accepted.

For Further Information Contact Ms. Kelly J. Vowels, Vice President for Advancement and Enrollment Management, Benedictine College, 1020 North 2nd Street, Atchison, KS 66002. *Telephone:* 913-367-5340 or 800-467-5340 (toll-free). *Fax:* 913-367-5462. *E-mail:* bcadmiss@benedictine. edu. *Web site:* http://www.benedictine.edu/.

BETHANY COLLEGE
Lindsborg, Kansas

Bethany College is a coed, private, Lutheran, four-year college, founded in 1881, offering degrees at the bachelor's level. It has an 80-acre campus in Lindsborg.

Academic Information The faculty has 81 members (51% full-time), 53% with terminal degrees. The student-faculty ratio is 10:1. The library holds 90,230 titles, 709 serial subscriptions, and 1,232 audiovisual materials. Special programs include academic remediation, services for learning-disabled students, an honors program, study abroad, advanced placement credit, accelerated degree programs, double majors, independent study, self-designed majors, summer session for credit, internships, and arrangement for off-campus study with 6 members of the Associated Colleges of Central Kansas. The most frequently chosen baccalaureate fields are business/marketing, biological/life sciences, education.

Student Body Statistics The student body is made up of 554 undergraduates (168 freshmen). 51 percent are women and 49 percent are men. Students come from 24 states and territories and 11 other countries. 56 percent are from Kansas. 2.8 percent are international students. 17 percent of the 2006 graduating class went on to graduate and professional schools.

Expenses for 2007–08 *Application fee:* $20. *Comprehensive fee:* $22,610 includes full-time tuition ($16,900), mandatory fees ($210), and college room and board ($5500). *College room only:* $3000. *Part-time tuition:* $300 per credit hour.

Financial Aid Forms of aid include need-based and non-need-based scholarships, athletic grants, and part-time jobs. The average aided 2006–07 undergraduate received an aid package worth an estimated $17,554. The application deadline for financial aid is continuous.

Freshman Admission Bethany College requires a high school transcript, a minimum 2.5 high school GPA, SAT or ACT scores, and TOEFL scores for international students. An essay, recommendations, and an interview are required for some. The application deadline for regular admission is rolling.

Transfer Admission The application deadline for admission is rolling.

Entrance Difficulty Bethany College assesses its entrance difficulty level as moderately difficult. For the fall 2006 freshman class, 60 percent of the applicants were accepted.

For Further Information Contact Mr. Anthony Booker, Director of Admissions, Bethany College, 335 East Swensson Street, Lindsborg, KS 67456. *Telephone:* 785-227-3311 Ext. 8110 or 800-826-2281 (toll-free). *Fax:* 785-227-8993. *E-mail:* admissions@bethanylb.edu. *Web site:* http://www. bethanylb.edu/.

BETHEL COLLEGE
North Newton, Kansas

Bethel College is a coed, private, four-year college, founded in 1887, affiliated with the Mennonite Church USA, offering degrees at the bachelor's level. It has a 60-acre campus in North Newton near Wichita.

Academic Information The faculty has 65 members (71% full-time), 54% with terminal degrees. The student-faculty ratio is 10:1. The library holds 162,327 titles, 38,356 serial subscriptions, and 3,665 audiovisual materials. Special programs include academic remediation, services for learning-disabled students, study abroad, advanced placement credit, double majors, independent study, summer session for credit, part-time degree programs (daytime, evenings, summer), internships, and arrangement for off-campus study with 6 members of the Associated Colleges of Central Kansas, Hesston College. The most frequently chosen baccalaureate fields are business/marketing, health professions and related sciences, public administration and social services.

Student Body Statistics The student body is made up of 539 undergraduates (104 freshmen). 48 percent are women and 52 percent are men. Students come from 19 states and territories and 14 other countries. 76 percent are from Kansas. 6.9 percent are international students.

Expenses for 2006–07 *Application fee:* $20. *Comprehensive fee:* $22,800 includes full-time tuition ($16,700) and college room and board ($6100). *College room only:* $3200. Full-time tuition varies according to course load. Room and board charges vary according to board plan and housing facility. *Part-time tuition:* $590 per credit hour. Part-time tuition varies according to course load.

Financial Aid Forms of aid include need-based and non-need-based scholarships, athletic grants, and part-time jobs. The average aided 2005–06 undergraduate received an aid package worth $16,476. The priority application deadline for financial aid is March 15.

Freshman Admission Bethel College requires a high school transcript, a minimum 2.5 high school GPA, SAT or ACT scores, and TOEFL scores for international students. An interview is recommended. An essay and 2 recommendations are required for some. The application deadline for regular admission is rolling.

Transfer Admission The application deadline for admission is rolling.

Entrance Difficulty Bethel College assesses its entrance difficulty level as moderately difficult. For the fall 2006 freshman class, 75 percent of the applicants were accepted.

For Further Information Contact Mr. Allan Bartel, Vice President for Admissions, Bethel College, 300 East 27th Street, North Newton, KS 67117-0531. *Telephone:* 316-284-5230 or 800-522-1887 Ext. 230 (toll-free). *Fax:* 316-284-5870. *E-mail:* admissions@bethelks.edu. *Web site:* http://www. bethelks.edu/.

CENTRAL CHRISTIAN COLLEGE OF KANSAS

McPherson, Kansas

Central Christian College of Kansas is a coed, private, Free Methodist, four-year college, founded in 1884, offering degrees at the associate and bachelor's levels. It has a 16-acre campus in McPherson.

Academic Information The faculty has 36 members (44% full-time), 11% with terminal degrees. The student-faculty ratio is 16:1. The library holds 45,357 titles, 91 serial subscriptions, and 1,218 audiovisual materials. Special programs include academic remediation, services for learning-disabled students, cooperative (work-study) education, study abroad, advanced placement credit, double majors, independent study, distance learning, self-designed majors, part-time degree programs (daytime, evenings), adult/continuing education programs, internships, and arrangement for off-campus study with McPherson College, Christian Center for Urban Studies, Focus on the Family Institute, CCCU. The most frequently chosen baccalaureate fields are business/marketing, liberal arts/general studies, theology and religious vocations.
Student Body Statistics The student body is made up of 349 undergraduates (123 freshmen). 48 percent are women and 52 percent are men. Students come from 28 states and territories and 3 other countries. 36 percent are from Kansas. 2.8 percent are international students. 6 percent of the 2006 graduating class went on to graduate and professional schools.
Expenses for 2007–08 *Application fee:* $20. *Comprehensive fee:* $20,500 includes full-time tuition ($15,100), mandatory fees ($200), and college room and board ($5200). *College room only:* $2400. *Part-time tuition:* $405 per credit hour.
Financial Aid Forms of aid include need-based and non-need-based scholarships, athletic grants, and part-time jobs. The priority application deadline for financial aid is March 1.
Freshman Admission Central Christian College of Kansas requires a high school transcript, a minimum 2.5 high school GPA, 2 recommendations, SAT or ACT scores, and TOEFL scores for international students. An essay and an interview are recommended. The application deadline for regular admission is rolling.
Transfer Admission The application deadline for admission is rolling.
Entrance Difficulty Central Christian College of Kansas assesses its entrance difficulty level as moderately difficult. For the fall 2006 freshman class, 98 percent of the applicants were accepted.
For Further Information Contact Dr. David Ferrell, Dean of Admissions, Central Christian College of Kansas, PO Box 1403, McPherson, KS 67460. *Telephone:* 620-241-0723 Ext. 380 or 800-835-0078 Ext. 337 (toll-free). *Fax:* 620-241-6032. *E-mail:* admissions@centralchristian.edu. *Web site:* http://www.centralchristian.edu/.

DONNELLY COLLEGE

Kansas City, Kansas

http://www.donnelly.edu/

EMPORIA STATE UNIVERSITY

Emporia, Kansas

Emporia State University is a coed, public, comprehensive unit of Kansas State Board of Education, founded in 1863, offering degrees at the bachelor's, master's, and doctoral levels and post-master's and postbachelor's certificates. It has a 207-acre campus in Emporia near Wichita.

Academic Information The faculty has 284 members (91% full-time), 78% with terminal degrees. The undergraduate student-faculty ratio is 18:1. The library holds 2 million titles, 15,645 serial subscriptions, and 8,551 audiovisual materials. Special programs include academic remediation, services for learning-disabled students, an honors program, study abroad, advanced placement credit, accelerated degree programs, ESL programs, double majors, independent study, distance learning,

summer session for credit, part-time degree programs (daytime, evenings, weekends, summer), adult/continuing education programs, internships, and arrangement for off-campus study. The most frequently chosen baccalaureate fields are business/marketing, education, social sciences.
Student Body Statistics The student body totals 6,473, of whom 4,458 are undergraduates (769 freshmen). 61 percent are women and 39 percent are men. Students come from 32 states and territories and 30 other countries. 93 percent are from Kansas. 5.9 percent are international students. 19 percent of the 2006 graduating class went on to graduate and professional schools.
Expenses for 2006–07 *Application fee:* $30. *State resident tuition:* $2862 full-time, $95 per credit hour part-time. *Nonresident tuition:* $10,214 full-time, $340 per credit hour part-time. *Mandatory fees:* $724 full-time, $44 per credit hour part-time. Both full-time and part-time tuition and fees vary according to degree level. *College room and board:* $5170. *College room only:* $2552. Room and board charges vary according to board plan and housing facility.
Financial Aid Forms of aid include need-based and non-need-based scholarships, athletic grants, and part-time jobs. The average aided 2005–06 undergraduate received an aid package worth $5955. The priority application deadline for financial aid is March 15.
Freshman Admission Emporia State University requires a high school transcript, SAT or ACT scores, and TOEFL scores for international students. A minimum 2.0 high school GPA is recommended. The application deadline for regular admission is rolling.
Transfer Admission The application deadline for admission is rolling.
Entrance Difficulty Emporia State University assesses its entrance difficulty level as noncompetitive; minimally difficult for transfers. For the fall 2006 freshman class, 80 percent of the applicants were accepted.
For Further Information Contact Ms. Laura Eddy, Director of Admissions, Emporia State University, 1200 Commercial Street, Campus Box 4034, Emporia, KS 66801-5087. *Telephone:* 620-341-5465, 877-GOTOESU (toll-free in-state), or 877-468-6378 (toll-free out-of-state). *Fax:* 620-341-5599. *E-mail:* go2esu@emporia.edu. *Web site:* http://www.emporia.edu/.

FORT HAYS STATE UNIVERSITY

Hays, Kansas

Fort Hays State University is a coed, public, comprehensive unit of Kansas State Board of Education, founded in 1902, offering degrees at the associate, bachelor's, and master's levels and post-master's certificates. It has a 200-acre campus in Hays.

Academic Information The faculty has 291 members (87% full-time), 66% with terminal degrees. The undergraduate student-faculty ratio is 17:1. The library holds 624,637 titles and 1,689 serial subscriptions. Special programs include academic remediation, services for learning-disabled students, study abroad, advanced placement credit, ESL programs, double majors, distance learning, self-designed majors, summer session for credit, part-time degree programs (daytime, evenings, weekends, summer), external degree programs, adult/continuing education programs, internships, and arrangement for off-campus study with members of the National Student Exchange.
Student Body Statistics The student body totals 7,403, of whom 5,920 are undergraduates (904 freshmen). 54 percent are women and 46 percent are men. Students come from 48 states and territories and 15 other countries. 90 percent are from Kansas. 16 percent are international students. 19 percent of the 2006 graduating class went on to graduate and professional schools.
Expenses for 2006–07 *Application fee:* $30. *State resident tuition:* $3192 full-time, $106.40 per credit hour part-time. *Nonresident tuition:* $10,032 full-time, $334.40 per credit hour part-time. Both full-time and part-time tuition varies according to course load and location. *College room and board:* $5553. *College room only:* $2823. Room and board charges vary according to board plan, housing facility, and student level.
Financial Aid Forms of aid include need-based and non-need-based scholarships, athletic grants, and part-time jobs.
Freshman Admission Fort Hays State University requires a high school transcript, ACT scores, SAT or ACT scores, and TOEFL scores for international students. The application deadline for regular admission is rolling.
Transfer Admission The application deadline for admission is rolling.

Entrance Difficulty Fort Hays State University assesses its entrance difficulty level as noncompetitive; minimally difficult for out-of-state applicants; minimally difficult for transfers; moderately difficult for radiological technology program, School of Nursing. For the fall 2006 freshman class, 94 percent of the applicants were accepted.

For Further Information Contact Ms. Susan Cochran, Office Manager/ Campus Visit Coordinator, Office of Admissions, Fort Hays State University, 600 Park Street, Hays, KS 67601-4099. *Telephone:* 785-628-5666 or 800-628-FHSU (toll-free). *Fax:* 800-432-0248. *E-mail:* tigers@ fhsu.edu. *Web site:* http://www.fhsu.edu/.

FRIENDS UNIVERSITY
Wichita, Kansas
http://www.friends.edu/

HASKELL INDIAN NATIONS UNIVERSITY
Lawrence, Kansas
http://www.haskell.edu/

HESSTON COLLEGE
Hesston, Kansas

Hesston College is a coed, private, Mennonite, two-year college, founded in 1909, offering degrees at the associate level. It has a 50-acre campus in Hesston near Wichita.

Academic Information The faculty has 44 members (43% full-time), 18% with terminal degrees. The student-faculty ratio is 11:1. The library holds 35,000 titles, 234 serial subscriptions, and 2,670 audiovisual materials. Special programs include academic remediation, services for learning-disabled students, cooperative (work-study) education, advanced placement credit, ESL programs, double majors, independent study, summer session for credit, part-time degree programs (daytime, evenings), and internships.

Student Body Statistics The student body is made up of 462 undergraduates (172 freshmen). 55 percent are women and 45 percent are men. Students come from 29 states and territories and 14 other countries. 47 percent are from Kansas. 9.1 percent are international students. 60 percent of the 2006 graduating class went on to four-year colleges.

Expenses for 2007–08 *Application fee:* $15. *Comprehensive fee:* $23,600 includes full-time tuition ($17,140), mandatory fees ($280), and college room and board ($6180). *Part-time tuition:* $714 per hour. *Part-time mandatory fees:* $70 per term.

Financial Aid Forms of aid include need-based scholarships and part-time jobs. The priority application deadline for financial aid is April 1.

Freshman Admission Hesston College requires a high school transcript, 2 recommendations, SAT or ACT scores, and TOEFL scores for international students. An interview is required for some. The application deadline for regular admission is rolling.

Transfer Admission The application deadline for admission is rolling.

Entrance Difficulty Hesston College has an open admission policy except for nursing and pastoral ministries programs. It assesses its entrance difficulty as moderately difficult for nursing program.

For Further Information Contact Joel Kauffman, Vice President for Admissions, Hesston College, Box 3000, Hesston, KS 67062. *Telephone:* 620-327-8222 or 800-995-2757 (toll-free). *Fax:* 620-327-8300. *E-mail:* admissions@hesston.edu. *Web site:* http://www.hesston.edu/.

KANSAS NEWMAN COLLEGE
See Newman University.

KANSAS STATE UNIVERSITY
Manhattan, Kansas

Kansas State University is a coed, public unit of Kansas State Board of Education, founded in 1863, offering degrees at the associate, bachelor's, master's, doctoral, and first professional levels. It has a 668-acre campus in Manhattan near Kansas City.

Academic Information The faculty has 1,047 members (88% full-time), 80% with terminal degrees. The undergraduate student-faculty ratio is 21:1. The library holds 2 million titles and 1,365 serial subscriptions. Special programs include academic remediation, services for learning-disabled students, an honors program, cooperative (work-study) education, study abroad, advanced placement credit, accelerated degree programs, Freshman Honors College, ESL programs, double majors, independent study, distance learning, summer session for credit, part-time degree programs (daytime, evenings, summer), adult/continuing education programs, internships, and arrangement for off-campus study with Manhattan Christian College, University of Missouri-Kansas City, 19 Kansas community colleges. The most frequently chosen baccalaureate fields are business/marketing, education, social sciences.

Student Body Statistics The student body totals 23,141, of whom 18,761 are undergraduates (3,385 freshmen). 49 percent are women and 51 percent are men. Students come from 50 states and territories and 100 other countries. 87 percent are from Kansas. 1.7 percent are international students. 18.3 percent of the 2006 graduating class went on to graduate and professional schools.

Expenses for 2006–07 *Application fee:* $30. *State resident tuition:* $4830 full-time, $172 per credit hour part-time. *Nonresident tuition:* $13,916 full-time, $497 per credit hour part-time. *Mandatory fees:* $604 full-time. *College room and board:* $5912. Room and board charges vary according to board plan.

Financial Aid Forms of aid include need-based and non-need-based scholarships, athletic grants, and part-time jobs. The priority application deadline for financial aid is March 1.

Freshman Admission Kansas State University requires a high school transcript, a minimum 2.0 high school GPA, SAT or ACT scores, and TOEFL scores for international students. The application deadline for regular admission is rolling.

Transfer Admission The application deadline for admission is rolling.

Entrance Difficulty Kansas State University assesses its entrance difficulty level as noncompetitive; moderately difficult for out-of-state applicants; moderately difficult for transfers; very difficult for architecture and design program. For the fall 2006 freshman class, 83 percent of the applicants were accepted.

For Further Information Contact Ms. Christy Crenshaw, Associate Director of Admissions, Kansas State University, 119 Anderson Hall, Manhattan, KS 66506. *Telephone:* 785-532-6250 or 800-432-8270 (toll-free in-state). *Fax:* 785-532-6393. *E-mail:* kstate@ksu.edu. *Web site:* http://www. ksu.edu/.

KANSAS WESLEYAN UNIVERSITY
Salina, Kansas
http://www.kwu.edu/

MANHATTAN CHRISTIAN COLLEGE
Manhattan, Kansas
http://www.mccks.edu/

McPHERSON COLLEGE
McPherson, Kansas
http://www.mcpherson.edu/

MIDAMERICA NAZARENE UNIVERSITY
Olathe, Kansas

MidAmerica Nazarene University is a coed, private, comprehensive institution, founded in 1966, affiliated with the Church of the Nazarene, offering degrees at the associate, bachelor's, and master's levels. It has a 105-acre campus in Olathe near Kansas City.

Expenses for 2006–07 *Application fee:* $25. *Comprehensive fee:* $21,798 includes full-time tuition ($14,968), mandatory fees ($1000), and college room and board ($5830). *Part-time tuition:* $500 per semester hour. *Part-time mandatory fees:* $500 per term.
For Further Information Contact Mr. Dennis Troyer, Director of Admissions, MidAmerica Nazarene University, 2030 East College Way, Olathe, KS 66062-1899. *Telephone:* 913-791-3380 Ext. 481 or 800-800-8887 (toll-free). *Fax:* 913-791-3481. *E-mail:* admissions@mnu.edu. *Web site:* http://www.mnu.edu/.

NATIONAL AMERICAN UNIVERSITY
Overland Park, Kansas

National American University is a coed, private, two-year college, offering degrees at the associate level.

Student Body Statistics The student body is made up of 156 undergraduates.
Expenses for 2006–07 *Application fee:* $25. *Tuition:* $13,322 full-time.
Entrance Difficulty National American University assesses its entrance difficulty level as noncompetitive.
For Further Information Contact Admissions Office, National American University, 10310 Mastin, Overland Park, KS 66212. *Telephone:* 913-981-8700. *Web site:* http://www.national.edu/.

NEWMAN UNIVERSITY
Wichita, Kansas

Newman University is a coed, private, Roman Catholic, comprehensive institution, founded in 1933, offering degrees at the associate, bachelor's, and master's levels. It has a 61-acre campus in Wichita.

Academic Information The faculty has 85 members (95% full-time), 58% with terminal degrees. The undergraduate student-faculty ratio is 14:1. The library holds 108,735 titles, 267 serial subscriptions, and 1,872 audiovisual materials. Special programs include academic remediation, services for learning-disabled students, cooperative (work-study) education, study abroad, advanced placement credit, accelerated degree programs, double majors, independent study, distance learning, summer session for credit, part-time degree programs (daytime, evenings, weekends, summer), external degree programs, adult/continuing education programs, internships, and arrangement for off-campus study with Friends University. The most frequently chosen baccalaureate fields are business/marketing, education, health professions and related sciences.
Student Body Statistics The student body totals 2,104, of whom 1,631 are undergraduates (162 freshmen). 62 percent are women and 38 percent are men. Students come from 19 states and territories and 20 other countries. 85 percent are from Kansas. 6.6 percent are international students.
Expenses for 2006–07 *Application fee:* $20. *Comprehensive fee:* $22,680 includes full-time tuition ($17,008), mandatory fees ($300), and college room and board ($5372). Full-time tuition and fees vary according to location and program. Room and board charges vary according to housing facility. *Part-time tuition:* $567 per credit hour. *Part-time mandatory fees:* $10 per credit hour. Part-time tuition and fees vary according to location and program.
Financial Aid Forms of aid include need-based and non-need-based scholarships, athletic grants, and part-time jobs. The average aided 2005–06 undergraduate received an aid package worth $10,323. The priority application deadline for financial aid is March 1.

Freshman Admission Newman University requires a high school transcript, a minimum 2.0 high school GPA, SAT or ACT scores, and TOEFL scores for international students. An interview is recommended. The application deadline for regular admission is rolling.
Transfer Admission The application deadline for admission is rolling.
Entrance Difficulty Newman University assesses its entrance difficulty level as minimally difficult; moderately difficult for nursing, occupational therapy programs. For the fall 2006 freshman class, 72 percent of the applicants were accepted.
For Further Information Contact Jann Reusser, Admissions Recruitment, Newman University, 3100 McCormick Avenue, Wichita, KS 67213. *Telephone:* 316-942-4291 Ext. 2144 or 877-NEWMANU Ext. 2144 (toll-free). *Fax:* 316-942-4483. *E-mail:* admissions@newmanu.edu. *Web site:* http://www.newmanu.edu/.

OTTAWA UNIVERSITY
Ottawa, Kansas

Ottawa University is a coed, private, American Baptist Churches in the USA, comprehensive institution, founded in 1865, offering degrees at the bachelor's level (also offers master's, adult, international and on-line education programs with significant enrollment not reflected in profile). It has a 60-acre campus in Ottawa near Kansas City.

Academic Information The faculty has 25 members (100% full-time), 48% with terminal degrees. The student-faculty ratio is 15:1. The library holds 75,401 titles, 808 serial subscriptions, and 15 audiovisual materials. Special programs include study abroad, advanced placement credit, double majors, independent study, distance learning, self-designed majors, summer session for credit, part-time degree programs (daytime), and internships. The most frequently chosen baccalaureate fields are business/marketing, biological/life sciences, education.
Student Body Statistics The student body is made up of 382 undergraduates (90 freshmen). 47 percent are women and 53 percent are men. Students come from 20 states and territories and 6 other countries. 71 percent are from Kansas. 1.8 percent are international students. 20 percent of the 2006 graduating class went on to graduate and professional schools.
Expenses for 2007–08 *Application fee:* $15. *Comprehensive fee:* $23,280 includes full-time tuition ($17,000), mandatory fees ($350), and college room and board ($5930). *College room only:* $2630. *Part-time tuition:* $515 per credit hour. *Part-time mandatory fees:* $15 per credit hour.
Financial Aid Forms of aid include need-based and non-need-based scholarships and part-time jobs. The priority application deadline for financial aid is March 15.
Freshman Admission Ottawa University requires a high school transcript, a minimum 2.5 high school GPA, 18 or higher ACT; rank in upper 50% of class, SAT or ACT scores, and TOEFL scores for international students. 2 recommendations and an interview are recommended. An essay is required for some. The application deadline for regular admission is rolling.
Transfer Admission The application deadline for admission is rolling.
Entrance Difficulty Ottawa University assesses its entrance difficulty level as moderately difficult. For the fall 2006 freshman class, 77 percent of the applicants were accepted.
For Further Information Contact Ms. Fola Akande, Director of Admissions, Ottawa University, 1001 South Cedar #17, Ottawa, KS 66067-3399. *Telephone:* 785-242-5200 Ext. 5561 or 800-755-5200 Ext. 5559 (toll-free). *Fax:* 785-229-1008. *E-mail:* admiss@ottawa.edu. *Web site:* http://www.ottawa.edu/.

PITTSBURG STATE UNIVERSITY
Pittsburg, Kansas

Pittsburg State University is a coed, public, comprehensive unit of Kansas State Board of Education, founded in 1903, offering degrees at the bachelor's and master's levels (associate, specialist in education). It has a 233-acre campus in Pittsburg.

Academic Information The faculty has 391 members (77% full-time), 62% with terminal degrees. The undergraduate student-faculty ratio is 18:1. The library holds 705,267 titles, 9,436 serial subscriptions, and 3,710 audiovisual materials. Special programs include academic remediation, services for learning-disabled students, an honors program, cooperative (work-study) education, study abroad, advanced placement credit, Freshman Honors College, ESL programs, double majors, independent study, distance learning, self-designed majors, summer session for credit, part-time degree programs (daytime, evenings, summer), external degree programs, adult/continuing education programs, internships, and arrangement for off-campus study with Southside Education Center, Wichita, KS, Kansas City Metro Center, Lenexa, KS. The most frequently chosen baccalaureate fields are business/marketing, education, science technologies.

Student Body Statistics The student body totals 6,859, of whom 5,747 are undergraduates (864 freshmen). 48 percent are women and 52 percent are men. Students come from 40 states and territories and 25 other countries. 77 percent are from Kansas. 3.5 percent are international students. 16 percent of the 2006 graduating class went on to graduate and professional schools.

Expenses for 2006–07 *Application fee:* $30. *State resident tuition:* $3036 full-time, $101 per credit hour part-time. *Nonresident tuition:* $10,366 full-time, $346 per credit hour part-time. *Mandatory fees:* $754 full-time, $34 per credit hour part-time. *College room and board:* $4844. Room and board charges vary according to board plan and housing facility.

Financial Aid Forms of aid include need-based and non-need-based scholarships, athletic grants, and part-time jobs. The average aided 2006–07 undergraduate received an aid package worth an estimated $7107. The priority application deadline for financial aid is March 1.

Freshman Admission Pittsburg State University requires a high school transcript, ACT scores, and TOEFL scores for international students. A minimum 2.0 high school GPA is required for some. The application deadline for regular admission is rolling.

Transfer Admission The application deadline for admission is rolling.

Entrance Difficulty Pittsburg State University has an open admission policy for state residents. It assesses its entrance difficulty as minimally difficult for out-of-state applicants; minimally difficult for transfers; moderately difficult for international students.

For Further Information Contact Director of Admission and Enrollment Services, Pittsburg State University, 1701 S. Broadway, Pittsburg, KS 66762. *Telephone:* 620-235-4251 or 800-854-7488 Ext. 1 (toll-free). *Fax:* 620-235-6003. *E-mail:* psuadmit@pittstate.edu. *Web site:* http://www.pittstate.edu/.

SOUTHWESTERN COLLEGE

Winfield, Kansas

Southwestern College is a coed, private, United Methodist, comprehensive institution, founded in 1885, offering degrees at the bachelor's and master's levels. It has a 70-acre campus in Winfield near Wichita.

Academic Information The faculty has 180 members (26% full-time), 17% with terminal degrees. The undergraduate student-faculty ratio is 10:1. The library holds 50,720 titles, 19,999 serial subscriptions, and 5,456 audiovisual materials. Special programs include an honors program, study abroad, double majors, independent study, distance learning, self-designed majors, part-time degree programs (daytime, evenings, weekends, summer), adult/continuing education programs, internships, and arrangement for off-campus study with Urban Life Center, Chicago. The most frequently chosen baccalaureate fields are business/marketing, education, health professions and related sciences.

Student Body Statistics The student body totals 1,557, of whom 1,373 are undergraduates (140 freshmen). 49 percent are women and 51 percent are men. Students come from 37 states and territories and 8 other countries. 65 percent are from Kansas. 1.3 percent are international students.

Expenses for 2006–07 *Application fee:* $20. *Comprehensive fee:* $22,338 includes full-time tuition ($16,800), mandatory fees ($100), and college room and board ($5438). *College room only:* $2428. Full-time tuition and fees vary according to course load, degree level, and location. Room and

board charges vary according to board plan, housing facility, and location. *Part-time tuition:* $700 per semester hour. Part-time tuition varies according to course load, degree level, and location.

Financial Aid Forms of aid include need-based and non-need-based scholarships, athletic grants, and part-time jobs. The priority application deadline for financial aid is April 1.

Freshman Admission Southwestern College requires SAT or ACT scores and TOEFL scores for international students. The application deadline for regular admission is August 25.

Transfer Admission The application deadline for admission is August 25.

Entrance Difficulty Southwestern College assesses its entrance difficulty level as moderately difficult. For the fall 2006 freshman class, 63 percent of the applicants were accepted.

For Further Information Contact Mr. Todd Moore, Director of Admission, Southwestern College, 100 College Street, Winfield, KS 67156. *Telephone:* 620-229-6236 or 800-846-1543 (toll-free). *Fax:* 620-229-6344. *E-mail:* scadmit@sckans.edu. *Web site:* http://www.sckans.edu/.

STERLING COLLEGE

Sterling, Kansas

Sterling College is a coed, private, Presbyterian, four-year college, founded in 1887, offering degrees at the bachelor's level. It has a 46-acre campus in Sterling.

Academic Information The faculty has 52 members (67% full-time), 31% with terminal degrees. The student-faculty ratio is 15:1. The library holds 76,637 titles and 350 serial subscriptions. Special programs include services for learning-disabled students, an honors program, study abroad, advanced placement credit, double majors, independent study, distance learning, self-designed majors, internships, and arrangement for off-campus study with 6 members of the Associated Colleges of Central Kansas.

Student Body Statistics The student body is made up of 607 undergraduates (199 freshmen). 45 percent are women and 55 percent are men. Students come from 32 states and territories and 3 other countries. 46 percent are from Kansas. 0.4 percent are international students.

Expenses for 2007–08 *Application fee:* $25. *Comprehensive fee:* $21,830 includes full-time tuition ($15,500), mandatory fees ($100), and college room and board ($6230). *Part-time tuition:* $300 per credit hour.

Financial Aid Forms of aid include need-based and non-need-based scholarships, athletic grants, and part-time jobs. The priority application deadline for financial aid is April 1.

Freshman Admission Sterling College requires a high school transcript, a minimum 2.2 high school GPA, SAT or ACT scores, and TOEFL scores for international students. An essay and an interview are recommended. 2 recommendations and audition required for fine arts majors are required for some. The application deadline for regular admission is July 15 and for early action it is November 15.

Transfer Admission The application deadline for admission is rolling.

Entrance Difficulty Sterling College assesses its entrance difficulty level as minimally difficult. For the fall 2006 freshman class, 65 percent of the applicants were accepted.

For Further Information Contact Mr. Dennis Dutton, Vice President for Enrollment Services, Sterling College, PO Box 98, Sterling, KS 67579-0098. *Telephone:* 620-278-4364 or 800-346-1017 (toll-free). *Fax:* 620-278-4416. *E-mail:* admissions@sterling.edu. *Web site:* http://www.sterling.edu/.

TABOR COLLEGE

Hillsboro, Kansas

Tabor College is a coed, private, Mennonite Brethren, comprehensive institution, founded in 1908, offering degrees at the associate, bachelor's, and master's levels. It has a 26-acre campus in Hillsboro near Wichita.

Academic Information The faculty has 57 members (61% full-time), 47% with terminal degrees. The undergraduate student-faculty ratio is 11:1. The library holds 80,099 titles, 265 serial subscriptions, and 1,109 audiovisual materials. Special programs include academic remediation, services for learning-disabled students, an honors program, cooperative

Tabor College (continued)

(work-study) education, study abroad, advanced placement credit, accelerated degree programs, double majors, independent study, distance learning, self-designed majors, part-time degree programs (evenings, weekends, summer), adult/continuing education programs, internships, and arrangement for off-campus study with Associated Colleges of Central Kansas.

Student Body Statistics The student body totals 603, of whom 599 are undergraduates (131 freshmen). 47 percent are women and 53 percent are men. Students come from 30 states and territories and 6 other countries. 64 percent are from Kansas. 1.4 percent are international students. 13 percent of the 2006 graduating class went on to graduate and professional schools.

Expenses for 2006–07 *Application fee:* $30. *Comprehensive fee:* $22,634 includes full-time tuition ($16,354), mandatory fees ($380), and college room and board ($5900). *College room only:* $2300. Full-time tuition and fees vary according to course load. Room and board charges vary according to board plan, housing facility, and location. *Part-time tuition:* $681 per credit hour. *Part-time mandatory fees:* $5 per credit hour. Part-time tuition and fees vary according to course load.

Financial Aid Forms of aid include need-based and non-need-based scholarships, athletic grants, and part-time jobs. The average aided 2005–06 undergraduate received an aid package worth $15,751. The application deadline for financial aid is August 15 with a priority deadline of March 1.

Freshman Admission Tabor College requires an essay, a high school transcript, a minimum 2.0 high school GPA, 2 recommendations, an interview, minimum ACT score of 18, SAT or ACT scores, and TOEFL scores for international students. A minimum 3.0 high school GPA is recommended. The application deadline for regular admission is August 1 and for early decision plan 1 it is January 1.

Transfer Admission The application deadline for admission is August 1.

Entrance Difficulty Tabor College assesses its entrance difficulty level as moderately difficult. For the fall 2006 freshman class, 99 percent of the applicants were accepted.

For Further Information Contact Mr. Rusty Allen, Dean of Enrollment Management, Tabor College, 400 South Jefferson, Hillsboro, KS 67063. *Telephone:* 620-947-3121 or 800-822-6799 (toll-free). *Fax:* 620-947-6276. *E-mail:* admissions@tabor.edu. *Web site:* http://www.tabor.edu/.

UNIVERSITY OF KANSAS
Lawrence, Kansas

University of Kansas is a coed, public university, founded in 1866, offering degrees at the bachelor's, master's, doctoral, and first professional levels and post-master's certificates (University of Kansas is a single institution with academic programs and facilities at two primary locations: Lawrence and Kansas City.). It has a 1,100-acre campus in Lawrence near Kansas City.

Academic Information The faculty has 1,283 members (93% full-time), 95% with terminal degrees. The undergraduate student-faculty ratio is 20:1. The library holds 5 million titles, 50,992 serial subscriptions, and 57,471 audiovisual materials. Special programs include academic remediation, services for learning-disabled students, an honors program, cooperative (work-study) education, study abroad, advanced placement credit, accelerated degree programs, ESL programs, double majors, independent study, distance learning, summer session for credit, part-time degree programs (daytime, evenings, summer), and internships. The most frequently chosen baccalaureate fields are business/marketing, English, health professions and related sciences.

Student Body Statistics The student body totals 28,924, of whom 21,353 are undergraduates (4,153 freshmen). 50 percent are women and 50 percent are men. Students come from 52 states and territories and 111 other countries. 74 percent are from Kansas. 2.8 percent are international students. 28 percent of the 2006 graduating class went on to graduate and professional schools.

Expenses for 2006–07 *Application fee:* $30. *State resident tuition:* $5513 full-time, $183.75 per credit hour part-time. *Nonresident tuition:* $14,483 full-time, $482.75 per credit hour part-time. *Mandatory fees:* $640 full-time, $53.33 per credit hour part-time. Both full-time and part-time tuition and fees vary according to program and reciprocity agreements. *College room and board:* $5747. *College room only:* $2997. Room and board charges vary according to board plan and housing facility.

Financial Aid Forms of aid include need-based and non-need-based scholarships, athletic grants, and part-time jobs. The average aided 2005–06 undergraduate received an aid package worth $7594. The priority application deadline for financial aid is March 1.

Freshman Admission University of Kansas requires a high school transcript, a minimum 2.0 high school GPA, Kansas Board of Regents admissions criteria with GPA of 2.0 resident, 2.5 nonresident; or upper third of high school class; or minimum ACT score 21 resident, 24 nonresident; or minimum SAT score 980 resident, 1090 nonresident, and SAT or ACT scores. TOEFL scores for international students are recommended. A minimum 2.5 high school GPA is required for some. The application deadline for regular admission is April 1.

Transfer Admission The application deadline for admission is May 1.

Entrance Difficulty University of Kansas assesses its entrance difficulty level as moderately difficult; very difficult for architecture, all engineering programs. For the fall 2006 freshman class, 77 percent of the applicants were accepted.

For Further Information Contact Ms. Lisa Pinamonti Kress, Director of Admissions and Scholarships, University of Kansas, KU Visitor Center, 1502 Iowa Street, Lawrence, KS 66045-7576. *Telephone:* 785-864-3911 or 888-686-7323 (toll-free in-state). *Fax:* 785-864-5006. *E-mail:* adm@ku.edu. *Web site:* http://www.ku.edu.

UNIVERSITY OF PHOENIX–WICHITA CAMPUS
Wichita, Kansas

University of Phoenix–Wichita Campus is a coed, proprietary, comprehensive institution, founded in 2003, offering degrees at the bachelor's and master's levels.

Academic Information The faculty has 68 members (9% full-time), 22% with terminal degrees. The undergraduate student-faculty ratio is 5:1. The library holds 1,759 titles and 692 serial subscriptions. Special programs include services for learning-disabled students, advanced placement credit, accelerated degree programs, independent study, distance learning, external degree programs, and adult/continuing education programs.

Student Body Statistics The student body totals 406, of whom 339 are undergraduates (34 freshmen). 56 percent are women and 44 percent are men. 99 percent are from Kansas. 8.6 percent are international students.

Expenses for 2006–07 *Application fee:* $45. *Tuition:* $10,770 full-time, $359 per credit part-time.

Financial Aid Forms of aid include need-based and non-need-based scholarships. The average aided 2005–06 undergraduate received an aid package worth $3923. The application deadline for financial aid is continuous.

Freshman Admission University of Phoenix–Wichita Campus requires 1 recommendation. A high school transcript is required for some. The application deadline for regular admission is rolling.

Transfer Admission The application deadline for admission is rolling.

Entrance Difficulty University of Phoenix–Wichita Campus has an open admission policy.

For Further Information Contact Ms. Beth Barilla, Associate Vice President, Student Admissions and Services, University of Phoenix–Wichita Campus, 4615 East Elwood Street, Mail Stop AA-K101, Phoenix, AZ 85040-1958. *Telephone:* 480-894-1758, 800-776-4867 (toll-free in-state), or 800-228-7240 (toll-free out-of-state). *Fax:* 480-643-1521. *E-mail:* beth.barilla@phoenix.edu. *Web site:* http://www.phoenix.edu/.

UNIVERSITY OF SAINT MARY
Leavenworth, Kansas

University of Saint Mary is a coed, private, Roman Catholic, comprehensive institution, founded in 1923, offering degrees at the associate, bachelor's, and master's levels. It has a 240-acre campus in Leavenworth near Kansas City.

Academic Information The faculty has 89 members (37% full-time), 39% with terminal degrees. The undergraduate student-faculty ratio is 11:1. The library holds 118,195 titles and 205 serial subscriptions. Special programs include an honors program, cooperative (work-study) education, study abroad, advanced placement credit, double majors, independent study, distance learning, self-designed majors, summer session for credit, part-time degree programs (daytime, evenings, summer), adult/continuing education programs, internships, and arrangement for off-campus study with University of Kansas, members of the Council of Independent Colleges. The most frequently chosen baccalaureate fields are business/marketing, education, psychology.

Student Body Statistics The student body totals 837, of whom 548 are undergraduates (82 freshmen). 58 percent are women and 42 percent are men. Students come from 27 states and territories and 4 other countries. 59 percent are from Kansas. 0.4 percent are international students.

Expenses for 2006–07 *Application fee:* $25. *Comprehensive fee:* $22,510 includes full-time tuition ($16,100), mandatory fees ($310), and college room and board ($6100). *College room only:* $2600. Full-time tuition and fees vary according to course load. Room and board charges vary according to student level. *Part-time tuition:* $310 per credit. *Part-time mandatory fees:* $108 per term. Part-time tuition and fees vary according to class time and course load.

Financial Aid Forms of aid include need-based and non-need-based scholarships and part-time jobs. The application deadline for financial aid is continuous.

Freshman Admission University of Saint Mary requires a high school transcript, a minimum 2.5 high school GPA, SAT or ACT scores, and TOEFL scores for international students. 1 recommendation and an interview are recommended. The application deadline for regular admission is rolling.

Transfer Admission The application deadline for admission is rolling.

Entrance Difficulty University of Saint Mary assesses its entrance difficulty level as moderately difficult. For the fall 2006 freshman class, 55 percent of the applicants were accepted.

For Further Information Contact Ms. Jessica Goffinet, Director of Admissions, University of Saint Mary, 4100 South Fourth Street, Leavenworth, KS 66048. *Telephone:* 913-758-6118 or 800-752-7043 (toll-free out-of-state). *Fax:* 913-758-6140. *E-mail:* admiss@stmary.edu. *Web site:* http://www.stmary.edu/.

WASHBURN UNIVERSITY

Topeka, Kansas

Washburn University is a coed, public, comprehensive institution, founded in 1865, offering degrees at the associate, bachelor's, master's, and first professional levels. It has a 160-acre campus in Topeka near Kansas City.

Academic Information The faculty has 536 members (49% full-time), 63% with terminal degrees. The undergraduate student-faculty ratio is 16:1. The library holds 345,642 titles, 1,672 serial subscriptions, and 3,141 audiovisual materials. Special programs include academic remediation, services for learning-disabled students, an honors program, cooperative (work-study) education, study abroad, advanced placement credit, ESL programs, double majors, independent study, distance learning, self-designed majors, summer session for credit, part-time degree programs, adult/continuing education programs, internships, and arrangement for off-campus study with Kansas City Kansas Community College, Johnson County Community College. The most frequently chosen baccalaureate fields are business/marketing, health professions and related sciences, security and protective services.

Student Body Statistics The student body totals 7,153, of whom 6,297 are undergraduates (908 freshmen). 61 percent are women and 39 percent are men. Students come from 49 states and territories and 45 other countries. 95 percent are from Kansas.

Expenses for 2006–07 *Application fee:* $20. *State resident tuition:* $5250 full-time, $175 per credit hour part-time. *Nonresident tuition:* $11,910 full-time, $397 per credit hour part-time. *Mandatory fees:* $62 full-time, $15 per term part-time. *College room and board:* $5170. *College room only:* $2910. Room and board charges vary according to board plan and housing facility.

Financial Aid Forms of aid include need-based and non-need-based scholarships and athletic grants. The priority application deadline for financial aid is March 1.

Freshman Admission Washburn University requires a high school transcript, ACT scores, and TOEFL scores for international students. The application deadline for regular admission is August 1.

Transfer Admission The application deadline for admission is August 1.

Entrance Difficulty Washburn University has an open admission policy except for nursing program. It assesses its entrance difficulty as minimally difficult for out-of-state applicants; minimally difficult for transfers; moderately difficult for nursing program.

For Further Information Contact Mr. Kirk R. Haskins, Director of Admission, Washburn University, 1700 SW College Avenue, Topeka, KS 66621. *Telephone:* 785-670-1030 or 800-332-0291 (toll-free in-state). *Fax:* 785-670-1089. *E-mail:* admissions@washburn.edu. *Web site:* http://www.washburn.edu/.

WICHITA STATE UNIVERSITY

Wichita, Kansas

Wichita State University is a coed, public unit of Kansas State Board of Education, founded in 1895, offering degrees at the associate, bachelor's, master's, and doctoral levels and post-master's and postbachelor's certificates. It has a 335-acre campus in Wichita.

Academic Information The faculty has 524 members (92% full-time), 77% with terminal degrees. The undergraduate student-faculty ratio is 17:1. The library holds 2 million titles, 3,697 serial subscriptions, and 21,829 audiovisual materials. Special programs include academic remediation, services for learning-disabled students, an honors program, cooperative (work-study) education, study abroad, advanced placement credit, accelerated degree programs, Freshman Honors College, ESL programs, double majors, independent study, distance learning, self-designed majors, summer session for credit, part-time degree programs (daytime, evenings, weekends, summer), internships, and arrangement for off-campus study with National Student Exchange, Midwest Student Exchange. The most frequently chosen baccalaureate fields are business/marketing, education, health professions and related sciences.

Student Body Statistics The student body totals 14,298, of whom 11,203 are undergraduates (1,259 freshmen). 56 percent are women and 44 percent are men. Students come from 49 states and territories and 91 other countries. 92 percent are from Kansas. 4.7 percent are international students.

Expenses for 2006–07 *Application fee:* $30. *State resident tuition:* $3673 full-time, $122.45 per credit hour part-time. *Nonresident tuition:* $11,020 full-time, $367.35 per credit hour part-time. *Mandatory fees:* $808 full-time, $26.95 per credit hour part-time, $17 per term part-time. Both full-time and part-time tuition and fees vary according to course load. *College room and board:* $5276. Room and board charges vary according to board plan and housing facility.

Financial Aid Forms of aid include need-based and non-need-based scholarships, athletic grants, and part-time jobs. The average aided 2005–06 undergraduate received an aid package worth $5160. The priority application deadline for financial aid is March 1.

Freshman Admission Wichita State University requires TOEFL scores for international students. A minimum 2.0 high school GPA, minimum ACT score of 21; rank in top 1/3 of high school class, or minimum of 2.00 high school GPA, and SAT or ACT scores are required for some. The application deadline for regular admission is rolling.

Transfer Admission The application deadline for admission is rolling.

Entrance Difficulty Wichita State University has an open admission policy for state residents who graduated from a Kansas high school before May 2001. It assesses its entrance difficulty as moderately difficult for out-of-state applicants; moderately difficult for transfers; very difficult for physical therapy, dental hygiene, nursing, physician assistant programs.

For Further Information Contact Ms. Gina Crabtree, Director of Admissions, Wichita State University, 1845 North Fairmount, Wichita, KS 67260-0124. *Telephone:* 316-978-3085 or 800-362-2594 (toll-free). *Fax:* 316-978-3174. *E-mail:* admissions@wichita.edu. *Web site:* http://www.wichita.edu/.

Michigan

ADRIAN COLLEGE

Adrian, Michigan

Adrian College is a coed, private, four-year college, founded in 1859, affiliated with the United Methodist Church, offering degrees at the associate and bachelor's levels. It has a 100-acre campus in Adrian near Detroit and Toledo.

Academic Information The faculty has 139 members (50% full-time), 50% with terminal degrees. The student-faculty ratio is 15:1. The library holds 150,595 titles, 571 serial subscriptions, and 1,597 audiovisual materials. Special programs include academic remediation, services for learning-disabled students, an honors program, cooperative (work-study) education, study abroad, advanced placement credit, ESL programs, double majors, independent study, self-designed majors, summer session for credit, part-time degree programs (daytime), adult/continuing education programs, internships, and arrangement for off-campus study with Urban Life Center (Chicago), The Washington Center.

Student Body Statistics The student body is made up of 1,051 undergraduates (364 freshmen). 50 percent are women and 50 percent are men. Students come from 15 states and territories and 5 other countries. 87 percent are from Michigan. 0.9 percent are international students. 45.5 percent of the 2006 graduating class went on to graduate and professional schools.

Expenses for 2007–08 *Application fee:* $0. *Comprehensive fee:* $26,680 includes full-time tuition ($19,800), mandatory fees ($100), and college room and board ($6780). *College room only:* $3000. *Part-time tuition:* $625 per credit hour. *Part-time mandatory fees:* $50 per year.

Financial Aid Forms of aid include need-based and non-need-based scholarships and part-time jobs. The average aided 2005–06 undergraduate received an aid package worth $17,074. The priority application deadline for financial aid is March 1.

Freshman Admission Adrian College requires a high school transcript, SAT or ACT scores, and TOEFL scores for international students. An interview and ACT scores are recommended. An essay is required for some. The application deadline for regular admission is March 15.

Transfer Admission The application deadline for admission is March 15.

Entrance Difficulty Adrian College assesses its entrance difficulty level as moderately difficult. For the fall 2006 freshman class, 66 percent of the applicants were accepted.

For Further Information Contact Ms. Carolyn Quinlan, Director of Admissions, Adrian College, 110 South Madison Street, Adrian, MI 49221. *Telephone:* 800-877-2246 or 800-877-2246 (toll-free). *Fax:* 517-264-3331. *E-mail:* admissions@adrian.edu. *Web site:* http://www.adrian.edu/.

ALBION COLLEGE

Albion, Michigan

Albion College is a coed, private, Methodist, four-year college, founded in 1835, offering degrees at the bachelor's level. It has a 565-acre campus in Albion near Detroit.

Academic Information The faculty has 170 members (78% full-time), 75% with terminal degrees. The student-faculty ratio is 13:1. The library holds 363,000 titles, 2,016 serial subscriptions, and 6,540 audiovisual materials. Special programs include services for learning-disabled students, an honors program, study abroad, advanced placement credit, double majors, independent study, self-designed majors, summer session for credit, part-time degree programs (daytime, evenings, summer), internships, and arrangement for off-campus study with Great Lakes Colleges Association. The most frequently chosen baccalaureate fields are psychology, biological/ life sciences, social sciences.

Student Body Statistics The student body is made up of 1,941 undergraduates (480 freshmen). 56 percent are women and 44 percent are men. Students come from 32 states and territories and 19 other countries. 89 percent are from Michigan. 0.9 percent are international students.

Expenses for 2006–07 *Application fee:* $20. *Comprehensive fee:* $33,528 includes full-time tuition ($25,668), mandatory fees ($454), and college room and board ($7406). *College room only:* $3622. Room and board charges vary according to housing facility. *Part-time tuition:* $1090 per semester hour.

Financial Aid Forms of aid include need-based and non-need-based scholarships and part-time jobs. The average aided 2006–07 undergraduate received an aid package worth an estimated $20,965. The priority application deadline for financial aid is March 1.

Freshman Admission Albion College requires an essay, a high school transcript, 1 recommendation, SAT or ACT scores, and TOEFL scores for international students. A minimum 3.2 high school GPA and SAT and SAT Subject Test or ACT scores are recommended. An interview is required for some. The application deadline for regular admission is March 1 and for early action it is December 1.

Transfer Admission The application deadline for admission is June 1.

Entrance Difficulty Albion College assesses its entrance difficulty level as moderately difficult. For the fall 2006 freshman class, 81 percent of the applicants were accepted.

For Further Information Contact Mr. Doug Kellar, Associate Vice President for Enrollment, Albion College, 611 East Porter Street, Albion, MI 49224. *Telephone:* 517-629-0321 or 800-858-6770 (toll-free). *Fax:* 517-629-0569. *E-mail:* admissions@albion.edu. *Web site:* http://www.albion.edu/.

See page 230 for the College Close-Up.

ALMA COLLEGE

Alma, Michigan

Alma College is a coed, private, Presbyterian, four-year college, founded in 1886, offering degrees at the bachelor's level. It has a 125-acre campus in Alma.

Academic Information The faculty has 117 members (74% full-time), 68% with terminal degrees. The student-faculty ratio is 12:1. The library holds 271,614 titles, 1,562 serial subscriptions, and 8,933 audiovisual materials. Special programs include academic remediation, services for learning-disabled students, an honors program, study abroad, advanced placement credit, double majors, independent study, self-designed majors, summer session for credit, internships, and arrangement for off-campus study with New York Arts program, Philadelphia Center Internship, Urban Life Center, Washington Semester. The most frequently chosen baccalaureate fields are biological/life sciences, business/marketing, health professions and related sciences.

Student Body Statistics The student body is made up of 1,215 undergraduates (313 freshmen). 59 percent are women and 41 percent are men. Students come from 22 states and territories and 7 other countries. 95 percent are from Michigan. 0.7 percent are international students. 30 percent of the 2006 graduating class went on to graduate and professional schools.

Expenses for 2006–07 *Application fee:* $25. *One-time mandatory fee:* $300. *Comprehensive fee:* $30,154 includes full-time tuition ($22,170), mandatory fees ($210), and college room and board ($7774). *College room only:* $3830. Room and board charges vary according to board plan and housing facility. *Part-time tuition:* $860 per credit. Part-time tuition varies according to course load.

Financial Aid Forms of aid include need-based and non-need-based scholarships and part-time jobs. The average aided 2006–07 undergraduate received an aid package worth an estimated $19,393. The priority application deadline for financial aid is March 1.

Freshman Admission Alma College requires a high school transcript, a minimum 3.0 high school GPA, minimum SAT score of 1030 or ACT score of 22, SAT or ACT scores, and TOEFL scores for international students. An interview is recommended. An essay and recommendations are required for some. The application deadline for regular admission is rolling.

Transfer Admission The application deadline for admission is rolling.

Entrance Difficulty Alma College assesses its entrance difficulty level as moderately difficult. For the fall 2006 freshman class, 70 percent of the applicants were accepted.

For Further Information Contact Mr. Evan Montague, Director of Admissions, Alma College, Admissions Office, Alma, MI 48801-1599. *Telephone:* 800-321-ALMA or 800-321-ALMA (toll-free). *Fax:* 989-463-7057. *E-mail:* admissions@alma.edu. *Web site:* http://www.alma.edu/.

ANDREWS UNIVERSITY
Berrien Springs, Michigan

Andrews University is a coed, private, Seventh-day Adventist university, founded in 1874, offering degrees at the associate, bachelor's, master's, doctoral, and first professional levels and post-master's certificates. It has a 1,650-acre campus in Berrien Springs.

Academic Information The faculty has 266 members (78% full-time), 64% with terminal degrees. The undergraduate student-faculty ratio is 11:1. The library holds 512,100 titles and 3,032 serial subscriptions. Special programs include academic remediation, an honors program, cooperative (work-study) education, study abroad, advanced placement credit, accelerated degree programs, Freshman Honors College, ESL programs, double majors, distance learning, self-designed majors, summer session for credit, part-time degree programs (daytime, evenings), adult/continuing education programs, internships, and arrangement for off-campus study. The most frequently chosen baccalaureate fields are business/marketing, health professions and related sciences, visual and performing arts.

Student Body Statistics The student body totals 3,195, of whom 1,733 are undergraduates (290 freshmen). 55 percent are women and 45 percent are men. Students come from 45 states and territories and 50 other countries. 51 percent are from Michigan. 13.2 percent are international students.

Expenses for 2007–08 *Application fee:* $32. *Comprehensive fee:* $26,278 includes full-time tuition ($18,968), mandatory fees ($560), and college room and board ($6750). *College room only:* $3250. *Part-time tuition:* $767 per credit hour.

Financial Aid Forms of aid include need-based and non-need-based scholarships. The average aided 2006–07 undergraduate received an aid package worth an estimated $21,664. The application deadline for financial aid is continuous.

Freshman Admission Andrews University requires an essay, a high school transcript, a minimum 2.25 high school GPA, 2 recommendations, and SAT or ACT scores. The application deadline for regular admission is rolling.

Transfer Admission The application deadline for admission is rolling.

Entrance Difficulty Andrews University assesses its entrance difficulty level as moderately difficult. For the fall 2006 freshman class, 47 percent of the applicants were accepted.

For Further Information Contact Mr. Delmus Pinkston, Undergraduate Admissions Coordinator, Andrews University, Berrien Springs, MI 49104. *Telephone:* 800-253-2874 or 800-253-2874 (toll-free). *Fax:* 269-471-3228. *E-mail:* enroll@andrews.edu. *Web site:* http://www.andrews.edu/.

AQUINAS COLLEGE
Grand Rapids, Michigan

Aquinas College is a coed, private, Roman Catholic, comprehensive institution, founded in 1886, offering degrees at the associate, bachelor's, and master's levels. It has a 107-acre campus in Grand Rapids near Detroit.

Academic Information The faculty has 151 members (62% full-time), 53% with terminal degrees. The undergraduate student-faculty ratio is 14:1. The library holds 112,458 titles and 14,725 serial subscriptions. Special programs include academic remediation, services for learning-disabled students, an honors program, cooperative (work-study) education, study abroad, advanced placement credit, accelerated degree programs, double majors, independent study, distance learning, self-designed majors, summer session for credit, part-time degree programs, external degree programs, adult/continuing education programs, internships, and arrangement for off-campus study with members of the Dominican College Interchange. The most frequently chosen baccalaureate fields are business/marketing, education, social sciences.

Student Body Statistics The student body totals 2,098, of whom 1,780 are undergraduates (387 freshmen). 64 percent are women and 36 percent are men. Students come from 20 states and territories and 6 other countries. 95 percent are from Michigan. 0.3 percent are international students. 13 percent of the 2006 graduating class went on to graduate and professional schools.

Expenses for 2007–08 *Application fee:* $0. *Comprehensive fee:* $26,470 includes full-time tuition ($20,048) and college room and board ($6422). *College room only:* $2966. *Part-time tuition:* $406 per credit.

Financial Aid Forms of aid include need-based and non-need-based scholarships, athletic grants, and part-time jobs. The application deadline for financial aid is August 15 with a priority deadline of March 1.

Freshman Admission Aquinas College requires a high school transcript, a minimum 2.5 high school GPA, SAT or ACT scores, and TOEFL scores for international students. An essay and an interview are required for some. The application deadline for regular admission is rolling.

Transfer Admission The application deadline for admission is rolling.

Entrance Difficulty Aquinas College assesses its entrance difficulty level as moderately difficult. For the fall 2006 freshman class, 81 percent of the applicants were accepted.

SPECIAL MESSAGE TO STUDENTS

Social Life Aquinas College, located in Grand Rapids, Michigan, has the advantages of a city that is the cultural, medical, business, and commercial center of western Michigan. Students involve themselves in the Community Senate, intramural and intercollegiate athletics, music performance groups, volunteer and service groups, and campus ministry. Some campus-sponsored events include white-water rafting, Spring Fling, Homecoming, dinner nightclubs, Murder Mystery Night, a cultural series, Welcome Week, movie nights, Winterfest, a film series, dances, and lectures. Off-campus events include theater, concerts, and musical performances by nationally known performers and a local IHL hockey team as well as minor league baseball.

Academic Highlights Aquinas offers more than sixty different majors. The College has three schools within this structure: the School of Education, the School of Liberal Arts and Sciences, and the School of Management. The study program in Ireland provides a semester abroad for 30 students during the second semester of each academic year. The curriculum centers on Irish studies and culture and provides independent travel opportunities to the British Isles and the continent. Other cultural immersion programs include Costa Rica, France, Germany, Japan, and Spain. A general education plan ensures that the student is equipped with the skills necessary for both life and a career. Aquinas also offers a semester of field experience in career-related employment through which the student earns college credit and a salary. The location of the College in Grand Rapids provides myriad experiences for students in medical, business, and commercial fields. More than 200 internships with leading firms and organizations are available.

Interviews and Campus Visits Although the admission interview is not a requirement, campus visits are highly recommended. Aquinas hosts AQ Days throughout the year. There are four General Visit Days and Athletics, Science, Math, Nursing, Leadership, and Fine Arts Days. This program gives the student the opportunity to tour the campus, meet with faculty members, participate in financial aid workshops, and enjoy a complimentary lunch. Parents are also welcome. Individual appointments with the Admissions Office are available. Students are encouraged to see the Holmdene Mansion, part of the original estate on which Aquinas is built, and the Art and Music Center, which houses recital halls, an art gallery, a sculpture studio, a photography lab, and a darkroom. The Albertus Magnus Hall of Science houses laboratories, a

Aquinas College (continued)

greenhouse, and an observatory. Campus visitors should also tour the Performing Arts Center, a state-of-the-art, $7-million facility. Jarecki Center provides the latest in classroom technology, and the Grace Hauenstein Library opened in fall 2006. The Ravine Apartments give students a living option beyond the traditional. For information about appointments and campus visits, students should call the Admissions Office at 616-732-4460 or 800-678-9593 (toll-free), Monday through Friday, 8:30 to 5, and Saturdays, 9 to 1. The office is located in Hruby Hall, 1760 Fulton Street, on the campus. The nearest commercial airport is Kent County International.

For Further Information Write to Paula Meehan, Dean of Admissions, Aquinas College, 1607 Robinson Road, SE, Grand Rapids, MI 49506-1799. *E-mail:* admissions@aquinas.edu. *Web site:* http://www.aquinas.edu.

AVE MARIA COLLEGE
Ypsilanti, Michigan
http://www.avemaria.edu/

BAKER COLLEGE OF ALLEN PARK
Allen Park, Michigan

Baker College of Allen Park is a coed, primarily women's, private, four-year college of Baker College System, founded in 2003, offering degrees at the associate and bachelor's levels. It has a 13-acre campus in Allen Park near Detroit.

Academic Information The faculty has 88 members (2% full-time), 12% with terminal degrees. The student-faculty ratio is 34:1.
Student Body Statistics The student body is made up of 1,923 undergraduates. 77 percent are women and 23 percent are men. Students come from 1 state or territory.
Expenses for 2007–08 *Application fee:* $0. *Tuition:* $6660 full-time, $185 per quarter hour part-time.
Freshman Admission Baker College of Allen Park requires a high school transcript and an interview. The application deadline for regular admission is September 24.
Entrance Difficulty For the fall 2006 freshman class, 100 percent of the applicants were accepted.
For Further Information Contact Mr. Steve Peterson, Vice President of Admissions, Baker College of Allen Park, 4500 Enterprise Drive, Allen Park, MI 48101. *Telephone:* 313-425-3700 or 800-767-4120 (toll-free in-state). *E-mail:* steve.peterson@baker.edu. *Web site:* http://www.baker.edu/.

BAKER COLLEGE OF AUBURN HILLS
Auburn Hills, Michigan

Baker College of Auburn Hills is a coed, private, four-year college of Baker College System, founded in 1911, offering degrees at the associate and bachelor's levels and postbachelor's certificates. It has a 7-acre campus in Auburn Hills near Detroit.

Academic Information The faculty has 155 members (7% full-time), 15% with terminal degrees. The student-faculty ratio is 41:1. The library holds 5,400 titles and 95 serial subscriptions. Special programs include academic remediation, services for learning-disabled students, cooperative (work-study) education, advanced placement credit, accelerated degree programs, double majors, independent study, distance learning, summer session for credit, part-time degree programs (daytime, evenings, summer), external degree programs, and internships.
Student Body Statistics The student body is made up of 3,740 undergraduates. 73 percent are women and 27 percent are men. Students come from 1 state or territory.

Expenses for 2007–08 *Application fee:* $20. *Tuition:* $6660 full-time, $185 per quarter hour part-time.
Freshman Admission Baker College of Auburn Hills requires a high school transcript and TOEFL scores for international students. The application deadline for regular admission is rolling.
Transfer Admission The application deadline for admission is rolling.
Entrance Difficulty Baker College of Auburn Hills has an open admission policy.
For Further Information Contact Ms. Jan Bohlen, Vice President for Admissions, Baker College of Auburn Hills, 1500 University Drive, Auburn Hills, MI 48326-1586. *Telephone:* 248-340-0600 or 888-429-0410 (toll-free in-state). *Fax:* 248-340-0608. *E-mail:* jan.bohlen@baker.edu. *Web site:* http://www.baker.edu/.

BAKER COLLEGE OF CADILLAC
Cadillac, Michigan

Baker College of Cadillac is a coed, private, four-year college of Baker College System, founded in 1986, offering degrees at the associate and bachelor's levels. It has a 40-acre campus in Cadillac.

Academic Information The faculty has 105 members (4% full-time), 5% with terminal degrees. The student-faculty ratio is 42:1. The library holds 4,000 titles and 78 serial subscriptions. Special programs include academic remediation, services for learning-disabled students, cooperative (work-study) education, advanced placement credit, double majors, independent study, distance learning, summer session for credit, part-time degree programs (daytime, evenings, weekends, summer), external degree programs, and internships.
Student Body Statistics The student body is made up of 1,640 undergraduates. 70 percent are women and 30 percent are men. Students come from 4 states and territories.
Expenses for 2007–08 *Application fee:* $20. *Tuition:* $6660 full-time, $185 per quarter hour part-time.
Freshman Admission Baker College of Cadillac requires a high school transcript and TOEFL scores for international students. An interview is recommended. SAT or ACT scores are required for some. The application deadline for regular admission is rolling.
Transfer Admission The application deadline for admission is rolling.
Entrance Difficulty Baker College of Cadillac has an open admission policy.
For Further Information Contact Mr. Mike Tisdale, Director of Admissions, Baker College of Cadillac, 9600 East 13th Street, Cadillac, MI 49601. *Telephone:* 231-876-3100 or 888-313-3463 (toll-free in-state). *Fax:* 231-775-8505. *E-mail:* mike.tisdale@baker.edu. *Web site:* http://www.baker.edu/.

BAKER COLLEGE OF CLINTON TOWNSHIP
Clinton Township, Michigan

Baker College of Clinton Township is a coed, private, four-year college of Baker College System, founded in 1990, offering degrees at the associate and bachelor's levels. It has a 25-acre campus in Clinton Township near Detroit.

Academic Information The faculty has 208 members (8% full-time), 12% with terminal degrees. The student-faculty ratio is 45:1. The library holds 8,000 titles and 97 serial subscriptions. Special programs include academic remediation, services for learning-disabled students, cooperative (work-study) education, advanced placement credit, summer session for credit, part-time degree programs (daytime, evenings, weekends, summer), external degree programs, and internships.
Student Body Statistics The student body is made up of 5,281 undergraduates. 75 percent are women and 25 percent are men. Students come from 2 states and territories.
Expenses for 2007–08 *Application fee:* $20. *Tuition:* $6660 full-time, $185 per quarter hour part-time.

Freshman Admission Baker College of Clinton Township requires a high school transcript and TOEFL scores for international students. SAT or ACT scores are required for some. The application deadline for regular admission is rolling.

Transfer Admission The application deadline for admission is rolling.

Entrance Difficulty Baker College of Clinton Township has an open admission policy.

For Further Information Contact Ms. Annette Looser, Vice President for Admissions, Baker College of Clinton Township, 34401 South Gratiot Avenue, Clinton Township, MI 48035. *Telephone:* 586-790-9580 or 888-272-2842 (toll-free). *Fax:* 586-791-6811. *E-mail:* annette.looser@baker.edu. *Web site:* http://www.baker.edu/.

BAKER COLLEGE OF FLINT

Flint, Michigan

Baker College of Flint is a coed, private, four-year college of Baker College System, founded in 1911, offering degrees at the associate and bachelor's levels. It has a 30-acre campus in Flint near Detroit.

Academic Information The faculty has 315 members (13% full-time), 12% with terminal degrees. The student-faculty ratio is 31:1. The library holds 168,700 titles. Special programs include academic remediation, services for learning-disabled students, cooperative (work-study) education, advanced placement credit, accelerated degree programs, double majors, independent study, distance learning, summer session for credit, part-time degree programs, external degree programs, and internships.

Student Body Statistics The student body is made up of 5,776 undergraduates. 70 percent are women and 30 percent are men. Students come from 5 states and territories. 99 percent are from Michigan.

Expenses for 2007–08 *Application fee:* $20. *Tuition:* $6660 full-time, $185 per quarter hour part-time. *College room only:* $2600.

Freshman Admission Baker College of Flint requires a high school transcript and TOEFL scores for international students. The application deadline for regular admission is September 20.

Transfer Admission The application deadline for admission is September 20.

Entrance Difficulty Baker College of Flint has an open admission policy.

For Further Information Contact Mr. Troy Crowe, Vice President for Admissions, Baker College of Flint, 1050 West Bristol Road, Flint, MI 48507-5508. *Telephone:* 810-766-4015 or 800-964-4299 (toll-free). *Fax:* 810-766-4049. *E-mail:* troy.crowe@baker.edu. *Web site:* http://www.baker.edu/.

BAKER COLLEGE OF JACKSON

Jackson, Michigan

Baker College of Jackson is a coed, private, four-year college of Baker College System, founded in 1994, offering degrees at the associate and bachelor's levels. It has a 42-acre campus in Jackson near Lansing.

Academic Information The faculty has 85 members (6% full-time), 13% with terminal degrees. The student-faculty ratio is 36:1. The library holds 7,000 titles and 150 serial subscriptions. Special programs include academic remediation, services for learning-disabled students, cooperative (work-study) education, advanced placement credit, accelerated degree programs, double majors, independent study, distance learning, summer session for credit, part-time degree programs (daytime, evenings, weekends, summer), external degree programs, and internships.

Student Body Statistics The student body is made up of 1,730 undergraduates. 76 percent are women and 24 percent are men. Students come from 2 states and territories. 99 percent are from Michigan.

Expenses for 2007–08 *Application fee:* $20. *Tuition:* $6660 full-time, $185 per quarter hour part-time.

Freshman Admission Baker College of Jackson requires a high school transcript. The application deadline for regular admission is September 19.

Transfer Admission The application deadline for admission is rolling.

Entrance Difficulty Baker College of Jackson has an open admission policy.

For Further Information Contact Ms. Kelli Stepka, Vice President for Admissions, Baker College of Jackson, 2800 Springport Road, Jackson, MI 49202. *Telephone:* 517-788-7800 or 888-343-3683 (toll-free). *Fax:* 517-789-7331. *E-mail:* kelli.stepka@baker.edu. *Web site:* http://www.baker.edu/.

BAKER COLLEGE OF MUSKEGON

Muskegon, Michigan

Baker College of Muskegon is a coed, private, four-year college of Baker College System, founded in 1888, offering degrees at the associate and bachelor's levels. It has a 40-acre campus in Muskegon near Grand Rapids.

Academic Information The faculty has 177 members (10% full-time), 8% with terminal degrees. The student-faculty ratio is 55:1. The library holds 32,000 titles and 140 serial subscriptions. Special programs include academic remediation, services for learning-disabled students, cooperative (work-study) education, advanced placement credit, accelerated degree programs, double majors, independent study, distance learning, summer session for credit, part-time degree programs (daytime, evenings, weekends), external degree programs, adult/continuing education programs, and internships.

Student Body Statistics The student body is made up of 5,022 undergraduates. 70 percent are women and 30 percent are men. Students come from 13 states and territories. 99 percent are from Michigan. 1 percent of the 2006 graduating class went on to graduate and professional schools.

Expenses for 2007–08 *Application fee:* $20. *Tuition:* $6660 full-time, $185 per quarter hour part-time. *College room only:* $2500.

Freshman Admission Baker College of Muskegon requires a high school transcript and TOEFL scores for international students. The application deadline for regular admission is September 24.

Transfer Admission The application deadline for admission is rolling.

Entrance Difficulty Baker College of Muskegon has an open admission policy.

For Further Information Contact Ms. Kathy Jacobson, Vice President of Admissions, Baker College of Muskegon, 1903 Marquette Avenue, Muskegon, MI 49442-3497. *Telephone:* 231-777-5207 or 800-937-0337 (toll-free in-state). *Fax:* 231-777-5201. *E-mail:* kathy.jacobson@baker.edu. *Web site:* http://www.baker.edu/.

BAKER COLLEGE OF OWOSSO

Owosso, Michigan

Baker College of Owosso is a coed, private, four-year college of Baker College System, founded in 1984, offering degrees at the associate and bachelor's levels. It has a 32-acre campus in Owosso.

Academic Information The faculty has 144 members (6% full-time), 15% with terminal degrees. The student-faculty ratio is 40:1. The library holds 35,424 titles and 215 serial subscriptions. Special programs include academic remediation, services for learning-disabled students, cooperative (work-study) education, advanced placement credit, accelerated degree programs, summer session for credit, part-time degree programs, external degree programs, adult/continuing education programs, and internships.

Student Body Statistics The student body is made up of 2,875 undergraduates. 68 percent are women and 32 percent are men. Students come from 4 states and territories.

Expenses for 2007–08 *Application fee:* $20. *Tuition:* $6660 full-time, $185 per quarter hour part-time. *College room only:* $2400.

Freshman Admission Baker College of Owosso requires a high school transcript and TOEFL scores for international students. The application deadline for regular admission is rolling.

Transfer Admission The application deadline for admission is rolling.

Baker College of Owosso (continued)

Entrance Difficulty Baker College of Owosso has an open admission policy.

For Further Information Contact Mr. Michael Konopacke, Vice President for Admissions, Baker College of Owosso, 1020 South Washington Street, Owosso, MI 48867-4400. *Telephone:* 989-729-3350 or 800-879-3797 (toll-free). *Fax:* 517-729-3359. *E-mail:* mike.konopacke@baker.edu. *Web site:* http://www.baker.edu/.

BAKER COLLEGE OF PORT HURON
Port Huron, Michigan

Baker College of Port Huron is a coed, private, four-year college of Baker College System, founded in 1990, offering degrees at the associate and bachelor's levels. It has a 10-acre campus in Port Huron near Detroit.

Academic Information The faculty has 126 members (10% full-time), 7% with terminal degrees. The student-faculty ratio is 28:1. The library holds 16,823 titles and 181 serial subscriptions. Special programs include academic remediation, services for learning-disabled students, cooperative (work-study) education, advanced placement credit, accelerated degree programs, double majors, independent study, distance learning, summer session for credit, part-time degree programs (daytime, evenings, weekends, summer), external degree programs, and internships.

Student Body Statistics The student body is made up of 1,598 undergraduates. 77 percent are women and 23 percent are men.

Expenses for 2007–08 *Application fee:* $20. *Tuition:* $6660 full-time, $185 per quarter hour part-time.

Freshman Admission Baker College of Port Huron requires a high school transcript, an interview, and TOEFL scores for international students. The application deadline for regular admission is September 24.

Transfer Admission The application deadline for admission is rolling.

Entrance Difficulty Baker College of Port Huron has an open admission policy.

For Further Information Contact Mr. Daniel Kenny, Vice President for Admissions, Baker College of Port Huron, 3403 Lapeer Road, Port Huron, MI 48060-2597. *Telephone:* 810-985-7000 or 888-262-2442 (toll-free). *Fax:* 810-985-7066. *E-mail:* kenny_d@porthuron.baker.edu. *Web site:* http://www.baker.edu/.

CALVIN COLLEGE
Grand Rapids, Michigan

Calvin College is a coed, private, comprehensive institution, founded in 1876, affiliated with the Christian Reformed Church, offering degrees at the bachelor's and master's levels and postbachelor's certificates. It has a 370-acre campus in Grand Rapids.

Academic Information The faculty has 411 members (76% full-time), 68% with terminal degrees. The undergraduate student-faculty ratio is 12:1. The library holds 824,806 titles, 14,464 serial subscriptions, and 26,191 audiovisual materials. Special programs include academic remediation, services for learning-disabled students, an honors program, study abroad, advanced placement credit, accelerated degree programs, double majors, independent study, self-designed majors, summer session for credit, part-time degree programs (daytime, evenings, summer), adult/continuing education programs, internships, and arrangement for off-campus study with Council for Christian Colleges and Universities, Central College, Trinity Christian College, Au Sable Institute. The most frequently chosen baccalaureate fields are business/marketing, education, health professions and related sciences.

Student Body Statistics The student body totals 4,187, of whom 4,130 are undergraduates (1,027 freshmen). 54 percent are women and 46 percent are men. Students come from 50 states and territories and 48 other countries. 57 percent are from Michigan. 7.3 percent are international students. 20 percent of the 2006 graduating class went on to graduate and professional schools.

Expenses for 2006–07 *Application fee:* $35. *Comprehensive fee:* $27,510 includes full-time tuition ($20,245), mandatory fees ($225), and college room and board ($7040). *College room only:* $3830. Full-time tuition and fees vary according to program. Room and board charges vary according to board plan. *Part-time tuition:* $480 per credit hour. Part-time tuition varies according to course load.

Financial Aid Forms of aid include need-based and non-need-based scholarships and part-time jobs. The average aided 2006–07 undergraduate received an aid package worth an estimated $14,200.

Freshman Admission Calvin College requires an essay, a high school transcript, a minimum 2.5 high school GPA, 1 recommendation, SAT and SAT Subject Test or ACT scores, and TOEFL scores for international students. An interview is recommended. The application deadline for regular admission is August 15.

Transfer Admission The application deadline for admission is rolling.

Entrance Difficulty Calvin College assesses its entrance difficulty level as moderately difficult. For the fall 2006 freshman class, 96 percent of the applicants were accepted.

For Further Information Contact Mr. Dale D. Kuiper, Director of Admissions, Calvin College, 3201 Burton Street, SE, Grand Rapids, MI 49546. *Telephone:* 616-526-6106 or 800-688-0122 (toll-free). *Fax:* 616-526-6777. *E-mail:* admissions@calvin.edu. *Web site:* http://www.calvin.edu/.

CENTER FOR CREATIVE STUDIES-COLLEGE OF ART AND DESIGN

See College for Creative Studies.

CENTRAL MICHIGAN UNIVERSITY
Mount Pleasant, Michigan

Central Michigan University is a coed, public university, founded in 1892, offering degrees at the bachelor's, master's, and doctoral levels and post-master's and postbachelor's certificates. It has an 854-acre campus in Mount Pleasant.

Academic Information The faculty has 1,119 members (65% full-time), 60% with terminal degrees. The undergraduate student-faculty ratio is 22:1. The library holds 1 million titles and 7,392 serial subscriptions. Special programs include academic remediation, an honors program, study abroad, advanced placement credit, accelerated degree programs, Freshman Honors College, ESL programs, double majors, independent study, distance learning, self-designed majors, summer session for credit, part-time degree programs (daytime, evenings, summer), external degree programs, adult/continuing education programs, internships, and arrangement for off-campus study. The most frequently chosen baccalaureate fields are business/marketing, education, social sciences.

Student Body Statistics The student body totals 26,710, of whom 20,129 are undergraduates (3,819 freshmen). 56 percent are women and 44 percent are men. Students come from 38 states and territories and 43 other countries. 97 percent are from Michigan. 1.2 percent are international students. 19 percent of the 2006 graduating class went on to graduate and professional schools.

Expenses for 2006–07 *Application fee:* $35. *State resident tuition:* $6753 full-time, $225.11 per credit part-time. *Nonresident tuition:* $15,915 full-time, $530.50 per credit part-time. Both full-time and part-time tuition varies according to student level. *College room and board:* $6824. *College room only:* $3412. Room and board charges vary according to board plan, housing facility, location, and student level. Costs at Central Michigan University are based upon a guaranteed undergraduate tuition plan called the CMU Promise. The CMU Promise to new and transfer undergraduate students is one unchanging tuition rate for up to five years. In addition to fixing the cost of tuition, the CMU Promise guaranteed tuition program eliminates all former mandatory fees, so there are no added fees. The CMU Promise also guarantees that the room and board rate for residence halls will not increase for two years from the date of a student's admission to CMU.

Financial Aid Forms of aid include need-based and non-need-based scholarships, athletic grants, and part-time jobs. The average aided 2006–07 undergraduate received an aid package worth an estimated $10,212.

Freshman Admission Central Michigan University requires a high school transcript, ACT scores, and TOEFL scores for international students. A minimum 3.0 high school GPA is recommended. An essay, recommendations, and an interview are required for some. The application deadline for regular admission is rolling.

Transfer Admission The application deadline for admission is rolling.

Entrance Difficulty Central Michigan University assesses its entrance difficulty level as moderately difficult.

For Further Information Contact Ms. Betty J. Wagner, Director of Admissions, Central Michigan University, Warriner Hall 102, Mt. Pleasant, MI 48859. *Telephone:* 989-774-3076 or 888-292-5366 (toll-free). *Fax:* 989-774-7267. *E-mail:* cmuadmit@cmich.edu. *Web site:* http://www.cmich.edu/.

CLEARY UNIVERSITY

Ann Arbor, Michigan

Cleary University is a coed, private, comprehensive institution, founded in 1883, offering degrees at the associate, bachelor's, and master's levels. It has a 32-acre campus in Ann Arbor near Detroit and Lansing.

Academic Information The faculty has 127 members (6% full-time), 13% with terminal degrees. The undergraduate student-faculty ratio is 10:1. The library holds 10,000 titles and 330 audiovisual materials. Special programs include cooperative (work-study) education, advanced placement credit, accelerated degree programs, independent study, distance learning, summer session for credit, part-time degree programs (daytime, evenings, summer), adult/continuing education programs, and internships.

Student Body Statistics The student body totals 691, of whom 626 are undergraduates. 54 percent are women and 46 percent are men. Students come from 4 states and territories and 2 other countries. 99 percent are from Michigan. 0.3 percent are international students.

Expenses for 2007–08 *Application fee:* $25. *Tuition:* $14,160 full-time, $295 per quarter hour part-time.

Financial Aid Forms of aid include need-based and non-need-based scholarships and part-time jobs. The average aided 2005–06 undergraduate received an aid package worth $10,287. The priority application deadline for financial aid is March 1.

Freshman Admission Cleary University requires a high school transcript and a minimum 2.0 high school GPA. An interview is recommended. An essay, 2 recommendations, SAT or ACT scores, SAT Subject Test scores, and TOEFL are required for some. The application deadline for regular admission is August 15.

Transfer Admission The application deadline for admission is August 15.

Entrance Difficulty Cleary University assesses its entrance difficulty level as moderately difficult. For the fall 2006 freshman class, 92 percent of the applicants were accepted.

For Further Information Contact Ms. Charlotte Paquette, Admissions Representative, Cleary University, 3750 Cleary Drive, Howell, MI 48843. *Telephone:* 517-548-3670 Ext. 2249 or 888-5-CLEARY Ext. 2249 (toll-free). *Fax:* 517-552-7805. *E-mail:* admissions@cleary.edu. *Web site:* http://www. cleary.edu/.

COLLEGE FOR CREATIVE STUDIES

Detroit, Michigan

College for Creative Studies is a coed, private, four-year college, founded in 1926, offering degrees at the bachelor's level. It has an 11-acre campus in Detroit.

Academic Information The faculty has 246 members (19% full-time). The student-faculty ratio is 11:1. The library holds 24,000 titles and 75 serial subscriptions. Special programs include academic remediation, services for learning-disabled students, cooperative (work-study) education, advanced placement credit, ESL programs, double majors, independent study, summer session for credit, part-time degree programs (daytime, evenings, weekends, summer), internships, and arrangement for off-campus study with Association of Independent Colleges of Art and Design. The most frequently chosen baccalaureate field is visual and performing arts.

Student Body Statistics The student body is made up of 1,302 undergraduates (197 freshmen). 41 percent are women and 59 percent are men. Students come from 35 states and territories and 18 other countries. 82 percent are from Michigan. 4.3 percent are international students.

Expenses for 2007–08 *Application fee:* $35. *Tuition:* $25,230 full-time, $841 per credit hour part-time. *Mandatory fees:* $1145 full-time. *College room only:* $3900.

Financial Aid Forms of aid include need-based and non-need-based scholarships and part-time jobs.

Freshman Admission College for Creative Studies requires an essay, a high school transcript, a portfolio, SAT or ACT scores, and TOEFL scores for international students. A minimum 2.5 high school GPA is recommended. An essay, recommendations, and an interview are required for some. The application deadline for regular admission is August 1.

Transfer Admission The application deadline for admission is rolling.

Entrance Difficulty College for Creative Studies assesses its entrance difficulty level as moderately difficult. For the fall 2006 freshman class, 36 percent of the applicants were accepted.

For Further Information Contact Office of Admissions, College for Creative Studies, 201 East Kirby, Detroit, MI 48202-4034. *Telephone:* 800-952-2787 or 800-952-ARTS (toll-free). *Fax:* 313-872-2739. *E-mail:* admissions@ccscad.edu. *Web site:* http://www.ccscad.edu/.

CONCORDIA UNIVERSITY

Ann Arbor, Michigan

Concordia University is a coed, private, comprehensive unit of Concordia University System, founded in 1963, affiliated with the Lutheran Church–Missouri Synod, offering degrees at the associate, bachelor's, and master's levels. It has a 187-acre campus in Ann Arbor near Detroit.

Academic Information The faculty has 85 members (46% full-time). The undergraduate student-faculty ratio is 12:1. The library holds 117,000 titles, 660 serial subscriptions, and 1,400 audiovisual materials. Special programs include academic remediation, services for learning-disabled students, cooperative (work-study) education, study abroad, advanced placement credit, accelerated degree programs, double majors, independent study, distance learning, self-designed majors, summer session for credit, part-time degree programs (daytime, evenings, weekends, summer), adult/continuing education programs, internships, and arrangement for off-campus study with Concordia University System. The most frequently chosen baccalaureate fields are business/marketing, education, security and protective services.

Student Body Statistics The student body totals 736, of whom 562 are undergraduates (112 freshmen). 57 percent are women and 43 percent are men. Students come from 17 states and territories and 3 other countries. 84 percent are from Michigan. 1.1 percent are international students.

Expenses for 2006–07 *Application fee:* $25. *Comprehensive fee:* $26,410 includes full-time tuition ($18,940), mandatory fees ($120), and college room and board ($7350). *College room only:* $5290. Full-time tuition and fees vary according to course load, degree level, program, and reciprocity agreements. *Part-time tuition:* $620 per credit hour. *Part-time mandatory fees:* $120 per year. Part-time tuition and fees vary according to course load, degree level, program, and reciprocity agreements.

Financial Aid Forms of aid include need-based and non-need-based scholarships, athletic grants, and part-time jobs. The average aided 2005–06 undergraduate received an aid package worth $16,827. The priority application deadline for financial aid is March 1.

Freshman Admission Concordia University requires a high school transcript and SAT or ACT scores. A minimum 2.5 high school GPA, 1 recommendation, and ACT scores are recommended. An essay and an interview are required for some. The application deadline for regular admission is rolling and for nonresidents it is rolling.

Transfer Admission The application deadline for admission is rolling.

Entrance Difficulty Concordia University assesses its entrance difficulty level as moderately difficult. For the fall 2006 freshman class, 69 percent of the applicants were accepted.

For Further Information Contact Jessica Greenwald, Associate Director of Admissions, Concordia University, 4090 Geddes Road, Ann Arbor, MI 48105. *Telephone:* 734-995-7319 or 800-253-0680 (toll-free). *Fax:* 734-995-4610. *E-mail:* greenj@cuaa.edu. *Web site:* http://www.cuaa.edu/.

CORNERSTONE UNIVERSITY
Grand Rapids, Michigan

Cornerstone University is a coed, private, nondenominational, comprehensive institution, founded in 1941, offering degrees at the associate, bachelor's, master's, and first professional levels. It has a 132-acre campus in Grand Rapids.

Academic Information The faculty has 136 members (46% full-time), 29% with terminal degrees. The undergraduate student-faculty ratio is 14:1. The library holds 109,376 titles and 1,073 serial subscriptions. Special programs include academic remediation, services for learning-disabled students, an honors program, study abroad, advanced placement credit, accelerated degree programs, ESL programs, double majors, independent study, distance learning, summer session for credit, part-time degree programs, adult/continuing education programs, internships, and arrangement for off-campus study with Calvin College, Reformed Bible College, Grace Bible College. The most frequently chosen baccalaureate fields are education, psychology, theology and religious vocations.
Student Body Statistics The student body totals 2,509, of whom 1,981 are undergraduates (367 freshmen). 61 percent are women and 39 percent are men. Students come from 29 states and territories and 3 other countries. 82 percent are from Michigan. 1.1 percent are international students. 15 percent of the 2006 graduating class went on to graduate and professional schools.
Expenses for 2006–07 *Application fee:* $25. *Comprehensive fee:* $22,940 includes full-time tuition ($16,780), mandatory fees ($300), and college room and board ($5860). Room and board charges vary according to board plan. *Part-time tuition:* $642 per hour. Part-time tuition varies according to course load.
Financial Aid Forms of aid include need-based and non-need-based scholarships, athletic grants, and part-time jobs. The application deadline for financial aid is March 1.
Freshman Admission Cornerstone University requires an essay, a high school transcript, a minimum 2.5 high school GPA, 1 recommendation, pastoral letter, SAT or ACT scores, and TOEFL scores for international students. An interview is recommended. The application deadline for regular admission is rolling.
Transfer Admission The application deadline for admission is rolling.
Entrance Difficulty Cornerstone University assesses its entrance difficulty level as minimally difficult. For the fall 2006 freshman class, 73 percent of the applicants were accepted.
For Further Information Contact Mr. Brent Rudin, Dean of Admissions and Marketing, Cornerstone University, 1001 East Beltline Avenue, NE, Grand Rapids, MI 49525. *Telephone:* 616-222-1426 or 800-787-9778 (toll-free). *Fax:* 616-222-1400. *E-mail:* admissions@cornerstone.edu. *Web site:* http://www.cornerstone.edu/.

DAVENPORT UNIVERSITY
Alma, Michigan
http://www.davenport.edu/

DAVENPORT UNIVERSITY
Bad Axe, Michigan
http://www.davenport.edu/

DAVENPORT UNIVERSITY
Bay City, Michigan
http://www.davenport.edu/

DAVENPORT UNIVERSITY
Caro, Michigan
http://www.davenport.edu/

DAVENPORT UNIVERSITY
Dearborn, Michigan

Davenport University is a coed, private, comprehensive institution, founded in 1985, offering degrees at the associate, bachelor's, and master's levels and postbachelor's certificates. It has a 50-acre campus in Dearborn near Detroit.

Academic Information The faculty has 1,157 members (10% full-time), 15% with terminal degrees. The undergraduate student-faculty ratio is 15:1. The library holds 132,595 titles, 434 serial subscriptions, and 10,256 audiovisual materials. Special programs include academic remediation, services for learning-disabled students, an honors program, cooperative (work-study) education, study abroad, advanced placement credit, accelerated degree programs, ESL programs, double majors, independent study, distance learning, self-designed majors, summer session for credit, part-time degree programs, and internships. The most frequently chosen baccalaureate fields are business/marketing, computer and information sciences, health professions and related sciences.
Student Body Statistics The student body totals 12,617, of whom 11,954 are undergraduates (1,230 freshmen). 75 percent are women and 25 percent are men. Students come from 40 states and territories. 98 percent are from Michigan. 0.1 percent are international students.
Expenses for 2007–08 *Application fee:* $25. *Comprehensive fee:* $14,406 includes full-time tuition ($9816), mandatory fees ($140), and college room and board ($4450). *Part-time tuition:* $409 per credit.
Financial Aid Forms of aid include need-based and non-need-based scholarships, athletic grants, and part-time jobs. The priority application deadline for financial aid is March 1.
Freshman Admission Davenport University requires a high school transcript and TOEFL scores for international students. An interview and SAT or ACT scores are recommended. The application deadline for regular admission is rolling.
Transfer Admission The application deadline for admission is rolling.
Entrance Difficulty Davenport University has an open admission policy.
For Further Information Contact Cathtyn Claerhout, Davenport University, 415 East Fulton Street, Grand Rapids, MI 49503. *Telephone:* 616-451-3511 or 800-632-9569 (toll-free). *Fax:* 616-732-1142. *E-mail:* gradmiss@davenport.edu. *Web site:* http://www.davenport.edu/.

DAVENPORT UNIVERSITY
Midland, Michigan
http://www.davenport.edu/

DAVENPORT UNIVERSITY
Saginaw, Michigan
http://www.davenport.edu/

EASTERN MICHIGAN UNIVERSITY
Ypsilanti, Michigan

Eastern Michigan University is a coed, public, comprehensive institution, founded in 1849, offering degrees at the bachelor's, master's, and doctoral levels and post-master's and postbachelor's certificates. It has a 460-acre campus in Ypsilanti near Detroit.

Academic Information The faculty has 1,242 members (62% full-time), 50% with terminal degrees. The undergraduate student-faculty ratio is 18:1. The library holds 658,648 titles, 4,457 serial subscriptions, and

11,524 audiovisual materials. Special programs include academic remediation, services for learning-disabled students, an honors program, cooperative (work-study) education, study abroad, advanced placement credit, accelerated degree programs, ESL programs, double majors, independent study, distance learning, self-designed majors, summer session for credit, part-time degree programs (daytime, evenings, weekends, summer), adult/continuing education programs, and internships.

Student Body Statistics The student body totals 22,821, of whom 18,172 are undergraduates (2,347 freshmen). 59 percent are women and 41 percent are men. Students come from 48 states and territories and 55 other countries. 93 percent are from Michigan. 1.5 percent are international students. 20 percent of the 2006 graduating class went on to graduate and professional schools.

Expenses for 2006–07 *Application fee:* $30. *State resident tuition:* $5835 full-time, $194.50 per credit hour part-time. *Nonresident tuition:* $17,190 full-time, $573 per credit hour part-time. *Mandatory fees:* $1100 full-time, $34 per credit hour part-time, $40 per term part-time. *College room and board:* $6610. *College room only:* $3104. Room and board charges vary according to board plan, housing facility, and location.

Financial Aid Forms of aid include need-based and non-need-based scholarships, athletic grants, and part-time jobs. The average aided 2005–06 undergraduate received an aid package worth $6584. The application deadline for financial aid is continuous.

Freshman Admission Eastern Michigan University requires a high school transcript, a minimum 2.0 high school GPA, TOEFL scores for international students, 1 recommendation, an interview, and ACT scores are required for some.

Transfer Admission The application deadline for admission is rolling.

Entrance Difficulty Eastern Michigan University assesses its entrance difficulty level as moderately difficult. For the fall 2006 freshman class, 79 percent of the applicants were accepted.

For Further Information Contact Ms. Judy Benfield-Tatum, Director of Admissions, Eastern Michigan University, 400 Pierce Hall, Ypsilanti, MI 48197. *Telephone:* 734-487-3060 or 800-GO TO EMU (toll-free). *Fax:* 734-487-1484. *E-mail:* admissions@emich.edu. *Web site:* http://www.emich.edu/.

FERRIS STATE UNIVERSITY
Big Rapids, Michigan

Ferris State University is a coed, public, comprehensive institution, founded in 1884, offering degrees at the associate, bachelor's, master's, and first professional levels (Associate). It has an 880-acre campus in Big Rapids near Grand Rapids.

Academic Information The faculty has 864 members (62% full-time). The undergraduate student-faculty ratio is 17:1. The library holds 354,173 titles and 1,049 serial subscriptions. Special programs include academic remediation, services for learning-disabled students, an honors program, cooperative (work-study) education, study abroad, advanced placement credit, accelerated degree programs, Ferris Honors College, ESL programs, double majors, independent study, distance learning, summer session for credit, part-time degree programs (daytime, evenings, summer), adult/continuing education programs, internships, and arrangement for off-campus study with Delta College, Henry Ford Community College (CC), Lansing CC, Mott CC, Macomb CC, Macomb CC, St. Clair County CC, North Central Michigan College, Northwestern Michigan College, University Center, Gaylord, Westshore Community College, Muskegon CC, Southwestern Michigan College. The most frequently chosen baccalaureate fields are business/marketing, engineering technologies, visual and performing arts.

Student Body Statistics The student body totals 12,575, of whom 11,409 are undergraduates (1,980 freshmen). 47 percent are women and 53 percent are men. Students come from 46 states and territories and 39 other countries. 95 percent are from Michigan. 1.1 percent are international students. 6 percent of the 2006 graduating class went on to graduate and professional schools.

Expenses for 2006–07 *Application fee:* $30. *State resident tuition:* $7200 full-time, $270 per credit hour part-time. *Nonresident tuition:* $14,640 full-time, $530 per credit hour part-time. *Mandatory fees:* $142 full-time. Full-time tuition and fees vary according to reciprocity agreements. *College room and board:* $7220. *College room only:* $3668. Room and board charges vary according to board plan and housing facility.

Financial Aid Forms of aid include need-based and non-need-based scholarships, athletic grants, and part-time jobs. The average aided 2005–06 undergraduate received an aid package worth $8000. The priority application deadline for financial aid is March 1.

Freshman Admission Ferris State University requires a high school transcript, a minimum 2.35 high school GPA, SAT or ACT scores, and TOEFL scores for international students. The application deadline for regular admission is August 1.

Transfer Admission The application deadline for admission is July 1.

Entrance Difficulty Ferris State University has an open admission policy. It assesses its entrance difficulty as moderately difficult for transfers; very difficult for pharmacy, optometry.

For Further Information Contact Dr. Craig Westman, Dean of Enrollment Services, Ferris State University, 1201 South State Street, CSS201, Big Rapids, MI 49307-2742. *Telephone:* 231-591-2797 or 800-433-7747 (toll-free). *Fax:* 231-591-3944. *E-mail:* admissions@ferris.edu. *Web site:* http://www.ferris.edu/.

FINLANDIA UNIVERSITY
Hancock, Michigan

Finlandia University is a coed, private, four-year college, founded in 1896, affiliated with the Evangelical Lutheran Church in America, offering degrees at the associate and bachelor's levels. It has a 25-acre campus in Hancock.

Academic Information The faculty has 78 members (56% full-time), 22% with terminal degrees. The student-faculty ratio is 13:1. The library holds 68,803 titles, 997 serial subscriptions, and 2,865 audiovisual materials. Special programs include academic remediation, services for learning-disabled students, cooperative (work-study) education, study abroad, advanced placement credit, accelerated degree programs, ESL programs, independent study, distance learning, summer session for credit, part-time degree programs (daytime, evenings, summer), adult/continuing education programs, internships, and arrangement for off-campus study. The most frequently chosen baccalaureate fields are business/marketing, education, liberal arts/general studies.

Student Body Statistics The student body is made up of 584 undergraduates (119 freshmen). 67 percent are women and 33 percent are men. Students come from 15 states and territories. 91 percent are from Michigan. 4.3 percent are international students.

Expenses for 2006–07 *Application fee:* $30. *Comprehensive fee:* $21,824 includes full-time tuition ($16,200), mandatory fees ($100), and college room and board ($5524). Full-time tuition and fees vary according to program. Room and board charges vary according to housing facility. *Part-time tuition:* $540 per credit. Part-time tuition varies according to course load, degree level, and program.

Financial Aid Forms of aid include need-based and non-need-based scholarships and part-time jobs. The priority application deadline for financial aid is March 1.

Freshman Admission Finlandia University requires an essay, a high school transcript, a minimum 2.0 high school GPA, and TOEFL scores for international students. SAT or ACT scores are recommended. Recommendations and an interview are required for some. The application deadline for regular admission is August 23 and for nonresidents it is August 23.

Transfer Admission The application deadline for admission is August 23.

Entrance Difficulty Finlandia University assesses its entrance difficulty level as minimally difficult. For the fall 2006 freshman class, 72 percent of the applicants were accepted.

For Further Information Contact Mr. Ben Larson, Dean of Enrollment Management, Finlandia University, 601 Quincy Street, Hancock, MI 49930. *Telephone:* 906-487-7311 or 877-202-5491 (toll-free). *Fax:* 906-487-7383. *E-mail:* admissions@finlandia.edu. *Web site:* http://www.finlandia.edu/.

GMI ENGINEERING & MANAGEMENT INSTITUTE

See Kettering University.

GRACE BIBLE COLLEGE
Grand Rapids, Michigan

Grace Bible College is a coed, private, four-year college, founded in 1945, affiliated with the Grace Gospel Fellowship, offering degrees at the associate and bachelor's levels. It has a 16-acre campus in Grand Rapids.

Academic Information The faculty has 28 members (29% full-time), 18% with terminal degrees. The student-faculty ratio is 11:1. The library holds 39,079 titles and 183 serial subscriptions. Special programs include academic remediation, advanced placement credit, ESL programs, independent study, internships, and arrangement for off-campus study with Grand Rapids Community College, Davenport University, Cornerstone University. The most frequently chosen baccalaureate fields are education, communication technologies, visual and performing arts.
Student Body Statistics The student body is made up of 173 undergraduates (42 freshmen). 46 percent are women and 54 percent are men. Students come from 15 states and territories and 1 other country. 75 percent are from Michigan. 0.6 percent are international students. 1 percent of the 2006 graduating class went on to graduate and professional schools.
Expenses for 2006–07 *Application fee:* $0. *Comprehensive fee:* $17,860 includes full-time tuition ($10,770), mandatory fees ($520), and college room and board ($6570). *College room only:* $2860. Room and board charges vary according to housing facility. *Part-time tuition:* $450 per semester hour. Part-time tuition varies according to course load.
Financial Aid Forms of aid include need-based and non-need-based scholarships and part-time jobs. The average aided 2006–07 undergraduate received an aid package worth an estimated $7762. The priority application deadline for financial aid is February 28.
Freshman Admission Grace Bible College requires a high school transcript, 2 recommendations, SAT and SAT Subject Test or ACT scores, and TOEFL scores for international students. A minimum 2.5 high school GPA is recommended. An interview is required for some. The application deadline for regular admission is July 15.
Entrance Difficulty Grace Bible College assesses its entrance difficulty level as minimally difficult. For the fall 2006 freshman class, 62 percent of the applicants were accepted.
For Further Information Contact Mr. Kevin Gilliam, Director of Enrollment, Grace Bible College, 1101 Aldon Street, SW, PO Box 910, Grand Rapids, MI 49509. *Telephone:* 616-538-2330 Ext. 239 or 800-968-1887 (toll-free). *Fax:* 616-538-0599. *E-mail:* gbc@gbcol.edu. *Web site:* http://www.gbcol.edu/.

GRAND VALLEY STATE UNIVERSITY
Allendale, Michigan

Grand Valley State University is a coed, public, comprehensive institution, founded in 1960, offering degrees at the bachelor's and master's levels and post-master's and postbachelor's certificates. It has a 900-acre campus in Allendale near Grand Rapids.

Academic Information The faculty has 1,414 members (65% full-time), 50% with terminal degrees. The undergraduate student-faculty ratio is 18:1. The library holds 634,000 titles and 5,000 serial subscriptions. Special programs include academic remediation, services for learning-disabled students, an honors program, cooperative (work-study) education, study abroad, advanced placement credit, accelerated degree programs, Freshman Honors College, ESL programs, double majors, independent study, distance learning, summer session for credit, part-time degree programs (daytime, evenings, weekends, summer), adult/continuing education programs, and internships. The most frequently chosen baccalaureate fields are business/marketing, health professions and related sciences, psychology.
Student Body Statistics The student body totals 23,295, of whom 19,578 are undergraduates (3,562 freshmen). 61 percent are women and 39 percent are men. Students come from 55 states and territories and 51 other countries. 96 percent are from Michigan. 0.7 percent are international students.
Expenses for 2006–07 *Application fee:* $30. *State resident tuition:* $6588 full-time, $287 per credit hour part-time. *Nonresident tuition:* $12,510

full-time, $532 per credit hour part-time. Full-time tuition varies according to program and student level. Part-time tuition varies according to course load, program, and student level. *College room and board:* $6600. *College room only:* $4700. Room and board charges vary according to board plan, housing facility, and location.
Financial Aid Forms of aid include need-based and non-need-based scholarships, athletic grants, and part-time jobs. The average aided 2006–07 undergraduate received an aid package worth an estimated $7753. The priority application deadline for financial aid is March 1.
Freshman Admission Grand Valley State University requires a high school transcript, SAT or ACT scores, and TOEFL scores for international students. An essay and an interview are required for some. The application deadline for regular admission is May 1.
Transfer Admission The application deadline for admission is July 28.
Entrance Difficulty Grand Valley State University assesses its entrance difficulty level as moderately difficult. For the fall 2006 freshman class, 70 percent of the applicants were accepted.
For Further Information Contact Ms. Jodi Chycinski, Director of Admissions, Grand Valley State University, 1 Campus Drive, Allendale, MI 49401. *Telephone:* 616-331-2025 or 800-748-0246 (toll-free). *Fax:* 616-331-2000. *E-mail:* go2gvsu@gvsu.edu. *Web site:* http://www.gvsu.edu/.

GREAT LAKES CHRISTIAN COLLEGE
Lansing, Michigan

Great Lakes Christian College is a coed, private, four-year college, founded in 1949, affiliated with the Christian Churches and Churches of Christ, offering degrees at the associate and bachelor's levels. It has a 50-acre campus in Lansing.

Academic Information The faculty has 30 members (30% full-time). The student-faculty ratio is 15:1. The library holds 60,244 titles and 8,942 serial subscriptions. Special programs include advanced placement credit, double majors, independent study, part-time degree programs (daytime, evenings), external degree programs, adult/continuing education programs, internships, and arrangement for off-campus study with Cornerstone College, Davenport College of Business.
Student Body Statistics The student body is made up of 207 undergraduates. Students come from 8 states and territories and 3 other countries. 2.4 percent are international students.
Expenses for 2007–08 *Application fee:* $30. *Comprehensive fee:* $16,658 includes full-time tuition ($9728), mandatory fees ($730), and college room and board ($6200). *Part-time tuition:* $304 per hour.
Financial Aid Forms of aid include non-need-based scholarships and part-time jobs.
Freshman Admission Great Lakes Christian College requires an essay, a high school transcript, a minimum 2.25 high school GPA, 3 recommendations, SAT or ACT scores, and TOEFL scores for international students. The application deadline for regular admission is August 1.
Transfer Admission The application deadline for admission is August 1.
Entrance Difficulty Great Lakes Christian College assesses its entrance difficulty level as moderately difficult.
For Further Information Contact Mr. Lloyd Scharer, Director of Admissions, Great Lakes Christian College, 6211 West Willow Highway, Lansing, MI 48917-1299. *Telephone:* 517-321-0242 or 800-YES-GLCC (toll-free). *Fax:* 517-321-5902. *E-mail:* lscharer@glcc.edu. *Web site:* http://www.glcc.edu/.

HILLSDALE COLLEGE
Hillsdale, Michigan

Hillsdale College is a coed, private, four-year college, founded in 1844, offering degrees at the bachelor's level. It has a 200-acre campus in Hillsdale.

Academic Information The faculty has 149 members (70% full-time), 72% with terminal degrees. The student-faculty ratio is 10:1. The library holds 240,000 titles, 1,650 serial subscriptions, and 8,000 audiovisual materials. Special programs include an honors program, study abroad, advanced placement credit, accelerated degree programs, double majors, independent study, summer session for credit, part-time degree programs (daytime, summer), and internships. The most frequently chosen baccalaureate fields are business/marketing, education, history.

Student Body Statistics The student body is made up of 1,346 undergraduates (381 freshmen). 52 percent are women and 48 percent are men. Students come from 48 states and territories and 13 other countries. 44 percent are from Michigan. 26 percent of the 2006 graduating class went on to graduate and professional schools.

Expenses for 2006–07 *Application fee:* $35. *Comprehensive fee:* $25,290 includes full-time tuition ($17,850), mandatory fees ($410), and college room and board ($7030). *College room only:* $3530. Room and board charges vary according to board plan. *Part-time tuition:* $700 per semester hour.

Financial Aid Forms of aid include need-based and non-need-based scholarships and athletic grants. The average aided 2006–07 undergraduate received an aid package worth an estimated $15,000. The application deadline for financial aid is April 1 with a priority deadline of February 1.

Freshman Admission Hillsdale College requires an essay, a high school transcript, 1 recommendation, SAT or ACT scores, and TOEFL scores for international students. A minimum 3.25 high school GPA, 2 recommendations, an interview, and SAT Subject Test scores are recommended. 2 recommendations and an interview are required for some. The application deadline for regular admission is February 15 and for nonresidents it is February 15. The application deadline for early decision is November 15 and for early action it is January 1.

Transfer Admission The application deadline for admission is February 15.

Entrance Difficulty Hillsdale College assesses its entrance difficulty level as very difficult. For the fall 2006 freshman class, 75 percent of the applicants were accepted.

For Further Information Contact Mr. Jeffrey S. Lantis, Director of Admissions, Hillsdale College, 33 East College Street, Hillsdale, MI 49242-1298. *Telephone:* 517-607-2327. *Fax:* 517-607-2223. *E-mail:* admissions@hillsdale.edu. *Web site:* http://www.hillsdale.edu/.

HOPE COLLEGE
Holland, Michigan

Hope College is a coed, private, four-year college, founded in 1866, affiliated with the Reformed Church in America, offering degrees at the bachelor's level. It has a 45-acre campus in Holland near Grand Rapids.

Academic Information The faculty has 322 members (67% full-time), 61% with terminal degrees. The library holds 358,329 titles, 2,878 serial subscriptions, and 13,263 audiovisual materials. Special programs include services for learning-disabled students, study abroad, advanced placement credit, ESL programs, double majors, independent study, self-designed majors, summer session for credit, part-time degree programs (daytime), internships, and arrangement for off-campus study with members of the Great Lakes Colleges Association, Associated Colleges of the Midwest, Institute of European Studies, Council for International Educational Exchange. The most frequently chosen baccalaureate fields are business/marketing, education, psychology.

Student Body Statistics The student body is made up of 3,203 undergraduates (778 freshmen). 60 percent are women and 40 percent are men. Students come from 47 states and territories and 33 other countries. 74 percent are from Michigan. 1.6 percent are international students. 28 percent of the 2006 graduating class went on to graduate and professional schools.

Expenses for 2006–07 *Application fee:* $35. *Comprehensive fee:* $29,552 includes full-time tuition ($22,430), mandatory fees ($140), and college room and board ($6982). Full-time tuition and fees vary according to course load. Room and board charges vary according to board plan.

Financial Aid Forms of aid include need-based and non-need-based scholarships and part-time jobs. The average aided 2006–07 undergraduate received an aid package worth an estimated $18,771. The priority application deadline for financial aid is March 1.

Freshman Admission Hope College requires an essay, a high school transcript, SAT or ACT scores, and TOEFL scores for international

students. An interview is recommended. 1 recommendation is required for some. The application deadline for regular admission is rolling.

Transfer Admission The application deadline for admission is rolling.

Entrance Difficulty Hope College assesses its entrance difficulty level as moderately difficult. For the fall 2006 freshman class, 81 percent of the applicants were accepted.

For Further Information Contact Dr. James R. Bekkering, Vice President for Admissions, Hope College, 69 East 10th Street, PO Box 9000, Holland, MI 49422-9000. *Telephone:* 616-395-7850 or 800-968-7850 (toll-free). *Fax:* 616-395-7130. *E-mail:* admissions@hope.edu. *Web site:* http://www.hope.edu/.

KALAMAZOO COLLEGE
Kalamazoo, Michigan

Kalamazoo College is a coed, private, four-year college, founded in 1833, affiliated with the American Baptist Churches in the U.S.A., offering degrees at the bachelor's level. It has a 60-acre campus in Kalamazoo.

Academic Information The faculty has 113 members (89% full-time), 81% with terminal degrees. The student-faculty ratio is 12:1. The library holds 342,939 titles and 1,495 serial subscriptions. Special programs include services for learning-disabled students, study abroad, advanced placement credit, double majors, independent study, internships, and arrangement for off-campus study with Western Michigan University. The most frequently chosen baccalaureate fields are biological/life sciences, English, social sciences.

Student Body Statistics The student body is made up of 1,345 undergraduates (390 freshmen). 57 percent are women and 43 percent are men. Students come from 38 states and territories and 13 other countries. 71 percent are from Michigan. 0.8 percent are international students. 33 percent of the 2006 graduating class went on to graduate and professional schools.

Expenses for 2006–07 *Application fee:* $35. *Comprehensive fee:* $33,969 includes full-time tuition ($27,054) and college room and board ($6915). *College room only:* $3372. Room and board charges vary according to board plan.

Financial Aid Forms of aid include need-based and non-need-based scholarships and part-time jobs. The average aided 2006–07 undergraduate received an aid package worth an estimated $22,820. The priority application deadline for financial aid is February 15.

Freshman Admission Kalamazoo College requires an essay, a high school transcript, 2 recommendations, SAT or ACT scores, and TOEFL scores for international students. A minimum 3.0 high school GPA and an interview are recommended. The application deadline for regular admission is February 15; for early decision it is November 15; and for early action it is December 1.

Transfer Admission The application deadline for admission is February 15.

Entrance Difficulty Kalamazoo College assesses its entrance difficulty level as very difficult. For the fall 2006 freshman class, 69 percent of the applicants were accepted.

For Further Information Contact Mrs. Linda Wirgau, Records Manager, Kalamazoo College, Mandelle Hall, 1200 Academy Street, Kalamazoo, MI 49006-3295. *Telephone:* 269-337-7166 or 800-253-3602 (toll-free). *Fax:* 269-337-7190. *E-mail:* admissions@kzoo.edu. *Web site:* http://www.kzoo.edu/.

KETTERING UNIVERSITY
Flint, Michigan

Kettering University is a coed, private, comprehensive institution, founded in 1919, offering degrees at the bachelor's and master's levels. It has an 85-acre campus in Flint near Detroit.

Academic Information The faculty has 146 members (91% full-time), 82% with terminal degrees. The undergraduate student-faculty ratio is 9:1. The library holds 122,360 titles, 525 serial subscriptions, and 1,280 audiovisual materials. Special programs include services for learning-disabled students, cooperative (work-study) education, study abroad, advanced placement credit, accelerated degree programs, double majors,

Kettering University (continued)

independent study, distance learning, and internships. The most frequently chosen baccalaureate fields are business/marketing, computer and information sciences, engineering.

Student Body Statistics The student body totals 2,809, of whom 2,290 are undergraduates (398 freshmen). 15 percent are women and 85 percent are men. Students come from 48 states and territories and 17 other countries. 67 percent are from Michigan. 1.8 percent are international students. 30 percent of the 2006 graduating class went on to graduate and professional schools.

Expenses for 2006–07 *Application fee:* $35. *Comprehensive fee:* $30,598 includes full-time tuition ($24,512), mandatory fees ($396), and college room and board ($5690). *College room only:* $3600. Full-time tuition and fees vary according to student level. *Part-time tuition:* $766 per credit hour.

Financial Aid Forms of aid include need-based and non-need-based scholarships and part-time jobs. The average aided 2005–06 undergraduate received an aid package worth $13,586.

Freshman Admission Kettering University requires a high school transcript, SAT or ACT scores, and TOEFL scores for international students. A minimum 3.0 high school GPA, an interview, and SAT Subject Test scores are recommended. An essay is required for some. The application deadline for regular admission is rolling.

Transfer Admission The application deadline for admission is rolling.

Entrance Difficulty Kettering University assesses its entrance difficulty level as very difficult. For the fall 2006 freshman class, 71 percent of the applicants were accepted.

For Further Information Contact Ms. Barbara Sosin, Director of Admissions, Kettering University, 1700 West Third Avenue, Flint, MI 48504-4898. *Telephone:* 810-762-7865, 800-955-4464 Ext. 7865 (toll-free in-state), or 800-955-4464 (toll-free out-of-state). *Fax:* 810-762-9837. *E-mail:* admissions@kettering.edu. *Web site:* http://www.kettering.edu/.

See page 262 for the College Close-Up.

KUYPER COLLEGE

Grand Rapids, Michigan

Kuyper College is a coed, private, four-year college, founded in 1939, offering degrees at the associate and bachelor's levels and postbachelor's certificates. It has a 34-acre campus in Grand Rapids.

Academic Information The faculty has 26 members (46% full-time), 42% with terminal degrees. The student-faculty ratio is 15:1. The library holds 56,177 titles and 254 serial subscriptions. Special programs include academic remediation, services for learning-disabled students, cooperative (work-study) education, study abroad, advanced placement credit, ESL programs, double majors, independent study, summer session for credit, part-time degree programs (daytime, evenings), internships, and arrangement for off-campus study with Grand Rapids Community College, Cornerstone University, Calvin College. The most frequently chosen baccalaureate fields are public administration and social services, education, theology and religious vocations.

Student Body Statistics The student body is made up of 290 undergraduates (51 freshmen). 52 percent are women and 48 percent are men. Students come from 16 states and territories and 8 other countries. 93 percent are from Michigan. 7.9 percent are international students.

Expenses for 2007–08 *Application fee:* $25. *Comprehensive fee:* $18,425 includes full-time tuition ($12,200), mandatory fees ($525), and college room and board ($5700). *Part-time tuition:* $585 per credit hour.

Financial Aid Forms of aid include need-based and non-need-based scholarships and part-time jobs. The average aided 2006–07 undergraduate received an aid package worth an estimated $10,860. The priority application deadline for financial aid is March 1.

Freshman Admission Kuyper College requires an essay, a high school transcript, a minimum 2.5 high school GPA, SAT or ACT scores, and TOEFL scores for international students. An interview is required for some. The application deadline for regular admission is rolling.

Entrance Difficulty Kuyper College assesses its entrance difficulty level as moderately difficult. For the fall 2006 freshman class, 89 percent of the applicants were accepted.

For Further Information Contact Kuyper College Admissions Office, Kuyper College, 3333 East Beltline Avenue, NE, Grand Rapids, MI 49525. *Telephone:* 616-222-3000 Ext. 632 or 800-511-3749 (toll-free). *Fax:* 616-222-3045. *E-mail:* admissions@kuyper.edu. *Web site:* http://www.kuyper.edu/.

LAKE SUPERIOR STATE UNIVERSITY

Sault Sainte Marie, Michigan

Lake Superior State University is a coed, public, four-year college, founded in 1946, offering degrees at the associate, bachelor's, and master's levels. It has a 115-acre campus in Sault Sainte Marie.

Academic Information The faculty has 202 members (56% full-time), 38% with terminal degrees. The undergraduate student-faculty ratio is 17:1. The library holds 200,449 titles, 850 serial subscriptions, and 592 audiovisual materials. Special programs include services for learning-disabled students, an honors program, cooperative (work-study) education, study abroad, advanced placement credit, Freshman Honors College, double majors, independent study, distance learning, self-designed majors, summer session for credit, part-time degree programs, adult/continuing education programs, and internships. The most frequently chosen baccalaureate fields are business/marketing, engineering, security and protective services.

Student Body Statistics The student body totals 2,919, of whom 2,916 are undergraduates (492 freshmen). 52 percent are women and 48 percent are men. Students come from 23 states and territories and 4 other countries. 86 percent are from Michigan. 11.1 percent are international students.

Expenses for 2006–07 *Application fee:* $35. *State resident tuition:* $6628 full-time, $273.25 per credit hour part-time. *Nonresident tuition:* $13,186 full-time, $546.50 per credit hour part-time. *Mandatory fees:* $70 full-time. Full-time tuition and fees vary according to reciprocity agreements. Part-time tuition varies according to course load and reciprocity agreements. *College room and board:* $6836. Room and board charges vary according to board plan and housing facility.

Financial Aid Forms of aid include need-based scholarships, athletic grants, and part-time jobs. The average aided 2005–06 undergraduate received an aid package worth $8157. The priority application deadline for financial aid is February 21.

Freshman Admission Lake Superior State University requires a high school transcript, SAT or ACT scores, and TOEFL scores for international students. A minimum 2.2 high school GPA is required for some. The application deadline for regular admission is August 15.

Transfer Admission The application deadline for admission is rolling.

Entrance Difficulty Lake Superior State University assesses its entrance difficulty level as moderately difficult. For the fall 2006 freshman class, 84 percent of the applicants were accepted.

For Further Information Contact Ms. Susan Camp, Director of Admissions, Lake Superior State University, 650 West Easterday Avenue, Sault Saint Marie, MI 49783-1699. *Telephone:* 906-635-2231 or 888-800-LSSU Ext. 2231 (toll-free). *Fax:* 906-635-6669. *E-mail:* admissions@lssu.edu. *Web site:* http://www.lssu.edu/.

LAWRENCE TECHNOLOGICAL UNIVERSITY

Southfield, Michigan

Lawrence Technological University is a coed, private university, founded in 1932, offering degrees at the associate, bachelor's, master's, and doctoral levels. It has a 115-acre campus in Southfield near Detroit.

Academic Information The faculty has 375 members (30% full-time), 51% with terminal degrees. The undergraduate student-faculty ratio is 12:1. The library holds 128,000 titles, 750 serial subscriptions, and 136 audiovisual materials. Special programs include academic remediation, services for learning-disabled students, cooperative (work-study) education, study abroad, advanced placement credit, ESL programs, double majors, independent study, distance learning, summer session for credit, part-time degree programs (daytime, evenings, weekends, summer), adult/continuing education programs, internships, and arrangement for off-campus study with Macomb University Center, Oakland Technical Center. The most frequently chosen baccalaureate fields are architecture, engineering, engineering technologies.

Student Body Statistics The student body totals 4,049, of whom 2,680 are undergraduates (329 freshmen). 23 percent are women and 77 percent are men. Students come from 26 states and territories and 25 other countries. 99 percent are from Michigan. 1.5 percent are international students.

Expenses for 2006–07 *Application fee:* $30. *Comprehensive fee:* $26,709 includes full-time tuition ($19,073), mandatory fees ($370), and college room and board ($7266). *College room only:* $5286. *Part-time tuition:* $635 per credit hour. *Part-time mandatory fees:* $185 per term.

Financial Aid Forms of aid include need-based and non-need-based scholarships and part-time jobs. The average aided 2005–06 undergraduate received an aid package worth $14,891. The priority application deadline for financial aid is April 1.

Freshman Admission Lawrence Technological University requires a high school transcript, a minimum 2.5 high school GPA, and SAT or ACT scores. TOEFL scores for international students are recommended. An essay, recommendations, and an interview are required for some. The application deadline for regular admission is August 15.

Transfer Admission The application deadline for admission is August 15.

Entrance Difficulty Lawrence Technological University assesses its entrance difficulty level as moderately difficult. For the fall 2006 freshman class, 66 percent of the applicants were accepted.

For Further Information Contact Ms. Jane Rohrback, Director of Admissions, Lawrence Technological University, 21000 West Ten Mile Road, Southfield, MI 48075. *Telephone:* 248-204-3160 or 800-225-5588 (toll-free). *Fax:* 248-204-3188. *E-mail:* admissions@ltu.edu. *Web site:* http://www.ltu.edu/.

LEWIS COLLEGE OF BUSINESS
Detroit, Michigan

Lewis College of Business is a coed, private, two-year college, founded in 1929, offering degrees at the associate level. It has an 11-acre campus in Detroit.

Academic Information The faculty has 36 members (25% full-time). The student-faculty ratio is 15:1. The library holds 3,355 titles and 90 serial subscriptions. Special programs include academic remediation, cooperative (work-study) education, summer session for credit, and part-time degree programs (daytime, evenings).

Student Body Statistics The student body is made up of 324 undergraduates.

Expenses for 2006–07 *Application fee:* $15. *Tuition:* $8130 full-time. Contact college directly for program costs.

Financial Aid Forms of aid include need-based scholarships and part-time jobs. The priority application deadline for financial aid is February 1.

Freshman Admission Lewis College of Business requires a high school transcript. The application deadline for regular admission is rolling.

Transfer Admission The application deadline for admission is August 1.

Entrance Difficulty Lewis College of Business has an open admission policy.

For Further Information Contact Ms. Frances Ambrose, Admissions Secretary, Lewis College of Business, 17370 Meyers Road, Detroit, MI 48235-1423. *Telephone:* 313-862-6300. *Fax:* 313-862-1027. *Web site:* http://www.lewiscollege.edu/.

MADONNA UNIVERSITY
Livonia, Michigan

Madonna University is a coed, private, Roman Catholic, comprehensive institution, founded in 1947, offering degrees at the associate, bachelor's, and master's levels and post-master's and postbachelor's certificates. It has a 49-acre campus in Livonia near Detroit.

Academic Information The faculty has 368 members (29% full-time), 32% with terminal degrees. The undergraduate student-faculty ratio is 13:1. The library holds 199,144 titles, 1,679 serial subscriptions, and 938 audiovisual materials. Special programs include academic remediation, services for learning-disabled students, cooperative (work-study) education, study abroad, advanced placement credit, accelerated degree programs, ESL programs, double majors, independent study, distance learning, self-designed majors, summer session for credit, part-time degree programs (daytime, evenings, weekends, summer), adult/continuing education programs, internships, and arrangement for off-campus study with 5 members of the Detroit Area Consortium of Catholic Colleges. The most frequently chosen baccalaureate fields are business/marketing, health professions and related sciences, security and protective services.

Student Body Statistics The student body totals 4,156, of whom 3,264 are undergraduates (285 freshmen). 76 percent are women and 24 percent are men. Students come from 9 states and territories and 36 other countries. 98 percent are from Michigan. 3.5 percent are international students. 40 percent of the 2006 graduating class went on to graduate and professional schools.

Expenses for 2006–07 *Application fee:* $25. *Comprehensive fee:* $16,906 includes full-time tuition ($10,860), mandatory fees ($100), and college room and board ($5946). *College room only:* $2652. Room and board charges vary according to board plan. *Part-time tuition:* $362 per credit hour. *Part-time mandatory fees:* $50 per term.

Financial Aid Forms of aid include need-based and non-need-based scholarships, athletic grants, and part-time jobs. The priority application deadline for financial aid is February 21.

Freshman Admission Madonna University requires an essay, a high school transcript, a minimum 2.75 high school GPA, SAT or ACT scores, and TOEFL scores for international students. An interview is recommended. 2 recommendations are required for some. The application deadline for regular admission is rolling.

Transfer Admission The application deadline for admission is rolling.

Entrance Difficulty Madonna University assesses its entrance difficulty level as moderately difficult. For the fall 2006 freshman class, 81 percent of the applicants were accepted.

For Further Information Contact Mr. Mike Quattro, Director of Enrollment Management, Madonna University, 36600 Schoolcraft Road, Livonia, MI 48150-1173. *Telephone:* 734-432-5317 or 800-852-4951 (toll-free). *Fax:* 734-432-5393. *E-mail:* muinfo@madonna.edu. *Web site:* http://www.madonna.edu.

MARYGROVE COLLEGE
Detroit, Michigan

Marygrove College is a coed, primarily women's, private, Roman Catholic, comprehensive institution, founded in 1905, offering degrees at the associate, bachelor's, and master's levels and postbachelor's certificates. It has a 50-acre campus in Detroit.

Academic Information The faculty has 64 members (88% full-time), 59% with terminal degrees. The undergraduate student-faculty ratio is 22:1. The library holds 86,268 titles and 72,048 serial subscriptions. Special programs include academic remediation, cooperative (work-study) education, advanced placement credit, double majors, distance learning, self-designed majors, summer session for credit, part-time degree programs (daytime, evenings, weekends, summer), internships, and arrangement for off-campus study with Detroit Area Consortium of Catholic Colleges. The most frequently chosen baccalaureate fields are social sciences, business/marketing, visual and performing arts.

Student Body Statistics The student body totals 2,953, of whom 780 are undergraduates (94 freshmen). 79 percent are women and 21 percent are men. Students come from 3 states and territories and 9 other countries. 100 percent are from Michigan. 2 percent are international students.

Expenses for 2006–07 *Application fee:* $25. *One-time mandatory fee:* $25. *Comprehensive fee:* $20,360 includes full-time tuition ($13,570), mandatory fees ($390), and college room and board ($6400). Room and board charges vary according to board plan. *Part-time tuition:* $488 per credit. Part-time tuition varies according to location.

Marygrove College (continued)

Financial Aid Forms of aid include non-need-based scholarships and part-time jobs.

Freshman Admission Marygrove College requires a high school transcript, a minimum 2.7 high school GPA, ACT scores, and TOEFL scores for international students. Recommendations and an interview are required for some. The application deadline for regular admission is August 15.

Transfer Admission The application deadline for admission is August 15.

Entrance Difficulty Marygrove College assesses its entrance difficulty level as moderately difficult. For the fall 2006 freshman class, 42 percent of the applicants were accepted.

For Further Information Contact Mr. John Ambrose, Director of Undergraduate Admissions, Marygrove College, Admissions Office, Detroit, MI 48221-2599. *Telephone:* 313-927-1236 or 866-313-1297 (toll-free). *Fax:* 313-927-1345. *E-mail:* info@marygrove.edu. *Web site:* http://www.marygrove.edu/.

MICHIGAN CHRISTIAN COLLEGE

See Rochester College.

MICHIGAN JEWISH INSTITUTE

Oak Park, Michigan

Michigan Jewish Institute is a coed, private, four-year college, founded in 1994, offering degrees at the associate and bachelor's levels.

Academic Information The faculty has 36 members (6% full-time). Special programs include academic remediation, services for learning-disabled students, cooperative (work-study) education, study abroad, advanced placement credit, accelerated degree programs, ESL programs, double majors, independent study, summer session for credit, adult/continuing education programs, and internships.

Expenses for 2006–07 *Application fee:* $50. *Tuition:* $7680 full-time, $320 per credit part-time. *Mandatory fees:* $100 full-time, $50 per semester hour part-time. Both full-time and part-time tuition and fees vary according to course load and program.

Freshman Admission Michigan Jewish Institute requires a high school transcript.

Entrance Difficulty Michigan Jewish Institute has an open admission policy.

For Further Information Contact Mr. Paul Levine, Michigan Jewish Institute, 25401 Coolidge Highway, Oak Park, MI 48237. *Telephone:* 248-414-6900 Ext. 16. *Fax:* 248-414-6907. *E-mail:* plevine@mji.edu. *Web site:* http://www.mji.edu/.

MICHIGAN STATE UNIVERSITY

East Lansing, Michigan

Michigan State University is a coed, public university, founded in 1855, offering degrees at the bachelor's, master's, doctoral, and first professional levels and post-master's certificates. It has a 5,192-acre campus in East Lansing near Detroit.

Academic Information The faculty has 2,910 members (87% full-time), 89% with terminal degrees. The undergraduate student-faculty ratio is 17:1. The library holds 5 million titles, 37,832 serial subscriptions, and 342,873 audiovisual materials. Special programs include academic remediation, services for learning-disabled students, an honors program, cooperative (work-study) education, study abroad, advanced placement credit, accelerated degree programs, Freshman Honors College, ESL programs, double majors, independent study, distance learning, self-designed majors, summer session for credit, part-time degree programs, adult/continuing education programs, internships, and arrangement for off-campus study with Committee on Institutional Cooperation. The most frequently chosen baccalaureate fields are business/marketing, communications/journalism, social sciences.

Student Body Statistics The student body totals 45,520, of whom 35,821 are undergraduates (7,440 freshmen). 54 percent are women and 46 percent are men. Students come from 54 states and territories and 100 other countries. 92 percent are from Michigan. 3.3 percent are international students.

Expenses for 2006–07 *Application fee:* $35. *State resident tuition:* $7665 full-time, $234.75 per credit hour part-time. *Nonresident tuition:* $20,310 full-time, $656.25 per credit hour part-time. *Mandatory fees:* $1178 full-time, $422 per term part-time. Both full-time and part-time tuition and fees vary according to course load, degree level, program, and student level. *College room and board:* $6044. *College room only:* $2618. Room and board charges vary according to board plan and housing facility.

Financial Aid Forms of aid include need-based and non-need-based scholarships, athletic grants, and part-time jobs. The average aided 2006–07 undergraduate received an aid package worth an estimated $9307. The application deadline for financial aid is continuous.

Freshman Admission Michigan State University requires an essay, a high school transcript, SAT or ACT scores, and TOEFL scores for international students. The application deadline for regular admission is rolling.

Transfer Admission The application deadline for admission is rolling.

Entrance Difficulty Michigan State University assesses its entrance difficulty level as moderately difficult. For the fall 2006 freshman class, 73 percent of the applicants were accepted.

For Further Information Contact James Cotter, Acting Director of Admissions, Michigan State University, 250 Administration Building, East Lansing, MI 48824. *Telephone:* 517-355-8332. *Fax:* 517-353-1647. *E-mail:* admis@msu.edu. *Web site:* http://www.msu.edu/.

MICHIGAN TECHNOLOGICAL UNIVERSITY

Houghton, Michigan

Michigan Technological University is a coed, public university, founded in 1885, offering degrees at the associate, bachelor's, master's, and doctoral levels and postbachelor's certificates. It has a 925-acre campus in Houghton.

Academic Information The faculty has 489 members (71% full-time), 80% with terminal degrees. The undergraduate student-faculty ratio is 12:1. The library holds 799,775 titles, 2,777 serial subscriptions, and 6,797 audiovisual materials. Special programs include services for learning-disabled students, an honors program, cooperative (work-study) education, study abroad, advanced placement credit, ESL programs, double majors, distance learning, self-designed majors, summer session for credit, part-time degree programs, internships, and arrangement for off-campus study with National Student Exchange. The most frequently chosen baccalaureate fields are business/marketing, engineering, engineering technologies.

Student Body Statistics The student body totals 6,550, of whom 5,634 are undergraduates (1,169 freshmen). 23 percent are women and 77 percent are men. Students come from 47 states and territories and 73 other countries. 74 percent are from Michigan. 4 percent are international students. 17 percent of the 2006 graduating class went on to graduate and professional schools.

Expenses for 2006–07 *Application fee:* $40. *State resident tuition:* $8271 full-time, $275.70 per credit hour part-time. *Nonresident tuition:* $20,040 full-time, $668 per credit hour part-time. *Mandatory fees:* $639 full-time, $319.54 per term part-time. Both full-time and part-time tuition and fees vary according to course load and program. *College room and board:* $6840. *College room only:* $3461. Room and board charges vary according to board plan and housing facility.

Financial Aid Forms of aid include need-based and non-need-based scholarships, athletic grants, and part-time jobs. The average aided 2006–07 undergraduate received an aid package worth an estimated $9065.

Freshman Admission Michigan Technological University requires a high school transcript, SAT or ACT scores, and TOEFL scores for international students. A minimum 2.75 high school GPA and an interview are recommended. The application deadline for regular admission is rolling.

Transfer Admission The application deadline for admission is rolling.

Entrance Difficulty Michigan Technological University assesses its entrance difficulty level as moderately difficult. For the fall 2006 freshman class, 82 percent of the applicants were accepted.

For Further Information Contact Ms. Allison Carter, Director of Admissions, Michigan Technological University, 1400 Townsend Drive, Houghton, MI 49931-1295. *Telephone:* 906-487-2335 or 888-MTU-1885 (toll-free). *Fax:* 906-487-2125. *E-mail:* mtu4u@mtu.edu. *Web site:* http://www.mtu.edu/.

NORTHERN MICHIGAN UNIVERSITY
Marquette, Michigan

Northern Michigan University is a coed, public, comprehensive institution, founded in 1899, offering degrees at the associate, bachelor's, and master's levels and post-master's and postbachelor's certificates. It has a 300-acre campus in Marquette near Sawyer International.

Academic Information The faculty has 471 members (68% full-time), 42% with terminal degrees. The undergraduate student-faculty ratio is 22:1. The library holds 615,406 titles, 4,573 serial subscriptions, and 8,251 audiovisual materials. Special programs include academic remediation, services for learning-disabled students, an honors program, study abroad, advanced placement credit, double majors, independent study, distance learning, self-designed majors, summer session for credit, part-time degree programs (daytime, evenings, weekends, summer), adult/continuing education programs, internships, and arrangement for off-campus study with other public institutions in Michigan. The most frequently chosen baccalaureate fields are business/marketing, education, social sciences.

Student Body Statistics The student body totals 9,353, of whom 8,702 are undergraduates (1,389 freshmen). 53 percent are women and 47 percent are men. Students come from 48 states and territories and 17 other countries. 80 percent are from Michigan. 0.7 percent are international students.

Expenses for 2006–07 *Application fee:* $30. *State resident tuition:* $5592 full-time, $233 per credit hour part-time. *Nonresident tuition:* $9528 full-time, $397 per credit hour part-time. *Mandatory fees:* $549 full-time, $30.26 per term part-time. Both full-time and part-time tuition and fees vary according to location. *College room and board:* $6874. *College room only:* $3366. Room and board charges vary according to board plan and housing facility.

Financial Aid Forms of aid include need-based and non-need-based scholarships, athletic grants, and part-time jobs. The average aided 2005–06 undergraduate received an aid package worth $6971. The priority application deadline for financial aid is March 1.

Freshman Admission Northern Michigan University requires a high school transcript, SAT or ACT scores, and TOEFL scores for international students. A minimum 2.25 high school GPA is required for some. The application deadline for regular admission is rolling.

Transfer Admission The application deadline for admission is rolling.

Entrance Difficulty Northern Michigan University assesses its entrance difficulty level as minimally difficult. For the fall 2006 freshman class, 80 percent of the applicants were accepted.

For Further Information Contact Ms. Gerri Daniels, Director of Admissions, Northern Michigan University, 1401 Preque Isle Avenue, Marquette, MI 49855. *Telephone:* 906-227-2650 or 800-682-9797 (toll-free). *Fax:* 906-227-1747. *E-mail:* admiss@nmu.edu. *Web site:* http://www.nmu.edu/.

NORTHWOOD UNIVERSITY
Midland, Michigan

Northwood University is a coed, private, comprehensive institution, founded in 1959, offering degrees at the associate, bachelor's, and master's levels. It has a 434-acre campus in Midland.

Academic Information The faculty has 82 members (57% full-time), 18% with terminal degrees. The undergraduate student-faculty ratio is 33:1. The library holds 40,063 titles and 335 serial subscriptions. Special programs include academic remediation, an honors program, cooperative (work-study) education, study abroad, advanced placement credit, accelerated degree programs, ESL programs, double majors, independent study, distance learning, summer session for credit, part-time degree programs (daytime, evenings, weekends, summer), external degree programs, adult/continuing education programs, internships, and arrangement for off-campus study. The most frequently chosen baccalaureate fields are business/marketing, communications/journalism, parks and recreation.

Student Body Statistics The student body totals 4,125, of whom 3,802 are undergraduates (504 freshmen). 44 percent are women and 56 percent are men. Students come from 34 states and territories and 26 other countries. 87 percent are from Michigan. 7.9 percent are international students.

Expenses for 2007–08 *Application fee:* $25. *Comprehensive fee:* $23,649 includes full-time tuition ($15,825), mandatory fees ($630), and college room and board ($7194). *College room only:* $3474. *Part-time tuition:* $330 per credit hour.

Financial Aid Forms of aid include need-based and non-need-based scholarships, athletic grants, and part-time jobs. The average aided 2006–07 undergraduate received an aid package worth an estimated $13,375. The application deadline for financial aid is continuous.

Freshman Admission Northwood University requires an essay, a high school transcript, SAT or ACT scores, and TOEFL scores for international students. A minimum 2.0 high school GPA, 1 recommendation, and an interview are recommended. The application deadline for regular admission is rolling.

Transfer Admission The application deadline for admission is rolling.

Entrance Difficulty Northwood University assesses its entrance difficulty level as moderately difficult. For the fall 2006 freshman class, 81 percent of the applicants were accepted.

For Further Information Contact Mr. Daniel F. Toland, Dean of Admission, Northwood University, 4000 Whiting Drive, Midland, MI 48640. *Telephone:* 989-837-4273 or 800-457-7878 (toll-free). *Fax:* 989-837-4490. *E-mail:* miadmit@northwood.edu. *Web site:* http://www.northwood.edu/.

OAKLAND UNIVERSITY
Rochester, Michigan

Oakland University is a coed, public university, founded in 1957, offering degrees at the bachelor's, master's, and doctoral levels and post-master's and postbachelor's certificates. It has a 1,444-acre campus in Rochester near Detroit.

Academic Information The faculty has 906 members (52% full-time), 60% with terminal degrees. The undergraduate student-faculty ratio is 22:1. The library holds 2 million titles, 11,896 serial subscriptions, and 18,767 audiovisual materials. Special programs include academic remediation, services for learning-disabled students, an honors program, cooperative (work-study) education, study abroad, advanced placement credit, accelerated degree programs, ESL programs, double majors, independent study, distance learning, self-designed majors, summer session for credit, part-time degree programs (daytime, evenings, weekends, summer), internships, and arrangement for off-campus study with Macomb Community College, Beaumont Hospital-Troy. The most frequently chosen baccalaureate fields are business/marketing, education, psychology.

Student Body Statistics The student body totals 17,737, of whom 13,701 are undergraduates (2,287 freshmen). 62 percent are women and 38 percent are men. Students come from 30 states and territories and 60 other countries. 99 percent are from Michigan. 1.1 percent are international students. 19 percent of the 2006 graduating class went on to graduate and professional schools.

Expenses for 2006–07 *Application fee:* $40. *State resident tuition:* $6638 full-time, $221.25 per credit part-time. *Nonresident tuition:* $15,472 full-time, $515.75 per credit part-time. Both full-time and part-time tuition varies according to program and student level. *College room and board:* $6354. Room and board charges vary according to housing facility.

Financial Aid Forms of aid include need-based and non-need-based scholarships, athletic grants, and part-time jobs. The priority application deadline for financial aid is February 15.

Freshman Admission Oakland University requires a high school transcript, a minimum 2.5 high school GPA, and TOEFL scores for international students. SAT or ACT scores are recommended. A minimum

Oakland University (continued)
3.0 high school GPA, recommendations, an interview, and audition are required for some. The application deadline for regular admission is rolling and for nonresidents it is rolling.

Transfer Admission The application deadline for admission is rolling.

Entrance Difficulty Oakland University assesses its entrance difficulty level as moderately difficult. For the fall 2006 freshman class, 79 percent of the applicants were accepted.

For Further Information Contact Ms. Eleanor Reynolds, Interim Assistant Vice President, Student Affairs, Oakland University, 101 North Foundation Hall, Rochester, MI 48309-4401. *Telephone:* 248-370-3364 or 800-OAK-UNIV (toll-free). *Fax:* 248-370-4462. *E-mail:* ouinfo@oakland.edu. *Web site:* http://www.oakland.edu/.

OLIVET COLLEGE
Olivet, Michigan

http://www.olivetcollege.edu/

ROCHESTER COLLEGE
Rochester Hills, Michigan

Rochester College is a coed, private, four-year college, founded in 1959, affiliated with the Church of Christ, offering degrees at the associate, bachelor's, and master's levels. It has an 83-acre campus in Rochester Hills near Detroit.

Academic Information The faculty has 135 members (33% full-time), 27% with terminal degrees. The undergraduate student-faculty ratio is 14:1. The library holds 55,000 titles and 200 serial subscriptions. Special programs include academic remediation, study abroad, advanced placement credit, accelerated degree programs, double majors, independent study, distance learning, summer session for credit, part-time degree programs (daytime, evenings, weekends, summer), external degree programs, adult/continuing education programs, internships, and arrangement for off-campus study with Madonna University, Macomb Community College, Oakland Community College, Mott Community College, Specs Howard School of Broadcasters. The most frequently chosen baccalaureate fields are business/marketing, education, psychology.

Student Body Statistics The student body totals 1,055, of whom 1,047 are undergraduates (137 freshmen). 61 percent are women and 39 percent are men. Students come from 24 states and territories and 8 other countries. 94 percent are from Michigan. 1.5 percent are international students.

Expenses for 2006–07 *Application fee:* $25. *Comprehensive fee:* $19,908 includes full-time tuition ($11,780), mandatory fees ($1308), and college room and board ($6820). *College room only:* $1890. Full-time tuition and fees vary according to course load. Room and board charges vary according to board plan and housing facility. *Part-time tuition:* $380 per credit hour. *Part-time mandatory fees:* $205 per term. Part-time tuition and fees vary according to course load.

Financial Aid Forms of aid include need-based and non-need-based scholarships, athletic grants, and part-time jobs. The priority application deadline for financial aid is March 15.

Freshman Admission Rochester College requires a high school transcript, a minimum 2.25 high school GPA, SAT or ACT scores, and TOEFL scores for international students. An essay and 2 recommendations are recommended. An interview is required for some. The application deadline for regular admission is rolling.

Transfer Admission The application deadline for admission is rolling.

Entrance Difficulty Rochester College assesses its entrance difficulty level as minimally difficult. For the fall 2006 freshman class, 87 percent of the applicants were accepted.

For Further Information Contact Mr. Kelvin Brown, Dean of Admissions, Rochester College, 800 West Avon Road, Rochester Hills, MI 48307-2764. *Telephone:* 248-218-2032 or 800-521-6010 (toll-free). *Fax:* 248-218-2035. *E-mail:* admissions@rc.edu. *Web site:* http://www.rc.edu/.

SACRED HEART MAJOR SEMINARY
Detroit, Michigan

Sacred Heart Major Seminary is a coed, private, Roman Catholic, comprehensive institution, founded in 1919, offering degrees at the associate, bachelor's, master's, and first professional levels and postbachelor's certificates. It has a 24-acre campus in Detroit.

Academic Information The faculty has 50 members (62% full-time), 74% with terminal degrees. The undergraduate student-faculty ratio is 4:1. The library holds 139,873 titles, 510 serial subscriptions, and 3,209 audiovisual materials. Special programs include academic remediation, services for learning-disabled students, advanced placement credit, independent study, part-time degree programs (daytime, evenings), and arrangement for off-campus study with Detroit Area Catholic Higher Education Consortium. The most frequently chosen baccalaureate fields are liberal arts/general studies, philosophy and religious studies.

Student Body Statistics The student body totals 498, of whom 322 are undergraduates (4 freshmen). 41 percent are women and 59 percent are men. Students come from 3 states and territories. 99 percent are from Michigan. 60 percent of the 2006 graduating class went on to graduate and professional schools.

Expenses for 2006–07 *Application fee:* $30. *Comprehensive fee:* $18,190 includes full-time tuition ($11,610), mandatory fees ($80), and college room and board ($6500). Full-time tuition and fees vary according to course load. *Part-time tuition:* $275 per credit hour. *Part-time mandatory fees:* $40 per term. Part-time tuition and fees vary according to course load.

Financial Aid Forms of aid include need-based and non-need-based scholarships and part-time jobs. The application deadline for financial aid is continuous.

Freshman Admission Sacred Heart Major Seminary requires an essay, a high school transcript, a minimum 2.0 high school GPA, 1 recommendation, and an interview. The application deadline for regular admission is July 31.

Transfer Admission The application deadline for admission is July 31.

Entrance Difficulty Sacred Heart Major Seminary assesses its entrance difficulty level as moderately difficult. For the fall 2006 freshman class, 100 percent of the applicants were accepted.

For Further Information Contact Fr. Michael Byrnes, Vice Rector, Sacred Heart Major Seminary, 2701 Chicago Boulevard, Detroit, MI 48206. *Telephone:* 313-883-8552. *Fax:* 313-868-6400. *Web site:* http://www.archdioceseofdetroit.org/shms/shms.htm.

SAGINAW CHIPPEWA TRIBAL COLLEGE
Mount Pleasant, Michigan

Saginaw Chippewa Tribal College is a coed, private, two-year college, founded in 1998, offering degrees at the associate level.

Academic Information The faculty has 17 members (24% full-time). The student-faculty ratio is 9:1.

Student Body Statistics The student body is made up of 123 undergraduates (36 freshmen). 75 percent are women and 25 percent are men.

Expenses for 2007–08 *Application fee:* $0. *Tuition:* $1320 full-time, $55 per credit hour part-time. *Mandatory fees:* $136 full-time, $68 per term part-time.

Freshman Admission Saginaw Chippewa Tribal College requires a high school transcript.

Entrance Difficulty Saginaw Chippewa Tribal College assesses its entrance difficulty level as noncompetitive. For the fall 2006 freshman class, 100 percent of the applicants were accepted.

For Further Information Contact Ms. Tracy Reed, Admissions Officer/Registrar/Financial Aid, Saginaw Chippewa Tribal College, 22747 Enterprise Drive, Mount Pleasant, MI 48858. *Telephone:* 989-775-4123. *Fax:* 989-775-4528. *E-mail:* treed@sagchip.org. *Web site:* http://www.sagchip.org/tribalcollege/.

SAGINAW VALLEY STATE UNIVERSITY
University Center, Michigan

Saginaw Valley State University is a coed, public, comprehensive institution, founded in 1963, offering degrees at the bachelor's and master's levels and post-master's certificates. It has a 782-acre campus in University Center.

Academic Information The faculty has 570 members (47% full-time). The undergraduate student-faculty ratio is 20:1. The library holds 641,190 titles, 11,770 serial subscriptions, and 6,380 audiovisual materials. Special programs include academic remediation, services for learning-disabled students, an honors program, cooperative (work-study) education, study abroad, advanced placement credit, accelerated degree programs, ESL programs, double majors, independent study, distance learning, self-designed majors, summer session for credit, part-time degree programs (daytime, evenings, summer), adult/continuing education programs, and internships. The most frequently chosen baccalaureate fields are business/marketing, education, health professions and related sciences.

Student Body Statistics The student body totals 9,543, of whom 7,933 are undergraduates (1,450 freshmen). 60 percent are women and 40 percent are men. Students come from 14 states and territories and 46 other countries. 100 percent are from Michigan. 2.7 percent are international students. 21.18 percent of the 2006 graduating class went on to graduate and professional schools.

Expenses for 2006–07 *Application fee:* $25. *State resident tuition:* $5130 full-time, $171 per credit hour part-time. *Nonresident tuition:* $12,128 full-time, $404.25 per credit hour part-time. *Mandatory fees:* $412 full-time, $13.75 per credit hour part-time. Both full-time and part-time tuition and fees vary according to course level, course load, location, and program. *College room and board:* $6380. *College room only:* $3830. Room and board charges vary according to board plan, housing facility, and student level.

Financial Aid Forms of aid include need-based and non-need-based scholarships, athletic grants, and part-time jobs. The priority application deadline for financial aid is February 14.

Freshman Admission Saginaw Valley State University requires a high school transcript, ACT scores, and TOEFL scores for international students. A minimum 2.5 high school GPA and minimum ACT score of 17 are recommended. The application deadline for regular admission is rolling.

Transfer Admission The application deadline for admission is rolling.

Entrance Difficulty Saginaw Valley State University assesses its entrance difficulty level as moderately difficult. For the fall 2006 freshman class, 89 percent of the applicants were accepted.

For Further Information Contact Mr. James P. Dwyer, Director of Admissions, Saginaw Valley State University, 7400 Bay Road, University Center, MI 48710-0001. *Telephone:* 989-964-4200 or 800-968-9500 (toll-free). *Fax:* 517-790-0180. *E-mail:* admissions@svsu.edu. *Web site:* http://www.svsu.edu/.

SIENA HEIGHTS UNIVERSITY
Adrian, Michigan

http://www.sienahts.edu

SPRING ARBOR UNIVERSITY
Spring Arbor, Michigan

Spring Arbor University is a coed, private, Free Methodist, comprehensive institution, founded in 1873, offering degrees at the associate, bachelor's, and master's levels. It has a 123-acre campus in Spring Arbor.

Academic Information The faculty has 133 members (62% full-time), 43% with terminal degrees. The undergraduate student-faculty ratio is 15:1. The library holds 111,736 titles, 665 serial subscriptions, and 3,775 audiovisual materials. Special programs include academic remediation, services for learning-disabled students, an honors program, study abroad, advanced placement credit, accelerated degree programs, ESL programs, double majors, independent study, distance learning, self-designed majors, summer session for credit, part-time degree programs (daytime, evenings, weekends, summer), external degree programs, adult/continuing education programs, internships, and arrangement for off-campus study with Christian College Consortium. The most frequently chosen baccalaureate fields are business/marketing, education, family and consumer sciences.

Student Body Statistics The student body totals 3,714, of whom 2,609 are undergraduates (335 freshmen). 67 percent are women and 33 percent are men. Students come from 30 states and territories and 7 other countries. 84 percent are from Michigan. 0.8 percent are international students. 30 percent of the 2006 graduating class went on to graduate and professional schools.

Expenses for 2006–07 *Application fee:* $30. *Comprehensive fee:* $23,456 includes full-time tuition ($16,990), mandatory fees ($396), and college room and board ($6070). *College room only:* $2850. Full-time tuition and fees vary according to course load and program. Room and board charges vary according to board plan, housing facility, and location. *Part-time tuition:* $400 per credit. *Part-time mandatory fees:* $153 per term. Part-time tuition and fees vary according to course load, program, and reciprocity agreements.

Financial Aid Forms of aid include need-based and non-need-based scholarships and part-time jobs. The average aided 2006–07 undergraduate received an aid package worth an estimated $15,163. The priority application deadline for financial aid is March 1.

Freshman Admission Spring Arbor University requires a high school transcript, SAT or ACT scores, and TOEFL scores for international students. A minimum 2.6 high school GPA, guidance counselor's evaluation form, and ACT scores are recommended. An essay, recommendations, and an interview are required for some. The application deadline for regular admission is August 1 and for nonresidents it is August 1.

Transfer Admission The application deadline for admission is rolling.

Entrance Difficulty Spring Arbor University assesses its entrance difficulty level as moderately difficult. For the fall 2006 freshman class, 74 percent of the applicants were accepted.

For Further Information Contact Mr. Randy Comfort, Director of Admissions, Spring Arbor University, 106 East Main Street, Spring Arbor, MI 49283-9799. *Telephone:* 517-750-1200 Ext. 1468 or 800-968-0011 (toll-free). *Fax:* 517-750-6620. *E-mail:* admissions@arbor.edu. *Web site:* http://www.arbor.edu/.

UNIVERSITY OF DETROIT MERCY
Detroit, Michigan

http://www.udmercy.edu/

UNIVERSITY OF MICHIGAN
Ann Arbor, Michigan

University of Michigan is a coed, public university, founded in 1817, offering degrees at the bachelor's, master's, doctoral, and first professional levels and post-master's and postbachelor's certificates. It has an 8,070-acre campus in Ann Arbor near Detroit.

Academic Information The faculty has 2,987 members (80% full-time), 89% with terminal degrees. The undergraduate student-faculty ratio is 15:1. The library holds 8 million titles, 67,554 serial subscriptions, and 92,392 audiovisual materials. Special programs include services for learning-disabled students, an honors program, cooperative (work-study) education, study abroad, advanced placement credit, accelerated degree programs, ESL programs, double majors, independent study, distance learning, self-designed majors, summer session for credit, part-time degree programs, adult/continuing education programs, internships, and arrangement for off-campus study with Committee on Institutional Cooperation. The most frequently chosen baccalaureate fields are engineering, psychology, social sciences.

Student Body Statistics The student body totals 40,025, of whom 25,555 are undergraduates (5,060 freshmen). 50 percent are women and 50 percent are men. Students come from 55 states and territories and 84 other

University of Michigan (continued)

countries. 69 percent are from Michigan. 4.7 percent are international students. 34 percent of the 2006 graduating class went on to graduate and professional schools.

Expenses for 2006–07 *Application fee:* $40. *State resident tuition:* $9609 full-time. *Nonresident tuition:* $28,381 full-time. *Mandatory fees:* $189 full-time. Full-time tuition and fees vary according to course load, degree level, location, program, and student level. *College room and board:* $7838. Room and board charges vary according to board plan and housing facility.

Financial Aid Forms of aid include need-based and non-need-based scholarships, athletic grants, and part-time jobs. The average aided 2005–06 undergraduate received an aid package worth $11,111. The application deadline for financial aid is April 30.

Freshman Admission University of Michigan requires an essay, a high school transcript, SAT or ACT scores, and TOEFL scores for international students. An interview and SAT Subject Test scores are required for some. The application deadline for regular admission is February 1.

Transfer Admission The application deadline for admission is March 1.

Entrance Difficulty University of Michigan assesses its entrance difficulty level as very difficult. For the fall 2006 freshman class, 47 percent of the applicants were accepted.

For Further Information Contact Mr. Ted Spencer, Director of Undergraduate Admissions, University of Michigan, 1220 Student Activities Building, 515 East Jefferson, Ann Arbor, MI 48109-1316. *Telephone:* 734-764-7433. *Fax:* 734-936-0740. *E-mail:* ugadmiss@umich.edu. *Web site:* http://www.umich.edu/.

UNIVERSITY OF MICHIGAN–DEARBORN

Dearborn, Michigan

University of Michigan–Dearborn is a coed, public, comprehensive unit of University of Michigan System, founded in 1959, offering degrees at the bachelor's and master's levels and postbachelor's certificates. It has a 210-acre campus in Dearborn near Detroit.

Academic Information The faculty has 481 members (60% full-time), 68% with terminal degrees. The undergraduate student-faculty ratio is 16:1. The library holds 340,897 titles and 1,099 serial subscriptions. Special programs include academic remediation, services for learning-disabled students, an honors program, cooperative (work-study) education, study abroad, advanced placement credit, accelerated degree programs, double majors, independent study, distance learning, self-designed majors, summer session for credit, part-time degree programs (daytime, evenings, weekends, summer), adult/continuing education programs, internships, and arrangement for off-campus study with University of Michigan. The most frequently chosen baccalaureate fields are business/marketing, education, engineering.

Student Body Statistics The student body totals 8,566, of whom 6,612 are undergraduates (802 freshmen). 53 percent are women and 47 percent are men. Students come from 11 states and territories and 27 other countries. 100 percent are from Michigan. 1.3 percent are international students. 22.8 percent of the 2006 graduating class went on to graduate and professional schools.

Expenses for 2006–07 *Application fee:* $30. *State resident tuition:* $7259 full-time, $267.70 per credit hour part-time. *Nonresident tuition:* $16,054 full-time, $628.30 per credit hour part-time. *Mandatory fees:* $133 full-time, $133.15 per term part-time. Both full-time and part-time tuition and fees vary according to course load, course level, program, and student level.

Financial Aid Forms of aid include need-based and non-need-based scholarships, athletic grants, and part-time jobs. The average aided 2006–07 undergraduate received an aid package worth an estimated $4390. The priority application deadline for financial aid is February 14.

Freshman Admission University of Michigan–Dearborn requires a high school transcript, a minimum 3.0 high school GPA, SAT or ACT scores, and TOEFL scores for international students. An interview is required for some. The application deadline for regular admission is rolling.

Transfer Admission The application deadline for admission is rolling.

Entrance Difficulty University of Michigan–Dearborn assesses its entrance difficulty level as moderately difficult. For the fall 2006 freshman class, 72 percent of the applicants were accepted.

For Further Information Contact Mr. Christopher Tremblay, Director of Admissions, University of Michigan–Dearborn, 4901 Evergreen Road, Dearborn, MI 48128-1491. *Telephone:* 313-593-5100. *Fax:* 313-436-9167. *E-mail:* admissions@umd.umich.edu. *Web site:* http://www.umd.umich.edu/.

UNIVERSITY OF MICHIGAN–FLINT

Flint, Michigan

University of Michigan–Flint is a coed, public, comprehensive unit of University of Michigan System, founded in 1956, offering degrees at the bachelor's, master's, and first professional levels. It has a 72-acre campus in Flint near Detroit.

Academic Information The faculty has 445 members (52% full-time), 43% with terminal degrees. The undergraduate student-faculty ratio is 14:1. The library holds 259,260 titles and 911 serial subscriptions. Special programs include academic remediation, services for learning-disabled students, an honors program, cooperative (work-study) education, study abroad, advanced placement credit, double majors, independent study, distance learning, self-designed majors, summer session for credit, part-time degree programs (daytime, evenings, weekends, summer), adult/continuing education programs, internships, and arrangement for off-campus study. The most frequently chosen baccalaureate fields are business/marketing, education, health professions and related sciences.

Student Body Statistics The student body totals 6,527, of whom 5,600 are undergraduates (524 freshmen). 63 percent are women and 37 percent are men. Students come from 31 states and territories and 26 other countries. 97 percent are from Michigan. 0.9 percent are international students. 9 percent of the 2006 graduating class went on to graduate and professional schools.

Expenses for 2006–07 *Application fee:* $30. *State resident tuition:* $6568 full-time, $259 per credit part-time. *Nonresident tuition:* $12,818 full-time, $518 per credit part-time. *Mandatory fees:* $334 full-time, $129 per term part-time. Full-time tuition and fees vary according to course level, course load, degree level, and program. Part-time tuition and fees vary according to course level, degree level, and program.

Financial Aid Forms of aid include need-based and non-need-based scholarships and part-time jobs. The average aided 2005–06 undergraduate received an aid package worth $7228. The priority application deadline for financial aid is March 1.

Freshman Admission University of Michigan–Flint requires a high school transcript, a minimum 2.0 high school GPA, SAT or ACT scores, and TOEFL scores for international students. An essay and recommendations are recommended. An essay and recommendations are required for some.

Transfer Admission The application deadline for admission is August 19.

Entrance Difficulty University of Michigan–Flint assesses its entrance difficulty level as moderately difficult. For the fall 2006 freshman class, 88 percent of the applicants were accepted.

For Further Information Contact Ms. Kimberley Buster-Williams, Director of Admissions, University of Michigan–Flint, 303 East Kearsley Street, 245 UPAV, Flint, MI 48502-1950. *Telephone:* 810-762-3300 or 800-942-5636 (toll-free in-state). *Fax:* 810-762-3272. *E-mail:* admissions@umflint.edu. *Web site:* http://www.umflint.edu/.

UNIVERSITY OF PHOENIX–METRO DETROIT CAMPUS

Troy, Michigan

University of Phoenix–Metro Detroit Campus is a coed, proprietary, comprehensive institution, offering degrees at the bachelor's and master's levels.

Academic Information The faculty has 772 members (2% full-time), 34% with terminal degrees. The undergraduate student-faculty ratio is 11:1. The library holds 1,759 titles and 692 serial subscriptions. Special programs include services for learning-disabled students, advanced placement credit, accelerated degree programs, independent study, distance learning, external degree programs, and adult/continuing education programs. The most frequently chosen baccalaureate fields are business/marketing, computer and information sciences, health professions and related sciences.

Student Body Statistics The student body totals 3,918, of whom 2,948 are undergraduates (275 freshmen). 70 percent are women and 30 percent are men. 2.8 percent are international students.

Expenses for 2006–07 *Application fee:* $45. *Tuition:* $11,700 full-time.

Financial Aid Forms of aid include need-based and non-need-based scholarships. The average aided 2005–06 undergraduate received an aid package worth $4337. The application deadline for financial aid is continuous.

Freshman Admission University of Phoenix–Metro Detroit Campus requires 1 recommendation and TOEFL scores for international students. A high school transcript is required for some. The application deadline for regular admission is rolling.

Transfer Admission The application deadline for admission is rolling.

Entrance Difficulty University of Phoenix–Metro Detroit Campus has an open admission policy.

For Further Information Contact Ms. Beth Barilla, Associate Vice President, Student Admissions and Services, University of Phoenix–Metro Detroit Campus, 4615 East Elwood Street, Mail Stop AA-K101, Phoenix, AZ 85040-1958. *Telephone:* 480-317-6000, 800-776-4867 (toll-free in-state), or 800-228-7240 (toll-free out-of-state). *Fax:* 480-894-1758. *E-mail:* beth.barilla@phoenix.edu. *Web site:* http://www.phoenix.edu/.

UNIVERSITY OF PHOENIX–WEST MICHIGAN CAMPUS
Walker, Michigan

University of Phoenix–West Michigan Campus is a coed, proprietary, comprehensive institution, founded in 2000, offering degrees at the bachelor's and master's levels.

Academic Information The faculty has 370 members (5% full-time), 22% with terminal degrees. The undergraduate student-faculty ratio is 6:1. The library holds 1,759 titles and 692 serial subscriptions. Special programs include services for learning-disabled students, advanced placement credit, accelerated degree programs, independent study, distance learning, external degree programs, and adult/continuing education programs. The most frequently chosen baccalaureate fields are business/marketing, computer and information sciences, health professions and related sciences.

Student Body Statistics The student body totals 1,004, of whom 812 are undergraduates (26 freshmen). 62 percent are women and 38 percent are men. 4.3 percent are international students.

Expenses for 2006–07 *Application fee:* $45. *Tuition:* $11,400 full-time.

Financial Aid Forms of aid include need-based and non-need-based scholarships. The average aided 2005–06 undergraduate received an aid package worth $4167. The application deadline for financial aid is continuous.

Freshman Admission University of Phoenix–West Michigan Campus requires 1 recommendation and TOEFL scores for international students. A high school transcript is required for some. The application deadline for regular admission is rolling.

Transfer Admission The application deadline for admission is rolling.

Entrance Difficulty University of Phoenix–West Michigan Campus has an open admission policy.

For Further Information Contact Ms. Beth Barilla, Associate Vice President, Student Admissions and Services, University of Phoenix–West Michigan Campus, 4615 East Elwood Street, Mail Stop AA-K101, Phoenix, AZ 85040-1958. *Telephone:* 480-317-6000, 800-776-4867 (toll-free in-state), or 800-228-7240 (toll-free out-of-state). *Fax:* 480-894-1758. *E-mail:* beth.barilla@phoenix.edu. *Web site:* http://www.phoenix.edu/.

WALSH COLLEGE OF ACCOUNTANCY AND BUSINESS ADMINISTRATION
Troy, Michigan
http://www.walshcollege.edu/

WAYNE STATE UNIVERSITY
Detroit, Michigan

Wayne State University is a coed, public university, founded in 1868, offering degrees at the bachelor's, master's, doctoral, and first professional levels and post-master's and postbachelor's certificates. It has a 203-acre campus in Detroit.

Expenses for 2006–07 *Application fee:* $30. *State resident tuition:* $6012 full-time, $200.40 per credit hour part-time. *Nonresident tuition:* $13,770 full-time, $459.50 per credit hour part-time. *Mandatory fees:* $800 full-time, $16.75 per semester hour part-time, $148.50 per term part-time. *College room and board:* $6575. Room and board charges vary according to housing facility.

For Further Information Contact Ms. Susan Zwieg, Executive Director, Undergraduate Admissions and Student Financial Aid, Wayne State University, The Welcome Center, WSU Main Campus, 42, W Warren, Detroit, MI 48202. *Telephone:* 313-577-3577, 877-978 Ext. 4636 (toll-free in-state), or 800-WSU-INFO (toll-free out-of-state). *Fax:* 313-577-7536. *E-mail:* admissions@wayne.edu. *Web site:* http://www.wayne.edu/.

WESTERN MICHIGAN UNIVERSITY
Kalamazoo, Michigan

Western Michigan University is a coed, public university, founded in 1903, offering degrees at the bachelor's, master's, and doctoral levels and postbachelor's certificates (specialist). It has a 1,200-acre campus in Kalamazoo.

Academic Information The faculty has 1,412 members (65% full-time). The undergraduate student-faculty ratio is 19:1. The library holds 4 million titles, 10,074 serial subscriptions, and 27,891 audiovisual materials. Special programs include academic remediation, services for learning-disabled students, an honors program, cooperative (work-study) education, study abroad, advanced placement credit, accelerated degree programs, Freshman Honors College, ESL programs, double majors, independent study, distance learning, self-designed majors, summer session for credit, part-time degree programs (daytime, evenings, weekends, summer), adult/continuing education programs, internships, and arrangement for off-campus study with Kalamazoo College, Kalamazoo Valley Community College, Davenport College of Business. The most frequently chosen baccalaureate fields are business/marketing, communications/journalism, education.

Student Body Statistics The student body totals 24,841, of whom 20,081 are undergraduates (3,556 freshmen). 51 percent are women and 49 percent are men. Students come from 51 states and territories and 84 other countries. 94 percent are from Michigan. 1.8 percent are international students.

Expenses for 2006–07 *Application fee:* $35. *State resident tuition:* $6176 full-time, $205.83 per credit hour part-time. *Nonresident tuition:* $16,116 full-time, $537.22 per credit hour part-time. *Mandatory fees:* $690 full-time, $181.25 per term part-time. Both full-time and part-time tuition and fees vary according to course load, location, and student level. *College room and board:* $6877. *College room only:* $3638. Room and board charges vary according to board plan.

Financial Aid Forms of aid include need-based and non-need-based scholarships, athletic grants, and part-time jobs. The application deadline for financial aid is continuous.

Freshman Admission Western Michigan University requires a high school transcript, a minimum X high school GPA, SAT or ACT scores, and TOEFL scores for international students. An interview is required for some. The application deadline for regular admission is rolling.

Transfer Admission The application deadline for admission is August 1.

Western Michigan University (continued)

Entrance Difficulty Western Michigan University assesses its entrance difficulty level as moderately difficult. For the fall 2006 freshman class, 86 percent of the applicants were accepted.

For Further Information Contact Director, Office of Admissions, Western Michigan University, 1903 West Michigan Avenue, Kalamazoo, MI 49008-5211. *Telephone:* 269-387-2000. *Fax:* 269-387-2096. *E-mail:* askwmu@wmich.edu. *Web site:* http://www.wmich.edu/.

See page 304 for the College Close-Up.

YESHIVA GEDDOLAH OF GREATER DETROIT RABBINICAL COLLEGE

Oak Park, Michigan

For Information Write to Yeshiva Geddolah of Greater Detroit Rabbinical College, Oak Park, MI 48237-1544.

Minnesota

ACADEMY COLLEGE

Minneapolis, Minnesota

Academy College is a coed, proprietary, primarily two-year college, founded in 1936, offering degrees at the associate and bachelor's levels.

Academic Information The faculty has 54 members (7% full-time). The student-faculty ratio is 8:1. The library holds 1,309 titles and 22 serial subscriptions. Special programs include academic remediation, services for learning-disabled students, an honors program, cooperative (work-study) education, advanced placement credit, accelerated degree programs, ESL programs, double majors, distance learning, summer session for credit, part-time degree programs (daytime, evenings, weekends, summer), adult/continuing education programs, and internships.

Student Body Statistics The student body is made up of 210 undergraduates (22 freshmen). 39 percent are women and 61 percent are men. Students come from 2 states and territories. 98 percent are from Minnesota.

Expenses for 2007–08 *Application fee:* $30. *Tuition:* $19,527 full-time, $305 per credit part-time. *Mandatory fees:* $250 full-time.

Financial Aid Forms of aid include need-based scholarships and part-time jobs. The application deadline for financial aid is continuous.

Freshman Admission Academy College requires a high school transcript and an interview. TOEFL scores for international students are recommended.

Entrance Difficulty Academy College has an open admission policy.

For Further Information Contact Ms. Jacinda Miller, Director, Academy College, 1101 East 78th Street, Suite 100, Minneapolis, MN 55420. *Telephone:* 952-851-0066 or 800-292-9149 (toll-free). *Fax:* 952-851-0094. *E-mail:* admissions@academycollege.edu. *Web site:* http://www.academycollege.edu/.

ARGOSY UNIVERSITY, TWIN CITIES

Eagan, Minnesota

Argosy University, Twin Cities is a coed, proprietary unit of Education Management Corporation, founded in 1961, offering degrees at the associate, bachelor's, master's, and doctoral levels and post-master's and first professional certificates. It is located in Eagan near Minneapolis–St. Paul, MN.

Academic Information The faculty has 140 members (38% full-time), 38% with terminal degrees. The undergraduate student-faculty ratio is 12:1. The library holds 9,000 titles and 160 serial subscriptions. Special programs include academic remediation, services for learning-disabled students, study abroad, accelerated degree programs, double majors, independent study, summer session for credit, part-time degree programs (daytime, evenings), and internships.

Student Body Statistics The student body totals 1,700, of whom 1,100 are undergraduates. Students come from 20 states and territories and 1 other country. 90 percent are from Minnesota.

Expenses for 2007–08 *Application fee:* $50. *Tuition:* $425 per credit part-time.

Financial Aid Forms of aid include need-based scholarships and part-time jobs. The application deadline for financial aid is continuous.

Freshman Admission Argosy University, Twin Cities requires a high school transcript, SAT or ACT scores, TOEFL scores for international students, and Wonderlic Scholastic Level Exam. SAT or ACT scores are recommended. An essay, recommendations, an interview, and additional requirements for some programs are required for some. The application deadline for regular admission is rolling and for nonresidents it is rolling.

Transfer Admission Argosy University, Twin Cities requires a college transcript. Standardized test scores are required for some. The application deadline for admission is rolling.

Entrance Difficulty Argosy University, Twin Cities assesses its entrance difficulty level as moderately difficult. For the fall 2006 freshman class, 86 percent of the applicants were accepted.

For Further Information Contact Admissions Director, Argosy University, Twin Cities, 1515 Central Parkway, Eagan, MN 55121. *Telephone:* 651-846-2882 or 888-844-2004 (toll-free). *E-mail:* auadmissions@argosyu.edu. *Web site:* http://www.argosyu.edu/.

THE ART INSTITUTES INTERNATIONAL MINNESOTA

Minneapolis, Minnesota

The Art Institutes International Minnesota is a coed, proprietary, four-year college of Education Management Corporation, founded in 1964, offering degrees at the associate and bachelor's levels.

Academic Information The faculty has 111 members (50% full-time). The student-faculty ratio is 20:1. The library holds 42,752 titles, 160 serial subscriptions, and 2,259 audiovisual materials. Special programs include academic remediation, services for learning-disabled students, cooperative (work-study) education, advanced placement credit, independent study, summer session for credit, part-time degree programs (daytime, evenings), and internships.

Student Body Statistics The student body is made up of 1,594 undergraduates. 54 percent are women and 46 percent are men. Students come from 10 states and territories and 6 other countries. 94 percent are from Minnesota.

Expenses for 2006–07 *Application fee:* $50. *Tuition:* $18,336 full-time, $6112 per term part-time.

Financial Aid Forms of aid include need-based scholarships and part-time jobs. The application deadline for financial aid is continuous.

Freshman Admission The Art Institutes International Minnesota requires an essay, a high school transcript, an interview, TOEFL scores for international students, and ACT COMPASS. ACT scores are recommended. The application deadline for regular admission is rolling.

Transfer Admission The application deadline for admission is rolling.

Entrance Difficulty The Art Institutes International Minnesota assesses its entrance difficulty level as minimally difficult. For the fall 2006 freshman class, 100 percent of the applicants were accepted.

For Further Information Contact Mr. Russ Gill, Director of Admissions, The Art Institutes International Minnesota, 15 South 9th Street, Minneapolis, MN 55402. *Telephone:* 612-332-3361 or 800-777-3643 (toll-free). *Fax:* 612-332-3934. *E-mail:* aimadm@aii.edu. *Web site:* http://www.aim.artinstitutes.edu/.

AUGSBURG COLLEGE

Minneapolis, Minnesota

Augsburg College is a coed, private, Lutheran, comprehensive institution, founded in 1869, offering degrees at the bachelor's and master's levels and post-master's and postbachelor's certificates. It has a 23-acre campus in Minneapolis.

Academic Information The faculty has 355 members (46% full-time), 48% with terminal degrees. The undergraduate student-faculty ratio is 15:1. The library holds 146,166 titles and 754 serial subscriptions. Special programs include academic remediation, services for learning-disabled students, an honors program, cooperative (work-study) education, study abroad, advanced placement credit, Freshman Honors College, ESL programs, double majors, independent study, self-designed majors, summer session for credit, part-time degree programs (daytime, weekends, summer), adult/continuing education programs, internships, and arrangement for off-campus study with Associated Colleges of the Twin Cities. The most frequently chosen baccalaureate fields are business/marketing, education, social sciences.

Student Body Statistics The student body totals 3,732, of whom 2,921 are undergraduates (401 freshmen). 57 percent are women and 43 percent are men. Students come from 39 states and territories and 24 other countries. 83 percent are from Minnesota. 1.3 percent are international students. 15.4 percent of the 2006 graduating class went on to graduate and professional schools.

Expenses for 2006–07 *Application fee:* $25. *Comprehensive fee:* $30,026 includes full-time tuition ($22,900), mandatory fees ($522), and college room and board ($6604). *College room only:* $3396. Room and board charges vary according to board plan and housing facility. *Part-time tuition:* $2860 per course. *Part-time mandatory fees:* $90 per term. Part-time tuition and fees vary according to course load.

Financial Aid Forms of aid include need-based and non-need-based scholarships and part-time jobs. The average aided 2005–06 undergraduate received an aid package worth $10,566. The application deadline for financial aid is August 15.

Freshman Admission Augsburg College requires an essay, a high school transcript, a minimum 2.5 high school GPA, an interview, and TOEFL scores for international students. SAT or ACT scores are recommended. 2 recommendations are required for some. The application deadline for regular admission is August 15.

Transfer Admission The application deadline for admission is August 15.

Entrance Difficulty Augsburg College assesses its entrance difficulty level as moderately difficult. For the fall 2006 freshman class, 71 percent of the applicants were accepted.

For Further Information Contact Ms. Carrie Carroll, Director of Undergraduate Day Admissions, Augsburg College, 2211 Riverside Avenue, Minneapolis, MN 55454-1351. *Telephone:* 612-330-1001 or 800-788-5678 (toll-free). *Fax:* 612-330-1590. *E-mail:* admissions@augsburg.edu. *Web site:* http://www.augsburg.edu/.

BEMIDJI STATE UNIVERSITY

Bemidji, Minnesota

Bemidji State University is a coed, public, comprehensive unit of Minnesota State Colleges and Universities System, founded in 1919, offering degrees at the associate, bachelor's, and master's levels. It has an 89-acre campus in Bemidji.

Academic Information The faculty has 362 members (68% full-time), 50% with terminal degrees. The undergraduate student-faculty ratio is 19:1. The library holds 554,087 titles and 991 serial subscriptions. Special programs include academic remediation, services for learning-disabled students, an honors program, cooperative (work-study) education, study abroad, advanced placement credit, ESL programs, double majors, independent study, distance learning, summer session for credit, part-time degree programs (daytime, evenings, summer), external degree programs, adult/continuing education programs, internships, and arrangement for off-campus study with other colleges in MNSCU system. The most frequently chosen baccalaureate fields are education, business/marketing, engineering technologies.

Student Body Statistics The student body totals 4,918, of whom 4,388 are undergraduates (657 freshmen). 54 percent are women and 46 percent are men. Students come from 35 states and territories and 41 other countries. 93 percent are from Minnesota. 6 percent are international students.

Expenses for 2006–07 *Application fee:* $20. *State resident tuition:* $5900 full-time, $199.50 per credit part-time. *Nonresident tuition:* $5900 full-time, $199.50 per credit part-time. *Mandatory fees:* $790 full-time, $360.26 per term part-time. Both full-time and part-time tuition and fees vary according to course load, program, and reciprocity agreements. *College room and board:* $5860. *College room only:* $3628. Room and board charges vary according to board plan and housing facility.

Financial Aid Forms of aid include need-based and non-need-based scholarships, athletic grants, and part-time jobs. The average aided 2006–07 undergraduate received an aid package worth an estimated $7856. The priority application deadline for financial aid is May 15.

Freshman Admission Bemidji State University requires a high school transcript, ACT scores, and TOEFL scores for international students. An essay, recommendations, and an interview are required for some. The application deadline for regular admission is rolling.

Transfer Admission The application deadline for admission is rolling.

Entrance Difficulty Bemidji State University assesses its entrance difficulty level as moderately difficult. For the fall 2006 freshman class, 71 percent of the applicants were accepted.

For Further Information Contact Mr. Russ Kreager, Director of Admissions, Bemidji State University, Deputy 102, Bemidji State University, 1500 Birchmont Drive NE, Bemidji, MN 56601. *Telephone:* 218-755-2040, 800-475-2001 (toll-free in-state), or 800-652-9747 (toll-free out-of-state). *Fax:* 218-755-2074. *E-mail:* admissions@bemidjistate.edu. *Web site:* http://www. bemidjistate.edu/.

BETHANY LUTHERAN COLLEGE

Mankato, Minnesota

Bethany Lutheran College is a coed, private, Lutheran, four-year college, founded in 1927, offering degrees at the associate and bachelor's levels. It has a 50-acre campus in Mankato near Minneapolis–St. Paul.

Academic Information The faculty has 68 members (56% full-time), 26% with terminal degrees. The student-faculty ratio is 11:1. The library holds 72,392 titles and 23,266 serial subscriptions. Special programs include academic remediation, services for learning-disabled students, an honors program, study abroad, advanced placement credit, double majors, independent study, and internships. The most frequently chosen baccalaureate fields are business/marketing, communications/journalism, liberal arts/general studies.

Student Body Statistics The student body is made up of 597 undergraduates (212 freshmen). 56 percent are women and 44 percent are men. Students come from 25 states and territories and 7 other countries. 67 percent are from Minnesota. 1.7 percent are international students.

Expenses for 2007–08 *Application fee:* $0. *Comprehensive fee:* $23,038 includes full-time tuition ($17,500), mandatory fees ($260), and college room and board ($5278). *College room only:* $1988. *Part-time tuition:* $750 per credit. *Part-time mandatory fees:* $130 per term.

Financial Aid Forms of aid include need-based and non-need-based scholarships and part-time jobs. The average aided 2005–06 undergraduate received an aid package worth $12,864. The priority application deadline for financial aid is April 15.

Freshman Admission Bethany Lutheran College requires an essay, a high school transcript, a minimum 2.4 high school GPA, SAT or ACT scores, and TOEFL scores for international students. A minimum 3.2 high school GPA and an interview are recommended. An interview is required for some. The application deadline for regular admission is July 15.

Entrance Difficulty Bethany Lutheran College assesses its entrance difficulty level as moderately difficult; minimally difficult for transfers. For the fall 2006 freshman class, 85 percent of the applicants were accepted.

For Further Information Contact Mr. Donald Westphal, Dean of Admissions, Bethany Lutheran College, 700 Luther Drive, Mankato, MN 56001. *Telephone:* 507-344-7320 or 800-944-3066 Ext. 331 (toll-free). *Fax:* 507-344-7376. *E-mail:* dwestpha@blc.edu. *Web site:* http://www.blc.edu/.

BETHEL UNIVERSITY
St. Paul, Minnesota

SPONSOR
See Front Insert
for Details!

Bethel University is a coed, private, comprehensive institution, founded in 1871, affiliated with the Baptist General Conference, offering degrees at the associate, bachelor's, and master's levels and post-master's and postbachelor's certificates. It has a 248-acre campus in St. Paul near Twin Cities.

Academic Information The faculty has 284 members (60% full-time), 62% with terminal degrees. The undergraduate student-faculty ratio is 13:1. The library holds 184,000 titles, 21,343 serial subscriptions, and 14,171 audiovisual materials. Special programs include academic remediation, services for learning-disabled students, an honors program, study abroad, advanced placement credit, accelerated degree programs, double majors, independent study, self-designed majors, summer session for credit, part-time degree programs (daytime, evenings, summer), adult/continuing education programs, internships, and arrangement for off-campus study with members of the Christian College Consortium, Au Sable Institute, Coalition for Christian Colleges and Universities. The most frequently chosen baccalaureate fields are business/marketing, education, health professions and related sciences.

Student Body Statistics The student body totals 5,185, of whom 3,321 are undergraduates (674 freshmen). 61 percent are women and 39 percent are men. Students come from 43 states and territories and 16 other countries. 74 percent are from Minnesota. 0.2 percent are international students.

Expenses for 2007–08 *Application fee:* $25. *Comprehensive fee:* $31,890 includes full-time tuition ($24,400), mandatory fees ($110), and college room and board ($7380). *College room only:* $4400. *Part-time tuition:* $935 per credit.

Financial Aid Forms of aid include need-based and non-need-based scholarships and part-time jobs. The average aided 2006–07 undergraduate received an aid package worth an estimated $16,609.

Freshman Admission Bethel University requires an essay, 2 recommendations, rank in upper 50% of high school class, minimum ACT score of 21 or SAT score of 920, SAT or ACT scores, and TOEFL scores for international students. An interview is recommended. A high school transcript is required for some. The application deadline for regular admission is August 1 and for early action it is November 1.

Transfer Admission The application deadline for admission is August 1.

Entrance Difficulty Bethel University assesses its entrance difficulty level as moderately difficult; very difficult for nursing program. For the fall 2006 freshman class, 85 percent of the applicants were accepted.

SPECIAL MESSAGE TO STUDENTS

Social Life The social atmosphere at Bethel is exciting, with many student-run campus activities. Bethel has excellent music performance groups, varsity and intramural sports, student government, theater productions, and a wide variety of student clubs and spiritual growth groups. Spiritual life is a priority at Bethel. Community chapel services, residence hall Bible studies, and discipleship programs offer opportunities for Christian growth. There are also many opportunities for students to get involved in ministry through campus outreach events, Habitat for Humanity, community service programs, inner-city projects, and missions trips.

Academic Highlights With sixty-six majors within eighty-two areas of study, Bethel ranks in the top Midwestern Universities category of *U.S. News & World Report's* "America's Best Colleges." Bethel's general education curriculum has become a model for many other institutions nationwide. General education courses give students a broad view of the world and their role as Christians in it. The courses are grouped around the following themes: personal development; biblical foundations; math, science, and technology; and global perspectives. Bethel strongly encourages and provides students with the opportunity to participate in a number of off-campus study programs, including Australia Term, England Term, Europe Term, Guatemala Term, South Africa Term, Spain Term, Thailand Term, the American Studies Program in Washington, D.C., the Los Angeles Film Studies Center, and the New York Center for Art and Media Studies.

Interviews and Campus Visits On-campus interviews are strongly encouraged but not required. An interview gives the prospective student the opportunity to learn more about the University, ask questions, and better determine if the University is a good fit. A campus visit at Bethel gives students opportunities to stay in a residence hall, attend classes and chapel, meet with professors and coaches, enjoy free meals with Bethel students, and attend on-campus events. Bethel's beautiful wooded campus is located on the shores of Lake Valentine in Arden Hills, Minnesota—just 15 minutes from downtown St. Paul and Minneapolis. The Bethel campus offers modern academic, housing, and recreation facilities. The Community Life Center houses the 1,700-seat Benson Great Hall, hailed as one of the best music performance halls in the upper Midwest. For more information about Bethel University or to arrange a campus visit, students can call the Office of Admissions at 651-638-6242 or 800-255-8706 (toll-free), Monday through Friday, 8:30 to 4:30. The fax number is 651-635-1490. The Office of Admissions is located on campus in RC 341, Robertson Center building. The nearest commercial airport is Minneapolis-St. Paul International.

For Further Information Write to the Office of Admissions, Bethel University, 3900 Bethel Drive, St. Paul, MN 55112. *E-mail:* BUadmissions-cas@bethel.edu. *Web site:* http://www.bethel.edu.

BROWN COLLEGE
Mendota Heights, Minnesota

Brown College is a coed, proprietary, primarily two-year college of Career Education Corporation, founded in 1946, offering degrees at the associate and bachelor's levels. It has a 20-acre campus in Mendota Heights near Minneapolis–St. Paul.

Expenses for 2006–07 *Application fee:* $50. *Tuition:* $18,540 full-time. *Mandatory fees:* $2200 full-time. Full-time tuition and fees vary according to degree level and program.

For Further Information Contact Mr. Mark Fredrichs, Registrar, Brown College, 1440 Northland Drive, Mendota Heights, MN 55120. *Telephone:* 651-905-3400 or 800-6BROWN6 (toll-free). *Fax:* 651-905-3550. *Web site:* http://www.browncollege.edu/.

CAPELLA UNIVERSITY
Minneapolis, Minnesota

Capella University is a coed, proprietary, upper-level institution, founded in 1993, offering degrees at the bachelor's, master's, doctoral, and first professional levels and first professional and postbachelor's certificates (offers only distance learning degree programs).

Academic Information The faculty has 796 members (14% full-time), 80% with terminal degrees. Special programs include services for learning-disabled students, advanced placement credit, double majors, independent study, distance learning, self-designed majors, summer session for credit, part-time degree programs, external degree programs, adult/continuing education programs, internships, and arrangement for off-campus study.

Student Body Statistics The student body totals 17,203, of whom 2,478 are undergraduates. 50 percent are women and 50 percent are men. 1.8 percent are international students.

Expenses for 2007–08 *Application fee:* $75. *Tuition:* $10,440 full-time, $870 per course part-time.

Financial Aid Forms of aid include need-based scholarships. The application deadline for financial aid is continuous.

Transfer Admission Capella University requires a college transcript and a minimum 2.0 college GPA. The application deadline for admission is rolling.

Entrance Difficulty Capella University assesses its entrance difficulty level as minimally difficult.

For Further Information Contact Learner Support, Capella University, 225 South Sixth Street, 9th Floor, Minneapolis, MN 55402. *Telephone:* 888-277-3552 or 888-CAPELLA (toll-free). *Fax:* 612-977-5060. *E-mail:* info@capella.edu. *Web site:* http://www.capella.edu/.

CARLETON COLLEGE
Northfield, Minnesota

Carleton College is a coed, private, four-year college, founded in 1866, offering degrees at the bachelor's level. It has a 955-acre campus in Northfield near Minneapolis–St. Paul.

Academic Information The faculty has 225 members (89% full-time), 92% with terminal degrees. The student-faculty ratio is 9:1. The library holds 1 million titles and 10,964 serial subscriptions. Special programs include services for learning-disabled students, study abroad, advanced placement credit, accelerated degree programs, double majors, independent study, self-designed majors, internships, and arrangement for off-campus study with Cooperative programs/St. Olaf College, memberships in Associated Colleges of the Midwest, Higher Education Consortium for Urban Affairs. The most frequently chosen baccalaureate fields are biological/life sciences, social sciences, visual and performing arts.

Student Body Statistics The student body is made up of 1,980 undergraduates (504 freshmen). 53 percent are women and 47 percent are men. Students come from 51 states and territories and 30 other countries. 27 percent are from Minnesota. 5.1 percent are international students. 23 percent of the 2006 graduating class went on to graduate and professional schools.

Expenses for 2006–07 *Application fee:* $30. *Comprehensive fee:* $42,864 includes full-time tuition ($34,083), mandatory fees ($189), and college room and board ($8592). *College room only:* $4299.

Financial Aid Forms of aid include need-based and non-need-based scholarships and part-time jobs. The average aided 2005–06 undergraduate received an aid package worth $29,116. The application deadline for financial aid is February 15 with a priority deadline of February 15.

Freshman Admission Carleton College requires an essay, a high school transcript, 2 recommendations, common application supplement, SAT or ACT scores, and TOEFL scores for international students. An interview and SAT Subject Test scores are recommended. The application deadline for regular admission is January 15; for early decision plan 1 it is November 15; and for early decision plan 2 it is January 15.

Transfer Admission The application deadline for admission is March 31.

Entrance Difficulty Carleton College assesses its entrance difficulty level as very difficult; most difficult for transfers. For the fall 2006 freshman class, 32 percent of the applicants were accepted.

For Further Information Contact Mr. Paul Thiboutot, Dean of Admissions, Carleton College, 100 South College Street, Northfield, MN 55057. *Telephone:* 507-646-4190 or 800-995-2275 (toll-free). *Fax:* 507-646-4526. *E-mail:* admissions@acs.carleton.edu. *Web site:* http://www.carleton.edu/.

COLLEGE OF SAINT BENEDICT
Saint Joseph, Minnesota

College of Saint Benedict is a coed, primarily women's, private, Roman Catholic, four-year college, founded in 1887, coordinate with Saint John's University (MN), offering degrees at the bachelor's level (coordinate with Saint John's University for men). It has a 315-acre campus in Saint Joseph near Minneapolis–St. Paul.

Academic Information The faculty has 178 members (84% full-time), 75% with terminal degrees. The student-faculty ratio is 13:1. The library holds 481,338 titles, 5,315 serial subscriptions, and 34,985 audiovisual materials. Special programs include services for learning-disabled students, an honors program, study abroad, advanced placement credit, accelerated degree programs, ESL programs, double majors, independent study, self-designed majors, internships, and arrangement for off-campus study

with Tri-College Exchange Program (MN), Saint John's University (MN). The most frequently chosen baccalaureate fields are business/marketing, English, psychology.

Student Body Statistics The student body is made up of 2,059 undergraduates (540 freshmen). 100 percent are women. Students come from 34 states and territories and 20 other countries. 82 percent are from Minnesota. 4.3 percent are international students. 23 percent of the 2006 graduating class went on to graduate and professional schools.

Expenses for 2006–07 *Application fee:* $0. *Comprehensive fee:* $31,822 includes full-time tuition ($24,448), mandatory fees ($476), and college room and board ($6898). *College room only:* $3546. Room and board charges vary according to board plan and housing facility. *Part-time tuition:* $1020 per credit. *Part-time mandatory fees:* $238 per term. Part-time tuition and fees vary according to course load.

Financial Aid Forms of aid include need-based and non-need-based scholarships and part-time jobs. The average aided 2005–06 undergraduate received an aid package worth $19,044. The priority application deadline for financial aid is March 15.

Freshman Admission College of Saint Benedict requires an essay, a high school transcript, 1 recommendation, SAT or ACT scores, and TOEFL scores for international students. A minimum 3.0 high school GPA and an interview are recommended. The application deadline for regular admission is rolling.

Transfer Admission The application deadline for admission is rolling.

Entrance Difficulty College of Saint Benedict assesses its entrance difficulty level as moderately difficult. For the fall 2006 freshman class, 84 percent of the applicants were accepted.

For Further Information Contact Ms. Karen Backes, Associate Dean of Admissions, College of Saint Benedict, 37 South College Avenue, St. Joseph, MN 56374. *Telephone:* 320-363-2196 or 800-544-1489 (toll-free). *Fax:* 320-363-2750. *E-mail:* admissions@csbsju.edu. *Web site:* http://www.csbsju.edu/.

COLLEGE OF ST. CATHERINE
St. Paul, Minnesota

College of St. Catherine is an undergraduate: women only; graduate: coed, private, Roman Catholic, comprehensive institution, founded in 1905, offering degrees at the associate, bachelor's, master's, and doctoral levels and postbachelor's certificates. It has a 110-acre campus in St. Paul near Minneapolis.

Academic Information The faculty has 483 members (54% full-time). The undergraduate student-faculty ratio is 11:1. The library holds 263,495 titles and 1,141 serial subscriptions. Special programs include academic remediation, services for learning-disabled students, an honors program, study abroad, advanced placement credit, double majors, independent study, self-designed majors, summer session for credit, part-time degree programs (daytime, weekends, summer), external degree programs, adult/continuing education programs, internships, and arrangement for off-campus study with Associated Colleges of the Twin Cities, Sisters of St. Joseph College Consortium, Higher Education Consortium for Urban Affairs. The most frequently chosen baccalaureate fields are business/marketing, education, health professions and related sciences.

Student Body Statistics The student body totals 5,246, of whom 3,831 are undergraduates (437 freshmen). 96 percent are women and 4 percent are men. Students come from 37 states and territories and 16 other countries. 90 percent are from Minnesota. 1.6 percent are international students. 14 percent of the 2006 graduating class went on to graduate and professional schools.

Expenses for 2006–07 *Application fee:* $0. *Comprehensive fee:* $29,312 includes full-time tuition ($22,620), mandatory fees ($260), and college room and board ($6432). *College room only:* $3592. Full-time tuition and fees vary according to class time. Room and board charges vary according to board plan and housing facility. *Part-time tuition:* $754 per credit. Part-time tuition varies according to class time.

Financial Aid Forms of aid include need-based and non-need-based scholarships and part-time jobs. The average aided 2006–07 undergraduate received an aid package worth an estimated $23,534. The priority application deadline for financial aid is April 15.

Freshman Admission College of St. Catherine requires a high school transcript, 1 recommendation, SAT or ACT scores, and TOEFL scores for

College of St. Catherine (continued)

international students. An interview is recommended. An essay and an interview are required for some. The application deadline for regular admission is rolling.

Transfer Admission The application deadline for admission is rolling.
Entrance Difficulty College of St. Catherine assesses its entrance difficulty level as moderately difficult. For the fall 2006 freshman class, 81 percent of the applicants were accepted.
For Further Information Contact Ms. Cory Piper-Hauswirth, Associate Director of Admission and Financial Aid, College of St. Catherine, 2004 Randolph Avenue, F-02, St. Paul, MN 55105. *Telephone:* 651-690-6047 or 800-656-5283 (toll-free in-state). *Fax:* 651-690-8824. *E-mail:* stkate@stkate. edu. *Web site:* http://www.stkate.edu/.

COLLEGE OF ST. CATHERINE–MINNEAPOLIS

Minneapolis, Minnesota

http://www.stkate.edu/

THE COLLEGE OF ST. SCHOLASTICA

Duluth, Minnesota

The College of St. Scholastica is a coed, private, comprehensive institution, founded in 1912, affiliated with the Roman Catholic Church, offering degrees at the bachelor's, master's, and first professional levels and post-master's and postbachelor's certificates. It has a 186-acre campus in Duluth.

Academic Information The faculty has 260 members (55% full-time), 42% with terminal degrees. The undergraduate student-faculty ratio is 13:1. The library holds 130,353 titles, 21,656 serial subscriptions, and 5,418 audiovisual materials. Special programs include services for learning-disabled students, an honors program, study abroad, advanced placement credit, accelerated degree programs, double majors, independent study, distance learning, self-designed majors, summer session for credit, part-time degree programs (evenings), external degree programs, adult/continuing education programs, internships, and arrangement for off-campus study with University of Wisconsin-Superior, University of Minnesota, Duluth. The most frequently chosen baccalaureate fields are business/marketing, computer and information sciences, health professions and related sciences.
Student Body Statistics The student body totals 3,304, of whom 2,648 are undergraduates (499 freshmen). 69 percent are women and 31 percent are men. Students come from 36 states and territories and 22 other countries. 88 percent are from Minnesota. 4 percent are international students. 21 percent of the 2006 graduating class went on to graduate and professional schools.
Expenses for 2006–07 *Application fee:* $25. *Comprehensive fee:* $30,088 includes full-time tuition ($23,434), mandatory fees ($140), and college room and board ($6514). *College room only:* $3708. Full-time tuition and fees vary according to class time. Room and board charges vary according to board plan and housing facility. *Part-time tuition:* $729 per credit hour. Part-time tuition varies according to class time and course load.
Financial Aid Forms of aid include need-based and non-need-based scholarships and part-time jobs. The average aided 2006–07 undergraduate received an aid package worth an estimated $17,801. The priority application deadline for financial aid is March 15.
Freshman Admission The College of St. Scholastica requires a high school transcript, SAT or ACT scores, and TOEFL scores for international students. An interview is recommended. A minimum 2.0 high school GPA and an interview are required for some. The application deadline for regular admission is rolling.
Transfer Admission The application deadline for admission is rolling.

Entrance Difficulty The College of St. Scholastica assesses its entrance difficulty level as moderately difficult. For the fall 2006 freshman class, 88 percent of the applicants were accepted.
For Further Information Contact Mr. Brian Dalton, Vice President for Enrollment Management, The College of St. Scholastica, 1200 Kenwood Avenue, Duluth, MN 55811-4199. *Telephone:* 218-723-6053 or 800-249-6412 (toll-free). *Fax:* 218-723-5991. *E-mail:* admissions@css.edu. *Web site:* http://www.css.edu/.

COLLEGE OF VISUAL ARTS

St. Paul, Minnesota

College of Visual Arts is a coed, private, four-year college, founded in 1924, offering degrees at the bachelor's level. It has a 2-acre campus in St. Paul near Minneapolis.

Academic Information The faculty has 46 members (15% full-time), 15% with terminal degrees. The student-faculty ratio is 8:1. The library holds 7,100 titles, 55 serial subscriptions, and 30,370 audiovisual materials. Special programs include academic remediation, an honors program, study abroad, advanced placement credit, double majors, independent study, summer session for credit, part-time degree programs (daytime, evenings, summer), and internships. The most frequently chosen baccalaureate field is visual and performing arts.
Student Body Statistics The student body is made up of 172 undergraduates (37 freshmen). 58 percent are women and 42 percent are men. Students come from 5 states and territories and 3 other countries. 92 percent are from Minnesota. 2.9 percent are international students.
Expenses for 2007–08 *Application fee:* $40. *Tuition:* $21,184 full-time, $1057 per credit part-time. *Mandatory fees:* $500 full-time, $50.
Financial Aid Forms of aid include need-based and non-need-based scholarships and part-time jobs. The average aided 2006–07 undergraduate received an aid package worth an estimated $7915. The application deadline for financial aid is June 1 with a priority deadline of April 1.
Freshman Admission College of Visual Arts requires an essay, a high school transcript, a minimum 2.7 high school GPA, a portfolio, SAT or ACT scores, and TOEFL scores for international students. A minimum 3.0 high school GPA, recommendations, and an interview are recommended. The application deadline for regular admission is rolling.
Transfer Admission The application deadline for admission is rolling.
Entrance Difficulty College of Visual Arts assesses its entrance difficulty level as moderately difficult. For the fall 2006 freshman class, 99 percent of the applicants were accepted.
For Further Information Contact Mr. Paul Gaines, Director of Student Life, College of Visual Arts, 344 Summit Avenue, St. Paul, MN 55102-2124. *Telephone:* 651-224-3416 or 800-224-1536 (toll-free). *Fax:* 651-224-8854. *E-mail:* pgaines@cva.edu. *Web site:* http://www.cva.edu/.

CONCORDIA COLLEGE

Moorhead, Minnesota

Concordia College is a coed, private, four-year college, founded in 1891, affiliated with the Evangelical Lutheran Church in America, offering degrees at the bachelor's and master's levels. It has a 120-acre campus in Moorhead.

Academic Information The faculty has 238 members (77% full-time), 59% with terminal degrees. The undergraduate student-faculty ratio is 14:1. The library holds 325,408 titles, 3,528 serial subscriptions, and 23,205 audiovisual materials. Special programs include services for learning-disabled students, an honors program, cooperative (work-study) education, study abroad, advanced placement credit, ESL programs, double majors, independent study, summer session for credit, part-time degree programs (daytime, evenings, summer), adult/continuing education programs, internships, and arrangement for off-campus study with Tri-College University.
Student Body Statistics The student body totals 2,764, of whom 2,759 are undergraduates (773 freshmen). 63 percent are women and 37 percent are men. Students come from 40 states and territories and 35 other

countries. 67 percent are from Minnesota. 4.4 percent are international students. 23 percent of the 2006 graduating class went on to graduate and professional schools.

Expenses for 2006–07 *Application fee:* $20. *Comprehensive fee:* $26,070 includes full-time tuition ($20,816), mandatory fees ($164), and college room and board ($5090). *College room only:* $2460. Room and board charges vary according to board plan and housing facility. *Part-time tuition:* $3273 per course. Part-time tuition varies according to course load.

Financial Aid Forms of aid include need-based and non-need-based scholarships and part-time jobs. The average aided 2006–07 undergraduate received an aid package worth an estimated $15,899. The application deadline for financial aid is continuous.

Freshman Admission Concordia College requires a high school transcript, 2 recommendations, references, SAT or ACT scores, and TOEFL scores for international students. The application deadline for regular admission is rolling.

Transfer Admission The application deadline for admission is rolling.

Entrance Difficulty Concordia College assesses its entrance difficulty level as moderately difficult. For the fall 2006 freshman class, 84 percent of the applicants were accepted.

For Further Information Contact Mr. Scott E. Ellingson, Director of Admissions, Concordia College, 901 8th Street South, Moorhead, MN 56562. *Telephone:* 218-299-3004 or 800-699-9897 (toll-free). *Fax:* 218-299-3947. *E-mail:* admissions@gloria.cord.edu. *Web site:* http://www.concordiacollege.edu/.

CONCORDIA UNIVERSITY, ST. PAUL

St. Paul, Minnesota

Concordia University, St. Paul is a coed, private, comprehensive institution, founded in 1893, affiliated with the Lutheran Church–Missouri Synod, offering degrees at the associate, bachelor's, and master's levels and postbachelor's certificates. It has a 37-acre campus in St. Paul.

Academic Information The faculty has 437 members (19% full-time), 29% with terminal degrees. The undergraduate student-faculty ratio is 12:1. The library holds 113,256 titles, 336 serial subscriptions, and 3,171 audiovisual materials. Special programs include academic remediation, services for learning-disabled students, an honors program, study abroad, advanced placement credit, accelerated degree programs, double majors, independent study, distance learning, self-designed majors, summer session for credit, part-time degree programs (daytime, evenings, summer), adult/continuing education programs, internships, and arrangement for off-campus study with University of Minnesota–Twin Cities Campus, University of St. Thomas, Oak Hill College. The most frequently chosen baccalaureate fields are business/marketing, education, family and consumer sciences.

Student Body Statistics The student body totals 2,046, of whom 1,683 are undergraduates (201 freshmen). 61 percent are women and 39 percent are men. Students come from 43 states and territories and 4 other countries. 79 percent are from Minnesota. 0.3 percent are international students.

Expenses for 2007–08 *Application fee:* $30. *Comprehensive fee:* $30,272 includes full-time tuition ($23,496) and college room and board ($6776). *Part-time tuition:* $490 per credit.

Financial Aid Forms of aid include need-based and non-need-based scholarships, athletic grants, and part-time jobs. The average aided 2006–07 undergraduate received an aid package worth an estimated $13,035. The priority application deadline for financial aid is May 1.

Freshman Admission Concordia University, St. Paul requires a high school transcript, 2 recommendations, and ACT scores. A minimum 2.0 high school GPA and an interview are recommended. An essay is required for some. The application deadline for regular admission is August 1.

Transfer Admission The application deadline for admission is August 1.

Entrance Difficulty Concordia University, St. Paul assesses its entrance difficulty level as minimally difficult. For the fall 2006 freshman class, 65 percent of the applicants were accepted.

For Further Information Contact Kristin Schoon, Director of Undergraduate Admission, Concordia University, St. Paul, 275 Syndicate North, St. Paul, MN 55104-5494. *Telephone:* 651-641-8230 or 800-333-4705 (toll-free). *Fax:* 651-603-6320. *E-mail:* admission@csp.edu. *Web site:* http://www.csp.edu/.

CROSSROADS COLLEGE

Rochester, Minnesota

Crossroads College is a coed, private, four-year college, founded in 1913, affiliated with the Christian Churches and Churches of Christ, offering degrees at the associate and bachelor's levels. It has a 40-acre campus in Rochester near Minneapolis–St. Paul.

Academic Information The faculty has 30 members (20% full-time), 20% with terminal degrees. The student-faculty ratio is 9:1. The library holds 33,697 titles and 300 serial subscriptions. Special programs include academic remediation, advanced placement credit, double majors, independent study, self-designed majors, external degree programs, adult/continuing education programs, and internships.

Student Body Statistics The student body is made up of 168 undergraduates (23 freshmen). 53 percent are women and 47 percent are men. Students come from 10 states and territories and 1 other country. 77 percent are from Minnesota. 0.6 percent are international students. 31 percent of the 2006 graduating class went on to graduate and professional schools.

Expenses for 2007–08 *Application fee:* $30. *Tuition:* $11,950 full-time, $365 per semester hour part-time. *Mandatory fees:* $320 full-time, $320 per year part-time. *College room only:* $3600.

Financial Aid Forms of aid include need-based and non-need-based scholarships and part-time jobs. The priority application deadline for financial aid is May 1.

Freshman Admission Crossroads College requires an essay, a high school transcript, 3 recommendations, SAT or ACT scores, and TOEFL scores for international students. An interview is recommended. The application deadline for regular admission is August 15.

Transfer Admission The application deadline for admission is August 15.

Entrance Difficulty Crossroads College assesses its entrance difficulty level as noncompetitive. For the fall 2006 freshman class, 78 percent of the applicants were accepted.

For Further Information Contact Mr. Scott Klaehn, Director of Admissions, Crossroads College, 920 Mayowood Road, SW, Rochester, MN 55902-2382. *Telephone:* 507-288-4563 Ext. 304 or 800-456-7651 (toll-free). *Fax:* 507-288-9046. *E-mail:* admissions@crossroadscollege.edu. *Web site:* http://www.crossroadscollege.edu/.

CROWN COLLEGE

St. Bonifacius, Minnesota

SPONSOR
See Front Insert for Details!

Crown College is a coed, private, comprehensive institution, founded in 1916, affiliated with The Christian and Missionary Alliance, offering degrees at the associate, bachelor's, and master's levels. It has a 215-acre campus in St. Bonifacius near Minneapolis–St. Paul.

Academic Information The faculty has 155 members (26% full-time), 29% with terminal degrees. The undergraduate student-faculty ratio is 13:1. The library holds 96,222 titles, 19,179 serial subscriptions, and 1,523 audiovisual materials. Special programs include academic remediation, services for learning-disabled students, an honors program, study abroad, advanced placement credit, accelerated degree programs, ESL programs, double majors, independent study, distance learning, summer session for credit, part-time degree programs (daytime, evenings, weekends, summer), adult/continuing education programs, and internships. The most frequently chosen baccalaureate fields are business/marketing, education, philosophy and religious studies.

Crown College (continued)

Student Body Statistics The student body totals 1,344, of whom 1,231 are undergraduates (156 freshmen). 59 percent are women and 41 percent are men. Students come from 41 states and territories and 4 other countries. 71 percent are from Minnesota. 0.2 percent are international students. 19 percent of the 2006 graduating class went on to graduate and professional schools.

Expenses for 2007–08 *Application fee:* $35. *Comprehensive fee:* $25,510 includes full-time tuition ($18,588) and college room and board ($6922). *College room only:* $3834. *Part-time tuition:* $777 per credit.

Financial Aid Forms of aid include need-based and non-need-based scholarships and part-time jobs. The average aided 2006–07 undergraduate received an aid package worth an estimated $12,720. The application deadline for financial aid is August 1 with a priority deadline of April 5.

Freshman Admission Crown College requires an essay, a high school transcript, a minimum 2.0 high school GPA, 2 recommendations, ACT 18/SAT 870, SAT or ACT scores, and TOEFL scores for international students. An interview is required for some. The application deadline for regular admission is rolling.

Transfer Admission The application deadline for admission is rolling.

Entrance Difficulty Crown College assesses its entrance difficulty level as minimally difficult. For the fall 2006 freshman class, 62 percent of the applicants were accepted.

SPECIAL MESSAGE TO STUDENTS

Social Life As a Christ-centered community committed to biblical education for Christian leadership, the environment at Crown encourages the formation of the whole person: body, mind, and spirit. To that end, Crown College offers many opportunities for growth both within the academic setting and beyond the classroom. These experiences contribute to community life, personal development and enjoyment, career preparation, leadership training, and spiritual development. Believing that "community" is the best context for this type of personal transformation, Crown College places a high priority on the residential experience. In addition, there are activities such as student government, student publications, community service, intercultural experiences, and music performance groups. Both men and women are involved in intercollegiate athletics at Crown and participate in baseball, basketball, cross-country, football, golf, soccer, and volleyball.

Academic Highlights Crown College offers a wide variety of majors and minors that prepare students for careers in fields such as business, Christian ministry, education, and nursing. Crown College is uncompromising in its commitment to high-quality education with a solid base of studies in the humanities and sciences integrated with enthusiastic biblical studies. Every baccalaureate degree includes a general studies core curriculum and a Christian studies core curriculum in addition to the chosen major. Practical hands-on experience is built into many of Crown's degrees. For example, business, ministry, and intercultural studies majors can take a six-month internship during their junior or senior year.

Interviews and Campus Visits The best way to become acquainted with Crown College is to visit the campus. Crown provides prospective students and their families with up to four meals in the College Dining Room or Storm Cafe, one night's lodging in a residence hall, and transportation to and from the airport or bus or train station. While on campus, students should visit the Student Center—the ultimate student gathering place on campus. Located in the Main Building near the Storm Cafe, the Student Center offers a coffee shop with a loft and booth-style seating. There is also a performance stage along with a double-sided fireplace, art gallery, and a climbing wall. For the best possible visit, guests should contact the Office of Admissions at least two weeks prior to their visit so that appointments (chapel, class visits, faculty/coach meetings, music auditions, etc.) and hospitality arrangements can be made. Admissions office hours are weekdays from 8:00 a.m. to 4:30 p.m. Students should call 800-68-CROWN (toll-free) for additional information. The nearest commercial airport is Minneapolis-St. Paul International.

For Further Information Write to Office of Admissions, Crown College, 8700 College View Drive, St. Bonifacius, MN 55375-9001. *E-mail:* info@crown.edu. *Web site:* http://www.crown.edu.

DEVRY UNIVERSITY
Edina, Minnesota

DeVry University is a coed, proprietary, comprehensive institution, offering degrees at the associate, bachelor's, and master's levels and postbachelor's certificates.

Academic Information The faculty has 3 members. The undergraduate student-faculty ratio is 68:1. Special programs include accelerated degree programs and distance learning.

Student Body Statistics The student body totals 162, of whom 117 are undergraduates (13 freshmen). 38 percent are women and 62 percent are men. 97 percent are from Minnesota.

Expenses for 2007–08 *Application fee:* $50. *Tuition:* $12,900 full-time, $490 per credit part-time. *Mandatory fees:* $120 full-time.

Freshman Admission DeVry University requires a high school transcript and an interview. The application deadline for regular admission is rolling.

Transfer Admission The application deadline for admission is rolling.

For Further Information Contact Admissions Office, DeVry University, 7700 France Avenue South, Suite 575, Edina, MN 55435-5876. *Telephone:* 952-838-1860. *Web site:* http://www.devry.edu/.

DUNWOODY COLLEGE OF TECHNOLOGY
Minneapolis, Minnesota

http://www.dunwoody.edu/

GLOBE COLLEGE
Oakdale, Minnesota

Globe College is a coed, proprietary, primarily two-year college, founded in 1885, offering degrees at the associate and bachelor's levels.

Expenses for 2006–07 *Application fee:* $50. *Tuition:* $15,750 full-time, $350 per credit part-time. *Mandatory fees:* $500 full-time. Full-time tuition and fees vary according to course load. Part-time tuition varies according to course load.

For Further Information Contact Ms. Christina Hilipipre, Director of Admissions, Globe College, 7166 10th Street North, Oakdale, MN 55128. *Telephone:* 651-730-5100. *Fax:* 651-730-5151. *E-mail:* admissions@globecollege.edu. *Web site:* http://www.globecollege.com/.

GUSTAVUS ADOLPHUS COLLEGE
St. Peter, Minnesota

Gustavus Adolphus College is a coed, private, four-year college, founded in 1862, affiliated with the Evangelical Lutheran Church in America, offering degrees at the bachelor's level. It has a 340-acre campus in St. Peter near Minneapolis–St. Paul.

Academic Information The faculty has 267 members (72% full-time), 70% with terminal degrees. The student-faculty ratio is 12:1. The library holds 297,861 titles, 17,078 serial subscriptions, and 17,359 audiovisual materials. Special programs include services for learning-disabled students, an honors program, cooperative (work-study) education, study abroad, advanced placement credit, accelerated degree programs, double majors, independent study, self-designed majors, summer session for credit, internships, and arrangement for off-campus study with Minnesota State University, Mankato. The most frequently chosen baccalaureate fields are business/marketing, biological/life sciences, social sciences.

Student Body Statistics The student body is made up of 2,618 undergraduates (685 freshmen). 57 percent are women and 43 percent are men. Students come from 47 states and territories and 14 other countries. 82 percent are from Minnesota. 1 percent are international students. 36 percent of the 2006 graduating class went on to graduate and professional schools.

Expenses for 2007–08 *Application fee:* $0. *Comprehensive fee:* $32,790 includes full-time tuition ($28,125), mandatory fees ($390), and college room and board ($4275). *College room only:* $2500. *Part-time tuition:* $3840 per course.

Financial Aid Forms of aid include need-based and non-need-based scholarships and part-time jobs. The average aided 2005–06 undergraduate received an aid package worth $18,100. The application deadline for financial aid is April 1 with a priority deadline of February 15.

Freshman Admission Gustavus Adolphus College requires an essay, a high school transcript, 2 recommendations, and TOEFL scores for international students. An interview is recommended. The application deadline for regular admission is April 1 and for early action it is November 1.

Transfer Admission The application deadline for admission is April 1.

Entrance Difficulty Gustavus Adolphus College assesses its entrance difficulty level as very difficult. For the fall 2006 freshman class, 78 percent of the applicants were accepted.

For Further Information Contact Mr. Mark Anderson, Vice President for Admission and Student Financial Aid, Gustavus Adolphus College, 800 West College Ave., St. Peter, MN 56082-1498. *Telephone:* 507-933-7676 or 800-GUSTAVU(S) (toll-free). *Fax:* 507-933-7474. *E-mail:* admission@gac.edu. *Web site:* http://www.gustavus.edu/.

HAMLINE UNIVERSITY
St. Paul, Minnesota

Hamline University is a coed, private, comprehensive institution, founded in 1854, affiliated with the United Methodist Church, offering degrees at the bachelor's, master's, doctoral, and first professional levels and postbachelor's certificates. It has a 50-acre campus in St. Paul.

Academic Information The faculty has 481 members (38% full-time), 46% with terminal degrees. The undergraduate student-faculty ratio is 13:1. The library holds 228,973 titles, 1,681 serial subscriptions, and 4,886 audiovisual materials. Special programs include academic remediation, services for learning-disabled students, an honors program, study abroad, advanced placement credit, ESL programs, double majors, independent study, self-designed majors, summer session for credit, part-time degree programs (daytime, evenings, summer), adult/continuing education programs, internships, and arrangement for off-campus study with members of the Associated Colleges of the Twin Cities, American University, Southern College Student Exchange Program, Higher Education Consortium for Urban Affairs, Drew University. The most frequently chosen baccalaureate fields are psychology, business/marketing, social sciences.

Student Body Statistics The student body totals 4,575, of whom 2,012 are undergraduates (424 freshmen). 59 percent are women and 41 percent are men. Students come from 30 states and territories and 35 other countries. 84 percent are from Minnesota. 3 percent are international students. 22 percent of the 2006 graduating class went on to graduate and professional schools.

Expenses for 2006–07 *Application fee:* $0. *Comprehensive fee:* $32,320 includes full-time tuition ($24,586), mandatory fees ($454), and college room and board ($7280). *College room only:* $3682. Full-time tuition and fees vary according to student level. Room and board charges vary according to board plan and housing facility. *Part-time tuition:* $768 per credit. Part-time tuition varies according to course load and student level.

Financial Aid Forms of aid include need-based and non-need-based scholarships and part-time jobs.

Freshman Admission Hamline University requires an essay, a high school transcript, 2 recommendations, SAT or ACT scores, and TOEFL scores for international students. An interview and activity resume are recommended. The application deadline for regular admission is rolling and for early action it is December 1.

Transfer Admission The application deadline for admission is rolling.

Entrance Difficulty Hamline University assesses its entrance difficulty level as moderately difficult. For the fall 2006 freshman class, 78 percent of the applicants were accepted.

For Further Information Contact Ms. Ann Kjorstad, Director of Undergraduate Admission, Hamline University, 1536 Hewitt Avenue, C1930, St. Paul, MN 55104-2458. *Telephone:* 651-523-2207 or 800-753-9753 (toll-free). *Fax:* 651-523-2458. *E-mail:* cla-admis@hamline.edu. *Web site:* http://www.hamline.edu/.

HERZING COLLEGE
Minneapolis, Minnesota

Herzing College is a coed, primarily women's, proprietary, primarily two-year college of Herzing College, founded in 1961, offering degrees at the associate and bachelor's levels. It has a 1-acre campus in Minneapolis.

Academic Information The faculty has 32 members (66% full-time), 25% with terminal degrees. The student-faculty ratio is 14:1. Special programs include distance learning, part-time degree programs (daytime, evenings, summer), adult/continuing education programs, and internships.

Student Body Statistics The student body is made up of 270 undergraduates (53 freshmen). 92 percent are women and 8 percent are men. Students come from 3 states and territories. 99 percent are from Minnesota.

Expenses for 2007–08 *Application fee:* $0. *Tuition:* $13,186 full-time, $440 per credit part-time. *Mandatory fees:* $25 full-time.

Freshman Admission Herzing College requires a high school transcript, an interview, and ACCUPLACER.

Entrance Difficulty Herzing College has an open admission policy.

For Further Information Contact Ms. Shelly Larson, Director of Admissions, Herzing College, 5700 West Broadway, Minneapolis, MN 55428. *Telephone:* 763-231-3155 or 800-878-DRAW (toll-free). *Fax:* 763-535-9205. *E-mail:* info@mpls.herzing.edu. *Web site:* http://www.herzing.edu/.

ITT TECHNICAL INSTITUTE
Eden Prairie, Minnesota

ITT Technical Institute is a coed, proprietary, primarily two-year college of ITT Educational Services, Inc, founded in 2003, offering degrees at the associate and bachelor's levels.

Expenses for 2006–07 *Application fee:* $100. Contact school for program costs.

Freshman Admission ITT Technical Institute requires a high school transcript, an interview, and Wonderlic aptitude test. Recommendations are recommended. The application deadline for regular admission is rolling.

Transfer Admission The application deadline for admission is rolling.

For Further Information Contact Mr. Paul Rozeski, ITT Technical Institute, 8911 Columbine Road, Eden Prairie, MN 55347. *Telephone:* 952-914-5300 or 888-488-9646 (toll-free in-state). *Web site:* http://www.itt-tech.edu/.

LEECH LAKE TRIBAL COLLEGE
Cass Lake, Minnesota

Leech Lake Tribal College is a coed, private, two-year college, founded in 1992, offering degrees at the associate level.

Student Body Statistics The student body is made up of 189 undergraduates.

Expenses for 2006–07 *Application fee:* $15. *State resident tuition:* $3240 full-time.

Leech Lake Tribal College (continued)

Entrance Difficulty Leech Lake Tribal College assesses its entrance difficulty level as noncompetitive.

For Further Information Contact Admissions Office, Leech Lake Tribal College, 6945 Littlewolf Road NW, Cass Lake, MN 56633. *Telephone:* 218-335-4247. *Fax:* 218-335-4209. *E-mail:* ejenkins@lltc.edu. *Web site:* http://www.lltc.org/.

LOWTHIAN COLLEGE

See The Art Institutes International Minnesota.

MACALESTER COLLEGE

St. Paul, Minnesota

Macalester College is a coed, private, Presbyterian, four-year college, founded in 1874, offering degrees at the bachelor's level. It has a 53-acre campus in St. Paul.

Academic Information The faculty has 215 members (72% full-time), 82% with terminal degrees. The student-faculty ratio is 11:1. The library holds 448,968 titles, 3,559 serial subscriptions, and 9,181 audiovisual materials. Special programs include an honors program, study abroad, double majors, independent study, self-designed majors, part-time degree programs (daytime), internships, and arrangement for off-campus study with College of St. Catherine, University of St. Thomas, Augsburg College, Hamline University, Minneapolis College of Art and Design. The most frequently chosen baccalaureate fields are interdisciplinary studies, foreign languages and literature, social sciences.

Student Body Statistics The student body is made up of 1,918 undergraduates (501 freshmen). 58 percent are women and 42 percent are men. Students come from 53 states and territories and 92 other countries. 21 percent are from Minnesota. 11.3 percent are international students. 28 percent of the 2006 graduating class went on to graduate and professional schools.

Expenses for 2007–08 *Application fee:* $40. *Comprehensive fee:* $41,914 includes full-time tuition ($33,494), mandatory fees ($200), and college room and board ($8220). *College room only:* $4334. *Part-time tuition:* $1045 per semester hour.

Financial Aid Forms of aid include need-based and non-need-based scholarships and part-time jobs. The average aided 2005–06 undergraduate received an aid package worth $25,238. The priority application deadline for financial aid is February 8.

Freshman Admission Macalester College requires an essay, a high school transcript, 3 recommendations, SAT or ACT scores, and TOEFL scores for international students. An interview is recommended. The application deadline for regular admission is January 15; for early decision plan 1 it is November 15; and for early decision plan 2 it is January 2.

Transfer Admission The application deadline for admission is April 15.

Entrance Difficulty Macalester College assesses its entrance difficulty level as very difficult. For the fall 2006 freshman class, 39 percent of the applicants were accepted.

For Further Information Contact Mr. Lorne T. Robinson, Dean of Admissions and Financial Aid, Macalester College, 1600 Grand Avenue, St. Paul, MN 55105-1899. *Telephone:* 651-696-6357 or 800-231-7974 (toll-free). *Fax:* 651-696-6724. *E-mail:* admissions@macalester.edu. *Web site:* http://www.macalester.edu/.

MANKATO STATE UNIVERSITY

See Minnesota State University Mankato.

MARTIN LUTHER COLLEGE

New Ulm, Minnesota

Martin Luther College is a coed, private, four-year college, founded in 1995, affiliated with the Wisconsin Evangelical Lutheran Synod, offering degrees at the bachelor's level. It has a 50-acre campus in New Ulm.

Academic Information The faculty has 74 members (78% full-time), 46% with terminal degrees. The student-faculty ratio is 14:1. The library holds 115,309 titles, 519 serial subscriptions, and 5,786 audiovisual materials. Special programs include academic remediation, advanced placement credit, ESL programs, double majors, independent study, summer session for credit, and internships.

Student Body Statistics The student body totals 820, of whom 786 are undergraduates (166 freshmen). 50 percent are women and 50 percent are men. Students come from 35 states and territories and 9 other countries. 16 percent are from Minnesota. 0.4 percent are international students.

Expenses for 2007–08 *Application fee:* $25. *Comprehensive fee:* $13,675 includes full-time tuition ($9850) and college room and board ($3825). *Part-time tuition:* $200 per credit hour.

Financial Aid Forms of aid include need-based and non-need-based scholarships and part-time jobs. The average aided 2005–06 undergraduate received an aid package worth $7789. The application deadline for financial aid is April 15.

Freshman Admission Martin Luther College requires a high school transcript, a minimum 2.0 high school GPA, recommendations, ACT scores, and TOEFL scores for international students. The application deadline for regular admission is April 15.

Transfer Admission The application deadline for admission is April 15.

Entrance Difficulty Martin Luther College assesses its entrance difficulty level as moderately difficult. For the fall 2006 freshman class, 98 percent of the applicants were accepted.

For Further Information Contact Prof. Ronald B. Brutlag, Associate Director of Admissions, Martin Luther College, 1995 Luther Court, New Ulm, MN 56073. *Telephone:* 507-354-8221 Ext. 280. *Fax:* 507-354-8225. *E-mail:* brutlaro@mlc-wels.edu. *Web site:* http://www.mlc-wels.edu/.

McNALLY SMITH COLLEGE OF MUSIC

Saint Paul, Minnesota

McNally Smith College of Music is a coed, proprietary, primarily two-year college, founded in 1985, offering degrees at the associate and bachelor's levels.

Academic Information The faculty has 61 members (54% full-time). The student-faculty ratio is 10:1. The library holds 4,500 titles, 50 serial subscriptions, and 4,000 audiovisual materials. Special programs include cooperative (work-study) education, advanced placement credit, independent study, summer session for credit, part-time degree programs (daytime), and internships.

Student Body Statistics The student body is made up of 474 undergraduates (146 freshmen). 15 percent are women and 85 percent are men. Students come from 36 states and territories and 6 other countries. 52 percent are from Minnesota. 2.1 percent are international students.

Expenses for 2007–08 *Application fee:* $75. *Tuition:* $16,770 full-time, $645 per credit part-time. *Mandatory fees:* $2805 full-time, $1365 per term part-time.

Freshman Admission McNally Smith College of Music requires an essay, a high school transcript, 2 recommendations, an interview, and TOEFL scores for international students. ACT scores are recommended. Audition and ACT scores are required for some. The application deadline for regular admission is August 1.

Entrance Difficulty McNally Smith College of Music has an open admission policy.

For Further Information Contact Mrs. Kathy Hawks, Director of Admissions, McNally Smith College of Music, 19 Exchange Street East, St. Paul, MN 55101. *Telephone:* 651-291-0177 Ext. 2373 or 800-594-9500 (toll-free). *Fax:* 651-291-0366. *E-mail:* khawks@mcnallysmith.edu. *Web site:* http://www.mcnallysmith.edu/.

MEDICAL INSTITUTE OF MINNESOTA

See Argosy University, Twin Cities.

METROPOLITAN STATE UNIVERSITY
St. Paul, Minnesota

Metropolitan State University is a coed, public, comprehensive unit of Minnesota State Colleges and Universities System, founded in 1971, offering degrees at the bachelor's and master's levels (offers primarily part-time evening degree programs).

Academic Information The faculty has 509 members (25% full-time), 44% with terminal degrees. The undergraduate student-faculty ratio is 27:1. The library holds 39,128 titles, 242 serial subscriptions, and 2,431 audiovisual materials. Special programs include advanced placement credit, ESL programs, double majors, independent study, distance learning, self-designed majors, summer session for credit, part-time degree programs (daytime, evenings, weekends, summer), external degree programs, adult/continuing education programs, internships, and arrangement for off-campus study with other colleges in the Minnesota State College and University System.
Student Body Statistics The student body totals 6,543, of whom 6,022 are undergraduates (52 freshmen). 60 percent are women and 40 percent are men. Students come from 18 states and territories and 53 other countries. 98 percent are from Minnesota. 1.6 percent are international students. 23 percent of the 2006 graduating class went on to graduate and professional schools.
Expenses for 2006–07 *Application fee:* $20. *State resident tuition:* $4830 full-time, $161 per credit part-time. *Nonresident tuition:* $9660 full-time, $322 per credit part-time. *Mandatory fees:* $252 full-time, $8.39 per credit part-time. Full-time tuition and fees vary according to program and reciprocity agreements. Part-time tuition and fees vary according to course load, program, and reciprocity agreements.
Financial Aid Forms of aid include need-based and non-need-based scholarships and part-time jobs. The priority application deadline for financial aid is June 1.
Freshman Admission Metropolitan State University requires a high school transcript, a minimum 2.0 high school GPA, and TOEFL scores for international students. SAT or ACT scores are required for some. The application deadline for regular admission is June 15 and for nonresidents it is June 15.
Transfer Admission The application deadline for admission is June 15.
Entrance Difficulty Metropolitan State University assesses its entrance difficulty level as minimally difficult. For the fall 2006 freshman class, 53 percent of the applicants were accepted.
For Further Information Contact Ms. Monir Johnson, Director, Metropolitan State University, 700 East 7th Street, St. Paul, MN 55106. *Telephone:* 651-793-1303. *Fax:* 651-793-1310. *E-mail:* monir.johnson@metrostate.edu. *Web site:* http://www.metrostate.edu.

MINNEAPOLIS COLLEGE OF ART AND DESIGN
Minneapolis, Minnesota

Minneapolis College of Art and Design is a coed, private, comprehensive institution, founded in 1886, offering degrees at the bachelor's and master's levels and postbachelor's certificates. It has a 7-acre campus in Minneapolis.

Academic Information The faculty has 105 members (36% full-time). The undergraduate student-faculty ratio is 13:1. The library holds 47,166 titles, 196 serial subscriptions, and 139,245 audiovisual materials. Special programs include services for learning-disabled students, cooperative (work-study) education, study abroad, advanced placement credit, independent study, distance learning, summer session for credit, part-time degree programs (daytime), adult/continuing education programs, internships, and arrangement for off-campus study with members of the Association of Independent Colleges of Art and Design, Macalester College. The most frequently chosen baccalaureate field is visual and performing arts.
Student Body Statistics The student body totals 749, of whom 702 are undergraduates (140 freshmen). 52 percent are women and 48 percent are men. Students come from 39 states and territories. 65 percent are from Minnesota. 1.7 percent are international students. 10 percent of the 2006 graduating class went on to graduate and professional schools.
Expenses for 2007–08 *Application fee:* $35. *Tuition:* $27,000 full-time, $900 per credit part-time. *Mandatory fees:* $200 full-time, $100 per term part-time. *College room only:* $4160.
Financial Aid Forms of aid include need-based and non-need-based scholarships and part-time jobs. The priority application deadline for financial aid is March 15.
Freshman Admission Minneapolis College of Art and Design requires an essay, a high school transcript, 1 recommendation, SAT or ACT scores, and TOEFL scores for international students. A minimum 2.75 high school GPA and an interview are recommended. A portfolio is required for some. The application deadline for regular admission is June 1.
Transfer Admission The application deadline for admission is June 1.
Entrance Difficulty Minneapolis College of Art and Design assesses its entrance difficulty level as moderately difficult. For the fall 2006 freshman class, 77 percent of the applicants were accepted.
For Further Information Contact Mr. William Mullen, Director of Admissions, Minneapolis College of Art and Design, 2501 Stevens Avenue South, Minneapolis, MN 55404. *Telephone:* 612-874-3762 or 800-874-6223 (toll-free). *E-mail:* admissions@mn.mcad.edu. *Web site:* http://www.mcad.edu/.

MINNESOTA BIBLE COLLEGE
See Crossroads College.

MINNESOTA SCHOOL OF BUSINESS
Rochester, Minnesota

Minnesota School of Business is a coed, proprietary, four-year college, offering degrees at the associate, bachelor's, and master's levels.

Academic Information The faculty has 41 members (5% full-time), 5% with terminal degrees. The undergraduate student-faculty ratio is 13:1. The library holds 6,369 titles, 69 serial subscriptions, and 12 audiovisual materials. Special programs include academic remediation, services for learning-disabled students, advanced placement credit, independent study, distance learning, summer session for credit, part-time degree programs, external degree programs, and internships.
Student Body Statistics The student body is made up of 535 undergraduates (191 freshmen). 76 percent are women and 24 percent are men. Students come from 2 states and territories. 99 percent are from Minnesota.
Expenses for 2006–07 *Application fee:* $50. *Tuition:* $15,750 full-time, $350 per credit hour part-time. Both full-time and part-time tuition varies according to course load.
Freshman Admission Minnesota School of Business requires a high school transcript, an interview, and CPAt. The application deadline for regular admission is October 6.
Entrance Difficulty For the fall 2006 freshman class, 82 percent of the applicants were accepted.
For Further Information Contact Mr. Shan Pollitt, Director of Admissions, Minnesota School of Business, 2521 Pennington Drive NW, Rochester, MN 55901. *Telephone:* 507-536-9500 or 888-662-8772 (toll-free). *Fax:* 507-535-8011. *E-mail:* spollitt@msbcollege.edu. *Web site:* http://www.msbcollege.edu/oncampus/rochester/.

MINNESOTA SCHOOL OF BUSINESS–BROOKLYN CENTER
Brooklyn Center, Minnesota

Minnesota School of Business–Brooklyn Center is a coed, proprietary, primarily two-year college, founded in 1989, offering degrees at the associate, bachelor's, and master's levels.

Academic Information The undergraduate student-faculty ratio is 13:1. The library holds 1,534 titles and 99 serial subscriptions. Special programs

Minnesota School of Business–Brooklyn Center (continued)
include academic remediation, cooperative (work-study) education, accelerated degree programs, distance learning, part-time degree programs (daytime, evenings, summer), adult/continuing education programs, and internships.
Student Body Statistics The student body is made up of 551 undergraduates.
Expenses for 2006–07 *Application fee:* $50. *Tuition:* $14,850 full-time, $350 per credit hour part-time.
Freshman Admission Minnesota School of Business–Brooklyn Center requires a high school transcript, an interview, and CPAt. An essay is required for some. The application deadline for regular admission is October 6.
Entrance Difficulty Minnesota School of Business–Brooklyn Center has an open admission policy.
For Further Information Contact Mr. Bruce Christman, Director of Admissions, Minnesota School of Business–Brooklyn Center, 5910 Shingle Creek Parkway, Brooklyn Center, MN 55430. *Telephone:* 763-585-7777. *Fax:* 763-566-7030. *Web site:* http://www.msbcollege.edu/.

MINNESOTA SCHOOL OF BUSINESS–PLYMOUTH

Minneapolis, Minnesota

Minnesota School of Business–Plymouth is a coed, proprietary, primarily two-year college, founded in 2002, offering degrees at the associate, bachelor's, and master's levels. It has a 3-acre campus in Minneapolis.

Academic Information The undergraduate student-faculty ratio is 10:1. The library holds 1,189 titles and 106 serial subscriptions. Special programs include academic remediation, cooperative (work-study) education, accelerated degree programs, distance learning, summer session for credit, part-time degree programs (daytime, evenings, summer), adult/continuing education programs, and internships.
Student Body Statistics The student body is made up of 445 undergraduates.
Expenses for 2006–07 *Application fee:* $50. *Tuition:* $14,850 full-time, $350 per credit part-time. Both full-time and part-time tuition varies according to course load.
Freshman Admission Minnesota School of Business–Plymouth requires a high school transcript, an interview, and CPAt. An essay is required for some. The application deadline for regular admission is October 6.
Entrance Difficulty Minnesota School of Business–Plymouth has an open admission policy.
For Further Information Contact Stacy Severson, Minnesota School of Business–Plymouth, 1455 County Road 101 North, Plymouth, MN 55447. *Telephone:* 763-476-2000. *Fax:* 763-476-1000. *Web site:* http://www.msbcollege.edu/.

MINNESOTA SCHOOL OF BUSINESS–RICHFIELD

Richfield, Minnesota

Minnesota School of Business–Richfield is a coed, proprietary, primarily two-year college, founded in 1877, offering degrees at the associate, bachelor's, and master's levels. It has a 3-acre campus in Richfield near Minneapolis–St. Paul.

Academic Information The undergraduate student-faculty ratio is 14:1. The library holds 2,420 titles and 93 serial subscriptions. Special programs include academic remediation, cooperative (work-study) education, accelerated degree programs, distance learning, summer session for credit, part-time degree programs (daytime, evenings, summer), adult/continuing education programs, and internships.
Student Body Statistics The student body is made up of 763 undergraduates. Students come from 5 states and territories.

Expenses for 2006–07 *Application fee:* $50. *Tuition:* $14,850 full-time, $350 per credit hour part-time.
Financial Aid Forms of aid include need-based scholarships. The application deadline for financial aid is continuous.
Freshman Admission Minnesota School of Business–Richfield requires a high school transcript, an interview, and CPAt. An essay is required for some. The application deadline for regular admission is October 6.
Entrance Difficulty Minnesota School of Business–Richfield has an open admission policy.
For Further Information Contact Ms. Patricia Murray, Director of Admissions, Minnesota School of Business–Richfield, 1401 West 76th Street, Richfield, MN 55430. *Telephone:* 612-861-2000 Ext. 720 or 800-752-4223 (toll-free in-state). *Fax:* 612-861-5548. *E-mail:* pmurray@msbcollege.com. *Web site:* http://www.msbcollege.edu/.

MINNESOTA SCHOOL OF BUSINESS–ST. CLOUD

Waite Park, Minnesota

Minnesota School of Business–St. Cloud is a coed, proprietary, primarily two-year college, founded in 2004, offering degrees at the associate, bachelor's, and master's levels.

Academic Information The undergraduate student-faculty ratio is 13:1. The library holds 724 titles and 88 serial subscriptions. Special programs include academic remediation, cooperative (work-study) education, accelerated degree programs, distance learning, summer session for credit, part-time degree programs (daytime, evenings, summer), adult/continuing education programs, and internships.
Student Body Statistics The student body is made up of 724 undergraduates.
Expenses for 2006–07 *Application fee:* $50. *Tuition:* $14,850 full-time, $350 per credit hour part-time.
Freshman Admission Minnesota School of Business–St. Cloud requires a high school transcript, an interview, and CPAt. An essay is required for some. The application deadline for regular admission is October 6.
Entrance Difficulty Minnesota School of Business–St. Cloud has an open admission policy.
For Further Information Contact Mr. Jim Beck, Director of Admissions, Minnesota School of Business–St. Cloud, 1201 2nd Street S, Waite Park, MN 56387. *Telephone:* 320-257-2000 or 866-403-3333 (toll-free out-of-state). *Fax:* 320-257-0131. *E-mail:* jbeck@msbcollege.edu. *Web site:* http://www.msbcollege.edu/.

MINNESOTA SCHOOL OF BUSINESS–SHAKOPEE

Shakopee, Minnesota

Minnesota School of Business–Shakopee is a coed, proprietary, primarily two-year college, founded in 2004, offering degrees at the associate, bachelor's, and master's levels.

Academic Information The undergraduate student-faculty ratio is 12:1. The library holds 919 titles and 95 serial subscriptions. Special programs include academic remediation, cooperative (work-study) education, accelerated degree programs, distance learning, summer session for credit, part-time degree programs (daytime, evenings, summer), adult/continuing education programs, and internships.
Student Body Statistics The student body is made up of 381 undergraduates.
Expenses for 2006–07 *Application fee:* $50. *Tuition:* $14,850 full-time, $350 per credit part-time. Both full-time and part-time tuition varies according to course load.
Freshman Admission Minnesota School of Business–Shakopee requires a high school transcript, an interview, and CPAt. An essay is required for some. The application deadline for regular admission is October 6.

Entrance Difficulty Minnesota School of Business–Shakopee has an open admission policy.

For Further Information Contact Ms. Gretchen Seifert, Director of Admissions, Minnesota School of Business–Shakopee, 1200 Shakopee Town Square, Shakopee, MN 55379. *Telephone:* 952-516-7015 or 866-766-1200 (toll-free out-of-state). *Fax:* 952-345-1201. *Web site:* http://www.msbcollege.edu/.

MINNESOTA STATE UNIVERSITY MANKATO

Mankato, Minnesota

Minnesota State University Mankato is a coed, public, comprehensive unit of Minnesota State Colleges and Universities System, founded in 1868, offering degrees at the associate, bachelor's, and master's levels and post-master's certificates. It has a 303-acre campus in Mankato near Minneapolis–St. Paul.

Academic Information The faculty has 717 members (68% full-time), 56% with terminal degrees. The undergraduate student-faculty ratio is 22:1. The library holds 474,252 titles and 3,400 serial subscriptions. Special programs include academic remediation, services for learning-disabled students, an honors program, study abroad, advanced placement credit, ESL programs, double majors, independent study, distance learning, self-designed majors, summer session for credit, part-time degree programs (daytime, evenings, weekends, summer), adult/continuing education programs, internships, and arrangement for off-campus study with other colleges in the Minnesota State College and University System. The most frequently chosen baccalaureate fields are business/marketing, education, health professions and related sciences.

Student Body Statistics The student body totals 14,148, of whom 12,534 are undergraduates (2,163 freshmen). 53 percent are women and 47 percent are men. Students come from 44 states and territories and 68 other countries. 87 percent are from Minnesota. 2.6 percent are international students. 8 percent of the 2006 graduating class went on to graduate and professional schools.

Expenses for 2006–07 *Application fee:* $20. *State resident tuition:* $5104 full-time, $204.10 per credit part-time. *Nonresident tuition:* $10,932 full-time, $436 per credit part-time. *Mandatory fees:* $736 full-time, $30.56 per credit part-time. Both full-time and part-time tuition and fees vary according to course load and reciprocity agreements. *College room and board:* $5099. Room and board charges vary according to board plan.

Financial Aid Forms of aid include need-based and non-need-based scholarships, athletic grants, and part-time jobs. The average aided 2006–07 undergraduate received an aid package worth an estimated $7058. The priority application deadline for financial aid is March 15.

Freshman Admission Minnesota State University Mankato requires a high school transcript, ACT scores, and TOEFL scores for international students. An essay, 3 recommendations, and personal statement are required for some. The application deadline for regular admission is rolling.

Transfer Admission The application deadline for admission is rolling.

Entrance Difficulty Minnesota State University Mankato assesses its entrance difficulty level as moderately difficult. For the fall 2006 freshman class, 90 percent of the applicants were accepted.

For Further Information Contact Office of Admissions, Minnesota State University Mankato, 122 Taylor Center, Mankato, MN 56001. *Telephone:* 507-389-1822 or 800-722-0544 (toll-free). *Fax:* 507-389-1511. *E-mail:* admissions@mnsu.edu. *Web site:* http://www.mnsu.edu/.

MINNESOTA STATE UNIVERSITY MOORHEAD

Moorhead, Minnesota

Minnesota State University Moorhead is a coed, public, comprehensive unit of Minnesota State Colleges and Universities System, founded in 1885, offering degrees at the associate, bachelor's, and master's levels and post-master's certificates. It has a 118-acre campus in Moorhead.

Expenses for 2006–07 *Application fee:* $20. *State resident tuition:* $4,888 full-time, $162.94 per credit part-time. *Nonresident tuition:* $4,888 full-time, $162.94 per credit part-time. *Mandatory fees:* $833 full-time, $34.60 per credit part-time. Both full-time and part-time tuition and fees vary according to reciprocity agreements. *College room and board:* $5420. *College room only:* $3348. Room and board charges vary according to board plan and housing facility.

For Further Information Contact Ms. Gina Monson, Director of Admissions, Minnesota State University Moorhead, Owens Hall, Moorhead, MN 56563-0002. *Telephone:* 218-477-2161 or 800-593-7246 (toll-free). *Fax:* 218-477-4374. *E-mail:* dragon@mnstate.edu. *Web site:* http://www.mnstate.edu/.

MUSICTECH COLLEGE

See McNally Smith College of Music.

NATIONAL AMERICAN UNIVERSITY

Roseville, Minnesota

http://www.national.edu/

NORTH CENTRAL UNIVERSITY

Minneapolis, Minnesota

http://www.northcentral.edu/

NORTHWESTERN COLLEGE

St. Paul, Minnesota

Northwestern College is a coed, private, nondenominational, four-year college, founded in 1902, offering degrees at the associate, bachelor's, and master's levels. It has a 107-acre campus in St. Paul.

Academic Information The faculty has 174 members (55% full-time), 44% with terminal degrees. The undergraduate student-faculty ratio is 14:1. The library holds 117,745 titles, 1,131 serial subscriptions, and 5,960 audiovisual materials. Special programs include academic remediation, services for learning-disabled students, an honors program, study abroad, advanced placement credit, double majors, independent study, distance learning, self-designed majors, summer session for credit, part-time degree programs (evenings, weekends), adult/continuing education programs, internships, and arrangement for off-campus study with Council for Christian Colleges and Universities, Focus on the Family Institute, William Mitchell College of Law. The most frequently chosen baccalaureate fields are business/marketing, education, theology and religious vocations.

Student Body Statistics The student body is made up of 1,781 undergraduates (487 freshmen). 60 percent are women and 40 percent are men. Students come from 35 states and territories and 23 other countries. 67 percent are from Minnesota. 0.7 percent are international students. 9 percent of the 2006 graduating class went on to graduate and professional schools.

Expenses for 2007–08 *Application fee:* $30. *Comprehensive fee:* $27,740 includes full-time tuition ($20,990) and college room and board ($6750). *College room only:* $3800. *Part-time tuition:* $895 per credit.

Financial Aid Forms of aid include need-based and non-need-based scholarships and part-time jobs. The average aided 2005–06 undergraduate received an aid package worth $14,551. The application deadline for financial aid is May 1 with a priority deadline of March 1.

Freshman Admission Northwestern College requires an essay, a high school transcript, a minimum 2.0 high school GPA, 2 recommendations, lifestyle agreement, statement of Christian faith, SAT or ACT scores, and

Northwestern College (continued)

TOEFL scores for international students. A minimum 3.0 high school GPA is recommended. An interview is required for some. The application deadline for regular admission is August 1.

Transfer Admission The application deadline for admission is August 1.

Entrance Difficulty Northwestern College assesses its entrance difficulty level as moderately difficult. For the fall 2006 freshman class, 90 percent of the applicants were accepted.

For Further Information Contact Mr. Kenneth K. Faffler, Director of Admissions, Northwestern College, Officer of Admissions, 3003 Snelling Avenue North, 212 Nazareth Hall, St. Paul, MN 55113-1598. *Telephone:* 651-631-5111 or 800-827-6827 (toll-free). *Fax:* 651-631-5680. *E-mail:* admissions@nwc.edu. *Web site:* http://www.nwc.edu/.

OAK HILLS CHRISTIAN COLLEGE

Bemidji, Minnesota

Oak Hills Christian College is a coed, private, interdenominational, four-year college, founded in 1946, offering degrees at the associate and bachelor's levels. It has a 180-acre campus in Bemidji.

Academic Information The faculty has 16 members (38% full-time), 38% with terminal degrees. The student-faculty ratio is 24:1. The library holds 24,410 titles and 86 serial subscriptions. Special programs include academic remediation, services for learning-disabled students, an honors program, advanced placement credit, double majors, independent study, part-time degree programs (daytime, evenings), internships, and arrangement for off-campus study. The most frequently chosen baccalaureate field is theology and religious vocations.

Student Body Statistics The student body is made up of 186 undergraduates (35 freshmen). 47 percent are women and 53 percent are men. Students come from 19 states and territories and 1 other country. 75 percent are from Minnesota. 1.6 percent are international students. 5 percent of the 2006 graduating class went on to graduate and professional schools.

Expenses for 2007–08 *Application fee:* $25. *Comprehensive fee:* $17,160 includes full-time tuition ($12,560) and college room and board ($4600). *Part-time tuition:* $113.60 per semester hour.

Financial Aid Forms of aid include need-based and non-need-based scholarships and part-time jobs. The application deadline for financial aid is continuous.

Freshman Admission Oak Hills Christian College requires an essay, a high school transcript, a minimum 2.0 high school GPA, 2 recommendations, and SAT or ACT scores. An interview and minimum ACT score of 18 are required for some. The application deadline for regular admission is rolling.

Transfer Admission The application deadline for admission is rolling.

Entrance Difficulty Oak Hills Christian College assesses its entrance difficulty level as minimally difficult. For the fall 2006 freshman class, 56 percent of the applicants were accepted.

For Further Information Contact Mr. Daniel Hovestol, Admissions Director, Oak Hills Christian College, 1600 Oak Hills Road, SW, Bemidji, MN 56601-8832. *Telephone:* 218-751-8670 Ext. 1220 or 888-751-8670 Ext. 285 (toll-free). *Fax:* 218-751-8825. *E-mail:* admissions@oakhills.edu. *Web site:* http://www.oakhills.edu/.

PILLSBURY BAPTIST BIBLE COLLEGE

Owatonna, Minnesota

http://www.pillsbury.edu/

ROCHESTER COMMUNITY AND TECHNICAL COLLEGE

Rochester, Minnesota

http://www.roch.edu/

ST. CLOUD STATE UNIVERSITY

St. Cloud, Minnesota

St. Cloud State University is a coed, public, comprehensive unit of Minnesota State Colleges and Universities System, founded in 1869, offering degrees at the associate, bachelor's, and master's levels and postbachelor's certificates. It has a 922-acre campus in St. Cloud near Minneapolis–St. Paul.

Academic Information The faculty has 934 members (71% full-time). The undergraduate student-faculty ratio is 17:1. The library holds 897,973 titles, 1,737 serial subscriptions, and 24,929 audiovisual materials. Special programs include academic remediation, services for learning-disabled students, an honors program, study abroad, advanced placement credit, accelerated degree programs, ESL programs, double majors, independent study, distance learning, self-designed majors, summer session for credit, part-time degree programs (daytime, evenings, weekends, summer), adult/continuing education programs, internships, and arrangement for off-campus study with members of the Tri-College Exchange Program, other colleges in the Minnesota State Colleges and University System. The most frequently chosen baccalaureate fields are business/marketing, education, social sciences.

Student Body Statistics The student body totals 15,964, of whom 14,486 are undergraduates (2,152 freshmen). 55 percent are women and 45 percent are men. Students come from 50 states and territories and 85 other countries. 92 percent are from Minnesota. 4.4 percent are international students.

Expenses for 2006–07 *Application fee:* $20. *State resident tuition:* $5045 full-time, $169 per credit part-time. *Nonresident tuition:* $10,952 full-time, $365 per credit part-time. *Mandatory fees:* $673 full-time, $27 per credit part-time. Both full-time and part-time tuition and fees vary according to course load and reciprocity agreements. *College room and board:* $5194. Room and board charges vary according to board plan and housing facility.

Financial Aid Forms of aid include need-based and non-need-based scholarships, athletic grants, and part-time jobs. The average aided 2006–07 undergraduate received an aid package worth an estimated $10,772. The application deadline for financial aid is continuous.

Freshman Admission St. Cloud State University requires a high school transcript, SAT or ACT scores, and TOEFL scores for international students. Recommendations are required for some. The application deadline for regular admission is June 1.

Transfer Admission The application deadline for admission is August 15.

Entrance Difficulty St. Cloud State University assesses its entrance difficulty level as moderately difficult; most difficult for honors program. For the fall 2006 freshman class, 78 percent of the applicants were accepted.

For Further Information Contact Pat Krueger, Associate Director of Admissions, St. Cloud State University, 115 AS Building, 720 4th Avenue South, St. Cloud, MN 56301-4498. *Telephone:* 320-308-2244 or 877-654-7278 (toll-free). *Fax:* 320-308-2243. *E-mail:* scsu4u@stcloudstate.edu. *Web site:* http://www.stcloudstate.edu/.

SAINT JOHN'S UNIVERSITY

Collegeville, Minnesota

Saint John's University is a coed, primarily men's, private, Roman Catholic, comprehensive institution, founded in 1857, coordinate with College of Saint Benedict, offering degrees at the bachelor's, master's, and first professional levels (coordinate with College of Saint Benedict for women). It has a 2,400-acre campus in Collegeville near Minneapolis–St. Paul.

Academic Information The faculty has 164 members (84% full-time), 75% with terminal degrees. The undergraduate student-faculty ratio is 13:1. The library holds 481,338 titles, 5,315 serial subscriptions, and 34,985 audiovisual materials. Special programs include services for learning-disabled students, an honors program, study abroad, advanced placement credit, accelerated degree programs, ESL programs, double majors, independent study, self-designed majors, internships, and arrangement for off-campus study with College of Saint Benedict, Tri-College Exchange Program. The most frequently chosen baccalaureate fields are business/marketing, English, social sciences.

Student Body Statistics The student body totals 2,044, of whom 1,919 are undergraduates (506 freshmen). 100 percent are men. Students come from 42 states and territories and 29 other countries. 81 percent are from Minnesota. 4.2 percent are international students. 24 percent of the 2006 graduating class went on to graduate and professional schools.

Expenses for 2006–07 *Application fee:* $0. *Comprehensive fee:* $31,420 includes full-time tuition ($24,448), mandatory fees ($476), and college room and board ($6496). *College room only:* $3262. Room and board charges vary according to board plan and housing facility. *Part-time tuition:* $1020 per credit. *Part-time mandatory fees:* $238 per term. Part-time tuition and fees vary according to course load.

Financial Aid Forms of aid include need-based and non-need-based scholarships and part-time jobs. The average aided 2006–07 undergraduate received an aid package worth an estimated $18,898. The priority application deadline for financial aid is March 15.

Freshman Admission Saint John's University requires an essay, a high school transcript, 1 recommendation, SAT or ACT scores, and TOEFL scores for international students. A minimum 3.0 high school GPA and an interview are recommended. The application deadline for regular admission is rolling.

Transfer Admission The application deadline for admission is rolling.

Entrance Difficulty Saint John's University assesses its entrance difficulty level as moderately difficult. For the fall 2006 freshman class, 89 percent of the applicants were accepted.

For Further Information Contact Mr. Matt Beirne, Director of Admission, Saint John's University, PO Box 7155, Collegeville, MN 56321-7155. *Telephone:* 320-363-2196 or 800-544-1489 (toll-free). *Fax:* 320-363-2750. *E-mail:* admissions@csbsju.edu. *Web site:* http://www.csbsju.edu/.

SAINT MARY'S UNIVERSITY OF MINNESOTA
Winona, Minnesota

Saint Mary's University of Minnesota is a coed, private, Roman Catholic, comprehensive institution, founded in 1912, offering degrees at the bachelor's, master's, and doctoral levels and post-master's and postbachelor's certificates. It has a 350-acre campus in Winona.

Academic Information The faculty has 569 members (18% full-time), 41% with terminal degrees. The undergraduate student-faculty ratio is 12:1. The library holds 222,153 titles, 19,948 serial subscriptions, and 8,650 audiovisual materials. Special programs include academic remediation, services for learning-disabled students, an honors program, cooperative (work-study) education, study abroad, advanced placement credit, accelerated degree programs, ESL programs, double majors, independent study, self-designed majors, summer session for credit, part-time degree programs (daytime, evenings, summer), external degree programs, adult/continuing education programs, internships, and arrangement for off-campus study with Winona State University. The most frequently chosen baccalaureate fields are business/marketing, computer and information sciences, visual and performing arts.

Student Body Statistics The student body totals 5,566, of whom 1,818 are undergraduates (378 freshmen). 53 percent are women and 47 percent are men. Students come from 31 states and territories and 13 other countries. 61 percent are from Minnesota. 1.3 percent are international students. 37 percent of the 2006 graduating class went on to graduate and professional schools.

Expenses for 2007–08 *Application fee:* $25. *Comprehensive fee:* $28,528 includes full-time tuition ($21,918), mandatory fees ($480), and college room and board ($6130). *College room only:* $3430. *Part-time tuition:* $730 per credit. *Part-time mandatory fees:* $460 per year.

Financial Aid Forms of aid include need-based and non-need-based scholarships and part-time jobs. The average aided 2006–07 undergraduate received an aid package worth an estimated $15,570. The priority application deadline for financial aid is March 15.

Freshman Admission Saint Mary's University of Minnesota requires an essay, a high school transcript, a minimum 2.5 high school GPA, SAT or ACT scores, and TOEFL scores for international students. 2 recommendations are recommended. An interview is required for some. The application deadline for regular admission is May 1.

Transfer Admission The application deadline for admission is rolling.

Entrance Difficulty Saint Mary's University of Minnesota assesses its entrance difficulty level as moderately difficult. For the fall 2006 freshman class, 78 percent of the applicants were accepted.

For Further Information Contact Mr. Anthony M. Piscitiello, Vice President for Admission, Saint Mary's University of Minnesota, 700 Terrace Heights, Winona, MN 55987-1399. *Telephone:* 507-457-1700 or 800-635-5987 (toll-free). *Fax:* 507-457-1722. *E-mail:* admissions@smumn.edu. *Web site:* http://www.smumn.edu/.

ST. OLAF COLLEGE
Northfield, Minnesota

St. Olaf College is a coed, private, Lutheran, four-year college, founded in 1874, offering degrees at the bachelor's level. It has a 300-acre campus in Northfield near Minneapolis-St. Paul.

Academic Information The faculty has 324 members (60% full-time), 82% with terminal degrees. The student-faculty ratio is 13:1. The library holds 1 million titles, 2,319 serial subscriptions, and 24,205 audiovisual materials. Special programs include services for learning-disabled students, study abroad, advanced placement credit, double majors, independent study, self-designed majors, summer session for credit, part-time degree programs (daytime), internships, and arrangement for off-campus study with Augsburg College, Minnesota Intercollegiate Nursing Consortium, Oak Ridge Science semester, Biosphere 2 Earth semester, HECUA programs, Environmental Science at Superior Studies site. The most frequently chosen baccalaureate fields are public administration and social services, English, visual and performing arts.

Student Body Statistics The student body is made up of 3,041 undergraduates (793 freshmen). 56 percent are women and 44 percent are men. Students come from 45 states and territories and 18 other countries. 58 percent are from Minnesota. 0.7 percent are international students. 29.3 percent of the 2006 graduating class went on to graduate and professional schools.

Expenses for 2007–08 *Application fee:* $40. *Comprehensive fee:* $38,500 includes full-time tuition ($30,600) and college room and board ($7900). *College room only:* $3650. *Part-time tuition:* $955 per credit hour.

Financial Aid Forms of aid include need-based and non-need-based scholarships and part-time jobs. The average aided 2006–07 undergraduate received an aid package worth an estimated $15,990. The application deadline for financial aid is April 15 with a priority deadline of January 15.

Freshman Admission St. Olaf College requires an essay, a high school transcript, 2 recommendations, SAT or ACT scores, and TOEFL scores for international students. An interview is recommended. The application deadline for regular admission is rolling; for early decision it is November 1; and for early action it is December 1.

Entrance Difficulty St. Olaf College assesses its entrance difficulty level as very difficult. For the fall 2006 freshman class, 65 percent of the applicants were accepted.

For Further Information Contact Mr. Jerry Pope, Director of Admissions, St. Olaf College, 1520 St. Olaf Avenue, Northfield, MN 55057. *Telephone:* 507-786-3025 or 800-800-3025 (toll-free). *Fax:* 507-786-3832. *E-mail:* admissions@stolaf.edu. *Web site:* http://www.stolaf.edu/.

SOUTHWEST MINNESOTA STATE UNIVERSITY
Marshall, Minnesota

Southwest Minnesota State University is a coed, public, comprehensive unit of Minnesota State Colleges and Universities System, founded in 1963, offering degrees at the associate, bachelor's, and master's levels. It has a 216-acre campus in Marshall.

Academic Information The faculty has 195 members (66% full-time), 59% with terminal degrees. The undergraduate student-faculty ratio is 23:1. The library holds 197,057 titles, 768 serial subscriptions, and 11,511 audiovisual materials. Special programs include academic remediation, services for learning-disabled students, an honors program, study abroad, advanced placement credit, accelerated degree programs, Freshman

Southwest Minnesota State University (continued)

Honors College, ESL programs, double majors, independent study, distance learning, self-designed majors, summer session for credit, part-time degree programs (daytime, evenings, weekends, summer), external degree programs, adult/continuing education programs, internships, and arrangement for off-campus study with other colleges in the Minnesota State College and University System.

Student Body Statistics The student body totals 6,126, of whom 5,605 are undergraduates (553 freshmen). 58 percent are women and 42 percent are men. Students come from 27 states and territories and 22 other countries. 92 percent are from Minnesota. 7.5 percent are international students. 4 percent of the 2006 graduating class went on to graduate and professional schools.

Expenses for 2006–07 *Application fee:* $20. *State resident tuition:* $5400 full-time, $174.25 per credit part-time. *Mandatory fees:* $840 full-time, $32.71 per credit part-time. Part-time tuition and fees vary according to class time and course load. *College room and board:* $5360. *College room only:* $3360. Room and board charges vary according to board plan and housing facility.

Financial Aid Forms of aid include need-based and non-need-based scholarships, athletic grants, and part-time jobs. The average aided 2006–07 undergraduate received an aid package worth an estimated $7381. The priority application deadline for financial aid is March 1.

Freshman Admission Southwest Minnesota State University requires an essay, a high school transcript, an interview, SAT or ACT scores, and TOEFL scores for international students. ACT scores are recommended. The application deadline for regular admission is rolling.

Transfer Admission The application deadline for admission is rolling.

Entrance Difficulty Southwest Minnesota State University assesses its entrance difficulty level as minimally difficult. For the fall 2006 freshman class, 72 percent of the applicants were accepted.

For Further Information Contact Mr. Richard Shearer, Director of Enrollment Services, Southwest Minnesota State University, 1501 State Street, Marshall, MN 56258. *Telephone:* 507-537-6286 or 800-642-0684 (toll-free). *Fax:* 507-537-7154. *E-mail:* shearerr@southwestmsu.edu. *Web site:* http://www.southwest.msus.edu/.

UNIVERSITY OF MINNESOTA, CROOKSTON

Crookston, Minnesota

University of Minnesota, Crookston is a coed, public, four-year college of University of Minnesota System, founded in 1966, offering degrees at the associate and bachelor's levels. It has a 237-acre campus in Crookston.

Academic Information The faculty has 108 members (49% full-time), 33% with terminal degrees. The student-faculty ratio is 21:1. The library holds 54,887 titles, 3,415 serial subscriptions, and 1,515 audiovisual materials. Special programs include academic remediation, services for learning-disabled students, study abroad, advanced placement credit, ESL programs, double majors, independent study, distance learning, self-designed majors, summer session for credit, part-time degree programs (daytime, evenings, summer), external degree programs, adult/continuing education programs, and internships. The most frequently chosen baccalaureate fields are agriculture, business/marketing, natural resources/environmental science.

Student Body Statistics The student body is made up of 2,414 undergraduates (216 freshmen). 52 percent are women and 48 percent are men. Students come from 33 states and territories and 13 other countries. 68 percent are from Minnesota. 4.2 percent are international students. 5 percent of the 2006 graduating class went on to graduate and professional schools.

Expenses for 2007–08 *Application fee:* $30. *State resident tuition:* $6525 full-time, $215 per credit part-time. *Nonresident tuition:* $6525 full-time, $215 per credit part-time. *Mandatory fees:* $2540 full-time. *College room and board:* $5750. *College room only:* $2725.

Financial Aid Forms of aid include need-based and non-need-based scholarships, athletic grants, and part-time jobs. The average aided 2006–07 undergraduate received an aid package worth an estimated $10,998. The priority application deadline for financial aid is February 15.

Freshman Admission University of Minnesota, Crookston requires a high school transcript and ACT scores. TOEFL scores for international students are recommended. The application deadline for regular admission is rolling and for nonresidents it is rolling.

Transfer Admission The application deadline for admission is rolling.

Entrance Difficulty University of Minnesota, Crookston assesses its entrance difficulty level as moderately difficult. For the fall 2006 freshman class, 83 percent of the applicants were accepted.

For Further Information Contact Ms. Pam Holsinger-Fuchs, Interim Director of Admissions, University of Minnesota, Crookston, 2900 University Avenue, Crookston, MN 56716-5001. *Telephone:* 218-281-8569 or 800-862-6466 (toll-free). *Fax:* 218-281-8575. *E-mail:* info@UMCrookston.edu. *Web site:* http://www.crk.umn.edu/.

UNIVERSITY OF MINNESOTA, DULUTH

Duluth, Minnesota

University of Minnesota, Duluth is a coed, public, comprehensive unit of University of Minnesota System, founded in 1947, offering degrees at the bachelor's, master's, and first professional levels. It has a 250-acre campus in Duluth.

Academic Information The faculty has 523 members (72% full-time), 69% with terminal degrees. The undergraduate student-faculty ratio is 22:1. The library holds 608,579 titles, 52,595 serial subscriptions, and 21,204 audiovisual materials. Special programs include academic remediation, services for learning-disabled students, an honors program, study abroad, advanced placement credit, ESL programs, double majors, independent study, distance learning, self-designed majors, summer session for credit, part-time degree programs (daytime, evenings, summer), adult/continuing education programs, internships, and arrangement for off-campus study with University of Wisconsin-Superior, College of St. Scholastica.

Student Body Statistics The student body totals 11,090, of whom 10,372 are undergraduates (2,315 freshmen). 48 percent are women and 52 percent are men. Students come from 36 states and territories and 38 other countries. 86 percent are from Minnesota. 2 percent are international students. 20 percent of the 2006 graduating class went on to graduate and professional schools.

Expenses for 2006–07 *Application fee:* $35. *State resident tuition:* $7605 full-time, $253 per credit part-time. *Nonresident tuition:* $18,712 full-time, $624 per credit part-time. *Mandatory fees:* $1834 full-time. Full-time tuition and fees vary according to course load, degree level, program, and reciprocity agreements. Part-time tuition varies according to course load, degree level, program, and reciprocity agreements. *College room and board:* $5722.

Financial Aid Forms of aid include need-based scholarships, athletic grants, and part-time jobs. The average aided 2005–06 undergraduate received an aid package worth $8139. The priority application deadline for financial aid is March 1.

Freshman Admission University of Minnesota, Duluth requires a high school transcript, SAT or ACT scores, and TOEFL scores for international students. The application deadline for regular admission is February 1.

Transfer Admission The application deadline for admission is August 1.

Entrance Difficulty University of Minnesota, Duluth assesses its entrance difficulty level as moderately difficult. For the fall 2006 freshman class, 76 percent of the applicants were accepted.

For Further Information Contact Admissions, University of Minnesota, Duluth, 23 Solon Campus Center, 1117 University Drive, Duluth, MN 55812-3000. *Telephone:* 218-726-7171 or 800-232-1339 (toll-free). *Fax:* 218-726-7040. *E-mail:* umdadmis@d.umn.edu. *Web site:* http://www.d.umn.edu/.

UNIVERSITY OF MINNESOTA, MORRIS

Morris, Minnesota

University of Minnesota, Morris is a coed, public, four-year college of University of Minnesota System, founded in 1959, offering degrees at the bachelor's level. It has a 130-acre campus in Morris.

Academic Information The faculty has 174 members (68% full-time), 72% with terminal degrees. The student-faculty ratio is 12:1. The library holds 191,469 titles and 9,042 serial subscriptions. Special programs include services for learning-disabled students, an honors program, study abroad, advanced placement credit, accelerated degree programs, Freshman Honors College, double majors, independent study, distance learning, self-designed majors, summer session for credit, part-time degree programs (daytime, summer), external degree programs, adult/continuing education programs, internships, and arrangement for off-campus study with other units of the University of Minnesota System, National Student Exchange. The most frequently chosen baccalaureate fields are English, biological/life sciences, social sciences.

Student Body Statistics The student body is made up of 1,740 undergraduates (377 freshmen). 58 percent are women and 42 percent are men. Students come from 30 states and territories and 11 other countries. 87 percent are from Minnesota. 1.9 percent are international students. 30 percent of the 2006 graduating class went on to graduate and professional schools.

Expenses for 2007–08 *Application fee:* $35. *State resident tuition:* $9112 full-time, $311.07 per credit part-time. *Nonresident tuition:* $9112 full-time, $311.07 per credit part-time. *College room and board:* $6260. *College room only:* $2980.

Financial Aid Forms of aid include need-based and non-need-based scholarships, athletic grants, and part-time jobs. The average aided 2005–06 undergraduate received an aid package worth $12,660.

Freshman Admission University of Minnesota, Morris requires an essay, a high school transcript, SAT or ACT scores, and TOEFL scores for international students. A minimum 3.0 high school GPA is recommended. 1 recommendation and an interview are required for some. The application deadline for regular admission is March 15.

Transfer Admission The application deadline for admission is May 1.

Entrance Difficulty University of Minnesota, Morris assesses its entrance difficulty level as moderately difficult. For the fall 2006 freshman class, 80 percent of the applicants were accepted.

For Further Information Contact Ms. Jaime Moquin, Director of Admissions, University of Minnesota, Morris, 600 East 4th Street, Morris, MN 56267-2199. *Telephone:* 320-539-6035 or 800-992-8863 (toll-free). *Fax:* 320-589-1673. *E-mail:* admissions@morris.umn.edu. *Web site:* http://www.mrs.umn.edu/.

UNIVERSITY OF MINNESOTA, TWIN CITIES CAMPUS

Minneapolis, Minnesota

University of Minnesota, Twin Cities Campus is a coed, public unit of University of Minnesota System, founded in 1851, offering degrees at the bachelor's, master's, doctoral, and first professional levels and post-master's, first professional, and postbachelor's certificates. It has a 2,000-acre campus in Minneapolis.

Academic Information The faculty has 1,974 members (86% full-time), 67% with terminal degrees. The undergraduate student-faculty ratio is 15:1. The library holds 6 million titles, 45,000 serial subscriptions, and 1 million audiovisual materials. Special programs include academic remediation, services for learning-disabled students, an honors program, cooperative (work-study) education, study abroad, advanced placement credit, accelerated degree programs, Freshman Honors College, ESL programs, double majors, independent study, distance learning, self-designed majors, summer session for credit, part-time degree programs (daytime, evenings, weekends, summer), external degree programs, adult/continuing education programs, internships, and arrangement for off-campus study with National Student Exchange, Minnesota Community College System. The most frequently chosen baccalaureate fields are engineering, business/marketing, social sciences.

Student Body Statistics The student body totals 50,402, of whom 32,113 are undergraduates (5,439 freshmen). 53 percent are women and 47 percent are men. Students come from 51 states and territories and 77 other countries. 73 percent are from Minnesota. 1.6 percent are international students.

Expenses for 2006–07 *Application fee:* $45. *State resident tuition:* $7588 full-time, $291.85 per credit part-time. *Nonresident tuition:* $19,218

full-time, $739.15 per credit part-time. *Mandatory fees:* $1585 full-time. Full-time tuition and fees vary according to program and reciprocity agreements. Part-time tuition varies according to course load, program, and reciprocity agreements. *College room and board:* $6996. *College room only:* $4042. Room and board charges vary according to board plan, housing facility, and location.

Financial Aid Forms of aid include need-based and non-need-based scholarships, athletic grants, and part-time jobs. The average aided 2006–07 undergraduate received an aid package worth an estimated $11,969. The application deadline for financial aid is continuous.

Freshman Admission University of Minnesota, Twin Cities Campus requires a high school transcript, SAT or ACT scores, and TOEFL scores for international students. A minimum 2.0 high school GPA is recommended. The application deadline for regular admission is rolling.

Transfer Admission The application deadline for admission is rolling.

Entrance Difficulty University of Minnesota, Twin Cities Campus assesses its entrance difficulty level as moderately difficult; very difficult for Institute of Technology, management, biological science programs. For the fall 2006 freshman class, 57 percent of the applicants were accepted.

For Further Information Contact Rachelle Hernandez, Associate Director of Admissions, University of Minnesota, Twin Cities Campus, 240 Williamson, Minneapolis, MN 55455-0213. *Telephone:* 612-625-2008 or 800-752-1000 (toll-free). *Fax:* 612-626-1693. *E-mail:* admissions@tc.umn.edu. *Web site:* http://www.umn.edu/tc/.

UNIVERSITY OF ST. THOMAS

St. Paul, Minnesota

University of St. Thomas is a coed, private, Roman Catholic university, founded in 1885, offering degrees at the bachelor's, master's, doctoral, and first professional levels and post-master's and postbachelor's certificates. It has a 78-acre campus in St. Paul near Minneapolis.

Academic Information The faculty has 776 members (51% full-time). The library holds 510,355 titles, 2,743 serial subscriptions, and 7,824 audiovisual materials. Special programs include services for learning-disabled students, an honors program, study abroad, advanced placement credit, ESL programs, double majors, independent study, self-designed majors, summer session for credit, part-time degree programs (daytime, evenings, weekends, summer), internships, and arrangement for off-campus study with 5 members of the Associated Colleges of the Twin Cities.

Student Body Statistics The student body totals 10,712, of whom 5,807 are undergraduates (1,299 freshmen). 50 percent are women and 50 percent are men. Students come from 44 states and territories and 7 other countries. 56 percent are from Minnesota. 1 percent are international students.

Expenses for 2006–07 *Application fee:* $0. *Comprehensive fee:* $31,690 includes full-time tuition ($24,368), mandatory fees ($440), and college room and board ($6882). *College room only:* $4042. Full-time tuition and fees vary according to class time, course load, and program. Room and board charges vary according to board plan, housing facility, and student level. *Part-time tuition:* $761 per credit hour. Part-time tuition varies according to class time, course load, and program.

Financial Aid Forms of aid include need-based and non-need-based scholarships and part-time jobs. The average aided 2006–07 undergraduate received an aid package worth an estimated $17,223. The application deadline for financial aid is continuous.

Freshman Admission University of St. Thomas requires an essay, a high school transcript, SAT or ACT scores, and TOEFL scores for international students. Recommendations and an interview are recommended. The application deadline for regular admission is rolling.

Transfer Admission The application deadline for admission is August 1.

Entrance Difficulty University of St. Thomas assesses its entrance difficulty level as moderately difficult. For the fall 2006 freshman class, 83 percent of the applicants were accepted.

For Further Information Contact Ms. Marla Friederichs, Associate Vice President of Enrollment Management, University of St. Thomas, 2115 Summit Avenue, Mail #32F-1, St. Paul, MN 55105-1096. *Telephone:* 651-962-6150 or 800-328-6819 Ext. 26150 (toll-free). *Fax:* 651-962-6160. *E-mail:* admissions@stthomas.edu. *Web site:* http://www.stthomas.edu/.

WALDEN UNIVERSITY
Minneapolis, Minnesota

Walden University is a coed, proprietary, upper-level unit of Laureate International Universities Network, founded in 1970, offering degrees at the bachelor's, master's, and doctoral levels.

Academic Information The faculty has 1,254 members. The undergraduate student-faculty ratio is 20:1. Special programs include distance learning. The most frequently chosen baccalaureate fields are business/marketing, computer and information sciences.

Student Body Statistics The student body totals 27,633, of whom 1,690 are undergraduates. 56 percent are women and 44 percent are men. Students come from 51 states and territories and 12 other countries. 1 percent are from Minnesota. 36 percent are international students.

Expenses for 2006–07 *Tuition:* $8640 full-time, $240 per quarter hour part-time.

For Further Information Contact Ms. Dawn Wolff, Director of Admissions, Walden University, 155 Fifth Avenue South, Minneapolis, MN 55401. *Telephone:* 800-925-3368 or 866-492-5336 (toll-free out-of-state). *Fax:* 410-843-8780. *E-mail:* request@walden.edu. *Web site:* http://www.waldenu.edu/.

WINONA STATE UNIVERSITY
Winona, Minnesota

Winona State University is a coed, public, comprehensive unit of Minnesota State Colleges and Universities System, founded in 1858, offering degrees at the associate, bachelor's, and master's levels and post-master's certificates. It has a 40-acre campus in Winona.

Academic Information The faculty has 456 members (71% full-time), 63% with terminal degrees. The undergraduate student-faculty ratio is 21:1. The library holds 350,000 titles, 1,000 serial subscriptions, and 8,000 audiovisual materials. Special programs include academic remediation, services for learning-disabled students, an honors program, study abroad, advanced placement credit, accelerated degree programs, ESL programs, double majors, independent study, distance learning, self-designed majors, summer session for credit, part-time degree programs (daytime, evenings, weekends, summer), external degree programs, adult/continuing education programs, internships, and arrangement for off-campus study with Saint Mary's University of Minnesota, other colleges in the Minnesota State Colleges and Universities System.

Student Body Statistics The student body totals 8,220, of whom 7,608 are undergraduates (1,727 freshmen). 62 percent are women and 38 percent are men. Students come from 21 states and territories and 48 other countries. 66 percent are from Minnesota. 4 percent are international students. 25 percent of the 2006 graduating class went on to graduate and professional schools.

Expenses for 2006–07 *Application fee:* $20. *State resident tuition:* $5386 full-time. *Nonresident tuition:* $9686 full-time. *Mandatory fees:* $1714 full-time. *College room and board:* $6300.

Financial Aid Forms of aid include need-based and non-need-based scholarships, athletic grants, and part-time jobs. The average aided 2005–06 undergraduate received an aid package worth $6066. The application deadline for financial aid is continuous.

Freshman Admission Winona State University requires a high school transcript, class rank, SAT or ACT scores, and TOEFL scores for international students. An essay, recommendations, and an interview are required for some. The application deadline for regular admission is rolling.

Transfer Admission The application deadline for admission is August 1.

Entrance Difficulty Winona State University assesses its entrance difficulty level as moderately difficult; minimally difficult for adult students. For the fall 2006 freshman class, 79 percent of the applicants were accepted.

For Further Information Contact Carl Stange, Director of Admissions, Winona State University, PO Box 5838, Winona, MN 55987. *Telephone:* 507-457-5100 or 800-DIAL WSU (toll-free). *Fax:* 507-457-5620. *E-mail:* admissions@winona.edu.

Missouri

AVILA UNIVERSITY
Kansas City, Missouri

Avila University is a coed, private, Roman Catholic, comprehensive institution, founded in 1916, offering degrees at the bachelor's and master's levels. It has a 50-acre campus in Kansas City.

Academic Information The faculty has 203 members (33% full-time), 37% with terminal degrees. The undergraduate student-faculty ratio is 12:1. The library holds 80,865 titles and 7,179 serial subscriptions. Special programs include academic remediation, services for learning-disabled students, cooperative (work-study) education, study abroad, advanced placement credit, accelerated degree programs, ESL programs, double majors, independent study, distance learning, summer session for credit, part-time degree programs (daytime, evenings, weekends, summer), adult/continuing education programs, internships, and arrangement for off-campus study with Sisters of St. Joseph Consortium, Council of Independent Colleges Exchange Program. The most frequently chosen baccalaureate fields are business/marketing, health professions and related sciences, psychology.

Student Body Statistics The student body totals 1,683, of whom 1,130 are undergraduates (138 freshmen). 67 percent are women and 33 percent are men. Students come from 25 states and territories and 30 other countries. 64 percent are from Missouri. 4.4 percent are international students.

Expenses for 2007–08 *Application fee:* $0. *Comprehensive fee:* $24,600 includes full-time tuition ($18,300), mandatory fees ($550), and college room and board ($5750). *College room only:* $2750. *Part-time tuition:* $465 per credit hour. *Part-time mandatory fees:* $19 per credit hour.

Financial Aid Forms of aid include need-based and non-need-based scholarships, athletic grants, and part-time jobs. The average aided 2005–06 undergraduate received an aid package worth $11,751. The application deadline for financial aid is continuous.

Freshman Admission Avila University requires a high school transcript, a minimum 2.5 high school GPA, minimum ACT score of 20, SAT or ACT scores, and TOEFL scores for international students. An interview is recommended. An essay and recommendations are required for some. The application deadline for regular admission is rolling.

Transfer Admission Avila University requires a college transcript. Standardized test scores are required for some. The application deadline for admission is rolling.

Entrance Difficulty Avila University assesses its entrance difficulty level as minimally difficult. For the fall 2006 freshman class, 57 percent of the applicants were accepted.

For Further Information Contact Ms. Patricia Harper, Director of Admission, Avila University, 11901 Wornall Road, Kansas City, MO 64145. *Telephone:* 816-501-2400 or 800-GO-AVILA (toll-free). *Fax:* 816-501-2453. *E-mail:* patti.harper@avila.edu. *Web site:* http://www.avila.edu/.

BAPTIST BIBLE COLLEGE
Springfield, Missouri

Baptist Bible College is a coed, private, Baptist, comprehensive institution, founded in 1950, offering degrees at the associate, bachelor's, master's, and first professional levels. It has a 38-acre campus in Springfield.

Academic Information The faculty has 53 members (49% full-time). The library holds 64,236 titles, 335 serial subscriptions, and 3,311 audiovisual materials. Special programs include academic remediation, summer session for credit, part-time degree programs (daytime, summer), and internships.

Student Body Statistics The student body totals 768, of whom 608 are undergraduates (142 freshmen). 42 percent are women and 58 percent are men. Students come from 46 states and territories and 5 other countries. 20 percent are from Missouri.

Expenses for 2006–07 *Application fee:* $40. *Comprehensive fee:* $18,960 includes full-time tuition ($13,460) and college room and board ($5500).
Financial Aid Forms of aid include need-based and non-need-based scholarships and part-time jobs. The application deadline for financial aid is continuous.
Freshman Admission Baptist Bible College requires a high school transcript, 1 recommendation, and SAT or ACT scores. The application deadline for regular admission is rolling.
Transfer Admission The application deadline for admission is rolling.
Entrance Difficulty Baptist Bible College has an open admission policy.
For Further Information Contact Mr. Terry Allcorn, Director of Admissions, Baptist Bible College, 628 East Kearney, Springfield, MO 65803-3498. *Telephone:* 417-268-6000. *Fax:* 417-268-6694. *Web site:* http://www.baptist.edu/index.htm.

BARNES-JEWISH COLLEGE OF NURSING AND ALLIED HEALTH

St. Louis, Missouri

Barnes-Jewish College of Nursing and Allied Health is a coed, primarily women's, private, comprehensive institution, founded in 1902, offering degrees at the associate, bachelor's, and master's levels and post-master's and postbachelor's certificates.

Academic Information The faculty has 43 members (77% full-time), 40% with terminal degrees. The undergraduate student-faculty ratio is 10:1. The library holds 3,765 titles, 232 serial subscriptions, and 400 audiovisual materials. Special programs include services for learning-disabled students, advanced placement credit, double majors, independent study, summer session for credit, part-time degree programs (daytime, evenings, weekends, summer), and arrangement for off-campus study with Washington University in St. Louis.
Student Body Statistics The student body totals 665, of whom 604 are undergraduates. 85 percent are women and 15 percent are men. Students come from 14 states and territories and 11 other countries. 78 percent are from Missouri. 5.1 percent are international students. 43 percent of the 2006 graduating class went on to graduate and professional schools.
Financial Aid Forms of aid include need-based and non-need-based scholarships and part-time jobs. The priority application deadline for financial aid is April 1.
Freshman Admission Barnes-Jewish College of Nursing and Allied Health requires a high school transcript, a minimum 2.0 high school GPA, 2 recommendations, SAT or ACT scores, and TOEFL scores for international students. The application deadline for regular admission is rolling.
Transfer Admission The application deadline for admission is rolling.
Entrance Difficulty Barnes-Jewish College of Nursing and Allied Health assesses its entrance difficulty level as moderately difficult. For the fall 2006 freshman class, 91 percent of the applicants were accepted.
For Further Information Contact Ms. Elaine Dempsey, Admissions Director, Barnes-Jewish College of Nursing and Allied Health, 306 South Kings Highway Boulevard, St. Louis, MO 63110. *Telephone:* 314-454-7538 or 800-832-9009 (toll-free in-state). *Fax:* 314-454-5239. *E-mail:* jhcollegeinquiry@bjc.org. *Web site:* http://www.barnesjewishcollege.edu/.

CALVARY BIBLE COLLEGE AND THEOLOGICAL SEMINARY

Kansas City, Missouri

Calvary Bible College and Theological Seminary is a coed, private, nondenominational, comprehensive institution, founded in 1932, offering degrees at the associate, bachelor's, master's, and first professional levels. It has a 55-acre campus in Kansas City.

Academic Information The faculty has 33 members (33% full-time), 27% with terminal degrees. The undergraduate student-faculty ratio is 12:1. The library holds 59,234 titles, 285 serial subscriptions, and 338 audiovisual materials. Special programs include academic remediation,

advanced placement credit, double majors, independent study, summer session for credit, part-time degree programs (daytime, evenings, weekends, summer), and adult/continuing education programs. The most frequently chosen baccalaureate fields are business/marketing, education, theology and religious vocations.
Student Body Statistics The student body totals 329, of whom 267 are undergraduates (47 freshmen). 49 percent are women and 51 percent are men. 0.4 percent are international students.
Expenses for 2006–07 *Application fee:* $25. *Comprehensive fee:* $12,100 includes full-time tuition ($7500), mandatory fees ($600), and college room and board ($4000). *College room only:* $1800. *Part-time tuition:* $250 per hour. *Part-time mandatory fees:* $20 per hour.
Financial Aid Forms of aid include need-based and non-need-based scholarships and part-time jobs. The application deadline for financial aid is April 1 with a priority deadline of March 1.
Freshman Admission Calvary Bible College and Theological Seminary requires an essay, a high school transcript, 2 recommendations, statement of faith, SAT or ACT scores, and TOEFL scores for international students. An interview is required for some. The application deadline for regular admission is July 15.
Transfer Admission The application deadline for admission is July 15.
Entrance Difficulty Calvary Bible College and Theological Seminary assesses its entrance difficulty level as minimally difficult. For the fall 2006 freshman class, 98 percent of the applicants were accepted.
For Further Information Contact Rev. Robert Reinsch, Director of Admissions, Calvary Bible College and Theological Seminary, 15800 Calvary Road, Kansas City, MO 64147-1341. *Telephone:* 816-322-0110 Ext. 1326 or 800-326-3960 (toll-free). *Fax:* 816-331-4474. *E-mail:* admissions@calvary.edu. *Web site:* http://www.calvary.edu/.

CENTRAL BIBLE COLLEGE

Springfield, Missouri

http://www.cbcag.edu/

CENTRAL CHRISTIAN COLLEGE OF THE BIBLE

Moberly, Missouri

Central Christian College of the Bible is a coed, private, four-year college, founded in 1957, affiliated with the Christian Churches and Churches of Christ, offering degrees at the associate and bachelor's levels. It has a 40-acre campus in Moberly.

For Further Information Contact Mr. Jason Rodenbeck, Director of Admissions, Central Christian College of the Bible, 911 Urbandale Drive East, Moberly, MO 65270-1997. *Telephone:* 660-263-3900 or 888-263-3900 (toll-free in-state). *Fax:* 660-263-3936. *E-mail:* iwant2be@cccb.edu. *Web site:* http://www.cccb.edu/.

CENTRAL METHODIST UNIVERSITY

Fayette, Missouri

Central Methodist University is a coed, private, Methodist, comprehensive institution, founded in 1854, offering degrees at the associate, bachelor's, and master's levels. It has an 80-acre campus in Fayette.

Academic Information The faculty has 83 members (69% full-time), 46% with terminal degrees. The undergraduate student-faculty ratio is 14:1. The library holds 97,793 titles, 316 serial subscriptions, and 379 audiovisual materials. Special programs include an honors program, study abroad, accelerated degree programs, double majors, independent study, distance learning, part-time degree programs (daytime, evenings, summer), internships, and arrangement for off-campus study with Mineral Area College, East Central College.

Central Methodist University (continued)

Student Body Statistics The student body is made up of 841 undergraduates (212 freshmen). 52 percent are women and 48 percent are men. Students come from 17 states and territories. 90 percent are from Missouri. 1 percent are international students.

Expenses for 2007–08 *Application fee:* $20. *Comprehensive fee:* $22,880 includes full-time tuition ($16,430), mandatory fees ($730), and college room and board ($5720). *Part-time tuition:* $170 per semester hour.

Financial Aid Forms of aid include need-based and non-need-based scholarships, athletic grants, and part-time jobs. The average aided 2006–07 undergraduate received an aid package worth an estimated $13,172.

Freshman Admission Central Methodist University requires a high school transcript, a minimum 2.5 high school GPA, SAT or ACT scores, and TOEFL scores for international students. ACT scores are recommended. 2 recommendations are required for some. The application deadline for regular admission is rolling.

Transfer Admission The application deadline for admission is rolling.

Entrance Difficulty Central Methodist University assesses its entrance difficulty level as moderately difficult. For the fall 2006 freshman class, 69 percent of the applicants were accepted.

For Further Information Contact Mr. Larry Anderson, Director of Admissions, Central Methodist University, 411 Central Methodist Square, Fayette, MO 65248-1198. *Telephone:* 660-248-6247 or 888-CMU-1854 (toll-free in-state). *Fax:* 660-248-1872. *E-mail:* admissions@ centralmethodist.edu. *Web site:* http://www.centralmethodist.edu/.

CENTRAL MISSOURI STATE UNIVERSITY

See University of Central Missouri.

CHAMBERLAIN COLLEGE OF NURSING

St. Louis, Missouri

http://www.chamberlain.edu/

CLEVELAND CHIROPRACTIC COLLEGE-KANSAS CITY CAMPUS

Kansas City, Missouri

Cleveland Chiropractic College-Kansas City Campus is a coed, private, upper-level institution, founded in 1922, offering degrees at the bachelor's and first professional levels. It has a 10-acre campus in Kansas City.

Academic Information The faculty has 47 members (83% full-time), 89% with terminal degrees. The undergraduate student-faculty ratio is 11:1. The library holds 15,000 titles, 6,100 serial subscriptions, and 12,300 audiovisual materials. Special programs include academic remediation, services for learning-disabled students, cooperative (work-study) education, advanced placement credit, accelerated degree programs, summer session for credit, and internships.

Student Body Statistics The student body totals 479, of whom 86 are undergraduates (50 in entering class). 30 percent are women and 70 percent are men. Students come from 17 states and territories and 1 other country. 22 percent are from Missouri. 1.2 percent are international students.

Expenses for 2006–07 *Application fee:* $50. *Tuition:* $12,512 full-time, $184 per credit hour part-time. *Mandatory fees:* $545 full-time. Full-time tuition and fees vary according to course load. Part-time tuition varies according to course load.

Transfer Admission Cleveland Chiropractic College-Kansas City Campus requires a college transcript and a minimum 2.5 college GPA.

Entrance Difficulty Cleveland Chiropractic College-Kansas City Campus has an open admission policy except cumulative college GPA of 2.0 or 2.0 high school GPA required to enter BS degree program.

For Further Information Contact Ms. Melissa Denton, Director of Admissions, Cleveland Chiropractic College-Kansas City Campus, 6401 Rockhill Road, Kansas City, MO 64131. *Telephone:* 816-501-0100 or 800-467-2252 (toll-free). *Fax:* 816-501-0205. *E-mail:* kc.admissions@cleveland. edu. *Web site:* http://www.cleveland.edu/.

COLLEGE OF THE OZARKS

Point Lookout, Missouri

College of the Ozarks is a coed, private, Presbyterian, four-year college, founded in 1906, offering degrees at the bachelor's level. It has a 1,000-acre campus in Point Lookout.

Academic Information The faculty has 133 members (59% full-time), 37% with terminal degrees. The student-faculty ratio is 16:1. The library holds 119,276 titles, 539 serial subscriptions, and 2,744 audiovisual materials. Special programs include academic remediation, an honors program, cooperative (work-study) education, advanced placement credit, accelerated degree programs, ESL programs, double majors, independent study, self-designed majors, part-time degree programs (daytime, evenings), and internships. The most frequently chosen baccalaureate fields are business/marketing, agriculture, education.

Student Body Statistics The student body is made up of 1,345 undergraduates (276 freshmen). 54 percent are women and 46 percent are men. Students come from 38 states and territories and 13 other countries. 65 percent are from Missouri. 1.3 percent are international students. 20 percent of the 2006 graduating class went on to graduate and professional schools.

Expenses for 2007–08 *Application fee:* $0. *Tuition:* $295 per credit hour part-time. *Mandatory fees:* $140 per term part-time.

Financial Aid Forms of aid include need-based and non-need-based scholarships, athletic grants, and part-time jobs. The average aided 2005–06 undergraduate received an aid package worth $17,013. The priority application deadline for financial aid is February 15.

Freshman Admission College of the Ozarks requires a high school transcript, 2 recommendations, an interview, medical history, financial statement, SAT or ACT scores, and TOEFL scores for international students. A minimum 3.0 high school GPA and ACT scores are recommended. The application deadline for regular admission is March 15.

Transfer Admission The application deadline for admission is March 15.

Entrance Difficulty College of the Ozarks assesses its entrance difficulty level as moderately difficult. For the fall 2006 freshman class, 12 percent of the applicants were accepted.

For Further Information Contact Mrs. Gayle Groves, Admissions Secretary, College of the Ozarks, PO Box 17, Point Lookout, MO 65726. *Telephone:* 417-334-6411 Ext. 4217 or 800-222-0525 (toll-free). *Fax:* 417-335-2618. *E-mail:* admiss4@cofo.edu. *Web site:* http://www.cofo.edu/.

COLUMBIA COLLEGE

Columbia, Missouri

SPONSOR
See Front Insert
for Details!

Columbia College is a coed, private, comprehensive institution, founded in 1851, affiliated with the Christian Church (Disciples of Christ), offering degrees at the associate, bachelor's, and master's levels (offers continuing education program with significant enrollment not reflected in profile). It has a 29-acre campus in Columbia.

Academic Information The faculty has 89 members (65% full-time), 62% with terminal degrees. The undergraduate student-faculty ratio is 13:1. The library holds 62,265 titles and 382 serial subscriptions. Special programs include an honors program, cooperative (work-study) education, study abroad, advanced placement credit, accelerated degree programs, ESL programs, double majors, independent study, distance learning, self-designed majors, summer session for credit, part-time degree programs (daytime, evenings, summer), adult/continuing education programs, internships, and arrangement for off-campus study with local institutions. The most frequently chosen baccalaureate fields are business/marketing, liberal arts/general studies, security and protective services.

Student Body Statistics The student body totals 1,186, of whom 1,036 are undergraduates (191 freshmen). 60 percent are women and 40 percent are men. Students come from 23 states and territories and 27 other countries. 87 percent are from Missouri. 6.1 percent are international students.

Expenses for 2006–07 *Application fee:* $25. *Comprehensive fee:* $17,578 includes full-time tuition ($12,414) and college room and board ($5164). *College room only:* $3248. Full-time tuition varies according to class time and course load. Room and board charges vary according to board plan. *Part-time tuition:* $266 per credit hour. Part-time tuition varies according to class time, course load, and location.

Financial Aid Forms of aid include need-based and non-need-based scholarships, athletic grants, and part-time jobs. The average aided 2006–07 undergraduate received an aid package worth an estimated $12,096. The priority application deadline for financial aid is March 1.

Freshman Admission Columbia College requires a high school transcript, a minimum 2.5 high school GPA, SAT or ACT scores, and TOEFL scores for international students. Rank in upper 50% of high school class is recommended. An essay, recommendations, and an interview are required for some. The application deadline for regular admission is rolling.

Transfer Admission The application deadline for admission is rolling.

Entrance Difficulty Columbia College assesses its entrance difficulty level as moderately difficult; minimally difficult for transfers. For the fall 2006 freshman class, 60 percent of the applicants were accepted.

SPECIAL MESSAGE TO STUDENTS

Social Life An influential Student Government Association plans and organizes social activities. There are more than forty clubs and organizations, ranging from academic associations to special interest groups, providing myriad choices for students to get involved and experience leadership opportunities. Strong athletics are a tradition at Columbia College with a history of nationally ranked NAIA Division I teams. One of three institutions of higher education in town, Columbia College provides a vibrant small campus environment within a larger college community.

Academic Highlights Columbia College is known for its excellence in teaching and learning. Among the nearly forty programs offered, those in criminal justice, forensic science, art, education, and business are quite distinctive. The Writing and Math Centers build on high-quality teaching in the classroom to provide opportunities for students to enhance their learning experience. INCC 111 Introduction to Columbia College is a popular freshman orientation course team-taught by a full-time professor and an upperclass student. Study-abroad opportunities are available, and internships can be obtained for a more hands-on experience in any field.

Interviews and Campus Visits Located in a small city consistently recognized by national magazines as an exceptional place to live, Columbia College welcomes visitors to its beautiful historic campus. The campus dates from 1851 and has several distinct architectural features in its older buildings. Williams Hall is the oldest building west of the Mississippi still in continuous use for education purposes. The entire campus is wireless. Visitors have the opportunity to sit in on a class and meet faculty members and students as well as financial aid officials. Campus visits may be arranged weekdays from 8 to 5 by calling the Admissions Office at 573-875-7352 or 800-231-2391 Ext. 7352 (toll-free). The nearest commercial airport is Columbia Regional.

For Further Information Write to Ms. Regina M. Morin, Director of Admissions, Columbia College, 1001 Rogers Street, Columbia, MO 65216. *E-mail:* admissions@ccis.edu. *Web site:* http://www.ccis.edu.

CONCEPTION SEMINARY COLLEGE
Conception, Missouri

Conception Seminary College is a men's, private, Roman Catholic, four-year college, founded in 1886, offering degrees at the bachelor's level. It has a 30-acre campus in Conception.

Academic Information The faculty has 26 members (92% full-time), 77% with terminal degrees. The student-faculty ratio is 3:1. The library holds 115,000 titles and 300 serial subscriptions. Special programs include academic remediation, advanced placement credit, ESL programs, double majors, independent study, and arrangement for off-campus study with Northwest Missouri State University.

Student Body Statistics The student body is made up of 85 undergraduates (13 freshmen). Students come from 13 states and territories and 3 other countries. 30 percent are from Missouri. 13.5 percent are international students. 77 percent of the 2006 graduating class went on to graduate and professional schools.

Expenses for 2006–07 *Application fee:* $0. *Comprehensive fee:* $20,254 includes full-time tuition ($12,844), mandatory fees ($180), and college room and board ($7230). *College room only:* $3228. *Part-time tuition:* $150 per credit.

Financial Aid Forms of aid include need-based and non-need-based scholarships and part-time jobs. The average aided 2005–06 undergraduate received an aid package worth $16,500. The application deadline for financial aid is continuous.

Freshman Admission Conception Seminary College requires an essay, a high school transcript, a minimum 2.0 high school GPA, 2 recommendations, church certificate, medical history, and ACT scores. The application deadline for regular admission is July 31.

Transfer Admission The application deadline for admission is July 31.

Entrance Difficulty Conception Seminary College assesses its entrance difficulty level as noncompetitive. For the fall 2006 freshman class, 87 percent of the applicants were accepted.

For Further Information Contact Br. Victor Schinstock, OSB, Director of Recruitment and Admissions, Conception Seminary College, PO Box 502, Highway 136 and VV, 37174 State Highway VV, Conception, MO 64433. *Telephone:* 660-944-2886. *Fax:* 660-944-2829. *E-mail:* vocations@conception.edu. *Web site:* http://www.conceptionabbey.org/.

COTTEY COLLEGE
Nevada, Missouri

Cottey College is a women's, private, two-year college, founded in 1884, offering degrees at the associate level. It has a 51-acre campus in Nevada.

Academic Information The faculty has 33 full-time members. The student-faculty ratio is 10:1. The library holds 54,200 titles and 246 serial subscriptions. Special programs include services for learning-disabled students, study abroad, advanced placement credit, independent study, distance learning, part-time degree programs (daytime), and internships.

Student Body Statistics The student body is made up of 318 undergraduates (171 freshmen). Students come from 44 states and territories and 15 other countries. 10 percent are from Missouri. 7.9 percent are international students. 95 percent of the 2006 graduating class went on to four-year colleges.

Expenses for 2007–08 *Application fee:* $20. *Comprehensive fee:* $18,710 includes full-time tuition ($12,800), mandatory fees ($710), and college room and board ($5200). *Part-time tuition:* $150 per credit hour. *Part-time mandatory fees:* $11 per credit hour, $25 per term.

Financial Aid Forms of aid include need-based scholarships and part-time jobs. The priority application deadline for financial aid is March 31.

Freshman Admission Cottey College requires an essay, a high school transcript, 1 recommendation, SAT or ACT scores, and TOEFL scores for international students. A minimum 2.6 high school GPA and an interview are recommended. The application deadline for regular admission is rolling and for nonresidents it is rolling.

Transfer Admission The application deadline for admission is rolling.

Cottey College (continued)

Entrance Difficulty Cottey College assesses its entrance difficulty level as moderately difficult. For the fall 2006 freshman class, 64 percent of the applicants were accepted.

For Further Information Contact Ms. Judi Steege, Director of Admission, Cottey College, 1000 West Austin Boulevard, Nevada, MO 64772. *Telephone:* 417-667-8181 or 888-526-8839 (toll-free). *Fax:* 417-667-8103. *E-mail:* enrollmgt@cottey.edu. *Web site:* http://www.cottey.edu/.

COX COLLEGE OF NURSING AND HEALTH SCIENCES

Springfield, Missouri

Cox College of Nursing and Health Sciences is a coed, primarily women's, private, four-year college, founded in 1994, offering degrees at the associate and bachelor's levels.

For Further Information Contact Ms. Stacy Danaher, Admission Coordinator, Cox College of Nursing and Health Sciences, 1423 North Jefferson, Springfield, MO 65802. *Telephone:* 417-269-3038 or 866-898-5355 (toll-free in-state). *Fax:* 417-269-3581. *E-mail:* admissions@coxcollege.edu. *Web site:* http://www.coxcollege.edu/.

CULVER-STOCKTON COLLEGE

Canton, Missouri

Culver-Stockton College is a coed, private, four-year college, founded in 1853, affiliated with the Christian Church (Disciples of Christ), offering degrees at the bachelor's level. It has a 143-acre campus in Canton.

Academic Information The faculty has 52 members (88% full-time), 63% with terminal degrees. The student-faculty ratio is 13:1. The library holds 162,680 titles, 16,233 serial subscriptions, and 3,688 audiovisual materials. Special programs include an honors program, study abroad, advanced placement credit, double majors, independent study, self-designed majors, summer session for credit, part-time degree programs, internships, and arrangement for off-campus study with Central College. The most frequently chosen baccalaureate fields are business/marketing, education, health professions and related sciences.

Student Body Statistics The student body is made up of 869 undergraduates (212 freshmen). 58 percent are women and 42 percent are men. Students come from 22 states and territories and 4 other countries. 52 percent are from Missouri. 0.6 percent are international students. 12 percent of the 2006 graduating class went on to graduate and professional schools.

Expenses for 2007–08 *Application fee:* $25. *Comprehensive fee:* $23,450 includes full-time tuition ($16,600) and college room and board ($6850). *College room only:* $3100. *Part-time tuition:* $450 per credit hour. *Part-time mandatory fees:* $125 per term.

Financial Aid Forms of aid include need-based and non-need-based scholarships, athletic grants, and part-time jobs. The average aided 2006–07 undergraduate received an aid package worth an estimated $12,632. The application deadline for financial aid is June 15 with a priority deadline of April 1.

Freshman Admission Culver-Stockton College requires a high school transcript, a minimum 2.0 high school GPA, rank in upper 50% of high school class, SAT or ACT scores, and TOEFL scores for international students. An essay, recommendations, and an interview are recommended. An interview is required for some. The application deadline for regular admission is rolling.

Transfer Admission The application deadline for admission is rolling.

Entrance Difficulty Culver-Stockton College assesses its entrance difficulty level as moderately difficult. For the fall 2006 freshman class, 74 percent of the applicants were accepted.

For Further Information Contact Mr. Melik Khoury, Vice President for Enrollment Management, Culver-Stockton College, One College Hill, Canton, MO 63435-1299. *Telephone:* 573-288-6312 or 800-537-1883 (toll-free). *Fax:* 573-288-6618. *E-mail:* enrollment@culver.edu. *Web site:* http://www.culver.edu/.

See page 246 for the College Close-Up.

DEACONESS COLLEGE OF NURSING

See Chamberlain College of Nursing.

DeVRY UNIVERSITY

Kansas City, Missouri

DeVry University is a coed, proprietary, four-year college of DeVry University, founded in 1931, offering degrees at the associate, bachelor's, and master's levels and postbachelor's certificates. It has a 12-acre campus in Kansas City.

Academic Information The faculty has 95 members (49% full-time). The undergraduate student-faculty ratio is 12:1. The library holds 15,000 titles and 68 serial subscriptions. Special programs include academic remediation, services for learning-disabled students, advanced placement credit, accelerated degree programs, distance learning, summer session for credit, part-time degree programs (daytime, evenings, weekends, summer), and adult/continuing education programs. The most frequently chosen baccalaureate fields are business/marketing, computer and information sciences, engineering technologies.

Student Body Statistics The student body totals 1,148, of whom 1,013 are undergraduates (177 freshmen). 29 percent are women and 71 percent are men. 66 percent are from Missouri. 0.4 percent are international students.

Expenses for 2007–08 *Application fee:* $50. *Tuition:* $12,900 full-time, $490 per credit part-time. *Mandatory fees:* $320 full-time.

Financial Aid Forms of aid include need-based and non-need-based scholarships and part-time jobs. The application deadline for financial aid is continuous.

Freshman Admission DeVry University requires a high school transcript, an interview, and TOEFL scores for international students. The application deadline for regular admission is rolling.

Transfer Admission The application deadline for admission is rolling.

Entrance Difficulty DeVry University assesses its entrance difficulty level as minimally difficult; moderately difficult for electronics engineering technology program.

For Further Information Contact Admissions Office, DeVry University, 11224 Holmes Road, Kansas City, MO 64131. *Telephone:* 819-941-0430. *Web site:* http://www.devry.edu/.

DeVRY UNIVERSITY

Kansas City, Missouri

http://www.devry.edu/

DeVRY UNIVERSITY

St. Louis, Missouri

http://www.devry.edu/

DRURY UNIVERSITY
Springfield, Missouri

Drury University is a coed, private, comprehensive institution, founded in 1873, offering degrees at the bachelor's and master's levels (also offers evening program with significant enrollment not reflected in profile). It has an 80-acre campus in Springfield.

Academic Information The faculty has 167 members (72% full-time), 74% with terminal degrees. The undergraduate student-faculty ratio is 12:1. The library holds 168,600 titles, 1,755 serial subscriptions, and 4,245 audiovisual materials. Special programs include services for learning-disabled students, an honors program, cooperative (work-study) education, study abroad, advanced placement credit, accelerated degree programs, ESL programs, double majors, independent study, distance learning, self-designed majors, summer session for credit, part-time degree programs (daytime, evenings, summer), adult/continuing education programs, internships, and arrangement for off-campus study. The most frequently chosen baccalaureate fields are biological/life sciences, business/marketing, communications/journalism.

Student Body Statistics The student body totals 2,053, of whom 1,606 are undergraduates (398 freshmen). 54 percent are women and 46 percent are men. Students come from 35 states and territories and 33 other countries. 83 percent are from Missouri. 4.5 percent are international students. 27.5 percent of the 2006 graduating class went on to graduate and professional schools.

Expenses for 2006–07 *Application fee:* $25. *Comprehensive fee:* $21,302 includes full-time tuition ($15,173), mandatory fees ($339), and college room and board ($5790). Room and board charges vary according to board plan and housing facility. *Part-time tuition:* $500 per semester hour.

Financial Aid Forms of aid include need-based and non-need-based scholarships, athletic grants, and part-time jobs. The average aided 2006–07 undergraduate received an aid package worth an estimated $7689. The priority application deadline for financial aid is March 15.

Freshman Admission Drury University requires an essay, a high school transcript, a minimum 2.7 high school GPA, 1 recommendation, minimum ACT score of 21, SAT or ACT scores, and TOEFL scores for international students. An interview is recommended. The application deadline for regular admission is August 1.

Transfer Admission The application deadline for admission is rolling.

Entrance Difficulty Drury University assesses its entrance difficulty level as moderately difficult. For the fall 2006 freshman class, 77 percent of the applicants were accepted.

For Further Information Contact Mr. Chip Parker, Director of Admission, Drury University, 900 North Benton, Bay Hall, Springfield, MO 65802. *Telephone:* 417-873-7205 or 800-922-2274 (toll-free). *Fax:* 417-866-3873. *E-mail:* druryad@drury.edu. *Web site:* http://www.drury.edu/.

EVANGEL UNIVERSITY
Springfield, Missouri

Evangel University is a coed, private, comprehensive institution, founded in 1955, affiliated with the Assemblies of God, offering degrees at the associate, bachelor's, and master's levels. It has an 80-acre campus in Springfield.

Academic Information The faculty has 156 members (65% full-time), 47% with terminal degrees. The undergraduate student-faculty ratio is 18:1. The library holds 100,691 titles and 1,060 serial subscriptions. Special programs include academic remediation, services for learning-disabled students, advanced placement credit, accelerated degree programs, double majors, summer session for credit, part-time degree programs (daytime, summer), adult/continuing education programs, and internships.

Student Body Statistics The student body totals 1,721, of whom 1,640 are undergraduates (367 freshmen). 60 percent are women and 40 percent are men. Students come from 47 states and territories and 6 other countries. 47 percent are from Missouri. 0.5 percent are international students.

Expenses for 2007–08 *Application fee:* $25. *Comprehensive fee:* $19,420 includes full-time tuition ($13,530), mandatory fees ($770), and college room and board ($5120). *College room only:* $2580. *Part-time tuition:* $528 per credit hour. *Part-time mandatory fees:* $384 per term.

Financial Aid Forms of aid include need-based and non-need-based scholarships, athletic grants, and part-time jobs. The average aided 2006–07 undergraduate received an aid package worth an estimated $8409. The priority application deadline for financial aid is March 1.

Freshman Admission Evangel University requires a high school transcript, SAT or ACT scores, and TOEFL scores for international students. A minimum 2.0 high school GPA is recommended. The application deadline for regular admission is August 1.

Transfer Admission The application deadline for admission is August 1.

Entrance Difficulty Evangel University assesses its entrance difficulty level as moderately difficult. For the fall 2006 freshman class, 79 percent of the applicants were accepted.

For Further Information Contact Ms. Charity Waltner, Director of Admissions, Evangel University, 1111 North Glenstone, Springfield, MO 65802. *Telephone:* 417-865-2811 Ext. 7262 or 800-382-6435 (toll-free in-state). *Fax:* 417-865-9599. *E-mail:* admissions@evangel.edu. *Web site:* http://www.evangel.edu/.

EVEREST COLLEGE
Springfield, Missouri

Everest College is a coed, proprietary, primarily two-year college, offering degrees at the associate and bachelor's levels.

Student Body Statistics The student body is made up of 548 undergraduates.

Expenses for 2006–07 *Tuition:* $9051 full-time.

Entrance Difficulty For the fall 2006 freshman class, 95 percent of the applicants were accepted.

For Further Information Contact Admissions Office, Everest College, 1010 West Sunshine Street, Springfield, MO 65807. *Telephone:* 417-864-7220. *Fax:* 417-864-5697. *Web site:* http://www.everest.edu/campus/springfield.

FONTBONNE UNIVERSITY
St. Louis, Missouri

Fontbonne University is a coed, private, Roman Catholic, comprehensive institution, founded in 1917, offering degrees at the bachelor's and master's levels and postbachelor's certificates. It has a 13-acre campus in St. Louis.

Academic Information The faculty has 339 members (22% full-time). The undergraduate student-faculty ratio is 14:1. The library holds 88,063 titles, 19,532 serial subscriptions, and 3,084 audiovisual materials. Special programs include academic remediation, services for learning-disabled students, an honors program, cooperative (work-study) education, study abroad, advanced placement credit, accelerated degree programs, ESL programs, double majors, independent study, distance learning, self-designed majors, summer session for credit, adult/continuing education programs, internships, and arrangement for off-campus study with Webster University, Maryville College, Lindenwood College, Missouri Baptist College. The most frequently chosen baccalaureate fields are business/marketing, education, visual and performing arts.

Student Body Statistics The student body totals 2,924, of whom 2,061 are undergraduates (198 freshmen). 72 percent are women and 28 percent are men. Students come from 21 states and territories and 1 other country. 91 percent are from Missouri. 0.5 percent are international students. 15 percent of the 2006 graduating class went on to graduate and professional schools.

Expenses for 2006–07 *Application fee:* $25. *Comprehensive fee:* $23,797 includes full-time tuition ($17,120), mandatory fees ($320), and college room and board ($6357). *Part-time tuition:* $465 per credit hour. *Part-time mandatory fees:* $16 per credit hour.

Financial Aid Forms of aid include need-based and non-need-based scholarships and part-time jobs. The priority application deadline for financial aid is April 30.

Freshman Admission Fontbonne University requires a high school transcript, a minimum 2.5 high school GPA, SAT or ACT scores, and

Fontbonne University (continued)

TOEFL scores for international students. 2 recommendations and an interview are recommended. The application deadline for regular admission is August 1.

Transfer Admission The application deadline for admission is rolling.

Entrance Difficulty Fontbonne University assesses its entrance difficulty level as moderately difficult. For the fall 2006 freshman class, 76 percent of the applicants were accepted.

For Further Information Contact Ms. Peggy Musen, Associate Dean for Enrollment Management, Fontbonne University, 6800 Wydown Boulevard, St. Louis, MO 63105-3098. *Telephone:* 314-889-1400. *Fax:* 314-719-8021. *E-mail:* pmusen@fontbonne.edu. *Web site:* http://www.fontbonne.edu/.

GLOBAL UNIVERSITY OF THE ASSEMBLIES OF GOD
Springfield, Missouri

Global University of the Assemblies of God is a coed, private, comprehensive institution, founded in 1948, affiliated with the Assemblies of God, offering degrees at the associate, bachelor's, master's, and first professional levels and postbachelor's certificates (offers only external degree programs).

Academic Information The faculty has 605 members (9% full-time), 48% with terminal degrees. The undergraduate student-faculty ratio is 21:1. The library holds 180 serial subscriptions. Special programs include an honors program, double majors, independent study, distance learning, part-time degree programs, external degree programs, adult/continuing education programs, internships, and arrangement for off-campus study. The most frequently chosen baccalaureate field is theology and religious vocations.

Student Body Statistics The student body totals 5,033, of whom 4,807 are undergraduates. 34 percent are women and 66 percent are men. Students come from 50 states and territories and 127 other countries. 2 percent are from Missouri.

Expenses for 2006–07 *Application fee:* $35. *Tuition:* $2376 full-time, $99 per hour part-time. Part-time tuition varies according to class time.

Freshman Admission Global University of the Assemblies of God requires a high school transcript. An essay is recommended. 1 recommendation is required for some. The application deadline for regular admission is rolling.

Transfer Admission The application deadline for admission is rolling.

Entrance Difficulty Global University of the Assemblies of God has an open admission policy.

For Further Information Contact Ms. Jessica Dorn, Director of US Enrollments, Global University of the Assemblies of God, 1211 South Glenstone Avenue, Springfield, MO 65804. *Telephone:* 417-862-9533 Ext. 2335 or 800-443-1083 (toll-free). *Fax:* 417-862-0863. *E-mail:* studentinfo@globaluniversity.edu. *Web site:* http://www.globaluniversity.edu/.

GRANTHAM UNIVERSITY
Kansas City, Missouri

Grantham University is a coed, proprietary, comprehensive institution, founded in 1951, offering degrees at the associate, bachelor's, and master's levels (offers only external degree programs).

Academic Information Special programs include advanced placement credit, accelerated degree programs, independent study, distance learning, part-time degree programs, external degree programs, and adult/continuing education programs.

Student Body Statistics The student body totals 9,500, of whom 9,000 are undergraduates. Students come from 52 states and territories.

Expenses for 2007–08 *Application fee:* $0. *Tuition:* $6360 full-time, $265 per credit hour part-time.

Freshman Admission Grantham University requires a high school transcript and TOEFL scores for international students. The application deadline for regular admission is rolling and for nonresidents it is rolling.

Transfer Admission The application deadline for admission is rolling.

Entrance Difficulty Grantham University has an open admission policy.

For Further Information Contact Ms. DeAnn Wandler, Director of Admissions, Grantham University, 7200 NW 86th Street, Kansas City, MO 64153. *Telephone:* 800-955-2527 Ext. 322 or 800-955-2527 (toll-free). *Fax:* 816-595-5757. *E-mail:* admissions@grantham.edu. *Web site:* http://www.grantham.edu/.

HANNIBAL-LaGRANGE COLLEGE
Hannibal, Missouri

Hannibal-LaGrange College is a coed, private, Southern Baptist, four-year college, founded in 1858, offering degrees at the associate and bachelor's levels. It has a 110-acre campus in Hannibal.

Academic Information The faculty has 99 members (62% full-time), 23% with terminal degrees. The student-faculty ratio is 12:1. The library holds 97,875 titles, 432 serial subscriptions, and 5,850 audiovisual materials. Special programs include academic remediation, services for learning-disabled students, an honors program, cooperative (work-study) education, study abroad, advanced placement credit, accelerated degree programs, double majors, independent study, distance learning, summer session for credit, part-time degree programs (daytime, evenings, weekends, summer), adult/continuing education programs, and internships. The most frequently chosen baccalaureate fields are business/marketing, education, law/legal studies.

Student Body Statistics The student body is made up of 1,091 undergraduates (132 freshmen). 52 percent are women and 48 percent are men. Students come from 24 states and territories and 12 other countries. 80 percent are from Missouri. 3.9 percent are international students. 31 percent of the 2006 graduating class went on to graduate and professional schools.

Expenses for 2006–07 *Application fee:* $25. *Comprehensive fee:* $17,538 includes full-time tuition ($12,220), mandatory fees ($388), and college room and board ($4930). Full-time tuition and fees vary according to course load and program. Room and board charges vary according to housing facility. *Part-time tuition:* $407 per hour. *Part-time mandatory fees:* $97 per term. Part-time tuition and fees vary according to course load and program.

Financial Aid Forms of aid include need-based and non-need-based scholarships, athletic grants, and part-time jobs. The application deadline for financial aid is continuous.

Freshman Admission Hannibal-LaGrange College requires a high school transcript, a minimum 2.0 high school GPA, SAT or ACT scores, and TOEFL scores for international students. GED is required for some. The application deadline for regular admission is rolling.

Transfer Admission The application deadline for admission is rolling.

Entrance Difficulty Hannibal-LaGrange College assesses its entrance difficulty level as moderately difficult.

For Further Information Contact Dr. Raymond Carty, Vice President for Enrollment Management, Hannibal-LaGrange College, 2800 Palmyra Road, Hannibal, MO 63401-1999. *Telephone:* 573-221-3113 or 800-HLG-1119 (toll-free). *E-mail:* admissio@hlg.edu. *Web site:* http://www.hlg.edu/.

HARRIS-STOWE STATE UNIVERSITY
St. Louis, Missouri

Harris-Stowe State University is a coed, public, four-year college of Missouri Coordinating Board for Higher Education, founded in 1857, offering degrees at the bachelor's level and postbachelor's certificates. It has a 22-acre campus in St. Louis.

Academic Information The faculty has 107 members (51% full-time), 36% with terminal degrees. The student-faculty ratio is 17:1. The library holds 60,000 titles and 340 serial subscriptions. Special programs include academic remediation, services for learning-disabled students, cooperative (work-study) education, advanced placement credit, self-designed majors, summer session for credit, part-time degree programs (daytime, evenings, weekends, summer), internships, and arrangement for off-campus study with Saint Louis University, University of Missouri–St. Louis. The most frequently chosen baccalaureate fields are business/marketing, education, interdisciplinary studies.

Student Body Statistics The student body is made up of 1,868 undergraduates (413 freshmen). 70 percent are women and 30 percent are men. Students come from 11 states and territories and 10 other countries. 90 percent are from Missouri. 0.6 percent are international students.

Expenses for 2006–07 *Application fee:* $15. *State resident tuition:* $4910 full-time, $152 per hour part-time. *Nonresident tuition:* $9,333 full-time, $299.44 per hour part-time. *Mandatory fees:* $300 full-time, $175 per term part-time. Both full-time and part-time tuition and fees vary according to course load. *College room only:* $4950.

Financial Aid Forms of aid include need-based and non-need-based scholarships, athletic grants, and part-time jobs. The priority application deadline for financial aid is April 1.

Freshman Admission Harris-Stowe State University requires a high school transcript and TOEFL scores for international students. SAT or ACT scores are recommended. The application deadline for regular admission is rolling.

Transfer Admission The application deadline for admission is rolling.

Entrance Difficulty Harris-Stowe State University has an open admission policy.

For Further Information Contact Ms. LaShanda Boone, Executive Director of Enrollment Management, Harris-Stowe State University, 3026 Laclede Avenue, St. Louis, MO 63103. *Telephone:* 314-340-3301. *Fax:* 314-340-3555. *E-mail:* admissions@hssu.edu. *Web site:* http://www.hssu.edu/.

HICKEY COLLEGE

St. Louis, Missouri

Hickey College is a coed, proprietary, primarily two-year college, founded in 1933, offering degrees at the associate and bachelor's levels.

For Further Information Contact Ms. Michelle Hayes, Director of Admissions, Hickey College, 940 West Port Plaza Drive, St. Louis, MO 63145. *Telephone:* 314-434-2212 Ext. 136 or 800-777-1544 (toll-free). *Fax:* 314-434-1974. *E-mail:* admin@hickeycollege.edu. *Web site:* http://www.hickeycollege.edu/.

IHM HEALTH STUDIES CENTER

St. Louis, Missouri

http://www.ihmhealthstudies.com/

ITT TECHNICAL INSTITUTE

Arnold, Missouri

ITT Technical Institute is a coed, proprietary, primarily two-year college of ITT Educational Services, Inc, founded in 1997, offering degrees at the associate and bachelor's levels.

Expenses for 2006–07 *Application fee:* $100. Contact school directly for program costs.

Financial Aid Forms of aid include need-based scholarships and part-time jobs. The application deadline for financial aid is continuous.

Freshman Admission ITT Technical Institute requires a high school transcript, an interview, and Wonderlic aptitude test. Recommendations are recommended. The application deadline for regular admission is rolling.

Transfer Admission The application deadline for admission is rolling.

Entrance Difficulty ITT Technical Institute assesses its entrance difficulty level as minimally difficult.

For Further Information Contact Mr. Brad Coleman, Director of Recruitment, ITT Technical Institute, 1930 Meyer Drury Drive, Arnold, MO 63010. *Telephone:* 636-464-6600 or 888-488-1082 (toll-free). *Fax:* 636-464-6611. *Web site:* http://www.itt-tech.edu/.

ITT TECHNICAL INSTITUTE

Earth City, Missouri

ITT Technical Institute is a coed, proprietary, primarily two-year college of ITT Educational Services, Inc, founded in 1936, offering degrees at the associate and bachelor's levels. It has a 2-acre campus in Earth City near St. Louis.

Expenses for 2006–07 *Application fee:* $100. Contact school for program costs.

Financial Aid Forms of aid include need-based scholarships and part-time jobs. The application deadline for financial aid is continuous.

Freshman Admission ITT Technical Institute requires a high school transcript, an interview, TOEFL scores for international students, and Wonderlic aptitude test. Recommendations are recommended. The application deadline for regular admission is rolling.

Transfer Admission The application deadline for admission is rolling.

Entrance Difficulty ITT Technical Institute assesses its entrance difficulty level as minimally difficult.

For Further Information Contact Mr. Arlen K. Freeman, Director of Recruitment, ITT Technical Institute, 3640 Corporate Trail Drive, Earth City, MO 63045. *Telephone:* 314-298-7800 or 800-235-5488 (toll-free). *Fax:* 314-298-0559. *Web site:* http://www.itt-tech.edu/.

ITT TECHNICAL INSTITUTE

Kansas City, Missouri

ITT Technical Institute is a coed, proprietary, primarily two-year college of ITT Educational Services, Inc, founded in 2004, offering degrees at the associate and bachelor's levels.

Expenses for 2006–07 *Application fee:* $100. Contact school for program costs.

Freshman Admission ITT Technical Institute requires a high school transcript, an interview, and Wonderlic aptitude test. Recommendations are recommended. The application deadline for regular admission is rolling.

Transfer Admission The application deadline for admission is rolling.

For Further Information Contact Mr. William Vinson, Director of Recruitment, ITT Technical Institute, 9150 East 41st Terrace, Kansas City, MO 64133. *Telephone:* 816-276-1400 or 877-488-1442 (toll-free). *Fax:* 816-276-1410. *Web site:* http://www.itt-tech.edu/.

JEWISH HOSPITAL COLLEGE OF NURSING AND ALLIED HEALTH

See Barnes-Jewish College of Nursing and Allied Health.

KANSAS CITY ART INSTITUTE

Kansas City, Missouri

Kansas City Art Institute is a coed, private, four-year college, founded in 1885, offering degrees at the bachelor's level. It has an 18-acre campus in Kansas City.

Academic Information The faculty has 112 members (45% full-time), 86% with terminal degrees. The student-faculty ratio is 12:1. The library holds 32,235 titles and 133 serial subscriptions. Special programs include academic remediation, services for learning-disabled students, cooperative (work-study) education, study abroad, advanced placement credit, ESL programs, double majors, independent study, summer session for credit, adult/continuing education programs, internships, and arrangement for off-campus study with New York Studio Program, AICAD School Exchange. The most frequently chosen baccalaureate field is visual and performing arts.

Student Body Statistics The student body is made up of 674 undergraduates (139 freshmen). 57 percent are women and 43 percent are men. Students come from 38 states and territories and 8 other countries.

Kansas City Art Institute (continued)

35 percent are from Missouri. 1.3 percent are international students. 20 percent of the 2006 graduating class went on to graduate and professional schools.

Expenses for 2007–08 *Application fee:* $35. *Comprehensive fee:* $33,554 includes full-time tuition ($25,680) and college room and board ($7874). *Part-time tuition:* $1070 per credit hour.

Financial Aid Forms of aid include need-based and non-need-based scholarships and part-time jobs. The average aided 2005–06 undergraduate received an aid package worth $15,004. The priority application deadline for financial aid is March 1.

Freshman Admission Kansas City Art Institute requires an essay, a high school transcript, a minimum 2.5 high school GPA, 2 recommendations, portfolio, statement of purpose, SAT or ACT scores, and TOEFL scores for international students. An interview is recommended. The application deadline for regular admission is rolling.

Transfer Admission The application deadline for admission is rolling.

Entrance Difficulty Kansas City Art Institute assesses its entrance difficulty level as moderately difficult. For the fall 2006 freshman class, 72 percent of the applicants were accepted.

For Further Information Contact Mr. Gerald Valet, Director of Admission Technology, Kansas City Art Institute, 4415 Warwick Boulevard, Kansas City, MO 64111-1874. *Telephone:* 816-474-5224 or 800-522-5224 (toll-free). *Fax:* 816-802-3309. *E-mail:* admiss@kcai.edu. *Web site:* http://www.kcai.edu/.

LINCOLN UNIVERSITY
Jefferson City, Missouri

Lincoln University is a coed, public, comprehensive unit of Missouri Coordinating Board for Higher Education, founded in 1866, offering degrees at the associate, bachelor's, and master's levels and post-master's certificates. It has a 165-acre campus in Jefferson City.

Academic Information The faculty has 199 members (58% full-time). The undergraduate student-faculty ratio is 17:1. The library holds 204,948 titles, 368 serial subscriptions, and 5,497 audiovisual materials. Special programs include academic remediation, services for learning-disabled students, an honors program, advanced placement credit, accelerated degree programs, double majors, independent study, distance learning, summer session for credit, part-time degree programs (daytime, evenings, weekends, summer), adult/continuing education programs, internships, and arrangement for off-campus study. The most frequently chosen baccalaureate fields are business/marketing, computer and information sciences, education.

Student Body Statistics The student body totals 3,224, of whom 2,927 are undergraduates (563 freshmen). 59 percent are women and 41 percent are men. Students come from 32 states and territories and 21 other countries. 84 percent are from Missouri. 4.6 percent are international students.

Expenses for 2007–08 *Application fee:* $17. *State resident tuition:* $4,633 full-time, $154.43 per credit hour part-time. *Nonresident tuition:* $8,462 full-time, $282.05 per credit hour part-time. *Mandatory fees:* $490 full-time, $15 per credit hour part-time, $20 per term part-time. *College room and board:* $3990. *College room only:* $2050.

Financial Aid Forms of aid include need-based and non-need-based scholarships, athletic grants, and part-time jobs. The average aided 2005–06 undergraduate received an aid package worth $8000.

Freshman Admission Lincoln University requires a high school transcript and TOEFL scores for international students. A minimum 2.0 high school GPA is required for some. The application deadline for regular admission is July 15 and for nonresidents it is July 15.

Transfer Admission The application deadline for admission is June 15.

Entrance Difficulty Lincoln University has an open admission policy for state residents. It assesses its entrance difficulty as minimally difficult for out-of-state applicants; minimally difficult for transfers.

For Further Information Contact Mr. Mike Kosher, Associate Director of Admissions, Lincoln University, Office of Admissions, 820 Chestnut Street, B-7 Young Hall, Jefferson City, MO 65102-0029. *Telephone:* 573-681-5599 or 800-521-5052 (toll-free). *Fax:* 573-681-5889. *E-mail:* enroll@lincolnu.edu. *Web site:* http://www.lincolnu.edu/.

LINDENWOOD UNIVERSITY
St. Charles, Missouri

Lindenwood University is a coed, private, Presbyterian, comprehensive institution, founded in 1827, offering degrees at the bachelor's and master's levels and post-master's certificates (education specialist). It has a 420-acre campus in St. Charles near St. Louis.

Academic Information The faculty has 453 members (36% full-time), 36% with terminal degrees. The undergraduate student-faculty ratio is 13:1. The library holds 122,358 titles, 28,732 serial subscriptions, and 1,342 audiovisual materials. Special programs include academic remediation, services for learning-disabled students, an honors program, cooperative (work-study) education, study abroad, advanced placement credit, accelerated degree programs, Freshman Honors College, double majors, independent study, self-designed majors, summer session for credit, part-time degree programs (daytime, evenings, weekends, summer), adult/continuing education programs, internships, and arrangement for off-campus study with St. Louis Private College Consortium, Washington University in St. Louis, University of Missouri–Columbia. The most frequently chosen baccalaureate fields are business/marketing, communications/journalism, education.

Student Body Statistics The student body totals 9,525, of whom 6,068 are undergraduates (871 freshmen). 57 percent are women and 43 percent are men. Students come from 42 states and territories and 65 other countries. 84 percent are from Missouri. 7.3 percent are international students. 14 percent of the 2006 graduating class went on to graduate and professional schools.

Expenses for 2007–08 *Application fee:* $30. *Comprehensive fee:* $18,900 includes full-time tuition ($12,400), mandatory fees ($300), and college room and board ($6200). *College room only:* $3100. *Part-time tuition:* $350 per credit hour.

Financial Aid Forms of aid include need-based and non-need-based scholarships and part-time jobs. The priority application deadline for financial aid is March 15.

Freshman Admission Lindenwood University requires a high school transcript, minimum ACT score of 20 or minimum SAT score of 900, SAT or ACT scores, and TOEFL scores for international students. A minimum 2.25 high school GPA and an interview are recommended. An essay, recommendations, and an interview are required for some. The application deadline for regular admission is rolling.

Transfer Admission The application deadline for admission is rolling.

Entrance Difficulty Lindenwood University assesses its entrance difficulty level as moderately difficult. For the fall 2006 freshman class, 64 percent of the applicants were accepted.

For Further Information Contact Mr. Joseph Parisi, Assistant Director of Undergraduate Admissions, Lindenwood University, 209 South Kings Highway, St. Charles, MO 6331-1695. *Telephone:* 636-949-4949. *Fax:* 636-949-4989. *E-mail:* admissions@lindenwood.edu. *Web site:* http://www.lindenwood.edu/.

LOGAN UNIVERSITY-COLLEGE OF CHIROPRACTIC
Chesterfield, Missouri

Logan University-College of Chiropractic is a coed, private, upper-level institution, founded in 1935, offering degrees at the bachelor's and first professional levels. It has a 111-acre campus in Chesterfield near St. Louis.

Academic Information The faculty has 85 members (51% full-time), 100% with terminal degrees. The library holds 14,001 titles, 163 serial subscriptions, and 2,366 audiovisual materials. Special programs include services for learning-disabled students, advanced placement credit, independent study, distance learning, part-time degree programs (daytime, summer), adult/continuing education programs, and internships. The most frequently chosen baccalaureate field is biological/life sciences.

Student Body Statistics The student body totals 1,098, of whom 123 are undergraduates. 42 percent are women and 58 percent are men. Students come from 28 states and territories and 2 other countries. 34 percent are from Missouri. 2.4 percent are international students.

Expenses for 2006–07 *Application fee:* $40. *Tuition:* $3420 full-time, $95 per credit hour part-time. *Mandatory fees:* $330 full-time, $110 per term part-time. Both full-time and part-time tuition and fees vary according to program.

Financial Aid Forms of aid include need-based and non-need-based scholarships and part-time jobs. The priority application deadline for financial aid is April 30.

Transfer Admission Logan University-College of Chiropractic requires a minimum 2.5 college GPA and a college transcript. The application deadline for admission is rolling.

Entrance Difficulty Logan University-College of Chiropractic assesses its entrance difficulty level as moderately difficult.

For Further Information Contact Robert Smith, Associate Director of Admissions, Logan University-College of Chiropractic, 1851 Schoettler Road, Chesterfield, MO 63006-1065. *Telephone:* 636-227-2100 or 800-533-9210 (toll-free). *Fax:* 636-207-2425. *E-mail:* loganadm@logan.edu. *Web site:* http://www.logan.edu/.

MARYVILLE UNIVERSITY OF SAINT LOUIS
St. Louis, Missouri

Maryville University of Saint Louis is a coed, private, comprehensive institution, founded in 1872, offering degrees at the bachelor's, master's, and doctoral levels. It has a 130-acre campus in St. Louis.

Academic Information The faculty has 355 members (30% full-time), 56% with terminal degrees. The undergraduate student-faculty ratio is 12:1. The library holds 213,053 titles and 14,110 serial subscriptions. Special programs include services for learning-disabled students, an honors program, cooperative (work-study) education, study abroad, advanced placement credit, accelerated degree programs, Freshman Honors College, double majors, independent study, distance learning, self-designed majors, summer session for credit, part-time degree programs (daytime, evenings, weekends, summer), adult/continuing education programs, internships, and arrangement for off-campus study with Fontbonne University, Lindenwood University, Webster University, Missouri Baptist University. The most frequently chosen baccalaureate fields are business/marketing, health professions and related sciences, psychology.

Student Body Statistics The student body totals 3,333, of whom 2,748 are undergraduates (292 freshmen). 77 percent are women and 23 percent are men. Students come from 23 states and territories and 14 other countries. 86 percent are from Missouri. 0.5 percent are international students.

Expenses for 2006–07 *Application fee:* $25. *Comprehensive fee:* $25,840 includes full-time tuition ($17,800), mandatory fees ($320), and college room and board ($7720). *College room only:* $6800. Full-time tuition and fees vary according to course load. Room and board charges vary according to housing facility. *Part-time tuition:* $540 per credit hour. *Part-time mandatory fees:* $80 per term. Part-time tuition and fees vary according to class time.

Financial Aid Forms of aid include need-based and non-need-based scholarships and part-time jobs. The average aided 2006–07 undergraduate received an aid package worth an estimated $13,522.

Freshman Admission Maryville University of Saint Louis requires a high school transcript, a minimum 2.5 high school GPA, SAT or ACT scores, and TOEFL scores for international students. An essay, recommendations, an interview, and audition, portfolio are required for some. The application deadline for regular admission is August 15.

Transfer Admission The application deadline for admission is rolling.

Entrance Difficulty Maryville University of Saint Louis assesses its entrance difficulty level as moderately difficult; very difficult for physical therapy, occupational therapy, education, actuarial science. For the fall 2006 freshman class, 70 percent of the applicants were accepted.

For Further Information Contact Ms. Shani Lenore, Admissions Director, Maryville University of Saint Louis, 650 Maryville University Drive, St. Louis, MO 63141-7299. *Telephone:* 314-529-9350 or 800-627-9855 (toll-free). *Fax:* 314-529-9927. *E-mail:* admissions@maryville.edu. *Web site:* http://www.maryville.edu/.

MESSENGER COLLEGE
Joplin, Missouri

Messenger College is a coed, private, Pentecostal, four-year college, founded in 1987, offering degrees at the associate and bachelor's levels. It has a 16-acre campus in Joplin near Springfield.

Academic Information The faculty has 14 members (29% full-time), 29% with terminal degrees. The student-faculty ratio is 8:1. The library holds 28,874 titles and 114 serial subscriptions. Special programs include academic remediation, an honors program, cooperative (work-study) education, double majors, independent study, distance learning, part-time degree programs (daytime, evenings), external degree programs, and internships.

Student Body Statistics The student body is made up of 96 undergraduates (19 freshmen). 42 percent are women and 58 percent are men. Students come from 17 states and territories. 51 percent are from Missouri.

Expenses for 2006–07 *Application fee:* $35. *Comprehensive fee:* $9760 includes full-time tuition ($5250), mandatory fees ($610), and college room and board ($3900). Room and board charges vary according to housing facility. *Part-time tuition:* $175 per credit hour. *Part-time mandatory fees:* $26 per credit hour.

Financial Aid Forms of aid include need-based and non-need-based scholarships and part-time jobs. The average aided 2005–06 undergraduate received an aid package worth $6000. The application deadline for financial aid is continuous.

Freshman Admission Messenger College requires an essay, a high school transcript, a minimum 2.0 high school GPA, 3 recommendations, a health form, SAT or ACT scores, and TOEFL scores for international students. An interview is required for some. The application deadline for regular admission is August 14.

Transfer Admission The application deadline for admission is August 14.

Entrance Difficulty Messenger College assesses its entrance difficulty level as moderately difficult. For the fall 2006 freshman class, 90 percent of the applicants were accepted.

For Further Information Contact Ron Cannon, Vice President of Academic Affairs, Messenger College, 300 East 50th, Joplin, MO 64804. *Telephone:* 417-624-7070 Ext. 108 or 800-385-8940 (toll-free in-state). *Fax:* 417-624-5070. *E-mail:* info@messengercollege.edu. *Web site:* http://www.messengercollege.edu/.

METRO BUSINESS COLLEGE
Cape Girardeau, Missouri
http://www.metrobusinesscollege.edu/

MIDWEST UNIVERSITY
Wentzville, Missouri
http://www.midwest.edu/

MISSOURI BAPTIST UNIVERSITY
St. Louis, Missouri

Missouri Baptist University is a coed, private, Southern Baptist, comprehensive institution, founded in 1964, offering degrees at the associate, bachelor's, and master's levels and postbachelor's certificates. It has a 65-acre campus in St. Louis.

Academic Information The faculty has 191 members (31% full-time). The undergraduate student-faculty ratio is 12:1. The library holds 71,634 titles, 452 serial subscriptions, and 2,155 audiovisual materials. Special programs include services for learning-disabled students, study abroad, advanced placement credit, accelerated degree programs, double majors, independent study, distance learning, self-designed majors, summer session for credit, part-time degree programs (daytime, evenings, summer), adult/continuing education programs, internships, and arrangement for

Missouri Baptist University (continued)

off-campus study with Maryville University of Saint Louis, Lindenwood University, Fontbonne College, Webster University. The most frequently chosen baccalaureate fields are business/marketing, education, psychology.

Student Body Statistics The student body totals 4,511, of whom 3,496 are undergraduates (195 freshmen). 62 percent are women and 38 percent are men. Students come from 29 states and territories and 20 other countries. 75 percent are from Missouri. 5.3 percent are international students.

Expenses for 2006–07 *Application fee:* $30. *Comprehensive fee:* $20,800 includes full-time tuition ($14,140), mandatory fees ($670), and college room and board ($5990). Full-time tuition and fees vary according to course load and location. Room and board charges vary according to housing facility. *Part-time tuition:* $490 per credit. *Part-time mandatory fees:* $11 per credit, $25 per term. Part-time tuition and fees vary according to course load and location.

Financial Aid Forms of aid include need-based and non-need-based scholarships, athletic grants, and part-time jobs. The average aided 2005–06 undergraduate received an aid package worth $8120. The priority application deadline for financial aid is April 1.

Freshman Admission Missouri Baptist University requires a high school transcript, a minimum 2.0 high school GPA, recommendations, an interview, and TOEFL scores for international students. SAT or ACT scores are required for some. The application deadline for regular admission is rolling.

Transfer Admission The application deadline for admission is rolling.

Entrance Difficulty Missouri Baptist University assesses its entrance difficulty level as moderately difficult. For the fall 2006 freshman class, 71 percent of the applicants were accepted.

For Further Information Contact Mr. Terry Dale Cruse, Director of Admissions, Missouri Baptist University, One College Park Drive, St. Louis, MO 63141-8660. *Telephone:* 314-392-2291 or 877-434-1115 Ext. 2290 (toll-free). *Fax:* 314-434-7596. *E-mail:* admissions@mobap.edu. *Web site:* http://www.mobap.edu/.

MISSOURI SOUTHERN STATE UNIVERSITY

Joplin, Missouri

Missouri Southern State University is a coed, public, four-year college, founded in 1937, offering degrees at the associate, bachelor's, and master's levels. It has a 350-acre campus in Joplin.

Academic Information The faculty has 307 members (68% full-time), 50% with terminal degrees. The undergraduate student-faculty ratio is 19:1. Special programs include academic remediation, services for learning-disabled students, an honors program, cooperative (work-study) education, study abroad, advanced placement credit, accelerated degree programs, ESL programs, double majors, independent study, distance learning, summer session for credit, part-time degree programs (daytime, evenings, weekends, summer), external degree programs, adult/continuing education programs, internships, and arrangement for off-campus study with Nevada Consortium. The most frequently chosen baccalaureate fields are business/marketing, education, health professions and related sciences.

Student Body Statistics The student body totals 5,675, of whom 5,666 are undergraduates (945 freshmen). 59 percent are women and 41 percent are men. Students come from 27 states and territories and 34 other countries. 85 percent are from Missouri. 1.5 percent are international students.

Expenses for 2007–08 *Application fee:* $15. *State resident tuition:* $4050 full-time, $135 per credit part-time. *Nonresident tuition:* $8100 full-time, $270 per credit part-time. *Mandatory fees:* $226 full-time. *College room and board:* $4720.

Financial Aid Forms of aid include need-based and non-need-based scholarships, athletic grants, and part-time jobs. The priority application deadline for financial aid is February 15.

Freshman Admission Missouri Southern State University requires a high school transcript, standardized test scores; class rank, SAT or ACT scores, and TOEFL scores for international students. ACT scores are recommended. 2 recommendations and Michigan Test of English Language Proficiency are required for some. The application deadline for regular admission is August 1.

Transfer Admission The application deadline for admission is August 1.

Entrance Difficulty Missouri Southern State University assesses its entrance difficulty level as moderately difficult; noncompetitive for transfers. For the fall 2006 freshman class, 98 percent of the applicants were accepted.

For Further Information Contact Mr. Derek Skaggs, Director of Enrollment Services, Missouri Southern State University, 3950 East Newman Road, Joplin, MO 64801-1595. *Telephone:* 417-625-9537 or 866-818-MSSU (toll-free). *Fax:* 417-659-4429. *E-mail:* admissions@mssu.edu. *Web site:* http://www.mssu.edu/.

MISSOURI STATE UNIVERSITY

Springfield, Missouri

Missouri State University is a coed, public, comprehensive institution, founded in 1905, offering degrees at the bachelor's, master's, and doctoral levels and post-master's and postbachelor's certificates. It has a 225-acre campus in Springfield.

Academic Information The faculty has 1,027 members (71% full-time), 61% with terminal degrees. The undergraduate student-faculty ratio is 18:1. The library holds 2 million titles, 4,238 serial subscriptions, and 33,547 audiovisual materials. Special programs include services for learning-disabled students, an honors program, cooperative (work-study) education, study abroad, advanced placement credit, accelerated degree programs, Freshman Honors College, ESL programs, double majors, independent study, distance learning, self-designed majors, summer session for credit, part-time degree programs, internships, and arrangement for off-campus study with National Student Exchange.

Student Body Statistics The student body totals 19,218, of whom 16,234 are undergraduates (2,775 freshmen). 56 percent are women and 44 percent are men. Students come from 47 states and territories and 81 other countries. 94 percent are from Missouri. 1.7 percent are international students. 20 percent of the 2006 graduating class went on to graduate and professional schools.

Expenses for 2007–08 *Application fee:* $30. *State resident tuition:* $5190 full-time, $173 per credit hour part-time. *Nonresident tuition:* $10,110 full-time, $337 per credit hour part-time. *Mandatory fees:* $548 full-time. *College room and board:* $5358. *College room only:* $3600.

Financial Aid Forms of aid include need-based and non-need-based scholarships, athletic grants, and part-time jobs. The average aided 2006–07 undergraduate received an aid package worth an estimated $6093.

Freshman Admission Missouri State University requires a high school transcript, SAT or ACT scores, and TOEFL scores for international students. An essay, recommendations, and an interview are required for some. The application deadline for regular admission is July 20.

Transfer Admission The application deadline for admission is July 20.

Entrance Difficulty Missouri State University assesses its entrance difficulty level as moderately difficult. For the fall 2006 freshman class, 77 percent of the applicants were accepted.

For Further Information Contact Ms. Jill Duncan, Associate Director of Admissions, Missouri State University, 901 South National, Springfield, MO 65804. *Telephone:* 417-836-5517 or 800-492-7900 (toll-free). *Fax:* 417-836-6334. *E-mail:* info@missouristate.edu. *Web site:* http://www.missouristate.edu/.

MISSOURI TECH

St. Louis, Missouri

http://www.motech.edu/

MISSOURI VALLEY COLLEGE

Marshall, Missouri

Missouri Valley College is a coed, private, four-year college, founded in 1889, affiliated with the Presbyterian Church, offering degrees at the associate and bachelor's levels. It has a 140-acre campus in Marshall near Kansas City.

Academic Information The faculty has 119 members (62% full-time), 39% with terminal degrees. The student-faculty ratio is 19:1. The library holds 71,203 titles, 338 serial subscriptions, and 2,456 audiovisual materials. Special programs include academic remediation, services for learning-disabled students, cooperative (work-study) education, study abroad, advanced placement credit, ESL programs, double majors, independent study, distance learning, self-designed majors, summer session for credit, part-time degree programs (daytime, evenings), adult/continuing education programs, and internships.

Student Body Statistics The student body is made up of 1,606 undergraduates (375 freshmen). 45 percent are women and 55 percent are men. Students come from 43 states and territories and 32 other countries. 71 percent are from Missouri. 11 percent are international students.

Expenses for 2007–08 *Application fee:* $15. *Comprehensive fee:* $21,300 includes full-time tuition ($14,950), mandatory fees ($500), and college room and board ($5850). *College room only:* $3000. *Part-time tuition:* $350 per credit hour.

Financial Aid Forms of aid include need-based and non-need-based scholarships and part-time jobs. The average aided 2006–07 undergraduate received an aid package worth an estimated $12,450. The application deadline for financial aid is September 15 with a priority deadline of March 15.

Freshman Admission Missouri Valley College requires a high school transcript and SAT or ACT scores. A minimum 2.0 high school GPA, an interview, and TOEFL scores for international students are recommended. An essay, 3 recommendations, and an interview are required for some. The application deadline for regular admission is rolling.

Transfer Admission The application deadline for admission is rolling.

Entrance Difficulty Missouri Valley College assesses its entrance difficulty level as minimally difficult. For the fall 2006 freshman class, 58 percent of the applicants were accepted.

For Further Information Contact Ms. Debi Bultmann, Admissions Office Manager, Missouri Valley College, Admissions Office, 500 East College, Marshall, MO 65340. *Telephone:* 660-831-4125. *Fax:* 660-831-4233. *E-mail:* admissions@moval.edu. *Web site:* http://www.moval.edu/.

MISSOURI WESTERN STATE UNIVERSITY
St. Joseph, Missouri

Missouri Western State University is a coed, public, four-year college, founded in 1915, offering degrees at the associate and bachelor's levels. It has a 744-acre campus in St. Joseph near Kansas City.

Academic Information The faculty has 308 members (58% full-time), 51% with terminal degrees. The student-faculty ratio is 19:1. The library holds 147,509 titles and 1,068 serial subscriptions. Special programs include academic remediation, an honors program, study abroad, advanced placement credit, accelerated degree programs, Freshman Honors College, double majors, distance learning, summer session for credit, part-time degree programs (daytime, evenings, weekends, summer), and internships. The most frequently chosen baccalaureate fields are business/marketing, education, security and protective services.

Student Body Statistics The student body is made up of 5,276 undergraduates (1,059 freshmen). 59 percent are women and 41 percent are men. Students come from 31 states and territories and 7 other countries. 93 percent are from Missouri. 0.3 percent are international students. 22 percent of the 2006 graduating class went on to graduate and professional schools.

Expenses for 2006–07 *Application fee:* $15. *State resident tuition:* $4650 full-time, $155 per credit part-time. *Nonresident tuition:* $8490 full-time, $283 per credit part-time. *Mandatory fees:* $518 full-time, $17 per credit part-time, $35 per term part-time. *College room and board:* $4756. Room and board charges vary according to board plan and housing facility.

Financial Aid Forms of aid include need-based and non-need-based scholarships and part-time jobs. The priority application deadline for financial aid is April 1.

Freshman Admission Missouri Western State University requires a high school transcript and TOEFL scores for international students. The application deadline for regular admission is June 1.

Transfer Admission The application deadline for admission is June 1.

Entrance Difficulty Missouri Western State University has an open admission policy. It assesses its entrance difficulty as moderately difficult

for nursing, computer science, education, criminal justice, leisure management, math, history, political science, social work programs.

For Further Information Contact Mr. Howard McCauley, Director of Admissions, Missouri Western State University, 4525 Downs Drive, St. Joseph, MO 64507-2294. *Telephone:* 816-271-4267 or 800-662-7041 Ext. 60 (toll-free). *Fax:* 816-271-5833. *E-mail:* admission@missouriwestern.edu. *Web site:* http://www.missouriwestern.edu/.

NATIONAL AMERICAN UNIVERSITY
Kansas City, Missouri

http://www.national.edu/

NORTHWEST MISSOURI STATE UNIVERSITY
Maryville, Missouri

Northwest Missouri State University is a coed, public, comprehensive unit of Missouri Coordinating Board for Higher Education, founded in 1905, offering degrees at the bachelor's and master's levels. It has a 240-acre campus in Maryville near Kansas City.

Academic Information The faculty has 284 members (88% full-time), 58% with terminal degrees. The undergraduate student-faculty ratio is 20:1. The library holds 371,026 titles, 24,054 serial subscriptions, and 6,253 audiovisual materials. Special programs include academic remediation, services for learning-disabled students, an honors program, study abroad, advanced placement credit, accelerated degree programs, ESL programs, double majors, independent study, distance learning, summer session for credit, part-time degree programs (daytime, evenings, summer), internships, and arrangement for off-campus study with Missouri Western State College, Truman State University, North Central Missouri College.

Student Body Statistics The student body totals 6,220, of whom 5,280 are undergraduates (1,270 freshmen). 56 percent are women and 44 percent are men. Students come from 17 states and territories and 6 other countries. 71 percent are from Missouri. 1.6 percent are international students. 18.7 percent of the 2006 graduating class went on to graduate and professional schools.

Expenses for 2006–07 *Application fee:* $25. *State resident tuition:* $4668 full-time, $194.50 per credit hour part-time. *Nonresident tuition:* $8064 full-time, $336 per credit hour part-time.

Financial Aid Forms of aid include need-based and non-need-based scholarships, athletic grants, and part-time jobs. The priority application deadline for financial aid is March 1.

Freshman Admission Northwest Missouri State University requires a high school transcript, a minimum 2.0 high school GPA, SAT or ACT scores, and TOEFL scores for international students. Recommendations and an interview are required for some. The application deadline for regular admission is rolling and for nonresidents it is rolling.

Transfer Admission The application deadline for admission is rolling.

Entrance Difficulty Northwest Missouri State University assesses its entrance difficulty level as moderately difficult; minimally difficult for transfers. For the fall 2006 freshman class, 75 percent of the applicants were accepted.

For Further Information Contact Ms. Tami Grow, Associate Director of Admission, Northwest Missouri State University, 800 University Drive, Maryville, MO 64468. *Telephone:* 660-562-1146 or 800-633-1175 (toll-free). *Fax:* 660-562-1121. *E-mail:* admissions@nwmissouri.edu. *Web site:* http://www.nwmissouri.edu/.

OZARK CHRISTIAN COLLEGE
Joplin, Missouri

Ozark Christian College is a coed, private, Christian, four-year college, founded in 1942, offering degrees at the associate and bachelor's levels. It has a 110-acre campus in Joplin.

Ozark Christian College (continued)

Academic Information The faculty has 60 members (50% full-time), 17% with terminal degrees. The student-faculty ratio is 19:1. The library holds 59,808 titles and 362 serial subscriptions. Special programs include academic remediation, services for learning-disabled students, ESL programs, double majors, distance learning, summer session for credit, part-time degree programs (daytime, evenings, summer), adult/continuing education programs, and internships.

Expenses for 2007–08 *Application fee:* $30. *One-time mandatory fee:* $32. *Comprehensive fee:* $12,870 includes full-time tuition ($7840), mandatory fees ($480), and college room and board ($4550). *College room only:* $2060. *Part-time tuition:* $245 per hour.

Financial Aid Forms of aid include need-based and non-need-based scholarships and part-time jobs. The application deadline for financial aid is April 1.

Freshman Admission Ozark Christian College requires an essay, a high school transcript, 2 recommendations, SAT or ACT scores, and TOEFL scores for international students. An interview is required for some. The application deadline for regular admission is August 5.

Transfer Admission The application deadline for admission is rolling.

Entrance Difficulty Ozark Christian College has an open admission policy.

For Further Information Contact Mr. Troy B. Nelson, Executive Director of Admissions, Ozark Christian College, 1111 North Main Street, Joplin, MO 64801-4804. *Telephone:* 417-624-2518 or 800-299-4622 (toll-free). *Fax:* 417-624-0090. *E-mail:* occadmin@occ.edu. *Web site:* http://www.occ.edu/.

PARK UNIVERSITY

Parkville, Missouri

Park University is a coed, private, comprehensive institution, founded in 1875, offering degrees at the associate, bachelor's, and master's levels. It has an 800-acre campus in Parkville near Kansas City.

Academic Information The faculty has 876 members (12% full-time). The undergraduate student-faculty ratio is 14:1. The library holds 150,503 titles and 591 serial subscriptions. Special programs include academic remediation, services for learning-disabled students, an honors program, advanced placement credit, ESL programs, double majors, independent study, distance learning, self-designed majors, summer session for credit, part-time degree programs, external degree programs, adult/continuing education programs, internships, and arrangement for off-campus study with members of the Kansas City Professional Development Council. The most frequently chosen baccalaureate fields are business/marketing, psychology, security and protective services.

Student Body Statistics The student body totals 13,182, of whom 12,629 are undergraduates (194 freshmen). 48 percent are women and 52 percent are men. Students come from 50 states and territories and 91 other countries. 19 percent are from Missouri. 1.9 percent are international students. 7 percent of the 2006 graduating class went on to graduate and professional schools.

Expenses for 2007–08 *Application fee:* $25. *Comprehensive fee:* $12,746 includes full-time tuition ($7280), mandatory fees ($60), and college room and board ($5406). *College room only:* $3180. *Part-time tuition:* $260 per credit hour. *Part-time mandatory fees:* $15 per term.

Financial Aid Forms of aid include need-based and non-need-based scholarships, athletic grants, and part-time jobs. The priority application deadline for financial aid is April 1.

Freshman Admission Park University requires a high school transcript, a minimum 2.0 high school GPA, and SAT or ACT scores. An essay is recommended. 2 recommendations and an interview are required for some. The application deadline for regular admission is August 1.

Transfer Admission The application deadline for admission is August 1.

Entrance Difficulty Park University assesses its entrance difficulty level as moderately difficult. For the fall 2006 freshman class, 76 percent of the applicants were accepted.

For Further Information Contact Cathy Colapietro, Director of Admissions and Student Financial Services, Park University, 8700 NW River Park Drive, Campus Box 1, Parkville, MO 64152. *Telephone:* 816-584-6728 or 800-745-7275 (toll-free). *Fax:* 816-741-4462. *E-mail:* admissions@mail.park.edu. *Web site:* http://www.park.edu/.

RANKEN TECHNICAL COLLEGE

St. Louis, Missouri

http://www.ranken.edu/

RESEARCH COLLEGE OF NURSING

Kansas City, Missouri

Research College of Nursing is a coed, primarily women's, private, comprehensive unit of Rockhurst University, founded in 1980, offering degrees at the bachelor's and master's levels (bachelor's degree offered jointly with Rockhurst College). It has a 66-acre campus in Kansas City.

Academic Information The faculty has 29 members (90% full-time), 14% with terminal degrees. The undergraduate student-faculty ratio is 7:1. The library holds 150,000 titles and 675 serial subscriptions. Special programs include services for learning-disabled students, an honors program, study abroad, advanced placement credit, accelerated degree programs, double majors, independent study, and summer session for credit.

Student Body Statistics The student body totals 406, of whom 339 are undergraduates (50 freshmen). 91 percent are women and 9 percent are men. Students come from 7 states and territories. 0.9 percent are international students.

Expenses for 2007–08 *Application fee:* $20. *Tuition:* $22,000 full-time.

Financial Aid Forms of aid include need-based and non-need-based scholarships. The priority application deadline for financial aid is March 15.

Freshman Admission Research College of Nursing requires a high school transcript, 1 recommendation, minimum ACT score of 21, SAT or ACT scores, and TOEFL scores for international students. A minimum 2.8 high school GPA and an interview are recommended. The application deadline for regular admission is June 30.

Transfer Admission The application deadline for admission is February 15.

Entrance Difficulty Research College of Nursing assesses its entrance difficulty level as moderately difficult. For the fall 2006 freshman class, 77 percent of the applicants were accepted.

For Further Information Contact Ms. Amy Johnson, Rockhurst College Admission Office, Research College of Nursing, 1100 Rockhurst Road, Kansas City, MO 64110. *Telephone:* 816-501-4100 Ext. 4654 or 800-842-6776 (toll-free). *Fax:* 816-501-4588. *E-mail:* mendenhall@vax2.rockhurst.edu. *Web site:* http://www.researchcollege.edu/.

ROCKHURST UNIVERSITY

Kansas City, Missouri

Rockhurst University is a coed, private, Roman Catholic (Jesuit), comprehensive institution, founded in 1910, offering degrees at the bachelor's, master's, and doctoral levels and postbachelor's certificates. It has a 35-acre campus in Kansas City.

Academic Information The faculty has 226 members (55% full-time), 61% with terminal degrees. The undergraduate student-faculty ratio is 11:1. The library holds 450,000 titles, 278,790 serial subscriptions, and 3,394 audiovisual materials. Special programs include academic remediation, services for learning-disabled students, an honors program, cooperative (work-study) education, study abroad, advanced placement credit, accelerated degree programs, Freshman Honors College, double majors, independent study, distance learning, summer session for credit, part-time degree programs (daytime, evenings, weekends, summer), adult/continuing education programs, internships, and arrangement for off-campus study with Kansas City Area Student Exchange. The most frequently chosen baccalaureate fields are business/marketing, health professions and related sciences, psychology.

Student Body Statistics The student body totals 3,066, of whom 2,222 are undergraduates (396 freshmen). 59 percent are women and 41 percent are men. Students come from 26 states and territories and 10 other countries. 63 percent are from Missouri. 0.9 percent are international students. 26.1 percent of the 2006 graduating class went on to graduate and professional schools.

Expenses for 2007–08 *Application fee:* $25. *Comprehensive fee:* $29,190 includes full-time tuition ($22,000), mandatory fees ($990), and college room and board ($6200). *Part-time tuition:* $733 per credit hour. *Part-time mandatory fees:* $30 per term.

Financial Aid Forms of aid include need-based and non-need-based scholarships, athletic grants, and part-time jobs. The average aided 2006–07 undergraduate received an aid package worth an estimated $20,314. The application deadline for financial aid is June 30 with a priority deadline of March 1.

Freshman Admission Rockhurst University requires a high school transcript, a minimum 2.0 high school GPA, 1 recommendation, SAT or ACT scores, and TOEFL scores for international students. An essay and an interview are required for some. The application deadline for regular admission is June 30.

Transfer Admission The application deadline for admission is rolling.

Entrance Difficulty Rockhurst University assesses its entrance difficulty level as moderately difficult. For the fall 2006 freshman class, 75 percent of the applicants were accepted.

For Further Information Contact Mr. Lane Ramey, Director of Freshman Admissions, Rockhurst University, 1100 Rockhurst Road, Kansas City, MO 64110-2561. *Telephone:* 816-501-4100 or 800-842-6776 (toll-free). *Fax:* 816-501-4142. *E-mail:* admission@rockhurst.edu. *Web site:* http://www.rockhurst.edu/.

ST. LOUIS CHRISTIAN COLLEGE
Florissant, Missouri
http://www.slcconline.edu/

ST. LOUIS COLLEGE OF PHARMACY
St. Louis, Missouri

St. Louis College of Pharmacy is a coed, private, comprehensive institution, founded in 1864, offering degrees at the master's and first professional levels. It has a 5-acre campus in St. Louis.

Academic Information The faculty has 101 members (63% full-time), 93% with terminal degrees. The undergraduate student-faculty ratio is 18:1. The library holds 73,411 titles, 153 serial subscriptions, and 50 audiovisual materials. Special programs include academic remediation, advanced placement credit, summer session for credit, and internships. The most frequently chosen baccalaureate field is health professions and related sciences.

Student Body Statistics The student body totals 1,126. Students come from 1 state or territory and 3 other countries. 54 percent are from Missouri. 0.5 percent are international students.

Expenses for 2007–08 *Application fee:* $50. *Comprehensive fee:* $27,573 includes full-time tuition ($19,425), mandatory fees ($325), and college room and board ($7823). *Part-time tuition:* $800 per credit.

Financial Aid Forms of aid include need-based and non-need-based scholarships and part-time jobs. The average aided 2005–06 undergraduate received an aid package worth $10,199. The priority application deadline for financial aid is March 15.

Freshman Admission St. Louis College of Pharmacy requires an essay, a high school transcript, a minimum 3.0 high school GPA, 2 recommendations, SAT or ACT scores, and TOEFL scores for

international students. An interview is required for some. The application deadline for regular admission is February 1 and for nonresidents it is February 1.

Transfer Admission The application deadline for admission is February 1.

Entrance Difficulty St. Louis College of Pharmacy assesses its entrance difficulty level as moderately difficult; most difficult for transfers. For the fall 2006 freshman class, 55 percent of the applicants were accepted.

For Further Information Contact Laurie Fitzgerald, Administrative Assistant, St. Louis College of Pharmacy, 4588 Parkview Place, St. Louis, MO 63110-1088. *Telephone:* 314-446-8328 or 800-278-5267 (toll-free in-state). *Fax:* 314-446-8310. *E-mail:* lfitzgerald@stlcop.edu. *Web site:* http://www.stlcop.edu/.

SAINT LOUIS UNIVERSITY
St. Louis, Missouri

Saint Louis University is a coed, private, Roman Catholic (Jesuit) university, founded in 1818, offering degrees at the bachelor's, master's, doctoral, and first professional levels and post-master's and postbachelor's certificates. It has a 244-acre campus in St. Louis.

Academic Information The faculty has 1,004 members (61% full-time), 62% with terminal degrees. The undergraduate student-faculty ratio is 12:1. The library holds 2 million titles, 14,395 serial subscriptions, and 174,702 audiovisual materials. Special programs include academic remediation, services for learning-disabled students, an honors program, cooperative (work-study) education, study abroad, advanced placement credit, accelerated degree programs, ESL programs, double majors, independent study, distance learning, self-designed majors, summer session for credit, part-time degree programs (daytime, evenings, weekends, summer), adult/continuing education programs, internships, and arrangement for off-campus study with Washington University in St. Louis. The most frequently chosen baccalaureate fields are business/marketing, health professions and related sciences, psychology.

Student Body Statistics The student body totals 12,034, of whom 7,479 are undergraduates (1,721 freshmen). 58 percent are women and 42 percent are men. Students come from 53 states and territories and 50 other countries. 47 percent are from Missouri. 2 percent are international students. 30.1 percent of the 2006 graduating class went on to graduate and professional schools.

Expenses for 2006–07 *Application fee:* $25. *Comprehensive fee:* $34,878 includes full-time tuition ($26,250), mandatory fees ($398), and college room and board ($8230). *College room only:* $4700. Full-time tuition and fees vary according to location and program. Room and board charges vary according to board plan, housing facility, and location. *Part-time tuition:* $915 per credit hour. *Part-time mandatory fees:* $120 per term. Part-time tuition and fees vary according to location and program.

Financial Aid Forms of aid include need-based and non-need-based scholarships, athletic grants, and part-time jobs. The average aided 2005–06 undergraduate received an aid package worth $19,034.

Freshman Admission Saint Louis University requires an essay, a high school transcript, a minimum 2.5 high school GPA, secondary school report form, SAT or ACT scores, and TOEFL scores for international students. 2 recommendations and an interview are recommended. The application deadline for regular admission is August 1.

Transfer Admission The application deadline for admission is rolling.

Entrance Difficulty Saint Louis University assesses its entrance difficulty level as moderately difficult. For the fall 2006 freshman class, 67 percent of the applicants were accepted.

For Further Information Contact Director, Saint Louis University, 221 North Grand Boulevard, St. Louis, MO 63103-2097. *Telephone:* 314-977-3415 or 800-758-3678 (toll-free out-of-state). *Fax:* 314-977-7136. *E-mail:* admitme@slu.edu. *Web site:* http://www.slu.edu.

SAINT LUKE'S COLLEGE
Kansas City, Missouri

Saint Luke's College is a coed, private, Episcopal, upper-level institution, founded in 1903, offering degrees at the bachelor's level. It has a 3-acre campus in Kansas City.

Academic Information The faculty has 16 members (100% full-time), 19% with terminal degrees. The student-faculty ratio is 8:1. Special programs include cooperative (work-study) education, summer session for credit, and part-time degree programs (daytime, summer).
Student Body Statistics The student body is made up of 109 undergraduates. 92 percent are women and 8 percent are men. Students come from 5 states and territories.
Expenses for 2006–07 *Application fee:* $35. *Tuition:* $8850 full-time, $295 per credit part-time. *Mandatory fees:* $670 full-time, $335 per term part-time.
Financial Aid Forms of aid include need-based and non-need-based scholarships and part-time jobs. The application deadline for financial aid is continuous.
Transfer Admission Saint Luke's College requires a college transcript and a minimum 2.7 college GPA. Standardized test scores are required for some. The application deadline for admission is December 31.
Entrance Difficulty Saint Luke's College assesses its entrance difficulty level as very difficult; moderately difficult for transfers.
For Further Information Contact Assistant Director of Admissions, Saint Luke's College, 8320 Ward Parkway, Suite 300, Kansas City, MO 64114. *Telephone:* 816-932-3372. *Fax:* 816-932-9064. *E-mail:* slc-admissions@saint-lukes.org. *Web site:* http://www.saintlukescollege.edu/.

SANFORD-BROWN COLLEGE
Fenton, Missouri

http://www.sanford-brown.edu/

SOUTHEAST MISSOURI HOSPITAL COLLEGE OF NURSING AND HEALTH SCIENCES
Cape Girardeau, Missouri

Southeast Missouri Hospital College of Nursing and Health Sciences is a coed, private, two-year college, founded in 1928, offering degrees at the associate level.

Academic Information Special programs include study abroad and advanced placement credit.
Student Body Statistics The student body is made up of 221 undergraduates (36 freshmen). 72 percent are women and 28 percent are men. 99 percent are from Missouri. 0.8 percent are international students. 50 percent of the 2006 graduating class went on to four-year colleges.
Expenses for 2007–08 *Application fee:* $40. *Tuition:* $10,192 full-time, $299.75 per credit hour part-time. *Mandatory fees:* $272 full-time, $8 per credit hour part-time.
Freshman Admission Southeast Missouri Hospital College of Nursing and Health Sciences requires a high school transcript, a minimum X high school GPA, recommendations, SAT or ACT scores, and ACT COMPASS. The application deadline for regular admission is rolling.
Entrance Difficulty Southeast Missouri Hospital College of Nursing and Health Sciences assesses its entrance difficulty level as moderately difficult.
For Further Information Contact Tonya L. Buttry, President, Southeast Missouri Hospital College of Nursing and Health Sciences, 2001 William Street, Cape Girardeau, MO 63701. *Telephone:* 573-334-6825. *Fax:* 573-339-7805. *E-mail:* tbuttry@sehosp.org. *Web site:* http://www.southeastmissourihospital.com/college/.

SOUTHEAST MISSOURI STATE UNIVERSITY
Cape Girardeau, Missouri

Southeast Missouri State University is a coed, public, comprehensive unit of Missouri Coordinating Board for Higher Education, founded in 1873, offering degrees at the associate, bachelor's, and master's levels and post-master's certificates. It has a 400-acre campus in Cape Girardeau near St. Louis.

Academic Information The faculty has 579 members (68% full-time), 59% with terminal degrees. The undergraduate student-faculty ratio is 18:1. The library holds 429,108 titles, 32,455 serial subscriptions, and 14,279 audiovisual materials. Special programs include academic remediation, services for learning-disabled students, an honors program, study abroad, advanced placement credit, accelerated degree programs, ESL programs, double majors, independent study, distance learning, self-designed majors, summer session for credit, part-time degree programs (daytime, evenings, summer), adult/continuing education programs, and internships. The most frequently chosen baccalaureate fields are business/marketing, education, liberal arts/general studies.
Student Body Statistics The student body totals 10,477, of whom 8,977 are undergraduates (1,518 freshmen). 60 percent are women and 40 percent are men. Students come from 36 states and territories and 33 other countries. 90 percent are from Missouri. 2 percent are international students.
Expenses for 2006–07 *Application fee:* $20. *State resident tuition:* $5034 full-time, $167.80 per credit hour part-time. *Nonresident tuition:* $9159 full-time, $305.30 per credit hour part-time. *Mandatory fees:* $471 full-time, $15.70 per credit hour part-time. Both full-time and part-time tuition and fees vary according to course load and location. *College room and board:* $5647. *College room only:* $3363. Room and board charges vary according to board plan and housing facility.
Financial Aid Forms of aid include need-based and non-need-based scholarships, athletic grants, and part-time jobs. The average aided 2005–06 undergraduate received an aid package worth $6522. The priority application deadline for financial aid is March 1.
Freshman Admission Southeast Missouri State University requires a high school transcript, a minimum 2.0 high school GPA, SAT or ACT scores, and TOEFL scores for international students.
Entrance Difficulty Southeast Missouri State University assesses its entrance difficulty level as moderately difficult; minimally difficult for transfers. For the fall 2006 freshman class, 69 percent of the applicants were accepted.
For Further Information Contact Dr. Deborah Below, Director of Admissions, Southeast Missouri State University, MS 3550, Cape Girardeau, MO 63701. *Telephone:* 573-651-2590. *Fax:* 573-651-5936. *E-mail:* admissions@semo.edu. *Web site:* http://www.semo.edu/.

SOUTHWEST BAPTIST UNIVERSITY
Bolivar, Missouri

Southwest Baptist University is a coed, private, Southern Baptist, comprehensive institution, founded in 1878, offering degrees at the associate, bachelor's, master's, and doctoral levels and post-master's certificates. It has a 152-acre campus in Bolivar.

Academic Information The faculty has 248 members (42% full-time), 34% with terminal degrees. The undergraduate student-faculty ratio is 14:1. The library holds 180,115 titles, 22,080 serial subscriptions, and 8,028 audiovisual materials. Special programs include academic remediation, services for learning-disabled students, an honors program, cooperative (work-study) education, study abroad, advanced placement credit, double majors, independent study, distance learning, self-designed majors, summer session for credit, part-time degree programs (daytime, evenings, summer), internships, and arrangement for off-campus study with Mountain View Center, Salem Center, Springfield Center. The most frequently chosen baccalaureate fields are education, business/marketing, psychology.
Student Body Statistics The student body totals 3,503, of whom 2,730 are undergraduates (508 freshmen). 66 percent are women and 34 percent

are men. Students come from 45 states and territories and 15 other countries. 70 percent are from Missouri. 0.8 percent are international students. 20 percent of the 2006 graduating class went on to graduate and professional schools.

Expenses for 2006–07 *Application fee:* $30. *Comprehensive fee:* $18,300 includes full-time tuition ($13,300), mandatory fees ($800), and college room and board ($4200). *College room only:* $2200. Room and board charges vary according to board plan and housing facility. *Part-time tuition:* $500 per hour. Part-time tuition varies according to course load.

Financial Aid Forms of aid include need-based and non-need-based scholarships, athletic grants, and part-time jobs. The average aided 2006–07 undergraduate received an aid package worth an estimated $10,617.

Freshman Admission Southwest Baptist University requires a high school transcript, SAT or ACT scores, and TOEFL scores for international students. An essay and an interview are recommended. 3 recommendations are required for some. The application deadline for regular admission is rolling.

Transfer Admission The application deadline for admission is rolling.

Entrance Difficulty Southwest Baptist University assesses its entrance difficulty level as moderately difficult. For the fall 2006 freshman class, 75 percent of the applicants were accepted.

For Further Information Contact Mr. Darren Crowder, Director of Admissions, Southwest Baptist University, 1600 University Avenue, Bolivar, MO 65613-2597. *Telephone:* 417-328-1817 or 800-526-5859 (toll-free). *Fax:* 417-328-1808. *E-mail:* dcrowder@sbuniv.edu. *Web site:* http://www.sbuniv.edu/.

SOUTHWEST MISSOURI STATE UNIVERSITY

See Missouri State University.

STEPHENS COLLEGE
Columbia, Missouri

Stephens College is an undergraduate: women only; graduate: coed, private, comprehensive institution, founded in 1833, offering degrees at the bachelor's and master's levels and postbachelor's certificates. It has an 86-acre campus in Columbia.

Academic Information The faculty has 91 members (48% full-time), 58% with terminal degrees. The undergraduate student-faculty ratio is 12:1. The library holds 125,000 titles, 7,393 serial subscriptions, and 850 audiovisual materials. Special programs include academic remediation, services for learning-disabled students, an honors program, cooperative (work-study) education, study abroad, advanced placement credit, accelerated degree programs, Freshman Honors College, ESL programs, double majors, independent study, distance learning, self-designed majors, part-time degree programs (daytime, weekends), external degree programs, adult/continuing education programs, internships, and arrangement for off-campus study with University of Missouri, Columbia College (MO). The most frequently chosen baccalaureate fields are communications/journalism, business/marketing, visual and performing arts.

Student Body Statistics The student body totals 964, of whom 845 are undergraduates (225 freshmen). 97 percent are women and 3 percent are men. Students come from 41 states and territories and 3 other countries. 45 percent are from Missouri. 0.5 percent are international students.

Expenses for 2006–07 *Application fee:* $25. *Comprehensive fee:* $28,475 includes full-time tuition ($20,500) and college room and board ($7975). *College room only:* $4760. Room and board charges vary according to board plan, gender, and housing facility. *Part-time tuition:* $235 per hour.

Financial Aid Forms of aid include need-based and non-need-based scholarships, athletic grants, and part-time jobs. The average aided 2006–07 undergraduate received an aid package worth an estimated $14,579. The priority application deadline for financial aid is March 15.

Freshman Admission Stephens College requires an essay, a high school transcript, a minimum 2.5 high school GPA, 1 recommendation, SAT or ACT scores, and TOEFL scores for international students. An interview is recommended. The application deadline for regular admission is August 1.

Entrance Difficulty Stephens College assesses its entrance difficulty level as moderately difficult. For the fall 2006 freshman class, 76 percent of the applicants were accepted.

For Further Information Contact Mr. David Adams, Director of Enrollment, Stephens College, 1200 East Broadway, Box 2121, Columbia, MO 65215-0002. *Telephone:* 573-876-7207 or 800-876-7207 (toll-free). *Fax:* 573-876-7237. *E-mail:* apply@stephens.edu. *Web site:* http://www.stephens.edu/.

See page 292 for the College Close-Up.

TRUMAN STATE UNIVERSITY
Kirksville, Missouri

Truman State University is a coed, public, comprehensive institution, founded in 1867, offering degrees at the bachelor's and master's levels. It has a 140-acre campus in Kirksville.

Academic Information The faculty has 363 members (93% full-time), 81% with terminal degrees. The undergraduate student-faculty ratio is 16:1. The library holds 499,536 titles, 3,340 serial subscriptions, and 24,802 audiovisual materials. Special programs include services for learning-disabled students, an honors program, study abroad, advanced placement credit, double majors, self-designed majors, summer session for credit, part-time degree programs (daytime, summer), internships, and arrangement for off-campus study with Gulf Coast Research Laboratory, Reis Biological Station. The most frequently chosen baccalaureate fields are business/marketing, biological/life sciences, social sciences.

Student Body Statistics The student body totals 5,762, of whom 5,524 are undergraduates (1,367 freshmen). 58 percent are women and 42 percent are men. Students come from 42 states and territories and 42 other countries. 78 percent are from Missouri. 3.5 percent are international students. 54.1 percent of the 2006 graduating class went on to graduate and professional schools.

Expenses for 2006–07 *Application fee:* $0. *State resident tuition:* $5970 full-time, $248 per credit part-time. *Nonresident tuition:* $10,400 full-time, $433 per credit part-time. *Mandatory fees:* $372 full-time. Part-time tuition varies according to course load. *College room and board:* $5570. Room and board charges vary according to housing facility.

Financial Aid Forms of aid include need-based and non-need-based scholarships, athletic grants, and part-time jobs. The average aided 2005–06 undergraduate received an aid package worth $6056. The priority application deadline for financial aid is April 1.

Freshman Admission Truman State University requires an essay, a high school transcript, SAT or ACT scores, and TOEFL scores for international students. A minimum 3.0 high school GPA, an interview, and ACT scores are recommended. The application deadline for regular admission is March 1 and for early action it is November 15.

Transfer Admission The application deadline for admission is rolling.

Entrance Difficulty Truman State University assesses its entrance difficulty level as moderately difficult. For the fall 2006 freshman class, 81 percent of the applicants were accepted.

For Further Information Contact Mr. Brad Chambers, Co-Director of Admissions, Truman State University, 205 McClain Hall, 100 East Normal Street, Kirksville, MO 63501-4221. *Telephone:* 660-785-4114 or 800-892-7792 (toll-free in-state). *Fax:* 660-785-7456. *E-mail:* admissions@truman.edu. *Web site:* http://www.truman.edu/.

See page 296 for the College Close-Up.

UNIVERSITY OF CENTRAL MISSOURI
Warrensburg, Missouri

University of Central Missouri is a coed, public, comprehensive institution, founded in 1871, offering degrees at the associate, bachelor's, and master's levels and post-master's and postbachelor's certificates. It has a 1,561-acre campus in Warrensburg near Kansas City.

Academic Information The faculty has 596 members (75% full-time), 55% with terminal degrees. The undergraduate student-faculty ratio is

University of Central Missouri (continued)

19:1. The library holds 2 million titles, 1,703 serial subscriptions, and 18,434 audiovisual materials. Special programs include academic remediation, services for learning-disabled students, an honors program, cooperative (work-study) education, study abroad, advanced placement credit, ESL programs, double majors, distance learning, self-designed majors, summer session for credit, part-time degree programs (daytime, evenings, weekends, summer), adult/continuing education programs, internships, and arrangement for off-campus study. The most frequently chosen baccalaureate fields are business/marketing, education, engineering technologies.

Student Body Statistics The student body totals 10,711, of whom 8,970 are undergraduates (1,592 freshmen). 56 percent are women and 44 percent are men. Students come from 48 states and territories and 53 other countries. 85 percent are from Missouri. 2 percent are international students. 14 percent of the 2006 graduating class went on to graduate and professional schools.

Expenses for 2006–07 *Application fee:* $30. *State resident tuition:* $5835 full-time, $195.50 per credit part-time. *Nonresident tuition:* $11,250 full-time, $375 per credit part-time. *Mandatory fees:* $14 per credit part-time. Full-time tuition varies according to course load and location. *College room and board:* $5109. *College room only:* $4606. Room and board charges vary according to board plan and housing facility.

Financial Aid Forms of aid include need-based and non-need-based scholarships, athletic grants, and part-time jobs. The average aided 2005–06 undergraduate received an aid package worth $7341. The priority application deadline for financial aid is April 1.

Freshman Admission University of Central Missouri requires a high school transcript, rank in upper two-thirds of high school class, minimum ACT score of 20, ACT scores, and TOEFL scores for international students. Recommendations are required for some. The application deadline for regular admission is rolling.

Transfer Admission The application deadline for admission is rolling.

Entrance Difficulty University of Central Missouri assesses its entrance difficulty level as moderately difficult; very difficult for business, teacher education, nursing programs. For the fall 2006 freshman class, 84 percent of the applicants were accepted.

For Further Information Contact Mr. Paul Orschlen, Chief Admission Officer, University of Central Missouri, 1401 Ward Edwards, Warrensburg, MO 64093. *Telephone:* 660-543-4170 or 800-729-2678 (toll-free in-state). *Fax:* 660-543-8517. *E-mail:* admit@cmsuvmb.cmsu.edu. *Web site:* http://www.ucmo.edu/.

UNIVERSITY OF MISSOURI–COLUMBIA

Columbia, Missouri

University of Missouri–Columbia is a coed, public unit of University of Missouri System, founded in 1839, offering degrees at the bachelor's, master's, doctoral, and first professional levels and post-master's and first professional certificates. It has a 1,358-acre campus in Columbia.

Academic Information The faculty has 1,126 members (94% full-time), 92% with terminal degrees. The undergraduate student-faculty ratio is 18:1. The library holds 3 million titles, 36,244 serial subscriptions, and 4,870 audiovisual materials. Special programs include services for learning-disabled students, an honors program, cooperative (work-study) education, study abroad, advanced placement credit, accelerated degree programs, Freshman Honors College, ESL programs, double majors, independent study, distance learning, self-designed majors, summer session for credit, part-time degree programs (daytime, evenings, summer), external degree programs, adult/continuing education programs, internships, and arrangement for off-campus study with Mid-Missouri Associated Colleges and Universities, National Student Exchange. The most frequently chosen baccalaureate fields are business/marketing, communications/journalism, engineering.

Student Body Statistics The student body totals 28,253, of whom 21,551 are undergraduates (4,838 freshmen). 51 percent are women and 49 percent are men. Students come from 53 states and territories and 92 other countries. 86 percent are from Missouri. 1.1 percent are international students.

Expenses for 2006–07 *Application fee:* $45. *State resident tuition:* $6364 full-time, $227.30 per credit hour part-time. *Nonresident tuition:* $15,946 full-time, $569.50 per credit hour part-time. *Mandatory fees:* $944 full-time, $33.60 per credit hour part-time. Both full-time and part-time tuition and fees vary according to course load, program, and reciprocity agreements. *College room and board:* $6977. *College room only:* $3837. Room and board charges vary according to board plan and housing facility.

Financial Aid Forms of aid include need-based and non-need-based scholarships, athletic grants, and part-time jobs. The average aided 2006–07 undergraduate received an aid package worth an estimated $11,452. The priority application deadline for financial aid is March 1.

Freshman Admission University of Missouri–Columbia requires a high school transcript, specific high school curriculum, SAT or ACT scores, and TOEFL scores for international students. ACT scores are recommended. The application deadline for regular admission is rolling.

Transfer Admission The application deadline for admission is rolling.

Entrance Difficulty University of Missouri–Columbia assesses its entrance difficulty level as moderately difficult. For the fall 2006 freshman class, 78 percent of the applicants were accepted.

For Further Information Contact Ms. Barbara Rupp, Director of Admissions, University of Missouri–Columbia, 230 Jesse Hall, Columbia, MO 65211. *Telephone:* 573-882-7786 or 800-225-6075 (toll-free in-state). *Fax:* 573-882-7887. *E-mail:* mu4u@missouri.edu. *Web site:* http://www.missouri.edu/.

UNIVERSITY OF MISSOURI–KANSAS CITY

Kansas City, Missouri

University of Missouri–Kansas City is a coed, public unit of University of Missouri System, founded in 1929, offering degrees at the bachelor's, master's, doctoral, and first professional levels and post-master's and first professional certificates. It has a 191-acre campus in Kansas City.

Academic Information The faculty has 1,100 members (60% full-time), 63% with terminal degrees. The undergraduate student-faculty ratio is 13:1. The library holds 1 million titles, 25,022 serial subscriptions, and 421,713 audiovisual materials. Special programs include services for learning-disabled students, an honors program, cooperative (work-study) education, study abroad, advanced placement credit, accelerated degree programs, ESL programs, double majors, independent study, distance learning, self-designed majors, summer session for credit, part-time degree programs (daytime, evenings, weekends, summer), adult/continuing education programs, internships, and arrangement for off-campus study with other campuses of the University of Missouri System. The most frequently chosen baccalaureate fields are business/marketing, education, liberal arts/general studies.

Student Body Statistics The student body totals 14,213, of whom 9,383 are undergraduates (956 freshmen). 59 percent are women and 41 percent are men. Students come from 47 states and territories and 63 other countries. 74 percent are from Missouri. 2.6 percent are international students.

Expenses for 2006–07 *Application fee:* $35. *State resident tuition:* $6819 full-time, $227.30 per credit hour part-time. *Nonresident tuition:* $17,085 full-time, $569.50 per credit hour part-time. *Mandatory fees:* $773 full-time, $29.72 per credit hour part-time. Both full-time and part-time tuition and fees vary according to course load, program, and student level. *College room and board:* $6823. Room and board charges vary according to board plan and housing facility.

Financial Aid Forms of aid include need-based and non-need-based scholarships, athletic grants, and part-time jobs. The average aided 2006–07 undergraduate received an aid package worth an estimated $9867. The priority application deadline for financial aid is March 1.

Freshman Admission University of Missouri–Kansas City requires a high school transcript, SAT or ACT scores, and TOEFL scores for international students. The application deadline for regular admission is rolling.

Transfer Admission The application deadline for admission is rolling.

Entrance Difficulty University of Missouri–Kansas City assesses its entrance difficulty level as moderately difficult. For the fall 2006 freshman class, 71 percent of the applicants were accepted.

For Further Information Contact Ms. Jennifer DeHaemers, Director of Admissions, University of Missouri–Kansas City, Office of Admissions, 5100 Rockhill Road, Kansas City, MO 64110-2499. *Telephone:* 816-235-1111 or 800-775-8652 (toll-free out-of-state). *Fax:* 816-235-5544. *E-mail:* admit@umkc.edu. *Web site:* http://www.umkc.edu/.

UNIVERSITY OF MISSOURI–ROLLA
Rolla, Missouri

University of Missouri–Rolla is a coed, public unit of University of Missouri System, founded in 1870, offering degrees at the bachelor's, master's, and doctoral levels and postbachelor's certificates. It has a 284-acre campus in Rolla.

Academic Information The faculty has 418 members (80% full-time), 78% with terminal degrees. The undergraduate student-faculty ratio is 14:1. The library holds 255,768 titles, 1,495 serial subscriptions, and 6,353 audiovisual materials. Special programs include academic remediation, services for learning-disabled students, an honors program, cooperative (work-study) education, study abroad, advanced placement credit, accelerated degree programs, Freshman Honors College, ESL programs, double majors, independent study, distance learning, summer session for credit, part-time degree programs, adult/continuing education programs, internships, and arrangement for off-campus study with University of Missouri–Columbia.

Student Body Statistics The student body totals 5,858, of whom 4,515 are undergraduates (962 freshmen). 23 percent are women and 77 percent are men. Students come from 47 states and territories and 25 other countries. 80 percent are from Missouri. 2.6 percent are international students. 17 percent of the 2006 graduating class went on to graduate and professional schools.

Expenses for 2006–07 *Application fee:* $35. *State resident tuition:* $6819 full-time, $227.30 per credit hour part-time. *Nonresident tuition:* $17,085 full-time, $569.50 per credit hour part-time. *Mandatory fees:* $1070 full-time, $313.36 per term part-time. Both full-time and part-time tuition and fees vary according to course load, degree level, and program. *College room and board:* $6185. Room and board charges vary according to board plan, housing facility, and location. Tuition and fees for Kansas, Michigan, Minnesota, Nebraska, North Dakota, and Wisconsin students: $10,998.

Financial Aid Forms of aid include need-based and non-need-based scholarships and part-time jobs. The priority application deadline for financial aid is March 1.

Freshman Admission University of Missouri–Rolla requires a high school transcript and SAT or ACT scores. TOEFL scores for international students are recommended. The application deadline for regular admission is July 1.

Transfer Admission The application deadline for admission is July 1.

Entrance Difficulty University of Missouri–Rolla assesses its entrance difficulty level as very difficult; moderately difficult for transfers. For the fall 2006 freshman class, 90 percent of the applicants were accepted.

For Further Information Contact Ms. Lynn Stichnote, Director of Admissions, University of Missouri–Rolla, 106 Parker Hall, Rolla, MO 65409. *Telephone:* 573-341-4164 or 800-522-0938 (toll-free). *Fax:* 573-341-4082. *E-mail:* admissions@umr.edu. *Web site:* http://www.umr.edu/.

UNIVERSITY OF MISSOURI–ST. LOUIS
St. Louis, Missouri

University of Missouri–St. Louis is a coed, public unit of University of Missouri System, founded in 1963, offering degrees at the bachelor's, master's, doctoral, and first professional levels and postbachelor's certificates. It has a 350-acre campus in St. Louis.

Academic Information The faculty has 811 members (52% full-time), 54% with terminal degrees. The undergraduate student-faculty ratio is 17:1. The library holds 1 million titles, 3,174 serial subscriptions, and 3,902 audiovisual materials. Special programs include services for learning-disabled students, an honors program, cooperative (work-study) education, study abroad, advanced placement credit, accelerated degree programs, Freshman Honors College, ESL programs, double majors, independent study, distance learning, self-designed majors, summer session for credit, part-time degree programs (daytime, evenings, weekends, summer), adult/continuing education programs, internships, and arrangement for off-campus study with Southern Illinois University, Saint Louis University, Washington University in St. Louis, St. Charles Community College, Mineral Area Community College, East Central Community College, Jefferson Community College. The most frequently chosen baccalaureate fields are business/marketing, education, social sciences.

Student Body Statistics The student body totals 15,540, of whom 12,470 are undergraduates (526 freshmen). 60 percent are women and 40 percent are men. Students come from 42 states and territories and 58 other countries. 94 percent are from Missouri. 1.9 percent are international students. 15 percent of the 2006 graduating class went on to graduate and professional schools.

Expenses for 2006–07 *Application fee:* $35. *State resident tuition:* $6819 full-time, $227.30 per credit hour part-time. *Nonresident tuition:* $17,085 full-time, $569.50 per credit hour part-time. *Mandatory fees:* $1149 full-time, $44.04 per credit hour part-time. Both full-time and part-time tuition and fees vary according to course load, program, and reciprocity agreements. *College room and board:* $7178. *College room only:* $5298. Room and board charges vary according to board plan and housing facility.

Financial Aid Forms of aid include need-based and non-need-based scholarships, athletic grants, and part-time jobs. The average aided 2006–07 undergraduate received an aid package worth an estimated $10,458. The priority application deadline for financial aid is April 1.

Freshman Admission University of Missouri–St. Louis requires a high school transcript, CBHE Core Requirements, SAT or ACT scores, and TOEFL scores for international students. The application deadline for regular admission is rolling and for nonresidents it is rolling.

Transfer Admission The application deadline for admission is rolling.

Entrance Difficulty University of Missouri–St. Louis assesses its entrance difficulty level as moderately difficult. For the fall 2006 freshman class, 52 percent of the applicants were accepted.

For Further Information Contact Mr. Dennis Saunders, Associate Director of Admissions, University of Missouri–St. Louis, 351 Millennium Student Center, One University Boulevard, St. Louis, MO 63121-4400. *Telephone:* 314-516-5451 or 888-GO2-UMSL (toll-free in-state). *Fax:* 314-516-5310. *E-mail:* admissions@umsl.edu. *Web site:* http://www.umsl.edu/.

UNIVERSITY OF PHOENIX–KANSAS CITY CAMPUS
Kansas City, Missouri

University of Phoenix–Kansas City Campus is a coed, proprietary, comprehensive institution, founded in 2002, offering degrees at the bachelor's and master's levels.

Academic Information The faculty has 241 members (6% full-time), 13% with terminal degrees. The undergraduate student-faculty ratio is 8:1. The library holds 1,759 titles and 692 serial subscriptions. Special programs include services for learning-disabled students, advanced placement credit, accelerated degree programs, independent study, distance learning, external degree programs, and adult/continuing education programs. The most frequently chosen baccalaureate fields are business/marketing, computer and information sciences.

Student Body Statistics The student body totals 1,201, of whom 928 are undergraduates (33 freshmen). 61 percent are women and 39 percent are men. 12.4 percent are international students.

Expenses for 2006–07 *Application fee:* $45. *Tuition:* $11,064 full-time, $373 per credit part-time.

Financial Aid Forms of aid include need-based and non-need-based scholarships. The average aided 2005–06 undergraduate received an aid package worth $4111. The application deadline for financial aid is continuous.

Freshman Admission University of Phoenix–Kansas City Campus requires 1 recommendation and TOEFL scores for international students. A high school transcript is required for some. The application deadline for regular admission is rolling.

University of Phoenix–Kansas City Campus (continued)

Transfer Admission The application deadline for admission is rolling.

Entrance Difficulty University of Phoenix–Kansas City Campus has an open admission policy.

For Further Information Contact Ms. Beth Barilla, Associate Vice President, Student Admissions and Services, University of Phoenix–Kansas City Campus, 4615 East Elwood Street, Mail Stop AA-K101, Phoenix, AZ 85040-1958. *Telephone:* 480-317-6000, 800-776-4867 (toll-free in-state), or 800-228-7240 (toll-free out-of-state). *Fax:* 480-894-1758. *E-mail:* beth. barilla@phoenix.edu. *Web site:* http://www.phoenix.edu/.

UNIVERSITY OF PHOENIX–ST. LOUIS CAMPUS

St. Louis, Missouri

University of Phoenix–St. Louis Campus is a coed, proprietary, comprehensive institution, founded in 2000, offering degrees at the bachelor's and master's levels.

Academic Information The faculty has 203 members (6% full-time), 18% with terminal degrees. The undergraduate student-faculty ratio is 7:1. The library holds 1,759 titles and 692 serial subscriptions. Special programs include services for learning-disabled students, advanced placement credit, accelerated degree programs, independent study, distance learning, external degree programs, and adult/continuing education programs. The most frequently chosen baccalaureate fields are business/marketing, computer and information sciences.

Student Body Statistics The student body totals 964, of whom 834 are undergraduates (26 freshmen). 59 percent are women and 41 percent are men. 6.4 percent are international students.

Expenses for 2006–07 *Application fee:* $45. *Tuition:* $11,910 full-time.

Financial Aid Forms of aid include need-based and non-need-based scholarships. The average aided 2005–06 undergraduate received an aid package worth $3888. The application deadline for financial aid is continuous.

Freshman Admission University of Phoenix–St. Louis Campus requires 1 recommendation and TOEFL scores for international students. A high school transcript is required for some. The application deadline for regular admission is rolling.

Transfer Admission The application deadline for admission is rolling.

Entrance Difficulty University of Phoenix–St. Louis Campus has an open admission policy.

For Further Information Contact Ms. Beth Barilla, Associate Vice President, Student Admissions and Services, University of Phoenix–St. Louis Campus, 4615 East Elwood Street, Mail Stop AA-K101, Phoenix, AZ 85040-1958. *Telephone:* 480-317-6000, 800-776-4867 (toll-free in-state), or 800-228-7240 (toll-free out-of-state). *Fax:* 480-894-1758. *E-mail:* beth. barilla@phoenix.edu. *Web site:* http://www.phoenix.edu/.

UNIVERSITY OF PHOENIX–SPRINGFIELD CAMPUS

Springfield, Missouri

University of Phoenix–Springfield Campus is a coed, proprietary, comprehensive institution, offering degrees at the bachelor's and master's levels.

Academic Information The faculty has 35 members (9% full-time), 9% with terminal degrees. The undergraduate student-faculty ratio is 5:1. The library holds 1,759 titles and 692 serial subscriptions. Special programs include services for learning-disabled students, advanced placement credit, accelerated degree programs, independent study, distance learning, external degree programs, and adult/continuing education programs.

Student Body Statistics The student body totals 305, of whom 265 are undergraduates (12 freshmen). 55 percent are women and 45 percent are men. 5.3 percent are international students.

Expenses for 2006–07 *Application fee:* $45. *Tuition:* $9750 full-time, $325 per credit part-time.

Financial Aid Forms of aid include need-based and non-need-based scholarships. The average aided 2005–06 undergraduate received an aid package worth $4044. The application deadline for financial aid is continuous.

Freshman Admission University of Phoenix–Springfield Campus requires 1 recommendation. A high school transcript is required for some. The application deadline for regular admission is rolling.

Transfer Admission The application deadline for admission is rolling.

Entrance Difficulty University of Phoenix–Springfield Campus has an open admission policy.

For Further Information Contact Ms. Beth Barilla, Associate Vice President, Student Admissions and Services, University of Phoenix–Springfield Campus, 4615 East Elwood Street, Phoenix, AZ 58040-1958. *Telephone:* 480-317-6000, 800-776-4867 (toll-free in-state), or 800-228-7240 (toll-free out-of-state). *Fax:* 480-894-1758. *E-mail:* beth.barilla@phoenix. edu. *Web site:* http://www.phoenix.edu/.

VATTEROTT COLLEGE

St. Ann, Missouri

http://www.vatterott-college.edu/

VATTEROTT COLLEGE

Sunset Hills, Missouri

http://www.vatterott-college.edu/

WASHINGTON UNIVERSITY IN ST. LOUIS

St. Louis, Missouri

Washington University in St. Louis is a coed, private university, founded in 1853, offering degrees at the bachelor's, master's, doctoral, and first professional levels and postbachelor's certificates. It has a 169-acre campus in St. Louis.

Academic Information The faculty has 1,076 members (80% full-time), 78% with terminal degrees. The undergraduate student-faculty ratio is 7:1. The library holds 2 million titles, 44,806 serial subscriptions, and 83,027 audiovisual materials. Special programs include services for learning-disabled students, cooperative (work-study) education, study abroad, advanced placement credit, accelerated degree programs, ESL programs, double majors, independent study, self-designed majors, summer session for credit, part-time degree programs, adult/continuing education programs, internships, and arrangement for off-campus study with Consortium on Financing Higher Education. The most frequently chosen baccalaureate fields are engineering, psychology, social sciences.

Student Body Statistics The student body totals 13,355, of whom 7,386 are undergraduates (1,470 freshmen). 52 percent are women and 48 percent are men. Students come from 54 states and territories and 59 other countries. 11 percent are from Missouri. 4.2 percent are international students. 33 percent of the 2006 graduating class went on to graduate and professional schools.

Expenses for 2007–08 *Application fee:* $55. *Comprehensive fee:* $46,776 includes full-time tuition ($34,500), mandatory fees ($1024), and college room and board ($11,252). *College room only:* $7102.

Financial Aid Forms of aid include need-based and non-need-based scholarships and part-time jobs. The average aided 2006–07 undergraduate received an aid package worth an estimated $27,310. The application deadline for financial aid is February 15.

Freshman Admission Washington University in St. Louis requires an essay, a high school transcript, 2 recommendations, SAT or ACT scores, and TOEFL scores for international students. A minimum 3.0 high school GPA and portfolio for art and architecture programs are recommended. The application deadline for regular admission is January 15 and for early decision plan 1 it is November 15.

Transfer Admission The application deadline for admission is April 15.

Entrance Difficulty Washington University in St. Louis assesses its entrance difficulty level as most difficult. For the fall 2006 freshman class, 21 percent of the applicants were accepted.

For Further Information Contact Ms. Nanette Tarbouni, Director of Admissions, Washington University in St. Louis, Campus Box 1089, One Brookings Drive, St. Louis, MO 63130-4899. *Telephone:* 314-935-6000 or 800-638-0700 (toll-free). *Fax:* 314-935-4290. *E-mail:* admissions@wustl.edu. *Web site:* http://www.wustl.edu/.

WEBSTER UNIVERSITY
St. Louis, Missouri

Webster University is a coed, private, comprehensive institution, founded in 1915, offering degrees at the bachelor's, master's, and doctoral levels and post-master's and postbachelor's certificates. It has a 47-acre campus in St. Louis.

Academic Information The faculty has 749 members (22% full-time), 38% with terminal degrees. The undergraduate student-faculty ratio is 13:1. The library holds 283,742 titles and 2,429 serial subscriptions. Special programs include academic remediation, services for learning-disabled students, cooperative (work-study) education, study abroad, advanced placement credit, accelerated degree programs, ESL programs, double majors, independent study, distance learning, self-designed majors, summer session for credit, part-time degree programs (daytime, evenings, summer), adult/continuing education programs, internships, and arrangement for off-campus study with Fontbonne College, Lindenwood College, Maryville University of Saint Louis, Eden Theological Seminary, Missouri Baptist College. The most frequently chosen baccalaureate fields are business/marketing, communications/journalism, visual and performing arts.

Student Body Statistics The student body totals 7,840, of whom 3,567 are undergraduates (444 freshmen). 59 percent are women and 41 percent are men. Students come from 39 states and territories and 38 other countries. 77 percent are from Missouri. 3.1 percent are international students. 20 percent of the 2006 graduating class went on to graduate and professional schools.

Expenses for 2006–07 *Application fee:* $25. *Comprehensive fee:* $25,643 includes full-time tuition ($18,240) and college room and board ($7403). *College room only:* $3944. Full-time tuition varies according to program. Room and board charges vary according to board plan and housing facility. *Part-time tuition:* $465 per credit hour. Part-time tuition varies according to location.

Financial Aid Forms of aid include need-based and non-need-based scholarships and part-time jobs. The average aided 2006–07 undergraduate received an aid package worth an estimated $17,988. The priority application deadline for financial aid is April 1.

Freshman Admission Webster University requires an essay, a high school transcript, a minimum 2.5 high school GPA, 1 recommendation, SAT or ACT scores, and TOEFL scores for international students. A minimum 3.0 high school GPA and an interview are recommended. A minimum 3.0 high school GPA and audition are required for some. The application deadline for regular admission is June 1.

Transfer Admission The application deadline for admission is August 1.

Entrance Difficulty Webster University assesses its entrance difficulty level as moderately difficult. For the fall 2006 freshman class, 57 percent of the applicants are accepted.

For Further Information Contact Mr. Andrew Laue, Associate Director of Undergraduate Admission, Webster University, 470 East Lockwood Avenue, St. Louis, MO 63119-3194. *Telephone:* 314-961-2660 or 800-75-ENROL (toll-free). *Fax:* 314-968-7115. *E-mail:* admit@webster.edu. *Web site:* http://www.webster.edu/.

WENTWORTH MILITARY ACADEMY AND JUNIOR COLLEGE
Lexington, Missouri

Wentworth Military Academy and Junior College is a coed, private, two-year college, founded in 1880, offering degrees at the associate level. It has a 130-acre campus in Lexington near Kansas City.

Expenses for 2006–07 *Application fee:* $100. *One-time mandatory fee:* $25. *Tuition:* $3480 full-time, $145 per hour part-time.

For Further Information Contact Dr. Roger Hamilton, Vice President for Academic Affairs, Wentworth Military Academy and Junior College, 1880 Washington Avenue, Lexington, MO 64067. *Telephone:* 660-259-2221. *Fax:* 660-259-2677. *E-mail:* admissions@wma1880.org. *Web site:* http://www.wma1880.org/.

WESTMINSTER COLLEGE
Fulton, Missouri

Westminster College is a coed, private, four-year college, founded in 1851, affiliated with the Presbyterian Church, offering degrees at the bachelor's level. It has an 80-acre campus in Fulton.

Academic Information The faculty has 82 members (71% full-time), 61% with terminal degrees. The student-faculty ratio is 13:1. The library holds 126,801 titles, 16,353 serial subscriptions, and 1,786 audiovisual materials. Special programs include academic remediation, services for learning-disabled students, an honors program, cooperative (work-study) education, study abroad, advanced placement credit, double majors, independent study, self-designed majors, summer session for credit, part-time degree programs (daytime), internships, and arrangement for off-campus study with Chicago Urban Studies Semester, American University. The most frequently chosen baccalaureate fields are business/marketing, education, social sciences.

Student Body Statistics The student body is made up of 953 undergraduates (278 freshmen). 43 percent are women and 57 percent are men. Students come from 26 states and territories and 50 other countries. 65 percent are from Missouri. 11.4 percent are international students. 30 percent of the 2006 graduating class went on to graduate and professional schools.

Expenses for 2006–07 *Application fee:* $0. *Comprehensive fee:* $21,170 includes full-time tuition ($14,600), mandatory fees ($430), and college room and board ($6140). *College room only:* $3170. Room and board charges vary according to board plan and housing facility. *Part-time tuition:* $750 per credit hour.

Financial Aid Forms of aid include need-based and non-need-based scholarships and part-time jobs. The average aided 2006–07 undergraduate received an aid package worth an estimated $14,264.

Freshman Admission Westminster College requires a high school transcript, 1 recommendation, minimum ACT score of 21 or minimum SAT score of 970, and SAT or ACT scores. An essay and a minimum 2.5 high school GPA are recommended. An interview is required for some.

Entrance Difficulty Westminster College assesses its entrance difficulty level as moderately difficult. For the fall 2006 freshman class, 79 percent of the applicants were accepted.

For Further Information Contact Dr. Patrick Kirby, Dean of Enrollment Services, Westminster College, 501 Westminster Avenue, Fulton, MO 65251-1299. *Telephone:* 573-592-5251 or 800-475-3361 (toll-free). *Fax:* 573-592-5255. *E-mail:* admissions@westminster-mo.edu. *Web site:* http://www.westminster-mo.edu/.

WILLIAM JEWELL COLLEGE
Liberty, Missouri

William Jewell College is a coed, private, Baptist, four-year college, founded in 1849, offering degrees at the bachelor's level (also offers evening program with significant enrollment not reflected in profile). It has a 200-acre campus in Liberty near Kansas City.

Academic Information The faculty has 154 members (50% full-time). The student-faculty ratio is 15:1. The library holds 255,750 titles, 527 serial subscriptions, and 20,010 audiovisual materials. Special programs include academic remediation, services for learning-disabled students, an honors program, cooperative (work-study) education, study abroad, advanced placement credit, double majors, independent study, self-designed majors, summer session for credit, part-time degree programs (daytime, evenings, weekends, summer), adult/continuing education programs,

William Jewell College *(continued)*

internships, and arrangement for off-campus study. The most frequently chosen baccalaureate fields are business/marketing, health professions and related sciences, psychology.

Student Body Statistics The student body is made up of 1,404 undergraduates (248 freshmen). 62 percent are women and 38 percent are men. Students come from 29 states and territories and 4 other countries. 74 percent are from Missouri. 0.6 percent are international students. 27 percent of the 2006 graduating class went on to graduate and professional schools.

Expenses for 2007–08 *Application fee:* $25. *Comprehensive fee:* $27,240 includes full-time tuition ($21,400) and college room and board ($5840). *College room only:* $2459. *Part-time tuition:* $700 per credit hour.

Financial Aid Forms of aid include need-based and non-need-based scholarships, athletic grants, and part-time jobs. The average aided 2006–07 undergraduate received an aid package worth an estimated $15,639. The priority application deadline for financial aid is March 1.

Freshman Admission William Jewell College requires an essay, a high school transcript, SAT or ACT scores, and TOEFL scores for international students. 2 recommendations and an interview are recommended. An interview is required for some. The application deadline for regular admission is August 15.

Transfer Admission The application deadline for admission is rolling.

Entrance Difficulty William Jewell College assesses its entrance difficulty level as moderately difficult. For the fall 2006 freshman class, 63 percent of the applicants were accepted.

For Further Information Contact Dr. Edwin Harris, Vice President for Enrollment, William Jewell College, 500 College Hill, Liberty, MO 64068. *Telephone:* 816-781-7700 Ext. 5570 or 888-2JEWELL (toll-free). *Fax:* 816-415-5040. *E-mail:* admission@william.jewell.edu. *Web site:* http://www.jewell.edu/.

WILLIAM WOODS UNIVERSITY
Fulton, Missouri

William Woods University is a coed, private, comprehensive institution, founded in 1870, affiliated with the Christian Church (Disciples of Christ), offering degrees at the associate, bachelor's, and master's levels and post-master's certificates. It has a 170-acre campus in Fulton near St. Louis.

Academic Information The faculty has 274 members (32% full-time), 22% with terminal degrees. The undergraduate student-faculty ratio is 14:1. The library holds 139,986 titles and 11,713 serial subscriptions. Special programs include academic remediation, an honors program, study abroad, advanced placement credit, accelerated degree programs, double majors, independent study, self-designed majors, summer session for credit, part-time degree programs (evenings, weekends), adult/continuing education programs, internships, and arrangement for off-campus study with University of Missouri–Columbia, Westminster College (MO), Stephens College, Lincoln University (MO). The most frequently chosen baccalaureate fields are business/marketing, agriculture, computer and information sciences.

Student Body Statistics The student body totals 2,893, of whom 1,162 are undergraduates (196 freshmen). 75 percent are women and 25 percent are men. Students come from 42 states and territories and 10 other countries. 73 percent are from Missouri. 2 percent are international students.

Expenses for 2006–07 *Application fee:* $25. *Comprehensive fee:* $21,670 includes full-time tuition ($15,150), mandatory fees ($420), and college room and board ($6100). Full-time tuition and fees vary according to program. Room and board charges vary according to board plan and housing facility. *Part-time tuition:* $505 per credit. *Part-time mandatory fees:* $15 per term. Part-time tuition and fees vary according to course load and program.

Financial Aid Forms of aid include need-based and non-need-based scholarships, athletic grants, and part-time jobs. The average aided 2005–06 undergraduate received an aid package worth $12,617. The application deadline for financial aid is continuous.

Freshman Admission William Woods University requires a high school transcript, a minimum 2.5 high school GPA, 16 hours college prep, SAT

or ACT scores, and TOEFL scores for international students. An interview is recommended. An essay and 2 recommendations are required for some. The application deadline for regular admission is rolling and for nonresidents it is rolling.

Transfer Admission The application deadline for admission is rolling.

Entrance Difficulty William Woods University assesses its entrance difficulty level as moderately difficult. For the fall 2006 freshman class, 81 percent of the applicants were accepted.

For Further Information Contact Ms. Sharon Horn, Admissions Data Analyst, William Woods University, One University Avenue, Fulton, MO 65251. *Telephone:* 573-592-4221 or 800-995-3159 Ext. 4221 (toll-free). *Fax:* 573-592-1146. *E-mail:* admissions@williamwoods.edu. *Web site:* http://www.williamwoods.edu/.

Nebraska

BELLEVUE UNIVERSITY
Bellevue, Nebraska

Bellevue University is a coed, private, comprehensive institution, founded in 1965, offering degrees at the bachelor's and master's levels. It has a 50-acre campus in Bellevue near Omaha.

Academic Information The faculty has 370 members (21% full-time). The undergraduate student-faculty ratio is 18:1. The library holds 100,904 titles and 12,468 serial subscriptions. Special programs include academic remediation, services for learning-disabled students, cooperative (work-study) education, advanced placement credit, accelerated degree programs, ESL programs, double majors, independent study, distance learning, summer session for credit, part-time degree programs, external degree programs, adult/continuing education programs, and internships. The most frequently chosen baccalaureate fields are business/marketing, health professions and related sciences, security and protective services.

Student Body Statistics The student body totals 6,808, of whom 4,900 are undergraduates (143 freshmen). 46 percent are women and 54 percent are men. Students come from 42 states and territories and 66 other countries. 5.9 percent are international students.

Expenses for 2007–08 *Application fee:* $50. *Tuition:* $5700 full-time, $190 per credit hour part-time. *Mandatory fees:* $95 full-time.

Financial Aid Forms of aid include need-based and non-need-based scholarships, athletic grants, and part-time jobs. The application deadline for financial aid is continuous.

Freshman Admission Bellevue University requires a high school transcript and TOEFL scores for international students. The application deadline for regular admission is rolling.

Transfer Admission The application deadline for admission is rolling.

Entrance Difficulty Bellevue University has an open admission policy.

For Further Information Contact Michelle Eppler, Dean of Students/Dean of Academic Services, Bellevue University, 1000 Galvin Road South, Bellevue, NE 68005-3098. *Telephone:* 402-557-7010 or 800-756-7920 (toll-free). *Fax:* 402-557-5404. *E-mail:* michelle.eppler@bellevue.edu. *Web site:* http://www.bellevue.edu/.

CHADRON STATE COLLEGE
Chadron, Nebraska

Chadron State College is a coed, public, comprehensive unit of Nebraska State College System, founded in 1911, offering degrees at the bachelor's and master's levels. It has a 281-acre campus in Chadron.

For Further Information Contact Ms. Tena Cook Gould, Director of Admissions, Chadron State College, 1000 Main Street, Chadron, NE 69337-2690. *Telephone:* 308-432-6263 or 800-242-3766 (toll-free in-state). *Fax:* 308-432-6229. *E-mail:* inquire@csc1.csc.edu. *Web site:* http://www.csc.edu/.

CLARKSON COLLEGE
Omaha, Nebraska
http://www.clarksoncollege.edu/

COLLEGE OF SAINT MARY
Omaha, Nebraska

College of Saint Mary is a women's, private, Roman Catholic, four-year college, founded in 1923, offering degrees at the associate, bachelor's, and master's levels. It has a 25-acre campus in Omaha.

Academic Information The faculty has 159 members (36% full-time), 30% with terminal degrees. The undergraduate student-faculty ratio is 10:1. The library holds 77,246 titles, 398 serial subscriptions, and 1,735 audiovisual materials. Special programs include academic remediation, services for learning-disabled students, study abroad, advanced placement credit, accelerated degree programs, double majors, independent study, summer session for credit, part-time degree programs, adult/continuing education programs, and internships. The most frequently chosen baccalaureate fields are business/marketing, education, health professions and related sciences.

Student Body Statistics The student body totals 960, of whom 921 are undergraduates (100 freshmen). Students come from 19 states and territories and 6 other countries. 90 percent are from Nebraska. 0.8 percent are international students. 13.3 percent of the 2006 graduating class went on to graduate and professional schools.

Expenses for 2007–08 *Application fee:* $30. *Comprehensive fee:* $26,307 includes full-time tuition ($19,635), mandatory fees ($420), and college room and board ($6252). *Part-time tuition:* $651 per credit hour. *Part-time mandatory fees:* $14 per credit hour.

Financial Aid Forms of aid include need-based and non-need-based scholarships, athletic grants, and part-time jobs. The average aided 2006–07 undergraduate received an aid package worth an estimated $12,301. The priority application deadline for financial aid is March 1.

Freshman Admission College of Saint Mary requires a high school transcript, a minimum 2.0 high school GPA, SAT or ACT scores, and TOEFL scores for international students. An essay, a minimum 3.0 high school GPA, 2 recommendations, and an interview are required for some. The application deadline for regular admission is rolling.

Transfer Admission The application deadline for admission is rolling.

Entrance Difficulty College of Saint Mary assesses its entrance difficulty level as minimally difficult. For the fall 2006 freshman class, 58 percent of the applicants were accepted.

For Further Information Contact Ms. Natalie Vrbka, Assistant Director of Admissions, College of Saint Mary, 7000 Mercy Road, Omaha, NE 68106. *Telephone:* 402-399-2405 or 800-926-5534 (toll-free). *Fax:* 402-399-2412. *E-mail:* enroll@csm.edu. *Web site:* http://www.csm.edu/.

CONCORDIA UNIVERSITY
Seward, Nebraska

Concordia University is a coed, private, comprehensive institution, founded in 1894, affiliated with the Lutheran Church–Missouri Synod, offering degrees at the bachelor's and master's levels. It has a 120-acre campus in Seward near Omaha.

Academic Information The faculty has 133 members (43% full-time), 52% with terminal degrees. The undergraduate student-faculty ratio is 14:1. The library holds 189,104 titles, 15,981 serial subscriptions, and 9,756 audiovisual materials. Special programs include academic remediation, services for learning-disabled students, study abroad, advanced placement credit, accelerated degree programs, ESL programs, double majors, independent study, distance learning, summer session for credit, part-time degree programs (daytime, evenings, summer), adult/continuing education programs, internships, and arrangement for off-campus study with University of Nebraska–Lincoln.

Student Body Statistics The student body totals 1,251, of whom 1,107 are undergraduates (302 freshmen). 54 percent are women and 46 percent are men. Students come from 41 states and territories and 8 other countries. 40 percent are from Nebraska. 0.6 percent are international students.

Expenses for 2007–08 *Application fee:* $25. *Comprehensive fee:* $24,860 includes full-time tuition ($19,670), mandatory fees ($120), and college room and board ($5070). *College room only:* $2170. *Part-time tuition:* $610 per credit.

Financial Aid Forms of aid include need-based and non-need-based scholarships, athletic grants, and part-time jobs. The average aided 2006–07 undergraduate received an aid package worth an estimated $14,097.

Freshman Admission Concordia University requires a high school transcript, a minimum 2.5 high school GPA, SAT or ACT scores, and TOEFL scores for international students. An interview is recommended. Recommendations are required for some. The application deadline for regular admission is August 1 and for nonresidents it is August 1.

Entrance Difficulty Concordia University assesses its entrance difficulty level as moderately difficult. For the fall 2006 freshman class, 78 percent of the applicants were accepted.

For Further Information Contact Mr. Chad Thies, Director of Admissions and Recruitment, Concordia University, 800 N Columbia Avenue, Seward, NE 68434. *Telephone:* 800-535-5494 Ext. 7233 or 800-535-5494 (toll-free). *Fax:* 402-643-4073. *E-mail:* admiss@seward.ccsn.edu. *Web site:* http://www.cune.edu/.

CREIGHTON UNIVERSITY
Omaha, Nebraska

Creighton University is a coed, private, Roman Catholic (Jesuit) university, founded in 1878, offering degrees at the associate, bachelor's, master's, doctoral, and first professional levels. It has a 110-acre campus in Omaha.

Academic Information The faculty has 654 members (75% full-time), 79% with terminal degrees. The undergraduate student-faculty ratio is 12:1. The library holds 466,556 titles, 27,144 serial subscriptions, and 9,502 audiovisual materials. Special programs include services for learning-disabled students, an honors program, study abroad, advanced placement credit, accelerated degree programs, Freshman Honors College, ESL programs, double majors, independent study, distance learning, summer session for credit, part-time degree programs (daytime, evenings, summer), adult/continuing education programs, internships, and arrangement for off-campus study with Creighton University; West Omaha Campus. The most frequently chosen baccalaureate fields are business/marketing, biological/life sciences, health professions and related sciences.

Student Body Statistics The student body totals 6,981, of whom 4,075 are undergraduates (965 freshmen). 60 percent are women and 40 percent are men. Students come from 51 states and territories and 33 other countries. 45 percent are from Nebraska. 1.1 percent are international students. 40 percent of the 2006 graduating class went on to graduate and professional schools.

Expenses for 2006–07 *Application fee:* $40. *Comprehensive fee:* $32,968 includes full-time tuition ($24,166), mandatory fees ($960), and college room and board ($7842). *College room only:* $4420. Full-time tuition and fees vary according to student level. Room and board charges vary according to board plan and housing facility. *Part-time tuition:* $756 per semester hour. *Part-time mandatory fees:* $78 per term. Part-time tuition and fees vary according to student level.

Financial Aid Forms of aid include need-based and non-need-based scholarships, athletic grants, and part-time jobs. The average aided 2006–07 undergraduate received an aid package worth an estimated $21,260. The priority application deadline for financial aid is May 15.

Freshman Admission Creighton University requires an essay, a high school transcript, a minimum 2.75 high school GPA, 1 recommendation, SAT or ACT scores, and TOEFL scores for international students. The application deadline for regular admission is August 1.

Transfer Admission The application deadline for admission is August 1.

Creighton University (continued)

Entrance Difficulty Creighton University assesses its entrance difficulty level as moderately difficult. For the fall 2006 freshman class, 89 percent of the applicants were accepted.

For Further Information Contact Ms. Mary Chase, Director of Admissions-Scholarships, Creighton University, 2500 California Plaza, Omaha, NE 68178-0001. *Telephone:* 402-280-3105 or 800-282-5835 (toll-free). *Fax:* 402-280-2685. *E-mail:* admissions@creighton.edu. *Web site:* http://www.creighton.edu/.

DANA COLLEGE
Blair, Nebraska

Dana College is a coed, private, four-year college, founded in 1884, affiliated with the Evangelical Lutheran Church in America, offering degrees at the bachelor's level. It has a 150-acre campus in Blair near Omaha.

Academic Information The faculty has 69 members (45% full-time), 42% with terminal degrees. The student-faculty ratio is 12:1. The library holds 177,500 titles and 5,000 serial subscriptions. Special programs include services for learning-disabled students, an honors program, study abroad, advanced placement credit, accelerated degree programs, ESL programs, double majors, independent study, self-designed majors, summer session for credit, part-time degree programs (daytime), adult/continuing education programs, internships, and arrangement for off-campus study with Consortium of Eastern Nebraska Colleges. The most frequently chosen baccalaureate fields are business/marketing, education, parks and recreation.

Student Body Statistics The student body is made up of 601 undergraduates (146 freshmen). 47 percent are women and 53 percent are men. Students come from 31 states and territories and 3 other countries. 58 percent are from Nebraska. 0.5 percent are international students. 12 percent of the 2006 graduating class went on to graduate and professional schools.

Expenses for 2006–07 *Application fee:* $0. *Comprehensive fee:* $24,040 includes full-time tuition ($17,850), mandatory fees ($800), and college room and board ($5390). *College room only:* $2160. Room and board charges vary according to board plan and housing facility. *Part-time tuition:* $520 per semester hour. *Part-time mandatory fees:* $35 per term. Part-time tuition and fees vary according to course load.

Financial Aid Forms of aid include need-based and non-need-based scholarships, athletic grants, and part-time jobs. The average aided 2006–07 undergraduate received an aid package worth an estimated $16,241. The priority application deadline for financial aid is March 15.

Freshman Admission Dana College requires a high school transcript, a minimum 2.0 high school GPA, SAT or ACT scores, and TOEFL scores for international students. ACT scores are recommended. An essay, 1 recommendation, and an interview are required for some. The application deadline for regular admission is rolling.

Entrance Difficulty Dana College assesses its entrance difficulty level as moderately difficult. For the fall 2006 freshman class, 72 percent of the applicants were accepted.

For Further Information Contact Duane Heffelfinger, Dean of Enrollment, Dana College, 2848 College Drive, Blair, NE 68008-1099. *Telephone:* 402-426-7220 or 800-444-3262 (toll-free). *Fax:* 402-426-7386. *E-mail:* admissions@dana.edu. *Web site:* http://www.dana.edu/.

DOANE COLLEGE
Crete, Nebraska

Doane College is a coed, private, comprehensive institution, founded in 1872, affiliated with the United Church of Christ, offering degrees at the bachelor's and master's levels (non-traditional undergraduate programs and graduate programs offered at Lincoln campus). It has a 300-acre campus in Crete near Omaha.

Academic Information The faculty has 139 members (53% full-time). The undergraduate student-faculty ratio is 9:1. The library holds 351,653 titles, 25,589 serial subscriptions, and 3,015 audiovisual materials. Special programs include an honors program, cooperative (work-study) education, study abroad, advanced placement credit, ESL programs, double majors, independent study, self-designed majors, summer session for credit, internships, and arrangement for off-campus study with Association of Nebraska Interterm Colleges. The most frequently chosen baccalaureate fields are business/marketing, biological/life sciences, education.

Student Body Statistics The student body is made up of 922 undergraduates (247 freshmen). 55 percent are women and 45 percent are men. Students come from 23 states and territories and 2 other countries. 83 percent are from Nebraska. 0.4 percent are international students. 22 percent of the 2006 graduating class went on to graduate and professional schools.

Expenses for 2007–08 *Application fee:* $15. *Comprehensive fee:* $24,560 includes full-time tuition ($18,800), mandatory fees ($350), and college room and board ($5410). *College room only:* $1950. *Part-time tuition:* $630 per credit hour. *Part-time mandatory fees:* $125 per term.

Financial Aid Forms of aid include need-based and non-need-based scholarships, athletic grants, and part-time jobs. The average aided 2006–07 undergraduate received an aid package worth an estimated $18,997.

Freshman Admission Doane College requires a high school transcript, 2 recommendations, SAT or ACT scores, and TOEFL scores for international students. A minimum 2.0 high school GPA is recommended. An interview is required for some. The application deadline for regular admission is rolling.

Transfer Admission The application deadline for admission is rolling.

Entrance Difficulty Doane College assesses its entrance difficulty level as moderately difficult. For the fall 2006 freshman class, 79 percent of the applicants were accepted.

For Further Information Contact Mr. Cezar Mesquita, Director of Admission, Doane College, 1014 Boswell Avenue, Crete, NE 68333-2430. *Telephone:* 402-826-8222 or 800-333-6263 (toll-free). *Fax:* 402-826-8600. *E-mail:* admissions@doane.edu. *Web site:* http://www.doane.edu/.

GRACE UNIVERSITY
Omaha, Nebraska

http://www.graceuniversity.edu/

HAMILTON COLLEGE-OMAHA
Omaha, Nebraska

http://www.hamiltonomaha.edu/

HASTINGS COLLEGE
Hastings, Nebraska

Hastings College is a coed, private, Presbyterian, comprehensive institution, founded in 1882, offering degrees at the bachelor's and master's levels. It has a 109-acre campus in Hastings.

Academic Information The faculty has 128 members (66% full-time), 52% with terminal degrees. The undergraduate student-faculty ratio is 12:1. The library holds 113,318 titles and 636 serial subscriptions. Special programs include services for learning-disabled students, study abroad, advanced placement credit, double majors, independent study, self-designed majors, summer session for credit, part-time degree programs (daytime, summer), adult/continuing education programs, internships, and arrangement for off-campus study. The most frequently chosen baccalaureate fields are business/marketing, education, psychology.

Student Body Statistics The student body totals 1,137, of whom 1,093 are undergraduates (263 freshmen). 49 percent are women and 51 percent are men. Students come from 27 states and territories and 4 other countries. 76 percent are from Nebraska. 0.7 percent are international students. 22 percent of the 2006 graduating class went on to graduate and professional schools.

Expenses for 2006–07 *Application fee:* $20. *Comprehensive fee:* $23,450 includes full-time tuition ($17,572), mandatory fees ($730), and college room and board ($5148). *College room only:* $2200. Full-time tuition and fees vary according to course level and program. Room and board charges vary according to board plan and housing facility. *Part-time tuition:* $728 per semester hour. *Part-time mandatory fees:* $193 per term. Part-time tuition and fees vary according to course level, course load, and program.

Financial Aid Forms of aid include need-based and non-need-based scholarships, athletic grants, and part-time jobs. The average aided 2005–06 undergraduate received an aid package worth $11,739. The application deadline for financial aid is September 1 with a priority deadline of May 1.

Freshman Admission Hastings College requires a high school transcript, a minimum 2.0 high school GPA, counselor's recommendation, SAT or ACT scores, and TOEFL scores for international students. An essay, 2 recommendations, and an interview are required for some. The application deadline for regular admission is August 1.

Transfer Admission The application deadline for admission is August 1.

Entrance Difficulty Hastings College assesses its entrance difficulty level as moderately difficult. For the fall 2006 freshman class, 81 percent of the applicants were accepted.

For Further Information Contact Ms. Mary Molliconi, Director of Admissions, Hastings College, 710 North Turner Avenue, Hastings, NE 68901-7621. *Telephone:* 402-461-7320 or 800-532-7642 (toll-free). *Fax:* 402-461-7490. *E-mail:* mmolliconi@hastings.edu. *Web site:* http://www.hastings.edu/.

ITT TECHNICAL INSTITUTE
Omaha, Nebraska

ITT Technical Institute is a coed, proprietary, primarily two-year college of ITT Educational Services, Inc, founded in 1991, offering degrees at the associate and bachelor's levels. It has a 1-acre campus in Omaha.

Expenses for 2006–07 *Application fee:* $100. Contact school for program costs.

Financial Aid Forms of aid include need-based scholarships. The application deadline for financial aid is continuous.

Freshman Admission ITT Technical Institute requires a high school transcript, an interview, TOEFL scores for international students, and Wonderlic aptitude test. Recommendations are recommended. The application deadline for regular admission is rolling.

Transfer Admission The application deadline for admission is rolling.

Entrance Difficulty ITT Technical Institute assesses its entrance difficulty level as minimally difficult.

For Further Information Contact Schon Nielson, Director of Recruitment, ITT Technical Institute, 9814 M Street, Omaha, NE 68127. *Telephone:* 402-331-2900 or 800-677-9260 (toll-free). *Fax:* 402-331-9495. *Web site:* http://www.itt-tech.edu/.

LITTLE PRIEST TRIBAL COLLEGE
Winnebago, Nebraska

http://www.lptc.bia.edu/

MIDLAND LUTHERAN COLLEGE
Fremont, Nebraska

Midland Lutheran College is a coed, private, Lutheran, four-year college, founded in 1883, offering degrees at the associate and bachelor's levels. It has a 27-acre campus in Fremont near Omaha.

Expenses for 2006–07 *Application fee:* $30. *Comprehensive fee:* $24,460 includes full-time tuition ($19,510) and college room and board ($4950). *College room only:* $2190.

For Further Information Contact Mr. Todd Hansen, Associate Director of Admissions, Midland Lutheran College, Admissions Office, Fremont, NE 68025-4200. *Telephone:* 402-941-6504 or 800-642-8382 Ext. 6501 (toll-free). *Fax:* 402-941-6513. *E-mail:* admissions@mlc.edu. *Web site:* http://www.mlc.edu/.

NEBRASKA CHRISTIAN COLLEGE
Norfolk, Nebraska

http://www.nechristian.edu/

NEBRASKA COLLEGE OF BUSINESS
See Hamilton College-Omaha.

NEBRASKA METHODIST COLLEGE
Omaha, Nebraska

Nebraska Methodist College is a coed, primarily women's, private, comprehensive institution, founded in 1891, affiliated with the United Methodist Church, offering degrees at the associate, bachelor's, and master's levels and post-master's certificates. It has a 5-acre campus in Omaha.

Academic Information The faculty has 57 members (58% full-time), 23% with terminal degrees. The undergraduate student-faculty ratio is 10:1. The library holds 8,656 titles and 475 serial subscriptions. Special programs include academic remediation, services for learning-disabled students, advanced placement credit, accelerated degree programs, independent study, distance learning, summer session for credit, and internships. The most frequently chosen baccalaureate field is health professions and related sciences.

Student Body Statistics The student body totals 512, of whom 446 are undergraduates (20 freshmen). 89 percent are women and 11 percent are men. Students come from 6 states and territories and 1 other country. 75 percent are from Nebraska. 0.2 percent are international students. 3 percent of the 2006 graduating class went on to graduate and professional schools.

Expenses for 2007–08 *Application fee:* $25. *Tuition:* $12,630 full-time, $421 per credit hour part-time. *Mandatory fees:* $600 full-time, $20 per credit hour part-time. *College room only:* $2384.

Financial Aid Forms of aid include need-based and non-need-based scholarships and part-time jobs. The average aided 2005–06 undergraduate received an aid package worth $6789. The priority application deadline for financial aid is May 1.

Freshman Admission Nebraska Methodist College requires an essay, a high school transcript, a minimum 2.0 high school GPA, 3 recommendations, an interview, SAT or ACT scores, and TOEFL scores for international students. The application deadline for regular admission is April 1.

Transfer Admission The application deadline for admission is April 1.

Entrance Difficulty Nebraska Methodist College assesses its entrance difficulty level as moderately difficult. For the fall 2006 freshman class, 39 percent of the applicants were accepted.

For Further Information Contact Ms. Deann Sterner, Director of Admissions, Nebraska Methodist College, 720 North 87th Street, Omaha, NE 68114. *Telephone:* 402-354-7200 or 800-335-5510 (toll-free). *Fax:* 402-354-7020. *E-mail:* deann.sterner@methodistcollege.edu. *Web site:* http://www.methodistcollege.edu/.

NEBRASKA WESLEYAN UNIVERSITY
Lincoln, Nebraska

Nebraska Wesleyan University is a coed, private, United Methodist, comprehensive institution, founded in 1887, offering degrees at the bachelor's and master's levels and post-master's certificates. It has a 50-acre campus in Lincoln near Omaha.

Academic Information The faculty has 217 members (50% full-time), 53% with terminal degrees. The undergraduate student-faculty ratio is 13:1. The library holds 178,531 titles and 743 serial subscriptions. Special programs include services for learning-disabled students, study abroad, advanced placement credit, double majors, independent study, summer session for credit, part-time degree programs (evenings, summer), adult/continuing education programs, internships, and arrangement for off-

Nebraska Wesleyan University (continued)

campus study with Chicago Urban Life Center, Capitol Hill Internship Program. The most frequently chosen baccalaureate fields are business/marketing, education, health professions and related sciences.

Student Body Statistics The student body totals 2,068, of whom 1,864 are undergraduates (414 freshmen). 57 percent are women and 43 percent are men. Students come from 25 states and territories and 13 other countries. 92 percent are from Nebraska. 0.2 percent are international students. 30 percent of the 2006 graduating class went on to graduate and professional schools.

Expenses for 2006–07 *Application fee:* $20. *Comprehensive fee:* $24,467 includes full-time tuition ($18,980), mandatory fees ($322), and college room and board ($5165). Full-time tuition and fees vary according to class time, course load, degree level, location, and program. Room and board charges vary according to board plan and housing facility. *Part-time tuition:* $715 per credit hour. Part-time tuition varies according to class time, course load, degree level, location, and program.

Financial Aid Forms of aid include need-based and non-need-based scholarships and part-time jobs. The average aided 2006–07 undergraduate received an aid package worth an estimated $13,419. The application deadline for financial aid is continuous.

Freshman Admission Nebraska Wesleyan University requires a high school transcript, a minimum 2.0 high school GPA, SAT or ACT scores, and TOEFL scores for international students. An interview is recommended. An essay and resume of activities are required for some. The application deadline for regular admission is August 15 and for early decision it is November 15.

Transfer Admission The application deadline for admission is August 15.

Entrance Difficulty Nebraska Wesleyan University assesses its entrance difficulty level as moderately difficult. For the fall 2006 freshman class, 84 percent of the applicants were accepted.

For Further Information Contact Ms. Patty Karthauser, Vice President for Enrollment and Marketing, Nebraska Wesleyan University, 5000 Saint Paul Avenue, Lincoln, NE 68504. *Telephone:* 402-465-2218 or 800-541-3818 (toll-free). *Fax:* 402-465-2177. *E-mail:* admissions@nebrwesleyan.edu. *Web site:* http://www.nebrwesleyan.edu/.

PERU STATE COLLEGE
Peru, Nebraska

Peru State College is a coed, public, comprehensive unit of Nebraska State College System, founded in 1867, offering degrees at the bachelor's and master's levels. It has a 104-acre campus in Peru.

Academic Information The faculty has 130 members (31% full-time). The undergraduate student-faculty ratio is 20:1. The library holds 177,373 titles and 232 serial subscriptions. Special programs include academic remediation, services for learning-disabled students, an honors program, cooperative (work-study) education, advanced placement credit, accelerated degree programs, Freshman Honors College, double majors, distance learning, summer session for credit, part-time degree programs (daytime, evenings, summer), external degree programs, adult/continuing education programs, internships, and arrangement for off-campus study. The most frequently chosen baccalaureate fields are business/marketing, education, engineering technologies.

Student Body Statistics The student body totals 1,677, of whom 1,487 are undergraduates (225 freshmen). 54 percent are women and 46 percent are men. Students come from 27 states and territories and 7 other countries. 88 percent are from Nebraska. 0.9 percent are international students. 21 percent of the 2006 graduating class went on to graduate and professional schools.

Expenses for 2006–07 *Application fee:* $0. *State resident tuition:* $3075 full-time, $102.50 per credit hour part-time. *Nonresident tuition:* $6150 full-time, $205 per credit hour part-time. *Mandatory fees:* $756 full-time. Full-time tuition and fees vary according to course load and location. Part-time tuition varies according to course load and location. *College room and board:* $4620. Room and board charges vary according to housing facility.

Financial Aid Forms of aid include need-based and non-need-based scholarships, athletic grants, and part-time jobs. The priority application deadline for financial aid is March 1.

Freshman Admission Peru State College requires a high school transcript and TOEFL scores for international students. A minimum 2.0 high school GPA and SAT or ACT scores are required for some. The application deadline for regular admission is rolling.

Transfer Admission The application deadline for admission is rolling.

Entrance Difficulty Peru State College has an open admission policy. It assesses its entrance difficulty as minimally difficult for out-of-state applicants.

For Further Information Contact Ms. Micki Willis, Director of Recruitment and Admissions, Peru State College, PO Box 10, Peru, NE 68421. *Telephone:* 402-872-2221 or 800-742-4412 (toll-free in-state). *Fax:* 402-872-2296. *E-mail:* mwillis@oakmail.peru.edu. *Web site:* http://www.peru.edu/.

UNION COLLEGE
Lincoln, Nebraska

Union College is a coed, private, Seventh-day Adventist, comprehensive institution, founded in 1891, offering degrees at the associate, bachelor's, and master's levels. It has a 26-acre campus in Lincoln near Omaha.

Academic Information The faculty has 102 members (57% full-time), 29% with terminal degrees. The undergraduate student-faculty ratio is 12:1. The library holds 147,813 titles and 1,357 serial subscriptions. Special programs include services for learning-disabled students, an honors program, cooperative (work-study) education, study abroad, advanced placement credit, accelerated degree programs, ESL programs, double majors, independent study, self-designed majors, summer session for credit, part-time degree programs (daytime, summer), adult/continuing education programs, internships, and arrangement for off-campus study with University of Nebraska, Southeast Community College. The most frequently chosen baccalaureate fields are business/marketing, education, health professions and related sciences.

Student Body Statistics The student body totals 982, of whom 912 are undergraduates (192 freshmen). 54 percent are women and 46 percent are men. Students come from 42 states and territories and 29 other countries. 21 percent are from Nebraska. 9.1 percent are international students.

Expenses for 2006–07 *Application fee:* $0. *Comprehensive fee:* $19,448 includes full-time tuition ($14,790), mandatory fees ($440), and college room and board ($4218). *College room only:* $2898. *Part-time tuition:* $625 per semester hour.

Financial Aid Forms of aid include non-need-based scholarships and part-time jobs. The average aided 2005–06 undergraduate received an aid package worth $12,234.

Freshman Admission Union College requires a high school transcript, a minimum 2.5 high school GPA, 3 recommendations, and SAT or ACT scores. An essay and an interview are required for some. The application deadline for regular admission is rolling.

Transfer Admission The application deadline for admission is rolling.

Entrance Difficulty Union College assesses its entrance difficulty level as moderately difficult. For the fall 2006 freshman class, 45 percent of the applicants were accepted.

For Further Information Contact Huda McClelland, Director of Admissions, Union College, 3800 South 48th Street, Lincoln, NE 68506. *Telephone:* 402-486-2504 or 800-228-4600 (toll-free out-of-state). *Fax:* 402-486-2895. *E-mail:* ucenroll@ucollege.edu. *Web site:* http://www.ucollege.edu/.

UNIVERSITY OF NEBRASKA AT KEARNEY
Kearney, Nebraska

University of Nebraska at Kearney is a coed, public, comprehensive unit of University of Nebraska System, founded in 1903, offering degrees at the bachelor's and master's levels and post-master's certificates. It has a 235-acre campus in Kearney.

Academic Information The faculty has 377 members (82% full-time), 67% with terminal degrees. The undergraduate student-faculty ratio is 16:1. The library holds 320,915 titles and 1,657 serial subscriptions. Special programs include academic remediation, services for learning-disabled students, an honors program, cooperative (work-study) education, study abroad, advanced placement credit, ESL programs, double majors, independent study, distance learning, summer session for credit, part-time degree programs (daytime, evenings, weekends, summer), internships, and arrangement for off-campus study with National Student Exchange. The most frequently chosen baccalaureate fields are business/marketing, communications/journalism, education.

Student Body Statistics The student body totals 6,468, of whom 5,276 are undergraduates (1,014 freshmen). 54 percent are women and 46 percent are men. Students come from 43 states and territories and 40 other countries. 94 percent are from Nebraska. 7 percent are international students.

Expenses for 2006–07 *Application fee:* $45. *State resident tuition:* $3885 full-time, $129.50 per hour part-time. *Nonresident tuition:* $7958 full-time, $265.25 per hour part-time. *Mandatory fees:* $880 full-time, $17.50 per hour part-time, $64 per term part-time. Both full-time and part-time tuition and fees vary according to course level, course load, degree level, and location. *College room and board:* $5686. Room and board charges vary according to board plan and housing facility.

Financial Aid Forms of aid include need-based and non-need-based scholarships, athletic grants, and part-time jobs. The average aided 2005–06 undergraduate received an aid package worth $7227.

Freshman Admission University of Nebraska at Kearney requires a high school transcript, rank in upper 50% of high school class, minimum SAT score of 950, or ACT score of 20, SAT and SAT Subject Test or ACT scores, and TOEFL scores for international students. 3 recommendations are required for some. The application deadline for regular admission is rolling.

Transfer Admission The application deadline for admission is rolling.

Entrance Difficulty University of Nebraska at Kearney assesses its entrance difficulty level as moderately difficult. For the fall 2006 freshman class, 83 percent of the applicants were accepted.

For Further Information Contact Mr. Dusty Newton, Director of Admissions, University of Nebraska at Kearney, 905 West 25th Street, Kearney, NE 68849-0001. *Telephone:* 308-865-8702 or 800-532-7639 (toll-free). *Fax:* 308-865-8987. *E-mail:* admissionsug@unk.edu. *Web site:* http://www.unk.edu/.

UNIVERSITY OF NEBRASKA AT OMAHA
Omaha, Nebraska

University of Nebraska at Omaha is a coed, public unit of University of Nebraska System, founded in 1908, offering degrees at the bachelor's, master's, and doctoral levels and post-master's and postbachelor's certificates. It has a 158-acre campus in Omaha.

Academic Information The faculty has 865 members (58% full-time), 59% with terminal degrees. The undergraduate student-faculty ratio is 17:1. The library holds 700,000 titles and 37,000 serial subscriptions. Special programs include services for learning-disabled students, an honors program, cooperative (work-study) education, study abroad, advanced placement credit, ESL programs, double majors, independent study, distance learning, self-designed majors, summer session for credit, part-time degree programs (daytime, evenings, summer), adult/continuing education programs, internships, and arrangement for off-campus study with other units of the University of Nebraska System. The most frequently chosen baccalaureate fields are business/marketing, education, security and protective services.

Student Body Statistics The student body totals 13,906, of whom 11,156 are undergraduates (1,708 freshmen). 52 percent are women and 48 percent are men. Students come from 40 states and territories and 75 other countries. 94 percent are from Nebraska. 2.1 percent are international students. 18 percent of the 2006 graduating class went on to graduate and professional schools.

Expenses for 2006–07 *Application fee:* $45. *State resident tuition:* $4380 full-time, $146 per semester hour part-time. *Nonresident tuition:* $12,908 full-time, $430.25 per semester hour part-time. *Mandatory fees:* $738 full-time, $24.50 per semester hour part-time, $89.20 per term part-time. Both full-time and part-time tuition and fees vary according to course load. *College room and board:* $6630. *College room only:* $4110. Room and board charges vary according to board plan.

Financial Aid Forms of aid include need-based and non-need-based scholarships and part-time jobs. The priority application deadline for financial aid is March 1.

Freshman Admission University of Nebraska at Omaha requires a high school transcript, minimum ACT score of 20 or rank in upper 50% of high school class, SAT or ACT scores, and TOEFL scores for international students. SAT or ACT scores are required for some. The application deadline for regular admission is August 1 and for nonresidents it is August 1.

Transfer Admission The application deadline for admission is August 1.

Entrance Difficulty University of Nebraska at Omaha assesses its entrance difficulty level as minimally difficult; moderately difficult for engineering program; noncompetitive for nontraditional, adult applicants. For the fall 2006 freshman class, 86 percent of the applicants were accepted.

For Further Information Contact Ms. Jolene Adams, Associate Director of Admissions, University of Nebraska at Omaha, 6001 Dodge Street, Omaha, NE 68182. *Telephone:* 402-554-2393 or 800-858-8648 (toll-free in-state). *Fax:* 402-554-3472. *E-mail:* jadams@mail.unomaha.edu. *Web site:* http://www.unomaha.edu/.

UNIVERSITY OF NEBRASKA–LINCOLN
Lincoln, Nebraska

University of Nebraska–Lincoln is a coed, public unit of University of Nebraska System, founded in 1869, offering degrees at the associate, bachelor's, master's, doctoral, and first professional levels and post-master's and postbachelor's certificates. It has a 623-acre campus in Lincoln near Omaha.

Academic Information The faculty has 1,060 members (98% full-time), 97% with terminal degrees. The undergraduate student-faculty ratio is 19:1. The library holds 3 million titles, 50,817 serial subscriptions, and 7,079 audiovisual materials. Special programs include services for learning-disabled students, an honors program, cooperative (work-study) education, study abroad, advanced placement credit, accelerated degree programs, ESL programs, double majors, independent study, distance learning, self-designed majors, summer session for credit, part-time degree programs (daytime, evenings, summer), adult/continuing education programs, internships, and arrangement for off-campus study with University of Missouri, Kansas State University, University of South Dakota. The most frequently chosen baccalaureate fields are business/marketing, education, engineering.

Student Body Statistics The student body totals 22,106, of whom 17,371 are undergraduates (3,849 freshmen). 46 percent are women and 54 percent are men. Students come from 52 states and territories and 112 other countries. 86 percent are from Nebraska. 2.6 percent are international students.

Expenses for 2006–07 *Application fee:* $45. *State resident tuition:* $4800 full-time, $160 per credit hour part-time. *Nonresident tuition:* $14,250 full-time, $475 per credit hour part-time. *Mandatory fees:* $1,067 full-time, $9 per credit hour part-time, $216.20 per term part-time. Both full-time and part-time tuition and fees vary according to course load. *College room and board:* $6183. *College room only:* $3262. Room and board charges vary according to board plan and housing facility.

Financial Aid Forms of aid include need-based and non-need-based scholarships, athletic grants, and part-time jobs. The application deadline for financial aid is continuous.

Freshman Admission University of Nebraska–Lincoln requires a high school transcript, SAT or ACT scores, and TOEFL scores for international students. ACT scores are recommended. Rank in upper 50% of high school class is required for some. The application deadline for regular admission is May 1.

Transfer Admission The application deadline for admission is June 30.

University of Nebraska–Lincoln (continued)

Entrance Difficulty University of Nebraska–Lincoln assesses its entrance difficulty level as moderately difficult; very difficult for architecture, engineering programs. For the fall 2006 freshman class, 73 percent of the applicants were accepted.

For Further Information Contact Pat McBride, Director, New Student Enrollment, University of Nebraska–Lincoln, 1410 Q Street, Lincoln, NE 68588-0256. *Telephone:* 402-472-2023 or 800-742-8800 (toll-free). *Fax:* 402-472-0670. *E-mail:* admissions@unl.edu. *Web site:* http://www.unl.edu/.

UNIVERSITY OF NEBRASKA MEDICAL CENTER

Omaha, Nebraska

University of Nebraska Medical Center is a coed, public, upper-level unit of University of Nebraska System, founded in 1869, offering degrees at the bachelor's, master's, doctoral, and first professional levels and post-master's, first professional, and postbachelor's certificates. It has a 51-acre campus in Omaha.

Academic Information The faculty has 1,007 members (78% full-time). The library holds 241,551 titles and 4,280 serial subscriptions. Special programs include services for learning-disabled students, an honors program, accelerated degree programs, distance learning, summer session for credit, part-time degree programs (daytime, summer), internships, and arrangement for off-campus study with University of Nebraska–Lincoln, University of Nebraska at Omaha, University of Nebraska at Kearney. The most frequently chosen baccalaureate field is health professions and related sciences.

Student Body Statistics The student body totals 2,995, of whom 851 are undergraduates. 90 percent are women and 10 percent are men. Students come from 15 states and territories and 6 other countries. 91 percent are from Nebraska. 1.1 percent are international students.

Expenses for 2006–07 *Application fee:* $45. *State resident tuition:* $4530 full-time, $151 per semester hour part-time. *Nonresident tuition:* $13,440 full-time, $448 per semester hour part-time. *Mandatory fees:* $300 full-time, $105 per semester hour part-time.

Financial Aid Forms of aid include need-based scholarships and part-time jobs. The average aided 2005–06 undergraduate received an aid package worth $7999. The priority application deadline for financial aid is March 15.

Transfer Admission University of Nebraska Medical Center requires a college transcript and a minimum 2.0 college GPA. Standardized test scores and a minimum 3.0 college GPA are required for some. The application deadline for admission is rolling.

Entrance Difficulty University of Nebraska Medical Center assesses its entrance difficulty level as moderately difficult.

For Further Information Contact Ms. Tymaree Tonjes, Administrative Technician, University of Nebraska Medical Center, 084230 Nebraska Medical Center, Omaha, NE 68198-4230. *Telephone:* 402-559-6468 or 800-626-8431 Ext. 6468 (toll-free). *Fax:* 402-559-6796. *E-mail:* ttonjes@unmc.edu. *Web site:* http://www.unmc.edu/.

WAYNE STATE COLLEGE

Wayne, Nebraska

Wayne State College is a coed, public, comprehensive unit of Nebraska State College System, founded in 1910, offering degrees at the bachelor's and master's levels and post-master's certificates. It has a 128-acre campus in Wayne.

Academic Information The faculty has 204 members (63% full-time), 53% with terminal degrees. The undergraduate student-faculty ratio is 18:1. The library holds 245,259 titles, 14,975 serial subscriptions, and 6,622 audiovisual materials. Special programs include services for learning-disabled students, an honors program, cooperative (work-study) education, study abroad, advanced placement credit, double majors, independent study, distance learning, self-designed majors, summer session for credit, part-time degree programs (daytime, evenings, weekends, summer), adult/continuing education programs, internships, and arrangement for off-campus study with Northeast Community College, Central Community College. The most frequently chosen baccalaureate fields are business/marketing, education, psychology.

Student Body Statistics The student body totals 3,407, of whom 2,748 are undergraduates (611 freshmen). 56 percent are women and 44 percent are men. Students come from 26 states and territories and 12 other countries. 86 percent are from Nebraska. 0.8 percent are international students.

Expenses for 2006–07 *Application fee:* $30. *State resident tuition:* $3075 full-time, $102.50 per credit hour part-time. *Nonresident tuition:* $6150 full-time, $205 per credit hour part-time. *Mandatory fees:* $938 full-time, $37.25 per credit hour part-time. Both full-time and part-time tuition and fees vary according to course level and course load. *College room and board:* $4470. *College room only:* $2170. Room and board charges vary according to board plan and housing facility.

Financial Aid Forms of aid include need-based and non-need-based scholarships, athletic grants, and part-time jobs. The average aided 2006–07 undergraduate received an aid package worth an estimated $4027.

Freshman Admission Wayne State College requires a high school transcript and TOEFL scores for international students. The application deadline for regular admission is rolling and for nonresidents it is rolling.

Transfer Admission The application deadline for admission is rolling.

Entrance Difficulty Wayne State College has an open admission policy. It assesses its entrance difficulty as minimally difficult for transfers.

For Further Information Contact Ms. Lois Ash, Interim Director of Admissions, Wayne State College, 1111 Main Street, Wayne, NE 68787. *Telephone:* 402-375-7234 or 800-228-9972 (toll-free in-state). *Fax:* 402-375-7204. *E-mail:* admit1@wsc.edu. *Web site:* http://www.wsc.edu/.

YORK COLLEGE

York, Nebraska

York College is a coed, private, four-year college, founded in 1890, affiliated with the Church of Christ, offering degrees at the associate and bachelor's levels. It has a 44-acre campus in York.

Academic Information The faculty has 65 members (57% full-time), 35% with terminal degrees. The student-faculty ratio is 10:1. The library holds 134,738 titles, 292 serial subscriptions, and 2,566 audiovisual materials. Special programs include academic remediation, services for learning-disabled students, an honors program, cooperative (work-study) education, study abroad, advanced placement credit, double majors, independent study, summer session for credit, part-time degree programs (daytime, evenings, summer), external degree programs, adult/continuing education programs, and internships. The most frequently chosen baccalaureate fields are business/marketing, biological/life sciences, engineering.

Student Body Statistics The student body is made up of 440 undergraduates (94 freshmen). 51 percent are women and 49 percent are men. Students come from 29 states and territories and 9 other countries. 28 percent are from Nebraska. 2.4 percent are international students. 4 percent of the 2006 graduating class went on to graduate and professional schools.

Expenses for 2006–07 *Application fee:* $20. *Comprehensive fee:* $17,800 includes full-time tuition ($12,000), mandatory fees ($1500), and college room and board ($4300). Full-time tuition and fees vary according to course load. Room and board charges vary according to board plan and housing facility. *Part-time tuition:* $375 per credit hour. *Part-time mandatory fees:* $212 per credit hour. Part-time tuition and fees vary according to course load.

Financial Aid Forms of aid include need-based and non-need-based scholarships, athletic grants, and part-time jobs. The priority application deadline for financial aid is April 30.

Freshman Admission York College requires a high school transcript, a minimum 2.0 high school GPA, 2 recommendations, SAT or ACT scores, and TOEFL scores for international students. The application deadline for regular admission is rolling.

Transfer Admission The application deadline for admission is rolling.

Entrance Difficulty York College assesses its entrance difficulty level as moderately difficult. For the fall 2006 freshman class, 99 percent of the applicants were accepted.

For Further Information Contact Ms. Kristin Mathews, Associate Director of Admissions, York College, 1125 East 8th Street, York, NE 68467-2699. *Telephone:* 402-363-5629 or 800-950-9675 (toll-free). *Fax:* 402-363-5623. *E-mail:* enroll@york.edu. *Web site:* http://www.york.edu/.

North Dakota

AAKERS COLLEGE

Fargo, North Dakota

Aakers College is a coed, proprietary, primarily two-year college, founded in 1902, offering degrees at the associate and bachelor's levels.

Academic Information The faculty has 31 members (26% full-time). The student-faculty ratio is 13:1. Special programs include academic remediation, cooperative (work-study) education, distance learning, and part-time degree programs.

Student Body Statistics The student body is made up of 643 undergraduates (189 freshmen). 75 percent are women and 25 percent are men. Students come from 8 states and territories. 75 percent are from North Dakota.

Expenses for 2006–07 *Application fee:* $60. *Tuition:* $10,410 full-time, $845 per course part-time.

Freshman Admission Aakers College requires a high school transcript. The application deadline for regular admission is October 1.

Transfer Admission The application deadline for admission is October 1.

Entrance Difficulty Aakers College assesses its entrance difficulty level as minimally difficult; noncompetitive for.

For Further Information Contact Ms. Elizabeth Largent, Director, Aakers College, 4012 19th Avenue, SW, Fargo, ND 58103. *Telephone:* 701-277-3889 or 800-817-0009 (toll-free). *Fax:* 701-277-5604. *E-mail:* blargent@aakers.edu. *Web site:* http://www.aakers.edu/.

DICKINSON STATE UNIVERSITY

Dickinson, North Dakota

Dickinson State University is a coed, public, four-year college of North Dakota University System, founded in 1918, offering degrees at the associate and bachelor's levels. It has a 100-acre campus in Dickinson.

Academic Information The faculty has 217 members (40% full-time), 25% with terminal degrees. The student-faculty ratio is 19:1. The library holds 105,713 titles and 823 serial subscriptions. Special programs include academic remediation, services for learning-disabled students, an honors program, cooperative (work-study) education, study abroad, advanced placement credit, accelerated degree programs, double majors, independent study, distance learning, self-designed majors, summer session for credit, part-time degree programs (daytime, evenings, weekends, summer), external degree programs, adult/continuing education programs, internships, and arrangement for off-campus study. The most frequently chosen baccalaureate fields are business/marketing, education, liberal arts/general studies.

Student Body Statistics The student body is made up of 2,572 undergraduates (358 freshmen). 59 percent are women and 41 percent are men. Students come from 27 states and 21 other countries. 68 percent are from North Dakota. 9.8 percent are international students. 13 percent of the 2006 graduating class went on to graduate and professional schools.

Expenses for 2006–07 *Application fee:* $35. *State resident tuition:* $4470 full-time, $186.25 per credit part-time. *Nonresident tuition:* $10,560 full-time, $440 per credit part-time. *Mandatory fees:* $825 full-time.

Full-time tuition and fees vary according to location, program, and reciprocity agreements. Part-time tuition varies according to course load, location, program, and reciprocity agreements. *College room and board:* $3882. Room and board charges vary according to board plan.

Financial Aid Forms of aid include need-based and non-need-based scholarships, athletic grants, and part-time jobs. The average aided 2005–06 undergraduate received an aid package worth $5174. The priority application deadline for financial aid is March 15.

Freshman Admission Dickinson State University requires a high school transcript, medical history, proof of measles-rubella shot, SAT or ACT scores, and TOEFL scores for international students. The application deadline for regular admission is rolling.

Transfer Admission The application deadline for admission is rolling.

Entrance Difficulty Dickinson State University has an open admission policy for all United States students. It assesses its entrance difficulty as moderately difficult for nursing program.

For Further Information Contact Mr. Steve Glasser, Director of Enrollment Services, Dickinson State University, Campus Box 169, Dickinson, ND 58601. *Telephone:* 701-483-2175 or 800-279-4295 (toll-free). *Fax:* 701-483-2409. *E-mail:* dsu.hawks@dsu.nodak.edu. *Web site:* http://www.dsu.nodak.edu/.

See page 248 for the College Close-Up.

FORT BERTHOLD COMMUNITY COLLEGE

New Town, North Dakota

Fort Berthold Community College is a coed, private, two-year college, founded in 1973, offering degrees at the associate level.

Academic Information The faculty has 42 members (29% full-time). The library holds 10,000 titles and 300 serial subscriptions. Special programs include academic remediation, cooperative (work-study) education, summer session for credit, part-time degree programs (daytime, evenings), internships, and arrangement for off-campus study with University of North Dakota, Minot State University.

Student Body Statistics The student body is made up of 416 undergraduates. 42 percent of the 2006 graduating class went on to four-year colleges.

Expenses for 2006–07 *Application fee:* $10. *Tuition:* $2640 full-time, $110 per credit part-time. *Mandatory fees:* $600 full-time, $25 per credit part-time, $25 per term part-time. Full-time tuition and fees vary according to course load.

Financial Aid Forms of aid include need-based scholarships and part-time jobs. The application deadline for financial aid is continuous.

Freshman Admission The application deadline for regular admission is rolling.

Entrance Difficulty Fort Berthold Community College has an open admission policy except for nursing program. It assesses its entrance difficulty as minimally difficult for nursing program.

For Further Information Contact Twila Aulaumea, Registrar/Admissions Director, Fort Berthold Community College, PO Box 490, 220 8th Avenue North, New Town, ND 58763-0490. *Telephone:* 701-627-4738 Ext. 286. *Fax:* 701-627-3609. *E-mail:* taulau@fbcc.bia.edu. *Web site:* http://www.fbcc.bia.edu/.

JAMESTOWN COLLEGE

Jamestown, North Dakota

Jamestown College is a coed, private, Presbyterian, four-year college, founded in 1883, offering degrees at the bachelor's level.

Academic Information The faculty has 77 members (74% full-time), 42% with terminal degrees. The student-faculty ratio is 15:1. The library holds 121,382 titles and 630 serial subscriptions. Special programs include services for learning-disabled students, an honors program, cooperative (work-study) education, study abroad, advanced placement credit, double majors, independent study, distance learning, self-designed majors, summer session for credit, part-time degree programs (daytime, evenings, summer),

Jamestown College (continued)

internships, and arrangement for off-campus study. The most frequently chosen baccalaureate fields are business/marketing, education, health professions and related sciences.

Student Body Statistics The student body is made up of 996 undergraduates (242 freshmen). 55 percent are women and 45 percent are men. Students come from 27 states and territories and 8 other countries. 58 percent are from North Dakota. 5 percent are international students. 12 percent of the 2006 graduating class went on to graduate and professional schools.

Expenses for 2007–08 *Application fee:* $20. *Comprehensive fee:* $15,855 includes full-time tuition ($11,235) and college room and board ($4620). *College room only:* $1970. *Part-time tuition:* $310 per credit. *Part-time mandatory fees:* $200 per year.

Financial Aid Forms of aid include need-based and non-need-based scholarships, athletic grants, and part-time jobs. The average aided 2006–07 undergraduate received an aid package worth an estimated $7939. The priority application deadline for financial aid is March 15.

Freshman Admission Jamestown College requires a high school transcript and TOEFL scores for international students. A minimum 2.5 high school GPA, minimum ACT score of 18 or minimum SAT score of 850, and SAT or ACT scores are recommended. Recommendations and minimum ACT score of 18 or minimum SAT score of 850 are required for some. The application deadline for regular admission is rolling.

Transfer Admission The application deadline for admission is rolling.

Entrance Difficulty Jamestown College assesses its entrance difficulty level as minimally difficult. For the fall 2006 freshman class, 94 percent of the applicants were accepted.

For Further Information Contact Mrs. Carol Schmeichel, Vice President of Student Affairs, Jamestown College, 6081 College Lane, Jamestown, ND 58405. *Telephone:* 701-252-3467 Ext. 2563 or 800-336-2554 (toll-free). *Fax:* 701-253-4318. *E-mail:* admissions@jc.edu. *Web site:* http://www.jc.edu/.

MAYVILLE STATE UNIVERSITY
Mayville, North Dakota

Mayville State University is a coed, public, four-year college of North Dakota University System, founded in 1889, offering degrees at the associate and bachelor's levels. It has a 60-acre campus in Mayville.

Academic Information The faculty has 74 members (49% full-time), 26% with terminal degrees. The student-faculty ratio is 13:1. The library holds 93,684 titles, 424 serial subscriptions, and 12,262 audiovisual materials. Special programs include academic remediation, services for learning-disabled students, an honors program, cooperative (work-study) education, advanced placement credit, accelerated degree programs, double majors, distance learning, self-designed majors, summer session for credit, part-time degree programs (daytime, evenings, summer), adult/continuing education programs, and internships. The most frequently chosen baccalaureate fields are business/marketing, computer and information sciences, education.

Student Body Statistics The student body is made up of 832 undergraduates (134 freshmen). 50 percent are women and 50 percent are men. Students come from 37 states and territories and 5 other countries. 68 percent are from North Dakota. 3.7 percent are international students. 8 percent of the 2006 graduating class went on to graduate and professional schools.

Expenses for 2006–07 *Application fee:* $35. *State resident tuition:* $3614 full-time, $150.58 per credit hour part-time. *Nonresident tuition:* $5421 full-time, $225.88 per credit hour part-time. *Mandatory fees:* $1643 full-time, $68.45 per hour part-time. Both full-time and part-time tuition and fees vary according to course load and reciprocity agreements. *College room and board:* $3884. *College room only:* $1576. Room and board charges vary according to board plan and housing facility.

Financial Aid Forms of aid include need-based and non-need-based scholarships, athletic grants, and part-time jobs. The average aided 2006–07 undergraduate received an aid package worth an estimated $4622. The application deadline for financial aid is continuous.

Freshman Admission Mayville State University requires a high school transcript, a minimum 2.0 high school GPA, SAT or ACT scores, and

TOEFL scores for international students. An interview is recommended. The application deadline for regular admission is rolling and for nonresidents it is rolling.

Transfer Admission Mayville State University requires a minimum 2.00 college GPA. The application deadline for admission is rolling.

Entrance Difficulty Mayville State University has an open admission policy. It assesses its entrance difficulty as minimally difficult for transfers.

For Further Information Contact Dr. Ray Gerszewski, Vice President, Student Affairs and International Research, Mayville State University, 330 3rd Street, NE, Mayville, ND 58257-1299. *Telephone:* 701-788-4842 or 800-437-4104 (toll-free). *Fax:* 701-788-4748. *E-mail:* admit@mayvillestate.edu. *Web site:* http://www.mayvillestate.edu/.

MEDCENTER ONE COLLEGE OF NURSING
Bismarck, North Dakota

Medcenter One College of Nursing is a coed, primarily women's, private, upper-level institution, founded in 1988, offering degrees at the bachelor's level. It has a 15-acre campus in Bismarck.

Academic Information The faculty has 12 members (83% full-time), 8% with terminal degrees. The student-faculty ratio is 9:1. The library holds 25,257 titles, 500 serial subscriptions, and 963 audiovisual materials. Special programs include independent study and internships.

Student Body Statistics The student body is made up of 93 undergraduates. 84 percent are women and 16 percent are men. Students come from 6 states and territories. 97 percent are from North Dakota.

Expenses for 2007–08 *Application fee:* $40. *Tuition:* $9258 full-time, $385.75 per credit part-time. *Mandatory fees:* $759 full-time, $15.01 per credit part-time, $199.50 per term part-time.

Financial Aid Forms of aid include need-based and non-need-based scholarships and part-time jobs. The average aided 2005–06 undergraduate received an aid package worth $13,343. The priority application deadline for financial aid is March 15.

Transfer Admission Medcenter One College of Nursing requires a college transcript and a minimum 2.5 college GPA. The application deadline for admission is November 7.

Entrance Difficulty Medcenter One College of Nursing assesses its entrance difficulty level as moderately difficult. For the fall 2006 entering class, 46 percent of the applicants were accepted.

For Further Information Contact Ms. Mary Smith, Director of Student Services, Medcenter One College of Nursing, 512 North 7th Street, Bismarck, ND 58501-4494. *Telephone:* 701-323-6271. *Fax:* 701-323-6289. *E-mail:* msmith@mohs.org. *Web site:* http://medcenterone.com/college/nursing.htm.

MINOT STATE UNIVERSITY
Minot, North Dakota

Minot State University is a coed, public, comprehensive unit of North Dakota University System, founded in 1913, offering degrees at the associate, bachelor's, and master's levels and post-master's certificates. It has a 103-acre campus in Minot.

Academic Information The faculty has 278 members (64% full-time). The undergraduate student-faculty ratio is 14:1. The library holds 428,407 titles, 693 serial subscriptions, and 123,173 audiovisual materials. Special programs include academic remediation, services for learning-disabled students, an honors program, cooperative (work-study) education, study abroad, advanced placement credit, accelerated degree programs, double majors, independent study, distance learning, self-designed majors, summer session for credit, part-time degree programs (daytime, evenings, summer), adult/continuing education programs, and internships. The most frequently chosen baccalaureate fields are business/marketing, education, health professions and related sciences.

Student Body Statistics The student body totals 3,712, of whom 3,433 are undergraduates (483 freshmen). 62 percent are women and 38 percent are men. Students come from 46 states and territories and 20 other countries. 88 percent are from North Dakota. 7.5 percent are international students. 11 percent of the 2006 graduating class went on to graduate and professional schools.

Expenses for 2006–07 *Application fee:* $35. *State resident tuition:* $3790 full-time, $187 per credit hour part-time. *Nonresident tuition:* $10,116 full-time, $450.74 per credit hour part-time. *Mandatory fees:* $702 full-time, $29 per credit hour part-time. Full-time tuition and fees vary according to class time, course load, location, program, and reciprocity agreements. Part-time tuition and fees vary according to class time, location, program, and reciprocity agreements. *College room and board:* $5294. *College room only:* $2600. Room and board charges vary according to board plan and housing facility.

Financial Aid Forms of aid include need-based and non-need-based scholarships, athletic grants, and part-time jobs. The average aided 2005–06 undergraduate received an aid package worth $4931. The priority application deadline for financial aid is March 15.

Freshman Admission Minot State University requires a high school transcript, SAT or ACT scores, and TOEFL scores for international students. A minimum 2.75 high school GPA and ACT composite score of 16 or higher or comparative SAT score (under age of 25) are required for some. The application deadline for regular admission is rolling.

Transfer Admission Minot State University requires standardized test scores and a college transcript. The application deadline for admission is rolling.

Entrance Difficulty Minot State University assesses its entrance difficulty level as minimally difficult. For the fall 2006 freshman class, 80 percent of the applicants were accepted.

For Further Information Contact Mr. Shane Larson, Director of Enrollment, Minot State University, 500 University Avenue West, Minot, ND 58707-0002. *Telephone:* 701-858-3126 or 800-777-0750 Ext. 3350 (toll-free). *Fax:* 701-858-3825. *E-mail:* askmsu@minotstateu.edu. *Web site:* http://www.minotstateu.edu/.

NORTH DAKOTA STATE UNIVERSITY

Fargo, North Dakota

North Dakota State University is a coed, public unit of North Dakota University System, founded in 1890, offering degrees at the bachelor's, master's, doctoral, and first professional levels and post-master's certificates. It has a 2,100-acre campus in Fargo.

Academic Information The faculty has 630 members (86% full-time), 76% with terminal degrees. The undergraduate student-faculty ratio is 19:1. The library holds 303,274 titles, 2,499 serial subscriptions, and 3,276 audiovisual materials. Special programs include academic remediation, services for learning-disabled students, an honors program, cooperative (work-study) education, study abroad, advanced placement credit, ESL programs, double majors, independent study, distance learning, self-designed majors, summer session for credit, part-time degree programs (daytime, evenings, summer), internships, and arrangement for off-campus study with members of the Tri-College University-Concordia College, Moorhead, MN, Minnesota State University Moorhead. The most frequently chosen baccalaureate fields are business/marketing, engineering, health professions and related sciences.

Student Body Statistics The student body totals 12,258, of whom 10,596 are undergraduates (2,073 freshmen). 45 percent are women and 55 percent are men. Students come from 37 states and territories and 70 other countries. 54 percent are from North Dakota. 2.5 percent are international students. 18.9 percent of the 2006 graduating class went on to graduate and professional schools.

Expenses for 2006–07 *Application fee:* $35. *One-time mandatory fee:* $45. *State resident tuition:* $4774 full-time, $198.92 per credit part-time. *Nonresident tuition:* $12,747 full-time, $531.11 per credit part-time. *Mandatory fees:* $948 full-time, $38.99 per credit part-time. Full-time tuition and fees vary according to reciprocity agreements. Part-time tuition and fees vary according to course load and reciprocity agreements. *College room and board:* $5477. *College room only:* $2277. Room and board charges vary according to board plan and housing facility.

Financial Aid Forms of aid include need-based and non-need-based scholarships, athletic grants, and part-time jobs. The average aided 2005–06 undergraduate received an aid package worth $4604. The priority application deadline for financial aid is March 15.

Freshman Admission North Dakota State University requires a high school transcript, a minimum 2.5 high school GPA, SAT or ACT scores, and TOEFL scores for international students. The application deadline for regular admission is August 15.

Transfer Admission The application deadline for admission is August 15.

Entrance Difficulty North Dakota State University assesses its entrance difficulty level as moderately difficult. For the fall 2006 freshman class, 87 percent of the applicants were accepted.

For Further Information Contact Jobey Lichtblau, Director of Admission, North Dakota State University, PO Box 5454, Fargo, ND 58105-5454. *Telephone:* 701-231-8643 or 800-488-NDSU (toll-free). *Fax:* 701-231-8802. *E-mail:* ndsu.admission@ndsu.edu. *Web site:* http://www.ndsu.edu/.

SITTING BULL COLLEGE

Fort Yates, North Dakota

Sitting Bull College is a coed, private, two-year college, founded in 1973, offering degrees at the associate level.

Academic Information The faculty has 32 members (50% full-time), 9% with terminal degrees. The student-faculty ratio is 6:1. The library holds 10,000 titles and 130 serial subscriptions. Special programs include academic remediation, part-time degree programs (daytime, evenings, weekends, summer), adult/continuing education programs, and arrangement for off-campus study with members of the American Indian Higher Education Consortium.

Student Body Statistics The student body is made up of 214 undergraduates. Students come from 2 states and territories.

Expenses for 2006–07 *Application fee:* $10. *State resident tuition:* $3540 full-time.

Financial Aid Forms of aid include need-based scholarships and part-time jobs. The priority application deadline for financial aid is May 15.

Freshman Admission Sitting Bull College requires a high school transcript, medical questionnaire, and TABE. The application deadline for regular admission is September 6.

Transfer Admission The application deadline for admission is September 6.

Entrance Difficulty Sitting Bull College has an open admission policy.

For Further Information Contact Ms. Melody Silk, Director of Registration and Admissions, Sitting Bull College, 1341 92nd Street, Fort Yates, ND 58538-9701. *Telephone:* 701-854-8000. *Fax:* 701-854-3403. *E-mail:* melodys@sbci.edu. *Web site:* http://www.sittingbull.edu/.

TRINITY BIBLE COLLEGE

Ellendale, North Dakota

http://www.trinitybiblecollege.edu/

TURTLE MOUNTAIN COMMUNITY COLLEGE

Belcourt, North Dakota

Turtle Mountain Community College is a coed, private, two-year college, founded in 1972, offering degrees at the associate level. It has a 10-acre campus in Belcourt.

Academic Information The faculty has 42 members (50% full-time). The library holds 20,500 titles and 150 serial subscriptions. Special programs include academic remediation, part-time degree programs (daytime, evenings), and adult/continuing education programs.

Student Body Statistics The student body is made up of 579 undergraduates (102 freshmen). 65 percent are women and 35 percent are men. Students come from 1 state or territory.

Expenses for 2006–07 *Tuition:* $2000 full-time.

Turtle Mountain Community College (continued)

Financial Aid Forms of aid include need-based scholarships and part-time jobs. The application deadline for financial aid is June 30 with a priority deadline of April 15.

Freshman Admission Turtle Mountain Community College requires a high school transcript and ACT scores. The application deadline for regular admission is rolling.

Transfer Admission The application deadline for admission is rolling.

Entrance Difficulty Turtle Mountain Community College has an open admission policy.

For Further Information Contact Ms. Joni LaFontaine, Admissions/Records Officer, Turtle Mountain Community College, Box 340, Belcourt, ND 58316-0340. *Telephone:* 701-477-7862. *Fax:* 701-477-8967. *E-mail:* jlafontaine@tm.edu. *Web site:* http://www.turtle-mountain.cc.nd.us/.

UNIVERSITY OF MARY
Bismarck, North Dakota

University of Mary is a coed, private, Roman Catholic, comprehensive institution, founded in 1959, offering degrees at the associate, bachelor's, master's, and doctoral levels. It has a 107-acre campus in Bismarck.

Academic Information The faculty has 313 members (32% full-time), 24% with terminal degrees. The undergraduate student-faculty ratio is 17:1. The library holds 78,137 titles, 567 serial subscriptions, and 7,866 audiovisual materials. Special programs include academic remediation, services for learning-disabled students, cooperative (work-study) education, study abroad, advanced placement credit, accelerated degree programs, double majors, independent study, distance learning, summer session for credit, part-time degree programs (daytime, evenings, weekends, summer), external degree programs, adult/continuing education programs, internships, and arrangement for off-campus study. The most frequently chosen baccalaureate fields are business/marketing, education, health professions and related sciences.

Student Body Statistics The student body totals 2,765, of whom 2,106 are undergraduates (343 freshmen). 60 percent are women and 40 percent are men. Students come from 35 states and territories and 14 other countries. 70 percent are from North Dakota. 1.1 percent are international students. 20 percent of the 2006 graduating class went on to graduate and professional schools.

Expenses for 2007–08 *Application fee:* $25. *Comprehensive fee:* $16,040 includes full-time tuition ($11,530), mandatory fees ($250), and college room and board ($4260). *College room only:* $1840. *Part-time tuition:* $365 per credit. *Part-time mandatory fees:* $7 per credit.

Financial Aid Forms of aid include need-based and non-need-based scholarships and part-time jobs. The priority application deadline for financial aid is May 1.

Freshman Admission University of Mary requires a high school transcript, 1 recommendation, SAT or ACT scores, and TOEFL scores for international students. A minimum 2.5 high school GPA is recommended. An essay and an interview are required for some. The application deadline for regular admission is rolling.

Transfer Admission The application deadline for admission is rolling.

Entrance Difficulty University of Mary assesses its entrance difficulty level as moderately difficult. For the fall 2006 freshman class, 81 percent of the applicants were accepted.

For Further Information Contact Dr. Dave Heringer, Vice President for Enrollment Services, University of Mary, 7500 University Drive, Bismarck, ND 58504-9652. *Telephone:* 701-355-8191 or 800-288-6279 (toll-free). *Fax:* 701-255-7687. *E-mail:* marauder@umary.edu. *Web site:* http://www.umary.edu/.

UNIVERSITY OF NORTH DAKOTA
Grand Forks, North Dakota

University of North Dakota is a coed, public unit of North Dakota University System, founded in 1883, offering degrees at the bachelor's, master's, doctoral, and first professional levels and post-master's certificates. It has a 550-acre campus in Grand Forks.

Academic Information The faculty has 627 members (90% full-time), 62% with terminal degrees. The undergraduate student-faculty ratio is 18:1. The library holds 1 million titles, 16,153 serial subscriptions, and 2,928 audiovisual materials. Special programs include services for learning-disabled students, an honors program, cooperative (work-study) education, study abroad, advanced placement credit, accelerated degree programs, ESL programs, double majors, independent study, distance learning, self-designed majors, summer session for credit, part-time degree programs, adult/continuing education programs, internships, and arrangement for off-campus study. The most frequently chosen baccalaureate fields are business/marketing, education, health professions and related sciences.

Student Body Statistics The student body totals 12,834, of whom 10,376 are undergraduates (1,900 freshmen). 46 percent are women and 54 percent are men. Students come from 57 states and territories and 27 other countries. 51 percent are from North Dakota. 2 percent are international students. 13 percent of the 2006 graduating class went on to graduate and professional schools.

Expenses for 2006–07 *Application fee:* $35. *State resident tuition:* $4786 full-time. *Nonresident tuition:* $12,780 full-time. *Mandatory fees:* $1006 full-time. Full-time tuition and fees vary according to degree level, program, and reciprocity agreements. *College room and board:* $5085. *College room only:* $2137. Room and board charges vary according to board plan and housing facility.

Financial Aid Forms of aid include need-based and non-need-based scholarships, athletic grants, and part-time jobs. The average aided 2006–07 undergraduate received an aid package worth an estimated $7032. The priority application deadline for financial aid is March 15.

Freshman Admission University of North Dakota requires a high school transcript, SAT or ACT scores, and TOEFL scores for international students. A minimum 2.5 high school GPA and ACT scores are recommended.

Transfer Admission Standardized test scores and a college transcript are required for some. The application deadline for admission is rolling.

Entrance Difficulty University of North Dakota assesses its entrance difficulty level as minimally difficult; moderately difficult for transfers. For the fall 2006 freshman class, 74 percent of the applicants were accepted.

For Further Information Contact Ms. Heidi Kippenhan, Director of Admissions, University of North Dakota, Box 8382, Grand Forks, ND 58202. *Telephone:* 701-777-3821 or 800-CALL UND (toll-free). *Fax:* 701-777-2721. *E-mail:* enrollment_services@mail.und.nodak.edu. *Web site:* http://www.und.nodak.edu/.

VALLEY CITY STATE UNIVERSITY
Valley City, North Dakota

Valley City State University is a coed, public, four-year college of North Dakota University System, founded in 1890, offering degrees at the bachelor's level. It has a 55-acre campus in Valley City.

Academic Information The faculty has 91 members (60% full-time), 38% with terminal degrees. The student-faculty ratio is 11:1. The library holds 94,450 titles and 7,500 serial subscriptions. Special programs include academic remediation, services for learning-disabled students, cooperative (work-study) education, double majors, distance learning, self-designed majors, summer session for credit, part-time degree programs (daytime, evenings, summer), internships, and arrangement for off-campus study with North Dakota State University, Mayville State University. The most frequently chosen baccalaureate fields are business/marketing, computer and information sciences, education.

Student Body Statistics The student body totals 1,037, of whom 959 are undergraduates (178 freshmen). 54 percent are women and 46 percent are men. Students come from 24 states and territories and 8 other countries. 75 percent are from North Dakota. 5.9 percent are international students.

Expenses for 2006–07 *Application fee:* $35. *State resident tuition:* $3753 full-time, $126 per semester hour part-time. *Nonresident tuition:* $10,021 full-time, $335 per semester hour part-time. *Mandatory fees:* $1554 full-time. Full-time tuition and fees vary according to course load, location, program, and reciprocity agreements. Part-time tuition varies according to course load, location, program, and reciprocity agreements. *College room and board:* $3716. *College room only:* $1436. Room and board charges vary according to board plan and housing facility.

Financial Aid Forms of aid include need-based and non-need-based scholarships, athletic grants, and part-time jobs. The average aided 2006–07 undergraduate received an aid package worth an estimated $5672. The priority application deadline for financial aid is March 15.

Freshman Admission Valley City State University requires a high school transcript and TOEFL scores for international students. SAT or ACT scores are required for some. The application deadline for regular admission is rolling.

Transfer Admission The application deadline for admission is rolling.

Entrance Difficulty Valley City State University has an open admission policy.

For Further Information Contact Ms. Charlene Stenson, Admission Counselor, Valley City State University, 101 College Street Southwest, Valley City, ND 58072. *Telephone:* 701-845-7105 or 800-532-8641 Ext. 37101 (toll-free). *Fax:* 701-845-7299. *E-mail:* enrollment.services@vcsu.edu. *Web site:* http://www.vcsu.edu/.

Ohio

ALLEGHENY WESLEYAN COLLEGE
Salem, Ohio

http://www.awc.edu/

ANTIOCH COLLEGE
Yellow Springs, Ohio

Antioch College is a coed, private, four-year college of Antioch University, founded in 1852, offering degrees at the bachelor's level. It has a 100-acre campus in Yellow Springs near Dayton.

Academic Information The faculty has 59 members (76% full-time), 71% with terminal degrees. The student-faculty ratio is 8:1. The library holds 300,000 titles, 10,504 serial subscriptions, and 6,259 audiovisual materials. Special programs include academic remediation, services for learning-disabled students, cooperative (work-study) education, study abroad, advanced placement credit, double majors, independent study, self-designed majors, summer session for credit, internships, and arrangement for off-campus study with members of the Great Lakes Colleges Association, Southwestern Ohio Council for Higher Education. The most frequently chosen baccalaureate fields are area and ethnic studies, interdisciplinary studies, liberal arts/general studies.

Student Body Statistics The student body totals 341, of whom 330 are undergraduates (98 freshmen). 61 percent are women and 39 percent are men. Students come from 43 states and territories and 2 other countries. 32 percent are from Ohio.

Expenses for 2007–08 *Application fee:* $0. *Comprehensive fee:* $35,904 includes full-time tuition ($27,800), mandatory fees ($750), and college room and board ($7354). *College room only:* $3597. *Part-time tuition:* $458 per credit hour.

Financial Aid Forms of aid include need-based and non-need-based scholarships and part-time jobs. The average aided 2006–07 undergraduate received an aid package worth an estimated $30,640.

Freshman Admission Antioch College requires an essay, a high school transcript, a minimum 2.5 high school GPA, 2 recommendations, and TOEFL scores for international students. An interview is recommended. The application deadline for regular admission is February 1 and for early action it is January 1.

Transfer Admission The application deadline for admission is rolling.

Entrance Difficulty Antioch College assesses its entrance difficulty level as moderately difficult. For the fall 2006 freshman class, 51 percent of the applicants were accepted.

For Further Information Contact Ms. Cathy Paige, Information Manager, Antioch College, 795 Livermore Street, Yellow Springs, OH 45387-1697. *Telephone:* 937-769-1100 Ext. 1119 or 800-543-9436 (toll-free). *Fax:* 937-769-1111. *E-mail:* admissions@college.antioch.edu. *Web site:* http://www.antioch-college.edu/.

ANTIOCH UNIVERSITY McGREGOR
Yellow Springs, Ohio

Antioch University McGregor is a coed, private, upper-level unit of Antioch University, founded in 1988, offering degrees at the bachelor's and master's levels and post-master's certificates. It has a 100-acre campus in Yellow Springs near Dayton.

Academic Information The faculty has 63 members (38% full-time), 56% with terminal degrees. The undergraduate student-faculty ratio is 11:1. The library holds 325,000 titles and 1,000 serial subscriptions. Special programs include cooperative (work-study) education, advanced placement credit, accelerated degree programs, double majors, independent study, distance learning, summer session for credit, part-time degree programs (evenings, weekends, summer), adult/continuing education programs, and internships. The most frequently chosen baccalaureate fields are liberal arts/general studies, business/marketing, psychology.

Student Body Statistics The student body totals 679, of whom 160 are undergraduates. 69 percent are women and 31 percent are men. Students come from 1 state or territory.

Expenses for 2006–07 *Application fee:* $45. *Tuition:* $12,912 full-time, $269 per credit hour part-time. *Mandatory fees:* $225 full-time, $75 per term part-time.

Financial Aid Forms of aid include need-based scholarships and part-time jobs. The average aided 2006–07 undergraduate received an aid package worth an estimated $6000. The application deadline for financial aid is continuous.

Transfer Admission Antioch University McGregor requires a college transcript and a minimum 2.0 college GPA. The application deadline for admission is rolling.

Entrance Difficulty Antioch University McGregor assesses its entrance difficulty level as noncompetitive.

For Further Information Contact Mr. Oscar Robinson, Director of Admissions, Antioch University McGregor, Student and Alumni Services Division, Enrollment Services, Yellow Springs, OH 45387. *Telephone:* 937-769-1823 or 937-769-1818 (toll-free). *Fax:* 937-769-1804. *E-mail:* sas@mcgregor.edu. *Web site:* http://www.mcgregor.edu/.

ART ACADEMY OF CINCINNATI
Cincinnati, Ohio

Art Academy of Cincinnati is a coed, private, comprehensive institution, founded in 1887, offering degrees at the associate, bachelor's, and master's levels. It has a 184-acre campus in Cincinnati.

Academic Information The faculty has 61 members (26% full-time), 74% with terminal degrees. The undergraduate student-faculty ratio is 12:1. The library holds 66,404 titles, 150 serial subscriptions, and 588 audiovisual materials. Special programs include services for learning-disabled students, an honors program, cooperative (work-study) education, study abroad, advanced placement credit, double majors, independent study, self-designed majors, summer session for credit, part-time degree programs (daytime, evenings, summer), adult/continuing education programs, internships, and arrangement for off-campus study with members of the Greater Cincinnati Consortium of Colleges and Universities, Association of Independent Colleges of Art and Design. The most frequently chosen baccalaureate field is visual and performing arts.

Student Body Statistics The student body totals 164, of whom 163 are undergraduates (52 freshmen). 55 percent are women and 45 percent are men. Students come from 15 states and territories and 7 other countries.

Art Academy of Cincinnati (continued)

65 percent are from Ohio. 2.5 percent are international students. 5 percent of the 2006 graduating class went on to graduate and professional schools.

Expenses for 2006–07 *Application fee:* $25. *Tuition:* $19,250 full-time, $810 per credit hour part-time. *Mandatory fees:* $350 full-time, $175 per term part-time.

Financial Aid Forms of aid include need-based and non-need-based scholarships and part-time jobs. The application deadline for financial aid is continuous.

Freshman Admission Art Academy of Cincinnati requires an essay, a high school transcript, a minimum 2.0 high school GPA, 1 recommendation, a portfolio, SAT or ACT scores, and TOEFL scores for international students. An interview is recommended. The application deadline for regular admission is June 30.

Transfer Admission The application deadline for admission is June 30.

Entrance Difficulty Art Academy of Cincinnati assesses its entrance difficulty level as moderately difficult. For the fall 2006 freshman class, 25 percent of the applicants were accepted.

For Further Information Contact Ms. Mary Jane Zumwalde, Director of Admissions, Art Academy of Cincinnati, 1212 Jackson Street, Cincinnati, OH 45202-7106. *Telephone:* 513-562-8744 or 800-323-5692 (toll-free in-state). *Fax:* 513-562-8778. *E-mail:* admissions@artacademy.edu. *Web site:* http://www.artacademy.edu/.

ASHLAND UNIVERSITY
Ashland, Ohio

Ashland University is a coed, private, comprehensive institution, founded in 1878, affiliated with the Brethren Church, offering degrees at the associate, bachelor's, master's, doctoral, and first professional levels. It has a 98-acre campus in Ashland near Cleveland.

Academic Information The faculty has 589 members (39% full-time), 50% with terminal degrees. The undergraduate student-faculty ratio is 12:1. The library holds 205,200 titles, 1,625 serial subscriptions, and 3,550 audiovisual materials. Special programs include academic remediation, services for learning-disabled students, an honors program, study abroad, advanced placement credit, ESL programs, double majors, independent study, self-designed majors, summer session for credit, part-time degree programs (daytime, evenings, weekends, summer), adult/continuing education programs, internships, and arrangement for off-campus study with Case Western Reserve University, Art Institute of Pittsburgh, Purdue University, Drew University, American University, Merrill-Palmer Institute, Hunter College of the City University of New York. The most frequently chosen baccalaureate fields are business/marketing, education, social sciences.

Student Body Statistics The student body totals 6,648, of whom 2,793 are undergraduates (564 freshmen). 55 percent are women and 45 percent are men. Students come from 31 states and territories and 23 other countries. 94 percent are from Ohio. 1.8 percent are international students. 13 percent of the 2006 graduating class went on to graduate and professional schools.

Expenses for 2007–08 *Application fee:* $0. *Comprehensive fee:* $31,364 includes full-time tuition ($22,216), mandatory fees ($774), and college room and board ($8374). *College room only:* $4498. *Part-time tuition:* $682 per credit hour.

Financial Aid Forms of aid include need-based and non-need-based scholarships, athletic grants, and part-time jobs. The application deadline for financial aid is continuous.

Freshman Admission Ashland University requires an essay, a high school transcript, a minimum 2.5 high school GPA, SAT or ACT scores, and TOEFL scores for international students. An interview is recommended. Recommendations and an interview are required for some. The application deadline for regular admission is rolling.

Transfer Admission The application deadline for admission is rolling.

Entrance Difficulty Ashland University assesses its entrance difficulty level as moderately difficult. For the fall 2006 freshman class, 71 percent of the applicants were accepted.

For Further Information Contact Mr. Thomas Mansperger, Director of Admission, Ashland University, 401 College Avenue, Ashland, OH 44805. *Telephone:* 419-289-5052 or 800-882-1548 (toll-free). *Fax:* 419-289-5999. *E-mail:* enrollme@ashland.edu. *Web site:* http://www.exploreashland.com.

BALDWIN-WALLACE COLLEGE
Berea, Ohio

Baldwin-Wallace College is a coed, private, Methodist, comprehensive institution, founded in 1845, offering degrees at the bachelor's and master's levels. It has a 100-acre campus in Berea near Cleveland.

Academic Information The faculty has 382 members (43% full-time), 47% with terminal degrees. The undergraduate student-faculty ratio is 15:1. The library holds 200,000 titles and 22,000 serial subscriptions. Special programs include academic remediation, services for learning-disabled students, an honors program, study abroad, advanced placement credit, accelerated degree programs, ESL programs, double majors, independent study, distance learning, self-designed majors, summer session for credit, part-time degree programs (daytime, evenings, weekends, summer), adult/continuing education programs, internships, and arrangement for off-campus study with Drew University, American University. The most frequently chosen baccalaureate fields are business/marketing, education, psychology.

Student Body Statistics The student body totals 4,365, of whom 3,625 are undergraduates (705 freshmen). 60 percent are women and 40 percent are men. Students come from 29 states and territories and 15 other countries. 90 percent are from Ohio. 1.2 percent are international students. 28.4 percent of the 2006 graduating class went on to graduate and professional schools.

Expenses for 2006–07 *Application fee:* $25. *Comprehensive fee:* $28,210 includes full-time tuition ($21,236) and college room and board ($6974). *College room only:* $3406. *Part-time tuition:* $674 per semester hour. Part-time tuition varies according to class time.

Financial Aid Forms of aid include need-based and non-need-based scholarships and part-time jobs. The average aided 2006–07 undergraduate received an aid package worth an estimated $16,700. The application deadline for financial aid is September 1 with a priority deadline of May 1.

Freshman Admission Baldwin-Wallace College requires an essay, a high school transcript, a minimum 2.7 high school GPA, 1 recommendation, and TOEFL scores for international students. A minimum 3.2 high school GPA and an interview are recommended. The application deadline for regular admission is rolling.

Transfer Admission The application deadline for admission is rolling.

Entrance Difficulty Baldwin-Wallace College assesses its entrance difficulty level as moderately difficult. For the fall 2006 freshman class, 80 percent of the applicants were accepted.

For Further Information Contact Ms. Grace B. Chalker, Interim Associate Director of Admissions, Baldwin-Wallace College, 275 Eastland Road, Berea, OH 44017-2088. *Telephone:* 440-826-2222 or 877-BWAPPLY (toll-free in-state). *Fax:* 440-826-3830. *E-mail:* admission@baldwinw.edu. *Web site:* http://www.bw.edu/.

See page 236 for the College Close-Up.

BLUFFTON UNIVERSITY
Bluffton, Ohio

Bluffton University is a coed, private, Mennonite, comprehensive institution, founded in 1899, offering degrees at the bachelor's and master's levels. It has a 65-acre campus in Bluffton near Toledo.

Academic Information The faculty has 113 members (60% full-time), 45% with terminal degrees. The undergraduate student-faculty ratio is 13:1. The library holds 168,888 titles and 263 serial subscriptions. Special programs include academic remediation, an honors program, study abroad, advanced placement credit, double majors, independent study, self-designed majors, summer session for credit, part-time degree programs (evenings), adult/continuing education programs, internships, and arrangement for off-campus study with Christian College Coalition, Council of Independent Colleges. The most frequently chosen baccalaureate fields are business/marketing, education, parks and recreation.

Student Body Statistics The student body totals 1,155, of whom 1,030 are undergraduates (244 freshmen). 54 percent are women and 46 percent are men. Students come from 11 states and territories and 17 other countries. 88 percent are from Ohio. 1.9 percent are international students.

Expenses for 2006–07 *Application fee:* $20. *Comprehensive fee:* $27,652 includes full-time tuition ($20,170), mandatory fees ($400), and college room and board ($7082). *College room only:* $3260. Full-time tuition and fees vary according to course load and program. Room and board charges vary according to board plan and housing facility. *Part-time tuition:* $840 per credit hour. Part-time tuition varies according to course load and program.

Financial Aid Forms of aid include need-based and non-need-based scholarships and part-time jobs. The average aided 2006–07 undergraduate received an aid package worth an estimated $18,847. The application deadline for financial aid is October 1 with a priority deadline of May 1.

Freshman Admission Bluffton University requires a high school transcript, 2 recommendations, rank in upper 50% of high school class or 2.3 high school GPA, SAT or ACT scores, and TOEFL scores for international students. An interview is recommended. An essay is required for some. The application deadline for regular admission is May 31.

Transfer Admission The application deadline for admission is rolling.

Entrance Difficulty Bluffton University assesses its entrance difficulty level as moderately difficult. For the fall 2006 freshman class, 65 percent of the applicants were accepted.

For Further Information Contact Mr. Chris Jebsen, Director of Admissions, Bluffton University, 1 University Drive, Bluffton, OH 45817. *Telephone:* 419-358-3254 or 800-488-3257 (toll-free). *Fax:* 419-358-3232. *E-mail:* admissions@bluffton.edu. *Web site:* http://www.bluffton.edu/.

BOHECKER'S BUSINESS COLLEGE
Ravenna, Ohio
http://www.boheckercollege.edu/

BOWLING GREEN STATE UNIVERSITY
Bowling Green, Ohio

Bowling Green State University is a coed, public university, founded in 1910, offering degrees at the bachelor's, master's, and doctoral levels and post-master's certificates. It has a 1,230-acre campus in Bowling Green near Toledo.

Academic Information The faculty has 1,032 members (85% full-time). The undergraduate student-faculty ratio is 19:1. Special programs include academic remediation, services for learning-disabled students, an honors program, cooperative (work-study) education, study abroad, advanced placement credit, accelerated degree programs, ESL programs, double majors, independent study, distance learning, self-designed majors, summer session for credit, part-time degree programs (daytime, evenings, summer), adult/continuing education programs, internships, and arrangement for off-campus study with University of Toledo, Medical College of Ohio. The most frequently chosen baccalaureate fields are business/marketing, education, visual and performing arts.

Student Body Statistics The student body totals 19,108, of whom 16,085 are undergraduates (3,598 freshmen). 55 percent are women and 45 percent are men. Students come from 50 states and territories and 47 other countries. 91 percent are from Ohio. 1.4 percent are international students.

Expenses for 2006–07 *Application fee:* $40. *State resident tuition:* $7778 full-time, $380 per credit hour part-time. *Nonresident tuition:* $15,086 full-time, $729 per credit hour part-time. *Mandatory fees:* $1282 full-time, $64 per credit hour part-time. Part-time tuition and fees vary according to course load. *College room and board:* $6684. *College room only:* $4084. Room and board charges vary according to board plan and housing facility.

Financial Aid Forms of aid include need-based and non-need-based scholarships, athletic grants, and part-time jobs. The average aided 2005–06 undergraduate received an aid package worth $10,507. The application deadline for financial aid is continuous.

Freshman Admission Bowling Green State University requires a high school transcript, a minimum 2.5 high school GPA, SAT and SAT Subject Test or ACT scores, and TOEFL scores for international students. An interview is recommended. The application deadline for regular admission is July 15 and for nonresidents it is July 15.

Transfer Admission The application deadline for admission is July 15.

Entrance Difficulty Bowling Green State University assesses its entrance difficulty level as moderately difficult. For the fall 2006 freshman class, 90 percent of the applicants were accepted.

For Further Information Contact Mr. Gary Swegan, Director of Admissions, Bowling Green State University, 110 McFall, Bowling Green, OH 43403. *Telephone:* 419-372-BGSU. *Fax:* 419-372-6955. *E-mail:* admissions@bgnet.bgsu.edu. *Web site:* http://www.bgsu.edu/.

BOWLING GREEN STATE UNIVERSITY–FIRELANDS COLLEGE
Huron, Ohio

Bowling Green State University–Firelands College is a coed, public, primarily two-year college of Bowling Green State University System, founded in 1968, offering degrees at the associate and bachelor's levels (also offers some upper-level and graduate courses). It has a 216-acre campus in Huron near Cleveland and Toledo.

Academic Information The faculty has 121 members (40% full-time), 35% with terminal degrees. The student-faculty ratio is 19:1. The library holds 31,262 titles and 223 serial subscriptions. Special programs include academic remediation, services for learning-disabled students, advanced placement credit, double majors, independent study, distance learning, self-designed majors, summer session for credit, part-time degree programs (daytime, evenings, summer), adult/continuing education programs, and internships.

Student Body Statistics The student body totals 2,024, of whom 1,984 are undergraduates (411 freshmen). 65 percent are women and 35 percent are men. Students come from 3 states and territories. 100 percent are from Ohio.

Expenses for 2006–07 *Application fee:* $35. *State resident tuition:* $4022 full-time, $196 per credit part-time. *Nonresident tuition:* $11,330 full-time, $545 per credit part-time. *Mandatory fees:* $206 full-time, $10 per credit part-time, $8 per term part-time. Both full-time and part-time tuition and fees vary according to course load and location.

Financial Aid Forms of aid include need-based scholarships and part-time jobs. The application deadline for financial aid is continuous.

Freshman Admission Bowling Green State University–Firelands College requires a high school transcript and TOEFL scores for international students. The application deadline for regular admission is August 13.

Transfer Admission The application deadline for admission is August 13.

Entrance Difficulty Bowling Green State University–Firelands College has an open admission policy. It assesses its entrance difficulty as minimally difficult for transfers.

For Further Information Contact Ms. Debralee Divers, Director of Admissions and Financial Aid, Bowling Green State University–Firelands College, One University Drive, Huron, OH 44839. *Telephone:* 419-433-5560 or 800-322-4787 (toll-free in-state). *Fax:* 419-372-0604. *E-mail:* divers@bgsu.edu. *Web site:* http://www.firelands.bgsu.edu/.

BRYANT AND STRATTON COLLEGE
Cleveland, Ohio

Bryant and Stratton College is a coed, proprietary, four-year college of Bryant and Stratton Business Institute, Inc, founded in 1929, offering degrees at the associate and bachelor's levels.

Academic Information The faculty has 37 members (35% full-time), 27% with terminal degrees. The student-faculty ratio is 10:1. The library

Bryant and Stratton College (continued)

holds 4,466 titles, 80 serial subscriptions, and 159 audiovisual materials. Special programs include academic remediation, services for learning-disabled students, cooperative (work-study) education, double majors, independent study, distance learning, summer session for credit, part-time degree programs (evenings, weekends, summer), adult/continuing education programs, and internships. The most frequently chosen baccalaureate field is business/marketing.

Student Body Statistics The student body is made up of 524 undergraduates. 63 percent are women and 37 percent are men. Students come from 2 states and territories.

Expenses for 2006–07 *Tuition:* $415 per credit hour part-time. *Mandatory fees:* $62.25 per term part-time.

Financial Aid Forms of aid include need-based and non-need-based scholarships and part-time jobs. The application deadline for financial aid is continuous.

Freshman Admission Bryant and Stratton College requires a high school transcript, an interview, entrance evaluation and placement evaluation, TOEFL scores for international students, and TABE. SAT or ACT scores are recommended. The application deadline for regular admission is rolling.

Transfer Admission The application deadline for admission is rolling.

Entrance Difficulty Bryant and Stratton College assesses its entrance difficulty level as minimally difficult.

For Further Information Contact Ted Hanson, Director of Admissions, Bryant and Stratton College, 1700 East 13th Street, Cleveland, OH 44114-3203. *Telephone:* 216-771-1700. *Fax:* 216-771-7787. *E-mail:* thanson@bryantstratton.edu. *Web site:* http://www.bryantstratton.edu/.

BRYANT AND STRATTON COLLEGE

Parma, Ohio

Bryant and Stratton College is a coed, proprietary, primarily two-year college of Bryant and Stratton Business Institute, Inc, founded in 1981, offering degrees at the associate and bachelor's levels. It has a 4-acre campus in Parma near Cleveland.

Expenses for 2006–07 *Tuition:* $415 per credit hour part-time. *Mandatory fees:* $62.25 per term part-time.

For Further Information Contact Mr. F. Lee Nelly, Director of Admissions, Bryant and Stratton College, 12955 Snow Road, Parma, OH 44130. *Telephone:* 216-265-3151 Ext. 229 or 800-327-3151 (toll-free in-state). *Fax:* 216-265-0325. *E-mail:* finelly@bryantstratton.edu. *Web site:* http://www.bryantstratton.edu/.

CAPITAL UNIVERSITY

Columbus, Ohio

Capital University is a coed, private, comprehensive institution, founded in 1830, affiliated with the Evangelical Lutheran Church in America, offering degrees at the bachelor's, master's, and first professional levels. It has a 48-acre campus in Columbus.

Academic Information The faculty has 419 members (54% full-time), 51% with terminal degrees. The undergraduate student-faculty ratio is 11:1. The library holds 196,000 titles, 7,055 serial subscriptions, and 16,000 audiovisual materials. Special programs include services for learning-disabled students, an honors program, cooperative (work-study) education, study abroad, advanced placement credit, accelerated degree programs, Freshman Honors College, ESL programs, double majors, independent study, self-designed majors, summer session for credit, part-time degree programs (evenings, weekends, summer), adult/continuing education programs, internships, and arrangement for off-campus study with members of the Higher Education Council of Columbus. The most frequently chosen baccalaureate fields are education, health professions and related sciences, interdisciplinary studies.

Student Body Statistics The student body totals 3,825, of whom 2,824 are undergraduates (696 freshmen). 62 percent are women and 38 percent are men. Students come from 26 states and territories and 15 other countries. 96 percent are from Ohio. 0.8 percent are international students. 16 percent of the 2006 graduating class went on to graduate and professional schools.

Expenses for 2006–07 *Application fee:* $25. *Comprehensive fee:* $31,652 includes full-time tuition ($25,100) and college room and board ($6552). Full-time tuition varies according to course load, degree level, program, and student level. Room and board charges vary according to board plan and housing facility. *Part-time tuition:* $786 per credit hour. Part-time tuition varies according to course load, degree level, program, and student level.

Financial Aid Forms of aid include need-based and non-need-based scholarships and part-time jobs. The average aided 2006–07 undergraduate received an aid package worth an estimated $17,938. The priority application deadline for financial aid is February 28.

Freshman Admission Capital University requires a high school transcript, a minimum 2.6 high school GPA, SAT or ACT scores, and TOEFL scores for international students. An interview is recommended. 1 recommendation and audition are required for some. The application deadline for regular admission is April 1.

Transfer Admission The application deadline for admission is rolling.

Entrance Difficulty Capital University assesses its entrance difficulty level as moderately difficult. For the fall 2006 freshman class, 77 percent of the applicants were accepted.

For Further Information Contact Mrs. Kimberly V. Ebbrecht, Director of Admission, Capital University, 2199 East Main Street, Columbus, OH 43209. *Telephone:* 614-236-6101 or 800-289-6289 (toll-free). *Fax:* 614-236-6926. *E-mail:* admissions@capital.edu. *Web site:* http://www.capital.edu/.

CASE WESTERN RESERVE UNIVERSITY

Cleveland, Ohio

Case Western Reserve University is a coed, private university, founded in 1826, offering degrees at the bachelor's, master's, doctoral, and first professional levels. It has a 150-acre campus in Cleveland.

Academic Information The faculty has 863 members (81% full-time), 86% with terminal degrees. The undergraduate student-faculty ratio is 9:1. The library holds 2 million titles, 20,265 serial subscriptions, and 56,916 audiovisual materials. Special programs include services for learning-disabled students, an honors program, cooperative (work-study) education, study abroad, advanced placement credit, accelerated degree programs, ESL programs, double majors, independent study, self-designed majors, summer session for credit, part-time degree programs (daytime, evenings), adult/continuing education programs, internships, and arrangement for off-campus study with Cleveland Institute of Art, Cleveland Institute of Music, 11 other Cleveland area institutions. The most frequently chosen baccalaureate fields are biological/life sciences, engineering, social sciences.

Student Body Statistics The student body totals 9,592, of whom 4,080 are undergraduates (1,015 freshmen). 42 percent are women and 58 percent are men. Students come from 52 states and territories and 28 other countries. 56 percent are from Ohio. 3.5 percent are international students. 43 percent of the 2006 graduating class went on to graduate and professional schools.

Expenses for 2006–07 *Comprehensive fee:* $41,018 includes full-time tuition ($31,090), mandatory fees ($648), and college room and board ($9280). *College room only:* $5440. Room and board charges vary according to board plan, housing facility, and student level. *Part-time tuition:* $1296 per credit hour. Part-time tuition varies according to course load.

Financial Aid Forms of aid include need-based and non-need-based scholarships and part-time jobs. The average aided 2006–07 undergraduate received an aid package worth an estimated $32,131. The priority application deadline for financial aid is February 15.

Freshman Admission Case Western Reserve University requires an essay, a high school transcript, 1 recommendation, SAT or ACT scores, and TOEFL scores for international students. An interview is recommended. The application deadline for regular admission is January 15 and for early action it is November 1.

Transfer Admission The application deadline for admission is May 15.

Entrance Difficulty Case Western Reserve University assesses its entrance difficulty level as very difficult. For the fall 2006 freshman class, 67 percent of the applicants were accepted.

For Further Information Contact Ms. Elizabeth Woyczynski, Director of Undergraduate Admission, Case Western Reserve University, 10900 Euclid Avenue, Cleveland, OH 44106. *Telephone:* 216-368-4450. *Fax:* 216-368-5111. *E-mail:* admission@case.edu. *Web site:* http://www.case.edu/.

CEDARVILLE UNIVERSITY
Cedarville, Ohio

Cedarville University is a coed, private, Baptist, comprehensive institution, founded in 1887, offering degrees at the bachelor's and master's levels. It has a 400-acre campus in Cedarville near Columbus and Dayton.

Academic Information The faculty has 262 members (79% full-time), 50% with terminal degrees. The undergraduate student-faculty ratio is 11:1. The library holds 170,561 titles, 6,400 serial subscriptions, and 15,868 audiovisual materials. Special programs include academic remediation, services for learning-disabled students, an honors program, study abroad, advanced placement credit, accelerated degree programs, double majors, independent study, distance learning, summer session for credit, part-time degree programs (daytime), internships, and arrangement for off-campus study with Au Sable Institute. The most frequently chosen baccalaureate fields are business/marketing, education, theology and religious vocations.

Student Body Statistics The student body totals 3,112, of whom 3,064 are undergraduates (713 freshmen). 55 percent are women and 45 percent are men. Students come from 49 states and territories and 16 other countries. 37 percent are from Ohio. 0.5 percent are international students. 10 percent of the 2006 graduating class went on to graduate and professional schools.

Expenses for 2006–07 *Application fee:* $30. *Comprehensive fee:* $24,810 includes full-time tuition ($18,400), mandatory fees ($1400), and college room and board ($5010). *College room only:* $2684. Room and board charges vary according to board plan. *Part-time tuition:* $575 per credit hour. Part-time tuition varies according to course load.

Financial Aid Forms of aid include need-based and non-need-based scholarships, athletic grants, and part-time jobs. The average aided 2006–07 undergraduate received an aid package worth an estimated $16,048. The priority application deadline for financial aid is March 1.

Freshman Admission Cedarville University requires an essay, a high school transcript, a minimum 3.0 high school GPA, 2 recommendations, SAT or ACT scores, and TOEFL scores for international students. SAT and SAT Subject Test or ACT scores are recommended. An interview is required for some. The application deadline for regular admission is rolling.

Transfer Admission The application deadline for admission is rolling.

Entrance Difficulty Cedarville University assesses its entrance difficulty level as moderately difficult. For the fall 2006 freshman class, 81 percent of the applicants were accepted.

For Further Information Contact Mr. Roscoe Smith, Director of Admissions, Cedarville University, 251 North Main Street, Cedarville, OH 45314-0601. *Telephone:* 937-766-7700 or 800-CEDARVILLE (toll-free). *Fax:* 937-766-7575. *E-mail:* admiss@cedarville.edu. *Web site:* http://www.cedarville.edu/.

CENTRAL STATE UNIVERSITY
Wilberforce, Ohio

Central State University is a coed, public, comprehensive unit of Ohio Board of Regents, founded in 1887, offering degrees at the bachelor's and master's levels and postbachelor's certificates. It has a 60-acre campus in Wilberforce near Dayton.

Academic Information The faculty has 179 members (57% full-time). The undergraduate student-faculty ratio is 13:1. The library holds 280,470 titles and 26,066 serial subscriptions. Special programs include services for learning-disabled students, an honors program, cooperative (work-study)

education, study abroad, double majors, independent study, summer session for credit, part-time degree programs (daytime, evenings, weekends, summer), adult/continuing education programs, internships, and arrangement for off-campus study with members of the Southwestern Ohio Council for Higher Education. The most frequently chosen baccalaureate fields are business/marketing, communications/journalism, education.

Student Body Statistics The student body totals 1,766, of whom 1,747 are undergraduates (546 freshmen). 50 percent are women and 50 percent are men. Students come from 32 states and territories and 8 other countries. 66 percent are from Ohio. 0.5 percent are international students. 19 percent of the 2006 graduating class went on to graduate and professional schools.

Expenses for 2006–07 *Application fee:* $20. *State resident tuition:* $5294 full-time, $218 per credit hour part-time. *Nonresident tuition:* $11,462 full-time, $496 per credit hour part-time. Full-time tuition varies according to course load. *College room and board:* $7402. *College room only:* $3978. Room and board charges vary according to board plan.

Financial Aid Forms of aid include need-based and non-need-based scholarships, athletic grants, and part-time jobs. The priority application deadline for financial aid is February 15.

Freshman Admission Central State University requires a high school transcript, SAT or ACT scores, and TOEFL scores for international students. An interview and ACT scores are recommended. An essay, a minimum 2.0 high school GPA, 2 recommendations, and 2.5 high school GPA for nonresidents are required for some. The application deadline for regular admission is June 15.

Transfer Admission The application deadline for admission is June 15.

Entrance Difficulty Central State University has an open admission policy for state residents. It assesses its entrance difficulty as moderately difficult for out-of-state applicants; moderately difficult for transfers.

For Further Information Contact Ms. Robin Rucker, Interim Associate Director, Admissions, Central State University, PO Box 1004, 1400 Blush Row Road, Wilberforce, OH 45384. *Telephone:* 937-376-6580 or 800-388-CSU1 (toll-free in-state). *Fax:* 937-376-6648. *E-mail:* admissions@centralstate.edu. *Web site:* http://www.centralstate.edu/.

CHATFIELD COLLEGE
St. Martin, Ohio

Chatfield College is a coed, primarily women's, private, two-year college, founded in 1970, affiliated with the Roman Catholic Church, offering degrees at the associate level. It has a 200-acre campus in St. Martin near Cincinnati and Dayton.

Expenses for 2006–07 *Application fee:* $10. *Tuition:* $3360 full-time, $280 per credit hour part-time. *Mandatory fees:* $80 full-time.

For Further Information Contact Ms. Anna Jones, Director of Admissions, Chatfield College, 20918 State Route 251, St. Martin, OH 45118-9705. *Telephone:* 513-875-3344. *Fax:* 513-875-3912. *E-mail:* chatfield@chatfield.edu. *Web site:* http://www.chatfield.edu/.

CINCINNATI CHRISTIAN UNIVERSITY
Cincinnati, Ohio

Cincinnati Christian University is a coed, private, comprehensive institution, founded in 1924, affiliated with the Church of Christ, offering degrees at the associate, bachelor's, master's, and first professional levels. It has a 40-acre campus in Cincinnati.

Academic Information The faculty has 68 members (49% full-time). The undergraduate student-faculty ratio is 19:1. The library holds 9,400 titles and 656 serial subscriptions. Special programs include academic remediation, advanced placement credit, double majors, independent study, summer session for credit, part-time degree programs (daytime, evenings, summer), adult/continuing education programs, internships, and arrangement for off-campus study with College of Mount St. Joseph, Greater Cincinnati Consortium of Colleges and Universities.

Student Body Statistics The student body totals 1,125, of whom 841 are undergraduates (227 freshmen). 48 percent are women and 52 percent

Cincinnati Christian University (continued)

are men. Students come from 34 states and territories and 65 other countries. 62 percent are from Ohio. 1.2 percent are international students. 15 percent of the 2006 graduating class went on to graduate and professional schools.

Expenses for 2006–07 *Application fee:* $40. *Comprehensive fee:* $17,380 includes full-time tuition ($11,420) and college room and board ($5960). *Part-time tuition:* $310 per credit hour.

Financial Aid Forms of aid include need-based and non-need-based scholarships and part-time jobs. The priority application deadline for financial aid is March 15.

Freshman Admission Cincinnati Christian University requires an essay, a high school transcript, 3 recommendations, SAT or ACT scores, and TOEFL scores for international students. A minimum 2.0 high school GPA and an interview are recommended. The application deadline for regular admission is July 1.

Transfer Admission The application deadline for admission is July 1.

Entrance Difficulty Cincinnati Christian University assesses its entrance difficulty level as minimally difficult. For the fall 2006 freshman class, 75 percent of the applicants were accepted.

For Further Information Contact Ms. Rachel Kitterman, Office Manager of Undergraduate Admissions, Cincinnati Christian University, 2700 Glenway Avenue, Cincinnati, OH 45204-1799. *Telephone:* 800-949-4222 Ext. 8610 or 800-949-4228 (toll-free in-state). *Fax:* 513-244-8140. *E-mail:* admissions@cincybible.edu. *Web site:* http://www.ccuniversity.edu/.

CINCINNATI COLLEGE OF MORTUARY SCIENCE

Cincinnati, Ohio

Cincinnati College of Mortuary Science is a coed, private, primarily two-year college, founded in 1882, offering degrees at the associate and bachelor's levels. It has a 10-acre campus in Cincinnati.

Expenses for 2006–07 *Application fee:* $25. *Tuition:* $13,500 full-time, $180 per credit part-time. *Mandatory fees:* $610 full-time.

For Further Information Contact Ms. Pat Leon, Director of Financial Aid, Cincinnati College of Mortuary Science, 645 West North Bend Road, Cincinnati, OH 45224-1462. *Telephone:* 513-761-2020. *Fax:* 513-761-3333. *Web site:* http://www.ccms.edu/.

CIRCLEVILLE BIBLE COLLEGE

See Ohio Christian University.

CLEVELAND COLLEGE OF JEWISH STUDIES

See Laura and Alvin Siegal College of Judaic Studies.

THE CLEVELAND INSTITUTE OF ART

Cleveland, Ohio

The Cleveland Institute of Art is a coed, private, comprehensive institution, founded in 1882, offering degrees at the bachelor's and master's levels. It has a 488-acre campus in Cleveland.

Academic Information The faculty has 101 members (47% full-time), 62% with terminal degrees. The undergraduate student-faculty ratio is 9:1. The library holds 42,000 titles and 250 serial subscriptions. Special programs include academic remediation, services for learning-disabled students, an honors program, study abroad, advanced placement credit, independent study, part-time degree programs (daytime), internships, and arrangement for off-campus study with Case Western Reserve University, Northeast Ohio Commission on Higher Education, Association of Independent Colleges of Art and Design.

Student Body Statistics The student body totals 610, of whom 604 are undergraduates (123 freshmen). 52 percent are women and 48 percent are men. Students come from 26 states and territories and 16 other countries. 68 percent are from Ohio. 2.6 percent are international students. 17 percent of the 2006 graduating class went on to graduate and professional schools.

Expenses for 2006–07 *Application fee:* $30. Contact Institute directly for tuition, fees, and room and board.

Financial Aid Forms of aid include need-based and non-need-based scholarships and part-time jobs. The average aided 2006–07 undergraduate received an aid package worth an estimated $16,642. The priority application deadline for financial aid is March 15.

Freshman Admission The Cleveland Institute of Art requires an essay, a high school transcript, a minimum 2.0 high school GPA, 2 recommendations, a portfolio, SAT or ACT scores, and TOEFL scores for international students. An interview is recommended. The application deadline for regular admission is rolling.

Transfer Admission The application deadline for admission is rolling.

Entrance Difficulty The Cleveland Institute of Art assesses its entrance difficulty level as moderately difficult. For the fall 2006 freshman class, 76 percent of the applicants were accepted.

For Further Information Contact Office of Admissions, The Cleveland Institute of Art, 11141 East Boulevard, Cleveland, OH 44106. *Telephone:* 216-421-7418 or 800-223-4700 (toll-free). *Fax:* 216-754-3634. *E-mail:* 74527.17@compuserve.com. *Web site:* http://www.cia.edu/.

CLEVELAND INSTITUTE OF MUSIC

Cleveland, Ohio

Cleveland Institute of Music is a coed, private, comprehensive institution, founded in 1920, offering degrees at the bachelor's, master's, and doctoral levels and postbachelor's certificates. It has a 488-acre campus in Cleveland.

Academic Information The faculty has 105 members (40% full-time), 4% with terminal degrees. The undergraduate student-faculty ratio is 7:1. The library holds 50,924 titles and 115 serial subscriptions. Special programs include academic remediation, study abroad, advanced placement credit, accelerated degree programs, ESL programs, double majors, independent study, distance learning, summer session for credit, internships, and arrangement for off-campus study with Case Western Reserve University. The most frequently chosen baccalaureate field is visual and performing arts.

Student Body Statistics The student body totals 426, of whom 234 are undergraduates (67 freshmen). 54 percent are women and 46 percent are men. Students come from 39 states and territories and 17 other countries. 36 percent are from Ohio. 12.9 percent are international students. 90 percent of the 2006 graduating class went on to graduate and professional schools.

Expenses for 2006–07 *Application fee:* $100. *Comprehensive fee:* $38,368 includes full-time tuition ($27,950), mandatory fees ($1084), and college room and board ($9334). *College room only:* $5440. Room and board charges vary according to board plan. *Part-time tuition:* $1165 per credit hour.

Financial Aid Forms of aid include need-based and non-need-based scholarships and part-time jobs. The average aided 2006–07 undergraduate received an aid package worth an estimated $18,324. The application deadline for financial aid is February 15 with a priority deadline of February 15.

Freshman Admission Cleveland Institute of Music requires an essay, a high school transcript, 2 recommendations, audition, and TOEFL scores for international students. An interview is recommended. SAT or ACT scores are required for some. The application deadline for regular admission is December 1.

Transfer Admission The application deadline for admission is December 1.

Entrance Difficulty Cleveland Institute of Music assesses its entrance difficulty level as very difficult. For the fall 2006 freshman class, 38 percent of the applicants were accepted.

For Further Information Contact Mr. William Fay, Director of Admission, Cleveland Institute of Music, 11021 East Boulevard, Cleveland, OH 44106-1776. *Telephone:* 216-795-3107. *Fax:* 216-791-1530. *E-mail:* cimadmission@po.cwru.edu. *Web site:* http://www.cim.edu/.

CLEVELAND STATE UNIVERSITY
Cleveland, Ohio

Cleveland State University is a coed, public university, founded in 1964, offering degrees at the bachelor's, master's, doctoral, and first professional levels and post-master's and postbachelor's certificates. It has a 70-acre campus in Cleveland near Akron.

Academic Information The faculty has 963 members (54% full-time), 63% with terminal degrees. The undergraduate student-faculty ratio is 14:1. The library holds 847,731 titles, 7,826 serial subscriptions, and 143,894 audiovisual materials. Special programs include academic remediation, an honors program, cooperative (work-study) education, study abroad, advanced placement credit, accelerated degree programs, Freshman Honors College, ESL programs, independent study, self-designed majors, summer session for credit, part-time degree programs, adult/continuing education programs, internships, and arrangement for off-campus study with 7 members of the Cleveland Commission on Higher Education, University of Akron, Baldwin-Wallace College, University of Toledo. The most frequently chosen baccalaureate fields are business/marketing, education, social sciences.

Student Body Statistics The student body totals 15,483, of whom 9,878 are undergraduates (1,040 freshmen). 56 percent are women and 44 percent are men. Students come from 23 states and territories and 75 other countries. 98 percent are from Ohio. 2.1 percent are international students.

Expenses for 2006–07 *Application fee:* $30. *State resident tuition:* $7920 full-time, $330 per semester hour part-time. *Nonresident tuition:* $10,664 full-time, $444.30 per semester hour part-time. Both full-time and part-time tuition varies according to program. *College room and board:* $7800. *College room only:* $5000. Room and board charges vary according to board plan and housing facility.

Financial Aid Forms of aid include need-based and non-need-based scholarships, athletic grants, and part-time jobs. The average aided 2006–07 undergraduate received an aid package worth an estimated $7679. The priority application deadline for financial aid is February 15.

Freshman Admission Cleveland State University requires a high school transcript, SAT or ACT scores, and TOEFL scores for international students. The application deadline for regular admission is August 15.

Transfer Admission The application deadline for admission is July 15.

Entrance Difficulty Cleveland State University has an open admission policy for state residents.

For Further Information Contact Undergraduate Admissions Office, Cleveland State University, 204 RTW, 1806 East 22nd Street, Cleveland, OH 44114. *Telephone:* 216-687-2100 or 888-CSU-OHIO (toll-free). *Fax:* 216-687-9210. *E-mail:* admissions@csuohio.edu. *Web site:* http://www.csuohio.edu/.

COLLEGE OF MOUNT ST. JOSEPH
Cincinnati, Ohio

College of Mount St. Joseph is a coed, private, Roman Catholic, comprehensive institution, founded in 1920, offering degrees at the associate, bachelor's, master's, and doctoral levels and postbachelor's certificates. It has a 92-acre campus in Cincinnati.

Academic Information The faculty has 238 members (48% full-time), 45% with terminal degrees. The undergraduate student-faculty ratio is 11:1. The library holds 97,172 titles, 9,000 serial subscriptions, and 1,818 audiovisual materials. Special programs include academic remediation, services for learning-disabled students, an honors program, cooperative (work-study) education, study abroad, advanced placement credit, accelerated degree programs, double majors, independent study, distance learning, summer session for credit, part-time degree programs (daytime, evenings, weekends, summer), adult/continuing education programs, internships, and arrangement for off-campus study with Greater Cincinnati Consortium of Colleges and Universities. The most frequently chosen baccalaureate fields are business/marketing, health professions and related sciences, personal and culinary services.

Student Body Statistics The student body totals 2,259, of whom 1,916 are undergraduates (322 freshmen). 68 percent are women and 32 percent are men. Students come from 24 states and territories and 7 other countries. 85 percent are from Ohio. 0.3 percent are international students. 13 percent of the 2006 graduating class went on to graduate and professional schools.

Expenses for 2007–08 *Application fee:* $25. *Comprehensive fee:* $26,350 includes full-time tuition ($19,650), mandatory fees ($400), and college room and board ($6300). *College room only:* $3100. *Part-time tuition:* $440 per semester hour. *Part-time mandatory fees:* $200 per semester hour.

Financial Aid Forms of aid include need-based and non-need-based scholarships and part-time jobs. The average aided 2005–06 undergraduate received an aid package worth $15,832. The priority application deadline for financial aid is March 1.

Freshman Admission College of Mount St. Joseph requires a high school transcript, SAT or ACT scores, and TOEFL scores for international students. A minimum 2.5 high school GPA and minimum SAT score of 960 or ACT score of 19 are recommended. 1 recommendation and an interview are required for some. The application deadline for regular admission is August 15.

Transfer Admission The application deadline for admission is August 1.

Entrance Difficulty College of Mount St. Joseph assesses its entrance difficulty level as moderately difficult. For the fall 2006 freshman class, 71 percent of the applicants were accepted.

For Further Information Contact Ms. Peggy Minnich, Director of Admission, College of Mount St. Joseph, 5701 Delhi Road, Cincinnati, OH 45233-1670. *Telephone:* 513-244-4531 or 800-654-9314 (toll-free). *Fax:* 513-244-4629. *E-mail:* admissions@mail.msj.edu. *Web site:* http://www.msj.edu/.

THE COLLEGE OF WOOSTER
Wooster, Ohio

The College of Wooster is a coed, private, four-year college, founded in 1866, affiliated with the Presbyterian Church (U.S.A.), offering degrees at the bachelor's level. It has a 240-acre campus in Wooster near Cleveland.

Academic Information The faculty has 202 members (68% full-time), 91% with terminal degrees. The student-faculty ratio is 11:1. The library holds 581,518 titles and 12,416 audiovisual materials. Special programs include services for learning-disabled students, cooperative (work-study) education, study abroad, advanced placement credit, double majors, independent study, self-designed majors, summer session for credit, internships, and arrangement for off-campus study. The most frequently chosen baccalaureate fields are history, English, social sciences.

Student Body Statistics The student body is made up of 1,819 undergraduates (493 freshmen). 51 percent are women and 49 percent are men. Students come from 46 states and territories and 37 other countries. 46 percent are from Ohio. 4.7 percent are international students. 42 percent of the 2006 graduating class went on to graduate and professional schools.

Expenses for 2006–07 *Application fee:* $40. *Comprehensive fee:* $37,580 includes full-time tuition ($30,060) and college room and board ($7520). *College room only:* $3420. Full-time tuition varies according to course load and reciprocity agreements. *Part-time tuition:* varies with course load.

Financial Aid Forms of aid include need-based and non-need-based scholarships. The average aided 2006–07 undergraduate received an aid package worth an estimated $24,981. The application deadline for financial aid is September 1 with a priority deadline of February 15.

Freshman Admission The College of Wooster requires an essay, a high school transcript, 2 recommendations, SAT or ACT scores, and TOEFL scores for international students. An interview is recommended. The application deadline for regular admission is February 15; for early decision plan 1 it is December 1; and for early decision plan 2 it is January 15.

Transfer Admission The application deadline for admission is June 1.

The College of Wooster (continued)

Entrance Difficulty The College of Wooster assesses its entrance difficulty level as moderately difficult. For the fall 2006 freshman class, 80 percent of the applicants were accepted.

For Further Information Contact Mr. Derek Gueldenzoph, Dean of Admissions, The College of Wooster, 847 College Avenue, Wooster, OH 44691. *Telephone:* 330-263-2270 Ext. 2118 or 800-877-9905 (toll-free). *Fax:* 330-263-2621. *E-mail:* admissions@wooster.edu. *Web site:* http://www.wooster.edu/.

See page 242 for the College Close-Up.

COLUMBUS COLLEGE OF ART & DESIGN

Columbus, Ohio

Columbus College of Art & Design is a coed, private, four-year college, founded in 1879, offering degrees at the bachelor's level. It has a 10-acre campus in Columbus.

Academic Information The faculty has 170 members (45% full-time), 44% with terminal degrees. The student-faculty ratio is 15:1. The library holds 50,920 titles, 275 serial subscriptions, and 540 audiovisual materials. Special programs include academic remediation, services for learning-disabled students, advanced placement credit, ESL programs, double majors, independent study, summer session for credit, part-time degree programs (daytime, evenings, summer), internships, and arrangement for off-campus study with members of the Higher Education Council of Columbus. The most frequently chosen baccalaureate field is visual and performing arts.

Student Body Statistics The student body is made up of 1,581 undergraduates (350 freshmen). 57 percent are women and 43 percent are men. Students come from 39 states and territories and 37 other countries. 79 percent are from Ohio. 6 percent are international students. 10 percent of the 2006 graduating class went on to graduate and professional schools.

Expenses for 2006–07 *Application fee:* $25. *Comprehensive fee:* $27,946 includes full-time tuition ($20,736), mandatory fees ($610), and college room and board ($6600). Room and board charges vary according to housing facility and student level. *Part-time tuition:* $864 per credit. *Part-time mandatory fees:* $305 per term. Part-time tuition and fees vary according to course load.

Financial Aid Forms of aid include need-based and non-need-based scholarships and part-time jobs. The average aided 2005–06 undergraduate received an aid package worth $14,993. The priority application deadline for financial aid is March 3.

Freshman Admission Columbus College of Art & Design requires an essay, a high school transcript, a minimum 2.0 high school GPA, 1 recommendation, a portfolio, SAT or ACT scores, and TOEFL scores for international students. An interview is recommended. The application deadline for regular admission is rolling.

Transfer Admission The application deadline for admission is rolling.

Entrance Difficulty Columbus College of Art & Design assesses its entrance difficulty level as moderately difficult. For the fall 2006 freshman class, 63 percent of the applicants were accepted.

For Further Information Contact Mr. Thomas E. Green, Director of Admissions, Columbus College of Art & Design, 107 North Ninth Street, Columbus, OH 43215-1758. *Telephone:* 614-224-9101 or 877-997-2223 (toll-free). *Fax:* 614-232-8344. *E-mail:* admissions@ccad.edu. *Web site:* http://www.ccad.edu/.

DAVID N. MYERS UNIVERSITY

See Myers University.

DEFIANCE COLLEGE

Defiance, Ohio

Defiance College is a coed, private, comprehensive institution, founded in 1850, affiliated with the United Church of Christ, offering degrees at the associate, bachelor's, and master's levels. It has a 150-acre campus in Defiance near Toledo.

Expenses for 2006–07 *Application fee:* $25. *Comprehensive fee:* $25,910 includes full-time tuition ($19,260), mandatory fees ($480), and college room and board ($6170). *College room only:* $3150. Full-time tuition and fees vary according to program. Room and board charges vary according to board plan and housing facility. *Part-time tuition:* $325 per credit hour. *Part-time mandatory fees:* $65 per term.

For Further Information Contact Mr. Michael Suzo, Vice President for Enrollment Management, Defiance College, 701 North Clinton Street, Defiance, OH 43512-1610. *Telephone:* 419-783-2361 or 800-520-4632 Ext. 2359 (toll-free). *Fax:* 419-783-2468. *E-mail:* admissions@defiance.edu. *Web site:* http://www.defiance.edu/.

DENISON UNIVERSITY

Granville, Ohio

Denison University is a coed, private, four-year college, founded in 1831, offering degrees at the bachelor's level. It has a 900-acre campus in Granville near Columbus.

Academic Information The faculty has 207 members (92% full-time), 96% with terminal degrees. The student-faculty ratio is 11:1. The library holds 767,118 titles, 6,616 serial subscriptions, and 32,745 audiovisual materials. Special programs include services for learning-disabled students, an honors program, cooperative (work-study) education, study abroad, advanced placement credit, double majors, independent study, self-designed majors, part-time degree programs (daytime), internships, and arrangement for off-campus study with American University, Great Lakes Colleges Association, Marine Science Consortium. The most frequently chosen baccalaureate fields are communications/journalism, psychology, social sciences.

Student Body Statistics The student body is made up of 2,263 undergraduates (573 freshmen). 57 percent are women and 43 percent are men. Students come from 50 states and territories and 27 other countries. 46 percent are from Ohio. 3.8 percent are international students. 22 percent of the 2006 graduating class went on to graduate and professional schools.

Expenses for 2006–07 *Application fee:* $40. *Comprehensive fee:* $39,220 includes full-time tuition ($29,860), mandatory fees ($800), and college room and board ($8560). *College room only:* $4740. Room and board charges vary according to housing facility. *Part-time tuition:* $930 per semester hour. Part-time tuition varies according to course load.

Financial Aid Forms of aid include need-based and non-need-based scholarships and part-time jobs. The average aided 2006–07 undergraduate received an aid package worth an estimated $26,424. The priority application deadline for financial aid is February 15.

Freshman Admission Denison University requires an essay, a high school transcript, 2 recommendations, and SAT or ACT scores. An interview and TOEFL scores for international students are recommended. The application deadline for regular admission is January 15 and for early decision plan 1 it is November 1.

Transfer Admission The application deadline for admission is July 1.

Entrance Difficulty Denison University assesses its entrance difficulty level as very difficult; moderately difficult for transfers. For the fall 2006 freshman class, 39 percent of the applicants were accepted.

For Further Information Contact Mr. Perry Robinson, Director of Admissions, Denison University, Box H, Granville, OH 43023. *Telephone:* 740-587-6276 or 800-DENISON (toll-free). *E-mail:* admissions@denison.edu. *Web site:* http://www.denison.edu/.

DeVRY UNIVERSITY

Cleveland, Ohio

http://www.devry.edu/

DeVRY UNIVERSITY
Columbus, Ohio

DeVry University is a coed, proprietary, comprehensive unit of DeVry University, founded in 1952, offering degrees at the associate, bachelor's, and master's levels and postbachelor's certificates. It has a 21-acre campus in Columbus.

Academic Information The faculty has 106 members (54% full-time). The undergraduate student-faculty ratio is 24:1. The library holds 30,000 titles and 5,892 serial subscriptions. Special programs include academic remediation, services for learning-disabled students, advanced placement credit, accelerated degree programs, distance learning, summer session for credit, part-time degree programs (daytime, evenings, weekends, summer), and adult/continuing education programs. The most frequently chosen baccalaureate fields are business/marketing, computer and information sciences, engineering technologies.
Student Body Statistics The student body totals 2,546, of whom 2,328 are undergraduates (483 freshmen). 35 percent are women and 65 percent are men. 98 percent are from Ohio. 0.3 percent are international students.
Expenses for 2007–08 *Application fee:* $50. *Tuition:* $12,900 full-time, $490 per credit part-time. *Mandatory fees:* $320 full-time.
Financial Aid Forms of aid include need-based and non-need-based scholarships and part-time jobs. The application deadline for financial aid is continuous.
Freshman Admission DeVry University requires a high school transcript, an interview, and TOEFL scores for international students. The application deadline for regular admission is rolling.
Transfer Admission The application deadline for admission is rolling.
Entrance Difficulty DeVry University assesses its entrance difficulty level as minimally difficult; moderately difficult for electronics engineering technology program.
For Further Information Contact Admissions Office, DeVry University, 1350 Alum Creek Drive, Columbus, OH 43209-2705. *Telephone:* 614-253-7291. *Web site:* http://www.devry.edu/.

DeVRY UNIVERSITY
Seven Hills, Ohio
http://www.devry.edu/

FRANCISCAN UNIVERSITY OF STEUBENVILLE
Steubenville, Ohio

Franciscan University of Steubenville is a coed, private, Roman Catholic, comprehensive institution, founded in 1946, offering degrees at the associate, bachelor's, and master's levels. It has a 124-acre campus in Steubenville near Pittsburgh.

Academic Information The faculty has 189 members (59% full-time), 49% with terminal degrees. The undergraduate student-faculty ratio is 15:1. The library holds 236,689 titles, 392 serial subscriptions, and 1,260 audiovisual materials. Special programs include services for learning-disabled students, an honors program, study abroad, advanced placement credit, accelerated degree programs, double majors, independent study, distance learning, summer session for credit, part-time degree programs (daytime, evenings, summer), adult/continuing education programs, and internships. The most frequently chosen baccalaureate fields are health professions and related sciences, education, theology and religious vocations.
Student Body Statistics The student body totals 2,387, of whom 1,982 are undergraduates (398 freshmen). 60 percent are women and 40 percent are men. Students come from 52 states and territories and 11 other countries. 23 percent are from Ohio. 0.9 percent are international students. 29 percent of the 2006 graduating class went on to graduate and professional schools.
Expenses for 2006–07 *Application fee:* $20. *Comprehensive fee:* $24,550 includes full-time tuition ($17,800), mandatory fees ($450), and college

room and board ($6300). *College room only:* $3600. Room and board charges vary according to board plan. *Part-time tuition:* $595 per credit hour. *Part-time mandatory fees:* $15 per credit hour. Part-time tuition and fees vary according to course load.
Financial Aid Forms of aid include need-based and non-need-based scholarships and part-time jobs. The priority application deadline for financial aid is April 15.
Freshman Admission Franciscan University of Steubenville requires an essay, a high school transcript, a minimum 2.4 high school GPA, SAT or ACT scores, and TOEFL scores for international students. An interview is recommended. Recommendations are required for some. The application deadline for regular admission is rolling.
Transfer Admission The application deadline for admission is rolling.
Entrance Difficulty Franciscan University of Steubenville assesses its entrance difficulty level as moderately difficult. For the fall 2006 freshman class, 80 percent of the applicants were accepted.
For Further Information Contact Mrs. Margaret Weber, Director of Admissions, Franciscan University of Steubenville, 1235 University Boulevard, Steubenville, OH 43952-1763. *Telephone:* 740-283-6226 or 800-783-6220 (toll-free). *Fax:* 740-284-5456. *E-mail:* admissions@franciscan.edu. *Web site:* http://www.franciscan.edu/.

FRANKLIN UNIVERSITY
Columbus, Ohio
http://www.franklin.edu/

GALLIPOLIS CAREER COLLEGE
Gallipolis, Ohio

Gallipolis Career College is a coed, primarily women's, private, two-year college, founded in 1962, offering degrees at the associate level.

Expenses for 2006–07 *Application fee:* $50. *Tuition:* $8640 full-time, $180 per credit hour part-time. *Mandatory fees:* $100 full-time.
For Further Information Contact Mr. Jack Henson, Director of Admissions, Gallipolis Career College, 11/6 Jackson Pike, Suite 312, Gallipolis, OH 45631. *Telephone:* 740-446-4367 or 800-214-0452 (toll-free). *Fax:* 740-446-4124. *E-mail:* admissions@gallipaliscareercollege.com. *Web site:* http://www.gallipoliscareercollege.com/.

GOD'S BIBLE SCHOOL AND COLLEGE
Cincinnati, Ohio

God's Bible School and College is a coed, private, interdenominational, four-year college, founded in 1900, offering degrees at the associate and bachelor's levels. It has a 14-acre campus in Cincinnati.

Academic Information The faculty has 29 members (41% full-time), 21% with terminal degrees. The student-faculty ratio is 13:1. The library holds 41,756 titles and 214 serial subscriptions. Special programs include academic remediation, advanced placement credit, independent study, summer session for credit, part-time degree programs (daytime), and internships. The most frequently chosen baccalaureate fields are family and consumer sciences, education, theology and religious vocations.
Student Body Statistics The student body is made up of 272 undergraduates (56 freshmen). 53 percent are women and 47 percent are men. Students come from 22 states and territories and 12 other countries. 42 percent are from Ohio. 12.1 percent are international students. 14 percent of the 2006 graduating class went on to graduate and professional schools.
Expenses for 2007–08 *Application fee:* $25. *Comprehensive fee:* $8280 includes full-time tuition ($4200), mandatory fees ($780), and college room and board ($3300). *Part-time tuition:* $162 per credit hour. *Part-time mandatory fees:* $28 per credit hour.

God's Bible School and College (continued)

Financial Aid Forms of aid include need-based and non-need-based scholarships. The application deadline for financial aid is continuous.
Freshman Admission God's Bible School and College requires a high school transcript, 3 recommendations, an interview, SAT or ACT scores, and TOEFL scores for international students. SAT scores are recommended. The application deadline for regular admission is August 18.
Transfer Admission The application deadline for admission is rolling.
Entrance Difficulty For the fall 2006 freshman class, 88 percent of the applicants were accepted.
For Further Information Contact Mrs. Lisa Profitt, Director of Admissions, God's Bible School and College, 1810 Young Street, Cincinnati, OH 45202-6838. *Telephone:* 513-721-7944 Ext. 205 or 800-486-4637 (toll-free). *Fax:* 513-721-3971. *E-mail:* lprofitt@gbs.edu. *Web site:* http://www.gbs.edu/.

HEIDELBERG COLLEGE

Tiffin, Ohio

Heidelberg College is a coed, private, comprehensive institution, founded in 1850, affiliated with the United Church of Christ, offering degrees at the bachelor's and master's levels. It has a 115-acre campus in Tiffin.

Academic Information The faculty has 159 members (35% full-time), 50% with terminal degrees. The undergraduate student-faculty ratio is 14:1. The library holds 268,702 titles and 513 serial subscriptions. Special programs include academic remediation, services for learning-disabled students, an honors program, study abroad, advanced placement credit, accelerated degree programs, ESL programs, double majors, summer session for credit, part-time degree programs (daytime, evenings, weekends, summer), adult/continuing education programs, internships, and arrangement for off-campus study with members of the East Central College Consortium. The most frequently chosen baccalaureate fields are business/marketing, communications/journalism, education.
Student Body Statistics The student body totals 1,569, of whom 1,330 are undergraduates (274 freshmen). 52 percent are women and 48 percent are men. Students come from 25 states and territories and 10 other countries. 92 percent are from Ohio. 2.2 percent are international students. 18 percent of the 2006 graduating class went on to graduate and professional schools.
Expenses for 2007–08 *Application fee:* $25. *Comprehensive fee:* $26,520 includes full-time tuition ($18,190), mandatory fees ($428), and college room and board ($7902). *College room only:* $3740.
Financial Aid Forms of aid include need-based and non-need-based scholarships and part-time jobs. The average aided 2006–07 undergraduate received an aid package worth an estimated $15,397. The priority application deadline for financial aid is March 1.
Freshman Admission Heidelberg College requires a high school transcript, a minimum 2.5 high school GPA, and SAT or ACT scores. An essay, an interview, and TOEFL scores for international students are recommended. Recommendations are required for some. The application deadline for regular admission is August 15 and for nonresidents it is August 15.
Transfer Admission The application deadline for admission is August 15.
Entrance Difficulty Heidelberg College assesses its entrance difficulty level as moderately difficult. For the fall 2006 freshman class, 72 percent of the applicants were accepted.
For Further Information Contact Ms. Lindsay Sooy, Director of Admission, Heidelberg College, 310 East Market Street, Tiffin, OH 44883. *Telephone:* 419-448-2330 or 800-434-3352 (toll-free). *Fax:* 419-448-2334. *E-mail:* adminfo@heidelberg.edu. *Web site:* http://www.heidelberg.edu/.

See page 252 for the College Close-Up.

HIRAM COLLEGE

Hiram, Ohio

Hiram College is a coed, private, four-year college, founded in 1850, affiliated with the Christian Church (Disciples of Christ), offering degrees at the bachelor's and master's levels. It has a 110-acre campus in Hiram near Cleveland.

Academic Information The faculty has 103 members (62% full-time), 75% with terminal degrees. The undergraduate student-faculty ratio is 12:1. The library holds 187,451 titles, 3,993 serial subscriptions, and 10,351 audiovisual materials. Special programs include services for learning-disabled students, study abroad, advanced placement credit, ESL programs, double majors, independent study, self-designed majors, summer session for credit, part-time degree programs (weekends), adult/continuing education programs, internships, and arrangement for off-campus study. The most frequently chosen baccalaureate fields are business/marketing, biological/life sciences, social sciences.
Student Body Statistics The student body totals 1,239, of whom 1,205 are undergraduates (312 freshmen). 56 percent are women and 44 percent are men. Students come from 29 states and territories and 19 other countries. 87 percent are from Ohio. 2.7 percent are international students.
Expenses for 2006–07 *Application fee:* $35. *Comprehensive fee:* $32,666 includes full-time tuition ($24,215), mandatory fees ($670), and college room and board ($7781). *College room only:* $3801. Full-time tuition and fees vary according to student level. Room and board charges vary according to housing facility. *Part-time tuition:* $784 per credit hour.
Financial Aid Forms of aid include need-based and non-need-based scholarships and part-time jobs. The priority application deadline for financial aid is February 15.
Freshman Admission Hiram College requires an essay, a high school transcript, 2 recommendations, SAT or ACT scores, and TOEFL scores for international students. 3 recommendations and an interview are recommended. An interview is required for some. The application deadline for regular admission is April 1.
Transfer Admission The application deadline for admission is July 15.
Entrance Difficulty Hiram College assesses its entrance difficulty level as moderately difficult. For the fall 2006 freshman class, 88 percent of the applicants were accepted.
For Further Information Contact Mr. Sherman C. Dean II, Director of Admission, Hiram College, PO Box 96, Hiram, OH 44234. *Telephone:* 330-569-5169 or 800-362-5280 (toll-free). *Fax:* 330-569-5944. *E-mail:* admission@hiram.edu. *Web site:* http://www.hiram.edu/.

JOHN CARROLL UNIVERSITY

University Heights, Ohio

http://www.jcu.edu/

KENT STATE UNIVERSITY

Kent, Ohio

Kent State University is a coed, public unit of Kent State University System, founded in 1910, offering degrees at the associate, bachelor's, master's, and doctoral levels and post-master's and postbachelor's certificates. It has a 1,347-acre campus in Kent near Cleveland.

Academic Information The faculty has 1,449 members (59% full-time), 45% with terminal degrees. The undergraduate student-faculty ratio is 18:1. The library holds 2 million titles, 12,000 serial subscriptions, and 15,578 audiovisual materials. Special programs include academic remediation, services for learning-disabled students, an honors program, cooperative (work-study) education, study abroad, advanced placement credit, accelerated degree programs, Freshman Honors College, ESL programs, double majors, independent study, distance learning, self-designed majors, summer session for credit, part-time degree programs (daytime, evenings, weekends, summer), external degree programs, adult/continuing education programs, internships, and arrangement for off-campus study with Cuyahoga Community College, Lorain County

Community College, Lakeland Community College. The most frequently chosen baccalaureate fields are business/marketing, education, health professions and related sciences.

Student Body Statistics The student body totals 22,697, of whom 18,136 are undergraduates (3,696 freshmen). 59 percent are women and 41 percent are men. Students come from 43 states and territories and 68 other countries. 91 percent are from Ohio. 1.3 percent are international students.

Expenses for 2006–07 *Application fee:* $30. *State resident tuition:* $8430 full-time, $384 per credit hour part-time. *Nonresident tuition:* $15,862 full-time, $722 per credit hour part-time. Both full-time and part-time tuition varies according to course load, program, and reciprocity agreements. *College room and board:* $6880. *College room only:* $4200. Room and board charges vary according to board plan and housing facility.

Financial Aid Forms of aid include need-based and non-need-based scholarships, athletic grants, and part-time jobs. The average aided 2006–07 undergraduate received an aid package worth an estimated $7685. The priority application deadline for financial aid is March 1.

Freshman Admission Kent State University requires a high school transcript, a minimum 2.5 high school GPA, SAT or ACT scores, and TOEFL scores for international students. The application deadline for regular admission is May 1.

Entrance Difficulty Kent State University assesses its entrance difficulty level as moderately difficult; minimally difficult for transfers; very difficult for architecture, 6-year medical program. For the fall 2006 freshman class, 84 percent of the applicants were accepted.

For Further Information Contact Mr. Christopher Buttenschon, Assistant Director of Admissions, Kent State University, 161 Michael Schwartz Center, Kent, OH 44242-0001. *Telephone:* 330-672-2444 or 800-988-KENT (toll-free). *Fax:* 330-672-2499. *E-mail:* admissions@kent.edu. *Web site:* http://www.kent.edu/.

See page 260 for the College Close-Up.

KENT STATE UNIVERSITY, ASHTABULA CAMPUS

Ashtabula, Ohio

Kent State University, Ashtabula Campus is a coed, public, primarily two-year college of Kent State University System, founded in 1958, offering degrees at the associate and bachelor's levels (also offers some upper-level and graduate courses). It has a 120-acre campus in Ashtabula near Cleveland.

Academic Information The faculty has 80 members (45% full-time). The library holds 51,884 titles and 225 serial subscriptions. Special programs include academic remediation, an honors program, advanced placement credit, Freshman Honors College, self-designed majors, summer session for credit, part-time degree programs (daytime, evenings, summer), and internships.

Student Body Statistics The student body is made up of 1,396 undergraduates. 0.4 percent are international students.

Expenses for 2006–07 *Application fee:* $30. *State resident tuition:* $4770 full-time. *Nonresident tuition:* $12,202 full-time.

Financial Aid Forms of aid include need-based scholarships and part-time jobs. The priority application deadline for financial aid is March 1.

Freshman Admission Kent State University, Ashtabula Campus requires TOEFL scores for international students. SAT or ACT scores are recommended. The application deadline for regular admission is August 1 and for nonresidents it is July 15.

Transfer Admission The application deadline for admission is July 15.

Entrance Difficulty Kent State University, Ashtabula Campus has an open admission policy except for nursing program. It assesses its entrance difficulty as moderately difficult for nursing program.

For Further Information Contact Ms. Kelly Sanford, Director, Enrollment Management and Student Services, Kent State University, Ashtabula Campus, 3300 Lake Road West, Ashtabula, OH 44004-2299. *Telephone:* 440-964-3322. *Fax:* 440-964-4269. *E-mail:* robinson@ashtabula.kent.edu. *Web site:* http://www.ashtabula.kent.edu/.

KENT STATE UNIVERSITY, GEAUGA CAMPUS

Burton, Ohio

Kent State University, Geauga Campus is a coed, public, primarily two-year college of Kent State University System, founded in 1964, offering degrees at the associate and bachelor's levels. It has an 87-acre campus in Burton near Cleveland.

Academic Information The faculty has 87 members (15% full-time), 15% with terminal degrees. The student-faculty ratio is 15:1. The library holds 8,300 titles and 6,600 serial subscriptions. Special programs include academic remediation, services for learning-disabled students, advanced placement credit, double majors, distance learning, self-designed majors, summer session for credit, part-time degree programs (daytime, evenings, weekends, summer), adult/continuing education programs, and internships.

Student Body Statistics The student body totals 1,062, of whom 1,057 are undergraduates (124 freshmen). 58 percent are women and 42 percent are men. Students come from 8 states and territories and 1 other country. 99 percent are from Ohio. 0.2 percent are international students.

Expenses for 2006–07 *Application fee:* $30. *State resident tuition:* $4770 full-time, $217 per credit hour part-time. *Nonresident tuition:* $12,202 full-time, $555 per credit hour part-time. Both full-time and part-time tuition varies according to course level.

Financial Aid Forms of aid include need-based scholarships and part-time jobs. The average aided 2006–07 undergraduate received an aid package worth an estimated $5960. The priority application deadline for financial aid is March 1.

Freshman Admission Kent State University, Geauga Campus requires a high school transcript and TOEFL scores for international students. SAT or ACT scores are recommended. SAT or ACT scores are required for some. The application deadline for regular admission is rolling.

Transfer Admission The application deadline for admission is rolling.

Entrance Difficulty Kent State University, Geauga Campus has an open admission policy.

For Further Information Contact Ms. Betty Landrus, Kent State University, Geauga Campus, 14111 Claridon-Troy Road, Burton, OH 44021. *Telephone:* 440-834-4187. *Fax:* 440-834-8846. *E-mail:* blandrus@kent.edu. *Web site:* http://www.geauga.kent.edu/.

KENT STATE UNIVERSITY, SALEM CAMPUS

Salem, Ohio

http://www.salem.kent.edu/

KENT STATE UNIVERSITY, STARK CAMPUS

Canton, Ohio

http://www.stark.kent.edu/

KENT STATE UNIVERSITY, TRUMBULL CAMPUS

Warren, Ohio

Kent State University, Trumbull Campus is a coed, public, primarily two-year college of Kent State University System, founded in 1954, offering degrees at the associate and bachelor's levels (also offers some upper-level and graduate courses). It has a 200-acre campus in Warren near Cleveland.

Academic Information The faculty has 123 members (48% full-time), 33% with terminal degrees. The student-faculty ratio is 16:1. The library

Kent State University, Trumbull Campus (continued)

holds 65,951 titles and 759 serial subscriptions. Special programs include academic remediation, services for learning-disabled students, an honors program, cooperative (work-study) education, advanced placement credit, Freshman Honors College, independent study, distance learning, self-designed majors, summer session for credit, part-time degree programs (daytime, evenings, weekends, summer), adult/continuing education programs, and internships.

Student Body Statistics The student body totals 2,015, of whom 1,996 are undergraduates (309 freshmen). 64 percent are women and 36 percent are men. Students come from 4 states and territories and 3 other countries. 99 percent are from Ohio. 0.2 percent are international students.

Expenses for 2006–07 *Application fee:* $30. *State resident tuition:* $4586 full-time, $217 per credit hour part-time. *Nonresident tuition:* $12,018 full-time, $555 per credit hour part-time. Both full-time and part-time tuition varies according to course level.

Financial Aid Forms of aid include need-based scholarships and part-time jobs. The priority application deadline for financial aid is March 1.

Freshman Admission Kent State University, Trumbull Campus requires a high school transcript and TOEFL scores for international students. SAT or ACT scores are recommended. SAT or ACT scores are required for some. The application deadline for regular admission is July 30.

Transfer Admission The application deadline for admission is rolling.

Entrance Difficulty Kent State University, Trumbull Campus has an open admission policy except for nursing program. It assesses its entrance difficulty as minimally difficult for transfers; moderately difficult for nursing program.

For Further Information Contact Ms. Patricia Davis, Clerical Specialist, Kent State University, Trumbull Campus, 4314 Mahoning Avenue NW, Warren, OH 44483. *Telephone:* 330-675-888. *Fax:* 330-847-6571. *E-mail:* pdavis1@kent.edu. *Web site:* http://www.trumbull.kent.edu/.

KENT STATE UNIVERSITY, TUSCARAWAS CAMPUS

New Philadelphia, Ohio

Kent State University, Tuscarawas Campus is a coed, public, primarily two-year college of Kent State University System, founded in 1962, offering degrees at the associate, bachelor's, and master's levels (also offers some upper-level and graduate courses). It has a 172-acre campus in New Philadelphia near Cleveland.

Academic Information The faculty has 115 members (41% full-time), 25% with terminal degrees. The undergraduate student-faculty ratio is 19:1. The library holds 63,880 titles, 208 serial subscriptions, and 1,179 audiovisual materials. Special programs include academic remediation, services for learning-disabled students, an honors program, advanced placement credit, accelerated degree programs, Freshman Honors College, double majors, independent study, distance learning, self-designed majors, summer session for credit, part-time degree programs (daytime, evenings, weekends, summer), adult/continuing education programs, and internships.

Student Body Statistics The student body totals 2,021, of whom 1,977 are undergraduates (380 freshmen). 60 percent are women and 40 percent are men. 0.2 percent are international students.

Expenses for 2006–07 *Application fee:* $30. *Area resident tuition:* $217 per credit hour part-time. *State resident tuition:* $5590 full-time. *Nonresident tuition:* $12,202 full-time.

Financial Aid Forms of aid include need-based scholarships and part-time jobs. The priority application deadline for financial aid is March 1.

Freshman Admission Kent State University, Tuscarawas Campus requires a high school transcript and TOEFL scores for international students. SAT or ACT scores are recommended. The application deadline for regular admission is September 1.

Transfer Admission The application deadline for admission is September 1.

Entrance Difficulty Kent State University, Tuscarawas Campus has an open admission policy except for business administration, education, nursing, fine and performing arts programs. It assesses its entrance

difficulty as moderately difficult for nursing, education, business administration, fine and performing arts programs.

For Further Information Contact Director of Admissions, Kent State University, Tuscarawas Campus, 330 University Drive NE, New Philadelphia, OH 44663-9403. *Telephone:* 330-339-3391 Ext. 47425. *Fax:* 330-339-3321. *Web site:* http://www.tusc.kent.edu/.

KENYON COLLEGE

Gambier, Ohio

Kenyon College is a coed, private, four-year college, founded in 1824, offering degrees at the bachelor's level. It has a 1,200-acre campus in Gambier near Columbus.

Academic Information The faculty has 186 members (81% full-time), 92% with terminal degrees. The student-faculty ratio is 10:1. The library holds 826,059 titles and 8,574 serial subscriptions. Special programs include services for learning-disabled students, an honors program, study abroad, advanced placement credit, accelerated degree programs, double majors, independent study, self-designed majors, internships, and arrangement for off-campus study. The most frequently chosen baccalaureate fields are English, social sciences, visual and performing arts.

Student Body Statistics The student body is made up of 1,661 undergraduates (440 freshmen). 53 percent are women and 47 percent are men. Students come from 46 states and territories and 28 other countries. 23 percent are from Ohio. 2.8 percent are international students. 25 percent of the 2006 graduating class went on to graduate and professional schools.

Expenses for 2006–07 *Application fee:* $50. *Comprehensive fee:* $41,950 includes full-time tuition ($34,990), mandatory fees ($1060), and college room and board ($5900). *College room only:* $2780. Room and board charges vary according to housing facility.

Financial Aid Forms of aid include need-based and non-need-based scholarships and part-time jobs. The average aided 2006–07 undergraduate received an aid package worth an estimated $27,275. The priority application deadline for financial aid is February 15.

Freshman Admission Kenyon College requires an essay, a high school transcript, 1 recommendation, counselor recommendation, SAT or ACT scores, and TOEFL scores for international students. A minimum 3.5 high school GPA, 2 recommendations, and an interview are recommended. The application deadline for regular admission is January 15 and for early decision plan 1 it is December 1.

Transfer Admission The application deadline for admission is April 1.

Entrance Difficulty Kenyon College assesses its entrance difficulty level as very difficult. For the fall 2006 freshman class, 36 percent of the applicants were accepted.

For Further Information Contact Ms. Jennifer Britz, Dean of Admissions, Kenyon College, Ransom Hall, Gambier, OH 43022. *Telephone:* 740-427-5778 or 800-848-2468 (toll-free). *Fax:* 740-427-5770. *E-mail:* admissions@kenyon.edu. *Web site:* http://www.kenyon.edu/.

KETTERING COLLEGE OF MEDICAL ARTS

Kettering, Ohio

Kettering College of Medical Arts is a coed, primarily women's, private, Seventh-day Adventist, primarily two-year college, founded in 1967, offering degrees at the associate and bachelor's levels and postbachelor's certificates. It has a 35-acre campus in Kettering.

Academic Information The faculty has 61 members (57% full-time), 39% with terminal degrees. The student-faculty ratio is 13:1. The library holds 29,390 titles and 266 serial subscriptions. Special programs include an honors program, study abroad, advanced placement credit, independent study, distance learning, summer session for credit, part-time degree programs (daytime, evenings), and arrangement for off-campus study with members of the Southwestern Ohio Council for Higher Education.

Student Body Statistics The student body totals 803, of whom 773 are undergraduates (69 freshmen). 80 percent are women and 20 percent are men. Students come from 18 states and territories and 10 other countries. 94 percent are from Ohio. 2.4 percent are international students.

Expenses for 2007–08 *Application fee:* $25. *Comprehensive fee:* $12,948 includes full-time tuition ($7008), mandatory fees ($540), and college room and board ($5400). *College room only:* $2400. *Part-time tuition:* $292 per credit hour. *Part-time mandatory fees:* $220 per term.

Financial Aid Forms of aid include need-based scholarships and part-time jobs. The priority application deadline for financial aid is March 31.

Freshman Admission Kettering College of Medical Arts requires a high school transcript, a minimum 2.0 high school GPA, 3 recommendations, ACT scores, and TOEFL scores for international students. A minimum 3.0 high school GPA and an interview are recommended. The application deadline for regular admission is rolling.

Transfer Admission The application deadline for admission is rolling.

Entrance Difficulty Kettering College of Medical Arts assesses its entrance difficulty level as moderately difficult; most difficult for physician's assistant program.

For Further Information Contact Mrs. Becky McDonald, Associate Director of Enrollment Services, Kettering College of Medical Arts, 3737 Southern Boulevard, Kettering, OH 45429-1299. *Telephone:* 937-395-8628 or 800-433-5262 (toll-free). *Fax:* 937-296-4238. *Web site:* http://www.kcma.edu/.

LAKE ERIE COLLEGE

Painesville, Ohio

Lake Erie College is a coed, private, comprehensive institution, founded in 1856, offering degrees at the bachelor's and master's levels. It has a 57-acre campus in Painesville near Cleveland.

For Further Information Contact Ms. Jennifer Calhoun, Director of Admissions, Lake Erie College, 391 West Washington Street, Painesville, OH 44077-3389. *Telephone:* 440-375-7050 or 800-916-0904 (toll-free). *Fax:* 440-375-7005. *E-mail:* admissions@lec.edu. *Web site:* http://www.lec.edu/.

LAURA AND ALVIN SIEGAL COLLEGE OF JUDAIC STUDIES

Beachwood, Ohio

http://www.siegalcollege.edu/

LOURDES COLLEGE

Sylvania, Ohio

Lourdes College is a coed, private, Roman Catholic, comprehensive institution, founded in 1958, offering degrees at the associate, bachelor's, and master's levels. It has a 90-acre campus in Sylvania near Toledo.

Academic Information The faculty has 178 members (38% full-time), 28% with terminal degrees. The undergraduate student-faculty ratio is 12:1. The library holds 62,222 titles, 6,200 serial subscriptions, and 170 audiovisual materials. Special programs include academic remediation, services for learning-disabled students, cooperative (work-study) education, study abroad, advanced placement credit, double majors, independent study, distance learning, self-designed majors, summer session for credit, part-time degree programs (daytime, evenings, weekends, summer), adult/continuing education programs, and internships.

Student Body Statistics The student body totals 1,881, of whom 1,733 are undergraduates (124 freshmen). 84 percent are women and 16 percent are men. Students come from 3 states and territories. 91 percent are from Ohio. 0.2 percent are international students.

Expenses for 2006–07 *Application fee:* $25. *Tuition:* $11,700 full-time, $390 per credit hour part-time. *Mandatory fees:* $1500 full-time, $50 per credit hour part-time. Both full-time and part-time tuition and fees vary according to course load and location.

Financial Aid Forms of aid include need-based and non-need-based scholarships and part-time jobs. The average aided 2006–07 undergraduate received an aid package worth an estimated $9373. The priority application deadline for financial aid is March 1.

Freshman Admission Lourdes College requires a high school transcript and TOEFL scores for international students. SAT or ACT scores are required for some. The application deadline for regular admission is rolling and for nonresidents it is rolling.

Transfer Admission The application deadline for admission is rolling.

Entrance Difficulty For the fall 2006 freshman class, 84 percent of the applicants were accepted.

For Further Information Contact Ms. Amy Mergen, Office of Admissions, Lourdes College, 6832 Convent Boulevard, Sylvania, OH 43560. *Telephone:* 419-885-5291 or 800-878-3210 Ext. 1299 (toll-free). *Fax:* 419-882-3987. *E-mail:* lcadmits@lourdes.edu. *Web site:* http://www.lourdes.edu/.

MALONE COLLEGE

Canton, Ohio

Malone College is a coed, private, comprehensive institution, founded in 1892, affiliated with the Evangelical Friends Church–Eastern Region, offering degrees at the bachelor's and master's levels and postbachelor's certificates. It has a 78-acre campus in Canton near Cleveland.

Academic Information The faculty has 209 members (52% full-time), 43% with terminal degrees. The undergraduate student-faculty ratio is 14:1. The library holds 245,530 titles, 6,869 serial subscriptions, and 13,354 audiovisual materials. Special programs include academic remediation, services for learning-disabled students, an honors program, study abroad, advanced placement credit, accelerated degree programs, double majors, independent study, distance learning, self-designed majors, summer session for credit, part-time degree programs (daytime, evenings, summer), adult/continuing education programs, internships, and arrangement for off-campus study with members of the Christian College Consortium, Council for Christian Colleges and Universities. The most frequently chosen baccalaureate fields are business/marketing, education, health professions and related sciences.

Student Body Statistics The student body totals 2,296, of whom 1,960 are undergraduates (345 freshmen). 61 percent are women and 39 percent are men. Students come from 27 states and territories and 8 other countries. 88 percent are from Ohio. 1.4 percent are international students. 21 percent of the 2006 graduating class went on to graduate and professional schools.

Expenses for 2006–07 *Application fee:* $20. *Comprehensive fee:* $24,190 includes full-time tuition ($17,520), mandatory fees ($270), and college room and board ($6400). *College room only:* $3300. Room and board charges vary according to board plan. *Part-time tuition:* $330 per semester hour. *Part-time mandatory fees:* $67.50 per term. Part-time tuition and fees vary according to course load.

Financial Aid Forms of aid include need-based and non-need-based scholarships, athletic grants, and part-time jobs. The average aided 2006–07 undergraduate received an aid package worth an estimated $12,794. The application deadline for financial aid is July 31 with a priority deadline of March 1.

Freshman Admission Malone College requires an essay, a high school transcript, a minimum 2.5 high school GPA, SAT or ACT scores, and TOEFL scores for international students. An interview is recommended. The application deadline for regular admission is July 1.

Transfer Admission The application deadline for admission is July 1.

Entrance Difficulty Malone College assesses its entrance difficulty level as moderately difficult. For the fall 2006 freshman class, 80 percent of the applicants were accepted.

For Further Information Contact Mr. John Russell, Director of Admissions, Malone College, 515 25th Street, NW, Canton, OH 44709-3897. *Telephone:* 330-471-8145 or 800-521-1146 (toll-free). *Fax:* 330-471-8149. *E-mail:* admissions@malone.edu. *Web site:* http://www.malone.edu/.

MARIETTA COLLEGE

Marietta, Ohio

Marietta College is a coed, private, comprehensive institution, founded in 1835, offering degrees at the associate, bachelor's, and master's levels. It has a 120-acre campus in Marietta.

Academic Information The faculty has 139 members (68% full-time), 66% with terminal degrees. The undergraduate student-faculty ratio is 12:1. The library holds 246,706 titles, 28,188 serial subscriptions, and 6,147 audiovisual materials. Special programs include academic remediation, services for learning-disabled students, an honors program, study abroad, advanced placement credit, accelerated degree programs, ESL programs, double majors, independent study, self-designed majors, summer session for credit, part-time degree programs (daytime, evenings, summer), adult/continuing education programs, internships, and arrangement for off-campus study with American University, Stillman College, Central College, Institute of European Studies, Institute of Asian Studies. The most frequently chosen baccalaureate fields are business/marketing, communications/journalism, liberal arts/general studies.

Student Body Statistics The student body totals 1,530, of whom 1,412 are undergraduates (402 freshmen). 51 percent are women and 49 percent are men. Students come from 43 states and territories and 14 other countries. 50 percent are from Ohio. 4.7 percent are international students. 30 percent of the 2006 graduating class went on to graduate and professional schools.

Expenses for 2006–07 *Application fee:* $25. *Comprehensive fee:* $30,845 includes full-time tuition ($23,200), mandatory fees ($615), and college room and board ($7030). *College room only:* $3900. Room and board charges vary according to board plan and housing facility. *Part-time tuition:* $770 per credit. Part-time tuition varies according to class time.

Financial Aid Forms of aid include need-based and non-need-based scholarships and part-time jobs. The priority application deadline for financial aid is March 1.

Freshman Admission Marietta College requires an essay, a high school transcript, a minimum 2.0 high school GPA, 1 recommendation, SAT or ACT scores, and TOEFL scores for international students. A minimum 3.0 high school GPA, an interview, and SAT Subject Test scores are recommended. The application deadline for regular admission is May 1.

Transfer Admission The application deadline for admission is rolling.

Entrance Difficulty Marietta College assesses its entrance difficulty level as moderately difficult. For the fall 2006 freshman class, 79 percent of the applicants were accepted.

For Further Information Contact Ms. Marke Vickers, Director of Admission, Marietta College, 215 Fifth Street, Marietta, OH 45750. *Telephone:* 740-376-4600 or 800-331-7896 (toll-free). *Fax:* 740-376-8888. *E-mail:* admit@marietta.edu. *Web site:* http://www.marietta.edu/.

THE McGREGOR SCHOOL OF ANTIOCH UNIVERSITY

See Antioch University McGregor.

MEDCENTRAL COLLEGE OF NURSING

Mansfield, Ohio

http://www.medcentral.edu/

MERCY COLLEGE OF NORTHWEST OHIO

Toledo, Ohio

Mercy College of Northwest Ohio is a coed, primarily women's, private, primarily two-year college, founded in 1993, affiliated with the Roman Catholic Church, offering degrees at the associate and bachelor's levels. It is located in Toledo near Detroit.

Academic Information The faculty has 100 members (54% full-time), 16% with terminal degrees. The student-faculty ratio is 11:1. The library holds 15,000 titles, 171 serial subscriptions, and 352 audiovisual materials. Special programs include academic remediation, services for learning-disabled students, advanced placement credit, double majors, independent study, distance learning, summer session for credit, part-time degree programs (daytime, evenings, summer), and internships. The most frequently chosen baccalaureate field is health professions and related sciences.

Student Body Statistics The student body is made up of 780 undergraduates (72 freshmen). 85 percent are women and 15 percent are men. Students come from 5 states and territories. 88 percent are from Ohio.

Expenses for 2007–08 *Application fee:* $25. *Tuition:* $8896 full-time, $310 per credit hour part-time. *Mandatory fees:* $650 full-time, $5 per credit hour part-time.

Financial Aid Forms of aid include need-based scholarships and part-time jobs. The application deadline for financial aid is continuous.

Freshman Admission Mercy College of Northwest Ohio requires a high school transcript. SAT or ACT scores are recommended. SAT or ACT scores are required for some. The application deadline for regular admission is rolling.

Transfer Admission The application deadline for admission is rolling.

Entrance Difficulty Mercy College of Northwest Ohio assesses its entrance difficulty level as moderately difficult. For the fall 2006 freshman class, 55 percent of the applicants were accepted.

For Further Information Contact Admissions Counselor, Mercy College of Northwest Ohio, 2221 Madison Avenue, Toledo, OH 43624-1197. *Telephone:* 419-251-1313 or 888-80-Mercy (toll-free). *Fax:* 419-251-1462. *E-mail:* admissions@mercycollege.edu. *Web site:* http://www.mercycollege.edu/.

MIAMI UNIVERSITY

Oxford, Ohio

Miami University is a coed, public unit of Miami University System, founded in 1809, offering degrees at the associate, bachelor's, master's, and doctoral levels and post-master's certificates. It has a 2,000-acre campus in Oxford near Cincinnati.

Academic Information The faculty has 1,272 members (64% full-time), 69% with terminal degrees. The undergraduate student-faculty ratio is 16:1. The library holds 3 million titles and 14,089 serial subscriptions. Special programs include services for learning-disabled students, an honors program, cooperative (work-study) education, study abroad, advanced placement credit, double majors, independent study, self-designed majors, summer session for credit, adult/continuing education programs, internships, and arrangement for off-campus study with Greater Cincinnati Consortium of Colleges and Universities. The most frequently chosen baccalaureate fields are business/marketing, education, social sciences.

Student Body Statistics The student body totals 16,329, of whom 14,551 are undergraduates (3,560 freshmen). 54 percent are women and 46 percent are men. Students come from 50 states and territories and 32 other countries. 71 percent are from Ohio. 0.7 percent are international students.

Expenses for 2006–07 *Application fee:* $45. *State resident tuition:* $8496 full-time, $349 per credit hour part-time. *Nonresident tuition:* $21,011 full-time, $884 per credit hour part-time. *Mandatory fees:* $2006 full-time, $43 per credit hour part-time. *College room and board:* $8140. *College room only:* $4160. Room and board charges vary according to board plan and housing facility.

Financial Aid Forms of aid include need-based and non-need-based scholarships, athletic grants, and part-time jobs. The average aided 2006–07 undergraduate received an aid package worth an estimated $17,573.

Freshman Admission Miami University requires a high school transcript, SAT or ACT scores, and TOEFL scores for international students. An essay and 1 recommendation are recommended. The application deadline for regular admission is January 31 and for early decision it is November 1.

Transfer Admission The application deadline for admission is May 1.

Entrance Difficulty Miami University assesses its entrance difficulty level as moderately difficult; noncompetitive for district residents. For the fall 2006 freshman class, 78 percent of the applicants were accepted.

For Further Information Contact Ann Larson, Interim Director of Undergraduate Admissions, Miami University, 301 South Campus Avenue, Oxford, OH 45056. *Telephone:* 513-529-2531. *Fax:* 513-529-1550. *E-mail:* admissions@muohio.edu. *Web site:* http://www.muohio.edu/.

MIAMI UNIVERSITY HAMILTON
Hamilton, Ohio

Miami University Hamilton is a coed, public, primarily two-year college of Miami University System, founded in 1968, offering degrees at the associate, bachelor's, and master's levels (degrees awarded by Miami University main campus). It has a 78-acre campus in Hamilton near Cincinnati.

Academic Information The faculty has 218 members (40% full-time). The undergraduate student-faculty ratio is 21:1. The library holds 68,000 titles and 400 serial subscriptions. Special programs include academic remediation, services for learning-disabled students, an honors program, cooperative (work-study) education, study abroad, advanced placement credit, ESL programs, double majors, distance learning, self-designed majors, summer session for credit, part-time degree programs (daytime, evenings, weekends, summer), adult/continuing education programs, and internships.

Student Body Statistics The student body totals 3,234, of whom 3,189 are undergraduates (600 freshmen). 56 percent are women and 44 percent are men.

Expenses for 2006–07 *Application fee:* $35. *State resident tuition:* $3954 full-time, $164.75 per credit part-time. *Nonresident tuition:* $16,085 full-time, $670.24 per credit part-time. *Mandatory fees:* $498 full-time, $15.25 per credit part-time, $22 per term part-time.

Financial Aid Forms of aid include need-based scholarships and part-time jobs. The application deadline for financial aid is continuous.

Freshman Admission Miami University Hamilton requires a high school transcript and TOEFL scores for international students. The application deadline for regular admission is rolling.

Entrance Difficulty Miami University Hamilton has an open admission policy except for nursing program, transfer students. It assesses its entrance difficulty as minimally difficult for transfers; moderately difficult for nursing program.

For Further Information Contact Mr. Archie Nelson, Director of Admission and Financial Aid, Miami University Hamilton, 1601 University Boulevard, Hamilton, OH 45011-3399. *Telephone:* 513-785-3111. *Fax:* 513-785-1807. *E-mail:* nelsona3@muohio.edu. *Web site:* http://www.ham.muohio.edu/.

MIAMI UNIVERSITY–MIDDLETOWN CAMPUS
Middletown, Ohio

Miami University–Middletown Campus is a coed, public, primarily two-year college of Miami University System, founded in 1966, offering degrees at the associate and bachelor's levels (also offers up to 2 years of most bachelor's degree programs offered at Miami University main campus). It has a 141-acre campus in Middletown near Cincinnati and Dayton.

Academic Information The faculty has 209 members (38% full-time). The student-faculty ratio is 13:1. The library holds 540 serial subscriptions and 4,857 audiovisual materials. Special programs include academic remediation, services for learning-disabled students, cooperative (work-study) education, study abroad, advanced placement credit, double majors, independent study, distance learning, self-designed majors, summer session for credit, part-time degree programs, adult/continuing education programs, internships, and arrangement for off-campus study with members of the Greater Cincinnati Consortium of Colleges and Universities.

Student Body Statistics The student body is made up of 2,660 undergraduates. 99 percent are from Ohio.

Expenses for 2006–07 *Application fee:* $25. *State resident tuition:* $3954 full-time. *Nonresident tuition:* $16,086 full-time. *Mandatory fees:* $498 full-time.

Financial Aid Forms of aid include need-based scholarships and part-time jobs. The priority application deadline for financial aid is February 15.

Freshman Admission Miami University–Middletown Campus requires a high school transcript and TOEFL scores for international students. SAT or ACT scores are recommended. The application deadline for regular admission is rolling.

Transfer Admission The application deadline for admission is rolling.

Entrance Difficulty Miami University–Middletown Campus has an open admission policy except for nursing program. It assesses its entrance difficulty as moderately difficult for nursing program.

For Further Information Contact Mrs. Mary Lou Flynn, Director of Enrollment Services, Miami University–Middletown Campus, 4200 East University Boulevard, Middletown, OH 45042. *Telephone:* 513-727-3346 or 866-426-4643 (toll-free). *Fax:* 513-727-3223. *E-mail:* flynnml@muohio.edu. *Web site:* http://www.mid.muohio.edu/.

MOUNT CARMEL COLLEGE OF NURSING
Columbus, Ohio

http://www.mccn.edu/

MOUNT UNION COLLEGE
Alliance, Ohio

Mount Union College is a coed, private, United Methodist, four-year college, founded in 1846, offering degrees at the bachelor's level. It has a 115-acre campus in Alliance near Cleveland.

Academic Information The faculty has 226 members (55% full-time), 51% with terminal degrees. The student-faculty ratio is 13:1. The library holds 220,601 titles, 39,000 serial subscriptions, and 4,929 audiovisual materials. Special programs include services for learning-disabled students, an honors program, cooperative (work-study) education, study abroad, advanced placement credit, accelerated degree programs, ESL programs, double majors, independent study, self-designed majors, summer session for credit, part-time degree programs (daytime, evenings, summer), adult/continuing education programs, internships, and arrangement for off-campus study with 6 members of the East Central College Consortium. The most frequently chosen baccalaureate fields are business/marketing, education, parks and recreation.

Student Body Statistics The student body is made up of 2,193 undergraduates (636 freshmen). 50 percent are women and 50 percent are men. Students come from 22 states and territories and 12 other countries. 90 percent are from Ohio. 1.9 percent are international students. 22 percent of the 2006 graduating class went on to graduate and professional schools.

Expenses for 2006–07 *Application fee:* $0. *Comprehensive fee:* $27,320 includes full-time tuition ($20,720), mandatory fees ($250), and college room and board ($6350). *College room only:* $2850. Room and board charges vary according to board plan and housing facility. *Part-time tuition:* $870 per semester hour. *Part-time mandatory fees:* $50 per term.

Financial Aid Forms of aid include need-based and non-need-based scholarships and part-time jobs. The average aided 2005–06 undergraduate received an aid package worth $15,618. The application deadline for financial aid is continuous.

Freshman Admission Mount Union College requires an essay, a high school transcript, a minimum 2.0 high school GPA, 1 recommendation, SAT or ACT scores, and TOEFL scores for international students. An interview is recommended. The application deadline for regular admission is rolling.

Transfer Admission The application deadline for admission is rolling.

Mount Union College (continued)

Entrance Difficulty Mount Union College assesses its entrance difficulty level as moderately difficult. For the fall 2006 freshman class, 79 percent of the applicants were accepted.
For Further Information Contact Mr. Vincent Heslop, Director of Enrollment Technology, Mount Union College, 1972 Clark Avenue, Alliance, OH 44601. *Telephone:* 330-823-2590, 800-334-6682 (toll-free in-state), or 800-992-6682 (toll-free out-of-state). *Fax:* 330-823-5097. *E-mail:* admission@muc.edu. *Web site:* http://www.muc.edu/.

MOUNT VERNON NAZARENE UNIVERSITY
Mount Vernon, Ohio

Mount Vernon Nazarene University is a coed, private, Nazarene, comprehensive institution, founded in 1964, offering degrees at the associate, bachelor's, and master's levels. It has a 401-acre campus in Mount Vernon near Columbus.

Academic Information The faculty has 244 members (46% full-time), 41% with terminal degrees. The undergraduate student-faculty ratio is 16:1. The library holds 99,914 titles, 7,341 serial subscriptions, and 3,472 audiovisual materials. Special programs include academic remediation, services for learning-disabled students, an honors program, study abroad, advanced placement credit, double majors, independent study, distance learning, summer session for credit, part-time degree programs (evenings), adult/continuing education programs, internships, and arrangement for off-campus study with Kenyon College, Capital University, Coalition for Christian Colleges and Universities. The most frequently chosen baccalaureate fields are business/marketing, education, philosophy and religious studies.
Student Body Statistics The student body totals 2,670, of whom 2,171 are undergraduates (347 freshmen). 59 percent are women and 41 percent are men. Students come from 23 states and territories and 5 other countries. 93 percent are from Ohio. 0.4 percent are international students. 18 percent of the 2006 graduating class went on to graduate and professional schools.
Expenses for 2007–08 *Application fee:* $25. *Comprehensive fee:* $23,350 includes full-time tuition ($17,544), mandatory fees ($520), and college room and board ($5286). *College room only:* $2954. *Part-time tuition:* $626 per semester hour. *Part-time mandatory fees:* $18 per semester hour.
Financial Aid Forms of aid include need-based and non-need-based scholarships, athletic grants, and part-time jobs. The average aided 2006–07 undergraduate received an aid package worth an estimated $13,283.
Freshman Admission Mount Vernon Nazarene University requires an essay, a high school transcript, a minimum 2.5 high school GPA, 2 recommendations, SAT or ACT scores, and TOEFL scores for international students. The application deadline for regular admission is May 1.
Entrance Difficulty Mount Vernon Nazarene University assesses its entrance difficulty level as moderately difficult. For the fall 2006 freshman class, 81 percent of the applicants were accepted.
For Further Information Contact Mr. Tim Eades, Director of Admissions and Student Recruitment, Mount Vernon Nazarene University, 800 Martinsburg Road, Mount Vernon, OH 43050. *Telephone:* 740-392-6868 Ext. 4511 or 866-462-6868 (toll-free). *Fax:* 740-393-0511. *E-mail:* admissions@mvnu.edu. *Web site:* http://www.mvnu.edu/.

MUSKINGUM COLLEGE
New Concord, Ohio
http://www.muskingum.edu/

MYERS UNIVERSITY
Cleveland, Ohio
http://www.myers.edu/

NORTHWESTERN COLLEGE
See University of Northwestern Ohio.

NOTRE DAME COLLEGE
South Euclid, Ohio

Notre Dame College is a coed, private, Roman Catholic, comprehensive institution, founded in 1922, offering degrees at the associate, bachelor's, and master's levels and postbachelor's certificates. It has a 53-acre campus in South Euclid near Cleveland.

Academic Information The faculty has 118 members (29% full-time), 52% with terminal degrees. The undergraduate student-faculty ratio is 13:1. The library holds 9,983 audiovisual materials. Special programs include academic remediation, services for learning-disabled students, cooperative (work-study) education, study abroad, advanced placement credit, accelerated degree programs, double majors, independent study, distance learning, self-designed majors, summer session for credit, part-time degree programs (daytime, evenings, weekends, summer), adult/continuing education programs, internships, and arrangement for off-campus study with members of the Northeast Ohio Commission on Higher Education.
Student Body Statistics The student body totals 1,393, of whom 1,240 are undergraduates (227 freshmen). 66 percent are women and 34 percent are men. Students come from 17 states and territories and 19 other countries. 89 percent are from Ohio. 4 percent are international students. 7 percent of the 2006 graduating class went on to graduate and professional schools.
Expenses for 2006–07 *Application fee:* $30. *Comprehensive fee:* $26,980 includes full-time tuition ($19,580), mandatory fees ($550), and college room and board ($6850). *College room only:* $3400. Full-time tuition and fees vary according to course load and degree level. Room and board charges vary according to board plan. *Part-time tuition:* $405 per credit. Part-time tuition varies according to course load and degree level.
Financial Aid Forms of aid include need-based and non-need-based scholarships, athletic grants, and part-time jobs. The application deadline for financial aid is continuous.
Freshman Admission Notre Dame College requires an essay, a high school transcript, a minimum 2.0 high school GPA, an interview, SAT or ACT scores, and TOEFL scores for international students. A minimum 2.5 high school GPA is recommended. The application deadline for regular admission is rolling.
Transfer Admission The application deadline for admission is rolling.
Entrance Difficulty Notre Dame College assesses its entrance difficulty level as moderately difficult. For the fall 2006 freshman class, 52 percent of the applicants were accepted.
For Further Information Contact Mr. David Armstrong, Dean of Admissions, Notre Dame College, 4545 College Road, South Euclid, OH 44121-4293. *Telephone:* 216-373-5214 or 800-632-1680 (toll-free). *Fax:* 216-381-3802. *E-mail:* admissinos@ndc.edu. *Web site:* http://www.notredamecollege.edu/.

OBERLIN COLLEGE
Oberlin, Ohio

Oberlin College is a coed, private, comprehensive institution, founded in 1833, offering degrees at the bachelor's and master's levels and postbachelor's certificates. It has a 440-acre campus in Oberlin near Cleveland.

Academic Information The faculty has 334 members (82% full-time). The undergraduate student-faculty ratio is 10:1. The library holds 2 million titles and 4,560 serial subscriptions. Special programs include services for learning-disabled students, an honors program, study abroad, advanced placement credit, ESL programs, double majors, independent study, self-designed majors, part-time degree programs (daytime), internships, and arrangement for off-campus study with Great Lakes Colleges Association.

Student Body Statistics The student body totals 2,841, of whom 2,829 are undergraduates (715 freshmen). 55 percent are women and 45 percent are men. Students come from 50 states and territories and 44 other countries. 9 percent are from Ohio. 5.6 percent are international students. 22 percent of the 2006 graduating class went on to graduate and professional schools.

Expenses for 2006–07 *Application fee:* $35. *Comprehensive fee:* $43,146 includes full-time tuition ($34,216), mandatory fees ($210), and college room and board ($8720). *College room only:* $4580. Full-time tuition and fees vary according to course load. Room and board charges vary according to board plan and housing facility. *Part-time tuition:* $1420 per credit. Part-time tuition varies according to course load.

Financial Aid Forms of aid include need-based and non-need-based scholarships and part-time jobs. The average aided 2006–07 undergraduate received an aid package worth an estimated $24,255. The priority application deadline for financial aid is January 15.

Freshman Admission Oberlin College requires an essay, a high school transcript, 2 recommendations, SAT or ACT scores, and TOEFL scores for international students. SAT Subject Test scores are recommended. An interview is required for some. The application deadline for regular admission is January 15 and for early decision it is November 15.

Transfer Admission The application deadline for admission is March 15.

Entrance Difficulty Oberlin College assesses its entrance difficulty level as very difficult. For the fall 2006 freshman class, 34 percent of the applicants were accepted.

For Further Information Contact Ms. Debra Chermonte, Dean of Admissions and Financial Aid, Oberlin College, Admissions Office, Carnegie Building, Oberlin, OH 44074-1090. *Telephone:* 440-775-8411 or 800-622-OBIE (toll-free). *Fax:* 440-775-6905. *E-mail:* college.admissions@oberlin.edu. *Web site:* http://www.oberlin.edu/.

OHIO CHRISTIAN UNIVERSITY
Circleville, Ohio
http://www.ohiochristian.edu/

OHIO COLLEGE OF MASSOTHERAPY
Akron, Ohio

Ohio College of Massotherapy is a coed, private, two-year college, founded in 1973, offering degrees at the associate level.

Student Body Statistics The student body is made up of 282 undergraduates.

Expenses for 2006–07 *Application fee:* $25. *Tuition:* $8140 full-time.

Entrance Difficulty Ohio College of Massotherapy assesses its entrance difficulty level as noncompetitive.

For Further Information Contact Mr. John Atkins, Director of Admissions and Marketing,, Ohio College of Massotherapy, 225 Heritage Woods Drive, Akron, OH 44321. *Telephone:* 330-665-1084 or 888-888-4325 (toll-free). *Fax:* 330-665-5021. *E-mail:* admissions@ocm.edu. *Web site:* http://www.ocm.edu/.

OHIO DOMINICAN UNIVERSITY
Columbus, Ohio

Ohio Dominican University is a coed, private, Roman Catholic, comprehensive institution, founded in 1911, offering degrees at the associate, bachelor's, and master's levels. It has a 62-acre campus in Columbus.

Academic Information The faculty has 217 members (32% full-time), 53% with terminal degrees. The undergraduate student-faculty ratio is 14:1. The library holds 104,739 titles, 511 serial subscriptions, and 3,470 audiovisual materials. Special programs include academic remediation, an honors program, study abroad, advanced placement credit, ESL programs, independent study, distance learning, self-designed majors, summer session for credit, part-time degree programs (daytime, evenings, weekends, summer), adult/continuing education programs, internships, and arrangement for off-campus study with members of the Higher Education Council of Columbus. The most frequently chosen baccalaureate fields are business/marketing, education, social sciences.

Student Body Statistics The student body totals 3,054, of whom 2,518 are undergraduates (365 freshmen). 62 percent are women and 38 percent are men. Students come from 19 states and territories and 10 other countries. 97 percent are from Ohio. 0.4 percent are international students.

Expenses for 2006–07 *Application fee:* $25. *Comprehensive fee:* $27,370 includes full-time tuition ($20,500), mandatory fees ($70), and college room and board ($6800). Room and board charges vary according to board plan and housing facility. *Part-time tuition:* $425 per credit hour.

Financial Aid Forms of aid include need-based and non-need-based scholarships, athletic grants, and part-time jobs. The priority application deadline for financial aid is April 1.

Freshman Admission Ohio Dominican University requires a high school transcript, a minimum 2.0 high school GPA, an interview, SAT or ACT scores, and TOEFL scores for international students. An essay and recommendations are required for some. The application deadline for regular admission is rolling.

Transfer Admission The application deadline for admission is rolling.

Entrance Difficulty Ohio Dominican University assesses its entrance difficulty level as moderately difficult. For the fall 2006 freshman class, 73 percent of the applicants were accepted.

For Further Information Contact Ms. Nicole A. Evans, Director of Admissions, Ohio Dominican University, 1216 Sunbury Road, Columbus, OH 43219. *Telephone:* 614-251-4500 or 800-854-2670 (toll-free). *Fax:* 614-251-0156. *E-mail:* admissions@ohiodominican.edu. *Web site:* http://www.ohiodominican.edu/.

OHIO NORTHERN UNIVERSITY
Ada, Ohio

SPONSOR
See Front Insert
for Details!

Ohio Northern University is a coed, private, comprehensive institution, founded in 1871, affiliated with the United Methodist Church, offering degrees at the bachelor's, master's, and first professional levels and postbachelor's certificates. It has a 300-acre campus in Ada.

Academic Information The faculty has 307 members (73% full-time), 64% with terminal degrees. The undergraduate student-faculty ratio is 13:1. Special programs include academic remediation, services for learning-disabled students, an honors program, cooperative (work-study) education, study abroad, advanced placement credit, ESL programs, double majors, independent study, distance learning, summer session for credit, part-time degree programs (daytime, evenings), internships, and arrangement for off-campus study. The most frequently chosen baccalaureate fields are business/marketing, education, engineering.

Student Body Statistics The student body totals 3,620, of whom 2,612 are undergraduates (760 freshmen). 47 percent are women and 53 percent are men. Students come from 42 states and territories and 15 other countries. 86 percent are from Ohio. 0.9 percent are international students.

Expenses for 2006–07 *Application fee:* $30. *Comprehensive fee:* $35,340 includes full-time tuition ($28,050), mandatory fees ($210), and college room and board ($7080). *College room only:* $3540. *Part-time tuition:* $780 per quarter hour. *Part-time mandatory fees:* $70 per year.

Financial Aid Forms of aid include need-based and non-need-based scholarships and part-time jobs. The average aided 2005–06 undergraduate received an aid package worth $22,130.

Freshman Admission Ohio Northern University requires a high school transcript, SAT or ACT scores, and TOEFL scores for international students. An essay, a minimum 2.5 high school GPA, and an interview are recommended. 2 recommendations are required for some. The application deadline for regular admission is August 15.

Transfer Admission The application deadline for admission is September 1.

Entrance Difficulty Ohio Northern University assesses its entrance difficulty level as moderately difficult; very difficult for pharmacy. For the fall 2006 freshman class, 87 percent of the applicants were accepted.

Ohio Northern University (continued)

SPECIAL MESSAGE TO STUDENTS

Social Life With more than 150 campus clubs and organizations available, life outside of the classroom at Ohio Northern University (ONU) is an enriched, rewarding experience. Activities are geared toward the more than 3,600 students on the residential campus and include sporting events, concerts, plays, and many other varieties of entertainment. Northern students are also encouraged to become involved in their campus through Greek life, religious groups, theater, music ensembles, student government, multicultural organizations, Habitat for Humanity, and other such organizations.

Academic Highlights Ohio Northern's distinctive, high-quality academic programs blend the liberal arts with professional and/or preprofessional training in its four undergraduate Colleges of Arts and Sciences, Business Administration, Engineering, and Pharmacy. Internships, cooperative education, and study-abroad programs are available in each of the four undergraduate colleges and provide invaluable hands-on experience to those entering the professional workplace after graduation. The beautiful and well-maintained 300-acre campus includes many exceptional facilities such as the Freed Center for the Performing Arts, a magnificent theater/concert hall; the new Dial-Robertson Stadium Outdoor All-Events Facility; the turf of the ONU Polar Bear's football team; and James F. Dicke Hall, which houses the College of Business Administration and is completely equipped with state-of-the-art technology. Another impressive facility is the ONU Sports Center. It has been the site of three NCAA Division III Indoor Track and Field Championships and three Division III Wrestling Championships. Students have recreational use of three gymnasiums, a wrestling room, a six-lane swimming pool, two racquetball courts, and gymnastics rooms. The center also includes a 200-meter indoor running track, two weight-training rooms, classrooms, athletic faculty/staff offices, and modern athletic training and fitness areas.

Interviews and Campus Visits While interviews are not required for admission to Ohio Northern, they are encouraged. Depending upon a student's preference, there are opportunities to attend class, tour campus, speak to a professor about a specific area of interest, meet an athletic coach, and meet with an admissions or financial aid representative. For information about appointments and campus visits, students should call the Office of Admissions at 888-408-4668 (toll-free) Monday through Friday, 8 to 4:30, or Saturday, 8 to noon. The fax number is 419-772-2313. The nearest commercial airport is Port Columbus International. The nearest commercial airport is Port Columbus International.

For Further Information Write to Karen P. Condeni, Vice President and Dean of Enrollment, Office of Admissions, Ohio Northern University, Ada, OH 45810. *E-mail:* admissions-ug@onu.edu. *Web site:* http://www.onu.edu.

THE OHIO STATE UNIVERSITY
Columbus, Ohio

The Ohio State University is a coed, public university, founded in 1870, offering degrees at the associate, bachelor's, master's, doctoral, and first professional levels and post-master's and postbachelor's certificates. It has a 6,191-acre campus in Columbus.

Academic Information The faculty has 4,031 members (75% full-time). The undergraduate student-faculty ratio is 13:1. The library holds 6 million titles, 43,086 serial subscriptions, and 68,454 audiovisual materials. Special programs include academic remediation, services for learning-disabled students, an honors program, cooperative (work-study) education, study abroad, advanced placement credit, accelerated degree programs, Freshman Honors College, ESL programs, double majors, independent study, distance learning, self-designed majors, summer session for credit, part-time degree programs (daytime, evenings, weekends, summer), adult/continuing education programs, internships, and arrangement for off-campus study with Higher Education Council of Columbus. The most frequently chosen baccalaureate fields are business/marketing, family and consumer sciences, social sciences.

Student Body Statistics The student body totals 51,818, of whom 38,479 are undergraduates (6,280 freshmen). 47 percent are women and 53 percent are men. Students come from 54 states and territories and 74 other countries. 90 percent are from Ohio. 2.5 percent are international students.

Expenses for 2006–07 *Application fee:* $40. *State resident tuition:* $8298 full-time. *Nonresident tuition:* $20,193 full-time. *Mandatory fees:* $261 full-time. Full-time tuition and fees vary according to course load, program, reciprocity agreements, and student level. *College room and board:* $6720. Room and board charges vary according to board plan and housing facility.

Financial Aid Forms of aid include need-based and non-need-based scholarships, athletic grants, and part-time jobs. The average aided 2006–07 undergraduate received an aid package worth an estimated $10,149. The priority application deadline for financial aid is March 1.

Freshman Admission The Ohio State University requires an essay, a high school transcript, SAT or ACT scores, and TOEFL scores for international students. The application deadline for regular admission is February 1 and for nonresidents it is February 1.

Transfer Admission The application deadline for admission is June 25.

Entrance Difficulty The Ohio State University assesses its entrance difficulty level as moderately difficult. For the fall 2006 freshman class, 68 percent of the applicants were accepted.

For Further Information Contact Dr. Mabel G. Freeman, Assistant Vice President for Undergraduate Admissions and First Year Experience, The Ohio State University, Enarson Hall, 154 West 12th Avenue, Columbus, OH 43210. *Telephone:* 614-247-6281. *Fax:* 614-292-4818. *E-mail:* askabuckeye@osu.edu. *Web site:* http://www.osu.edu/.

THE OHIO STATE UNIVERSITY AT LIMA
Lima, Ohio

The Ohio State University at Lima is a coed, public, comprehensive unit of Ohio State University, founded in 1960, offering degrees at the associate, bachelor's, and master's levels. It has a 565-acre campus in Lima.

Academic Information The faculty has 79 members (47% full-time). The undergraduate student-faculty ratio is 21:1. The library holds 73,180 titles, 508 serial subscriptions, and 2,279 audiovisual materials. Special programs include academic remediation, services for learning-disabled students, an honors program, advanced placement credit, accelerated degree programs, ESL programs, summer session for credit, part-time degree programs, and adult/continuing education programs.

Student Body Statistics The student body totals 1,214, of whom 1,136 are undergraduates (364 freshmen). 55 percent are women and 45 percent are men. Students come from 5 states and territories.

Expenses for 2006–07 *Application fee:* $40. *State resident tuition:* $6240 full-time. *Nonresident tuition:* $18,153 full-time. Full-time tuition varies according to course load and student level.

Freshman Admission The Ohio State University at Lima requires an essay and a high school transcript. SAT or ACT scores are required for some. The application deadline for regular admission is February 1 and for nonresidents it is February 1.

Transfer Admission The application deadline for admission is June 25.

Entrance Difficulty The Ohio State University at Lima has an open admission policy for state residents. It assesses its entrance difficulty as moderately difficult for out-of-state applicants; moderately difficult for transfers.

For Further Information Contact Ms. Beth Keehn, Director of Admissions, The Ohio State University at Lima, 4240 Campus Drive, Lima, OH 45804. *Telephone:* 419-995-8434. *Fax:* 419-995-8483. *E-mail:* admissions@lima.ohio-state.edu. *Web site:* http://www.lima.osu.edu/.

THE OHIO STATE UNIVERSITY AT MARION
Marion, Ohio

The Ohio State University at Marion is a coed, public, comprehensive unit of Ohio State University, founded in 1958, offering degrees at the associate, bachelor's, and master's levels. It has a 180-acre campus in Marion near Columbus.

Academic Information The faculty has 112 members (32% full-time). The undergraduate student-faculty ratio is 22:1. The library holds 40,000 titles, 400 serial subscriptions, and 3,800 audiovisual materials. Special programs include academic remediation, services for learning-disabled students, an honors program, advanced placement credit, accelerated degree programs, ESL programs, summer session for credit, part-time degree programs (daytime, evenings, summer), and adult/continuing education programs.

Student Body Statistics The student body totals 1,538, of whom 1,432 are undergraduates (426 freshmen). 56 percent are women and 44 percent are men. Students come from 4 states and territories and 3 other countries. 0.2 percent are international students.

Expenses for 2006–07 *Application fee:* $40. *State resident tuition:* $6240 full-time. *Nonresident tuition:* $18,153 full-time. Full-time tuition varies according to course load and student level.

Freshman Admission The Ohio State University at Marion requires an essay, a high school transcript, and TOEFL scores for international students. The application deadline for regular admission is February 1 and for nonresidents it is February 1.

Transfer Admission The application deadline for admission is June 25.

Entrance Difficulty The Ohio State University at Marion has an open admission policy for state residents. It assesses its entrance difficulty as minimally difficult for transfers.

For Further Information Contact Mr. Matthew Moreau, Admissions and Financial Aid Coordinator, The Ohio State University at Marion, 1465 Mount Vernon Avenue, Marion, OH 43302. *Telephone:* 740-725-6337. *Fax:* 740-386-2439. *E-mail:* moreau.1@osu.edu. *Web site:* http://www.marion.ohio-state.edu/.

THE OHIO STATE UNIVERSITY–MANSFIELD CAMPUS
Mansfield, Ohio

The Ohio State University–Mansfield Campus is a coed, public, comprehensive unit of The Ohio State University, founded in 1958, offering degrees at the associate, bachelor's, and master's levels. It has a 644-acre campus in Mansfield near Columbus and Cleveland.

Academic Information The faculty has 91 members (52% full-time). The undergraduate student-faculty ratio is 19:1. The library holds 45,977 titles and 453 serial subscriptions. Special programs include academic remediation, services for learning-disabled students, an honors program, advanced placement credit, accelerated degree programs, ESL programs, summer session for credit, part-time degree programs (daytime, evenings, summer), and adult/continuing education programs.

Student Body Statistics The student body totals 1,464, of whom 1,383 are undergraduates (393 freshmen). 62 percent are women and 38 percent are men. Students come from 5 states and territories. 99 percent are from Ohio.

Expenses for 2006–07 *Application fee:* $40. *State resident tuition:* $6240 full-time. *Nonresident tuition:* $18,153 full-time. Full-time tuition varies according to course load and student level. *College room and board:* $4803. Room and board charges vary according to housing facility.

Freshman Admission The Ohio State University–Mansfield Campus requires an essay and a high school transcript. SAT or ACT scores are required for some. The application deadline for regular admission is February 1 and for nonresidents it is February 1.

Transfer Admission The application deadline for admission is June 25.

Entrance Difficulty The Ohio State University–Mansfield Campus has an open admission policy for state residents. It assesses its entrance difficulty as moderately difficult for out-of-state applicants; moderately difficult for transfers.

For Further Information Contact Mr. Henry D. Thomas, Coordinator of Admissions and Financial Aid, The Ohio State University–Mansfield Campus, 1760 University Drive, Mansfield, OH 44906. *Telephone:* 419-755-4225. *Fax:* 419-755-4241. *E-mail:* admissions@mansfield.ohio-state.edu. *Web site:* http://www.mansfield.osu.edu/.

THE OHIO STATE UNIVERSITY–NEWARK CAMPUS
Newark, Ohio

The Ohio State University–Newark Campus is a coed, public, comprehensive unit of Ohio State University, founded in 1957, offering degrees at the associate, bachelor's, and master's levels. It has a 106-acre campus in Newark near Columbus.

Academic Information The faculty has 135 members (37% full-time). The undergraduate student-faculty ratio is 26:1. The library holds 49,000 titles, 423 serial subscriptions, and 2,680 audiovisual materials. Special programs include academic remediation, services for learning-disabled students, an honors program, advanced placement credit, accelerated degree programs, ESL programs, summer session for credit, part-time degree programs (daytime, evenings, summer), and adult/continuing education programs.

Student Body Statistics The student body totals 2,310, of whom 2,240 are undergraduates (932 freshmen). 54 percent are women and 46 percent are men. Students come from 13 states and territories and 12 other countries. 99 percent are from Ohio. 0.1 percent are international students.

Expenses for 2006–07 *Application fee:* $40. *State resident tuition:* $6240 full-time. *Nonresident tuition:* $18,153 full-time. *College room only:* $4989.

Freshman Admission The Ohio State University–Newark Campus requires an essay and a high school transcript. The application deadline for regular admission is February 1 and for nonresidents it is February 1.

Transfer Admission The application deadline for admission is June 25.

Entrance Difficulty The Ohio State University–Newark Campus has an open admission policy for state residents. It assesses its entrance difficulty as moderately difficult for out-of-state applicants; moderately difficult for transfers.

For Further Information Contact Mr. Claude R. Barclay, Admissions Counselor/Staff Assistant, The Ohio State University–Newark Campus, 1179 University Drive, Newark, OH 43055. *Telephone:* 614-366-9396. *Fax:* 740-364-9645. *E-mail:* barclay.3@osu.edu. *Web site:* http://www.newark.osu.edu/.

OHIO UNIVERSITY
Athens, Ohio

Ohio University is a coed, public unit of Ohio Board of Regents, founded in 1804, offering degrees at the associate, bachelor's, master's, doctoral, and first professional levels. It has a 1,700-acre campus in Athens.

Academic Information The faculty has 1,188 members (73% full-time), 81% with terminal degrees. The undergraduate student-faculty ratio is 19:1. The library holds 3 million titles, 27,606 serial subscriptions, and 93,337 audiovisual materials. Special programs include academic remediation, services for learning-disabled students, an honors program, cooperative (work-study) education, study abroad, advanced placement credit, accelerated degree programs, ESL programs, double majors, independent study, distance learning, self-designed majors, summer session for credit, part-time degree programs, external degree programs, adult/continuing education programs, internships, and arrangement for off-campus study. The most frequently chosen baccalaureate fields are business/marketing, communications/journalism, education.

Student Body Statistics The student body totals 20,593, of whom 17,176 are undergraduates (4,075 freshmen). 51 percent are women and 49

Ohio University (continued)

percent are men. Students come from 35 states and territories and 109 other countries. 92 percent are from Ohio. 1.3 percent are international students. 25 percent of the 2006 graduating class went on to graduate and professional schools.

Expenses for 2006–07 *Application fee:* $45. *State resident tuition:* $8847 full-time, $277 per quarter hour part-time. *Nonresident tuition:* $17,811 full-time, $572 per quarter hour part-time. *College room and board:* $7839. *College room only:* $4008. Room and board charges vary according to board plan.

Financial Aid Forms of aid include need-based and non-need-based scholarships, athletic grants, and part-time jobs. The average aided 2006–07 undergraduate received an aid package worth an estimated $6785. The priority application deadline for financial aid is March 15.

Freshman Admission Ohio University requires a high school transcript and SAT or ACT scores. 2 recommendations are recommended. An essay and an interview are required for some. The application deadline for regular admission is February 1.

Transfer Admission The application deadline for admission is May 15.

Entrance Difficulty Ohio University assesses its entrance difficulty level as moderately difficult; very difficult for transfers; very difficult for business, journalism, honors tutorial college. For the fall 2006 freshman class, 85 percent of the applicants were accepted.

For Further Information Contact Ms. Candace Boeninger, Assistant Director, Communications and Tech Operations, Ohio University, Athens, OH 45701-2979. *Telephone:* 740-593-4113. *Fax:* 740-593-0560. *E-mail:* admissions@ohio.edu. *Web site:* http://www.ohio.edu/.

OHIO UNIVERSITY–CHILLICOTHE

Chillicothe, Ohio

http://www.ohio.edu/chillicothe/

OHIO UNIVERSITY–EASTERN

St. Clairsville, Ohio

http://www.eastern.ohiou.edu/

OHIO UNIVERSITY–LANCASTER

Lancaster, Ohio

http://www.ohiou.edu/lancaster/

OHIO UNIVERSITY–SOUTHERN CAMPUS

Ironton, Ohio

http://www.ohiou.edu/

OHIO UNIVERSITY–ZANESVILLE

Zanesville, Ohio

Ohio University–Zanesville is a coed, public, comprehensive unit of Ohio Board of Regents, founded in 1946, offering degrees at the associate, bachelor's, and master's levels (offers first 2 years of most bachelor's degree programs available at the main campus in Athens; also offers several bachelor's degree programs that can be completed at this campus; also offers some graduate courses). It has a 179-acre campus in Zanesville near Columbus.

Academic Information The faculty has 130 members (24% full-time), 25% with terminal degrees. The undergraduate student-faculty ratio is 23:1. The library holds 64,227 titles and 489 serial subscriptions. Special programs include academic remediation, services for learning-disabled students, advanced placement credit, self-designed majors, summer session

for credit, part-time degree programs, external degree programs, adult/continuing education programs, and arrangement for off-campus study with Muskingum Area Technical College.

Student Body Statistics The student body is made up of 1,679 undergraduates (248 freshmen). 72 percent are women and 28 percent are men. Students come from 4 states and territories. 99 percent are from Ohio. 0.3 percent are international students.

Expenses for 2006–07 *Application fee:* $20. *State resident tuition:* $4596 full-time, $144 per quarter hour part-time. *Nonresident tuition:* $8919 full-time. Both full-time and part-time tuition varies according to student level.

Financial Aid Forms of aid include need-based and non-need-based scholarships and part-time jobs. The average aided 2006–07 undergraduate received an aid package worth an estimated $6827. The priority application deadline for financial aid is March 15.

Freshman Admission Ohio University–Zanesville requires a high school transcript. SAT or ACT scores are required for some. The application deadline for regular admission is rolling.

Transfer Admission The application deadline for admission is rolling.

Entrance Difficulty Ohio University–Zanesville has an open admission policy except for nursing, engineering, business, communications programs, education. It assesses its entrance difficulty as moderately difficult for nursing, business, engineering, communications programs.

For Further Information Contact Mrs. Karen Ragsdale, Student Services Secretary, Ohio University–Zanesville, Office of Student Services, 1425 Newark Road, Zanesville, OH 43701. *Telephone:* 740-588-1440. *Fax:* 740-588-1444. *E-mail:* ouzservices@ohio.edu. *Web site:* http://www.zanesville.ohiou.edu/.

OHIO WESLEYAN UNIVERSITY

Delaware, Ohio

Ohio Wesleyan University is a coed, private, United Methodist, four-year college, founded in 1842, offering degrees at the bachelor's level. It has a 200-acre campus in Delaware near Columbus.

Academic Information The faculty has 182 members (74% full-time), 85% with terminal degrees. The student-faculty ratio is 13:1. The library holds 441,912 titles and 1,073 serial subscriptions. Special programs include services for learning-disabled students, an honors program, study abroad, advanced placement credit, Freshman Honors College, double majors, independent study, self-designed majors, summer session for credit, part-time degree programs (daytime, summer), internships, and arrangement for off-campus study with Great Lakes Colleges Association, New York City Arts Program, Wesleyan in Washington, Philadelphia Center. The most frequently chosen baccalaureate fields are biological/life sciences, business/marketing, social sciences.

Student Body Statistics The student body is made up of 1,935 undergraduates (565 freshmen). 52 percent are women and 48 percent are men. Students come from 40 states and territories and 45 other countries. 54 percent are from Ohio. 8.2 percent are international students. 41 percent of the 2006 graduating class went on to graduate and professional schools.

Expenses for 2006–07 *Application fee:* $35. *Comprehensive fee:* $38,080 includes full-time tuition ($29,870), mandatory fees ($420), and college room and board ($7790). *College room only:* $3880. Room and board charges vary according to board plan. *Part-time tuition:* $3250 per course.

Financial Aid Forms of aid include need-based and non-need-based scholarships and part-time jobs. The average aided 2006–07 undergraduate received an aid package worth an estimated $20,854. The application deadline for financial aid is May 1 with a priority deadline of March 1.

Freshman Admission Ohio Wesleyan University requires an essay, a high school transcript, a minimum 2.5 high school GPA, 1 recommendation, SAT or ACT scores, and TOEFL scores for international students. 2 recommendations, an interview, and SAT Subject Test scores are recommended. The application deadline for regular admission is March 1; for early decision it is December 1; and for early action it is December 15.

Transfer Admission The application deadline for admission is May 15.

Entrance Difficulty Ohio Wesleyan University assesses its entrance difficulty level as very difficult; most difficult for honors program. For the fall 2006 freshman class, 63 percent of the applicants were accepted.

For Further Information Contact Ms. Carol DelPropost, Assistant Vice President of Admission and Financial Aid, Ohio Wesleyan University, 61 South Sandusky Street, Delaware, OH 43015. *Telephone:* 740-368-3059 or 800-922-8953 (toll-free). *Fax:* 740-368-3314. *E-mail:* cjdelpro@owu.edu. *Web site:* http://www.owu.edu/.

See page 278 for the College Close-Up.

OTTERBEIN COLLEGE
Westerville, Ohio

SPONSOR
See Front Insert
for Details!

Otterbein College is a coed, private, United Methodist, comprehensive institution, founded in 1847, offering degrees at the bachelor's and master's levels. It has a 142-acre campus in Westerville near Columbus.

Academic Information The faculty has 275 members (58% full-time). The undergraduate student-faculty ratio is 12:1. The library holds 182,629 titles and 1,012 serial subscriptions. Special programs include academic remediation, services for learning-disabled students, an honors program, study abroad, advanced placement credit, double majors, self-designed majors, summer session for credit, part-time degree programs (daytime, evenings, weekends, summer), adult/continuing education programs, internships, and arrangement for off-campus study with American University, University of Pittsburgh (Semester at Sea), members of the Higher Education Council of Columbus.

Student Body Statistics The student body totals 3,176, of whom 2,804 are undergraduates (658 freshmen). 64 percent are women and 36 percent are men. Students come from 34 states and territories and 12 other countries. 92 percent are from Ohio.

Expenses for 2006–07 *Application fee:* $25. *Comprehensive fee:* $30,660 includes full-time tuition ($23,871) and college room and board ($6789). *College room only:* $3174. Full-time tuition varies according to course load and program. Room and board charges vary according to housing facility. *Part-time tuition:* $285 per credit. Part-time tuition varies according to course load and program.

Financial Aid Forms of aid include need-based and non-need-based scholarships and part-time jobs. The priority application deadline for financial aid is April 1.

Freshman Admission Otterbein College requires a high school transcript, SAT or ACT scores, and TOEFL scores for international students. A minimum 2.5 high school GPA and an interview are recommended. The application deadline for regular admission is March 1.

Transfer Admission The application deadline for admission is rolling.

Entrance Difficulty Otterbein College assesses its entrance difficulty level as moderately difficult. For the fall 2006 freshman class, 77 percent of the applicants were accepted.

SPECIAL MESSAGE TO STUDENTS

Social Life Students participate in more than 100 campus organizations, from music performance groups, such as the marching band, concert choir, and orchestra, to student government to student-run radio and television studios to intramural sports. Twenty-seven percent join one of the five fraternities and six sororities. Many students are involved in campus service organizations, such as Habitat for Humanity. Religious activities are also available for students in most denominations. Cultural activities on campus include a Professional Artist Series, the Otterbein College Theatre, and musical performances. Off-campus activities in nearby Columbus include many social, sports, and cultural offerings.

Academic Highlights The curriculum revolves around Otterbein's nationally recognized liberal arts curriculum, Integrative Studies, combined with professional and career preparation. Otterbein offers

forty-nine majors and seven baccalaureate and four graduate degrees. Internships are encouraged in order to give students hands-on work experience to complement their course work. Programs in theater and equine science have each achieved national recognition.

Interviews and Campus Visits Individual interviews are not required of all applicants, but campus visits are strongly recommended for all accepted students. The visit is structured so students can gain a thorough understanding of the campus from a variety of perspectives. Faculty conferences, student-conducted tours, admission and financial aid conferences, and classroom observation are part of each campus visit. Roush Hall, the multipurpose, state-of-the-art classroom building; Battelle Fine Arts Center; the Rike Physical Education Building; the Science Hall–Observatory; the campus center; residence halls; Towers Hall; the computer center; Courtright Memorial Library; and the new Clements Recreation Center should not be missed. For information about appointments and campus visits, students should call the Office of Admission at 614-823-1500 (collect) or 800-488-8144 (toll-free), Monday through Friday, 8:30 to 5, or Saturday, 9:30 to 1. The office is located in the Clippinger Administration Building on the campus. The nearest commercial airport is Port Columbus International.

For Further Information Write to Dr. Cass Johnson, Director of Admission, Otterbein College, Westerville, OH 43081. *Web site:* http://www.otterbein.edu.

PONTIFICAL COLLEGE JOSEPHINUM
Columbus, Ohio

Pontifical College Josephinum is a coed, primarily men's, private, Roman Catholic, comprehensive institution, founded in 1888, offering degrees at the bachelor's, master's, and first professional levels. It has a 100-acre campus in Columbus.

Academic Information The faculty has 50 members (46% full-time), 58% with terminal degrees. The undergraduate student-faculty ratio is 6:1. The library holds 137,883 titles and 465 serial subscriptions. Special programs include academic remediation, services for learning-disabled students, an honors program, advanced placement credit, ESL programs, double majors, internships, and arrangement for off-campus study with 2 members of the Theological Cluster. The most frequently chosen baccalaureate fields are English, area and ethnic studies, philosophy and religious studies.

Student Body Statistics The student body totals 153, of whom 104 are undergraduates (25 freshmen). 100 percent are men. Students come from 20 states and territories and 1 other country. 27 percent are from Ohio. 7.7 percent are international students. 90 percent of the 2006 graduating class went on to graduate and professional schools.

Expenses for 2007–08 *Application fee:* $25. *Comprehensive fee:* $23,178 includes full-time tuition ($14,997), mandatory fees ($683), and college room and board ($7498). *Part-time tuition:* $606 per credit hour.

Financial Aid Forms of aid include need-based and non-need-based scholarships and part-time jobs. The priority application deadline for financial aid is September 2.

Freshman Admission Pontifical College Josephinum requires an essay, a high school transcript, 3 recommendations, an interview, SAT and SAT Subject Test or ACT scores, and TOEFL scores for international students. The application deadline for regular admission is July 31.

Transfer Admission The application deadline for admission is rolling.

Entrance Difficulty Pontifical College Josephinum assesses its entrance difficulty level as minimally difficult. For the fall 2006 freshman class, 83 percent of the applicants were accepted.

For Further Information Contact Mrs. Arminda Crawford, PhD, Secretary for Admissions, Pontifical College Josephinum, 7825 North High Street, Columbus, OH 43235. *Telephone:* 614-985-2241 or 888-252-5812 (toll-free). *Fax:* 614-885-2307. *E-mail:* acrawford@pcj.edu. *Web site:* http://www.pcj.edu/.

RABBINICAL COLLEGE OF TELSHE

Wickliffe, Ohio

For Information Write to Rabbinical College of Telshe, Wickliffe, OH 44092-2523.

ROSEDALE BIBLE COLLEGE

Irwin, Ohio

Rosedale Bible College is a coed, private, Mennonite, two-year college, founded in 1952, offering degrees at the associate level.

Student Body Statistics The student body is made up of 89 undergraduates.

Expenses for 2006–07 *Application fee:* $50. *Tuition:* $5370 full-time.

Freshman Admission Rosedale Bible College requires recommendations. SAT or ACT scores are recommended.

Entrance Difficulty For the fall 2006 freshman class, 94 percent of the applicants were accepted.

For Further Information Contact Mr. John Showalter, Director of Enrollment Services, Rosedale Bible College, 2270 Rosedale Road, Irwin, OH 43029-9501. *Telephone:* 740-857-1311. *Fax:* 877-857-1312. *E-mail:* pweber@rosedale.edu. *Web site:* http://www.rosedalebible.org/.

SHAWNEE STATE UNIVERSITY

Portsmouth, Ohio

Shawnee State University is a coed, public, four-year college of Ohio Board of Regents, founded in 1986, offering degrees at the associate and bachelor's levels. It has a 52-acre campus in Portsmouth.

Academic Information The faculty has 317 members (45% full-time). The student-faculty ratio is 17:1. The library holds 150,957 titles and 56,172 serial subscriptions. Special programs include academic remediation, services for learning-disabled students, an honors program, study abroad, advanced placement credit, double majors, independent study, distance learning, summer session for credit, part-time degree programs (daytime, evenings, summer), adult/continuing education programs, internships, and arrangement for off-campus study. The most frequently chosen baccalaureate fields are business/marketing, education, social sciences.

Student Body Statistics The student body totals 3,889, of whom 3,880 are undergraduates (492 freshmen). 60 percent are women and 40 percent are men. Students come from 18 states and territories and 12 other countries. 92 percent are from Ohio. 0.7 percent are international students.

Expenses for 2006–07 *Application fee:* $0. *State resident tuition:* $5202 full-time, $162 per credit hour part-time. *Nonresident tuition:* $9342 full-time, $277 per credit hour part-time. *Mandatory fees:* $630 full-time, $1705 per credit hour part-time. Both full-time and part-time tuition and fees vary according to course load, reciprocity agreements, and student level. *College room and board:* $6939. *College room only:* $4551. Room and board charges vary according to board plan and housing facility.

Financial Aid Forms of aid include need-based and non-need-based scholarships, athletic grants, and part-time jobs. The priority application deadline for financial aid is April 1.

Freshman Admission Shawnee State University requires a high school transcript and TOEFL scores for international students. ACT scores are recommended. Recommendations, an interview, and ACT scores are required for some. The application deadline for regular admission is rolling.

Transfer Admission The application deadline for admission is rolling.

Entrance Difficulty Shawnee State University has an open admission policy except for allied health programs, nonresident aliens. It assesses its entrance difficulty as moderately difficult for allied health programs.

For Further Information Contact Mr. Bob Trusz, Director of Admission, Shawnee State University, 940 Second Street, Commons Building, Portsmouth, OH 45662. *Telephone:* 740-351-3610 Ext. 610 or 800-959-2SSU (toll-free). *Fax:* 740-351-3111. *E-mail:* to_ssu@shawnee.edu. *Web site:* http://www.shawnee.edu/.

SOUTHEASTERN BUSINESS COLLEGE

See Gallipolis Career College.

TEMPLE BAPTIST COLLEGE

Cincinnati, Ohio

http://www.templebaptistcollege.com/

TIFFIN UNIVERSITY

Tiffin, Ohio

Tiffin University is a coed, private, comprehensive institution, founded in 1888, offering degrees at the associate, bachelor's, and master's levels. It has a 110-acre campus in Tiffin near Toledo.

Academic Information The faculty has 137 members (39% full-time), 37% with terminal degrees. The undergraduate student-faculty ratio is 15:1. The library holds 29,779 titles, 250 serial subscriptions, and 536 audiovisual materials. Special programs include an honors program, study abroad, advanced placement credit, accelerated degree programs, ESL programs, double majors, independent study, distance learning, summer session for credit, external degree programs, adult/continuing education programs, and internships.

Student Body Statistics The student body totals 1,977, of whom 1,437 are undergraduates (332 freshmen). 53 percent are women and 47 percent are men. Students come from 21 states and territories and 16 other countries. 88 percent are from Ohio. 3.8 percent are international students.

Expenses for 2006–07 *Application fee:* $20. *Comprehensive fee:* $22,645 includes full-time tuition ($15,870) and college room and board ($6775). *College room only:* $3525. *Part-time tuition:* $529 per credit hour.

Financial Aid Forms of aid include need-based and non-need-based scholarships and part-time jobs. The average aided 2006–07 undergraduate received an aid package worth an estimated $13,044. The priority application deadline for financial aid is January 1.

Freshman Admission Tiffin University requires a high school transcript, SAT or ACT scores, and TOEFL scores for international students. An essay, a minimum 3.00 high school GPA, an interview, and minimum score of 19 on ACT or 890 on SAT are recommended. An essay, recommendations, and an interview are required for some. The application deadline for regular admission is rolling.

Entrance Difficulty Tiffin University assesses its entrance difficulty level as minimally difficult. For the fall 2006 freshman class, 74 percent of the applicants were accepted.

For Further Information Contact Ms. Dawn Shores, Director of Undergraduate Admissions, Tiffin University, 155 Miami Street, Tiffin, OH 44883. *Telephone:* 419-448-3301 or 800-968-6446 (toll-free). *Fax:* 419-443-5006. *E-mail:* admiss@tiffin.edu. *Web site:* http://www.tiffin.edu/.

TRI-STATE BIBLE COLLEGE

South Point, Ohio

http://www.tsbc.edu/

UNION INSTITUTE & UNIVERSITY

Cincinnati, Ohio

Union Institute & University is a coed, private university, founded in 1969, offering degrees at the bachelor's, master's, and doctoral levels and post-master's certificates. It has a 5-acre campus in Cincinnati.

For Further Information Contact Dr. Emily Harbold, Associate Vice President, Academic Affairs, Union Institute & University, 440 East McMillan Street, Cincinnati, OH 45206. *Telephone:* 513-861-6400 or 800-486-3116 (toll-free). *E-mail:* admissions@tui.edu. *Web site:* http://www.tui.edu/.

THE UNIVERSITY OF AKRON

Akron, Ohio

The University of Akron is a coed, public university, founded in 1870, offering degrees at the bachelor's, master's, doctoral, and first professional levels and first professional and postbachelor's certificates (associate). It has a 218-acre campus in Akron near Cleveland.

Academic Information The faculty has 1,497 members (47% full-time), 54% with terminal degrees. The undergraduate student-faculty ratio is 18:1. The library holds 1 million titles, 13,677 serial subscriptions, and 46,248 audiovisual materials. Special programs include academic remediation, services for learning-disabled students, an honors program, cooperative (work-study) education, study abroad, advanced placement credit, accelerated degree programs, Freshman Honors College, ESL programs, double majors, independent study, distance learning, self-designed majors, summer session for credit, part-time degree programs (daytime, evenings, weekends, summer), external degree programs, adult/continuing education programs, and internships. The most frequently chosen baccalaureate fields are business/marketing, education, health professions and related sciences.

Student Body Statistics The student body totals 21,882, of whom 18,016 are undergraduates (3,763 freshmen). 52 percent are women and 48 percent are men. Students come from 34 states and territories and 47 other countries. 96 percent are from Ohio. 1 percent are international students.

Expenses for 2006–07 *Application fee:* $30. *State resident tuition:* $7218 full-time, $301 per credit part-time. *Nonresident tuition:* $16,467 full-time, $609 per credit part-time. *Mandatory fees:* $1164 full-time, $49 per credit part-time. Both full-time and part-time tuition and fees vary according to course load, degree level, and location. *College room and board:* $7640. *College room only:* $4764. Room and board charges vary according to board plan and housing facility.

Financial Aid Forms of aid include need-based and non-need-based scholarships, athletic grants, and part-time jobs. The average aided 2005–06 undergraduate received an aid package worth $6632. The priority application deadline for financial aid is February 1.

Freshman Admission The University of Akron requires a high school transcript, SAT or ACT scores, and TOEFL scores for international students. An essay, 3 recommendations, and an interview are required for some. The application deadline for regular admission is August 1 and for early action it is November 15.

Transfer Admission The application deadline for admission is rolling.

Entrance Difficulty The University of Akron assesses its entrance difficulty level as moderately difficult; noncompetitive for Community and Technical College. For the fall 2006 freshman class, 79 percent of the applicants were accepted.

For Further Information Contact Ms. Diane Raybuck, Director of Admissions, The University of Akron, The University of Akron, Akron, OH 44325-2001. *Telephone:* 330-972-6427 or 800-655-4884 (toll-free). *Fax:* 330-972-7022. *E-mail:* admissions@uakron.edu. *Web site:* http://www.uakron.edu/.

UNIVERSITY OF CINCINNATI

Cincinnati, Ohio

University of Cincinnati is a coed, public university, founded in 1819, offering degrees at the associate, bachelor's, master's, doctoral, and first professional levels and postbachelor's certificates. It has a 137-acre campus in Cincinnati.

Academic Information The faculty has 1,241 members (97% full-time), 66% with terminal degrees. The undergraduate student-faculty ratio is 14:1. The library holds 3 million titles and 16,560 serial subscriptions. Special programs include academic remediation, services for learning-disabled students, an honors program, cooperative (work-study) education, study abroad, advanced placement credit, accelerated degree programs, ESL programs, double majors, independent study, distance learning, summer session for credit, part-time degree programs, adult/continuing education programs, internships, and arrangement for off-campus study with Greater Cincinnati Consortium of Colleges and Universities. The most frequently chosen baccalaureate fields are business/marketing, engineering, visual and performing arts.

Student Body Statistics The student body totals 27,932, of whom 19,512 are undergraduates (3,914 freshmen). 50 percent are women and 50 percent are men. Students come from 52 states and territories and 123 other countries. 91 percent are from Ohio. 1.3 percent are international students. 36 percent of the 2006 graduating class went on to graduate and professional schools.

Expenses for 2006–07 *Application fee:* $40. *State resident tuition:* $7896 full-time, $220 per credit hour part-time. *Nonresident tuition:* $22,419 full-time, $623 per credit hour part-time. *Mandatory fees:* $1503 full-time, $42 per credit hour part-time. Both full-time and part-time tuition and fees vary according to course load, degree level, location, program, and reciprocity agreements. *College room and board:* $9246. *College room only:* $5874. Room and board charges vary according to board plan and housing facility.

Financial Aid Forms of aid include need-based and non-need-based scholarships, athletic grants, and part-time jobs. The average aided 2005–06 undergraduate received an aid package worth $7787. The application deadline for financial aid is continuous.

Freshman Admission University of Cincinnati requires a high school transcript and SAT or ACT scores. An interview is recommended. 2 recommendations and audition are required for some. The application deadline for regular admission is rolling.

Transfer Admission The application deadline for admission is rolling.

Entrance Difficulty University of Cincinnati assesses its entrance difficulty level as moderately difficult; most difficult for engineering, architecture programs. For the fall 2006 freshman class, 76 percent of the applicants were accepted.

For Further Information Contact Mr. Thomas Canepa, Assistant Vice President, Admissions, University of Cincinnati, 340 University Pavillion, Cincinnati, OH 45221-0091. *Telephone:* 513-556-1100. *Fax:* 513-556-1105. *E-mail:* admissions@uc.edu. *Web site:* http://www.uc.edu/.

UNIVERSITY OF DAYTON

Dayton, Ohio

SPONSOR
See Front Insert
for Details!

University of Dayton is a coed, private, Roman Catholic university, founded in 1850, offering degrees at the bachelor's, master's, doctoral, and first professional levels and post-master's certificates. It has a 259-acre campus in Dayton near Cincinnati.

Academic Information The faculty has 914 members (50% full-time). The undergraduate student-faculty ratio is 13:1. The library holds 973,842 titles, 10,481 serial subscriptions, and 2,186 audiovisual materials. Special programs include academic remediation, services for learning-disabled students, an honors program, cooperative (work-study) education, study abroad, advanced placement credit, accelerated degree programs, ESL programs, double majors, independent study, distance learning, self-designed majors, summer session for credit, part-time degree programs (daytime, evenings, summer), adult/continuing education programs, internships, and arrangement for off-campus study with Southwestern Ohio Council for Higher Education, Chaminade University of Honolulu, St. Mary's University. The most frequently chosen baccalaureate fields are business/marketing, education, engineering.

Student Body Statistics The student body totals 10,503, of whom 7,473 are undergraduates (1,738 freshmen). 50 percent are women and 50 percent are men. Students come from 49 states and territories and 25 other countries. 66 percent are from Ohio. 0.7 percent are international students.

Expenses for 2006–07 *Application fee:* $0. *Comprehensive fee:* $31,160 includes full-time tuition ($23,000), mandatory fees ($970), and college room and board ($7190). *College room only:* $4300. Full-time tuition and fees vary according to program. Room and board charges vary according to board plan, housing facility, and student level. *Part-time tuition:* $767 per credit hour. *Part-time mandatory fees:* $25 per term. Part-time tuition and fees vary according to course load and program.

Financial Aid Forms of aid include need-based and non-need-based scholarships, athletic grants, and part-time jobs. The average aided 2005–06 undergraduate received an aid package worth $11,850. The priority application deadline for financial aid is March 31.

Freshman Admission University of Dayton requires a high school transcript, 1 recommendation, SAT or ACT scores, and TOEFL scores for

University of Dayton (continued)

international students. An essay and an interview are recommended. Audition required for music, music therapy, music education programs is required for some. The application deadline for regular admission is rolling.

Transfer Admission The application deadline for admission is June 15.

Entrance Difficulty University of Dayton assesses its entrance difficulty level as moderately difficult. For the fall 2006 freshman class, 79 percent of the applicants were accepted.

SPECIAL MESSAGE TO STUDENTS

Social Life The residential character of the University of Dayton (UD) campus supports a stimulating academic and extracurricular life for approximately 6,900 full-time undergraduate students, of whom more than 92 percent choose to live on campus. Participation in clubs and organizations—whether athletic, performance, professional, service, or social—is a distinguishing characteristic of the active UD student body. More than 180 clubs and organizations are active on campus. One of the most notable interests of students, however, is service to others. Virtually every organization offers some type of service.

Academic Highlights The University of Dayton is a place where students are encouraged and challenged to reach their full potential in and out of the classroom. Students are the most important part of UD, and teaching and advising are the University's highest priorities. The University of Dayton provides cooperative education, internships, study abroad, and the University Honors and John W. Berry Sr. Scholars programs as well as opportunities in undergraduate research to supplement academic course work. UD's campus is completely wired, providing 24-hour access to the library, the Internet, and administrative services such as course registration. All University-owned housing is fully wired for the Internet, and a wireless network offers more than 800 access points covering academic buildings, the library, residential buildings, the student union, and outdoor plazas. It expands each year to include more areas.

Interviews and Campus Visits The campus interview is not required for admission but is recommended as a means of sharing information. Campus visits include an appointment with an admission counselor, a campus tour, and a residence hall tour. An appointment with a financial aid counselor, meeting with a faculty member, attending class, or accompanying a UD student through his or her day can also be arranged. A limited number of hosted overnight visits are available during the winter semester for accepted students. The University of Dayton urges visitors to see new and renovated campus facilities, including ArtStreet, an innovative living and learning center in the heart of the south student neighborhood; Marycrest Complex and Marianist Hall, residential facilities for first- and second-year students; the Science Center, home to the University's science and mathematics programs; the Arena Sports Complex, including the recently renovated University of Dayton Arena; and the new fitness and recreation complex, the RecPlex, which opened in January 2006. Renovations are underway in Kettering Laboratories, location of the School of Engineering and part of the University of Dayton Research Institute. Visitors are also encouraged to visit Roesch Library, which holds more than 1.3 million volumes; the Ryan C. Harris Learning Teaching Center; and the Davis Center for Portfolio Management. More information about appointments and campus visits can be found online at http://admission.udayton.edu/visitud/ or by calling the Office of Admission at 937-229-4411 or 800-837-7433 (toll-free), Monday through Friday, 8:30 to 4:30. Open house programs are available in the fall, and group appointments may be scheduled on Saturday mornings from January through May. The nearest commercial airport is Dayton International.

For Further Information Write to Mr. Robert Durkle, Director of Admission, University of Dayton, 300 College Park, Dayton, OH 45469-1300. *E-mail:* admission@udayton.edu. *Web site:* http://admission.udayton.edu.

THE UNIVERSITY OF FINDLAY
Findlay, Ohio

The University of Findlay is a coed, private, comprehensive institution, founded in 1882, affiliated with the Church of God, offering degrees at the associate, bachelor's, and master's levels. It has a 200-acre campus in Findlay near Toledo.

Academic Information The faculty has 299 members (57% full-time), 33% with terminal degrees. The undergraduate student-faculty ratio is 18:1. The library holds 132,052 titles and 23,128 serial subscriptions. Special programs include academic remediation, services for learning-disabled students, an honors program, cooperative (work-study) education, study abroad, advanced placement credit, accelerated degree programs, ESL programs, double majors, independent study, distance learning, self-designed majors, summer session for credit, part-time degree programs (daytime, evenings, weekends, summer), adult/continuing education programs, internships, and arrangement for off-campus study. The most frequently chosen baccalaureate fields are business/marketing, education, health professions and related sciences.

Student Body Statistics The student body totals 6,182, of whom 4,926 are undergraduates (673 freshmen). 61 percent are women and 39 percent are men. Students come from 45 states and territories and 34 other countries. 87 percent are from Ohio. 5.6 percent are international students.

Expenses for 2006–07 *Application fee:* $0. *Comprehensive fee:* $30,588 includes full-time tuition ($21,836), mandatory fees ($960), and college room and board ($7792). *College room only:* $3906. Full-time tuition and fees vary according to location and program. *Part-time tuition:* $481 per semester hour. *Part-time mandatory fees:* $130 per term. Part-time tuition and fees vary according to location and program.

Financial Aid Forms of aid include need-based and non-need-based scholarships, athletic grants, and part-time jobs. The average aided 2006–07 undergraduate received an aid package worth an estimated $14,900. The application deadline for financial aid is March 1.

Freshman Admission The University of Findlay requires an essay, a high school transcript, a minimum 2.3 high school GPA, recommendations, and SAT or ACT scores. TOEFL scores for international students are recommended. An interview is required for some. The application deadline for regular admission is rolling.

Transfer Admission The application deadline for admission is August 1.

Entrance Difficulty The University of Findlay assesses its entrance difficulty level as moderately difficult. For the fall 2006 freshman class, 72 percent of the applicants were accepted.

For Further Information Contact Mr. Randall Langston, Executive Director of Enrollment Services, The University of Findlay, 1000 North Main Street, Findlay, OH 45840-3653. *Telephone:* 419-434-4732 or 800-548-0932 (toll-free). *Fax:* 419-434-4898. *E-mail:* admissions@findlay.edu. *Web site:* http://www.findlay.edu/.

See page 298 for the College Close-Up.

UNIVERSITY OF NORTHWESTERN OHIO
Lima, Ohio

University of Northwestern Ohio is a coed, private, primarily two-year college, founded in 1920, offering degrees at the associate and bachelor's levels. It has a 35-acre campus in Lima near Dayton and Toledo.

For Further Information Contact Mr. Dan Klopp, Vice President for Enrollment Management, University of Northwestern Ohio, 1441 North Cable Road, Lima, OH 45805-1498. *Telephone:* 419-227-3141. *Fax:* 419-229-6926. *E-mail:* info@nc.edu. *Web site:* http://www.unoh.edu/.

UNIVERSITY OF PHOENIX–CINCINNATI CAMPUS

West Chester, Ohio

University of Phoenix–Cincinnati Campus is a coed, proprietary, comprehensive institution, founded in 2003, offering degrees at the bachelor's and master's levels.

Academic Information The faculty has 198 members (12% full-time), 18% with terminal degrees. The undergraduate student-faculty ratio is 6:1. The library holds 1,759 titles and 692 serial subscriptions. Special programs include services for learning-disabled students, advanced placement credit, accelerated degree programs, independent study, distance learning, external degree programs, and adult/continuing education programs. The most frequently chosen baccalaureate field is business/marketing.

Student Body Statistics The student body totals 646, of whom 462 are undergraduates (32 freshmen). 65 percent are women and 35 percent are men. 4.8 percent are international students.

Expenses for 2006–07 *Application fee:* $45. *Tuition:* $11,910 full-time, $397 per credit part-time.

Financial Aid Forms of aid include need-based and non-need-based scholarships. The average aided 2005–06 undergraduate received an aid package worth $3974. The application deadline for financial aid is continuous.

Freshman Admission University of Phoenix–Cincinnati Campus requires 1 recommendation. A high school transcript is required for some. The application deadline for regular admission is rolling.

Transfer Admission The application deadline for admission is rolling.

Entrance Difficulty University of Phoenix–Cincinnati Campus has an open admission policy.

For Further Information Contact Ms. Beth Barilla, Associate Vice President, Student Admissions and Services, University of Phoenix–Cincinnati Campus, 4615 East Elwood Street, Mail Stop AA-K101, Phoenix, AZ 85040-1958. *Telephone:* 480-317-6000, 800-776-4867 (toll-free in-state), or 800-228-7240 (toll-free out-of-state). *Fax:* 480-894-1758. *E-mail:* beth.barilla@phoenix.edu. *Web site:* http://www.phoenix.edu/.

UNIVERSITY OF PHOENIX–CLEVELAND CAMPUS

Independence, Ohio

University of Phoenix–Cleveland Campus is a coed, proprietary, comprehensive institution, founded in 2000, offering degrees at the bachelor's and master's levels.

Academic Information The faculty has 201 members (4% full-time), 13% with terminal degrees. The undergraduate student-faculty ratio is 6:1. The library holds 1,759 titles and 692 serial subscriptions. Special programs include services for learning-disabled students, advanced placement credit, accelerated degree programs, independent study, distance learning, external degree programs, and adult/continuing education programs. The most frequently chosen baccalaureate fields are business/marketing, computer and information sciences, health professions and related sciences.

Student Body Statistics The student body totals 865, of whom 663 are undergraduates (41 freshmen). 69 percent are women and 31 percent are men. 9.4 percent are international students.

Expenses for 2006–07 *Application fee:* $45. *Tuition:* $11,910 full-time.

Financial Aid Forms of aid include need-based and non-need-based scholarships. The average aided 2005–06 undergraduate received an aid package worth $4211. The application deadline for financial aid is continuous.

Freshman Admission University of Phoenix–Cleveland Campus requires 1 recommendation and TOEFL scores for international students. A high school transcript is required for some. The application deadline for regular admission is rolling.

Transfer Admission The application deadline for admission is rolling.

Entrance Difficulty University of Phoenix–Cleveland Campus has an open admission policy.

For Further Information Contact Ms. Beth Barilla, Associate Vice President, Student Admissions and Services, University of Phoenix–Cleveland Campus, 4615 East Elwood Street, Mail Stop AA-K101, Phoenix, AZ 85040-1958. *Telephone:* 480-317-6000, 800-776-4867 (toll-free in-state), or 800-228-7240 (toll-free out-of-state). *Fax:* 480-594-1758. *E-mail:* beth.barilla@phoenix.edu. *Web site:* http://www.phoenix.edu/.

UNIVERSITY OF PHOENIX–COLUMBUS OHIO CAMPUS

Columbus, Ohio

University of Phoenix–Columbus Ohio Campus is a coed, proprietary, comprehensive institution, founded in 2003, offering degrees at the bachelor's and master's levels.

Academic Information The faculty has 75 members (7% full-time), 28% with terminal degrees. The undergraduate student-faculty ratio is 7:1. The library holds 1,756 titles and 692 serial subscriptions. Special programs include services for learning-disabled students, advanced placement credit, accelerated degree programs, independent study, distance learning, external degree programs, and adult/continuing education programs. The most frequently chosen baccalaureate fields are business/marketing, computer and information sciences.

Student Body Statistics The student body totals 471, of whom 326 are undergraduates (13 freshmen). 56 percent are women and 44 percent are men. 5.8 percent are international students.

Expenses for 2006–07 *Application fee:* $45. *Tuition:* $10,080 full-time.

Financial Aid Forms of aid include need-based and non-need-based scholarships. The average aided 2005–06 undergraduate received an aid package worth $3460. The application deadline for financial aid is continuous.

Freshman Admission University of Phoenix–Columbus Ohio Campus requires 1 recommendation. A high school transcript is required for some. The application deadline for regular admission is rolling.

Transfer Admission The application deadline for admission is rolling.

Entrance Difficulty University of Phoenix–Columbus Ohio Campus has an open admission policy.

For Further Information Contact Ms. Beth Barilla, Associate Vice President, Student Admissions and Services, University of Phoenix–Columbus Ohio Campus, 8415 Pulsar Place, Columbus, OH 43240-4032. *Telephone:* 480-317-6000, 800-776-4867 (toll-free in-state), or 800-228-7240 (toll-free out-of-state). *Fax:* 480-894-1758. *E-mail:* beth.barilla@phoenix. edu. *Web site:* http://www.phoenix.edu/.

UNIVERSITY OF RIO GRANDE

Rio Grande, Ohio

University of Rio Grande is a coed, private, comprehensive institution, founded in 1876, offering degrees at the associate, bachelor's, and master's levels. It has a 170-acre campus in Rio Grande.

Academic Information The faculty has 308 members (30% full-time), 14% with terminal degrees. The undergraduate student-faculty ratio is 18:1. The library holds 96,731 titles and 850 serial subscriptions. Special programs include academic remediation, services for learning-disabled students, an honors program, cooperative (work-study) education, study abroad, advanced placement credit, accelerated degree programs, Freshman Honors College, ESL programs, double majors, independent study, distance learning, self-designed majors, summer session for credit, part-time degree programs (daytime, evenings), adult/continuing education programs, and internships. The most frequently chosen baccalaureate fields are business/marketing, education, health professions and related sciences.

Student Body Statistics The student body totals 2,429, of whom 2,107 are undergraduates (408 freshmen). 59 percent are women and 41 percent are men. Students come from 7 states and territories and 7 other countries. 95 percent are from Ohio. 0.3 percent are international students.

University of Rio Grande (continued)

Expenses for 2006–07 *Application fee:* $25. *Area resident tuition:* $2880 full-time, $96 per credit hour part-time. *State resident tuition:* $13,290 full-time, $560 per hour part-time. *Nonresident tuition:* $14,670 full-time, $605 per hour part-time. Both full-time and part-time tuition varies according to course load, degree level, and program. *College room and board:* $6788. Room and board charges vary according to board plan, housing facility, and student level.

Financial Aid Forms of aid include need-based and non-need-based scholarships, athletic grants, and part-time jobs. The application deadline for financial aid is continuous.

Freshman Admission University of Rio Grande requires a high school transcript, medical history, and TOEFL scores for international students. ACT scores are recommended. The application deadline for regular admission is rolling.

Transfer Admission The application deadline for admission is rolling.

Entrance Difficulty University of Rio Grande has an open admission policy except for nursing, red tech, education, social work.

For Further Information Contact Tammy McCain, Admissions, University of Rio Grande, PO Box 500, Rio Grande, OH 45674. *Telephone:* 740-245-7208 or 800-282-7201 (toll-free in-state). *Fax:* 740-245-7260. *E-mail:* admissions@rio.edu. *Web site:* http://www.rio.edu/.

THE UNIVERSITY OF TOLEDO
Toledo, Ohio

The University of Toledo is a coed, public university, founded in 1872, offering degrees at the associate, bachelor's, master's, doctoral, and first professional levels and post-master's and postbachelor's certificates. It has a 407-acre campus in Toledo near Detroit.

Academic Information The faculty has 1,145 members (65% full-time). The undergraduate student-faculty ratio is 19:1. The library holds 2 million titles and 6,500 serial subscriptions. Special programs include academic remediation, services for learning-disabled students, an honors program, cooperative (work-study) education, study abroad, advanced placement credit, ESL programs, double majors, independent study, distance learning, self-designed majors, summer session for credit, part-time degree programs (daytime, evenings, weekends, summer), adult/continuing education programs, internships, and arrangement for off-campus study with Bowling Green State University, Medical College of Ohio, Consortium for Health Education, The Central States Universities, Inc.

Student Body Statistics The student body totals 19,374, of whom 16,067 are undergraduates (3,432 freshmen). 49 percent are women and 51 percent are men. Students come from 43 states and territories and 88 other countries. 90 percent are from Ohio. 1.6 percent are international students.

Expenses for 2006–07 *Application fee:* $40. *State resident tuition:* $6816 full-time, $284 per semester hour part-time. *Nonresident tuition:* $15,627 full-time, $651 per semester hour part-time. *Mandatory fees:* $1111 full-time, $46.30 per semester hour part-time. Both full-time and part-time tuition and fees vary according to course load, program, and reciprocity agreements. *College room and board:* $7894. *College room only:* $5044. Room and board charges vary according to board plan, housing facility, and location.

Financial Aid Forms of aid include need-based and non-need-based scholarships, athletic grants, and part-time jobs. The average aided 2005–06 undergraduate received an aid package worth $6979. The priority application deadline for financial aid is April 1.

Freshman Admission The University of Toledo requires a high school transcript and SAT or ACT scores. TOEFL scores for international students are recommended. A minimum 2.0 high school GPA and CORE high school curriculum are required for some. The application deadline for regular admission is rolling.

Transfer Admission The application deadline for admission is rolling.

Entrance Difficulty The University of Toledo has an open admission policy for state residents. It assesses its entrance difficulty as moderately difficult for out-of-state applicants; moderately difficult for transfers; very difficult for physical therapy, engineering, pharmacy, legal assisting technology, pre-medicine, pre-dentistry programs.

For Further Information Contact William Pierce, Director, The University of Toledo, 2801 West Bancroft, Toledo, OH 43606-3398. *Telephone:* 419-530-5705 or 800-5TOLEDO (toll-free in-state). *Fax:* 419-530-5713. *E-mail:* william.pierce@utoledo.edu. *Web site:* http://www.utoledo.edu/.

URBANA UNIVERSITY
Urbana, Ohio

Urbana University is a coed, private, comprehensive institution, founded in 1850, affiliated with the Church of the New Jerusalem, offering degrees at the associate, bachelor's, and master's levels. It has a 128-acre campus in Urbana near Columbus and Dayton.

Expenses for 2006–07 *Application fee:* $25. *Comprehensive fee:* $22,866 includes full-time tuition ($16,254) and college room and board ($6612). *College room only:* $2234. *Part-time tuition:* $337 per semester hour.

For Further Information Contact Ms. Paula Brown, Director of Admissions, Urbana University, 579 College Way, Urbana, OH 43078. *Telephone:* 937-484-1356 or 800-7-URBANA (toll-free). *Fax:* 937-652-6871. *E-mail:* admiss@urbana.edu. *Web site:* http://www.urbana.edu/.

URSULINE COLLEGE
Pepper Pike, Ohio

Ursuline College is an undergraduate: women only; graduate: coed, private, Roman Catholic, comprehensive institution, founded in 1871, offering degrees at the bachelor's and master's levels and post-master's certificates (applications from men are also accepted). It has a 112-acre campus in Pepper Pike near Cleveland.

Academic Information The faculty has 213 members (34% full-time), 41% with terminal degrees. The undergraduate student-faculty ratio is 10:1. The library holds 129,621 titles, 14,198 serial subscriptions, and 8,719 audiovisual materials. Special programs include academic remediation, services for learning-disabled students, cooperative (work-study) education, advanced placement credit, accelerated degree programs, double majors, independent study, distance learning, summer session for credit, part-time degree programs (daytime, evenings, weekends, summer), adult/continuing education programs, internships, and arrangement for off-campus study with Baldwin-Wallace College, Case Western Reserve University, Cleveland State University, Cuyahoga Community College, David N. Myers College, Notre Dame College of Ohio, John Carroll University. The most frequently chosen baccalaureate fields are business/marketing, education, health professions and related sciences.

Student Body Statistics The student body totals 1,639, of whom 1,180 are undergraduates (125 freshmen). 93 percent are women and 7 percent are men. Students come from 7 states and territories and 9 other countries. 95 percent are from Ohio. 0.7 percent are international students.

Expenses for 2006–07 *Application fee:* $25. *Comprehensive fee:* $26,774 includes full-time tuition ($19,860), mandatory fees ($230), and college room and board ($6684). *College room only:* $3414. Room and board charges vary according to board plan and housing facility. *Part-time tuition:* $662 per credit hour. *Part-time mandatory fees:* $190 per term.

Financial Aid Forms of aid include need-based and non-need-based scholarships, athletic grants, and part-time jobs.

Freshman Admission Ursuline College requires an essay, a high school transcript, SAT or ACT scores, and TOEFL scores for international students. A minimum 2.0 high school GPA, recommendations, and an interview are recommended. The application deadline for regular admission is rolling and for early action it is November 15.

Transfer Admission The application deadline for admission is rolling.

Entrance Difficulty Ursuline College assesses its entrance difficulty level as minimally difficult. For the fall 2006 freshman class, 92 percent of the applicants were accepted.

For Further Information Contact Director of Admissions, Ursuline College, 2550 Lander Road, Pepper Pike, OH 44124. *Telephone:* 440-449-4203 or 888-URSULINE (toll-free). *Fax:* 440-684-6138. *E-mail:* admission@ursuline.edu. *Web site:* http://www.ursuline.edu/.

WALSH UNIVERSITY
North Canton, Ohio

Walsh University is a coed, private, Roman Catholic, comprehensive institution, founded in 1958, offering degrees at the associate, bachelor's, and master's levels. It has a 134-acre campus in North Canton near Cleveland.

Academic Information The faculty has 217 members (42% full-time), 41% with terminal degrees. The undergraduate student-faculty ratio is 15:1. The library holds 199,543 titles, 5,586 serial subscriptions, and 2,369 audiovisual materials. Special programs include academic remediation, services for learning-disabled students, an honors program, study abroad, advanced placement credit, accelerated degree programs, ESL programs, double majors, independent study, summer session for credit, part-time degree programs (daytime, evenings, weekends, summer), adult/continuing education programs, internships, and arrangement for off-campus study with University of Michigan, Case Western Reserve University, Stark State College of Technology, Cooperative Center for Study Abroad. The most frequently chosen baccalaureate fields are business/marketing, education, health professions and related sciences.

Student Body Statistics The student body totals 2,396, of whom 2,078 are undergraduates (479 freshmen). 64 percent are women and 36 percent are men. Students come from 17 states and territories and 13 other countries. 98 percent are from Ohio. 1.1 percent are international students. 28 percent of the 2006 graduating class went on to graduate and professional schools.

Expenses for 2007–08 *Application fee:* $25. *Comprehensive fee:* $26,330 includes full-time tuition ($18,300), mandatory fees ($600), and college room and board ($7430). *College room only:* $5100. *Part-time tuition:* $600 per credit hour. *Part-time mandatory fees:* $20 per credit hour.

Financial Aid Forms of aid include need-based and non-need-based scholarships, athletic grants, and part-time jobs. The average aided 2006–07 undergraduate received an aid package worth an estimated $11,262. The application deadline for financial aid is continuous.

Freshman Admission Walsh University requires a high school transcript, a minimum 2.3 high school GPA, SAT or ACT scores, and TOEFL scores for international students. An interview is recommended. An essay, a minimum 3.0 high school GPA, and 2 recommendations are required for some. The application deadline for regular admission is rolling and for nonresidents it is rolling.

Transfer Admission The application deadline for admission is rolling.

Entrance Difficulty Walsh University assesses its entrance difficulty level as moderately difficult. For the fall 2006 freshman class, 80 percent of the applicants were accepted.

For Further Information Contact Mr. Brett D. Freshour, Vice President of Enrollment Management, Walsh University, 2020 East Maple, North Canton, OH 44720. *Telephone:* 330-490-7171, 800-362-9846 (toll-free in-state), or 800-362-8846 (toll-free out-of-state). *Fax:* 330-490-7165. *E-mail:* admissions@walsh.edu. *Web site:* http://www.walsh.edu/.

WILBERFORCE UNIVERSITY
Wilberforce, Ohio

http://www.wilberforce.edu/

WILMINGTON COLLEGE
Wilmington, Ohio

Wilmington College is a coed, private, Friends, comprehensive institution, founded in 1870, offering degrees at the bachelor's and master's levels. It has a 1,465-acre campus in Wilmington near Cincinnati and Columbus.

Academic Information The faculty has 122 members (59% full-time), 41% with terminal degrees. The undergraduate student-faculty ratio is 14:1. The library holds 103,706 titles, 408 serial subscriptions, and 1,280 audiovisual materials. Special programs include academic remediation, services for learning-disabled students, an honors program, study abroad, advanced placement credit, accelerated degree programs, double majors, self-designed majors, summer session for credit, part-time degree programs (daytime, evenings, summer), adult/continuing education programs, internships, and arrangement for off-campus study with members of the Southwestern Ohio Council for Higher Education, Greater Cincinnati Consortium of Colleges and Universities. The most frequently chosen baccalaureate fields are business/marketing, education, social sciences.

Student Body Statistics The student body totals 1,704, of whom 1,666 are undergraduates (360 freshmen). 55 percent are women and 45 percent are men. Students come from 15 states and territories and 6 other countries. 95 percent are from Ohio. 0.8 percent are international students.

Expenses for 2006–07 *Comprehensive fee:* $28,062 includes full-time tuition ($20,166), mandatory fees ($490), and college room and board ($7406). *College room only:* $3496. Room and board charges vary according to board plan and housing facility. *Part-time tuition:* $825 per credit. Part-time tuition varies according to course load.

Financial Aid Forms of aid include need-based and non-need-based scholarships and part-time jobs.

Freshman Admission Wilmington College requires a high school transcript, SAT or ACT scores, and TOEFL scores for international students. A minimum 2.5 high school GPA, 1 recommendation, and an interview are recommended. The application deadline for regular admission is rolling.

Transfer Admission The application deadline for admission is rolling.

Entrance Difficulty Wilmington College assesses its entrance difficulty level as moderately difficult. For the fall 2006 freshman class, 98 percent of the applicants were accepted.

For Further Information Contact Ms. Tina Garland, Director of Admission and Financial Aid, Wilmington College, Pyle Center Box 1325, 251 Ludovic Street, Wilmington, OH 45177. *Telephone:* 937-382-6661 Ext. 426 or 800-341-9318 (toll-free). *Fax:* 937-383-8542. *E-mail:* admissions@wilmington.edu. *Web site:* http://www.wilmington.edu/.

WITTENBERG UNIVERSITY
Springfield, Ohio

Wittenberg University is a coed, private, comprehensive institution, founded in 1845, affiliated with the Evangelical Lutheran Church, offering degrees at the bachelor's and master's levels. It has a 71-acre campus in Springfield near Columbus and Dayton.

Academic Information The faculty has 195 members (73% full-time), 73% with terminal degrees. The undergraduate student-faculty ratio is 12:1. The library holds 407,502 titles and 958 serial subscriptions. Special programs include academic remediation, an honors program, cooperative (work-study) education, study abroad, advanced placement credit, Freshman Honors College, ESL programs, double majors, independent study, self-designed majors, summer session for credit, part-time degree programs (daytime, evenings, summer), adult/continuing education programs, internships, and arrangement for off-campus study with 21 members of the Southwestern Ohio Council for Higher Education. The most frequently chosen baccalaureate fields are business/marketing, education, social sciences.

Student Body Statistics The student body totals 2,089, of whom 2,059 are undergraduates (574 freshmen). 55 percent are women and 45 percent are men. Students come from 39 states and territories and 23 other countries. 74 percent are from Ohio. 2 percent are international students.

Wittenberg University (continued)

Expenses for 2007–08 *Application fee:* $40. *Comprehensive fee:* $39,270 includes full-time tuition ($31,100), mandatory fees ($300), and college room and board ($7870). *College room only:* $4110.

Financial Aid Forms of aid include need-based and non-need-based scholarships and part-time jobs. The average aided 2005–06 undergraduate received an aid package worth $20,155. The priority application deadline for financial aid is March 15.

Freshman Admission Wittenberg University requires an essay, a high school transcript, an interview, SAT or ACT scores, and TOEFL scores for international students. Recommendations are recommended. The application deadline for for early decision it is November 15 and for early action it is December 1.

Transfer Admission The application deadline for admission is rolling.

Entrance Difficulty Wittenberg University assesses its entrance difficulty level as moderately difficult; very difficult for International United Nations Scholars Program, Institute of International Education Program. For the fall 2006 freshman class, 82 percent of the applicants were accepted.

For Further Information Contact Mr. Brad Pochard, Director of Admission, Wittenberg University, PO Box 720, Springfield, OH 45501-0720. *Telephone:* 877-206-0332 Ext. 6377 or 800-677-7558 Ext. 6314 (toll-free). *Fax:* 937-327-6379. *E-mail:* admission@wittenberg.edu. *Web site:* http://www.wittenberg.edu/.

WRIGHT STATE UNIVERSITY
Dayton, Ohio

Wright State University is a coed, public university, founded in 1964, offering degrees at the associate, bachelor's, master's, doctoral, and first professional levels and post-master's certificates. It has a 557-acre campus in Dayton near Cincinnati.

Academic Information The faculty has 647 members (95% full-time). The undergraduate student-faculty ratio is 25:1. The library holds 703,000 titles, 443,200 serial subscriptions, and 29,800 audiovisual materials. Special programs include academic remediation, services for learning-disabled students, an honors program, cooperative (work-study) education, study abroad, advanced placement credit, ESL programs, self-designed majors, summer session for credit, part-time degree programs, adult/continuing education programs, internships, and arrangement for off-campus study with members of the Southwestern Ohio Council for Higher Education. The most frequently chosen baccalaureate fields are business/marketing, education, health professions and related sciences.

Student Body Statistics The student body totals 16,207, of whom 12,268 are undergraduates (2,336 freshmen). 56 percent are women and 44 percent are men. Students come from 49 states and territories and 66 other countries. 96 percent are from Ohio. 1.5 percent are international students.

Expenses for 2007–08 *Application fee:* $30. *State resident tuition:* $7278 full-time, $219 per hour part-time. *Nonresident tuition:* $14,004 full-time, $425 per hour part-time. *College room and board:* $7180.

Financial Aid Forms of aid include need-based and non-need-based scholarships and part-time jobs. The priority application deadline for financial aid is February 15.

Freshman Admission Wright State University requires a high school transcript, SAT or ACT scores, and TOEFL scores for international students. A minimum 2.0 high school GPA is recommended. The application deadline for regular admission is rolling.

Transfer Admission The application deadline for admission is rolling.

Entrance Difficulty Wright State University assesses its entrance difficulty level as minimally difficult; moderately difficult for out-of-state applicants. For the fall 2006 freshman class, 87 percent of the applicants were accepted.

For Further Information Contact Ms. Cathy Davis, Director of Undergraduate Admissions, Wright State University, 3640 Colonel Glenn Highway, Dayton, OH 45435. *Telephone:* 937-775-5700 or 800-247-1770 (toll-free). *Fax:* 937-775-5795. *E-mail:* admissions@wright.edu. *Web site:* http://www.wright.edu/.

XAVIER UNIVERSITY
Cincinnati, Ohio

Xavier University is a coed, private, Roman Catholic, comprehensive institution, founded in 1831, offering degrees at the associate, bachelor's, master's, and doctoral levels and post-master's and postbachelor's certificates. It has a 140-acre campus in Cincinnati.

Academic Information The faculty has 601 members (50% full-time), 51% with terminal degrees. The undergraduate student-faculty ratio is 13:1. The library holds 227,200 titles, 21,650 serial subscriptions, and 5,870 audiovisual materials. Special programs include academic remediation, services for learning-disabled students, an honors program, cooperative (work-study) education, study abroad, advanced placement credit, ESL programs, double majors, independent study, summer session for credit, part-time degree programs (daytime, evenings, weekends, summer), adult/continuing education programs, internships, and arrangement for off-campus study with 13 members of the Greater Cincinnati Consortium of Colleges and Universities. The most frequently chosen baccalaureate fields are business/marketing, communications/journalism, liberal arts/general studies.

Student Body Statistics The student body totals 6,666, of whom 3,910 are undergraduates (813 freshmen). 57 percent are women and 43 percent are men. Students come from 46 states and territories and 45 other countries. 60 percent are from Ohio. 1.3 percent are international students. 28 percent of the 2006 graduating class went on to graduate and professional schools.

Expenses for 2006–07 *Application fee:* $35. *Comprehensive fee:* $32,520 includes full-time tuition ($23,270), mandatory fees ($610), and college room and board ($8640). *College room only:* $4710. Full-time tuition and fees vary according to course load, program, and student level. Room and board charges vary according to board plan and housing facility. *Part-time tuition:* $446 per credit hour. Part-time tuition varies according to course load.

Financial Aid Forms of aid include need-based and non-need-based scholarships, athletic grants, and part-time jobs. The average aided 2006–07 undergraduate received an aid package worth an estimated $15,224. The priority application deadline for financial aid is February 15.

Freshman Admission Xavier University requires an essay, a high school transcript, 1 recommendation, SAT or ACT scores, and TOEFL scores for international students. An interview is recommended. The application deadline for regular admission is February 1 and for early action it is December 1.

Transfer Admission The application deadline for admission is rolling.

Entrance Difficulty Xavier University assesses its entrance difficulty level as moderately difficult; very difficult for occupational therapy program; dual enrollment medical program with University of Cincinnati. For the fall 2006 freshman class, 72 percent of the applicants were accepted.

For Further Information Contact Marueen Mathis, Interim Director of Admission, Xavier University, 3800 Victory Parkway, Cincinnati, OH 45207-5311. *Telephone:* 513-745-3301 or 800-344-4698 (toll-free). *Fax:* 513-745-4319. *E-mail:* xuadmit@xavier.edu. *Web site:* http://www.xu.edu/.

YOUNGSTOWN STATE UNIVERSITY
Youngstown, Ohio

Youngstown State University is a coed, public, comprehensive institution, founded in 1908, offering degrees at the associate, bachelor's, master's, and doctoral levels and postbachelor's certificates. It has a 200-acre campus in Youngstown near Cleveland and Pittsburgh.

Academic Information The faculty has 969 members (44% full-time), 49% with terminal degrees. The undergraduate student-faculty ratio is 17:1. The library holds 868,835 titles, 22,277 serial subscriptions, and 21,119 audiovisual materials. Special programs include academic remediation, services for learning-disabled students, an honors program, cooperative (work-study) education, study abroad, advanced placement credit, accelerated degree programs, ESL programs, double majors, distance learning, self-designed majors, summer session for credit, part-time degree programs (daytime, evenings, weekends, summer), adult/

continuing education programs, internships, and arrangement for off-campus study with Lorain County Community College, Cuyahoga Community College, North Central State. The most frequently chosen baccalaureate fields are business/marketing, education, health professions and related sciences.

Student Body Statistics The student body totals 13,178, of whom 11,987 are undergraduates (2,352 freshmen). 55 percent are women and 45 percent are men. Students come from 35 states and territories and 55 other countries. 91 percent are from Ohio. 0.5 percent are international students.

Expenses for 2006–07 *Application fee:* $30. *Area resident tuition:* $269 per credit part-time. *State resident tuition:* $6468 full-time. *Nonresident tuition:* $11,976 full-time, $498.98 per credit part-time. *Mandatory fees:* $229 full-time, $9.54 per credit part-time. Both full-time and part-time tuition and fees vary according to course load. *College room and board:* $6490. Room and board charges vary according to board plan and housing facility.

Financial Aid Forms of aid include need-based and non-need-based scholarships, athletic grants, and part-time jobs. The priority application deadline for financial aid is February 15.

Freshman Admission Youngstown State University requires a high school transcript, SAT or ACT scores, and TOEFL scores for international students. An interview is required for some. The application deadline for regular admission is August 15 and for early action it is February 15.

Transfer Admission The application deadline for admission is August 15.

Entrance Difficulty Youngstown State University has an open admission policy for state residents, students from Mercer and Lawrence Counties in Pennsylvania. It assesses its entrance difficulty as minimally difficult for out-of-state applicants; minimally difficult for transfers; moderately difficult for nursing, engineering, engineering technology, health occupations programs.

For Further Information Contact Ms. Sue Davis, Director of Undergraduate Admissions, Youngstown State University, One University Plaza, Youngstown, OH 44555-0001. *Telephone:* 330-941-2000 or 877-468-6978 (toll-free). *Fax:* 330-941-3674. *E-mail:* enroll@ysu.edu. *Web site:* http://www.ysu.edu/.

Oklahoma

BACONE COLLEGE
Muskogee, Oklahoma
http://www.bacone.edu/

BARTLESVILLE WESLEYAN COLLEGE
See Oklahoma Wesleyan University.

CAMERON UNIVERSITY
Lawton, Oklahoma

Cameron University is a coed, public, comprehensive unit of Oklahoma State Regents for Higher Education, founded in 1908, offering degrees at the bachelor's and master's levels. It has a 160-acre campus in Lawton.

Academic Information The faculty has 313 members (50% full-time), 42% with terminal degrees. The undergraduate student-faculty ratio is 20:1. The library holds 262,835 titles, 4,272 serial subscriptions, and 2,868 audiovisual materials. Special programs include academic remediation, services for learning-disabled students, an honors program, advanced placement credit, accelerated degree programs, ESL programs, double majors, independent study, distance learning, summer session for credit, part-time degree programs (daytime, evenings, weekends, summer), adult/continuing education programs, internships, and arrangement for off-campus study with University of Oklahoma, East Central University,

Oklahoma State University. The most frequently chosen baccalaureate fields are business/marketing, computer and information sciences, education.

Student Body Statistics The student body totals 5,734, of whom 5,327 are undergraduates (924 freshmen). 62 percent are women and 38 percent are men. Students come from 51 states and territories and 44 other countries. 85 percent are from Oklahoma. 2.2 percent are international students.

Expenses for 2006–07 *Application fee:* $15. *State resident tuition:* $2352 full-time, $78.40 per semester hour part-time. *Nonresident tuition:* $7218 full-time, $240.60 per semester hour part-time. *Mandatory fees:* $1080 full-time, $36 per semester hour part-time. Both full-time and part-time tuition and fees vary according to course load. *College room and board:* $3282. Room and board charges vary according to board plan.

Financial Aid Forms of aid include need-based and non-need-based scholarships, athletic grants, and part-time jobs. The application deadline for financial aid is continuous.

Freshman Admission Cameron University requires a high school transcript, a minimum 2.7 high school GPA, SAT or ACT scores, and TOEFL scores for international students. The application deadline for regular admission is rolling.

Transfer Admission The application deadline for admission is rolling.

Entrance Difficulty Cameron University has an open admission policy.

For Further Information Contact Ms. Brenda Dally, Assistant Director of Admissions, Cameron University, Admissions, 2800 West Gore Boulevard, Lawton, OK 73505. *Telephone:* 580-581-2837 or 888-454-7600 (toll-free). *Fax:* 580-581-5514. *E-mail:* admiss@cua.cameron.edu. *Web site:* http://www.cameron.edu/.

DeVRY UNIVERSITY
Oklahoma City, Oklahoma

DeVry University is a coed, proprietary, comprehensive institution, offering degrees at the associate, bachelor's, and master's levels and postbachelor's certificates.

Academic Information The faculty has 7 members. The undergraduate student-faculty ratio is 13:1. Special programs include accelerated degree programs and distance learning.

Student Body Statistics The student body totals 57, of whom 39 are undergraduates (14 freshmen). 31 percent are women and 69 percent are men.

Expenses for 2007–08 *Application fee:* $50. *Tuition:* $12,900 full-time, $490 per credit part-time. *Mandatory fees:* $120 full-time.

Freshman Admission The application deadline for regular admission is rolling.

Transfer Admission The application deadline for admission is rolling.

For Further Information Contact Admissions Office, DeVry University, 4013 NW Expressway Street, Suite 100, Oklahoma City, OK 73116. *Telephone:* 405-767-9516. *Web site:* http://www.devry.edu/.

EAST CENTRAL UNIVERSITY
Ada, Oklahoma

East Central University is a coed, public, comprehensive unit of Oklahoma State Regents for Higher Education, founded in 1909, offering degrees at the bachelor's and master's levels. It has a 140-acre campus in Ada near Oklahoma City.

Academic Information The faculty has 246 members (64% full-time), 51% with terminal degrees. The undergraduate student-faculty ratio is 17:1. The library holds 182,126 titles, 25,076 serial subscriptions, and 906 audiovisual materials. Special programs include academic remediation, services for learning-disabled students, an honors program, advanced placement credit, double majors, independent study, distance learning, summer session for credit, part-time degree programs (daytime, evenings, weekends, summer), adult/continuing education programs, internships, and arrangement for off-campus study with Ardmore Higher Education Center. The most frequently chosen baccalaureate fields are business/marketing, education, public administration and social services.

East Central University (continued)

Student Body Statistics The student body totals 4,506, of whom 3,761 are undergraduates (615 freshmen). 58 percent are women and 42 percent are men. Students come from 24 states and territories and 28 other countries. 95 percent are from Oklahoma. 1.9 percent are international students.

Expenses for 2006–07 *Application fee:* $20. *State resident tuition:* $2,422 full-time, $80.75 per semester hour part-time. *Nonresident tuition:* $7,402 full-time, $246.75 per semester hour part-time. *Mandatory fees:* $1074 full-time, $34.50 per semester hour part-time, $36 per term part-time. Both full-time and part-time tuition and fees vary according to course load. *College room and board:* $3190. *College room only:* $1200. Room and board charges vary according to board plan and housing facility.

Financial Aid Forms of aid include need-based and non-need-based scholarships, athletic grants, and part-time jobs. The average aided 2006–07 undergraduate received an aid package worth an estimated $6628. The priority application deadline for financial aid is March 1.

Freshman Admission East Central University requires a high school transcript, SAT or ACT scores, and TOEFL scores for international students. ACT scores are recommended. A minimum 2.7 high school GPA and rank in upper 50% of high school class are required for some.

Entrance Difficulty East Central University assesses its entrance difficulty level as minimally difficult. For the fall 2006 freshman class, 97 percent of the applicants were accepted.

For Further Information Contact Ms. Pam Denny, Freshman Admissions Officer, East Central University, PMBJ8, 1100 East 14th Street, Ada, OK 74820-6999. *Telephone:* 580-310-5233 Ext. 233. *Fax:* 580-310-5432. *E-mail:* pdenny@ecok.edu. *Web site:* http://www.ecok.edu/.

HILLSDALE FREE WILL BAPTIST COLLEGE
Moore, Oklahoma

Hillsdale Free Will Baptist College is a coed, private, Free Will Baptist, comprehensive institution, founded in 1959, offering degrees at the associate, bachelor's, and master's levels. It has a 41-acre campus in Moore near Oklahoma City.

Academic Information The faculty has 42 members (48% full-time), 40% with terminal degrees. The undergraduate student-faculty ratio is 8:1. The library holds 28,000 titles, 200 serial subscriptions, and 541 audiovisual materials. Special programs include academic remediation, advanced placement credit, accelerated degree programs, ESL programs, independent study, summer session for credit, part-time degree programs (daytime, evenings, summer), adult/continuing education programs, and internships.

Student Body Statistics The student body totals 230, of whom 207 are undergraduates (57 freshmen). 43 percent are women and 57 percent are men. Students come from 10 states and territories and 4 other countries. 86 percent are from Oklahoma. 5.3 percent are international students.

Expenses for 2007–08 *Application fee:* $20. *Comprehensive fee:* $12,528 includes full-time tuition ($6900), mandatory fees ($1170), and college room and board ($4458). *Part-time tuition:* $270 per credit hour. *Part-time mandatory fees:* $17 per credit hour, $170 per term.

Financial Aid Forms of aid include need-based and non-need-based scholarships and part-time jobs. The application deadline for financial aid is continuous.

Freshman Admission Hillsdale Free Will Baptist College requires an essay, a high school transcript, Biblical foundation statement, student conduct pledge; medical form required for some, SAT or ACT scores, and TOEFL scores for international students. A minimum 2.0 high school GPA is recommended. An interview is required for some. The application deadline for regular admission is June 1.

Transfer Admission The application deadline for admission is May 1.

Entrance Difficulty Hillsdale Free Will Baptist College assesses its entrance difficulty level as noncompetitive. For the fall 2006 freshman class, 95 percent of the applicants were accepted.

For Further Information Contact Ms. Sue Chaffin, Registrar, Hillsdale Free Will Baptist College, PO Box 7208, Moore, OK 73160. *Telephone:* 405-912-9005. *Fax:* 405-912-9050. *E-mail:* schaffin@hc.edu. *Web site:* http://www.hc.edu/.

ITT TECHNICAL INSTITUTE
Oklahoma City, Oklahoma

ITT Technical Institute is a coed, proprietary, four-year college, founded in 2006, offering degrees at the associate and bachelor's levels.

Expenses for 2006–07 Contact school directly for program costs.

For Further Information Contact Mr. Ron Gross, Director of Recruitment, ITT Technical Institute, 50 Penn Place—Suite 305, Oklahoma City, OK 73118. *Telephone:* 405-810-4100 or 800-518-1612 (toll-free in-state). *Web site:* http://www2.itt-tech.edu/dnm/campus/.

ITT TECHNICAL INSTITUTE
Tulsa, Oklahoma

ITT Technical Institute is a coed, proprietary, primarily two-year college, founded in 2005, offering degrees at the associate and bachelor's levels.

Expenses for 2006–07 *Application fee:* $100. Contact school for program costs.

Freshman Admission ITT Technical Institute requires a high school transcript, an interview, and Wonderlic aptitude test. Recommendations are recommended. The application deadline for regular admission is rolling.

Transfer Admission The application deadline for admission is rolling.

For Further Information Contact Gigi Braecklein, Director of Recruitment, ITT Technical Institute, 4943 South 78th East Avenue, Tulsa, OK 74145. *Telephone:* 918-619-8700. *Fax:* 918-619-8799. *Web site:* http://www.itt-tech.edu/.

LANGSTON UNIVERSITY
Langston, Oklahoma

Langston University is a coed, public, comprehensive unit of Oklahoma State Regents for Higher Education, founded in 1897, offering degrees at the associate, bachelor's, and master's levels. It has a 40-acre campus in Langston near Oklahoma City.

Academic Information The undergraduate student-faculty ratio is 30:1. The library holds 97,565 titles, 1,235 serial subscriptions, and 4,974 audiovisual materials. Special programs include academic remediation, services for learning-disabled students, an honors program, cooperative (work-study) education, advanced placement credit, accelerated degree programs, summer session for credit, part-time degree programs (daytime, evenings, weekends, summer), adult/continuing education programs, and internships.

Student Body Statistics The student body is made up of 2,526 undergraduates. Students come from 37 states and territories and 8 other countries.

Expenses for 2007–08 Contact university directly for tuition costs.

Financial Aid Forms of aid include need-based and non-need-based scholarships, athletic grants, and part-time jobs. The average aided 2006–07 undergraduate received an aid package worth an estimated $7986. The priority application deadline for financial aid is March 15.

Freshman Admission Langston University requires a high school transcript, a minimum 2.70 high school GPA, SAT or ACT scores, and TOEFL scores for international students. Recommendations are required for some. The application deadline for regular admission is rolling.

Transfer Admission The application deadline for admission is rolling.

Entrance Difficulty Langston University has an open admission policy. It assesses its entrance difficulty as moderately difficult for out-of-state applicants; moderately difficult for transfers.

For Further Information Contact Maurice Osborne, Assistant Director of Admission, Langston University, PO Box 667, Langston, OK 73050. *Telephone:* 405-466-2984 or 405-466-3428 (toll-free in-state). *Fax:* 405-466-3391. *Web site:* http://www.lunet.edu/.

MID-AMERICA CHRISTIAN UNIVERSITY
Oklahoma City, Oklahoma
http://www.macu.edu/

NORTHEASTERN STATE UNIVERSITY
Tahlequah, Oklahoma

Northeastern State University is a coed, public, comprehensive unit of Regional University System of Oklahoma, founded in 1846, offering degrees at the bachelor's, master's, and first professional levels. It has a 160-acre campus in Tahlequah near Tulsa.

Academic Information The faculty has 459 members (67% full-time), 54% with terminal degrees. The undergraduate student-faculty ratio is 23:1. The library holds 466,526 titles, 17,570 serial subscriptions, and 7,871 audiovisual materials. Special programs include academic remediation, services for learning-disabled students, an honors program, cooperative (work-study) education, advanced placement credit, double majors, independent study, distance learning, self-designed majors, summer session for credit, part-time degree programs, adult/continuing education programs, and internships.
Student Body Statistics The student body totals 9,540, of whom 8,499 are undergraduates (1,202 freshmen). 61 percent are women and 39 percent are men. Students come from 31 states and territories and 41 other countries. 97 percent are from Oklahoma. 3 percent are international students.
Expenses for 2006–07 *Application fee:* $0. *State resident tuition:* $2700 full-time. *Nonresident tuition:* $7800 full-time. *Mandatory fees:* $789 full-time. Full-time tuition and fees vary according to course level, course load, and location. *College room and board:* $3600. Room and board charges vary according to board plan and housing facility.
Financial Aid Forms of aid include need-based and non-need-based scholarships, athletic grants, and part-time jobs. The average aided 2006–07 undergraduate received an aid package worth an estimated $7570. The priority application deadline for financial aid is April 1.
Freshman Admission Northeastern State University requires a high school transcript, a minimum 2.7 high school GPA, rank in upper 50% of high school class or minimum ACT composite score of 20, ACT scores, and TOEFL scores for international students. The application deadline for regular admission is August 1.
Transfer Admission The application deadline for admission is August 1.
Entrance Difficulty Northeastern State University assesses its entrance difficulty level as moderately difficult; minimally difficult for transfers. For the fall 2006 freshman class, 74 percent of the applicants were accepted.
For Further Information Contact Mr. Jason Jessie, Director of High School and College Relations, Northeastern State University, 600 North Grand Avenue, Tahlequah, OK 74464. *Telephone:* 918-456-5511 Ext. 4675 or 800-722-9614 (toll-free in-state). *Fax:* 918-458-2326. *E-mail:* jessiejb@nsuok.edu. *Web site:* http://www.nsuok.edu/.

NORTHWESTERN OKLAHOMA STATE UNIVERSITY
Alva, Oklahoma

Northwestern Oklahoma State University is a coed, public, comprehensive unit of Oklahoma State Regents for Higher Education, founded in 1897, offering degrees at the bachelor's and master's levels and post-master's and postbachelor's certificates. It has a 70-acre campus in Alva.

Academic Information The faculty has 144 members (50% full-time), 33% with terminal degrees. The undergraduate student-faculty ratio is 17:1. The library holds 344,640 titles, 3,990 serial subscriptions, and 3,609 audiovisual materials. Special programs include academic remediation, services for learning-disabled students, study abroad, advanced placement credit, double majors, independent study, distance learning, summer session for credit, part-time degree programs (daytime, evenings, weekends, summer), adult/continuing education programs, internships, and

arrangement for off-campus study with Northern Oklahoma College, Southwestern Oklahoma State University. The most frequently chosen baccalaureate fields are business/marketing, education, health professions and related sciences.
Student Body Statistics The student body totals 2,024, of whom 1,778 are undergraduates (261 freshmen). 59 percent are women and 41 percent are men. Students come from 31 states and territories and 30 other countries. 79 percent are from Oklahoma. 2.7 percent are international students.
Expenses for 2006–07 *Application fee:* $15. *State resident tuition:* $3450 full-time, $115 per credit hour part-time. *Nonresident tuition:* $8550 full-time, $285 per credit hour part-time. Both full-time and part-time tuition varies according to course load, location, and program. *College room and board:* $3310. *College room only:* $1250. Room and board charges vary according to board plan.
Financial Aid Forms of aid include need-based and non-need-based scholarships, athletic grants, and part-time jobs. The average aided 2005–06 undergraduate received an aid package worth $5512. The priority application deadline for financial aid is March 1.
Freshman Admission Northwestern Oklahoma State University requires a high school transcript, SAT or ACT scores, and TOEFL scores for international students. An essay, a minimum 2.7 high school GPA, and 3 recommendations are required for some. The application deadline for regular admission is rolling.
Transfer Admission The application deadline for admission is rolling.
Entrance Difficulty Northwestern Oklahoma State University assesses its entrance difficulty level as moderately difficult. For the fall 2006 freshman class, 99 percent of the applicants were accepted.
For Further Information Contact Mr. Matt Adair, Director of Recruitment, Northwestern Oklahoma State University, 709 Oklahoma Boulevard, Alva, OK 73717-2799. *Telephone:* 580-327-8545. *Fax:* 580-327-8699. *E-mail:* wmadair@nwosu.edu. *Web site:* http://www.nwosu.edu/.

OKLAHOMA BAPTIST UNIVERSITY
Shawnee, Oklahoma
http://www.okbu.edu/

OKLAHOMA CHRISTIAN UNIVERSITY
Oklahoma City, Oklahoma

Oklahoma Christian University is a coed, private, comprehensive institution, founded in 1950, affiliated with the Church of Christ, offering degrees at the bachelor's and master's levels. It has a 200-acre campus in Oklahoma City.

Academic Information The faculty has 181 members (50% full-time), 53% with terminal degrees. The undergraduate student-faculty ratio is 11:1. The library holds 125,841 titles, 8,139 serial subscriptions, and 6,248 audiovisual materials. Special programs include academic remediation, services for learning-disabled students, an honors program, study abroad, advanced placement credit, accelerated degree programs, ESL programs, double majors, independent study, distance learning, summer session for credit, internships, and arrangement for off-campus study with University of Central Oklahoma. The most frequently chosen baccalaureate fields are business/marketing, education, liberal arts/general studies.
Student Body Statistics The student body totals 2,120, of whom 1,874 are undergraduates. 51 percent are women and 49 percent are men. 41 percent are from Oklahoma.
Expenses for 2007–08 *Application fee:* $25. *Comprehensive fee:* $21,856 includes full-time tuition ($14,020), mandatory fees ($1776), and college room and board ($6060). *Part-time tuition:* $585 per credit hour. *Part-time mandatory fees:* $855 per term.
Financial Aid Forms of aid include need-based and non-need-based scholarships, athletic grants, and part-time jobs. The application deadline for financial aid is August 31 with a priority deadline of March 15.
Freshman Admission Oklahoma Christian University requires a high school transcript, SAT or ACT scores, and TOEFL scores for international students. The application deadline for regular admission is rolling.

Oklahoma

Oklahoma Christian University (continued)

Transfer Admission The application deadline for admission is rolling.
Entrance Difficulty Oklahoma Christian University has an open admission policy.
For Further Information Contact Ms. Risa Forrester, Dean of Admissions and Marketing, Oklahoma Christian University, Box 11000, Oklahoma City, OK 73136-1100. *Telephone:* 405-425-5050 or 800-877-5010 (toll-free in-state). *Fax:* 405-425-5208. *E-mail:* info@oc.edu. *Web site:* http://www.oc.edu/.

OKLAHOMA CITY UNIVERSITY
Oklahoma City, Oklahoma

Oklahoma City University is a coed, private, United Methodist, comprehensive institution, founded in 1904, offering degrees at the bachelor's, master's, and first professional levels. It has a 75-acre campus in Oklahoma City.

Academic Information The faculty has 285 members (58% full-time). The undergraduate student-faculty ratio is 14:1. The library holds 520,953 titles, 14,000 serial subscriptions, and 1,611 audiovisual materials. Special programs include academic remediation, services for learning-disabled students, an honors program, cooperative (work-study) education, study abroad, advanced placement credit, accelerated degree programs, ESL programs, double majors, independent study, self-designed majors, summer session for credit, part-time degree programs (daytime, evenings, summer), external degree programs, adult/continuing education programs, internships, and arrangement for off-campus study with American University. The most frequently chosen baccalaureate fields are liberal arts/general studies, business/marketing, visual and performing arts.
Student Body Statistics The student body totals 3,713, of whom 2,100 are undergraduates (360 freshmen). 63 percent are women and 37 percent are men. Students come from 43 states and territories and 43 other countries. 64 percent are from Oklahoma. 20.3 percent are international students.
Expenses for 2006–07 *Application fee:* $30. *Comprehensive fee:* $25,960 includes full-time tuition ($17,900), mandatory fees ($1500), and college room and board ($6560). *College room only:* $3215. Full-time tuition and fees vary according to program. Room and board charges vary according to board plan and housing facility. *Part-time tuition:* $610 per semester hour. *Part-time mandatory fees:* $120 per term. Part-time tuition and fees vary according to program.
Financial Aid Forms of aid include need-based and non-need-based scholarships, athletic grants, and part-time jobs. The priority application deadline for financial aid is March 1.
Freshman Admission Oklahoma City University requires an essay, a high school transcript, a minimum 3.0 high school GPA, SAT or ACT scores, and TOEFL scores for international students. An interview and audition for music and dance programs are required for some. The application deadline for regular admission is August 20.
Transfer Admission The application deadline for admission is rolling.
Entrance Difficulty Oklahoma City University assesses its entrance difficulty level as moderately difficult. For the fall 2006 freshman class, 81 percent of the applicants were accepted.
For Further Information Contact Linc Morris, Director, Undergraduate Admissions, Oklahoma City University, 2501 North Blackwelder, Oklahoma City, OK 73106. *Telephone:* 405-208-5340 or 800-633-7242 (toll-free). *Fax:* 405-208-5916. *E-mail:* lmorris@okcu.edu. *Web site:* http://www.okcu.edu/.

OKLAHOMA PANHANDLE STATE UNIVERSITY
Goodwell, Oklahoma

Oklahoma Panhandle State University is a coed, public, four-year college of Oklahoma State Regents for Higher Education, founded in 1909, offering degrees at the associate and bachelor's levels. It has a 40-acre campus in Goodwell.

Academic Information The faculty has 92 members (65% full-time), 23% with terminal degrees. The student-faculty ratio is 12:1. Special programs include academic remediation, advanced placement credit, ESL programs, double majors, distance learning, summer session for credit, and internships. The most frequently chosen baccalaureate fields are agriculture, biological/life sciences, education.
Student Body Statistics The student body is made up of 1,136 undergraduates (255 freshmen). 53 percent are women and 47 percent are men. Students come from 36 states and territories and 12 other countries. 60 percent are from Oklahoma. 2 percent are international students.
Expenses for 2006–07 *Application fee:* $0. *State resident tuition:* $2274 full-time, $75.80 per hour part-time. *Nonresident tuition:* $2274 full-time, $75.80 per hour part-time. *Mandatory fees:* $1247 full-time, $34.50 per hour part-time, $61 per term part-time. Full-time tuition and fees vary according to course level and program. Part-time tuition and fees vary according to course level. *College room and board:* $3200. *College room only:* $900. Room and board charges vary according to board plan, housing facility, and student level.
Financial Aid Forms of aid include need-based and non-need-based scholarships and part-time jobs.
Freshman Admission Oklahoma Panhandle State University requires TOEFL scores for international students. A high school transcript and SAT or ACT scores are required for some. The application deadline for regular admission is rolling and for nonresidents it is rolling.
Transfer Admission The application deadline for admission is rolling.
Entrance Difficulty Oklahoma Panhandle State University has an open admission policy.
For Further Information Contact Mr. Bobby Jenkins, Registrar and Director of Admissions, Oklahoma Panhandle State University, PO Box 430, 323 Eagle Boulevard, Goodwell, OK 73939-0430. *Telephone:* 580-349-1376 or 800-664-6778 (toll-free). *Fax:* 580-349-1371. *E-mail:* opsu@opsu.edu. *Web site:* http://www.opsu.edu/.

OKLAHOMA STATE UNIVERSITY
Stillwater, Oklahoma

Oklahoma State University is a coed, public unit of Oklahoma State University, founded in 1890, offering degrees at the bachelor's, master's, doctoral, and first professional levels and post-master's certificates. It has an 840-acre campus in Stillwater near Oklahoma City and Tulsa.

Academic Information The faculty has 1,245 members (82% full-time), 78% with terminal degrees. The undergraduate student-faculty ratio is 19:1. The library holds 3 million titles, 38,745 serial subscriptions, and 19,510 audiovisual materials. Special programs include academic remediation, services for learning-disabled students, an honors program, study abroad, advanced placement credit, accelerated degree programs, Freshman Honors College, ESL programs, double majors, independent study, distance learning, self-designed majors, summer session for credit, part-time degree programs (daytime, evenings, weekends, summer), adult/continuing education programs, internships, and arrangement for off-campus study with National Student Exchange. The most frequently chosen baccalaureate fields are business/marketing, education, engineering.
Student Body Statistics The student body totals 23,307, of whom 18,737 are undergraduates (3,236 freshmen). 49 percent are women and 51 percent are men. Students come from 50 states and territories and 82 other countries. 84 percent are from Oklahoma. 3.2 percent are international students.
Expenses for 2006–07 *Application fee:* $40. *State resident tuition:* $3,262 full-time, $108.75 per credit hour part-time. *Nonresident tuition:* $11,835 full-time, $394.50 per credit hour part-time. *Mandatory fees:* $1,734 full-time, $57.81 per credit hour part-time. Both full-time and part-time tuition and fees vary according to program and student level. *College room and board:* $6015. *College room only:* $3015. Room and board charges vary according to board plan and housing facility.
Financial Aid Forms of aid include need-based and non-need-based scholarships, athletic grants, and part-time jobs. The average aided 2006–07 undergraduate received an aid package worth an estimated $9296. The application deadline for financial aid is continuous.
Freshman Admission Oklahoma State University requires a high school transcript, a minimum 3.0 high school GPA, class rank, SAT or ACT

scores, and TOEFL scores for international students. An interview is required for some. The application deadline for regular admission is rolling.

Transfer Admission The application deadline for admission is rolling.
Entrance Difficulty Oklahoma State University assesses its entrance difficulty level as moderately difficult. For the fall 2006 freshman class, 87 percent of the applicants were accepted.
For Further Information Contact Karen Lucas, Director of Undergraduate Admissions, Oklahoma State University, 219 Student Union, Stillwater, OK 74078. *Telephone:* 405-744-1234, 800-233-5019 Ext. 1 (toll-free in-state), or 800-852-1255 (toll-free out-of-state). *Fax:* 405-744-7092. *E-mail:* admissions@okstate.edu. *Web site:* http://osu.okstate.edu/.

OKLAHOMA WESLEYAN UNIVERSITY
Bartlesville, Oklahoma

Oklahoma Wesleyan University is a coed, private, comprehensive institution, founded in 1909, affiliated with the Wesleyan Church, offering degrees at the associate, bachelor's, and master's levels. It has a 127-acre campus in Bartlesville near Tulsa.

Academic Information The faculty has 35 members (94% full-time), 43% with terminal degrees. The undergraduate student-faculty ratio is 14:1. The library holds 124,722 titles and 300 serial subscriptions. Special programs include academic remediation, cooperative (work-study) education, study abroad, advanced placement credit, accelerated degree programs, ESL programs, double majors, independent study, distance learning, self-designed majors, summer session for credit, part-time degree programs (daytime, evenings, summer), external degree programs, adult/continuing education programs, internships, and arrangement for off-campus study with Tri-County Technical College, Coalition for Christian Colleges and Universities.
Student Body Statistics The student body totals 1,159, of whom 1,113 are undergraduates (155 freshmen). 64 percent are women and 36 percent are men. Students come from 33 states and territories and 12 other countries. 68 percent are from Oklahoma. 1.5 percent are international students. 10 percent of the 2006 graduating class went on to graduate and professional schools.
Expenses for 2007–08 *Application fee:* $25. *Comprehensive fee:* $21,300 includes full-time tuition ($14,650), mandatory fees ($850), and college room and board ($5800). *College room only:* $3050. *Part-time tuition:* $575 per credit. *Part-time mandatory fees:* $50 per credit.
Financial Aid Forms of aid include need-based and non-need-based scholarships, athletic grants, and part-time jobs. The priority application deadline for financial aid is March 31.
Freshman Admission Oklahoma Wesleyan University requires an essay, a high school transcript, minimum ACT of 18 or SAT 860, and SAT or ACT scores. A minimum 2.0 high school GPA and TOEFL scores for international students are recommended. The application deadline for regular admission is rolling.
Transfer Admission The application deadline for admission is rolling.
Entrance Difficulty Oklahoma Wesleyan University assesses its entrance difficulty level as minimally difficult. For the fall 2006 freshman class, 77 percent of the applicants were accepted.
For Further Information Contact Audrey Kelleher, Associate Vice President for Enrollment Services, Oklahoma Wesleyan University, 2201 Silver Lake Drive, Bartlesville, OK 74006. *Telephone:* 866-222-8226 or 866-222-8226 (toll-free in-state). *Fax:* 918-335-6229. *E-mail:* admissions@okwu.edu. *Web site:* http://www.okwu.edu/.

ORAL ROBERTS UNIVERSITY
Tulsa, Oklahoma

Oral Roberts University is a coed, private, interdenominational, comprehensive institution, founded in 1963, offering degrees at the bachelor's, master's, doctoral, and first professional levels. It has a 263-acre campus in Tulsa.

Academic Information The faculty has 291 members (68% full-time), 50% with terminal degrees. The undergraduate student-faculty ratio is

13:1. The library holds 216,691 titles and 600 serial subscriptions. Special programs include academic remediation, services for learning-disabled students, an honors program, study abroad, advanced placement credit, Freshman Honors College, ESL programs, double majors, independent study, distance learning, self-designed majors, summer session for credit, part-time degree programs, external degree programs, adult/continuing education programs, internships, and arrangement for off-campus study with Christian College Coalition.
Student Body Statistics The student body totals 3,244, of whom 2,758 are undergraduates (553 freshmen). 59 percent are women and 41 percent are men. 38 percent are from Oklahoma. 5.4 percent are international students.
Expenses for 2007–08 *Application fee:* $35. *Comprehensive fee:* $24,750 includes full-time tuition ($17,000), mandatory fees ($400), and college room and board ($7350). *Part-time tuition:* $710 per credit hour.
Financial Aid Forms of aid include need-based and non-need-based scholarships and part-time jobs. The average aided 2006–07 undergraduate received an aid package worth an estimated $18,350. The priority application deadline for financial aid is March 15.
Freshman Admission Oral Roberts University requires an essay, a high school transcript, a minimum 2.0 high school GPA, 1 recommendation, proof of immunization, SAT or ACT scores, and TOEFL scores for international students. An interview is required for some. The application deadline for regular admission is rolling and for early action it is September 1.
Transfer Admission The application deadline for admission is rolling.
Entrance Difficulty Oral Roberts University assesses its entrance difficulty level as moderately difficult; noncompetitive for transfers. For the fall 2006 freshman class, 74 percent of the applicants were accepted.
For Further Information Contact Chris Belcher, Oral Roberts University, 7777 South Lewis Avenue, Tulsa, OK 74171. *Telephone:* 800-678-8876 or 800-678-8876 (toll-free). *Fax:* 918-495-6222. *E-mail:* admissions@oru.edu. *Web site:* http://www.oru.edu/.

ROGERS STATE UNIVERSITY
Claremore, Oklahoma

Rogers State University is a coed, public, four-year college of Oklahoma State Regents for Higher Education, founded in 1909, offering degrees at the associate and bachelor's levels. It has a 40-acre campus in Claremore near Tulsa.

Academic Information The faculty has 204 members (45% full-time), 36% with terminal degrees. The student-faculty ratio is 22:1. The library holds 71,771 titles, 683 serial subscriptions, and 5,415 audiovisual materials. Special programs include academic remediation, services for learning-disabled students, an honors program, cooperative (work-study) education, advanced placement credit, double majors, independent study, distance learning, summer session for credit, part-time degree programs (daytime, evenings, weekends, summer), external degree programs, adult/continuing education programs, internships, and arrangement for off-campus study with Northeast Technology Centers, Claremore and Pryor, OK; Tri-County Technology Center, Bartlesville, OK; University Learning Center of Northern Oklahoma; Central Technology Center, Drumright, OK.
Student Body Statistics The student body is made up of 3,952 undergraduates (788 freshmen). 63 percent are women and 37 percent are men. Students come from 9 states and territories and 5 other countries. 97 percent are from Oklahoma. 0.2 percent are international students.
Expenses for 2007–08 *Application fee:* $0. *State resident tuition:* $2280 full-time, $76 per credit hour part-time. *Nonresident tuition:* $6840 full-time, $228 per credit hour part-time. *Mandatory fees:* $1260 full-time, $41 per credit hour part-time, $15 per term part-time. *College room and board:* $6300. *College room only:* $4140.
Financial Aid Forms of aid include need-based scholarships and part-time jobs. The application deadline for financial aid is continuous.
Freshman Admission Rogers State University requires a high school transcript, SAT or ACT scores, and TOEFL scores for international students. ACT scores are recommended. A minimum 2.7 high school GPA and ACT COMPASS (for students over 21) are required for some. The application deadline for regular admission is rolling and for nonresidents it is rolling.

Rogers State University (continued)

Transfer Admission The application deadline for admission is rolling.

Entrance Difficulty Rogers State University has an open admission policy for applicants to the Associate's degree program or the Certificate program.

For Further Information Contact Ms. Lindsay Fields, Director of Enrollment Management, Rogers State University, 1701 W. Will Rogers Blvd., Claremore, OK 74017. *Telephone:* 918-343-7545 or 800-256-7511 (toll-free). *Fax:* 918-343-7595. *E-mail:* lfields@rsu.edu. *Web site:* http://www.rsu.edu/.

ST. GREGORY'S UNIVERSITY
Shawnee, Oklahoma

St. Gregory's University is a coed, private, Roman Catholic, four-year college, founded in 1875, offering degrees at the associate and bachelor's levels. It has a 640-acre campus in Shawnee near Oklahoma City.

Academic Information The faculty has 46 members (59% full-time), 37% with terminal degrees. The student-faculty ratio is 25:1. The library holds 85,622 titles, 2,060 serial subscriptions, and 1,009 audiovisual materials. Special programs include services for learning-disabled students, an honors program, study abroad, advanced placement credit, accelerated degree programs, ESL programs, double majors, independent study, distance learning, self-designed majors, summer session for credit, part-time degree programs (daytime, evenings, summer), external degree programs, adult/continuing education programs, internships, and arrangement for off-campus study. The most frequently chosen baccalaureate fields are business/marketing, parks and recreation, social sciences.

Student Body Statistics The student body totals 860, of whom 823 are undergraduates (100 freshmen). 56 percent are women and 44 percent are men. Students come from 13 states and territories and 16 other countries. 88 percent are from Oklahoma. 7.2 percent are international students. 20 percent of the 2006 graduating class went on to graduate and professional schools.

Expenses for 2006–07 *Application fee:* $25. *Comprehensive fee:* $19,408 includes full-time tuition ($12,922), mandatory fees ($850), and college room and board ($5636). *College room only:* $3200. Room and board charges vary according to board plan. *Part-time tuition:* $430 per hour. *Part-time mandatory fees:* $35 per hour. Part-time tuition and fees vary according to course load and reciprocity agreements.

Financial Aid Forms of aid include need-based and non-need-based scholarships, athletic grants, and part-time jobs. The average aided 2005–06 undergraduate received an aid package worth $10,686. The application deadline for financial aid is continuous.

Freshman Admission St. Gregory's University requires a high school transcript, a minimum 2.75 high school GPA, SAT or ACT scores, and TOEFL scores for international students. An essay, recommendations, and an interview are required for some. The application deadline for regular admission is rolling.

Transfer Admission The application deadline for admission is rolling.

Entrance Difficulty St. Gregory's University assesses its entrance difficulty level as minimally difficult. For the fall 2006 freshman class, 77 percent of the applicants were accepted.

For Further Information Contact Mr. Bill Halbach, Director of Admissions, St. Gregory's University, 1900 West MacArthur Drive, Shawnee, OK 74804. *Telephone:* 405-878-5447 or 888-STGREGS (toll-free). *Fax:* 405-878-5198. *E-mail:* admissions@stgregorys.edu. *Web site:* http://www.stgregorys.edu/.

SOUTHEASTERN OKLAHOMA STATE UNIVERSITY
Durant, Oklahoma

Southeastern Oklahoma State University is a coed, public, comprehensive unit of Oklahoma State Regents for Higher Education, founded in 1909, offering degrees at the bachelor's and master's levels and post-master's certificates. It has a 177-acre campus in Durant.

Academic Information The faculty has 229 members (62% full-time), 54% with terminal degrees. The undergraduate student-faculty ratio is 19:1. The library holds 277,902 titles, 930 serial subscriptions, and 5,082 audiovisual materials. Special programs include academic remediation, services for learning-disabled students, an honors program, advanced placement credit, accelerated degree programs, double majors, independent study, distance learning, summer session for credit, part-time degree programs (daytime, evenings), adult/continuing education programs, internships, and arrangement for off-campus study with Ardmore Higher Education Center, E.T. Dunlap Higher Education Center, Tinker AFB, OKCCC. The most frequently chosen baccalaureate fields are business/marketing, education, engineering technologies.

Student Body Statistics The student body totals 3,872, of whom 3,533 are undergraduates (616 freshmen). 56 percent are women and 44 percent are men. Students come from 21 states and territories and 27 other countries. 77 percent are from Oklahoma. 1.1 percent are international students. 14 percent of the 2006 graduating class went on to graduate and professional schools.

Expenses for 2006–07 *Application fee:* $20. *State resident tuition:* $2897 full-time. *Nonresident tuition:* $8169 full-time. *Mandatory fees:* $677 full-time. Full-time tuition and fees vary according to course level. *College room and board:* $5348. *College room only:* $2566.

Financial Aid Forms of aid include need-based and non-need-based scholarships, athletic grants, and part-time jobs. The average aided 2005–06 undergraduate received an aid package worth $1368.

Freshman Admission Southeastern Oklahoma State University requires a high school transcript, SAT or ACT scores, and TOEFL scores for international students. An interview is required for some. The application deadline for regular admission is rolling.

Transfer Admission The application deadline for admission is rolling.

Entrance Difficulty Southeastern Oklahoma State University has an open admission policy for adults over 21. It assesses its entrance difficulty as minimally difficult for transfers; very difficult for honors program.

For Further Information Contact Mr. Kyle Stafford, Director of Admissions and Enrollment Services, Southeastern Oklahoma State University, 1405 North 4th Avenue PMB 4225, Durant, OK 74701-0609. *Telephone:* 580-745-2060 or 800-435-1327 (toll-free). *Fax:* 580-745-7502. *E-mail:* admissions@sosu.edu. *Web site:* http://www.sosu.edu/.

SOUTHERN NAZARENE UNIVERSITY
Bethany, Oklahoma

Southern Nazarene University is a coed, private, Nazarene, comprehensive institution, founded in 1899, offering degrees at the associate, bachelor's, and master's levels. It has a 40-acre campus in Bethany near Oklahoma City.

Expenses for 2006–07 *Application fee:* $25. *One-time mandatory fee:* $350. *Comprehensive fee:* $20,402 includes full-time tuition ($14,400), mandatory fees ($624), and college room and board ($5378). *College room only:* $2458. *Part-time tuition:* $507 per credit hour. *Part-time mandatory fees:* $23 per credit hour.

For Further Information Contact Mr. Larry Hess, Director of Admissions, Southern Nazarene University, 6729 Northwest 39th Expressway, Bethany, OK 73008. *Telephone:* 405-491-6324 or 800-648-9899 (toll-free). *Fax:* 405-491-6320. *E-mail:* admiss@snu.edu. *Web site:* http://www.snu.edu/.

SOUTHWESTERN CHRISTIAN UNIVERSITY
Bethany, Oklahoma

http://www.swcu.edu/

SOUTHWESTERN OKLAHOMA STATE UNIVERSITY

Weatherford, Oklahoma

Southwestern Oklahoma State University is a coed, public, comprehensive unit of Southwestern Oklahoma State University, founded in 1901, offering degrees at the bachelor's, master's, and first professional levels. It has a 73-acre campus in Weatherford near Oklahoma City.

Academic Information The faculty has 225 members (94% full-time). The undergraduate student-faculty ratio is 21:1. The library holds 217,051 titles, 1,230 serial subscriptions, and 6,718 audiovisual materials. Special programs include academic remediation, services for learning-disabled students, cooperative (work-study) education, advanced placement credit, accelerated degree programs, double majors, independent study, distance learning, self-designed majors, summer session for credit, part-time degree programs (daytime, evenings, summer), adult/continuing education programs, internships, and arrangement for off-campus study with Academic Common Market.

Student Body Statistics The student body totals 5,164, of whom 4,397 are undergraduates (831 freshmen). 58 percent are women and 42 percent are men. Students come from 32 states and territories and 32 other countries. 88 percent are from Oklahoma. 3.2 percent are international students.

Expenses for 2006–07 *Application fee:* $15. *State resident tuition:* $2700 full-time, $90 per hour part-time. *Nonresident tuition:* $7200 full-time, $240 per hour part-time. *Mandatory fees:* $750 full-time, $25 per hour part-time. Both full-time and part-time tuition and fees vary according to program. *College room and board:* $3330. *College room only:* $1450. Room and board charges vary according to board plan.

Financial Aid Forms of aid include non-need-based scholarships.

Freshman Admission Southwestern Oklahoma State University requires a high school transcript, a minimum 2.0 high school GPA, ACT scores, and TOEFL scores for international students.

Entrance Difficulty Southwestern Oklahoma State University assesses its entrance difficulty level as minimally difficult. For the fall 2006 freshman class, 89 percent of the applicants were accepted.

For Further Information Contact Ms. Connie Phillips, Admission Counselor, Southwestern Oklahoma State University, 100 Campus Drive, Weatherford, OK 73096. *Telephone:* 580-774-3009. *Fax:* 580-774-3795. *E-mail:* ropers@swosu.edu. *Web site:* http://www.swosu.edu/.

SPARTAN COLLEGE OF AERONAUTICS AND TECHNOLOGY

Tulsa, Oklahoma

http://www.spartan.edu/

UNIVERSITY OF CENTRAL OKLAHOMA

Edmond, Oklahoma

University of Central Oklahoma is a coed, public, comprehensive unit of Oklahoma State Regents for Higher Education, founded in 1890, offering degrees at the bachelor's and master's levels. It has a 200-acre campus in Edmond near Oklahoma City.

Academic Information The faculty has 803 members (52% full-time), 42% with terminal degrees. The undergraduate student-faculty ratio is 23:1. The library holds 582,547 titles, 3,130 serial subscriptions, and 28,555 audiovisual materials. Special programs include services for learning-disabled students, an honors program, advanced placement credit, accelerated degree programs, ESL programs, double majors, independent study, distance learning, summer session for credit, part-time degree programs (daytime, evenings, weekends, summer), adult/continuing education programs, and internships. The most frequently chosen baccalaureate fields are business/marketing, education, liberal arts/general studies.

Student Body Statistics The student body totals 15,723, of whom 14,429 are undergraduates (2,193 freshmen). 58 percent are women and 42 percent are men. Students come from 47 states and territories and 76 other countries. 95 percent are from Oklahoma. 7.4 percent are international students.

Expenses for 2006–07 *Application fee:* $25. *State resident tuition:* $3027 full-time, $100.90 per semester hour part-time. *Nonresident tuition:* $8412 full-time, $280.40 per semester hour part-time. *Mandatory fees:* $512 full-time, $17.05 per semester hour part-time. Both full-time and part-time tuition and fees vary according to course load, degree level, program, and student level. *College room and board:* $4763. *College room only:* $2383. Room and board charges vary according to board plan and housing facility.

Financial Aid Forms of aid include need-based and non-need-based scholarships, athletic grants, and part-time jobs. The average aided 2005–06 undergraduate received an aid package worth $6005.

Freshman Admission University of Central Oklahoma requires a high school transcript, a minimum 2.7 high school GPA, rank in upper 50% of high school class, SAT or ACT scores, and TOEFL scores for international students. ACT scores are recommended. The application deadline for regular admission is rolling and for nonresidents it is rolling.

Transfer Admission The application deadline for admission is rolling.

Entrance Difficulty University of Central Oklahoma assesses its entrance difficulty level as minimally difficult. For the fall 2006 freshman class, 94 percent of the applicants were accepted.

For Further Information Contact Ms. Linda Lofton, Director, Admissions and Records Processing, University of Central Oklahoma, Office of Enrollment Services, 100 North University Drive, Box 151, Edmond, OK 73034-5209. *Telephone:* 405-974-2338 Ext. 2338 or 800-254-4215 (toll-free). *Fax:* 405-341-4964. *E-mail:* admituco@ucok.edu. *Web site:* http://www.ucok.edu/.

UNIVERSITY OF OKLAHOMA

Norman, Oklahoma

University of Oklahoma is a coed, public university, founded in 1890, offering degrees at the bachelor's, master's, doctoral, and first professional levels and post-master's certificates. It has a 3,762-acre campus in Norman near Oklahoma City.

Academic Information The faculty has 1,296 members (82% full-time), 77% with terminal degrees. The undergraduate student-faculty ratio is 20:1. The library holds 5 million titles, 58,399 serial subscriptions, and 6,703 audiovisual materials. Special programs include academic remediation, services for learning-disabled students, an honors program, cooperative (work-study) education, study abroad, advanced placement credit, accelerated degree programs, Freshman Honors College, ESL programs, double majors, independent study, distance learning, self-designed majors, summer session for credit, part-time degree programs (daytime, evenings, weekends, summer), external degree programs, adult/continuing education programs, internships, and arrangement for off-campus study with Oklahoma State University, Langston University, Northeastern State University, Rose State College, Oklahoma City Community College, Rogers University, Cameron University. The most frequently chosen baccalaureate fields are business/marketing, communications/journalism, social sciences.

Student Body Statistics The student body totals 26,002, of whom 19,600 are undergraduates (3,342 freshmen). 49 percent are women and 51 percent are men. Students come from 49 states and territories and 80 other countries. 76 percent are from Oklahoma. 1.8 percent are international students.

Expenses for 2006–07 *Application fee:* $40. *State resident tuition:* $3006 full-time, $100.20 per credit hour part-time. *Nonresident tuition:* $11,295 full-time, $376.50 per credit hour part-time. *Mandatory fees:* $2104 full-time, $62.40 per credit hour part-time, $116.50 per term part-time. Both full-time and part-time tuition and fees vary according to course load, location, program, and reciprocity agreements. *College room and board:* $6863. *College room only:* $3753. Room and board charges vary according to board plan and housing facility.

Financial Aid Forms of aid include need-based and non-need-based scholarships, athletic grants, and part-time jobs. The average aided 2005–06 undergraduate received an aid package worth $9316. The application deadline for financial aid is continuous.

Oklahoma

University of Oklahoma (continued)

Freshman Admission University of Oklahoma requires a high school transcript, a minimum 3.0 high school GPA, SAT or ACT scores, and TOEFL scores for international students. An essay is required for some. The application deadline for regular admission is April 1.

Transfer Admission The application deadline for admission is April 1.

Entrance Difficulty University of Oklahoma assesses its entrance difficulty level as moderately difficult; most difficult for honors college program. For the fall 2006 freshman class, 91 percent of the applicants were accepted.

For Further Information Contact Mr. Craig Hayes, Executive Director of Recruitment Services, University of Oklahoma, 550 Parrington Oval, L-1, Norman, OK 73019-3032. *Telephone:* 405-325-2151 or 800-234-6868 (toll-free). *Fax:* 405-325-7478. *E-mail:* ou-pss@ou.edu. *Web site:* http://www.ou.edu/.

UNIVERSITY OF OKLAHOMA HEALTH SCIENCES CENTER

Oklahoma City, Oklahoma

University of Oklahoma Health Sciences Center is a coed, public, upper-level unit of University of Oklahoma, founded in 1890, offering degrees at the bachelor's, master's, doctoral, and first professional levels and post-master's, first professional, and postbachelor's certificates. It has a 200-acre campus in Oklahoma City near Oklahoma City.

Academic Information The faculty has 423 members (68% full-time), 71% with terminal degrees. The undergraduate student-faculty ratio is 9:1. The library holds 300,260 titles and 4,028 serial subscriptions. Special programs include an honors program, advanced placement credit, distance learning, summer session for credit, part-time degree programs (daytime, evenings, summer), and internships. The most frequently chosen baccalaureate fields are biological/life sciences, health professions and related sciences, interdisciplinary studies.

Student Body Statistics The student body totals 3,726, of whom 992 are undergraduates. 87 percent are women and 13 percent are men. Students come from 18 states and territories and 1 other country. 88 percent are from Oklahoma. 0.9 percent are international students.

Expenses for 2006–07 *State resident tuition:* $3006 full-time, $100.20 per credit hour part-time. *Nonresident tuition:* $11,295 full-time, $376.50 per credit hour part-time. *Mandatory fees:* $1422 full-time, $39.15 per credit hour part-time, $123.50 per term part-time. Both full-time and part-time tuition and fees vary according to program.

Financial Aid Forms of aid include non-need-based scholarships.

Transfer Admission The application deadline for admission is rolling.

For Further Information Contact Mr. Heath Burge, Director of Admissions, University of Oklahoma Health Sciences Center, BSE-200, PO Box 26901, 941 S.L. Young Boulevard, Oklahoma City, OK 73190. *Telephone:* 405-271-2359 Ext. 48902. *Fax:* 405-271-2480. *E-mail:* admissions@ouhsc.edu. *Web site:* http://www.ouhsc.edu/.

UNIVERSITY OF PHOENIX–OKLAHOMA CITY CAMPUS

Oklahoma City, Oklahoma

University of Phoenix–Oklahoma City Campus is a coed, proprietary, comprehensive institution, founded in 1976, offering degrees at the bachelor's and master's levels.

Academic Information The faculty has 265 members (4% full-time), 29% with terminal degrees. The undergraduate student-faculty ratio is 7:1. The library holds 1,759 titles and 692 serial subscriptions. Special programs include services for learning-disabled students, advanced placement credit, accelerated degree programs, independent study, distance learning, external degree programs, and adult/continuing education programs. The most frequently chosen baccalaureate fields are business/marketing, computer and information sciences, security and protective services.

Student Body Statistics The student body totals 1,080, of whom 915 are undergraduates (76 freshmen). 63 percent are women and 37 percent are men. 4.9 percent are international students.

Expenses for 2006–07 *Application fee:* $45. *Tuition:* $9750 full-time.

Financial Aid Forms of aid include need-based and non-need-based scholarships. The average aided 2005–06 undergraduate received an aid package worth $4443. The application deadline for financial aid is continuous.

Freshman Admission University of Phoenix–Oklahoma City Campus requires 1 recommendation and TOEFL scores for international students. A high school transcript is required for some. The application deadline for regular admission is rolling.

Transfer Admission The application deadline for admission is rolling.

Entrance Difficulty University of Phoenix–Oklahoma City Campus has an open admission policy.

For Further Information Contact Ms. Beth Barilla, Associate Vice President, Student Admissions and Services, University of Phoenix–Oklahoma City Campus, 4615 East Elwood Street, Mail Stop AA-K101, Phoenix, AZ 85040-1958. *Telephone:* 480-317-6000, 800-776-4867 (toll-free in-state), or 800-228-7240 (toll-free out-of-state). *Fax:* 480-894-1758. *E-mail:* beth.barilla@phoenix.edu. *Web site:* http://www.phoenix.edu/.

UNIVERSITY OF PHOENIX–TULSA CAMPUS

Tulsa, Oklahoma

University of Phoenix–Tulsa Campus is a coed, proprietary, comprehensive institution, founded in 1998, offering degrees at the bachelor's and master's levels.

Academic Information The faculty has 309 members (4% full-time), 35% with terminal degrees. The undergraduate student-faculty ratio is 6:1. The library holds 1,759 titles and 692 serial subscriptions. Special programs include services for learning-disabled students, advanced placement credit, accelerated degree programs, independent study, distance learning, external degree programs, and adult/continuing education programs. The most frequently chosen baccalaureate fields are business/marketing, computer and information sciences, security and protective services.

Student Body Statistics The student body totals 1,169, of whom 1,018 are undergraduates (60 freshmen). 59 percent are women and 41 percent are men. 24.5 percent are international students.

Expenses for 2006–07 *Application fee:* $45. *Tuition:* $9750 full-time.

Financial Aid Forms of aid include need-based and non-need-based scholarships. The average aided 2005–06 undergraduate received an aid package worth $4528. The application deadline for financial aid is continuous.

Freshman Admission University of Phoenix–Tulsa Campus requires 1 recommendation and TOEFL scores for international students. A high school transcript is required for some. The application deadline for regular admission is rolling.

Transfer Admission The application deadline for admission is rolling.

Entrance Difficulty University of Phoenix–Tulsa Campus has an open admission policy.

For Further Information Contact Ms. Beth Barilla, Associate Vice President, Student Admissions and Services, University of Phoenix–Tulsa Campus, 4615 East Elwood Street, Mail Stop AA-K101, Phoenix, AZ 85040-1958. *Telephone:* 480-317-6000, 800-776-4867 (toll-free in-state), or 800-228-7240 (toll-free out-of-state). *Fax:* 480-894-1758. *E-mail:* beth.barilla@phoenix.edu. *Web site:* http://www.phoenix.edu/.

UNIVERSITY OF SCIENCE AND ARTS OF OKLAHOMA

Chickasha, Oklahoma

University of Science and Arts of Oklahoma is a coed, public, four-year college of Oklahoma State Regents for Higher Education, founded in 1908, offering degrees at the bachelor's level. It has a 75-acre campus in Chickasha near Oklahoma City.

Academic Information The faculty has 89 members (60% full-time), 65% with terminal degrees. The student-faculty ratio is 18:1. The library holds 72,304 titles, 10,277 serial subscriptions, and 4,816 audiovisual materials. Special programs include academic remediation, services for learning-disabled students, advanced placement credit, accelerated degree programs, double majors, independent study, self-designed majors, summer session for credit, part-time degree programs (daytime, evenings, summer), adult/continuing education programs, internships, and arrangement for off-campus study. The most frequently chosen baccalaureate fields are business/marketing, education, visual and performing arts.

Student Body Statistics The student body is made up of 1,492 undergraduates (246 freshmen). 65 percent are women and 35 percent are men. Students come from 24 states and territories and 13 other countries. 91 percent are from Oklahoma. 2.6 percent are international students. 35 percent of the 2006 graduating class went on to graduate and professional schools.

Expenses for 2006–07 *Application fee:* $15. *State resident tuition:* $2640 full-time, $88 per hour part-time. *Nonresident tuition:* $7740 full-time, $258 per hour part-time. *Mandatory fees:* $1080 full-time, $36 per hour part-time. *College room and board:* $4360. *College room only:* $2290. Room and board charges vary according to board plan and housing facility.

Financial Aid Forms of aid include need-based and non-need-based scholarships, athletic grants, and part-time jobs. The average aided 2006–07 undergraduate received an aid package worth an estimated $7300.

Freshman Admission University of Science and Arts of Oklahoma requires SAT or ACT scores and TOEFL scores for international students. Graduated in top half of high school class is recommended. A high school transcript, a minimum 3.0 high school GPA, and graduated in top half of high school class are required for some. The application deadline for regular admission is August 31.

Transfer Admission The application deadline for admission is August 31.

Entrance Difficulty University of Science and Arts of Oklahoma assesses its entrance difficulty level as moderately difficult. For the fall 2006 freshman class, 65 percent of the applicants were accepted.

For Further Information Contact Office of Admissions, University of Science and Arts of Oklahoma, 1727 West Alabama, Office of Admissions, Chickasha, OK 73018-5322. *Telephone:* 405-574-1357 or 800-933-8726 Ext. 1212 (toll-free). *Fax:* 405-574-1220. *E-mail:* usao-admissions@usao.edu. *Web site:* http://www.usao.edu/.

UNIVERSITY OF TULSA

Tulsa, Oklahoma

University of Tulsa is a coed, private university, founded in 1894, affiliated with the Presbyterian Church (U.S.A.), offering degrees at the bachelor's, master's, doctoral, and first professional levels and first professional and postbachelor's certificates. It has a 2,090-acre campus in Tulsa near Tulsa.

Academic Information The faculty has 376 members (82% full-time), 96% with terminal degrees. The undergraduate student-faculty ratio is 11:1. The library holds 1 million titles, 26,228 serial subscriptions, and 18,905 audiovisual materials. Special programs include services for learning-disabled students, an honors program, study abroad, advanced placement credit, accelerated degree programs, ESL programs, double majors, independent study, self-designed majors, summer session for credit, part-time degree programs (daytime, evenings, summer), adult/continuing education programs, and internships. The most frequently chosen baccalaureate fields are business/marketing, engineering, visual and performing arts.

Student Body Statistics The student body totals 4,125, of whom 2,882 are undergraduates (660 freshmen). 50 percent are women and 50 percent are men. Students come from 42 states and territories and 48 other countries. 64 percent are from Oklahoma. 8.9 percent are international students. 38 percent of the 2006 graduating class went on to graduate and professional schools.

Expenses for 2007–08 *Application fee:* $35. *Comprehensive fee:* $29,174 includes full-time tuition ($21,690), mandatory fees ($80), and college room and board ($7404). *College room only:* $4090. *Part-time tuition:* $778 per credit hour. *Part-time mandatory fees:* $3 per credit hour.

Financial Aid Forms of aid include need-based and non-need-based scholarships, athletic grants, and part-time jobs. The average aided 2005–06 undergraduate received an aid package worth $22,586.

Freshman Admission University of Tulsa requires an essay, a high school transcript, 1 recommendation, an interview, SAT or ACT scores, and TOEFL scores for international students. An essay and a minimum 3.0 high school GPA are recommended. The application deadline for regular admission is rolling.

Transfer Admission The application deadline for admission is rolling.

Entrance Difficulty University of Tulsa assesses its entrance difficulty level as very difficult; moderately difficult for transfers. For the fall 2006 freshman class, 76 percent of the applicants were accepted.

For Further Information Contact Mr. John Corso and Mr. Earl Johnson, Associate Vice President for Enrollment and Student Services/Dean of Admission, University of Tulsa, 600 South College Avenue, Tulsa, OK 74104. *Telephone:* 918-631-2307 or 800-331-3050 (toll-free). *Fax:* 918-631-5003. *E-mail:* admission@utulsa.edu. *Web site:* http://www.utulsa.edu/.

South Dakota

AUGUSTANA COLLEGE

Sioux Falls, South Dakota

Augustana College is a coed, private, comprehensive institution, founded in 1860, affiliated with the Evangelical Lutheran Church in America, offering degrees at the bachelor's and master's levels. It has a 100-acre campus in Sioux Falls.

Academic Information The faculty has 186 members (60% full-time), 53% with terminal degrees. The undergraduate student-faculty ratio is 13:1. The library holds 279,918 titles and 595 serial subscriptions. Special programs include academic remediation, services for learning-disabled students, an honors program, cooperative (work-study) education, study abroad, advanced placement credit, accelerated degree programs, Freshman Honors College, double majors, independent study, self-designed majors, summer session for credit, part-time degree programs (daytime, evenings, summer), internships, and arrangement for off-campus study with 10 other colleges in the upper Midwest. The most frequently chosen baccalaureate fields are education, business/marketing, history.

Student Body Statistics The student body totals 1,768, of whom 1,747 are undergraduates (442 freshmen). 63 percent are women and 37 percent are men. Students come from 29 states and territories and 7 other countries. 46 percent are from South Dakota. 1.7 percent are international students. 28 percent of the 2006 graduating class went on to graduate and professional schools.

Expenses for 2006–07 *Application fee:* $0. *Comprehensive fee:* $25,650 includes full-time tuition ($19,750), mandatory fees ($236), and college room and board ($5664). *College room only:* $2700. Room and board charges vary according to board plan and housing facility. *Part-time tuition:* $290 per credit. Part-time tuition varies according to course load.

Financial Aid Forms of aid include need-based and non-need-based scholarships, athletic grants, and part-time jobs. The average aided 2006–07 undergraduate received an aid package worth an estimated $15,938. The priority application deadline for financial aid is March 1.

Freshman Admission Augustana College requires a high school transcript, a minimum 2.5 high school GPA, 1 recommendation, minimum ACT score of 20, SAT or ACT scores, and TOEFL scores for international students. An interview is recommended. An essay is required for some. The application deadline for regular admission is August 1.

Transfer Admission The application deadline for admission is rolling.

Entrance Difficulty Augustana College assesses its entrance difficulty level as moderately difficult; minimally difficult for transfers. For the fall 2006 freshman class, 83 percent of the applicants were accepted.

For Further Information Contact Ms. Nancy Davidson, Dean of Admission, Augustana College, 2001 S. Summit Avenue, Sioux Falls, SD 57197. *Telephone:* 605-274-5516, 800-727-2844 Ext. 5516 (toll-free in-state), or 800-727-2844 (toll-free out-of-state). *Fax:* 605-274-5518. *E-mail:* admission@augie.edu. *Web site:* http://www.augie.edu/.

BLACK HILLS STATE UNIVERSITY
Spearfish, South Dakota

Black Hills State University is a coed, public, comprehensive unit of South Dakota State University System, founded in 1883, offering degrees at the associate, bachelor's, and master's levels and post-master's and postbachelor's certificates. It has a 123-acre campus in Spearfish.

Academic Information The faculty has 190 members (62% full-time), 57% with terminal degrees. The undergraduate student-faculty ratio is 21:1. The library holds 310,210 titles and 485 serial subscriptions. Special programs include academic remediation, services for learning-disabled students, an honors program, cooperative (work-study) education, advanced placement credit, accelerated degree programs, double majors, independent study, distance learning, summer session for credit, part-time degree programs (daytime, evenings, summer), internships, and arrangement for off-campus study with South Dakota State University.
Student Body Statistics The student body totals 3,896, of whom 3,733 are undergraduates (658 freshmen). 64 percent are women and 36 percent are men. Students come from 44 states and territories and 7 other countries. 79 percent are from South Dakota. 0.5 percent are international students.
Expenses for 2006–07 *Application fee:* $20. *State resident tuition:* $2541 full-time, $79.40 per credit part-time. *Nonresident tuition:* $8074 full-time, $252.30 per credit part-time. *Mandatory fees:* $2794 full-time, $87.30 per credit part-time. Both full-time and part-time tuition and fees vary according to course load and reciprocity agreements. *College room and board:* $3988. *College room only:* $2202. Room and board charges vary according to board plan and housing facility.
Financial Aid Forms of aid include need-based and non-need-based scholarships, athletic grants, and part-time jobs. The average aided 2005–06 undergraduate received an aid package worth $4337. The priority application deadline for financial aid is March 1.
Freshman Admission Black Hills State University requires a high school transcript, minimum 2.0 high school GPA in core curriculum, SAT or ACT scores, and TOEFL scores for international students. The application deadline for regular admission is July 18.
Transfer Admission The application deadline for admission is July 18.
Entrance Difficulty Black Hills State University assesses its entrance difficulty level as minimally difficult. For the fall 2006 freshman class, 93 percent of the applicants were accepted.
For Further Information Contact Lisa Jenner, Black Hills State University, 1200 University ST USB 9502, Spearfish, SD 57799-9502. *Telephone:* 605-642-6343 or 800-255-2478 (toll-free). *Fax:* 605-642-6254. *E-mail:* admissions@bhsu.edu. *Web site:* http://www.bhsu.edu/.

COLORADO TECHNICAL UNIVERSITY SIOUX FALLS CAMPUS
Sioux Falls, South Dakota

http://www.ctu-siouxfalls.com/

DAKOTA STATE UNIVERSITY
Madison, South Dakota

Dakota State University is a coed, public, comprehensive unit of South Dakota Board of Regents, founded in 1881, offering degrees at the associate, bachelor's, and master's levels. It has a 40-acre campus in Madison near Sioux Falls.

Academic Information The faculty has 105 members (76% full-time), 54% with terminal degrees. The undergraduate student-faculty ratio is 18:1. The library holds 95,819 titles and 350 serial subscriptions. Special programs include academic remediation, services for learning-disabled students, an honors program, cooperative (work-study) education, advanced placement credit, ESL programs, double majors, independent study, distance learning, summer session for credit, part-time degree programs (daytime, evenings, summer), adult/continuing education programs,

internships, and arrangement for off-campus study with South Dakota State University, University of Sioux Falls, University of South Dakota. The most frequently chosen baccalaureate fields are business/marketing, computer and information sciences, education.
Student Body Statistics The student body totals 2,392, of whom 2,144 are undergraduates (317 freshmen). 54 percent are women and 46 percent are men. Students come from 23 states and territories and 4 other countries. 78 percent are from South Dakota. 0.9 percent are international students.
Expenses for 2006–07 *Application fee:* $20. *State resident tuition:* $2382 full-time, $79 per credit hour part-time. *Nonresident tuition:* $3573 full-time, $119 per credit hour part-time. *Mandatory fees:* $3317 full-time, $89 per credit hour part-time. Both full-time and part-time tuition and fees vary according to location and reciprocity agreements. *College room and board:* $3927. *College room only:* $1924. Room and board charges vary according to board plan and housing facility.
Financial Aid Forms of aid include need-based and non-need-based scholarships, athletic grants, and part-time jobs. The average aided 2005–06 undergraduate received an aid package worth $6360. The priority application deadline for financial aid is March 1.
Freshman Admission Dakota State University requires a high school transcript, a minimum 2.7 high school GPA, rank in upper two-thirds of high school class, and SAT or ACT scores. TOEFL scores for international students are recommended. The application deadline for regular admission is rolling and for nonresidents it is rolling.
Transfer Admission The application deadline for admission is rolling.
Entrance Difficulty Dakota State University assesses its entrance difficulty level as minimally difficult; moderately difficult for out-of-state applicants; moderately difficult for transfers. For the fall 2006 freshman class, 96 percent of the applicants were accepted.
For Further Information Contact Ms. Dana Hoff, Admissions Secretary, Dakota State University, 820 North Washington, Madison, SD 57042-1799. *Telephone:* 605-256-5139 or 888-DSU-9988 (toll-free). *Fax:* 605-256-5020. *E-mail:* yourfuture@dsu.edu. *Web site:* http://www.dsu.edu/.

DAKOTA WESLEYAN UNIVERSITY
Mitchell, South Dakota

Dakota Wesleyan University is a coed, private, United Methodist, comprehensive institution, founded in 1885, offering degrees at the associate, bachelor's, and master's levels. It has a 50-acre campus in Mitchell.

Academic Information The faculty has 80 members (65% full-time), 45% with terminal degrees. The undergraduate student-faculty ratio is 12:1. The library holds 76,997 titles, 742 serial subscriptions, and 3,929 audiovisual materials. Special programs include academic remediation, services for learning-disabled students, an honors program, study abroad, advanced placement credit, double majors, independent study, distance learning, self-designed majors, summer session for credit, part-time degree programs (daytime, evenings, summer), adult/continuing education programs, internships, and arrangement for off-campus study. The most frequently chosen baccalaureate fields are business/marketing, education, law/legal studies.
Student Body Statistics The student body totals 776, of whom 735 are undergraduates (215 freshmen). 57 percent are women and 43 percent are men. Students come from 29 states and territories and 9 other countries. 66 percent are from South Dakota. 0.8 percent are international students.
Expenses for 2007–08 *Application fee:* $25. *Comprehensive fee:* $22,900 includes full-time tuition ($17,500) and college room and board ($5400). *College room only:* $2200. *Part-time tuition:* $367.50 per credit.
Financial Aid Forms of aid include athletic grants and part-time jobs. The average aided 2006–07 undergraduate received an aid package worth an estimated $12,000. The priority application deadline for financial aid is April 15.
Freshman Admission Dakota Wesleyan University requires a high school transcript, SAT or ACT scores, and TOEFL scores for international students. A minimum 2.0 high school GPA is recommended. The application deadline for regular admission is August 27.
Transfer Admission The application deadline for admission is August 27.

Entrance Difficulty Dakota Wesleyan University assesses its entrance difficulty level as moderately difficult. For the fall 2006 freshman class, 75 percent of the applicants were accepted.

For Further Information Contact Mrs. Amy Novak, Vice President for Enrollment Management, Dakota Wesleyan University, 1200 West University Avenue, Mitchell, SD 57301-4398. *Telephone:* 605-995-2600 Ext. 2661 or 800-333-8506 (toll-free). *Fax:* 605-995-2699. *E-mail:* admissions@ dwu.edu. *Web site:* http://www.dwu.edu/.

KILIAN COMMUNITY COLLEGE

Sioux Falls, South Dakota

Kilian Community College is a coed, private, two-year college, founded in 1977, offering degrees at the associate level. It has a 2-acre campus in Sioux Falls.

Academic Information The faculty has 55 members (11% full-time), 5% with terminal degrees. The student-faculty ratio is 10:1. The library holds 78,000 titles and 395 serial subscriptions. Special programs include academic remediation, services for learning-disabled students, an honors program, cooperative (work-study) education, ESL programs, double majors, independent study, summer session for credit, part-time degree programs (daytime, evenings, summer), and internships.

Student Body Statistics The student body is made up of 477 undergraduates (64 freshmen). 74 percent are women and 26 percent are men. Students come from 3 states and territories. 95 percent are from South Dakota.

Expenses for 2006–07 *Application fee:* $25. *Tuition:* $7416 full-time, $206 per credit hour part-time. *Mandatory fees:* $180 full-time, $60 per term part-time.

Financial Aid Forms of aid include need-based scholarships and part-time jobs. The application deadline for financial aid is continuous.

Freshman Admission Kilian Community College requires a high school transcript and TOEFL scores for international students. The application deadline for regular admission is rolling.

Transfer Admission The application deadline for admission is rolling.

Entrance Difficulty Kilian Community College has an open admission policy.

For Further Information Contact Ms. Amy Modrell, Director of Admissions, Kilian Community College, 300 East 6th Street, Sioux Falls, SD 57103. *Telephone:* 605-221-3100 or 800-888-1147 (toll-free). *Fax:* 605-336-2606. *E-mail:* info@killian.edu. *Web site:* http://www.kilian.edu/.

MOUNT MARTY COLLEGE

Yankton, South Dakota

Mount Marty College is a coed, private, Roman Catholic, comprehensive institution, founded in 1936, offering degrees at the associate, bachelor's, and master's levels and postbachelor's certificates. It has an 80-acre campus in Yankton.

Academic Information The faculty has 97 members (92% full-time), 35% with terminal degrees. The undergraduate student-faculty ratio is 11:1. The library holds 76,571 titles and 424 serial subscriptions. Special programs include academic remediation, services for learning-disabled students, an honors program, cooperative (work-study) education, advanced placement credit, accelerated degree programs, double majors, independent study, distance learning, self-designed majors, summer session for credit, part-time degree programs (daytime, evenings), adult/continuing education programs, internships, and arrangement for off-campus study with members of the Colleges of Mid-America. The most frequently chosen baccalaureate fields are education, business/marketing, health professions and related sciences.

Student Body Statistics The student body totals 1,220, of whom 1,083 are undergraduates (152 freshmen). 67 percent are women and 33 percent are men. Students come from 12 states and territories and 3 other countries. 70 percent are from South Dakota. 8 percent of the 2006 graduating class went on to graduate and professional schools.

Expenses for 2006–07 *Application fee:* $35. *Comprehensive fee:* $21,540 includes full-time tuition ($14,752), mandatory fees ($1830), and college

room and board ($4958). Full-time tuition and fees vary according to course load and location. *Part-time tuition:* $239 per credit hour. *Part-time mandatory fees:* $25 per credit hour. Part-time tuition and fees vary according to course load and location.

Financial Aid Forms of aid include need-based and non-need-based scholarships, athletic grants, and part-time jobs. The average aided 2005–06 undergraduate received an aid package worth $13,253. The priority application deadline for financial aid is March 1.

Freshman Admission Mount Marty College requires a high school transcript, a minimum 2.0 high school GPA, SAT or ACT scores, and TOEFL scores for international students. An interview and ACT scores are recommended. Recommendations are required for some. The application deadline for regular admission is rolling.

Transfer Admission The application deadline for admission is rolling.

Entrance Difficulty Mount Marty College assesses its entrance difficulty level as moderately difficult. For the fall 2006 freshman class, 83 percent of the applicants were accepted.

For Further Information Contact Ms. Brandi Tschumper, Vice President for Enrollment Management, Mount Marty College, 1105 West 8th Street, Yankton, SD 57078. *Telephone:* 605-668-1545 or 800-658-4552 (toll-free). *Fax:* 605-668-1607. *E-mail:* mmcadmit@mtmc.edu. *Web site:* http://www. mtmc.edu/.

NATIONAL AMERICAN UNIVERSITY

Rapid City, South Dakota

National American University is a coed, proprietary, comprehensive unit of National College, founded in 1941, offering degrees at the associate, bachelor's, and master's levels. It has an 8-acre campus in Rapid City.

Academic Information The faculty has 47 members (28% full-time), 17% with terminal degrees. The undergraduate student-faculty ratio is 26:1. The library holds 31,018 titles and 268 serial subscriptions. Special programs include academic remediation, services for learning-disabled students, cooperative (work-study) education, advanced placement credit, accelerated degree programs, ESL programs, independent study, distance learning, summer session for credit, part-time degree programs (daytime, evenings, summer), external degree programs, adult/continuing education programs, and internships. The most frequently chosen baccalaureate fields are business/marketing, computer and information sciences, health professions and related sciences.

Student Body Statistics The student body totals 475, of whom 447 are undergraduates (32 freshmen). 64 percent are women and 36 percent are men. Students come from 28 states and territories and 5 other countries. 70 percent are from South Dakota. 5.5 percent are international students.

Expenses for 2006–07 *Application fee:* $25. *Comprehensive fee:* $15,423 includes full-time tuition ($11,520), mandatory fees ($50), and college room and board ($3853). *College room only:* $1938. *Part-time tuition:* $240 per credit hour. *Part-time mandatory fees:* $90 per credit hour.

Financial Aid Forms of aid include need-based and non-need-based scholarships and part-time jobs. The application deadline for financial aid is continuous.

Freshman Admission National American University requires TOEFL scores for international students. An interview and ACT scores are recommended. A high school transcript is required for some. The application deadline for regular admission is rolling and for nonresidents it is rolling.

Transfer Admission The application deadline for admission is rolling.

Entrance Difficulty National American University has an open admission policy.

For Further Information Contact Ms. Angela Beck, Director of Enrollment Management, National American University, 321 Kansas City Street, Rapid City, SD 57701. *Telephone:* 605-394-4902 or 800-843-8892 (toll-free). *Fax:* 605-394-4871. *E-mail:* abeck@national.edu. *Web site:* http://www. rapid.national.edu/.

NATIONAL AMERICAN UNIVERSITY–SIOUX FALLS BRANCH
Sioux Falls, South Dakota
http://www.national.edu/

NORTHERN STATE UNIVERSITY
Aberdeen, South Dakota

Northern State University is a coed, public, comprehensive unit of South Dakota Board of Regents, founded in 1901, offering degrees at the associate, bachelor's, and master's levels and postbachelor's certificates. It has a 52-acre campus in Aberdeen.

Academic Information The faculty has 93 members (100% full-time), 83% with terminal degrees. The undergraduate student-faculty ratio is 20:1. The library holds 192,007 titles and 882 serial subscriptions. Special programs include academic remediation, services for learning-disabled students, an honors program, cooperative (work-study) education, study abroad, advanced placement credit, accelerated degree programs, ESL programs, distance learning, self-designed majors, summer session for credit, part-time degree programs, adult/continuing education programs, internships, and arrangement for off-campus study with National Student Exchange. The most frequently chosen baccalaureate fields are business/marketing, education, social sciences.
Student Body Statistics The student body totals 2,407, of whom 2,183 are undergraduates (376 freshmen). 59 percent are women and 41 percent are men. Students come from 33 states and territories and 13 other countries. 80 percent are from South Dakota. 5.5 percent are international students.
Expenses for 2006–07 *Application fee:* $15. *State resident tuition:* $2382 full-time, $79.40 per credit hour part-time. *Nonresident tuition:* $7589 full-time, $252.30 per credit hour part-time. *Mandatory fees:* $2580 full-time, $86 per credit hour part-time. Both full-time and part-time tuition and fees vary according to course level, course load, and reciprocity agreements. *College room and board:* $4102. *College room only:* $2145. Room and board charges vary according to board plan.
Financial Aid Forms of aid include need-based and non-need-based scholarships, athletic grants, and part-time jobs. The average aided 2006–07 undergraduate received an aid package worth an estimated $7318. The priority application deadline for financial aid is March 1.
Freshman Admission Northern State University requires a high school transcript, a minimum 2.6 high school GPA, SAT or ACT scores, and TOEFL scores for international students. Recommendations are required for some. The application deadline for regular admission is September 1.
Transfer Admission The application deadline for admission is September 1.
Entrance Difficulty Northern State University assesses its entrance difficulty level as minimally difficult; moderately difficult for transfers. For the fall 2006 freshman class, 94 percent of the applicants were accepted.
For Further Information Contact Mr. Allan Vogel, Director of Admissions-Campus, Northern State University, 1200 South Jay Street, Aberdeen, SD 57401. *Telephone:* 605-626-2544 or 800-678-5330 (toll-free). *Fax:* 605-626-2587. *E-mail:* admissions1@northern.edu. *Web site:* http://www.northern.edu/.

OGLALA LAKOTA COLLEGE
Kyle, South Dakota

Oglala Lakota College is a coed, public, comprehensive institution, founded in 1970, offering degrees at the associate level.

Academic Information The library holds 15,000 titles and 150 serial subscriptions. Special programs include academic remediation, cooperative (work-study) education, accelerated degree programs, summer session for credit, part-time degree programs (daytime, evenings, summer), adult/continuing education programs, internships, and arrangement for off-campus study with American Indian Higher Education Consortium.

Student Body Statistics The student body totals 1,000. Students come from 2 states and territories. 10 percent of the 2006 graduating class went on to graduate and professional schools.
Financial Aid Forms of aid include need-based and non-need-based scholarships and part-time jobs. The application deadline for financial aid is continuous.
Entrance Difficulty Oglala Lakota College has an open admission policy.
For Further Information Contact Director of Admissions, Oglala Lakota College, 490 Piya Wiconi Road, Kyle, SD 57752-0490. *Telephone:* 605-455-2321 Ext. 236. *E-mail:* lmeseteth@olc.edu. *Web site:* http://www.olc.edu/.

PRESENTATION COLLEGE
Aberdeen, South Dakota

Presentation College is a coed, private, Roman Catholic, four-year college, founded in 1951, offering degrees at the associate and bachelor's levels. It has a 100-acre campus in Aberdeen.

Academic Information The faculty has 97 members (46% full-time), 22% with terminal degrees. The student-faculty ratio is 9:1. The library holds 40,000 titles and 430 serial subscriptions. Special programs include academic remediation, cooperative (work-study) education, advanced placement credit, accelerated degree programs, double majors, distance learning, summer session for credit, part-time degree programs (daytime, evenings, summer), external degree programs, adult/continuing education programs, and internships. The most frequently chosen baccalaureate fields are health professions and related sciences, business/marketing, public administration and social services.
Student Body Statistics The student body is made up of 786 undergraduates (94 freshmen). 83 percent are women and 17 percent are men. Students come from 17 states and territories and 3 other countries. 63 percent are from South Dakota. 0.9 percent are international students.
Expenses for 2006–07 *Application fee:* $0. *Comprehensive fee:* $17,075 includes full-time tuition ($12,300) and college room and board ($4775). *College room only:* $3975. Full-time tuition varies according to course load, location, and program. Room and board charges vary according to board plan, housing facility, and student level. *Part-time tuition:* $450 per credit. Part-time tuition varies according to course load, location, and program.
Financial Aid Forms of aid include need-based and non-need-based scholarships and part-time jobs. The average aided 2005–06 undergraduate received an aid package worth $7442. The priority application deadline for financial aid is March 1.
Freshman Admission Presentation College requires a high school transcript, SAT or ACT scores, and TOEFL scores for international students. A minimum 2.0 high school GPA is recommended. 2 recommendations are required for some. The application deadline for regular admission is rolling.
Transfer Admission The application deadline for admission is rolling.
Entrance Difficulty Presentation College has an open admission policy except for allied health programs, nursing. It assesses its entrance difficulty as minimally difficult for allied health programs.
For Further Information Contact Ms. Jo Ellen Lindner, Vice President for Enrollment and Student Retention, Presentation College, 1500 North Main Street, Aberdeen, SD 57401. *Telephone:* 605-229-8492 or 800-437-6060 (toll-free). *Fax:* 605-229-8425. *E-mail:* admit@presentation.edu. *Web site:* http://www.presentation.edu/.

SINTE GLESKA UNIVERSITY
Rosebud, South Dakota
http://www.sinte.edu/

SOUTH DAKOTA SCHOOL OF MINES AND TECHNOLOGY
Rapid City, South Dakota

South Dakota School of Mines and Technology is a coed, public unit of South Dakota State University System, founded in 1885, offering degrees at the associate, bachelor's, master's, and doctoral levels. It has a 120-acre campus in Rapid City.

Academic Information The faculty has 137 members (79% full-time), 77% with terminal degrees. The undergraduate student-faculty ratio is 15:1. The library holds 273,243 titles, 13,633 serial subscriptions, and 2,190 audiovisual materials. Special programs include academic remediation, services for learning-disabled students, cooperative (work-study) education, study abroad, advanced placement credit, ESL programs, double majors, independent study, distance learning, summer session for credit, part-time degree programs (daytime, evenings), adult/continuing education programs, and internships. The most frequently chosen baccalaureate fields are engineering, computer and information sciences, interdisciplinary studies.

Student Body Statistics The student body totals 2,124, of whom 1,870 are undergraduates (285 freshmen). 31 percent are women and 69 percent are men. Students come from 34 states and territories and 11 other countries. 66 percent are from South Dakota. 0.9 percent are international students.

Expenses for 2006–07 *Application fee:* $20. *State resident tuition:* $2380 full-time, $79.40 per credit hour part-time. *Nonresident tuition:* $3570 full-time, $119.10 per credit hour part-time. *Mandatory fees:* $2950 full-time, $86.90 per credit hour part-time. Both full-time and part-time tuition and fees vary according to course load, program, and reciprocity agreements. *College room and board:* $4410. *College room only:* $2240. Room and board charges vary according to board plan and housing facility.

Financial Aid Forms of aid include need-based and non-need-based scholarships, athletic grants, and part-time jobs.

Freshman Admission South Dakota School of Mines and Technology requires a high school transcript and TOEFL scores for international students. A minimum 2.75 high school GPA and SAT or ACT scores are recommended. SAT or ACT scores are required for some. The application deadline for regular admission is rolling.

Transfer Admission The application deadline for admission is rolling.

Entrance Difficulty South Dakota School of Mines and Technology assesses its entrance difficulty level as moderately difficult. For the fall 2006 freshman class, 82 percent of the applicants were accepted.

For Further Information Contact Mr. Tex Claymore, Director of Admissions, South Dakota School of Mines and Technology, 501 East Saint Joseph, Rapid City, SD 57701-3995. *Telephone:* 605-394-2414 Ext. 1266 or 800-544-8162 Ext. 2414 (toll-free). *Fax:* 605-394-1268. *E-mail:* admissions@sdsmut.edu. *Web site:* http://www.sdsmt.edu/.

SOUTH DAKOTA STATE UNIVERSITY
Brookings, South Dakota

South Dakota State University is a coed, public university, founded in 1881, offering degrees at the associate, bachelor's, master's, doctoral, and first professional levels and post-master's and postbachelor's certificates. It has a 272-acre campus in Brookings.

Academic Information The faculty has 598 members (71% full-time), 62% with terminal degrees. The undergraduate student-faculty ratio is 17:1. The library holds 1 million titles, 29,255 serial subscriptions, and 13,123 audiovisual materials. Special programs include academic remediation, services for learning-disabled students, an honors program, cooperative (work-study) education, study abroad, advanced placement credit, accelerated degree programs, Freshman Honors College, ESL programs, double majors, independent study, distance learning, summer session for credit, part-time degree programs (daytime, evenings, summer), adult/continuing education programs, internships, and arrangement for off-campus study with National Student Exchange. The most frequently chosen baccalaureate fields are agriculture, health professions and related sciences, social sciences.

Student Body Statistics The student body totals 11,303, of whom 9,897 are undergraduates (1,917 freshmen). 52 percent are women and 48 percent are men. Students come from 36 states and territories and 26 other countries. 70 percent are from South Dakota. 0.4 percent are international students.

Expenses for 2006–07 *Application fee:* $20. *State resident tuition:* $2382 full-time, $79.40 per credit part-time. *Nonresident tuition:* $3573 full-time, $119.10 per credit part-time. *Mandatory fees:* $2670 full-time, $89 per credit part-time. Both full-time and part-time tuition and fees vary according to course load, location, program, and reciprocity agreements. *College room and board:* $5029. *College room only:* $2240. Room and board charges vary according to board plan and housing facility. Note: as of fall 2006, new non-resident freshman and transfer students will be paying less; 30 credits for these students will be $3573, or $119.10 per credit. Fees are the same for all students.

Financial Aid Forms of aid include need-based and non-need-based scholarships, athletic grants, and part-time jobs. The average aided 2006–07 undergraduate received an aid package worth an estimated $7714. The priority application deadline for financial aid is March 15.

Freshman Admission South Dakota State University requires a high school transcript, a minimum 2.6 high school GPA, minimum ACT score of 18, SAT or ACT scores, and TOEFL scores for international students. The application deadline for regular admission is rolling.

Transfer Admission The application deadline for admission is rolling.

Entrance Difficulty South Dakota State University assesses its entrance difficulty level as minimally difficult. For the fall 2006 freshman class, 94 percent of the applicants were accepted.

For Further Information Contact Ms. Michelle Kuebler, Assistant Director of Admissions, South Dakota State University, PO Box 2201, Brookings, SD 57007. *Telephone:* 605-688-4121 or 800-952-3541 (toll-free). *Fax:* 605-688-6891. *E-mail:* sdsu.admissions@sdstate.edu. *Web site:* http://www.sdstate.edu/.

UNIVERSITY OF SIOUX FALLS
Sioux Falls, South Dakota

University of Sioux Falls is a coed, private, American Baptist Churches in the USA, comprehensive institution, founded in 1883, offering degrees at the associate, bachelor's, master's, and doctoral levels. It has a 22-acre campus in Sioux Falls.

Academic Information The faculty has 140 members (43% full-time). The undergraduate student-faculty ratio is 17:1. The library holds 85,713 titles and 378 serial subscriptions. Special programs include academic remediation, services for learning-disabled students, an honors program, study abroad, advanced placement credit, accelerated degree programs, double majors, independent study, distance learning, self-designed majors, summer session for credit, part-time degree programs (daytime, evenings, weekends, summer), adult/continuing education programs, internships, and arrangement for off-campus study with Colleges of Mid-America, Augustana College (SD), North American Baptist Seminary, Christian College Coalition. The most frequently chosen baccalaureate fields are business/marketing, education, health professions and related sciences.

Student Body Statistics The student body totals 1,675, of whom 1,270 are undergraduates (233 freshmen). 55 percent are women and 45 percent are men. Students come from 24 states and territories and 3 other countries. 67 percent are from South Dakota. 0.2 percent are international students. 12 percent of the 2006 graduating class went on to graduate and professional schools.

Expenses for 2007–08 *Application fee:* $25. *Comprehensive fee:* $23,340 includes full-time tuition ($17,540), mandatory fees ($400), and college room and board ($5400). *College room only:* $2450. *Part-time tuition:* $270 per semester hour.

Financial Aid Forms of aid include need-based and non-need-based scholarships, athletic grants, and part-time jobs. The priority application deadline for financial aid is March 1.

Freshman Admission University of Sioux Falls requires a high school transcript, SAT or ACT scores, and TOEFL scores for international students. An essay and a minimum 2.5 high school GPA are recommended. 2 recommendations and an interview are required for some. The application deadline for regular admission is rolling.

Transfer Admission The application deadline for admission is rolling.

University of Sioux Falls (continued)

Entrance Difficulty University of Sioux Falls assesses its entrance difficulty level as moderately difficult. For the fall 2006 freshman class, 73 percent of the applicants were accepted.

For Further Information Contact Ms. Amanda Anderson, Director of Recruitment and Retention, University of Sioux Falls, 1101 West 22nd Street, Sioux Falls, SD 57105. *Telephone:* 605-331-6600 or 800-888-1047 (toll-free). *Fax:* 605-331-6615. *E-mail:* admissions@usiouxfalls.edu. *Web site:* http://www.usiouxfalls.edu/.

THE UNIVERSITY OF SOUTH DAKOTA
Vermillion, South Dakota

The University of South Dakota is a coed, public university, founded in 1862, offering degrees at the associate, bachelor's, master's, doctoral, and first professional levels and post-master's and postbachelor's certificates. It has a 216-acre campus in Vermillion.

Academic Information The faculty has 335 members (86% full-time), 73% with terminal degrees. The undergraduate student-faculty ratio is 15:1. The library holds 645,672 titles and 2,647 serial subscriptions. Special programs include academic remediation, services for learning-disabled students, an honors program, study abroad, advanced placement credit, ESL programs, double majors, independent study, distance learning, summer session for credit, part-time degree programs, internships, and arrangement for off-campus study with National Student Exchange. The most frequently chosen baccalaureate fields are business/marketing, education, health professions and related sciences.

Student Body Statistics The student body totals 8,746, of whom 6,468 are undergraduates (1,128 freshmen). 62 percent are women and 38 percent are men. Students come from 48 states and territories and 31 other countries. 74 percent are from South Dakota. 0.5 percent are international students. 35 percent of the 2006 graduating class went on to graduate and professional schools.

Expenses for 2006–07 *Application fee:* $20. *State resident tuition:* $2,690 full-time, $79.40 per credit hour part-time. *Nonresident tuition:* $7569 full-time, $252.30 per credit hour part-time. *Mandatory fees:* $2,690 full-time, $89.65 per credit hour part-time. Both full-time and part-time tuition and fees vary according to course load and reciprocity agreements. *College room and board:* $4,964. *College room only:* $2,389. Room and board charges vary according to board plan and housing facility.

Financial Aid Forms of aid include need-based and non-need-based scholarships, athletic grants, and part-time jobs. The average aided 2005–06 undergraduate received an aid package worth $5500. The priority application deadline for financial aid is March 15.

Freshman Admission The University of South Dakota requires a high school transcript, test scores, SAT or ACT scores, and TOEFL scores for international students. A minimum 2.0 high school GPA is recommended. Recommendations are required for some. The application deadline for regular admission is rolling.

Transfer Admission The application deadline for admission is rolling.

Entrance Difficulty The University of South Dakota assesses its entrance difficulty level as moderately difficult. For the fall 2006 freshman class, 86 percent of the applicants were accepted.

For Further Information Contact Ms. Stephanie Moser, Director of Admissions, The University of South Dakota, 414 East Clark Street, Vermillion, SD 57069. *Telephone:* 605-677-5434 or 877-269-6837 (toll-free). *Fax:* 605-677-6753. *E-mail:* admiss@usd.edu. *Web site:* http://www.usd.edu/.

Wisconsin

ALVERNO COLLEGE
Milwaukee, Wisconsin

Alverno College is an undergraduate: women only; graduate: coed, private, Roman Catholic, comprehensive institution, founded in 1887, offering degrees at the associate, bachelor's, and master's levels and postbachelor's certificates (also offers weekend program with significant enrollment not reflected in profile). It has a 46-acre campus in Milwaukee.

Academic Information The faculty has 226 members (47% full-time), 70% with terminal degrees. The undergraduate student-faculty ratio is 13:1. The library holds 95,622 titles, 3,932 serial subscriptions, and 4,191 audiovisual materials. Special programs include academic remediation, services for learning-disabled students, study abroad, advanced placement credit, double majors, independent study, self-designed majors, summer session for credit, part-time degree programs (daytime, evenings, weekends, summer), adult/continuing education programs, and internships. The most frequently chosen baccalaureate fields are business/marketing, education, health professions and related sciences.

Student Body Statistics The student body totals 2,480, of whom 2,245 are undergraduates (283 freshmen). 100 percent are women and 0 percent are men. 98 percent are from Wisconsin. 0.7 percent are international students. 12 percent of the 2006 graduating class went on to graduate and professional schools.

Expenses for 2007–08 *Application fee:* $20. *Comprehensive fee:* $23,402 includes full-time tuition ($16,896), mandatory fees ($400), and college room and board ($6106). *Part-time tuition:* $704 per credit. *Part-time mandatory fees:* $200 per term.

Financial Aid Forms of aid include need-based and non-need-based scholarships and part-time jobs.

Freshman Admission Alverno College requires an essay, a high school transcript, SAT or ACT scores, and TOEFL scores for international students. An interview is recommended. The application deadline for regular admission is rolling.

Transfer Admission The application deadline for admission is rolling.

Entrance Difficulty Alverno College assesses its entrance difficulty level as moderately difficult. For the fall 2006 freshman class, 59 percent of the applicants were accepted.

For Further Information Contact Ms. Mary Kay Farrell, Director of Admissions, Alverno College, 3400 South 43 Street, PO Box 343922, Milwaukee, WI 53234-3922. *Telephone:* 414-382-6031 or 800-933-3401 (toll-free). *Fax:* 414-382-6354. *E-mail:* admissions@alverno.edu. *Web site:* http://www.alverno.edu/.

See page 232 for the College Close-Up.

BELLIN COLLEGE OF NURSING
Green Bay, Wisconsin

http://www.bcon.edu/

BELOIT COLLEGE
Beloit, Wisconsin

Beloit College is a coed, private, four-year college, founded in 1846, offering degrees at the bachelor's level. It has a 65-acre campus in Beloit near Chicago and Milwaukee.

Academic Information The faculty has 136 members (77% full-time), 93% with terminal degrees. The student-faculty ratio is 12:1. The library holds 183,736 titles and 946 serial subscriptions. Special programs include services for learning-disabled students, study abroad, advanced placement credit, ESL programs, double majors, independent study, self-designed majors, summer session for credit, adult/continuing education programs, internships, and arrangement for off-campus study with University of Wisconsin-Madison, University of Chicago, Spelman College, Morehouse College, Associated Colleges of the Midwest. The most frequently chosen baccalaureate fields are social sciences, English, visual and performing arts.

Student Body Statistics The student body is made up of 1,432 undergraduates (347 freshmen). 59 percent are women and 41 percent are men. Students come from 47 states and territories and 43 other countries. 18 percent are from Wisconsin. 6.1 percent are international students. 33 percent of the 2006 graduating class went on to graduate and professional schools.

Expenses for 2006–07 *Application fee:* $35. *Comprehensive fee:* $34,512 includes full-time tuition ($28,130), mandatory fees ($220), and college room and board ($6162). *College room only:* $3006. Room and board charges vary according to board plan. *Part-time tuition:* $3517 per course.

Financial Aid Forms of aid include need-based and non-need-based scholarships and part-time jobs. The average aided 2006–07 undergraduate received an aid package worth an estimated $22,781. The priority application deadline for financial aid is March 1.

Freshman Admission Beloit College requires an essay, a high school transcript, 1 recommendation, SAT or ACT scores, and TOEFL scores for international students. An interview is recommended. An interview is required for some. The application deadline for regular admission is January 15 and for early action it is December 15.

Transfer Admission The application deadline for admission is rolling.

Entrance Difficulty Beloit College assesses its entrance difficulty level as very difficult. For the fall 2006 freshman class, 67 percent of the applicants were accepted.

For Further Information Contact Mr. James S. Zielinski, Director of Admissions, Beloit College, 700 College Street, Beloit, WI 53511-5596. *Telephone:* 608-363-2500 or 800-9-BELOIT (toll-free). *Fax:* 608-363-2075. *E-mail:* admiss@beloit.edu. *Web site:* http://www.beloit.edu/.

BRYANT AND STRATTON COLLEGE

Milwaukee, Wisconsin

Bryant and Stratton College is a coed, proprietary, primarily two-year college of Bryant and Stratton Business Institute, Inc, founded in 1863, offering degrees at the associate and bachelor's levels. It has a 2-acre campus in Milwaukee.

Expenses for 2006–07 *Tuition:* $415 per credit hour part-time. *Mandatory fees:* $62.25 per term part-time.

For Further Information Contact Ms. Kathryn Cotey, Director of Admissions, Bryant and Stratton College, 310 West Wisconsin Avenue, Milwaukee, WI 53203-2214. *Telephone:* 414-276-5200. *Web site:* http://www.bryantstratton.edu/.

BRYANT AND STRATTON COLLEGE, WAUWATOSA CAMPUS

Wauwatosa, Wisconsin

Bryant and Stratton College, Wauwatosa Campus is a coed, proprietary, four-year college, offering degrees at the associate and bachelor's levels.

Expenses for 2006–07 *Tuition:* $415 per credit hour part-time. *Mandatory fees:* $62.25 per term part-time.

For Further Information Contact Mr. Cori Prohaska, Campus Director, Bryant and Stratton College, Wauwatosa Campus, 10950 W. Potter Road, Wauwatosa, WI 53226. *Telephone:* 414-302-7000. *Web site:* http://www.bryantstratton.edu/.

CARDINAL STRITCH UNIVERSITY

Milwaukee, Wisconsin

Cardinal Stritch University is a coed, private, Roman Catholic, comprehensive institution, founded in 1937, offering degrees at the associate, bachelor's, master's, and doctoral levels and postbachelor's certificates. It has a 40-acre campus in Milwaukee.

Academic Information The faculty has 449 members (22% full-time). The undergraduate student-faculty ratio is 16:1. The library holds 124,897 titles and 667 serial subscriptions. Special programs include academic remediation, services for learning-disabled students, an honors program, cooperative (work-study) education, advanced placement credit, accelerated degree programs, ESL programs, double majors, independent study, distance learning, self-designed majors, summer session for credit, part-time degree programs (daytime, evenings, weekends, summer), external degree programs, adult/continuing education programs, internships, and arrangement for off-campus study with Concordia University Wisconsin, Saint Francis Seminary, Sacred Heart School of Theology.

Student Body Statistics The student body totals 6,000, of whom 3,237 are undergraduates (257 freshmen). 69 percent are women and 31 percent are men. Students come from 10 states and territories and 17 other countries. 82 percent are from Wisconsin. 2.2 percent are international students.

Expenses for 2006–07 *Application fee:* $25. *Comprehensive fee:* $23,590 includes full-time tuition ($17,600), mandatory fees ($400), and college room and board ($5590). Full-time tuition and fees vary according to course load. Room and board charges vary according to board plan. *Part-time tuition:* $550 per credit. *Part-time mandatory fees:* $150 per term. Part-time tuition and fees vary according to course load.

Financial Aid Forms of aid include need-based and non-need-based scholarships and part-time jobs. The application deadline for financial aid is continuous.

Freshman Admission Cardinal Stritch University requires an essay, a high school transcript, a minimum 2.0 high school GPA, SAT or ACT scores, and TOEFL scores for international students. An interview is recommended. Recommendations are required for some. The application deadline for regular admission is August 1.

Transfer Admission The application deadline for admission is rolling.

Entrance Difficulty Cardinal Stritch University assesses its entrance difficulty level as moderately difficult. For the fall 2006 freshman class, 93 percent of the applicants were accepted.

For Further Information Contact Kristine Bueno, Director of Admissions, Cardinal Stritch University, 6801 North Yates Road, Milwaukee, WI 53217. *Telephone:* 414-410-4040 or 800-347-8822 Ext. 4040 (toll-free). *Fax:* 414-410-4058. *E-mail:* admityou@stritch.edu. *Web site:* http://www.stritch.edu/.

CARROLL COLLEGE

Waukesha, Wisconsin

Carroll College is a coed, private, Presbyterian, comprehensive institution, founded in 1846, offering degrees at the bachelor's and master's levels. It has a 52-acre campus in Waukesha near Milwaukee.

Academic Information The faculty has 283 members (39% full-time), 38% with terminal degrees. The undergraduate student-faculty ratio is 16:1. The library holds 150,000 titles, 18,000 serial subscriptions, and 1,025 audiovisual materials. Special programs include academic remediation, services for learning-disabled students, an honors program, study abroad, advanced placement credit, double majors, independent study, distance learning, self-designed majors, summer session for credit, part-time degree programs (daytime, evenings, weekends, summer), adult/continuing education programs, and internships. The most frequently chosen baccalaureate fields are business/marketing, education, health professions and related sciences.

Student Body Statistics The student body totals 3,292, of whom 3,017 are undergraduates (685 freshmen). 67 percent are women and 33 percent are men. Students come from 23 states and territories and 32 other countries. 81 percent are from Wisconsin. 1.6 percent are international students.

Expenses for 2007–08 *Application fee:* $0. *Comprehensive fee:* $27,180 includes full-time tuition ($20,400), mandatory fees ($430), and college room and board ($6350). *College room only:* $3450. *Part-time tuition:* $250 per credit.

Carroll College (continued)

Financial Aid Forms of aid include need-based and non-need-based scholarships and part-time jobs. The average aided 2006–07 undergraduate received an aid package worth an estimated $14,979. The application deadline for financial aid is continuous.

Freshman Admission Carroll College requires a high school transcript, a minimum 2.0 high school GPA, 1 recommendation, SAT or ACT scores, and TOEFL scores for international students. An interview and ACT scores are recommended. An essay is required for some. The application deadline for regular admission is rolling.

Transfer Admission The application deadline for admission is rolling.

Entrance Difficulty Carroll College assesses its entrance difficulty level as moderately difficult. For the fall 2006 freshman class, 74 percent of the applicants were accepted.

For Further Information Contact Mr. James Wiseman, Vice President of Enrollment, Carroll College, 100 North East Avenue, Waukesha, WI 53186-5593. *Telephone:* 262-524-7221 or 800-CARROLL (toll-free). *Fax:* 262-524-7139. *E-mail:* cc.info@ccadmin.cc.edu. *Web site:* http://www.cc.edu/.

CARTHAGE COLLEGE
Kenosha, Wisconsin

Carthage College is a coed, private, comprehensive institution, founded in 1847, affiliated with the Evangelical Lutheran Church in America, offering degrees at the bachelor's and master's levels. It has a 72-acre campus in Kenosha near Chicago and Milwaukee.

Expenses for 2006–07 *Application fee:* $25. *Comprehensive fee:* $30,450 includes full-time tuition ($23,650) and college room and board ($6800). Room and board charges vary according to board plan. *Part-time tuition:* $345 per credit hour. Part-time tuition varies according to class time and course load.

For Further Information Contact Ms. Brenda Poggendorf, Vice President for Enrollment, Carthage College, 2001 Alford Park Drive, Kenosha, WI 53140. *Telephone:* 262-551-5850 or 800-351-4058 (toll-free). *Fax:* 262-551-5762. *E-mail:* admissions@carthage.edu. *Web site:* http://www.carthage.edu/.

COLLEGE OF MENOMINEE NATION
Keshena, Wisconsin

College of Menominee Nation is a coed, private, two-year college, founded in 1993, offering degrees at the associate level.

Academic Information The faculty has 14 full-time members.

Student Body Statistics The student body is made up of 499 undergraduates. 76 percent are women and 24 percent are men.

Expenses for 2006–07 *Application fee:* $10. *Tuition:* $4524 full-time.

Financial Aid Forms of aid include need-based scholarships and part-time jobs. The application deadline for financial aid is continuous.

Freshman Admission College of Menominee Nation requires TABE. The application deadline for regular admission is August 14.

Entrance Difficulty College of Menominee Nation has an open admission policy.

For Further Information Contact Ms. Cynthia Norton, Admissions Representative, College of Menominee Nation, PO Box 1179, Keshena, WI 54135. *Telephone:* 715-799-5600 or 800-567-2344 (toll-free in-state). *Fax:* 715-799-1326. *Web site:* http://www.menominee.edu/.

COLUMBIA COLLEGE OF NURSING
Milwaukee, Wisconsin

http://www.ccon.edu/

CONCORDIA UNIVERSITY WISCONSIN
Mequon, Wisconsin

Concordia University Wisconsin is a coed, private, comprehensive unit of Concordia University System, founded in 1881, affiliated with the Lutheran Church–Missouri Synod, offering degrees at the associate, bachelor's, master's, and doctoral levels and postbachelor's certificates. It has a 192-acre campus in Mequon near Milwaukee.

Academic Information The faculty has 204 members (43% full-time), 40% with terminal degrees. The undergraduate student-faculty ratio is 14:1. The library holds 79,341 titles, 4,440 serial subscriptions, and 4,352 audiovisual materials. Special programs include academic remediation, services for learning-disabled students, an honors program, study abroad, advanced placement credit, accelerated degree programs, ESL programs, double majors, independent study, distance learning, self-designed majors, summer session for credit, part-time degree programs, adult/continuing education programs, internships, and arrangement for off-campus study with Milwaukee Area Technical College, Milwaukee Institute of Art and Design, Cardinal Stritch University, Mount Mary College. The most frequently chosen baccalaureate fields are business/marketing, education, health professions and related sciences.

Student Body Statistics The student body totals 5,574, of whom 3,782 are undergraduates (395 freshmen). 62 percent are women and 38 percent are men. Students come from 41 states and territories and 23 other countries. 71 percent are from Wisconsin. 1 percent are international students.

Expenses for 2006–07 *Application fee:* $35. *Comprehensive fee:* $25,000 includes full-time tuition ($18,050), mandatory fees ($90), and college room and board ($6860). Full-time tuition and fees vary according to program. Room and board charges vary according to board plan. *Part-time tuition:* $752 per credit hour. Part-time tuition varies according to class time and program.

Financial Aid Forms of aid include need-based and non-need-based scholarships and part-time jobs. The average aided 2006–07 undergraduate received an aid package worth an estimated $17,399. The priority application deadline for financial aid is April 1.

Freshman Admission Concordia University Wisconsin requires a high school transcript, a minimum 2.0 high school GPA, ACT scores, and TOEFL scores for international students. An interview is recommended. An essay, a minimum 3.0 high school GPA, and 3 recommendations are required for some. The application deadline for regular admission is August 15.

Entrance Difficulty Concordia University Wisconsin assesses its entrance difficulty level as moderately difficult; minimally difficult for transfers. For the fall 2006 freshman class, 70 percent of the applicants were accepted.

For Further Information Contact Ms. Julie Schroeder, Concordia University Wisconsin, Admissions Office, 12800 N. Lake Drive, Mequon, WI 53097. *Telephone:* 262-243-5700 or 888-628-9472 (toll-free). *Fax:* 262-243-4351. *E-mail:* admission@cuw.edu. *Web site:* http://www.cuw.edu/.

DeVRY UNIVERSITY
Milwaukee, Wisconsin

DeVry University is a coed, proprietary, comprehensive unit of DeVry University, offering degrees at the bachelor's and master's levels and postbachelor's certificates.

Academic Information The faculty has 1 members. The undergraduate student-faculty ratio is 55:1. Special programs include academic remediation, services for learning-disabled students, advanced placement credit, accelerated degree programs, distance learning, summer session for credit, part-time degree programs (daytime, evenings, weekends, summer), and adult/continuing education programs.

Student Body Statistics The student body totals 227, of whom 98 are undergraduates (18 freshmen). 68 percent are women and 32 percent are men.

Expenses for 2007–08 *Application fee:* $50. *Tuition:* $12,900 full-time, $490 per credit part-time. *Mandatory fees:* $120 full-time.

Freshman Admission DeVry University requires a high school transcript and an interview. The application deadline for regular admission is rolling.

Transfer Admission The application deadline for admission is rolling.
Entrance Difficulty DeVry University assesses its entrance difficulty level as minimally difficult.
For Further Information Contact Admissions Office, DeVry University, 100 East Wisconsin Avenue, Suite 2550, Milwaukee, WI 53202-4107. *Telephone:* 414-278-7677. *Web site:* http://www.devry.edu/.

DEVRY UNIVERSITY
Waukesha, Wisconsin
http://www.devry.edu/

EDGEWOOD COLLEGE
Madison, Wisconsin

Edgewood College is a coed, private, Roman Catholic, comprehensive institution, founded in 1927, offering degrees at the associate, bachelor's, master's, and doctoral levels. It has a 55-acre campus in Madison.

Academic Information The faculty has 270 members (37% full-time), 46% with terminal degrees. The undergraduate student-faculty ratio is 12:1. The library holds 90,253 titles, 447 serial subscriptions, and 4,359 audiovisual materials. Special programs include academic remediation, services for learning-disabled students, advanced placement credit, independent study, summer session for credit, part-time degree programs (daytime, evenings, weekends, summer), adult/continuing education programs, and arrangement for off-campus study with University of Wisconsin-Madison. The most frequently chosen baccalaureate fields are business/marketing, education, health professions and related sciences.
Student Body Statistics The student body totals 2,565, of whom 1,989 are undergraduates (296 freshmen). 72 percent are women and 28 percent are men. Students come from 16 states and territories and 22 other countries. 94 percent are from Wisconsin. 1.5 percent are international students. 8 percent of the 2006 graduating class went on to graduate and professional schools.
Expenses for 2007-08 *Application fee:* $25. *Comprehensive fee:* $25,615 includes full-time tuition ($19,080) and college room and board ($6535). *College room only:* $3335. *Part-time tuition:* $601 per credit.
Financial Aid Forms of aid include need-based and non-need-based scholarships and part-time jobs. The average aided 2005-06 undergraduate received an aid package worth $12,859. The priority application deadline for financial aid is March 15.
Freshman Admission Edgewood College requires a high school transcript, a minimum 2.5 high school GPA, SAT or ACT scores, and TOEFL scores for international students. An interview is recommended. An essay, 2 recommendations, and an interview are required for some. The application deadline for regular admission is rolling.
Transfer Admission The application deadline for admission is rolling.
Entrance Difficulty Edgewood College assesses its entrance difficulty level as moderately difficult. For the fall 2006 freshman class, 79 percent of the applicants were accepted.
For Further Information Contact Ms. Christine Benedict, Director of Undergraduate Admission, Edgewood College, 1000 Edgewood College Drive, Madison, WI 53711-1997. *Telephone:* 608-663-2294 or 800-444-4861 Ext. 2294 (toll-free). *Fax:* 608-663-2214. *E-mail:* admissions@edgewood.edu. *Web site:* http://www.edgewood.edu/.

HERZING COLLEGE
Madison, Wisconsin

Herzing College is a coed, primarily men's, proprietary, primarily two-year college of Herzing Institutes, Inc, founded in 1948, offering degrees at the associate and bachelor's levels. It is located in Madison near Milwaukee.

Academic Information The faculty has 46 members (33% full-time), 15% with terminal degrees. The student-faculty ratio is 13:1. The library holds 1,500 titles and 15 serial subscriptions. Special programs include academic remediation, services for learning-disabled students, an honors program, cooperative (work-study) education, advanced placement credit, accelerated degree programs, double majors, independent study, distance learning, part-time degree programs (daytime, evenings, summer), adult/continuing education programs, and internships.
Student Body Statistics The student body is made up of 650 undergraduates. Students come from 5 states and territories and 2 other countries. 67 percent are from Wisconsin. 20 percent of the 2006 graduating class went on to four-year colleges.
Expenses for 2006-07 *Application fee:* $0. *Tuition:* $10,720 full-time, $335 per credit hour part-time. *Mandatory fees:* $48 full-time. Full-time tuition and fees vary according to course load, location, and program. Part-time tuition varies according to course load, location, and program.
Financial Aid Forms of aid include need-based scholarships and part-time jobs. The application deadline for financial aid is June 30.
Freshman Admission Herzing College requires a high school transcript, an interview, and TOEFL scores for international students. The application deadline for regular admission is rolling.
Transfer Admission The application deadline for admission is October 10.
Entrance Difficulty Herzing College has an open admission policy.
For Further Information Contact Ms. Rebecca M. Abrams, Admissions Director, Herzing College, 5218 East Terrace Drive, Madison, WI 53718. *Telephone:* 608-663-0804 or 800-582-1227 (toll-free). *Fax:* 608-249-8593. *E-mail:* info@msn.herzing.edu. *Web site:* http://www.herzing.edu/madison.

ITT TECHNICAL INSTITUTE
Green Bay, Wisconsin

ITT Technical Institute is a coed, proprietary, primarily two-year college of ITT Educational Services, Inc, founded in 2000, offering degrees at the associate and bachelor's levels.

Expenses for 2006-07 *Application fee:* $100. Contact school for program costs.
Financial Aid Forms of aid include need-based scholarships and part-time jobs. The application deadline for financial aid is continuous.
Freshman Admission ITT Technical Institute requires a high school transcript, an interview, and Wonderlic aptitude test. Recommendations are recommended. The application deadline for regular admission is rolling.
Transfer Admission The application deadline for admission is rolling.
Entrance Difficulty ITT Technical Institute assesses its entrance difficulty level as minimally difficult.
For Further Information Contact Ms. Marnie Glanner, Director of Recruitment, ITT Technical Institute, 470 Security Boulevard, Green Bay, WI 54313. *Telephone:* 920-662-9000 or 888-884-3626 (toll-free out-of-state). *Fax:* 920-662-9384. *Web site:* http://www.itt-tech.edu/.

ITT TECHNICAL INSTITUTE
Greenfield, Wisconsin

ITT Technical Institute is a coed, proprietary, primarily two-year college of ITT Educational Services, Inc, founded in 1968, offering degrees at the associate and bachelor's levels. It is located in Greenfield near Milwaukee.

Student Body Statistics The student body is made up of 548 undergraduates.
Expenses for 2006-07 *Application fee:* $100. Contact school for program costs.
Financial Aid Forms of aid include need-based scholarships and part-time jobs. The application deadline for financial aid is continuous.
Freshman Admission ITT Technical Institute requires a high school transcript, an interview, and Wonderlic aptitude test. Recommendations are recommended. The application deadline for regular admission is rolling.
Transfer Admission The application deadline for admission is rolling.

ITT Technical Institute (continued)

Entrance Difficulty ITT Technical Institute assesses its entrance difficulty level as minimally difficult.

For Further Information Contact Ms. Geraldine Purcell, Director of Recruitment, ITT Technical Institute, 6300 West Layton avenue, Greenfield, WI 53220. *Telephone:* 414-282-9494. *Fax:* 414-282-9698. *Web site:* http://www.itt-tech.edu/.

LAKELAND COLLEGE

Sheboygan, Wisconsin

Lakeland College is a coed, private, comprehensive institution, founded in 1862, affiliated with the United Church of Christ, offering degrees at the bachelor's and master's levels. It has a 240-acre campus in Sheboygan near Milwaukee.

Academic Information The faculty has 71 members (80% full-time), 61% with terminal degrees. The undergraduate student-faculty ratio is 17:1. The library holds 64,970 titles and 317 serial subscriptions. Special programs include academic remediation, services for learning-disabled students, an honors program, study abroad, advanced placement credit, ESL programs, independent study, distance learning, summer session for credit, part-time degree programs (evenings, summer), adult/continuing education programs, internships, and arrangement for off-campus study. The most frequently chosen baccalaureate fields are business/marketing, computer and information sciences, education.

Student Body Statistics The student body totals 4,047, of whom 3,298 are undergraduates (220 freshmen). 62 percent are women and 38 percent are men. Students come from 41 states and territories and 30 other countries. 85 percent are from Wisconsin. 4.1 percent are international students. 15 percent of the 2006 graduating class went on to graduate and professional schools.

Expenses for 2007–08 *Application fee:* $20. *Comprehensive fee:* $23,740 includes full-time tuition ($16,845), mandatory fees ($750), and college room and board ($6145). *Part-time tuition:* $1686 per course.

Financial Aid Forms of aid include need-based and non-need-based scholarships and part-time jobs. The average aided 2006–07 undergraduate received an aid package worth an estimated $11,728. The application deadline for financial aid is July 1 with a priority deadline of March 31.

Freshman Admission Lakeland College requires an essay, a high school transcript, a minimum 2.0 high school GPA, SAT or ACT scores, and TOEFL scores for international students. Recommendations are recommended. An interview is required for some. The application deadline for regular admission is rolling.

Transfer Admission The application deadline for admission is rolling.

Entrance Difficulty Lakeland College assesses its entrance difficulty level as minimally difficult. For the fall 2006 freshman class, 50 percent of the applicants were accepted.

For Further Information Contact Mr. Nathan Dehne, Director of Admissions, Lakeland College, PO Box 359, Nash Visitors Center, Sheboygan, WI 53082-0359. *Telephone:* 920-565-1588 or 800-242-3347 (toll-free in-state). *Fax:* 920-565-1206. *E-mail:* admissions@lakeland.edu. *Web site:* http://www.lakeland.edu/.

LAWRENCE UNIVERSITY

Appleton, Wisconsin

Lawrence University is a coed, private, four-year college, founded in 1847, offering degrees at the bachelor's level. It has an 84-acre campus in Appleton.

Academic Information The faculty has 182 members (82% full-time), 86% with terminal degrees. The student-faculty ratio is 9:1. The library holds 395,000 titles, 2,816 serial subscriptions, and 20,500 audiovisual materials. Special programs include services for learning-disabled students, study abroad, advanced placement credit, double majors, independent study, self-designed majors, internships, and arrangement for off-campus study with Associated Colleges of the Midwest, Great Lakes Colleges Association. The most frequently chosen baccalaureate fields are social sciences, foreign languages and literature, visual and performing arts.

Student Body Statistics The student body is made up of 1,480 undergraduates (372 freshmen). 55 percent are women and 45 percent are men. Students come from 43 states and territories and 42 other countries. 43 percent are from Wisconsin. 6.6 percent are international students. 22 percent of the 2006 graduating class went on to graduate and professional schools.

Expenses for 2006–07 *Application fee:* $40. *Comprehensive fee:* $36,480 includes full-time tuition ($29,376), mandatory fees ($222), and college room and board ($6882). *College room only:* $2934.

Financial Aid Forms of aid include need-based and non-need-based scholarships and part-time jobs. The average aided 2006–07 undergraduate received an aid package worth an estimated $23,900. The priority application deadline for financial aid is March 15.

Freshman Admission Lawrence University requires an essay, a high school transcript, 2 recommendations, and audition for music program. A minimum 3.0 high school GPA, an interview, and TOEFL scores for international students are recommended. The application deadline for regular admission is January 15; for early decision it is November 15; and for early action it is December 1.

Transfer Admission The application deadline for admission is May 1.

Entrance Difficulty Lawrence University assesses its entrance difficulty level as very difficult. For the fall 2006 freshman class, 56 percent of the applicants were accepted.

For Further Information Contact Mr. Steven T. Syverson, Dean of Admissions and Financial Aid, Lawrence University, PO Box 599, Appleton, WI 54912-0599. *Telephone:* 920-832-6500 or 800-227-0982 (toll-free). *Fax:* 920-832-6782. *E-mail:* excel@lawrence.edu. *Web site:* http://www.lawrence.edu/.

MARANATHA BAPTIST BIBLE COLLEGE

Watertown, Wisconsin

Maranatha Baptist Bible College is a coed, private, Baptist, comprehensive institution, founded in 1968, offering degrees at the associate, bachelor's, and master's levels. It has a 60-acre campus in Watertown near Milwaukee.

Academic Information The faculty has 72 members (62% full-time), 21% with terminal degrees. The undergraduate student-faculty ratio is 15:1. The library holds 122,251 titles and 502 serial subscriptions. Special programs include academic remediation, accelerated degree programs, double majors, independent study, distance learning, summer session for credit, part-time degree programs (daytime, evenings, summer), internships, and arrangement for off-campus study with Madison Area Technical College.

Student Body Statistics The student body totals 876, of whom 811 are undergraduates (212 freshmen). 54 percent are women and 46 percent are men. Students come from 41 states and territories and 4 other countries. 33 percent are from Wisconsin. 0.1 percent are international students. 25 percent of the 2006 graduating class went on to graduate and professional schools.

Expenses for 2006–07 *Application fee:* $50. *Comprehensive fee:* $14,180 includes full-time tuition ($8160), mandatory fees ($870), and college room and board ($5150). *Part-time tuition:* $255 per semester hour.

Financial Aid Forms of aid include need-based and non-need-based scholarships and part-time jobs. The average aided 2005–06 undergraduate received an aid package worth $6765. The priority application deadline for financial aid is March 1.

Freshman Admission Maranatha Baptist Bible College requires an essay, a high school transcript, 4 recommendations, ACT scores, and TOEFL scores for international students. The application deadline for regular admission is rolling and for nonresidents it is rolling.

Transfer Admission The application deadline for admission is rolling.

Entrance Difficulty Maranatha Baptist Bible College has an open admission policy.

For Further Information Contact Dr. James H. Harrison, Director of Admissions, Maranatha Baptist Bible College, 745 West Main Street, Watertown, WI 53094. *Telephone:* 920-206-2327 or 800-622-2947 (toll-free). *Fax:* 920-261-9109. *E-mail:* admissions@mbbc.edu. *Web site:* http://www.mbbc.edu/.

MARIAN COLLEGE OF FOND DU LAC
Fond du Lac, Wisconsin

Marian College of Fond du Lac is a coed, private, Roman Catholic, comprehensive institution, founded in 1936, offering degrees at the bachelor's, master's, and doctoral levels. It has a 77-acre campus in Fond du Lac near Milwaukee.

Academic Information The faculty has 278 members (29% full-time), 28% with terminal degrees. The undergraduate student-faculty ratio is 12:1. The library holds 94,217 titles, 952 serial subscriptions, and 1,320 audiovisual materials. Special programs include academic remediation, services for learning-disabled students, an honors program, cooperative (work-study) education, study abroad, advanced placement credit, accelerated degree programs, ESL programs, double majors, independent study, distance learning, self-designed majors, summer session for credit, part-time degree programs (daytime, evenings, weekends, summer), external degree programs, adult/continuing education programs, and internships. The most frequently chosen baccalaureate fields are business/marketing, education, health professions and related sciences.

Student Body Statistics The student body totals 3,040, of whom 2,126 are undergraduates (245 freshmen). 73 percent are women and 27 percent are men. Students come from 11 states and territories and 5 other countries. 95 percent are from Wisconsin. 0.7 percent are international students.

Expenses for 2006–07 *Application fee:* $20. *Comprehensive fee:* $22,825 includes full-time tuition ($17,300), mandatory fees ($325), and college room and board ($5200). *College room only:* $3420. Full-time tuition and fees vary according to class time, course load, and program. Room and board charges vary according to board plan and housing facility. *Part-time tuition:* $290 per credit. *Part-time mandatory fees:* $80 per term. Part-time tuition and fees vary according to class time, course load, and program.

Financial Aid Forms of aid include need-based and non-need-based scholarships and part-time jobs. The average aided 2006–07 undergraduate received an aid package worth an estimated $17,973. The priority application deadline for financial aid is March 1.

Freshman Admission Marian College of Fond du Lac requires a high school transcript, SAT or ACT scores, and TOEFL scores for international students. A minimum 2.0 high school GPA and recommendations are recommended. An interview is required for some. The application deadline for regular admission is rolling.

Transfer Admission The application deadline for admission is rolling.

Entrance Difficulty Marian College of Fond du Lac assesses its entrance difficulty level as moderately difficult. For the fall 2006 freshman class, 85 percent of the applicants were accepted.

For Further Information Contact Mr. Eric Peterson, Dean of Admissions, Marian College of Fond du Lac, 45 South National Avenue, Fond du Lac, WI 54935-4699. *Telephone:* 800-262-7426 or 800-2-MARIAN Ext. 7652 (toll-free in-state). *Fax:* 920-923-8755. *E-mail:* admit@mariancollege.edu. *Web site:* http://www.mariancollege.edu/.

MARQUETTE UNIVERSITY
Milwaukee, Wisconsin

Marquette University is a coed, private, Roman Catholic (Jesuit) university, founded in 1881, offering degrees at the associate, bachelor's, master's, doctoral, and first professional levels and post-master's certificates. It has an 80-acre campus in Milwaukee.

Academic Information The faculty has 1,054 members (57% full-time), 70% with terminal degrees. The undergraduate student-faculty ratio is 15:1. The library holds 1 million titles and 23,039 serial subscriptions. Special programs include services for learning-disabled students, an honors program, cooperative (work-study) education, study abroad, advanced placement credit, ESL programs, double majors, summer session for credit, part-time degree programs (daytime, evenings, weekends, summer), adult/continuing education programs, internships, and arrangement for off-campus study with Milwaukee Institute of Art and Design, Les Aspin Center for Government, Washington, DC. The most frequently chosen baccalaureate fields are business/marketing, communications/journalism, engineering.

Student Body Statistics The student body totals 11,548, of whom 8,048 are undergraduates (1,854 freshmen). 54 percent are women and 46 percent are men. Students come from 50 states and territories and 48 other countries. 47 percent are from Wisconsin. 2 percent are international students. 31 percent of the 2006 graduating class went on to graduate and professional schools.

Expenses for 2006–07 *Application fee:* $30. *Comprehensive fee:* $33,194 includes full-time tuition ($24,670), mandatory fees ($404), and college room and board ($8120). *College room only:* $5278. Full-time tuition and fees vary according to course load and program. Room and board charges vary according to board plan and housing facility. *Part-time tuition:* $725 per credit. *Part-time mandatory fees:* $725 per credit. Part-time tuition and fees vary according to program.

Financial Aid Forms of aid include need-based and non-need-based scholarships, athletic grants, and part-time jobs. The average aided 2006–07 undergraduate received an aid package worth an estimated $18,248. The application deadline for financial aid is continuous.

Freshman Admission Marquette University requires an essay, a high school transcript, a minimum 2.5 high school GPA, 1 recommendation, SAT or ACT scores, and TOEFL scores for international students. A minimum 3.4 high school GPA is recommended. The application deadline for regular admission is December 1.

Transfer Admission The application deadline for admission is December 1.

Entrance Difficulty Marquette University assesses its entrance difficulty level as moderately difficult; very difficult for physical therapy and athletic training. For the fall 2006 freshman class, 70 percent of the applicants were accepted.

For Further Information Contact Mr. Robert Blust, Dean of Undergraduate Admissions, Marquette University, PO Box 1881, Milwaukee, WI 53201-1881. *Telephone:* 414-288-7004 or 800-222-6544 (toll-free). *Fax:* 414-288-3764. *E-mail:* admissions@marquette.edu. *Web site:* http://www.marquette.edu/.

MILWAUKEE INSTITUTE OF ART AND DESIGN
Milwaukee, Wisconsin

Milwaukee Institute of Art and Design is a coed, private, four-year college, founded in 1974, offering degrees at the bachelor's level.

Expenses for 2006–07 *Application fee:* $25. *Comprehensive fee:* $30,400 includes full-time tuition ($23,100), mandatory fees ($300), and college room and board ($7000). *Part-time tuition:* $770 per credit hour.

For Further Information Contact Mr. Mark Fetherston, Director of Admissions, Milwaukee Institute of Art and Design, 273 East Erie Street, Milwaukee, WI 53202. *Telephone:* 414-847-3259 or 888-749-MIAD (toll-free). *Fax:* 414-291-8077. *E-mail:* admissions@miad.edu. *Web site:* http://www.miad.edu/.

MILWAUKEE SCHOOL OF ENGINEERING
Milwaukee, Wisconsin

Milwaukee School of Engineering is a coed, private, comprehensive institution, founded in 1903, offering degrees at the bachelor's and master's levels. It has a 15-acre campus in Milwaukee.

Academic Information The faculty has 224 members (54% full-time), 50% with terminal degrees. The undergraduate student-faculty ratio is 12:1. The library holds 72,192 titles, 376 serial subscriptions, and 1,421 audiovisual materials. Special programs include academic remediation, services for learning-disabled students, study abroad, advanced placement credit, ESL programs, double majors, independent study, distance learning, summer session for credit, part-time degree programs (daytime, evenings, weekends, summer), adult/continuing education programs, and internships. The most frequently chosen baccalaureate fields are business/marketing, engineering, engineering technologies.

Student Body Statistics The student body totals 2,427, of whom 2,203 are undergraduates (560 freshmen). 18 percent are women and 82 percent

Milwaukee School of Engineering (continued)

are men. Students come from 35 states and territories and 19 other countries. 73 percent are from Wisconsin. 2 percent are international students. 6 percent of the 2006 graduating class went on to graduate and professional schools.

Expenses for 2007–08 *Application fee:* $25. *Comprehensive fee:* $32,481 includes full-time tuition ($25,980) and college room and board ($6501). *College room only:* $4170. *Part-time tuition:* $450 per quarter hour.

Financial Aid Forms of aid include need-based and non-need-based scholarships and part-time jobs. The average aided 2005–06 undergraduate received an aid package worth $16,915.

Freshman Admission Milwaukee School of Engineering requires a high school transcript, a minimum 2.5 high school GPA, SAT or ACT scores, and TOEFL scores for international students. An essay and an interview are required for some. The application deadline for regular admission is rolling.

Transfer Admission The application deadline for admission is rolling.

Entrance Difficulty Milwaukee School of Engineering assesses its entrance difficulty level as moderately difficult. For the fall 2006 freshman class, 68 percent of the applicants were accepted.

For Further Information Contact Paul Borens, Director of Admissions, Milwaukee School of Engineering, 1025 North Broadway, Milwaukee, WI 53202-3109. *Telephone:* 414-277-6765 or 800-332-6763 (toll-free). *Fax:* 414-277-7475. *E-mail:* borens@msoe.edu. *Web site:* http://www.msoe.edu/.

See page 268 for the College Close-Up.

MOUNT MARY COLLEGE
Milwaukee, Wisconsin

Mount Mary College is an undergraduate: women only; graduate: coed, private, Roman Catholic, comprehensive institution, founded in 1913, offering degrees at the bachelor's and master's levels and postbachelor's certificates. It has an 80-acre campus in Milwaukee.

Academic Information The faculty has 213 members (31% full-time), 36% with terminal degrees. The undergraduate student-faculty ratio is 10:1. The library holds 103,450 titles, 22,210 serial subscriptions, and 8,104 audiovisual materials. Special programs include academic remediation, services for learning-disabled students, an honors program, study abroad, advanced placement credit, accelerated degree programs, double majors, independent study, distance learning, self-designed majors, summer session for credit, part-time degree programs (daytime, evenings, weekends, summer), and internships. The most frequently chosen baccalaureate fields are health professions and related sciences, business/marketing, visual and performing arts.

Student Body Statistics The student body totals 1,732, of whom 1,459 are undergraduates (139 freshmen). 97 percent are women and 3 percent are men. Students come from 9 states and territories and 9 other countries. 97 percent are from Wisconsin. 0.7 percent are international students. 10 percent of the 2006 graduating class went on to graduate and professional schools.

Expenses for 2007–08 *Application fee:* $25. *Comprehensive fee:* $25,399 includes full-time tuition ($18,994), mandatory fees ($210), and college room and board ($6195). *Part-time tuition:* $510 per credit. *Part-time mandatory fees:* $57.50 per term.

Financial Aid Forms of aid include need-based and non-need-based scholarships and part-time jobs. The average aided 2006–07 undergraduate received an aid package worth an estimated $11,918. The priority application deadline for financial aid is March 1.

Freshman Admission Mount Mary College requires a high school transcript, a minimum 2.5 high school GPA, SAT or ACT scores, and TOEFL scores for international students. An interview is recommended. An essay and 2 recommendations are required for some. The application deadline for regular admission is rolling.

Transfer Admission The application deadline for admission is rolling.

Entrance Difficulty Mount Mary College assesses its entrance difficulty level as moderately difficult. For the fall 2006 freshman class, 60 percent of the applicants were accepted.

For Further Information Contact Ms. Mary Ellen Stepanski, Admission Counselor Assistant/Receptionist, Mount Mary College, 2900 North Menomonee River Parkway, Milwaukee, WI 53222-4597. *Telephone:* 414-258-4810 Ext. 219. *Fax:* 414-256-0180. *E-mail:* admiss@mtmary.edu. *Web site:* http://www.mtmary.edu/.

See page 272 for the College Close-Up.

NORTHLAND COLLEGE
Ashland, Wisconsin

Northland College is a coed, private, four-year college, founded in 1892, affiliated with the United Church of Christ, offering degrees at the bachelor's level. It has a 130-acre campus in Ashland.

Academic Information The faculty has 73 members (56% full-time), 58% with terminal degrees. The student-faculty ratio is 12:1. The library holds 75,000 titles and 260 serial subscriptions. Special programs include services for learning-disabled students, an honors program, cooperative (work-study) education, study abroad, advanced placement credit, accelerated degree programs, double majors, independent study, distance learning, self-designed majors, summer session for credit, part-time degree programs (daytime, evenings, summer), adult/continuing education programs, internships, and arrangement for off-campus study with members of the May Term Consortium, Allegheny College, Beloit College, Ecoleaglue. The most frequently chosen baccalaureate fields are education, business/marketing, natural resources/environmental science.

Student Body Statistics The student body is made up of 692 undergraduates (181 freshmen). 57 percent are women and 43 percent are men. Students come from 44 states and territories and 4 other countries. 44 percent are from Wisconsin. 1.3 percent are international students.

Expenses for 2007–08 *Application fee:* $0. *Comprehensive fee:* $28,061 includes full-time tuition ($21,300), mandatory fees ($601), and college room and board ($6160). *College room only:* $2490. *Part-time tuition:* $410 per credit.

Financial Aid Forms of aid include need-based and non-need-based scholarships and part-time jobs. The average aided 2006–07 undergraduate received an aid package worth an estimated $16,008. The priority application deadline for financial aid is April 15.

Freshman Admission Northland College requires an essay, a high school transcript, 1 recommendation, SAT or ACT scores, and TOEFL scores for international students. A minimum 2.0 high school GPA and an interview are recommended. The application deadline for regular admission is May 1.

Transfer Admission The application deadline for admission is May 1.

Entrance Difficulty Northland College assesses its entrance difficulty level as moderately difficult. For the fall 2006 freshman class, 57 percent of the applicants were accepted.

For Further Information Contact Mr. Jason Turley, Director of Admission, Northland College, 1411 Ellis Avenue, Ashland, WI 54806. *Telephone:* 715-682-1224, 800-753-1840 (toll-free in-state), or 800-753-1040 (toll-free out-of-state). *Fax:* 715-682-1258. *E-mail:* admit@northland.edu. *Web site:* http://www.northland.edu/.

RIPON COLLEGE
Ripon, Wisconsin

Ripon College is a coed, private, four-year college, founded in 1851, offering degrees at the bachelor's level. It has a 250-acre campus in Ripon near Milwaukee.

Academic Information The faculty has 91 members (55% full-time), 70% with terminal degrees. The student-faculty ratio is 13:1. The library holds 160,988 titles, 939 serial subscriptions, and 227 audiovisual materials. Special programs include services for learning-disabled students, study abroad, advanced placement credit, accelerated degree programs, double majors, self-designed majors, part-time degree programs (daytime), internships, and arrangement for off-campus study with American

University, Newberry Library, Oak Ridge National Laboratory, University of Chicago, Associated Colleges of the Midwest Wilderness Field Station. The most frequently chosen baccalaureate fields are education, biological/life sciences, social sciences.

Student Body Statistics The student body is made up of 977 undergraduates (264 freshmen). 54 percent are women and 46 percent are men. Students come from 30 states and territories and 10 other countries. 75 percent are from Wisconsin. 0.9 percent are international students. 24 percent of the 2006 graduating class went on to graduate and professional schools.

Expenses for 2006–07 *Application fee:* $30. *Comprehensive fee:* $28,497 includes full-time tuition ($22,162), mandatory fees ($275), and college room and board ($6060). *College room only:* $3030. *Part-time tuition:* $890 per credit.

Financial Aid Forms of aid include need-based and non-need-based scholarships and part-time jobs. The average aided 2006–07 undergraduate received an aid package worth an estimated $19,019. The priority application deadline for financial aid is March 1.

Freshman Admission Ripon College requires an essay, a high school transcript, a minimum 2.0 high school GPA, 1 recommendation, SAT or ACT scores, and TOEFL scores for international students. An interview is recommended. The application deadline for regular admission is rolling.

Transfer Admission The application deadline for admission is rolling.

Entrance Difficulty Ripon College assesses its entrance difficulty level as moderately difficult. For the fall 2006 freshman class, 78 percent of the applicants were accepted.

For Further Information Contact Office of Admission, Ripon College, 300 Seward Street, PO Box 248, Ripon, WI 54971. *Telephone:* 920-748-8114 or 800-947-4766 (toll-free). *Fax:* 920-748-8335. *E-mail:* adminfo@ripon.edu. *Web site:* http://www.ripon.edu/.

ST. NORBERT COLLEGE
De Pere, Wisconsin

St. Norbert College is a coed, private, Roman Catholic, comprehensive institution, founded in 1898, offering degrees at the bachelor's and master's levels. It has a 92-acre campus in De Pere.

Academic Information The faculty has 179 members (61% full-time), 71% with terminal degrees. The undergraduate student-faculty ratio is 14:1. The library holds 223,096 titles, 580 serial subscriptions, and 6,640 audiovisual materials. Special programs include academic remediation, services for learning-disabled students, an honors program, study abroad, advanced placement credit, ESL programs, double majors, independent study, self-designed majors, summer session for credit, part-time degree programs (daytime, summer), internships, and arrangement for off-campus study with Higher Education Consortium for Urban Affairs, American University. The most frequently chosen baccalaureate fields are business/marketing, communications/journalism, education.

Student Body Statistics The student body totals 2,072, of whom 2,015 are undergraduates (552 freshmen). 56 percent are women and 44 percent are men. Students come from 23 states and territories and 27 other countries. 74 percent are from Wisconsin. 1.7 percent are international students. 13 percent of the 2006 graduating class went on to graduate and professional schools.

Expenses for 2006–07 *Application fee:* $25. *Comprehensive fee:* $29,816 includes full-time tuition ($23,097), mandatory fees ($400), and college room and board ($6319). *College room only:* $3349. Full-time tuition and fees vary according to course load. Room and board charges vary according to board plan, housing facility, and student level. *Part-time tuition:* $722 per credit. Part-time tuition varies according to course load.

Financial Aid Forms of aid include need-based and non-need-based scholarships and part-time jobs. The average aided 2006–07 undergraduate received an aid package worth an estimated $17,303. The priority application deadline for financial aid is March 1.

Freshman Admission St. Norbert College requires a high school transcript, 1 recommendation, SAT or ACT scores, and TOEFL scores for international students. An essay is recommended. An interview is required for some. The application deadline for regular admission is rolling and for early decision it is December 1.

Transfer Admission The application deadline for admission is rolling.

Entrance Difficulty St. Norbert College assesses its entrance difficulty level as moderately difficult. For the fall 2006 freshman class, 88 percent of the applicants were accepted.

For Further Information Contact Ms. Bridget O'Connor, Interim Vice President for Enrollment Management and Communications, St. Norbert College, 100 Grant Street, De Pere, WI 54115-2099. *Telephone:* 920-403-3005 or 800-236-4878 (toll-free). *Fax:* 920-403-4072. *E-mail:* admit@snc.edu. *Web site:* http://www.snc.edu/.

SILVER LAKE COLLEGE
Manitowoc, Wisconsin

Silver Lake College is a coed, private, Roman Catholic, comprehensive institution, founded in 1869, offering degrees at the associate, bachelor's, and master's levels and postbachelor's certificates. It has a 30-acre campus in Manitowoc near Milwaukee.

Academic Information The faculty has 278 members (15% full-time), 15% with terminal degrees. The undergraduate student-faculty ratio is 9:1. The library holds 61,574 titles, 277 serial subscriptions, and 8,631 audiovisual materials. Special programs include academic remediation, cooperative (work-study) education, advanced placement credit, accelerated degree programs, ESL programs, double majors, independent study, distance learning, self-designed majors, summer session for credit, part-time degree programs (daytime, evenings, weekends, summer), adult/continuing education programs, and internships. The most frequently chosen baccalaureate fields are business/marketing, education, psychology.

Student Body Statistics The student body totals 939, of whom 628 are undergraduates (31 freshmen). 73 percent are women and 27 percent are men. Students come from 4 states and territories and 3 other countries. 96 percent are from Wisconsin. 1.1 percent are international students. 8.3 percent of the 2006 graduating class went on to graduate and professional schools.

Expenses for 2007–08 *Application fee:* $35. *Tuition:* $17,980 full-time, $565 per credit part-time. *Mandatory fees:* $308 full-time. *College room only:* $4650.

Financial Aid Forms of aid include need-based and non-need-based scholarships, athletic grants, and part-time jobs. The average aided 2006–07 undergraduate received an aid package worth an estimated $12,054. The priority application deadline for financial aid is March 15.

Freshman Admission Silver Lake College requires a high school transcript, a minimum 2.0 high school GPA, SAT or ACT scores, and TOEFL scores for international students. An interview and audition are required for some. The application deadline for regular admission is August 1.

Transfer Admission The application deadline for admission is August 1.

Entrance Difficulty Silver Lake College assesses its entrance difficulty level as minimally difficult. For the fall 2006 freshman class, 76 percent of the applicants were accepted.

For Further Information Contact Ms. Janis Algozine, Vice President, Dean of Students, Silver Lake College, 2406 South Alverno Road, Manitowoc, WI 54220. *Telephone:* 920-686-6192 Ext. 192 or 800-236-4752 Ext. 175 (toll-free in-state). *Fax:* 920-684-7082. *E-mail:* admslc@silver.sl.edu. *Web site:* http://www.sl.edu/.

STRATTON COLLEGE
See Bryant and Stratton College.

UNIVERSITY OF PHOENIX–WISCONSIN CAMPUS
Brookfield, Wisconsin

University of Phoenix–Wisconsin Campus is a coed, proprietary, comprehensive institution, founded in 2001, offering degrees at the bachelor's and master's levels.

University of Phoenix–Wisconsin Campus (continued)

Academic Information The faculty has 238 members (5% full-time). The undergraduate student-faculty ratio is 6:1. The library holds 1,959 titles and 692 serial subscriptions. Special programs include services for learning-disabled students, advanced placement credit, accelerated degree programs, independent study, distance learning, external degree programs, and adult/continuing education programs. The most frequently chosen baccalaureate fields are business/marketing, computer and information sciences.

Student Body Statistics The student body totals 1,132, of whom 883 are undergraduates (15 freshmen). 59 percent are women and 41 percent are men. 4.3 percent are international students.

Expenses for 2006–07 *Application fee:* $45. *Tuition:* $11,010 full-time, $367 per credit part-time.

Financial Aid Forms of aid include need-based and non-need-based scholarships. The average aided 2005–06 undergraduate received an aid package worth $3918. The application deadline for financial aid is continuous.

Freshman Admission University of Phoenix–Wisconsin Campus requires 1 recommendation and TOEFL scores for international students. A high school transcript is required for some. The application deadline for regular admission is rolling.

Transfer Admission The application deadline for admission is rolling.

Entrance Difficulty University of Phoenix–Wisconsin Campus has an open admission policy.

For Further Information Contact Ms. Beth Barilla, Associate Vice President, Student Admissions and Services, University of Phoenix–Wisconsin Campus, 4615 East Elwood Street, Mail Stop AA-K101, Phoenix, AZ 85040-1958. *Telephone:* 480-317-6000, 800-776-4867 (toll-free in-state), or 800-228-7240 (toll-free out-of-state). *Fax:* 480-894-1758. *E-mail:* beth.barilla@phoenix.edu. *Web site:* http://www.phoenix.edu/.

UNIVERSITY OF WISCONSIN–EAU CLAIRE

Eau Claire, Wisconsin

University of Wisconsin–Eau Claire is a coed, public, comprehensive unit of University of Wisconsin System, founded in 1916, offering degrees at the associate, bachelor's, and master's levels and post-master's and postbachelor's certificates. It has a 333-acre campus in Eau Claire.

Academic Information The faculty has 518 members (80% full-time), 74% with terminal degrees. The undergraduate student-faculty ratio is 19:1. The library holds 764,275 titles and 2,448 serial subscriptions. Special programs include academic remediation, services for learning-disabled students, an honors program, cooperative (work-study) education, study abroad, advanced placement credit, ESL programs, double majors, independent study, distance learning, summer session for credit, part-time degree programs (daytime, evenings, summer), adult/continuing education programs, internships, and arrangement for off-campus study with National Student Exchange. The most frequently chosen baccalaureate fields are business/marketing, education, health professions and related sciences.

Student Body Statistics The student body totals 10,505, of whom 10,031 are undergraduates (2,024 freshmen). 59 percent are women and 41 percent are men. Students come from 31 states and territories and 40 other countries. 78 percent are from Wisconsin. 1 percent are international students. 9 percent of the 2006 graduating class went on to graduate and professional schools.

Expenses for 2006–07 *Application fee:* $35. *State resident tuition:* $5502 full-time, $229.08 per credit part-time. *Nonresident tuition:* $12,977 full-time, $540.52 per credit part-time. Both full-time and part-time tuition varies according to reciprocity agreements. *College room and board:* $4936. *College room only:* $2640. Room and board charges vary according to board plan.

Financial Aid Forms of aid include need-based and non-need-based scholarships and part-time jobs. The priority application deadline for financial aid is April 15.

Freshman Admission University of Wisconsin–Eau Claire requires a high school transcript, rank in upper 50% of high school class, SAT or ACT scores, and TOEFL scores for international students. The application deadline for regular admission is rolling.

Transfer Admission The application deadline for admission is July 1.

Entrance Difficulty University of Wisconsin–Eau Claire assesses its entrance difficulty level as moderately difficult. For the fall 2006 freshman class, 69 percent of the applicants were accepted.

For Further Information Contact Ms. Kristina Anderson, Executive Director of Enrollment Management and Director of Admissions, University of Wisconsin–Eau Claire, PO Box 4004, Eau Claire, WI 54702-4004. *Telephone:* 715-836-5415. *Fax:* 715-836-2409. *E-mail:* admissions@uwec.edu. *Web site:* http://www.uwec.edu/.

UNIVERSITY OF WISCONSIN–GREEN BAY

Green Bay, Wisconsin

University of Wisconsin–Green Bay is a coed, public, comprehensive unit of University of Wisconsin System, founded in 1968, offering degrees at the associate, bachelor's, and master's levels and postbachelor's certificates. It has a 700-acre campus in Green Bay.

Academic Information The faculty has 285 members (62% full-time). The undergraduate student-faculty ratio is 24:1. The library holds 333,482 titles and 5,512 serial subscriptions. Special programs include academic remediation, services for learning-disabled students, study abroad, advanced placement credit, double majors, independent study, distance learning, self-designed majors, summer session for credit, part-time degree programs (daytime, evenings, weekends, summer), external degree programs, adult/continuing education programs, internships, and arrangement for off-campus study with National Student Exchange. The most frequently chosen baccalaureate fields are business/marketing, biological/life sciences, psychology.

Student Body Statistics The student body totals 5,803, of whom 5,661 are undergraduates (1,025 freshmen). 65 percent are women and 35 percent are men. Students come from 31 states and territories and 24 other countries. 95 percent are from Wisconsin. 0.5 percent are international students. 20 percent of the 2006 graduating class went on to graduate and professional schools.

Expenses for 2006–07 *Application fee:* $35. *State resident tuition:* $4568 full-time, $190 per credit part-time. *Nonresident tuition:* $12,042 full-time, $502 per credit part-time. *Mandatory fees:* $1148 full-time, $75 per credit part-time. *College room and board:* $4700. *College room only:* $3000.

Financial Aid Forms of aid include need-based and non-need-based scholarships, athletic grants, and part-time jobs. The average aided 2006–07 undergraduate received an aid package worth an estimated $8095. The priority application deadline for financial aid is April 15.

Freshman Admission University of Wisconsin–Green Bay requires a high school transcript, SAT or ACT scores, and TOEFL scores for international students. An essay is recommended. Recommendations and an interview are required for some.

Entrance Difficulty University of Wisconsin–Green Bay assesses its entrance difficulty level as moderately difficult. For the fall 2006 freshman class, 70 percent of the applicants were accepted.

For Further Information Contact Ms. Pam Harvey-Jacobs, Director of Admissions, University of Wisconsin–Green Bay, 2420 Nicolet Drive, Green Bay, WI 54311-7001. *Telephone:* 920-465-2111 or 888-367-8942 (toll-free out-of-state). *Fax:* 920-465-5754. *E-mail:* uwgb@uwgb.edu. *Web site:* http://www.uwgb.edu/.

UNIVERSITY OF WISCONSIN–LA CROSSE

La Crosse, Wisconsin

University of Wisconsin–La Crosse is a coed, public, comprehensive unit of University of Wisconsin System, founded in 1909, offering degrees at the associate, bachelor's, and master's levels. It has a 121-acre campus in La Crosse.

Academic Information The faculty has 443 members (77% full-time), 63% with terminal degrees. The undergraduate student-faculty ratio is 24:1. The library holds 687,207 titles and 1,181 serial subscriptions. Special programs include academic remediation, services for learning-disabled students, an honors program, cooperative (work-study) education, study abroad, advanced placement credit, Freshman Honors College, ESL programs, double majors, distance learning, summer session for credit, part-time degree programs (daytime, summer), adult/continuing education programs, internships, and arrangement for off-campus study with Viterbo College. The most frequently chosen baccalaureate fields are business/marketing, parks and recreation, social sciences.

Student Body Statistics The student body totals 9,818, of whom 8,306 are undergraduates (1,743 freshmen). 59 percent are women and 41 percent are men. Students come from 27 states and territories and 42 other countries. 85 percent are from Wisconsin. 0.8 percent are international students. 23 percent of the 2006 graduating class went on to graduate and professional schools.

Expenses for 2006–07 *Application fee:* $35. *State resident tuition:* $5555 full-time, $244.17 per credit hour part-time. *Nonresident tuition:* $12,873 full-time, $555.61 per credit hour part-time. Full-time tuition varies according to program and reciprocity agreements. Part-time tuition varies according to course load, program, and reciprocity agreements. *College room and board:* $4970. *College room only:* $2840. Room and board charges vary according to board plan.

Financial Aid Forms of aid include need-based and non-need-based scholarships and part-time jobs. The average aided 2005–06 undergraduate received an aid package worth $5461.

Freshman Admission University of Wisconsin–La Crosse requires a high school transcript and SAT or ACT scores. An essay, ACT scores, and TOEFL scores for international students are recommended. An interview is required for some. The application deadline for regular admission is rolling.

Transfer Admission The application deadline for admission is rolling.

Entrance Difficulty University of Wisconsin–La Crosse assesses its entrance difficulty level as moderately difficult. For the fall 2006 freshman class, 64 percent of the applicants were accepted.

For Further Information Contact Ms. Kathryn Kiefer, Director of Admissions, University of Wisconsin–La Crosse, 1725 State Street, LaCrosse, WI 54601. *Telephone:* 608-785-8939. *Fax:* 608-785-8940. *E-mail:* admissions@uwlax.edu. *Web site:* http://www.uwlax.edu.

UNIVERSITY OF WISCONSIN–MADISON
Madison, Wisconsin

University of Wisconsin–Madison is a coed, public unit of University of Wisconsin System, founded in 1848, offering degrees at the bachelor's, master's, doctoral, and first professional levels and post-master's and first professional certificates. It has a 1,050-acre campus in Madison near Milwaukee.

Academic Information The faculty has 2,975 members (79% full-time), 87% with terminal degrees. The undergraduate student-faculty ratio is 13:1. Special programs include services for learning-disabled students, an honors program, cooperative (work-study) education, study abroad, advanced placement credit, accelerated degree programs, ESL programs, double majors, independent study, distance learning, self-designed majors, summer session for credit, part-time degree programs (daytime, evenings), adult/continuing education programs, and internships. The most frequently chosen baccalaureate fields are biological/life sciences, engineering, social sciences.

Student Body Statistics The student body totals 41,466, of whom 30,055 are undergraduates (5,643 freshmen). 53 percent are women and 47 percent are men. Students come from 54 states and territories and 110 other countries. 69 percent are from Wisconsin. 4 percent are international students. 69 percent of the 2006 graduating class went on to graduate and professional schools.

Expenses for 2006–07 *Application fee:* $35. *State resident tuition:* $6000 full-time, $282 per credit part-time. *Nonresident tuition:* $20,000 full-time, $866 per credit part-time. *Mandatory fees:* $726 full-time, $32.25 per credit part-time. Full-time tuition and fees vary according to degree level and reciprocity agreements. Part-time tuition and fees vary according to course load, degree level, and reciprocity agreements. *College room and board:* $6920. Room and board charges vary according to board plan, housing facility, and location.

Financial Aid Forms of aid include need-based and non-need-based scholarships, athletic grants, and part-time jobs. The average aided 2006–07 undergraduate received an aid package worth an estimated $11,818. The application deadline for financial aid is continuous.

Freshman Admission University of Wisconsin–Madison requires an essay, a high school transcript, SAT or ACT scores, and TOEFL scores for international students. The application deadline for regular admission is February 1.

Transfer Admission The application deadline for admission is February 1.

Entrance Difficulty University of Wisconsin–Madison assesses its entrance difficulty level as very difficult. For the fall 2006 freshman class, 58 percent of the applicants were accepted.

For Further Information Contact Office of Undergraduate Admissions, University of Wisconsin–Madison, 716 Langdon Street, Madison, WI 53706-1481. *Telephone:* 608-262-3961. *Fax:* 608-262-7706. *E-mail:* onwisconsin@admissions.wisc.edu. *Web site:* http://www.wisc.edu/.

UNIVERSITY OF WISCONSIN–MILWAUKEE
Milwaukee, Wisconsin

University of Wisconsin–Milwaukee is a coed, public unit of University of Wisconsin System, founded in 1956, offering degrees at the bachelor's, master's, and doctoral levels and post-master's and postbachelor's certificates. It has a 90-acre campus in Milwaukee.

Academic Information The faculty has 1,444 members (75% full-time), 67% with terminal degrees. The undergraduate student-faculty ratio is 20:1. The library holds 1 million titles and 8,240 serial subscriptions. Special programs include academic remediation, services for learning-disabled students, an honors program, cooperative (work-study) education, study abroad, advanced placement credit, accelerated degree programs, ESL programs, double majors, independent study, distance learning, self-designed majors, summer session for credit, part-time degree programs, adult/continuing education programs, internships, and arrangement for off-campus study with University of Wisconsin-Parkside. The most frequently chosen baccalaureate fields are business/marketing, education, health professions and related sciences.

Student Body Statistics The student body totals 28,309, of whom 23,595 are undergraduates (4,090 freshmen). 53 percent are women and 47 percent are men. Students come from 53 states and territories and 40 other countries. 97 percent are from Wisconsin. 0.6 percent are international students.

Expenses for 2006–07 *Application fee:* $35. *State resident tuition:* $6630 full-time, $244.50 per credit part-time. *Nonresident tuition:* $16,232 full-time, $644.58 per credit part-time. *Mandatory fees:* $762 full-time. Full-time tuition and fees vary according to location, program, and reciprocity agreements. Part-time tuition varies according to course load, location, program, and reciprocity agreements. *College room and board:* $5314. *College room only:* $3304. Room and board charges vary according to board plan and housing facility.

Financial Aid Forms of aid include need-based and non-need-based scholarships, athletic grants, and part-time jobs. The average aided 2006–07 undergraduate received an aid package worth an estimated $6266. The priority application deadline for financial aid is March 1.

Freshman Admission University of Wisconsin–Milwaukee requires a high school transcript, SAT or ACT scores, TOEFL scores for international students, and ACT for state residents. An essay is recommended. The application deadline for regular admission is August 1.

Transfer Admission The application deadline for admission is August 1.

Entrance Difficulty University of Wisconsin–Milwaukee assesses its entrance difficulty level as moderately difficult. For the fall 2006 freshman class, 78 percent of the applicants were accepted.

For Further Information Contact Ms. Jan Ford, Director, Recruitment and Outreach, University of Wisconsin–Milwaukee, PO Box 749, Milwaukee, WI 53201. *Telephone:* 414-229-4397. *Fax:* 414-229-6940. *E-mail:* uwmlook@uwm.edu. *Web site:* http://www.uwm.edu/.

UNIVERSITY OF WISCONSIN–OSHKOSH
Oshkosh, Wisconsin

University of Wisconsin–Oshkosh is a coed, public, comprehensive unit of University of Wisconsin System, founded in 1871, offering

University of Wisconsin–Oshkosh (continued)
degrees at the associate, bachelor's, and master's levels. It has a 192-acre campus in Oshkosh near Milwaukee.

Academic Information The faculty has 560 members (67% full-time), 66% with terminal degrees. The undergraduate student-faculty ratio is 22:1. The library holds 446,774 titles and 5,219 serial subscriptions. Special programs include academic remediation, services for learning-disabled students, an honors program, cooperative (work-study) education, study abroad, advanced placement credit, accelerated degree programs, ESL programs, double majors, independent study, distance learning, self-designed majors, summer session for credit, part-time degree programs (daytime, evenings, weekends, summer), adult/continuing education programs, and internships. The most frequently chosen baccalaureate fields are business/marketing, education, health professions and related sciences.

Student Body Statistics The student body totals 11,080, of whom 9,780 are undergraduates (1,769 freshmen). 59 percent are women and 41 percent are men. Students come from 30 states and territories and 32 other countries. 98 percent are from Wisconsin. 0.7 percent are international students.

Expenses for 2006–07 *Application fee:* $35. *State resident tuition:* $5364 full-time, $225 per credit hour part-time. *Nonresident tuition:* $12,838 full-time, $537 per credit hour part-time. *College room and board:* $5164. *College room only:* $3034.

Financial Aid Forms of aid include need-based and non-need-based scholarships and part-time jobs. The priority application deadline for financial aid is March 15.

Freshman Admission University of Wisconsin–Oshkosh requires a high school transcript, rank in upper 50% of high school class or ACT composite score of 23 or above, SAT or ACT scores, TOEFL scores for international students, and ACT required for state residents. An essay is recommended. The application deadline for regular admission is rolling.

Transfer Admission The application deadline for admission is rolling.

Entrance Difficulty University of Wisconsin–Oshkosh assesses its entrance difficulty level as moderately difficult. For the fall 2006 freshman class, 80 percent of the applicants were accepted.

For Further Information Contact Mr. Richard Hillman, Associate Director of Admissions, University of Wisconsin–Oshkosh, 800 Algoma Boulevard, Oshkosh, WI 54901. *Telephone:* 920-424-0202. *E-mail:* oshadmuw@uwosh.edu. *Web site:* http://www.uwosh.edu/.

UNIVERSITY OF WISCONSIN–PARKSIDE
Kenosha, Wisconsin

University of Wisconsin–Parkside is a coed, public, comprehensive unit of University of Wisconsin System, founded in 1968, offering degrees at the bachelor's and master's levels. It has a 700-acre campus in Kenosha near Chicago and Milwaukee.

Academic Information The faculty has 271 members (60% full-time), 53% with terminal degrees. The undergraduate student-faculty ratio is 20:1. The library holds 400,000 titles and 1,590 serial subscriptions. Special programs include academic remediation, services for learning-disabled students, an honors program, study abroad, advanced placement credit, accelerated degree programs, ESL programs, double majors, independent study, distance learning, summer session for credit, part-time degree programs (daytime, evenings, weekends, summer), external degree programs, internships, and arrangement for off-campus study with Carthage College. The most frequently chosen baccalaureate fields are business/marketing, security and protective services, social sciences.

Student Body Statistics The student body totals 4,914, of whom 4,802 are undergraduates (906 freshmen). 56 percent are women and 44 percent are men. Students come from 23 states and territories and 12 other countries. 91 percent are from Wisconsin. 1.1 percent are international students. 15.2 percent of the 2006 graduating class went on to graduate and professional schools.

Expenses for 2006–07 *Application fee:* $35. *One-time mandatory fee:* $107. *State resident tuition:* $4568 full-time, $190 per credit part-time. *Nonresident tuition:* $12,042 full-time, $502 per credit part-time. *Mandatory fees:* $818 full-time, $34 per credit part-time. Full-time tuition and fees vary according to course load and reciprocity agreements. Part-time tuition and fees vary according to course load. *College room and board:* $5277. *College room only:* $3217. Room and board charges vary according to board plan and housing facility.

Financial Aid Forms of aid include need-based and non-need-based scholarships and athletic grants. The average aided 2005–06 undergraduate received an aid package worth $8377. The application deadline for financial aid is continuous.

Freshman Admission University of Wisconsin–Parkside requires a high school transcript, minimum of 17 high school units distributed as specified in the UW-Parkside catalog, and TOEFL scores for international students. SAT or ACT scores are required for some. The application deadline for regular admission is August 1.

Transfer Admission The application deadline for admission is August 1.

Entrance Difficulty University of Wisconsin–Parkside assesses its entrance difficulty level as moderately difficult; very difficult for international students. For the fall 2006 freshman class, 81 percent of the applicants were accepted.

For Further Information Contact Mr. Matthew Jensen, Director of Admissions, University of Wisconsin–Parkside, PO Box 2000, 900 Wood Road, Kenosha, WI 53141-2000. *Telephone:* 262-595-2784. *Fax:* 262-595-2008. *E-mail:* matthew.jensen@uwp.edu. *Web site:* http://www.uwp.edu/.

UNIVERSITY OF WISCONSIN–PLATTEVILLE
Platteville, Wisconsin

University of Wisconsin–Platteville is a coed, public, comprehensive unit of University of Wisconsin System, founded in 1866, offering degrees at the associate, bachelor's, and master's levels. It has a 380-acre campus in Platteville.

Academic Information The faculty has 356 members (74% full-time), 65% with terminal degrees. The undergraduate student-faculty ratio is 20:1. The library holds 362,247 titles and 2,116 serial subscriptions. Special programs include academic remediation, services for learning-disabled students, an honors program, cooperative (work-study) education, study abroad, advanced placement credit, ESL programs, double majors, independent study, distance learning, self-designed majors, summer session for credit, part-time degree programs (daytime, evenings, weekends, summer), external degree programs, adult/continuing education programs, internships, and arrangement for off-campus study with Westfield State College. The most frequently chosen baccalaureate fields are business/marketing, education, engineering.

Student Body Statistics The student body totals 6,732, of whom 6,084 are undergraduates (1,384 freshmen). 36 percent are women and 64 percent are men. Students come from 15 states and territories and 13 other countries. 90 percent are from Wisconsin. 0.4 percent are international students.

Expenses for 2006–07 *Application fee:* $35. *State resident tuition:* $4568 full-time, $190.33 per credit part-time. *Nonresident tuition:* $12,042 full-time, $501.77 per credit part-time. *Mandatory fees:* $882 full-time, $36.75 per credit part-time, $2 per term part-time. Both full-time and part-time tuition and fees vary according to course load, degree level, and reciprocity agreements. *College room and board:* $4880. *College room only:* $2624. Room and board charges vary according to board plan.

Financial Aid Forms of aid include need-based and non-need-based scholarships and part-time jobs. The priority application deadline for financial aid is March 15.

Freshman Admission University of Wisconsin–Platteville requires a high school transcript, SAT or ACT scores, and TOEFL scores for international students. An essay is recommended. Recommendations and an interview are required for some. The application deadline for regular admission is rolling.

Transfer Admission The application deadline for admission is rolling.

Entrance Difficulty University of Wisconsin–Platteville assesses its entrance difficulty level as moderately difficult. For the fall 2006 freshman class, 84 percent of the applicants were accepted.

For Further Information Contact Ms. Angela Udelhofen, Director of Admissions and Enrollment Management, University of Wisconsin–Platteville, 1 University Plaza, 120 Brigham Hall, Platteville, WI 53818-3099. *Telephone:* 608-342-1125 or 800-362-5515 (toll-free). *Fax:* 608-342-1122. *E-mail:* admit@uwplatt.edu. *Web site:* http://www.uwplatt.edu/.

UNIVERSITY OF WISCONSIN–RIVER FALLS

River Falls, Wisconsin

University of Wisconsin–River Falls is a coed, public, comprehensive unit of University of Wisconsin System, founded in 1874, offering degrees at the bachelor's and master's levels and post-master's certificates. It has a 225-acre campus in River Falls near Minneapolis–St. Paul.

Academic Information The faculty has 330 members (71% full-time). The undergraduate student-faculty ratio is 17:1. The library holds 448,088 titles, 1,660 serial subscriptions, and 7,500 audiovisual materials. Special programs include academic remediation, services for learning-disabled students, an honors program, cooperative (work-study) education, study abroad, advanced placement credit, accelerated degree programs, double majors, independent study, distance learning, self-designed majors, summer session for credit, part-time degree programs (daytime, summer), external degree programs, adult/continuing education programs, internships, and arrangement for off-campus study with National Student Exchange.

Student Body Statistics The student body totals 5,862, of whom 5,275 are undergraduates (1,296 freshmen). 60 percent are women and 40 percent are men. Students come from 40 states and territories and 18 other countries. 58 percent are from Wisconsin. 0.3 percent are international students. 19 percent of the 2006 graduating class went on to graduate and professional schools.

Expenses for 2006–07 *Application fee:* $35. *State resident tuition:* $5728 full-time, $284.13 per credit part-time. *Nonresident tuition:* $13,202 full-time, $595.57 per credit part-time. Both full-time and part-time tuition varies according to course load. *College room and board:* $4586. *College room only:* $2716. Tuition for Minnesota residents: $6320.

Financial Aid Forms of aid include need-based and non-need-based scholarships and part-time jobs. The priority application deadline for financial aid is March 15.

Freshman Admission University of Wisconsin–River Falls requires a high school transcript, ACT scores, and TOEFL scores for international students. Rank in upper 40% of high school class is recommended. The application deadline for regular admission is rolling.

Transfer Admission The application deadline for admission is rolling.

Entrance Difficulty University of Wisconsin–River Falls assesses its entrance difficulty level as moderately difficult; very difficult for elementary education majors. For the fall 2006 freshman class, 81 percent of the applicants were accepted.

For Further Information Contact Dr. Alan Tuchtenhagen, Director of Admissions, University of Wisconsin–River Falls, 410 South Third Street, 112 South Hall, River Falls, WI 54022-5001. *Telephone:* 715-425-3500. *Fax:* 715-425-0676. *E-mail:* admit@uwrf.edu. *Web site:* http://www.uwrf.edu/.

UNIVERSITY OF WISCONSIN–STEVENS POINT

Stevens Point, Wisconsin

University of Wisconsin–Stevens Point is a coed, public, comprehensive unit of University of Wisconsin System, founded in 1894, offering degrees at the associate, bachelor's, and master's levels. It has a 335-acre campus in Stevens Point.

Academic Information The faculty has 439 members (81% full-time), 78% with terminal degrees. The undergraduate student-faculty ratio is 22:1. The library holds 1 million titles, 18,428 serial subscriptions, and 8,850 audiovisual materials. Special programs include academic remediation, services for learning-disabled students, study abroad, advanced placement credit, accelerated degree programs, ESL programs, double majors, independent study, distance learning, self-designed majors, summer session for credit, part-time degree programs (daytime, evenings, summer), adult/continuing education programs, internships, and arrangement for off-campus study with University of Wisconsin campuses at Oshkosh, Eau Claire, Fond du Lac, Marinette, Marshfield, and Marathon. The most frequently chosen baccalaureate fields are business/marketing, natural resources/environmental science, social sciences.

Student Body Statistics The student body totals 8,842, of whom 8,612 are undergraduates (1,638 freshmen). 54 percent are women and 46 percent are men. Students come from 31 states and territories and 32 other countries. 94 percent are from Wisconsin. 1.6 percent are international students. 11 percent of the 2006 graduating class went on to graduate and professional schools.

Expenses for 2006–07 *Application fee:* $35. *State resident tuition:* $4568 full-time, $190 per credit part-time. *Nonresident tuition:* $12,042 full-time, $502 per credit part-time. *Mandatory fees:* $891 full-time, $79 per credit part-time. Both full-time and part-time tuition and fees vary according to course load and reciprocity agreements. *College room and board:* $4542. *College room only:* $2726.

Financial Aid Forms of aid include need-based and non-need-based scholarships and part-time jobs. The average aided 2005–06 undergraduate received an aid package worth $6887. The priority application deadline for financial aid is June 15.

Freshman Admission University of Wisconsin–Stevens Point requires a high school transcript, SAT or ACT scores, and TOEFL scores for international students. Campus visit is recommended. The application deadline for regular admission is rolling.

Transfer Admission The application deadline for admission is rolling.

Entrance Difficulty University of Wisconsin–Stevens Point assesses its entrance difficulty level as moderately difficult. For the fall 2006 freshman class, 79 percent of the applicants were accepted.

For Further Information Contact Ms. Catherine Glennon, Director of Admissions, University of Wisconsin–Stevens Point, 2100 Main Street, Stevens Point, WI 54481. *Telephone:* 715-346-2441. *Fax:* 715-346-3296. *E-mail:* admiss@uwsp.edu. *Web site:* http://www.uwsp.edu/.

UNIVERSITY OF WISCONSIN–STOUT

Menomonie, Wisconsin

University of Wisconsin–Stout is a coed, public, comprehensive unit of University of Wisconsin System, founded in 1891, offering degrees at the bachelor's and master's levels and post-master's certificates. It has a 120-acre campus in Menomonie near Minneapolis–St. Paul.

Academic Information The faculty has 390 members (84% full-time), 65% with terminal degrees. The undergraduate student-faculty ratio is 19:1. The library holds 229,986 titles, 1,784 serial subscriptions, and 16,142 audiovisual materials. Special programs include an honors program, cooperative (work-study) education, study abroad, accelerated degree programs, double majors, independent study, distance learning, part-time degree programs, external degree programs, adult/continuing education programs, internships, and arrangement for off-campus study with Fashion Institute of Technology, University of Wisconsin–Eau Claire. The most frequently chosen baccalaureate fields are business/marketing, education, visual and performing arts.

Student Body Statistics The student body totals 8,327, of whom 7,492 are undergraduates (1,506 freshmen). 49 percent are women and 51 percent are men. Students come from 26 states and territories. 69 percent are from Wisconsin. 1.1 percent are international students.

Expenses for 2007–08 *Application fee:* $35. *State resident tuition:* $5087 full-time, $170 per credit part-time. *Nonresident tuition:* $12,737 full-time, $425 per credit part-time. *Mandatory fees:* $1876 full-time. *College room and board:* $4884. *College room only:* $2990.

Financial Aid Forms of aid include need-based and non-need-based scholarships and part-time jobs. The average aided 2006–07 undergraduate received an aid package worth an estimated $8113.

Freshman Admission University of Wisconsin–Stout requires a high school transcript, SAT or ACT scores, and TOEFL scores for international students. A minimum 2.50 high school GPA is recommended. A minimum 2.75 high school GPA is required for some.

Transfer Admission The application deadline for admission is rolling.

University of Wisconsin–Stout (continued)

Entrance Difficulty University of Wisconsin–Stout assesses its entrance difficulty level as moderately difficult. For the fall 2006 freshman class, 78 percent of the applicants were accepted.

For Further Information Contact Dr. Cynthia S. Gilberts, Executive Director of Enrollment Services, University of Wisconsin–Stout, Admissions UW-Stout, Bowman Hall, Menomonie, WI 54751. *Telephone:* 715-232-2639 or 800-HI-STOUT (toll-free in-state). *Fax:* 715-232-2639. *E-mail:* admissions@uwstout.edu. *Web site:* http://www.uwstout.edu/.

UNIVERSITY OF WISCONSIN–SUPERIOR

Superior, Wisconsin

University of Wisconsin–Superior is a coed, public, comprehensive unit of University of Wisconsin System, founded in 1893, offering degrees at the bachelor's and master's levels (associate, educational specialist). It has a 230-acre campus in Superior.

Academic Information The faculty has 173 members (64% full-time), 57% with terminal degrees. The undergraduate student-faculty ratio is 18:1. The library holds 467,700 titles and 753 serial subscriptions. Special programs include academic remediation, services for learning-disabled students, an honors program, cooperative (work-study) education, study abroad, advanced placement credit, Freshman Honors College, ESL programs, double majors, independent study, distance learning, self-designed majors, summer session for credit, part-time degree programs (daytime, evenings, weekends, summer), external degree programs, adult/continuing education programs, internships, and arrangement for off-campus study with College of St. Scholastica, Northland College, University of Minnesota, Duluth. The most frequently chosen baccalaureate fields are business/marketing, communications/journalism, education.

Student Body Statistics The student body totals 2,924, of whom 2,626 are undergraduates (312 freshmen). 58 percent are women and 42 percent are men. Students come from 24 states and territories and 30 other countries. 57 percent are from Wisconsin. 4.4 percent are international students. 13 percent of the 2006 graduating class went on to graduate and professional schools.

Expenses for 2006–07 *Application fee:* $35. *State resident tuition:* $4558 full-time, $340 per credit part-time. *Nonresident tuition:* $12,043 full-time, $652 per credit part-time. *Mandatory fees:* $1009 full-time, $287.66 per unit part-time. Both full-time and part-time tuition and fees vary according to reciprocity agreements. *College room and board:* $4576. *College room only:* $2668. Room and board charges vary according to board plan and housing facility.

Financial Aid Forms of aid include need-based and non-need-based scholarships and part-time jobs. The average aided 2006–07 undergraduate received an aid package worth an estimated $6809.

Freshman Admission University of Wisconsin–Superior requires a high school transcript, SAT or ACT scores, and TOEFL scores for international students. An interview is recommended. An essay and recommendations are required for some. The application deadline for regular admission is rolling.

Transfer Admission The application deadline for admission is rolling.

Entrance Difficulty University of Wisconsin–Superior assesses its entrance difficulty level as moderately difficult. For the fall 2006 freshman class, 73 percent of the applicants were accepted.

For Further Information Contact Lee Parker, Admissions Advisor, University of Wisconsin–Superior, Belknap and Catlin, PO Box 2000, Superior, WI 54880-4500. *Telephone:* 715-394-8217 or 715-394-8230 (toll-free in-state). *Fax:* 715-394-8407. *E-mail:* admissions@uwsuper.edu. *Web site:* http://www.uwsuper.edu/.

UNIVERSITY OF WISCONSIN–WHITEWATER

Whitewater, Wisconsin

University of Wisconsin–Whitewater is a coed, public, comprehensive unit of University of Wisconsin System, founded in 1868, offering degrees at the associate, bachelor's, and master's levels. It has a 385-acre campus in Whitewater near Milwaukee.

Academic Information The faculty has 502 members (78% full-time), 74% with terminal degrees. The undergraduate student-faculty ratio is 22:1. The library holds 701,086 titles, 4,589 serial subscriptions, and 19,427 audiovisual materials. Special programs include academic remediation, services for learning-disabled students, an honors program, cooperative (work-study) education, study abroad, advanced placement credit, accelerated degree programs, ESL programs, double majors, independent study, distance learning, self-designed majors, summer session for credit, part-time degree programs (daytime, evenings, weekends, summer), external degree programs, adult/continuing education programs, and internships. The most frequently chosen baccalaureate fields are business/marketing, communications/journalism, education.

Student Body Statistics The student body totals 10,502, of whom 9,210 are undergraduates (1,805 freshmen). 51 percent are women and 49 percent are men. Students come from 23 states and territories and 25 other countries. 95 percent are from Wisconsin. 0.5 percent are international students. 10 percent of the 2006 graduating class went on to graduate and professional schools.

Expenses for 2006–07 *Application fee:* $35. *One-time mandatory fee:* $100. *State resident tuition:* $5568 full-time, $232 per credit part-time. *Nonresident tuition:* $13,042 full-time, $543 per credit part-time. *Mandatory fees:* $839 full-time, $35 per credit part-time. Full-time tuition and fees vary according to degree level and reciprocity agreements. *College room and board:* $4190. *College room only:* $2440. Room and board charges vary according to board plan.

Financial Aid Forms of aid include need-based and non-need-based scholarships and part-time jobs. The average aided 2006–07 undergraduate received an aid package worth an estimated $6773. The priority application deadline for financial aid is March 15.

Freshman Admission University of Wisconsin–Whitewater requires a high school transcript and TOEFL scores for international students. SAT or ACT scores are recommended. Recommendations, ACT scores, and SAT or ACT scores are required for some. The application deadline for regular admission is rolling.

Transfer Admission The application deadline for admission is rolling.

Entrance Difficulty University of Wisconsin–Whitewater assesses its entrance difficulty level as moderately difficult. For the fall 2006 freshman class, 76 percent of the applicants were accepted.

For Further Information Contact Mr. Stephen J. McKellips, Director of Admissions, University of Wisconsin–Whitewater, 800 West Main Street, Whitewater, WI 53190-1790. *Telephone:* 262-472-1440 Ext. 1512. *Fax:* 262-472-1515. *E-mail:* uwwadmit@uww.edu. *Web site:* http://www.uww.edu/.

VITERBO UNIVERSITY

La Crosse, Wisconsin

Viterbo University is a coed, private, Roman Catholic, comprehensive institution, founded in 1890, offering degrees at the bachelor's and master's levels. It has a 72-acre campus in La Crosse.

Academic Information The faculty has 205 members (54% full-time), 34% with terminal degrees. The undergraduate student-faculty ratio is 13:1. The library holds 92,036 titles, 466 serial subscriptions, and 6,531 audiovisual materials. Special programs include academic remediation, services for learning-disabled students, an honors program, study abroad, advanced placement credit, accelerated degree programs, double majors, independent study, distance learning, self-designed majors, summer session for credit, part-time degree programs (daytime, evenings, weekends, summer), adult/continuing education programs, internships, and arrangement for off-campus study with University of Wisconsin-La Crosse, Western Wisconsin Technical College, Viterbo Centers: West Demoine, West Allis, WI. The most frequently chosen baccalaureate fields are business/marketing, education, health professions and related sciences.

Student Body Statistics The student body totals 2,991, of whom 1,980 are undergraduates (313 freshmen). 72 percent are women and 28 percent are men. Students come from 16 states and territories and 15 other countries. 79 percent are from Wisconsin. 1.5 percent are international students. 6.5 percent of the 2006 graduating class went on to graduate and professional schools.

Expenses for 2007–08 *Application fee:* $25. *Comprehensive fee:* $24,730 includes full-time tuition ($18,170), mandatory fees ($420), and college room and board ($6140). *College room only:* $3340. *Part-time tuition:* $535 per credit. *Part-time mandatory fees:* $8 per credit.

Financial Aid Forms of aid include need-based and non-need-based scholarships, athletic grants, and part-time jobs. The priority application deadline for financial aid is March 15.

Freshman Admission Viterbo University requires a high school transcript, a minimum 2.0 high school GPA, ACT scores, and TOEFL scores for international students. An essay, 1 recommendation, an interview, and audition for theater and music; portfolio for art are required for some. The application deadline for regular admission is rolling.

Transfer Admission The application deadline for admission is rolling.

Entrance Difficulty Viterbo University assesses its entrance difficulty level as moderately difficult; most difficult for nursing programs. For the fall 2006 freshman class, 89 percent of the applicants were accepted.

For Further Information Contact Mr. Wayne Wojciechowski, Assistant Academic Vice President, Viterbo University, 900 Viterbo Drive, LaCrosse, WI 54601. *Telephone:* 608-796-3085 or 800-VITERBO Ext. 3010 (toll-free). *Fax:* 608-796-3020. *E-mail:* admission@viterbo.edu. *Web site:* http://www.viterbo.edu/.

WISCONSIN LUTHERAN COLLEGE
Milwaukee, Wisconsin

Wisconsin Lutheran College is a coed, private, four-year college, founded in 1973, affiliated with the Wisconsin Evangelical Lutheran Synod, offering degrees at the bachelor's level. It has a 48-acre campus in Milwaukee.

Academic Information The faculty has 97 members (60% full-time). The student-faculty ratio is 10:1. Special programs include services for learning-disabled students, study abroad, advanced placement credit, double majors, independent study, self-designed majors, summer session for credit, part-time degree programs (daytime, evenings), and internships.

Student Body Statistics The student body is made up of 741 undergraduates (198 freshmen). 59 percent are women and 41 percent are men. Students come from 28 states and territories and 8 other countries. 81 percent are from Wisconsin. 1.4 percent are international students.

Expenses for 2007–08 *Application fee:* $20. *Comprehensive fee:* $26,474 includes full-time tuition ($19,430), mandatory fees ($134), and college room and board ($6910). *College room only:* $3680.

Financial Aid Forms of aid include need-based and non-need-based scholarships and part-time jobs. The average aided 2006–07 undergraduate received an aid package worth an estimated $14,709. The priority application deadline for financial aid is March 1.

Freshman Admission Wisconsin Lutheran College requires a high school transcript, a minimum 2.70 high school GPA, minimum ACT score of 21, SAT or ACT scores, and TOEFL scores for international students. 1 recommendation is recommended. An interview is required for some.

Entrance Difficulty Wisconsin Lutheran College assesses its entrance difficulty level as moderately difficult. For the fall 2006 freshman class, 85 percent of the applicants were accepted.

For Further Information Contact Ms. Amanda Delaney, Wisconsin Lutheran College, 8800 West Bluemound Road, Milwaukee, WI 53226-9942. *Telephone:* 414-443-8726 or 888-WIS LUTH (toll-free). *Fax:* 414-443-8514. *E-mail:* amanda.delaney@wlc.edu. *Web site:* http://www.wlc.edu/.

Close-Ups of Colleges in the Midwest

ALBION COLLEGE
ALBION, MICHIGAN

The College

Albion College offers the powerful combination of a traditional liberal arts curriculum coupled with a strong professional focus in business, medicine, law, education, and the sciences. "Liberal Arts at Work" aptly characterizes Albion's commitment to preparing students for admission into top graduate schools and their first career assignments. All students have an opportunity to enhance their education through value-added programming in one or more academic institutes, including America's first higher education program named after the late President Gerald R. Ford, the Ford Institute for Public Service; the Carl A. Gerstacker Liberal Arts Program in Professional Management; the Pre-Med/Allied Health Institute; the Honors Institute; the Fritz Shurmur Education Institute; and the Institute for the Study of the Environment.

Albion is a national leader for the percentage of students involved in undergraduate research. It is ranked fourth in Princeton Review's *The Best 361 Colleges* for More to Do on Campus, and first among colleges and universities in Michigan. In addition, 50 percent of Albion's alumni regularly support the College, the highest percentage among schools in Michigan and among the top fifteen in the nation. Albion is among the top eighty-five private, liberal arts colleges for the number of alumni who are corporate executives, including top executives and CEOs of *Newsweek,* the Lahey Clinic (MA), PricewaterhouseCoopers, Dow Chemical, the NCAA, Avon, and the Financial Accounting Standards Board (FASB). Albion's 2005 graduate school placement was 98 percent for law, 96 percent for dental, and 94 percent for medical schools, including Harvard, Michigan, Columbia, Northwestern, Notre Dame, Vanderbilt, and Wisconsin.

Albion's 2006 fall enrollment was 1,950 students. Approximately 87 percent of Albion's students are from Michigan; the rest come from twenty-eight states and nineteen countries. Albion is a residential college and campus life is important for every student. Campus lecturers and other recent performers and speakers include James Earl Jones, Salman Rushdie, Kurt Vonnegut, Duke University basketball coach Mike Krzyzewski, Gloria Steinem, Three Doors Down, Shawn Colvin, and various federal and state legislators. The Kellogg Center, completed in 1996, provides space for concerts and dances, meeting rooms and offices for student organizations, the College bookstore, and a snack bar. The College also offers the full-service, 350-acre Nancy G. Held Equestrian Center, featuring indoor and outdoor arenas, boarding in College stables, and riding trails. The more than 100 student organizations include clubs in academic departments, student publications, a campus radio station, religious fellowship groups, the Black Student Alliance, intercollegiate and intramural athletics, and national fraternities and sororities.

Ninety-six percent of students live on campus. Residence halls, located within walking distance of other campus buildings, are coed, with separate sections for men and women. A comprehensive student services program includes a career development office that assists students in exploring career options and arranges on-campus interviews with employers and graduate schools. More than 40 percent of Albion graduates go directly to graduate or professional school each year; virtually everyone seeking immediate employment has found a position within six months of graduation. Within five years of graduation, more than 75 percent of Albion alumni have enrolled for graduate work.

Location

A 1½-hour drive west of Detroit and a 3-hour drive east of Chicago, the College is located on I-94 in the small city of Albion (population 10,000). Eight other colleges and universities, including Michigan State and the University of Michigan, are located within an hour's drive. The 225-acre main campus is a few blocks from the downtown business section. The 350-acre equestrian center is a ½ mile

from campus. Students and faculty members are very involved in community activities and regional volunteer efforts and internships.

Majors and Degrees

Albion College awards the Bachelor of Arts and Bachelor of Fine Arts degrees. Majors include American studies, anthropology and sociology, art, art history, athletic training, biology, chemistry, computer science, earth sciences, economics and management, English, French, geological sciences, German, history, human services, international studies, mathematics, music, philosophy, physical education, physics, political science, psychology, public policy, religious studies, Spanish, and speech communication and theater. Individually designed majors, created with faculty approval, are also offered. Students may be certified in secondary education and for grades K–12 in art, music, and physical education.

Preprofessional programs include business management, dentistry, law, medicine, the ministry, and veterinary medicine. Combined three-year preprofessional programs, involving three years of study at Albion and additional work at other institutions, are available in engineering, health services and nursing, natural resources management, and public policy. Students in these programs are awarded the bachelor's degree from Albion after completing one additional year of study at the participating institutions.

Academic Programs

Albion expects its students to gain a broad knowledge in the arts and sciences while also developing an area of specialization. To graduate with the Bachelor of Arts degree, students must complete 32 units (128 semester hours); to earn the Bachelor of Fine Arts degree, art majors must complete 34 units (136 semester hours). All students must pass a writing examination.

To introduce students to important areas of knowledge, Albion has a core curriculum requirement for study in the natural sciences and mathematics, the social sciences, the humanities, interdisciplinary studies, and the fine arts, together with additional studies in environmental science, ethnic studies, neuroscience, and prelaw. The core curriculum and the requirements for a major total about one half to two thirds of a student's program at Albion. The remainder can be used for electives, to complete a second major, or for a six-to eight-course sequence in business management, computer science, human services, mass communication, public service, or women's studies. Independent study and on-the-job internships for academic credit are also available. College credit can be obtained through Advanced Placement exams, College-Level Examination Program (CLEP) tests, or Albion departmental exams.

Off-Campus Programs

Albion College, together with other leading educational institutions, offers off-campus study in Australia, China, Costa Rica, the Dominican Republic, France, Germany, Great Britain, India, Ireland, Israel, Italy, Japan, Mexico, New Zealand, Russia, Spain, and several African countries. Semester-long programs are available in the United States through the Washington (D.C.) Center for Learning Alternatives, the New York City Arts Program, the Philadelphia Center, the Chicago Urban Life Center, the Newberry Library Program in the Humanities (Chicago), and the Oak Ridge National Laboratory (Tennessee). All arrangements are supervised by the Director of Off-Campus Programs.

Academic Facilities

Kresge Hall, a $45-million science and research complex, opened in fall 2006. Ferguson Hall, opened in 2003, features 24-hour computer labs and one-stop student administrative services. In the Stockwell/Mudd Libraries, researchers are helped by an online catalog of the College's book and periodical collections and by access to national databases in many different academic areas. Other prominent campus facilities include the Herrick Center for Speech and Theatre and the 144-acre Whitehouse Nature Center, used for both science instruction and recreation. The Dow Recreation and Wellness Center offers a 1/9-mile indoor track, canoe and kayak livery, multipurpose court space, indoor tennis courts, a swimming pool, weight-training facilities for physical education courses, intramural sports, individual conditioning, and wellness programs. Albion students also have access to Digital Equipment Corporation VAX 4000-200 computers and to the Internet through PCs located throughout the campus and in individual rooms. More than 500 microcomputers are available for various research activities. Albion is a leader in Michigan for wireless networking across campus, digital imaging and digital video editing capabilities, and satellite downlink services and is a member of the Internet2 group, the fastest computing and transmission system in the nation, restricted to use by the higher education and nonprofit community.

Costs

Costs for the 2006–07 academic year were $25,668 for tuition, $7406 for room and board, and $304 for the student activity fee. Laboratory fees and music lessons were additional, as were personal expenses and travel. Costs were the same for both in-state and out-of-state students.

Financial Aid

Every student admitted to Albion College receives financial assistance if need is determined from the Free Application for Federal Student Aid (FAFSA). Families should file the FAFSA as soon as possible after January 1 so that the College receives the analysis from the federal government by February 15. For each student, Albion builds a financial aid package using federal grants and loans and College aid funds. Many Michigan residents are eligible for state scholarships and grants of more than $2000 that are reserved for people attending private colleges and universities in the state. More than 50 percent of Albion students also have jobs on campus. Students must apply for admission and be accepted before a financial aid package is prepared. Students with strong academic records are also eligible for academic scholarships. These range from $9000 to full tuition. The scholarship application deadline is February 1. Students with special talent in art, music, and theater may qualify for scholarships in these areas of up to $4000.

Faculty

Ninety-two percent of Albion's faculty members hold the doctorate or terminal degree in their field. There are 135 full-time faculty members. Courses and laboratories are taught by regular faculty members and not by graduate teaching assistants. The average class size is 19. First- and second-year courses have average enrollments of 24 students, with the exception of special First Year Experience courses, which limit enrollment to 16 students. Upper-level courses average 15 students.

Albion's faculty members are dedicated to teaching at a liberal arts college. Faculty members know their students personally and are available outside class hours for discussion and counseling. They are also active scholars and researchers, as shown by the grants that they receive from the National Science Foundation, the National Endowment for the Humanities, and many other sources.

Student Government

An elected Student Senate oversees the operation of campus organizations and disburses student activity fee funds to these groups. The Board of Trustees invites Student Senate members to sit on its committees for academic and student affairs, institutional advancement, and buildings and grounds. Student representatives also sit on the faculty's Educational Policies Committee, which reviews the College curriculum.

Admission Requirements

Albion is a selective national liberal arts college, and admission is mainly based on the applicant's academic record in high school with special attention to the college-preparatory courses completed. Standard test scores from either the ACT or SAT are also an important factor but may be waived for certain students who are in the top of their class or who have special circumstances, e.g., learning disabilities. Personal qualifications and accomplishments outside the classroom are also very important. The College seeks a diverse enrollment without regard to race, religion, or national origin. In 2005, entering freshmen had an average GPA of 3.6, with an average ACT score of 25 and SAT score of 1200. Prospective freshmen can take either the SAT or ACT. These exams are not required of transfer students who have earned at least a semester of college credit. Candidates for admission are expected to be graduates of an accredited high school or preparatory school and have at least 15 acceptable credit units. Applicants should have a strong background in English, mathematics, and the laboratory and social sciences. Homeschooled applicants are reviewed on an individual basis and need to complete either the SAT or ACT. International applicants are welcome and must have a minimum TOEFL score of 550 on the paper-based test or 270 on the computer-based test and submit a Statement of Personal Finances form to show adequate financial resources beyond any Albion College scholarship that may be offered. An interview may be required. Arrangements for a personal campus visit should be made in advance in writing, by phone, or by e-mail.

Application and Information

Applications for admission are accepted at any time, but most students apply after September 1 of their senior year in high school. Before a decision is made, applicants must submit an application form and $20 application fee (there is no fee for Web applications), high school transcripts, test score results, and recommendations. Students should submit all materials by April 1. Albion is also a member of the Common Application group and accepts applications completed on its Web site. Students who wish to receive an admission decision before Albion's regular decision candidates may apply under the early application program.

Early applications need to be completed by December 1, and notification of an admission decision is mailed prior to January 1. Students do not have to make a final commitment to Albion until May 1, when the $300 enrollment deposit is required to reserve a place in the class. The deposit may be refunded if the admissions office receives a written request before May 1. Students who apply after December 1 are considered for regular decision. Notification of an admission decision is made on a regular basis beginning February 1. All applicants are encouraged to submit their application for admission prior to March 1, as students who apply after this date are considered for admission on a space-available basis. For further information, students should contact:

Albion College
611 East Porter Street
Albion, Michigan 49224

Phone: 800-858-6770 (toll-free)
Fax: 517-629-0569
E-mail: admissions@albion.edu
Web site: http://www.albion.edu

Students at Albion's Astronomical Observatory.

ALVERNO COLLEGE
MILWAUKEE, WISCONSIN

The College

Alverno College is a college like no other. Its creative hands-on learning style has gained national and worldwide praise and emulation. Hundreds of educators representing more than 200 institutions—from the United States and abroad—visit Alverno each year to study Alverno's teaching methods. The College's unique approach to evaluation and assessment provides students with a comprehensive education that takes them from the classroom to the community to a career where they can make their mark. Students receive individual attention and demonstrate what they have learned through assessments, not traditional examinations. Classes are small, and projects are student centered.

Internationally known for its innovative, abilities-based, assessment-as-learning approach to education, Alverno College is an award-winning, four-year, independent liberal arts college for women. Founded in 1887 by the School Sisters of St. Francis, Alverno has one of the most diverse student bodies in the nation. Currently, there are more than 2,370 students enrolled. The College offers bachelor's degree programs in weekday and weekend time frames, initial teacher certification programs for postgraduates, a Master of Arts in education for teachers and business professionals, a Master of Science in Nursing, and a Master of Business Administration. Alverno also offers educational licensure programs and a licensure-to-master's program.

Alverno College is accredited by the Higher Learning Commission of the North Central Association of Colleges and Schools, National Council for Accreditation of Teacher Education, Wisconsin Department of Public Instruction, Wisconsin Board of Nursing, Commission on Collegiate Nursing Education, and National Association of Schools of Music. In *U.S. News & World Report*'s 2007 edition of *America's Best Colleges*, Alverno ranked in six of eight categories within the "Programs to Look For" section.

Alverno's mission is to promote the personal and professional development of women through four areas: creating a community of learning, creating a curriculum, creating ties to the community, and creating relationships with higher education. Alverno accomplishes this by remaining focused on the student and higher education. The hallmark of an Alverno education is to prepare students for real life, not just for finals. Faculty members develop curricula that meet today's challenges.

In every class, students learn to analyze issues from a variety of perspectives, make value decisions, engage in meaningful discussion, and apply creative solutions in problem solving, abilities needed in today's changing world. Students are able to follow their own progress through Alverno's patented Diagnostic Digital Portfolio (DDP), the first-of-its-kind Web-based system. It enables each student to access feedback from faculty members, external assessors, and peers, thus developing a more reflective and autonomous learner.

Each student is required to complete one off-campus professional internship. These internships are designed to complement the classroom experience and expose each student to real-life work situations by providing insight into career options. Alverno's Career Education Center is fully integrated into the learning process, providing students with numerous services, resources, training opportunities, and tools to assist them with their career planning. Nearly 90 percent of Alverno graduates report that they are working in their chosen fields within six months of graduation.

Students take advantage of a wide variety of athletic, social, cultural, and cocurricular academic activities on- and off-campus. There are more than thirty student organizations, including service, professional, musical, cultural, and other interest groups. The Student Activities Planning Team gives students an active voice and leadership role in what happens on campus. Programming opportunities include events such as the Metropolitan Milwaukee Leadership Conference and the National Collegiate Alcohol Awareness Week.

The College's NCAA Division III athletics program provides students with five competitive sports: basketball, cross-country, soccer, softball, and volleyball. Intramural sports are also available. Alverno Presents is one of the longest-running performing arts series in the Midwest, offering such top-notch performers as Dianne Reeves, Mariza, Irma Thomas, Wynton Marsalis, Arnie Zane Dance Company, McCoy Tyner, and others. Austin Hall, the main residence hall, features the Mug Coffeehouse, run by students for students, as a place to relax and study with a latte and enjoy live music, lively discussions, large-screen TVs, and movie nights.

Alverno College features several extracurricular and cocurricular facilities on campus. Pitman Theatre is a beautiful art deco–style theater with seating for 930. The theater is the home of Alverno Presents and numerous concerts and special events each season. Wehr Hall, with seating for 375, is a state-of-the-art presentation hall designed for multimedia presentations as well as smaller performances. Alverno's Conference Center can accommodate seated dinners for up to 300 and is host to countless alumnae weddings and other celebrations each year.

The residence hall features high-speed Internet access and cable television capability in each room.

Location

Alverno's 46-acre campus is nestled in the residential Jackson Park area of Milwaukee, just minutes from downtown and the parks and beaches along the beautiful Lake Michigan shoreline. Students are only minutes away from the world-famous Milwaukee Art Museum and its Calatrava addition as well as the Marcus Center for the Performing Arts and Lakefront festival grounds, the gallery and theater districts, and Miller Park, home of the Milwaukee Brewers. The city offers a mix of trendy nightspots and chic coffee bars and has a highly eclectic dining scene.

Majors and Degrees

Alverno College is a fully accredited four-year baccalaureate institution conferring Bachelor of Arts, Bachelor of Science, Master of Arts, Master of Business Administration, and Master of Science in Nursing degrees.

Alverno offers more than sixty majors and minors, including accounting, art, art therapy, biology, business, chemistry, computer science, education, English, environmental science, global studies, history, international business, liberal studies, management, marketing, mathematics, music therapy, nursing, philosophy, political science, professional communication, psychology, religious studies, sociology, Spanish, a host of preprofessional training programs, and many other areas of study.

Academic Programs

Alverno's learning process prepares students for success. The curriculum includes academic course work as well as external experiences and develops the student's abilities in eight specific core areas: *communication, analysis, problem solving, valuing in decision making, social interaction, developing a global perspective, effective citizenship,* and *aesthetic engagement.* Each student acquires the knowledge that is needed to demonstrate learning in each of these areas, tying her studies to her personal and professional goals.

Alverno is home to Wisconsin's original Weekend College program, one of the first in the nation. The program, which began in 1977, allows students to earn their degrees in professional communication, communication management and technology, community leadership and development, international business, management, management accounting, marketing management, and nursing (RN to B.S.N.) by attending classes on alternate weekends.

Off-Campus Programs

Alverno's travel-abroad program provides students with the opportunity to study for a semester or a shorter term in such places as England, France, Japan, Mexico, Northern Ireland, and South Korea. International internship programs are continually being developed to accommodate Alverno's diverse student body. Travel courses that culminate in a trip are also available.

The students' learning experiences are enhanced by opportunities in the community and abroad through internships and international-studies programs. Students are able to apply their knowledge to real-life situations by working with mentors on site. Local organizations that regularly participate include Harley-Davidson, Miller Brewing, Milwaukee Art Museum, the mayor's office, and scores of others.

Academic Facilities

Alverno College remains one of the most technologically advanced campuses in the region, featuring a state-of-the-art Media Hub, a videoconferencing center that allows for long-distance learning, and multiple computer labs and smart classrooms. Smart rooms are equipped with a computer, TV, VCR, DVD player, document camera, overhead projector, and electronic projector screen. Portable equipment is also available.

Alverno's library provides on-site and remote access to its print, audiovisual, and electronic collection of more than 250,000 items, as well as access to worldwide resources available through technology. The library's resources and services are further enhanced through a consortium of seven local college and university libraries.

The Teaching, Learning and Technology Center is a 73,000-square-foot facility that features cutting-edge science labs, computer and multimedia centers, and an on-campus digital production facility. The center houses hundreds of networked high-tech computers plus writing devices, the latest software, digital cameras, scanners, laptops, and more. The production facility houses nonlinear digital editing equipment, allowing students to produce and edit their own projects. All of these service areas are staff supported to assist students.

The Nursing Education Building provides resources dedicated to meeting the needs of nursing students, including a library and a clinical nursing resource center. The center allows students to practice their nursing therapeutic skills and to participate in simulated clinical experiences. Computers are equipped with interactive nursing software and registered nurses serve as mentors and assessors.

Costs

For 2006–07, the tuition was $15,984–$16,728 per year, and the room and board rate was $5954 per year. Books vary by course load but average $300 per semester for full-time students. Personal expenses vary greatly by student.

Financial Aid

Financial aid is readily available based on student need, academic performance, and other criteria. Aid can take the form of scholarships, grants, loans, and campus work-study programs. Approximately 88 percent of Alverno students receive some form of financial assistance, with an average award of $11,853 per student per year. More than 100 Alverno-sponsored scholarships are available.

Faculty

Alverno's coed faculty is made up of 104 full-time members, 89 percent of whom have earned the highest degree available in their field. Faculty members also serve as academic advisers to students in their major areas of concentration. Class sizes average 20 to 25 students, and the student-faculty ratio is 13:1.

Admission Requirements

Candidates applying for admission to Alverno College directly after high school must have completed at least 17 academic units. These units should include at least 4 units in English, with the rest distributed among foreign languages, history and the social sciences, mathematics, and natural sciences. All students must have satisfactory scores on the ACT or SAT and complete an evaluation of their abilities through the Communication Placement Assessment before beginning classes.

Application and Information

Students who wish to apply for admission can apply online, or they can write, call, or e-mail the Admission Office for the necessary forms. An application is considered complete upon receipt of the application form, the application fee (waived if students apply online), a high school transcript, and SAT or ACT scores. Students may submit any additional evidence that they believe might help the College determine their capacity to benefit from an Alverno education. Alverno's admission policy permits notification of acceptance within three weeks of receipt of all credentials. Acceptance is contingent upon satisfactory completion of the secondary school courses.

For more information about Alverno College, interested students should contact:

Admission Office
Alverno College
3400 South 43rd Street
P.O. Box 343922
Milwaukee, Wisconsin 53234-3922
Phone: 414-382-6100
      800-933-3401 (toll-free)
E-mail: admissions@alverno.edu
Web site: http://www.alverno.edu

Students demonstrate panel discussion skills.

AURORA UNIVERSITY
AURORA, ILLINOIS

The University

Aurora University was founded in 1893. The school has grown substantially over the years and has taken on many new challenges. In 1938, it was one of the first small colleges to achieve regional accreditation. In 1947, the college's evening program was instituted—one of the nation's first adult education programs at a liberal arts college. In 1985, Aurora College was reorganized as Aurora University, reflecting both the increased size of the institution and the needs associated with its many new programs. In addition to the College of Arts and Sciences, the University comprises the College of Education and the College of Professional Studies (social work, nursing, and business). Today, the University enrolls 4,000 students in more than forty undergraduate programs and eleven graduate degree programs in business, social work, and education. An Ed.D. degree is offered in educational leadership. Degree programs are also offered on the shores of Geneva Lake in Williams Bay, Wisconsin. Degree programs include the B.S. in communication, marketing, organizational leadership, and recreation administration; the RN to B.S.N.; the Master of Arts in Teaching; the M.A. in Reading Instruction; the M.S. in Recreation Administration; the M.B.A.; and a weekend M.S.W. program.

The University's student body includes 600 on-campus, traditional-age students; 1,400 undergraduate commuters; 1,800 graduate students; and more than 300 students at the George Williams College campus. The majority of Aurora's students come from the upper-Midwest region, but twenty states are also represented.

Social life is based on campus, and most activities are campus-wide. Aurora has more than sixty musical, literary, religious, social, and service clubs and organizations. There are also opportunities to be involved in theater and the highly regarded University Chorale. Aurora University has a long history of excellence in both intercollegiate and intramural athletics. A member of the NCAA Division III, Aurora fields intercollegiate teams in baseball, basketball, cross country, football, golf, indoor track, soccer, softball, tennis, track, and volleyball, often with championship results.

Aurora University is accredited at the bachelor's, master's, and doctoral degree levels by the Higher Learning Commission of the North Central Association of Colleges and Schools, and its programs are accredited by the Commission on Collegiate Nursing Education, National League for Nursing Accrediting Commission, Illinois Department of Professional Regulation, Council on Social Work Education, National Recreation and Park Association/American Association of Leisure and Recreation, and Association of Collegiate Business Schools and Programs.

Location

Aurora University is located in an attractive residential neighborhood on the southwest side of Aurora, Illinois, which has a population of more than 162,000 and is the state's second-largest city. The 30-acre main campus is located only minutes from the Illinois Research and Development Corridor, the site of dozens of nationally and internationally based businesses and industries. Located within an hour's drive or train ride is Chicago, one of the most vibrant cities in the world.

Majors and Degrees

The Bachelor of Arts degree is awarded in accounting, biology, business administration, communication (media studies and professional practice), computer science, criminal justice, elementary education, English, history, management and innovation, management information technology, marketing, physical education (K–12 teacher certification), political science, professional selling and sales management, psychology, sociology, and Spanish. The Bachelor of Science degree is awarded in accounting, biology, business administration, computer science, health science (allied health, predentistry, premedicine, pre–physical therapy, and pre–veterinary studies), management and innovation, management information technology, marketing, mathematics, and physical education (athletic training and fitness and health promotion). The Bachelor of Science in Nursing and the Bachelor of Science in Social Work are also offered. The University offers supplemental majors in prelaw and secondary education as well as the YMCA Senior Director Certificate Program.

Academic Programs

Aurora University prides itself on its first-year program, which ensures that entering students can make a successful transition to college. The only private college in Illinois selected to be part of a national project to create a model of excellence for the first college year, Aurora University recognizes the unique needs of freshmen.

Aurora University offers academic programs combining a liberal arts foundation with majors emphasizing career preparation and selected concentrations. Graduates are educated to be purposeful, ethical, and proficient—equipped for worthwhile careers and productive lives and for venturing forth into a changing world.

To earn a bachelor's degree, students are required to fulfill the general degree requirements of the University and the major requirements for an approved major; complete at least 120 semester hours with a GPA of at least 2.0 on a 4.0 scale, including at least 52 semester hours at a senior college; and complete at least 30 semester hours, including the last 24 for the degree and at least 18 semester hours in the major, at Aurora University.

Entering freshmen who qualify and are highly motivated are invited to join the Honors Program. Students with an ACT of 25 and above and a high school GPA of 3.5 on a 4.0 scale are invited to join. Those in the program participate in innovative seminars, service learning, advanced course work, and other special and cultural events.

Aurora University accepts credits earned through the CLEP, DANTES, ACT-PREP, and NLN Mobility testing programs. In addition, credit based on portfolio assessment is available to students who have significant prior learning from career experience or individual study.

The University observes a semester calendar (two 16-week semesters), with classes beginning in late August and concluding in early May. A three-week May Term offers exciting course work, including international study /travel and unique intensive courses.

Off-Campus Programs

Aurora University offers travel-study programs abroad and within the United States. Recent travel/study destinations included Paris, London, Italy, South Africa, Mexico, and Hungary. The University also has off-campus classes in various locations in Illinois and Wisconsin and several degree programs at the University's George Williams campus near Lake Geneva, Wisconsin.

Academic Facilities

The major buildings at Aurora are marked by the distinctive, red-tiled roofs specified by Charles Eckhart in his donation for the original campus. Dunham Hall houses state-of-the-art computer facilities as well as the Schingoethe Center for Native American Cultures. The newest classroom building houses the Institute for Collaboration, which brings together education, health and human services, business, and government to facilitate the development of collaborative leadership. Other facilities include the fully equipped Perry Theatre, science labs, flora-fauna complex, and the College Commons. Music practice rooms, piano labs, and a spacious art studio are housed in the Parolini Center. The Charles B. Phillips Library has more than 99,000 volumes, 7,000 multimedia materials, and approximately 518 current periodical subscriptions. In addition, the library provides access to approximately 3,700 journals in electronic full text and interfaces with sixty-four other universities.

Costs

Tuition for the 2006–07 school year was $16,090 for full-time students (24–34 semester hours per year), and yearly room and board costs average $6590.

Financial Aid

Aurora University's financial aid program has been designed to make it possible for any academically qualified student to afford the benefits of a private education. The University works with students to determine the amount of their costs and to identify all available resources so that students can meet these expenses. Financial aid is awarded based on financial need as reported on the FAFSA. In addition to need-based financial aid, Aurora University offers academic scholarships, including the Board of Trustees Scholarship, Crimi Scholarship, Deans' Scholarship, Solon B. Cousins Scholarship, Aurora University Opportunity Grant, and transfer scholarships.

Faculty

The favorable student-faculty ratio of 16:1 ensures that students receive plenty of individual attention in class. Instructors also make time for students outside of class, acting as mentors and advisers, and they are eager to answer questions and join students in campus activities.

Student Government

The student body is represented by the AUSA (Aurora University Student Association), which provides funding for sixty-three student groups on campus. Students are also active members of committees ranging from faculty searches to ad hoc task forces and are provided with certain voting privileges.

Admission Requirements

The Aurora University Committee on Admission considers the complete record of a candidate for admission. The University seeks qualified students from varied geographical, cultural, economic, racial, and religious backgrounds. Admission requirements include an ACT of 20 or above, a high school GPA of 2.5 or above, and a college-preparatory curriculum. Two general qualities are considered in each candidate: academic ability, enabling the student to benefit from a high-quality academic program, and a diversity of talents and interests that can contribute to making the campus community a better and more interesting place for learning. An application for admission to Aurora University is considered on the basis of the academic ability, achievements, activities, and motivation of the student. Candidates for the Honors Program must have an ACT of 25 or higher and a high school GPA of at least 3.5 on a 4.0 scale. Transfer students with fewer than 30 semester hours of credit should apply in the same manner as freshman applicants. Transfer students with more than 15 semester hours may be admitted to Aurora University if they have a transferable overall GPA of 2.5 or higher. Aurora accepts a maximum of 90 semester hours of transfer credits from a combination of two- and four-year schools. A maximum of 68 semester hours may be transferred from two-year schools. For further information, students should contact a transfer counselor in the Office of Admission and Financial Aid.

Application and Information

To apply for admission to Aurora University, the following items should be sent to the Office of Admission and Financial Aid: a completed application form, an official transcript from the guidance counselor, and official ACT or SAT scores. Transfer students should submit official transcripts from each college or university attended, along with the completed application.

For applications and further information, students may contact:

Office of Admission and Financial Aid
Aurora University
347 South Gladstone Avenue
Aurora, Illinois 60506
Phone: 630-844-5533
      800-742-5281 (toll-free)
E-mail: admission@aurora.edu
Web site: http://www.aurora.edu

An aerial view of Aurora University in Aurora, Illinois.

BALDWIN-WALLACE COLLEGE

BEREA, OHIO

The College

Founded in 1845, Baldwin-Wallace College (B-W) in Berea, Ohio, is an accredited institution affiliated with the United Methodist Church that blends the hallmarks of a traditional liberal arts education with an emphasis on professional preparation. Baldwin-Wallace celebrates a long history of diversity and prides itself as being one of the first colleges in Ohio to admit students without regard to race or gender. That spirit of inclusiveness has flourished and evolved into a personalized approach to education—one that stresses individual growth as students learn to learn, respond to new ideas, adapt to new situations, and prepare for the certainty of change.

B-W's reputation as one of the most respected independent colleges in Ohio has led to consistent growth over the past decade and enrollment of approximately 3,000 full-time undergraduate students. The student profile shows that 30 percent of incoming freshmen come from the top 10 percent of their high school classes, with more than 60 percent in the top quarter. In addition to the traditional-aged college student, Baldwin-Wallace has helped adult learners for more than fifty years to develop skills, redirect careers, and enhance lives. Today, 600 adult learners of all ages participate in evening and weekend classes in a variety of programs that are designed to accommodate the varying learning styles and schedules of busy adult learners. Another 800 students are enrolled in part-time graduate programs in education and business administration.

Baldwin-Wallace College is an academic community committed to the liberal arts and sciences as the foundation for lifelong learning. The College fulfills this mission through a rigorous academic program that is characterized by excellence in teaching and learning within a challenging, supportive environment that enhances students' intellectual and personal growth. Baldwin-Wallace College is committed to the success of their students. In addition to receiving a top-notch liberal arts education, students also enjoy numerous opportunities for internships, faculty-directed research, and service-learning programs. Moreover, students work with their faculty advisers to develop personal action plans that are designed to help each individual student prepare fully for life after college. These programs and approaches are enhanced by B-W's student-focused faculty, close-knit community, and rich college traditions. In all, Baldwin-Wallace College provides a truly unique place to study and prepare for future success that has been the heart of B-W for more than 150 years.

More than 90 percent of Baldwin-Wallace graduates find employment or enter graduate or professional school within nine months of graduation. Recent Baldwin-Wallace graduates have been accepted at some of the finest graduate schools in the world, including Boston University, Carnegie Mellon, College of William and Mary, Eastman School of Music, Harvard, Oxford, Peabody Conservatory of Music, Pepperdine, University of Chicago, and Yale.

Location

B-W students enjoy the best of both worlds. Berea, Ohio, with its tree-lined streets, picturesque homes, and population of 19,000, is an ideal college town. At the same time, students are only 20 minutes from the heart of Cleveland, which is home to Fortune 500 companies as well as unique recreational and cultural opportunities. Cleveland is home to outstanding museums and galleries, professional sporting events, a world-class orchestra, exciting nightlife, and an extensive park system.

Majors and Degrees

Baldwin-Wallace offers the Bachelor of Arts (B.A.), Bachelor of Science (B.S.), Bachelor of Science in Education (B.S.E.), Bachelor of Music (B.M.), and the Bachelor of Music in Education (B.M.E.) degrees. Majors include accounting, art, art history, athletic training, biology, broadcasting and mass communications, business, chemistry, communication disorders, communication studies, computer information systems, computer science, criminal justice, economics, education, English, exercise science, film studies, finance, foreign languages, health and physical education, history, human resource management, international studies, management, marketing, mathematics, medical technology, neuroscience, philosophy, physics, political science, psychology, public relations, religion, sociology, sport management, and theater. Minors are available in Asian studies, diversity studies, environmental studies, geology, and leadership studies. The Conservatory of Music offers majors in arts management, music composition, music education, music history and literature, music management, music performance, music theory, music therapy, and musical theater.

Academic Programs

More than fifty majors and several 3-2 cooperative and preprofessional programs are available to traditional B-W undergraduates. Evening and weekend programs include thirteen majors and six certificate programs.

Off-Campus Programs

Baldwin-Wallace College has institutional partnerships with several other universities around the globe: Edge Hill College (England), University of the Sunshine Coast (Australia), Ewha University (Korea), Bohme Jesus (Brazil), University of Osnabrück (Germany), Kansai Gaidai University (Japan), Hong Kong Baptist University (China), University of Hull (England), Athlone Institute of Technology (Ireland), Galway May Institute of Technology (Ireland), American Business School in Paris, York St John University (England), Washington Center, New York Media Institute at Marist College, Christ College, and American University (Washington, D.C.).

In addition to traditional study-abroad programs, with students studying and living on a particular campus for the semester, B-W features a series of focused-study tours that are led by B-W faculty and staff members and examine specific topics or geographic regions. Some programs involve home-stays, while others use hostels and hotels. Quite literally, students learn while on the road. Study tours are offered on alternating academic years.

B-W often sponsors faculty-led two- to three-week seminars for credit in May, which is perfect for students who seek an international experience but do not want to be away for extended periods. Destinations in 2006 include Vienna, Prague, and Budapest. 2007 spring trips include Ecuador, Iceland, and Switzerland, and there is a Seminar in Europe and an environmental excursion to Ecuador. Most locations for study-abroad programs offered during the academic year—such as Australia, England, Italy, Korea, and Spain—are also offered during the summer term. The Semester at Sea program sends students to ten different countries—such as Brazil, Egypt, India, Japan, and Vietnam—aboard a 23,000-ton ship with 600 other college undergraduates.

Academic Facilities

The Ritter Library offers special programs, including instruction in how to use the library and a reference service to help students find specific information quickly. The library's convenient online databases, 36 million OhioLINK books, and 20,000 electronic and print periodicals offer a wealth of information. The Jones Music Library is located on the lower level of Merner-Pfeiffer Hall. Jones is the only lending music library on campus, and its collection of nearly 40,000 items composes a significant portion of Baldwin-Wallace College's music holdings. The Riemenschneider Bach Institute, located on the floor above the Jones Music Library, is the other music library at B-W and functions primarily as a research library. The Institute is a world-renowned Bach center—the guardian of priceless Bach-related manuscripts and first editions and the publisher of BACH: Journal of the Riemenschneider Bach Institute, an international journal. The Institute's facilities include a research library and a vault for manuscripts and rare books. Other resources include twenty campus computer labs; a 4,000-watt campus radio station; a multimedia lab for video digitizing and editing, Web site development, computer animation, and more; an on-campus gallery showcasing the work of student, faculty, and area artists; and the Burrell Memorial Observatory. The neuroscience lab includes a two-room vivarium, a small-animal surgery room, a neurophysical laboratory, and several rooms dedicated to behavioral observation and computer analysis.

Costs

In 2006–07, full-time (12–18 credit hours) liberal arts students paid $28,270 per academic year in tuition, room, board, and fees. Conservatory students paid $29,980 per academic year.

Financial Aid

Baldwin-Wallace's tuition ranks among the lowest and most affordable of private colleges in Ohio. To help students and their families meet the cost of a high-quality education, B-W awards more than $50 million annually to students in the form of scholarships, grants, loans, and work-study opportunities. B-W is committed to working with students and their families to offer financial support in terms of scholarships, grants, loans from government and private sources, and an array of campus employment opportunities. More than 90 percent of Baldwin-Wallace students receive some sort of financial assistance.

Merit scholarships are offered in the amounts of $6000, $8500, and $11,000 to academically exceptional incoming freshmen. The College also offers competitive awards, ranging from $1000 to $4000. Baldwin-Wallace provides scholarships for transfer students. More information is available from the Office of Financial Aid.

Faculty

Close relationships are at the heart of the B-W experience. Most classes average only 18 students, and the student-faculty ratio is 15:1. Professors share their wisdom and experience on a one-to-one basis, helping students choose classes or assisting students in their search for the perfect internship. Faculty members regularly give out their home phone numbers. From corporate executives and lifelong educators to environmentalists and practicing psychologists, B-W's more than 300 full-time and part-time faculty members bring impressive credentials in their fields. Nearly 80 percent have earned the highest degrees in their field. They are dedicated and talented teachers who want to provide an educational experience that goes well beyond the textbook.

Student Government

Student Government consists of three branches—the legislative, the executive, and the judicial. The Student Senate is the official representative body of the students of Baldwin-Wallace College. All meetings are open, and all students are welcome to participate. Senators meet with College administrators and faculty members to express the opinions of the student body in matters affecting student life and to establish and fund official student organizations. The president and vice president of the student body lead the executive branch of student government and work closely with the Senate to express student body views to the College faculty and administration. The judicial branch of the student government consists of the supreme court of the student body, which hears cases pertaining to student government and the clubs it funds. Elections for student body government occur each February. All class officers are elected by the student body and help in planning various events on campus including Homecoming, April Reign, and senior class events.

Admission Requirements

Applicants must submit the completed application (electronic or paper), a high school transcript, ACT or SAT scores, a teacher recommendation, the Secondary School Record Request Form, and the $25 application fee (waived if applying online). Transfer applicants also must submit college or university transcripts. Candidates applying to the Conservatory of Music also must complete the Conservatory Audition Portfolio.

Application and Information

The deadline for undergraduate admission is May 1. Priority admission is March 1. Applicants are notified on a rolling basis within four to six weeks of receipt of a completed application.

Office of Admission
Baldwin-Wallace College
275 Eastland Road
Berea, Ohio 44017-2088
Phone: 440-826-2222
          877-BW-APPLY (toll-free)
Fax: 440-826-3830
E-mail: info@bw.edu
Web site: http://www.bw.edu/admission

BALL STATE UNIVERSITY
MUNCIE, INDIANA

The University

Ball State University began as a small, private teacher-training school that opened in 1899. The early campus and buildings were purchased by the Ball brothers, 5 Muncie industrialists best known for making canning jars, and given to the state of Indiana in 1918. In 1922, in recognition of the generosity of the Ball family, the Indiana General Assembly changed the school's name to Ball Teachers College. The institution became a university in 1965 in recognition of its growth in enrollment, physical facilities, and the variety and quality of its educational programs.

There are 20,030 total students, and 17,082 are undergraduates. Ball State has students enrolled from forty-nine states, two territories, seventy-eight other countries, and every county in Indiana. Fifty-five percent of the students are women, and 45 percent are men. The average class size is 31 students.

There are more than 300 student organizations that provide extracurricular activities. These include leadership programs, departmental organizations, honorary societies, music groups, religious organizations, fraternities, sororities, governing groups, special-interest organizations, and service groups. The University Health Service staff members offer health education, provide care in cases of acute illness and injury while a student is in attendance, and serve as medical advisers for the University.

Location

The Ball State campus is in the mid-sized city of Muncie, Indiana, an industrial city of 70,000 people in east-central Indiana—one hour northeast of Indianapolis. The city's cultural features include the Muncie Symphony Orchestra, the Civic Theater, Minnetrista Cultural Center, and the Artists Series and Concert Series presented in the John R. Emens University–Community Auditorium located on the Ball State campus.

Majors and Degrees

Ball State offers majors in advertising, anthropology*, architecture and planning (architecture, environmental design, landscape architecture, urban planning and development), art (ceramics, drawing, general, metals, painting, photography, printmaking, sculpture, visual arts education, visual communication (graphic design)), athletic training, biology (aquatic biology and fisheries, botany, cellular and molecular, ecology, general, genetics, microbiology, wildlife, zoology), business (accounting*, business administration*, business and marketing education, economics (business*, financial analyst*, liberal arts), finance* (corporate finance management, financial institutions, financial planning), management (entrepreneurship*, human resource and organizational behavior* information systems*, operations management*), marketing*, risk management and insurance*), business administration (two-year), business information technology (two-year), chemical technology (two-year), chemistry (biochemistry and chemistry education), classical culture, classical languages, communication studies*, computer science (cooperative education, hardware systems, information systems), criminal justice and criminology*, criminal justice and criminology (two-year), dance, dietetic technology (two-year), dietetics, early childhood education, earth science (earth/space science education), elementary education, English (English/language arts education), exceptional needs (early childhood special education, hearing impaired/deaf, mild interventions, severe interventions), exercise science (aquatics, sport administration), family and consumer sciences (apparel design, family and child, family and consumer sciences education, family and consumer science–general, fashion merchandising, hospitality and food management, hospitality and food management (two-year), interior design, residential property management), French (French education), general studies, geography (comprehensive, geographic information processing and mapping, operational meteorology and climatology, travel and tourism), geology, German (German education), graphic arts management, health science (school health education), history*, industrial supervision (two-year), industrial technology (career and technical education, construction technology, technology education), international business*, Japanese (Japanese education), journalism (graphics, journalism education, magazine, news-editorial, photojournalism), Latin-American studies, Latin (Latin education), legal assistance (two-year), legal studies (business, public law), library media and computer education, life science education, manufacturing engineering technology, manufacturing technology (two-year), mathematical economics, mathematical sciences (actuarial science, applied mathematics–physics, financial mathematics, mathematics, mathematics education, statistics), mechanical engineering technology (two-year cooperative program with Purdue University), medical technology, military science (minor only), music (guitar, music composition, music education, instrumental and general music, vocal and general music, music technology, organ, piano, symphonic instruments, voice), natural resources and environmental management (environmental communication/interpretation, environmental management, land management, natural resource studies, occupational/industrial hygiene, park and recreation management), nuclear medicine technology (two-year), nursing*, philosophy*, physical education, physical science education, physics (physics education), political science*, printing technology (two-year), psychology*, public relations, public service (two-year), radiation therapy (two-year), radiography (two-year), religious studies*, respiratory therapy, social studies education, social work (B.S.W.)*, sociology*, Spanish (Spanish education), special education (also see exceptional needs), speech-language pathology, telecommunications (media studies, multimedia, news, production, sales and promotion), theater (acting, design and technology, musical theater, theater education, theatrical studies), and women's studies*.

Ball State also offers preprofessional programs in audiology, dental hygiene, dental preparation*, engineering preparation (chemical, general, and metallurgical), law, medical preparation, optometry, pharmacy, physical therapy, physician's assistant, and veterinary medicine.

The majors and preprofessional programs noted above with an asterisk (*) may be taken as part of an accelerated track, which allows students to earn a bachelor's degree in three years.

Academic Programs

Undergraduate programs combine general studies with majors and minors. Most degrees require 126 semester hours, at least a 2.0 grade point average, and the last year in residence. The academic calendar consists of fall, spring, and summer semesters and two shorter summer sessions.

The Honors College, a four-year University-wide program featuring special course offerings, colloquia, seminars, and independent study, is especially designed to challenge the talented student. University College is organized to provide support services to students who are undecided about their majors. The Learning Center provides free peer tutoring, small-group study sessions, and academic workshops to all Ball State students. Each year, freshmen through graduate students use the Learning Center's service. Freshmen who attend tutoring or study groups earn higher grade point averages than those who do not.

The University, which recognizes that there are other ways to obtain an education beside regular enrollment in a class, grants credit through any combination of credit for successful scores on Advanced Placement (AP) tests, IB, and College-Level Examination Program (CLEP) tests; credit for military service; credit by departmental examination; and credit by departmental authorization.

Off-Campus Programs

Study-abroad programs are open to all Ball State students. It gives students the opportunity to explore intercultural issues outside the classroom. Programs vary in length, location, and cost, and credit is offered for most programs so that students who participate are not required to delay graduation.

Summer programs are a popular option for students seeking short-term international experiences. The center works in coordination with the various colleges to develop discipline-specific field studies and special tours in all price ranges that appeal to students in all majors. Students receive course credit for most programs, and financial aid is applicable. Programs range in focus from ethnographic studies in British Columbia, student teaching in England, and business in Turkey or England, to architecture and urban planning in Germany and Italy.

Academic Facilities

Bracken library is one of the largest libraries in the state, with more than 1.5 million volumes, professional librarians, and wireless connectivity. Separate materials in the main library are the music collection, special collections, archives, government publications, maps, and educational resources.

Facilities on the campus also include an art museum, an observatory and planetarium, outdoor laboratories, a solar-energy research center, fully equipped science laboratories, a human-performance laboratory, state-of-the-art teaching classrooms, and music laboratories. University Computing Services provides a full range of computing and systems services for students, faculty members, and the administration.

Costs

For full-time students in 2006–07, tuition/fees (12–18 hours) were $6360 for Indiana residents or $16,736 for out-of-state residents. Room and board started at $6898; the University technology fee was $312; the Health Center fee was $138; and the residence hall technology fee was $110. The total cost was $13,818 for Indiana residents and $24,194 for out-of-state students.

Additional expenses included course fees ($2 per course for 100- and 200-level courses or $4 per course for 300- and 400-level courses); books and supplies, estimated at $800; and personal expenses and transportation, estimated at $1800–

$2100. For detailed cost information, such as special fees, prospective students should visit the Bursar's Office Web site at http://www.bsu.edu/bursar. Current Ball State students may paid their bills online at Cardinal QuickPay.

Financial Aid

Through a program of scholarships, grants, loans, and employment, Ball State's Office of Scholarships and Financial Aid provides aid for 75 percent of its students. The Free Application for Federal Student Aid (FAFSA), obtainable from a high school guidance counselor or online, should be filed no later than March 10.

Faculty

Ball State's instructional programs are carried out by 910 full-time faculty members. Over 91 percent of tenure-track faculty members have terminal degrees. Faculty members serve on the University Senate and on numerous senate and campus committees. Full-time academic advisers work with freshmen. Seven advising centers around the campus work with departments and their faculty advisers.

Student Government

The all-campus student governing group is the Ball State University Student Association, composed of executive, legislative, and judicial branches. All students are encouraged to participate in such activities as proposing changes in University policy, working for expanded and improved educational programs at Ball State, and lobbying at the city and state levels. One student is appointed to serve on the University's Board of Trustees. In addition, representatives from the Student Association are appointed to serve on numerous boards, committees, and councils on campus, including the University Senate and its committees.

Admission Requirements

Admission to Ball State is based on the strength of the student's high school curriculum, including successful completion of 4 years of English, 3 years of college-prep math (2 of algebra and 1 of geometry), 3 years of science (2 with a lab), and 3 years of social studies. A foreign language is not required but is highly recommended. Performance is measured by grades in the above courses or by the GED score. Ball State uses an Academic Index, a grade point average on a 4.0 scale computed by Ball State, based only on college-prep and academic course work completed. In addition, curricular patterns and grading trends in the above courses are considered. SAT or ACT scores must be submitted.

Transfer admission is considered if the student has a cumulative GPA of 2.0 or higher (on a 4.0 scale). Other conditions may apply. Prospective students should visit the Web site at http://www.bsu.edu/admissions for more information.

Application and Information

High school students should complete an application in the fall of their senior year. Application materials must be submitted by March 1 for priority consideration for the fall semester and by December 1 for the spring semester. Requests for visits and information should be addressed to:

Office of Admissions
Ball State University
Muncie, Indiana 47306
Phone: 765-285-8300
        800-482-4BSU (toll-free)
E-mail: askus@bsu.edu
Web site: http://www.bsu.edu/admissions

BENEDICTINE UNIVERSITY
LISLE, ILLINOIS

The University

Benedictine University was founded in 1887 as St. Procopius College. One hundred nineteen years later, the University remains committed to providing a high-quality, Catholic, liberal education for men and women. The undergraduate enrollment is more than 2,600 students. The student body comprises students of diverse ages, religions, races, and national origins. Twenty-five percent of the full-time students reside on campus.

Benedictine University is situated on a rolling, tree-covered 108-acre campus of ten major buildings with air-conditioned classrooms and modern, well-equipped laboratories. A student athletic center features three full-size basketball courts, a competition-size swimming pool, three tennis courts, and training facilities. All of the residence halls are comfortable and spacious and have access to the Internet. On-campus apartments offer one-, two-, and four-bedroom residences. Other features include a scenic lake; a student center with dining halls, lounges, a chapel, a bookstore, and meeting rooms; and the Village of Lisle–Benedictine University Sports Complex, featuring a lighted multipurpose football/soccer stadium with a nine-lane track and lighted baseball and softball fields.

Benedictine University is highly competitive in varsity sports with a total of sixteen sports. Men's varsity sports are baseball, basketball, cross-country, football, golf, soccer, swimming and diving, and track and field (indoor and outdoor). Women's varsity sports are basketball, cross-country, soccer, softball, swimming and diving, tennis, track and field (indoor and outdoor), and volleyball. Aside from varsity and intramural athletic programs, thirty-five organizations and clubs exist on campus, including student government, a student newspaper, an orchestra, a jazz group, an African-American Student Union, a Muslim Student Association, the Association of Latin American Students, campus ministry, a drama club, and various other extracurricular and academic organizations.

Benedictine University and Springfield College in Illinois became permanent partners in 2003 to bring Benedictine programs and services to the Springfield area, Illinois' state capital. Benedictine recently opened the Moser Center in nearby Naperville to meet the needs of adult students and area businesses.

At Benedictine University, the environment is strengthened by success, not size. Renowned faculty members know students by name and care as much about each student's progress as they do about their own research. Those personal relationships have produced superb results. Benedictine graduates are accepted into some of the most prestigious graduate programs in the country. Approximately two thirds of Benedictine graduates who apply to medical school are accepted, in addition to similar ratios for other health-related professional schools (optometry, pharmacy, physical therapy, and podiatry). The liberal arts curriculum has helped place the University among some of the finest small private schools in the nation.

U.S. News & World Report's 2007 rankings listed Benedictine University as a Best School in the Midwest and eighth in the region for campus diversity.

The graduate division offers the following graduate degrees in the business, education, and health areas: the Doctor of Philosophy (Ph.D.) in organization development; the Doctor of Education (Ed.D.) degree in higher education and organizational change; the Master of Business Administration (M.B.A.); the Master of Arts in Education (M.A.Ed.); the Master of Education (M.Ed.); the Master of Science (M.S.) in clinical psychology, clinical exercise physiology, management and organizational behavior, management information systems, nutrition and wellness, and science content and process; and the Master of Public Health (M.P.H.).

Adult undergraduate accelerated programs, taught by distinguished faculty members, are available in the following areas: accounting (B.B.A.), business and economics (B.A.), computer information systems (B.S.), computer science (B.S.), finance (B.A.), health administration (B.B.A.), management (B.A.M.), management and organizational behavior (B.B.A.), marketing (B.A.), nursing and health (B.S.), organizational leadership (B.A.), and psychology (B.A.). The University also offers an Associate of Arts degree in business administration in an accelerated format.

Location

Benedictine University is 25 miles west of Chicago, in suburban Lisle near Naperville, and is easily accessible from the city and suburbs via the interstate highway system. Metra trains stop in Lisle, and O'Hare International Airport is only a 30-minute drive away. In addition to the many social and cultural offerings of the Chicago metropolitan area, the University enjoys the proximity and use of Argonne National Laboratory, Fermi National Accelerator Laboratory, the Morton Arboretum, a ski hill, a riding stable, and several golf courses. The University's location in the high-tech East-West Tollway corridor gives students opportunities for internships and employment.

Majors and Degrees

Benedictine University offers programs leading to the Bachelor of Arts, Bachelor of Business Administration, and Bachelor of Science degrees. Programs are offered in accounting, biochemistry/molecular biology, biology, business and economics (concentration in sports management), chemistry, clinical laboratory science, communication arts (concentration in sports communication), computer information systems, computer science, diagnostic medical sonography, economics, elementary education, engineering science, English language and literature, environmental science, finance, health science, history, international business and economics, international studies (concentration in business and political science), management and organizational behavior, marketing, mathematics (concentration in actuarial science), music (concentration in chamber music), nuclear medicine technology, nutrition (concentration in dietetics), philosophy, physics (concentration in biological physics, engineering physics and physics), political science (concentration in prelaw), prenursing, prepharmacy, preprofessional health programs (concentration in chiropractic, dentistry, medicine, occupational therapy, optometry, physical therapy, podiatry, and veterinary medicine), psychology, radiation therapy, secondary education, social science, sociology (concentration in criminal justice), Spanish, special education, studio art, and writing and publishing.

In many areas of study, students may opt for a double major. Preprofessional health programs include chiropractic, dentistry, medicine, occupational therapy, optometry, physical therapy, podiatry, and veterinary medicine. Combined professional programs are available with cooperating institutions in clinical laboratory science, nuclear medicine technology, and engineering. A joint engineering program is offered with the Illinois Institute of Technology. A nursing program is offered in cooperation with Rush University in Chicago and the College of DuPage; a registered nurse may earn a Bachelor of Science degree in nursing. Teacher certification is available in the following majors: biology, business and economics, chemistry, English language and literature, mathematics, physics, social science, and Spanish.

Academic Programs

For graduation, a student must earn at least 120 semester hours, 55 of which must be completed at a four-year regionally accredited college. At least the final 45 semester hours must be completed at Benedictine University. The University makes selective exceptions to the normal academic residency requirement of 45 semester hours for adults who are eligible for the Degree Completion Program.

Eligibility is limited to those who have nearly completed their undergraduate studies but, for reasons of employment, career change, or family situation, found it necessary to interrupt their studies.

The Second Major Program is designed for people who already have a degree in one area and would like to gain expertise in another. This program allows the student to concentrate on courses that fulfill the requirements of a second major. The student receives a certificate upon completion.

Each year, a select number of talented and motivated prospective students are invited to participate in the Scholars Program. The program is designed to enhance the college experience by developing students' international awareness and strengthening their leadership ability.

Off-Campus Programs

Benedictine University is a member of a three-school consortium in the west suburban Chicago area through which students are able to take classes at the other member colleges. Study abroad and internships abroad are encouraged to complement a liberal education.

Academic Facilities

The Kindlon Hall of Learning and the Birck Hall of Science bring science and technology to new levels. The Birck Hall of Science houses state-of-the art computer labs, specialized science labs, a research center, and the Jurica Nature Museum.

The Kindlon Hall of Learning houses computer labs, classrooms, multimedia labs, offices, and student lounges. It is also home to the Benedictine Library, which houses more than 180,000 volumes and can be found in the building's impressive four-story tower. The library is also equipped with eleven group study rooms, a computer lab, and an instruction room.

Benedictine University has distance education classrooms that provide students with the capability to interact globally with other colleges and universities in a classroom setting. Scholl Hall houses classrooms and faculty and administrative offices.

Costs

The cost of tuition for the 2006–07 academic year was $19,800. The average cost of room and board was $6773. Mandatory fees totaled $510 and included health, technology, and student activity fees.

Financial Aid

In 2005–06, Benedictine University freshmen received approximately $4.5 million from financial aid sources that included loans, scholarship and grants, tuition remission, and employment opportunities. Ninety-eight percent of the freshman class received financial aid. The average package was $14,682. Benedictine University has dedicated more than $8 million of the annual budget to providing grants and scholarships to its students. Students who wish to apply for aid must complete the Free Application for Federal Student Aid (FAFSA), the Benedictine University application for financial aid, and the Benedictine University application for admission.

Faculty

The 12:1 student-faculty ratio allows for close interaction between students and faculty members. Of the 94 full-time faculty members, 86 percent hold a Ph.D. or the terminal professional degree in their respective fields. All students are assigned a faculty member as an adviser to help plan programs of study.

Student Government

All full-time enrolled students are automatically members of the student government. The Student Government Association (SGA) is a representative body elected annually by the students to represent their interests. The SGA is responsible for the annual allocation of the student activity fee.

Admission Requirements

The Benedictine University admission philosophy is to select students who are expected to perform successfully in the University's academic programs and become active members of the University community. Typically, Benedictine University's freshman students are in the top third of their high school graduating class, with about 50 percent in the top quarter, and report better-than-average ACT or SAT scores. A minimum of 16 units in academic subjects is required, including 4 units of English, 1 unit of algebra, 1 unit of geometry, 1 unit of history, 1 unit of laboratory science, and 2 units of foreign language. Benedictine University does admit some students who fall below these standards. These applicants receive individual consideration by the Academic Admissions Committee. When appropriate, the committee will place conditions and/or restrictions upon students to help them reach their academic potential.

Students interested in transferring to Benedictine University must have a minimum cumulative average of C (2.0 on a 4.0 scale) or better from all colleges previously attended. Official transcripts from high school and all colleges attended must be submitted directly to the Enrollment Center for evaluation. If fewer than 20 semester hours of transfer credit are submitted, an official high school transcript and SAT or ACT scores are required, and the general admission high school curriculum requirements must also be satisfied. High school information is not required with A.A. or A.S. degrees. Credits transferred from other institutions are evaluated on the basis of their equivalent at Benedictine University. Grades of D are accepted as transfer credit but do not satisfy Benedictine University requirements, which demand a minimum grade of C.

Requests for admission are considered without regard to the applicant's race, religion, gender, age, or disability.

Application and Information

Applications are reviewed on a rolling basis. Students are encouraged to apply for admission at any time after completing their junior year of high school. Transfer students may apply for admission during their last semester or quarter before anticipated transfer to Benedictine University. Earlier applications are encouraged for scholarship and financial aid opportunities.

For further information, students should contact:

Enrollment Center
Benedictine University
5700 College Road
Lisle, Illinois 60532
Phone: 630-829-6300
      888-829-6363 (toll-free outside Illinois)
Fax: 630-829-6301
E-mail: admissions@ben.edu
Web site: http://www.ben.edu

The Birck Hall of Science houses science labs, classrooms, offices, a lecture hall, and the Jurica Nature Museum.

THE COLLEGE OF WOOSTER
WOOSTER, OHIO

The College

The College of Wooster engages every student in a process of learning that places the student at its center. This ability to democratize excellence—and to infuse students with self-reliance—gives Wooster incomparable value. Some colleges reserve that heightened experience for honors students; Wooster honors every student with personal attention and the tools to develop his or her own vision. The College of Wooster acts on the conviction that everyone can benefit from an honors education. At Wooster, that philosophy enhances the entire college experience. Small classes and an accessible faculty committed to teaching ensure individual attention for every student, from First-Year Seminar to senior year, when students work one-on-one with a faculty adviser on an Independent Study project that pulls together everything they have learned in their first three years at Wooster.

Founded as a Presbyterian college in 1866, Wooster has been an independent, residential college of the liberal arts and sciences since 1969. With small classes (70 percent have fewer than 20 students) and a 11:1 student-faculty ratio, students receive close attention both in and out of the classroom.

Wooster's 1,800 students come from forty-six states and thirty countries from all backgrounds and life experiences. They are serious about their academic lives, but they are just as intense about exploring their other interests—and having fun.

Ninety-nine percent of Wooster students live on campus. First-year students can choose to live with their First-Year Seminar classmates or a mix of students from all years. After the first year, the options multiply. Wooster's thirty program houses allow students to live with a group of 7 to 14 others who share their interests. Together, they might work on a service project in the community throughout the year, from Habitat for Humanity to the Humane Society.

Close to a third of Wooster students follow their passion for making music through three choirs, a symphony orchestra, symphonic and marching bands, a jazz ensemble, four a cappella groups, and other ensembles. Three in 10 participate in intercollegiate athletics and regularly earn All-American and Academic All-American honors. In the past dozen years, 10 Wooster athletes have won the prestigious NCAA Postgraduate Scholarship.

From the improv group Don't Throw Shoes to the student-run investment club (managing a $1-million portfolio for the College's endowment) and the equestrian team to the radio station, there is something for just about every interest.

Location

The College is located in Wooster, Ohio, a city of approximately 26,000. Wooster is 55 miles southwest of Cleveland and 30 miles west of Akron. An unusually close relationship exists between the College and the community. College-community activities include the Wooster Symphony, the Ambassador Program, and a variety of volunteer and internship experiences.

Majors and Degrees

The College of Wooster offers the degrees of Bachelor of Arts, Bachelor of Music, and Bachelor of Music Education. A student may choose from more than fifty majors and programs of study, including Africana studies, anthropology, archaeology, art history, art–studio, biochemistry and molecular biology, biology, business economics, chemical physics, chemistry, classical studies (Greek, Latin, classical civilization), communication sciences and disorders, communication studies, comparative literature, computer science, cultural area studies (African studies; Latin American studies; modern Western Europe, Russia, and East Europe studies; South Asia studies), economics, English, French, geology, German (language, literature, culture), history, international relations, mathematics, music, music education, music history and literature, music performance, music theory–composition, music therapy, philosophy, physics, political science, psychology, religious studies, Russian studies, sociology, Spanish, student-designed major (e.g., journalism, neuroscience, sports medicine), theater and dance, urban studies, and women's studies. In addition, minors are available in most areas as well as Chinese, education (with licensure in elementary or secondary teaching), film studies, international business, and physical education.

Wooster offers dual-degree programs in cooperation with other institutions; such programs lead to either two bachelor's degrees (one from each institution) or a bachelor's degree from Wooster and a master's from the cooperating institution. The dual-degree programs are in the areas of architecture, dentistry, engineering, forestry and environmental studies, nursing, and social work.

The College also offers a preprofessional advising program to support those students who want to combine the study of liberal arts with preparation for a specific profession. The preprofessional advising programs provide students with advice on the development of an appropriate academic program, cocurricular and volunteer experiences, guidance on summer research opportunities, lectures by leaders in the various professions, and information about the process of selecting and applying to graduate and professional schools. Wooster's preprofessional programs are in the areas of business, medicine, veterinary medicine, law, and seminary studies.

Academic Programs

A student's academic journey begins with First-Year Seminar, a writing-intensive course that exercises their intellect and sharpens their critical faculties. In a class of no more than 15, with a professor who is also their academic adviser, students approach a wide range of texts, questioning and analyzing them to tease out meaning and then formulating arguments through extensive writing and discussion.

To ensure that they are conversant with forms of inquiry and discourse in a range of disciplines, students select courses in each of three areas: arts and humanities, history and social sciences, and mathematical and natural sciences. They also gain insight into other cultures through a course in global and cultural perspectives and another in religious perspectives.

Once a major is selected, students engage with the scholarship of that field, master its particular methodologies, and prepare to participate in the creation of knowledge themselves. There are numerous opportunities to work with faculty members on research projects (as early as the second semester of the first year), participate in internships, or study abroad.

It all culminates in the senior Independent Study (I.S.) project. Working one-on-one with a faculty adviser over the course of a year, students conduct research, create art, or shape a performance that demonstrates their understanding of a discipline and their ability to communicate that knowledge to others. It is called Independent Study, but it is a journey that the student and the faculty adviser take together. In weekly, hour-long, one-on-one meetings, the adviser helps refine and focus the topic, suggests areas for exploration, asks questions that provoke thought and creativity, and evaluates progress. Students, in turn, review and synthesize literature related to the subject, plan and conduct research in the lab, or work to realize a creative vision in the studio, recital hall, or theater. Students present drafts of their work to their advisers, who offer extensive thoughtful feedback as close collaborators.

If the I.S. project requires travel or special equipment or supplies, the College's Henry J. Copeland Fund for Independent Study can help. In a typical year, the fund disburses more than $90,000 to support a diverse array of student projects, from studying the lives of West African immigrants in Paris or producing a documentary on survivors of Hiroshima to researching ways to purify methane gas to permit its use as a renewable energy source. When the I.S. is complete, students may find themselves presenting the results at a national conference in their discipline or coauthoring papers with their advisers. (Geology professor Mark Wilson has published articles with more than 40 student coauthors.)

Throughout the I.S. project, students learn not just about a specific topic but also about how to break down any complex project into manageable pieces, develop a plan of action, and follow it through. Students learn how to analyze a problem, gather and evaluate information, propose a solution, test its validity, and communicate the results clearly and persuasively. The completed I.S. gives employers tangible proof of resourcefulness, creativity, and communication skills. It also marks the student as an independent scholar who is ready to take on graduate-level research wherever his or her interests lead.

To get a full sense of the range of possibilities, students should check out the I.S. database or read student I.S. profiles at http://academics.wooster.edu/is/.

Off-Campus Programs

Students who wish to enrich their undergraduate experience by overseas study may choose from a variety of fully accredited programs. Wooster sponsors a number of off-campus programs in the United States and abroad, and, as a member of the Great Lakes Colleges Association, offers off-campus study opportunities in more than fifty countries spanning the globe.

A variety of off-campus opportunities within the United States provide both academic and internship experiences. The Washington Semester and the Semester at the United Nations offer extensive possibilities in national and international government. Urban studies centers in Philadelphia and Portland provide many different experiential options. There is also a fine-arts semester in New York City. Other internship possibilities exist in business, the humanities, the natural sciences, and psychology.

Academic Facilities

The College libraries consist of the Andrews Library, the adjacent Flo K. Gault Library for Independent Study, and the nearby Timken Science Library in Frick Hall. Together, they contain more than 1 million books, periodicals, microforms, electronic journals, videotapes, and audio recordings. As a member of CONSORT and OhioLINK, the libraries can provide almost any book from Ohio's academic libraries within two to three days. The libraries subscribe to a wide variety of electronic databases and to some 5,000 periodicals in electronic form, all available campuswide via the computing network. The libraries house more than 300 study carrels, each of which is equipped with electrical and data connections.

Computing is an important part of Wooster's academic environment. All academic buildings and residence hall rooms are connected to the campus network. The Taylor Hall computer center houses fifty-two terminals for student use while the Wired Scot, a cyber café, features twenty-two PC workstations with Internet access, two large plasma-screen TVs, and wireless Internet access throughout the building.

The College's science facilities contain the most up-to-date laboratory equipment, libraries, computer terminals, and instrumentation, including ultraviolet, visible, fluorescence, and infrared spectrometers; a scanning electron microscope; an atomic force microscope; a nuclear magnetic resonance spectrometer; a mass spectrometer; an X-ray diffractometer; and various chromatographs.

Wooster's Learning Center provides academic support for students, and priority is given to students with identified learning disabilities. Adult tutors work with individual students on time management, organization skills, and effective study strategies. Wooster's Writing Center provides writing assistance through one-to-one tutorial sessions and group workshops covering all aspects of the writing process.

The Freedlander Theatre complex contains excellent technical equipment and a separate theater for students' experimental pro-

ductions. The speech facility houses a radio station and a speech and hearing clinic that also serves the community.

The Scheide Music Center, a 35,000-square-foot complex, contains five classrooms, eleven teaching studios, twenty-three soundproof practice rooms, a music library, and a listening lab. The Timken Rehearsal Hall and the acoustically balanced Gault Recital Hall are "tunable" so that the halls can be rendered "live" to greater or lesser degrees.

The Ebert Art Center has expansive space for studio art and art history. The building includes classrooms, individual studios for senior studio art majors, and the Sussel Art Gallery.

Costs

The comprehensive fee (room, board, tuition, and fees) for 2007–08 is $40,022.

Financial Aid

Financial assistance is awarded on merit and/or need. Need-based aid is determined by the Free Application for Federal Student Aid (FAFSA). Aid is allocated when students are admitted to the College. Applications for need-based aid should be submitted by February 15.

The College of Wooster believes in recognizing individual talent and hard work. Thus, Wooster offers merit-based scholarships that range from $2500 to $23,500 in a number of academic, performance, and leadership areas. All scholarship awards are applicable only toward tuition and are renewable for four years. Each year the College awards about $17 million in competitive scholarship funds. Students should call the Office of Admissions to request detailed information about scholarship opportunities.

Faculty

The faculty, 97 percent of whom hold a doctoral degree or terminal degree in their field, are dedicated to meeting the educational needs of individual students; they strive to help them realize their inherent potential. The student-faculty ratio is 11:1.

Student Government

The Campus Council, which consists of representatives from the student body, faculty, and administration, is the main legislative body in the areas of student life and cocurricular affairs. The Student Government Association, the Black Students Association, and the International Student Association also contribute to policymaking at Wooster. Students may attend open meetings of the faculty and are represented on virtually all faculty committees.

Admission Requirements

A candidate for admission to the College should have earned a minimum of 16 academic units in high school, with emphases in English, foreign language, mathematics, natural science, and social studies. The student must present satisfactory scores on either the SAT or the ACT. No College Board Subject Test scores are required.

The deadline for regular admission is February 15. Students are notified of the decision by April 1 and must reply by May 1. Early Decision I applicants must apply by December 1 and are notified on December 15. Early Decision II candidates must apply by January 15 and are notified by February 1. Students are encouraged to visit the campus and have a personal interview.

The College of Wooster does not discriminate on the basis of age, sex, race, creed, national origin, handicap, sexual orientation, or political affiliation in the admission of students or in their participation in College educational programs, activities, financial aid, or employment.

Application and Information

Dean of Admissions
The College of Wooster
Wooster, Ohio 44691
Phone: 330-263-2000 Ext. 2270 or 2322
        800-877-9905 (toll-free)
Fax: 330-263-2621
E-mail: admissions@wooster.edu
Web site: http://www.wooster.edu

COLUMBIA COLLEGE CHICAGO
CHICAGO, ILLINOIS

The College

Columbia College Chicago is the nation's largest and most diverse visual, performing, and media arts college. The foundation of a Columbia education features small class sizes that ensure close interaction with a faculty of working professionals, abundant internship opportunities with major employers in the Chicago and national marketplaces, and outstanding professional facilities that foster learning by doing. All students are encouraged to begin course work in their chosen fields during their freshman year, allowing them four full years in which to master their craft and build professional portfolios, audition tapes, resumes, and clip books. The College provides a strong liberal arts background for the developing artist or communicator and supports student employment goals through a full range of career services.

Columbia's enrollment of more than 11,500 students is drawn from Chicago and its suburbs, the Midwest, across the United States, and more than forty-five other countries. The student body is almost equally divided between men and women. Creative students who enjoy a supportive but challenging environment thrive at Columbia.

Columbia College Chicago's five residence halls extend the supportive philosophy of the College. There are a wide variety of available housing options, all with access to computer and study rooms, drawing and painting studio space, music practice space, fitness rooms, an indoor heated pool, lake views, and a laundry room. Apartments, suites, and rooms are fully furnished. All facilities are conveniently located steps from the main campus buildings and close to public transportation, all in the heart of downtown Chicago. Students have access to a wide range of services, including the student health center, counseling, and a broad host of artistic and academic events. Columbia College students are immersed in a creative environment both in and out of the classroom.

Outside the classroom, students participate in activities that include the College's award-winning student newspaper, radio station, electronic newsletter, two student magazines, cable television soap opera, three theaters, dance center, photography and art museums, and film and video festival. Many of the fifty student clubs on campus are linked to an academic discipline and offer opportunities to expand social and professional networking experiences. Several gallery/café environments allow students to relax or study between classes. These centers feature a variety of activities, including art exhibits, film screenings, lectures, and live performances of music, comedy, readings, or dance.

At the graduate level, Columbia awards the Master of Arts (M.A.) in arts, entertainment, and media management; creative writing and writing instruction; dance/movement therapy; interdisciplinary arts; journalism; photography; photography–museum studies; and writing instruction. The College awards the Master of Fine Arts (M.F.A.) in architectural studies, creative writing, creative writing and writing instruction, film and video, interdisciplinary book and paper arts, interior architecture, and photography. The Master of Arts in Teaching (M.A.T.) is also offered in elementary education (K–9), interdisciplinary arts education (K–12), and urban teaching.

Location

Columbia's campus is set in Chicago's dynamic South Loop neighborhood, across from Grant Park and Lake Michigan. Close to the Art Institute, Navy Pier, the Adler Planetarium, the Field Museum, the Chicago Symphony, and several other colleges and universities, Columbia's faculty members and students utilize the city of Chicago as a social, educational, and professional resource. Convenient public transportation makes all cultural and educational opportunities easily accessible.

Majors and Degrees

Columbia College grants the Bachelor of Arts (B.A.) and the Bachelor of Fine Arts (B.F.A.) degrees and the Bachelor of Music (B.M.) degree in composition. The School of Fine and Performing Arts offers majors in art and design (advertising art direction, art history, fashion design, fine arts, graphic design, illustration, interior architecture, and product design); arts, entertainment, and media management (small business/arts entrepreneurship, fashion/retail, media, music business, performing arts, sports management, and visual arts); dance; fiction writing; music (instrumental performance, vocal performance, instrumental jazz, and vocal jazz); photography; and theater (acting, directing, musical theater performance, technical theater, and theater design). The School of Media Arts offers majors in audio arts and acoustics (acoustics, audio for visual media, sound contracting, and sound reinforcement), digital media technology, film and video (alternative forms, audio for visual media, cinematography, computer animation, critical studies, directing, documentary, editing, producing, screenwriting, and traditional animation), game design, interactive arts and media, interdisciplinary (self-designed major), journalism (broadcast, magazine writing and editing, news reporting and writing, and reporting on health, science, and the environment), marketing communication (advertising, creative sports marketing, marketing, and public relations), radio (business, broadcast journalism, and talent/production), and television (broadcast journalism, interactive television, effects/postproduction, directing/production, and writing/producing). The School of Liberal Arts and Sciences offers majors in American Sign Language–English interpretation, cultural studies, early childhood education, and poetry.

Academic Programs

Columbia supports creative and integrated approaches to education and encourages interdisciplinary study. The B.A. degree is awarded to students who successfully complete 120 semester hours, and the B.F.A. degree is awarded to students who successfully complete 128 semester hours of study in designated programs. Of the required hours, 48 are distributed among courses in the humanities and literature, science and mathematics, English composition, oral communications, social sciences, and computer applications.

The College continues to expand its extensive internship program. Columbia's location allows students to intern with major employers in Chicago. Chicago provides professional settings, classrooms, and internship opportunities for Columbia students.

Columbia College Chicago's Portfolio Center is uniquely geared to provide students with professional-grade portfolio development. The Portfolio Center links industry professionals and alumni with current students through workshops, portfolio development sessions, and networking events. The center also maintains an online Portfolio Archive that serves as an invaluable resource and inspiration for students.

Off-Campus Programs

Columbia has an affiliation agreement with the American Institute for Foreign Study, which enables students to participate in study-abroad programs in numerous countries. Columbia also sponsors and participates in a variety of its own study-abroad programs. These programs include trips to Moscow and Prague. Summer programs are also offered with Dartington College in Dartington, England; the Santa Reparata International School of Art in Florence, Italy; and the University of Guadalajara in Mexico. Open to all Columbia students, the Semester in Los Angeles program is a five-week immersion program in which the student maintains full-time status while gaining invaluable real-world experience. Located in Bungalow 25 on the CBS Studio Lot in Culver City, Columbia is the only institution of higher learning to be permanently located on a studio lot.

Students are given Lot ID badges and enter the gates of the lot every day, just like working producers, directors, stars, and craft personnel.

Academic Facilities

Columbia College consists of seventeen campus buildings that are located primarily in the historic South Loop neighborhood of downtown Chicago. Advanced facilities for radio, television, art, computer graphics, photography, interactive multimedia, fashion design, and film are state-of-the-industry and include professionally equipped color and black-and-white darkrooms, digital imaging computer facilities, photography and film stages, film and video editing suites, and studios for painting, drawing, and 3-D design. The campus also includes the Museum of Contemporary Photography, one of only a few such facilities in the United States, and the Audio Technology Center, a recording production and research facility. In addition, Columbia has extensive computer facilities that are used by basic computer classes as well as dedicated computer facilities that are utilized by the departments. The centers for dance, music, and theater are separate but conveniently located and are designed for their specific performance needs, including individual and group rehearsal and specialized performance spaces.

The College's 200,000-volume library and instructional service center provides comprehensive information and study facilities. Reading/study rooms and special audiovisual equipment are available for use in individual projects and research. As a member of a statewide online computer catalog and resource-sharing network, Columbia's library provides students with access to the resources of forty-five academic institutions in Illinois, effectively creating an information base of several million volumes. The library also houses special collections, such as the George S. Lurie Memorial Collection of books and resource materials on art, photography, and film; the Black Music Resource Center of books and sound recordings; the Screenwriters' Collection of film and television manuscripts; the History of Photography microfilm collection of books and periodicals; and a nonprint collection of 100,000 slides and more than 7,300 videotapes and films. The latest addition to the library is the Albert P. Weisman Center for the Study of Contemporary Issues in Chicago Journalism. The center includes a print and audiovisual collection and a learning center that explores the development of Chicago's political and social history.

Costs

For the 2006–07 academic year, full tuition (12 to 16 credit hours) was $8164 for each fifteen-week semester, or $16,328 per year. Part-time tuition (up to 11 credit hours) was $565 per credit hour. Summer school tuition was $440 per credit hour. Some courses require additional service or laboratory fees.

To enroll at Columbia College Chicago, applicants were required to confirm their decision by submitting a $250 tuition deposit (nonrefundable after May 1, 2006). Required nonrefundable fees that were charged each semester included the registration fee, $50; the student activity fee, $60 ($30 for part-time students); the U-Pass, $75 (for unlimited access to the public transportation system); and a health center fee, $25 ($10 for part-time students). There was also a one-time $30 library deposit that was refunded when the student leaves the College.

Financial Aid

Columbia College makes every effort to help students obtain financial assistance, including grants, on-campus work, and loans. The Office of Student Financial Services administers federal and state grant and loan programs. The College also provides information for students seeking part-time employment both on and off campus. On-campus jobs are available in technical, clerical, secretarial, and food service areas. Columbia offers institution-based scholarships, such as Presidential Scholarships for freshmen, scholarships for transfer students, academic excellence awards, leadership awards, and housing grants. The Fischetti Scholarships support the efforts of outstanding Columbia journalism students, and the Weisman

Scholarships support special communication-related projects. Appropriate scholarship and applications forms for financial aid are available through the Office of Undergraduate Admissions.

Faculty

Many of Columbia's 1,340 full- and part-time faculty members are working professionals (artists, writers, filmmakers, dancers, etc.) with national reputations. The College is constantly seeking individuals who are both gifted teachers and talented professionals. Many faculty members work nearby in the disciplines in which they teach and share practical expertise with students in informal workshop settings and in the classroom. Interaction with faculty members who are practicing professionals provides students with invaluable access to the latest information in their fields. Students also begin developing their own professional network as faculty members share contacts and information on how to break into the market.

Student Government

Through the Student Government Association (SGA) and the Student Organization Council (SOC), students are able to address College-wide and departmental issues and sponsor services and activities. SGA and SOC work closely with the Office of Student Affairs and serve as liaisons to the administration and departments. The fifty campus clubs and organizations reflect the interests and the diversity of Columbia's student body. Film screenings, student-produced television shows, dance recitals, poetry readings, plays, campus radio, music concerts, and a national award–winning newspaper are just some of the campus events and activities that are available to students.

Admission Requirements

Columbia College invites applications from all students with creative ability in or inclination to the arts, media, and communication disciplines in which the College specializes. To apply for admission, students must submit high school transcripts, college transcripts (if applicable), a letter of recommendation, a personal essay, and a $35 application fee. ACT Assessment or SAT scores are not required but are strongly encouraged. Graduation from high school or an earned GED certificate is required prior to enrollment. Freshman applicants whose application materials suggest they are likely to be underprepared to meet the College's standards are required to successfully complete the Bridge Program to be admitted to the College. Columbia has a liberal transfer policy.

Application and Information

Students are strongly advised to apply early. The priority date is May 1 for the fall semester, November 15 for the spring semester, and April 15 for the summer term. Applicants are notified within two to four weeks after the College receives all the required information and documents. Students who want to live in campus housing are strongly advised to apply early. Housing assignments are offered on a first-come, first-served basis until full occupancy is achieved.

All students are invited to tour the College and meet with an admissions counselor. To arrange for a tour and an appointment with an admissions counselor, students should call the Office of Undergraduate Admissions.

For more information, students should contact:

Office of Undergraduate Admissions
Columbia College Chicago
600 South Michigan Avenue
Chicago, Illinois 60605
Phone: 312-344-7130
Fax: 312-344-8024
E-mail: admissions@colum.edu
Web site: http://www.colum.edu

CULVER-STOCKTON COLLEGE

CANTON, MISSOURI

The College

Students at Culver-Stockton College (C-SC) receive a superb education that extends far beyond the classroom. The four-year experience at C-SC expands not only the student's academic knowledge but also an awareness of the world in which they live. Besides achieving their academic goals, students receive an opportunity to develop their leadership skills, discover new interests, and form lasting relationships with classmates and faculty and staff members. These opportunities play a major part in the College's goal of creating visions of success for each student.

C-SC was founded in 1853 as the first institution of higher learning west of the Mississippi River chartered expressly for coeducation. Affiliated with the Christian Church (Disciples of Christ), the College is personal (870 students) and provides a strong career-oriented education within a liberal arts setting.

Principally residential in character, the College offers a full array of extracurricular activities, including course-related clubs and organizations, an active national fraternity and sorority system, a fine intramural program, and a strong intercollegiate athletics program featuring men's teams in baseball, basketball, football, golf, and soccer and women's teams in basketball, golf, soccer, softball, and volleyball. The College also features a coed spirit squad team and an award-winning dance team. Performance opportunities in the fine arts include outstanding choral and instrumental ensembles as well as several theater productions each year.

Culver-Stockton College has more than 10,000 living alumni, many of whom have achieved distinction in the arts, government, medicine, law, education, and other professional fields. With more than 150 years of history, Culver-Stockton College moves into the twenty-first century as one of the truly distinctive small liberal arts colleges in the Midwest.

Culver-Stockton College is fully accredited by the Higher Learning Commission of the North Central Association of Colleges and Schools, the Missouri Department of Elementary and Secondary Education, the International Assembly for Collegiate Business Education, the National Association of Schools of Music, the Commission on Accreditation of Allied Health Education Programs, the National League of Nursing, and the Commission on Collegiate Nursing Education.

Location

Canton, Missouri, a quaint town of 2,600 on the Mississippi River, sits in the rolling farmland of northeast Missouri. The College has close ties with Quincy, Illinois, a progressive, arts-oriented community of approximately 45,000. Canton is located on U.S. 61, 30 miles north of historic Hannibal, Missouri, the boyhood home of the famous American author Mark Twain. St. Louis is within a 2½-hour drive, and Chicago and Kansas City are close enough to be significant factors in the cultural life of the College. Culver-Stockton sits atop a hill that overlooks Canton and the Mississippi River. Canton exhibits a strong sense of community pride, civic involvement, and a very low crime rate.

Majors and Degrees

Culver-Stockton offers bachelor's degrees in twenty-five areas: the Bachelor of Fine Arts in art, arts management, and theater; the Bachelor of Music Education; and the Bachelor of Science in Nursing. Study areas include accounting, art, art education, arts management, athletic training, biology, business administration, communication, criminal justice, early childhood development, elementary education, English, finance, history and political science, management, management information systems, mathematics, music, music education, nursing, physical education, psychology, recreation management, religion and philosophy, secondary education, speech and theater education, and theater. Preprofes-

sional programs are available in health sciences, law, occupational therapy, and physical therapy. The College has cooperative arrangements with Washington University in occupational therapy.

Academic Programs

The Culver-Stockton emphasis on career preparation is enhanced by the liberal arts. The development of student skills in writing, speaking, critical thinking, and problem solving is a critical element in the liberal arts emphasis. In addition, core courses in composition, religious studies, and speech combine with student choices from among five areas to ensure a wide breadth of study. Students must complete 124 credit hours for the bachelor's degree. Major programs require from 30 to 62 credits. Double majors and minors are encouraged, adding further diversity and breadth to graduates' qualifications as they approach the job market.

The College has committed itself to academic distinction. Students are challenged to achieve their maximum potential in learned skills, breadth and depth of knowledge, and understanding their own values. Students are assigned an academic adviser, who is prepared to assist students in achieving their educational goals. An individualized plan is developed and then updated each semester until graduation.

For highly motivated students, including freshmen, the Honors Scholars Program provides the opportunity to participate in certain specially designated courses and events, culminating in an opportunity for independent study or research in an area of the student's special interest. The program is especially helpful for students planning for graduate programs.

Exploratory and professional internships are available in all majors and are viewed as an important part of the career selection process. More than 700 internship sites are available. Combined with an active career counseling and placement service that includes computerized interest and preference testing, on- and off-campus internships are a key element in the Culver-Stockton approach to preparing students for employment after graduation.

Work completed at other colleges and universities is transferable toward Culver-Stockton graduation requirements, and various testing procedures (e.g., CLEP, AP, PEP) allow credit for equivalent knowledge or experience. Individualized learning options are plentiful; they range from individually negotiated independent study to the option of developing an individualized major.

The College operates on a two-semester calendar, with the first semester concluding before Christmas and the spring semester ending in early to mid-May. Summer sessions of varying lengths are also available to students. All programs and classes are characterized by individual attention to the needs and interests of the student.

In January 2006, the College began offering online courses for nontraditional students through the Connected Campus program. Degree-completion programs include the Bachelor of Science in business administration and Bachelor of Science in management information systems.

Off-Campus Programs

Students at Culver-Stockton College may pursue a variety of study-abroad opportunities. For example, each January students and faculty members travel together on study-abroad trips. Recent trips have included such destinations as Austria, Greece, Great Britain, and Italy. C-SC also offers a Semester Study and International Program in London in association with the Missouri Consortium for International Programs and Studies and International Enrichment Inc. The College's wind ensemble and concert choir also take concert tours each year.

Academic Facilities

At C-SC, computer network connections are available for each student in every residence hall room and provide connections for students' personal computers for continuous access to the Internet, e-mail, the College's network, laser printers, and library holdings. Culver-Stockton offers Pentium computer clusters in every residence hall and maintains four general computer labs with Pentium workstations, the Windows operating system, and Microsoft Office as well as four specialized labs. Faculty members have integrated computers into the classroom in almost every field, using dedicated computer labs equipped with major-specific software.

The computerized Johann Memorial Library has a collection of 151,979 volumes and also presents comprehensive collections of periodicals, journals, and other materials in both hard copy and microform. Extensive interlibrary loan and electronic bibliographical search capabilities are available to both students and the faculty. C-SC belongs to the MOBIUS Consortium, which provides open access to the holdings of every academic library in Missouri. Students also have access to more than 6 million volumes through the College's link to a statewide library database.

The Robert W. Brown Performing Arts Center and Mabee Art Gallery house professional-quality art and performance studios, computer laboratories, and three performance stages where 200 to nearly 1,000 guests can attend theater and music performances.

The four-year-old Science Center is the home of the departments of biology, chemistry, computer science, physics, and mathematics. Students can benefit from its state-of-the-art labs and technology, classrooms with full multimedia capabilities, and facilities designed specifically for student research.

Costs

The 2006–07 school year costs at Culver-Stockton College were $15,250 for tuition, $6550 for room and board, approximately $800 for books and supplies, and a $200 technology fee. With the exception of students who were married or living with parents, all students receiving college financial aid were required to participate in the College's room and board plan. Variable board plans were available for the dining hall and Cat's Pause, the campus snack bar and cybercafé.

Financial Aid

Culver-Stockton College understands the financial needs of students and their families and works to make a C-SC education affordable. The College assists every qualified student to meet the costs of earning a C-SC degree. Through scholarships, grants, work-study opportunities, and loans, the College helps to offset the cost of a college education for qualified students. Through careful tuition pricing and a variety of financial aid options, C-SC is a great value for a superb educational experience.

The College participates in all federal and state financial aid programs, presenting aid packages that are based on need and merit. Merit awards are based on academic achievement as well as performance—theater, music, art, leadership, and athletics. The College requires the Free Application for Federal Student Aid (FAFSA). Pillars for Excellence full-tuition scholarships are awarded on a competitive basis each year for high-achieving students who meet certain GPA and ACT criteria.

Faculty

The strength of the College's academic program is the outstanding faculty. Faculty members provide instruction of high quality and individualized attention to students. Faculty members are active in scholarship, professional activity, and service. Faculty members also take an active role in many aspects of college life, including the advising and sponsorship of student organizations.

Student Government

An active Student Government Association deals with significant issues of student interest and communicates information about them to the faculty and administration. Students have voting representation on key faculty committees, such as the Academic Council, the Student Development Council, the Academic and Cultural Events Committee, and others that have a direct impact upon the nature and quality of student life. The Student Government Association president also serves as the student representative on the College's board of trustees. An active Campus Programming Council regularly plans student events.

Admission Requirements

Prospective students are expected to have completed a college-preparatory course of study of 15 units at an accredited secondary school. A proper foundation to facilitate success in college studies includes 4 units of English, 3 units of history, at least 2 units of mathematics (algebra and geometry), and 2 to 4 units of science. Students who intend to major in the science disciplines may wish to select additional high school courses in science and mathematics, and those interested in the humanities and social studies areas typically present additional course work in literature, foreign language, and history. Applicants must submit ACT or SAT scores. Each applicant for admission is given personal attention and is considered on the basis of academic performance, test scores, and personal attributes. An electronic application is available on the College's Web site.

Application and Information

Early application is recommended, as residence halls and classroom space may be limited. For further information, students should contact:

Admissions Office
Culver-Stockton College
One College Hill
Canton, Missouri 63435

Phone: 800-537-1883 (toll-free)
E-mail: admissions@culver.edu
Web site: http://www.culver.edu

Students on the Culver-Stockton College campus.

DICKINSON STATE UNIVERSITY
DICKINSON, NORTH DAKOTA

The University

Student success, both inside and outside the classroom, has been the focus of Dickinson State University since 1918, when the University was established as Dickinson Normal School and Model High. The tradition continues today, allowing easy access to and meaningful relationships with qualified professors, supportive and comfortable living arrangements on campus, and student activities that provide something for everyone.

Dickinson State, with an enrollment of approximately 2,570 students, is the only comprehensive, four-year public university in West River North Dakota. The University is proud of its safe campus. Its location offers students a secure environment in which to pursue their educational and social interests.

The University's mission, as dictated by the North Dakota University System, is to provide high-quality, accessible programs; to promote excellence in teaching and learning; to support scholarly and creative activities; and to provide service that is relevant to the economy, health, and quality of life of the citizens of North Dakota. With a wide range of academic programs, Dickinson State University prepares students to live, learn, and lead in the twenty-first century.

Dickinson State University is accredited by the North Central Association of Colleges and Schools (NCA), the North Central Association for Teacher Education (NCATE), and the National League for Nursing Accrediting Commission (NLNAC).

At Dickinson State, there are approximately forty-five different organizations to help every student find a niche. Students choose from intramural sports, band, chorus, drama, art, student government, honorary societies, academic clubs, and cheerleading, to name just a few.

Living in a residence hall at Dickinson State offers many conveniences and countless opportunities to build friendships in an exciting environment that is close to classes and University activities. Meal plans are available on campus for five or seven days per week. For added ease, students can also opt to purchase meals at the snack bar. Rooms have free access to the campus computer network and cable television. Features in each hall include a game room, exercise equipment, computer stations, free laundry facilities, and a kitchenette. Students can select to live in women's, men's, or coed halls or student apartments. Family student housing complexes provide apartments at reasonable housing rates to nontraditional students.

Location

Dickinson State is located in Dickinson, North Dakota, near the rugged and beautiful Badlands. With a population of more than 17,000, Dickinson is the hub of West River North Dakota. The community lies only 30 miles from Theodore Roosevelt National Park, and it is just 1 hour's drive south of Lake Sakakawea. Dickinson is served by commercial air transportation.

Dickinson's location provides abundant opportunities for people to enjoy outdoor recreational activities year-round. The area's picturesque rivers, lakes, and Badlands are ideal for hiking, fishing, boating, hunting, cross-country skiing, and much more.

As the state's fifth-largest community, Dickinson offers a wide array of restaurants, shopping malls, specialty stores, historic landmarks, museums, movie theaters, and other entertainment outlets. The region offers abundant dinosaur fossils and geological phenomena for explorers of all ages. Many of these treasures are displayed in Dickinson's impressive Dakota Dinosaur Museum.

Health-care services are provided by a 109-bed acute-care hospital, two major clinics, and numerous specialty clinics. The University's Student Health Service provides prompt care on campus for routine health concerns.

Majors and Degrees

Programs offered at Dickinson State University include liberal arts along with specialized programs in education, business, health services, agriculture, and computer science. There are opportunities for preprofessional study and vocational training in selected areas as well.

Dickinson State offers Bachelor of Arts and Bachelor of Science degrees in ten departments, including majors and/or minors (indicated with a *) in accounting, agriculture (with options in business/marketing, equine studies, integrated ranch management, natural resource management, and range management), applied science in technology, art, biology, business administration (with concentrations in accounting, agribusiness, banking and finance, entrepreneurship, human resource management, management, management information systems, manufacturing technology, marketing, office administration, and organizational psychology), business education, chemistry, coaching*, communications, computer science, dance*, earth science*, elementary education, English, entrepreneurship*, environmental health, geography*, graphic design*, history, human resource management*, journalism*, leadership studies*, mathematics, music, music education, nursing, physical education, political science, psychology, science composite, secondary education, social science composite, social science (elementary education)*, sociology*, social work (linked with University of North Dakota), Spanish, technology education, theater, university studies, and writing.

Associate degree and certificate programs include agriculture, with specialty areas in agriculture sales and service (with options in agriculture business management, equine management, and technology in agriculture) or farm and ranch management; nursing; office administration (with concentrations in accounting, agribusiness, computer science, graphic design, legal studies, management, and medical studies); and university studies.

Preprofessional programs include athletic training, chiropractic, criminal justice, dentistry, dental hygiene, dietetics, law, medicine, medical/lab technology, mortuary science, occupational therapy, optometry, pharmacy, physical therapy, veterinary studies, and wildlife management.

Academic Programs

While many of the majors that Dickinson State University offers have unique academic requirements, the basic baccalaureate degree academic curriculum consists of approximately 39 semester hours of general education courses from the areas of communications, scientific inquiry, expression of human civilization, understanding human civilization, multicultural studies, and physical education; a specific major core curriculum of 32 to 60 or more semester hours; approximately 24 semester hours of credit in a minor field of study (when a minor is required); and professional education course work for those students entering the teaching profession. Students seeking a Bachelor of Arts degree must also complete a minimum of 16 semester hours of a foreign language. A minimum of 128 semester hours is required for graduation in a baccalaureate degree program. Associate degree programs require 64 credit hours for graduation.

Academic Facilities

The commitment to technology at Dickinson State is evident in the number of cutting-edge computers that are provided for student use. There is an outstanding student–personal computer ratio, resulting in easy access to the type of technology students need to excel. Computer labs are located in academic areas, the library, and all residence halls. Students also have free access to e-mail and the Internet, including the World Wide Web.

Stoxen Library is proud of its highly sophisticated automated library. The On-line Dakota Information Network allows students to access resources from across the United States.

Murphy Hall, which houses the Department of Natural Sciences, has been under construction as part of a $9-million expansion and renovation project. The new-look Murphy Hall includes classrooms, state-of-the-art laboratories, faculty offices, and John Thompson Auditorium. The project is expected to be completed by January 2007.

Costs

In 2006–07, tuition and fees were $2235 per semester for North Dakota residents; $2400 per semester for Minnesota residents; $2691 per semester for residents of Montana, South Dakota, Manitoba (Canada), and Saskatchewan (Canada); and $3147 per semester for residents of Alaska, Arizona, California, Colorado, Hawaii, Idaho, Kansas, Michigan, Missouri, Nebraska, Nevada, New Mexico, Oregon, Utah, Washington, and Wyoming. For residents of other states, tuition and fees were $5280 per semester. Room and board costs average $1941 per semester. Books are approximately $400 per semester. These figures reflect current costs, which are subject to change.

Financial Aid

College is a valuable investment in the future, and Dickinson State realizes financing it can be challenging. One of the best college buys in the region, Dickinson State's tuition and housing rates are among the lowest in the upper Midwest. In addition, attractive tuition rates are offered for students living in states and provinces bordering on North Dakota. Special rates also exist for students who live in those states participating in the Western Undergraduate Exchange (WUE) and the Midwest Student Exchange Program (MSEP). These include Alaska, Arizona, California, Colorado, Hawaii, Idaho, Kansas, Michigan, Missouri, Nebraska, Nevada, New Mexico, Oregon, Utah, Washington, and Wyoming.

The Office of Financial Aid is ready to help ease the cost of a college education through a number of financial aid programs, including scholarships, grants, loans, student employment opportunities, cultural diversity awards, and international awards. More than 80 percent of Dickinson State's students received financial assistance last year.

Faculty

Dickinson State University has 93 full-time and 70 part-time faculty members. Students develop close relationships with their teachers since three fourths of the classes have fewer than 30 students.

Student Government

The Student Senate is the governing body and official voice of Dickinson State University students. The Senate is composed of a cross-section of students who have been elected by the campus community. The Campus Activity Board (CAB) offers a broad range of social and recreational activities, including dances, films, comedians, and other special events. The Campus Programming Committee (CPC) provides a variety of educational, instructional, and cultural programs. Residence Hall Councils are made up of elected student residents and deal with matters relating to campus housing. The Student Policies Council is composed of students and faculty and staff members. The council recommends policies and programs related to student affairs.

Admission Requirements

Dickinson State's admission policy allows students to enroll if they are high school graduates or have successfully completed the GED examination, along with completion of the ACT or SAT. The completion of a high school college-preparatory course core curriculum is also required for admission into a baccalaureate program.

The nursing program has special enrollment and admission requirements. Students should apply early for this program.

All students under the age of 21 who have not completed 60 semester hours are required to live on campus. Exceptions to this policy include married students; students living locally with parents, grandparents, or a legal guardian; students who live with a brother or sister who is a head of a household; and single parents with one or more dependents.

Application and Information

The enrollment services staff is anxious to discuss the variety of programs the University has to offer and give a tour of the beautiful campus and its classrooms, facilities, and residence halls. When students are on campus, they should meet with the financial aid staff to discuss concerns about financing an education. Enrollment counselors are available Monday through Friday, 8 a.m. to 4:30 p.m., Mountain Time. Students should contact:

Office of Enrollment Services
Dickinson State University
Dickinson, North Dakota 58601-4896
Phone: 701-483-2175
       800-279-HAWK Ext. 2175 (toll-free)
E-mail: dsu.hawks@dickinsonstate.edu
Web site: http://www.dickinsonstate.edu

Dickinson State University ensures student success with flexible schedules and by providing numerous group activities, allowing students to live, learn, and lead as they grow together.

GRACELAND UNIVERSITY
LAMONI, IOWA

GRACELAND
UNIVERSITY

The University

Graceland University (GU) offers a strong academic program firmly rooted in the liberal arts tradition with an emphasis on career preparation. Since its founding in 1895 as a private, coeducational university, Graceland has maintained a tradition of academic excellence based on a commitment to the Christian view of the wholeness, worth, and dignity of every person. The University, sponsored by Community of Christ, is nonsectarian and offers a varied religious life program for those who wish to participate. Of Graceland's fall 2005 freshman class on the Lamoni campus, 26 percent came from Iowa. The remaining 74 percent represent forty-five states and forty-one countries.

Graceland believes that an important part of a student's learning experience is achieved through association with other students in residence hall living. This belief is supported by an on-campus housing system that provides students with the camaraderie of a fraternity or sorority without the competition. Within the residence halls, there are men's and women's "houses." Members of each house elect a house council to plan social, intramural athletic, religious, and academic support activities. Residence halls are equipped with voice mail, e-mail, Internet connections, and cable TV.

Graceland University is a member of the North Central Association of Colleges and Schools (NCA) and is accredited by the Higher Learning Commission (30 North LaSalle Street, Suite 2400, Chicago, Illinois 60602-2504; 800-621-7440 (toll-free); http://www.ncahigherlearning-commission.org). All teacher-education programs at GU are approved by the Iowa Department of Education and are accredited by the National Council for Accreditation of Teacher Education (NCATE; 2010 Massachusetts Avenue NW, Suite 500, Washington, D.C. 20036; 202-466-7496; http://www.ncate.org). All GU nursing programs are accredited by the National League for Nursing Accreditation Commission, Inc. (NLNAC; 61 Broadway, 33rd Floor, New York, New York 10006; 800-669-1656 (toll-free); http://www.nlnac.org) and the Commission on Collegiate Nursing Education (CCNE; One Dupont Circle NW, Suite 530, Washington, D.C. 20036; http://www.aacn.nche.edu). The athletic training program is accredited by the Commission on Accreditation of Athletic Training Education Programs (CAATE; 2201 Double Creek Drive, Suite 5006, Round Rock, Texas 78664; 512-733-9700; http://www.caate.net). These academic standards ensure that a degree from Graceland University is recognized by educational, business, and professional communities.

Graduate programs include the Master of Arts in Christian Ministries, Master of Arts in Religion, Master of Education, and Master of Science in Nursing. Certificates are offered in American humanics nonprofit management, post-master's family nurse practitioner, post-master's nurse educator, and post-master's health-care administration.

In addition to its traditional programs Graceland offers many options for distance learners. Several programs are offered online by the School of Nursing. These include Bachelor in Healthcare Management, RN-B.S.N., RN-M.S.N., and M.S.N. programs. The M.S.N. program has three tracks: family nurse practitioner, nurse educator, and health-care administrator. The Graceland University School of Education offers a Master of Education with an emphasis in collaborative learning and teaching and special education. The Community of Christ Seminary also offers master's programs in religion and Christian ministries at a distance. The Master of Education program is offered in Cedar Rapids, Des Moines, and Lamoni, Iowa; Independence, Missouri; and online.

The Community of Christ Seminary offers a Master of Arts in Religion and a Master of Arts in Christian Ministries in blended delivery systems. The Community of Christ Seminary also offers master's programs in religion and Christian ministries at a distance.

Location

Lamoni, in south-central Iowa, is on Interstate 35. It is 3 miles north of the Missouri border, 1 hour from Des Moines, 2 hours from Kansas City, and 3 hours from Omaha. Lamoni is the home of Liberty Hall Historic Center, a 6-mile bike trail, an annual Civil War Days Re-Enactment and Living History Event, numerous hometown eateries, and several unique gift and antique shops. A county lake, Slip Bluff County Park, and Nine Eagles State Park are within 10 miles.

Majors and Degrees

Graceland awards the degrees of Bachelor of Arts, Bachelor of Science, and Bachelor of Science in Nursing. These degrees represent study in liberal arts with a concentration of courses in a major.

The majors and concentrations offered in the Bachelor of Arts programs are accounting, art (studio or visual communication), athletic training, business administration (emphases in entrepreneurship and free enterprise, finance, management, marketing, and pre-M.B.A.), chemistry, communications, economics, elementary education, English (concentrations in cinema studies, literature, and writing), fitness leadership, health, health-care administration, history, information technology, international business, international studies, liberal studies, mathematics, modern foreign language, music, music education, philosophy and religion, physical education and health, psychology, publications design, recreation, religion, social science, sociology (emphases in criminology, general sociology, and human services), Spanish, theater, visual communications (see: art), and wellness program management.

Bachelor of Science programs and majors are basic science, biology (options in general, preprofessional, and secondary school teaching), chemistry, clinical laboratory science/medical technology, and computer science.

The first two years of the Bachelor of Science in Nursing program are offered on the Lamoni campus, while the junior and senior years are on the Independence, Missouri, campus.

Graceland also offers degree programs at extended campus locations. Through a partnership with North Central Missouri College, Graceland offers undergraduate degrees in liberal arts and education. Through a partnership with Indian Hills Community College, Graceland offers an undergraduate degree in education. The undergraduate education program is offered at the Graceland Independence campus location.

Academic Programs

Graceland is committed to helping develop the lives of its students—intellectually, socially, physically, and ethically—through a curriculum that is strongly rooted in the liberal arts. General education requirements are based on ten core competencies and can be satisfied by course selections, internships, portfolios, proficiency exams, work experience, independent studies, performance, and achievement. Graceland offers majors that foster conceptual thinking, encourage team building, develop communication skills, and accommodate growth and enrichment.

Two programs at Graceland give attention to the special needs of students. The Honors Program is designed for highly motivated students who want to expand their learning beyond the regular academic curriculum. Honors students are required to develop and complete an honors thesis or project. Chance is a program for bright students who have the aptitude for university education but have experienced learning difficulties. The Lindamood and Bell clinical models are used for remediation in reading, spelling, and language comprehension.

The University operates on a 4-1-4 academic calendar. The regular semesters are separated by a one-month winter term in January. Full tuition for either the fall or the spring semester includes the winter term. This program is geared toward innovative and exceptional approaches and action-oriented learning experiences. On-campus programs vary from dance basics to science fiction to philosophy. Off-campus winter term experiences range from scuba diving in Grand Cayman to touring Italy. Winter term is also the ideal time to explore career interests through an internship.

Off-Campus Programs

Many students see the world during the winter term by visiting such places as Australia, China, England, France, Grand Cayman Island in the British West Indies, Hungary, Italy, India, Israel, Japan, and Mexico. Students who major in a foreign language may study abroad during their junior or senior year under the auspices of a recognized study program. Graceland sponsors an International Health Center that provides opportunities for students to interact with health workers in villages in Africa and Asia.

Academic Facilities

The Helene Center for the Visual Arts includes 29,000 square feet for classrooms, studios, and exhibits. The large north-facing windows, an important feature, provide optimum light for artists.

The Shaw Center for the Performing Arts includes an 800-seat auditorium, a 150-seat studio theater, a 40-foot proscenium stage with orchestra pit, a Casavant pipe organ, a full fly gallery, a spacious scene shop, an art gallery, classrooms, rehearsal rooms, and faculty offices.

Computer facilities include three primary microcomputer laboratories with Macintosh and IBM-compatible computers. Students have access to equipment of commercial quality for desktop publishing and graphics design and to a music laboratory that provides computer-assisted tutoring, synthesis, and composition as well as professional-quality manuscript printing. The centerpiece of this laboratory is the Kurzweil synthesizer. Graceland's Enter.Net.C@fe provides 24-hour Internet access for student research and recreation.

The Frederick Madison Smith Library uses the latest technologies to provide the information services that students need. Ten fully networked computer workstations offer access to the Internet and many research databases, including 2 databases that provide full-text newspaper articles and periodicals for online reading. Access to LIBBIE, the computerized library catalog, is available from residence hall rooms. Articles and books may be ordered from a worldwide network of research libraries. Students log on to the library's home page to ask reference questions. Holdings include 118,004 books and bound journals, 3,858 audiovisual materials, 73,041 government documents, 851 magazine and newspaper subscriptions, and 5,006 items in the Teacher Curriculum Lab. Three microcomputer labs and the Iowa Communications Network (ICN) classroom are located in the library. Students across the state take classes from Graceland via the ICN.

The Charles F. Grabske, Sr. Library on the Independence campus provides resources for both on-campus and distance students in the nursing and education departments. The library contains 2,879 nursing, education, and medical books, 282 audiovisual items, and 1,400 journal titles. Grabske Library has one of the largest collections of nursing journals in the greater Kansas City area, with current subscriptions to 169 journals. Books, videos, journal articles, and interlibrary loan services are available to both on-campus and distance students. More than 1,500 journal articles were interlibrary-loaned to distance students alone during the previous year.

Students have the opportunity to use the ABT 52 scanning electron microscope, nuclear magnetic resonance spectroscope, Fourier-transform infrared spectroscope, and a computer lab with PCs that provide access to a multiple-operating system environment in the Platz-Mortimore Science Hall.

The Eugene E. and Judy Travis Closson Physical Education Center includes an indoor junior Olympic-size pool; an indoor track; a weight room; basketball, tennis, and volleyball courts; and a racquetball court. The Bruce Jenner Sports Complex contains the outdoor track, the football stadium, three soccer fields, five intramural fields, and eight tennis courts. The campus borders on a nine-hole golf course and two small ponds for fishing and canoeing. Disc golf courses are in locations throughout the community.

Costs

Full-time tuition for 2006–07 was $16,850. Freshmen and sophomores were required to live on campus.

Financial Aid

Graceland's financial aid program is designed to assist qualified students attending the University. More than 94 percent of Graceland's students receive financial aid such as academic scholarships, performance grants, work-study, federal and state grants, and government loans. Academic scholarships are based on the high school GPA and composite ACT or combined SAT scores for entering freshmen and on cumulative GPA for transfer and continuing students. Grants are available for achievement in athletics and performing arts and for international students. The University matches a grant up to $1000 annually for a contribution made by a congregation and designated for a student attending Graceland. Some financial aid is available for dis-

tance learning programs; interested students should contact the Graceland University Financial Aid Services Office for specific information.

Faculty

The majority of faculty members have earned a doctorate or the highest degree in their field. Faculty members are active in their professional fields but consider teaching their primary responsibility. The student-faculty ratio is 15:1.

Student Government

Students are actively involved in the decision-making process of the University. Student-elected executive members of the Graceland Student Government attend faculty meetings and participate with voice and vote. Each academic department has student representatives who participate in business sessions and serve on faculty search committees. Students provide leadership for the housing system and for the campus social program. These and many other avenues are available allowing students to gain practical leadership experience.

Admission Requirements

Admission to Graceland is selective. To be considered, high school graduates must qualify in two of the following three areas: (1) rank in the upper 50 percent of their class; (2) have a minimum 2.5 GPA, based on a 4.0 system; and (3) have either a minimum composite ACT score of 21 or a minimum SAT combined score (Critical Reading and Math) of 960. Applicants who do not meet the above criteria may be considered individually. If accepted, they will be required to take developmental courses. Some applicants may be requested to test for the Chance Program prior to being considered for acceptance. Transfer, international, and home-schooled students should refer to the requirements listed in the catalog on the University's Web site. No one is denied admission to the University on the basis of race, color, religion, age, sex, national origin, disability, or sexual orientation. Prospective students and their families are encouraged to visit the campus.

Application and Information

Students are encouraged to apply as early as possible. For more information and application materials, students should contact:

Admissions Office
Graceland University
1 University Place
Lamoni, Iowa 50140
Phone: 641-784-5196
   866-GRACELAND (toll-free in the United States and
    Canada)
Fax: 641-784-5480
E-mail: admissions@graceland.edu
Web site: http://www.admissions.graceland.edu

Higdon Administration Building on Graceland's Lamoni Campus.

HEIDELBERG COLLEGE

TIFFIN, OHIO

The College

Heidelberg College provides a unique blend of liberal arts and professional studies that prepares students for a world where goals and careers frequently change. Since 1850, Heidelberg has been providing students with a high-quality education at an affordable price. Ranked by *U.S. News & World Report* as one of the Midwest's top colleges for nineteen consecutive years, Heidelberg is also listed in the magazine's "Great School at a Great Price" category.

The current undergraduate enrollment is about 1,100 men and women. Students come to Heidelberg from twenty-two states and fourteen other countries. This cross-cultural mix helps to keep the campus diverse and broaden students' knowledge and understanding of ethnic and cultural differences.

Heidelberg has more than sixty campus organizations that offer opportunities for leadership, service, and fellowship. Included in these organizations are thirteen departmental clubs and fifteen departmental honorary societies that sponsor discussions, lectures, and field trips. Other cocurricular activities include a student-edited and student-managed newspaper, a television station that broadcasts daily news, forensic programs, choral and instrumental groups, and intramural sports. The Communication and Theatre Arts Department presents four or more dramatic productions each year.

A member of the Ohio Athletic Conference, NCAA Division III, Heidelberg offers nine varsity men's sports: baseball, basketball, cross-country, football, golf, soccer, tennis, track and field, and wrestling. The women's varsity sports program, among the first in Ohio to be affiliated with the NCAA Division III, fields eight intercollegiate teams: basketball, cheerleading, cross-country, soccer, softball, tennis, track and field, and volleyball. Athletic facilities include a weight room, handball/racquetball courts, locker rooms, and an eight-lane, all-weather track, which is considered one of the finest in Ohio.

Heidelberg also offers Master of Arts degree programs in counseling and education as well as a Master of Business Administration (M.B.A.) degree program.

Location

Heidelberg's 110-acre campus is located in Tiffin, Ohio, a town of 20,000. It is the center of a prosperous agricultural and business area. Downtown Tiffin, within half a mile of the campus, is traditional in appearance; its charming brickwork stores and large lampposts trimmed in wrought iron resemble an old German town. Four metropolitan areas are within easy driving distance: Toledo, 50 miles; Columbus, 86 miles; Cleveland, 92 miles; and Detroit, 103 miles.

Majors and Degrees

Heidelberg offers a wide variety of undergraduate majors and several preprofessional programs within nineteen academic departments. It awards Bachelor of Arts, Bachelor of Science, and Bachelor of Music degrees. Majors are available in accounting, anthropology (archaeology, cultural anthropology), athletic training, biology (forensic science, general), business administration, chemistry, communication and theater arts (communication studies, communication/media, musical theater, theater), computer information systems, computer science, education (early childhood, middle childhood, adolescence/young adult, intervention specialist studies, multiage health and physical education, multiage music education, multiage Spanish), English (literature, writing), environmental biology, forensic science, German, health and physical education, history, international studies (cross-cultural studies, international relations), mathematics, music (music education, music performance, music theory/composition), philosophy, physics, political science, psychology (biopsychology, child/adolescent, general, mental health), public relations, religion, Spanish, sports management, and water resources (biology, chemistry, geology). Preprofessional and cooperative degree programs include dentistry, engineering, environmental management, law, medical technology, medicine, nursing, occupational therapy, optometry, osteopathy, physical therapy, physician assistant studies, podiatry, and veterinary science.

Academic Programs

To graduate, a student must complete 120 academic semester hours, comprising 32–56 semester hours of general education, 40 semester hours in a selected major, and 26–50 hours of electives. Two credits in health and physical education and 1 credit for First-Year Seminar are also required.

Off-Campus Programs

To supplement their course work, students may choose from a variety of off-campus study programs that provide practical, career-related experience. For example, students interested in studying habitats not found in northwestern Ohio may do on-site field research in the Caribbean, study biogeography in Belize, and do on-site field research in the Appalachian mountains of West Virginia. Students may also participate in the excavation of an archaeological site.

Opportunities for practical experience in research are also available through Heidelberg's National Center for Water Quality Research, which has ongoing research in water-quality studies involving both northern Ohio streams and Lake Erie. Heidelberg's internship program also enables students to participate in on-the-job internships in several area businesses and industries.

Students interested in studying in Washington, D.C., may take part in the Washington Semester at American University; those interested in studying abroad may participate in Heidelberg's own programs in Germany (at Heidelberg University) and Spain or may participate in programs arranged cooperatively with other colleges and universities in such locations as England, Latin America, Africa, and the Far East.

Academic Facilities

Gillmor Science Hall, Heidelberg's new 42,000-square-foot science hall, opened in January 2005. Gillmor, the cornerstone of the science complex at Heidelberg, features state-of-the-art technology and laboratories. The new science hall is home to the chemistry, biology, physics, anthropology, and forensic science departments as well as National Center for Water Quality Research. Known for their work over the past thirty years, the lab's staff members help protect the aquatic resources of Ohio, the Midwest, Lake Erie, and the Great Lakes ecosystems. In addition, the $17-million project includes complete renovations to the College's two existing science halls, Bareis and Laird, which are expected to be complete in January 2006.

Beeghly Library, containing 154,000 volumes, is the intellectual heart of Heidelberg College. The three-story circular library holds a seventy-seat audiovisual room, a seminar and computer room, the Rickard-Mayer Rare Books Room, and the Besse Collection of Letters. The computer center provides access to Macintosh and PC-compatible computers. In addition, wireless technology is available throughout the Library as well as several other locations throughout campus. All of these systems are connected to a campus-wide network providing e-mail, file transfer, World Wide Web, and full access to the Internet. The high number of computers available for student use, in addition to the convenience of the computer center hours, are outstanding strengths of the College. Additional computer facilities are located in Brenneman Music Hall, the Pfleiderer Center for Religion and the Humanities, and the Aigler Alumni Building. Founders Hall houses a 250-seat performance theater and a rehearsal theater; an FM radio station, WHEI; television studio WHEI-TV; video taping rooms; costume rooms; a dance studio; and offices and classrooms for the Departments of Communication and Theatre Arts and the Languages.

Costs

Tuition for 2006–07 was $17,000 plus $7530 for room and board.

Financial Aid

About 97 percent of the undergraduate student body at Heidelberg receives financial aid. College and government programs—including scholarships, grants, loans, and jobs—total about $16 million annually. Government assistance includes the Federal Pell Grant, direct loan programs, the Federal Supplemental Educational Opportunity Grant, and the Federal Work-Study Program. Heidelberg offers students who meet various academic requirements a number of grants and scholarships that are renewable if eligibility is maintained.

Faculty

Close personal interaction between students and professors is one of Heidelberg's primary strengths. Seventy-nine full-time professors serve the student body, and the student-faculty ratio is 13:1. More than 80 percent of the faculty members hold doctoral degrees in their disciplines. Heidelberg's faculty members are readily available to answer questions and meet with students outside of the classroom.

Student Government

Because students are voting members of 90 percent of the faculty committees, their concerns are heard and have an impact on academic standards, athletics, educational policies, and religious life. Heidelberg's Student Senate is made up of 25 students and a Student Affairs adviser.

Admission Requirements

Heidelberg's selective admission policy seeks to admit those students who will benefit from the educational offerings of the College and who will contribute to the shared life of the campus community. The Admission Committee considers each applicant individually to determine if the student will be able to successfully fulfill the academic responsibilities of a Heidelberg student. The applicant's high school achievement record is the single most important factor considered. Other factors considered are ACT or SAT scores, cocurricular involvement, character, talent, and teacher recommendations.

Application and Information

Although Heidelberg follows a rolling admission policy, applicants are strongly encouraged to complete this process before January 1. Once all admission credentials are received, applicants are notified of the College's admission decision within two weeks.

For additional information, students should contact:

Office of Admission
Heidelberg College
310 East Market Street
Tiffin, Ohio 44883
Phone: 419-448-2330
        800-HEIDELBERG (toll-free)
Fax: 419-448-2334
E-mail: adminfo@heidelberg.edu
Web site: http://www.heidelberg.edu

Heidelberg College's newest building, the 42,000-square-foot Gillmor Science Hall, is a state-of-the-art facility that completes the science complex.

THE ILLINOIS INSTITUTE OF ART–CHICAGO

CHICAGO, ILLINOIS

The Institute

The Illinois Institute of Art–Chicago offers a stimulating learning environment where committed and talented students, led by dedicated and professional faculty members, may develop their creativity and acquire the skills and knowledge needed to pursue an entry-level job in the creative arts. The Illinois Institute of Art–Chicago offers eleven bachelor's degree and six associate degree programs.

There are nearly 2,700 students at The Illinois Institute of Art–Chicago; they come from throughout the United States and abroad. The student population includes recent high school graduates, transfer students, and those who have left a previous employment situation to study and train for a new career. Students are creative, competitive, and open to new ideas. They place great value on an education that prepares them for an exciting entry-level position in the arts.

Orientation events provide students with an introduction to the school's academic environment, extracurricular life, residence life, and campus surroundings. Student organizations include the American Marketing Association (AMA), Textile Surface Design Club, American Society of Interior Designers (ASID), International Student Association (ISA), and American Institute of Graphic Arts (AIGA).

The school provides opportunities outside of the classroom that enhance students' personal development, including a wide variety of social and educational activities. On-campus activities include student organizations, leadership workshops, special guest presentations, heritage celebrations, holiday events, and unique contests.

Dedicated Career Services staff members offer a range of services to support students' efforts in career planning. With employer contacts and resources across the country, Career Services provides students with proven tips and techniques to start a job search. Of all 2005 Illinois Institute of Art–Chicago graduates who were available for employment, 91.9 percent were working in a field related to their program of study within six months of graduation and earning an average salary of $31,165.

The school maintains master-lease apartments in downtown Chicago that offer convenient and comfortable living. School-sponsored housing offers studio apartments that house 2 students. Basic utilities, Internet, basic cable, local phone service, and furnishings are included in the rent price.

The Illinois Institute of Art–Chicago is accredited by the Accrediting Commission of Career Schools and Colleges of Technology (ACCSCT). The school is licensed by the Illinois State Board of Education and is authorized by the Illinois Board of Higher Education to award associate and bachelor's degrees. The Bachelor of Fine Arts program in interior design is accredited by the Council for Interior Design Accreditation.

The Associate of Applied Science degree in culinary arts is accredited by the Accrediting Commission of the American Culinary Federation (ACF).

Location

Chicago is one of the five most visited cities in the country, with the Museum of Contemporary Art, the Mexican Fine Arts Center Museum, and the Terra Museum of American Art. Neighborhood street fairs and festivals throughout the year celebrate art, food, and creativity. Other attractions include the Sears Tower, Navy Pier, Shedd Aquarium, Field Museum, Adler Planetarium, Lincoln Park Zoo, and a lakefront with beautiful beaches. Music lovers enjoy the Lyric Opera and Chicago Symphony, while sports fans watch the Cubs, White Sox, Bulls, Blackhawks, and Bears.

Majors and Degrees

The Illinois Institute of Art–Chicago offers bachelor's degree programs in advertising, culinary management, digital filmmaking and video production, fashion design, fashion marketing and management, game art and design, interactive media design, interior design, media arts and animation, visual communications, and visual effects and motion graphics. Associate degree programs include accessory design, culinary arts, fashion merchandising, fashion production, graphic design, and interactive media production.

Academic Programs

The Illinois Institute of Art–Chicago offers bachelor's degree programs (180 academic credits), associate degree programs (96 credits), and certificate programs.

Academic Facilities

The Illinois Institute of Art–Chicago library includes computer workstations; online databases; nearly 11,000 volumes; 286 subscriptions; 6,430 slides of art history, interior architecture, furniture, and fashion; and a CD sound library. There are eleven computer labs with high-speed Internet access—six PC-based labs and five Macintosh labs. Applied software includes Microsoft Office 2000, Adobe Photoshop, Macromedia Flash, Discreet 3D StudioMax, AutoCAD, and QuarkXPress. Digital media production studios include editing stations, an audio production studio, and a video production studio.

Culinary facilities include five kitchens, two storage rooms, and a forty-five-seat restaurant. The Fashion Department contains power sewing machines, large cutting tables, steamers, and computer labs. Fashion marketing classes utilize a walk-in window, props, mannequins, and other display materials. The Interior Design Resource Center contains a variety of contemporary fabrics, wall- and floor-covering samples, manufacturers' furniture catalogs, a new lighting lab, and other design tools.

The 180 North Wabash facility is a satellite location of The Illinois Institute of Art–Chicago.

Costs

Full-time tuition for 2007–08 is $19,968. Housing costs an additional $11,512. Other charges include a starting kit for all first-quarter students. Kits vary in price, depending on the program of study. Part-time tuition is $416 per credit.

Financial Aid

Financial aid is available for those who qualify. Students who require financial assistance should first complete and submit a Free Application for Federal Student Aid (FAFSA) and meet with a financial aid officer. The officer determines the level of need based on a required federal formula, the cost of education, and other factors. Gift aid is available in the form of Federal Pell Grants, Federal Supplemental Educational Opportunity Grants, and veterans' benefits. Loans include Federal Stafford Student Loans, Federal PLUS loans, and alternative loans. Other scholarships are available from the school and private sources. Application deadlines and eligibility requirements vary by program.

Faculty

The Illinois Institute of Art–Chicago faculty includes 175 full-time and part-time instructors, many of whom have advanced degrees and experience in their respective fields. The student-faculty ratio is 24:1.

Admission Requirements

An assistant director of admissions personally interviews prospective students to assess their potential for success at The Illinois Institute of Art–Chicago. Applicants are required to submit an essay of 150 words (associate degree programs) or 300 words (bachelor's degree programs) describing how they may benefit from an education at The Illinois Institute of Art–Chicago. Proof of high school graduation or equivalency is required for final admission to the school. Applicants must also provide current immunization records. Scores on the SAT or ACT may be considered for admission but are not required. The school reserves the right to request any additional information necessary to evaluate an applicant's potential for academic success. The application for admission and enrollment agreement must be completed and signed by the applicant and parent or guardian (if applicable). There is a $50 application fee.

Application and Information

To obtain an application, make arrangements for an interview, or tour the school, students should contact:

The Illinois Institute of Art–Chicago
350 North Orleans Street
Chicago, Illinois 60654-1593
Phone: 312-280-3500
          800-351-3450 (toll-free)
Fax: 312-280-8562
Web site: http://www.artinstitutes.edu/chicago

The Art Institute of Atlanta®, GA; The Art Institute of California℠–Inland Empire; The Art Institute of California℠–Los Angeles; The Art Institute of California℠–Orange County; The Art Institute of California℠–San Diego; The Art Institute of California℠–San Francisco; The Art Institute of Charleston℠, SC, A branch of The Art Institute of Atlanta, GA; The Art Institute of Charlotte®, NC; The Art Institute of Colorado® (Denver); The Art Institute of Dallas®, TX; The Art Institute of Fort Lauderdale®, FL; The Art Institute of Houston®, TX; The Art Institute of Indianapolis℠, IN*; The Art Institute of Jacksonville℠, A branch of Miami International University of Art & Design, FL; The Art Institute of Las Vegas®, NV; The Art Institute of New York City®, NY; The Art Institute of Ohio℠–Cincinnati**; The Art Institute of Philadelphia®, PA; The Art Institute of Phoenix®, AZ; The Art Institute of Pittsburgh®, PA; The Art Institute of Portland®, OR; The Art Institute of Seattle®, WA; The Art Institute of Tampa℠, FL, A branch of Miami International University of Art & Design; The Art Institute of Tennessee℠–Nashville, A branch of The Art Institute of Atlanta, GA; The Art Institute of Toronto℠, ON; The Art Institute of Vancouver℠, BC (Burnaby location, Downtown location, Dubrulle Culinary Arts location); The Art Institute of Washington® (Arlington, VA), A branch of The Art Institute of Atlanta, GA; The Art Institute Online℠, A division of The Art Institute of Pittsburgh, PA; The Art Institutes International Minnesota℠ (Minneapolis); Bradley Academy for the Visual Arts℠ (York, PA); California Design College℠ (Wilshire Boulevard, Los Angeles); The Illinois Institute of Art®–Chicago; The Illinois Institute of Art®–Schaumburg; Miami International University of Art & Design℠, FL; The New England Institute of Art℠ (Boston, MA).

*The Art Institute of Indianapolis is licensed by the Indiana Commission on Proprietary Education, 302 West Washington Street, Room E201, Indianapolis, IN 46204, AC-0080.

**The Art Institute of Ohio–Cincinnati, 8845 Governors Hill Drive, Suite 100, Cincinnati, OH 45249-3317, Reg. #04-01-1698B.

ILLINOIS INSTITUTE OF TECHNOLOGY
CHICAGO, ILLINOIS

The Institute

Illinois Institute of Technology (IIT) is a private, Ph.D.-granting research university with undergraduate programs in architecture, business, engineering, humanities, psychology, and science. One of the select institutions in the Association of Independent Technological Universities (AITU), IIT offers exceptional preparation for professions that require technological sophistication. Through a committed faculty and close personal attention, IIT provides a challenging academic program focused on the rigor of the real world. The internationally famous main campus is based on a master plan developed by the late Ludwig Mies van der Rohe, one of the most influential architects of the century, who served for twenty years as director of IIT's College of Architecture. An independent university, the Institute includes the College of Architecture, the Armour College of Engineering, the College of Science and Letters, the Institute of Business and Interprofessional Studies, the Institute of Psychology, the Stuart Graduate School of Business, the Institute of Design, and the Chicago-Kent College of Law.

The more than 6,000 students at IIT (more than 2,000 of whom are undergraduates) are encouraged to participate in the many social, cultural, and athletic opportunities available. Student activities include the campus newspaper *(TechNews)*, the radio station (WIIT), special interest clubs, theater groups, intramural and varsity athletics, fraternities and sororities, honor societies, professional societies, student government, residence hall organizations, and the student-run Union Board. The VanderCook College of Music is also located on the IIT campus for students interested in studying music or participating in musical performances. Campus facilities include the McCormick Tribune Campus Center, a convenience store and campus book store, a coffee shop, a gymnasium, outdoor tennis and volleyball courts, thirteen residence halls, two resident sorority houses, and six resident fraternity houses. Counseling, job placement, and student health services are included in the various campus services.

Location

IIT stands in the midst of a developing urban area. It is 1 mile west of Lake Michigan and one block from the recent world-champion White Sox ballpark. The campus is located approximately 3 miles south of the Chicago Loop, offering students unlimited opportunities to enjoy art, music, theater, movies, museums, shopping, and other entertainment. Also convenient to the campus are a number of recreational areas, including McCormick Place exhibition hall, Soldier Field, Grant Park, Millennium Park, Lincoln Park Zoo, various bicycle paths, and lakefront beaches. IIT is easily accessible to the rest of Chicago via two major expressways. Bus and elevated train lines have stops on the campus, and the IIT shuttle bus provides free transportation between the campus and the university's Downtown Campus in Chicago's West Loop area.

Majors and Degrees

The Armour College of Engineering offers the Bachelor of Science in aerospace, architectural, biomedical, chemical, civil, computer, electrical, mechanical, and materials science engineering. The College of Science and Letters offers the Bachelor of Science in applied mathematics, biology, chemistry, computer information systems, computer science, humanities, Internet communication, journalism, molecular biochemistry and biophysics, physics, political science, and professional and technical communication.

The College of Architecture awards the Bachelor of Architecture degree through its five-year professional degree program.

There are various options and minors available within each curriculum, such as artificial intelligence, bioengineering, business, computer-aided drafting, law, management, manufacturing technology, military science, psychology, public administration, and technical communications. Other individualized specializations may be arranged with approval of the dean. Combined undergraduate/graduate degrees include those offered in conjunction with business administration (B.S./M.B.A.), law (B.S./J.D.), and public administration (B.S./M.P.A.).

IIT has also established combined-degree programs in medicine (B.S./M.D. or D.O.), law (B.S./J.D.), pharmacy (B.S./Pharm.D.), and optometry (B.S./O.D.). Students interested in a combined-degree program must submit an undergraduate application and a supplemental application for the graduate portion of the program.

Academic Programs

While requirements vary according to the major, all IIT students complete a general education core, which includes a minimum of 7 semester hours in mathematics and computer science, 11 semester hours in natural science or engineering, 12 semester hours in the humanities, and 12 semester hours in the social sciences. Students pursuing a Bachelor of Science in an engineering field or in the physical sciences take, in addition, a program that includes further study in mathematics and computer science, chemistry, and physics.

IIT's mission is to educate students for complex professional roles in a changing world and to advance knowledge through research and scholarship. The Institute is committed to the educational ideal of small undergraduate classes and individual mentoring. IIT's signature Introduction to the Professions (IPRO) program brings students and senior faculty members together each week in small groups, where students interact with their advisers as both teachers and mentors. Throughout the curricula, the IIT interprofessional projects provide a learning environment in which interdisciplinary teams of students apply theoretical knowledge gained in the classroom and laboratory to real-world projects sponsored by industry and government. Many IIT students further enhance their education through a wide variety of research and entrepreneurial projects.

Cooperative education is encouraged. This career development program begins with a freshman year of full-time study and then alternates semesters of study and employment in industry for approximately four additional years. Placement services are provided by the university. More than 90 percent of recent graduates were placed in jobs in the fields of their majors or went on to graduate or professional schools.

Study abroad is available in several academic disciplines through the International Center at IIT.

Academic Facilities

As the central library, the Paul V. Galvin Library provides a broad range of services, including information on engineering, business, science, mathematics, the humanities, architecture, and design via the Internet; numerous electronic and paper-based databases; a document delivery service; interlibrary loan; and special collections. The main campus operates DEC minicomputers, a Silicon Graphics Challenge UNIX multiprocessor, and local UNIX servers. Terminals and microcomputers are located in most academic buildings across the campus, in residence halls, and in Galvin Library. Seminars, tutorials, and computer lab work are conducted in microcomputer classrooms. Among IIT's thirty-two research centers are the Center for Synchrotron Radiation Research, the Fluid Dynamics Research Center, and the Research Laboratory in Human Biomechanics. Most research centers offer undergraduates opportunities to participate on their projects.

Costs

Annual tuition for 2005–06 was $23,329. Other expenses were $8050 for room and board and $764 for fees. The estimated annual total for freshmen is $31,379. Annual tuition covers the fall and spring semesters.

Financial Aid

Most full-time undergraduates at IIT receive financial aid from a variety of sources. IIT participates in the Federal Perkins Loan, Federal Work-Study, Federal Pell Grant, Federal Supplemental Educational Opportunity Grant, federally insured student loan, Illinois State Scholarship Commission Monetary Award, Illinois Guaranteed Loan, and Federal PLUS Loan programs and similar programs. In addition, IIT provides generous merit-based and need-based scholarships and loans from its own funds and from those supported by a number of companies and other organizations. The Camras Scholarships award up to full tuition for the study of any major. All admitted students are automatically reviewed for tuition scholarships. More than 500 are awarded each year. Athletic scholarships are also available for qualified students. Two other programs may be utilized by students working to supplement their financial aid: on-campus employment and the cooperative education program. IIT requires the Free Application for Federal Student Aid (FAFSA). No additional applications or forms are required.

Army, Naval, and Air Force ROTC programs are offered. ROTC scholarship winners receive supplemental scholarships from IIT.

Faculty

There are 303 full-time faculty members and 277 industry professionals as part-time faculty members. The student-faculty ratio is approximately 13:1. All members of the senior teaching faculty instruct in both upper- and lower-division courses. Eighty-six percent hold doctoral degrees or the highest professional degree in their area.

Student Government

The Student Government Association (SGA) is a vital force in the IIT community. It acts as the students' official voice in communications with faculty and administration, and it plans, develops, and supervises most of the activities pertaining to campus life. In addition to having its own standing committees, SGA is represented on seven of the ten institutional committees pertaining to undergraduates.

Admission Requirements

Admission evaluation is a thorough, personal process. Of paramount consideration is the student's academic performance in high school, specifically in areas that are vital to the student's major at IIT. Minimum high school preparation includes 16 units of credit, including at least 4 units in English, 4 units in mathematics through precalculus, and 3 units of science with 2 lab sciences. Calculus is encouraged but not required. Chemistry and physics are strongly recommended.

A completed application, recommendations, test scores (either SAT or ACT), and an official high school transcript are required for admission. Although not required, interviews and a campus visit are encouraged.

Application and Information

Applications are reviewed on a rolling basis. Students should apply as early as possible, starting in the senior year of high school; an online application is available at http://www.iit.edu/~apply. In general, applicants can expect notification within two weeks after their completed applications are received.

For further information, students should contact:

Office of Undergraduate Admission
Perlstein Hall 101
Illinois Institute of Technology
10 West 33rd Street
Chicago, Illinois 60616-3793
Phone: 312-567-3025 (in Chicago)
       800-448-2329 (toll-free outside Chicago)
Fax: 312-567-6939
E-mail: admission@iit.edu
Web site: http://www.iit.edu

INTERNATIONAL ACADEMY OF DESIGN & TECHNOLOGY

CHICAGO, ILLINOIS

The Academy

The International Academy of Design & Technology is a postsecondary degree-granting institution with career-based curricula and professional staff members who contribute to students' development in their chosen fields. The Academy provides a high-quality education, prepares students for positions in fields related to their area of study, provides students with a professional environment that fosters cultural enrichment and personal development, maintains high-quality curricula that are sensitive to industry needs as defined by the Academy's advisory board, and offers career-planning services leading to employment opportunities for graduates to allow them to utilize their knowledge, skills, and talents.

The International Academy of Design & Technology was founded in 1977 by Clem Stein Jr. as a private coeducational institution. In 1983, the Academy opened a campus in Toronto, Canada. The Tampa, Florida, campus was opened in 1984, and in 1987, the fourth campus was opened in Montreal, Canada. In 1997, Career Education Corporation acquired the Academy. Career Education Corporation operates postsecondary institutions throughout the U.S. and abroad. In 2001, the Academy changed its name from the International Academy of Merchandising & Design to the International Academy of Design & Technology, which better reflects the infusion of technology into all of the program curricula.

There are various associations and clubs for Academy students. The Fashion Council is for fashion design students. Additional clubs are Behind the Scene, the merchandising management club; S7UDIO, computer graphic organization; the Information Technology Organization; Playback, the interactive media organization; International Interior Design Association, the interior design club; Game On, the game design club; the Movie Club; the International Club; Resident's Life; IADT Ballerz Athletic Club; Anime Student Alliance; American Institute of Graphic Arts; and the XI Beta Sigma Fraternal Organization, a coed fraternity. These clubs are organized by and for students. GLBT@IADT Community is the Academy's outreach to gay, lesbian, bisexual, and transgender students. The Academy also has a student-produced magazine, *Mixed Media*. The Student Ambassador Program assists new students with their transition to the Academy and college life.

The Academy is incorporated under the laws of the state of Illinois and accredited by the Accrediting Council for Independent Colleges and Schools (ACICS). The interior design program is accredited by the Council for Interior Design Accreditation.

Location

The Academy is located in Chicago's Loop at historic One North State Street. The campus is close to some of Chicago's famous and world-renowned landmarks. Within walking distance of the campus are the Merchandise Mart and the Apparel Center complex in historic River North and the retail shops of North Michigan Avenue. Along the revitalized State Street are Macy's, Sear's, and a multitude of nationally advertised retail outlets. More importantly, IADT Chicago is conveniently located in a region known for its internationally prominent advertising, graphic design, and interior design firms.

Nearby cultural and educational resources include the Art Institute of Chicago, the Harold Washington Library, the Chicago Cultural Center, the Athenaeum Museum of Architecture and Design, the Chicago Architecture Foundation, and the Goodman Theatre.

The natural beauty of Grant Park and the numerous public art works that are located throughout the Loop are the ideal complement to IADT Chicago's exciting urban location.

Majors and Degrees

The Academy is authorized by the Illinois Board of Higher Education to grant a Bachelor of Arts degree in merchandising management (tracks in fashion merchandising and retail operations management), a Bachelor of Applied Science in information technology, and a Bachelor of Fine Arts degree in fashion design, interior design, and visual communications (tracks in advertising communication, advertising design, game design, graphic design, multimedia and Web design, and video and animation production). The Academy is also authorized to grant Associate of Applied Science degrees in fashion design, merchandising management (tracks in fashion merchandising and retail operations management), information technology, and visual communication (tracks in advertising communication, advertising design, graphic design, multimedia and Web design, and video and animation production).

All degree programs provide students with the opportunity for in-depth career preparation and a firm foundation in general education studies. In the bachelor's degree programs, students benefit from advanced career courses and have the option of choosing elective courses to complete their general education requirements.

Academic Programs

The programs of the Academy involve both classroom education and supervised activities off campus that are designed to prepare students for entry-level positions in their chosen field. Students must take a minimum of 180 quarter hours of study to earn the baccalaureate degree. Transfer credits are acceptable in all programs. Students must take a minimum of 96 quarter hours to earn the Associate of Applied Science degree and must complete all prescribed courses satisfactorily with a minimum grade point average of 2.0.

The curriculum for each program is reviewed periodically by faculty members, program directors, and members of the program advisory boards. Members of the Advisory Boards are experienced professionals in their fields. The Advisory Boards provide the Academy with input on a variety of subjects related to their specific industry. These successful practitioners form an essential link between the academic world and the world that students enter upon graduation.

The Academy's programs are arranged into four quarters of eleven weeks each in a calendar year. A normal full-time load is 12 credit hours per quarter. As a result of the career-oriented emphasis of the Academy, course work is highly specialized and prepares students for entry into a career field. From the point at which they begin their studies at the Academy, and continuing through graduation, students are given personal one-on-one academic guidance. Students are regularly advised by the Academy's academic advisers regarding their progress in classes.

Academic Facilities

Classrooms are designed to facilitate learning and consist of lecture rooms, textile labs, drafting labs, design studios, and sewing and pattern-making rooms. Computer labs equipped with Macintosh and IBM-compatible personal computers are used for instruction and practice.

The library houses a growing collection of approximately 6,500 book volumes and 90 periodical subscriptions to support the major programs of study as well as general education courses. The library's multimedia resources consist of more than 600 videos, DVDs, and CDs with image and sound files. Other components of the collection are electronic resources with access to e-books, full-text journals, magazines, and newspaper articles. A professional librarian manages the site and assists students in the use of the library's print collection and online databases. The librarian also facilitates student access to local libraries that participate in the INFOPASS program.

The bookstore sells books and supplies used in the courses taught at the Academy. The bookstore attempts to keep a balance of inventory between new and used books whenever possible. School-specific merchandise and clothing are also available for purchase. The bookstore coordinates book buy-back periods at the end of each quarter.

Costs

Full-time tuition for the 2006–07 academic year was $16,800 for all programs. Books and supplies were additional.

Financial Aid

The Academy helps students find the financial resources they need to achieve their educational goals. The Academy participates in the Federal Pell Grant, Federal Supplemental Education Opportunity Grant (SEOG), Federal Stafford Student Loan, and the Federal PLUS Program. In addition to state and federal aid, the Academy has its own scholarship programs.

Faculty

Faculty members of the Academy possess extensive academic and professional credentials. Their experience enables them to teach theoretical principles while emphasizing current practices in the field. Faculty members are sought and retained because they are committed to teaching at the undergraduate level. In and out of the classroom, the faculty is an integral part of the students' career preparation.

Admission Requirements

Pursuant to the mission of the institution, the Academy desires to admit students who possess appropriate credentials and have demonstrated the capacity or potential for successfully completing the educational programs offered by the institution. To that end, the institution evaluates all students and makes admission decisions on an individual basis. To assist the admissions personnel in making informed decisions, an admissions interview is required.

Transfer students meeting admission requirements are accepted. Students must have an official transcript from postsecondary institutions previously attended forwarded to the Academy. Credit may be given for a course taken at the previous institution, if it is comparable in scope and length to an International Academy course, as stated in the Academy's Transfer Credit Guidelines.

Application and Information

Prospective students should apply for admission as soon as possible in order to be officially accepted for a specific program and its starting date. Prospective students must have an admissions interview and are given an opportunity to tour the Academy with their families to see its equipment and facilities, during which time, there is also an opportunity to ask questions relating to the Academy's curricula and a student's possible career goals.

At the time of application, the student must complete an enrollment agreement, pay a $50 application fee, and complete an attestation of high school graduation or its equivalency or provide proof of high school graduation or its equivalency. Once an applicant has completed and submitted the enrollment agreement, the school reviews the information and informs the applicant of its decision.

For further information, students should contact:

Cecily Arroyo, Vice President of Admissions
International Academy of Design & Technology
One North State Street, Suite 500
Chicago, Illinois 60602-3300

Phone: 888-704-2111 (toll-free)
Fax: 312-541-3929
E-mail: info@iadtchicago.com
Web site: http://www.iadtchicago.edu

KENT STATE UNIVERSITY

KENT, OHIO

The University

Kent State University has experienced tremendous growth since its founding in 1910. Today, Kent State is a multicampus network serving more than 33,000 students at eight locations throughout northeastern Ohio. The eight-campus network is anchored by a classic residential campus in Kent, Ohio. Throughout the network, students can pursue certificate, associate, bachelor's, master's, and doctoral degrees. The Kent Campus, serving 17,787 undergraduates and 4,530 graduates, offers 282 undergraduate study areas and numerous graduate degrees. Kent State's seven regional campuses are located in Ashtabula, Geauga, Stark, Trumbull, and Tuscarawas counties and the cities of Salem and East Liverpool.

As a residential campus, Kent State requires students to reside in one of thirty-four residence halls until junior academic standing is achieved. Exceptions include commuting and nontraditional students. Students can easily walk to any of the more than 100 academic, residential, administrative, and recreational buildings. The University has an eighteen-hole golf course, a 291-acre airport, a two-rink indoor ice arena, three on-campus theaters, and a new student recreation and wellness center. There are more than 230 student organizations, nineteen fraternities, ten sororities, and eighteen varsity sports. The Career Service Center provides career counseling and job placement assistance for students and alumni.

Location

Kent, Ohio, a city with a population of 28,000, is within easy traveling distance of the major metropolitan areas of northeastern Ohio. Within a 20-mile radius are concerts, cultural events, numerous amusement parks, museums, nature preserves, recreational areas, and year-round sports.

Majors and Degrees

The College of Architecture and Environmental Design offers the Bachelor of Science and Master of Architecture degrees. The School of Interior Design offers a Bachelor of Arts in interior design.

The College of the Arts offers the degrees of B.A., B.F.A., Bachelor of Music, and B.S. The college also offers multiple-degree programs. The academic divisions are the Schools of Art, Fashion Design and Merchandising, Integrated Health Studies, Music, and Theatre and Dance.

The College of Arts and Sciences awards Bachelor of Arts (B.A.), Bachelor of Science (B.S.), and Bachelor of General Studies degrees. Major fields of concentration are American Sign Language, American studies, anthropology, applied conflict management, applied mathematics, biology, biological chemistry, biology, biotechnology, botany, chemistry, classics, computer science, conservation, (criminal) justice studies, earth science, economics, English, ethnic heritage studies, French, French translation, geography, geology, German, German translation, history, international relations, Latin, Latin American studies, mathematics, medical technology, Pan-African studies, paralegal studies, philosophy, physics, political science, psychology, Russian, Russian translation, sociology, Soviet and East European studies, Spanish, Spanish translation, and zoology. Numerous interdisciplinary and preprofessional programs are available, including general studies, integrated life sciences, predentistry, pre-engineering, prelaw, premedicine, preosteopathy, prepharmacy, and pre–veterinary medicine. Students may also design their own individualized major.

The College of Business Administration awards the Bachelor of Business Administration degree. Major fields of concentration are accounting, business management, computer information systems, economics, finance, marketing, and operations management. Students can choose a minor in any of these programs as well as international business.

The College of Communication and Information offers the B.A., Bachelor of Fine Arts (B.F.A.), and the B.S. degrees. Major fields of concentration are advertising, communication studies, electronic media, news, photo illustration, public relations, radio-television, visual communication design, and visual journalism.

The College and Graduate School of Education, Health, and Human Services offers the Bachelor of Science in Education, B.A. and B.S. degrees, and Master of Arts degrees, with licensure programs available in adolescence/young adult education, early childhood education, intervention specialist studies (majors include deaf education, educational interpreter studies, gifted education, mild/moderate educational needs, and moderate/intensive educational needs), middle childhood education, multi-age education, and career technical teacher education (vocational education). In addition, separate degree programs are offered in the Schools of Exercise, Leisure, and Sport; Family and Consumer Studies; and Speech Pathology and Audiology.

The College of Nursing awards the Bachelor of Science in Nursing degree. The four-year program includes clinical practicums in the Cleveland-Akron-Warren-Youngstown areas.

The School of Technology offers associate, bachelor's, and master's degree programs throughout Kent State's eight-campus system. Students can select from a number of specialized academic programs in aeronautics, industrial, electrical, manufacturing, or educational technologies.

Academic Programs

Kent State's colleges and schools all maintain separate academic programs; completion of 36 to 37 credits of liberal education course work is a University requirement for all students. The number of credit hours required for graduation varies but is generally 121 semester hours. Credits can be transferred from previous college work satisfactorily completed or earned through courses taken at one of Kent State's regional campuses. Credit by examination is available. Generally, to earn a degree, students must earn at least 30 semester hours in residence.

The Honors College provides opportunities for students and faculty members to develop and implement special learning experiences. It offers four-year programs of undergraduate study with concurrent enrollment in one of the University's degree-granting programs. In addition, the Honors College awards Advanced Placement and International Baccalaureate credit, early admission to high school students, and specialized academic advising. Its Experimental and Integrative Studies Division offers nontraditional learning experiences for students and faculty members of the entire University community.

Support services are available for students needing assistance to ensure a successful college experience. The Academic Success Center program offers tutoring, and Student Disability Services provides assistance to students with various physical disabilities and specific learning disabilities.

Army and Air Force ROTC programs are offered on campus.

Off-Campus Programs

Through the Center for International and Comparative Programs, Kent State offers students a variety of overseas academic programs that provide a balance of academic, linguistic, and cross-cultural experiences and learning opportunities. Credit is granted toward degrees.

Academic Facilities

The collections of the University libraries total more than 2.7 million bound volumes, 14,560 periodicals, and 1.36 million microform pieces. The Department of Computer Science operates computer laboratories with Windows and UNIX workstations. These are connected to the campus network, which includes macrocomputer and microcomputer facilities. The Honors Center is a living-learning residential complex that houses undergraduate students as well as staff offices, a library-seminar room, a student computer facility, and an audiovisual center. The Center for Applied Conflict Management is an academic unit offering programs of study, research, and service activities that focus on the dynamics of change in human systems. The Instructional Television Service operates a closed-circuit, campuswide network and a production center for NETO, Inc., Channels 45 and 49, northeastern Ohio's public television stations. Audiovisual services support regularly scheduled classes with films and other educational materials. The Instructional Resources Center assists students in the production of educational media materials. The Language Laboratory provides tapes and other tools to assist students in foreign language studies. The Academic Testing Services Office offers test administration, test scoring, and research activities. The School of Fashion Design and Merchandising sponsors a working museum of fashion for students and the general public. This school houses classrooms, labs, a library, and a collection of costumes donated from the Silverman-Rogers estate for hands-on study.

As a recognized leader in liquid crystal technology, Kent State's Glenn H. Brown Liquid Crystal Institute is the nation's only center devoted solely to liquid crystal research. With a recent grant from the National Science Foundation, Kent State became the home of Ohio's first Science and Technology Research Center for the Study of Advanced Liquid Crystalline Optical Materials.

Costs

Instructional and other fees for Ohio residents for 2006–07 were $8430 per year. For students residing outside Ohio, instructional and other fees were $15,862 per year. Although room rates vary, costs for board and a double room averaged $6880 per year. The average student spends $1030 per year for books and supplies and should budget extra money for personal needs and expenses. All fees and charges are subject to change.

First-time freshmen from California, Delaware, Florida, Georgia, Illinois, Indiana, Kentucky, Maryland, Michigan, New Jersey, New York, North Carolina, Pennsylvania, South Carolina, Texas, Virginia, and West Virginia were eligible for a $3700 University Award. Students should visit http://www.sfa.kent.edu for details.

Financial Aid

The University's financial aid program assists promising students who lack the funds necessary to finance a college education. This program, which serves more than two thirds of Kent State's student body, consists of four basic sources of financial aid: scholarships, loans, grants-in-aid, and part-time employment. To be considered for financial aid awards, students must be admitted to the University and must submit the Free Application for Federal Student Aid (FAFSA). Ohio students should also check the Ohio Instructional Grant (OIG) box on the FAFSA if they are interested in being considered. Students planning to attend the fall semester as freshmen should apply for financial aid after January 1 and before March 1 of the same year. In order to meet the March 1 priority deadline, it is recommended that all financial aid forms be completed and mailed no later than February 1. Applications received after March 1 are considered, but sufficient funds to assist all late applicants may be lacking. Additional information and forms are available from the Student Financial Aid Office, P.O. Box 5190.

Kent State's Honors College awards merit scholarships to selected individuals who have the potential for superior scholarly and creative work at the University as determined by academic performance and creative artist competitions. For additional information, students should write to the Dean of the Honors College at P.O. Box 5190.

The Student Financial Aid Office also administers numerous private scholarships, including the President's Scholarship for out-of-state

students, the President's Grant for out-of-state students who are children of alumni, and various departmental scholarships. Kent State also administers the Oscar Ritchie Memorial Scholarship competition for qualified high school seniors who are members of underrepresented minority groups, including African Americans, Hispanics and Latinos, and Native Americans. Kent State offers the Founders Scholarship Program for academically talented freshmen entering the University in the fall. Qualified students are invited to campus to participate in an examination and meetings with faculty members. Scholarships range from full tuition, fees, room, and board to partial scholarships of varying amounts.

To be considered for freshman scholarships at the Kent Campus, students must complete an application for admission by February 1. Freshmen applying after this date are considered for scholarships if funds are available.

Faculty

The University's commitment to scholarship and teaching excellence is enhanced by a full-time faculty of approximately 2,100 members. Some of the faculty members are research oriented, and others publish widely.

Student Government

Students have leadership opportunities through residence hall and Greek organizations and the Undergraduate Student Senate. The senate is responsible for allocating student activity fees to registered undergraduate organizations, appointing undergraduates to all University committees and to other positions, conducting elections, and polling student opinion. Two students serve on Kent State's Board of Trustees.

Admission Requirements

Kent State's freshman admission policy differs for students with varying degrees of preparation for college studies. The students most likely to be admitted and to succeed at the Kent campus are those who have graduated with at least 16 units of the recommended college-preparatory curriculum in high school, achieved a high school grade point average of 2.5 or higher, and acquired an ACT score of 21 or better (or a combined SAT score of 980 or better).

Because special facilities and available faculties are limited, admission to certain academic programs requires special procedures and superior credentials. For freshmen, selective admission requirements apply to aeronautics flight technology, architecture, dance, education, fashion design and merchandising, interior design, journalism and mass communication, music, nursing, theater, and the six-year B.S./M.D. medical program with the Northeastern Ohio Universities College of Medicine (NEOUCOM). For transfer students, selective requirements apply to all of the preceding and to art and business. Students should contact the Admissions Office for information.

Application and Information

Application forms are available from the Admissions Office upon request. A $30 nonrefundable application fee is required. Application early in the senior year helps ensure priority consideration for fall registration, residence hall preference, and financial aid. Students may also access Kent State's online application at http://www.admissions.kent.edu. Applications are processed on a rolling basis.

Nancy J. DellaVecchia
Director, Admissions Office
Kent State University
P.O. Box 5190
Kent, Ohio 44242-0001
Phone: 330-672-2444
        800-988-KENT (toll-free)
E-mail: kentadm@kent.edu
Web site: http://www.kent.edu
          http://www.admissions.kent.edu

KETTERING UNIVERSITY

FLINT, MICHIGAN

The University

Kettering University offers education for the real world. Traditionally, nearly 100 percent of Kettering's students receive a job offer or are accepted by graduate schools before receiving their diplomas. Kettering University has a unique partnership that offers students, business, and industry an opportunity found at few undergraduate colleges in America. Kettering, a professional cooperative engineering, business, applied science, and math university, is the only institution that assists incoming freshmen to be selected by companies for cooperative employment, a process initiated for all accepted students. Through academics and the professional co-op program, Kettering is preparing a workforce for the knowledge economy.

Kettering University successfully integrates the practical aspects of the workplace into the world of higher education through its more than 700 corporate partners, corporations, and agencies located throughout the United States, Canada, and selected countries. Kettering's corporate partners represent most major industrial groups; many are recognized as worldwide leaders in business innovation, information, and manufacturing technology. These corporations share a commitment to "grow their own" engineers, leaders, and managers by employing exceptionally talented young men and women in one of the ten baccalaureate degree programs. Kettering's corporate partners invest in students' futures by providing a program of progressive work experience that exposes them to processes, products, corporate culture, and the technology necessary to compete in tomorrow's business environment.

Founded in 1919, Kettering University is private and enrolls nearly 2,400 undergraduate students. The University is accredited by the North Central Association of Colleges and Schools. Its engineering curricula are accredited by the Accreditation Board for Engineering and Technology, Inc. (ABET). The business program is accredited by the Association of Collegiate Business Schools and Programs (ACBSP). Kettering is also a member of the National Commission of Cooperative Education (NCCE).

The combination of academics and professional, paid work experience offered through Kettering University is not only highly effective, it is without equal, even among other cooperative education programs. The advantages of a Kettering education have enabled thousands of graduates to rise to key executive leadership positions in the world's finest corporations. Many graduates have also become entrepreneurs.

A 445-student residence hall and a new apartment complex are located on campus. Kettering University students enjoy an active college life with a wide range of clubs and organizations and an exciting intramural athletic program. Eleven professional societies are active on campus, and there are fourteen national fraternities and six sororities. More than half of all students are active in fraternities and sororities. Kettering students tend to enjoy competition, whether it be in service activities or on the athletic field.

A varied program of sports, fitness, and recreational activities is offered. Recreation facilities include athletic fields, tennis courts, and a recreation center with an Olympic-size, six-lane swimming pool, aerobic fitness rooms, a full line of Nautilus equipment, and basketball, tennis, and racquetball courts. A public golf course is adjacent to the campus.

Professional counseling, support services, and health care are available.

In addition to its undergraduate degrees, Kettering also offers Master of Science degree programs in engineering, engineering management, information technology, manufacturing management, manufacturing operations, and operations management.

Location

Located in east-central Michigan, 60 miles west of Lake Huron and Canada and 60 miles north of Detroit, Flint is a city of 135,000 residents with a metropolitan area population of 450,000. Flint is particularly proud of its distinctive College and Cultural Center Complex, which is about 1½ miles from campus. Built and endowed entirely by the gifts of private citizens, the center includes the Alfred P. Sloan Museum; the Whiting Auditorium, home of the Flint Symphony and host to leading stage shows and entertainers; the Robert T. Longway Planetarium, Michigan's largest and best-equipped sky show facility; the Flint Institute of Arts; the F. A. Bower Theatre; the Dort Institute of Music; the University of Michigan–Flint Campus; the C. S. Mott Community College; and the Flint Public Library.

Outdoor and indoor recreational opportunities are abundant. Within a few minutes' drive are downhill and cross-country skiing facilities, several fine lakes for the entire range of water sports, a wide selection of good golf courses open to the public, and excellent indoor and outdoor skating rinks.

Majors and Degrees

Kettering University offers a 4½-year, professional cooperative education program with curricula leading to designated Bachelor of Science degrees in Computer Engineering, Electrical Engineering (specialties in electronics, communication systems, control systems, and power systems), Industrial Engineering (specialties in computer systems integration, human factors and work design, quality assurance and reliability, production control systems, and manufacturing systems design), and Mechanical Engineering (specialties in bioengineering applications, automotive power train, automotive body and chassis, mechanical systems design, design for durability, and plastic product design) degrees; a designated Bachelor of Science in Business Management degree, with concentrations in accounting/finance, information systems, manufacturing management, marketing, and materials management; and designated Bachelor of Science degrees in applied mathematics (minors in applied and computational mathematics and applied statistics), applied physics (concentrations in acoustics, applied optics, and materials science), computer science, biochemistry, and chemistry.

Minors are available in acoustics, applied and computational mathematics, bioengineering, computer engineering, computer science, economics, electrical engineering, chemistry, fuel cell, history, international studies, literature, management, manufacturing engineering, materials science, physics, and statistics.

Academic Programs

Although each program at Kettering University has its own sequence requirements, 160 credit hours are generally required, including thesis credit hours. The program involves nine academic terms and nine co-op terms, two of which are focused on the capstone thesis project, which is done on behalf of the student's co-op employer. Students alternate between eleven-week periods of academic study on the campus in Flint and twelve-week periods of related work experience with their corporate employer. The academic year consists of two 3–month academic terms on campus and two 3–month terms of paid work experience. A typical Kettering University cooperative student may earn up to $65,000 in co-op wages through the complete program.

Academic Facilities

The C.S. Mott Engineering and Science Center—a $42-million facility—opened in summer 2003. This state-of-the-art facility houses a fuel-cell lab, an emissions lab, bioengineering labs, chemistry labs, and much more. Kettering University is one of the only universities to offer crash safety courses in its new Crash Safety Center, which includes hands-on laboratory instruction about safety testing of vehicles. Kettering University also has the traditional laboratory facilities expected of any top engineering school but also has labs to demonstrate and experiment with a wide range of technologies found in industry—from basic machining to emerging technologies.

The instrumentation in some labs is generally found only in graduate school facilities at other colleges. There are manufacturing, laser, radioisotope, heat transfer, electricity and solid-state electronics, metallurgy, computer-aided design (CAD), computer-integrated manufacturing (CIM), acoustics, mechatronics, human factors, digital and analog computer, robotics, holography, and electron microscopy laboratories as well as the Polymer Optimization Center.

The campus is fully networked and allows access to computer resources from dormitory rooms, dedicated labs, and other locations. Course materials are offered online through Blackboard. Each student has unlimited 24-hour access to computer resources. The library contains more than 94,000 cataloged volumes and currently subscribes to more than 540 periodicals and various online services. Special facilities include a microfilm area, database search services, record and tape listening and videocassette viewing facilities, and a special collection of SAE, SME, and ASME technical papers.

Costs

Tuition in 2007–08 is $25,248, and board is $3708.

Financial Aid

In addition to all traditional sources of aid, all Kettering students benefit from co-op earnings. One of the many advantages of attending Kettering University is the opportunity for students to earn a salary during their co-op work terms. Co-op income is substantial and can help cover part of the cost of a Kettering education by supplementing the family contribution and the standard forms of need-based and merit-based financial aid. The typical range of co-op earnings over the five-year program is $40,000 to $65,000.

Kettering University offers all the traditional forms of financial aid, both need- and merit-based. In 2006, 99 percent of the entering class received some form of scholarship or financial aid. The Kettering Scholarship program rewards all qualified applicants. Because of their talents, many students win scholarships from agencies and organizations from their local communities. Michigan residents are often recipients of the Michigan Competitive Scholarship/Tuition Grant. Traditionally, more than 92 percent of the entering class receives some form of financial aid, making a private education at Kettering very affordable.

The primary purpose of financial aid at Kettering University is to supplement a student's unmet financial need after cooperative earnings and parents' contributions. Students who wish to apply for financial aid should complete the Free Application for Federal Student Aid (FAFSA) and request that a copy of the analysis be sent to Kettering University. Aid is given as grants, scholarships, loans, and work-study awards.

Faculty

Kettering University's 144 full-time faculty members have teaching as their prime responsibility. Most professors in degree disciplines have industrial experience in addition to academic credentials and maintain contact with industry through consulting, sponsored research, and advising on student thesis projects. More than 80 percent of faculty members hold a doctorate. Because only half of the students are on campus at any one time, class sizes are small and opportunities for enrichment and extra help are readily available. Kettering faculty members find the challenge of teaching talented students who share their experiences from co-op especially refreshing and rewarding.

Student Government

The student government at Kettering represents the interests and needs of the students and contributes to their educational development in the areas of leadership skills, self-confidence, interpersonal relations, and organizational operations.

Admission Requirements

Admission to Kettering University is competitive and based on scholastic achievement and nonscholastic interests, activities, and achievements. Applicants are required to have earned the following credits (a credit represents two semesters or one year of study): algebra, 2 credits; geometry, 1 credit; trigonometry, ½ credit; laboratory science, 2 credits (physics and chemistry are strongly recommended for all students; at least 1 credit of chemistry or physics is required); and English, 3 credits. A minimum of 16 credits is required; however, the University encourages students to complete at least 20 credits. Applicants must submit results of the SAT or ACT. (Kettering's ACT code number is 1998; the SAT code number is 1246.) The staff of the Cooperative Education and Career Services Office assists all enrolled students with the process of securing cooperative employment. The process begins upon confirmation of enrollment and continues until each student is employed.

Most Kettering University students achieve at or near the top 10 percent of their graduating class on traditional criteria such as grades, rank, and test scores. Corporate employers are also very interested in activities, career goals, experiences, leadership, and other personal qualities. Kettering University also welcomes students wishing to transfer from other colleges and universities. The transfer alternative is an excellent way to gain admission for students who do not enroll as freshmen.

Application and Information

Prospective freshmen are encouraged to file their application early in their senior year. Admission decisions for transfer applicants are based on college record for those who have completed at least 30 credits. Applications are accepted all year long; however, early application greatly increases visibility for early employment possibilities in the co-op search process. The application fee is $35. Students can also apply online at the Admissions Office's Web site.

Admissions Office
Kettering University
1700 West Third Avenue
Flint, Michigan 48504-4898
Phone: 810-762-7865
　　　800-955-4464 (toll-free in the United States and Canada)
E-mail: admissions@kettering.edu
Web site: http://www.admissions.kettering.edu

Kettering has the experts, the labs, and the programs that bring theory and practice together.

LOYOLA UNIVERSITY CHICAGO
CHICAGO, ILLINOIS

The University

Consistently ranked a top national university by *U.S. News & World Report*, Loyola University Chicago is one of the largest of the twenty-eight Jesuit Catholic universities in the United States, with a total enrollment of 15,194 students from fifty states and eighty-two other countries. Loyola offers a total of 185 programs of study—sixty-nine undergraduate, seventy-seven master's, thirty-six doctoral, and three professional programs. Loyola prepares people to lead extraordinary lives by building upon its Jesuit tradition with an innovative Core Curriculum, which equips students with lifelong skills for success, and a strong commitment to develop the whole person—intellectually, socially, physically, and spiritually.

Loyola gives students the best of campus and city life with diverse living and learning opportunities in world-class Chicago. Located off North Michigan Avenue, Chicago's Magnificent Mile, Loyola's dynamic Water Tower Campus is home to the Schools of Business Administration, Continuing and Professional Studies, Education, Law, and Social Work and connects students to the heart of the city for myriad internship, job, and service opportunities. Loyola's Lake Shore Campus, home to the College of Arts and Sciences, the Graduate School, and the Marcella Niehoff School of Nursing, is located on the picturesque shores of Lake Michigan and offers students a traditional residential campus.

Loyola's student-faculty ratio of 14:1, well below the national average, ensures personal attention. Nearly all of Loyola's 940 full-time faculty members hold Ph.D.'s, and they are routinely called upon as experts in their fields.

Loyola students annually receive more than $180 million in financial assistance from numerous sources, including more than $45 million in Loyola-funded scholarships. Students gain practical experience and leadership, organizational, and life skills by participating in internships, engaging in service opportunities, and joining any of the school's 125 academic, social, cultural, or professional student organizations.

For information about admission, academics, housing, financial assistance, student life, and more, students should visit http://www.luc.edu/undergrad.

Location

Loyola's tranquil, residential Lake Shore Campus sits on the shores of Lake Michigan, just 8 miles north of downtown Chicago. The dynamic Water Tower Campus is located just off North Michigan Avenue, Chicago's Magnificent Mile, a fashionable area in the heart of the city, near theaters, museums, major corporate and financial institutions, and Chicago's most elegant shops and boutiques. A University-operated shuttle bus and convenient public transportation help students easily get back and forth from the two campuses.

Majors and Degrees

Loyola students may choose from sixty-nine undergraduate majors and sixty-nine minors. Undergraduate degrees offered include the Bachelor of Arts (B.A.), Bachelor of Science (B.S.), Bachelor of Business Administration (B.B.A.), Bachelor of Science in Education (B.S.Ed.), Bachelor of Science in Nursing (B.S.N.), and Bachelor of Social Work (B.S.W.) degrees.

The College of Arts and Sciences offers undergraduate majors in advertising and public relations, anthropology, biochemistry, bio-informatics, biology, black world studies, chemistry, classical civilization, communication, communications networks and security, computer science, criminal justice, ecology, economics, English, environmental sciences (chemistry), environmental studies, fine arts, forensic science, French, Greek (ancient), history, human services, information technology, international film and media studies, international studies, Italian, journalism, Latin, mathematics, mathematics and computer science, molecular biology, music, philosophy, physics, physics and computer science, physics and engineering, political science, psychology, religious studies, sociology, sociology and anthropology, software development, Spanish, statistical science, theater, theology, theoretical physics and applied mathematics, and women's studies (as a second major only).

The School of Business Administration offers majors in accounting, economics, finance, human resource management, information systems, international business, marketing, operations management, and sport management.

The School of Education offers majors in bilingual/bicultural education, elementary education, science education, and special education, along with an expanded secondary education dual-degree program.

The Marcella Niehoff School of Nursing offers the Bachelor of Science in Nursing, a health systems management major, and an accelerated B.S.N. program, which is available to students who have already completed a baccalaureate degree.

The School of Social Work offers an undergraduate major in social work and a combined bachelor's and master's degree in social work, which may be completed in five years.

Other special academic opportunities include preprofessional programs for law and health professions, eighteen 5-year (bachelor's/master's) degree programs, nineteen interdisciplinary programs, six-year early admission to Loyola's School of Law, early assurance to Loyola's Stritch School of Medicine, and the Loyola/Midwestern University Dual-Acceptance Pharmacy Program.

Academic Programs

Loyola's Core Curriculum sets goals for undergraduate education that focus on skills, values, and results that prepare students for the realities of living and working in today's world. The Core Curriculum gives students who have not yet selected an academic major the opportunity to explore many courses before deciding on a field of study.

Most degrees require 128 credit hours for graduation. Exceptionally well-qualified students may apply to the Interdisciplinary Honors Program. Students may receive credit through the Advanced Placement Program (AP) tests and the International Baccalaureate (I.B.). Certain College-Level Examination Program (CLEP) tests are accepted. Loyola students may participate in Army and Navy ROTC programs through neighboring universities.

Off-Campus Programs

Loyola's John Felice Rome Center in Italy is both one of the largest American university programs in Western Europe and the most popular study-abroad destination for Loyola students. Students may attend the Beijing Center for Chinese Studies or one of sixty other study-abroad programs in twenty-nine countries.

Academic Facilities

Loyola's state-of-the-art Michael R. and Marilyn C. Quinlan Life Sciences Education and Research Center houses laboratories used for biology, bioinformatics, chemistry, ecology, and other life science courses. It also provides numerous opportunities for undergraduates to engage in scientific research alongside their professors. The Sullivan Center for Student Services, which opened in 2006, consolidates a dozen student services offices into one convenient location. The University's library system, including the Cudahy Library at the Lake Shore Campus and the Lewis Library at the Water Tower Campus, contains more than 1 million books, 2,800 periodical subscriptions, and access to 18,000 online periodicals. The Loyola University Museum of Art, which recently opened at the Water Tower Campus, displays the University's medieval and Renaissance collection, along with other museum permanent collections and rotating exhibitions of professional and student work. The Information Commons, which is scheduled to open in spring 2008, is a new four-story lakeside research facility that will be open 24 hours daily and provide a large individual and group study space for students, state-of-the-art technology with more than 250 computers, wireless Internet connections, and a café.

The Medical Center Campus in Maywood, a suburb of Chicago, consists of the Foster G. McGaw Hospital and the Stritch School of Medicine as well as the Mulcahy Outpatient Center, the Russo Surgical Pavilion, and the Cardinal Bernardin Cancer Center.

Other key academic facilities include a nursing resource center and multiple computing centers on all campuses, including WiFi access in most areas. The Theatre Department's facilities include the Mullady Theatre, which hosts the annual main-stage performance series, and the Studio Theatre, an experimental black-box facility that is used for student productions. An FM-radio station affiliated with Loyola provides communication majors with on-campus production experience.

Costs

For undergraduate students entering in 2007–08, tuition is $27,200. Room and board costs are dependent on a student's selection of residence hall and meal plan.

Financial Aid

Loyola attempts to meet the financial need of as many students as possible. Ninety-four percent of Loyola freshmen receive some form of aid, including University-funded scholarships and grants, federal and state grants, work-study, and loans. Students are encouraged to file the Free Application for Federal Student Aid (FAFSA) before Loyola's March 1 priority date to be considered for as many sources of aid as possible.

Merit scholarships are awarded to entering freshmen who have outstanding academic records. Presidential, Damen, Loyola, and Trustee Scholarships are awarded to students who rank at the top of their high school graduating class and score well on the ACT or SAT. Scholarship amounts for these programs range from $5000 to $12,500 per year. Transfer students who have completed 30 hours of college credit with an outstanding record of academic achievement may receive a Transfer Academic Scholarship. These awards are all renewable for up to three years. Students must be admitted to Loyola prior to March 1 to be considered for scholarships that are automatically awarded with admission.

Students may also look for additional scholarships, which require separate applications. A great place to start is Loyola's list of more than seventy-five types of additional scholarships, twenty of which are awarded without considering financial need. For more information, students should visit http://www.luc.edu/finaid/scholarships.

Faculty

Nearly all of Loyola's full-time faculty members hold the Ph.D. or the highest degree in their field. Faculty members teach both graduate and undergraduate students, and senior faculty members often teach Core Curriculum courses. With a student-faculty ratio of 14:1, far below the national average, Loyola students have access to faculty members both as teachers and as advisers.

Student Government

Student government at Loyola provides a liaison between students and the administration, emphasizes concerns for student rights, and provides a forum for debate, recommendation, and action on issues that pertain to students. Students also take an active role in University policy and advisory committees and as elected representatives in the residence halls.

Admission Requirements

Students seeking admission to Loyola University Chicago are evaluated on their overall academic record, including ACT or SAT scores. For the freshman class entering in fall 2006, the middle 50 percent of ACT scores ranges between 22 and 28, the middle 50 percent of SAT verbal scores ranges between 530 and 640, the middle 50 percent of SAT math scores ranges between 520 and 640, and the average GPA is 3.63. Most Loyola students rank in the upper quarter of their graduating class, but consideration is given to students in the upper half. Candidates should be graduating from an accredited secondary school with a college-preparatory curriculum, including courses in English, math, social studies, and science. Study of a foreign language is strongly recommended. Students must submit the application for admission along with high school transcripts, test scores, a writing sample, and a secondary school counselor recommendation. Admission counselors are available to meet and talk with students individually either before or after the application is submitted.

Transfer students with 20 semester hours or more of acceptable credit are evaluated on the basis of their college work only. The minimum acceptable GPA is 2.0 (C) for the College of Arts and Sciences and the School of Social Work. A GPA of at least 2.5 (C+) is required for admission to the School of Business Administration, the School of Education, and the Marcella Niehoff School of Nursing. Candidates must also be in good standing at the last college attended.

Application and Information

Applicants are notified of the admission decision three to four weeks after the application, supporting credentials, secondary school counselor recommendation, and $25 application fee are received. The application fee is waived for students who apply online.

Prospective students are encouraged to visit the campus. Undergraduate Admission encourages students to schedule individual appointments and campus tours up to two weeks in advance or to participate in one of the many campus programs offered throughout the year.

To obtain an application and further information and to arrange a visit, students should contact:

Undergraduate Admission Office
Loyola University Chicago
820 North Michigan Avenue
Chicago, Illinois 60611
Phone: 312-915-6500
      800-262-2373 (toll-free)
E-mail: admission@luc.edu
Web site: http://www.luc.edu/undergrad

MANCHESTER COLLEGE
NORTH MANCHESTER, INDIANA

The College

Manchester College, founded in 1889, is an independent, coeducational, liberal arts college of the Church of the Brethren. Throughout its history, the College has held that values are central in the study of all majors and that the liberal arts provide a foundation of critical skills and sound scholarship.

An emphasis on service produces exceptional graduates who possess both professional ability and personal convictions, prepared for responsible lives that make a difference in the world.

Located at the edge of North Manchester, Indiana, Manchester College is primarily a residential school; 75 percent of the students live on the beautiful 124-acre campus. The academic buildings are constructed around a tree-lined central mall, and manicured flower gardens dot the campus. In addition, the resource-rich 100-acre Koinonia Environmental Retreat Center is located 12 miles from the academic campus.

The undergraduate enrollment is 1,050. Most students are between the ages of 18 and 22. Approximately 85 percent of the full-time students are from Indiana. Students from twenty-two states and twenty-three countries were also enrolled during 2006–07. Eleven percent of the students are members of the Church of the Brethren, but many different religious backgrounds are represented, and all are welcomed.

At Manchester, students get to know the members of the College's well-trained, concerned faculty on both a personal and an academic level. Faculty members take the time to assist students in a caring way, both in the classroom and as advisers.

There are five residence halls on campus that provide a variety of living experiences for students to choose from.

Manchester is a member of the National Collegiate Athletic Association Division III and offers nine men's and eight women's sports. The Physical Education and Recreation Center houses physical education classes, a fitness center, intercollegiate and intramural sports, and recreational activities. The College has a very strong intramural program that involves about 80 percent of its students.

Location

Located in the heart of Indiana's beautiful lake country, North Manchester is a thriving community of 6,000 people. It is within a half hour's drive of the Fort Wayne metropolitan area and is only 3½ hours from Chicago. Wide streets with large shade trees, graceful homes, and a beautiful park combine to provide a setting for classic college living.

Majors and Degrees

Manchester College grants Bachelor of Arts and Bachelor of Science degrees. Areas of study include accounting, adapted physical education, art, athletic training, biochemistry, biology, biotechnology, business, chemistry, coaching, communication studies, computer science, corporate finance, criminal justice, early childhood education, economics, elementary education, engineering science, English, environmental studies, exercise science, finance, fitness and sport management, French, gender studies, German, gerontology, history, journalism, manage-

ment, marketing, mathematics, media studies, medical technology, music, nonprofit management, peace studies, philosophy, physical education, physics, political science, prelaw, premedicine, prenursing, pre–occupational therapy, pre–physical therapy, psychology, public relations, religion, secondary education, social work, sociology, Spanish, sports management, and theater arts. Individualized interdisciplinary majors can also be arranged to meet a student's particular goals.

Academic Programs

The curriculum reflects a commitment to sound training in a specific area of study, the major, and broad development of skills and understanding through the liberal arts. In addition, students may explore interests different from specific career or professional areas through elective courses. This combination prepares students for careers or graduate school immediately after graduation and equips them for the challenges and changes of the coming century.

Manchester College operates on a 4-1-4 calendar and offers three summer sessions. Qualifying scores on the Advanced Placement Program and College-Level Examination Program tests of the College Board are recognized for college credit or advanced placement.

Off-Campus Programs

Manchester College students may study abroad for a semester or year in thirteen countries: at Philipps-Universität Marburg in Marburg/Lahn (Germany), the Institut International d'Études Françaises of the University of Strasbourg (France), the University of Nancy (France), the University of Barcelona (Spain), St. Mary's College in Cheltenham (England), Hokkai Gakuen University in Sapporo (Japan), the Dalian Institute of Foreign Languages in Dalian (People's Republic of China), the Athens Center (Greece), the Catholic University of Ecuador, the Federal University of Ouro Preto (Brazil), Satya Wacana University (Indonesia), Marmara University (Turkey), Cochin (India), and Universidad Veracruzana (Mexico).

During January session, numerous classes are held off campus. In the past several years, professors have taken classes to India, Kenya, England, Mexico, Russia, France, Jamaica, Ghana, Vietnam, Nicaragua, Haiti, Germany, Costa Rica, Cuba, and Hawaii as well as destinations in the continental United States.

Field experiences and internships are offered for credit in accounting, broadcasting, business, criminal justice, early childhood education, elementary education, forensic chemistry, gerontology, health sciences practicum, journalism, peace studies, physical education, political science, psychology, secondary education, and social work.

Academic Facilities

Manchester College has more than 160 personal computers in student labs, one for every 6 students. In addition, the Clark Computer Center houses file servers, three computer labs, and an AS400 for student use. PC labs tied to the network are located in each residence hall and the library. A 45-Mbs DS3 line provides high-speed Internet access.

Cordier Auditorium seats 1,300 people and has modern facilities for staging, lighting, and sound.

The $17-million Science Center, opened in fall 2005, provides state-of-the-art laboratories and fully wired classrooms. Students in astronomy use the 10-inch Newtonian reflector telescope in the Charles S. Morris Observatory.

The Funderburg Library is a newly renovated, three-story building that houses more than 170,000 books, 800 periodicals, and 4,500 audio recordings available for student use. Computer connections allow access to major libraries across the country.

Costs

Tuition and fees for 2006–07 were $19,800 for full-time students. Room and board costs for the residence halls (double occupancy) were $7320. The totaled charges with fees were $27,760 for the academic year.

Financial Aid

Manchester offers extensive scholarship and grant assistance through institutional resources. Academic awards include Honors, Trustee, Presidential, and Dean's Scholarships. Special scholarships based on academic merit and interest are awarded in art, broadcasting, journalism, music, theater, and the video arts. Service scholarships and modern language scholarships are also awarded. International students can receive scholarships based on academic accomplishments and financial need. Manchester awards significant need-based grants. More than $10.5 million in College funds were awarded in 2006–07.

Approximately 98 percent of Manchester's students have some type of financial assistance, whether it is a scholarship, a grant, a loan, or campus employment. Questions about financial aid should be referred to the Office of Admissions.

Faculty

Manchester's faculty consists of 72 full-time and 26 part-time members. Ninety percent of full-time faculty members hold the highest degrees in their fields, and 94 percent of all courses are taught by full-time faculty members. The primary emphasis of the faculty members is teaching, but many are actively engaged in research as well. Faculty members serve as academic advisers, with a specially trained group of faculty members acting as primary advisers for new students. There is a 14:1 student-faculty ratio.

Student Government

Students at Manchester assume responsibility for the governmental and judicial activities of the College. The Student Government Association provides a forum for discussion and investigation of community concerns and a channel for evaluating and solving community problems.

Each of the residence halls elects a governing body, which is responsible for providing leadership.

The judicial system of the College includes three courts: the Judicial Board, the Community Court, and an administrative hearing panel. The Student Budget Board is charged with responsibility for receiving requests for funds to support the activity program of the College and for making the necessary appropriations.

The Manchester Activities Council organizes programming of student events. Students are offered a wide variety of leadership and participation opportunities as part of the College's student development program.

Admission Requirements

Manchester College seeks to enroll students whose scholastic record, test scores, and personality give promise of success in college. Graduation from an accredited high school or its equivalent is required.

The College recommends that students take 4 years of English, 3 years of laboratory science, 3 years of mathematics, 2 years of foreign language, and 2 years of social studies in high school. Students may take either the ACT or the SAT, and personal recommendations from a high school principal or guidance counselor are required.

For transfer students, transcripts of all previous college work are required.

Application and Information

Students may apply for admission prior to each term. Applications are accepted on a rolling basis. There is a nonrefundable $25 application fee.

Interested students and their parents are encouraged to visit Manchester College and meet faculty members, coaches, and current students; sit in on classes; and take a campus tour. Arrangements can be made by writing or calling the Office of Admissions.

For application forms and further information, students may contact:

Office of Admissions
Manchester College
North Manchester, Indiana 46962-0365

Phone: 800-852-3648 (toll-free)
E-mail: admitinfo@manchester.edu
Web site: http://www.manchester.edu

Students lead Tai Chi activities with residents of Peabody Retirement Community.

MILWAUKEE SCHOOL OF ENGINEERING
MILWAUKEE, WISCONSIN

The School

Advancing beyond acquisition to the highly sophisticated application of knowledge has been the foundation of the Milwaukee School of Engineering's (MSOE) educational philosophy for more than 100 years. This approach, the university's educational niche, produces graduates who are fully prepared to begin their first jobs and pursue challenging careers. MSOE graduates start their careers as work-ready problem solvers and develop into leaders: creating new products, starting or heading companies, and working to better their communities. MSOE is governed by a Board of Regents of more than 50 members who are elected from leaders in business and industry nationwide who are members of the 200-member MSOE Corporation.

The student body of 2,400 men and women comes from throughout the United States and numerous countries. Since its founding, the university has encouraged the enrollment of students of any race, color, creed, or gender. Approximately half of the full-time students live in three high-rise residence halls.

Representatives from hundreds of firms from throughout the country, including representatives from Fortune 500 companies, visit MSOE during the academic year to interview graduating students for employment and to discuss career opportunities. The University has had a 95 percent placement rate over the past five years.

MSOE's Counseling Services Office provides individual assistance for students with educational, personal, or vocational concerns. Free, on-campus tutoring is provided by the Learning Resource Center and Tau Omega Mu, an honorary fraternity founded in 1953 for the purpose of aiding students who need extra help with their studies.

The Student Life and Campus Center provides on-campus recreational activities. This facility houses student activity rooms, student organization offices, a TV viewing area, a marketplace eatery, and a game room. Additional recreation areas can be found in the residence halls. The Kern Center, a new 210,000-square-foot health, wellness, and fitness facility, opened in fall 2004. The center houses a 1,600-seat ice arena, fitness center, 1,200-seat basketball arena, field house, recreational running track, and wrestling area.

There are more than sixty professional societies, fraternities, and other special-interest groups on campus. Many students participate in intramural sports programs. MSOE is a member of the National Collegiate Athletic Association (NCAA) Division III and the Northern Athletics Conference (NAC). The Athletic Department sponsors NCAA varsity teams in men's baseball, basketball, cross-country, golf, ice hockey, soccer, tennis, indoor and outdoor track and field, volleyball, and wrestling and women's basketball, cross-country, golf, soccer, softball, tennis, indoor and outdoor track and field, and volleyball that compete with teams from other private colleges and universities in the Midwest.

In addition to its undergraduate degree programs, MSOE offers seven Master of Science degree programs: cardiovascular studies, engineering, engineering management (accelerated option available), environmental engineering, medical informatics (jointly offered with the Medical College of Wisconsin), perfusion, and structural engineering.

Milwaukee School of Engineering (MSOE) is a member of, and accredited by, the North Central Association of Colleges and Schools. Program-specific accrediting agencies are identified in the MSOE academic catalogs.

Location

The MSOE campus is located in the East Town section of downtown Milwaukee. Nearby are the Bradley Center, the Midwest Airlines Center, the Marcus Center for the Performing Arts, the theater district, churches of most denominations, major hotels and office buildings, restaurants, and department stores. Famous for its friendly atmosphere, Milwaukee offers students many opportunities for educational, cultural, and professional growth as well as ample employment opportunities. The metropolitan area has more than 15,000 acres of parks and river parkways and miles of bike trails. A few blocks east of the MSOE campus is Lake Michigan, a place of year-round natural beauty. MSOE also offers classes in other locations in Wisconsin for students who wish to pursue select programs in the evening on a part-time basis.

Majors and Degrees

Four-year programs are offered that lead to Bachelor of Science degrees in business, construction management, engineering and specific areas of engineering (architectural, biomedical, computer, electrical, industrial, mechanical and software), engineering technology—transfer programs only (electrical and mechanical), international business, management, management information systems, and nursing. A Bachelor of Science or Bachelor of Arts degree is offered in technical communication. A five-year, double-major option is available in a combination of engineering, business, construction management, and technical communication programs. An engineering/environmental engineering dual degree (B.S./M.S. combination) is also available. An RN-to-B.S.N. program is available through the MSOE School of Nursing. International study opportunities also exist.

Academic Programs

MSOE guarantees that the classes needed to graduate in four years will be available for full-time undergraduate students who start and stay on track and meet academic requirements.

The degree programs at MSOE combine study in degree specialty courses with basic study in sciences, communication, mathematics, and humanities in a high-technology, applications-oriented atmosphere. Students who are admitted with advanced credit to a program leading to a bachelor's degree must complete at least 50 percent of the curriculum in residence at MSOE. MSOE operates on a quarter system. Students average between 16 and 19 credits per quarter, which represent a combination of lecture and laboratory courses. Undergraduate students average 600 hours of laboratory experience.

MSOE offers students the opportunity to participate in the Air Force Reserve Officer Training Corps (AFROTC) program, the Army ROTC program, or the Navy ROTC program.

Academic Facilities

The Fred Loock Engineering Center adjoins the Allen-Bradley Hall of Science, forming a prime technical education and applied research complex. Rosenberg Hall houses the Rader

School of Business faculty and technology-integrated classrooms. The Walter Schroeder Library houses more than 60,000 volumes, with collections that represent the specialized curricula of the university. Electronic technology enables the library to offer electronic books and journals, provide access to a wide variety of databases, and connect with libraries, government agencies, and other sources of information throughout the world. Full-time freshmen are required to participate in a Technology Package program that includes a notebook computer and affiliated services. A full range of software is available on these systems and via the local area network linked by a fiber-optic ring around the campus. Many areas also have wireless capability for laptop use. State-of-the-art electrical, mechanical, industrial, and nursing laboratories complement the respective areas of study. The Applied Technology Center™ (ATC) utilizes faculty and student expertise to solve technological problems confronting business and industry. The ATC is heavily involved in the transferring of new technologies into real business practice through the Rapid Prototyping Center (MSOE is the only university in the world to possess the five leading rapid prototyping technologies), the Fluid Power Institute™, the NanoEngineering Laboratory, the Photonics and Applied Optics Center, the Construction Science and Engineering Center, and the Center for BioMolecular Modeling.

There are more laboratories than classrooms at MSOE, many with industrial sponsorship from such companies as Johnson Controls, Harley-Davidson, Rockwell Automation/Allen-Bradley, Master Lock, Snap-On, General Electric, and Outboard Marine Corporation.

Costs

For 2006–07, tuition was $24,960 per year plus $1140 for the Technology Package (notebook computer, software, insurance, maintenance, Internet access, and user services). The cost of room and board in the residence halls was approximately $6189 per year. Books and supplies average $400 per quarter but may be somewhat higher for the first quarter.

Financial Aid

Qualified students are assisted by a comprehensive financial aid program, including MSOE and industry-supported scholarships, student loans, and part-time employment; Federal Perkins Loan, Federal Stafford Student Loan, Federal Work-Study, Federal Pell Grant, and Federal Supplemental Educational Opportunity Grant Programs; and state-supported grant programs. Students can also visit MSOE's Web site for a financial aid estimate.

Faculty

There are more than 200 men and women on the MSOE faculty (full-time and part-time). Many are registered professional engineers, architects, and nurses in Wisconsin and other states. They and their colleagues in nontechnical academic areas are active in related professional societies. Faculty members all have relevant experience in their area of expertise. The student-faculty ratio is 12:1. MSOE does not utilize teaching assistants.

Student Government

The MSOE Student Government Association (SGA) represents clubs and fraternities as well as residence halls and commuting students. SGA appoints representatives to the Campus Security and Disciplinary Hearing committees, the Executive Educational Council, and the Alumni Association's Board of Directors.

Admission Requirements

Each applicant to MSOE is reviewed individually on the basis of his or her potential for success as determined by academic preparation. Admission may be gained by submitting an application for admission and the appropriate transcripts. High school students are encouraged to complete math through precalculus (including algebra and geometry), chemistry, biology (nursing), physics, and four years of English. All entering freshmen are also required to provide results from the ACT or the SAT.

Transfer opportunities exist into the junior year of the Bachelor of Science in electrical engineering technology, management, mechanical engineering technology, and technical communication programs with the appropriate associate degree or equivalent credits.

Application and Information

Classes start in September, November, March, and late May. Freshmen and transfer students may enter at the beginning of any quarter; however, entry in the fall quarter is recommended. An application for admission may be obtained by contacting the address below or by visiting MSOE's Web site. Applicants are encouraged to visit MSOE and have a preadmission counseling interview. Transfer students are required to submit transcripts from all prior institutions attended. An applicant's prior course work is reviewed to determine eligibility for admission. Required course work varies depending on the desired course of study.

Admission Office
Milwaukee School of Engineering
1025 North Broadway
Milwaukee, Wisconsin 53202-3109
Phone: 414-277-6763
       800-332-6763 (toll-free)
E-mail: explore@msoe.edu
Web site: http://www.msoe.edu

MSOE's undergraduate students average 600 hours of laboratory experience—just one more advantage to an MSOE education.

MORNINGSIDE COLLEGE
SIOUX CITY, IOWA

The College

The Morningside College experience cultivates a passion for lifelong learning and a dedication to ethical leadership and civic responsibility. For more than 110 years, the goal of Morningside College has been to provide students with an education of the highest quality. Morningside is rooted in a strong church-related, liberal arts tradition, and its challenge is to prepare students to be flexible in thought, open in attitude, and confident in themselves.

Founded in 1894, Morningside College is a private, four-year, coeducational, liberal arts institution affiliated with the United Methodist Church. The College seeks both students and faculty members representing diverse social, cultural, ethnic, racial, and national backgrounds.

At the graduate level, Morningside confers a Master of Arts in Teaching, with professional educator or special education tracks.

Morningside College's approximately 1,100 full-time students are encouraged to participate in a wide variety of activities, including departmental, professional, and religious organizations; honor societies; and sororities and fraternities. A newspaper, literary magazine, yearbook, and campus radio station are all student directed. These activities provide students with many opportunities to develop leadership, interpersonal, and social skills. Since nearly all activities on campus are student initiated and student directed, ample opportunities for leadership development exist. Music recitals and concerts, theater productions, and an academic and cultural arts and lecture series are held each semester. Intercollegiate athletics are available for men in baseball, basketball, cross-country, football, golf, soccer, swimming, tennis, track and field, and wrestling and for women in basketball, cross-country, golf, soccer, softball, swimming, tennis, track, and volleyball. A variety of intramural activities are available.

The Hindman-Hobbs Center includes a pool, saunas, racquetball courts, a weight room, basketball courts, a wrestling room, and a jogging track as well as classroom facilities and offices.

Location

Morningside College is located on a 68-acre campus in Sioux City, the fourth-largest city in Iowa. The campus is based in a residential section of the community, adjacent to a city park, swimming pool, and tennis courts and within 5 minutes of a major regional shopping mall. The Sioux City metropolitan area offers a blend of urban shopping, commerce, and recreation in a scenic setting. Students find Morningside's Sioux City location to be advantageous in seeking internship opportunities and full- or part-time employment.

Majors and Degrees

The five undergraduate degrees conferred by Morningside College are the Bachelor of Arts, Bachelor of Science, Bachelor of Science in Nursing, Bachelor of Music, and Bachelor of Music Education. Career programs consist of accounting, advertising, art, biology, business administration, chemistry, computer science, corporate communications, elementary education, engineering physics, English, graphic arts, history, interdisciplinary studies, marketing, mass communications, mathematics, music, nursing, philosophy, photography, political science, psychology, religious studies, Spanish, special education, and theater. Students choosing to teach in secondary school may be certified in most academic majors.

In cooperation with other institutions, Morningside offers preprofessional programs in dentistry, engineering, law, medical technology, medicine, the ministry, optometry, pharmacy, physical therapy, physician assistant studies, and veterinary medicine.

Academic Programs

Morningside operates on a two-semester system; sessions are held from late August to December and from January to early May. Evening classes are offered each semester. A 3-week May Term and two 5-week summer sessions are also available.

The Morningside College experience provides an education that develops the whole person through an emphasis on critical thinking, effective communication, cultural understanding, practical wisdom, spiritual discernment, and ethical action. By working with talented faculty members in a large number of majors, caring college staff members who provide numerous opportunities for valuable cocurricular experiences, and other exceptional and interesting students with whom they will form lifelong connections, Morningside students gain the knowledge, skills, and personal dispositions that will ensure their success.

Special opportunities include a voluntary Interdepartmental Honors Program, in which students meet weekly to discuss ideas that have shaped history from the ancient world into the future. Friday is Writing Day, a weekly discussion format that allows students and faculty members to read aloud and react to one another's writing.

Every entering full-time student is provided with a notebook computer that is used in classroom work. Student technology services include high-speed Internet connection, ports in all residence halls and classrooms, Web-accessible personal e-mail accounts, a digital library accessible day and night, specialized computer labs to support academic programs, and wireless network access points across campus.

Off-Campus Programs

Morningside students who qualify have the opportunity to take advantage of special programs for off-campus study. Programs are available for a semester or the entire school year. The College has agreements with schools in England, Japan, and Northern Ireland.

Students participate in exchange programs with Kansai Gaidai University in Japan, Queen's University, the University of Ulster, and Belfast Institute for Further and Higher Education in Northern Ireland.

In addition, Morningside has opportunities for students to enroll for a semester at American University to study the U.S. government in action. Students may also be nominated for a semester at Drew University to study the United Nations. Students who participate in these programs maintain their enrollment at Morningside College.

Academic Facilities

The Hickman-Johnson-Furrow Learning Center is the home of the library and the Academic Support Services Center. The library has more than 114,000 volumes, more than 5,000 audio recordings and video materials, and nearly 600 current print periodical subscriptions. Online accessibility includes student/faculty access to more than 15,000 full-text journals. The library's Web-based, integrated online system allows seamless access to numerous subscription databases as well as other online catalogs and Web sites. The library building also houses the

Spoonholder Café, classrooms, the Mass Communication Department, a media center, and a computer lab.

Charles City College Hall is listed individually on the National Register of Historic Places and houses classrooms and offices for the History and Political Science, Philosophy, Religious Studies, and Theatre Departments.

The Eugene C. Eppley Fine Arts Building is one of the finest music and art facilities in the Midwest. The auditorium seats 1,400 and is noted for its acoustical qualities and the majestic Sanford Memorial Organ. The MacCollin Classroom Building, adjoining the auditorium, houses offices, art studios, practice rooms, and classrooms for music and art students.

The Helen Levitt Art Gallery adjoins the Eppley Auditorium and is home to the Levitt art collection, which includes work by internationally famous artists.

Lewis Hall, the second-oldest building on campus, is the site of the Education, English, Modern Languages, and Nursing Departments as well as administrative offices and Student Services.

The Robert M. Lincoln Center houses the College's division of business administration and economics and contains a library, auditorium, a conference room, several classrooms, and the newly remodeled Center for Entrepreneurship Education.

The James and Sharon Walker Science Center, completely renovated in 2001, features up-to-date laboratories and classrooms and houses offices for the Natural Sciences and Mathematics Division.

Costs

Tuition and fees for 2006–07 were $19,000, and room and board were $5930. These figures do not included books and personal expenses.

Financial Aid

In 2005–06, more than $22.2 million was awarded in financial aid to Morningside students, with an average financial aid package of $19,897. The financial aid resources of federal, state, and College programs are available to Morningside students through a combination of scholarships, grants, loans, and work-study employment. Morningside values students who achieve both in and out of the classroom—people who are thinkers and doers. Morningside Celebration of Excellence Scholarships recognize academic excellence and outstanding service, and awards of up to $10,000 per year are renewable for four years. Morningside also values its ties with alumni and the United Methodist Church, and those awards are also renewable for four years.

Students are encouraged to submit the Free Application for Federal Student Aid (FAFSA) as early as possible. The College's code number is 001879. The annual priority deadline for need-based financial aid is March 1.

Faculty

Eighty percent of Morningside College's 66 full-time faculty members have earned the terminal degree in their chosen field. The College also employs 66 part-time instructors and has a 16:1 student-faculty ratio.

Student Government

Student government is directly responsible for regulation, supervision, and coordination of student campus activities. The president of the student body is a voting member of the Board of Directors, allowing for student input in decisions facing the Board.

Admission Requirements

Morningside College selects students for admission whose scholastic achievement and personal abilities provide a foundation for success at the college level. While the College seeks students who rank in the upper half of their graduating class, each application is considered on an individual basis. The student's academic record, class rank, and test scores are considered. Transfer students must have earned 24 transferable semester hours of a 2.25 or better cumulative GPA on previous college work to qualify for automatic admission. It is the policy and practice of Morningside College to not discriminate against persons on the basis of age, sex, religion, creed, race, color, national or ethnic origin, sexual orientation, or physical or mental disability.

Application and Information

Rolling admission allows for flexibility; however, prospective students are encouraged to apply as early as possible before the semester in which they wish to enroll. Transfer and international students are welcome. Catalogs, application forms, and financial aid forms are available from the Office of Admissions.

For further information, students should contact:

Office of Admissions
Morningside College
1501 Morningside Avenue
Sioux City, Iowa 51106
Phone: 712-274-5111
      800-831-0806 (toll-free)
E-mail: mscadm@morningside.edu
Web site: http://www.morningside.edu

Morningside College provides a welcoming environment for art majors.

MOUNT MARY COLLEGE
MILWAUKEE, WISCONSIN

The College

Mount Mary College, Wisconsin's first Catholic college for women, was founded at Prairie du Chien on the Mississippi River in 1913 and moved to Milwaukee in 1929. Mount Mary is sponsored by the School Sisters of Notre Dame, traditionally recognized as excellent educators. More than 1,600 undergraduate and graduate students from a variety of backgrounds attend Mount Mary. Students at Mount Mary are fully engaged in the classroom, learning not just the subject matter but also how to express opinions and develop leadership skills. Students are inspired, challenged, and motivated by excellent teaching. Through exciting internships, club activities, community service, and campus ministry programs, students explore their interests and discover their skills. Special and professional interests are served by affiliates of national societies.

The College is situated on a beautiful 80-acre wooded campus with stately stone buildings. Caroline Hall, the student residence hall, provides accommodations for private occupancy and single and double suites. Every floor in Caroline Hall has a kitchen and a mini–computer lab with laser printers. All residence halls are wired for cable, telephone, and Internet connections.

Physical fitness and an interest in athletics are fostered through various activities, fitness programs, health and dance courses, and intramural and intercollegiate athletics. Mount Mary College is independent and a provisional member of the NCAA Division III. The Blue Angels compete against NCAA and NAIA schools in soccer, softball, volleyball, basketball, and tennis. Facilities include a gymnasium, an indoor swimming pool, outdoor soccer fields, a fitness center, and a sand volleyball court. Bordering the campus is a large parkway for biking, jogging, cross-country skiing, and much more.

Of special note, Mount Mary has completed its first comprehensive capital campaign having raised $28 million. Funds raised go toward the development of two new buildings—the Gerhardinger Center, which houses the science and nursing programs and student areas such as the cyber café and electronic lecture lab, and the Eileen Wirtz Bloechi Recreation Center, which features a new gymnasium, fitness center, and locker rooms—as well as toward scholarships, new and upgraded technology, women's leadership, and faculty development.

Mount Mary College sponsors many social activities, including performances by musicians and comedians, dances, and all-campus picnics. These events are sponsored by the Mount Mary Programming and Activities Council (MMPAC), Student Government, Residence Hall Association, and other groups on campus. Other events include films, concerts, and lectures. Mount Mary students also attend social functions at area colleges and universities and invite students from those institutions to Mount Mary events.

Academic and professional student services are available to all Mount Mary students, including tutoring and assistance with tests through the Academic Resource Center, advising, resume writing, career planning through the Advising and Career Development Center, and personal counseling through the Counseling Center.

In addition to undergraduate programs, Mount Mary College offers six graduate programs: the Master of Arts in education and gerontology and the Master of Science in art therapy, community counseling, dietetics, and occupational therapy.

Location

Mount Mary College is located in a residential area in northwestern Milwaukee, just 15 minutes from downtown and less than 5 minutes from a major shopping mall. Students can access public transportation right in front of the campus. Milwaukee offers a symphony, well-respected dance and theater companies, a beautiful lakefront, a newly expanded art museum, and a well-known zoo. Numerous professional and collegiate sports teams are based in Milwaukee.

Majors and Degrees

Mount Mary offers nearly thirty undergraduate degree programs leading to bachelor's degrees in accounting, art, art therapy, behavioral science (anthropology, psychology, sociology), biology, business administration, business/professional communication, chemistry, communication, dietetics, English, English professional writing, fashion: apparel product development, fashion: merchandise management, French, graphic design, history, interior design, international studies, justice, liberal studies, mathematics, occupational therapy, philosophy, psychology/behavioral science, public relations, religious education, social work, Spanish, student designed, teacher education, and theology. Columbia College of Nursing and Mount Mary College jointly offer a Bachelor of Science in Nursing (B.S.N.) degree. Special services for undeclared students help them find and focus on a major suited to their interests and talents. Preprofessional programs are also available in chiropractic medicine, dentistry, law, medicine, optometry, osteopathic medicine, and veterinary medicine. Mount Mary also provides a variety of minors to accompany any major.

Academic Programs

Mount Mary's curriculum integrates leadership skills into each student's educational experience, developing leaders who take individual responsibility for social justice. The curriculum and cocurricular activities promote self-knowledge and competence, an entrepreneurial sense of vision, effective oral and written communication skills, and the ability to strengthen leadership in others. In their professions, churches, and communities, Mount Mary students model collaborative leadership, enabling them to work effectively both in leadership positions and as supportive team members.

Mount Mary faculty members incorporate technology into the classroom through group projects and presentations. Students have access to the latest software and hardware in classrooms, labs, and the residence hall. Internet access is available throughout the campus.

The core curriculum consists of studies in five areas of the liberal arts: synoptics (12 credits in theology and philosophy), symbolics (8 credits in communication arts and mathematics), esthetics (12 credits in fine art), humanistics (12 credits in history and behavioral or social science), and empirics (4 credits of science). To qualify for graduation, baccalaureate degree students must complete a minimum of 128 credits that consist of 48 in core courses (a minimum of 24 in the major) and electives, with a minimum grade point average (GPA) of 2.0. Each academic department establishes its own requirements for the major and GPA needed for graduation.

Two signature courses at Mount Mary College are Leadership Seminar and Search for Meaning. Leadership Seminar is a 3-credit course designed to introduce students to Mount Mary's mission and the College's leadership model. This interactive and reflective course focuses on leadership and issues of social justice and includes a justice-in-action component. The course emphasizes critical thinking, reading, writing, and speaking skills and provides both a context for subsequent courses and a foundation for Search for Meaning. Search for Meaning, a 4-credit course offering 2 credits in theology and 2 credits in philosophy, includes reading and discussion of classical and contemporary authors from philosophical and theological viewpoints and reflection on such elemental human concern as the possible sources of happiness, the role of conscience in personal integrity, the meaning of suffering and death, and the transcendent dimension of reality.

Many academic programs at Mount Mary College offer internships, which allow students to relate theory to practice and interact with professionals while learning life skills. The process encourages students to reflect on the skills and knowledge they hope to gain and allows them to tailor their practical experience to the career goals they have set for the future. Many of the programs incorporate a work experience into the curriculum. Work experience includes student teaching, clinicals, fieldwork, practicum, and internships.

Mount Mary College is committed to the academic success of each student and strives to meet all adult students' needs, whether they are first-time college students or returning to complete or enhance a college degree.

Off-Campus Programs

Mount Mary encourages its students to take advantage of a variety of study abroad opportunities. Accordingly, Mount Mary College sponsors trips to China, England, France, Guatemala, Ireland, Italy, Nicaragua, and Peru. In addition to these study-abroad programs, the College maintains affiliate relationships with numerous international colleges and universities, including the American College, Dublin, Ireland; the American Intercontinental University, London and Dubai; Nanzan College, Japan; Universidad Cathólica de Santa Maria (UCSM), Arequipa, Peru; and Notre Dame College, Kyoto, Japan. Mount Mary College is part of a consortium directed by the Wisconsin Association of Independent Colleges and Universities that enables member institutions to share study-abroad opportunities.

The Office of International Studies also aids students in finding an accredited program that meets their individual needs.

Academic Facilities

Located on 80 beautiful acres, Mount Mary offers students unlimited space to grow. Facilities include the Marian Art Gallery, the Walter and Olive Stiemke Memorial Hall and Conference Center, Macintosh computer laboratories, two chapels, a fitness center, and an 800-seat theater. The Patrick and Beatrice Haggerty Library collection includes more than 110,000 volumes and 500 subscription periodical titles, along with a significant collection of audio-visual materials. As a member of the SWITCH library consortium, Haggerty Library is connected to six college and university libraries in the greater Milwaukee area. The consortium shares a common catalog, with complete exchange privileges for students and faculty members of member institutions; comprehensive subscription databases are available as well. The Web-based online catalog and an interactive library Web site provide services on and off campus.

Costs

For the 2006–07 academic year, undergraduate tuition was $17,938 for full-time students and $485 per credit for part-time students. The undergraduate fee (including matriculation, student activities, library, computer lab, parking, and health services) for full-time students was $190 per year; part-time students paid $95 per year. Room and board costs averaged $6103. All costs are subject to change.

Financial Aid

The financial aid office at Mount Mary College develops a financial package on an individual basis for all qualified students. More than 90 percent of Mount Mary's full-time students receive some form of financial assistance. Students filing for financial aid should complete the Free Application for Federal Student Aid (FAFSA) and an early financial aid estimate, both available through the Financial Aid Office. Additional information on numerous merit-based scholarships, grants, and work-study opportunities are available for incoming freshmen as well as transfer students.

Faculty

Faculty members holding advanced degrees do all the teaching; no classes are taught by teaching assistants. Faculty members are available to provide academic counseling. Mount Mary has 70 full-time and 90 part-time faculty members. With a total enrollment of 1,600, Mount Mary offers a low faculty-to-student ratio.

Student Government

Students are encouraged to participate in the governance of the College. Student Government makes recommendations about College policies and other matters of importance to students and serves as a liaison to the Mount Mary administration, faculty, and staff.

Admission Requirements

Candidates for admission are considered on the basis of academic preparation, scholarship, and evidence of the ability to do college work and benefit from it. Sixteen secondary school units are required; of these, 11 must be academic (3 in English, 2 in college-preparatory mathematics, 2 in science, 4 in history, language, or social science) and 4 in electives. Students must have achieved a minimum composite score of 18 on the ACT (870 on the SAT) and rank in the top 40 percent of their high school graduating class or have a minimum GPA of 2.5 (on a 4.0 scale). Students who do not meet the admission requirements are reviewed by an admission committee. International students must take the Test of English as a Foreign Language (TOEFL) and achieve a minimum score of 500. Mount Mary does not discriminate against any individual for reasons of race, color, religion, age, national or ethnic origin, or disability.

Application and Information

Mount Mary has a rolling admission policy. Early acceptance is available, and advanced placement is honored. An admission decision is sent as soon as all required materials, including a $25 application fee, have been received and reviewed by the Admission Office. After notification of acceptance, students wishing to enroll need to submit the $200 nonrefundable tuition deposit.

For further information, students should contact:

The Admission Office
Mount Mary College
2900 North Menomonee River Parkway
Milwaukee, Wisconsin 53222-4597
Phone: 414-256-1219
      800-321-6265 (toll-free)
Fax: 414-256-0180
E-mail: admiss@mtmary.edu
Web site: http://www.mtmary.edu

Mount Mary College is located on 80 acres in a convenient Milwaukee neighborhood. Students have a safe, secure environment in which to live and learn.

MOUNT MERCY COLLEGE
CEDAR RAPIDS, IOWA

The College

Mount Mercy College prepares students for life and work in the twenty-first century with its unique blend of career preparation and liberal arts, strengthened by a strong emphasis on leadership and service. A Catholic, coeducational four-year college, Mount Mercy is fully accredited by the North Central Association of Colleges and Schools.

Although the College offers a number of professional programs, its career preparation is not limited to those areas. Students majoring in English or history, for example, are just as likely to benefit from internships as students in business or social work. There is a focus on workplace skills such as group process and presentations—competencies that help graduates begin their careers. Mount Mercy believes strongly in a firm liberal arts foundation of analysis, critical thinking, and communication—skills that help graduates adapt to a changing world and find long-term career success.

Through its Emerging Leaders and Campus Ministry programs, the College supports the concept of servant leadership. This tradition of service is a legacy of the Sisters of Mercy, who founded the College in 1928. The College welcomes students of all faiths.

Mount Mercy's high academic quality and its relatively moderate cost make it one of the best values in Midwest higher education. The College offers thirty-five major fields of study, including several interdisciplinary majors. In the College's Partnership program, professors are paired with freshman students to support their transition to college and to enhance the intellectual growth needed to ensure academic success.

Student activities include more than thirty clubs and organizations, a student newspaper, a choir, and a pom squad and cheerleaders, along with such annual events as Hillfest and Spring Fling. Each May, commencement exercises are followed by a celebration for graduates and their families on Mount Mercy's hilltop. During the school year, many student activities—including Club Friday, a Friday afternoon gathering of students, faculty members, and staff members—take place in the Lundy Commons, which houses a game room, a fitness center, conference rooms, student organization offices, the *Mount Mercy Times* office, lounge areas, and a bookstore.

Mount Mercy College is a member of the National Association of Intercollegiate Athletics (NAIA) and the Midwest Classic Conference. The College offers intercollegiate competition in men's baseball, basketball, cross-country, golf, soccer, and track and field. In women's sports, the College offers basketball, cross-country, golf, soccer, softball, track and field, and volleyball. These programs have combined for more than thirty conference championships. Mount Mercy teams and individuals regularly qualify for regional and national championship events, and Mount Mercy student-athletes are annually recognized as NAIA academic all-Americans. Intramural activities include basketball, cross-country, flag football, golf, softball, and volleyball.

About 400 of Mount Mercy's 1,482 students live in campus housing. The College offers a variety of living arrangements. Mount Mercy's newest residence, Andreas House, houses 144 students in eight home-like, four-bedroom suites. A network of tunnels connects campus buildings; many students wear shorts all winter.

Location

Mount Mercy is just minutes from Cedar Rapids' many museums, malls, movie theaters, and restaurants. Local businesses offer numerous internships and employment opportunities. The 40-acre, tree-lined campus is tucked into a residential neighborhood of well-kept homes, neat lawns, and good neighbors. Mount Mercy's hilltop, with its sweeping view of the city skyline, is said to be the highest point in Linn County. The city bus stops at the College's "front door," providing convenient in-town transportation. Cedar Rapids is served by six major airlines and is just a 4- or 5-hour drive from Chicago, Minneapolis–St. Paul, Omaha, and St. Louis. Mount Mercy's location in a thriving Midwestern city helps students explore career possibilities and, when they graduate, find promising opportunities. Both economically and culturally, Cedar Rapids offers an outstanding quality of life.

Majors and Degrees

Mount Mercy awards the Bachelor of Arts, Bachelor of Science, Bachelor of Business Administration, Bachelor of Applied Science, Bachelor of Applied Arts, and Bachelor of Science in Nursing degrees.

The Bachelor of Arts degree is awarded to graduates who major in applied philosophy, art, biology, communication, criminal justice, criminal justice/business administration–interdisciplinary, English, English/business administration–interdisciplinary, English–language arts (teacher education program), history, international studies, mathematics, music, music education (teacher education program), political science, political science/business administration–interdisciplinary, psychology, psychology/business administration–interdisciplinary, religious studies, secondary education, social science–American government (teacher education program), social science–psychology (teacher education program), social work, sociology, sociology/business administration–interdisciplinary, speech/drama, and visual arts/business administration–interdisciplinary.

The Bachelor of Science degree is awarded to graduates who major in biology, biology–education (teacher education program), business, computer information systems, computer science, elementary education, health services administration, mathematics, mathematics–education (teacher education program), medical technology, and secondary education. The Bachelor of Science in Nursing degree is awarded to graduates who major in nursing.

The Bachelor of Business Administration is awarded to graduates who major in accounting, administrative management, business–general (teacher education program), marketing, and secondary education.

The Bachelor of Applied Science and Bachelor of Applied Arts degree programs are designed for students with technical training who wish to broaden their specialized background to include a liberal arts education. The Bachelor of Applied Science degree is awarded to graduates who major in accounting, administrative management, biology, business, computer information systems, computer science, health services administration, marketing, and mathematics. The Bachelor of Applied Arts degree is awarded to graduates who major in art, biology, criminal justice, history, mathematics, music, political science, psychology, religious studies, sociology, and speech/drama.

Elementary education majors may choose from a range of subject-area endorsements, such as reading, early childhood, and special education. Original endorsements, coupled with a secondary education major, may also be completed in a number of subject-area endorsements, ranging from art to speech-communication.

Academic Programs

Mount Mercy College requires 123 semester hours for graduation, with a cumulative grade point average of at least 2.0 (on a 4.0 scale). General education requirements include two courses in English, two in social sciences, and one each in fine arts, history, mathematics, multicultural studies, natural science, philosophy, religious studies, and speech. Students apply for admission to their major program in the spring of the sophomore year. The College gives credit for related experience based on portfolio presentations and for independent study arranged by the student and the instructor. Graduation requirements may vary according to the major field of study.

Special academic opportunities are offered to outstanding students through special honors sections of general education courses. Students graduating in the honors program receive special recognition at commencement.

Mount Mercy's academic year consists of fall and spring semesters, plus a winter term. This four-week term offers required courses as well as exploratory electives, allowing students to make more rapid progress toward their degrees. In addition, two 5-week summer sessions are held.

Off-Campus Programs

Mount Mercy College has an exchange program with the University of Palacky in Olomouc, Czech Republic.

Academic Facilities

The Busse Library provides an inviting study and research environment and access to numerous online databases. Internet access opens other major libraries to students as well. The library houses the computer center; a computer classroom that is used for instruction in writing, accounting, and computer skills; a media center; individual study carrels; group study rooms; and a variety of other comfortable study areas.

Basile Hall is an up-to-date business and biology building that opened in summer 2003, providing thirteen technology-ready classrooms and teaching labs, four seminar rooms, and a computer teaching laboratory.

All on-campus student rooms and faculty/staff offices are connected to a campus network. The College also has an ICN (Iowa Communications Network) fiber-optics classroom, making it possible for students in more than one location to take the same course, interacting with other students and with the instructor.

Costs

Full-time tuition for the 2006–07 academic year was $18,930, about the midpoint for costs among Iowa private colleges. Major fees were included in this figure. Room and board costs average $5970.

Financial Aid

Nearly all Mount Mercy's new, full-time freshmen receive some form of financial aid, including Mount Mercy scholarships or grants, federal or state grants, loans, on-campus employment, or a combination of these sources. The College awards a number of academic scholarships based on academic achievement, including Presidential Scholarships of up to $9200 per year to students with a minimum ACT score of 26 and a minimum 3.5 high school GPA, Distinguished Honor Scholarships of up to $8000 per year to high school students with a minimum 3.0 GPA and ACT score of 20, and Honor Scholarships of up to $6300 to high school students, based upon a combination of their high school GPA and ACT score. Each year, students who have been admitted to Mount Mercy and identified as Presidential Scholars are invited to the campus to compete for the Holland Scholarship, a full-tuition award named for the first president of Mount Mercy. Three Holland Scholarships were awarded for the 2005–06 school year. Students may also apply for the Merit Award, which is given to entering freshman and transfer students on the basis of their demonstrated leadership in school and community activities. In addition to these scholarships, other awards are available to students with records of achievement in art, drama, and music and to those who are planning to major in social work. Transfer students also qualify for academic awards, including Presidential Scholarships of up to $7500 per year for a transfer GPA of 3.5 or higher, Distinguished Honor Scholarships of up to $6000 per year for a transfer GPA of 3.0 to 3.49, and Honor Scholarships of up to $4500 per year, based on transfer GPA. Transfer students may qualify for an additional Phi Theta Kappa Scholarship. In 2006–07, the College awarded more than $6.2 million in institutional scholarships and grants to qualified students.

Students who show financial need may be eligible for the Federal Pell Grant, Iowa Tuition Grant, Federal Stafford Student Loan, and on-campus employment. Students in work-study positions typically earn from $1000 to $1500 per year.

To apply for Mount Mercy scholarships and grants, students must first be admitted to the College. Early application is advised. The priority deadline for filing the Free Application for Federal Student Aid (FAFSA) is March 1. Students should check other deadlines with their high school counselors or call the Mount Mercy financial aid office.

Faculty

Most of Mount Mercy's 73 full-time and 78 part-time faculty members hold the terminal degree in their fields. Many have been recognized for their achievements. Several faculty members have been Fulbright Fellows or have received grants from the National Endowment for the Humanities and the National Endowment for the Arts; many others have been recognized by their professional organizations. With a student-faculty ratio of 12:1, Mount Mercy offers students the opportunity to know their teachers well and to learn from them in an informal, friendly, and supportive environment.

Student Government

The official voice of the student at Mount Mercy is the Student Government Association (SGA). Its officers serve on College committees, and SGA is represented at regular faculty meetings. An SGA petition to the faculty resulted in adding a fall break to the academic calendar. SGA is the body through which all other campus organizations are formed and funded.

Admission Requirements

Mount Mercy admits students whose academic preparation, abilities, interests, and personal qualities give promise of success in college. Applicants are considered on the basis of academic record, class rank, test scores, and recommendations. An Admission Committee reviews the applications of students with minimum qualifications. To apply, freshman students must submit an application for admission, a transcript of high school credits, scores from ACT or SAT examinations, and a $20 application fee. Transfer students must submit an application for admission, official transcripts from all colleges attended, official transcripts from their high school (if not possessing an associate degree), and a $20 application fee. Students who wish to apply online should visit the College's Web site (http://www.mtmercy.edu). Mount Mercy College has an agreement with several two-year colleges in Iowa through which degree graduates of these colleges may be admitted to Mount Mercy with junior standing.

Prospective students are encouraged to visit the campus and meet with a faculty member in their area of interest. Special campus visit days are scheduled each year, and individual appointments also may be made. Overnight accommodations in residence halls can be arranged.

Application and Information

Students who wish to be considered for Mount Mercy scholarships and grants should submit their applications for admission as early as possible after their junior year in high school. Admission decisions are made on a rolling basis, and the College notifies students of its decision within ten days of receiving the necessary forms.

Application forms are available online at http://www.mtmercy.edu and may be completed online or printed and mailed. Students may also contact:

Office of Admissions
Mount Mercy College
1330 Elmhurst Drive, NE
Cedar Rapids, Iowa 52402
Phone: 319-368-6460 or 363-5270
      800-248-4504 (toll-free)
E-mail: admission@mtmercy.edu
Web site: http://www.mtmercy.edu

Student Government Association steering committee meeting.

NORTH CENTRAL COLLEGE
NAPERVILLE, ILLINOIS

The College

Founded in 1861, North Central College has a distinctive heritage as a comprehensive college that educates students in both the liberal arts and sciences and in preprofessional fields.

A private, United Methodist–affiliated institution, the College has long been recognized for academic excellence, with its educational philosophy of incorporating leadership, ethics, and values into academic and cocurricular activities. North Central's 2,500 students include traditional-age undergraduate, part-time, and graduate students. Master's degree programs are offered in business administration, computer science, education, leadership studies, liberal studies, and management information systems. Graduate certificates are available in business foundations, change management, dispute resolution, finance, gender studies, history and nature of science, human resource management, investments and financial planning, leadership studies, management, marketing, multicultural studies, organizational ethics, teacher leadership, and technology in education.

North Central's 59-acre campus has more than twenty major buildings. Facilities include the historic Old Main, built in 1870 and renovated in 1998; the state-of-the-art Cardinal Stadium, which seats 5,500 and is the home to football, soccer, and track; and Pfeiffer Hall, a 1,050-seat auditorium. Kaufman Dining Hall serves the entire campus.

Thirty-five states and twenty-four other countries are represented, and thirteen percent of the members of the 2006 freshman class are members of minority groups.

Cocurricular programs parallel many academic majors and include the nationally acclaimed Students in Free Enterprise, Cardinals in Action (a community service organization), campus radio station WONC-89.1 FM, Mock Trial, Model United Nations, and forensics. North Central student athletes compete in nineteen NCAA Division III intercollegiate varsity sports within the College Conference of Illinois and Wisconsin. The varsity sports include baseball, basketball, cross-country, football, golf, soccer, swimming, tennis, track and field, and wrestling for men. Women participate in basketball, cross-country, golf, soccer, softball, swimming, tennis, track and field, and volleyball. Students have many options for social activities: programmed events through the College Union Activities Board, residence life activities, an active intramural program, and travel to both downtown Naperville and Chicago. Student services include centers for academic advising, counseling, writing, foreign language, and career development.

Location

North Central is located in a charming historic district in the heart of Naperville, Illinois, a fast growing community of more than 140,000 residents in the west-suburban area of metropolitan Chicago. The city is a residential community with excellent community services and has become the Midwest center of scientific research and development. It is in the "Silicon Prairie" center of the high-technology Illinois Research and Development Corridor, where some of the nation's largest companies (e.g., BP Amoco, Metropolitan Life, and Nalco Chemical Company) are located. Nearby are Argonne National Laboratory, Fermi National Accelerator Laboratory, and Morton Arboretum. All of these facilities and industries represent unique resources for North Central students—for internships, jobs, and joint research opportunities.

Chicago is just 29 miles away, and the cultural, artistic, and entertainment venues in this great city make it a rich resource for a North Central education. Students can catch the Burlington Northern Railroad just two blocks from the campus for an easy commute.

Majors and Degrees

North Central College awards the Bachelor of Arts (B.A.) degree in accounting, anthropology, art, art education, athletic training, biochemistry, biology, broadcast communication, chemistry, classical civilization, computer science, East Asian studies, economics, education (elementary and secondary), English, entrepreneurship and small business management, exercise science, finance, French, German, global studies, history, human resource management, humanities, interactive media studies, international business, Japanese, management, management information systems, marketing, mathematics, music, musical theater, music education, nuclear medicine technology, organizational communication, philosophy, physical education, physics, political science, print journalism, psychology, radiation therapy, religious studies, science, social science, sociology, sociology and anthropology, Spanish, speech communication, sport management, and theater. The Bachelor of Science (B.S.) degree is awarded in accounting, actuarial science, applied mathematics, biochemistry, biology, chemistry, computer science, mathematics, nuclear medicine technology, psychology, radiation therapy, and in all economics and business areas.

Preprofessional-professional programs are offered in engineering, health sciences, medical physics, medical technology, nursing, and law. A 3-2 engineering program is offered in cooperation with the University of Illinois at Urbana-Champaign, Washington University in St. Louis, Missouri, Iowa State University, and the University of Minnesota. Both 2-2 and 3-2 programs in nursing are available in cooperation with Rush University in Chicago. Students may also design other majors that bridge two or more areas of study.

Academic Programs

North Central provides a comprehensive education with the goal of preparing students to live free, ethically responsible, and intellectually rewarding lives. Each student must complete a minimum of 120 credit hours, including all general education requirements and an approved major. CLEP, AP, and IB exams are considered for college credit and/or advanced course placement.

The academic year comprises three 10½-week terms and a six-week Interim Term between Thanksgiving and the beginning of the new calendar year. Students usually take three courses during each term, while the Interim Term is used for independent study, taking courses, travel, research, work, or simply relaxation. The College actively supports internships as part of career preparation, and the College Scholars Honors Program is open to select students.

Off-Campus Programs

North Central College provides many opportunities for students to study abroad. Students interested in engaging in intensive Spanish study may travel to Costa Rica each fall term for thirteen weeks. The fifteen-week London term allows students to explore European history and understand the changing contemporary English and continental cultures. The fifteen-week China/Japan term begins in Beijing and then moves to Kyoto, allowing students to live and study in both countries. Other study-abroad possibilities include exchange programs to China, England, France, Japan, Korea, Northern Ireland, and Sweden.

North Central is also one of only twelve colleges and universities in the nation to offer the distinctive Richter Independent Study Fellowship Program, which provides funds of up to $5000 for a single specialized project. Richter Independent Study projects have included travel and research on every continent.

Academic Facilities

WONC (89.1 FM), the College's 1,500-watt radio station, is one of the most powerful student-staffed stations in the Midwest. The station, with three state-of-the-art studios for on-air and audio production work, has won twenty Marconi Awards—more than any other college radio station in the country.

All students and faculty and staff members have access to a voice, video, and data network, including full Internet access from their residence halls, classrooms, computer laboratories, and offices.

Science equipment available for student research projects includes a fourteen-CPU LINUX parallel processor, computer networking and multimedia labs, a 300-MHz magnetic resonance spectrometer, a gas chromatograph/mass spectrometer, a liquid chromatograph, a pulsed nitrogen laser, a phase-contract video microscope, PCR thermal cyclers, and environmental chambers. North Central also has state-of-the-art language and market research laboratories.

Costs

For 2006–07, tuition at North Central College was $22,710. Room and board were $7440. Resident students paid a $225 technology fee. The student activity fee was $180, and estimated additional expenses were $425 for books and supplies. Students should also budget personal expenses and transportation costs.

Financial Aid

The Offices of Administration and Financial Aid are committed to assisting students throughout the process of applying for financial aid. Scholarships, loans, grants, and work-study assistance are awarded on the basis of demonstrated financial need and the academic record. Students are required to submit the Free Application for Federal Student Aid (FAFSA). Funds are also available through the Illinois State Monetary Award Program (for Illinois residents only), the Federal Pell Grant program, Federal Supplemental Educational Opportunity Grant, and the Federal Stafford Student Loan program. The College awarded more than $12 million from institutional sources for 2006–07. Merit scholarships range from $6000 to full tuition, renewable annually. Students may also interview and/or audition for scholarships in international business/global studies, science, theater, forensics, and vocal and instrumental music, as well as submit art portfolios.

Faculty

Members of the North Central faculty, 87 percent of whom hold the Ph.D. or another terminal degree, are first—and foremost—teachers. A student-faculty ratio of 14:1 and an average class size of 19 students ensure opportunities for a stimulating exchange of ideas. All faculty members also serve as academic advisers to provide guidance and counseling for students. Students get to know their professors on a personal basis, and the list of independent study projects is extensive. Faculty members teach both undergraduate and graduate courses.

Student Government

The Student Governing Association takes an active role in the development and implementation of policies concerning student life on campus. Representatives of the student body have a voice on faculty, trustee, and administrative committees, while the College Union Activities Board plans social and service events.

Admission Requirements

New students are accepted individually on the basis of their overall academic preparation, character, and potential for success at North Central College. Graduation from an accredited secondary school is a basic requirement for admission. Other criteria used in the selection of prospective students are the high school academic record, personal recommendations of high school counselors, ACT or SAT scores, and involvement in extracurricular activities. Members of the North Central freshman class of 2006–07 scored an average of 24.6 on the ACT. North Central does not discriminate on the basis of sex, race, ethnic background, age, or physical handicap.

Application and Information

North Central College operates on a rolling admission basis, which allows students to apply at any time during or after their senior year in high school. Students can complete and submit an application for admission on the College's Web site. Applicants receive notification within three weeks after the College receives all documentation. Early application is recommended to ensure availability of campus housing. The application must be accompanied by a $25 fee, an official high school transcript, and official reports of ACT or SAT scores from the testing agency. For additional information or application forms, students should contact:

Office of Admission
North Central College
30 North Brainard Street
Naperville, Illinois 60540
Phone: 630-637-5800
      800-411-1861 (toll-free)
Fax: 630-637-5819
E-mail: ncadm@noctrl.edu
Web site: http://www.northcentralcollege.edu

Historic Old Main, built in 1870 and renovated in 1998, houses the Offices of Admission, Financial Aid, and the Registrar.

OHIO WESLEYAN UNIVERSITY

DELAWARE, OHIO

The University

An unusual synthesis of liberal arts learning and preprofessional preparation has set Ohio Wesleyan University (OWU) apart. Founded by the United Methodist Church in 1842, the University is strongly committed to developing the service ethic in students, to fusing theory with its practical applications, and to confronting specific issues of long-range public importance.

Undergraduate enrollment is about 1,850 men and women. Students come to Ohio Wesleyan from forty-three states and forty countries, and most reside on the attractive 200-acre campus. Housing options include six large residence halls with special-interest corridors; a number of smaller special-interest units, such as the Tree House and the Peace and Justice House; and eleven fraternity houses. The five sorority houses are nonresidential.

There is a wide range of cocurricular activities. Students initiate discussion groups, service projects, and intramural athletics. Other activities include a fully independent student newspaper, cultural- and ethnic-interest groups such as the Student Union on Black Awareness and the Christian Fellowship, crisis intervention work, the College Republicans and Young Democrats, and prelaw and premed clubs. In the course of a year, students may enjoy more than 100 concerts, plays, dance programs, films, exhibits, and timely speakers. The Theatre and Dance Department stages four major productions and much additional studio work each year, while the Music Department sponsors four large groups and other small ensembles. An impressive campus center is the hub of cocurricular life on campus.

There are twenty-two varsity athletic teams—eleven for men and eleven for women. Many teams often earn NCAA Division III national ranking; recent rankings have included the men's teams in baseball, golf, lacrosse, and soccer and the women's teams in soccer and track and field. In 2001 and 2002, the OWU women's soccer team was the NCAA Division III national champion. In recent years, individual All-Americans have been named in these sports and in football and men's and women's track and field. In 2004, Chad Poling won the NCAA Division III individual men's golf championship. Intramural programs are extensive, and all students have access to racquet sports, swimming, and weight-lifting facilities in the Branch Rickey Physical Education Center. Fitness equipment and health services are housed in the Health and Wellness Center, conveniently located near the residence halls. Off-campus opportunities for backpacking, boating, camping, golf, skiing, and swimming are abundant.

Location

Delaware combines the small-town pace and maple-lined streets of the county seat (population 26,000) with easy access to the state capital, Columbus, the fifteenth-largest city in America. Thirty minutes south of the campus, Columbus provides rich internship opportunities, international research centers, fine dining and shopping, and cultural events that complement campus life. Delaware, founded in 1808, retains a stately, post-Colonial charm in many of its sections. Because the campus is in the town, students find a degree of solitude but not a sense of isolation. About half of the faculty members live a short walk from campus.

Majors and Degrees

Ohio Wesleyan offers the Bachelor of Arts degree in accounting, astronomy, biological sciences (botany, genetics, microbiology, and zoology), chemistry, computer science, economics (including accounting, international business, and management), education (elementary and secondary licensing in seventeen areas), English literature and writing, environmental science, fine arts, French, geography, geology, German, history, humanities-classics, journalism, mathematics, music (applied or history/literature), neurosci-

ence, philosophy, physical education, physics, politics and government, psychology, religion, sociology/anthropology, Spanish, and theater and dance. Fifteen interdisciplinary majors include black world studies, East Asian studies, environmental studies, international studies, Latin American studies, urban studies, and women's and gender studies, as well as prelaw and premedicine. Students may also design majors in topical, period, or regional studies.

Two professional degrees are awarded: the Bachelor of Fine Arts in art history, arts education, and studio art, and the Bachelor of Music in music education and performance. Combined-degree (generally 3-2) programs are offered in engineering, medical technology, optometry, and physical therapy.

Academic Programs

Ohio Wesleyan provides opportunities for students to acquire not only depth in a major area but also knowledge about their cultural past through the insight provided by a broad curriculum. At Ohio Wesleyan, education is placed in a context of values, and students are encouraged to develop the intellectual skills of effective communication, independent and logical thought, and creative problem solving. To these ends, students are required to demonstrate competence in English composition and a foreign language (often through placement testing) and to complete distributional study in the natural and social sciences, the humanities, and the arts. With few exceptions, the major requires the completion of eight to fifteen courses; double majors and minors are encouraged. Completion of thirty-four courses is required for graduation.

Advanced placement is available with or without credit. Under the four-year honors program, first-year students may be named Merit Scholars and work individually with faculty mentors on research, directed readings, or original creative work. Upperclass students are also encouraged to participate in independent study. Phi Beta Kappa is one of more than twenty scholastic honorary societies with chapters on campus.

The objectives of an Ohio Wesleyan education are crystallized in the distinctive Sagan National Colloquium, a program focused annually on one issue of compelling public importance, such as "Connected: How Science Influences Who We Are." Through weekly speakers and semester-long seminars, the colloquium stimulates campuswide dialogue and encourages students to integrate knowledge from many different disciplines and apply what is studied to life. Participants should discover not only what they think about the issue but also why they think as they do and how to make important decisions based on their beliefs.

Off-Campus Programs

Full-semester internships and apprenticeships, as well as programs of advanced research, are actively developed through most departments. Many are approved by the Great Lakes Colleges Association, Inc. (GLCA), a highly regarded academic consortium of twelve independent institutions. Programs include the Philadelphia Center, the GLCA Arts Program in New York, and the Oak Ridge National Laboratory Science Semester. Other cooperative arrangements include the Newberry Library Program, Wesleyan in Washington, and the Drew University United Nations Semester. Research is done locally at the U.S. Department of Agriculture (USDA) Laboratories in Delaware, the nearby Columbus Zoo, and several other sites.

Ohio Wesleyan has been long committed to education for a global society. Consequently, the curriculum has an international perspective, a significant portion of the student body is drawn from other countries, and a wide variety of opportunities are offered overseas. Individual work may be arranged elsewhere, but formal programs are offered in more than twenty countries. These include Ohio Wesleyan's affiliation with the University of Salamanca in Salamanca,

Spain, and its program in Strasbourg, France, as well as programs in Africa, China, Colombia, England, India/Nepal, Japan, Russia, and Scotland.

Academic Facilities

The Beeghly Library houses more than 550,000 holdings, one of the largest collections in the country for a private university of Ohio Wesleyan's size. The library's federal documents depository is among the nation's oldest and largest, providing an additional 200,000 reference publications. Beeghly also offers the Online Computer Library Center's most advanced cataloging system. The collection is enhanced by OhioLINK and CONSORT membership. A new Internet Café recently opened in Beeghly, providing students with a 24-hour study area. The café has eight computer workstations and wireless capabilities and serves Starbucks coffee and other assorted sandwiches and snacks.

The comprehensive academic computing system is accessible to students 24 hours per day, and all residence hall rooms are wired for campus network and global Internet access on a "one-port-per-pillow" basis. University-wide computing systems at Ohio Wesleyan include Red Hat Linux-based IBM xSeries and pSeries servers for e-mail, administrative data processing, Web hosting, and timesharing as well as Windows 2003 file server applications. Approximately 300 Windows-based microcomputers in more than a half-dozen public computer laboratories—including a state-of-the-art Information Commons area in the main library—are accessible to the campus community. Having begun in 2004, OWU is making gradual progress in developing Wi-Fi Internet access for select campus buildings, with the goal of making the entire campus wirelessly enabled in the near future.

The first phase of the $35-million new Conrades-Wetherell Science Center opened in January 2003. Now completed, it includes a 145,000-square-foot three-level building that houses a wide variety of state-of-the-art instrumentation, including a scanning electron microscope and scanning and transmission electron microscopes, which are co-owned by the USDA Labs. Located in the Science Center is the new Science Library, which consolidates all of OWU's science holdings. The Woltemade Center for Economics, Business, and Entrepreneurship; the Department of Economics; the Learning Resource Center; and Information Systems are located in the R. W. Corns Building. The University has a state-of-the-art Geographic Information Systems Computer Laboratory. Perkins Observatory houses a 32-inch reflecting telescope and two smaller instruments. Two University wilderness preserves cover a total of 100 acres. Other special facilities are the multistage Chappelear Drama Center; Sanborn Hall, home to the Music Department; and Gray Chapel, which houses a Klais concert organ.

Costs

The general fee for 2006–07 was $37,660. This amount covers tuition ($29,870), room and board ($7790), and fees ($420). Books and personal expenses average $1100. Nominal fees were charged for some studio art courses, off-campus study, private music lessons for students who were not majoring in music, and student teaching.

Financial Aid

Nearly all first-year students who demonstrate need have been awarded an aid package. Packages include grant, loan, and employment assistance from Ohio Wesleyan and the standard federal and state programs (such as Federal Pell Grant, Federal Stafford Student Loan, Federal Perkins Loan, and Federal Work-Study). More than two thirds of the student body receive some form of need-based aid, and another quarter receive merit- or non-need-based aid. More than 75 percent of all aid is provided by grants and scholarships. On the average, students on financial aid at Ohio Wesleyan receive more scholarship and grant assistance and rely less on loan support than do students at most other institutions.

Several merit scholarship programs worth as much as $29,870 per year, private loan programs, and flexible payment plans are available without regard to financial need. This year, more than 140 enrolling first-year students received merit awards.

Faculty

The full-time faculty numbers 130, providing a student-faculty ratio of approximately 13:1. All of the full-time faculty members hold the highest degree in their fields. Although committed first to teaching and advising, most faculty members maintain active research programs and publish important articles and books. Some members of the faculty are practicing artists whose contributions include the creation and exhibition of original works of art and theater.

Student Government

Students have a significant voice in the government of campus life. The Wesleyan Council on Student Affairs, more than two thirds of whose members are students, formulates basic policy. Students also sit on judicial boards and nine faculty committees and are represented at all meetings of the Board of Trustees.

Admission Requirements

The admission process is competitive. Each application is carefully studied on an individual basis. Although the applicant's academic record is most important, followed closely by teacher and counselor evaluations and SAT or ACT scores, many other factors are considered, such as evidence of creativity, community service, and leadership. A sixteen-course preparatory program is required. Four units of English and 3 each of mathematics, social studies, science, and foreign language are recommended, but variations of this program are considered. SAT Subject Tests are not required but may qualify students for advanced placement. Candidates for the B.Mus. degree must audition (tapes are accepted). Early action, early decision, and transfer admission are offered. Campus interviews are strongly recommended but not required. In 2005–06, approximately 3,000 applications were received; about 2,065 of the applicants gained admission.

Application and Information

Students are urged to complete the application process as early as possible in the senior year of secondary school, especially if they are applying for financial aid. Once complete credentials (application, transcript, recommendations, and SAT or ACT scores) are received, decisions are made on a rolling basis after January 1. The student's response is required by May 1. The deadline for early decision application is December 1; the deadline for early action application is December 15. Notification is given within four weeks. After April 1, students are admitted on a space-available, rolling admission basis.

For further information, students should contact:

Office of Admission
Ohio Wesleyan University
Delaware, Ohio 43015
Phone: 800-922-8953 (toll-free)
Fax: 740-368-3314
E-mail: owuadmit@owu.edu
Web site: http://www.owu.edu

The Hamilton-Williams Campus Center is a magnificent meeting place for the campus community.

OLIVET NAZARENE UNIVERSITY

BOURBONNAIS, ILLINOIS

The University

Olivet Nazarene University (ONU) is a private, Christian, liberal arts university with a strong emphasis on both academic excellence and Christ-centered living. ONU offers one of the finest liberal arts educations in the Midwest, world-class facilities for learning and entertainment, and an atmosphere that promotes fun, relationship building, and spiritual growth.

Olivet's high retention, graduation, and employment/placement rates demonstrate the University's commitment to students' success. The members of the faculty, staff, and administration are dedicated to teaching, encouraging, and mentoring each student as a whole person—academically, socially, and spiritually.

With 4,400 students (2,400 undergraduates), Olivet offers an ideal student population for a private institution, maintaining diversity without sacrificing personalized attention. Half of the student body comes from the Nazarene denomination, while the others come from some thirty other denominations. Most U.S. states are represented, as are over twenty countries.

The campus offers a championship-caliber athletics department (seventeen intercollegiate men's and women's sports in all) and a large intramural sports program. Music and drama groups involve hundreds of students, and many clubs are organized for a wide variety of interests. Olivet students are also heavily involved in dozens of ministry groups and volunteer efforts, small-group Bible studies, and weekly student-led services.

The University recently completed a number of campus improvements, including the renovation of the lower level of Ludwig Center, the student union, to include a glass-enclosed gaming room featuring plasma TV screens, a convenience store, and new student leadership offices. In addition, the first floor of Nesbitt Hall, a residence hall, was converted into a fourth dining option for students, and the Department of Communication moved to a new, technologically advanced facility in Benner Library, which also houses some of the University's Art programs, representing a partnership between Communication and Art. Future plans call for a new chapel and a performing arts center.

The University is home to the Chicago Bears' summer training camp and Shine.fm, a 35,000-watt station ranked among the top stations in the nation and staffed by Olivet's broadcasting students.

In addition to its undergraduate programs, Olivet offers eight master's degree programs and four adult degree-completion programs. The School of Graduate and Continuing Studies strives to meet the needs of the ever-expanding number of adults returning to school. Adult degree-completion programs are designed to assist working adults so they can complete their degree requirements without an interruption to their employment. The School of Graduate and Continuing Studies serves as a resource for adults striving to enhance their personal and professional lives in a constantly changing world.

Location

The University is located just 50 minutes south of Chicago's Loop in the historic Village of Bourbonnais. The area includes malls, restaurants, entertainment, and natural recreation centered on the Kankakee River State Park system. Olivet students enjoy many activities nearby and often make the quick trip north for the limitless offerings of Chicago and its surroundings.

In addition to recreation, students find numerous opportunities for employment and internships in the area, which is ranked as one of the top locations in the nation for small businesses, and the vast professional resources of Chicago. Students, faculty members, and staff members also find themselves working side by side in local and regional ministry projects. Olivet students are recognized professionally and ministerially as a valuable commodity by area businesses, churches, and parachurch organizations.

Majors and Degrees

Olivet confers Bachelor of Arts (B.A.) and/or Bachelor of Science (B.S.) degrees in the following fields of study (includes all majors, minors, and concentrations): accounting, art, art (education), athletic coaching, athletic training, Biblical languages, Biblical studies, biochemistry, biology, biology (education), business administration, chemistry, chemistry (education), child development, children's ministry, Christian education, church music, clinical laboratory science, communication studies, communication studies (education), computer science, corporate communication, counseling, criminal justice, cross-cultural ministries, dietetics, digital media: graphics, digital media: photography, digital production, drawing/illustration, early childhood education, earth and space science, earth and space science (education), economics/finance, electrical engineering, elementary education, engineering, English, English (education), environmental science, exercise science, family and consumer sciences, family and consumer sciences (education), fashion merchandising, film studies, finance, French, general science, general science (education), general studies, geological sciences, Greek, health education, history, history (education), hospitality, housing and environmental design, information systems, international business, journalism, journalism (education), literature, management, marketing, mass communication, mathematics, mathematics (education), mechanical engineering, military science, music, music education, music performance, nursing, painting, philosophy, physical education/health, physical science, physical science (education), physics, political science, practical ministries, pre-dentistry, prelaw, premedicine, preoptometry, prepharmacy, pre-physical therapy, pre–physician's assistant studies, pre–veterinarian studies, psychology, psychology (education), public policy, radio, religion, religion and philosophy, science (education), secondary education, social science, social science (education), social work, sociology, Spanish, Spanish (education), sports management, systems programming, television/video production, theater, youth ministry, and zoology.

Academic Programs

Olivet seeks to offer an "Education with a Christian Purpose." The University believes this commitment to Christ mandates nothing less than the highest-quality academic programs. Olivet's liberal arts curriculum requires that students complete 45 to 58 hours of general education courses. With the addition of major and minor programs of study, students must complete a minimum of 128 credit hours to obtain a bachelor's degree. Credit may be earned through AP and CLEP tests. Students may also participate in ROTC.

Olivet operates on a two-semester schedule, from August to May. Two summer sessions are also available.

Off-Campus Programs

Olivet students are encouraged to participate in the various off-campus study programs offered each semester. International locations include Beijing, China; San José, Costa Rica; Cairo, Egypt;

Drummoyne, Australia; Oxford, England; western Europe; Irian Jaya, Indonesia; Tokyo, Japan; Moscow, Nizhni Novgorod, and St. Petersburg, Russia; Mukono, Uganda; and Sighisoara, Transylvania (Romania). Domestic opportunities include the American Studies Program in Washington, D.C.; the Los Angeles Film Studies Program in Burbank, California; Focus on the Family Institute in Colorado Springs, Colorado; Contemporary Music Center on Martha's Vineyard; and the AuSable Institute (environmental science) in northern Michigan. Costs are usually comparable to a semester at Olivet, and credit is given for these programs. In addition, financial aid is applicable.

In addition, many Olivet students participate in numerous educational and missions-oriented short-term trips, which are available during the Christmas, spring, and summer breaks.

Academic Facilities

Olivet's 250-acre, $150-million campus offers leading-edge academic facilities. These include high-quality performance halls and athletic venues; excellent natural science, engineering, and nursing laboratories; SMART classrooms in most departments; and an observatory. It is one of only a handful of small college campuses in the nation to have a planetarium. Each department uses the top software in its field. More than a dozen campus computer labs are available for student use, and two network ports in each dorm room and the recently added campuswide wireless network give students access to e-mail, the Internet, and classroom applications 24 hours a day.

Benner Library and Resource Center provides unlimited access to any material a student needs, either on-site from its more than 170,000 books, 350,000 other items in various formats, 1,000 periodicals, over 10,000 full-text electronic journals, and more than 250,000 government documents and CD-ROMs or through the interlibrary loan system.

Costs

Tuition, based on 12 to 18 credit hours, was $8375 per semester in 2006–07. Room and board, based on double occupancy and the twenty-one-meals-per-week plan, cost $3200 per semester.

Financial Aid

Approximately 96 percent of traditional undergraduates receive a total of $24.9 million in scholarships and grants, of which $15.5 million comes from Olivet scholarships and grants.

Olivet's cost is below average for private colleges nationwide. The University also participates in all federal and state financial aid programs. The priority deadline for filing the Free Application for Federal Student Aid (FAFSA) is March 1. To apply for aid, students must fill out the FAFSA as well as Olivet's application for financial aid. The student must be an accepted applicant before a financial aid package can be created. Olivet offers a monthly installment plan in addition to the traditional three-payment plan. Olivet believes funding a student's education is a partnership between each family, Olivet, and the state and federal governments. The friendly staff is committed to making an Olivet education affordable to every young person.

Faculty

Olivet's more than 100 full-time faculty members are the key to excellence in and out of the classroom. Teaching is a ministry for these dedicated Christian individuals, and Olivet's student-faculty ratio gives them an opportunity to teach, mentor, and encourage students on a personal level. To that end, the faculty is heavily involved in campus life, whether sponsoring social organizations or participating in talent shows.

Within the traditional liberal arts curriculum, more than 75 percent of Olivet's faculty members have earned a Ph.D. or terminal degree in their fields.

Student Government

The Associated Student Council is the student government organization on campus. Its Executive Council consists of a president, vice president of finance, vice president of spiritual life, vice president of social affairs, vice president of women's residential life, vice president of men's residential life, vice president of office management, the *GlimmerGlass* (student newspaper) editor, and the *Aurora* (yearbook) editor. They work alongside the University's administrative team to ensure the health and promotion of campus activities and organizations.

Admission Requirements

Admission to the University is moderately difficult. Students are considered for admission on the basis of their high school GPA, ACT or SAT scores, and personal recommendations. An ACT score is required for placement in courses. For international students, TOEFL results are an additional factor in the admission decision. Students with low test scores and GPAs may be admitted on a provisional basis. A campus visit and interview are strongly recommended for all prospective students.

Application and Information

Admission is on a rolling basis until the application deadline of May 15. An early decision is required for some scholarships. Students may apply via Olivet's home page online or in print. The application process includes the written (or electronic) application, high school transcripts, ACT or SAT scores, and a health form. There is a $25 application fee, and an Enrollment Deposit is collected to prioritize both student housing and class registration.

For more information or to arrange a campus visit, students should contact:

Office of Admissions
Olivet Nazarene University
One University Avenue
Bourbonnais, Illinois 60914
Phone: 800-648-1463 (toll-free)
E-mail: admissions@olivet.edu
Web site: http://www.olivet.edu

Students on the campus of Olivet Nazarene University.

QUINCY UNIVERSITY
QUINCY, ILLINOIS

The University

Quincy University is a private Roman Catholic university of the liberal arts and sciences. It was founded in 1860 by the Franciscan Friars, who have influenced the world by caring about people as people and urging them to fulfill their potential. This spirit is still maintained at Quincy University today. The University prides itself on its personal approach to learning. Small classes, a dedicated faculty, close faculty-student relationships, and a comfortable atmosphere on campus all create an environment that is conducive to personal growth and development. The University offers courses on both its 52-acre main campus and the 23-acre North Campus, which is located ten blocks away. Shuttle bus service moves students between these campuses regularly.

The 900 students come from diverse social and economic backgrounds. Although the majority are from the Midwest, twenty-four states and ten countries are represented in the student body. Quincy University is a residential campus, with more than 70 percent of the students living on campus. Campus housing options are varied and include single-sex and coed residence halls, apartments, and houses. Numerous campus organizations offer unlimited opportunities for students to participate in both University and community activities. A National Public Radio station, music performance groups, publications, honor and service societies, a lecture series, and concerts are a few of the many extracurricular opportunities available to students. Eighty percent of the students participate in intramural sports. Quincy University also maintains membership in the NCAA and the Great Lakes Valley Conference. Intercollegiate sports for men are baseball, basketball, football, golf, soccer, tennis, and volleyball. Women's intercollegiate sports are basketball, golf, soccer, softball, tennis, and volleyball.

Career planning and placement counseling is available to students throughout their academic career. Quincy University has an outstanding placement record; more than 94 percent of graduates are placed in jobs or graduate schools within 180 days of graduation. Individual assistance with academic planning, study skills, and tutorial work, as well as personal and vocational counseling, is provided free of charge.

At the graduate level, Quincy University offers programs of study leading to the M.B.A., M.S.Ed., M.S.E. in counseling, and M.S.T. (theological studies) degrees.

Location

The University is located in a residential section of Quincy, a city of 50,000 people, which is situated on the bluffs of the Mississippi River. It is within easy traveling time of St. Louis (2 hours), Kansas City (4 hours), and Chicago (4½ hours). Good highways and bus, train, and air service make the area easily accessible from any part of the nation. Quincy has a rich and distinguished tradition in the arts. It is noted for its fine architecture and extensive park system.

Majors and Degrees

Quincy University awards the Bachelor of Arts (B.A.), Bachelor of Fine Arts (B.F.A.), and Bachelor of Science (B.S.) degrees. Programs of study include accounting, art, art/graphic design, aviation, aviation management, biology, biological sciences, biological sciences education, business administration, chemis-try, clinical laboratory science, communication, computer information systems, computer science, criminal justice, elementary education, English, English education, finance, history, history education, humanities (interdisciplinary), human services, management, marketing, math, music, music education, nursing, physical education, political science, psychology, social work, special education–learning disabilities, sport management, and theology and philosophy. A Bachelor of Science in Nursing (B.S.N.) is available through a cooperative program with Blessing-Riemann College of Nursing.

Minors are available in most programs; concentrations are offered in physics and reading. A certificate program in business and a coaching specialty in physical education are also available.

Preprofessional programs include dentistry, engineering, law, medicine, physical therapy, and veterinary medicine.

Academic Programs

The academic program at Quincy University is based on the belief that liberal arts is the most functional and exciting tradition in education. The curriculum is designed to provide students with the fundamentals of a liberal arts education and at the same time prepare them for a rewarding professional and personal life. The flexible curriculum design allows for double majors or major-minor combinations, student-designed majors, and interdepartmental majors. An honors program, independent studies, special-topics courses, independent research, practicums, and internships are also available to meet the special needs of students.

To be eligible for a baccalaureate degree, a student must complete a minimum of 124 semester hours of university courses with at least a C average. The degree program requires 43 semester hours in general education and "tools" courses, 30–33 hours in a major, and at least 36 hours each in distributed electives and upper-level course work.

Quincy University accepts credit earned through the Advanced Placement Program, the College-Level Examination Program, challenge examinations, and, in some cases, academically related experience.

Off-Campus Programs

Arrangements are made with area schools, health facilities, businesses, and industries for such credit-bearing activities as student teaching, clinical training, internships, and practicums. The University also promotes the Early Exploratory Internship Program to its first- and second-year students, allowing them to gain preprofessional experience with area businesses and agencies. Study abroad is possible through many options, with the academic credit for this study preplanned and integrated into the degree program.

Academic Facilities

The Brenner Library, which is considered one of the top three private-college libraries in the state of Illinois, houses more than 260,000 volumes and 182,000 microtext items and subscribes to 725 periodicals. Among the outstanding holdings are a rare-book collection, the 75,000-volume Bonaventure Collection of early Christian and medieval history and theology, and the 4,000-volume Fraborese Collection on Spanish-American history. Through the University's membership in the Online Computer Library Center, Quincy University students have access to millions of books in libraries throughout the Midwest and the nation. The library is also equipped with a computerized reference service.

A modern academic complex located at North Campus houses laboratories for chemistry, physics, biology, engineering, and psychology as well as lecture halls and faculty offices. Six computer labs and more than 200 workstations are available for student use. Students also have unlimited access to personal computers, various networks, Internet, and UNIX. Additional special facilities are a radio station; a fully equipped television studio; the Ameritech Center for Communication, a state-of-the-art computer writing lab and classroom; and the Student Health and Fitness Center.

Costs

The costs for the 2006–07 academic year were $18,450 for tuition (12–18 credit hours), $560 for the student activity/computer fee, $3750 for room (double occupancy), and $3230 for board.

Financial Aid

More than 95 percent of the students at Quincy University receive some form of financial assistance. The University participates in the Federal Pell Grant, Federal Supplemental Educational Opportunity Grant (FSEOG), Federal Perkins Loan, Federal Work-Study (FWS), and Federal Stafford Student Loan programs. Illinois State Grants are available for qualified Illinois residents. Quincy University awards academic scholarships ranging from $1500 to full tuition. Need-based grants are also available. Students who wish to apply for aid must complete the Free Application for Federal Student Aid (FAFSA) as well as the brief QU Application for Financial Aid. Notification of financial aid awards is made on a rolling basis. Early application is recommended, and priority is given to students who apply before February 15. Transfer applicants are required to submit a transcript from each college or university attended.

Faculty

The Quincy University faculty is composed of 115 professionals, who are highly qualified in their respective fields. Although many are engaged in research, teaching is the top priority at Quincy University. The University's favorable student-faculty ratio of 12:1 and its experienced faculty members, many of whom have had actual work experience in their field, bring an added dimension to the classroom. Eighty-eight percent of the faculty members have the highest degree possible in their field.

Student Government

Students participate in University governance through representation on most University committees, including the Academic Affairs Committee, Athletic Advisory Committee, Student Life Committee, and University Judicial Board. The Student Senate provides for effective student participation in all aspects of University life.

Admission Requirements

Quincy University encourages applications from students who are serious about enrolling in a coeducational university of the liberal arts and sciences and who have demonstrated through their previous academic work an ability to profit from and contribute to the University. Each applicant for admission is evaluated individually. Primary consideration is given to the student's previous academic record. Quincy University recommends that prospective students take a strong college-preparatory program in high school. The Office of Admissions evaluates the prospective freshman's high school record in the following areas: number of academic courses taken, level of difficulty of courses attempted, type of high school attended, grade point average, standardized test scores, class rank, and extracurricular activities. All freshmen are required to submit SAT or ACT scores along with an application for admission, a $25 application fee, high school transcripts, a counselor recommendation, and a personal statement on why they would like to attend Quincy University.

Transfer students who have earned fewer than 24 semester hours must submit a high school transcript in addition to their college transcripts and should have maintained an overall grade point average of at least 2.0 (C) during their collegiate years. All transfer students are required to submit an application for admission, transcripts from every college or university attended, and a personal statement on why they would like to attend Quincy University. Transfer students may enter at three times during the year: August, January, or June.

International students must submit a transcript from each secondary and collegiate institution they have attended. All non-English transcripts must be translated into English before submission to the Office of Admissions. All international students must also submit TOEFL scores or demonstrate proficiency in the English language.

Application and Information

All students seeking admission are encouraged to apply early. Applications are evaluated after all required application materials have been received. Notification of admission decisions is made on a rolling basis.

Parents, students, and student groups are always welcome to visit the University. The Office of Admissions welcomes visitors from 9 a.m. to 3 p.m., Monday through Friday. Saturday visitors are welcome by appointment. If possible, campus visits should be scheduled during the academic year, when classes are in session. Accepted students may stay overnight in residence halls with prior arrangements.

For more information about the University's 146-year tradition of excellence, students should contact:

Director of Admissions
Quincy University
1800 College Avenue
Quincy, Illinois 62301-2699
Phone: 217-228-5210
      800-688-HAWK (4295) (toll-free)
E-mail: admissions@quincy.edu
Web site: http://www.quincy.edu

Quincy University's $12-million Student Health and Fitness Center.

ROBERT MORRIS COLLEGE

CHICAGO, BENSENVILLE, DUPAGE, ORLAND PARK, LAKE COUNTY, PEORIA, AND SPRINGFIELD, ILLINOIS

The College

As an accredited, private, not-for-profit institution, Robert Morris College (RMC) grants associate, bachelor's, and master's degrees to more than 3,000 students each year. Its mission is to offer professional, career-focused education in a collegiate setting to diverse communities. Associate degrees in twelve different fields of study, the Bachelor of Business Administration degree, the Bachelor of Applied Science degree in graphic design, the Bachelor of Applied Science degree in computer studies, the Master of Business Administration, and the Master of Information degrees are awarded. Robert Morris College is accredited by the Higher Learning Commission and is a member of the North Central Association of Colleges and Schools (30 North LaSalle Street, Suite 2400, Chicago, Illinois 60602; 312-263-0456; http://www.ncahigherlearningcommission.org).

The history of Robert Morris College dates back to the founding of the Moser School, one of the outstanding independent business schools in Chicago, in 1913. Robert Morris College also has origins in Illinois at the site of the former Carthage College. Here, Robert Morris College was chartered and offered associate degrees in both liberal and vocational arts from 1965 to 1974. With the acquisition of the Moser School in 1975, RMC expanded to include business and allied health. The College now provides students with a choice of seven locations: Chicago, Bensenville, DuPage, Orland Park, Lake County, Peoria, and Springfield, Illinois.

RMC offers programs in the School of Business Administration, the School of Health Studies, the School of Computer Studies, the Institute of Culinary Arts, the School of Professional Studies, Institute of Art and Design, and the School of Graduate Studies. Each of these divisions uses the most modern computer technology. Acquisition of such technology is imperative to providing real-world, educational experiences that are relevant to the evolving workplace.

RMC's unique five-quarter system is designed for continuous learning. It enables students to accelerate their education, completing a bachelor's degree in as little as three years and an associate degree in fifteen months.

The student body of approximately 8,630 is a cross-cultural, ethnic, and racial mix representative of the communities served. Each student works with a team of program directors, instructors, and placement specialists in an effort to achieve educational and career goals. The records of the College's students and graduates are the best indicators of what a prospective student can expect. More than 72 percent of RMC students graduate from the programs they begin, compared to significantly lower percentages at other private and public colleges and universities.

The Career Services Department, which has offices at each of the College's campuses, continuously cultivates employment opportunities for RMC graduates, with representatives in the business, allied health, art, culinary, art and design, and computer industries. Last year, 86 percent of RMC bachelor's degree candidates had jobs at the time of graduation.

Robert Morris College is a member of the National Association of Intercollegiate Athletics (NAIA) and the Chicagoland Collegiate Athletic Conference (CCAC), Division II. RMC athletic teams compete in top-level facilities located near each campus. The College offers men's and women's basketball, cross-country, golf, soccer, and club hockey. It also offers men's baseball, women's softball, volleyball, tennis, and bowling.

Housing is available within walking distance of the main campus at 320 North Michigan. Student housing provides a wealth of amenities, shopping, entertainment and events that bring the community together in apartment-style student living.

Location

Located in the heart of Chicago's bustling cultural and financial districts, the College's main campus is minutes from all that Chicago offers, including the Chicago Board of Trade, Art Institute, Field Museum, Merchandise Mart, lakefront, sports arenas, theaters, and all forms of public transportation. The Chicago campus is readily accessible from all parts of the city and suburbs by bus lines and trains. Parking is available in the immediate vicinity. Robert Morris Center is across the street from the renowned Harold Washington Public Library.

The Bensenville campus opened to better serve the residents of western Cook and DuPage Counties and to meet the demands of employers in the area. The recently expanded Orland Park campus now includes a technology center with the latest computer facilities available to industry and education. In September 2005, the College opened the Institute of Culinary Arts at the Orland Park campus. The campus is adjacent to the Orland Square Mall, approximately 30 miles southwest of Chicago. It is accessible via public transportation and I-80 and I-55, which run parallel on the south and north ends of the campus, respectively. Orland Park is becoming a corporate center of the southwest Chicago suburbs, offering students opportunity for professional growth through internships and employment.

The DuPage campus opened on the border between Naperville and Aurora and serves students as well as employers along the East-West High Tech Corridor—the heart of rapid technological development and close to a wide range of employers. The RMC Institute of Culinary Arts started at the DuPage campus and grew so significantly so quickly, the program expanded to the main campus in downtown Chicago and Orland Park. The Lake County campus in Waukegan opened in summer 2003, serving students in northeastern Illinois and southeastern Wisconsin. Within a year, the Lake County campus was the fastest growing campus in the RMC system.

The Springfield campus—initiated as the first step of the College's commitment to serve central Illinois—is located just east of White Oaks Mall and is accessible by bus; ample parking is also available. This campus has also expanded to a second building at the same location due to expansion of programs and increases in enrollment. The RMC presence in Illinois has further extended to a campus in Peoria, with a busy downtown location.

All RMS campuses provide students with access to the unlimited variety of business services and enhance the students' understanding of the world of work, the employment process, and an appreciation for the attributes of each community.

Majors and Degrees

The Bachelor of Business Administration degree at Robert Morris College offers concentrations in accounting, health/fitness management, hospitality management, and management. The Bachelor of Applied Science degree in graphic design offers a concentration in graphic arts. The Bachelor of Applied Science degree in computer studies offers concentrations in systems integration and networking. RMC also awards associate degrees in accounting, business administration, CAD drafting (architectural/mechanical), computer networking, culinary arts, fitness and exercise, graphic design, interior design, medical assisting, paralegal studies, and surgical technology.

More than twenty-six transfer agreements have been established between RMC and community colleges, allowing students who have earned associate degrees elsewhere to complete their bachelor's degrees at RMC by transferring in as a junior. Robert Morris College is the fifth-largest private undergraduate college in Illinois and the state's top provider of associate degrees to women in the field of computer studies, as well as the state's number one private college provider of bachelor's degrees in business management. RMC's tuition rate is among the lowest of Illinois' private colleges/universities.

Academic Programs

The College's academic calendar consists of five quarters, each of which is ten weeks long. The program of study is designed so that students can complete their course work and enter their careers in the shortest time possible: in as little as three years for a bachelor's degree and fifteen months for an associate degree.

By concentrating on the specialized subjects related to the student's chosen career field, the College's curricula provide students with the skills and knowledge necessary to enter the job market. Each major consists of courses prescribed by the College to lead to this objective.

An associate degree requires at least 92 quarter hours of credit with a minimum of 36 hours of credit in general education in the areas of communications, humanities, math and science, and social and behavioral science. A minimum of 52 quarter hours of credit are required in career courses, and the remaining hours are electives split between general education and career courses. A bachelor's degree requires a minimum of 188 quarter hours of credit. A minimum of 76 hours of credit are required in general education courses; 100 to 104 hours are required in major course work.

The Honors Program at Robert Morris College recognizes a higher level of achievement in students and offers a unique track for specialized attention and educational opportunities. The students are enrolled in bachelor's or associate degree cohorts (teams of students working together in the same program) in which every class they take is honors or their general education core is all honors.

Robert Morris College offers students the opportunity to gain experience in their majors and improve their skills through internships and externships. Placement personnel work closely with students to secure positions related to their fields of study. Internships offer many educational and professional benefits and provide students with the opportunity to earn academic credit for participating in a career-specific work experience.

Off-Campus Programs

Robert Morris College offers students the opportunity to study abroad at the Institute of European Studies in Vienna, Austria; at Regent's College in London, England; in Florence, Italy, the Apicius Culinary Institute of Florence for culinary students and the Florence University of the Arts for graphic design students.

Academic Facilities

General purpose classrooms; high-tech equipment; specialized laboratories; study, practice, and leisure lounges; fitness centers; and student centers are among the facilities the College provides at each campus. The technology-based library has online capabilities that connect the College's various campuses. Online Internet access offers students advanced research capabilities, sizable collections of reference and resource volumes, and periodical subscriptions. Vertical file information is available in addition to numerous computer and audio resources and a job search center.

Costs

Robert Morris College has one of the lowest tuition rates of any baccalaureate degree–granting private college in the state. Tuition for 2005–06 was $5125 per quarter. Book and supply costs vary by major from $400 to $450 per quarter. Housing and program fees are also applicable.

Financial Aid

Robert Morris College participates in the following federal and state financial aid programs: the Federal Pell Grant, Illinois Monetary Award (SSIG/IMA), Federal Supplemental Educational Opportunity Grant (FSEOG), Federal Stafford Student Loan, Federal Perkins Loan, Federal PLUS Loan, and Federal Work-Study (FWS) programs. In addition, the College awards institutional grants on the basis of need, scholarship, residence, academic major, or a combination of these factors. All students must complete a financial planning interview with their admissions counselor, and all are urged to complete the Free Application for Federal Student Aid (FAFSA). Approximately 92 percent of the student body receives some financial assistance. In the 2004–05 academic year, the College awarded more than $16 million in institutional aid.

Robert Morris College also provides scholarship opportunities for students who are admitted to the Honors Program.

Faculty

The faculty members at Robert Morris College are selected on the basis of their academic credentials, career experiences in their field, and dedication to giving special attention to every student. All faculty members possess a master's degree in their chosen field, and many possess a Ph.D. in their area of specialization. In addition to teaching courses, faculty members promote the progress of their students through the individualized academic, employment, and personal development counseling they provide.

Student Government

Robert Morris College has no formal student government. Student representatives serve on committees that make recommendations about campus issues. Student organizations and activities are available.

Admission Requirements

All graduates of accredited high schools or the equivalent (GED) are eligible for admission to the College. All candidates are encouraged to have a personal interview with an admissions representative and to have a tour of the campus.

A variety of materials are considered for various applicants. Freshman applicants just graduating from high school must submit their high school record or GED score and test results from the ACT, SAT, Applied Education Skills Assessment (AESA), Advanced Placement, and SAT Subject Area tests.

Applicants to the Honors Program must have a minimum high school GPA of 3.0 and/or a high school GPA of at least 2.5 and an ACT score of 21 or higher.

Those enrolling as an adult (age 23 and above) must submit their high school record or GED score; test results from the ACT, SAT, Applied Education Skills Assessment (AESA), College Level Examination Program (CLEP), and Dantes; and evidence of a successful employment experience.

Transfer students must present a minimum of 12 transferable credit hours from an accredited institution and their academic records from any high schools and colleges previously attended.

International students must forward their official education records, the results from either TOEFL or AESA, and an affidavit of financial support.

Home-schooled students must submit a complete transcript of all classes they have taken, curriculum documentation and its state certification, and results from any standardized exams they have taken.

Application and Information

Applications can be obtained by contacting the Admissions Office at any of the College's campuses. The completed application and the $30 nonrefundable application fee ($100 nonrefundable application fee for international students) should be sent to the Admissions Office. The College operates on a rolling admissions basis, and students can enroll during any one of the five times offered during the year. For further information, prospective students should visit the Web site or contact:

Robert Morris College
Chicago–Main Campus
401 South State Street
Chicago, Illinois 60605
Phone: 800-RMC-5960 (toll-free)
Web site: http://www.robertmorris.edu

Robert Morris College
Bensenville Campus
1000 Tower Lane
Bensenville, Illinois 60106

Robert Morris College
DuPage Campus
905 Meridian Lake Drive
Aurora, Illinois 60504

Robert Morris College
Orland Park Campus
82 Orland Square
Orland Park, Illinois 60462

Robert Morris College
Lake County Campus
1507 South Waukegan Road
Waukegan, Illinois 60085

Robert Morris College
Peoria Campus
211 Fulton Street
Peoria, Illinois 61602

Robert Morris College
Springfield Campus
3101 Montvale Drive
Springfield, Illinois 62704

SAINT MARY'S COLLEGE
NOTRE DAME, INDIANA

The College

One of the oldest Catholic colleges for women in the United States, Saint Mary's College was founded in 1844 and continues to be sponsored by the Sisters of the Holy Cross. The College has long been recognized as a pioneer in exploring with integrity and imagination the roles of women in society. Today, Saint Mary's enjoys a national reputation for academic excellence and vitality of campus life.

With more than 1,500 students from forty-five states and nine countries, Saint Mary's brings together women from a wide range of geographical areas, social backgrounds, and educational experiences. International and minority students compose 9 percent of the student body.

Saint Mary's College's liberal arts emphasis enhances a comprehensive curriculum. Strong programs in the humanities and sciences are complemented by professional programs in business administration, education, nursing, and social work; majors in the fine and performing arts; and courses of preprofessional study that prepare students for law school, medical school, or advanced study in other health professions.

Small classes (median size: 16) and a low student-faculty ratio (11:1) encourage student participation in class discussions, collaboration with faculty members, and preparation for real-world challenges. The College enjoys a unique co-exchange program with the University of Notre Dame.

Approximately 80 percent of Saint Mary's students live on campus in five residence halls, each with its own distinctive character. Upperclass students may live off-campus while seniors may choose to live in Opus Hall, apartment-style living on campus. Residence halls offer a full calendar of activities, from twice-yearly dances to discussions with professors. The College has a new student center, a dining hall, and a clubhouse for extracurricular activities. All residence halls have chapels, and the Church of Loretto is on campus.

As an NCAA Division III school and a member of the Michigan Intercollegiate Athletic Association, Saint Mary's sponsors varsity teams in basketball, cross-country, golf, soccer, softball, swimming and diving, tennis, and volleyball. Club sports, cosponsored with Notre Dame, include equestrian, gymnastics, lacrosse, skiing, and synchronized swimming. In addition, Saint Mary's offers many intramural sports.

The College's Angela Athletic Facility contains multipurpose courts for tennis, volleyball, and basketball; a training and fitness center; and racquetball courts. The campus has an indoor swimming pool, outdoor tennis courts, and athletic fields for both soccer and softball.

Location

Saint Mary's 275-acre campus, set alongside the Saint Joseph River, has great natural beauty. The College, located just across the street from the University of Notre Dame, just north of the city of South Bend, and just 90 miles from Chicago, is at the hub of much activity. Students from Saint Mary's and Notre Dame form a dynamic intercollegiate community. South Bend provides sites for internships and practicums and opportunities for volunteer service.

Majors and Degrees

Saint Mary's College offers programs leading to the Bachelor of Arts, Bachelor of Science, Bachelor of Fine Arts, Bachelor of Business Administration, and Bachelor of Music degrees.

For a Bachelor of Arts degree, students may choose majors in art, biology, chemistry, communication studies, economics, elementary education, English literature, English writing, French, history, humanistic studies, Italian, mathematics, music, philosophy, political science, psychology, religious studies, social work, sociology, Spanish, statistics and actuarial mathematics, studio art, and theater.

A Bachelor of Science degree may be obtained in biology (with concentrations in cellular/molecular biology, environmental biology, and general biology), chemistry, computational mathematics/computer science, mathematics, nursing, and statistics and actuarial mathematics.

The Bachelor of Music degree program, which is a member of the National Association of Schools of Music, offers concentrations in music education and music performance. For talented art students, Saint Mary's offers a Bachelor of Fine Arts degree with concentrations in several media.

The Bachelor of Business Administration degree program offers a major in accounting, business administration (with concentrations in accounting, finance, international business, management, and marketing) and a major in management information systems.

Superior students who are candidates for either a Bachelor of Arts or a Bachelor of Science degree may design a program of study outside the traditional department structure.

For women interested in engineering fields, a dual-degree program offered in cooperation with the University of Notre Dame leads to a bachelor's degree from Saint Mary's College and a Bachelor of Science in Engineering degree from Notre Dame in one of seven areas.

Saint Mary's education department, accredited by the National Council for Accreditation of Teacher Education, offers certification in elementary and secondary education.

In addition, the College offers more than forty minors in a variety of fields, including American studies, information science, justice studies, Latin American studies, urban studies, and women's studies.

Academic Programs

Graduation from Saint Mary's College requires successful completion of at least 128 semester hours of credit with a minimum quality point average of 2.0. Every student must also complete a comprehensive examination in her major, which may take the form of a thesis, a research or creative project, or a written or oral examination, depending on the discipline. All students must demonstrate writing proficiency by satisfactorily completing a writing-intensive "W" course, usually in the first year, and an advanced portfolio of writings in the major discipline, usually as seniors.

Students spend approximately one third of their time in general education courses in humanities, fine arts, foreign language, natural and social sciences, theology, and philosophy. Remaining course hours are devoted to their major and electives or minors. The College assists those students interested in pursuing independent study or research and internships.

Off-Campus Programs

Through Saint Mary's international study programs, students can study with Irish students at the National University of Ireland Maynooth, just outside Dublin. They can absorb Italian art and culture on Saint Mary's campus in the center of Rome, or experience Southeast Asia and the Far East with the India-based Semester Around the World Program.

Saint Mary's students may also enroll in the Spanish language programs of the Center for Cross-Cultural Study in Seville, Spain, or in the French language and culture study in Dijon, France. A new exchange program with the Australian University of Notre Dame based in Freemantle is also available, as is a program based in Pietermaritzburg, South Africa.

Saint Mary's students may study in Austria and other countries through a cooperative program with the University of Notre Dame.

A student majoring in political science has the opportunity to spend a semester at the American University in Washington, D.C. Saint Mary's also participates in student- and faculty-member exchange programs with the University of Notre Dame and members of the Northern Indiana Consortium for Education.

Academic Facilities

Students have abundant access to technology systems, software, and services. Residence halls and classrooms are wired for network access and secure wireless network access is available in many public areas on campus. Computer labs for students are available in several campus buildings, as well as computer "collaboratories" where students and faculty members can conduct online research in groups in a classroom setting. Extensive support services are available to students and faculty and staff members for instructional, administrative, and network systems. Faculty members make significant use of information technology resources for teaching, research, and scholarship.

The modern Cushwa-Leighton Library houses an outstanding collection of more than 228,000 volumes. It includes offices, study areas, an after-hours study lounge, a media center, computer facilities, the College archives, and a rare-book room.

In addition to extensive biology, chemistry, and physics lab facilities, laboratories for psychology research and for foreign language study and practice are available to students. Art studios, music practice rooms, the O'Laughlin Auditorium, and Moreau's Little Theatre provide ample space for fine arts creation, practice, and performance.

The professionally staffed Early Childhood Development Center on campus provides education and psychology majors with an unusual opportunity to work with young children. Other facilities include the Madeleva classroom building, Science Hall, Havican nursing facility, and Moreau Art Galleries.

Costs

Expenses for the 2006–07 academic year included tuition and fees, $25,580; room and board, $8425 (double occupancy); and miscellaneous expenses (books, transportation, and living costs), $2625.

Financial Aid

The College strives to make a Saint Mary's education available for every student by offering eligible students financial aid packages that may include grants, scholarships, work-study, and loans. Competitive scholarships, awarded solely on academic merit, as well as those determined by a combination of financial need and academic achievement are available. Last year, more than 87 percent of Saint Mary's students received more than $25 million in financial assistance, more than $11 million from the College alone.

All applicants for financial assistance must complete the Financial Aid PROFILE and the Free Application for Federal Student Aid (FAFSA) each year that they desire assistance. Applications for assistance must be received at the processing center by March 1 to be given priority consideration. Decisions concerning financial aid are made as soon as possible after a student has been accepted.

Faculty

Saint Mary's has 128 full-time and 80 part-time faculty members. About 92 percent of the faculty members hold earned doctorates or other terminal degrees; of these, most teach first-year students as well as upper-division students. Faculty members work with students in all phases of college life, including academic counseling.

Student Government

Students are active at every level of campus governance and share in community decision making. There are voting representatives on the president's two highest advisory boards, the Student Affairs Council and the Academic Affairs Council. A student is a voting member of the College Board of Trustees. Student government sponsors many extracurricular and cocurricular activities.

Admission Requirements

Applicants for admission to Saint Mary's College should be graduates of an accredited high school and should ordinarily have completed a four-year program of 16 or more academic units. These academic units must include 4 units of English, 3 units of college-preparatory mathematics, 2 units of one foreign language, 2 units of social science, and 2 units of laboratory science. The remaining units should be in college-preparatory courses in the previous areas. An applicant's credentials should include an academic transcript showing current rank and senior-year subjects, a counselor/administrator recommendation, SAT or ACT scores (at least one test should include the new writing portion), and an essay.

Home-schooled students are encouraged to apply for admission and should contact the Admission Office for details.

An interview with an admission officer is recommended. Saint Mary's encourages students to visit the campus. The Admission Office can make arrangements for students who wish to attend classes or stay overnight.

Superior students who have studied for advanced placement may begin sophomore-level courses in their first year. Mature, well-qualified students who wish to enter college after three years of high school may apply for early admission. Saint Mary's College also grants deferred admission upon request to candidates who are accepted in the normal application process.

Application and Information

Saint Mary's has two application and notification programs: early decision and modified rolling admission. Highly qualified students who have selected Saint Mary's as their first choice for admission may apply under the early decision program. The application deadline is November 15, and the notification date is December 15. Students who apply for modified rolling admission and whose application files are complete on or before December 1 are notified of the admission decision in mid-January. Candidates are encouraged to apply by the end of their junior year of high school or in the fall of their senior year. Applications are accepted, however, as long as space is available.

Interested students are encouraged to contact:

Director of Admission
Saint Mary's College
Notre Dame, Indiana 46556-5001
Phone: 574-284-4587
      800-551-7621 (toll-free)
Fax: 574-284-4841
E-mail: admission@saintmarys.edu
Web site: http://www.saintmarys.edu

SIMPSON COLLEGE
INDIANOLA, IOWA

The College

Simpson College was founded in 1860. The institution was named Simpson College to honor Bishop Matthew Simpson (1811–1884), one of the best-known and most influential religious leaders of his day. The College is coeducational; although it is affiliated with the United Methodist Church, it is nonsectarian in spirit and accepts students without regard to race, color, creed, national origin, religion, sex, age, or disability.

For more than a century, Simpson has played a vital role in the educational, cultural, intellectual, political, and religious life of the nation. The College has thirty-five buildings on 85 acres of beautiful campus and enrolls more than 2,000 students.

Extracurricular activities at Simpson are designed to supplement and reinforce the academic program and contribute toward a total learning experience. Students may participate in student government, publications, music, theater, and social groups. Simpson competes in eighteen intercollegiate sports and has an extensive intramural program for both men and women. Men's and women's athletics at Simpson are governed by the NCAA. Simpson also has chapters of three national fraternities, one local fraternity, and four national sororities.

Location

Simpson is located in the city of Indianola, a residential community of 14,100 people. Indianola is 12 miles south of Des Moines, Iowa's capital city; 12 miles east of Interstate 35; and 15 miles south of Interstates 80 and 235. The Des Moines International Airport is 20 minutes from campus. Five miles south of Indianola is Lake Ahquabi State Park, where swimming and other recreational facilities are available. Every summer, Indianola is the home of the National Hot Air Balloon Classic and of the Des Moines Metropolitan Summer Opera Festival. The location of the residential campus provides the best of both metropolitan and suburban activities.

Majors and Degrees

Simpson College grants Bachelor of Arts and Bachelor of Music degrees in major and career programs, including accounting, art, athletic training, biochemistry, biology, chemistry, computer information systems, computer science, corporate communication, criminal justice, economics, education, English, environmental science, forensic science/biochemistry, French, German, history, international management, international relations, journalism and mass communication, management, marketing, mathematics, music, music education, music performance, philosophy, physical education, physics, political science, psychology, religion, rhetoric and speech communication, sociology, Spanish, sports administration, and theater arts.

Simpson also offers preprofessional programs in dentistry, engineering, law, medicine, optometry, physical therapy, theology, and veterinary medicine.

Academic Programs

Simpson College operates on a 4-4-1 academic calendar. The first semester starts in late August and ends in mid-December; the second semester starts in mid-January and ends in late April. A three-week session takes place during the month of May. During this period, students have the opportunity to take one class that focuses on a single subject, to study abroad, or to participate in a field experience or internship.

Students must participate in one May Term class or program for each year of full-time study at Simpson College. All students must complete the requirements of the cornerstone studies in liberal arts and competencies in foreign language, math, and writing. To earn the Bachelor of Arts degree, students may take no more than 42 hours in the major department, excluding May Term programs, and 84 hours in the division of the major, including May Term programs. At least 128 semester hours of course work must be accumulated with a grade point average of C (2.0) or better.

For a Bachelor of Music degree, the same requirements apply, except that 84 hours must be earned in the major, excluding May Terms, and the candidate is limited to 12 additional hours in the division of fine arts. A minimum of 132 hours of course work must be completed with a cumulative grade point average of C (2.0) or better.

The First Year Program is a broadly inclusive program of orientation, group-building, mentoring, community service, advising, and classroom work structured to help new students adapt to their first year of college. The program begins with summer registration and extends throughout the full year.

The academic component of the First Year Program is the Liberal Arts Seminar, a joint classroom and advising concept that is unique among first-year programs. The seminars are small in size—no more than 18 first-year students each—and all are taught by students' faculty advisers.

Off-Campus Programs

A variety of programs are offered for off-campus study. Simpson's semester-long study-abroad programs include London, England; Schorndorf, Germany; and Central America. Students also have the opportunity to study abroad in semester-long programs in France, Spain, Italy, and Australia.

Simpson is an affiliate of the American Institute for Foreign Study, which provides access to carefully planned semester or academic-year study programs in France and Spain. Additional international travel programs are offered on a regular basis during the May Term, including such destinations as Central America, Great Britain, France, Greece, Ireland, New Zealand, Thailand, and Scandinavia.

The Capitol Hill Internship Program (CHIP) provides students with the opportunity to spend either the fall or spring semester in Washington, D.C., working in an internship. In addition, students participate in two seminars for credit. Also available is the United Nations Semester with Drew University in Madison, New Jersey. Students undertake a course of study at Drew and at the United Nations.

Academic Facilities

The George Washington Carver Science Center provides state-of-the-art research facilities, computer labs, and classrooms.

Simpson has a campuswide Ethernet fiber-optic network and high-speed Internet access as well as wireless access in designated areas. There are numerous computer labs distributed across the campus where students can use standard office suite applications or specialized, discipline-specific applications.

The Henry H. and Thomas H. McNeill Hall houses classrooms for management, accounting, economics, and communication studies. In addition, the hall houses a seminar room and the Pioneer Hi-Bred International Conference Center.

The Amy Robertson Music Center houses the music department and contains the Sven and Mildred Lekberg Recital Hall, ten studios, twenty-two practice rooms, a music computer lab, and the band rehearsal room. The Salsbury Wing includes a choral rehearsal room, a classroom, and studios.

Dunn Library, a contemporary learning resource center, contains approximately 153,670 volumes, 500 current periodicals, 14,000 electronic journals, 2,560 DVDs and videotapes, 1,030 music CDs, and access to more than 7,485 e-books. Additional materials for research can be obtained through a national computer-based interlibrary loan network. The library also provides audiovisual equipment and services to the campus.

The A. H. and Theo Blank Performing Arts Center accommodates Simpson's well-known programs in theater arts and opera and includes the magnificent 500-seat Pote Theatre, with both proscenium and hydraulically controlled thrust stages; a studio theater; the Barborka Gallery; technical facilities and shops; and classrooms.

Wallace Hall reopened in 1996 after a complete internal renovation. Named to the National Register of Historic Places in 1991, Wallace Hall contains facilities for education, psychology, sociology, applied social science, and a biofeedback/psychology laboratory.

Costs

Tuition and fees for 2006–07 were $22,266; room charges were $3013; and board was $3265. These figures did not included books, music fees, or personal expenses.

Financial Aid

Simpson College seeks to make it financially possible for qualified students to experience the advantages of a Simpson education. Generous gifts from alumni, trustees, and friends of the College—in addition to state and federal student aid programs—make this opportunity possible. Simpson offers financial aid on both a need and non-need basis. Need is determined by filing the Free Application for Federal Student Aid.

Financial aid granted on a non-need basis includes academic scholarships, which are awarded on the basis of prior academic records, and talent scholarships, which are available in theater, music, and art. The talent scholarships are determined by audition/portfolio.

Faculty

Ninety-two percent of Simpson's 89 full-time faculty members have earned their terminal degrees. At Simpson, faculty members serve as academic advisers as well as teachers and often attend College plays, operas, and athletic events, reinforcing their sincere interest in students. The student-faculty ratio is 16:1.

Student Government

Student involvement in College governance is an integral part of the organization of the College. Students annually elect a president and vice president of the Student Government. The members of each housing unit and the off-campus students elect representatives to the Student Senate. The Student Senate appoints student members to all College committees in which students hold membership. The senate also appoints 3 students-at-large who attend plenary sessions of the Board of Trustees as members on the Student Affairs Committee.

Admission Requirements

Admission to Simpson College is selective and competitive. A strong academic record is essential. Applications are acted upon by an admissions committee, which is elected by the faculty and represents the five academic divisions of the College. These faculty members consider the college-preparatory courses taken, the grades received in those courses, rank in class, and standardized test scores (ACT and/or SAT), including test subscores. A short time after all required credentials are received, the application is reviewed by the Admissions Committee.

Transfer applicants are accepted on the basis of successful completion of academic work at an accredited college or university. In addition, transfer applicants are required to submit official high school transcripts and ACT/SAT results.

Application and Information

Simpson's rolling admission policy allows flexibility; however, early application is recommended. Transfer and international students are welcome. Students are strongly encouraged to visit the campus.

For additional information or to obtain application materials, students should contact:

Office of Admissions
Simpson College
701 North C Street
Indianola, Iowa 50125
Phone: 515-961-1624
       800-362-2454 (toll-free)
E-mail: admiss@simpson.edu
Web site: http://www.simpson.edu

The George Washington Carver Science Center provides Simpson students with state-of-the-art labs and research facilities.

SOUTHERN ILLINOIS UNIVERSITY CARBONDALE

CARBONDALE, ILLINOIS

The University

Southern Illinois University Carbondale (SIUC), chartered in 1869, is a comprehensive state-supported institution with nationally and internationally recognized instructional, research, and service programs. SIUC is fully accredited by the North Central Association of Colleges and Schools.

SIUC offers more than 150 undergraduate majors, specializations, and minors; two associate degree programs; ninety baccalaureate degree programs; sixty master's degree programs; thirty-two doctoral programs; and professional degrees in law and medicine. SIUC is a multicampus university and includes the Carbondale campus as well as the SIUC School of Medicine at Springfield.

During the 2006–07 academic year, SIUC's enrollment reached 21,003, which included 16,294 undergraduate students, 4,060 graduate students, and 649 professional students. The average age of undergraduates is 24. Five and one half percent of SIUC's enrolled students are international students. Of U.S. students, 15 percent are African American, .5 percent are American Indian/Alaskan, 2 percent are Asian or Pacific Islander, and 3 percent are Hispanic.

Students who are ready to start college but not ready to commit to a specific major can enroll in SIUC's Pre-Major Program. Premajor advisers and career counselors help premajor students plan their education and careers. SIUC faculty members, staff members, and alumni help students arrange internships, cooperative education programs, and work-study programs.

All single freshmen under the age of 21 are required to live on campus unless they are living at home. SIUC University Housing offers four on-campus residential areas for single students. Each area includes a dining hall, post office, and laundry facilities. Learning Resource Centers are available on both sides of campus and offer writing centers, computer labs, and student lounges. University Housing Residence Hall Dining provides a variety of meal plans, with all-you-care-to-eat meals and late night dining. Residence Hall Dining offers a variety of menus, vegetarian and light entrees, display cooking, and a full-time dietitian to help students who have special dietary needs.

Apartment housing is available for upperclass undergraduates, graduate students, and students with families.

SIUC intercollegiate sports teams compete at the NCAA Division I level (football is Division I-AA). Conference affiliations include the Missouri Valley and Gateway Conferences. Intercollegiate sports teams include men's and women's basketball, cross-country, diving, golf, swimming, tennis, and track and field; men's baseball and football; and women's softball and volleyball. The campus holds various playfields, several tennis courts, and a campus lake with a beach and a boat dock. SIUC's Student Recreation Center houses an Olympic-size pool; indoor tracks; handball/racquetball and squash courts; a climbing wall; weight rooms; and basketball, volleyball, and tennis courts. It also offers outdoor equipment rental, an aerobic area, walleyball, martial arts, and dance and cardio studios.

The Student Center is one of the largest student centers in the U.S. without a hotel. It contains a bookstore, several restaurants, a craft shop, a bakery, and facilities for bowling and billiards. It is headquarters for 400 active student organizations and the student government office. It holds four ballrooms and an auditorium. On-campus events throughout the year include concerts, plays, festivals, guest speakers, and musicals.

Location

Carbondale is 6 hours south of Chicago, 2 hours southeast of St. Louis, and 3 hours north of Nashville. Four large recreational lakes, the two great rivers (the Mississippi and the Ohio), and the spectacular 270,000-acre Shawnee National Forest are within minutes of the campus. The mid-South climate is ideal for year-round outdoor activities.

Carbondale is a small city of 26,000 people that supports one large enclosed mall, several mini-malls, theaters, and restaurants. Students frequent the shops and restaurants that line Illinois and Grand Avenues.

Majors and Degrees

The University offers associate in applied science degree programs at the College of Applied Sciences and Arts in aviation flight and physical therapist assistant studies.

The College of Applied Sciences and Arts offers bachelor's degree programs in advanced technical studies, architectural studies, automotive technology, aviation management, aviation technologies, dental hygiene, electronics systems technologies, fashion design and merchandising, fire service management (off campus only), health-care management, information systems technologies, interior design, mortuary science and funeral service, and radiologic sciences.

The College of Agriculture offers bachelor's degree programs in agribusiness economics, agricultural systems, animal science, food and nutrition, forestry, and plant and soil science.

The College of Business and Administration offers bachelor's degree programs in accounting, business and administration, business economics, finance, management, and marketing.

The College of Education and Human Services offers bachelor's degree programs in communication disorders and sciences, early childhood education, elementary education, health education, kinesiology, recreation, rehabilitation services, social work, special education, and workforce education and development. Teacher preparation is available in art, biological sciences, English, French, German, health education, mathematics, music, physical education, secondary education, social sciences with designations in history and social studies, Spanish, and special education.

The College of Engineering offers bachelor's degree programs in civil engineering, computer engineering, electrical engineering, engineering technology, industrial technology, mechanical engineering, and mining engineering.

The College of Liberal Arts offers bachelor's degrees in administration of justice, anthropology, art, classics, design, economics, English, foreign language and international trade, French, geography and environmental resources, German, history, linguistics, mathematics, music, paralegal studies, philosophy, political science, psychology, sociology, Spanish, speech communication, theater, and university studies.

The College of Mass Communication and Media Arts offers bachelor's degrees in cinema and photography, journalism, and radio-television.

The College of Science offers bachelor's degree programs in biological sciences, chemistry and biochemistry, computer science, environmental studies, geology, mathematics, microbiology, physics, physiology, plant biology, zoology, and preprofessional programs in dentistry, medicine, nursing, optometry, pharmacy, physical therapy, physician assistant studies, podiatry, and veterinary medicine.

In addition to many majors offered at SIUC, specializations are offered in all colleges in many areas.

Academic Programs

Each bachelor's degree candidate must earn a minimum of 120 semester hours of credit, including at least 60 at a senior-level institution and the last 30 at SIUC. Each student must maintain at least a C average in all course work at SIUC. Each student must fulfill the University core curriculum and the specific requirements of their degree programs. SIUC awards credit through qualifying extension and correspondence programs, military experience, the High School Advanced Placement Program, the College-Level Examination Program (CLEP), SIUC's proficiency examination program, and work experience.

SIUC offers honors course work and special recognition for students who demonstrate exceptional academic achievement. The Air Force and Army offer ROTC programs at SIUC. SIUC offers three semesters: fall, spring, and summer.

Off-Campus Programs

At Southern Illinois University Carbondale, distance education courses are offered in interactive, print-based and Web-based formats. Print-based (correspondence) and Web-based courses are offered by the

Individualized Learning Program (ILP). Web-based courses and Two-Way Interactive Video courses are offered through the Office of Distance Education. Many of the courses offered through the ILP and other distance education courses can be taken to complete the University Studies Degree (B.A.) in the College of Liberal Arts.

Off-campus credit programs are designed to meet the educational needs of adults wishing to pursue a degree but who are unable to travel to the Carbondale campus. Faculty members who teach off-campus courses travel to distant sites to teach SIUC courses.

Contractual services are provided and include specialized educational services to groups, organizations, governmental agencies, and businesses on a cost-recovery basis. These services are provided regionally, nationally, and internationally.

All credit courses offered through these programs carry full SIUC academic credit and are taught by faculty members appointed by the academic departments of the University. Additional information can be found on the Web (http://www.dce.siu.edu/siuconnected).

Academic Facilities

In addition to the 2.5 million volumes, 3.6 million microfilms, and more than 12,500 periodicals currently available in Morris Library, students and faculty members have access to more than 27,000 full-text electronic journals. SIUC students have access to several computer learning centers that are equipped, in all, with more than 1,600 microcomputers. Additional information can be found on the Web (http://www.lib.siu.edu).

Students learn and practice in the Southern Illinois Airport, outdoor laboratories, the student-run *Daily Egyptian* newspaper, WSIU-TV, WSIU-FM, art and natural history museums, a literary magazine, McCleod Theater, Memorial Hospital, a vivarium, the plant biology greenhouses, the University Farms, and the Touch of Nature Environmental Center.

Costs

Tuition and fee charges for the 2006–07 academic year (fall and spring) for students enrolled in 15 or more semester hours were $7794.90 for Illinois residents and $16,506.90 for out-of-state residents, including international students. Room and board were $6138. All costs are subject to change. The cost of books and school supplies varies among programs. The average cost is $900 per academic year. Some courses require that students purchase special materials.

Financial Aid

More than $189 million in financial aid was distributed to more than 77 percent of SIUC students in fiscal year 2006 through federal, state, and institutionally funded financial aid programs.

To apply for financial aid at SIUC, students should complete a Free Application for Federal Student Aid (FAFSA). Applications that are filed before April 1 receive priority consideration for campus-based aid. The FAFSA can be completed electronically at the U.S. Department of Education's Web site (http://www.fafsa.ed.gov). When completing the FAFSA, students should list Southern Illinois University Carbondale (Federal School Code 001758) as a school of choice.

SIUC has one of the largest student employment programs in the country, with approximately 5,400 students employed each year in a wide variety of job classifications. SIUC offers competitive scholarships based on talent and academic achievement.

Faculty

Faculty members are dedicated to excellence in teaching and to their advancement of knowledge in a wide variety of disciplines and professions. Many faculty members are well-known both nationally and internationally for their varied research contributions. The undergraduate student-faculty ratio is 17:1. There are 1,333 full-time and 220 part-time instructional faculty members.

Teaching assistants at SIUC are graduate students who assist faculty members in teaching. While some teach introductory undergraduate classes, others provide support to faculty members by assisting in laboratories, monitoring tests, and helping students.

Student Government

The undergraduate student government consists of a president, vice president, executive assistant, and chief of staff. Under the vice president, there are 43 senators: 1 senator per 388 students. Each student has at least 2 representatives: 1–6 for their residential area, and 1–6

for the college in which they are enrolled. Under the 6 commissioners are a list of committees on which a varying number of students sit to represent the student body. The student government writes and passes legislation on University policies, funding, student organizations, and other matters that affect the students and the University.

Admission Requirements

Freshman applicants whose ACT or SAT scores are at or above the 66th percentile and class rank is in the upper three quarters are admitted. Applicants can also be admitted with an ACT or SAT score at or above the 50th percentile and class rank in the upper half. Finally, applicants can be admitted with an ACT or SAT score at or above the 33rd percentile and class rank in the top quarter. Admission standards are subject to change. Freshman applicants must meet course pattern requirements: 4 years of English, 3 years of mathematics, 3 years of laboratory science, 3 years of social science, and 2 years of electives.

Transfer applicants must have an overall grade point average of at least 2.0 on a 4.0 scale, based on work attempted at all institutions and calculated by SIUC grading policies. Transfer applicants must also be eligible to continue at the last institution attended.

Some programs have higher admission requirements or require additional screening for admission. Undergraduates can apply online (http://salukinet.siu.edu/admit/).

Application and Information

Admission is granted on a rolling basis. Application priority deadlines for freshmen are: June 1 for the summer 2007 term; May 1 for the fall 2007 term; and December 1, 2007, for the spring 2008 term. Application priority deadlines for transfer students are: June 1 for the summer 2007 term; July 1 for the fall 2007 term; and December 1, 2007, for the spring 2008 term. The application fee is $30.

Undergraduate Admissions MC 4710
425 Clocktower Drive
Southern Illinois University Carbondale
Carbondale, Illinois 62901

Phone: 618-536-4405
Fax: 618-453-3250
E-mail: joinsiuc@siu.edu
Web site: http://www.siuc.edu

SIUC's Pulliam Hall.

STEPHENS COLLEGE
COLUMBIA, MISSOURI

The College

Stephens College was founded in 1833 as the nation's second-oldest women's college. Stephens is ranked nationally in *U.S. News & World Report* and has repeatedly been selected to the *Princeton Review*'s list of the best colleges in the country (listed one of the Best in the Midwest, 2006, and sixth on the list of best college theater programs in the nation).

Students from around the globe enrich Stephens with their varied talents, interests, and backgrounds. Stephens students may choose to join one of ten honorary societies on campus, including Psi Chi, Alpha Epsilon Rho, and Mortar Board, or become involved in student government. Leadership experience is emphasized in all aspects of life at Stephens.

Stephens' residence halls provide much of the focus for campus activity. The Honors House Plan offers a living/learning environment in the humanities to a select group of freshmen each year. Since it began in the 1960s as an experiment funded by the Ford Foundation, the program has served as a model for similar living/learning communities in colleges and universities across the nation.

In addition to undergraduate degrees, Stephens offers master's degrees.

Location

Stephens College is located in Columbia, Missouri. Situated halfway between Kansas City and St. Louis, Columbia is the cultural, medical, and business center of mid-Missouri. Often called "College Town, USA," Columbia is also the home of Columbia College and the University of Missouri. Stephens students have easy access to Columbia's shopping, dining, and entertainment offerings.

Majors and Degrees

Stephens College awards the Associate in Arts, Bachelor of Arts, Bachelor of Fine Arts, and Bachelor of Science. Majors include accounting; biology; creative writing; dance; digital filmmaking; education; English; entrepreneurship and business management; equestrian business management; equestrian science; fashion communication; fashion design and product development; fashion marketing and management; graphic design; human development; interior design; legal studies; liberal studies; marketing: public relations and advertising; mass media (electronic media production, print media production, or public relations); psychology; student-initiated majors; theater arts; theater management; and theatrical costume design. The B.F.A. program includes professional-level work in the fine or performing arts plus a strong component in liberal studies.

Academic Programs

The B.A. degree is generally completed in four years. Students pursue depth of study in an academic area, breadth in liberal arts study, and elective course work with guidance from faculty advisers. Academic departments require relevant internships and often provide opportunities for research projects in field settings. Stephens has introduced many innovative educational concepts into its programs. Stephens emphasizes personalized teaching and development of the individual. Small classes are offered, and most departments offer tutorial projects and readings.

Students in the bachelor's degree programs—B.A., B.F.A., or B.S.—must complete the residency requirement of seven semesters. Students take a total of 30 hours in the liberal arts program throughout their three or four years at the College. These courses provide an interdisciplinary platform for the study of the behavioral/social sciences, literature, humanities, history, science, ethics, math, and digital literacy. All liberal arts courses, regardless of the topics they cover, provide opportunities for students to sharpen their critical thinking and communication skills.

Degree requirements for the Bachelor of Arts include completion of at least 24 semester hours in a department. At least 15 of these hours must be at or above the 300 level. As many as 45 semester hours may be required in the major, but no more than 45 may count toward a 120-semester-hour degree program. Students also may elect to design an interdisciplinary student-initiated Bachelor of Arts major.

The Bachelor of Science degree program requires completion of 45 to 57 hours, including a minimum of 15 hours at or above the 300 level. Bachelor of Science candidates may elect additional courses in the major, but no more than 60 hours may count toward a 120-semester-hour degree program. Students also may elect to design an interdisciplinary student-initiated Bachelor of Science major.

Degree requirements for the Bachelor of Fine Arts include completion of 60 to 75 semester hours, including at least 15 hours at or above the 300 level. B.F.A. candidates may elect additional courses in their major, up to a maximum of 78 hours within a 120-semester-hour degree program. The B.F.A. degree programs in theater and in dance are completed in three years and two summers. Students also may elect to design an interdisciplinary student-initiated Bachelor of Fine Arts major.

Through Stephens College Division of Graduate and Continuing Studies, nontraditional students have the opportunity to complete degrees through programs that build on prior and current learning. The Division of Graduate and Continuing Studies offers undergraduate programs in business administration, and health information administration (the first accredited external degree program in medical record administration in the country). In addition, Stephens offers a Master of Business Administration (M.B.A.) and a Master of Education (M.Ed.) in counseling. Undergraduates in accounting, entrepreneurship and business management, fashion marketing/management, equestrian business management, and marketing: public relations and advertising may apply for a tuition-paid fellowship to complete the M.B.A degree. Certain requirements apply.

Stephens also offers numerous partnerships with other institutions wherein students may earn a bachelor's degree from Stephens in three years and a master's degree from another college or university after two or three additional years. Partnerships currently exist in occupational therapy, physical therapy, physician assistant studies, accounting, and law.

Off-Campus Programs

Stephens sponsors summer seminars in several countries, including France, Italy, and Japan, as extensions of courses that are regularly offered at the College. Summer-study programs include drama and musical theater at Lake Okoboji, Spirit Lake,

Iowa. Stephens also offers study opportunities in Ireland, Sweden, Ecuador, Korea, and Cambridge, England.

Many other study opportunities are available through global partnerships with other universities.

Academic Facilities

The Hugh Stephens Resources Library contains more than 120,000 volumes. The library is the central building of a quadrangle that includes the Helis Communication Center and the Patricia Barry Television Studio. The E. S. Pillsbury Science Center houses science and mathematics classrooms and laboratories, and the Ellis Learning Laboratories provide modern equipment for individual and group study of foreign languages. Other working laboratories include the student-run Warehouse Theatre, the Johnson Plant Laboratory, and the Audrey Webb Child Study Center, which has an enrollment of approximately 100 children in preschool through fifth grade.

Costs

For 2006–07, tuition was $20,500; room and board were $7974. Costs for room and board are subject to change. Additional costs for books, supplies, and personal expenses range between $750 and $1000. The enrollment deposit is $100.

Financial Aid

More than 95 percent of the student body receive some form of assistance through scholarships, grants, loans, or employment. Stephens participates in the Federal Pell Grant, Federal Supplemental Educational Opportunity Grant, Federal Perkins Loan, Federal Stafford Student Loan, and Federal Work-Study programs. Missouri residents are encouraged to apply for aid under the Missouri Student Grant Program. The Free Application for Federal Student Aid (FAFSA) is required for financial aid consideration. Applications for financial aid should be received by March 15. Stephens also offers an early financial aid estimate service.

Faculty

Though most faculty members have come to college teaching via the recognized route of graduate study and scholarship, some have prepared for teaching through work experience, particularly those in applied and performing arts with careers as actors, dancers, musicians, and artists. The faculty is primarily a teaching faculty, and many of the instructors include students in independent scholarly research. Men and women join the Stephens faculty with a commitment to individualized education. They are actively engaged in academic advising and tutorial relationships and frequently spend many more hours working with students outside the classroom than in formal teaching situations. The student-faculty ratio is 13:1.

Student Government

Each student is a member of the Student Government Association (SGA). Working in the SGA provides women with experience in planning and administering cultural, social, and recreational activities and in dealing with academic, residential, and community concerns. The association has executive and legislative powers to govern student activities and to develop and maintain group-living standards. Students also serve as voting members of established faculty committees and in advisory capacities to committees of the Board of Trustees. Stephens has been nationally recognized for the many leadership opportunities it provides for students.

Admission Requirements

Applicants are considered by the Dean of Enrollment Management and the Admission Committee on an individual basis without regard to race, religion, geographic origin, or handicap. Major factors for admission consideration are the recommendations and academic record, including rank in class, subjects studied, grade point average, proficiency in English, and test scores (SAT and ACT).

Application and Information

Candidates for admission should submit the application with the $25 application fee and arrange to have transcripts and recommendations mailed to the Office of Admission. Students who apply online at http://www.stephens.edu/admission/apply can waive the application fee. Upon receipt of the application, any additional material is mailed to the student. Qualified students are accepted on a rolling admission basis upon receipt of all necessary credentials.

Office of Admission
Campus Box 2121
Stephens College
Columbia, Missouri 65215
Phone: 573-876-7207
        800-876-7207 (toll-free)
Fax: 573-876-7237
E-mail: apply@stephens.edu
Web site: http://www.stephens.edu

On the Stephens College campus.

TRI-STATE UNIVERSITY
ANGOLA, INDIANA

The University

Tri-State University (TSU) is a private, independent, coeducational institution offering associate and baccalaureate degrees in more than forty programs to students in engineering, mathematics, science, computer science, business administration, teacher education, communications, and criminal justice. In 2002, TSU was elevated to a graduate-degree-granting institution and now offers an accelerated, five-year Bachelor of Science/Master of Engineering dual-degree program. In the spring of 2005, TSU introduced an interdisciplinary minor in entrepreneurship.

Since its founding in 1884, TSU's emphasis has been on providing an affordable, comprehensive, career-oriented, hands-on education. With a worldwide reputation for being "job-ready," TSU graduates are in demand. That is why each year more than 90 percent of TSU graduates are employed in major-related positions within six months of graduation.

TSU's current undergraduate enrollment is more than 1,100. Approximately 600 of these students live on campus in one of six residence halls. The University's 485-acre campus includes an eighteen-hole championship golf course. Currently under construction, the $15.5 million University Center and Center for Online Technology will house a new dining hall, deli, bakery, bookstore, game room, climbing wall, sports and wellness center, movie theater, post office, radio station, and library.

The University's campus offers an informal and friendly atmosphere, which complements the seriousness and determination with which TSU students pursue their academic goals. While focused on pursuing their goals, TSU students enjoy many opportunities to develop friendships and to build leadership and teamwork skills through their participation in athletics and a range of campus organizations.

Men's intercollegiate sports include baseball, basketball, cross-country, football, golf, lacrosse, soccer, tennis, track, and wrestling. Women's sports include basketball, cross-country, golf, lacrosse, soccer, softball, tennis, track, and volleyball. Intramural sports are also a big part of recreational life at TSU.

Student organizations that offer opportunities for participation include the student senate, honor societies, professional organizations, the campus newspaper, the FM radio station, the yearbook, the drama club, and more. In addition, there are a total of twelve social fraternities and sororities on campus, in which approximately 20 percent of the student body participate after their freshman year.

Tri-State University is accredited by the Higher Learning Commission and a member of the North Central Association of Colleges and Schools (Web site: http://www.ncahigherlearning-commission.org; phone: 312-263-0456). TSU's programs in chemical engineering, civil engineering, electrical engineering, and mechanical engineering are accredited by the Engineering Accreditation Commission of the Accreditation Board for Engineering and Technology, Inc. (ABET). ABET's national office is located at 111 Market Place, Suite 1050, Baltimore, Maryland, 21202-4012; phone: 410-347-7700. All teacher preparation programs are accredited by the National Council for Accreditation of Teacher Education (NCATE) and the Indiana Professional Standards Board.

Location

TSU is located in Angola, Indiana, the heart of northeast Indiana's scenic lake resort region and about halfway between the metropolitan areas of Chicago, Illinois, and Cleveland, Ohio. Just a 45-minute drive from Fort Wayne, Indiana, TSU offers the safety and ease of a small-town environment while being close to some of the nation's most vital cities. Pokagon State Park provides year-round recreational opportunities for the community and is just 5 miles from TSU's campus.

Majors and Degrees

The Allen School of Engineering and Technology awards Bachelor of Science degrees in chemical, civil, computer, electrical, and mechanical engineering; design engineering technology (CADD); and engineering administration. It awards associate degrees in construction management technology, design engineering technology (CADD), and manufacturing technology. An interdisciplinary minor in entrepreneurship is available.

Well-qualified high school graduates may be admitted directly into a five-year mechanical engineering program. Mechanical engineers with the skills necessary to lead the designing of a complex system are highly sought by industry professionals; therefore, the degree is a practice-oriented degree with a heavy design emphasis, as opposed to the research emphasis of a traditional Master of Science degree. On completion of this program, both the Bachelor of Science in Mechanical Engineering and the Master of Engineering degree are awarded.

The Ketner School of Business awards the Bachelor of Science in Business Administration degree in accounting, business/arts and sciences, finance, management, management information systems, and marketing and the Bachelor of Science degree in golf management. Associate degrees are awarded in accounting and business administration. An interdisciplinary minor in entrepreneurship is available.

The Franks School of Education awards Bachelor of Science degrees in elementary education, physical education, and secondary education. Secondary education majors can specialize in English, mathematics, science, and social studies.

The Jannen School of Arts and Sciences awards Bachelor of Arts degrees in communication and psychology. Bachelor of Science degrees are awarded in biology, chemistry, English education, forensic science, health education (K–12), health education (9–12), health promotion and recreational programming, mathematics, mathematics education, physical education (K–12), physical education (5–12), physical education (9–12), physical science, premed, science education, social studies education, and sport management; a Bachelor of Science in computer science; and a Bachelor of Science in criminal justice. Associate degrees are awarded in arts, computer technology, criminal justice, and science.

Academic Programs

The graduation requirements for a bachelor's degree are a cumulative grade point average of not less than 2.0 (on a 4.0 scale) and the completion of 120 to 132 semester hours, depending upon the major.

TSU's engineering programs concentrate on providing a fundamental, application-oriented engineering education. In addition to concentrating in a specialized area, students are required to successfully complete courses in communication skills, sociohumanistic studies, and analysis and design.

The University's business programs include a broad range of hands-on practical experience that acquaints the student with the practices, procedures, and problems of the contemporary business professional. Guest lecturers are frequent visitors to the campus, and field trips are considered vital to the total educational experience.

Off-Campus Programs

Co-op and internship opportunities are available. Semesters of classroom study are alternated with professional work experience, giving students the opportunity to integrate theory with practice and gain a competitive edge in the job market. The length of a co-op program depends upon the student's class status when entering the program. Work-study schedules require from three to six semesters on work assignments. During the semesters worked, students are paid directly by the employer.

Academic Facilities

Fawick Hall of Engineering reopened in 1997 after a yearlong $5-million complete interior demolition to load-bearing walls and then full reconstruction to house the University's Departments of Chemical Engineering, Civil and Environmental Engineering, Electrical and Computer Engineering, Mechanical and Aerospace Engineering, and Technology. Because of the University's commitment to a high-quality education, TSU's students use sophisticated equipment such as a scanning electron microscope in their cast metals laboratories and in projects related to industrial consulting. Each department has a computer lab with pertinent software for their students.

Named in honor of John G. Best, a distinguished alumnus and former member of the Board of Trustees, the John G. Best Hall of Science contains classrooms and science laboratories. Best Hall also houses the Fairfield Lecture Room, the Department of Mathematics and Computer Science, the Department of Science, the science laboratories, the Computer Center, the telephone services, and the Department of Criminal Justice, Psychology, and Social Sciences.

The University Computer Center houses an academic computer system that consists of Pentium microcomputers running Windows NT Workstation and Windows 2000. The academic system is an Internet site supporting Telnet, the Web, and e-mail to other Internet sites. A Microsoft Exchange server handles the e-mail. There are more than 200 computers dedicated to student access in labs across campus. Every room in each dorm is wired to the University network and the Internet.

Costs

Tuition for the academic year (two semesters) in 2006–07 was $21,210. Room and board for the academic year was $6240.

Financial Aid

Financial aid may be awarded in the form of scholarships, grants, loans, or employment. Any of these aids or any combination may be necessary to supplement family and student resources to meet basic educational expenses. Tri-State requires the use of the Free Application for Federal Student Aid (FAFSA) and recommends its submission by March 1.

Faculty

TSU has a full-time faculty of 70 members, most of whom have doctoral degrees and/or are registered professional engineers. The central mission of the faculty members is teaching. The student-faculty ratio is 13:1.

Student Government

The student senate is organized for the purpose of promoting and coordinating campus activities for students. Representatives elected from campus organizations form the senate, which sponsors social activities and campus projects and aids in formulating policies for student organizations.

Admission Requirements

Graduation from an approved high school or equivalent preparation is required for admission. TSU gives careful consideration to the caliber of the academic records. Selection is made without regard to race, religion, or color. The University requires that applicants for admission arrange to take the ACT or SAT prior to approval for admission (writing sections are optional).

Admission requirements for engineering include 4 years of English, 1 year of chemistry, 1 year of physics, 1 year of social studies, 2 years of algebra, 1 year of geometry, and ½ year of trigonometry. Preparatory courses are available for students who have not completed all the high school subjects normally required for admission.

All other applicants must have the following high school credits: 4 years of English, 3 years of mathematics, 3 years of science, and 3 years of social studies.

Graduates of preprofessional or college-parallel programs at approved community or junior colleges are eligible for transfer into TSU's baccalaureate programs. Qualified graduates of these programs may be granted junior standing upon transfer. In general, credit may be allowed for subjects equivalent to those in the program at TSU, provided that the student earned a C or better in the course.

Application and Information

TSU admits applicants on the basis of scholastic achievement and academic potential. Admission decisions are made on a rolling basis, without regard to race, religion, color, gender, sexual orientation, or age. Applicants are notified of their status within two weeks after the online application and high school record have been received. Transfer students must also submit an official copy of their college transcript(s).

Interested students and their parents are encouraged to visit the campus. Arrangements can be made by writing or calling the Office of Admission.

For additional information, students should call or write:

Office of Admission
Tri-State University
1 University Avenue
Angola, Indiana 46703-1764
Phone: 260-665-4100
      800-347-4TSU (toll-free within continental U.S.)
E-mail: admit@tristate.edu
Web site: http://www.tristate.edu

TRUMAN STATE UNIVERSITY
KIRKSVILLE, MISSOURI

The University

Truman has forged a national reputation for offering an exceptionally high-quality undergraduate education at a competitive price. For the tenth consecutive year, *U.S. News & World Report* has ranked Truman as the number one master's-level public institution in the Midwest offering bachelor's and master's degrees. In addition, Truman is ranked as the fourth-best public college value in the nation by Princeton Review's 2007 edition of *America's Best Value Colleges.*

A commitment to student achievement and learning is at the core of everything Truman does. This commitment is evidenced by faculty and staff members who recognize the importance of providing students with the opportunity to interact with their professors both in and out of the classroom. With class sizes averaging only 22 students and 93 percent of freshman-level academic courses being taught by professors, students find ample opportunity to ask questions of professors as well as interact with their multitalented peers. Truman's academic environment is enhanced by a student body that achieves at remarkable levels. The 2006 freshman class had an ACT midrange of 25 to 30 and an average GPA of 3.78 on a 4.00 scale. In addition, numerous opportunities exist for students to engage in undergraduate research. Each year, approximately 1,200 students work side by side with professors on University research projects, gaining greater confidence, knowledge, and skill in their chosen disciplines. The University offers these students the opportunity to present the results of their research at the annual Student Research Conference. In addition, selected students travel to the National Undergraduate Research Symposium to present their research findings. Undergraduate research stipends are also available.

The teaching degree at Truman is the Master of Arts in Education. Students wishing to pursue a teaching career first complete a bachelor's degree in an academic discipline and then apply for admission into professional study at the master's level. Through this program, certification can be achieved for early childhood education, middle school education, special education, elementary education, and secondary education.

With more than 250 University organizations available to students, encompassing service, Greek, honorary, professional, religious, social, political, and recreational influences, Truman students have tremendous opportunities to become involved while enrolled at the University. Truman's Student Activities Board provides special events such as Mythbusters: Adam and Jamie, comic acts such as Lewis Black and the Laughing Irish Comedy Tour, and musical artists like Cake, Yellowcard, and MXPX. In addition, admission to all varsity athletic events, Truman theater productions, and Lyceum Series events is free to Truman students. Recent theater productions have included *Cabaret, One Flew Over the Cuckoo's Nest,* and *The Real Inspector Hound.*

Location

Truman is located in Kirksville, a town of approximately 17,000 nestled in the northeast corner of Missouri. The town square, located within walking distance of the Truman campus, provides a connection to Kirksville's past. A multiplex movie theater is located on the town square; local merchants operate specialized gift, book, and clothing stores; and several restaurants offer a wide selection of American and international cuisine.

The Kirksville Aquatic Center is a great place to have fun and get fit. This indoor/outdoor pool complex offers a variety of activities, classes, and programs designed to appeal to people of all ages. Inside the complex is a six-lane indoor swimming pool, perfect for swimming, relaxing, or playing a game of water-basketball. The outdoor pool is designed with a zero-depth entry, a 1-meter diving board, and four 25-yard outdoor lap lanes as well as a 20-foot water slide.

The northeast region of Missouri is also home to Thousand Hills State Park. A 3,252-acre state park and 573-acre lake for camping, hiking, biking, fishing, swimming, boating, and water skiing is located within 10 minutes of the Truman campus.

Majors and Degrees

Undergraduate degrees offered by Truman include the Bachelor of Arts (B.A.), Bachelor of Science (B.S.), Bachelor of Music: Performance (B.M.), Bachelor of Fine Arts (B.F.A.), and Bachelor of Science in Nursing (B.S.N.). Truman offers more than forty areas of study in the following disciplines: accounting, agricultural science, art, art history, biology, business administration, chemistry, classics, communication, communication disorders, computer science, economics, English, exercise science, French, German, health science, history, interdisciplinary studies, justice systems, linguistics, mathematics, music, music: performance, nursing, philosophy and religion, physics, political science, psychology, Russian, sociology/anthropology, Spanish, and theater.

Professional paths include but are not limited to dentistry, engineering, law, medicine, optometry, pharmacy, physical therapy, and veterinary medicine.

Academic Programs

Truman is Missouri's premier liberal arts and sciences university and the only highly selective public institution in the state. The Liberal Studies Program is the heart of Truman's curriculum and is intended to serve as a foundation for all major programs of study offered by the University. Truman's mission is to "offer an exemplary undergraduate education, grounded in the liberal arts and sciences, in the context of a public institution of higher learning." Therefore, Truman is providing the kind of education in the liberal arts and sciences that has historically been offered only at private colleges. The program is a blend of two intellectual traditions in higher education, one that emphasizes the traditional thought and learning of the culture as reflected in the classical works produced by it, and the other that emphasizes personal investigation and freedom of discovery. The philosophy behind the Liberal Studies Program is based upon a commitment that Truman has made to provide students with essential skills needed for lifelong learning, breadth across the traditional liberal arts and sciences through exposure to various discipline-based modes of inquiry, and interconnecting perspectives that stress interdisciplinary thinking and integration as well as linkage to other cultures and experiences. All students graduating from Truman must complete 63 or more credit hours in liberal arts and sciences courses.

Truman's Residential College Program brings the University learning community inside the student residence halls. Historically, residential colleges have been places where faculty members and students join together as "friends of learning." At Truman, this living/learning tradition is honored as one means of furthering its specific goals as a public liberal arts university. The Residential College Program seeks to make liberal arts education personally vital and engaging to the whole person.

Truman also offers an especially challenging General Honors Program. This program provides students with the opportunity to select the most rigorous honors courses to satisfy the liberal arts component of their respective programs. Students who successfully complete this program not only benefit from an even richer academic experience at Truman but also receive special recognition at graduation. Departmental honors are also available in several disciplines.

Off-Campus Programs

Each year, approximately 500 Truman students participate in enriching and life-changing study-abroad experiences. Truman's own study-abroad programs, combined with programs offered through Truman's membership in the College Consortium for International Studies, International Student Exchange Program, Australearn, and the Council on International Educational Exchange, provide students with study-abroad opportunities in more than forty countries worldwide, including Australia, China, England, Finland, France, Italy, Russia, Spain, and Thailand.

In addition, there are two cooperative programs affiliated with biology. Truman is affiliated with the Gulf Coast Research Laboratory at Ocean Springs, Mississippi. Marine biology courses may be taken at the laboratory during the summer with credit awarded at Truman. In-depth study of the Ozark habitats is also available through Truman's affiliation with Reis Biological Station located near Steelville, Missouri.

In cooperation with the Washington Center for Internships and Academic Seminars, Truman offers a wide variety of experiential internships in Washington, D.C. Included are work-experience opportunities in such areas as public administration, the fine and performing arts, foreign affairs/diplomacy, government affairs, criminal justice, international relations, health and human services, environmental policy, business administration, and communications as well as other areas. Placement sites include nonprofit groups, media organizations, the State Department, Congress, museums, and much more.

Truman requires internships in education, health science, and exercise science and annually offers internship opportunities with the Missouri State Legislature. In recent years, students have completed internships with United States senators, the governor of Missouri, business and industry managers, zoos, broadcast and print media professionals, accountants, advertising agencies, physical therapists, musicians, artists, and the United States Supreme Court.

Academic Facilities

The Truman campus is beautifully situated on an expanse of 140 acres near downtown Kirksville. Featured among the forty facilities on campus is Pickler Memorial Library. This 460,116-volume facility provides a state-of-the-art library resource for students and faculty members alike. Materials not available in Pickler Memorial Library can be obtained through the Interlibrary Loan Office and MOBIUS.

Improvements to campus facilities recently include the $20-million renovation and 80,000-square-foot addition to the Ophelia Parrish Building that transformed this facility into the new Fine Arts Center housing art studios, practice facilities, a performing arts center, and a black-box theater. The $20-million renovation and expansion of Truman's science facility, Magruder Hall, was completed for the Spring 2006 semester and included new research labs, a greenhouse, classrooms, meeting areas, and a cyber café. The brand new West Campus Suites opened to students in fall 2006. Each suite is equipped with a living room, two bedrooms housing two students each, closet space, a large bathroom, and central air conditioning. Renovations have also begun on Missouri Hall. Improvements include a 2,500-square-foot addition, laundry facilities on every floor, and individually controlled heating and cooling in each room.

Additional facilities include a student media center with a TV studio, a radio station, print media production facilities, a speech-and-hearing clinic for students in communication disorders, a biofeedback laboratory, an organic chemistry lab, an analytical chemistry lab, an independent learning center for nursing students, an observatory, a greenhouse, a 5,000-seat football stadium, a soccer field, tennis and racquetball courts, softball and baseball diamonds, a 3,000-seat arena with three basketball courts, an Olympic-size swimming pool, a multicultural affairs center, a writing center, and a career center.

Costs

Tuition for Missouri residents for the 2006–07 academic year was $5970; out-of-state tuition was $10,400. Room and board totals for both Missouri residents and nonresidents start at $5240. Additional fees included a $250 freshman orientation fee, an annual $72 activities fee, $50 Student Health Center fee, a $50 parking fee for those with a vehicle, and the costs of books and personal expenses.

Financial Aid

Truman offers automatic scholarships ranging from $1000 to $2000. Competitive scholarship awards vary from $500 up to full tuition, room, and board plus a $4000 study-abroad stipend. The application for admission also serves as the application for the automatic and competitive scholarship programs.

Several scholarships are awarded to students for excellence in music, theater, or art. These scholarships are available for instrumental, strings, or vocal music; acting or dramatic production; and studio art or art history. Of special interest to piano students is the Truman Piano Fellowship Competition.

The National Collegiate Athletic Association and the University authorize a limited number of grants to outstanding athletes. The value of this aid may vary with each individual recipient.

Truman accepts the Free Application for Federal Student Aid (FAFSA) and participates in all Federal Title IV financial aid programs. Financial aid estimates are available upon request.

Faculty

Truman State University is committed to teaching the academically talented undergraduate student. The University has 353 full-time faculty members and 25 part-time faculty members. Of these, 98 percent teach undergraduates and 83 percent hold a doctoral degree or the highest terminal degree in their discipline. Most major graduate institutions are represented among the Truman faculty, including Harvard, Princeton, Yale, Berkeley, Oxford, and the Sorbonne. The student-faculty ratio at Truman is 15:1.

Student Government

Student Senate is the official elected governing body of the Student Association representing approximately 5,800 students. Its mission is to represent the views of the Student Association in the formulation of the University policy through legislation and membership on all University committees; to facilitate communication and mutual understanding among the Student Association, faculty and staff members, and administration; to maintain a cohesive vision for the future of the University; and to actively participate in the fulfillment of the University's mission as an exemplary public liberal arts and sciences university.

Admission Requirements

Admission to Truman is competitive. Each applicant is evaluated for admission based upon academic and cocurricular record, ACT or SAT results, and the admission essay. Truman requires the following high school core: 4 units of English, 3 units of mathematics (4 recommended), 3 units of social studies/history, 3 units of natural science, 1 unit of fine arts, and 2 units of the same foreign language.

Application and Information

Students interested in early admission must submit an application by November 15. Early admission applicants are considered for all applicable competitive scholarships. Applications received after November 15 are processed on a rolling basis. The recommended final deadline to apply for the fall semester is March 1. There is no application fee. Students may apply online at the University's Web site. For further information or to schedule a campus visit, students should contact:

Admission Office
Truman State University
205 McClain Hall
100 East Normal
Kirksville, Missouri 63501
Phone: 660-785-4114
        800-892-7792 (toll-free, Missouri only)
Fax: 660-785-7456
E-mail: admissions@truman.edu
Web site: http://admissions.truman.edu

THE UNIVERSITY OF FINDLAY
FINDLAY, OHIO

The University

The University of Findlay (UF) is a private coeducational institution with more than 4,600 full- and part-time students. Founded in 1882 by the Churches of God, General Conference, it emphasizes preparation for careers and professions in an educational program that blends liberal arts and career education. Students of many denominations attend Findlay, and religious participation is a matter of personal choice.

Bachelor of Arts degree programs are available in more than sixty-five different majors. Master's degrees are offered in athletic training; business administration; education; environmental, safety, and health management; liberal studies; occupational therapy; physical therapy; and teaching English to speakers of other languages (TESOL).

The largest programs at Findlay are in business, education, equestrian studies, health professions, and pre–veterinary medicine. Majors in the sciences and health professions include athletic training, chemistry, computer science, equestrian studies (English, Western, and equine management), nuclear medicine, occupational therapy, physical therapy, physician assistant studies, premedicine, and pre–veterinary medicine. Business degrees are founded in a comprehensive core program with eleven different majors, including an individualized major option.

Opportunities for internships and work-related experiences are available in most major fields through the Professional Experiences Program (PEP).

Most of Findlay's students come from Ohio and the surrounding states of Michigan, Indiana, and Pennsylvania. More than thirty other states are also represented. UF also has a strong international-student population, with more than 440 international students from thirty countries.

Resident students live in eight modern residence halls and several town-house-style apartments. Social life at Findlay centers on student organizations, fraternities, and sororities. Findlay has three officially recognized fraternities: Alpha Sigma Phi, Tau Kappa Epsilon, and Theta Chi; there are two sororities: Phi Sigma Sigma and Sigma Kappa. Organizations include department and special interest clubs, the newspaper, musical groups, a radio and TV station, Circle K, and Aristos Eklektos (honors).

Athletic programs are affiliated with NCAA Division II and the Great Lakes Intercollegiate Athletic Conference. Findlay offers twelve intercollegiate sports for men: baseball, basketball, cross-country, equestrian, football, golf, indoor track and field, outdoor track and field, soccer, swimming and diving, tennis, and wrestling. It has eleven varsity sports for women: basketball, cross-country, equestrian, golf, indoor track and field, outdoor track and field, soccer, softball, swimming and diving, tennis, track, and volleyball. Club sport teams include the dressage and ice hockey teams. Athletic scholarships are available.

Croy Physical Education Center has a 25-meter swimming pool, exercise areas, a gymnasium, offices, and classrooms. The Gardner Fitness Center is a state-of-the-art facility. The 130,000-square-foot Koehler Recreation and Fitness Complex, opened in 1999, contains the Malcolm Athletic Center, with a six-lane, NCAA regulation track and four multipurpose courts; the Clauss Ice Arena; locker rooms; and offices for the athletic department.

Student services include career and placement counseling, the Cosiano Health Center, academic tutoring and personal counseling, and study skills assistance through the Academic Support Center.

Location

Findlay was voted the most livable micropolitan city in Ohio and scored among the top twelve in the United States. It is within easy driving distance of Toledo, Columbus, Detroit, and Fort Wayne. Interstate 75 and the Ohio Turnpike (Interstates 80 and 90) are major highways serving the area. Airports in Toledo, Columbus, and Detroit are convenient. The town of Findlay has more than 39,000 residents and is home to Marathon Oil Corporation and Cooper Tire and Rubber Company. The Findlay campus consists of more than 200 acres on several sites. A 72-acre campus-owned farm houses the pre–veterinary medicine and English equestrian studies programs. A second 32-acre facility houses the English riding program. Many opportunities exist for students who want business-related and social service agency experience. The University has established strong relationships with the community, which supports athletic and cultural events on the campus. Besides the full program of on-campus activities, off-campus trips to cultural and entertainment events are scheduled. The city of Findlay, which has an excellent business climate, offers part-time job opportunities, volunteer service organizations, and the chance to be involved with the larger civic community. Findlay's campus is attractive, safe, comfortable, and friendly.

Majors and Degrees

The Bachelor of Arts (B.A.) degree is awarded in the following majors: adolescent/young adult/integrated English/language arts, adolescent/young adult/integrated social studies, art, children's book illustration, criminal justice administration, English, English as an international language, forensic science, general social studies, graphic communication, health communication, history, interpersonal communication, Japanese, journalism, law and the liberal arts, middle childhood/language arts and social studies, multi-age/drama/theater, multi-age/Japanese, multi-age/Spanish, multi-age/visual arts, philosophy/applied philosophy, political science, psychology, public relations, religious studies, social work, sociology, Spanish, studio art, teaching English to speakers of other languages, and theater. Minors are offered in numerous areas.

The Bachelor of Science (B.S.) degree is granted in accounting; adolescent/young adult/earth science; adolescent/young adult/integrated mathematics; adolescent/young adult/life science; biology; chemistry; business administration; business management; computer science; early childhood; economics; environmental, safety, and occupational health management; equestrian studies (English and Western emphases); equine business management; finance; health education; health studies; hospitality management; human resource management; international business; intervention specialist/mild to moderate disabilities; language and international business; marketing; mathematics; medical technology; middle childhood/language arts/math; middle childhood/language arts/science; middle childhood/math/science; middle childhood/math/social studies; middle childhood/science/social studies; multi-age/health education; multi-age/physical education; nuclear medicine technology; occupational therapy; operations and logistics; physical education; physician assistant; physical therapy; premedicine; prenursing; pre–veterinary medicine; recreation therapy; entrepreneurship; and strength and conditioning.

The Associate of Arts degree is available in accounting, computer science, criminal justice administration (corrections or law enforcement emphases), English as an international language, equestrian studies, financial management, general social studies, human resource management, humanities, management information systems, massage therapy, nuclear medicine technology, office administration, personal training, religious studies, sales/retail management, and entrepreneurship. Certificate programs are available in a variety of areas.

Academic Programs

Findlay operates on the semester system. Students must complete at least 124 semester hours with a minimum overall grade point average of 2.0 to earn a bachelor's degree. General education requirements and competency requirements in English, reading, computer literacy, speech, and library use must be fulfilled. The First Year Experience introduces students to living and learning at Findlay and gives them the opportunity to work with the same teachers and student group in two related courses. The Foundations Program offers students the chance to develop those skills in writing, reading, and thinking needed for their success as college students. Study skills, time management, and academic advising are included. Students are selected for this program at the time of admission. The Honors Program provides additional challenge to those students who qualify on the basis of academic credentials. Study- and travel-abroad programs are offered by various departments. Credit and/or placement can be earned through Advanced Placement (AP) exams.

The Equestrian Program is a well-recognized program of its kind and serves approximately 250 students from throughout the United States and abroad. Majors in equine business management and in English and Western riding are offered. The instruction, both in the classroom and on horseback, makes use of the expertise of recognized national equestrian champions. The pre–veterinary medicine program, using the farm facilities, offers the advantages of hands-on experience with livestock and an internship program in a distinctive curriculum. The pre–veterinary medicine program has a placement rate into veterinary schools at 60 percent; the national average is 33 percent.

The Nuclear Medicine Institute provides the training necessary to qualify students for careers in nuclear medicine technology, a growing health-related career field.

Academic Facilities

The focal point of the Findlay campus is Old Main, which houses classrooms, faculty and administrative offices, the computer center, facilities for various student activities, and the Ritz Auditorium. Shafer Library is a member of a consortium that provides extensive resources to students. The Gardner Fine Arts Pavilion, dedicated in 1994, houses the Mazza Museum of International Art from Children's Books. The University has numerous computer labs. Other academic buildings include the Frost Science Center, with a greenhouse and the Newhard Planetarium, and the Egner Center for the Performing Arts, which houses a 200-seat theater and the student-operated radio and television stations. A 101,000-square-foot athletic complex was completed in 1999. This facility houses a six-lane indoor track, sand pits for long jump, a state-of-the-art timing system, and a wrestling room. Also under the same roof is an ice arena with a seating capacity of 1,200. Approximately 450 horses are stabled and trained at the equestrian facilities, which offer barns and indoor and outdoor riding arenas.

Costs

Tuition for the 2006–07 academic year totaled $21,836 for most programs. Room and board cost $7792. The estimated cost for transportation, books, and supplies is $1500. There were additional program surcharges for equestrian studies and pre-veterinary medicine.

Financial Aid

Eighty-seven percent of Findlay students receive financial aid. Assistance is based on need as well as scholastic achievement. In 2005, UF students received approximately $23.3 million in intuitional financial aid from the University. The average freshman in 2005 was awarded $10,400 in institutional aid. Merit scholarships at UF range from $7000 to $12,000 a year. Notification of aid awards is made on a rolling basis. Work-study jobs are available. Scholarships for high-achieving students and student athletes are offered.

Faculty

The 16:1 student-faculty ratio results in small classes—usually fewer than 30 students. Professors know their students, and every student has a faculty adviser.

Student Government

The Student Government Association (SGA) and the Campus Program Board are involved in planning and implementing student activities. SGA provides leadership experience for students and enhances cooperation among faculty members, the administration, and students. A representative from SGA sits on the Board of Trustees. The Campus Program Board plans activities for recreation and cultural enrichment.

Admission Requirements

The University of Findlay considers each applicant on an individualized basis. The University accepts applications on a rolling basis, but it encourages students to complete applications by January 15, as the class fills rapidly. Application deadlines are August 1 for the fall semester and December 15 for the spring semester. Major factors associated with rendering a decision include GPA, standardized test scores, and strength of curriculum. Although it is not required, a campus admission visit is encouraged. Applicants to Findlay should have a college-preparatory high school background, including 4 years of English, 3 to 4 years of mathematics, 2 to 3 years of social studies, and 2 years of sciences. A foreign language is recommended but not required. Results of the ACT or SAT should be submitted with the application for admission. Transfer students must be eligible to return to the institution last attended and must submit transcripts of all college work. For students not meeting regular minimum admission requirements, Findlay has a Foundations Program, which provides skill building and academic support during the first semester of the freshman year. Findlay is an equal opportunity institution in admission and employment.

Application and Information

For application forms and other information, students may contact:

Office of Undergraduate Admissions
The University of Findlay
1000 North Main Street
Findlay, Ohio 45840
Phone: 419-434-4732
      800-548-0932 (toll-free)
E-mail: admissions@findlay.edu
Web site: http://www.findlay.edu

Old Main.

UNIVERSITY OF ST. FRANCIS
JOLIET, ILLINOIS

The University

Committed to the success of its students, the University of St. Francis (USF) offers a global perspective, strong career preparation, a liberal arts base, and the self-confidence to take on the world. About 93 percent of USF graduates find employment or enter graduate school within six months of graduation.

The University of St. Francis offers an intimate, personalized college experience, and all students—residents, commuters, adult learners, and graduate students—benefit from an innovative student-centered approach. The University serves approximately 1,600 students at its Joliet campus and more than 2,100 students throughout the nation via off-site locations and online.

Some interesting facts about The University of St. Francis include the following: 73 percent of the University's science graduates are women; nearly 25 percent of all students are involved in volunteer programs; 76 percent of students are transfer students; the University has provided Illinois schools with more than 1,000 teachers; the average undergraduate class size is 13; the University offers more than twenty-five student organizations and thirteen honor societies; and prominent Chicago-based and national companies recruit on the campus each year.

More than sixty areas of undergraduate study are offered in the arts and sciences, business, education, nursing, and social work. The University also offers undergraduate programs designed for adult learners, such as the Bachelor of Science in professional arts/applied organizational management, the RN-B.S.N. Fast Track program for registered nurses, and the health-care leadership and organizational leadership programs.

Twelve graduate programs are offered, including the M.B.A., M.S. in educational leadership, M.S. in health services administration, M.S. in management, M.S. in physician assistant studies, M.S. in reading, M.S. in teaching and learning, M.S. in training and development, M.S.N. in nursing, M.S.W. in social work, and M.Ed. in education with certification along with a major in special education.

USF offers programming nationwide at on-site locations, online, and through faculty-directed distance tutorials. USF is committed to teaching and to providing students with the challenges and support essential to meeting their potential. Small class sizes ensure that students get the individual attention they need. The University's writing and math centers and tutoring programs provide an important support network. Programs for scholars, such as the Biology Fellows Program and various honor societies, provide challenging and relevant educational experiences beyond classroom learning. USF is at the forefront of technology, providing a variety of online research work and experiences.

USF is committed to educating the student as a whole. A variety of student clubs and organizations are available, as are volunteer activities. Student Affairs sponsors many entertainment events as well as the Student Government Association. Schola, the student choir, and *Loquitur*, the University's literary magazine, are popular activities. The University is also host to the annual Undergraduate Conference on English Language and Literature, which draws student presenters from prestigious colleges and universities throughout the nation. Cultural musical events, which bring internationally and nationally acclaimed performers to the University, are sponsored through the Fine Arts Performance series, and exhibits that bring the works of regionally recognized artists to the campus are planned.

Athletics flourish at USF. During the past twenty years, USF teams have won sixty conference championships, have had sixty-two national tournament appearances, and have won one national championship. USF has six sports programs for men and eight programs for women, as well as ten intramural programs.

Location

The University of St. Francis has an amazing location in the midst of a historic residential area known as Joliet's Cathedral area. The University is 35 miles southwest of Chicago (about 45 minutes) and is easily accessible by major roadways and trains. USF is also conveniently located between Argonne National Laboratory and Midewin National Tallgrass Prairie. Both sites provide excellent opportunities for research, internships, and paid cooperative job programs with professionals in many disciplines, including math, natural sciences, education, computer science, and mass communication.

The University also offers classes at a variety of health-care facilities throughout the nation and maintains a regional center in Albuquerque, New Mexico, where the M.S. in physician assistant studies and the Master of Science in Nursing with a family nurse practitioner track are offered.

USF's Regional Education Academy for Leadership (REAL), an initiative of the College of Education, is housed on Jefferson Street in the Twin Oaks Office Center, approximately 10 minutes from the campus. In partnership with area school districts, REAL offers educational opportunities for area educators at convenient locations throughout the region.

Majors and Degrees

Undergraduate programs include accounting, actuarial science, advertising/public relations, American politics, applied organizational management, art, arts–management, arts–marketing, biology, broadcasting/audio-video, commercial/public recreation, computer science, computer science/electronics, elementary education, English, environmental science, finance, general management, health arts, history, human resource management, information technology, library science, management, marketing, mass communications, mathematics, media arts, medical technology, music, music education, nuclear medicine technology, nursing, pastoral ministry, political science, professional arts/applied organizational management, psychology, public policy, radiation therapy, radiography, recreation administration, secondary education (biology, language arts/English, mathematics , social science), social work, special education, studio art, teaching ministry, theology, therapeutic recreation, visual arts, visual arts/graphic design, and Web application development. Preprofessional programs are available for dentistry, medicine, pharmacy, physical therapy, and veterinary medicine,

Academic Programs

The University of St. Francis offers a comprehensive education to its students. The core curriculum includes interdisciplinary courses taken in the freshman through junior years. The relationship of the major to the liberal education courses is addressed in a senior capstone experience in the major. For a baccalaureate degree, a student must earn 128 semester hours. Thirty-two semester hours must be earned at USF. In addition to the overall requirement of at least a 2.0 GPA, a student must achieve a grade of C or better in every course required for the major program. The University also offers Prior Learning Assessment (PLAP), College-Level Examination Program (CLEP), and advanced placement opportunities. Various honors and internship programs are available.

Academic Facilities

The University's oldest building, Tower Hall, is the focal point of activities, housing interactive learning classrooms, state-of-the-art laboratories, offices, residence wings, dining facilities, the chapel, the bookstore, and the radio and television stations. St. Albert Hall is home to the Natural Science Learning Center and the University's main computing lab. Newly remodeled Marian Hall is a residence hall housing 185 students, a residence wing for science students, lounges, a game room, a computing lab, and Information Services offices.

The main campus also includes the three-story library, which offers Internet access. Online and off-campus students may fully utilize USF library services through the University's Web site. The recreation center, with seating for 1,500, is a three-level facility that includes basketball, volleyball, and racquetball courts; a Nautilus training and exercise room; a conference room; and a classroom. The Moser Performing Arts Center houses an auditorium, art gallery, studio theater, and music and choir practice rooms.

Costs

In 2007–08, tuition and fees for full-time undergraduates are $20,440 per year; room and board are $7610 for double occupancy. Tuition for part-time students is $680 per credit hour; RN-B.S.N. Fast Track, $450 per credit hour; professional arts/applied organizational management, $450 per credit hour; and health-care leadership and organizational leadership, $450 per credit hour.

Financial Aid

USF is committed to assisting students in obtaining a high-quality private education. The University spends $10 million in institutional aid and scholarships, in addition to nearly $6 million in federal and state assistance, to enable students to attend USF. In order to apply for all forms of federal, state, and USF assistance, students must complete a financial aid application form. USF prefers that students complete the Free Application for Federal Student Aid (FAFSA).

Faculty

The University of St. Francis faculty is committed to providing students with the best learning experience possible by challenging students academically and offering a personal, caring support system. The University has 75 full-time faculty members, 63 percent of whom have terminal degrees. Adjunct faculty members bring a variety of academic and professional experience to the classroom. Faculty advisers are an integral part of the USF experience. Nursing faculty members are strong clinicians with an intense commitment to the health-care field and to individual patient health. The USF faculty is invested in the success of its students, both academically and personally.

Admission Requirements

Although each applicant is considered individually, there are four general requirements for admission to the University of St. Francis as an incoming freshman: satisfactory ACT or SAT scores; rank in the upper half of their graduating class; at least 16 high school units in academic subjects, or the equivalent of a high school diploma, including 4 units of English, 2 units of mathematics (algebra and geometry), 2 units of social studies, 2 units of science (one with lab), 3 units total with courses from two of three areas (foreign language, computer science, or music/art), and 3 units of electives; and satisfactory scores on the TOEFL from applicants for whom English is a second language.

A $100 registration deposit is required thirty days after acceptance. This deposit is credited to the applicant's bill and is fully refundable until May 1 for students entering in the fall semester or January 1 for students entering in the spring semester.

Students attending other colleges may transfer to the University of St. Francis at any time during their academic careers. A minimum 2.0 GPA and demonstration of college-ready proficiency in math and English are required of transfer students for admission. Students attending community colleges are not required to earn an associate degree to enter. The University has outstanding services for transfer students. Articulation agreements with community colleges ensure a smooth transition to USF.

Application and Information

Freshmen are admitted in the fall and spring. Students should take the ACT or SAT and visit the campus for an interview by April 1. Entrance exams should be taken in the spring of the junior year or the fall of the senior year in high school. Applications, including a high school transcript and an application fee, should be filed by July 15 for fall entry and December 1 for spring entry. Notification is on a rolling basis. Students transferring from a community college or another senior college or university may seek admission for either the fall or spring semester. Transfer students anticipating enrollment as nursing majors should submit an application for admission and have transcripts forwarded to the Admissions Office from one year to one semester before their projected entry date.

Registered nurses seeking admission to the RN-B.S.N. Fast Track degree completion program must submit the application for admission with the fee, official transcripts from each school attended, a copy of current licensure as an RN, and two letters of reference. Specific prerequisite and major supportive courses are also required.

Health-care professionals (dental hygienists, radiologic technologists, registered nurses, respiratory therapists, and other qualified health-care professionals) seeking admission as a health-care leadership major must submit an application; transcripts of academic credit from all colleges, universities, or diploma programs; proof of current licensure; prior learning documentation of appropriate work experience, as specified; and applicable fees. For information about admissions, prospective students should contact:

University of St. Francis
500 Wilcox Street
Joliet, Illinois 60435
Phone: 815-740-3400
         800-735-7500 (toll-free)
E-mail: admissions@stfrancis.edu
Web site: http://www.stfrancis.edu

Tower Hall, on the campus of the University of St. Francis.

VALPARAISO UNIVERSITY
VALPARAISO, INDIANA

The University

Valparaiso University was founded in 1859 by citizens of Valparaiso, Indiana, but its recent history dates from 1925, when it was purchased by the Lutheran University Association. Valpo is one of the nation's largest Lutheran-affiliated universities, yet it remains independent and is open to individuals of all faiths. The University's 4,000 students represent most states and more than forty countries; 66 percent come from outside of Indiana. Valparaiso University is a residential community in which activities outside the classroom form an important part of campus life; more than 67 percent of its students live on campus. Approximately 100 extracurricular and cocurricular programs are open to all, including various NCAA Division I intercollegiate and intramural sports teams for men and women. Approximately 35 percent of the students are members of the University's nine national fraternities and six national sororities. Both in and out of the classroom, students and professors operate a student-initiated honor code in which integrity is assumed to be the norm. When violations occur, they are handled by peers through a student-composed Honor Council. Because of these structures and the University philosophy as a whole, relationships among students, faculty, and administration are remarkably collaborative.

Major divisions at Valparaiso University include the Colleges of Arts and Sciences, Business Administration, Engineering, and Nursing; Christ College (the Honors College); the School of Law; and the Graduate Division. Graduates earned a 96.7 percent job placement rate last year.

Location

Valparaiso University is located in Valparaiso, a safe community of 31,000 in Indiana. Only 1 hour west, Chicago and its theaters, museums, restaurants, and cultural and sports offerings are accessible by auto, train, or bus. The campus is within walking distance of a vibrant town square and commercial/entertainment center with national chain stores and restaurants. Just 15 miles north is the Indiana Dunes National Lakeshore on Lake Michigan, a famous recreational area and home of finest ecological laboratory in the nation. Air service is available from Chicago's O'Hare and Midway International Airports and South Bend's Michiana Regional Airport.

Majors and Degrees

Valparaiso University offers the following undergraduate degrees: Associate of Arts, Associate in Science, Bachelor of Arts, Bachelor of Music, Bachelor of Music Education, Bachelor of Science, Bachelor of Science in Accounting, Bachelor of Science in Business Administration, Bachelor of Science in Civil Engineering, Bachelor of Science in Computer Engineering, Bachelor of Science in Education, Bachelor of Science in Electrical Engineering, Bachelor of Science in Fine Arts, Bachelor of Science in Mechanical Engineering, Bachelor of Science in Nursing, Bachelor of Science in Physical Education, and Bachelor of Social Work. The B.A. or B.S. degree may be earned in accounting, actuarial science, American studies, art, athletic training, biochemistry, biology, business administration, chemistry, Chinese and Japanese studies, church music, civil engineering, classics, communication, communication law, computer engineering, computer science, creative writing, economics, economics and computer analysis, education (elementary, middle, or secondary), electrical engineering, engineering, English, environmental science, exercise science, finance, French, geography, geology, geoscience, German, history, information and decision sciences, international business, international economics and cultural affairs, international service, management, marketing, mathematics, mechanical engineering, meteorology, modern European studies, music, music composition, music education, music performance, new media-journalism, nursing, philosophy, physical education, physics, political science, professional writing, psychology, public and corporate communication, public relations, social work, sociology, Spanish, sports management, television-radio, theater, theology, and youth, family, and education ministry.

Academic Programs

Valparaiso University has a long tradition of combining professional colleges with a strong commitment to the values and broadening experiences of the liberal arts. The University helps students of varied interests and objectives to clarify their goals and explore new possibilities. Connections between students' lives and the classroom are encouraged through an emphasis on hands-on learning programs, including the Valpo Core. Programs are structured to provide a solid base for exploration in various fields, while offering students the freedom to develop depth in a specific interest. This philosophy is extended through the upper division, where students have three options when completing a degree: an individual plan of study involving the major and complementary courses from related fields of study, the election of a second academic major in addition to the first, or a special minor in connection with the major. Career planning is aided through the professional programs and the University's Career Center. Many students also gain professional work experience in their chosen field before graduation by participating in the cooperative education program and internships.

Valparaiso operates on the semester system; the fall semester begins in late August and ends before Christmas, and the spring semester starts in early January and ends during the second week in May. Valpo also has two summer terms that further extend opportunities for study on campus or at various off-campus locations.

The University participates in the Advanced Placement Program, the College-Level Examination Program, and the International Baccalaureate Program. In addition, Valparaiso provides its own placement testing in several academic areas.

All departments of the University offer opportunities for honors work through independent study, seminars, and research. Christ College, the Honors College of Valparaiso, has a well-established but continuously evolving program designed to challenge gifted students. Christ College students enroll concurrently in any other Valpo college.

Off-Campus Programs

Valparaiso University sponsors study-abroad programs in Reutlingen and Tübingen, Germany; Puebla, Mexico; Paris, France; Hangzhou, China; Granada, Spain; and Cambridge, England. Valparaiso also sponsors semester-long study opportunities at two universities in Japan, one in Namibia, and another in Greece. Valpo students may study at other overseas locations through Valparaiso's membership in the Central States College Association. In addition, Valpo grants credit for the following cooperative programs: Urban Studies Semester (Chicago), Urban Affairs Semester and Washington Semester (Washington, D.C.), and Semester on the United Nations (Madison, New Jersey).

Academic Facilities

Opened in fall 2004, the 115,000-square-foot Christopher Center for Library Information Services is a state-of-the-art facility, which boasts a robotic book-retrieval system. In addition to library resources, the four-story structure houses a 91-seat tiered classroom; three fireplace lounges; a 60-seat computer lab; a snack bar; twenty-four stations for listening, viewing, and developing multimedia projects; reading rooms; a writing center; electronic information services; and much more. The Neils Science Center houses an astronomical observatory, a greenhouse, and other facilities that have earned the University a citation from the Atomic Energy Commission for having a model undergraduate physics laboratory. The Kade-Duesenberg German House and Cultural Center, the Virtual Nursing Learning Center, weather station (which includes Dopplar Radar), Center for the Arts, Vis-Box 3-D scientific learning system, and nonlinear (digital) video editing lab are state-of-the-art facilities.

Costs

Tuition for the 2006–07 academic year at Valparaiso University was $23,200; room was $4140, and board was $2500. General fees were $800. The total cost of tuition, room, board, and fees was $30,640. Students spend approximately $2370 per year for books, supplies, and such miscellaneous expenses as laundry and travel.

Financial Aid

Ninety percent of Valparaiso's undergraduate students receive financial aid, totaling more than $55 million. Many scholarships and awards are determined by the admissions application. Students are also encouraged to file the Free Application for Federal Student Aid (FAFSA) to apply for need-based grants, loans, and employment. Valpo awards federal, state, and University need-based aid based on FAFSA results, attempting to make up the difference between the cost of attending Valpo and the amount a family can afford. Early application is recommended for Valpo assistance, since the awarding of aid begins in January of the year of enrollment.

Faculty

Valparaiso's 351 full-time faculty members share a common interest—teaching in ways that encourage students and faculty members to get to know one another. The majority of the faculty members are full-time, and a considerable number serve as advisers to the various academic and social organizations on campus. Classes are led by professors, not teaching assistants. Almost 90 percent of the full-time professors have terminal degrees, and this figure reaches 100 percent in many departments. Each department has a full advising system to help students with course and program selection.

Student Government

Students and faculty members alike are involved in the internal governance of the institution. House Councils in each of the residence halls are composed of representatives elected by the residents. Each council makes decisions and sets standards within the guidelines established by the University. Students in the living units and off-campus students elect representatives to the Student Senate (composed entirely of students) and the University Senate (made up of an equal number of representatives from the student body, faculty, and administration). The functions of these two separate bodies cover most phases of student life.

Admission Requirements

Valparaiso admits candidates who exhibit the potential for academic success at the University. The freshman retention rate averaged 86 percent over the past five years, reflecting in part the high quality of the admission program. Qualified students are admitted without regard to race, color, gender, disability, national origin, or ancestry. The credentials of each applicant are individually and personally evaluated, and consideration is given not only to ACT or SAT scores, but also to grades and trends in the student's record, the nature of the high school and the program followed, outside interests, and recommendations. A campus visit and an interview with an admission counselor are recommended but not required. Students who have taken the ACT or SAT in their junior year and have submitted their high school transcripts, complete through the eleventh grade, may be considered for admission.

Application and Information

An applicant must complete a formal University admission application or the Common Application to be considered for admission. In addition, Valpo requires a high school transcript (complete through the junior year), ACT or SAT scores, a counselor evaluation form, and college transcripts (when applicable). Valpo's nonbinding early action option requires applicants to submit their applications no later than November 1. Regular admission notification begins on a rolling basis after December 1. First priority for scholarship consideration is given to those who apply for admission by the early action deadline; preference is then given to those who apply by January 15.

Information and application forms for admission and financial aid may be obtained from:

Office of Admission
Kretzmann Hall
1700 Chapel Drive
Valparaiso University
Valparaiso, Indiana 46383-6493
Phone: 219-464-5011
       888-GO-VALPO (toll-free)
Fax: 219-464-6898
E-mail: undergrad.admissions@valpo.edu
Web site: http://www.valpo.edu

Students on the campus of Valparaiso University.

WESTERN MICHIGAN UNIVERSITY

KALAMAZOO, MICHIGAN

The University

Western Michigan University (WMU) is one of the country's top public universities and enjoys global recognition for its outstanding programs in aviation, fine arts, communications, and business marketing. WMU is also home to Lee Honors College, which has been in continuous operation longer than almost any other honors program in the country. More than 1,200 undergraduates are currently enrolled in Lee Honors College. With an increasing student demand for honors programs, the University plans to continue to enlarge Lee Honors College over the next three years.

Western Michigan University is focused on preparing its graduates for the competitive world of work as well as graduate and professional school. WMU is one of only ninety-seven public universities in the United States to have a chapter of Phi Beta Kappa, the nation's premier honor society. In addition, *U.S. News & World Report* has ranked WMU among America's top 100 public universities for the past seven years.

With 24,841 students, WMU is Michigan's fourth-largest university and one of the nation's fifty largest public universities in the country. Even though it is a large university with a broad range of program offerings at both the undergraduate and graduate level, WMU maintains a comfortable student-faculty ratio of 19:1, although some lectures in general education courses can be larger. Despite its size, complexity, and variety of offerings, WMU is one of the most affordable of Michigan's fifteen public universities.

Founded in 1903, WMU has seven degree-granting colleges: Arts and Sciences, Aviation, the Haworth College of Business, Education, Engineering and Applied Sciences, Fine Arts, and Health and Human Services as well as the Graduate College, to assist students pursuing advanced degrees, and the Lee Honors College. Students have 237 academic programs from which to choose, 141 of them at the undergraduate level. Because it has a vibrant graduate component that includes twenty-nine doctoral programs, the University attracts faculty members who not only enjoy teaching at the undergraduate level but have distinguished themselves nationally through their research.

WMU has focused on enhancing its out-of-class opportunities by expanding its internship opportunities and student engagement in research and service. The Haenicke Institute for Global Education provides access to study-abroad programs all over the world and supports international students coming to study at WMU.

The University is home to a diverse student body that includes students from nearly every state across the United States as well as some 975 international students from eighty-five countries. Minority students also are well represented and make up nearly 6 percent of the student population. The University's main campus enrollment of nearly 24,400 includes approximately 5,000 students who live in twenty-two campus residence halls that offer a variety of living arrangements.

There are more than 275 registered student organizations, including a wide range of Greek, academic honorary, and professional organizations. In addition, the University has nationally recognized arts programs, a lively cultural calendar, and NCAA Division I-A Mid-American and Central Collegiate Hockey Association sports teams. Its six men's and ten women's varsity sports, intramural teams, and club sports add vitality to campus life.

Location

For more than 100 years, Kalamazoo has been home to WMU. From the dedication of East Hall—the first building on campus—the community has supported Western's growth. Kalamazoo is an ideal college town, where business leaders recognize Western as their second-largest employer and where students and employees contribute more than $500 million annually to the economy of the region. Located just 40 miles from the beautiful eastern shoreline of Lake Michigan, the area embraces all four seasons with cool, sunny summers and moderate winters. Outdoor recreation abounds, from downhill skiing in winter months to every imaginable water sport available from late spring through early fall. Unlike much of eastern Michigan, southwest Michigan is composed of gently rolling hills, small recreational lakes, and dense woodlands. Fall is a particularly beautiful time to enjoy the variety of color while hiking or riding a bike on the Kal-Haven trail that connects Kalamazoo to the Lake Michigan resort town of South Haven. Nearly every weekend throughout the year Kalamazoo has something to offer its students and local residents. It is not unusual on a Saturday afternoon to find faculty members rubbing elbows with students at the annual Art Hop, Blues Festival, or Taste of Kalamazoo.

Kalamazoo, a city of more than 75,000, offers a wide array of lively entertainment including sports, such as professional baseball, hockey, and soccer; music, from jazz to heavy metal; intimate coffee houses and comedy clubs; and dining, from fast food to international cuisine. West Michigan is also home to numerous prosperous businesses, industries, and Fortune 500 companies including Haworth Inc., the Whirlpool Corporation, and the Kellogg Company. Many of these companies offer internships to WMU students.

Majors and Degrees

WMU offers a range of academic majors and programs to meet nearly everyone's needs. The College of Arts and Sciences offers undergraduate degrees in Africana studies; anthropology; biochemistry; biology; biomedical sciences; business-oriented chemistry; chemistry; communication studies; criminal justice; earth science; economics; English; film, video, and media studies; French; geochemistry; geography; geology; geophysics; German; global and international studies; history; hydrogeology; interpersonal communication; journalism; Latin; mathematics; organizational communication; philosophy; physics; political science; psychology; public history; public relations; religion; sociology; Spanish; statistics; student-planned major; telecommunications and information management; tourism and travel; preprofessional programs (dentistry, law, medicine); and coordinate majors (environmental studies, women's studies).

The College of Aviation offers programs in aviation flight science, aviation maintenance technology, and aviation science and administration.

The Haworth College of Business offers programs in accountancy, advertising and promotion, computer information systems, electronic business design, finance, food and consumer package goods marketing, human resource management, integrated supply matrix management, management, marketing, personal financial planning, sales and business marketing, and telecommunications and information management.

The College of Education offers programs in elementary education that emphasize language arts, mathematics, science, and social science. Secondary education students may major in art, biology, business, chemistry, earth science, English, family and consumer science, French, geography, German, health education, history, industrial technology, Latin, marketing, mathematics, music, physical education, physics, political science, school health education, Spanish, and technology and design. Other programs include athletic training, community health education, dietetics, exercise science, family studies, food service administration, industrial technology, interior design, recreation, special education, and textile and apparel studies.

The College of Engineering and Applied Sciences offers programs in aeronautical engineering, chemical engineering, civil engineering, computer engineering, computer science, construction engineering, electrical engineering, engineering graphics and design technology, engineering management technology, imaging, industrial design, industrial engineering, manufacturing engineering, manufacturing engineering technology, mechanical engineering, paper engineering, and paper science.

The College of Fine Arts offers programs in art, art education, art history, dance, graphic design, jazz studies, music, music composition, music education, music history, music performance, music theater performance, music therapy, theater design, theater performance, and theater technology.

The College of Health and Human Services offers programs in interdisciplinary health services, occupational therapy, nursing, nursing (RN), social work, speech pathology and audiology, and travel instruction.

Academic Programs

WMU is committed to student academic success, beginning with the new First-Year Experience program, which utilizes small-group seminars led by senior faculty members and upperclass student mentors. The University's college advisers help students plan their courses of study and consider program options, while advisers in University Curriculum assist undecided students in exploring academic programs and their relationships to various careers and professions. A comprehensive general education program provides the foundation for all fields of study. The Lee Honors College provides an atmosphere of small seminar classes, opportunities for research alongside faculty members, and the chance to explore new horizons through independent study. Student academic success is recognized through University, college, and department honor societies and through the prestigious Presidential Scholar Award given to outstanding graduating seniors.

Off-Campus Programs

A host of U.S. business-industry partnerships and exchange agreements with universities and other organizations around the world provide training, research, and study-abroad opportunities for graduate and undergraduate students. In addition, the University actively assists students seeking internships in their chosen fields of study.

Academic Facilities

Number two on Intel's list of the nation's 100 most wireless college campuses, WMU's network provides access to the University libraries, the Internet, and extensive campus information services. Computer labs are available across the campus, including many residence halls. Specialized labs support the work of students in engineering, graphic arts, teacher education, business, and other fields. New construction is continuously transforming the campus while giving students access to acclaimed fine arts performance spaces, a new center for visual arts, new science laboratories, world-class aviation facilities, a leading-edge building for the College of Health and Human Services, and an innovative College of Engineering and Applied Sciences building that is located in a thriving business and research park.

Costs

A college education is one of the best investments a person can make, and, best of all, it never depreciates over time. Over a lifetime of work, WMU's graduates can expect to earn nearly $2 million—more than twice that of someone with a high school diploma. WMU is committed to keeping costs as low as possible to ensure that all qualified students have access to the University. WMU's tuition and fees are among the lowest in the state. For 2006–07, tuition and fee costs were $6866, and room and board costs were $6877. Books and supplies and personal and travel expenses vary based on individual factors.

Financial Aid

The University annually awards more than $200 million in financial assistance to undergraduate students. Students who are qualified for need-based aid usually receive assistance through a combination of gift-aid (grants and scholarships), self-help (student loans), and employment (work-study).

A variety of academic achievement scholarships are available to students who have demonstrated academic success while in high school. These awards vary from $1000 to full tuition, and, in some instances, a combination of awards can be sufficient to cover nearly all direct costs of attendance at WMU. Most merit awards are renewable by enrolling full-time and earning a minimum 3.0 cumulative grade point average while at WMU. The two most recognized awards are the Medallion Scholarship and the Dean's Scholarship. The Dean's Scholarship is awarded to the top academic students (based on high school grades and standardized test scores) who apply for admission in early December, compete in the Medallion competition in January, and enroll the following fall semester as new, first-time students. Medallion recipients receive $10,000 annually, and the scholarship is renewable for up to four years of full-time enrollment.

There are also scholarships for students who have earned associate degrees from state and regional community colleges and who have earned high grade point averages while completing degree requirements.

Faculty

WMU's commitment to academic excellence means that many of its 924 full-time and 488 part-time faculty members conduct research. Tenured professors teach freshman-level courses, and full-time faculty members teach the majority of all courses. Plus, hundreds of these scholars have academic or research experience outside of the United States, bringing a global perspective into the classroom.

Student Government

Governance structures include the Western Student Association and its Student Senate and the Residence Hall Association. Each provides students with a wide variety of opportunities for leadership.

Admission Requirements

Admission to the University is based primarily on a combination of high school cumulative grade point average and standardized test scores (either ACT or SAT). When admission is not conclusive or admission is sought to selective or highly competitive programs, consideration is given to academic rigor of courses taken and counselor/principal recommendations, in addition to grade point averages and test scores.

To ensure academic success at WMU, all students should have completed a minimum of 4 years of English, 3 years of mathematics (through intermediate algebra), 3 years of social sciences, 2 years of natural sciences, and 2 years of the same foreign language.

Offers of admission made to students still in high school are conditional, pending graduation from high school and the University's review of final senior-year grades.

Transfer students with a minimum of 26 transferable hours (39 quarter hours) at the time of application and a grade point average of at least 2.0 (C average) are considered for admission. The trend of the most recent grades is also taken into account. Applicants with fewer than 26 transferable hours (39 quarter hours) at the time of application also must submit a high school transcript. In such cases, admission is based on both college and high school records.

Application and Information

For an application or more information, students should contact:

Office of Admissions and Orientation
Western Michigan University
1903 West Michigan Avenue
Kalamazoo, Michigan 49008-5211

Phone: 269-387-2000
Web site: http://www.wmich.edu/admissions

This impressive Stewart Clock Tower joins Waldo Library, on the right, with the high-tech University Computing Center.

Profiles and Close-Ups of Other Colleges to Consider

Florida

UNIVERSITY OF WEST FLORIDA
Pensacola, Florida

University of West Florida is a coed, public, comprehensive unit of State University System of Florida, founded in 1963, offering degrees at the associate, bachelor's, master's, and doctoral levels (specialists). It has a 1,600-acre campus in Pensacola.

Academic Information The faculty has 575 members (60% full-time). The undergraduate student-faculty ratio is 18:1. The library holds 792,733 titles, 5,122 serial subscriptions, and 10,061 audiovisual materials. Special programs include services for learning-disabled students, an honors program, cooperative (work-study) education, study abroad, advanced placement credit, ESL programs, independent study, distance learning, summer session for credit, part-time degree programs (daytime, evenings, summer), internships, and arrangement for off-campus study with other members of the State University System of Florida. The most frequently chosen baccalaureate fields are business/marketing, communications/journalism, education.

Student Body Statistics The student body totals 9,819, of whom 8,254 are undergraduates (1,186 freshmen). 60 percent are women and 40 percent are men. Students come from 51 states and territories and 78 other countries. 87 percent are from Florida. 1.1 percent are international students.

Expenses for 2006–07 *Application fee:* $30. *State resident tuition:* $2211 full-time, $110.39 per semester hour part-time. *Nonresident tuition:* $14,778 full-time, $527.27 per semester hour part-time. *Mandatory fees:* $1100 full-time. Full-time tuition and fees vary according to location and reciprocity agreements. Part-time tuition varies according to location and reciprocity agreements. *College room and board:* $6600. Room and board charges vary according to housing facility.

Financial Aid Forms of aid include need-based and non-need-based scholarships, athletic grants, and part-time jobs. The application deadline for financial aid is continuous.

Freshman Admission University of West Florida requires a high school transcript, a minimum 2.0 high school GPA, SAT or ACT scores, and TOEFL scores for international students. The application deadline for regular admission is June 30.

Transfer Admission The application deadline for admission is June 30.

Entrance Difficulty University of West Florida assesses its entrance difficulty level as moderately difficult; noncompetitive for applicants with associate degrees from Florida public junior colleges. For the fall 2006 freshman class, 72 percent of the applicants were accepted.

For Further Information Contact Director of Admissions, University of West Florida, Admissions, 11000 University Parkway, Pensacola, FL 32514. *Telephone:* 850-474-2230 or 800-263-1074 (toll-free). *Fax:* 850-474-3460. *E-mail:* admissions@uwf.edu. *Web site:* http://uwf.edu/.

See page 332 for the College Close-Up.

Kentucky

TRANSYLVANIA UNIVERSITY
Lexington, Kentucky

Transylvania University is a coed, private, four-year college, founded in 1780, affiliated with the Christian Church (Disciples of Christ), offering degrees at the bachelor's level. It has a 40-acre campus in Lexington near Cincinnati and Louisville.

Academic Information The faculty has 97 members (85% full-time), 81% with terminal degrees. The student-faculty ratio is 13:1. The library holds 125,000 titles, 500 serial subscriptions, and 1,200 audiovisual materials. Special programs include study abroad, advanced placement credit, double majors, independent study, self-designed majors, summer session for credit, part-time degree programs (daytime), internships, and arrangement for off-campus study with Washington Center for Internships and Academic Seminars, Kentucky Institute for International Studies. The most frequently chosen baccalaureate fields are business/marketing, biological/life sciences, social sciences.

Student Body Statistics The student body is made up of 1,117 undergraduates (293 freshmen). 58 percent are women and 42 percent are men. Students come from 31 states and territories. 82 percent are from Kentucky. 32 percent of the 2006 graduating class went on to graduate and professional schools.

Expenses for 2007–08 *Application fee:* $30. *Comprehensive fee:* $29,430 includes full-time tuition ($22,300) and college room and board ($7130). *Part-time tuition:* $2385 per course. *Part-time mandatory fees:* $80 per course.

Financial Aid Forms of aid include need-based and non-need-based scholarships and part-time jobs. The average aided 2006–07 undergraduate received an aid package worth an estimated $17,629. The priority application deadline for financial aid is March 1.

Freshman Admission Transylvania University requires an essay, a high school transcript, a minimum 2.75 high school GPA, 2 recommendations, SAT or ACT scores, and TOEFL scores for international students. An interview is recommended. An interview is required for some. The application deadline for regular admission is February 1 and for early action it is December 1.

Transfer Admission The application deadline for admission is rolling.

Entrance Difficulty Transylvania University assesses its entrance difficulty level as very difficult. For the fall 2006 freshman class, 83 percent of the applicants were accepted.

For Further Information Contact Mr. Bradley Goan, Director of Admissions, Transylvania University, 300 North Broadway, Lexington, KY 40508-1797. *Telephone:* 859-233-4242 or 800-872-6798 (toll-free). *Fax:* 859-233-8797. *E-mail:* admissions@transy.edu. *Web site:* http://www.transy.edu/.

See page 324 for the College Close-Up.

Louisiana

UNIVERSITY OF NEW ORLEANS
New Orleans, Louisiana

University of New Orleans is a coed, public unit of Louisiana State University System, founded in 1958, offering degrees at the bachelor's, master's, and doctoral levels and postbachelor's certificates. It has a 345-acre campus in New Orleans.

Academic Information The faculty has 654 members (73% full-time), 56% with terminal degrees. The undergraduate student-faculty ratio is 17:1. The library holds 896,000 titles, 4,950 serial subscriptions, and 22,775 audiovisual materials. Special programs include academic remediation, services for learning-disabled students, an honors program, cooperative (work-study) education, study abroad, advanced placement credit, ESL programs, double majors, independent study, distance learning, self-designed majors, summer session for credit, part-time degree programs, adult/continuing education programs, internships, and arrangement for off-campus study with Southern University at New Orleans, Delgado Community College, Nunez Community College.

Student Body Statistics The student body totals 11,747, of whom 9,156 are undergraduates (1,021 freshmen). 54 percent are women and 46 percent are men. Students come from 46 states and territories and 74 other countries. 96 percent are from Louisiana. 2.8 percent are international students.

Expenses for 2007–08 *Application fee:* $40. *State resident tuition:* $3292 full-time, $521 per course part-time. *Nonresident tuition:* $10,336 full-time, $1859 per course part-time. *Mandatory fees:* $518 full-time, $53 per hour part-time. *College room and board:* $4734.

University of New Orleans (continued)

Financial Aid Forms of aid include need-based and non-need-based scholarships, athletic grants, and part-time jobs. The average aided 2006–07 undergraduate received an aid package worth an estimated $7119. The priority application deadline for financial aid is May 15.

Freshman Admission University of New Orleans requires a high school transcript, SAT or ACT scores, and TOEFL scores for international students. An essay, a minimum 2.0 high school GPA, 3 recommendations, an interview, and 2.0 high school GPA on high school core program are required for some. The application deadline for regular admission is rolling.

Transfer Admission The application deadline for admission is August 28.

Entrance Difficulty University of New Orleans assesses its entrance difficulty level as moderately difficult. For the fall 2006 freshman class, 77 percent of the applicants were accepted.

For Further Information Contact Mr. Robert Hensley, Director of Admissions, University of New Orleans, Lake Front, New Orleans, LA 70148. *Telephone:* 504-280-7013 or 800-256-5866 (toll-free out-of-state). *Fax:* 504-280-5522. *E-mail:* admissions@uno.edu. *Web site:* http://www.uno.edu/.

See page 330 for the College Close-Up.

New York

CLARKSON UNIVERSITY

Potsdam, New York

SPONSOR
See Front Insert for Details!

Clarkson University is a coed, private university, founded in 1896, offering degrees at the bachelor's, master's, and doctoral levels. It has a 640-acre campus in Potsdam.

Academic Information The faculty has 198 members (88% full-time), 89% with terminal degrees. The undergraduate student-faculty ratio is 16:1. The library holds 269,059 titles, 1,778 serial subscriptions, and 2,128 audiovisual materials. Special programs include services for learning-disabled students, an honors program, cooperative (work-study) education, study abroad, advanced placement credit, accelerated degree programs, ESL programs, double majors, independent study, self-designed majors, summer session for credit, part-time degree programs (daytime, summer), internships, and arrangement for off-campus study with Associated Colleges of the St. Lawrence Valley. The most frequently chosen baccalaureate fields are business/marketing, engineering, interdisciplinary studies.

Student Body Statistics The student body totals 2,964, of whom 2,545 are undergraduates (646 freshmen). 26 percent are women and 74 percent are men. Students come from 35 states and territories and 22 other countries. 75 percent are from New York. 2.5 percent are international students. 25 percent of the 2006 graduating class went on to graduate and professional schools.

Expenses for 2006–07 *Application fee:* $50. *Comprehensive fee:* $36,738 includes full-time tuition ($26,650), mandatory fees ($440), and college room and board ($9648). *College room only:* $5058. Full-time tuition and fees vary according to course load. Room and board charges vary according to housing facility. *Part-time tuition:* $889 per credit. Part-time tuition varies according to course load.

Financial Aid Forms of aid include need-based and non-need-based scholarships, athletic grants, and part-time jobs. The average aided 2006–07 undergraduate received an aid package worth an estimated $19,993. The priority application deadline for financial aid is February 15.

Freshman Admission Clarkson University requires a high school transcript, 2 recommendations, SAT or ACT scores, and TOEFL scores for international students. An interview and SAT Subject Test scores are recommended. The application deadline for regular admission is January 15 and for early decision plan 1 it is December 1.

Entrance Difficulty Clarkson University assesses its entrance difficulty level as very difficult. For the fall 2006 freshman class, 84 percent of the applicants were accepted.

SPECIAL MESSAGE TO STUDENTS

Social Life Clarkson's 640-acre wooded campus, more than eighty active clubs and organizations, and major cultural and educational events afford enormous extracurricular opportunities for students. The 6-million-acre Adirondack Park is only minutes away, and within 2 hours of campus are Lake Placid and the cosmopolitan Canadian cities of Montreal and Ottawa.

Academic Highlights Academics at Clarkson emphasize rigorous professional preparation; dynamic, real-world learning; flexibility and adaptability; and teamwork that spans disciplines. Clarkson's award-winning programs in engineering, arts, sciences, business, and health sciences also develop communication and collaboration skills, with a focus on practical application of knowledge and creative, open-ended problem solving. Every student majoring in business, for example, gains firsthand experience by actually running a business. Undergraduates customize programs through specialized concentrations and minors that broaden career options. Clarkson's relatively small size encourages personal attention and interactions between students and faculty members, and Clarkson students enjoy extraordinary opportunities to pursue faculty-mentored research. They gain professional experience through internships and co-ops with corporations and government organizations and can broaden their perspectives through a wide range of study-abroad opportunities. The University offers an honors program and an accelerated three-year bachelor's degree.

Interviews and Campus Visits Although an interview is not required, Clarkson strongly recommends that students visit the campus for a tour and meeting with representatives. This meeting provides an opportunity for an informal exchange of information between the student and an admission staff member. Students who visit the campus for an interview with an admission counselor receive a fee-waived voucher for a Clarkson application. Clarkson is located in the friendly community of Potsdam, between the beautiful Adirondack Mountains and the St. Lawrence River. The scenic, open campus features more than forty-six buildings, offering a blend of old and new architecture. New buildings include a state-of-the-art building for business and liberal arts, which features fully networked classrooms and collaborative centers with wireless network access and videoconferencing capabilities and state-of-the-art laboratories, and the centrally located Cheel Student Center, which is a combination student union and multipurpose arena facility. For information about appointments and campus visits, students should call the Office of Undergraduate Admission at 315-268-6480 or 800-527-6577 (toll-free), Monday through Friday 8 to 4:30 or Saturday by appointment. The office is located in Holcroft House on the campus. The nearest commercial airport is Syracuse-Hancock International.

For Further Information Write to Mr. Brian Grant, Director of Admission, Clarkson University, P.O. Box 5605, Potsdam, NY 13699-5605. *E-mail:* admission@clarkson.edu. *Web site:* http://www.clarkson.edu.

See page 314 for the College Close-Up.

North Carolina

NORTH CAROLINA AGRICULTURAL AND TECHNICAL STATE UNIVERSITY
Greensboro, North Carolina

North Carolina Agricultural and Technical State University is a coed, public unit of University of North Carolina System, founded in 1891, offering degrees at the bachelor's, master's, and doctoral levels. It has an 800-acre campus in Greensboro.

Academic Information The faculty has 495 members (74% full-time). The undergraduate student-faculty ratio is 24:1. The library holds 597,093 titles, 40,425 serial subscriptions, and 37,886 audiovisual materials. Special programs include academic remediation, services for learning-disabled students, an honors program, cooperative (work-study) education, study abroad, advanced placement credit, summer session for credit, part-time degree programs (daytime, evenings, summer), adult/continuing education programs, internships, and arrangement for off-campus study with University of North Carolina at Greensboro, Guilford College, Bennett College, High Point University, Greensboro College. The most frequently chosen baccalaureate fields are business/marketing, engineering, engineering technologies.

Student Body Statistics The student body totals 11,098, of whom 9,687 are undergraduates (2,094 freshmen). 53 percent are women and 47 percent are men. Students come from 43 states and territories. 75 percent are from North Carolina. 0.4 percent are international students.

Expenses for 2006–07 *Application fee:* $45. *One-time mandatory fee:* $10. *State resident tuition:* $1994 full-time. *Nonresident tuition:* $11,436 full-time. *Mandatory fees:* $1878 full-time. Full-time tuition and fees vary according to student level. *College room and board:* $6686. Room and board charges vary according to board plan and housing facility.

Financial Aid Forms of aid include need-based and non-need-based scholarships, athletic grants, and part-time jobs. The average aided 2005–06 undergraduate received an aid package worth $5898. The priority application deadline for financial aid is March 15.

Freshman Admission North Carolina Agricultural and Technical State University requires a high school transcript, a minimum 2.0 high school GPA, and TOEFL scores for international students. SAT or ACT scores are recommended. The application deadline for regular admission is rolling.

Transfer Admission The application deadline for admission is rolling.

Entrance Difficulty North Carolina Agricultural and Technical State University assesses its entrance difficulty level as moderately difficult. For the fall 2006 freshman class, 84 percent of the applicants were accepted.

For Further Information Contact Mr. Lee Young, Director of Admissions, North Carolina Agricultural and Technical State University, 1601 East Market Street, Webb Hall, Greensboro, NC 27411. *Telephone:* 336-334-7946 or 800-443-8964 (toll-free in-state). *Fax:* 336-334-7478. *E-mail:* uadmit@ncat.edu. *Web site:* http://www.ncat.edu/.

See page 320 for the College Close-Up.

Pennsylvania

GANNON UNIVERSITY
Erie, Pennsylvania

SPONSOR
See Front Insert
for Details!

Gannon University is a coed, private, Roman Catholic, comprehensive institution, founded in 1925, offering degrees at the bachelor's, master's, and doctoral levels and post-master's and postbachelor's certificates (associate). It has a 13-acre campus in Erie near Cleveland.

Academic Information The faculty has 312 members (58% full-time), 49% with terminal degrees. The undergraduate student-faculty ratio is 11:1. The library holds 270,590 titles, 14,301 serial subscriptions, and 3,523 audiovisual materials. Special programs include academic remediation, services for learning-disabled students, an honors program, cooperative (work-study) education, study abroad, accelerated degree programs, ESL programs, double majors, independent study, distance learning, summer session for credit, part-time degree programs (daytime, evenings, weekends, summer), external degree programs, adult/continuing education programs, internships, and arrangement for off-campus study with Mercyhurst College and Edinboro University. The most frequently chosen baccalaureate fields are business/marketing, education, health professions and related sciences.

Student Body Statistics The student body totals 3,815, of whom 2,675 are undergraduates (615 freshmen). 59 percent are women and 41 percent are men. Students come from 27 states and territories and 11 other countries. 79 percent are from Pennsylvania. 1.3 percent are international students. 27 percent of the 2006 graduating class went on to graduate and professional schools.

Expenses for 2006–07 *Application fee:* $25. *Comprehensive fee:* $27,876 includes full-time tuition ($19,500), mandatory fees ($496), and college room and board ($7880). *College room only:* $4310. Full-time tuition and fees vary according to class time and program. Room and board charges vary according to board plan and housing facility. *Part-time tuition:* $605 per credit hour. *Part-time mandatory fees:* $16 per credit hour. Part-time tuition and fees vary according to class time and program.

Financial Aid Forms of aid include need-based and non-need-based scholarships, athletic grants, and part-time jobs. The average aided 2006–07 undergraduate received an aid package worth an estimated $16,261. The priority application deadline for financial aid is March 15.

Freshman Admission Gannon University requires a high school transcript, a minimum 2.0 high school GPA, counselor's recommendation, SAT or ACT scores, and TOEFL scores for international students. An essay is recommended. A minimum 3.0 high school GPA, 3 recommendations, and an interview are required for some. The application deadline for regular admission is rolling.

Transfer Admission The application deadline for admission is rolling.

Entrance Difficulty Gannon University assesses its entrance difficulty level as moderately difficult. For the fall 2006 freshman class, 86 percent of the applicants were accepted.

SPECIAL MESSAGE TO STUDENTS

Social Life Gannon's location on the shores of Lake Erie in Pennsylvania's fourth-largest city, Erie, provides something for everyone to enjoy. On Gannon's campus, students can attend everything from plays, movies, and dances to athletic events. They can also take advantage of cultural events and local entertainment in Erie. Students may also participate in fraternities and sororities, governing groups, academic clubs, media organizations, intercollegiate and intramural sports programs, and special interest clubs.

Academic Highlights Gannon's friendly environment, coupled with a low student-faculty ratio of 14:1, fosters achievement. Students can choose from a variety of majors offered in business, education, health

Pennsylvania

Gannon University (continued)

sciences, humanities, and science and engineering. Gannon's strategic vision ensures that the University deploys advanced technologies where students and faculty and staff members benefit most. At Gannon, students can enrich their education with professional experience offered through summer field courses; studies abroad; local, regional, and national co-ops; and internships.

Interviews and Campus Visits Choosing a college is one of the most important decisions a student will ever make. To help make that decision easier, Gannon invites students to visit the campus. The Office of Admissions schedules individual appointments year-round, Monday through Friday, from 9 to 3 and group presentations on select Saturday mornings at 10:30. During weekday campus visits, students have the opportunity to meet with a member of the Admissions staff, professors in their intended major, and financial aid representatives. Campus visits also include a campus tour. To schedule a campus visit, students should call 800-GANNON-U Ext. 7407 (toll-free). After visiting, many students decide that Gannon University is the right place for them—personally, academically, professionally, socially, and spiritually. The nearest commercial airport is Erie International.

For Further Information Write to the Office of Admissions, Gannon University, 109 University Square, Erie, PA 16541. *E-mail:* admissions@gannon.edu.

See page 318 for the College Close-Up.

Texas

SOUTHERN METHODIST UNIVERSITY

Dallas, Texas

Southern Methodist University is a coed, private university, founded in 1911, affiliated with the United Methodist Church, offering degrees at the bachelor's, master's, doctoral, and first professional levels and postbachelor's certificates. It has a 210-acre campus in Dallas.

Academic Information The faculty has 924 members (66% full-time), 73% with terminal degrees. The undergraduate student-faculty ratio is 12:1. The library holds 3 million titles, 11,701 serial subscriptions, and 45,168 audiovisual materials. Special programs include academic remediation, services for learning-disabled students, an honors program, cooperative (work-study) education, study abroad, advanced placement credit, accelerated degree programs, ESL programs, double majors, independent study, distance learning, self-designed majors, summer session for credit, part-time degree programs, adult/continuing education programs, and internships. The most frequently chosen baccalaureate fields are business/marketing, communications/journalism, social sciences.

Student Body Statistics The student body totals 10,941, of whom 6,296 are undergraduates (1,371 freshmen). 55 percent are women and 45 percent are men. Students come from 50 states and territories and 66 other countries. 62 percent are from Texas. 5 percent are international students.

Expenses for 2007–08 *Application fee:* $60. *Comprehensive fee:* $41,705 includes full-time tuition ($27,400), mandatory fees ($3480), and college room and board ($10,825). *College room only:* $6730. *Part-time tuition:* $1145 per credit hour. *Part-time mandatory fees:* $146 per credit hour.

Financial Aid Forms of aid include need-based and non-need-based scholarships, athletic grants, and part-time jobs. The average aided 2006–07 undergraduate received an aid package worth an estimated $24,824. The priority application deadline for financial aid is February 15.

Freshman Admission Southern Methodist University requires an essay, a high school transcript, 1 recommendation, SAT or ACT scores, and TOEFL scores for international students. SAT Subject Test scores are required for some. The application deadline for regular admission is January 15 and for early action it is November 1.

Transfer Admission The application deadline for admission is July 1.

Entrance Difficulty Southern Methodist University assesses its entrance difficulty level as moderately difficult. For the fall 2006 freshman class, 54 percent of the applicants were accepted.

For Further Information Contact Mr. Ron Moss, Director of Admission and Enrollment Management, Southern Methodist University, PO Box 750181, Dallas, TX 75275-0181. *Telephone:* 214-768-3417 or 800-323-0672 (toll-free). *Fax:* 214-768-0202. *E-mail:* enrol_serv@smu.edu. *Web site:* http://www.smu.edu/.

See page 322 for the College Close-Up.

UNIVERSITY OF DALLAS

Irving, Texas

University of Dallas is a coed, private, Roman Catholic university, founded in 1955, offering degrees at the bachelor's, master's, and doctoral levels and post-master's and postbachelor's certificates. It has a 750-acre campus in Irving near Dallas–Fort Worth.

Academic Information The faculty has 233 members (52% full-time), 64% with terminal degrees. The undergraduate student-faculty ratio is 11:1. The library holds 223,350 titles and 691 serial subscriptions. Special programs include services for learning-disabled students, study abroad, advanced placement credit, double majors, independent study, self-designed majors, summer session for credit, part-time degree programs (daytime, summer), internships, and arrangement for off-campus study. The most frequently chosen baccalaureate fields are English, biological/life sciences, social sciences.

Student Body Statistics The student body totals 2,941, of whom 1,188 are undergraduates (315 freshmen). 56 percent are women and 44 percent are men. Students come from 47 states and territories and 12 other countries. 56 percent are from Texas. 1.4 percent are international students. 40 percent of the 2006 graduating class went on to graduate and professional schools.

Expenses for 2007–08 *Application fee:* $40. *Comprehensive fee:* $30,882 includes full-time tuition ($21,819), mandatory fees ($1448), and college room and board ($7615). *College room only:* $4240. *Part-time tuition:* $975 per credit hour. *Part-time mandatory fees:* $1448 per year.

Financial Aid Forms of aid include need-based and non-need-based scholarships and part-time jobs. The average aided 2005–06 undergraduate received an aid package worth $17,668. The priority application deadline for financial aid is March 1.

Freshman Admission University of Dallas requires an essay, a high school transcript, 2 recommendations, SAT or ACT scores, and TOEFL scores for international students. An interview is recommended. An interview is required for some. The application deadline for regular admission is August 1 and for early action it is November 1.

Transfer Admission The application deadline for admission is July 1.

Entrance Difficulty University of Dallas assesses its entrance difficulty level as moderately difficult. For the fall 2006 freshman class, 85 percent of the applicants were accepted.

For Further Information Contact Sr. Mary Brian Bole, Assistant Dean of Enrollment Management, University of Dallas, 1845 East Northgate Drive, Irving, TX 75062-4799. *Telephone:* 972-721-5266 or 800-628-6999 (toll-free). *Fax:* 972-721-5017. *E-mail:* ugadmis@udallas.edu. *Web site:* http://www.udallas.edu/.

See page 328 for the College Close-Up.

West Virginia

CONCORD UNIVERSITY
Athens, West Virginia

Concord University is a coed, public, four-year college of State College System of West Virginia, founded in 1872, offering degrees at the associate, bachelor's, and master's levels. It has a 100-acre campus in Athens.

Academic Information The faculty has 197 members (49% full-time), 37% with terminal degrees. The undergraduate student-faculty ratio is 20:1. The library holds 150,151 titles and 227 serial subscriptions. Special programs include academic remediation, services for learning-disabled students, an honors program, study abroad, advanced placement credit, accelerated degree programs, ESL programs, double majors, independent study, distance learning, self-designed majors, summer session for credit, part-time degree programs (daytime, evenings, weekends, summer), external degree programs, internships, and arrangement for off-campus study. The most frequently chosen baccalaureate fields are business/marketing, education, social sciences.

Student Body Statistics The student body totals 2,928, of whom 2,805 are undergraduates (603 freshmen). 57 percent are women and 43 percent are men. Students come from 24 states and territories and 15 other countries. 83 percent are from West Virginia.

Expenses for 2006–07 *Application fee:* $0. *State resident tuition:* $4084 full-time, $170 per credit hour part-time. *Nonresident tuition:* $9218 full-time, $385 per credit hour part-time. Both full-time and part-time tuition varies according to course load. *College room and board:* $6070. *College room only:* $3106.

Financial Aid Forms of aid include need-based and non-need-based scholarships, athletic grants, and part-time jobs. The average aided 2005–06 undergraduate received an aid package worth $7652. The priority application deadline for financial aid is April 15.

Freshman Admission Concord University requires a high school transcript, a minimum 2.0 high school GPA, SAT or ACT scores, and TOEFL scores for international students. An interview and ACT scores are recommended. An essay and an interview are required for some. The application deadline for regular admission is rolling and for nonresidents it is January 15.

Transfer Admission The application deadline for admission is rolling.

Entrance Difficulty Concord University assesses its entrance difficulty level as minimally difficult. For the fall 2006 freshman class, 70 percent of the applicants were accepted.

For Further Information Contact Mr. Michael Curry, Vice President of Admissions and Financial Aid, Concord University, 1000 Vermillion Street, Athens, WV 24712. *Telephone:* 304-384-5248 or 888-384-5249 (toll-free). *Fax:* 304-384-9044. *E-mail:* admissions@concord.edu. *Web site:* http://www.concord.edu/.

See page 316 for the College Close-Up.

UNIVERSITY OF CHARLESTON
Charleston, West Virginia

University of Charleston is a coed, private, comprehensive institution, founded in 1888, offering degrees at the associate, bachelor's, and master's levels. It has a 40-acre campus in Charleston.

Academic Information The faculty has 90 members (66% full-time), 33% with terminal degrees. The undergraduate student-faculty ratio is 15:1. The library holds 164,457 titles, 14,192 serial subscriptions, and 3,759 audiovisual materials. Special programs include academic remediation, services for learning-disabled students, study abroad, advanced placement credit, accelerated degree programs, ESL programs, double majors, independent study, distance learning, self-designed majors, summer session for credit, part-time degree programs (daytime, evenings, summer), adult/continuing education programs, and internships. The most frequently chosen baccalaureate fields are business/marketing, education, health professions and related sciences.

Student Body Statistics The student body totals 1,202, of whom 1,074 are undergraduates (315 freshmen). 59 percent are women and 41 percent are men. Students come from 34 states and territories and 15 other countries. 72 percent are from West Virginia. 7.5 percent are international students. 19.6 percent of the 2006 graduating class went on to graduate and professional schools.

Expenses for 2006–07 *Application fee:* $25. *Comprehensive fee:* $28,600 includes full-time tuition ($21,000) and college room and board ($7600). *College room only:* $4175. Room and board charges vary according to board plan and housing facility. *Part-time tuition:* $380 per credit. *Part-time mandatory fees:* $75 per term. Part-time tuition and fees vary according to program.

Financial Aid Forms of aid include need-based and non-need-based scholarships, athletic grants, and part-time jobs. The average aided 2006–07 undergraduate received an aid package worth an estimated $18,300.

Freshman Admission University of Charleston requires a high school transcript, a minimum 2.25 high school GPA, minimum scores ACT 19; SAT 900, SAT or ACT scores, and TOEFL scores for international students. An essay and recommendations are recommended. An interview is required for some. The application deadline for regular admission is rolling and for nonresidents it is rolling.

Transfer Admission The application deadline for admission is rolling.

Entrance Difficulty University of Charleston assesses its entrance difficulty level as moderately difficult. For the fall 2006 freshman class, 73 percent of the applicants were accepted.

For Further Information Contact Mr. Brad Parrish, Associate Vice President for Enrollment, University of Charleston, 2300 MacCorkle Avenue, SE, Charleston, WV 25304. *Telephone:* 304-357-4750 or 800-995-GOUC (toll-free). *Fax:* 304-357-4781. *E-mail:* admissions@ucwv.edu. *Web site:* http://www.ucwv.edu/.

See page 326 for the College Close-Up.

CLARKSON UNIVERSITY

POTSDAM, NEW YORK

The University

Founded in 1896, Clarkson stands out among America's private, nationally ranked research institutions because of its dynamic collaborative learning environment, innovative degree and research programs, and unmatched track record for producing leaders and innovators.

The University attracts 3,000 enterprising students from diverse backgrounds (including some 400 graduate students) who thrive in rigorous programs in engineering, arts, sciences, business, and health sciences and in the University's close-knit, residential living/learning community. Clarkson defies convention in the classroom, in its laboratories, and by the impact its graduates have in the world. The University is the eighth-smallest Carnegie-classified research institution. However, size is actually Clarkson's advantage—fostering leadership and problem-solving skills and readily affording students and faculty members the flexibility to span the boundaries of traditional academic areas.

Clarkson students also enjoy extraordinary opportunities to pursue faculty-mentored research. They gain professional experience through internships and co-ops with corporations and government organizations and can broaden their perspectives through a wide range of study-abroad opportunities.

Top graduate schools welcome Clarkson graduates to study medicine, law, and other professions. Johns Hopkins, MIT, Princeton, Yale, Caltech, Rice, and Stanford are just some of the schools chosen by Clarkson students.

Clarkson's placement rates are among the nation's highest, with the most recent starting salaries averaging more than $45,000. Clarkson is a key recruitment source for many of America's industry leaders, including General Electric, Alcoa, Xerox, Accenture, IBM, and Procter & Gamble. In fact, 1 in 12 Clarkson alumni is already a CEO, president, vice president, or company owner.

Clarkson's active campus also offers a wide variety of extracurricular activities, including more than eighty clubs and interest groups. Students publish a lively campus newspaper and run campus radio and television stations. Active professional and honor societies enrich the campus experience.

There are Division I men's and women's hockey teams as well as seventeen Division III intercollegiate athletic teams for women and men. Recreational facilities include a field house and gym with racquetball, basketball, and indoor tennis courts; a state-of-the-art fitness center; and a swimming pool.

Location

Clarkson is located in Potsdam, the quintessential "college town," nestled in the foothills of the northern Adirondack region of New York. The beautiful northeast corner of the state is the home of the 6-million-acre Adirondack Park. Within 2 hours of the campus are Lake Placid and the cosmopolitan Canadian cities of Montreal and Ottawa.

Majors and Degrees

Undergraduate degree programs offered are aeronautical engineering, American studies, applied mathematics and statistics, Areté (liberal arts/business), biology, biomolecular engineering, biomolecular science, business and technology management, chemical engineering, chemistry, civil engineering, communication, computer engineering, computer science, digital arts and sciences, e-business, electrical engineering, engineering and management, environmental engineering, environmental health

science (industrial hygiene), environmental science and policy, financial information and analysis, history, humanities, information systems and business processes, liberal studies, mathematics, mechanical engineering, physical therapy (pre–physical therapy leading to a doctorate), physics, political science, psychology, social sciences, software engineering, and technical communications.

First-year students who are still deciding on a major may begin in a general program in business studies, engineering studies, science studies, or university studies.

Clarkson offers a University honors program, a three-year bachelor's degree option, a five-year B.S./M.S. in chemistry/biochemistry, a five-year B.S./M.B.A., and preprofessional programs in dentistry, law, medicine, physical therapy, and veterinary science.

Academic Programs

Clarkson's historic strengths in business, engineering, liberal arts, and science remain at the core of the curriculum. These programs have also been combined into cutting-edge, cross-disciplinary majors: biomolecular science, digital arts and sciences, environmental science and policy, information technology, interdisciplinary engineering and management, and software engineering.

A dynamic, hands-on approach to learning is one of the hallmarks of a Clarkson education. Clarkson students learn about business by actually starting a business. They conduct scientific research alongside distinguished faculty mentors in state-of-the-art laboratories. The University's undergraduate research program has produced 9 Goldwater Scholars in six years.

National rankings and honors include the following: among the 125 "Best National Universities–Doctoral," *U.S. News & World Report,* 2006; among the "Best Undergraduate Engineering Programs," *U.S. News & World Report,* 2007; among the "Top 25 Most Connected Campuses," in the *Princeton Review* and *Forbes,* 2006; among the "Top 10 Supply Chain Management Programs," *U.S. News & World Report,* 2007; and among the best business schools in the nation, the *Princeton Review's Best 237 Business Schools,* 2006 edition. The undergraduate program in innovation and entrepreneurship is ranked number twenty-two among 700 U.S. higher educational institutions by the *Princeton Review* and *Entrepreneur* magazine, 2006.

Clarkson was also ranked among the top 100 graduate schools in environmental engineering (23) and civil engineering (54) by *U.S. News & World Report's* "Best Graduate Programs," 2006.

In addition, Clarkson's award-winning Student Projects for Engineering Experience and Design (SPEED) program promotes multidisciplinary, project-based extracurricular learning opportunities for more than 400 undergraduates annually. Some fifteen design teams compete in national and regional collegiate competitions that involve design and analysis, teamwork, and communication skills.

Off-Campus Programs

Students benefit from the resources of the Associated Colleges of the St. Lawrence Valley, which comprises Clarkson University, St. Lawrence University, SUNY Canton, and SUNY Potsdam. Benefits for students include opportunities to participate in activities ranging from clubs to concerts, interlibrary exchange, and cross-registration that allows students to pursue two courses per year at member colleges at no extra cost.

Academic Facilities

The University's 640-acre wooded campus is the site of forty-six buildings that comprise 1,224,583 square feet of assignable space. Dedicated exclusively to instructional programs are 371,114 square feet, including 52,713 square feet of traditional classrooms and 166,334 square feet assigned as laboratory areas. In the Center for Advanced Materials Processing (a New York State Center for Advanced Technology), there are seventy state-of-the-art research labs, including many related to nanotechnology and environmental research. Others include a multidisciplinary engineering and project laboratory for team-based projects, such as the mini-Baja and Formulae SAE racers; a robotics laboratory; a high-voltage lab; electron microscopy; a Class 10 clean room; a polymer fabrication lab; crystal growth labs; and a structural testing lab. School of Arts and Sciences facilities include a virtual-reality laboratory, a molecular design laboratory, a human brain electrophysiology laboratory, and other specialized facilities.

Bertrand H. Snell Hall houses the School of Business and the School of Arts and Sciences administrative offices as well as fully networked classrooms and study spaces and collaborative centers that feature wireless network access and videoconferencing capabilities. The facility includes three academic centers, which are available to all students: the Shipley Center for Leadership and Entrepreneurship, the Center for Global Competitiveness, and the Eastman Kodak Center for Excellence in Communication. The Center for Health Sciences at Clarkson is a regional center of excellence for education, treatment, and research in physical rehabilitation and other health sciences.

Costs

Tuition was $26,650 for the 2006–07 year, room (2-person) was $5068, and the meal plan was $4580. Student fees totaled $440. In addition, students usually spend about $2000 annually on books, supplies, travel, and personal expenses.

Financial Aid

The University offers a variety of scholarships and loans, including state and federal student loans, state scholarships and awards, individual scholarships, federal grants, and federal work-study programs. More than half of the incoming class receives scholarships or grants from Clarkson.

Faculty

Clarkson's 190 full-time faculty members teach undergraduate and graduate classes, with graduate students assisting only in undergraduate lab sciences. With an excellent student-faculty ratio of 16:1, undergraduates benefit from regular interaction with the school's faculty members and small class sizes (especially at the upper levels). The University attracts teacher/scholars who are also highly regarded scholars in their fields. Ninety-six percent hold a doctorate.

Student Government

The Student Senate and the Interfraternity Council combine to form the student government at Clarkson University. The former supervises all extracurricular activities (except athletics) and has responsibility for the allocation of student activity funds and for other appropriate business. The latter prescribes standards and rules for fraternities. Students are involved in the formation of University policies through membership, with faculty and staff representatives, on all important committees.

Admission Requirements

Clarkson recommends that prospective students follow a challenging secondary school curriculum that includes mathematics, science, and English. Candidates for entrance to the Wallace H. Coulter School of Engineering or students pursuing a degree in the sciences or an interdisciplinary engineering and management degree should have successfully completed secondary school courses in physics and chemistry. All candidates for admission are required to take the SAT or ACT. SAT Subject Tests are optional. The high school record is the most important factor in an admission decision. International students for whom English is a second language must submit a minimum TOEFL score of 550 (paper-based) or 212 (computer-based). All applicants must include a personal statement of 250 to 500 words describing a special interest, experience, or achievement.

Students achieving scores of 4 or better on the College Board's Advanced Placement examinations are considered for advanced placement and credit in virtually all academic areas. Advanced standing is most common in English, mathematics, and science.

An early decision plan is offered on a "first-choice" basis; this plan does not prohibit the student from making other applications, but it does commit the student to withdrawing other applications if accepted at Clarkson.

Although not required, a personal interview with a member of the Office of Admission is highly recommended, especially for early decision candidates. Interviews on campus should be arranged by letter or telephone at least one week prior to the intended visit. The Office of Admission is open Monday through Friday, from 8 a.m. to 4:30 p.m., and Saturday by appointment. The University welcomes visitors to the campus and makes arrangements, as requested, for families to tour and meet with academic and other departments on campus.

Application and Information

Office of Undergraduate Admission
Holcroft House
Clarkson University
P.O. Box 5605
Potsdam, New York 13699-5605
Phone: 315-268-6479 or 6480
 800-527-6577 (toll-free)
Fax: 315-268-7647
E-mail: admission@clarkson.edu
Web site: http://www.clarkson.edu

Clarkson is a leader in project-based learning, providing students with strong communication skills, leadership ability, and technological skill in their fields.

CONCORD UNIVERSITY

ATHENS, WEST VIRGINIA

The University

Concord University, a highly respected liberal arts university, was founded more than 134 years ago. Concord features accredited career-oriented undergraduate and graduate programs in education with a strong liberal arts base and focusing on the needs of the individual student. The beautiful 123-acre campus stands on a ridge of the Appalachian Mountains. Five residence halls and apartments house up to 1,000 students from twenty-seven states, predominantly from the East, South, and Midwest. Concord also has a large international student population, with fifteen nations represented. With a total student population of more than 2,900, Concord serves the needs of active commuter students who join the residential students in following courses of study in the arts and sciences, business administration, teacher education, and such fields as advertising/graphic design and social work. Preparation for advanced and professional study is a Concord hallmark. In 2003, *The Wall Street Journal* rated Concord University 13th in the nation of best undergraduate public colleges and universities for admission of their alumni to the nation's most selective graduate schools. Concord is placing students in graduate programs at twice the rate of the national average. In 2004, 2005, and 2006 Concord's outstanding premed program placed 100 percent of its graduates in medical schools. One big reason for this achievement is the new, state-of-the-art DNA lab that serves the preprofessional science students.

Each year, the Alexander Fine Arts Center presents the Artist-Lecture Series, which includes recitals, plays, art exhibitions, and guest speakers. Special events have included the North Carolina Dance Theatre; the West Virginia Symphony; lecturers Dr. Homer Hickam, NASA scientist and author of the book *Rocket Boys* (which was later made into the hit movie *October Sky)*, and Dr. Cornel West, a preeminent African-American scholar from Princeton University; and professional art exhibits. Theatrical productions range from Shakespeare and Chekhov to Woody Allen.

Students participate in special interest organizations, honor societies, religious organizations, interfaith organizations, five fraternities, four sororities, the yearbook, and the newspaper and enjoy many student activities, which include comedians, musicians, magicians, and other entertainers. Students participate in intramural and intercollegiate sports. Intercollegiate sports for men include baseball, basketball, cross-country, football, golf, tennis, and track and field. Intercollegiate sports for women include basketball, soccer, softball, tennis, track and field, and volleyball. Concord's Phi Alpha Delta prelaw mock trial team won the national championship in 2006–07, defeating such schools as Texas Tech; University of Miami (Florida); University of California, Northridge; Temple; and three-time champion, Arizona.

Counseling and tutoring are strongly supported through Student Support Services; faculty-supervised developmental labs in English, reading, and mathematics; and twice-a-year individual counseling with faculty advisers. International students who need help mastering English may enroll in the English as a second language program. Once they successfully complete the ESL program and meet admission criteria, they may be admitted into the regular undergraduate program of study.

In addition to its undergraduate programs, Concord also offers a Master of Education degree with content specialization.

Location

Athens is a small town in southern West Virginia near the Virginia border. Located near Princeton, Beckley, and Bluefield, West Virginia, Athens is 6 miles from I-77 and not far from I-64 and I-81. Athens has easy access to thriving population centers, such as Roanoke, Virginia; Charleston, West Virginia; and Charlotte, North Carolina. Shopping malls and entertainment are also available nearby, and Pipestem State Park Resort offers many recreational opportunities. The WinterPlace ski resort is approximately 20 minutes north of the campus, and world-class white-water rafting is also nearby.

Majors and Degrees

Concord offers more than eighty majors, minors, and programs. The degrees offered at Concord are the Bachelor of Science in Computer Information Systems; the Bachelor of Arts in Communication Arts; the Bachelor of Arts/Bachelor of Science in Interdisciplinary Studies; the Bachelor of Social Work; the Bachelor of Science in Education (with a wide selection of teaching fields); the Bachelor of Science in Medical Technology; the Bachelor of Science in Business Administration; the Bachelor of Science, with majors in athletic training, biology, comprehensive chemistry, GIS and cartography, mathematics, mathematics comprehensive, mathematics/computer science, preprofessional biology, and preprofessional chemistry; and the Bachelor of Arts, with majors in advertising/graphic design, English (with emphases in journalism, literature, and writing), geography, history, history with a concentration in philosophy, political science, preprofessional mentoring programs for law and premed, psychology, sociology, and studio art. A new 2+2 program is being planned for students interested in engineering degrees. Concord offers the Regents Bachelor of Arts degree for adults who cannot interrupt their normal activities to attend college but have gained comparable knowledge outside the classroom. Concord also offers a two-year degree, the Associate of Arts in Office Supervision, and five structured interdisciplinary options, including environmental geosciences, health-care management, leadership and entrepreneurial studies, public administration, and sports management. A wide array of preprofessional fields, including premed, prepharmacy, predental, prelaw, pre–physical therapy, preoptometry, preveterinary, and others, are available.

Academic Programs

All students must complete a minimum of 128 semester hours with a grade point average of 2.0 (C) or better to receive a degree. A program of general studies, required of all students, includes courses in communication and literature, fine arts, social sciences, natural sciences, teacher education, mathematics, foreign languages (optional in most majors), athletic training, recombinant gene technology, and physical education. Credit is awarded for satisfactory scores on the College-Level Examination Program (CLEP), Advanced Placement (AP), and International Baccalaureate (I.B.) tests. An outstanding honors program is also available to qualifying students. Honors courses and independent study projects are available in most departments. Semesters begin in late August and mid-January; there are summer terms as well. The NcNair Scholars Program offers opportunities to selected students to conduct primary research for publication.

Off-Campus Programs

The Concord University Beckley Center offers a wide range of academic opportunities, from freshman-level courses to the four-year degrees in business administration, education, and social work, to students in Raleigh County, West Virginia. Summer internships, which provide valuable professional contacts and experience, are part of the program of study for students majoring in communication arts and advertising/graphic design. Medical technology students must complete a twelve-month internship at an approved hospital. An internship program is available for travel industry management students, education, prelaw, and premed. Professional field-work placements form part of the social work program.

Academic Facilities

An open-stack library and a modern center for academic technologies facilitate research. Students have access to twenty-two computer labs, port-per-pillow fiber optics in the residence halls, the observatory, two spacious theaters, and physical education facilities, including gymnasiums, an indoor swimming pool, a dance studio, well-equipped weight rooms, and squash, handball, and racquetball courts. Concord was rated in the top-fifty best-wired campuses by yahoo/zd-net. Laboratories are integral components of programs in the natural sciences, psychology, and geography. The University offers its students multimedia, graphic, and DNA Tech labs. The student-run television and radio stations offer top quality programming; they are aired on PBS twice monthly. The Alexander Fine Arts Center houses facilities for art, music, communications, and dramatic arts studies. The brand-new Rahall Technology Center is planned to house the Entrepreneurial Studies Program, the Computer Center, and the small-business incubator. Ground has been broken for a beautiful new interfaith chapel that should be completed by summer 2008.

Costs

Concord offers high quality at affordable prices. For the 2006–07 academic year, the tuition, fees, and room and board for West Virginia residents were $10,274, and books and supplies cost approximately $500. Personal expenses vary but are approximately $1000 for the year. For nonresidents, tuition, fees, and room and board were $15,408 per academic year. These figures are subject to change.

Financial Aid

Concord University has one of the most generous scholarship programs in both the West Virginia State Higher Education System and the mid-Atlantic region. Merit awards, athletic and talent scholarships, transfer scholarships, Entrepreneurial Scholarships, Bonner Scholarships for Community Service, and scholarships for nontraditional students are readily available for qualifying students. Federal Pell Grants, Federal Supplemental Educational Opportunity Grants, Federal Perkins Loans, West Virginia Higher Education Grants, Federal PLUS loans, and Federal Stafford Student Loans are available through the University. The State Student Assistance Program and the Federal Work-Study Program offer opportunities for student employment. To receive priority, the Free Application for Federal Student Aid (FAFSA) must be on file by March 1. Concord offers scholarships to qualifying international students.

Incoming freshmen who are willing to perform community service may apply for the Bonner Scholars Program. Funded by the Corella and Bertram F. Bonner Foundation of Princeton, New Jersey, the award is primarily based on need and prior service. The University offers an Entrepreneurial Scholars Program that provides students with the skills and knowledge to help them become entrepreneurs. These students begin to build their own businesses during their college years, with coaching by professional mentors working in their field. They establish their business plan, run it in the incubator, and then "spin it off" upon graduation to become the CEO of their own corporation.

Approximately 90 percent of freshman students receive scholarships, financial aid, or both. In addition, 85 percent of the entire student body receives some form of financial aid.

Faculty

All members of the faculty teach courses in the program of general studies, and all counsel and advise students. Of the more than 100 full-time faculty members, 70 percent hold the highest degree in their disciplines. In addition, the University employs adjunct instructors who are experts in their fields. The average class size is 22 students.

Student Government

Concord's Student Government Association (SGA) budgets the student activity fee and plans entertainment. The SGA names students to voting membership on administrative councils and committees. Students also fund the SGA Memorial Scholarship. The Student Activities Committee provides on-campus movies, dances, and special programs. The Concord Office of Housing and Residential Life offers numerous programs and activities in residence halls.

Admission Requirements

Applicants must have an overall grade point average of at least 2.0 (C) at an approved secondary school or a composite score of at least 18 on the ACT examination (or an equivalent SAT score), complete an application form, and send a high school transcript. Applicants may gain admission with advanced standing if they obtain qualifying scores on the College Board's AP tests, CLEP tests, or International Baccalaureate tests. GED test scores may be considered in lieu of the high school diploma. International applicants may seek admission in one of the following ways: meet all normally required admission criteria, enroll in the English as a second language program and successfully complete the program, or enroll for up to 15 credit hours as a non–degree-seeking student and, while taking those classes, successfully complete the regular requirements for admission. Most international students are required to pass the TOEFL exam and have sufficient SAT scores. However, the ESL entry path and the fact that Concord offers a residual SAT test may enable some international students to enroll who otherwise would have been denied admission.

Applicants must have completed the following secondary units: 4 in English, 3 in social studies (including U.S. history), 4 in mathematics (three units must be algebra I and higher), 3 in laboratory sciences, and 2 in a single foreign language.

Transfer students are encouraged to apply for admission and may be eligible for transfer scholarships. In addition, a limited number of talented high school students can be admitted to the summer school to earn college credit. Talented students who have completed the junior year of high school may be eligible for the University's early admission program.

Application and Information

Applications should be submitted by January 1 for early admission consideration and by August 1 for admission for the fall semester, which begins in late August and ends in December.

For further information, students may contact:

Michael Curry
Vice President for Admissions and Financial Aid
Concord University
P.O. Box 1000
Athens, West Virginia 24712
Phone: 304-384-5248 or 5249
　　　　888-384-5249 (toll-free)
E-mail: admissions@concord.edu
Web site: http://www.concord.edu

The Administration Building at Concord University.

GANNON UNIVERSITY
ERIE, PENNSYLVANIA

The University

Gannon University, which is consistently named one of America's Best Colleges by *U.S. News & World Report,* is dedicated to excellence in holistic education. The oldest part of the University is Villa Maria College, which was founded in 1925 by the Sisters of St. Joseph. In 1933, Archbishop John Mark Gannon established Cathedral College, a two-year institution, which by 1941 had evolved into a four-year college, the Gannon School of Arts and Sciences. The name Gannon College was adopted in 1944, and Gannon achieved university status in 1979. Villa Maria College subsequently merged with Gannon University in 1989.

Gannon's campus is located in the heart of downtown Erie, giving students the benefit of internships with businesses, law and law-enforcement agencies, health-care facilities, industries, and social service organizations. It is also within walking distance of stores, shops, restaurants, and theaters. The campus consists of more than thirty buildings located within six city blocks. Among these buildings is the Carneval Athletic Pavilion, which has a pool; three gyms; a running track; a weight room; courts for racquetball, handball, volleyball and basketball; and other facilities. Also on campus are two residence halls, eight apartment buildings, classroom and faculty office buildings, an administration building, and a multipurpose chapel building. The Waldron Campus Center is a focal point that gives students the opportunity to meet and socialize between classes with faculty members and other students.

Gannon offers students a broad intramural sports program that runs throughout the entire year. In Division II intercollegiate athletics, Gannon offers men's baseball, basketball, cross-country, football, golf, soccer, water polo, and wrestling and women's basketball, cross-country, golf, lacrosse, soccer, softball, volleyball, and water polo. There is also an intercollegiate coed swimming and diving team. Gannon's athletes utilize the Gannon University Field, a multipurpose athletic facility that is conveniently located on campus.

There are approximately 3,800 students at Gannon, more than 2,500 of whom are undergraduates. The ratio of commuters to resident students is approximately 1:4. The University has a Career Development and Employment Services Office to aid students in locating internships and part-time work during school and full-time work after graduation.

Location

Erie is Pennsylvania's fourth-largest city and is located in the northwestern corner of the state on the shore of Lake Erie. Erie is approximately 120 miles north of Pittsburgh, Pennsylvania; 90 miles east of Cleveland, Ohio; and 90 miles southwest of Buffalo, New York. The campus is within 5 miles of Interstates 79 and 90 and 5 miles from Erie International Airport. Erie is also serviced by rail and bus transportation.

Majors and Degrees

The College of Humanities, Business and Education awards the Bachelor of Arts and Bachelor of Science degrees.

In the School of Humanities, the areas of study from which students may select a major are communication arts, criminal justice, English (with concentrations in applied communications, literature, and writing), foreign language and international studies, foreign language and literature, foreign language teaching (Spanish only), history, journalism communications, legal studies, liberal arts, mortuary science, philosophy, political science, prelaw,

a 3+3 prelaw program that includes early admission to Duquesne University, psychology, social work, theater, theater and communication arts, and theology.

In the School of Business, students may choose to major in accounting, advertising communications, business administration, finance, international business, management, marketing, risk management, and sports management and marketing.

In the School of Education, the areas of study from which students may select a major are early childhood education, elementary education, secondary education (in biology, English, foreign language (Spanish only), mathematics, and social studies), and special education.

The College of Sciences, Engineering and Health Sciences awards the Bachelor of Science degree.

In the School of Sciences and Engineering, students may choose to major in bioinformatics, biology, biotechnology, chemistry, chemical engineering, computer science, electrical engineering, electrical engineering (five-year co-op program), environmental engineering, environmental science, management information systems, mathematics, mechanical engineering, mechanical engineering (five-year co-op program), science, scientific and technical sales, and software engineering. A minor is offered in environmental and occupational science and health. Preprofessional programs of study are offered in chiropractic, dentistry, medicine, optometry, osteopathy, pharmacy, physical therapy, podiatry, and veterinary medicine; seven-year accelerated programs are offered in optometry and podiatry. Additional accelerated programs include accelerated pharmacy options through Duquesne University (2+4), the University of Charleston (2+4 and 3+4), and the Lake Erie College of Osteopathic Medicine (LECOM) (2+3) and a conditionally guaranteed medical school 4+4 program with LECOM and the Philadelphia College of Osteopathic Medicine (PCOM). There are also accelerated options in allopathic medicine and veterinary medicine through Ross University in the Bahamas. Students who are interested in earning their Doctor of Physical Therapy degree can complete an accelerated (3+3) program at Gannon.

In the School of Health Sciences and the Villa Maria School of Nursing, the areas of study from which students may select a major are medical technology, nursing, occupational therapy, physician assistant studies, radiologic sciences, respiratory care, and sport and exercise science. A minor is also offered in athletic coaching.

The associate degree program offers Associate of Science and Associate of Arts degrees. Areas of study in which students may major are accounting, business administration, criminal justice, early childhood education, legal studies, radiologic sciences, and respiratory care.

Academic Programs

Each undergraduate program has its own sequence of requirements. Students in all programs must complete credits in liberal studies. A faculty adviser is assigned to each student to assist with academic planning. A department chairperson and faculty adviser also assist each student in selecting courses that fulfill requirements and best meet the student's desired career objectives. The basic graduation requirements for bachelor's degree candidates are 128 credit hours, including completion of requirements for their major and the liberal studies program. To earn an associate degree, students must usually complete 60 to 68 credit hours, depending on the program. Students may receive credit through the Advanced Placement Program.

Gannon offers a program for students with learning disabilities (PSLD) and an Army ROTC program that is open to interested students.

Gannon's academic calendar consists of two full semesters, running from August to December and from January to May. There are also optional summer classes.

Academic Facilities

The Nash Library currently has more than 250,000 bound volumes. The library subscribes to more than 1,000 periodicals and has book and periodical materials on various forms of microfilms and microcards. The wireless library contains a personal computer lab; a lecture room; a curriculum library; the Founder's Room for fine and rare books; the Cyber Café, containing personal computers, laptop ports, and cappuccino and juice machines; lounges; study rooms; typing rooms; an information-retrieval system; a TV studio; the latest audiovisual and tape equipment; and a multimedia studio classroom. In addition, students may use the facilities and resources of the Erie County Law Library and the Erie County Library. For specialized research projects, an efficient interlibrary loan service is available.

The A. J. Palumbo Academic Center houses the Schools of Health Sciences, Education, and Humanities. It offers some of the finest laboratories, technology, and classrooms available today. From education to nursing and foreign language programs, the faculty members and facilities in Palumbo provide high-quality education. The University's Honors Program also has a home in the Palumbo Center.

The Zurn Science Center has laboratories for research in biology, anatomy, physics, chemistry, and engineering. The building also houses three computer laboratories, including the Computer Integrated Enterprise Center and an IBM PC lab. There are numerous classrooms and two auditoriums in the building. Among other University facilities are additional classroom buildings, a radio station, and a theater. All academic buildings are wireless.

Costs

For 2006–07, full-time tuition was $9750 per semester ($10,340 for engineering and health sciences), or $19,500 per academic year ($20,680 for engineering and health sciences). Tuition for part-time students was $565 to $600 per credit hour. Room and board were approximately $3895 per semester. The total cost for the academic year at Gannon was between $19,996 and $21,856 for commuting students and $27,786 and $29,464 for resident students, depending on the program of study.

Financial Aid

In order to bring a Gannon education to qualified students who could not otherwise afford it, the University offers an integrated financial aid program of scholarships, grants, loans, and employment. Gannon's financial aid program is open to all full-time students attending classes during the period from August to May. It is highly recommended that all students seeking financial aid should file the admissions and financial aid applications no later than March 15.

Faculty

Gannon's faculty consists of 312 lay and religious men and women. Fifty-eight percent of the full-time faculty members have doctoral degrees. The student-faculty ratio is about 14:1, and there are approximately 25 students in each class. Most faculty members assist in the faculty adviser program, giving each student individual attention and counseling on academic and personal matters.

Student Government

The Student Government Association (SGA) is composed of students elected by members of their class. Through the SGA, students can play a responsible role in the planning and working of the University. SGA has voting representatives on all of the standing committees of the University. Members of the SGA not only research existing policies and problems, they also look for new ways to improve the academic life of students. The SGA also plans social events for the student body.

Admission Requirements

Gannon University actively recruits students of all races, creeds, and ages from all geographic regions. Transfer and international students are encouraged to seek admission. Applicants are required to submit scores (including senior-year scores) on either the SAT or ACT; an up-to-date transcript of the high school record, showing rank in class (plus a college transcript for transfer applicants); a completed application form; and a nonrefundable $25 fee. Admission decisions are based upon numerous factors, central of which is the strength of the high school record, as demonstrated through grades and relative class standing and SAT and/or ACT scores and other test scores that may be available. Recommendations and personal statements also affect admission decisions. Transfer and international students should check with the admissions office for special application procedures.

Application and Information

Students applying for admission in the fall semester should start the application process at the beginning of their senior year in high school. Gannon operates on a rolling admissions basis, which means that there is no deadline for filing applications, with the exceptions of the LECOM and PCOM 4+4 Medical Programs and the accelerated pharmacy options, which have a deadline of January 15 for the fall semester. Due to the competitiveness of the program, students who are interested in the physician's assistant studies program are highly encouraged to file their applications in September. Early applications are recommended, as are enrollment deposits.

For further information, students should contact:

Office of Admissions
Gannon University
109 University Square
Erie, Pennsylvania 16541
Phone: 814-871-7240
       800-GANNON-U (426-6668, toll-free)
Fax: 814-871-5803
E-mail: admissions@gannon.edu
Web site: http://www.gannon.edu

Gannon University's faculty advisers are always available to help students chart their personal, educational, and professional accomplishments and potential.

NORTH CAROLINA AGRICULTURAL AND TECHNICAL STATE UNIVERSITY
GREENSBORO, NORTH CAROLINA

The University

North Carolina Agricultural and Technical State University (A&T) was founded in 1891 as one of two land-grant institutions in the state. Originally, it was established to provide postsecondary education and training for black students. Today, the University is a comprehensive institution of higher education with an integrated faculty and student body, and it has been designated a constituent institution of the University of North Carolina, offering degrees at the baccalaureate, master's, and doctoral levels. Located on a 191-acre campus, the University has 110 buildings, including single-sex and coeducational residence halls. Of a total of 10,475 undergraduates, 4,925 are men and 5,550 are women. The total population is 11,082.

North Carolina Agricultural and Technical State University provides outstanding academic programs through five undergraduate schools, two colleges, and a graduate school.

The mission of the University is to provide an intellectual setting in which students may find a sense of belonging, responsibility, and achievement that prepares them for roles of leadership and service in the communities where they will live and work. In this sense, the University serves as a laboratory for the development of excellence in teaching, research, and public service. As a result, A&T today stands as an example of well-directed higher education for all students.

Student life at the University is active and purposeful. The broad objective of the program provided by Student Development Services is to aid students in attaining the attitudes, understandings, insights, and skills that enable them to be socially competent. The program places special emphasis on campus relationships and experiences that complement formal instruction. Some of the services available are counseling, housing, health, and placement services. There is a University Student Union, and there are special services for international and minority students, veterans, and handicapped students. The University also provides a well-balanced program of activities to foster the moral, spiritual, cultural, and physical development of its students.

Location

Greensboro, North Carolina, is 300 miles south of Washington, D.C., and 349 miles north of Atlanta. It is readily accessible by air, bus, and automobile. The city offers a variety of cultural and recreational activities and facilities. These include sports events, concerts, bowling, boating, fishing, tennis, golf, and other popular forms of recreation. There are major shopping centers, churches, theaters, and medical facilities near the University. The heavy concentration of factories, service industries, government agencies, and shopping centers provides many job opportunities for students who desire part-time employment.

Majors and Degrees

North Carolina Agricultural and Technical State University grants the following degrees: Bachelor of Arts, Bachelor of Science, Bachelor of Fine Arts, Bachelor of Science in Nursing, and Bachelor of Social Work.

The School of Agriculture and Environmental Sciences offers programs in agricultural economics, agricultural economics (agricultural business), agricultural education, agricultural education (agricultural extension), agricultural science–earth and environmental science (earth and environmental science, landscape horticulture design, plant science, and soil science), agricultural science–natural resources (plant science), animal science, animal science (animal industry), child development, child development–early education and family studies B–K (teaching), family and consumer science (fashion merchandising and design), family and consumer science education, food and nutritional sciences, laboratory animal science, and landscape architecture.

In the College of Arts and Sciences, programs are available in applied mathematics, biology, biology–secondary education, broadcast production, chemistry, chemistry–secondary education, criminal justice, electronic/media journalism, English, English–secondary education, history, history–secondary education, journalism and mass communications, liberal studies–African-American studies, liberal studies–business, liberal studies–cultural change and social development, liberal studies-dance, liberal studies–interdisciplinary, liberal studies–international studies, liberal studies–prelaw, liberal studies–women's studies, mathematics, mathematics–secondary education, media management, music education, music–general, music-performance, physics, physics–secondary education, political science, print journalism, professional theater, psychology, public relations, sociology, social work, Romance languages and literatures–French, Romance languages and literatures–French secondary education, Romance languages and literatures–Spanish, Romance languages and literatures–Spanish secondary education, speech, speech (speech pathology/audiology), visual arts–art education, and visual arts–design.

The School of Business and Economics offers programs in accounting, business administration, business education, business education (administrative systems, vocational business education, and vocational business education–data processing), economics, finance, management, management (management information systems), marketing, and transportation.

In the School of Education, programs are available in elementary education, human performance and leisure studies (fitness/wellness management), human performance and leisure studies (teaching), human performance and leisure studies (sports science and fitness management), recreation administration, and special education.

In the College of Engineering, programs are offered in architectural engineering, bioenvironmental engineering, chemical engineering, civil engineering, computer engineering, computer science, electrical engineering, industrial engineering, and mechanical engineering.

The School of Nursing grants the Bachelor of Science in Nursing (B.S.N.) degree.

The School of Technology has programs in computer-aided drafting and design, construction management, electronics technology, electronics technology (computational technology), electronics technology (information technology), graphic communication systems, integrated Internet technologies, manufacturing systems, manufacturing systems (motor sports), occupational safety and health, printing and publishing, technology education (teaching), trade and industrial education (teaching), and training and development for industry.

Academic Programs

Students must complete a minimum of 124 semester hours to earn a bachelor's degree; the exact number varies with the program. Students are also required to demonstrate competence in English and mathematics.

As complements to the academic programs, the University's Army and Air Force ROTC programs and cooperative education program provide excellent opportunities for students to enrich their educational experiences. The ROTC programs are designed to prepare college graduates for military service careers. The cooperative education program provides an opportunity for qualified students to alternate periods of study on campus and meaningful employment off campus in private industrial or business firms or government agencies.

Academic Facilities

The University library has current holdings that include 507,036 book volumes and bound periodicals, as well as 5,446 current serials. As a select depository in North Carolina for U.S. government documents, the library contains a collection of more than 250,000 official publications. Among the library's other holdings are a collection of audiovisuals and 1,038,474 microforms, archives, and special collections in black studies and teacher-education materials. Special services are provided through formal and informal library instruction, interlibrary loans, and photocopying facilities.

The University's educational support centers are the Learning Assistance Center, the Audiovisual Center, the Closed Circuit Television Facility, a 1,000-watt student-operated educational radio station, the Computer Center, the Reading Center, the Language Laboratory, and the Center for Manpower Research and Training. The H. Clinton Taylor Art Gallery and the African Heritage Center are two exceptional art museums on campus. Throughout the year, these museums have on display a number of special exhibits of sculpture, paintings, graphics, and other media.

Costs

In 2006–07, tuition and fees for North Carolina residents were $3872 per year; for nonresidents of the state, they were $13,314. Board and lodging for the academic year were approximately $6650.

Financial Aid

Through the student financial aid program, the University makes every effort to ensure that no qualified student is denied the opportunity to attend because of a lack of funds. Students who demonstrate financial need and have the potential to achieve academic success at the University may obtain assistance to meet their expenses in accordance with the funds available. Financial aid is awarded without regard to race, religion, color, national origin, or sex. The University provides financial aid for students from four basic sources: grants, scholarships, loans, and employment. To apply for aid, students must submit the Free Application for Federal Student Aid (FAFSA). The priority filing deadline is March 15 for the fall semester. North Carolina residents may call 800-443-0835 (toll-free).

Faculty

The University's teaching faculty consists of more than 600 highly qualified members. Approximately 90 percent of them hold the doctoral degree or the first professional degree in their discipline. Faculty members are recruited from many areas and backgrounds, thereby bringing together a diverse cadre of academic professionals from many nations.

Student Government

The Student Government Association (SGA), which is composed of senators elected from the student body, is primarily a policy-recommending group and represents the views and concerns of the students. The president of the SGA reports directly to the vice-chancellor for student affairs. In addition, each student organization is represented by a senator, and these senators sit on the Faculty Senate.

Admission Requirements

Applicants for undergraduate admission are considered individually and in accordance with criteria applied flexibly to ensure that applicants with unusual qualifications are not denied admission. However, admission for out-of-state freshman students is competitive due to an 18 percent out-of-state enrollment cap. Students who are applying for admission as freshmen are expected to have completed a college-preparatory program in high school and to have taken the SAT or the ACT. General requirements include graduation from an accredited high school, including 4 units of English, 2 units of the same foreign language, 4 units of college-preparatory mathematics, 3 units of natural sciences, 2 units of social sciences, and American history; a satisfactory score on the SAT or ACT; and a respectable GPA and/or class rank. The General Educational Development (GED) test score results or a high school equivalency certificate from the state Department of Education may be submitted in lieu of the high school transcript for applicants receiving equivalency before January 1988.

North Carolina A&T State University welcomes applications from graduates of accredited community, technical, and junior colleges and from students who wish to transfer from other senior colleges.

Application and Information

The suggested application deadline for students who expect to live on campus is February 1; for commuting students, it is June 1. Applications are processed upon the receipt of the completed application form with the $45 application fee, official transcripts, and SAT or ACT scores. Out-of-state admission is limited; therefore, applications for admission should be filed by February 1.

To arrange an interview or a visit to the campus, students should contact:

Office of Admissions
B. C. Webb Hall
North Carolina Agricultural and Technical State University
Greensboro, North Carolina 27411
Phone: 336-334-7946 or 7947
 800-443-8964 (toll-free in North Carolina)
Web site: http://www.ncat.edu

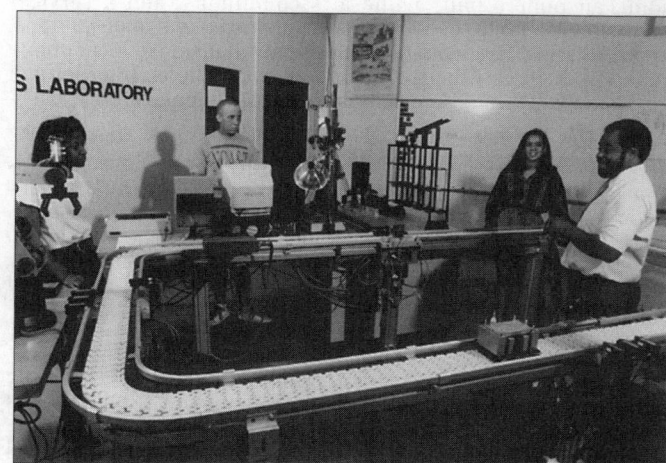

A professor and students in the chemical engineering lab.

SOUTHERN METHODIST UNIVERSITY

DALLAS, TEXAS

The University

Southern Methodist University (SMU) is a small, caring academic community in the heart of a vibrant city, where excellence is the standard and the goal is helping students succeed. SMU prepares students for life and leadership in the twenty-first century by educating them to meet the challenges of a rapidly changing world, intellectually equipping them for lifelong learning, and preparing them for successful careers. The broad-based curriculum provides a strong foundation in the humanities and sciences. SMU's four undergraduate schools offer nearly eighty majors in business, engineering, the arts, and humanities and sciences. Learning at SMU includes opportunities for mentoring relationships, internships, leadership development, research experience, international study, and community service.

Founded in 1911, SMU welcomes students of every religion, race, color, ethnic origin, and economic status. Students come from all fifty states and more than ninety countries. Total University enrollment is 10,901; 6,208 are undergraduates. Sixty percent of all undergraduate lecture sections have fewer than 25 students. Academically promising students are invited into the University Honors Program.

The life of a student's education is enriched at SMU, where there are nearly 200 student activities and organizations. From debate club to intramural sports, campus events to marching band, academic interests to community service, students have many options. There are also a large number of academic honorary societies.

SMU hosts more than 400 public arts events each year. The world-renowned Willis M. Tate Distinguished Lecture Series brings guests, such as Secretary of State Colin Powell, actor Julie Andrews, and former President George Bush to campus. SMU is a member of the National Collegiate Athletic Association and participates in the Western Athletic Conference, Division I-A. Nineteen Division I-A teams include basketball, football, golf, soccer, swimming/diving, and tennis and women's cross-country, equestrian, rowing, track and field, and volleyball.

SMU offers fourteen residence halls and living communities, including an honors hall, a fine arts community, and a service-learning house. First-year students are required to live on campus, except in special circumstances. Residence halls have local phone service, voice-mail, Ethernet computer connections, Internet and e-mail, air conditioning, and community computer and lounge areas.

Location

SMU's parklike campus, located north of downtown Dallas in a traditional and upscale residential neighborhood, features Georgian-style architecture and enjoys a pleasant Sun Belt climate. Dallas, often ranked as one of the world's most livable cities, is home to more than 6,000 corporate headquarters and offers outstanding opportunities for internships and future employment. A convenient light rail and bus system is located near the campus.

Majors and Degrees

SMU offers nearly eighty degrees through its four undergraduate schools, with flexible options such as double majors, minors, and dual degrees. Dedman College offers a Bachelor of Arts (B.A.) degree with a major in a department of the College and a Bachelor of Science (B.S.) degree with a major in mathematics, a natural science, or selected social sciences. The College also offers two part-time multidisciplinary evening degrees: the Bachelor of Humanities (B.Hum.) and the Bachelor of Social Science (B.Soc.Sci.). The Cox School of Business awards the Bachelor of Business Administration (B.B.A.) degree. The Meadows School of Arts awards the Bachelor of Fine Arts (B.F.A.) in art, art history, dance, and theater; the Bachelor of Arts (B.A.) in advertising, art history, cinema-television, jour-

nalism, music, corporate communications and public affairs; and the Bachelor of Music (B.M.) degrees. The School of Engineering offers the Bachelor of Arts (B.A.) degree in computer science and the Bachelor of Science (B.S.) degree in the fields of computer engineering, computer science, electrical engineering, environmental engineering, management science, and mechanical engineering, with specializations and biomedical and premed options.

Academic Programs

All undergraduates enter SMU through Dedman College. The College provides the University's general education curriculum, which is designed to help students develop analytical and communication skills, the ability to explore ethical issues, and a broad understanding of the world. The curriculum includes courses in such categories as cultural formation, perspectives, human diversity, and information technology. Students who know their career interest can select courses in their planned major while in Dedman College. Students majoring in the humanities, mathematics, the natural sciences, and the social or behavioral sciences remain in Dedman College. Requirements for graduation vary according to the major program.

SMU grants both credit and advanced placement for satisfactory completion of Advanced Placement (AP) courses in high school. Credit up to 6 semester hours is given for each course in which a score of 4 or 5 was earned; 12 to 14 hours of credit can be granted for foreign languages with a score of 4 or 5. SMU also gives credit for departmental examination. Credit also is awarded for scores from 5 to 7 on higher-level exams in transferable subjects for the International Baccalaureate. Credit is not awarded for subsidiary-level exams. High school students may earn dual credit by attending off-campus colleges. A maximum of 32 advanced credits can be awarded. The academic year at SMU is composed of two semesters, plus an optional summer session that comprises two 5-week terms. A May term is also available.

Off-Campus Programs

SMU Study Abroad offers twenty-two programs in Australia, China, Denmark, France, Germany, Great Britain, Italy, Japan, Mexico, Russia, Southeast Asia, Spain, and Taiwan. SMU-in-Taos is the University's summer campus in northern New Mexico.

Academic Facilities

Newer facilities include the Meadows Museum of Art, which houses one of the world's largest collections of Spanish art; an addition to the Fondren Library Center; the Dedman Life Sciences Building; the Jerry R. Junkins Electrical Engineering Building; and the Gerald R. Ford Stadium and Paul B. Loyd Jr. All-Sports Center. SMU's Dedman Center for Lifetime Sports recently expanded to offer students more new and renovated indoor and outdoor facilities.

SMU libraries contain more than 3 million volumes. Fondren Library contains a catalog of all holdings and major works of a general nature. Other collections are located in the Science Information Center, the Underwood Law Library, the Bridwell Library (a component of Perkins School of Theology), Hamon Arts Library, DeGolyer Library, and the Business Information Center. The Altshuler Learning Enhancement Center, known as the A-LEC, offers students individual tutoring, study groups, and techniques to enhance study and time management skills and test-taking strategies.

SMU has high-quality facilities campuswide, including specialized laboratories in the Dallas Seismological Observatory and the electron microscopy laboratory. The Institute for the Study of Earth and Man houses specialized laboratories for archeology, ethnology, geology, and physical anthropology. The Dedman Life Sciences Building and the new Junkins Electrical Engineering Building feature state-of-the-art research, teaching, and computer labs.

Costs

The comprehensive fee for full-time undergraduate students for the 2005–06 academic year was $36,088. This amount included tuition and fees totaling $26,880 and a room and board charge of $9208. SMU offers a monthly payment plan and other resources and plans to help students manage their investment in a college education.

Financial Aid

About 78 percent of first-year students receive some form of financial assistance. The SMU financial aid program includes University, state, and federal scholarships; merit- and need-based scholarships; grants; part-time jobs; payment plans; and/or low-interest loans. Most students who demonstrate financial need are awarded an aid package that combines SMU funds with government resources. The University assists all qualified students who cannot afford an SMU education. Financial aid decisions are based on academic performance and financial need. Accepted students interested in federal or state financial aid must file the Free Application for Federal Student Aid (FAFSA). SMU's code is 003136. Students may file online at http://www.fafsa.ed.gov. Students should complete the FAFSA by February 15 to receive primary consideration.

Students who also wish to be considered for SMU need-based assistance must complete the College Scholarship Service Financial Aid PROFILE (CSS PROFILE) in addition to the FAFSA. The PROFILE is available online at http://profileonline.collegeboard.com.

Financial aid, such as grants, low-interest loans, and campus employment, is also available to transfer students who demonstrate financial need based on the FAFSA and the CSS PROFILE, both of which should be filed each year. SMU offers transfer students a range of merit scholarships. For details, students should contact a transfer admission counselor at the telephone number listed below.

SMU's merit-based scholarships have been named among the best in the United States by *America's Best College Scholarships 2001*. SMU's most prestigious scholarship programs include the President's Scholars, the Nancy Ann and Ray L. Hunt Leadership Scholars, Dean's Scholars, SMU Distinguished Scholars, and University Scholars. National Merit Scholarships are available only to finalists who name SMU as their first college choice. Students must apply for merit scholarships by January 15.

Faculty

The undergraduate student-faculty ratio is 12:1, which allows students to interact closely with faculty members. Sixty percent of all undergraduate lecture sections have fewer than 25 students. Almost 90 percent of the full-time faculty members hold a Ph.D. or the highest degrees in their field. Regular, full-time faculty members teach most undergraduate classes (74 percent). SMU has more than 500 full-time faculty members.

Student Government

The SMU Student Senate is a comprehensive governing body that meets weekly to initiate and facilitate action on student affairs. The Senate is composed of 4 student body officers, 40 senators, and ten committees.

Admission Requirements

The Office of Admission bases selection of applicants on several criteria: the strength of the high school program and the grades received, SAT or ACT scores, teacher and counselor recommendations, an essay, and optional input from parents and peers. Applicants should present a college-preparatory program and are expected to complete a minimum of 4 years of English, 3 of mathematics (including algebra I and II and plane geometry), 3 of a natural science (including two lab sciences), 3 of social studies, and 2 of a foreign language. SMU places value on personal accomplishment, and an attempt is made to get to know the individual and the academic record beyond standardized scores.

Although the average GPA of successful transfer applicants who have completed 30 or more transferable hours is considerably higher than a 2.7 GPA (on a 4.0 scale), applicants with a GPA below this threshold are not typically successful in gaining admission. Candidates with a transferable GPA below 2.0 are not admitted to the University. For all candidates who have completed 30 or more college hours, the Admission Committee considers the rigorous nature of the courses attempted; in particular, applicants should have completed at least one course in English composition, a lab science, a math course beyond college algebra, and a course pertaining to the intended major. The committee weighs overall academic performance as well as evidence of recent improvement. For some applicants, the high school performance is also a factor. Candidates with fewer than 30 hours are considered on an individual basis and may be required to submit additional information, including high school records.

As a privately endowed institution, SMU has no limits on enrollment based solely on geography, and it makes no distinctions in tuition, fees, or other costs based on the home state of the student. Southern Methodist University does not discriminate on the basis of race, color, religion, national origin, sex, age, disability, or veteran status. SMU's commitment to equal opportunity includes nondiscrimination on the basis of sexual orientation.

Application and Information

Students should apply soon after completing the junior year of high school. Online applications are available at http://www.smu.edu/apply. The nonbinding early action deadline is November 1, with notification by December 30. For regular decision and priority merit scholarship application consideration, the deadline is January 15, with notification by March 15. SMU offers a spring decision deadline of March 15 on a space-available basis.

Transfer application deadlines are April 1 for the summer term entry, June 1 for fall term and merit scholarship consideration, and November 1 for spring term (including scholarship applicants).

For admission information, students should contact:

Division of Enrollment Services
Southern Methodist University
P.O. Box 750181
Dallas, Texas 75275-0181

Phone: 214-768-2058
   800-323-0672 (toll-free)
E-mail: ugadmission@smu.edu
Web site: http://www.smu.edu/admission/

Dallas Hall is the landmark building of SMU, reflecting the neo-Georgian architecture of the campus.

TRANSYLVANIA UNIVERSITY
LEXINGTON, KENTUCKY

The University

Transylvania, a small, private liberal arts college of about 1,120 men and women, is consistently ranked among the best of its kind in the nation. The name—from the Latin that means across the woods—refers to the heavily forested Transylvania settlement in which the University was founded in 1780. Transylvania was the first college west of the Allegheny Mountains and the sixteenth in the nation. The University established the first schools of medicine and law in what was then the West and educated the doctors, lawyers, ministers, political leaders, and others who helped shape the young nation. Transylvania also founded the first college literary magazine in the West, *The Transylvanian*, still published by students today. Transylvania's link with early Lexington is symbolized by its administration building, Old Morrison, a registered National Historic Landmark and the central feature on the official seal of the city of Lexington.

Transylvania continues as a pioneer in higher education, preparing future leaders in business, government, education, the sciences, and the arts. Students work closely with professors in small classes, many with fewer than 10 students. Due in large part to these close collaborations with faculty members, a high percentage of graduates attend excellent medical, law, and other graduate and professional programs.

Transylvania offers more than fifty cocurricular organizations, covering a range of student interests, and most students participate in several of these. The Lampas Circle of the national leadership honorary society Omicron Delta Kappa, which recently moved its national headquarters to Transylvania, recognizes students for academic excellence and campus leadership. The athletics program includes seven varsity sports for men, nine for women, and more than a dozen intramural sports. Transylvania also has four national sororities and four national fraternities.

Location

Transylvania is located in Lexington, Kentucky, a city of 270,000 and a growing center of commerce, culture, research, and education. Known as the horse capital of the world, Lexington is surrounded by the rolling green pastures of the famous Bluegrass region of central Kentucky. The area is also home to over 30,000 college students. Transylvania's parklike campus is just a 5-minute walk from downtown, with easy access to restaurants, shops, and entertainment. The proximity to downtown is also an advantage for students who want convenient part-time jobs and internship opportunities in law offices, accounting firms, hospitals, and other organizations. Transylvania offers its students a shuttle service between the modern Transylvania library and the University of Kentucky libraries every day, and the Lexington Public Library is a few blocks from the campus. Lexington is served by major airlines, and Louisville and Cincinnati are only 80 miles away.

Majors and Degrees

The Bachelor of Arts degree is awarded in the following majors: accounting, anthropology, art history, art studio, biology, business administration (concentrations in finance, hospitality management, management, and marketing), chemistry, classics, computer science, drama, economics, education, English, exercise science, French, history, mathematics, music, music technology, philosophy, physical education, physics, political science, psychology, religion, sociology, and Spanish. Individually designed majors also may be arranged. Minors are available in most majors and in classical studies, communication, environmental studies, German, hospitality management, international affairs, multicultural studies, and women's studies. Advising and undergraduate preparation are provided for preprofessional programs in dentistry, engineering, law, medicine, ministry, pharmacy, physical therapy, and veterinary medi-

cine. A cooperative program in engineering allows students to earn a B.A. in physics or liberal studies from Transylvania in three years and a B.S. in engineering from the University of Kentucky, Vanderbilt University, or Washington University in two years. A cooperative program in accounting allows students to earn a B.A. in accounting from Transylvania in four years and an M.S. in accounting from the University of Kentucky in one year; graduates qualify to take the CPA exam.

Academic Programs

The academic year is based on a 4-4-1 academic calendar, with two 14-week terms (fall and winter) and a one-month May term. The fall term begins in early September and ends in mid-December. The winter term begins in mid-January and ends in late April. During the May term, students may participate in a variety of programs on or off campus. Students normally take four courses in each of the fall and winter terms and one course in the May term. Thirty-six courses are required to graduate. Freshmen participate in a two-term program called Foundations of the Liberal Arts, which features small-group discussions with a faculty leader; lectures, films, concerts, and other presentations; and a tutorial program in basic communication, critical thinking, and study skills. Special study-skills clinics and workshops are offered on an optional basis. Students must complete requirements designed to ensure broad familiarity with the major areas of learning and human endeavor in the humanities and fine arts, social sciences, natural sciences and mathematics, logic, and languages.

Transylvania grants credit for scores of 4 or 5 on the Advanced Placement examinations of the College Board and at least 5 on the International Baccalaureate program. Detailed information may be obtained from the Office of the Registrar.

Off-Campus Programs

Experiencing diverse cultures through international study is a vital part of a Transylvania education. It is common for Transylvania students to study abroad for a summer, a term, or a year. A program at Regent's College, London, allows students to study there for the same cost and course credit as a semester at Transylvania. Scholarships are available for both semester-long and summer study abroad. Summer study programs, including those in Austria, Brazil, China, Costa Rica, Ecuador, France, Germany, Italy, Japan, Mexico, and Spain, are available through Transylvania's affiliation with the Kentucky Institute for International Studies. Transylvania also cooperates with the English-Speaking Union to offer advanced students scholarships for summer study at Cambridge and Oxford Universities. Students may participate in seminars or internships in Washington, D.C., through the Washington Center and in the Canadian Parliamentary Internship Program in Ottawa. Internships with congressional offices, Kentucky state government, city government, and local firms are easily arranged. Participation in Reserve Officers' Training Corps (Air Force and Army ROTC) is offered in cooperation with the University of Kentucky.

Academic Facilities

Two new Georgian-style buildings combine elegance with high-tech facilities to offer the latest advances in teaching and learning. The Cowgill Center for Business, Economics, and Education includes a multimedia classroom where professors from any discipline can use a large display screen to show the entire class information from one of the twenty-five networked student computers or from a TV, video, CD-ROM, or satellite. A specialized area for education majors includes a laboratory classroom for teacher training. The new Lucille C. Little Theater, used for faculty- and student-directed productions and drama classes, is a technically innovative facility that includes computerized lighting and sound, flexible staging options, and movable seating. The Frances Carrick Thomas/J.

Douglas Gay, Jr. Library offers sophisticated computerized databases, which are invaluable for research and can be accessed from any computer connected to Transylvania's server, including PCs in dorm rooms. The Mitchell Fine Arts Center provides music program facilities, including practice rooms, a recital hall, and an auditorium. It also houses the Career Development Center, which provides free interest testing and helps students research careers, improve job search skills, arrange internships and part-time jobs, and apply to graduate schools. Mitchell also houses a teaching laboratory for the hospitality management program. The recently acquired Shearer Art Building is dedicated to instructional space, student and faculty studios, and a student gallery. Other modern facilities include the newly renovated L. A. Brown Science Center, the Haupt Humanities Building, and the Clive M. Beck Athletic and Recreation Center, which opened in January 2002. About 80 percent of students live on campus in six residence halls—two for men, one for women, and three for men and women. These include traditional-style accommodations, apartment-style living for upperclass students, and suite-style rooms. All rooms are air-conditioned and completely furnished and offer private telephone service with voice mail and access to Transylvania's cable television and computer networks. Each residence hall has ample lounge and study space and easy access to computer labs and recreational facilities. The William T. Young Campus Center offers a competition-size indoor pool, a gymnasium, a fitness center, and other facilities.

Costs

Transylvania charges an annual tuition that covers fall, winter, and May terms for a normal full-time schedule of courses. Special instruction fees are charged in addition for certain designated courses, such as applied music and May Term travel courses. For 2006–07, tuition and fees were $20,950 and room and board (double occupancy) were $6850.

Financial Aid

Transylvania is committed to providing financial aid to students and their families. Four types of financial assistance are available. Scholarships are based on academic performance, leadership, and citizenship. Grants, loans, and work-study are based on financial need. About 90 percent of Transylvania students receive some form of financial assistance and many receive more than one type of aid. Outstanding entering freshmen may qualify for one of twenty William T. Young Scholarships—each worth more than $80,000 over four years—that cover tuition and fees. Submission of Transylvania's Application for Admission and Scholarships by the appropriate deadline is all that is necessary to be considered for all scholarships at Transylvania. Students who are interested in need-based aid must file the Free Application for Federal Student Aid (FAFSA).

Faculty

Transylvania's relatively small size and low student-faculty ratio of 13:1 allow for close, personal attention in teaching and advising. Ninety-seven percent of full-time faculty members hold a doctorate or the highest degree in their field, and they have come to Transylvania from a variety of graduate and professional schools. Many faculty members are recognized for their scholarship and professional activities, but their central concern is teaching and advising students. In the last five years, four Transylvania professors have been named Kentucky Professor of the Year by the Carnegie Foundation and the Council for the Advancement and Support of Education. In 2006, a Transylvania professor received the Acorn Award as Kentucky's outstanding professor from the Kentucky Advocates for Higher Education and the Council on Postsecondary Education. Transylvania's commitment to outstanding teaching is reflected in its nationally recognized Bingham Program for Excellence in Teaching, the first of its type in the nation to attract and retain gifted teachers through an evaluation process and financial incentives.

Student Government

Students at Transylvania have a high degree of access to the administration and governing board of the University. The Student Government Association serves as a representative government, and students also hold positions on standing committees of the faculty and the Board of Trustees.

Admission Requirements

Each applicant is considered individually on the basis of academic records, SAT scores and/or ACT scores, activities, interests, essays, and recommendations. Admission is also offered to transfer students, international students, and nontraditional students. High school students who graduate at the end of their junior year may also be considered for admission.

Transylvania enrolled 309 new students for the 2006–07 academic year. The middle 50 percent composite ACT score for the freshman class was 23 to 28; the middle 50 percent combined SAT score was 1070 to 1250. Fifty percent were in the top 10 percent of their high school class.

Application and Information

Submission of a Transylvania Application for Admission and Scholarships or submission of the Common Application is all that is necessary to be considered for admission and most merit scholarships at Transylvania. Application deadlines vary with particular scholarships and types of financial aid.

The early action deadline is December 1 for applicants who wish to learn of their acceptance by January 15 and who want to be considered for all Transylvania scholarships. February 1 is the regular admission and scholarships deadline for applicants who wish to be considered for all Transylvania scholarships except the William T. Young Scholarship. Applicants who apply after February 1 are considered on a space-available basis. The deadline for applications for the winter term, which begins in January, is December 1. The same deadlines apply to electronic applications, which may be submitted on the Internet at the Web address listed below.

Students considering Transylvania are urged to visit the campus, and high school seniors are encouraged to stay overnight in a dorm with a student admissions assistant. Weekday visits may include a customized campus tour and opportunities to attend classes; talk with professors, coaches, students, and admissions and financial aid counselors; and enjoy meals on campus. Visits should be arranged with the Office of Admissions, preferably one to two weeks in advance. Open houses are held in the fall and winter, and a college planning workshop for high school juniors and sophomores is held in the spring.

For more information and application materials, students should contact:

Office of Admissions
Transylvania University
300 North Broadway
Lexington, Kentucky 40508-1797
Phone: 859-233-8242
       800-872-6798 (toll-free)
E-mail: admissions@transy.edu
Web site: http://www.transy.edu

Small class sizes at Transylvania give professors and students the opportunity to work closely together, and many are directly involved in student research projects.

UNIVERSITY OF CHARLESTON
CHARLESTON, WEST VIRGINIA

The University

The University of Charleston (UC) strives to educate each student for a life of productive work, enlightened living, and community involvement. The University is very serious about its responsibility to provide students with the knowledge, abilities, and character necessary for them to have successful careers and to be productive and active citizens.

Founded in 1888 and formerly known as Morris Harvey College, the University of Charleston acquired its new name in 1979 to signify its importance as the leading higher education option in the capital. Today, UC proudly represents the capital city of Charleston and the surrounding Kanawha Valley. Currently, more than 1,000 students representing thirty states and twenty countries enjoy the University's 40-acre riverfront campus overlooking the State Capitol Complex and the beautiful city of Charleston.

The University of Charleston has been recognized as a national model for the freshman-year experience, which includes faculty mentoring, University transitions, and living/learning communities. The Collegiate Learning Assessment also recognizes the University for its outstanding commitment to student learning. In addition, *U.S. News & World Report* named UC as a Top 20 Comprehensive College offering bachelor's degrees in the South and as the Top Ranked Comprehensive College in West Virginia in its "Best Colleges for 2007" rankings. Students at UC also score among the highest in the country on the National Survey of Student Engagement.

The UC educational program focuses on "learning your way." The focus is on students, allowing them to demonstrate what they have learned in order to earn the credits necessary for graduation. Students are expected to demonstrate knowledge and skills in the areas of communication, critical thinking, citizenship, ethical practice, science, and creativity. These attributes are integrated with knowledge and skills in a chosen field of study. Future employers and graduate schools consistently seek and employ college graduates with these abilities, and it is imperative that all University graduates have a strong foundation in these skills. Therefore, the University of Charleston has designed this program to help students master the knowledge and skills that are necessary for success.

Students are encouraged to demonstrate mastery and earn credits at their own pace. Many students earn more than the traditional 15–18 credits per semester and graduate within three years, double major, or earn a master's degree in four years.

Housing facilities for residential students are very modern and student-friendly. Brotherton Hall, the oldest residence hall, was built in 2000 and houses 220 students; New Hall, built in 2003, houses 183 students; and Middle Hall, built in 2005 and 2006, houses 240 students. An expansion was completed for Middle Hall in August 2006 to accommodate increased student housing numbers, allowing the campus to house approximately 650 students.

Because the University believes that students learn from their involvement in community and campus activities, students are strongly encouraged to participate in one or more of the forty cocurricular organizations found at the University. There are academic clubs, publications, fraternities, sororities, religious organizations, intramural sports, honorary societies, drama clubs, cheerleading, chorus and band programs, and many student leadership organizations. The University's Welch Colleague program integrates student involvement, the academic curriculum, community service, and leadership. The Community Service program provides opportunities for students to participate both on campus and in the Charleston area. In addition, there are numerous civic, political, social, and charitable organizations easily accessible in the community.

The varsity sports program for men and women has become one of the University's most valuable assets. Men and women may participate in basketball, cheerleading, cross-country, soccer, tennis, and track and field. Men may also participate in baseball, football, and golf, and women in crew, softball, and volleyball. The University's athletic teams compete in Division II of the NCAA. In recent years, men's and women's teams have been contenders in the WVIAC tournaments, with several teams winning conference championships and attending national championship tournaments. The women's basketball team participated in the Elite 8 in 2005 and 2006, and the men's football team had the largest one-season turnaround in conference history in 2005.

The University of Charleston is accredited by the North Central Association of Colleges and Schools, National Council for Accreditation of Teacher Education, National Athletic Trainers Association, Commission on the Accreditation of Allied Health Education Programs–Athletic Training, Joint Review Committee on Education in Radiological Technology, and the National League for Nursing Accrediting Commission. The University holds a variety of professional recognitions, approvals, and memberships, including the International Assembly of Collegiate Business Education, West Virginia Academy of Sciences, Interior Design Educator's Council, and the American Council on Education.

The University offers master's degrees in business administration: an Executive M.B.A. and a plus-one M.B.A. for full-time study, one year beyond the bachelor's degree. The University of Charleston School of Pharmacy, which offers the University's first doctoral-level program, is now open and has enrolled its first class of 80 students.

Location

Charleston, West Virginia's vibrant state capital, is a cultural, social, political, and economic hub. Located in the Kanawha Valley near the foothills of the Appalachian Mountains, it offers scenic tranquility as well as the convenience and excitement of a modern city. With a metropolitan population of 200,000, Charleston has grown to be West Virginia's finest city. Accessibility to the city is quite easy via plane, car, bus, and train. A large civic center, historic sites, libraries, movie theaters, shopping malls, and a symphony orchestra are all highlights of the Charleston business district. The rapport between the University and the community is excellent, and many events are cosponsored annually.

Downtown Charleston, just a short ride from the campus by campus shuttle or city bus, offers the kind of social and cultural opportunities that can be found only in a large city. In addition, fishing, hunting, horseback riding, waterskiing, snow skiing, mountain biking, and white-water rafting are just a few of the many recreational activities to be found within a short distance of the campus.

Majors and Degrees

The University of Charleston offers undergraduate degree programs through its various divisions: the Morris Harvey Division of Arts and Sciences, the Herbert Jones Division of Business, and the Bert Bradford Division of Health Sciences.

The Morris Harvey Division of Arts and Sciences offers the Bachelor of Arts degree with the following majors: art, communications, education (various certifications), general studies, interior design, public policy, and psychology. The Bachelor of Science degree is offered with majors in biology, chemistry, and a biology/chemistry preprofessional program focused on the health sciences. The Division of Arts and Sciences is also home to the popular 2+4 Pre-Pharmacy program. This program is segmented into the Pre-Pharmacy Scholars track and the Traditional Pre-Pharmacy track. Students who excel in this unique program have preferential entry into the Pharm.D. program.

The Jones Division of Business offers Bachelor of Science degree programs in accounting, athletic administration, business administration, computer information technology systems, and finance. Associate of Science degree programs are offered in accounting, business administration, and computer information technology systems.

The Division of Health Sciences offers the Bachelor of Science degree in athletic training, nursing, and radiologic science. An Associate of Arts degree in nursing is also offered at the University.

Students may pursue directed independent study and internships in most majors. Army ROTC is offered to interested men and women. The Byrd Institute of Government Studies offers special opportunities to work with state and local governments.

Academic Programs

Candidates for a bachelor's degree from UC are required to complete a minimum of 120 semester hours and have a cumulative grade point average of at least 2.0 on all college work attempted. This must include 30 hours in upper division courses; demonstration of learning in the required outcomes of communication, critical thinking, ethical practice, creativity, science, and citizenship; and advanced work leading to a major in a department or a division. The minimum requirement for an associate degree is 60 semester hours and a cumulative grade point average of at least a 2.0 on all college work attempted, including completion of a prescribed program of general education and specialized work in a department.

The University follows a semester academic calendar and offers summer terms for students who wish to accelerate their college program. Students may enroll in as many credit hours per academic semester as they wish without additional tuition costs.

Academic Facilities

A large number of support facilities and programs supplement the various academic opportunities at the University of Charleston. The Schoenbaum Library serves as the center of the learning experience. Located in the new, technologically advanced Clay Tower Building, the library has a collection of more than 120,000 books, 200,000 microforms, and 3,600 audiovisual items. More than 8,000 journal titles are available either in print or electronically and are accessible from any Web-enabled computer, on or off campus. In addition, numerous specialized collections, CD-ROM-based electronic indexes, and online electronic search services are at the students' disposal for specialized research and study. The library also offers wireless technology and laptop computer check-out.

The University has numerous computer labs for student and faculty use: the Cabot Apple Lab, the IBM-PC combination classroom labs, an IBM-PC network lab, and an IBM-PC open lab. Wireless access is also available on much of the campus, including the scenic riverbank. The Learning Support Center provides a variety of services and classes to help students achieve academic, personal, and professional success. The Communication Resource Center provides support for students and faculty members through consultation services, workshops, and electronic access to a variety of writing resources.

The Clay Tower Building houses state-of-the-art science, technology, and information resource facilities. Riggleman Hall, the main college building, houses classrooms, a 976-seat auditorium and stage, education and language laboratories, the Carleton Varney Department of Art and Design, and administrative offices.

Costs

For the 2006–07 academic year, tuition was $21,000, and room (double occupancy) and board were $7600, for a total of $28,600. This does not included the cost of books, supplies, or other incidental charges.

Financial Aid

The University of Charleston provides generous financial assistance that may include a combination of scholarships, grants, loans, and work-study. In 2006–07, more than 90 percent of full-time students and 80 percent of part-time students received some form of financial aid. Special academic scholarships and grants are awarded to outstanding full-time students. The University also offers grants to qualified athletes and to students who are involved in leadership, community service, band, school newspaper, or vocal music.

Faculty

The University has 61 full-time and 38 part-time undergraduate faculty members. At the University of Charleston, faculty members provide academic, career, and in some cases, personal advice to students. They encourage active learning through collaborative projects and faculty/student research. Small classes through a 13:1 faculty-student ratio allow for individual attention for students.

Student Government

The Student Government Association is a policymaking body composed of students representing most campus organizations and student classes. Both the Student Government Association and the University believe that students should have the privilege, along with the faculty and administration, of participating in the governance of the University.

Admission Requirements

Admission to the University of Charleston is based on the academic records and potential for leadership and involvement. A qualified applicant's credentials must strongly suggest ability and motivation to succeed in higher education and in the University community. Candidates for admission must present a transcript of work from an accredited secondary school showing at least 16 academic units, grades indicating intellectual ability and promise, and proof of graduation or a GED. The pattern of courses should show purpose and continuity and furnish a background for the liberal learning outcomes curriculum offered by the University.

Since the unique and student-friendly curriculum emphasizes communication, critical thinking, and citizenship, secondary school courses should emphasize courses in English, mathematics, sciences, and social sciences. Candidates are also required to submit scores on the ACT or SAT. Students must have an above-average academic profile that includes a minimum 2.25 academic grade point average and a minimum ACT composite score of 19 or SAT score (combined math and critical reading) of 900. Applicants for admission are considered on an individual basis without regard to race, religion, geographic origin, or handicap. Letters of recommendation and a personal visit to the campus scheduled with the Office of Admissions are highly recommended.

Application and Information

For more information, interested students should contact:

Office of Admissions
University of Charleston
2300 MacCorkle Avenue, SE
Charleston, West Virginia 25304
Phone: 304-357-4750
　　　　 800-995-GO UC (4682) (toll-free)
Fax: 304-357-4781
E-mail: admissions@ucwv.edu
Web site: http://www.ucwv.edu

The Clay Tower Building houses state-of-the-art science facilities and a library with lounges overlooking the Kanawha River. The campus is directly across the river from the State Capitol.

UNIVERSITY OF DALLAS
IRVING, TEXAS, AND ROME, ITALY

The University

In 1955, the Roman Catholic Diocese of Dallas/Fort Worth purchased land for a university on a 1,000-acre tract of rolling hills northwest of Dallas, and in 1956, the University of Dallas (UD) opened. His Excellency Bishop Thomas K. Gorman, Chancellor of the new university, announced that it would be a coeducational institution, welcoming students of all faiths and ethnic backgrounds. Headed by a lay president and a lay academic dean, the faculty was composed of laymen, diocesan and Cistercian priests, and sisters of the Order of St. Mary of Namur.

Current undergraduate enrollment is about 1,200 men and women. Undergraduates come from all fifty states and thirty-three other countries. Although approximately 71 percent are Catholic, twenty faiths are represented on campus.

The University of Dallas was the first Catholic institution to have a board of trustees made up of both lay and religious members. Since its founding, many other universities and colleges have followed its example. The first class, a group of individuals who won significant honors, such as Fulbright and Woodrow Wilson fellowships, was graduated in 1960. There is a Phi Beta Kappa chapter on campus.

Through a $6-million endowment provided by the Blakley-Braniff Foundation, the Braniff Graduate School was established in 1966. Twelve graduate programs are now in existence, including doctoral programs in philosophy, politics, and literature and the M.F.A. program in art. The College of Business houses the Graduate School of Management, which is distinguished by its practice-oriented education, close ties with leading companies and professionals, and a global student body. In addition to its undergraduate programs, the College of Business offers Master of Business Administration (M.B.A.) and Master of Management degrees. The M.B.A. includes sixteen concentrations in the areas of finance, health care, information technology, management, marketing, and telecommunications.

The University of Dallas is a center of learning, and the experience on campus is intensive and highly directed. People choose to come to the University because they are serious students. While they engage in a full complement of extracurricular activities and independent study, it is the act of learning in association with their professors that shapes their college years. Because the undergraduate college is small and largely residential, it forms a close-knit community. The University sponsors a number of lectures, concerts, and art exhibits, ranging from the old masters to the UD international printmaking invitational. The Student Government sponsors weekly events and current and classic films. The *University News* has consistently won awards for excellence in writing and design. Collegium Cantorum, the a cappella liturgical choir, performs both nationally and internationally. Intercollegiate NCAA Division III sports include baseball, basketball, cross-country, golf, lacrosse, soccer, softball, tennis, track, and volleyball. Rugby is very popular at the club level. Eighty-five percent of the on-campus students are involved in intramurals: basketball, flag football, soccer, softball, paintball, and other sports. Traditional events include coffeehouses featuring student entertainment, Charity Week, Mallapalooza, Oktoberfest, Spring Olympics, and Groundhog.

For Catholic students, daily and weekly Mass, Reconciliation, and rosary are held in the 500-seat Church of the Incarnation. Transportation is arranged for students of other faiths to attend services nearby. Campus Ministry provides numerous volunteer opportunities, including annual service projects in Appalachia and Ecuador.

Location

Irving, Texas, a city of 195,000 on the northwest side of the city of Dallas, is about 15 minutes from downtown Dallas, 10 minutes from Love Field airport, and 15 minutes from DFW airport. The Dallas–Fort Worth Metroplex offers a diverse mix of cultural and entertainment attractions, including the Dallas Museum of Modern Art, the new Nasher Sculpture Center, and the Kimbell Museum in Fort Worth. The Dallas Theater Center and Stage One have built reputations as top-notch theaters and as proving grounds for Broadway-bound productions. Texas Stadium, home of the Dallas Cowboys, is just three blocks from the University. Dallas is home to professional sports teams in hockey, soccer, and basketball. Nearby Arlington is home to the Texas Rangers.

Majors and Degrees

The Constantin College of Liberal Arts offers programs leading to the Bachelor of Arts (B.A.) degree in art and art history, biology, business, chemistry, classics, computer science, drama, economics, economics and finance, education, English, history, mathematics, modern languages (French, German, and Spanish), philosophy, physics, politics, psychology, and theology. The Bachelor of Science degree is awarded in biochemistry, biology, chemistry, mathematics, and physics.

The College of Business offers Bachelor of Arts degrees in business leadership.

The University offers twenty-seven concentrations, or minors, including applied math, applied physics, art history, business, Christian contemplative studies, computer science, entrepreneurship, environmental science, international studies, journalism, math, medieval and Renaissance studies, modern language, music, and pure math.

Preprofessional programs in architecture, business, dentistry, engineering, law, medicine, and physical therapy are carefully integrated with the Core Curriculum of the Constantin College. The rate of acceptance and enrollment of the college's students by professional schools is exceptional. More than 60 percent go on to graduate school, and the rate of acceptance for medical and law school applicants is more than 90 percent.

A five-year, dual-degree program allows students to combine any undergraduate major with the graduate program in business management. Upon completion of the program, a student will have earned both the B.A. and M.B.A. degrees.

Academic Programs

The Core Curriculum is a shared series of specific courses that outline the development of Western thought and culture from classical to modern times. Every student becomes familiar with the same works of literature and the same great books and concepts, fostering a natural understanding and exchange of ideas. All students then go on to pursue their chosen major discipline, reaching a level of maturity and competence in the discipline that they could not have attained in the absence of a broad general foundation. The student body has an active and personal involvement with the Core Curriculum.

The University observes a two-semester calendar, with the semester examinations occurring before the monthlong Christmas break. An interterm session and three summer sessions are also offered.

Off-Campus Programs

All undergraduates, regardless of major, are encouraged to spend one semester on the University's campus in Rome. While not compulsory, the Rome experience is an important part of the undergraduate education; to seek one's heritage in the liberal arts and to be a student of the Western world is, in a sense, to be a citizen of Rome. Courses offered in Rome are from the Core Curriculum and are taught by professors from the Texas campus. The Rome campus is located just outside of downtown Rome. Transfer students who need courses offered on the Rome campus may participate after one semester on the main campus. The cost for tuition, room, and board for all participants is roughly equivalent to that on the main campus. More than 80 percent of University of Dallas graduates have participated in the Rome program.

Academic Facilities

The Science Center, a $6-million, state-of-the-art facility, houses some of the most advanced tools for scientific research available, including a working observatory. The Haggerty Arts Village has established the University as a leading center for ceramics and fine arts in the Southwest. Drama productions are staged in the Margaret Jonsson Theater. Blakely Library holds more than 275,000 volumes, including the personal library of the late political philosopher Wilmoore Kendall.

Costs

Annual tuition and fees for 2007–08 are $23,222; room and board costs average $7615. Costs are the same for in-state and out-of-state students.

Financial Aid

Tuition, fees, room, and board are substantially lower at the University of Dallas than at many other nationally recognized universities. In addition, all high school seniors who apply for admission by the freshman scholarship priority deadline of January 15 receive priority consideration for all of the University's achievement-based awards. The University currently offers four types of achievement-based awards: academic achievements, community achievements, leadership achievements, and special talents. Talent areas that are currently recognized include art, business, chemistry, classics (Latin and Greek), German, French, math, physics, and Spanish. Students who apply for admission between January 16 and March 1 receive regular consideration for achievement-based awards. Those who apply for admission after March 1 are considered for achievement-based awards dependent on the availability of funding.

All students who submit a Free Application for Federal Student Aid (FAFSA) are considered for all forms of financial assistance based on their family's finances. These forms of assistance include scholarships, grants, loans, and work-study programs. Priority is given to applicants whose FAFSA is received by the University of Dallas on or before March 1. The school code for sending a FAFSA to the University of Dallas is 003651.

Faculty

The University prides itself on its teaching faculty. Ninety-two percent hold terminal degrees. There are no graduate assis-tants. With a faculty-student ratio of 1:12, extensive consultation and direction are possible. The average class size is 19. The faculty is characterized by authority in the various disciplines, and its members have published more than 1,000 books and articles and secured major research grants.

Student Government

The Student Government Association and various departmental and special clubs, such as the social, film, lecture, and fine arts committees, encourage an extracurricular life created by the students themselves.

Admission Requirements

Although no rigid cutoff point is adhered to in admission, 52 percent of the students who enter as freshmen rank in the top 10 percent of their high school class. General admission requirements include SAT or ACT scores, rank in the upper third of the high school class, and 16 college-preparatory units, including 4 in English, 3 in mathematics, 2 in the same foreign language, 2 in social science, and 2 in a laboratory science. Interviews are not required but are strongly recommended. Through the Office of Undergraduate Admission, counseling appointments, tours, and overnight accommodations on campus may be arranged. Transfer students are welcome.

Application and Information

A transcript, official rank in class, and SAT or ACT scores must be submitted along with a letter of recommendation and a completed application form, which is obtainable online or via mail or phone from the Office of Admission. Transfer students should submit all transcripts from colleges previously attended. A $40 application fee should accompany the application; the other material may follow as ready. The Early Action I deadline is November 1; the Early Action II deadline is December 1. The freshman priority scholarship deadline is January 15. The regular admission deadline is March 1. Rolling admission is March 2–August 1.

For applications or further information, students should contact:

Office of Undergraduate Admission and Financial Aid
University of Dallas
1845 East Northgate Drive
Irving, Texas 75062
Phone: 972-721-5266
        800-628-6999 (toll-free)
Web site: http://www.udallas.edu

University of Dallas students learning on-site at Sicily, Italy.

UNIVERSITY OF NEW ORLEANS

NEW ORLEANS, LOUISIANA

The University

The University of New Orleans (UNO) is part of the rich cultural tapestry of its hometown, which is one of the most extraordinary cities in the world. Established in 1956 to bring publicly supported higher education to the New Orleans area, UNO is fully accredited by the Commission on Colleges of the Southern Association of Colleges and Schools. With an enrollment of 11,800 (9,200 undergraduates and 2,600 graduate students) in fall 2006, UNO offers both undergraduate and graduate degrees through the doctoral level.

UNO derives its strength from its urban setting and strives to enhance the economic, social, and cultural amenities of New Orleans through its numerous research projects, outreach programs, and special cooperative agreements. The University of New Orleans attracts students from forty-eight states (approximately 10 percent) and 102 countries, with a majority of the students Louisiana residents (approximately 90 percent). The diverse student population (42 percent of students are members of ethnic minorities) provides an excellent opportunity for personal growth and understanding.

For students who are interested in on-campus housing, UNO offers three unique styles living. Privateer Place overlooks beautiful Lake Pontchartrain and includes a swimming pool and Jacuzzi. Privateer Place contains seventy-two 2-person unfurnished efficiency apartments, 216 furnished two-bedroom apartments, and sixty furnished four-bedroom apartments. Bienville Hall is a coeducational dormitory for single students and has 306 two-person rooms, including seventy-eight rooms that were recently remodeled. In fall 2007, UNO plans to open a new $38.5-million residence hall complex, composed of two 4-story buildings totaling about 220,000 square feet. The facility will include 236 suite-style units that can accommodate 749 students, as well as TV and recreation rooms, study lounges, laundry facilities, and a convenience store. All complexes have disability-accessible rooms available.

Campus dining facilities are conveniently located near all on-campus housing facilities and heavily populated student areas, with various hours of operation. Other student services include six on-campus computer labs that provide free Internet access, a learning resource center that offers additional tutoring services, student counseling services, an on-campus medical office and pharmacy, student legal counseling, and religious centers.

UNO has more than 100 active student organizations on campus, including academic, professional, Greek, social, political, and religious organizations. UNO's newest addition is the University pep band, the UNO Blue Zoo, which performs at all UNO home basketball games and other University-related events. *Bayou* is UNO's annual national literary magazine that collects submissions from writers worldwide. UNO's student newspaper, *Driftwood*, is published weekly, and *Ellipsis*, a literary magazine, is published annually.

As a Division I member of the National Collegiate Athletic Association (NCAA), UNO fields men's teams in basketball, baseball, and tennis and women's teams in basketball, volleyball, and tennis. UNO students can also participate in many recreational and intramural sports. Students have access to a new 85,000-square-foot Recreation and Fitness Center, which features a 12,000-square-foot cardiovascular, circuit, and free weight training room; an indoor track; a lap pool; racquetball courts; outdoor sundeck; juice bar; and social lounge.

Location

The University's 195-acre main campus is set in one of the most beautiful residential areas on the south shore of Lake Pontchartrain, only minutes from the fun and excitement of downtown New Orleans and the French Quarter. New Orleans is a cosmopolitan city, known for its great Southern hospitality and its unique tourist attractions. Renowned for Creole and Cajun cuisine, Mardi Gras, and jazz music festivals, New Orleans culture offers a unique environment for students to grow, both socially and academically. Whether exploring the art galleries of the Warehouse District or strolling down stately St. Charles Avenue, New Orleans has something for everyone, and the University of New Orleans is a part of it all.

Many of UNO's hotel, restaurant, and tourism administration majors find internships in the city's best hotels and restaurants. Film students have the opportunity to work at the Nims Center film studio complex as New Orleans becomes the "Hollywood of the South." Naval architecture students have access to the nation's largest undergraduate program in naval architecture and marine engineering as well as to the UNO–Avondale Maritime Center. As New Orleans continues to attract computer technology–based businesses to what has been called "the Silicon Bayou," the UNO Research and Technology Park continues to expand, producing more than 8,000 new jobs. Computer science majors are able to network with potential employers in one of the fastest-growing computer technology markets in the country.

Majors and Degrees

Bachelor of Science degrees are offered in accounting; biological sciences; chemistry; civil and environmental engineering; computer science; earth and environmental science; electrical engineering; entrepreneurship; finance; general business administration; hotel, restaurant, and tourism administration; management; marketing; mathematics; mechanical engineering; naval architecture and marine engineering; physics; psychology; transportation studies; urban studies and planning; and preprofessional programs in dentistry; medicine (with biology, chemistry, and psychology tracks); nursing; pharmacy; physical therapy studies; and veterinary medicine.

Bachelor of Arts degrees are offered in anthropology; early childhood education; elementary education; English; English education; film, theater, and communication arts; fine arts–history; fine arts–studio (with options that include digital media, painting, photography, and sculpture); French; geography; history; international studies; mathematics education; music (with options including instrumental, jazz studies, theory and composition, and vocal); music education; philosophy; political science; secondary education; social science education; sociology; Spanish; and women's studies.

A four-year Bachelor of General Studies degree program is available for students who wish to design individual curricula. Credit programs in paralegal studies, medical coding, and medical transcripts are also offered. Additional interdisciplinary minors are offered in interdisciplinary studies in African studies, Asian studies, entrepreneurship, environmental studies, Latin American and Caribbean studies, medical coding, Native American studies, paralegal studies, and print journalism.

Academic Programs

All baccalaureate degree programs require a minimum of 128 semester hours with a minimum grade point average of 2.0 (C) in all work attempted in the college major. Also, all students must successfully complete an approved course demonstrating computer literacy. Other course requirements vary according to program. Programs leading to degrees with honors are offered in most academic majors. Credit for selected courses may be earned either through advanced-standing exams administered by the academic departments or through the College Board's Advanced Placement and College-Level Examination Program tests. College credit may also be gained for certain armed services and other nonacademic training. The academic year is composed of sixteen-week fall and spring semesters and three summer sessions.

Off-Campus Programs

The University of New Orleans Metropolitan College coordinates international study programs in Austria, Costa Rica, the Czech Republic, Ecuador, France, Greece, Honduras, and Italy. UNO's partnership with the University of Innsbruck, Austria, affords students an opportunity to participate in the largest international summer school of any American university in Europe. UNO offers college-credit exchange programs in Brazil and Canada. Students may also attend another school within the continental United States via the National Student Exchange (NSE) for one semester or one year.

UNO offers several off-campus facilities throughout the metropolitan New Orleans area, demonstrating UNO's commitment to community outreach. Off-campus locations offer both credit and noncredit courses, with hours varying from sunrise to evening and weekend classes.

Academic Facilities

The Earl K. Long Library's 1.5-million-volume collection includes approximately 12,000 journals, of which 3,800 are current subscriptions. Microform holdings include microfilm, microcard, and microfiche formats; microtext readers and reader-printers are also available. Other facilities include individual study carrels, a music listening room, computer terminals connected to the Computer Research Center, a Kurzweil reader for the visually impaired, and photocopy services. The Office of Educational Support Services includes a media resources center, which provides important media aids for the instructional staff in classroom presentations, and Television Resources, which coordinates a closed-circuit cable system and TV production studio. WWNO, the first public radio station in Louisiana, is located on the UNO campus.

All enrolled students and faculty and staff members receive a LAN and e-mail account. The University's computer network provides connections to approximately 5,000 locations campuswide as well as wireless connections in select buildings. High-speed ResNet service is available to students living in Privateer Place, and a free dial-up Internet modem pool provides access for all off-campus enrolled students and faculty and staff members.

The UNO Lee Circle Center for the Arts includes the Ogden Museum, which houses the largest collection of Southern art in the world. The center also houses the National D-Day Museum, which includes the world's largest collection of World War II color film. The 70,000-square-foot Nims Center, located 20 minutes from the main campus, houses a professional-quality sound stage, including a 10,000-square-foot studio for University film projects. The Nims Center is also available for professional film projects.

Costs

In 2006–07, combined undergraduate fees for full-time students for the fall and spring semesters were $3820 for Louisiana residents and $10,864 for nonresidents; summer session fees for full-time students were $1080 for Louisiana residents and $1630 for nonresidents. Residence hall and board fees totaled $3800 (double occupancy) for the fall and spring semesters. Costs of books and supplies totaled $800 per year. Additional charges included a $40 application fee, a $10 registration fee, field service and laboratory fees (usually $10 to $35) for some courses, an $80 car registration fee (includes parking pass), a $30 late application fee, a $30 late registration fee, a $5 per-credit-hour (maximum $75) technology fee, and a $10 per-credit-hour (maximum $120) academic enhancement fee. All fees are subject to change and can be confirmed by calling the Office of Admissions.

Financial Aid

The Office of Student Financial Aid develops financial aid packages to assist students with their educational expenses. This package is usually a combination of grants, loans, student employment, and/or scholarships, which, along with family contribution, help to finance the student's education. To be eligible for most federal financial aid programs, students must enroll for at least 6 credit hours (half-time) in an eligible program (one that leads to a degree or certificate). Approximately 90 percent of all freshmen in fall 2006 who showed financial need and took at least 6 credit hours were offered some form of financial aid. The priority date for the financial aid application is May 1. All applications postmarked on or before March 1 are considered for UNO's numerous academic scholarships, including those of international students. The University of New Orleans also offers scholarships in jazz studies; classical music; fine arts; film, theater, and communication arts; and creative writing. These scholarships require either an audition or the submission of a portfolio or manuscript along with the scholarship application.

Faculty

UNO has 525 full-time and 175 part-time faculty members, most of whom participate in both graduate and undergraduate instruction and research activity. Graduate students serve as teaching assistants in laboratory courses under the close supervision of the faculty. Approximately 80 percent of the faculty members hold doctorates. Most full-time faculty members devote themselves exclusively to University-related pursuits and are integrally involved in student affairs through counseling, teaching, research, and social activities. The student-faculty ratio is 17:1.

Student Government

Every student enrolled at UNO is a member of the Student Government (SG). SG offers students a way to create effective change, express opinions and concerns, and utilize resources to enhance their educational experiences. Some of the programs SG currently offers and/or sponsors are Student Legal Services, the Academic Travel Fund, 24-hour study hall during finals week, UNO pep band (The Blue Zoo), UNO Soccer Club, the Mechanical Engineering Mini Baja Competition, UNO Jazz Night at the University Center, musical excursions, UNO Ambassadors Fishing Rodeo, the UNO student literary magazine (Ellipsis), recreation and intramural sports, cheerleaders, and the Privateer dance team.

Admission Requirements

Students seeking admission to the University of New Orleans should submit their application as early as possible in their senior year. Admission requirements for Louisiana residents and nonresidents for fall 2007 include the completion of the Board of Regents core curriculum (in years): English (4), mathematics (3), science (3), social studies (3), foreign language (2), fine arts (1), and computer science (½). Residents must also have either a high school cumulative GPA of at least 2.5 or an ACT composite score of at least 23 (1060 SAT) or rank in the top 25 percent of their high school graduating class, and students must not require more than one developmental/remedial course. Out-of-state students who do not meet the GPA, test score, and rank requirements must have a minimum ACT composite score of 26 (SAT 1170) for automatic admission.

Transfer requirements include the completion of 18 semester hours of nondevelopmental work, a minimum 2.25 cumulative GPA, and completion of all developmental course work before transferring. Students with fewer than 18 semester hours must meet both freshman and transfer requirements.

Application and Information

The University of New Orleans has a rolling admissions policy. The application fee is $40. Priority deadlines for application are as follows: July 1 for the fall semester, November 15 for the spring semester, and May 1 for the summer semester. Deadlines for international students are June 1, October 1, and March 1, respectively.

Office of Admissions
103 Administration Building
University of New Orleans
2000 Lakeshore Drive
New Orleans, Louisiana 70148
Phone: 504-280-6595
      800-256-5-UNO (toll-free)
Fax: 504-280-5522
Web site: http://www.uno.edu

UNIVERSITY OF WEST FLORIDA
PENSACOLA, FLORIDA

The University

One of the eleven state universities of Florida, the University of West Florida (UWF) enrolls approximately 9,880 students in its Colleges of Arts and Sciences, Business, and Professional Studies. The University of West Florida, which opened in fall 1967, is located on a 1,600-acre nature preserve 10 miles north of downtown Pensacola. The University's facilities, which are valued at more than $81 million, have been designed to complement the natural beauty of the site.

The University currently enrolls students from forty-nine states and ninety-one countries. Students and professors enjoy a relationship that is more common at a small, private college. Approximately 970 freshmen began their studies at UWF last year. The middle 50 percent statistics for the class are as follows: high school grade point average ranged from 3.1 to 4.1; SAT total score ranged from 1000 to 1190; and ACT composite ranged from 21 to 26.

In addition to its undergraduate programs, UWF also offers the master's degree in thirty-three areas of study and specialist and Ed.D. degrees in education.

UWF operates centers in downtown Pensacola and at Eglin Air Force Base and a branch campus in Fort Walton Beach (in conjunction with a local community college). In addition, UWF owns 152 acres of beachfront property on nearby Santa Rosa Island, adjacent to the Gulf Islands National Seashore. Available for both recreation and research, this property provides special opportunities for students pursuing degrees in marine biology, maritime studies, and coastal zone studies.

The University of West Florida is a member of the NCAA Division II. Men's sports include baseball, basketball, cross-country, golf, soccer, and tennis. Women's sports include basketball, cross-country, golf, soccer, softball, tennis, track, and volleyball. Students also participate in more than nineteen intramural sports and twenty club sports. The Program Council and the Residence Hall Advisory Council provide activities and events that are open to the entire campus community. UWF hosts fourteen national sororities and fraternities; 136 professional, academic, and religious organizations are open to UWF students.

A natatorium housing an Olympic-size pool adjoins the Health, Leisure, Exercise, and Sports Facility, which is the center for indoor sports and large-group activities and events. Soccer fields, tennis courts, handball and racquetball courts, jogging trails, picnic areas, and sites for canoeing are available on campus. Baseball and softball fields and a lighted track complete the UWF sports complex. Sailing and waterskiing facilities are nearby, and campus nature trails attract thousands of visitors annually.

Students may choose to live on or off campus. The Office of Housing oversees 1,450 total residence hall spaces that include low-rise residence halls, two- or four-bedroom residence hall apartments that are equipped with modern conveniences, and three new residence halls, one with 300 spaces and the other two with 200 spaces.

There are also various apartment complexes conveniently located just beyond the campus.

Location

Students and visitors alike delight in the beauty of the campus, which is nestled in the rolling hills outside Pensacola, Florida. Wide verandas, massive moss-draped oaks, and spacious lawns capture the traditional charm and grace of the South, while modern architecture and state-of-the-art facilities blend in naturally among loblolly pines and meandering walkways.

Only minutes from the campus gate are the emerald waters and white beaches of the Gulf of Mexico and the Gulf Islands National Seashore, one of the nation's most beautiful beaches. The Pensacola area attracts vacationers from all around the country to its historic Seville Square, golf tournaments, sailing regattas, restaurants on the bay, and a variety of art and music festivals. WUWF, the University's public radio station, produces a monthly live program, Gulf Coast RadioLive. UWF is 3½ hours from New Orleans, 1 hour from Mobile, 3 hours from Tallahassee, and 5 hours from Atlanta.

Majors and Degrees

The University of West Florida awards the bachelor's degree in forty-nine undergraduate programs with many areas of specialization. Undergraduate majors are available in the College of Arts and Sciences in anthropology, art, biology, career and technical studies, chemistry, clinical laboratory sciences, communication arts, computer engineering, computer science, electrical engineering, English, environmental studies, fine arts, history, interdisciplinary humanities studies, interdisciplinary information technology, interdisciplinary science, international studies, leisure studies, marine biology, mathematics, medical technology, music, nursing, oceanography, philosophy, physics, preprofessional studies, political science, psychology, science (interdisciplinary), social sciences (interdisciplinary), studio art, and theater as well as a seven-year predental B.S./D.M.D. program with the University of Florida.

Undergraduate majors in the College of Business include accounting, economics, finance, management, management information systems, and marketing. The College of Business is accredited by AACSB International—The Association to Advance Collegiate Schools of Business.

The College of Professional Studies, which includes education programs that are accredited by the National Council for Accreditation of Teacher Education (NCATE), offers professional training and majors leading to bachelor's degrees in the following areas: community health; criminal justice; elementary education; engineering technology; exceptional student education; health education; health sciences; health, leisure, and exercise science; hospitality, recreation, and resort management; legal studies; middle school education; prekindergarten/primary education; prelaw; and social work. There are specialist programs in educational leadership and in curriculum and instruction and a doctoral program in curriculum and instruction.

Academic Programs

A general curriculum is required for entering freshmen and for transfer students without an Associate in Arts degree from a Florida public community college. General studies provide students with a broad foundation in the liberal arts, science, and career and life planning. The academic skills of reading, writing, discourse, critical inquiry, logical thinking, and mathematical reasoning are central elements of the general studies curriculum.

Students of high ability may enter an honors program offering intensive instruction in a more individualized setting. Cooperative education programs are available in nearly every field, allowing UWF students to get a head start on their careers while paying for their education. Army and Air Force ROTC programs and scholarships are also available.

Off-Campus Programs

The Office of International Education and Programs arranges more than twenty study-abroad and student exchange programs on every continent except Antarctica. Participants may study in Austria, Canada, England, Finland, France, Germany, Japan, Mexico, the Netherlands, and Portugal.

Academic Facilities

The main campus consists of more than 100 buildings. One of the most prominent of these is the five-floor John C. Pace Library, which houses a collection of more than 2.3 million bound volumes and micropieces. Interconnected through computer linkages with state and national libraries for research purposes, the UWF library contains one of the finest special collections about the Gulf Coast area. Some of the items in this collection date back to the fourteenth century, and there are also a manuscript letter signed by Thomas Jefferson, books autographed by Albert Einstein, and materials carried aboard the space shuttle by UWF alumni.

Excellent science and technology laboratories for preprofessional majors, extensive video and film equipment, desktop publishing labs, an AP wire service, and computer science facility also support students' scholarly endeavors. Microcomputers, minicomputers, a diverse inventory of software, a real-time laboratory, modem linkages to residence halls, and 24-hour-a-day access to the computer center all are available to students in every field of study. Other major facilities include a Center for Fine and Performing Arts; a College of Professional Studies Complex; a Student Services Complex; a Health, Leisure, Exercise, and Sports Facility; and a Commons.

Expansion and renovation continue to enhance the main campus. The Commons feature a bookstore, post office, and snack bar. An archaeology building and museum opened in 1999.

Costs

For fall 2006, tuition was $110.39 per credit for Florida residents and $527.27 per credit for out-of-state students. Legal residents of Alabama can qualify for the Alabama Tuition Differential Program, which has a tuition rate that is only slightly higher than the in-state rate. Room and board total $6600, and the cost of books and supplies is estimated at $1000. Transportation and personal expenses vary according to students' individual needs.

Financial Aid

About 65 percent of UWF students receive some form of financial aid and scholarships. UWF is committed to meeting a student's financial need. Aid is awarded on a first-come, first-served basis.

The Scholarship Program for outstanding freshmen allows students to receive early scholarship commitments as soon as they have decided to enroll in UWF. The John C. Pace Jr. scholarships are awarded to meritorious freshmen and transfers with A.A. degrees from Florida's community colleges. Awards are between $1000 and $5000 per year. Special scholarships for students with talent in the arts are awarded. Non-Florida tuition grants that reduce the amount of out-of-state fees are awarded to outstanding freshman and transfer students.

Faculty

Faculty members at the University of West Florida include published authors, scientists engaged in a wide range of research projects, and journalists who are skilled in advertising and filmmaking. Eighty-five percent of the faculty members hold doctoral degrees from major institutions throughout the United States.

Student Government

The Student Government Association is authorized to represent the student body in all matters concerning student life. The basic purposes of the student government are to provide students with an opportunity to participate in the decision-making process of the University; to review, evaluate, and allocate all student activity and service fee monies as allowed by state law (annually, some $1 million is allocated by students); to consider and make recommendations on all phases of student life; and to serve as the principal forum for discussion of matters of broad concern to the students.

Admission Requirements

The University of West Florida admits freshman applicants based on high school GPA, completion of college-preparatory courses, and test scores (either the ACT or the SAT is accepted). Special consideration is given to applicants with special talents. College-preparatory courses should include 4 years of English; 3 each of math, social science, and natural science; 2 of the same foreign language; and 4 academic electives.

Transfer applicants with fewer than 60 hours are required to submit SAT or ACT test scores and official transcripts from both the college(s) and the high school attended. Students transferring with 60 hours or more must submit their college transcript(s) only.

Application and Information

Students are encouraged to apply early in order to allow time for receipt of transcripts and to receive full consideration for financial aid, scholarships, and housing. Admissions decisions are made on a rolling basis. The University encourages visits to its beautiful campus and offers riding tours Monday through Friday at 10 a.m. and 1 p.m. Central Standard Time. Among the available features on the University's Web site (http://www.uwf.edu) are the catalog, Saturday Open House dates, applications for admission, and the course guide for the current term. The Lighthouse Information System allows applicants to view their admission and financial aid status via the Internet.

Additional information and application materials may be obtained by writing or calling:

Office of Admissions
University of West Florida
11000 University Parkway
Pensacola, Florida 32514-5750
Phone: 850-474-2230
       800-263-1074 (toll-free)
E-mail: admissions@uwf.edu
Web site: http://uwf.edu

The UWF Sailing Club goes out for a day of sun and recreation on Pensacola Bay.

Indexes

Majors and Degrees

Accounting

Aakers Coll, Fargo, ND — A
Academy Coll, MN — A
Adrian Coll, MI — B
AIB Coll of Business, IA — A
Alma Coll, MI — B
Anderson U, IN — B
Andrews U, MI — B
Aquinas Coll, MI — B
Ashford U, IA — B
Ashland U, OH — B
Augsburg Coll, MN — B
Augustana Coll, IL — B
Augustana Coll, SD — B
Aurora U, IL — B
Avila U, MO — B
Baker Coll of Allen Park, MI — A
Baker Coll of Auburn Hills, MI — A,B
Baker Coll of Cadillac, MI — A,B
Baker Coll of Clinton Township, MI — A
Baker Coll of Flint, MI — A,B
Baker Coll of Jackson, MI — A,B
Baker Coll of Muskegon, MI — A,B
Baker Coll of Owosso, MI — A,B
Baker Coll of Port Huron, MI — A,B
Baker U, KS — B
Baldwin-Wallace Coll, OH — B
Ball State U, IN — B
Bellevue U, NE — B
Bemidji State U, MN — B
Benedictine Coll, KS — B
Benedictine U, IL — B
Bethany Coll, KS — B
Blackburn Coll, IL — B
Black Hills State U, SD — B
Bluffton U, OH — B
Bowling Green State U, OH — B
Bradley U, IL — B
Briar Cliff U, IA — B
Buena Vista U, IA — B
Butler U, IN — B
Calumet Coll of Saint Joseph, IN — A,B
Calvin Coll, MI — B
Cameron U, OK — B
Capital U, OH — B
Cardinal Stritch U, WI — B
Carroll Coll, WI — B
Case Western Reserve U, OH — B
Cedarville U, OH — B
Central Christian Coll of Kansas, KS — B
Central Coll, IA — B
Central Methodist U, MO — B
Central Michigan U, MI — B
Central State U, OH — B
Chicago State U, IL — B
Clarke Coll, IA — B
Clarkson U, NY — B
Cleary U, MI — B
Cleveland State U, OH — B
Coe Coll, IA — B
Coll of Mount St. Joseph, OH — A,B
Coll of Saint Benedict, MN — B
Coll of St. Catherine, MN — B
Coll of Saint Mary, NE — A

The Coll of St. Scholastica, MN — B
Coll of the Ozarks, MO — B
Columbia Coll, MO — B
Concordia Coll, MN — B
Concordia U, IL — B
Concordia U, NE — B
Concordia U, St. Paul, MN — B
Concordia U Wisconsin, WI — B
Concord U, WV — B
Cornerstone U, MI — B
Creighton U, NE — B
Culver-Stockton Coll, MO — B
Dakota State U, SD — B
Dakota Wesleyan U, SD — B
Dana Coll, NE — B
Davenport U, Dearborn, MI — A,B
DePaul U, IL — B
Dickinson State U, ND — B
Doane Coll, NE — B
Dominican U, IL — B
Dordt Coll, IA — B
Drake U, IA — B
Drury U, MO — B
East Central U, OK — B
Eastern Illinois U, IL — B
Eastern Michigan U, MI — B
East-West U, IL — B
Edgewood Coll, WI — B
Elmhurst Coll, IL — B
Emporia State U, KS — B
Evangel U, MO — A,B
Everest Coll, Springfield, MO — A,B
Ferris State U, MI — A,B
Fontbonne U, MO — B
Fort Berthold Comm Coll, ND — A
Fort Hays State U, KS — B
Franciscan U of Steubenville, OH — A,B
Franklin Coll, IN — B
Gannon U, PA — B
Goshen Coll, IN — B
Grace Bible Coll, MI — B
Grace Coll, IN — B
Graceland U, IA — B
Grand Valley State U, MI — B
Grand View Coll, IA — B
Greenville Coll, IL — B
Gustavus Adolphus Coll, MN — B
Harris-Stowe State U, MO — B
Hastings Coll, NE — B
Heidelberg Coll, OH — B
Hillsdale Coll, MI — B
Hope Coll, MI — B
Huntington U, IN — B
Illinois Coll, IL — B
Illinois State U, IL — B
Illinois Wesleyan U, IL — B
Indiana State U, IN — B
Indiana Tech, IN — A,B
Indiana U Bloomington, IN — B
Indiana U Northwest, IN — B
Indiana U–Purdue U Fort Wayne, IN — B
Indiana Wesleyan U, IN — A,B
International Business Coll, Fort Wayne, IN — A,B

Iowa State U of Science and Technology, IA — B
Iowa Wesleyan Coll, IA — B
Jamestown Coll, ND — B
Judson Coll, IL — B
Kansas State U, KS — B
Kaplan U, IA — A
Kent State U, OH — B
Kent State U, Ashtabula Campus, OH — A
Kent State U, Tuscarawas Campus, OH — A
Kettering U, MI — B
Kilian Comm Coll, SD — A
Kuyper Coll, MI — B
Lakeland Coll, WI — B
Lake Superior State U, MI — A,B
Langston U, OK — B
Lewis Coll of Business, MI — A
Lewis U, IL — B
Lincoln U, MO — B
Lindenwood U, MO — B
Loras Coll, IA — B
Lourdes Coll, OH — B
Loyola U Chicago, IL — B
Luther Coll, IA — B
MacMurray Coll, IL — B
Madonna U, MI — B
Malone Coll, OH — B
Manchester Coll, IN — A,B
Marian Coll, IN — A,B
Marian Coll of Fond du Lac, WI — B
Marietta Coll, OH — B
Marquette U, WI — B
Marygrove Coll, MI — A
Maryville U of Saint Louis, MO — B
McKendree Coll, IL — B
Metropolitan State U, MN — B
Miami U, OH — B
Miami U Hamilton, OH — B
Miami U–Middletown Campus, OH — A
Michigan State U, MI — B
Michigan Technological U, MI — B
Millikin U, IL — B
Minnesota School of Business, MN — A,B
Minnesota School of Business–Brooklyn Center, MN — A,B
Minnesota School of Business–Plymouth, MN — A,B
Minnesota School of Business–Richfield, MN — A,B
Minnesota School of Business–St. Cloud, MN — A,B
Minnesota School of Business–Shakopee, MN — A,B
Minnesota State U Mankato, MN — B
Minot State U, ND — B
Missouri Baptist U, MO — B
Missouri Southern State U, MO — A,B
Missouri State U, MO — B
Missouri Valley Coll, MO — B

Missouri Western State U, MO — B
Morningside Coll, IA — B
Mount Marty Coll, SD — A,B
Mount Mary Coll, WI — B
Mount Mercy Coll, IA — B
Mount Union Coll, OH — B
Mount Vernon Nazarene U, OH — B
National American U, Rapid City, SD — A,B
Nebraska Wesleyan U, NE — B
Newman U, KS — B
North Carolina Ag and Tech State U, NC — B
North Central Coll, IL — B
North Dakota State U, ND — B
Northeastern Illinois U, IL — B
Northeastern State U, OK — B
Northern Illinois U, IL — B
Northern Michigan U, MI — B
Northern State U, SD — B
Northwestern Coll, IA — B
Northwestern Coll, MN — B
Northwestern Oklahoma State U, OK — B
Northwest Missouri State U, MO — B
Northwood U, MI — A,B
Notre Dame Coll, OH — B
Oakland U, MI — B
Oglala Lakota Coll, SD — A
Ohio Dominican U, OH — B
Ohio Northern U, OH — B
The Ohio State U, OH — B
Ohio Wesleyan U, OH — B
Oklahoma Christian U, OK — B
Oklahoma City U, OK — B
Oklahoma Panhandle State U, OK — B
Oklahoma State U, OK — B
Oklahoma Wesleyan U, OK — A,B
Oral Roberts U, OK — B
Otterbein Coll, OH — B
Park U, MO — B
Peru State Coll, NE — B
Pittsburg State U, KS — B
Purdue U, IN — B
Purdue U Calumet, IN — B
Purdue U North Central, IN — A
Quincy U, IL — B
Rochester Coll, MI — B
Rockford Business Coll, IL — A
Rockford Coll, IL — B
Rogers State U, OK — A
Roosevelt U, IL — B
Saginaw Valley State U, MI — B
St. Ambrose U, IA — B
St. Cloud State U, MN — B
St. Gregory's U, Shawnee, OK — B
Saint John's U, MN — B
Saint Joseph's Coll, IN — B
Saint Mary-of-the-Woods Coll, IN — B
Saint Mary's U of Minnesota, MN — B
St. Norbert Coll, WI — B
Saint Xavier U, IL — B

A—associate degree; B—bachelor's degree

Majors and Degrees
Administrative Assistant and Secretarial Science

Shawnee State U, OH	A
Silver Lake Coll, WI	B
Simpson Coll, IA	B
Southeastern Oklahoma State U, OK	B
Southeast Missouri State U, MO	B
Southern Illinois U Carbondale, IL	B
Southern Illinois U Edwardsville, IL	B
Southern Methodist U, TX	B
Southwest Baptist U, MO	A,B
Southwestern Oklahoma State U, OK	B
Southwest Minnesota State U, MN	A,B
Spring Arbor U, MI	B
Stephens Coll, MO	B
Tabor Coll, KS	B
Taylor U, IN	B
Tiffin U, OH	A,B
Transylvania U, KY	B
Trinity Christian Coll, IL	B
Trinity International U, IL	B
Tri-State U, IN	A,B
Truman State U, MO	B
Union Coll, NE	A,B
The U of Akron, OH	B
U of Central Oklahoma, OK	B
U of Charleston, WV	A,B
U of Cincinnati, OH	A,B
U of Dayton, OH	B
U of Evansville, IN	B
The U of Findlay, OH	A,B
U of Illinois at Chicago, IL	B
U of Illinois at Springfield, IL	B
U of Illinois at Urbana–Champaign, IL	B
U of Indianapolis, IN	B
The U of Iowa, IA	B
U of Kansas, KS	B
U of Mary, ND	A,B
U of Michigan–Dearborn, MI	B
U of Michigan–Flint, MI	B
U of Minnesota, Crookston, MN	A,B
U of Minnesota, Duluth, MN	B
U of Minnesota, Twin Cities Campus, MN	B
U of Missouri–Columbia, MO	B
U of Missouri–Kansas City, MO	B
U of Missouri–St. Louis, MO	B
U of Nebraska at Omaha, NE	B
U of Nebraska–Lincoln, NE	B
U of New Orleans, LA	B
U of North Dakota, ND	B
U of Northern Iowa, IA	B
U of Notre Dame, IN	B
U of Oklahoma, OK	B
U of Phoenix–Chicago Campus, IL	B
U of Phoenix–Cincinnati Campus, OH	B
U of Phoenix–Cleveland Campus, OH	A,B
U of Phoenix–Columbus Ohio Campus, OH	A,B
U of Phoenix–Indianapolis Campus, IN	A,B
U of Phoenix–Kansas City Campus, MO	B
U of Phoenix–Metro Detroit Campus, MI	B

U of Phoenix–Oklahoma City Campus, OK	B
U of Phoenix–St. Louis Campus, MO	A,B
U of Phoenix–Springfield Campus, MO	A,B
U of Phoenix–Tulsa Campus, OK	B
U of Phoenix–West Michigan Campus, MI	B
U of Phoenix–Wisconsin Campus, WI	B
U of Rio Grande, OH	A,B
U of St. Francis, IL	B
U of Saint Francis, IN	B
U of Saint Mary, KS	B
U of St. Thomas, MN	B
U of Sioux Falls, SD	B
The U of South Dakota, SD	B
U of Southern Indiana, IN	B
The U of Toledo, OH	A,B
U of Tulsa, OK	B
U of West Florida, FL	B
U of Wisconsin–Eau Claire, WI	B
U of Wisconsin–Green Bay, WI	B
U of Wisconsin–La Crosse, WI	B
U of Wisconsin–Madison, WI	B
U of Wisconsin–Milwaukee, WI	B
U of Wisconsin–Oshkosh, WI	B
U of Wisconsin–Parkside, WI	B
U of Wisconsin–Platteville, WI	B
U of Wisconsin–River Falls, WI	B
U of Wisconsin–Stevens Point, WI	B
U of Wisconsin–Superior, WI	B
U of Wisconsin–Whitewater, WI	B
Upper Iowa U, IA	B
Ursuline Coll, OH	B
Valparaiso U, IN	B
Viterbo U, WI	B
Walsh U, OH	A,B
Wartburg Coll, IA	B
Washburn U, KS	B
Washington U in St. Louis, MO	B
Wayne State Coll, NE	B
Webster U, MO	B
Western Illinois U, IL	B
Western Michigan U, MI	B
Westminster Coll, MO	B
Wichita State U, KS	B
William Jewell Coll, MO	B
William Penn U, IA	B
William Woods U, MO	B
Wilmington Coll, OH	B
Winona State U, MN	B
Wright State U, OH	B
Xavier U, OH	B
York Coll, NE	B
Youngstown State U, OH	A,B

Accounting and Business/Management
Central Christian Coll of Kansas, KS	A,B
Illinois State U, IL	B
ITT Tech Inst, Kansas City, MO	

Accounting and Finance
Drake U, IA	B
Hiram Coll, OH	B

Kettering U, MI	B
U of North Dakota, ND	B

Accounting Related
Central Michigan U, MI	B
Maryville U of Saint Louis, MO	B
Park U, MO	A,B
Saint Mary-of-the-Woods Coll, IN	B

Accounting Technology and Bookkeeping
Baker Coll of Flint, MI	A
Bowling Green State U–Firelands Coll, OH	A
Cleary U, MI	A
Gannon U, PA	A
ITT Tech Inst, Fort Wayne, IN	B
ITT Tech Inst, Indianapolis, IN	B
ITT Tech Inst, Arnold, MO	B
ITT Tech Inst, Earth City, MO	B
ITT Tech Inst, Kansas City, MO	B
ITT Tech Inst, NE	B
Kent State U, Geauga Campus, OH	A
Ohio U, OH	A
Robert Morris Coll, IL	A
St. Augustine Coll, IL	A
Turtle Mountain Comm Coll, ND	A
The U of Akron, OH	A
U of Rio Grande, OH	A
Wright State U, OH	A

Acting
Bowling Green State U, OH	B
Central Christian Coll of Kansas, KS	A
Coe Coll, IA	B
Coll of the Ozarks, MO	B
Columbia Coll Chicago, IL	B
DePaul U, IL	B
Drake U, IA	B
Kent State U, OH	B
Ohio U, OH	B
St. Cloud State U, MN	B
The U of Akron, OH	B
U of Northern Iowa, IA	B
Western Michigan U, MI	B

Actuarial Science
Ball State U, IN	B
Bradley U, IL	B
Butler U, IN	B
Carroll Coll, WI	B
Central Michigan U, MI	B
Drake U, IA	B
Eastern Michigan U, MI	B
Elmhurst Coll, IL	B
Ferris State U, MI	B
Indiana U Northwest, IN	B
Jamestown Coll, ND	B
Maryville U of Saint Louis, MO	B
Michigan Technological U, MI	B
North Central Coll, IL	B
Northwestern Coll, IA	B
The Ohio State U, OH	B
Roosevelt U, IL	B
Tabor Coll, KS	B
U of Central Oklahoma, OK	B
U of Illinois at Urbana–Champaign, IL	B
The U of Iowa, IA	B
U of Michigan–Flint, MI	B

U of Minnesota, Duluth, MN	B
U of Minnesota, Twin Cities Campus, MN	B
U of Nebraska–Lincoln, NE	B
U of Northern Iowa, IA	B
U of St. Thomas, MN	B
U of Wisconsin–Madison, WI	B
U of Wisconsin–Stevens Point, WI	B
Valparaiso U, IN	B

Administrative Assistant and Secretarial Science
AIB Coll of Business, IA	A
Baker Coll of Auburn Hills, MI	A
Baker Coll of Cadillac, MI	A
Baker Coll of Clinton Township, MI	A
Baker Coll of Flint, MI	A,B
Baker Coll of Jackson, MI	A
Baker Coll of Muskegon, MI	A,B
Baker Coll of Owosso, MI	A,B
Baker Coll of Port Huron, MI	A,B
Ball State U, IN	B
Baptist Bible Coll, MO	A,B
Black Hills State U, SD	A
Bryant and Stratton Coll, Cleveland, OH	A
Cedarville U, OH	B
Davenport U, Dearborn, MI	A
Dickinson State U, ND	A
Dordt Coll, IA	A
East-West U, IL	B
Evangel U, MO	A,B
Faith Baptist Bible Coll and Theological Seminary, IA	A
Fort Berthold Comm Coll, ND	A
Fort Hays State U, KS	A,B
God's Bible School and Coll, OH	A
Grace Coll, IN	A
International Business Coll, Fort Wayne, IN	A,B
Kent State U, Ashtabula Campus, OH	A
Kent State U, Tuscarawas Campus, OH	A
Kilian Comm Coll, SD	A
Kuyper Coll, MI	A
Langston U, OK	B
Lewis Coll of Business, MI	A
Maranatha Baptist Bible Coll, WI	A,B
Mayville State U, ND	A,B
Miami U–Middletown Campus, OH	A
Minnesota School of Business, MN	A
Minnesota School of Business–Brooklyn Center, MN	
Minnesota School of Business–Plymouth, MN	A
Minnesota School of Business–Richfield, MN	A
Minnesota School of Business–St. Cloud, MN	A
North Carolina Ag and Tech State U, NC	B
Northern State U, SD	A,B
Northwest Missouri State U, MO	B
Oglala Lakota Coll, SD	A
Ohio U, OH	A
Oklahoma Wesleyan U, OK	A
Robert Morris Coll, IL	A
Rogers State U, OK	A
St. Augustine Coll, IL	A

Sitting Bull Coll, ND	A
Southeast Missouri State U, MO	B
Tabor Coll, KS	A,B
Turtle Mountain Comm Coll, ND	A
The U of Akron, OH	A
U of Central Missouri, MO	A
U of Cincinnati, OH	A
The U of Findlay, OH	A
U of Rio Grande, OH	A
U of Sioux Falls, SD	A,B
The U of Toledo, OH	A
Washburn U, KS	A
Wright State U, OH	A

Adult and Continuing Education

Dakota Wesleyan U, SD	B
DePaul U, IL	B
Iowa Wesleyan Coll, IA	B
Tabor Coll, KS	B
U of Central Oklahoma, OK	B
The U of Toledo, OH	B

Adult Development and Aging

Bowling Green State U, OH	B
Madonna U, MI	A,B
Saint Mary-of-the-Woods Coll, IN	A,B
The U of Toledo, OH	A

Adult Health Nursing

Wright State U, OH	B

Advertising

Ball State U, IN	B
Bradley U, IL	B
Central Michigan U, MI	B
Clarke Coll, IA	B
Columbia Coll Chicago, IL	B
Concordia Coll, MN	B
DePaul U, IL	B
Drake U, IA	B
Drury U, MO	B
East Central U, OK	B
Ferris State U, MI	B
Fontbonne U, MO	B
Gannon U, PA	B
Grand Valley State U, MI	B
Hastings Coll, NE	B
The Illinois Inst of Art–Schaumburg, IL	B
Iowa State U of Science and Technology, IA	B
Kent State U, OH	B
Marquette U, WI	B
Metropolitan State U, MN	B
Michigan State U, MI	B
Minneapolis Coll of Art and Design, MN	B
Northwest Missouri State U, MO	B
Northwood U, MI	A,B
Ohio U, OH	B
Oklahoma Christian U, OK	B
Oklahoma City U, OK	B
St. Ambrose U, IA	B
St. Cloud State U, MN	B
Simpson Coll, IA	B
Southern Methodist U, TX	B
Stephens Coll, MO	B
U of Central Oklahoma, OK	B
U of Illinois at Urbana–Champaign, IL	B
U of Missouri–Columbia, MO	B
U of Nebraska–Lincoln, NE	B

U of Oklahoma, OK	B
U of Southern Indiana, IN	B
U of Wisconsin–Madison, WI	B
Washington U in St. Louis, MO	B
Wayne State Coll, NE	B
Webster U, MO	B
William Woods U, MO	B
Winona State U, MN	B
Xavier U, OH	A,B
Youngstown State U, OH	B

Aeronautical/Aerospace Engineering Technology

Ohio U, OH	B
Purdue U, IN	A
Saint Louis U, MO	B
U of Central Missouri, MO	B

Aeronautics/Aviation/Aerospace Science and Technology

Augsburg Coll, MN	B
Hesston Coll, KS	A
Indiana State U, IN	A
Kansas State U, KS	B
Kent State U, OH	B
Ohio U, OH	B
Oklahoma State U, OK	B
Purdue U, IN	A,B
U of Nebraska at Omaha, NE	B
U of North Dakota, ND	B
U of Oklahoma, OK	B

Aerospace, Aeronautical and Astronautical Engineering

Case Western Reserve U, OH	B
Clarkson U, NY	B
Illinois Inst of Technology, IL	B
Iowa State U of Science and Technology, IA	B
Miami U, OH	B
The Ohio State U, OH	B
Oklahoma State U, OK	B
Purdue U, IN	B
Saint Louis U, MO	B
U of Cincinnati, OH	B
U of Illinois at Urbana–Champaign, IL	B
U of Kansas, KS	B
U of Michigan, MI	B
U of Minnesota, Twin Cities Campus, MN	B
U of Missouri–Rolla, MO	B
U of Notre Dame, IN	B
U of Oklahoma, OK	B
Washington U in St. Louis, MO	B
Western Michigan U, MI	B
Wichita State U, KS	B

African-American/Black Studies

Antioch Coll, OH	B
Chicago State U, IL	B
Coe Coll, IA	B
The Coll of Wooster, OH	B
Denison U, OH	B
DePaul U, IL	B
DePauw U, IN	B
Earlham Coll, IN	B
Eastern Illinois U, IL	B
Eastern Michigan U, MI	B
Indiana State U, IN	B
Indiana U Bloomington, IN	B
Indiana U Northwest, IN	B

Kent State U, OH	B
Kenyon Coll, OH	B
Knox Coll, IL	B
Luther Coll, IA	B
Marquette U, WI	B
Miami U, OH	B
Northwestern U, IL	B
Oberlin Coll, OH	B
The Ohio State U, OH	B
Ohio U, OH	B
Ohio Wesleyan U, OH	B
Purdue U, IN	B
Roosevelt U, IL	B
Southern Methodist U, TX	B
U of Chicago, IL	B
U of Cincinnati, OH	B
U of Illinois at Chicago, IL	B
The U of Iowa, IA	B
U of Kansas, KS	B
U of Michigan, MI	B
U of Michigan–Flint, MI	B
U of Minnesota, Twin Cities Campus, MN	B
U of Nebraska at Omaha, NE	B
U of Oklahoma, OK	B
The U of Toledo, OH	B
U of Wisconsin–Madison, WI	B
U of Wisconsin–Milwaukee, WI	B
Washington U in St. Louis, MO	B
Western Illinois U, IL	B
Wright State U, OH	B
Youngstown State U, OH	B

African Languages

Ohio U, OH	B
U of Wisconsin–Madison, WI	B

African Studies

Antioch Coll, OH	B
Bowling Green State U, OH	B
Carleton Coll, MN	B
DePaul U, IL	B
Illinois Wesleyan U, IL	B
Indiana U Bloomington, IN	B
Kenyon Coll, OH	B
Northwestern U, IL	B
The Ohio State U, OH	B
Ohio U, OH	B
U of Chicago, IL	B
The U of Iowa, IA	B
U of Kansas, KS	B
U of Minnesota, Twin Cities Campus, MN	B
U of Wisconsin–Madison, WI	B
Washington U in St. Louis, MO	B
Western Michigan U, MI	B

Agribusiness

Andrews U, MI	B
Coll of the Ozarks, MO	B
Illinois State U, IL	B
Lindenwood U, MO	B
Missouri State U, MO	B
North Dakota State U, ND	B
Northwestern Coll, IA	B
Sitting Bull Coll, ND	A
South Dakota State U, SD	B
Southeast Missouri State U, MO	B
U of Central Missouri, MO	B
U of Illinois at Urbana–Champaign, IL	B

Agricultural and Food Products Processing

Kansas State U, KS	B
The Ohio State U, OH	B

Agricultural/Biological Engineering and Bioengineering

Dordt Coll, IA	B
Iowa State U of Science and Technology, IA	B
Kansas State U, KS	B
Michigan State U, MI	B
North Dakota State U, ND	B
The Ohio State U, OH	B
Purdue U, IN	B
South Dakota State U, SD	B
U of Illinois at Urbana–Champaign, IL	B
U of Minnesota, Twin Cities Campus, MN	B
U of Missouri–Rolla, MO	B
U of Nebraska–Lincoln, NE	B
U of Wisconsin–Madison, WI	B
U of Wisconsin–River Falls, WI	B

Agricultural Business and Management

Andrews U, MI	A,B
Capital U, OH	B
Central Christian Coll of Kansas, KS	A
Dickinson State U, ND	A,B
Dordt Coll, IA	A,B
Fort Hays State U, KS	B
Iowa State U of Science and Technology, IA	B
Kansas State U, KS	B
Lincoln U, MO	B
Michigan State U, MI	B
North Carolina Ag and Tech State U, NC	B
North Dakota State U, ND	B
Northwestern Oklahoma State U, OK	B
Northwest Missouri State U, MO	B
The Ohio State U, OH	B
Oklahoma Panhandle State U, OK	B
Oklahoma State U, OK	B
Rogers State U, OK	A
Southwest Minnesota State U, MN	A,B
Tabor Coll, KS	B
Truman State U, MO	B
U of Central Missouri, MO	B
U of Minnesota, Crookston, MN	A,B
U of Minnesota, Twin Cities Campus, MN	B
U of Missouri–Columbia, MO	B
U of Nebraska at Kearney, NE	B
U of Nebraska–Lincoln, NE	B
U of Wisconsin–Madison, WI	B
U of Wisconsin–Platteville, WI	B
U of Wisconsin–River Falls, WI	B
Upper Iowa U, IA	B
Wayne State Coll, NE	B
Wilmington Coll, OH	B

Agricultural Communication/Journalism

Michigan State U, MI	B

A—associate degree; B—bachelor's degree

Oklahoma State U, OK — B
U of Illinois at Urbana–
  Champaign, IL — B
U of Missouri–Columbia, MO — B
U of Nebraska–Lincoln, NE — B

Agricultural Economics
Kansas State U, KS — B
Langston U, OK — B
Michigan State U, MI — B
North Carolina Ag and Tech
  State U, NC — B
North Dakota State U, ND — B
Northwest Missouri State U,
  MO — B
The Ohio State U, OH — B
Oklahoma State U, OK — B
Purdue U, IN — B
South Dakota State U, SD — B
Southern Illinois U
  Carbondale, IL — B
Truman State U, MO — B
U of Central Missouri, MO — B
U of Illinois at Urbana–
  Champaign, IL — B
U of Missouri–Columbia, MO — B
U of Nebraska–Lincoln, NE — B
U of Wisconsin–Madison, WI — B

Agricultural Mechanization
Andrews U, MI — A,B
Coll of the Ozarks, MO — B
Iowa State U of Science and
  Technology, IA — B
Kansas State U, KS — B
North Carolina Ag and Tech
  State U, NC — B
North Dakota State U, ND — B
Northwest Missouri State U,
  MO — B
Purdue U, IN — B
South Dakota State U, SD — B
U of Illinois at Urbana–
  Champaign, IL — B
U of Missouri–Columbia, MO — B
U of Nebraska–Lincoln, NE — B

Agricultural Mechanization Related
Coll of the Ozarks, MO — B

Agricultural Power Machinery Operation
U of Minnesota, Crookston,
  MN — B

Agricultural Sciences
Cameron U, OK — B

Agricultural Teacher Education
Andrews U, MI — B
Coll of the Ozarks, MO — B
Dordt Coll, IA — B
Iowa State U of Science and
  Technology, IA — B
Langston U, OK — B
Missouri State U, MO — B
North Carolina Ag and Tech
  State U, NC — B
North Dakota State U, ND — B
Northwest Missouri State U,
  MO — B
The Ohio State U, OH — B
Oklahoma Panhandle State U,
  OK — B
Oklahoma State U, OK — B
Purdue U, IN — B
South Dakota State U, SD — B
The U of Akron, OH — B

U of Illinois at Urbana–
  Champaign, IL — B
U of Minnesota, Crookston,
  MN — B
U of Minnesota, Twin Cities
  Campus, MN — B
U of Missouri–Columbia, MO — B
U of Nebraska–Lincoln, NE — B
U of Wisconsin–Madison, WI — B
U of Wisconsin–Platteville, WI — B
U of Wisconsin–River Falls,
  WI — B
Wilmington Coll, OH — B

Agriculture
Andrews U, MI — A,B
Dordt Coll, IA — B
Fort Hays State U, KS — B
Illinois State U, IL — B
Iowa State U of Science and
  Technology, IA — B
Lincoln U, MO — B
Missouri State U, MO — B
North Carolina Ag and Tech
  State U, NC — B
North Dakota State U, ND — B
Northwestern Oklahoma State
  U, OK — B
Northwest Missouri State U,
  MO — B
Oglala Lakota Coll, SD — A
Oklahoma Panhandle State U,
  OK — A
Oklahoma State U, OK — B
Purdue U, IN — A,B
South Dakota State U, SD — A,B
Southeast Missouri State U,
  MO — B
Southern Illinois U
  Carbondale, IL — B
Truman State U, MO — B
U of Illinois at Urbana–
  Champaign, IL — B
U of Minnesota, Crookston,
  MN — A,B
U of Minnesota, Twin Cities
  Campus, MN — B
U of Missouri–Columbia, MO — B
U of Nebraska–Lincoln, NE — B
U of Wisconsin–Madison, WI — B
U of Wisconsin–River Falls,
  WI — B
Western Illinois U, IL — B
Wilmington Coll, OH — B

Agriculture and Agriculture Operations Related
Michigan State U, MI — B

Agronomy and Crop Science
Andrews U, MI — A,B
Coll of the Ozarks, MO — B
Fort Hays State U, KS — B
Iowa State U of Science and
  Technology, IA — B
Kansas State U, KS — B
Missouri State U, MO — B
Northwest Missouri State U,
  MO — B
The Ohio State U, OH — B
Oklahoma Panhandle State U,
  OK — B
Purdue U, IN — B
South Dakota State U, SD — B
Southwest Minnesota State U,
  MN — B
Truman State U, MO — B

U of Illinois at Urbana–
  Champaign, IL — B
U of Minnesota, Crookston,
  MN — A,B
U of Minnesota, Twin Cities
  Campus, MN — B
U of Nebraska–Lincoln, NE — B
U of Wisconsin–Madison, WI — B
U of Wisconsin–Platteville, WI — B
U of Wisconsin–River Falls,
  WI — B

Air Force ROTC/Air Science
The U of Iowa, IA — B

Airframe Mechanics and Aircraft Maintenance Technology
Kansas State U, KS — A
Lewis U, IL — A,B

Airline Flight Attendant
The U of Akron, OH — A

Airline Pilot and Flight Crew
Academy Coll, MN — A
Andrews U, MI — A,B
Baker Coll of Flint, MI — A
Baker Coll of Muskegon, MI — A
Central Christian Coll of
  Kansas, KS — A
Cornerstone U, MI — B
Eastern Michigan U, MI — B
Indiana State U, IN — B
Kansas State U, KS — A,B
Lewis U, IL — B
Quincy U, IL — B
St. Cloud State U, MN — B
Saint Louis U, MO — B
Southeastern Oklahoma State
  U, OK — B
Southern Illinois U
  Carbondale, IL — A
U of Illinois at Urbana–
  Champaign, IL — B
Western Michigan U, MI — B

Air Traffic Control
St. Cloud State U, MN — B
U of North Dakota, ND — B

Allied Health and Medical Assisting Services Related
Washburn U, KS — A,B

Allied Health Diagnostic, Intervention, and Treatment Professions Related
Cameron U, OK — A
The U of Akron, OH — A
The U of Toledo, OH — A

American Government and Politics
Drury U, MO — B
Oklahoma Christian U, OK — B
The U of Akron, OH — B

American Indian/Native American Studies
Bemidji State U, MN — B
Black Hills State U, SD — B
Creighton U, NE — B
Northeastern State U, OK — B
Northland Coll, WI — B
Oglala Lakota Coll, SD — A,B
Rogers State U, OK — A
Saginaw Chippewa Tribal Coll,
  MI — A
Sitting Bull Coll, ND — A

The U of Iowa, IA — B
U of Minnesota, Duluth, MN — B
U of Minnesota, Twin Cities
  Campus, MN — B
U of North Dakota, ND — B
U of Oklahoma, OK — B
U of Science and Arts of
  Oklahoma, OK — B
The U of South Dakota, SD — B
U of Wisconsin–Eau Claire,
  WI — B
U of Wisconsin–Milwaukee,
  WI — B

American Literature
Washington U in St. Louis,
  MO — B

American Native/Native American Education
The Coll of St. Scholastica,
  MN — B

American Native/Native American Languages
Bemidji State U, MN — B

American Sign Language (ASL)
Augustana Coll, SD — B
Madonna U, MI — A,B

American Sign Language Related
The U of Iowa, IA — B

American Studies
Albion Coll, MI — B
Ashland U, OH — B
Bowling Green State U, OH — B
Carleton Coll, MN — B
Case Western Reserve U, OH — B
Cedarville U, OH — B
Coe Coll, IA — B
Creighton U, NE — B
DePaul U, IL — B
Dominican U, IL — B
Elmhurst Coll, IL — B
Franklin Coll, IN — B
Hillsdale Coll, MI — B
Illinois Wesleyan U, IL — B
Kent State U, OH — B
Kenyon Coll, OH — B
Knox Coll, IL — B
Lake Forest Coll, IL — B
Lewis U, IL — B
Miami U, OH — B
Miami U Hamilton, OH — B
Michigan State U, MI — B
Mount Union Coll, OH — B
Northwestern U, IL — B
Oakland U, MI — B
Oklahoma City U, OK — B
Oklahoma State U, OK — B
St. Cloud State U, MN — B
Saint Louis U, MO — B
St. Olaf Coll, MN — B
Southeast Missouri State U,
  MO — B
U of Chicago, IL — B
U of Dayton, OH — B
The U of Iowa, IA — B
U of Kansas, KS — B
U of Michigan, MI — B
U of Michigan–Dearborn, MI — B
U of Minnesota, Twin Cities
  Campus, MN — B
U of Missouri–Kansas City,
  MO — B
U of Northern Iowa, IA — B

U of Notre Dame, IN	B
U of Rio Grande, OH	B
The U of Toledo, OH	B
U of Wisconsin–Madison, WI	B
Ursuline Coll, OH	B
Valparaiso U, IN	B
Washington U in St. Louis, MO	B
Western Michigan U, MI	B
Wittenberg U, OH	B
Youngstown State U, OH	B

Anatomy

Andrews U, MI	B
Minnesota State U Mankato, MN	B
Wright State U, OH	B

Ancient/Classical Greek

Carleton Coll, MN	B
Creighton U, NE	B
DePauw U, IN	B
Indiana U Bloomington, IN	B
Kenyon Coll, OH	B
Lawrence U, WI	B
Loyola U Chicago, IL	B
Miami U, OH	B
Ohio U, OH	B
Rockford Coll, IL	B
St. Olaf Coll, MN	B
U of Chicago, IL	B
The U of Iowa, IA	B
U of Nebraska–Lincoln, NE	B
U of Notre Dame, IN	B
U of St. Thomas, MN	B
Washington U in St. Louis, MO	B

Ancient Near Eastern and Biblical Languages

Concordia U, IL	B
Concordia U, MI	B
Concordia U Wisconsin, WI	B
Cornerstone U, MI	B
Hope Coll, MI	B
Indiana Wesleyan U, IN	A,B
Ozark Christian Coll, MO	B
Taylor U, IN	B
U of Chicago, IL	B
York Coll, NE	B

Ancient Studies

Michigan State U, MI	B
Missouri State U, MO	B
Ohio Wesleyan U, OH	B
Rockford Coll, IL	B
St. Olaf Coll, MN	B
The U of Iowa, IA	B
U of Kansas, KS	B

Animal Behavior and Ethology

Carroll Coll, WI	B

Animal Genetics

Ball State U, IN	B
Missouri Southern State U, MO	B
The Ohio State U, OH	B
Ohio Wesleyan U, OH	B
U of Minnesota, Twin Cities Campus, MN	B
U of Wisconsin–Madison, WI	B

Animal/Livestock Husbandry and Production

Dordt Coll, IA	B
Saint Mary-of-the-Woods Coll, IN	A,B

Animal Physiology

Minnesota State U Mankato, MN	B
The U of Akron, OH	B
U of Minnesota, Twin Cities Campus, MN	B

Animal Sciences

Coll of the Ozarks, MO	B
Dordt Coll, IA	B
Fort Hays State U, KS	B
Iowa State U of Science and Technology, IA	B
Kansas State U, KS	B
Langston U, OK	B
Michigan State U, MI	B
Missouri State U, MO	B
North Carolina Ag and Tech State U, NC	B
North Dakota State U, ND	B
Northwest Missouri State U, MO	B
The Ohio State U, OH	B
Oklahoma Panhandle State U, OK	B
Oklahoma State U, OK	B
Purdue U, IN	B
South Dakota State U, SD	B
Southern Illinois U Carbondale, IL	B
Truman State U, MO	B
U of Illinois at Urbana–Champaign, IL	B
U of Minnesota, Crookston, MN	A,B
U of Minnesota, Twin Cities Campus, MN	B
U of Missouri–Columbia, MO	B
U of Nebraska–Lincoln, NE	B
U of Wisconsin–Madison, WI	B
U of Wisconsin–Platteville, WI	B
U of Wisconsin–River Falls, WI	B

Animation, Interactive Technology, Video Graphics and Special Effects

The Art Insts International Minnesota, MN	B
The Illinois Inst of Art–Chicago, IL	A,B
The Illinois Inst of Art–Schaumburg, IL	B
ITT Tech Inst, Fort Wayne, IN	B
ITT Tech Inst, Newburgh, IN	B
ITT Tech Inst, MN	B
ITT Tech Inst, Arnold, MO	B
ITT Tech Inst, Earth City, MO	B
ITT Tech Inst, NE	B
ITT Tech Inst, Green Bay, WI	B
ITT Tech Inst, Greenfield, WI	B
Kent State U, Tuscarawas Campus, OH	A
North Central Coll, IL	B
School of the Art Inst of Chicago, IL	B

Anthropology

Albion Coll, MI	B
Alma Coll, MI	B
Antioch Coll, OH	B
Augustana Coll, IL	B
Ball State U, IN	B
Beloit Coll, WI	B
Butler U, IN	B
Carleton Coll, MN	B
Case Western Reserve U, OH	B
Central Michigan U, MI	B
Cleveland State U, OH	B
Cornell Coll, IA	B
Denison U, OH	B
DePaul U, IL	B
DePauw U, IN	B
Drake U, IA	B
Eastern Michigan U, MI	B
Franciscan U of Steubenville, OH	B
Grand Valley State U, MI	B
Grinnell Coll, IA	B
Gustavus Adolphus Coll, MN	B
Hamline U, MN	B
Hanover Coll, IN	B
Heidelberg Coll, OH	B
Illinois State U, IL	B
Indiana State U, IN	B
Indiana U Bloomington, IN	B
Indiana U–Purdue U Fort Wayne, IN	B
Indiana U–Purdue U Indianapolis, IN	B
Iowa State U of Science and Technology, IA	B
Judson Coll, IL	B
Kalamazoo Coll, MI	B
Kansas State U, KS	B
Kent State U, OH	B
Kenyon Coll, OH	B
Knox Coll, IL	B
Lake Forest Coll, IL	B
Lawrence U, WI	B
Loyola U Chicago, IL	B
Luther Coll, IA	B
Macalester Coll, MN	B
Marquette U, WI	B
Miami U, OH	B
Miami U Hamilton, OH	B
Miami U–Middletown Campus, OH	A
Michigan State U, MI	B
Minnesota State U Mankato, MN	B
Missouri State U, MO	B
North Central Coll, IL	B
Northeastern Illinois U, IL	B
Northern Illinois U, IL	B
Northwestern U, IL	B
Oakland U, MI	B
Oberlin Coll, OH	B
The Ohio State U, OH	B
Ohio U, OH	B
Ohio Wesleyan U, OH	B
Ripon Coll, WI	B
Rockford Coll, IL	B
St. Cloud State U, MN	B
Southeast Missouri State U, MO	B
Southern Illinois U Carbondale, IL	B
Southern Illinois U Edwardsville, IL	B
Southern Methodist U, TX	B
Transylvania U, KY	B
U of Chicago, IL	B
U of Cincinnati, OH	B
U of Illinois at Chicago, IL	B
U of Illinois at Springfield, IL	B
U of Illinois at Urbana–Champaign, IL	B
U of Indianapolis, IN	B
The U of Iowa, IA	B
U of Kansas, KS	B
U of Michigan, MI	B
U of Michigan–Dearborn, MI	B
U of Michigan–Flint, MI	B
U of Minnesota, Duluth, MN	B
U of Minnesota, Morris, MN	B
U of Minnesota, Twin Cities Campus, MN	B
U of Missouri–Columbia, MO	B
U of Missouri–St. Louis, MO	B
U of Nebraska–Lincoln, NE	B
U of New Orleans, LA	B
U of North Dakota, ND	B
U of Northern Iowa, IA	B
U of Notre Dame, IN	B
U of Oklahoma, OK	B
The U of South Dakota, SD	B
The U of Toledo, OH	B
U of Tulsa, OK	B
U of West Florida, FL	B
U of Wisconsin–Madison, WI	B
U of Wisconsin–Milwaukee, WI	B
U of Wisconsin–Oshkosh, WI	B
Washburn U, KS	B
Washington U in St. Louis, MO	B
Webster U, MO	B
Western Michigan U, MI	B
Westminster Coll, MO	B
Wheaton Coll, IL	B
Wichita State U, KS	B
Wright State U, OH	B
Youngstown State U, OH	B

Apparel and Accessories Marketing

Bluffton U, OH	B
The Illinois Inst of Art–Chicago, IL	B

Apparel and Textiles

Coll of the Ozarks, MO	B
The Illinois Inst of Art–Chicago, IL	A
Indiana State U, IN	B
Indiana U Bloomington, IN	B
Iowa State U of Science and Technology, IA	B
Kansas State U, KS	B
Michigan State U, MI	B
Missouri State U, MO	B
North Dakota State U, ND	B
Northern Illinois U, IL	B
The Ohio State U, OH	B
Ohio U, OH	B
Purdue U, IN	B
Southern Illinois U Carbondale, IL	B
The U of Akron, OH	B
U of Central Missouri, MO	B
U of Illinois at Urbana–Champaign, IL	B
U of Missouri–Columbia, MO	B
U of Nebraska–Lincoln, NE	B
U of Northern Iowa, IA	B
U of Wisconsin–Stout, WI	B
Western Michigan U, MI	B

Applied Art

Bemidji State U, MN	B
Chicago State U, IL	B
Cleveland State U, OH	B
DePaul U, IL	B
Indiana U Bloomington, IN	B
Lindenwood U, MO	B
Marygrove Coll, MI	B

A—associate degree; B—bachelor's degree

Minnesota State U Mankato, MN — B
Peru State Coll, NE — B
St. Cloud State U, MN — B
Truman State U, MO — B
The U of Akron, OH — B
U of Dayton, OH — B
U of Sioux Falls, SD — B
The U of Toledo, OH — B
U of Wisconsin–Madison, WI — B
Washington U in St. Louis, MO — B
Winona State U, MN — B

Applied Economics
The Coll of St. Scholastica, MN — B
Michigan State U, MI — B
Southern Methodist U, TX — B
U of Northern Iowa, IA — B

Applied Horticulture
Coll of the Ozarks, MO — B
Iowa State U of Science and Technology, IA — B
Kent State U, Geauga Campus, OH — A
South Dakota State U, SD — B

Applied Mathematics
Bowling Green State U, OH — B
Case Western Reserve U, OH — B
Central Methodist U, MO — A
Clarkson U, NY — B
Coll of Mount St. Joseph, OH — B
Creighton U, NE — B
DePaul U, IL — B
Ferris State U, MI — B
Grand Valley State U, MI — B
Grand View Coll, IA — B
Illinois Inst of Technology, IL — B
Indiana U South Bend, IN — B
Jamestown Coll, ND — B
Kent State U, OH — B
Kettering U, MI — B
Maryville U of Saint Louis, MO — B
Metropolitan State U, MN — B
Michigan State U, MI — B
Michigan Technological U, MI — B
Millikin U, IL — B
North Carolina Ag and Tech State U, NC — B
North Central Coll, IL — B
Northern Illinois U, IL — B
Northland Coll, WI — B
Northwestern U, IL — B
Ohio U, OH — B
Shawnee State U, OH — B
The U of Akron, OH — B
U of Central Oklahoma, OK — B
U of Chicago, IL — B
U of Michigan, MI — B
U of Missouri–Rolla, MO — B
U of Missouri–St. Louis, MO — B
U of Northern Iowa, IA — B
U of Sioux Falls, SD — B
U of Tulsa, OK — B
U of Wisconsin–Madison, WI — B
U of Wisconsin–Milwaukee, WI — B
U of Wisconsin–Stout, WI — B
Washington U in St. Louis, MO — B
Wayne State Coll, NE — B
Western Michigan U, MI — B
Winona State U, MN — B
Wright State U, OH — B

Applied Mathematics Related
Carroll Coll, WI — B
Saint Mary's Coll, IN — B
The U of Akron, OH — B
U of Dayton, OH — B
The U of Iowa, IA — B

Arabic
The Ohio State U, OH — B
U of Chicago, IL — B
U of Michigan, MI — B
U of Notre Dame, IN — B
Washington U in St. Louis, MO — B

Archeology
The Coll of Wooster, OH — B
Lawrence U, WI — B
Oberlin Coll, OH — B
U of Evansville, IN — B
U of Indianapolis, IN — B
U of Missouri–Columbia, MO — B
U of Wisconsin–La Crosse, WI — B
Washington U in St. Louis, MO — B
Wheaton Coll, IL — B

Architectural Drafting and CAD/CADD
Baker Coll of Flint, MI — A
Baker Coll of Muskegon, MI — A
Indiana State U, IN — A
Indiana U–Purdue U Indianapolis, IN — A
The U of Toledo, OH — A

Architectural Engineering
Andrews U, MI — B
Illinois Inst of Technology, IL — B
Kansas State U, KS — B
Milwaukee School of Engineering, WI — B
North Carolina Ag and Tech State U, NC — B
Oklahoma State U, OK — B
U of Cincinnati, OH — B
U of Kansas, KS — B
U of Missouri–Rolla, MO — B
U of Nebraska at Omaha, NE — B
U of Nebraska–Lincoln, NE — B

Architectural Engineering Technology
Baker Coll of Cadillac, MI — A
Baker Coll of Clinton Township, MI — A
Baker Coll of Owosso, MI — A
Baker Coll of Port Huron, MI — A
Ferris State U, MI — A
Indiana State U, IN — B
Indiana U–Purdue U Fort Wayne, IN — A
Indiana U–Purdue U Indianapolis, IN — B
Purdue U, IN — A,B
Purdue U Calumet, IN — A
Purdue U North Central, IN — A
U of Cincinnati, OH — A,B
Washington U in St. Louis, MO — B

Architectural History and Criticism
Miami U Hamilton, OH — B
U of Kansas, KS — B

Architectural Technology
Washington U in St. Louis, MO — B

Architecture
Andrews U, MI — B
Ball State U, IN — B
Central Christian Coll of Kansas, KS — A
Coe Coll, IA — B
Cornell Coll, IA — B
Drury U, MO — B
Eastern Michigan U, MI — B
Hope Coll, MI — B
Illinois Inst of Technology, IL — B
Iowa State U of Science and Technology, IA — B
Judson Coll, IL — B
Kansas State U, KS — B
Kent State U, OH — B
Lawrence Technological U, MI — B
Miami U, OH — B
Miami U Hamilton, OH — B
North Dakota State U, ND — B
The Ohio State U, OH — B
Oklahoma State U, OK — B
Southern Illinois U Carbondale, IL — B
U of Cincinnati, OH — B
U of Illinois at Chicago, IL — B
U of Kansas, KS — B
U of Michigan, MI — B
U of Minnesota, Twin Cities Campus, MN — B
U of Nebraska–Lincoln, NE — B
U of Notre Dame, IN — B
U of Oklahoma, OK — B
U of Wisconsin–Milwaukee, WI — B
Washington U in St. Louis, MO — B
Western Michigan U, MI — B

Architecture Related
School of the Art Inst of Chicago, IL — B
U of Illinois at Urbana–Champaign, IL — B
U of Oklahoma, OK — B
Washington U in St. Louis, MO — B

Area, Ethnic, Cultural, and Gender Studies Related
Bethel U, MN — B
Coe Coll, IA — B
The Coll of Wooster, OH — B
Columbia Coll Chicago, IL — B
Kent State U, OH — B
U of Chicago, IL — B
Washington U in St. Louis, MO — B

Area Studies
Denison U, OH — B
Hope Coll, MI — B
U of Oklahoma, OK — B

Area Studies Related
Gannon U, PA — B
Illinois Wesleyan U, IL — B
Kent State U, OH — B
Lewis U, IL — B
Northwestern U, IL — B
U of Illinois at Urbana–Champaign, IL — B
U of Michigan–Dearborn, MI — B
U of Oklahoma, OK — B
Washington U in St. Louis, MO — B
Wright State U, OH — B

Army ROTC/Military Science
Minnesota State U Mankato, MN — B
Northwest Missouri State U, MO — B
The U of Iowa, IA — B

Art
Adrian Coll, MI — A,B
Albion Coll, MI — B
Alma Coll, MI — B
Alverno Coll, WI — B
Andrews U, MI — B
Aquinas Coll, MI — B
Art Academy of Cincinnati, OH — B
Ashland U, OH — A,B
Augsburg Coll, MN — B
Augustana Coll, IL — B
Augustana Coll, SD — B
Ball State U, IN — B
Bemidji State U, MN — B
Benedictine Coll, KS — B
Bethany Coll, KS — B
Bethany Lutheran Coll, MN — B
Bethel U, MN — B
Blackburn Coll, IL — B
Black Hills State U, SD — B
Bluffton U, OH — B
Bradley U, IL — B
Briar Cliff U, IA — B
Buena Vista U, IA — B
Calvin Coll, MI — B
Cameron U, OK — B
Capital U, OH — B
Cardinal Stritch U, WI — B
Carroll Coll, WI — B
Central Christian Coll of Kansas, KS — A
Central Coll, IA — B
Central Michigan U, MI — B
Central State U, OH — B
Clarke Coll, IA — B
Cleveland State U, OH — B
Coe Coll, IA — B
Coll of Mount St. Joseph, OH — A,B
Coll of Saint Benedict, MN — B
Coll of St. Catherine, MN — B
Coll of Saint Mary, NE — B
Coll of the Ozarks, MO — B
Columbia Coll, MO — B
Columbia Coll Chicago, IL — B
Concordia Coll, MN — B
Concordia U, IL — B
Concordia U, MI — B
Concordia U, NE — B
Concordia U Wisconsin, WI — B
Cornell Coll, IA — B
Creighton U, NE — B
Culver-Stockton Coll, MO — B
Dakota Wesleyan U, SD — B
Dana Coll, NE — B
Denison U, OH — B
DePaul U, IL — B
Dickinson State U, ND — B
Doane Coll, NE — B
Drake U, IA — B
Drury U, MO — B
Earlham Coll, IN — B
East Central U, OK — B
Eastern Illinois U, IL — B
Eastern Michigan U, MI — B
Edgewood Coll, WI — B
Elmhurst Coll, IL — B
Emporia State U, KS — B
Evangel U, MO — B
Finlandia U, MI — B

Majors and Degrees

Art

Fontbonne U, MO	B	Northwestern Coll, IA	B	U of Northern Iowa, IA
Fort Hays State U, KS	B	Northwestern U, IL	B	U of Oklahoma, OK
Goshen Coll, IN	B	Northwest Missouri State U,		U of Rio Grande, OH

<table>
<tr><td>Fontbonne U, MO</td><td>B</td><td>Northwestern Coll, IA</td><td>B</td><td>U of Northern Iowa, IA</td><td>B</td><td>Dominican U, IL</td><td>B</td></tr>
<tr><td>Fort Hays State U, KS</td><td>B</td><td>Northwestern U, IL</td><td>B</td><td>U of Oklahoma, OK</td><td>B</td><td>Drake U, IA</td><td>B</td></tr>
<tr><td>Goshen Coll, IN</td><td>B</td><td>Northwest Missouri State U, MO</td><td>B</td><td>U of Rio Grande, OH</td><td>A,B</td><td>Drury U, MO</td><td>B</td></tr>
<tr><td>Grace Coll, IN</td><td>B</td><td>Notre Dame Coll, OH</td><td>B</td><td>U of Saint Francis, IN</td><td>B</td><td>Eastern Michigan U, MI</td><td>B</td></tr>
<tr><td>Graceland U, IA</td><td>B</td><td>Oberlin Coll, OH</td><td>B</td><td>U of Saint Mary, KS</td><td>B</td><td>Grand Valley State U, MI</td><td>B</td></tr>
<tr><td>Grand Valley State U, MI</td><td>B</td><td>Ohio Northern U, OH</td><td>B</td><td>U of Science and Arts of</td><td></td><td>Gustavus Adolphus Coll, MN</td><td>B</td></tr>
<tr><td>Grand View Coll, IA</td><td>B</td><td>The Ohio State U, OH</td><td>B</td><td>Oklahoma, OK</td><td>B</td><td>Hamline U, MN</td><td>B</td></tr>
<tr><td>Greenville Coll, IL</td><td>B</td><td>Oklahoma Christian U, OK</td><td>B</td><td>The U of South Dakota, SD</td><td>B</td><td>Hanover Coll, IN</td><td>B</td></tr>
<tr><td>Grinnell Coll, IA</td><td>B</td><td>Oklahoma State U, OK</td><td>B</td><td>U of Southern Indiana, IN</td><td>B</td><td>Hastings Coll, NE</td><td>B</td></tr>
<tr><td>Gustavus Adolphus Coll, MN</td><td>B</td><td>Ottawa U, KS</td><td>B</td><td>The U of Toledo, OH</td><td>A,B</td><td>Hiram Coll, OH</td><td>B</td></tr>
<tr><td>Hamline U, MN</td><td>B</td><td>Otterbein Coll, OH</td><td>B</td><td>U of West Florida, FL</td><td>B</td><td>Hope Coll, MI</td><td>B</td></tr>
<tr><td>Hannibal-LaGrange Coll, MO</td><td>B</td><td>Peru State Coll, NE</td><td>B</td><td>U of Wisconsin–Eau Claire, WI</td><td>B</td><td>Indiana U Bloomington, IN</td><td>B</td></tr>
<tr><td>Hanover Coll, IN</td><td>B</td><td>Pittsburg State U, KS</td><td>B</td><td>U of Wisconsin–Green Bay, WI</td><td>A,B</td><td>Indiana U–Purdue U Indianapolis, IN</td><td>B</td></tr>
<tr><td>Hastings Coll, NE</td><td>B</td><td>Purdue U, IN</td><td>B</td><td>U of Wisconsin–La Crosse, WI</td><td>B</td><td>Kalamazoo Coll, MI</td><td>B</td></tr>
<tr><td>Hillsdale Coll, MI</td><td>B</td><td>Ripon Coll, WI</td><td>B</td><td>U of Wisconsin–Madison, WI</td><td>B</td><td>Kansas City Art Inst, MO</td><td>B</td></tr>
<tr><td>Hiram Coll, OH</td><td>B</td><td>Rogers State U, OK</td><td>A</td><td>U of Wisconsin–Milwaukee, WI</td><td>B</td><td>Kent State U, OH</td><td>B</td></tr>
<tr><td>Huntington U, IN</td><td>B</td><td>Roosevelt U, IL</td><td>B</td><td>U of Wisconsin–Oshkosh, WI</td><td>B</td><td>Kenyon Coll, OH</td><td>B</td></tr>
<tr><td>Illinois Coll, IL</td><td>B</td><td>Saginaw Valley State U, MI</td><td>B</td><td>U of Wisconsin–Parkside, WI</td><td>B</td><td>Knox Coll, IL</td><td>B</td></tr>
<tr><td>Illinois State U, IL</td><td>B</td><td>St. Ambrose U, IA</td><td>B</td><td>U of Wisconsin–Platteville, WI</td><td>B</td><td>Lake Forest Coll, IL</td><td>B</td></tr>
<tr><td>Illinois Wesleyan U, IL</td><td>B</td><td>St. Cloud State U, MN</td><td>B</td><td>U of Wisconsin–River Falls, WI</td><td>B</td><td>Lawrence U, WI</td><td>B</td></tr>
<tr><td>Indiana State U, IN</td><td>B</td><td>St. Gregory's U, Shawnee, OK</td><td>A</td><td>U of Wisconsin–Whitewater, WI</td><td>B</td><td>Lindenwood U, MO</td><td>B</td></tr>
<tr><td>Indiana U Bloomington, IN</td><td>B</td><td>Saint John's U, MN</td><td>B</td><td>Upper Iowa U, IA</td><td>B</td><td>Lourdes Coll, OH</td><td>A,B</td></tr>
<tr><td>Indiana U Northwest, IN</td><td>B</td><td>Saint Mary-of-the-Woods Coll, IN</td><td>B</td><td>Valley City State U, ND</td><td>B</td><td>Macalester Coll, MN</td><td>B</td></tr>
<tr><td>Indiana U South Bend, IN</td><td>B</td><td>Saint Mary's Coll, IN</td><td>B</td><td>Valparaiso U, IN</td><td>B</td><td>MacMurray Coll, IL</td><td>B</td></tr>
<tr><td>Indiana U Southeast, IN</td><td>B</td><td>St. Norbert Coll, WI</td><td>B</td><td>Viterbo U, WI</td><td>B</td><td>Marian Coll, IN</td><td>B</td></tr>
<tr><td>Indiana Wesleyan U, IN</td><td>A,B</td><td>St. Olaf Coll, MN</td><td>B</td><td>Wabash Coll, IN</td><td>B</td><td>Miami U, OH</td><td>B</td></tr>
<tr><td>Iowa State U of Science and Technology, IA</td><td>B</td><td>Saint Xavier U, IL</td><td>B</td><td>Wartburg Coll, IA</td><td>B</td><td>Michigan State U, MI</td><td>B</td></tr>
<tr><td>Iowa Wesleyan Coll, IA</td><td>B</td><td>School of the Art Inst of Chicago, IL</td><td>B</td><td>Washburn U, KS</td><td>B</td><td>Minnesota State U Mankato, MN</td><td>B</td></tr>
<tr><td>Jamestown Coll, ND</td><td>B</td><td>Shawnee State U, OH</td><td>A,B</td><td>Washington U in St. Louis, MO</td><td>B</td><td>Northern Illinois U, IL</td><td>B</td></tr>
<tr><td>Judson Coll, IL</td><td>B</td><td>Silver Lake Coll, WI</td><td>B</td><td>Wayne State Coll, NE</td><td>B</td><td>Northwestern U, IL</td><td>B</td></tr>
<tr><td>Kalamazoo Coll, MI</td><td>B</td><td>Simpson Coll, IA</td><td>B</td><td>Webster U, MO</td><td>B</td><td>Oakland U, MI</td><td>B</td></tr>
<tr><td>Kansas State U, KS</td><td>B</td><td>South Dakota State U, SD</td><td>B</td><td>Western Illinois U, IL</td><td>B</td><td>Oberlin Coll, OH</td><td>B</td></tr>
<tr><td>Kenyon Coll, OH</td><td>B</td><td>Southeastern Oklahoma State U, OK</td><td>B</td><td>Western Michigan U, MI</td><td>B</td><td>The Ohio State U, OH</td><td>B</td></tr>
<tr><td>Knox Coll, IL</td><td>B</td><td>Southeast Missouri State U, MO</td><td>B</td><td>Wheaton Coll, IL</td><td>B</td><td>Ohio U, OH</td><td>B</td></tr>
<tr><td>Lakeland Coll, WI</td><td>B</td><td>Southern Illinois U Carbondale, IL</td><td>B</td><td>Wichita State U, KS</td><td>B</td><td>Ohio Wesleyan U, OH</td><td>B</td></tr>
<tr><td>Langston U, OK</td><td>B</td><td>Southern Illinois U Edwardsville, IL</td><td>B</td><td>William Jewell Coll, MO</td><td>B</td><td>Oklahoma City U, OK</td><td>B</td></tr>
<tr><td>Lewis U, IL</td><td>B</td><td>Southern Methodist U, TX</td><td>B</td><td>William Woods U, MO</td><td>B</td><td>Rockford Coll, IL</td><td>B</td></tr>
<tr><td>Lindenwood U, MO</td><td>B</td><td>Southwest Baptist U, MO</td><td>B</td><td>Winona State U, MN</td><td>B</td><td>Roosevelt U, IL</td><td>B</td></tr>
<tr><td>Lourdes Coll, OH</td><td>A,B</td><td>Southwest Minnesota State U, MN</td><td>B</td><td>Wisconsin Lutheran Coll, WI</td><td>B</td><td>St. Cloud State U, MN</td><td>B</td></tr>
<tr><td>Luther Coll, IA</td><td>B</td><td>Spring Arbor U, MI</td><td>B</td><td>Wittenberg U, OH</td><td>B</td><td>Saint Louis U, MO</td><td>B</td></tr>
<tr><td>MacMurray Coll, IL</td><td>B</td><td>Sterling Coll, KS</td><td>B</td><td>Wright State U, OH</td><td>B</td><td>St. Olaf Coll, MN</td><td>B</td></tr>
<tr><td>Madonna U, MI</td><td>A,B</td><td>Taylor U, IN</td><td>B</td><td>Xavier U, OH</td><td>B</td><td>School of the Art Inst of Chicago, IL</td><td>B</td></tr>
<tr><td>Manchester Coll, IN</td><td>A,B</td><td>Transylvania U, KY</td><td>B</td><td>Youngstown State U, OH</td><td>B</td><td>Southern Methodist U, TX</td><td>B</td></tr>
<tr><td>Marian Coll, IN</td><td>A,B</td><td>Trinity Christian Coll, IL</td><td>B</td><td></td><td></td><td>Transylvania U, KY</td><td>B</td></tr>
<tr><td>Marietta Coll, OH</td><td>B</td><td>Truman State U, MO</td><td>B</td><td colspan="2">Art History, Criticism and Conservation</td><td>Truman State U, MO</td><td>B</td></tr>
<tr><td>Marygrove Coll, MI</td><td>B</td><td>Turtle Mountain Comm Coll, ND</td><td>A</td><td>Andrews U, MI</td><td>B</td><td>The U of Akron, OH</td><td>B</td></tr>
<tr><td>McKendree Coll, IL</td><td>B</td><td>Union Coll, NE</td><td>A</td><td>Aquinas Coll, MI</td><td>B</td><td>U of Chicago, IL</td><td>B</td></tr>
<tr><td>Miami U, OH</td><td>B</td><td>The U of Akron, OH</td><td>B</td><td>Art Academy of Cincinnati, OH</td><td>B</td><td>U of Cincinnati, OH</td><td>B</td></tr>
<tr><td>Miami U Hamilton, OH</td><td>B</td><td>U of Central Oklahoma, OK</td><td>B</td><td>Augsburg Coll, MN</td><td>B</td><td>U of Dallas, TX</td><td>B</td></tr>
<tr><td>Miami U–Middletown Campus, OH</td><td>A</td><td>U of Charleston, WV</td><td>B</td><td>Augustana Coll, IL</td><td>B</td><td>U of Dayton, OH</td><td>B</td></tr>
<tr><td>Michigan State U, MI</td><td>B</td><td>U of Chicago, IL</td><td>B</td><td>Baker U, KS</td><td>B</td><td>U of Evansville, IN</td><td>B</td></tr>
<tr><td>Minnesota State U Mankato, MN</td><td>B</td><td>U of Cincinnati, OH</td><td>B</td><td>Baldwin-Wallace Coll, OH</td><td>B</td><td>U of Illinois at Chicago, IL</td><td>B</td></tr>
<tr><td>Minot State U, ND</td><td>B</td><td>U of Dallas, TX</td><td>B</td><td>Beloit Coll, WI</td><td>B</td><td>U of Illinois at Urbana–Champaign, IL</td><td>B</td></tr>
<tr><td>Missouri State U, MO</td><td>B</td><td>U of Evansville, IN</td><td>B</td><td>Blackburn Coll, IL</td><td>B</td><td>The U of Iowa, IA</td><td>B</td></tr>
<tr><td>Missouri Valley Coll, MO</td><td>B</td><td>The U of Findlay, OH</td><td>B</td><td>Bowling Green State U, OH</td><td>B</td><td>U of Kansas, KS</td><td>B</td></tr>
<tr><td>Missouri Western State U, MO</td><td>B</td><td>U of Indianapolis, IN</td><td>B</td><td>Bradley U, IL</td><td>B</td><td>U of Michigan, MI</td><td>B</td></tr>
<tr><td>Morningside Coll, IA</td><td>B</td><td>The U of Iowa, IA</td><td>B</td><td>Calvin Coll, MI</td><td>B</td><td>U of Michigan–Dearborn, MI</td><td>B</td></tr>
<tr><td>Mount Mary Coll, WI</td><td>B</td><td>U of Minnesota, Duluth, MN</td><td>B</td><td>Carleton Coll, MN</td><td>B</td><td>U of Minnesota, Duluth, MN</td><td>B</td></tr>
<tr><td>Mount Mercy Coll, IA</td><td>B</td><td>U of Minnesota, Twin Cities Campus, MN</td><td>B</td><td>Case Western Reserve U, OH</td><td>B</td><td>U of Minnesota, Morris, MN</td><td>B</td></tr>
<tr><td>Mount Union Coll, OH</td><td>B</td><td>U of Missouri–Columbia, MO</td><td>B</td><td>Clarke Coll, IA</td><td>B</td><td>U of Minnesota, Twin Cities Campus, MN</td><td>B</td></tr>
<tr><td>Mount Vernon Nazarene U, OH</td><td>B</td><td>U of Missouri–Kansas City, MO</td><td>B</td><td>Coll of St. Catherine, MN</td><td>B</td><td>U of Missouri–Columbia, MO</td><td>B</td></tr>
<tr><td>Nebraska Wesleyan U, NE</td><td>B</td><td>U of Nebraska at Kearney, NE</td><td>B</td><td>The Coll of Wooster, OH</td><td>B</td><td>U of Missouri–Kansas City, MO</td><td>B</td></tr>
<tr><td>Newman U, KS</td><td>B</td><td>U of Nebraska at Omaha, NE</td><td>B</td><td>Concordia Coll, MN</td><td>B</td><td>U of Missouri–St. Louis, MO</td><td>B</td></tr>
<tr><td>North Central Coll, IL</td><td>B</td><td>U of North Dakota, ND</td><td>B</td><td>Cornell Coll, IA</td><td>B</td><td>U of Nebraska at Omaha, NE</td><td>B</td></tr>
<tr><td>North Dakota State U, ND</td><td>B</td><td></td><td></td><td>Denison U, OH</td><td>B</td><td>U of Nebraska–Lincoln, NE</td><td>B</td></tr>
<tr><td>Northeastern Illinois U, IL</td><td>B</td><td></td><td></td><td>DePaul U, IL</td><td>B</td><td>U of New Orleans, LA</td><td>B</td></tr>
<tr><td>Northeastern State U, OK</td><td>B</td><td></td><td></td><td>DePauw U, IN</td><td>B</td><td>U of Northern Iowa, IA</td><td>B</td></tr>
<tr><td>Northern Illinois U, IL</td><td>B</td><td></td><td></td><td></td><td></td><td>U of Notre Dame, IN</td><td>B</td></tr>
<tr><td>Northern Michigan U, MI</td><td>B</td><td></td><td></td><td></td><td></td><td>U of Oklahoma, OK</td><td>B</td></tr>
<tr><td>Northern State U, SD</td><td>B</td><td></td><td></td><td></td><td></td><td></td><td></td></tr>
<tr><td>Northland Coll, WI</td><td>B</td><td></td><td></td><td></td><td></td><td></td><td></td></tr>
</table>

A—associate degree; B—bachelor's degree

U of St. Thomas, MN | B
The U of Toledo, OH | B
U of Tulsa, OK | B
U of Wisconsin–Madison, WI | B
U of Wisconsin–Milwaukee, WI | B
U of Wisconsin–Superior, WI | B
U of Wisconsin–Whitewater, WI | B
Ursuline Coll, OH | B
Washburn U, KS | B
Washington U in St. Louis, MO | B
Webster U, MO | B
Western Michigan U, MI | B
Wichita State U, KS | B
Wright State U, OH | B
Youngstown State U, OH | B

Artificial Intelligence and Robotics
U of Cincinnati, OH | A

Arts Management
Adrian Coll, MI | B
Aquinas Coll, MI | B
Benedictine Coll, KS | B
Benedictine U, IL | B
Bethany Coll, KS | B
Buena Vista U, IA | B
Butler U, IN | B
Columbia Coll Chicago, IL | B
Culver-Stockton Coll, MO | B
DePaul U, IL | B
Drury U, MO | B
Eastern Michigan U, MI | B
Fontbonne U, MO | B
Luther Coll, IA | B
Millikin U, IL | B
Oklahoma City U, OK | B
Quincy U, IL | B
Tiffin U, OH | B
The U of Iowa, IA | B
U of Tulsa, OK | B
U of Wisconsin–Stevens Point, WI | B
Upper Iowa U, IA | B
Viterbo U, WI | B
Wartburg Coll, IA | B
Wright State U, OH | B

Art Teacher Education
Adrian Coll, MI | B
Alma Coll, MI | B
Alverno Coll, WI | B
Anderson U, IN | B
Andrews U, MI | B
Aquinas Coll, MI | B
Ashland U, OH | B
Augsburg Coll, MN | B
Augustana Coll, IL | B
Augustana Coll, SD | B
Baker U, KS | B
Baldwin-Wallace Coll, OH | B
Ball State U, IN | B
Beloit Coll, WI | B
Bemidji State U, MN | B
Bethany Coll, KS | B
Bethel U, MN | B
Bowling Green State U, OH | B
Buena Vista U, IA | B
Calumet Coll of Saint Joseph, IN | B
Calvin Coll, MI | B
Capital U, OH | B
Cardinal Stritch U, WI | B
Carroll Coll, WI | B
Case Western Reserve U, OH | B

Central Christian Coll of Kansas, KS | A
Central Michigan U, MI | B
Central State U, OH | B
Chicago State U, IL | B
Clarke Coll, IA | B
Coe Coll, IA | B
Coll of Mount St. Joseph, OH | B
Coll of St. Catherine, MN | B
Coll of the Ozarks, MO | B
Concordia Coll, MN | B
Concordia U, IL | B
Concordia U, MI | B
Concordia U, NE | B
Concordia U Wisconsin, WI | B
Concord U, WV | B
Culver-Stockton Coll, MO | B
Dakota Wesleyan U, SD | B
Dana Coll, NE | B
Dickinson State U, ND | B
East Central U, OK | B
Eastern Michigan U, MI | B
Edgewood Coll, WI | B
Elmhurst Coll, IL | B
Evangel U, MO | B
Fontbonne U, MO | B
Fort Hays State U, KS | B
Goshen Coll, IN | B
Grace Coll, IN | B
Graceland U, IA | B
Grand Valley State U, MI | B
Gustavus Adolphus Coll, MN | B
Hannibal-LaGrange Coll, MO | B
Hastings Coll, NE | B
Hope Coll, MI | B
Huntington U, IN | B
Indiana State U, IN | B
Indiana U Bloomington, IN | B
Indiana U–Purdue U Fort Wayne, IN | B
Indiana U–Purdue U Indianapolis, IN | B
Indiana Wesleyan U, IN | B
Iowa Wesleyan Coll, IA | B
Kent State U, OH | B
Langston U, OK | B
Lawrence U, WI | B
Lewis U, IL | B
Lincoln U, MO | B
Lindenwood U, MO | B
Loras Coll, IA | B
Madonna U, MI | B
Malone Coll, OH | B
Manchester Coll, IN | A
Marian Coll, IN | B
Marian Coll of Fond du Lac, WI | B
Maryville U of Saint Louis, MO | B
McKendree Coll, IL | B
Miami U, OH | B
Miami U Hamilton, OH | B
Michigan State U, MI | B
Millikin U, IL | B
Minnesota State U Mankato, MN | B
Minot State U, ND | B
Missouri State U, MO | B
Missouri Western State U, MO | B
Morningside Coll, IA | B
Mount Mary Coll, WI | B
Mount Mercy Coll, IA | B
Mount Vernon Nazarene U, OH | B
North Carolina Ag and Tech State U, NC | B

North Central Coll, IL | B
Northeastern State U, OK | B
Northern Illinois U, IL | B
Northern Michigan U, MI | B
Northern State U, SD | B
Northland Coll, WI | B
Northwestern Coll, IA | B
Northwestern Coll, MN | B
Northwest Missouri State U, MO | B
Notre Dame Coll, OH | B
Ohio Dominican U, OH | B
Ohio Northern U, OH | B
The Ohio State U, OH | B
Ohio U, OH | B
Ohio Wesleyan U, OH | B
Oklahoma City U, OK | B
Oral Roberts U, OK | B
Ottawa U, KS | B
Otterbein Coll, OH | B
Peru State Coll, NE | B
Pittsburg State U, KS | B
Saginaw Valley State U, MI | B
St. Ambrose U, IA | B
St. Cloud State U, MN | B
Saint Joseph's Coll, IN | B
Saint Mary-of-the-Woods Coll, IN | B
Saint Mary's Coll, IN | B
Saint Xavier U, IL | B
School of the Art Inst of Chicago, IL | B
Shawnee State U, OH | B
Silver Lake Coll, WI | B
Simpson Coll, IA | B
South Dakota State U, SD | B
Southeastern Oklahoma State U, OK | B
Southeast Missouri State U, MO | B
Southwest Baptist U, MO | B
Southwestern Oklahoma State U, OK | B
Southwest Minnesota State U, MN | B
Tabor Coll, KS | B
Taylor U, IN | B
Transylvania U, KY | B
Trinity Christian Coll, IL | B
Union Coll, NE | B
The U of Akron, OH | B
U of Central Missouri, MO | B
U of Central Oklahoma, OK | B
U of Cincinnati, OH | B
U of Dallas, TX | B
U of Dayton, OH | B
U of Evansville, IN | B
The U of Findlay, OH | B
U of Illinois at Chicago, IL | B
U of Illinois at Urbana–Champaign, IL | B
U of Indianapolis, IN | B
The U of Iowa, IA | B
U of Kansas, KS | B
U of Michigan, MI | B
U of Michigan–Flint, MI | B
U of Minnesota, Duluth, MN | B
U of Minnesota, Twin Cities Campus, MN | B
U of Missouri–Columbia, MO | B
U of Nebraska–Lincoln, NE | B
U of North Dakota, ND | B
U of Northern Iowa, IA | B
U of Rio Grande, OH | B
U of Saint Francis, IN | B
U of Sioux Falls, SD | B

The U of South Dakota, SD | B
The U of Toledo, OH | B
U of Wisconsin–Madison, WI | B
U of Wisconsin–Milwaukee, WI | B
U of Wisconsin–Oshkosh, WI | B
U of Wisconsin–River Falls, WI | B
U of Wisconsin–Stout, WI | B
U of Wisconsin–Superior, WI | B
U of Wisconsin–Whitewater, WI | B
Upper Iowa U, IA | B
Ursuline Coll, OH | B
Valley City State U, ND | B
Valparaiso U, IN | B
Viterbo U, WI | B
Waldorf Coll, IA | B
Wartburg Coll, IA | B
Washington U in St. Louis, MO | B
Wayne State Coll, NE | B
Western Michigan U, MI | B
Wichita State U, KS | B
William Woods U, MO | B
Wilmington Coll, OH | B
Winona State U, MN | B
Wright State U, OH | B
York Coll, NE | B
Youngstown State U, OH | B

Art Therapy
Alverno Coll, WI | B
Capital U, OH | B
Edgewood Coll, WI | B
Goshen Coll, IN | B
Marian Coll of Fond du Lac, WI | B
Marygrove Coll, MI | B
Millikin U, IL | B
Mount Mary Coll, WI | B
Ohio Wesleyan U, OH | B
U of Indianapolis, IN | B
U of Wisconsin–Superior, WI | B
Webster U, MO | B
Wright State U, OH | B

Asian-American Studies
The Ohio State U, OH | B

Asian Studies
Augustana Coll, IL | B
Beloit Coll, WI | B
Bowling Green State U, OH | B
Calvin Coll, MI | B
Carleton Coll, MN | B
Case Western Reserve U, OH | B
Coe Coll, IA | B
Hamline U, MN | B
Illinois Wesleyan U, IL | B
Indiana U Bloomington, IN | B
Kenyon Coll, OH | B
Lake Forest Coll, IL | B
Macalester Coll, MN | B
Mount Union Coll, OH | B
Northwestern U, IL | B
Ohio U, OH | B
St. Olaf Coll, MN | B
U of Chicago, IL | B
U of Cincinnati, OH | B
The U of Iowa, IA | B
U of Michigan, MI | B
U of Northern Iowa, IA | B
The U of Toledo, OH | B
U of Wisconsin–Madison, WI | B
Washington U in St. Louis, MO | B
Western Michigan U, MI | B

Asian Studies (East)

Augsburg Coll, MN	B
Denison U, OH	B
DePaul U, IL	B
DePauw U, IN	B
Hamline U, MN	B
Indiana U Bloomington, IN	B
Lawrence U, WI	B
North Central Coll, IL	B
Oakland U, MI	B
Oberlin Coll, OH	B
The Ohio State U, OH	B
Ohio Wesleyan U, OH	B
U of Chicago, IL	B
U of Illinois at Urbana–Champaign, IL	B
U of Minnesota, Twin Cities Campus, MN	B
U of Missouri–Columbia, MO	B
U of St. Thomas, MN	B
Valparaiso U, IN	B
Washington U in St. Louis, MO	B
Wittenberg U, OH	B

Asian Studies (South)

U of Chicago, IL	B
U of Michigan, MI	B
U of Minnesota, Twin Cities Campus, MN	B
U of Missouri–Columbia, MO	B

Asian Studies (Southeast)

Ohio U, OH	B
U of Chicago, IL	B
U of Michigan, MI	B
U of Wisconsin–Madison, WI	B

Astronomy

Benedictine Coll, KS	B
Case Western Reserve U, OH	B
Central Michigan U, MI	B
Drake U, IA	B
Indiana U Bloomington, IN	B
Minnesota State U Mankato, MN	B
Mount Union Coll, OH	B
Northwestern U, IL	B
The Ohio State U, OH	B
Ohio Wesleyan U, OH	B
U of Illinois at Urbana–Champaign, IL	B
The U of Iowa, IA	B
U of Kansas, KS	B
U of Michigan, MI	B
U of Minnesota, Twin Cities Campus, MN	B
U of Oklahoma, OK	B
The U of Toledo, OH	B
U of Wisconsin–Madison, WI	B
Valparaiso U, IN	B
Youngstown State U, OH	B

Astrophysics

Augsburg Coll, MN	B
Indiana U Bloomington, IN	B
Michigan State U, MI	B
Ohio U, OH	B
Ohio Wesleyan U, OH	B
U of Minnesota, Twin Cities Campus, MN	B
U of Oklahoma, OK	B

Athletic Training

Anderson U, IN	B
Aquinas Coll, MI	B
Ashford U, IA	B

Ashland U, OH	B
Augsburg Coll, MN	B
Augustana Coll, SD	B
Baldwin-Wallace Coll, OH	B
Ball State U, IN	B
Benedictine Coll, KS	B
Bethany Coll, KS	B
Bethel Coll, KS	B
Bethel U, MN	B
Bowling Green State U, OH	B
Buena Vista U, IA	B
Capital U, OH	B
Carroll Coll, WI	B
Cedarville U, OH	B
Central Christian Coll of Kansas, KS	A
Central Methodist U, MO	B
Central Michigan U, MI	B
Clarke Coll, IA	B
Coe Coll, IA	B
Coll of Mount St. Joseph, OH	B
Concordia U Wisconsin, WI	B
Creighton U, NE	B
Culver-Stockton Coll, MO	B
Dakota Wesleyan U, SD	B
DePauw U, IN	B
Eastern Michigan U, MI	B
Emporia State U, KS	B
Franklin Coll, IN	B
Gannon U, PA	B
Graceland U, IA	B
Grand Valley State U, MI	B
Gustavus Adolphus Coll, MN	B
Hamline U, MN	B
Heidelberg Coll, OH	B
Hope Coll, MI	B
Illinois State U, IL	B
Indiana State U, IN	B
Indiana U Bloomington, IN	B
Indiana Wesleyan U, IN	B
Kansas State U, KS	B
Kent State U, OH	B
Lake Superior State U, MI	B
Lindenwood U, MO	B
Loras Coll, IA	B
Luther Coll, IA	B
Manchester Coll, IN	B
Marietta Coll, OH	B
Marquette U, WI	B
McKendree Coll, IL	B
Miami U, OH	B
Miami U Hamilton, OH	B
Millikin U, IL	B
Minnesota State U Mankato, MN	B
Missouri State U, MO	B
Missouri Valley Coll, MO	B
Mount Union Coll, OH	B
National American U, Rapid City, SD	B
Nebraska Wesleyan U, NE	B
North Central Coll, IL	B
North Dakota State U, ND	B
Northern Michigan U, MI	B
Northwestern Coll, IA	B
Ohio Northern U, OH	B
The Ohio State U, OH	B
Oklahoma State U, OK	B
Oklahoma Wesleyan U, OK	B
Otterbein Coll, OH	B
Park U, MO	B
Saginaw Valley State U, MI	B
Shawnee State U, OH	B
Simpson Coll, IA	B
South Dakota State U, SD	B

Southwest Baptist U, MO	B
Southwestern Coll, KS	B
Sterling Coll, KS	B
Tabor Coll, KS	B
Taylor U, IN	B
Trinity International U, IL	B
The U of Akron, OH	B
U of Charleston, WV	B
U of Evansville, IN	B
The U of Findlay, OH	B
U of Illinois at Urbana–Champaign, IL	B
U of Indianapolis, IN	B
The U of Iowa, IA	B
U of Mary, ND	B
U of Michigan, MI	B
U of Nebraska–Lincoln, NE	B
U of Northern Iowa, IA	B
U of Tulsa, OK	B
U of Wisconsin–Eau Claire, WI	B
U of Wisconsin–La Crosse, WI	B
U of Wisconsin–Stevens Point, WI	B
Upper Iowa U, IA	B
Walsh U, OH	B
Washburn U, KS	B
Wayne State Coll, NE	B
Western Michigan U, MI	B
William Woods U, MO	B
Wilmington Coll, OH	B
Winona State U, MN	B
Xavier U, OH	B
Youngstown State U, OH	B

Athletic Training/Sports Medicine

U of North Dakota, ND	B

Atmospheric Sciences and Meteorology

Creighton U, NE	B
Iowa State U of Science and Technology, IA	B
Northern Illinois U, IL	B
Northland Coll, WI	B
Ohio U, OH	B
St. Cloud State U, MN	B
Saint Louis U, MO	B
U of Kansas, KS	B
U of Michigan, MI	B
U of Missouri–Columbia, MO	B
U of Nebraska–Lincoln, NE	B
U of North Dakota, ND	B
U of Oklahoma, OK	B
U of Wisconsin–Milwaukee, WI	B
Valparaiso U, IN	B

Atomic/Molecular Physics

Ohio U, OH	B
The U of Akron, OH	B

Audio Engineering

Cleveland Inst of Music, OH	B
Michigan Technological U, MI	B

Audiology and Hearing Sciences

Cleveland State U, OH	B
Indiana U Bloomington, IN	B
Indiana U–Purdue U Fort Wayne, IN	B
Northwestern U, IL	B
Ohio U, OH	A
The U of Akron, OH	B

The U of Iowa, IA	B
U of Oklahoma Health Sciences Center, OK	

Audiology and Speech-Language Pathology

Andrews U, MI	B
Augustana Coll, SD	B
Ball State U, IN	B
Butler U, IN	B
Calvin Coll, MI	B
Central Michigan U, MI	B
Elmhurst Coll, IL	B
Fontbonne U, MO	B
Fort Hays State U, KS	B
Illinois State U, IL	B
Indiana State U, IN	B
Indiana U Bloomington, IN	B
Kent State U, OH	B
Marquette U, WI	B
Miami U, OH	B
Miami U Hamilton, OH	B
Michigan State U, MI	B
Minnesota State U Mankato, MN	B
Missouri State U, MO	B
Northeastern State U, OK	B
Northern Michigan U, MI	B
Northern State U, SD	B
Northwestern U, IL	B
The Ohio State U, OH	B
Ohio U, OH	B
Otterbein Coll, OH	B
Purdue U, IN	B
St. Cloud State U, MN	B
Southern Illinois U Edwardsville, IL	B
Southern Methodist U, TX	B
The U of Akron, OH	B
U of Central Oklahoma, OK	B
U of Cincinnati, OH	B
U of Illinois at Urbana–Champaign, IL	B
The U of Iowa, IA	B
U of Minnesota, Duluth, MN	B
U of Minnesota, Twin Cities Campus, MN	B
U of North Dakota, ND	B
U of Oklahoma Health Sciences Center, OK	B
The U of Toledo, OH	B
U of Tulsa, OK	B
U of Wisconsin–Milwaukee, WI	B
U of Wisconsin–Oshkosh, WI	B
U of Wisconsin–Stevens Point, WI	B
Western Michigan U, MI	B
Wichita State U, KS	B

Audiovisual Communications Technologies Related

Greenville Coll, IL	B

Automobile/Automotive Mechanics Technology

Baker Coll of Flint, MI	A
Ferris State U, MI	A,B
Kent State U, Trumbull Campus, OH	A
Northern Michigan U, MI	A
Pittsburg State U, KS	A,B

Automotive Engineering Technology

Central Michigan U, MI	B

A—associate degree; B—bachelor's degree

Indiana State U, IN — B
Minnesota State U Mankato, MN — B
Southern Illinois U Carbondale, IL — B
The U of Akron, OH — A

Aviation/Airway Management
Academy Coll, MN — A
Baker Coll of Muskegon, MI — B
Bowling Green State U, OH — B
Eastern Michigan U, MI — B
Indiana State U, IN — B
Kent State U, OH — B
Lewis U, IL — B
Minnesota State U Mankato, MN — B
The Ohio State U, OH — B
Ohio U, OH — B
Park U, MO — A,B
Quincy U, IL — B
St. Cloud State U, MN — B
Saint Louis U, MO — B
Southeastern Oklahoma State U, OK — B
Southern Illinois U Carbondale, IL — B
The U of Akron, OH — A
U of Illinois at Urbana–Champaign, IL — B
U of Minnesota, Crookston, MN — A,B
U of Nebraska at Kearney, NE — B
U of North Dakota, ND — B
Western Michigan U, MI — B
Winona State U, MN — B

Avionics Maintenance Technology
Andrews U, MI — A,B
Baker Coll of Flint, MI — A
Coll of the Ozarks, MO — B
Lewis U, IL — A,B
Northern Michigan U, MI — A
The Ohio State U, OH — B
Southern Illinois U Carbondale, IL — B
U of Minnesota, Crookston, MN — A
Western Michigan U, MI — B

Ayurvedic Medicine
Maharishi U of Management, IA — B

Baking and Pastry Arts
Kendall Coll, IL — A

Banking and Financial Support Services
Buena Vista U, IA — B
Central Michigan U, MI — B
Northwood U, MI — A,B
Pittsburg State U, KS — B
The U of Akron, OH — A
U of Illinois at Urbana–Champaign, IL — B
U of Indianapolis, IN — A,B
U of Nebraska at Omaha, NE — B
U of North Dakota, ND — B
Washburn U, KS — A

Behavioral Sciences
Andrews U, MI — B
Antioch Coll, OH — B
Augsburg Coll, MN — B
Bemidji State U, MN — B
Concordia U, NE — B
Dakota Wesleyan U, SD — B

East-West U, IL — B
Evangel U, MO — B
Grand Valley State U, MI — B
Indiana U Kokomo, IN — B
Minnesota State U Mankato, MN — B
Mount Mary Coll, WI — B
Northern Michigan U, MI — B
Northwest Missouri State U, MO — B
Oklahoma Wesleyan U, OK — A,B
Purdue U Calumet, IN — B
Rochester Coll, MI — B
St. Cloud State U, MN — B
Sterling Coll, KS — B
The U of Akron, OH — B
U of Chicago, IL — B
U of Kansas, KS — B
U of Missouri–Columbia, MO — B
U of Sioux Falls, SD — B
Ursuline Coll, OH — B
Walsh U, OH — B

Bengali
U of Chicago, IL — B

Biblical Studies
Anderson U, IN — B
Andrews U, MI — B
Barclay Coll, KS — A,B
Bethel U, MN — B
Calvary Bible Coll and Theological Seminary, MO — A,B
Calvin Coll, MI — B
Cedarville U, OH — B
Central Christian Coll of Kansas, KS — B
Cincinnati Christian U, OH — A,B
Cornerstone U, MI — B
Crossroads Coll, MN — B
Crown Coll, MN — A,B
Evangel U, MO — B
Faith Baptist Bible Coll and Theological Seminary, IA — A,B
Global U of the Assemblies of God, MO — B
God's Bible School and Coll, OH — A
Goshen Coll, IN — B
Grace Bible Coll, MI — B
Grace Coll, IN — A,B
Great Lakes Christian Coll, MI — B
Hannibal-LaGrange Coll, MO — B
Hesston Coll, KS — A
Hillsdale Free Will Baptist Coll, OK — A
Huntington U, IN — B
Indiana Wesleyan U, IN — B
Judson Coll, IL — B
Kuyper Coll, MI — A,B
Malone Coll, OH — B
Maranatha Baptist Bible Coll, WI — B
Messenger Coll, MO — B
Mount Vernon Nazarene U, OH — B
Northwestern Coll, MN — B
Oak Hills Christian Coll, MN — A,B
Oklahoma Christian U, OK — B
Oral Roberts U, OK — B
Ozark Christian Coll, MO — B
Rochester Coll, MI — B
Rosedale Bible Coll, OH — A
Southwest Baptist U, MO — B
Tabor Coll, KS — A,B
Taylor U, IN — B
Trinity International U, IL — B

U of Evansville, IN — B
Vennard Coll, IA — B
Wheaton Coll, IL — B
York Coll, NE — B

Bilingual and Multilingual Education
Adrian Coll, MI — B
Calvin Coll, MI — B
Chicago State U, IL — B
Goshen Coll, IN — B
Indiana U Bloomington, IN — B
Mount Mary Coll, WI — B
Northeastern Illinois U, IL — B
Oglala Lakota Coll, SD — B
The U of Akron, OH — B
The U of Findlay, OH — B
U of Wisconsin–Milwaukee, WI — B
Western Illinois U, IL — B

Biochemistry
Alma Coll, MI — B
Andrews U, MI — B
Beloit Coll, WI — B
Benedictine Coll, KS — B
Benedictine U, IL — B
Bradley U, IL — B
Calvin Coll, MI — B
Capital U, OH — B
Carroll Coll, WI — B
Case Western Reserve U, OH — B
Chicago State U, IL — B
Clarkson U, NY — B
Coe Coll, IA — B
Coll of Mount St. Joseph, OH — B
Coll of Saint Benedict, MN — B
Coll of St. Catherine, MN — B
The Coll of St. Scholastica, MN — B
The Coll of Wooster, OH — B
Cornell Coll, IA — B
Dakota Wesleyan U, SD — B
Denison U, OH — B
DePaul U, IL — B
DePauw U, IN — B
Dominican U, IL — B
Drake U, IA — A
Eastern Michigan U, MI — B
Grand Valley State U, MI — B
Grinnell Coll, IA — B
Gustavus Adolphus Coll, MN — B
Hamline U, MN — B
Illinois State U, IL — B
Indiana U Bloomington, IN — B
Iowa State U of Science and Technology, IA — B
Jamestown Coll, ND — B
Kansas State U, KS — B
Kenyon Coll, OH — B
Kettering U, MI — B
Knox Coll, IL — B
Lakeland Coll, WI — B
Lawrence Technological U, MI — B
Lawrence U, WI — B
Lewis U, IL — B
Loras Coll, IA — B
Loyola U Chicago, IL — B
Madonna U, MI — B
Marietta Coll, OH — B
Marquette U, WI — B
Miami U, OH — B
Miami U Hamilton, OH — B
Michigan State U, MI — B
Michigan Technological U, MI — B
Minnesota State U Mankato, MN — B

Missouri Western State U, MO — B
Nebraska Wesleyan U, NE — B
North Central Coll, IL — B
Northern Michigan U, MI — B
Northwestern U, IL — B
Notre Dame Coll, OH — B
Oakland U, MI — B
Oberlin Coll, OH — B
Ohio Northern U, OH — B
The Ohio State U, OH — B
Oklahoma Christian U, OK — B
Oklahoma City U, OK — B
Oklahoma State U, OK — B
Oral Roberts U, OK — B
Otterbein Coll, OH — B
Purdue U, IN — B
Ripon Coll, WI — B
Rockford Coll, IL — B
Rockhurst U, MO — B
Saginaw Valley State U, MI — B
Saint John's U, MN — B
Saint Joseph's Coll, IN — A,B
Saint Louis U, MO — B
Saint Mary's U of Minnesota, MN — B
Simpson Coll, IA — B
South Dakota State U, SD — B
Southern Methodist U, TX — B
Southwestern Coll, KS — B
Spring Arbor U, MI — B
Union Coll, NE — B
U of Chicago, IL — B
U of Cincinnati, OH — B
U of Dallas, TX — B
U of Dayton, OH — B
U of Evansville, IN — B
U of Illinois at Chicago, IL — B
U of Illinois at Urbana–Champaign, IL — B
The U of Iowa, IA — B
U of Michigan, MI — B
U of Michigan–Dearborn, MI — B
U of Minnesota, Duluth, MN — B
U of Minnesota, Twin Cities Campus, MN — B
U of Missouri–Columbia, MO — B
U of Nebraska–Lincoln, NE — B
U of Northern Iowa, IA — B
U of Notre Dame, IN — B
U of St. Thomas, MN — B
U of Tulsa, OK — B
U of Wisconsin–Madison, WI — B
U of Wisconsin–Milwaukee, WI — B
U of Wisconsin–River Falls, WI — B
Valparaiso U, IN — B
Viterbo U, WI — B
Wartburg Coll, IA — B
Washington U in St. Louis, MO — B
Western Michigan U, MI — B
William Jewell Coll, MO — B
Wisconsin Lutheran Coll, WI — B
Wright State U, OH — B

Biochemistry/Biophysics and Molecular Biology
Illinois Inst of Technology, IL — B
Michigan State U, MI — B
Nebraska Wesleyan U, NE — B
North Dakota State U, ND — B
U of Kansas, KS — B
Wittenberg U, OH — B

Biochemistry, Biophysics and Molecular Biology Related

Mount Union Coll, OH	B
Oklahoma State U, OK	B

Bioethics/Medical Ethics

Cleveland State U, OH	B

Bioinformatics

Gannon U, PA	B
Michigan Technological U, MI	B
Rockhurst U, MO	B
U of Northern Iowa, IA	B

Biological and Biomedical Sciences Related

Capital U, OH	B
Hiram Coll, OH	B
Kent State U, OH	B
Park U, MO	B
U of Illinois at Urbana–Champaign, IL	B
U of Kansas, KS	B
U of North Dakota, ND	B
U of Wisconsin–Parkside, WI	B
Ursuline Coll, OH	B
Washington U in St. Louis, MO	B

Biological and Physical Sciences

Alma Coll, MI	B
Antioch Coll, OH	B
Augsburg Coll, MN	B
Avila U, MO	B
Bemidji State U, MN	B
Bowling Green State U–Firelands Coll, OH	A
Buena Vista U, IA	B
Calvin Coll, MI	B
Cedarville U, OH	B
Central Christian Coll of Kansas, KS	A
Coe Coll, IA	B
Coll of Saint Benedict, MN	B
Concordia U, IL	B
Concordia U, MI	B
Concordia U, St. Paul, MN	B
Cottey Coll, MO	A
Crown Coll, MN	A
Eastern Michigan U, MI	B
Fort Berthold Comm Coll, ND	A
Fort Hays State U, KS	B
Gannon U, PA	B
Grand Valley State U, MI	B
Huntington U, IN	B
Indiana U East, IN	A
Indiana U Kokomo, IN	B
Iowa Wesleyan Coll, IA	B
Judson Coll, IL	B
Madonna U, MI	A,B
Marian Coll of Fond du Lac, WI	B
Marygrove Coll, MI	B
Maryville U of Saint Louis, MO	B
Miami U–Middletown Campus, OH	A
Michigan State U, MI	B
Minnesota State U Mankato, MN	
Mount Vernon Nazarene U, OH	B
North Central Coll, IL	B
Northern State U, SD	B
Northland Coll, WI	B

Northwestern U, IL	B
Northwest Missouri State U, MO	B
Ohio U, OH	A
Ohio U–Zanesville, OH	A
Oklahoma City U, OK	B
Oklahoma Panhandle State U, OK	B
Oklahoma Wesleyan U, OK	B
Palmer Coll of Chiropractic, IA	B
Peru State Coll, NE	B
Purdue U, IN	B
Purdue U Calumet, IN	B
Rochester Coll, MI	B
Rockford Coll, IL	B
Saint Mary-of-the-Woods Coll, IN	B
St. Norbert Coll, WI	B
Saint Xavier U, IL	B
Shawnee State U, OH	B
Simpson Coll, IA	B
Tabor Coll, KS	B
Tri-State U, IN	A
Turtle Mountain Comm Coll, ND	A
The U of Akron, OH	B
U of Cincinnati, OH	A
The U of Findlay, OH	B
U of Northern Iowa, IA	B
U of Saint Francis, IN	B
U of Southern Indiana, IN	B
The U of Toledo, OH	B
U of West Florida, FL	B
U of Wisconsin–Platteville, WI	B
U of Wisconsin–Superior, WI	B
U of Wisconsin–Whitewater, WI	B
Upper Iowa U, IA	B
Valparaiso U, IN	A
Walsh U, OH	B
Washington U in St. Louis, MO	B
Wilmington Coll, OH	B
Winona State U, MN	B
Wright State U, OH	B
Xavier U, OH	B
York Coll, NE	B

Biology/Biological Sciences

Adrian Coll, MI	A,B
Albion Coll, MI	B
Alma Coll, MI	B
Alverno Coll, WI	B
Anderson U, IN	B
Andrews U, MI	B
Antioch Coll, OH	B
Aquinas Coll, MI	B
Ashford U, IA	B
Ashland U, OH	B
Augsburg Coll, MN	B
Augustana Coll, IL	B
Augustana Coll, SD	B
Aurora U, IL	B
Avila U, MO	B
Baker U, KS	B
Baldwin-Wallace Coll, OH	B
Ball State U, IN	B
Beloit Coll, WI	B
Bemidji State U, MN	B
Benedictine Coll, KS	B
Benedictine U, IL	B
Bethany Coll, KS	B
Bethany Lutheran Coll, MN	B
Bethel Coll, KS	B
Bethel U, MN	B

Blackburn Coll, IL	B
Black Hills State U, SD	B
Bluffton U, OH	B
Bowling Green State U, OH	B
Bradley U, IL	B
Briar Cliff U, IA	B
Buena Vista U, IA	B
Butler U, IN	B
Calvin Coll, MI	B
Cameron U, OK	B
Capital U, OH	B
Cardinal Stritch U, WI	B
Carleton Coll, MN	B
Carroll Coll, WI	B
Case Western Reserve U, OH	B
Cedarville U, OH	B
Central Coll, IA	B
Central Methodist U, MO	B
Central Michigan U, MI	B
Central State U, OH	B
Chicago State U, IL	B
Clarke Coll, IA	B
Clarkson U, NY	B
Cleveland Chiropractic Coll-Kansas City Campus, MO	A,B
Cleveland State U, OH	B
Coe Coll, IA	B
Coll of Mount St. Joseph, OH	B
Coll of Saint Benedict, MN	B
Coll of St. Catherine, MN	B
Coll of Saint Mary, NE	B
The Coll of St. Scholastica, MN	B
Coll of the Ozarks, MO	B
The Coll of Wooster, OH	B
Columbia Coll, MO	B
Concordia Coll, MN	B
Concordia U, IL	B
Concordia U, MI	B
Concordia U, NE	B
Concordia U, St. Paul, MN	B
Concordia U Wisconsin, WI	B
Concord U, WV	B
Cornell Coll, IA	B
Cornerstone U, MI	B
Creighton U, NE	B
Crown Coll, MN	A,B
Culver-Stockton Coll, MO	B
Dakota State U, SD	B
Dakota Wesleyan U, SD	B
Dana Coll, NE	B
Denison U, OH	B
DePaul U, IL	B
DePauw U, IN	B
Dickinson State U, ND	B
Doane Coll, NE	B
Dominican U, IL	B
Dordt Coll, IA	B
Drake U, IA	B
Drury U, MO	B
Earlham Coll, IN	B
East Central U, OK	B
Eastern Illinois U, IL	B
Eastern Michigan U, MI	B
East-West U, IL	B
Edgewood Coll, WI	B
Elmhurst Coll, IL	B
Emporia State U, KS	B
Evangel U, MO	B
Ferris State U, MI	B
Fontbonne U, MO	B
Fort Hays State U, KS	B
Franciscan U of Steubenville, OH	B

Franklin Coll, IN	B
Gannon U, PA	B
Goshen Coll, IN	B
Grace Coll, IN	B
Graceland U, IA	B
Grand Valley State U, MI	B
Grand View Coll, IA	B
Greenville Coll, IL	B
Grinnell Coll, IA	B
Gustavus Adolphus Coll, MN	B
Hamline U, MN	B
Hannibal-LaGrange Coll, MO	B
Hanover Coll, IN	B
Hastings Coll, NE	B
Heidelberg Coll, OH	B
Hillsdale Coll, MI	B
Hiram Coll, OH	B
Hope Coll, MI	B
Huntington U, IN	B
Illinois Coll, IL	B
Illinois Inst of Technology, IL	B
Illinois State U, IL	B
Illinois Wesleyan U, IL	B
Indiana State U, IN	B
Indiana U Bloomington, IN	B
Indiana U East, IN	B
Indiana U Kokomo, IN	B
Indiana U Northwest, IN	B
Indiana U–Purdue U Fort Wayne, IN	A,B
Indiana U–Purdue U Indianapolis, IN	B
Indiana U South Bend, IN	A,B
Indiana U Southeast, IN	B
Indiana Wesleyan U, IN	A,B
Iowa State U of Science and Technology, IA	B
Iowa Wesleyan Coll, IA	B
Jamestown Coll, ND	B
Judson Coll, IL	B
Kalamazoo Coll, MI	B
Kansas State U, KS	B
Kent State U, OH	B
Kenyon Coll, OH	B
Knox Coll, IL	B
Lake Forest Coll, IL	B
Lakeland Coll, WI	B
Langston U, OK	B
Lawrence U, WI	B
Lewis U, IL	B
Lincoln U, MO	B
Lindenwood U, MO	B
Logan U-Coll of Chiropractic, MO	B
Loras Coll, IA	B
Lourdes Coll, OH	A,B
Loyola U Chicago, IL	B
Luther Coll, IA	B
Macalester Coll, MN	B
MacMurray Coll, IL	B
Madonna U, MI	B
Malone Coll, OH	B
Manchester Coll, IN	B
Marian Coll, IN	B
Marian Coll of Fond du Lac, WI	B
Marietta Coll, OH	B
Marquette U, WI	B
Marygrove Coll, MI	B
Maryville U of Saint Louis, MO	B
Mayville State U, ND	B
McKendree Coll, IL	B
Metropolitan State U, MN	B
Miami U, OH	B

A—associate degree; B—bachelor's degree

Michigan State U, MI	B
Michigan Technological U, MI	B
Millikin U, IL	B
Minnesota State U Mankato, MN	B
Minot State U, ND	B
Missouri Baptist U, MO	B
Missouri Southern State U, MO	B
Missouri State U, MO	B
Missouri Valley Coll, MO	B
Missouri Western State U, MO	B
Morningside Coll, IA	B
Mount Marty Coll, SD	B
Mount Mary Coll, WI	B
Mount Mercy Coll, IA	B
Mount Union Coll, OH	B
Mount Vernon Nazarene U, OH	B
Nebraska Wesleyan U, NE	B
Newman U, KS	B
North Carolina Ag and Tech State U, NC	B
North Central Coll, IL	B
North Dakota State U, ND	B
Northeastern Illinois U, IL	B
Northeastern State U, OK	B
Northern Illinois U, IL	B
Northern Michigan U, MI	B
Northern State U, SD	B
Northland Coll, WI	B
Northwestern Coll, IA	B
Northwestern Coll, MN	B
Northwestern Oklahoma State U, OK	B
Northwestern U, IL	B
Northwest Missouri State U, MO	B
Notre Dame Coll, OH	B
Oakland U, MI	B
Oberlin Coll, OH	B
Ohio Dominican U, OH	B
Ohio Northern U, OH	B
The Ohio State U, OH	B
The Ohio State U at Lima, OH	B
Ohio U, OH	B
Ohio Wesleyan U, OH	B
Oklahoma Christian U, OK	B
Oklahoma City U, OK	B
Oklahoma Panhandle State U, OK	B
Oklahoma State U, OK	B
Oklahoma Wesleyan U, OK	A,B
Oral Roberts U, OK	B
Ottawa U, KS	B
Otterbein Coll, OH	B
Park U, MO	B
Peru State Coll, NE	B
Pittsburg State U, KS	B
Presentation Coll, SD	A,B
Purdue U, IN	B
Purdue U Calumet, IN	B
Purdue U North Central, IN	B
Quincy U, IL	B
Ripon Coll, WI	B
Rockford Coll, IL	B
Rockhurst U, MO	B
Rogers State U, OK	A,B
Roosevelt U, IL	B
Rose-Hulman Inst of Technology, IN	B
Saginaw Valley State U, MI	B
St. Ambrose U, IA	B
St. Cloud State U, MN	B
St. Gregory's U, Shawnee, OK	B

Saint John's U, MN	B
Saint Joseph's Coll, IN	B
Saint Louis U, MO	B
Saint Mary-of-the-Woods Coll, IN	B
Saint Mary's Coll, IN	B
Saint Mary's U of Minnesota, MN	B
St. Norbert Coll, WI	B
St. Olaf Coll, MN	B
Saint Xavier U, IL	B
Shawnee State U, OH	A,B
Silver Lake Coll, WI	B
Simpson Coll, IA	B
South Dakota State U, SD	B
Southeastern Oklahoma State U, OK	B
Southeast Missouri State U, MO	B
Southern Illinois U Carbondale, IL	B
Southern Illinois U Edwardsville, IL	B
Southern Methodist U, TX	B
Southwest Baptist U, MO	B
Southwestern Coll, KS	B
Southwestern Oklahoma State U, OK	B
Southwest Minnesota State U, MN	B
Spring Arbor U, MI	B
Stephens Coll, MO	B
Sterling Coll, KS	B
Tabor Coll, KS	B
Taylor U, IN	B
Transylvania U, KY	B
Trinity Christian Coll, IL	B
Trinity International U, IL	B
Tri-State U, IN	B
Truman State U, MO	B
Turtle Mountain Comm Coll, ND	A
Union Coll, NE	B
The U of Akron, OH	B
U of Central Missouri, MO	B
U of Central Oklahoma, OK	B
U of Charleston, WV	B
U of Chicago, IL	B
U of Cincinnati, OH	B
U of Dallas, TX	B
U of Dayton, OH	B
U of Evansville, IN	B
The U of Findlay, OH	B
U of Illinois at Chicago, IL	B
U of Illinois at Springfield, IL	B
U of Illinois at Urbana–Champaign, IL	B
U of Indianapolis, IN	B
The U of Iowa, IA	B
U of Kansas, KS	B
U of Mary, ND	B
U of Michigan, MI	B
U of Michigan–Dearborn, MI	B
U of Michigan–Flint, MI	B
U of Minnesota, Duluth, MN	B
U of Minnesota, Morris, MN	B
U of Minnesota, Twin Cities Campus, MN	B
U of Missouri–Columbia, MO	B
U of Missouri–Kansas City, MO	B
U of Missouri–Rolla, MO	B
U of Missouri–St. Louis, MO	B
U of Nebraska at Kearney, NE	B
U of Nebraska at Omaha, NE	B
U of Nebraska–Lincoln, NE	B

U of New Orleans, LA	B
U of North Dakota, ND	B
U of Northern Iowa, IA	B
U of Notre Dame, IN	B
U of Rio Grande, OH	A,B
U of St. Francis, IL	B
U of Saint Francis, IN	B
U of Saint Mary, KS	B
U of St. Thomas, MN	B
U of Science and Arts of Oklahoma, OK	B
U of Sioux Falls, SD	B
The U of South Dakota, SD	B
U of Southern Indiana, IN	B
The U of Toledo, OH	A,B
U of Tulsa, OK	B
U of West Florida, FL	B
U of Wisconsin–Green Bay, WI	A,B
U of Wisconsin–La Crosse, WI	B
U of Wisconsin–Madison, WI	B
U of Wisconsin–Milwaukee, WI	B
U of Wisconsin–Oshkosh, WI	B
U of Wisconsin–Platteville, WI	B
U of Wisconsin–River Falls, WI	B
U of Wisconsin–Stevens Point, WI	B
U of Wisconsin–Superior, WI	B
U of Wisconsin–Whitewater, WI	B
Upper Iowa U, IA	B
Ursuline Coll, OH	B
Valley City State U, ND	B
Valparaiso U, IN	B
Viterbo U, WI	B
Wabash Coll, IN	B
Walsh U, OH	B
Wartburg Coll, IA	B
Washburn U, KS	B
Washington U in St. Louis, MO	B
Wayne State Coll, NE	B
Webster U, MO	B
Western Illinois U, IL	B
Western Michigan U, MI	B
Westminster Coll, MO	B
Wheaton Coll, IL	B
Wichita State U, KS	B
William Jewell Coll, MO	B
William Penn U, IA	B
William Woods U, MO	B
Wilmington Coll, OH	B
Winona State U, MN	B
Wisconsin Lutheran Coll, WI	B
Wittenberg U, OH	B
Wright State U, OH	A,B
Xavier U, OH	B
York Coll, NE	B
Youngstown State U, OH	B

Biology/Biotechnology Laboratory Technician

Cleveland State U, OH	B
Ferris State U, MI	A
Gannon U, PA	B
Michigan Technological U, MI	B
Minnesota State U Mankato, MN	B
Purdue U Calumet, IN	B
St. Cloud State U, MN	B

Biology Teacher Education

Alma Coll, MI	B
Bethany Coll, KS	B
Bethel U, MN	B

Bowling Green State U, OH	B
Buena Vista U, IA	B
Capital U, OH	B
Carroll Coll, WI	B
Cedarville U, OH	B
Central Christian Coll of Kansas, KS	A
Central Methodist U, MO	B
Central Michigan U, MI	B
Chicago State U, IL	B
Coll of St. Catherine, MN	B
Coll of the Ozarks, MO	B
Concordia Coll, MN	B
Concordia U, IL	B
Concordia U, MI	B
Concordia U, NE	B
Concordia U, St. Paul, MN	B
Cornerstone U, MI	B
Dakota State U, SD	B
Dakota Wesleyan U, SD	B
Dordt Coll, IA	B
East Central U, OK	B
Eastern Michigan U, MI	B
Elmhurst Coll, IL	B
Evangel U, MO	B
Franklin Coll, IN	B
Greenville Coll, IL	B
Gustavus Adolphus Coll, MN	B
Hastings Coll, NE	B
Hope Coll, MI	B
Illinois Wesleyan U, IL	B
Indiana U Bloomington, IN	B
Indiana U Northwest, IN	B
Indiana U–Purdue U Fort Wayne, IN	B
Indiana U South Bend, IN	B
Indiana U Southeast, IN	B
Jamestown Coll, ND	B
Lincoln U, MO	B
Lindenwood U, MO	B
Marian Coll of Fond du Lac, WI	B
Maryville U of Saint Louis, MO	B
Mayville State U, ND	B
McKendree Coll, IL	B
Miami U, OH	B
Michigan Technological U, MI	B
Minot State U, ND	B
Missouri State U, MO	B
Mount Mary Coll, WI	B
North Dakota State U, ND	B
Northwestern Coll, IA	B
Ohio Northern U, OH	B
Ohio U, OH	B
Ohio Wesleyan U, OH	B
Pittsburg State U, KS	B
Rochester Coll, MI	B
St. Ambrose U, IA	B
St. Gregory's U, Shawnee, OK	B
Saint Mary's U of Minnesota, MN	B
Saint Xavier U, IL	B
Southwest Minnesota State U, MN	B
Taylor U, IN	B
Trinity Christian Coll, IL	B
Union Coll, NE	B
The U of Akron, OH	B
U of Charleston, WV	B
U of Evansville, IN	B
U of Illinois at Chicago, IL	B
The U of Iowa, IA	B
U of Mary, ND	B
U of Michigan–Flint, MI	B
U of Missouri–Columbia, MO	B

Biology Teacher Education

U of Missouri–St. Louis, MO — B
U of Nebraska–Lincoln, NE — B
U of Rio Grande, OH — B
U of Saint Francis, IN — B
U of St. Thomas, MN — B
The U of South Dakota, SD — B
U of Wisconsin–River Falls, WI — B
U of Wisconsin–Superior, WI — B
Valley City State U, ND — B
Valparaiso U, IN — B
Viterbo U, WI — B
Washington U in St. Louis, MO — B
Wayne State Coll, NE — B
Xavier U, OH — B
York Coll, NE — B
Youngstown State U, OH — B

Biomedical/Medical Engineering
Case Western Reserve U, OH — B
Illinois Inst of Technology, IL — B
Indiana U–Purdue U Indianapolis, IN — B
Kettering U, MI — B
Lawrence Technological U, MI — B
Marquette U, WI — B
Michigan State U, MI — B
Michigan Technological U, MI — B
Milwaukee School of Engineering, WI — B
Northwestern U, IL — B
Oklahoma State U, OK — B
Oral Roberts U, OK — B
Rose-Hulman Inst of Technology, IN — B
Saint Louis U, MO — B
The U of Akron, OH — B
U of Central Oklahoma, OK — B
U of Illinois at Chicago, IL — B
U of Illinois at Urbana–Champaign, IL — B
The U of Iowa, IA — B
U of Nebraska–Lincoln, NE — B
U of Oklahoma, OK — B
The U of Toledo, OH — B
U of Wisconsin–Madison, WI — B
Washington U in St. Louis, MO — B
Wright State U, OH — B

Biomedical Sciences
Antioch Coll, OH — B
Grand Valley State U, MI — B
Marquette U, WI — B
Maryville U of Saint Louis, MO — B
St. Cloud State U, MN — B
St. Gregory's U, Shawnee, OK — B
Stephens Coll, MO — B
U of Michigan, MI — B
U of Wisconsin–Eau Claire, WI — B
U of Wisconsin–Green Bay, WI — B
Western Michigan U, MI — B

Biomedical Technology
Andrews U, MI — B
Baker Coll of Flint, MI — A
DeVry U, Addison, IL — B
DeVry U, Chicago, IL — B
DeVry U, Tinley Park, IL — B
DeVry U, Kansas City, MO — B

Indiana U–Purdue U Indianapolis, IN — A
Northwest Missouri State U, MO — B
Oral Roberts U, OK — B
Washburn U, KS — B
Wright State U, OH — B

Biophysics
Andrews U, MI — B
Clarkson U, NY — B
Illinois Inst of Technology, IL — B
Iowa State U of Science and Technology, IA — B
Oklahoma City U, OK — B
Saint Mary's U of Minnesota, MN — B
Southwestern Oklahoma State U, OK — B
U of Illinois at Urbana–Champaign, IL — B
U of Michigan, MI — B
U of Southern Indiana, IN — B
Washington U in St. Louis, MO — B

Biopsychology
Hastings Coll, NE — B
Morningside Coll, IA — B
Nebraska Wesleyan U, NE — B
Washington U in St. Louis, MO — B

Biotechnology
Calvin Coll, MI — B
Clarkson U, NY — B
Kent State U, OH — B
Missouri Southern State U, MO — B
North Dakota State U, ND — B
The Ohio State U, OH — B
Roosevelt U, IL — B
Southeastern Oklahoma State U, OK — B
U of Illinois at Urbana–Champaign, IL — B
U of Nebraska at Omaha, NE — B
U of Northern Iowa, IA — B
U of Wisconsin–River Falls, WI — B
Ursuline Coll, OH — B

Biotechnology Research
Missouri Western State U, MO — B

Botany/Plant Biology
Andrews U, MI — B
Ball State U, IN — B
Iowa State U of Science and Technology, IA — B
Kent State U, OH — B
Miami U, OH — B
Miami U–Middletown Campus, OH — A
Michigan State U, MI — B
Minnesota State U Mankato, MN — B
North Dakota State U, ND — B
Northern Michigan U, MI — B
Northwest Missouri State U, MO — B
The Ohio State U, OH — B
Ohio U, OH — B
Ohio Wesleyan U, OH — B
Oklahoma State U, OK — B
Purdue U, IN — B
St. Cloud State U, MN — B

Saint Xavier U, IL — B
Southeastern Oklahoma State U, OK — B
Southern Illinois U Carbondale, IL — B
The U of Akron, OH — B
U of Illinois at Urbana–Champaign, IL — B
U of Michigan, MI — B
U of Minnesota, Twin Cities Campus, MN — B
U of Oklahoma, OK — B
U of Wisconsin–Madison, WI — B

Botany/Plant Biology Related
Miami U Hamilton, OH — B

Broadcast Journalism
Adrian Coll, MI — B
Baldwin-Wallace Coll, OH — B
Bemidji State U, MN — B
Bowling Green State U, OH — B
Bradley U, IL — B
Calvary Bible Coll and Theological Seminary, MO — B
Cedarville U, OH — B
Coll of the Ozarks, MO — B
Columbia Coll Chicago, IL — B
Concordia Coll, MN — B
Cornerstone U, MI — A
Drake U, IA — B
Drury U, MO — B
Evangel U, MO — A,B
Fontbonne U, MO — B
Goshen Coll, IN — B
Grand Valley State U, MI — B
Hastings Coll, NE — B
Huntington U, IN — B
Indiana U Bloomington, IN — B
Kuyper Coll, MI — B
Langston U, OK — B
Lewis U, IL — B
Lindenwood U, MO — B
Manchester Coll, IN — A
Marquette U, WI — B
Mount Vernon Nazarene U, OH — B
Northern Michigan U, MI — B
Northwest Missouri State U, MO — B
Ohio U, OH — B
Ohio U–Zanesville, OH — A
Ohio Wesleyan U, OH — B
Oklahoma Christian U, OK — B
Oklahoma City U, OK — B
Oklahoma State U, OK — B
Rogers State U, OK — A
St. Cloud State U, MN — B
St. Gregory's U, Shawnee, OK — B
Southern Methodist U, TX — B
Stephens Coll, MO — B
The U of Akron, OH — B
U of Central Oklahoma, OK — B
U of Cincinnati, OH — B
U of Dayton, OH — B
The U of Findlay, OH — B
U of Illinois at Urbana–Champaign, IL — B
U of Missouri–Columbia, MO — B
U of Nebraska at Omaha, NE — B
U of Nebraska–Lincoln, NE — B
U of Northern Iowa, IA — B
U of Oklahoma, OK — B
U of St. Thomas, MN — B
U of Wisconsin–Madison, WI — B

U of Wisconsin–Milwaukee, WI — B
U of Wisconsin–Oshkosh, WI — B
U of Wisconsin–Platteville, WI — B
U of Wisconsin–River Falls, WI — B
U of Wisconsin–Superior, WI — B
Waldorf Coll, IA — B
Wartburg Coll, IA — B
Webster U, MO — B
William Woods U, MO — B
Winona State U, MN — B

Building/Property Maintenance and Management
Park U, MO — A

Business Administration and Management
Aakers Coll, Fargo, ND — A,B
Academy Coll, MN — A,B
Adrian Coll, MI — A,B
AIB Coll of Business, IA — A
Albion Coll, MI — B
Alma Coll, MI — B
Alverno Coll, WI — B
Anderson U, IN — B
Andrews U, MI — A,B
Antioch Coll, OH — B
Antioch U McGregor, OH — B
Aquinas Coll, MI — B
Argosy U, Twin Cities, Eagan, MN — B
Ashford U, IA — B
Ashland U, OH — B
Augsburg Coll, MN — B
Augustana Coll, IL — B
Augustana Coll, SD — B
Baker Coll of Allen Park, MI — A
Baker Coll of Auburn Hills, MI — A,B
Baker Coll of Cadillac, MI — A,B
Baker Coll of Clinton Township, MI — A,B
Baker Coll of Flint, MI — A,B
Baker Coll of Jackson, MI — A,B
Baker Coll of Muskegon, MI — A,B
Baker Coll of Owosso, MI — A,B
Baker Coll of Port Huron, MI — A,B
Baldwin-Wallace Coll, OH — B
Ball State U, IN — A,B
Baptist Bible Coll, MO — A,B
Barclay Coll, KS — B
Bellevue U, NE — B
Beloit Coll, WI — B
Bemidji State U, MN — B
Benedictine Coll, KS — B
Benedictine U, IL — A
Bethany Coll, KS — B
Bethany Lutheran Coll, MN — B
Bethel U, MN — B
Blackburn Coll, IL — B
Black Hills State U, SD — B
Bluffton U, OH — B
Bradley U, IL — B
Briar Cliff U, IA — B
Bryant and Stratton Coll, Cleveland, OH — B
Butler U, IN — B
Calumet Coll of Saint Joseph, IN — A,B
Calvin Coll, MI — B
Cameron U, OK — A,B
Capital U, OH — B
Cardinal Stritch U, WI — A,B
Carroll Coll, WI — B
Case Western Reserve U, OH — B

A—associate degree; B—bachelor's degree

Cedarville U, OH	B
Central Christian Coll of Kansas, KS	A,B
Central Coll, IA	B
Central Methodist U, MO	B
Central Michigan U, MI	B
Central State U, OH	B
Chicago State U, IL	B
Clarke Coll, IA	B
Clarkson U, NY	B
Cleary U, MI	A,B
Cleveland State U, OH	B
Coe Coll, IA	B
Coll of Menominee Nation, WI	A
Coll of Mount St. Joseph, OH	A,B
Coll of Saint Benedict, MN	B
Coll of St. Catherine, MN	B
Coll of Saint Mary, NE	A,B
The Coll of St. Scholastica, MN	B
Coll of the Ozarks, MO	B
Columbia Coll, MO	A,B
Columbia Coll Chicago, IL	B
Concordia Coll, MN	B
Concordia U, IL	B
Concordia U, MI	B
Concordia U, NE	B
Concordia U, St. Paul, MN	B
Concordia U Wisconsin, WI	B
Concord U, WV	A,B
Cornerstone U, MI	B
Crown Coll, MN	A,B
Culver-Stockton Coll, MO	B
Dakota State U, SD	A,B
Dakota Wesleyan U, SD	A,B
Dana Coll, NE	B
Davenport U, Dearborn, MI	A,B
DePaul U, IL	B
DeVry U, Chicago, IL	B
DeVry U, Naperville, IL	B
DeVry U, Indianapolis, IN	B
DeVry U, MN	B
DeVry U, Columbus, OH	B
DeVry U, OK	B
DeVry U, Milwaukee, WI	B
Dickinson State U, ND	B
Doane Coll, NE	B
Dominican U, IL	B
Dordt Coll, IA	B
Drake U, IA	B
Drury U, MO	B
Earlham Coll, IN	B
East Central U, OK	B
Eastern Illinois U, IL	B
Eastern Michigan U, MI	B
East-West U, IL	A,B
Edgewood Coll, WI	B
Elmhurst Coll, IL	B
Emporia State U, KS	B
Evangel U, MO	B
Everest Coll, Springfield, MO	B
Ferris State U, MI	B
Finlandia U, MI	B
Fontbonne U, MO	B
Fort Berthold Comm Coll, ND	A
Fort Hays State U, KS	B
Franciscan U of Steubenville, OH	A,B
Gannon U, PA	B
Goshen Coll, IN	B
Grace Bible Coll, MI	A,B
Grace Coll, IN	B
Graceland U, IA	B
Grand Valley State U, MI	B
Grand View Coll, IA	B
Grantham U, MO	A,B
Greenville Coll, IL	B
Gustavus Adolphus Coll, MN	B
Hamline U, MN	B
Hannibal-LaGrange Coll, MO	B
Hanover Coll, IN	B
Harris-Stowe State U, MO	B
Hastings Coll, NE	B
Heidelberg Coll, OH	B
Hesston Coll, KS	A
Hillsdale Coll, MI	B
Hiram Coll, OH	B
Hope Coll, MI	B
Huntington U, IN	B
Illinois Coll, IL	B
Illinois State U, IL	B
Illinois Wesleyan U, IL	B
Indiana State U, IN	B
Indiana Tech, IN	A,B
Indiana U Bloomington, IN	B
Indiana U Northwest, IN	A,B
Indiana U–Purdue U Fort Wayne, IN	A,B
Indiana Wesleyan U, IN	A,B
International Business Coll, Fort Wayne, IN	A,B
Iowa State U of Science and Technology, IA	B
Iowa Wesleyan Coll, IA	B
ITT Tech Inst, Fort Wayne, IN	B
ITT Tech Inst, Indianapolis, IN	B
ITT Tech Inst, Newburgh, IN	B
ITT Tech Inst, Arnold, MO	B
ITT Tech Inst, Earth City, MO	B
ITT Tech Inst, Kansas City, MO	B
ITT Tech Inst, NE	B
ITT Tech Inst, Tulsa, OK	B
ITT Tech Inst, Green Bay, WI	B
ITT Tech Inst, Greenfield, WI	B
Jamestown Coll, ND	B
Judson Coll, IL	B
Kansas State U, KS	B
Kaplan U, IA	A,B
Kendall Coll, IL	B
Kent State U, OH	A,B
Kent State U, Ashtabula Campus, OH	A
Kent State U, Geauga Campus, OH	A,B
Kent State U, Trumbull Campus, OH	A,B
Kent State U, Tuscarawas Campus, OH	A,B
Kettering U, MI	B
Kilian Comm Coll, SD	A
Kuyper Coll, MI	B
Lakeland Coll, WI	B
Lake Superior State U, MI	A,B
Langston U, OK	B
Lawrence Technological U, MI	B
Lewis Coll of Business, MI	A
Lewis U, IL	B
Lincoln U, MO	B
Lindenwood U, MO	B
Loras Coll, IA	B
Lourdes Coll, OH	A,B
Loyola U Chicago, IL	B
Luther Coll, IA	B
MacMurray Coll, IL	A,B
Madonna U, MI	A,B
Maharishi U of Management, IA	B
Malone Coll, OH	B
Manchester Coll, IN	A,B
Maranatha Baptist Bible Coll, WI	B
Marian Coll, IN	A,B
Marian Coll of Fond du Lac, WI	B
Marietta Coll, OH	A,B
Marquette U, WI	B
Marygrove Coll, MI	B
Maryville U of Saint Louis, MO	B
Mayville State U, ND	A,B
McKendree Coll, IL	B
Messenger Coll, MO	B
Metropolitan State U, MN	B
Miami U, OH	B
Miami U Hamilton, OH	A
Miami U–Middletown Campus, OH	A
Michigan State U, MI	B
Michigan Technological U, MI	B
Milwaukee School of Engineering, WI	B
Minnesota School of Business, MN	A,B
Minnesota School of Business–Brooklyn Center, MN	A,B
Minnesota School of Business–Plymouth, MN	A,B
Minnesota School of Business–Richfield, MN	A,B
Minnesota School of Business–St. Cloud, MN	B
Minnesota School of Business–Shakopee, MN	A,B
Minnesota State U Mankato, MN	B
Minot State U, ND	B
Missouri Baptist U, MO	A,B
Missouri State U, MO	B
Missouri Valley Coll, MO	A,B
Missouri Western State U, MO	A,B
Morningside Coll, IA	B
Mount Marty Coll, SD	A,B
Mount Mary Coll, WI	B
Mount Mercy Coll, IA	B
Mount Union Coll, OH	B
National American U, Rapid City, SD	A,B
Nebraska Wesleyan U, NE	B
Newman U, KS	A,B
North Carolina Ag and Tech State U, NC	B
North Central Coll, IL	B
North Dakota State U, ND	B
Northeastern Illinois U, IL	B
Northeastern State U, OK	B
Northern Illinois U, IL	B
Northern Michigan U, MI	B
Northern State U, SD	A,B
Northland Coll, WI	B
Northwestern Coll, IA	B
Northwestern Coll, MN	B
Northwestern Oklahoma State U, OK	B
Northwest Missouri State U, MO	B
Northwood U, MI	A,B
Notre Dame Coll, OH	A,B
Oglala Lakota Coll, SD	A,B
Ohio Dominican U, OH	A,B
Ohio Northern U, OH	B
The Ohio State U, OH	B
The Ohio State U at Lima, OH	B
The Ohio State U at Marion, OH	B
The Ohio State U–Mansfield Campus, OH	B
The Ohio State U–Newark Campus, OH	B
Ohio U, OH	A,B
Ohio Wesleyan U, OH	B
Oklahoma Christian U, OK	B
Oklahoma City U, OK	B
Oklahoma Panhandle State U, OK	A,B
Oklahoma Wesleyan U, OK	A,B
Oral Roberts U, OK	B
Ottawa U, KS	B
Otterbein Coll, OH	B
Park U, MO	A,B
Peru State Coll, NE	B
Pittsburg State U, KS	B
Presentation Coll, SD	A,B
Purdue U, IN	B
Purdue U Calumet, IN	B
Purdue U North Central, IN	A,B
Quincy U, IL	B
Ripon Coll, WI	B
Robert Morris Coll, IL	A,B
Rochester Coll, MI	B
Rockford Business Coll, IL	A
Rockford Coll, IL	B
Rockhurst U, MO	B
Rogers State U, OK	A
Roosevelt U, IL	B
Saginaw Valley State U, MI	B
St. Ambrose U, IA	B
St. Augustine Coll, IL	A
St. Cloud State U, MN	B
St. Gregory's U, Shawnee, OK	A,B
Saint John's U, MN	B
Saint Louis U, MO	B
Saint Mary-of-the-Woods Coll, IN	B
Saint Mary's Coll, IN	B
Saint Mary's U of Minnesota, MN	B
St. Norbert Coll, WI	B
Shawnee State U, OH	A,B
Silver Lake Coll, WI	B
Simpson Coll, IA	B
Sitting Bull Coll, ND	A
Southeastern Oklahoma State U, OK	B
Southeast Missouri State U, MO	B
Southern Illinois U Carbondale, IL	B
Southern Illinois U Edwardsville, IL	B
Southern Methodist U, TX	B
Southwestern Coll, KS	B
Southwestern Oklahoma State U, OK	B
Southwest Minnesota State U, MN	A,B
Spring Arbor U, MI	B
Stephens Coll, MO	B
Sterling Coll, KS	B
Tabor Coll, KS	B
Taylor U, IN	A,B
Tiffin U, OH	A,B
Transylvania U, KY	B
Trinity Christian Coll, IL	B
Trinity International U, IL	B
Tri-State U, IN	A,B
Truman State U, MO	B
Turtle Mountain Comm Coll, ND	A
Union Coll, NE	A,B
The U of Akron, OH	B

U of Central Missouri, MO	B
U of Central Oklahoma, OK	B
U of Charleston, WV	A,B
U of Cincinnati, OH	A,B
U of Dayton, OH	B
U of Evansville, IN	B
The U of Findlay, OH	A,B
U of Illinois at Chicago, IL	B
U of Illinois at Springfield, IL	B
U of Illinois at Urbana–Champaign, IL	B
U of Indianapolis, IN	A,B
The U of Iowa, IA	B
U of Mary, ND	A,B
U of Michigan, MI	B
U of Michigan–Dearborn, MI	B
U of Michigan–Flint, MI	B
U of Minnesota, Crookston, MN	A,B
U of Minnesota, Duluth, MN	B
U of Minnesota, Morris, MN	B
U of Missouri–Columbia, MO	B
U of Missouri–Kansas City, MO	B
U of Missouri–Rolla, MO	B
U of Missouri–St. Louis, MO	B
U of Nebraska at Kearney, NE	B
U of Nebraska at Omaha, NE	B
U of Nebraska–Lincoln, NE	B
U of New Orleans, LA	B
U of Northern Iowa, IA	B
U of Oklahoma, OK	B
U of Phoenix–Chicago Campus, IL	B
U of Phoenix–Cincinnati Campus, OH	B
U of Phoenix–Cleveland Campus, OH	B
U of Phoenix–Columbus Ohio Campus, OH	B
U of Phoenix–Indianapolis Campus, IN	B
U of Phoenix–Kansas City Campus, MO	B
U of Phoenix–Metro Detroit Campus, MI	B
U of Phoenix–Oklahoma City Campus, OK	B
U of Phoenix–St. Louis Campus, MO	B
U of Phoenix–Springfield Campus, MO	B
U of Phoenix–Tulsa Campus, OK	B
U of Phoenix–West Michigan Campus, MI	B
U of Phoenix–Wichita Campus, KS	B
U of Phoenix–Wisconsin Campus, WI	B
U of Rio Grande, OH	A,B
U of St. Francis, IL	B
U of Saint Francis, IN	A,B
U of Saint Mary, KS	B
U of St. Thomas, MN	B
U of Sioux Falls, SD	A,B
The U of South Dakota, SD	B
U of Southern Indiana, IN	B
The U of Toledo, OH	A,B
U of Tulsa, OK	B
U of West Florida, FL	B
U of Wisconsin–Eau Claire, WI	B
U of Wisconsin–Green Bay, WI	A,B

U of Wisconsin–La Crosse, WI	B
U of Wisconsin–Madison, WI	B
U of Wisconsin–Milwaukee, WI	B
U of Wisconsin–Oshkosh, WI	B
U of Wisconsin–Parkside, WI	B
U of Wisconsin–Platteville, WI	B
U of Wisconsin–River Falls, WI	B
U of Wisconsin–Stevens Point, WI	B
U of Wisconsin–Stout, WI	B
U of Wisconsin–Superior, WI	B
U of Wisconsin–Whitewater, WI	B
Upper Iowa U, IA	A,B
Ursuline Coll, OH	B
Valley City State U, ND	B
Vennard Coll, IA	B
Viterbo U, WI	B
Waldorf Coll, IA	B
Walsh U, OH	A,B
Wartburg Coll, IA	B
Washburn U, KS	B
Washington U in St. Louis, MO	B
Wayne State Coll, NE	B
Webster U, MO	B
Western Illinois U, IL	B
Western Michigan U, MI	B
Westminster Coll, MO	B
Wichita State U, KS	B
William Jewell Coll, MO	B
William Penn U, IA	B
William Woods U, MO	B
Wilmington Coll, OH	B
Winona State U, MN	B
Wittenberg U, OH	B
Wright State U, OH	B
Xavier U, OH	A,B
York Coll, NE	B
Youngstown State U, OH	A,B

Business Administration, Management and Operations Related

Alverno Coll, WI	B
Capital U, OH	B
Central Michigan U, MI	B
Cleveland State U, OH	B
Cornerstone U, MI	B
DePaul U, IL	B
DeVry U, Addison, IL	B
DeVry U, Tinley Park, IL	B
DeVry U, Kansas City, MO	B
Leech Lake Tribal Coll, MN	A
Malone Coll, OH	B
Mayville State U, ND	B
Miami U Hamilton, OH	B
Missouri Baptist U, MO	B
National American U, KS	A
St. Augustine Coll, IL	A
Saint Mary-of-the-Woods Coll, IN	B
Trinity Christian Coll, IL	B
U of Charleston, WV	B
U of Illinois at Springfield, IL	B
U of Michigan–Dearborn, MI	B
U of Notre Dame, IN	B
U of St. Thomas, MN	B
The U of Toledo, OH	B
Ursuline Coll, OH	B
Viterbo U, WI	B
Washington U in St. Louis, MO	B

Business Automation/Technology/Data Entry

Baker Coll of Clinton Township, MI	A
Central Christian Coll of Kansas, KS	A
East Central U, OK	B
The U of Akron, OH	A
U of Rio Grande, OH	A
The U of Toledo, OH	A

Business/Commerce

Academy Coll, MN	A
Anderson U, IN	A
Aurora U, IL	B
Avila U, MO	B
Baker Coll of Flint, MI	A
Baker Coll of Jackson, MI	B
Baker U, KS	B
Benedictine U, IL	B
Bethel Coll, KS	B
Bowling Green State U, OH	B
Bryant and Stratton Coll, Cleveland, OH	A
Capella U, MN	B
Capital U, OH	B
Central Christian Coll of Kansas, KS	B
Central Michigan U, MI	B
Concordia Coll, MN	B
Concordia U, NE	B
Crown Coll, MN	A
Davenport U, Dearborn, MI	B
DePaul U, IL	B
Drake U, IA	B
Eastern Michigan U, MI	B
Franklin Coll, IN	B
Gannon U, PA	A
God's Bible School and Coll, OH	A
Grace Coll, IN	B
Harris-Stowe State U, MO	B
Hillsdale Free Will Baptist Coll, OK	A,B
Illinois Inst of Technology, IL	B
Indiana U Bloomington, IN	B
Indiana U East, IN	A,B
Indiana U Kokomo, IN	A,B
Indiana U–Purdue U Indianapolis, IN	B
Indiana U South Bend, IN	A,B
Indiana U Southeast, IN	A,B
Kaplan U, IA	B
Kendall Coll, IL	A,B
Loras Coll, IA	B
Manchester Coll, IN	B
Marygrove Coll, MI	A,B
Maryville U of Saint Louis, MO	B
Miami U, OH	B
Miami U Hamilton, OH	B
Miami U–Middletown Campus, OH	A
Milwaukee School of Engineering, WI	B
Missouri State U, MO	B
Mount Vernon Nazarene U, OH	A,B
Northeastern Illinois U, IL	B
Northern Illinois U, IL	B
Northern Michigan U, MI	A
Ohio Northern U, OH	B
Ohio U, OH	B
Oklahoma Christian U, OK	B
Oklahoma City U, OK	B

Oklahoma State U, OK	B
Roosevelt U, IL	B
Saginaw Chippewa Tribal Coll, MI	A
St. Ambrose U, IA	B
Saint Joseph's Coll, IN	B
Saint Mary's U of Minnesota, MN	B
Saint Xavier U, IL	B
Southern Methodist U, TX	B
Southwest Baptist U, MO	A
Trinity Christian Coll, IL	B
The U of Akron, OH	B
U of Central Oklahoma, OK	B
U of Evansville, IN	B
U of Illinois at Urbana–Champaign, IL	B
U of Kansas, KS	B
U of Missouri–Rolla, MO	B
U of Missouri–St. Louis, MO	B
U of Nebraska at Omaha, NE	B
U of North Dakota, ND	B
U of Notre Dame, IN	B
U of Phoenix–Cincinnati Campus, OH	B
U of Phoenix–Cleveland Campus, OH	A
U of Phoenix–Columbus Ohio Campus, OH	A
U of Phoenix–Indianapolis Campus, IN	A
U of Phoenix–St. Louis Campus, MO	A
U of Phoenix–Springfield Campus, MO	A
U of Science and Arts of Oklahoma, OK	B
U of Southern Indiana, IN	B
The U of Toledo, OH	A,B
U of Wisconsin–Whitewater, WI	B
Washington U in St. Louis, MO	B
Webster U, MO	B
Western Michigan U, MI	B
Wright State U, OH	B
Youngstown State U, OH	A,B

Business/Corporate Communications

Aquinas Coll, MI	B
Augustana Coll, SD	B
Calvin Coll, MI	B
Central Christian Coll of Kansas, KS	A
Marietta Coll, OH	B
Morningside Coll, IA	B
Ohio Dominican U, OH	B
Rochester Coll, MI	B
Rockhurst U, MO	B
Simpson Coll, IA	B
Southwestern Coll, KS	B
The U of Findlay, OH	B
U of Mary, ND	B
U of Phoenix–Cincinnati Campus, OH	B
U of Phoenix–Cleveland Campus, OH	B
U of Phoenix–Columbus Ohio Campus, OH	B
U of Phoenix–Indianapolis Campus, IN	B
U of Phoenix–Oklahoma City Campus, OK	B

A—associate degree; B—bachelor's degree

U of Phoenix–Springfield Campus, MO — B
U of Phoenix–Tulsa Campus, OK — B
U of Rio Grande, OH — B
U of St. Thomas, MN — B

Business Family and Consumer Sciences/Human Sciences
The Ohio State U, OH — B

Business, Management, and Marketing Related
Benedictine U, IL — B
Bowling Green State U, OH — B
Central Michigan U, MI — B
Coll of Mount St. Joseph, OH — B
Iowa State U of Science and Technology, IA — B
Nebraska Wesleyan U, NE — B
Ohio U, OH — B
Park U, MO — B
Taylor U Fort Wayne, IN — A,B
The U of Akron, OH — A
U of Phoenix–Kansas City Campus, MO — B
U of Southern Indiana, IN — A
The U of Toledo, OH — B
U of Wisconsin–Stout, WI — B

Business/Managerial Economics
Anderson U, IN — B
Andrews U, MI — B
Augsburg Coll, MN — B
Aurora U, IL — B
Ball State U, IN — B
Beloit Coll, WI — B
Benedictine U, IL — B
Bethany Coll, KS — B
Bowling Green State U, OH — B
Bradley U, IL — B
Buena Vista U, IA — B
Butler U, IN — B
Capital U, OH — B
Cardinal Stritch U, WI — B
Central Christian Coll of Kansas, KS — A
Cleveland State U, OH — B
Coll of the Ozarks, MO — B
The Coll of Wooster, OH — B
DePaul U, IL — B
East Central U, OK — B
Eastern Michigan U, MI — B
Ferris State U, MI — B
Fort Hays State U, KS — B
Gustavus Adolphus Coll, MN — B
Hope Coll, MI — B
Huntington U, IN — B
Illinois Coll, IL — B
Indiana U Bloomington, IN — B
Indiana U–Purdue U Fort Wayne, IN — B
Indiana U Southeast, IN — B
Jamestown Coll, ND — B
Kalamazoo Coll, MI — B
Kent State U, OH — B
Lake Forest Coll, IL — B
Lake Superior State U, MI — B
Lewis U, IL — B
Loyola U Chicago, IL — B
Marian Coll of Fond du Lac, WI — B
Marquette U, WI — B
Miami U, OH — B
Miami U Hamilton, OH — B

Miami U–Middletown Campus, OH — A
Michigan Technological U, MI — B
Northern State U, SD — B
Northland Coll, WI — B
Northwest Missouri State U, MO — B
Northwood U, MI — A,B
The Ohio State U, OH — B
Ohio Wesleyan U, OH — B
Oklahoma City U, OK — B
Oklahoma State U, OK — B
Otterbein Coll, OH — B
Park U, MO — B
Roosevelt U, IL — B
Saginaw Valley State U, MI — B
Southeast Missouri State U, MO — B
Southern Illinois U Carbondale, IL — B
Southern Illinois U Edwardsville, IL — B
U of Central Oklahoma, OK — B
U of Dayton, OH — B
U of Evansville, IN — B
U of Indianapolis, IN — B
The U of Iowa, IA — B
U of Missouri–Columbia, MO — B
U of Nebraska at Omaha, NE — B
U of Nebraska–Lincoln, NE — B
U of New Orleans, LA — B
U of North Dakota, ND — B
U of Oklahoma, OK — B
The U of South Dakota, SD — B
The U of Toledo, OH — B
U of West Florida, FL — B
U of Wisconsin–Platteville, WI — B
U of Wisconsin–Superior, WI — B
U of Wisconsin–Whitewater, WI — B
Washington U in St. Louis, MO — B
Wayne State Coll, NE — B
Western Illinois U, IL — B
Western Michigan U, MI — B
Wheaton Coll, IL — B
William Woods U, MO — B
Wilmington Coll, OH — B
Winona State U, MN — B
Wisconsin Lutheran Coll, WI — B
Wittenberg U, OH — B
Wright State U, OH — B
Xavier U, OH — B
Youngstown State U, OH — B

Business Operations Support and Secretarial Services Related
Bowling Green State U–Firelands Coll, OH — A
The U of Akron, OH — A

Business Statistics
Cleveland State U, OH — B
U of Central Missouri, MO — B
Western Michigan U, MI — B

Business Systems Analysis/Design
U of North Dakota, ND — B

Business Teacher Education
Adrian Coll, MI — B
Ashford U, IA — B
Ball State U, IN — B
Bethany Coll, KS — B
Black Hills State U, SD — B
Bowling Green State U, OH — B

Buena Vista U, IA — B
Calumet Coll of Saint Joseph, IN — B
Central Christian Coll of Kansas, KS — A
Central Michigan U, MI — B
Chicago State U, IL — B
Coll of the Ozarks, MO — B
Concordia Coll, MN — B
Concordia U, NE — B
Concordia U Wisconsin, WI — B
Concord U, WV — B
Dakota State U, SD — B
Dakota Wesleyan U, SD — B
Dana Coll, NE — B
Dickinson State U, ND — B
Doane Coll, NE — B
Dordt Coll, IA — B
East Central U, OK — B
Eastern Michigan U, MI — B
Evangel U, MO — B
Ferris State U, MI — B
Fort Hays State U, KS — B
Gannon U, PA — B
Goshen Coll, IN — B
Hannibal-LaGrange Coll, MO — B
Hastings Coll, NE — B
Huntington U, IN — B
Illinois State U, IL — B
Indiana State U, IN — B
Kent State U, OH — B
Lakeland Coll, WI — B
Lincoln U, MO — B
Lindenwood U, MO — B
Maranatha Baptist Bible Coll, WI — B
Mayville State U, ND — B
McKendree Coll, IL — B
Michigan Technological U, MI — B
Minot State U, ND — B
Missouri Baptist U, MO — B
Missouri State U, MO — B
Morningside Coll, IA — B
Mount Mary Coll, WI — B
Mount Vernon Nazarene U, OH — B
North Carolina Ag and Tech State U, NC — B
Northeastern State U, OK — B
Northern Michigan U, MI — B
Northern State U, SD — B
Northwestern Coll, IA — B
Northwestern Oklahoma State U, OK — B
Northwest Missouri State U, MO — B
Ohio Wesleyan U, OH — B
Oklahoma Panhandle State U, OK — B
Oklahoma Wesleyan U, OK — B
St. Ambrose U, IA — B
Saint Mary's Coll, IN — B
Southeast Missouri State U, MO — B
Tabor Coll, KS — B
Trinity Christian Coll, IL — B
Union Coll, NE — B
The U of Akron, OH — B
U of Central Missouri, MO — B
U of Central Oklahoma, OK — B
The U of Findlay, OH — B
U of Illinois at Urbana–Champaign, IL — B
U of Indianapolis, IN — B
U of Minnesota, Twin Cities Campus, MN — B

U of Missouri–Columbia, MO — B
U of Missouri–St. Louis, MO — B
U of Nebraska at Kearney, NE — B
U of Nebraska–Lincoln, NE — B
U of North Dakota, ND — B
U of Northern Iowa, IA — B
U of Rio Grande, OH — B
U of Saint Francis, IN — B
U of Southern Indiana, IN — B
The U of Toledo, OH — B
U of Wisconsin–Superior, WI — B
U of Wisconsin–Whitewater, WI — B
Upper Iowa U, IA — B
Valley City State U, ND — B
Viterbo U, WI — B
Washburn U, KS — B
Wayne State Coll, NE — B
Western Michigan U, MI — B
William Penn U, IA — B
Wilmington Coll, OH — B
Winona State U, MN — B
Wright State U, OH — B
York Coll, NE — B
Youngstown State U, OH — B

CAD/CADD Drafting/Design Technology
Eastern Michigan U, MI — B
ITT Tech Inst, Mount Prospect, IL — A
ITT Tech Inst, Orland Park, IL — A
ITT Tech Inst, Fort Wayne, IN — A
ITT Tech Inst, Indianapolis, IN — A
ITT Tech Inst, Newburgh, IN — A
ITT Tech Inst, MN — A
ITT Tech Inst, Arnold, MO — A
ITT Tech Inst, Earth City, MO — A
ITT Tech Inst, Kansas City, MO — A
ITT Tech Inst, NE — A
ITT Tech Inst, Tulsa, OK — A
ITT Tech Inst, Green Bay, WI — A
ITT Tech Inst, Greenfield, WI — A
Morrison Inst of Technology, IL — A
Shawnee State U, OH — A

Canadian Studies
Franklin Coll, IN — B

Cardiovascular Technology
Nebraska Methodist Coll, NE — A,B
The U of Toledo, OH — A

Caribbean Studies
Northwestern U, IL — B

Carpentry
Oglala Lakota Coll, SD — A
Sitting Bull Coll, ND — A
Turtle Mountain Comm Coll, ND — A

Cartography
Ball State U, IN — B
East Central U, OK — B
Missouri State U, MO — B
The U of Akron, OH — B
U of Wisconsin–Madison, WI — B
U of Wisconsin–Platteville, WI — B

Cell and Molecular Biology
Grand Valley State U, MI — B
Missouri State U, MO — B
Oklahoma State U, OK — B
U of Illinois at Urbana–Champaign, IL — B

Cell Biology and Histology

Ball State U, IN	B
Beloit Coll, WI	B
Clarkson U, NY	B
Lindenwood U, MO	B
Northeastern State U, OK	B
Northwestern U, IL	B
Ohio U, OH	B
U of Illinois at Urbana–Champaign, IL	B
U of Michigan, MI	B
U of Minnesota, Duluth, MN	B
U of Minnesota, Twin Cities Campus, MN	B
U of Wisconsin–Madison, WI	B
William Jewell Coll, MO	B

Ceramic Arts and Ceramics

Aquinas Coll, MI	B
Ball State U, IN	B
Bethany Coll, KS	B
The Cleveland Inst of Art, OH	B
Coe Coll, IA	B
Concord U, WV	B
Finlandia U, MI	B
Grand Valley State U, MI	B
Indiana U Bloomington, IN	B
Indiana Wesleyan U, IN	B
Kansas City Art Inst, MO	B
Kent State U, OH	B
Minnesota State U Mankato, MN	B
Ohio Northern U, OH	B
The Ohio State U, OH	B
Ohio U, OH	B
St. Cloud State U, MN	B
School of the Art Inst of Chicago, IL	B
Shawnee State U, OH	B
Trinity Christian Coll, IL	B
The U of Akron, OH	B
U of Dallas, TX	B
The U of Iowa, IA	B
U of Kansas, KS	B
U of Michigan, MI	B
U of Michigan–Flint, MI	B
U of Wisconsin–Milwaukee, WI	B
Washington U in St. Louis, MO	B

Ceramic Sciences and Engineering

The Ohio State U, OH	B
U of Missouri–Rolla, MO	B

Chemical Engineering

Ball State U, IN	A
Calvin Coll, MI	B
Case Western Reserve U, OH	B
Clarkson U, NY	B
Cleveland State U, OH	B
Ferris State U, MI	A
Illinois Inst of Technology, IL	B
Iowa State U of Science and Technology, IA	B
Kansas State U, KS	B
Miami U, OH	B
Miami U–Middletown Campus, OH	A
Michigan State U, MI	B
Michigan Technological U, MI	B
North Carolina Ag and Tech State U, NC	B
Northwestern U, IL	B
The Ohio State U, OH	B

Ohio U, OH	B
Oklahoma State U, OK	B
Purdue U, IN	B
Rose-Hulman Inst of Technology, IN	B
South Dakota School of Mines and Technology, SD	B
Tri-State U, IN	B
The U of Akron, OH	B
U of Cincinnati, OH	B
U of Dayton, OH	B
U of Illinois at Chicago, IL	B
U of Illinois at Urbana–Champaign, IL	B
The U of Iowa, IA	B
U of Kansas, KS	B
U of Michigan, MI	B
U of Minnesota, Duluth, MN	B
U of Minnesota, Twin Cities Campus, MN	B
U of Missouri–Columbia, MO	B
U of Missouri–Rolla, MO	B
U of Nebraska–Lincoln, NE	B
U of North Dakota, ND	B
U of Notre Dame, IN	B
U of Oklahoma, OK	B
The U of Toledo, OH	B
U of Tulsa, OK	B
U of Wisconsin–Madison, WI	B
Waldorf Coll, IA	B
Washington U in St. Louis, MO	B
Western Michigan U, MI	B
Winona State U, MN	B
Xavier U, OH	B
Youngstown State U, OH	B

Chemical Physics

Michigan State U, MI	B
Michigan Technological U, MI	B
Saginaw Valley State U, MI	B

Chemical Technology

Dakota State U, SD	B
Indiana U–Purdue U Fort Wayne, IN	A
Lawrence Technological U, MI	A
The U of Akron, OH	A
The U of Toledo, OH	A

Chemistry

Adrian Coll, MI	A,B
Albion Coll, MI	B
Alma Coll, MI	B
Alverno Coll, WI	B
Anderson U, IN	B
Antioch Coll, OH	B
Aquinas Coll, MI	B
Ashland U, OH	B
Augsburg Coll, MN	B
Augustana Coll, IL	B
Augustana Coll, SD	B
Aurora U, IL	B
Avila U, MO	B
Baker U, KS	B
Baldwin-Wallace Coll, OH	B
Ball State U, IN	B
Beloit Coll, WI	B
Bemidji State U, MN	B
Benedictine Coll, KS	B
Benedictine U, IL	B
Bethany Coll, KS	B
Bethany Lutheran Coll, MN	B
Bethel Coll, KS	B
Bethel U, MN	B

Blackburn Coll, IL	B
Black Hills State U, SD	B
Bluffton U, OH	B
Bowling Green State U, OH	B
Bradley U, IL	B
Briar Cliff U, IA	B
Buena Vista U, IA	B
Butler U, IN	B
Calvin Coll, MI	B
Cameron U, OK	B
Capital U, OH	B
Cardinal Stritch U, WI	B
Carleton Coll, MN	B
Carroll Coll, WI	B
Case Western Reserve U, OH	B
Cedarville U, OH	B
Central Coll, IA	B
Central Methodist U, MO	A,B
Central Michigan U, MI	B
Central State U, OH	B
Chicago State U, IL	B
Clarke Coll, IA	B
Clarkson U, NY	B
Cleveland State U, OH	B
Coe Coll, IA	B
Coll of Mount St. Joseph, OH	B
Coll of Saint Benedict, MN	B
Coll of St. Catherine, MN	B
Coll of Saint Mary, NE	B
The Coll of St. Scholastica, MN	B
Coll of the Ozarks, MO	B
The Coll of Wooster, OH	B
Columbia Coll, MO	B
Concordia Coll, MN	B
Concordia U, IL	B
Concordia U, NE	B
Concord U, WV	B
Cornell Coll, IA	B
Creighton U, NE	B
Dana Coll, NE	B
Denison U, OH	B
DePaul U, IL	B
DePauw U, IN	B
Dickinson State U, ND	B
Doane Coll, NE	B
Dominican U, IL	B
Dordt Coll, IA	B
Drake U, IA	B
Drury U, MO	B
Earlham Coll, IN	B
East Central U, OK	B
Eastern Illinois U, IL	B
Eastern Michigan U, MI	B
Edgewood Coll, WI	B
Elmhurst Coll, IL	B
Emporia State U, KS	B
Evangel U, MO	B
Ferris State U, MI	B
Fort Hays State U, KS	B
Franciscan U of Steubenville, OH	B
Franklin Coll, IN	B
Gannon U, PA	B
Goshen Coll, IN	B
Graceland U, IA	B
Grand Valley State U, MI	B
Greenville Coll, IL	B
Grinnell Coll, IA	B
Gustavus Adolphus Coll, MN	B
Hamline U, MN	B
Hannibal-LaGrange Coll, MO	A
Hanover Coll, IN	B
Hastings Coll, NE	B
Heidelberg Coll, OH	B

Hillsdale Coll, MI	B
Hiram Coll, OH	B
Hope Coll, MI	B
Huntington U, IN	B
Illinois Coll, IL	B
Illinois Inst of Technology, IL	B
Illinois State U, IL	B
Illinois Wesleyan U, IL	B
Indiana State U, IN	B
Indiana U Bloomington, IN	B
Indiana U Northwest, IN	B
Indiana U–Purdue U Fort Wayne, IN	B
Indiana U–Purdue U Indianapolis, IN	B
Indiana U South Bend, IN	A,B
Indiana U Southeast, IN	B
Indiana Wesleyan U, IN	A,B
Iowa State U of Science and Technology, IA	B
Iowa Wesleyan Coll, IA	B
Jamestown Coll, ND	B
Judson Coll, IL	B
Kalamazoo Coll, MI	B
Kansas State U, KS	B
Kent State U, OH	B
Kenyon Coll, OH	B
Kettering U, MI	B
Knox Coll, IL	B
Lake Forest Coll, IL	B
Lakeland Coll, WI	B
Lake Superior State U, MI	A
Langston U, OK	B
Lawrence Technological U, MI	B
Lawrence U, WI	B
Lewis U, IL	B
Lincoln U, MO	B
Lindenwood U, MO	B
Loras Coll, IA	B
Lourdes Coll, OH	A,B
Loyola U Chicago, IL	B
Luther Coll, IA	B
Macalester Coll, MN	B
MacMurray Coll, IL	B
Madonna U, MI	A,B
Malone Coll, OH	B
Manchester Coll, IN	B
Marian Coll, IN	B
Marian Coll of Fond du Lac, WI	B
Marietta Coll, OH	B
Marquette U, WI	B
Marygrove Coll, MI	B
Maryville U of Saint Louis, MO	B
Mayville State U, ND	B
McKendree Coll, IL	B
Miami U, OH	B
Miami U Hamilton, OH	B
Miami U–Middletown Campus, OH	A
Michigan State U, MI	B
Michigan Technological U, MI	B
Millikin U, IL	B
Minnesota State U Mankato, MN	B
Minot State U, ND	B
Missouri Baptist U, MO	B
Missouri Southern State U, MO	B
Missouri State U, MO	B
Missouri Western State U, MO	B
Morningside Coll, IA	B
Mount Marty Coll, SD	B
Mount Mary Coll, WI	B

A—associate degree; B—bachelor's degree

Mount Union Coll, OH	B
Mount Vernon Nazarene U, OH	B
Nebraska Wesleyan U, NE	B
Newman U, KS	B
North Carolina Ag and Tech State U, NC	B
North Central Coll, IL	B
North Dakota State U, ND	B
Northeastern Illinois U, IL	B
Northeastern State U, OK	B
Northern Illinois U, IL	B
Northern Michigan U, MI	B
Northern State U, SD	B
Northland Coll, WI	B
Northwestern Coll, IA	B
Northwestern Oklahoma State U, OK	B
Northwestern U, IL	B
Northwest Missouri State U, MO	B
Notre Dame Coll, OH	B
Oakland U, MI	B
Oberlin Coll, OH	B
Ohio Dominican U, OH	A,B
Ohio Northern U, OH	B
The Ohio State U, OH	B
Ohio U, OH	B
Ohio Wesleyan U, OH	B
Oklahoma Christian U, OK	B
Oklahoma City U, OK	B
Oklahoma Panhandle State U, OK	B
Oklahoma State U, OK	B
Oklahoma Wesleyan U, OK	A,B
Oral Roberts U, OK	B
Otterbein Coll, OH	B
Park U, MO	B
Peru State Coll, NE	B
Pittsburg State U, KS	B
Presentation Coll, SD	A
Purdue U, IN	B
Purdue U Calumet, IN	B
Purdue U North Central, IN	B
Quincy U, IL	B
Ripon Coll, WI	B
Rockford Coll, IL	B
Rockhurst U, MO	B
Rogers State U, OK	A
Roosevelt U, IL	B
Rose-Hulman Inst of Technology, IN	B
Saginaw Valley State U, MI	B
St. Ambrose U, IA	B
St. Cloud State U, MN	B
St. Gregory's U, Shawnee, OK	B
Saint John's U, MN	B
Saint Joseph's Coll, IN	B
Saint Louis U, MO	B
Saint Mary's Coll, IN	B
Saint Mary's U of Minnesota, MN	B
St. Norbert Coll, WI	B
St. Olaf Coll, MN	B
Saint Xavier U, IL	B
Shawnee State U, OH	B
Simpson Coll, IA	B
South Dakota School of Mines and Technology, SD	B
South Dakota State U, SD	B
Southeastern Oklahoma State U, OK	B
Southeast Missouri State U, MO	B
Southern Illinois U Carbondale, IL	B

Southern Illinois U Edwardsville, IL	B
Southern Methodist U, TX	B
Southwest Baptist U, MO	B
Southwestern Coll, KS	B
Southwestern Oklahoma State U, OK	B
Southwest Minnesota State U, MN	B
Spring Arbor U, MI	B
Tabor Coll, KS	B
Taylor U, IN	B
Transylvania U, KY	B
Trinity Christian Coll, IL	B
Trinity International U, IL	B
Tri-State U, IN	B
Truman State U, MO	B
Union Coll, NE	B
The U of Akron, OH	B
U of Central Missouri, MO	B
U of Central Oklahoma, OK	B
U of Charleston, WV	B
U of Chicago, IL	B
U of Cincinnati, OH	B
U of Dallas, TX	B
U of Dayton, OH	B
U of Evansville, IN	B
U of Illinois at Chicago, IL	B
U of Illinois at Springfield, IL	B
U of Illinois at Urbana–Champaign, IL	B
U of Indianapolis, IN	A,B
The U of Iowa, IA	B
U of Kansas, KS	B
U of Michigan, MI	B
U of Michigan–Dearborn, MI	B
U of Michigan–Flint, MI	B
U of Minnesota, Duluth, MN	B
U of Minnesota, Morris, MN	B
U of Minnesota, Twin Cities Campus, MN	B
U of Missouri–Columbia, MO	B
U of Missouri–Kansas City, MO	B
U of Missouri–Rolla, MO	B
U of Missouri–St. Louis, MO	B
U of Nebraska at Kearney, NE	B
U of Nebraska at Omaha, NE	B
U of Nebraska–Lincoln, NE	B
U of New Orleans, LA	B
U of North Dakota, ND	B
U of Northern Iowa, IA	B
U of Notre Dame, IN	B
U of Oklahoma, OK	B
U of Rio Grande, OH	A,B
U of Saint Francis, IN	B
U of Saint Mary, KS	B
U of St. Thomas, MN	B
U of Science and Arts of Oklahoma, OK	B
U of Sioux Falls, SD	B
The U of South Dakota, SD	B
U of Southern Indiana, IN	B
The U of Toledo, OH	B
U of Tulsa, OK	B
U of West Florida, FL	B
U of Wisconsin–Eau Claire, WI	B
U of Wisconsin–Green Bay, WI	A,B
U of Wisconsin–La Crosse, WI	B
U of Wisconsin–Madison, WI	B
U of Wisconsin–Milwaukee, WI	B
U of Wisconsin–Oshkosh, WI	B
U of Wisconsin–Parkside, WI	B

U of Wisconsin–River Falls, WI	B
U of Wisconsin–Stevens Point, WI	B
U of Wisconsin–Superior, WI	B
U of Wisconsin–Whitewater, WI	B
Upper Iowa U, IA	B
Valley City State U, ND	B
Valparaiso U, IN	B
Viterbo U, WI	B
Wabash Coll, IN	B
Walsh U, OH	B
Wartburg Coll, IA	B
Washburn U, KS	B
Washington U in St. Louis, MO	B
Wayne State Coll, NE	B
Western Illinois U, IL	B
Western Michigan U, MI	B
Westminster Coll, MO	B
Wheaton Coll, IL	B
Wichita State U, KS	B
William Jewell Coll, MO	B
Wilmington Coll, OH	B
Winona State U, MN	B
Wisconsin Lutheran Coll, WI	B
Wittenberg U, OH	B
Wright State U, OH	A,B
Xavier U, OH	B
Youngstown State U, OH	B

Chemistry Related

Lawrence Technological U, MI	B
Ohio Northern U, OH	B
Saginaw Valley State U, MI	B
U of Northern Iowa, IA	B
U of Notre Dame, IN	B
U of Wisconsin–Eau Claire, WI	B
U of Wisconsin–Whitewater, WI	B
Washington U in St. Louis, MO	B
Western Michigan U, MI	B

Chemistry Teacher Education

Alma Coll, MI	B
Bethany Coll, KS	B
Bethel U, MN	B
Buena Vista U, IA	B
Capital U, OH	B
Carroll Coll, WI	B
Central Christian Coll of Kansas, KS	A
Central Methodist U, MO	B
Central Michigan U, MI	B
Coll of St. Catherine, MN	B
Coll of the Ozarks, MO	B
Concordia Coll, MN	B
Concordia U, NE	B
Concordia U, St. Paul, MN	B
Dordt Coll, IA	B
East Central U, OK	B
Eastern Michigan U, MI	B
Elmhurst Coll, IL	B
Evangel U, MO	B
Franklin Coll, IN	B
Greenville Coll, IL	B
Gustavus Adolphus Coll, MN	B
Hastings Coll, NE	B
Hope Coll, MI	B
Illinois Wesleyan U, IL	B
Indiana U Bloomington, IN	B
Indiana U Northwest, IN	B
Indiana U–Purdue U Fort Wayne, IN	B

Indiana U South Bend, IN	B
Kent State U, OH	B
Lincoln U, MO	B
Lindenwood U, MO	B
Marian Coll of Fond du Lac, WI	B
Maryville U of Saint Louis, MO	B
Mayville State U, ND	B
Miami U Hamilton, OH	B
Michigan State U, MI	B
Millikin U, IL	B
Minot State U, ND	B
Missouri State U, MO	B
Mount Marty Coll, SD	B
Mount Mary Coll, WI	B
North Dakota State U, ND	B
Ohio Dominican U, OH	B
Ohio Northern U, OH	B
Ohio Wesleyan U, OH	B
Pittsburg State U, KS	B
St. Ambrose U, IA	B
Saint Mary's U of Minnesota, MN	B
Southwest Baptist U, MO	B
Southwest Minnesota State U, MN	B
Taylor U, IN	B
Trinity Christian Coll, IL	B
Union Coll, NE	B
The U of Akron, OH	B
U of Evansville, IN	B
U of Illinois at Chicago, IL	B
U of Illinois at Urbana–Champaign, IL	B
The U of Iowa, IA	B
U of Michigan–Dearborn, MI	B
U of Michigan–Flint, MI	B
U of Missouri–Columbia, MO	B
U of Missouri–St. Louis, MO	B
U of Nebraska–Lincoln, NE	B
U of Saint Francis, IN	B
U of St. Thomas, MN	B
U of Wisconsin–River Falls, WI	B
U of Wisconsin–Superior, WI	B
Valley City State U, ND	B
Valparaiso U, IN	B
Viterbo U, WI	B
Washington U in St. Louis, MO	B
Wayne State Coll, NE	B
Western Michigan U, MI	B
Xavier U, OH	B

Child-Care and Support Services Management

Cameron U, OK	A
Central Michigan U, MI	B
Concordia U, St. Paul, MN	B
Mayville State U, ND	B
Mount Vernon Nazarene U, OH	A
St. Augustine Coll, IL	A
Saint Mary-of-the-Woods Coll, IN	B
Sitting Bull Coll, ND	A
Southeast Missouri State U, MO	A
Youngstown State U, OH	A

Child Care/Guidance

Coll of the Ozarks, MO	B

Child-Care Provision

Mayville State U, ND	A

Saint Mary-of-the-Woods Coll,
IN A
Wayne State Coll, NE B

Child-Care Services Management
Cameron U, OK A

Child Development
Ashland U, OH B
Bowling Green State U, OH B
Coll of the Ozarks, MO B
Concordia Coll, MN B
Evangel U, MO A
Franciscan U of Steubenville,
OH A
Goshen Coll, IN B
Indiana U Bloomington, IN B
Kansas State U, KS B
Kuyper Coll, MI A,B
Madonna U, MI A,B
Miami U, OH B
Michigan State U, MI B
Minnesota State U Mankato,
MN B
Missouri Baptist U, MO B
North Carolina Ag and Tech
State U, NC A,B
Northern Michigan U, MI A,B
Northwest Missouri State U,
MO B
Ohio U, OH A,B
Oklahoma Christian U, OK B
Pittsburg State U, KS B
Purdue U Calumet, IN A
St. Cloud State U, MN B
South Dakota State U, SD B
Stephens Coll, MO B
The U of Akron, OH B
U of Central Oklahoma, OK B
U of Cincinnati, OH A
U of Illinois at Urbana–
Champaign, IL B
U of Saint Mary, KS B
U of Wisconsin–Madison, WI B
Western Michigan U, MI B
Youngstown State U, OH A,B

Child Guidance
Coll of the Ozarks, MO B
U of Central Oklahoma, OK B

Chinese
Augustana Coll, IL B
Grinnell Coll, IA B
Indiana U Bloomington, IN B
Lawrence U, WI B
The Ohio State U, OH B
U of Chicago, IL B
The U of Iowa, IA B
U of Michigan, MI B
U of Minnesota, Twin Cities
Campus, MN B
U of Notre Dame, IN B
U of Oklahoma, OK B
U of Wisconsin–Madison, WI B
Washington U in St. Louis,
MO B

Christian Studies
Bethany Coll, KS B
Crown Coll, MN B
God's Bible School and Coll,
OH A,B
Hillsdale Coll, MI B
Lindenwood U, MO B

Ursuline Coll, OH B
Vennard Coll, IA A,B

Cinematography and Film/Video Production
Antioch Coll, OH B
Bowling Green State U, OH B
Columbia Coll Chicago, IL B
Grand Valley State U, MI B
The Illinois Inst of Art–
Chicago, IL B
Maharishi U of Management,
IA B
Minneapolis Coll of Art and
Design, MN B
Ohio U, OH B
Oklahoma City U, OK B
School of the Art Inst of
Chicago, IL B
Southern Illinois U
Carbondale, IL B
U of Illinois at Chicago, IL B
The U of Iowa, IA B
U of Oklahoma, OK B
Waldorf Coll, IA B
Webster U, MO B

City/Urban, Community and Regional Planning
Ball State U, IN B
DePaul U, IL B
Eastern Michigan U, MI B
Indiana U Bloomington, IN B
Iowa State U of Science and
Technology, IA B
Miami U, OH B
Miami U Hamilton, OH B
Michigan State U, MI B
Minnesota State U Mankato,
MN B
Missouri State U, MO B
The Ohio State U, OH B
St. Cloud State U, MN B
Saint Louis U, MO B
U of Cincinnati, OH B
U of Illinois at Urbana–
Champaign, IL B
Wright State U, OH B

Civil Engineering
Bradley U, IL B
Calvin Coll, MI B
Case Western Reserve U, OH B
Clarkson U, NY B
Cleveland State U, OH B
Dordt Coll, IA B
Illinois Inst of Technology, IL B
Iowa State U of Science and
Technology, IA B
Kansas State U, KS B
Lawrence Technological U, MI B
Lincoln U, MO B
Marquette U, WI B
Michigan State U, MI B
Michigan Technological U, MI B
Minnesota State U Mankato,
MN B
North Carolina Ag and Tech
State U, NC B
North Dakota State U, ND B
Northwestern U, IL B
Ohio Northern U, OH B
The Ohio State U, OH B
Ohio U, OH B
Oklahoma State U, OK B
Purdue U, IN B

Rose-Hulman Inst of
Technology, IN B
South Dakota School of Mines
and Technology, SD B
South Dakota State U, SD B
Southern Illinois U
Carbondale, IL B
Southern Illinois U
Edwardsville, IL B
Southern Methodist U, TX B
Tri-State U, IN B
The U of Akron, OH B
U of Cincinnati, OH B
U of Dayton, OH B
U of Evansville, IN B
U of Illinois at Chicago, IL B
U of Illinois at Urbana–
Champaign, IL B
The U of Iowa, IA B
U of Kansas, KS B
U of Michigan, MI B
U of Minnesota, Twin Cities
Campus, MN B
U of Missouri–Columbia, MO B
U of Missouri–Kansas City,
MO B
U of Missouri–Rolla, MO B
U of Missouri–St. Louis, MO B
U of Nebraska at Omaha, NE B
U of Nebraska–Lincoln, NE B
U of New Orleans, LA B
U of North Dakota, ND B
U of Notre Dame, IN B
U of Oklahoma, OK B
The U of Toledo, OH B
U of Wisconsin–Madison, WI B
U of Wisconsin–Milwaukee,
WI B
U of Wisconsin–Platteville, WI B
Valparaiso U, IN B
Washington U in St. Louis,
MO B
Western Michigan U, MI B
Youngstown State U, OH B

Civil Engineering Related
Bradley U, IL B
Ohio Northern U, OH B

Civil Engineering Technology
Ferris State U, MI A
Fontbonne U, MO B
Indiana U–Purdue U Fort
Wayne, IN A
Indiana U–Purdue U
Indianapolis, IN A
Michigan Technological U, MI A
Missouri Western State U, MO A,B
Purdue U Calumet, IN A
Purdue U North Central, IN A
U of Cincinnati, OH A,B
The U of Toledo, OH A,B
Washington U in St. Louis,
MO B
Youngstown State U, OH A,B

Classical, Ancient Mediterranean and Near Eastern Studies and Archaeology
Creighton U, NE B

Classics
Pontifical Coll Josephinum,
OH B

Rockford Coll, IL B
U of North Dakota, ND B

Classics and Classical Languages Related
Concordia Coll, MN B
Lawrence U, WI B
Saint Louis U, MO B
U of St. Thomas, MN B

Classics and Languages, Literatures and Linguistics
Augustana Coll, IL B
Ball State U, IN B
Beloit Coll, WI B
Bowling Green State U, OH B
Calvin Coll, MI B
Carleton Coll, MN B
Case Western Reserve U, OH B
Coe Coll, IA B
Coll of Saint Benedict, MN B
The Coll of Wooster, OH B
Cornell Coll, IA B
Denison U, OH B
DePauw U, IN B
Earlham Coll, IN B
Franciscan U of Steubenville,
OH B
Grand Valley State U, MI B
Grinnell Coll, IA B
Gustavus Adolphus Coll, MN B
Hanover Coll, IN B
Hillsdale Coll, MI B
Hiram Coll, OH B
Hope Coll, MI B
Illinois Wesleyan U, IL B
Indiana U Bloomington, IN B
Kalamazoo Coll, MI B
Kent State U, OH B
Kenyon Coll, OH B
Knox Coll, IL B
Lawrence U, WI B
Loyola U Chicago, IL B
Luther Coll, IA B
Macalester Coll, MN B
Marquette U, WI B
Miami U, OH B
Miami U Hamilton, OH B
North Central Coll, IL B
North Dakota State U, ND B
Northwestern U, IL B
Oberlin Coll, OH B
The Ohio State U, OH B
Ohio U, OH B
Ohio Wesleyan U, OH B
Rockford Coll, IL B
Saint John's U, MN B
St. Olaf Coll, MN B
Southern Illinois U
Carbondale, IL B
Truman State U, MO B
The U of Akron, OH B
U of Chicago, IL B
U of Cincinnati, OH B
U of Dallas, TX B
U of Evansville, IN B
U of Illinois at Chicago, IL B
U of Illinois at Urbana–
Champaign, IL B
The U of Iowa, IA B
U of Kansas, KS B
U of Michigan, MI B
U of Missouri–Columbia, MO B
U of Nebraska–Lincoln, NE B
U of Notre Dame, IN B
U of Oklahoma, OK B

A—associate degree; B—bachelor's degree

U of St. Thomas, MN	B
The U of South Dakota, SD	B
The U of Toledo, OH	B
U of Wisconsin–Madison, WI	B
U of Wisconsin–Milwaukee, WI	B
Valparaiso U, IN	B
Wabash Coll, IN	B
Washington U in St. Louis, MO	B
Wright State U, OH	B
Xavier U, OH	B

Clinical Laboratory Science/ Medical Technology

Anderson U, IN	B
Andrews U, MI	B
Aquinas Coll, MI	B
Augustana Coll, SD	B
Aurora U, IL	B
Ball State U, IN	B
Barnes-Jewish Coll of Nursing and Allied Health, MO	B
Bemidji State U, MN	B
Benedictine U, IL	B
Blackburn Coll, IL	B
Bowling Green State U, OH	B
Bradley U, IL	B
Cameron U, OK	B
Carroll Coll, WI	B
Cedarville U, OH	B
Central Michigan U, MI	B
Coll of Mount St. Joseph, OH	B
Coll of St. Catherine, MN	B
Coll of Saint Mary, NE	B
Coll of the Ozarks, MO	B
Concordia Coll, MN	B
Concord U, WV	B
DePaul U, IL	B
Dominican U, IL	B
Dordt Coll, IA	B
Eastern Illinois U, IL	B
Eastern Michigan U, MI	B
Edgewood Coll, WI	B
Elmhurst Coll, IL	B
Evangel U, MO	B
Ferris State U, MI	B
Fort Hays State U, KS	B
Gannon U, PA	B
Graceland U, IA	B
Grand Valley State U, MI	B
Illinois Coll, IL	B
Illinois State U, IL	B
Indiana State U, IN	B
Indiana U East, IN	A,B
Indiana U Kokomo, IN	B
Indiana U–Purdue U Fort Wayne, IN	B
Indiana U–Purdue U Indianapolis, IN	B
Indiana U Southeast, IN	B
Indiana Wesleyan U, IN	B
Jamestown Coll, ND	B
Kansas State U, KS	B
Kent State U, OH	B
Lake Superior State U, MI	B
Langston U, OK	B
Lewis U, IL	B
Lincoln U, MO	B
Lindenwood U, MO	B
Loras Coll, IA	B
Madonna U, MI	B
Malone Coll, OH	B
Manchester Coll, IN	B
Marian Coll of Fond du Lac, WI	B

Maryville U of Saint Louis, MO	B
McKendree Coll, IL	B
Miami U, OH	B
Miami U Hamilton, OH	B
Michigan State U, MI	B
Michigan Technological U, MI	B
Minnesota State U Mankato, MN	B
Minot State U, ND	B
Missouri Southern State U, MO	B
Missouri State U, MO	B
Missouri Western State U, MO	B
Morningside Coll, IA	B
Mount Marty Coll, SD	B
Mount Mercy Coll, IA	B
Mount Vernon Nazarene U, OH	B
North Dakota State U, ND	B
Northeastern State U, OK	B
Northern Illinois U, IL	B
Northern State U, SD	B
Northwestern Coll, IA	B
Northwest Missouri State U, MO	B
Ohio Northern U, OH	B
The Ohio State U, OH	B
Oklahoma Christian U, OK	B
Oklahoma Panhandle State U, OK	B
Peru State Coll, NE	B
Purdue U, IN	B
Purdue U Calumet, IN	B
Quincy U, IL	B
Roosevelt U, IL	B
Saginaw Valley State U, MI	B
St. Cloud State U, MN	B
Saint Joseph's Coll, IN	B
Saint Louis U, MO	B
Saint Mary-of-the-Woods Coll, IN	B
Saint Mary's Coll, IN	B
Saint Mary's U of Minnesota, MN	B
Simpson Coll, IA	B
South Dakota State U, SD	B
Southeast Missouri State U, MO	B
Southwest Baptist U, MO	B
Southwestern Oklahoma State U, OK	B
Tabor Coll, KS	B
Taylor U, IN	B
Turtle Mountain Comm Coll, ND	A
Union Coll, NE	B
U of Central Missouri, MO	B
U of Central Oklahoma, OK	B
U of Cincinnati, OH	B
The U of Findlay, OH	B
U of Indianapolis, IN	B
The U of Iowa, IA	B
U of Kansas, KS	B
U of Mary, ND	B
U of Michigan, MI	B
U of Michigan–Flint, MI	B
U of Minnesota, Twin Cities Campus, MN	B
U of Missouri–St. Louis, MO	B
U of Nebraska Medical Center, NE	B
U of New Orleans, LA	B
U of North Dakota, ND	B
U of Rio Grande, OH	B
U of St. Francis, IL	B

U of Saint Francis, IN	B
U of Sioux Falls, SD	B
The U of Toledo, OH	A,B
U of West Florida, FL	B
U of Wisconsin–La Crosse, WI	B
U of Wisconsin–Madison, WI	B
U of Wisconsin–Milwaukee, WI	B
U of Wisconsin–Oshkosh, WI	B
U of Wisconsin–Stevens Point, WI	B
Wartburg Coll, IA	B
Wayne State Coll, NE	B
Western Illinois U, IL	B
Wichita State U, KS	B
William Jewell Coll, MO	B
Winona State U, MN	B
Wright State U, OH	B
Xavier U, OH	B
Youngstown State U, OH	B

Clinical/Medical Laboratory Assistant

Argosy U, Twin Cities, Eagan, MN	A
Northern Michigan U, MI	A

Clinical/Medical Laboratory Science and Allied Professions Related

Roosevelt U, IL	B
Saint Louis U, MO	B
The U of Akron, OH	A
U of North Dakota, ND	B

Clinical/Medical Laboratory Technology

Baker Coll of Owosso, MI	A
Cameron U, OK	B
DePaul U, IL	B
East Central U, OK	B
Ferris State U, MI	A,B
Indiana U Northwest, IN	A
Madonna U, MI	A,B
Marquette U, WI	B
Northern Michigan U, MI	B
Northern State U, SD	B
Northwest Missouri State U, MO	B
Oral Roberts U, OK	B
Pittsburg State U, KS	B
Presentation Coll, SD	A
Purdue U Calumet, IN	B
Shawnee State U, OH	A
Turtle Mountain Comm Coll, ND	A
U of Cincinnati, OH	A
U of Missouri–Kansas City, MO	B
U of Oklahoma, OK	B
U of Rio Grande, OH	A
U of Science and Arts of Oklahoma, OK	B
Winona State U, MN	B
Youngstown State U, OH	A

Clinical/Medical Social Work

U of St. Thomas, MN	B

Clinical Psychology

Blackburn Coll, IL	B
U of Michigan–Flint, MI	B

Clothing/Textiles

Bluffton U, OH	B
Bowling Green State U, OH	B
Indiana U Bloomington, IN	A,B
Minnesota State U Mankato, MN	B

North Carolina Ag and Tech State U, NC	B
Northwest Missouri State U, MO	B
The Ohio State U, OH	B
The U of Akron, OH	B
U of Central Oklahoma, OK	B
U of Minnesota, Twin Cities Campus, MN	B
U of Wisconsin–Madison, WI	B

Cognitive Psychology and Psycholinguistics

Indiana U Bloomington, IN	B
Lawrence U, WI	B
Northwestern U, IL	B
U of Kansas, KS	B
Washington U in St. Louis, MO	B

Cognitive Science

Case Western Reserve U, OH	B
Lawrence U, WI	B
U of Evansville, IN	B

Commercial and Advertising Art

Academy Coll, MN	A
Anderson U, IN	B
Andrews U, MI	A,B
The Art Insts International Minnesota, MN	A,B
Ashland U, OH	B
Baker Coll of Auburn Hills, MI	A
Baker Coll of Clinton Township, MI	A
Baker Coll of Flint, MI	A,B
Baker Coll of Muskegon, MI	B
Baker Coll of Owosso, MI	A,B
Baker Coll of Port Huron, MI	A
Ball State U, IN	B
Bemidji State U, MN	B
Black Hills State U, SD	B
Buena Vista U, IA	B
Cardinal Stritch U, WI	B
Carroll Coll, WI	B
Central Michigan U, MI	B
The Cleveland Inst of Art, OH	B
Columbia Coll Chicago, IL	B
Concordia U, IL	B
Concordia U, NE	B
Concordia U Wisconsin, WI	B
Concord U, WV	B
DePaul U, IL	B
Dominican U, IL	B
Dordt Coll, IA	B
Drake U, IA	B
Edgewood Coll, WI	B
Ferris State U, MI	A
Fontbonne U, MO	B
Fort Hays State U, KS	B
Grace Coll, IN	B
Graceland U, IA	B
Grand Valley State U, MI	B
Huntington U, IN	B
The Illinois Inst of Art– Chicago, IL	A,B
Indiana U Bloomington, IN	B
Indiana U–Purdue U Fort Wayne, IN	A,B
International Academy of Design & Technology, IL	A,B
International Business Coll, Fort Wayne, IN	A,B
Iowa State U of Science and Technology, IA	B
Judson Coll, IL	B

Majors and Degrees
Commercial and Advertising Art

Kansas City Art Inst, MO	B
Kent State U, OH	B
Lewis U, IL	B
Marietta Coll, OH	B
Millikin U, IL	B
Minneapolis Coll of Art and Design, MN	
Minnesota State U Mankato, MN	B
Missouri Southern State U, MO	B
Morningside Coll, IA	B
Mount Mary Coll, WI	B
Northeastern State U, OK	B
Northern Michigan U, MI	A,B
Northern State U, SD	A
Northwest Missouri State U, MO	B
Ohio Northern U, OH	B
The Ohio State U, OH	B
Ohio U, OH	B
Oklahoma Christian U, OK	B
Oklahoma City U, OK	B
Oral Roberts U, OK	B
Peru State Coll, NE	B
Robert Morris Coll, IL	A
Rogers State U, OK	A
St. Norbert Coll, WI	B
School of the Art Inst of Chicago, IL	B
Silver Lake Coll, WI	A
Simpson Coll, IA	B
Southwest Baptist U, MO	B
Southwestern Oklahoma State U, OK	B
Taylor U, IN	B
Trinity Christian Coll, IL	B
Truman State U, MO	B
Union Coll, NE	B
The U of Akron, OH	B
U of Central Missouri, MO	B
U of Central Oklahoma, OK	B
U of Cincinnati, OH	B
U of Dayton, OH	B
U of Illinois at Chicago, IL	B
U of Indianapolis, IN	B
U of Michigan, MI	B
U of Minnesota, Duluth, MN	B
U of Minnesota, Twin Cities Campus, MN	B
U of Saint Francis, IN	A,B
U of Sioux Falls, SD	B
U of Wisconsin–Platteville, WI	B
U of Wisconsin–Stevens Point, WI	B
Upper Iowa U, IA	B
Wartburg Coll, IA	B
Washington U in St. Louis, MO	B
Western Michigan U, MI	B
Wichita State U, KS	B
William Woods U, MO	B
Winona State U, MN	B

Commercial Photography
Harrington Coll of Design, IL	A
The U of Akron, OH	A

Communication and Journalism Related
Ashford U, IA	B
Bowling Green State U, OH	B
Bradley U, IL	B
Coll of the Ozarks, MO	B
Hannibal-LaGrange Coll, MO	B
Illinois Inst of Technology, IL	B
Indiana State U, IN	B
Loyola U Chicago, IL	B
Luther Coll, IA	B
Malone Coll, OH	B
Marquette U, WI	B
Milwaukee School of Engineering, WI	
Ohio Northern U, OH	B
The Ohio State U, OH	B
Ohio U, OH	B
Saint Louis U, MO	B
Southeastern Oklahoma State U, OK	B
Sterling Coll, KS	B
Taylor U Fort Wayne, IN	B
The U of Akron, OH	B
U of Illinois at Urbana–Champaign, IL	B
U of Oklahoma, OK	B
U of Wisconsin–Green Bay, WI	B
Valparaiso U, IN	B
Washington U in St. Louis, MO	B
Webster U, MO	B
Wisconsin Lutheran Coll, WI	B

Communication and Media Related
Alma Coll, MI	B
Bellevue U, NE	B
Calumet Coll of Saint Joseph, IN	B
Crown Coll, MN	B
Greenville Coll, IL	B
Indiana U–Purdue U Fort Wayne, IN	B
Northwestern U, IL	B
St. Gregory's U, Shawnee, OK	B
Southwestern Coll, KS	B
Trinity International U, IL	B
U of Central Missouri, MO	B
U of Illinois at Springfield, IL	B
Walsh U, OH	B
Western Michigan U, MI	B

Communication Disorders
Baldwin-Wallace Coll, OH	B
Bowling Green State U, OH	B
Case Western Reserve U, OH	B
Eastern Illinois U, IL	B
Kansas State U, KS	B
Minnesota State U Mankato, MN	B
Minot State U, ND	B
Northern Illinois U, IL	B
Northwestern U, IL	B
Oklahoma State U, OK	B
St. Cloud State U, MN	B
Southeast Missouri State U, MO	B
Southern Illinois U Carbondale, IL	B
Truman State U, MO	B
The U of Akron, OH	B
U of Kansas, KS	B
U of Nebraska at Kearney, NE	B
U of North Dakota, ND	B
The U of South Dakota, SD	B
U of Wisconsin–Eau Claire, WI	B
U of Wisconsin–River Falls, WI	B
Western Illinois U, IL	B

Communication Disorders Sciences and Services Related
Ohio U, OH	B
St. Cloud State U, MN	B
U of Missouri–Columbia, MO	B
U of Oklahoma Health Sciences Center, OK	B

Communication/Speech Communication and Rhetoric
Alverno Coll, WI	B
Antioch Coll, OH	B
Aquinas Coll, MI	B
Augustana Coll, SD	B
Aurora U, IL	B
Avila U, MO	B
Baker Coll of Jackson, MI	A
Baker U, KS	B
Baldwin-Wallace Coll, OH	B
Benedictine U, IL	B
Bethany Coll, KS	B
Bethany Lutheran Coll, MN	B
Bethel U, MN	B
Blackburn Coll, IL	B
Bluffton U, OH	B
Bowling Green State U, OH	B
Bradley U, IL	B
Buena Vista U, IA	B
Calumet Coll of Saint Joseph, IN	B
Calvin Coll, MI	B
Cameron U, OK	A,B
Capital U, OH	B
Cardinal Stritch U, WI	B
Carroll Coll, WI	B
Cedarville U, OH	B
Central Christian Coll of Kansas, KS	A,B
Central Coll, IA	B
Central Methodist U, MO	B
Clarkson U, NY	B
Cleveland State U, OH	B
Coll of Mount St. Joseph, OH	A,B
The Coll of St. Scholastica, MN	B
The Coll of Wooster, OH	B
Concordia Coll, MN	B
Concordia U, IL	B
Concordia U, MI	B
Concordia U, NE	B
Creighton U, NE	B
Dana Coll, NE	B
DePaul U, IL	B
Doane Coll, NE	B
Drury U, MO	B
Elmhurst Coll, IL	B
Emporia State U, KS	B
Fontbonne U, MO	B
Franciscan U of Steubenville, OH	B
Hannibal-LaGrange Coll, MO	B
Hastings Coll, NE	B
Hope Coll, MI	B
Huntington U, IN	B
Indiana State U, IN	B
Indiana U Bloomington, IN	B
Indiana U East, IN	B
Indiana U Kokomo, IN	B
Indiana U–Purdue U Indianapolis, IN	B
Indiana U Southeast, IN	B
Indiana Wesleyan U, IN	A,B
Jamestown Coll, ND	B
Kansas State U, KS	B
Kuyper Coll, MI	B

Lake Forest Coll, IL	B
Loyola U Chicago, IL	B
Macalester Coll, MN	B
Marian Coll of Fond du Lac, WI	B
Marietta Coll, OH	B
Marquette U, WI	B
Metropolitan State U, MN	B
Miami U Hamilton, OH	B
Miami U–Middletown Campus, OH	A
Michigan State U, MI	B
Michigan Technological U, MI	B
Millikin U, IL	B
Missouri Baptist U, MO	B
Missouri Southern State U, MO	B
Missouri State U, MO	B
Mount Mary Coll, WI	B
Mount Mercy Coll, IA	B
Mount Union Coll, OH	B
Mount Vernon Nazarene U, OH	B
Nebraska Wesleyan U, NE	B
Northern Illinois U, IL	B
Northern Michigan U, MI	B
Northwestern Coll, MN	B
Northwestern U, IL	B
Notre Dame Coll, OH	B
Oakland U, MI	B
Ohio Dominican U, OH	B
Ohio Northern U, OH	B
The Ohio State U, OH	B
Ohio U, OH	B
Oral Roberts U, OK	B
Park U, MO	B
Pittsburg State U, KS	B
Presentation Coll, SD	A,B
Purdue U, IN	B
Quincy U, IL	B
Ripon Coll, WI	B
Rochester Coll, MI	B
Rockhurst U, MO	B
Roosevelt U, IL	B
Saginaw Valley State U, MI	B
Saint Louis U, MO	B
Saint Mary's Coll, IN	B
St. Norbert Coll, WI	B
Saint Xavier U, IL	B
Southeastern Oklahoma State U, OK	B
Southeast Missouri State U, MO	B
Southwest Baptist U, MO	B
Southwest Minnesota State U, MN	B
Spring Arbor U, MI	B
Tabor Coll, KS	B
Taylor U, IN	B
Tiffin U, OH	B
Trinity Christian Coll, IL	B
Tri-State U, IN	A,B
Truman State U, MO	B
The U of Akron, OH	B
U of Central Oklahoma, OK	B
U of Evansville, IN	B
U of Indianapolis, IN	B
The U of Iowa, IA	B
U of Michigan–Dearborn, MI	B
U of Michigan–Flint, MI	B
U of Missouri–Columbia, MO	B
U of Missouri–Kansas City, MO	B
U of Missouri–St. Louis, MO	B
U of Nebraska at Omaha, NE	B

A—associate degree; B—bachelor's degree

U of Nebraska–Lincoln, NE	B
U of New Orleans, LA	B
U of North Dakota, ND	B
U of Northern Iowa, IA	B
U of Oklahoma, OK	B
U of Rio Grande, OH	A,B
U of Saint Francis, IN	B
U of St. Thomas, MN	B
U of Science and Arts of Oklahoma, OK	B
U of Southern Indiana, IN	B
The U of Toledo, OH	B
U of Tulsa, OK	B
U of West Florida, FL	B
U of Wisconsin–Eau Claire, WI	B
U of Wisconsin–La Crosse, WI	B
U of Wisconsin–Parkside, WI	B
U of Wisconsin–Stevens Point, WI	B
U of Wisconsin–Whitewater, WI	B
Washburn U, KS	B
Washington U in St. Louis, MO	B
Western Illinois U, IL	B
Western Michigan U, MI	B
Wheaton Coll, IL	B
Wichita State U, KS	B
William Penn U, IA	B
William Woods U, MO	B
Wisconsin Lutheran Coll, WI	B
Wittenberg U, OH	B
Wright State U, OH	A,B

Communications Technologies and Support Services Related

Alverno Coll, WI	B
Bowling Green State U–Firelands Coll, OH	A
Saint Mary-of-the-Woods Coll, IN	B

Communications Technology

Cedarville U, OH	B
Eastern Michigan U, MI	B
Ferris State U, MI	A
Hastings Coll, NE	B
ITT Tech Inst, Fort Wayne, IN	B
ITT Tech Inst, Arnold, MO	B
ITT Tech Inst, NE	B
ITT Tech Inst, Green Bay, WI	B
Kent State U, Tuscarawas Campus, OH	A
Lawrence Technological U, MI	B
Saint Mary-of-the-Woods Coll, IN	B
Vennard Coll, IA	A

Community Health and Preventive Medicine

U of Illinois at Urbana–Champaign, IL	B

Community Health Services Counseling

Bethel U, MN	B
Cleveland State U, OH	B
Indiana State U, IN	B
Indiana U–Purdue U Fort Wayne, IN	B
Northeastern Illinois U, IL	B
U of Kansas, KS	B
U of Nebraska at Omaha, NE	B
U of Nebraska–Lincoln, NE	B
U of Northern Iowa, IA	B
U of West Florida, FL	B
Youngstown State U, OH	B

Community Organization and Advocacy

Alverno Coll, WI	B
Bemidji State U, MN	B
Central Michigan U, MI	B
Cleveland State U, OH	B
Eastern Michigan U, MI	B
Northern State U, SD	B
Northwestern U, IL	B
Rockhurst U, MO	B
Roosevelt U, IL	B
The U of Akron, OH	A,B
The U of Findlay, OH	A
U of Saint Mary, KS	B
The U of Toledo, OH	B

Community Psychology

Northwestern U, IL	B
U of Saint Mary, KS	B
Wright State U, OH	B

Comparative Literature

Antioch Coll, OH	B
Beloit Coll, WI	B
Benedictine U, IL	B
Case Western Reserve U, OH	B
The Coll of Wooster, OH	B
DePaul U, IL	B
Hillsdale Coll, MI	B
Indiana U Bloomington, IN	B
Northwestern U, IL	B
Oakland U, MI	B
Oberlin Coll, OH	B
The Ohio State U, OH	B
Roosevelt U, IL	B
St. Cloud State U, MN	B
U of Chicago, IL	B
U of Cincinnati, OH	B
U of Illinois at Urbana–Champaign, IL	B
The U of Iowa, IA	B
U of Michigan, MI	B
U of Minnesota, Twin Cities Campus, MN	B
U of Wisconsin–Madison, WI	B
U of Wisconsin–Milwaukee, WI	B
Washington U in St. Louis, MO	B
William Woods U, MO	B

Computational Mathematics

Indiana U–Purdue U Fort Wayne, IN	B
Marquette U, WI	B
Michigan State U, MI	B
Michigan Technological U, MI	B
Northern Illinois U, IL	B

Computer and Information Sciences

Academy Coll, MN	A
Alverno Coll, WI	B
Andrews U, MI	B
Aquinas Coll, MI	B
Ashford U, IA	B
Aurora U, IL	B
Avila U, MO	B
Baker Coll of Allen Park, MI	A
Baker Coll of Muskegon, MI	B
Bellevue U, NE	B
Bethel U, MN	B
Black Hills State U, SD	A
Bowling Green State U, OH	B
Bradley U, IL	B
Cameron U, OK	B
Carroll Coll, WI	B
Central Michigan U, MI	B

Central State U, OH	B
Clarkson U, NY	B
Cleveland State U, OH	B
Coll of St. Catherine, MN	B
The Coll of St. Scholastica, MN	B
Coll of the Ozarks, MO	B
Columbia Coll, MO	A,B
Concordia U, MI	B
Concordia U, NE	B
Dakota State U, SD	B
Davenport U, Dearborn, MI	A,B
DePaul U, IL	B
DeVry U, Addison, IL	B
DeVry U, Chicago, IL	B
DeVry U, Naperville, IL	B
DeVry U, Tinley Park, IL	B
DeVry U, Indianapolis, IN	B
DeVry U, MN	B
DeVry U, Kansas City, MO	B
DeVry U, Columbus, OH	B
DeVry U, OK	B
DeVry U, Milwaukee, WI	B
Doane Coll, NE	B
Drury U, MO	B
Eastern Michigan U, MI	B
Emporia State U, KS	B
Everest Coll, Springfield, MO	B
Franciscan U of Steubenville, OH	B
Franklin Coll, IN	B
Gannon U, PA	B
Grace Bible Coll, MI	B
Grand Valley State U, MI	B
Hannibal-LaGrange Coll, MO	B
Hastings Coll, NE	B
Herzing Coll, MN	A
Herzing Coll, WI	A,B
Indiana State U, IN	B
Indiana U Bloomington, IN	B
Indiana U–Purdue U Indianapolis, IN	B
Indiana Wesleyan U, IN	A,B
Iowa State U of Science and Technology, IA	B
Kansas State U, KS	B
Kaplan U, IA	A,B
Knox Coll, IL	B
Kuyper Coll, MI	B
Madonna U, MI	A,B
Marygrove Coll, MI	B
Mayville State U, ND	B
Miami U, OH	B
Miami U–Middletown Campus, OH	A
Michigan State U, MI	B
Millikin U, IL	B
Missouri Baptist U, MO	B
Missouri Southern State U, MO	B
Missouri Western State U, MO	B
Mount Mercy Coll, IA	B
Mount Vernon Nazarene U, OH	B
Northeastern Illinois U, IL	B
Northern Michigan U, MI	B
Northwestern U, IL	B
Northwood U, MI	B
Ohio Dominican U, OH	B
The Ohio State U, OH	B
Oklahoma Panhandle State U, OK	A
Park U, MO	B
Purdue U, IN	B
Purdue U Calumet, IN	B
Quincy U, IL	B

Rockford Business Coll, IL	A
Saginaw Valley State U, MI	B
St. Augustine Coll, IL	A
Saint Joseph's Coll, IN	B
Saint Louis U, MO	B
Saint Mary-of-the-Woods Coll, IN	B
St. Norbert Coll, WI	B
Saint Xavier U, IL	B
Silver Lake Coll, WI	B
South Dakota State U, SD	B
Southeastern Oklahoma State U, OK	B
Southeast Missouri State U, MO	B
Southwestern Oklahoma State U, OK	B
Sterling Coll, KS	B
Tri-State U, IN	A
U of Central Missouri, MO	B
U of Charleston, WV	A,B
U of Cincinnati, OH	A,B
U of Evansville, IN	B
U of Illinois at Chicago, IL	B
The U of Iowa, IA	B
U of Kansas, KS	B
U of Mary, ND	B
U of Michigan–Dearborn, MI	B
U of Missouri–Columbia, MO	B
U of Missouri–St. Louis, MO	B
U of Nebraska at Kearney, NE	B
U of Nebraska–Lincoln, NE	B
U of North Dakota, ND	B
U of Notre Dame, IN	B
U of Oklahoma, OK	B
U of Phoenix–Kansas City Campus, MO	B
U of Phoenix–Metro Detroit Campus, MI	B
U of Saint Mary, KS	B
U of St. Thomas, MN	B
U of Science and Arts of Oklahoma, OK	B
The U of South Dakota, SD	B
U of Southern Indiana, IN	B
U of West Florida, FL	B
U of Wisconsin–Eau Claire, WI	B
U of Wisconsin–La Crosse, WI	B
U of Wisconsin–River Falls, WI	B
U of Wisconsin–Stevens Point, WI	B
U of Wisconsin–Superior, WI	B
U of Wisconsin–Whitewater, WI	B
Valley City State U, ND	B
Viterbo U, WI	B
Washburn U, KS	B
Washington U in St. Louis, MO	B
Wayne State Coll, NE	B
Western Illinois U, IL	B
Western Michigan U, MI	B
Wichita State U, KS	B
William Woods U, MO	B
Winona State U, MN	B
Wright State U, OH	B

Computer and Information Sciences and Support Services Related

Academy Coll, MN	A
Cleary U, MI	A
Coll of Mount St. Joseph, OH	B
Columbia Coll Chicago, IL	B

Majors and Degrees
Computer and Information Sciences and Support Services Related

International Academy of
 Design & Technology, IL — B
Mayville State U, ND — B
Park U, MO — B
Purdue U, IN — B
Saint Louis U, MO — B
Tiffin U, OH — B
U of Evansville, IN — B
U of Missouri–Rolla, MO — B
U of Northern Iowa, IA — B
U of Notre Dame, IN — B
Valley City State U, ND — B
Washington U in St. Louis,
 MO — B

Computer and Information Sciences Related
Baldwin-Wallace Coll, OH — B
Bellevue U, NE — B
Central Michigan U, MI — B
DePaul U, IL — B
Eastern Illinois U, IL — B
Madonna U, MI — A
Miami U Hamilton, OH — B
National American U, KS — A
U of Northern Iowa, IA — B
Washburn U, KS — A

Computer and Information Systems Security
Academy Coll, MN — A
Dakota State U, SD — B
Davenport U, Dearborn, MI — B
ITT Tech Inst, Burr Ridge, IL — B
ITT Tech Inst, Mount
 Prospect, IL — B
ITT Tech Inst, Fort Wayne, IN — B
ITT Tech Inst, Indianapolis,
 IN — B
ITT Tech Inst, Newburgh, IN — B
ITT Tech Inst, MN — B
ITT Tech Inst, Arnold, MO — B
ITT Tech Inst, Earth City, MO — B
ITT Tech Inst, Kansas City,
 MO — B
ITT Tech Inst, NE — B
ITT Tech Inst, Oklahoma City,
 OK — B
ITT Tech Inst, Tulsa, OK — B
ITT Tech Inst, Green Bay, WI — B
ITT Tech Inst, Greenfield, WI — B
U of Phoenix–Cincinnati
 Campus, OH — B
U of Phoenix–Cleveland
 Campus, OH — B
U of Phoenix–Columbus Ohio
 Campus, OH — B
U of Phoenix–Indianapolis
 Campus, IN — B
U of Phoenix–St. Louis
 Campus, MO — B
U of Phoenix–Springfield
 Campus, MO — B

Computer Engineering
Capital U, OH — B
Case Western Reserve U, OH — B
Cedarville U, OH — B
Clarkson U, NY — B
Cleveland State U, OH — B
Dominican U, IL — B
Dordt Coll, IA — B
Grand Valley State U, MI — B
Illinois Inst of Technology, IL — B
Indiana Tech, IN — B

Indiana U–Purdue U Fort
 Wayne, IN — B
Indiana U–Purdue U
 Indianapolis, IN — B
Iowa State U of Science and
 Technology, IA — B
Kansas State U, KS — B
Kettering U, MI — B
Lawrence Technological U, MI — B
Marquette U, WI — B
Miami U Hamilton, OH — B
Michigan State U, MI — B
Michigan Technological U, MI — B
Milwaukee School of
 Engineering, WI — B
Minnesota State U Mankato,
 MN — B
Missouri Western State U, MO — A,B
North Dakota State U, ND — B
Northwestern U, IL — B
Oakland U, MI — B
Ohio Northern U, OH — B
The Ohio State U, OH — B
Ohio U, OH — B
Oklahoma Christian U, OK — B
Oral Roberts U, OK — B
Purdue U, IN — B
Purdue U Calumet, IN — B
Rose-Hulman Inst of
 Technology, IN — B
St. Cloud State U, MN — B
Saint Mary's U of Minnesota,
 MN — B
South Dakota School of Mines
 and Technology, SD — B
Southern Illinois U
 Carbondale, IL — B
Southern Illinois U
 Edwardsville, IL — B
Southern Methodist U, TX — B
Taylor U, IN — B
Tri-State U, IN — B
The U of Akron, OH — B
U of Cincinnati, OH — B
U of Dayton, OH — B
U of Evansville, IN — B
U of Illinois at Chicago, IL — B
U of Illinois at Urbana–
 Champaign, IL — B
U of Indianapolis, IN — B
U of Kansas, KS — B
U of Michigan, MI — B
U of Minnesota, Duluth, MN — B
U of Missouri–Columbia, MO — B
U of Missouri–Rolla, MO — B
U of Nebraska at Omaha, NE — B
U of Nebraska–Lincoln, NE — B
U of Notre Dame, IN — B
U of Oklahoma, OK — B
The U of Toledo, OH — B
U of West Florida, FL — B
U of Wisconsin–Madison, WI — B
Valparaiso U, IN — B
Washington U in St. Louis,
 MO — B
Western Michigan U, MI — B
Wichita State U, KS — B
Wright State U, OH — B

Computer Engineering Related
Ohio Northern U, OH — B

Computer Engineering Technology
Andrews U, MI — A,B
Baker Coll of Owosso, MI — A

Bowling Green State U–
 Firelands Coll, OH — A
Central Michigan U, MI — B
DeVry U, Addison, IL — B
DeVry U, Chicago, IL — B
DeVry U, Tinley Park, IL — B
DeVry U, Kansas City, MO — B
DeVry U, Columbus, OH — B
Eastern Michigan U, MI — B
East-West U, IL — B
Grantham U, MO — A,B
Indiana State U, IN — B
Indiana U–Purdue U Fort
 Wayne, IN — B
International Business Coll,
 Fort Wayne, IN — A,B
ITT Tech Inst, Burr Ridge, IL — A
ITT Tech Inst, Mount
 Prospect, IL — B
ITT Tech Inst, Orland Park, IL — A
ITT Tech Inst, Fort Wayne, IN — A
ITT Tech Inst, Indianapolis,
 IN — A
ITT Tech Inst, Newburgh, IN — A
ITT Tech Inst, MN — A
ITT Tech Inst, Arnold, MO — A
ITT Tech Inst, Earth City, MO — A
ITT Tech Inst, Kansas City,
 MO — A
ITT Tech Inst, NE — A
ITT Tech Inst, Oklahoma City,
 OK — A
ITT Tech Inst, Tulsa, OK — A
ITT Tech Inst, Green Bay, WI — A
ITT Tech Inst, Greenfield, WI — A
Kent State U, Ashtabula
 Campus, OH — A
Kent State U, Trumbull
 Campus, OH — A
Kent State U, Tuscarawas
 Campus, OH — A
Lake Superior State U, MI — A,B
Madonna U, MI — A
Miami U–Middletown Campus,
 OH — A
Minnesota State U Mankato,
 MN — B
National American U, Rapid
 City, SD — A
Purdue U Calumet, IN — A,B
Purdue U North Central, IN — A,B
Rogers State U, OK — A
Shawnee State U, OH — B
U of Cincinnati, OH — A
U of Dayton, OH — B

Computer Graphics
Academy Coll, MN — A
The Art Insts International
 Minnesota, MN — B
Baker Coll of Cadillac, MI — B
Baker Coll of Flint, MI — B
Capella U, MN — B
Dakota State U, SD — B
DePaul U, IL — B
The Illinois Inst of Art–
 Chicago, IL — B
Indiana Wesleyan U, IN — B
International Academy of
 Design & Technology, IL — A
Judson Coll, IL — B
School of the Art Inst of
 Chicago, IL — B
South Dakota State U, SD — B
Taylor U, IN — B

Computer/Information Technology Services Administration Related
Bellevue U, NE — B
Capella U, MN — B
Dordt Coll, IA — B
Eastern Illinois U, IL — B
Hesston Coll, KS — A
Kettering U, MI — B
Lindenwood U, MO — B
Saint Mary's U of Minnesota,
 MN — B
The U of Akron, OH — A
U of Phoenix–Indianapolis
 Campus, IN — B
Vennard Coll, IA — A
Washington U in St. Louis,
 MO — B

Computer Management
AIB Coll of Business, IA — A
Lewis Coll of Business, MI — A
Luther Coll, IA — B
National American U, Rapid
 City, SD — B
Northwest Missouri State U,
 MO — B
Northwood U, MI — A,B
Oklahoma State U, OK — B
Rochester Coll, MI — B
Simpson Coll, IA — B
U of Cincinnati, OH — B
Webster U, MO — B

Computer Programming
Academy Coll, MN — A
Andrews U, MI — B
Baker Coll of Flint, MI — A,B
Baker Coll of Muskegon, MI — A
Baker Coll of Owosso, MI — A,B
Baker Coll of Port Huron, MI — A
Black Hills State U, SD — A
Bowling Green State U–
 Firelands Coll, OH — A
Dakota State U, SD — A
DePaul U, IL — B
Dordt Coll, IA — B
East-West U, IL — B
Ferris State U, MI — B
Gannon U, PA — B
Grand Valley State U, MI — B
Indiana U East, IN — A
International Business Coll,
 Fort Wayne, IN — A,B
Iowa Wesleyan Coll, IA — B
ITT Tech Inst, Mount
 Prospect, IL — A
ITT Tech Inst, Orland Park, IL — A
Kent State U, OH — A,B
Lewis Coll of Business, MI — A
Michigan Technological U, MI — B
Minnesota State U Mankato,
 MN — B
National American U, Rapid
 City, SD — A,B
Northwest Missouri State U,
 MO — B
Purdue U Calumet, IN — A
Purdue U North Central, IN — A
Rockhurst U, MO — B
Rogers State U, OK — A
Southeast Missouri State U,
 MO — B
Southwestern Coll, KS — B
Taylor U, IN — B
Tiffin U, OH — A

A—associate degree; B—bachelor's degree

College	Degree
U of Cincinnati, OH	A,B
U of Michigan–Dearborn, MI	B
The U of Toledo, OH	A,B
Winona State U, MN	B
Youngstown State U, OH	A,B

Computer Programming Related

College	Degree
Herzing Coll, WI	A

Computer Programming (Specific Applications)

College	Degree
AIB Coll of Business, IA	A
DePaul U, IL	B
DeVry U, Tinley Park, IL	B
Kaplan Coll–Indianapolis, IN	A
Kent State U, OH	A,B
Robert Morris Coll, IL	A
The U of Toledo, OH	A

Computer Programming (Vendor/Product Certification)

College	Degree
Davenport U, Dearborn, MI	B

Computer Science

College	Degree
Academy Coll, MN	B
Albion Coll, MI	B
Alma Coll, MI	B
Alverno Coll, WI	B
Anderson U, IN	B
Andrews U, MI	B
Antioch Coll, OH	B
Aquinas Coll, MI	B
Ashland U, OH	B
Augsburg Coll, MN	B
Augustana Coll, IL	B
Augustana Coll, SD	B
Baker Coll of Allen Park, MI	A
Baker Coll of Muskegon, MI	B
Baker Coll of Owosso, MI	A,B
Baker U, KS	B
Baldwin-Wallace Coll, OH	B
Ball State U, IN	B
Beloit Coll, WI	B
Bemidji State U, MN	B
Benedictine Coll, KS	B
Benedictine U, IL	B
Bethel Coll, KS	B
Blackburn Coll, IL	B
Black Hills State U, SD	A
Bluffton U, OH	B
Buena Vista U, IA	B
Butler U, IN	B
Calumet Coll of Saint Joseph, IN	A,B
Calvin Coll, MI	B
Capital U, OH	B
Cardinal Stritch U, WI	B
Carleton Coll, MN	B
Carroll Coll, WI	B
Case Western Reserve U, OH	B
Cedarville U, OH	B
Central Christian Coll of Kansas, KS	A
Central Coll, IA	B
Central Methodist U, MO	A,B
Chicago State U, IL	B
Clarke Coll, IA	B
Clarkson U, NY	B
Cleveland State U, OH	B
Coe Coll, IA	B
Coll of Menominee Nation, WI	A
Coll of Mount St. Joseph, OH	B
Coll of Saint Benedict, MN	B
Coll of the Ozarks, MO	B
The Coll of Wooster, OH	B
Columbia Coll, MO	B

College	Degree
Concordia Coll, MN	B
Concordia U, IL	B
Concordia U, NE	B
Concordia U Wisconsin, WI	B
Concord U, WV	B
Cornell Coll, IA	B
Creighton U, NE	A,B
Dana Coll, NE	B
Denison U, OH	B
DePaul U, IL	B
DePauw U, IN	B
Dickinson State U, ND	B
Doane Coll, NE	B
Dominican U, IL	B
Dordt Coll, IA	B
Drake U, IA	B
Drury U, MO	B
Earlham Coll, IN	B
East Central U, OK	B
Eastern Michigan U, MI	B
East-West U, IL	A,B
Elmhurst Coll, IL	B
Evangel U, MO	B
Fontbonne U, MO	B
Franciscan U of Steubenville, OH	B
Franklin Coll, IN	B
Goshen Coll, IN	B
Graceland U, IA	B
Grand Valley State U, MI	B
Grand View Coll, IA	B
Grantham U, MO	A,B
Greenville Coll, IL	B
Grinnell Coll, IA	B
Gustavus Adolphus Coll, MN	B
Hanover Coll, IN	B
Hastings Coll, NE	B
Heidelberg Coll, OH	B
Hillsdale Coll, MI	B
Hiram Coll, OH	B
Hope Coll, MI	B
Huntington U, IN	B
Illinois Coll, IL	B
Illinois Inst of Technology, IL	B
Illinois Wesleyan U, IL	B
Indiana Tech, IN	B
Indiana U–Purdue U Fort Wayne, IN	A,B
Indiana U South Bend, IN	A,B
Indiana U Southeast, IN	A,B
Iowa Wesleyan Coll, IA	B
Jamestown Coll, ND	B
Judson Coll, IL	B
Kalamazoo Coll, MI	B
Kent State U, OH	B
Kettering U, MI	B
Kilian Comm Coll, SD	A
Lake Forest Coll, IL	B
Lakeland Coll, WI	B
Lake Superior State U, MI	B
Langston U, OK	B
Lawrence Technological U, MI	B
Lawrence U, WI	B
Lewis Coll of Business, MI	A
Lewis U, IL	B
Lincoln U, MO	A
Lindenwood U, MO	B
Loras Coll, IA	B
Loyola U Chicago, IL	B
Luther Coll, IA	B
Macalester Coll, MN	B
Madonna U, MI	A,B
Maharishi U of Management, IA	B
Malone Coll, OH	B
Manchester Coll, IN	A,B

College	Degree
Marietta Coll, OH	B
Marquette U, WI	B
Maryville U of Saint Louis, MO	B
McKendree Coll, IL	B
Metropolitan State U, MN	B
Miami U Hamilton, OH	B
Miami U–Middletown Campus, OH	A
Michigan Technological U, MI	B
Minnesota State U Mankato, MN	B
Minot State U, ND	B
Missouri Southern State U, MO	A,B
Missouri State U, MO	B
Missouri Valley Coll, MO	B
Morningside Coll, IA	B
Mount Marty Coll, SD	B
Mount Mary Coll, WI	B
Mount Mercy Coll, IA	B
Mount Union Coll, OH	B
Nebraska Wesleyan U, NE	B
North Carolina Ag and Tech State U, NC	B
North Central Coll, IL	B
North Dakota State U, ND	B
Northeastern Illinois U, IL	B
Northeastern State U, OK	B
Northern Illinois U, IL	B
Northern Michigan U, MI	B
Northwestern Coll, IA	B
Northwestern Oklahoma State U, OK	B
Northwestern U, IL	B
Northwest Missouri State U, MO	B
Oakland U, MI	B
Oberlin Coll, OH	B
Oglala Lakota Coll, SD	A
Ohio Dominican U, OH	B
Ohio Northern U, OH	B
The Ohio State U, OH	B
Ohio U, OH	B
Ohio Wesleyan U, OH	B
Oklahoma Christian U, OK	B
Oklahoma City U, OK	B
Oklahoma State U, OK	B
Oral Roberts U, OK	B
Otterbein Coll, OH	B
Park U, MO	A,B
Pittsburg State U, KS	B
Purdue U Calumet, IN	B
Quincy U, IL	B
Ripon Coll, WI	B
Rockford Coll, IL	B
Rockhurst U, MO	B
Rogers State U, OK	A
Roosevelt U, IL	B
Rose-Hulman Inst of Technology, IN	B
St. Ambrose U, IA	B
St. Cloud State U, MN	B
Saint John's U, MN	B
Saint Mary's U of Minnesota, MN	B
St. Olaf Coll, MN	B
Saint Xavier U, IL	B
Simpson Coll, IA	B
South Dakota School of Mines and Technology, SD	B
Southern Illinois U Carbondale, IL	B
Southern Illinois U Edwardsville, IL	B
Southern Methodist U, TX	B

College	Degree
Southwest Baptist U, MO	A,B
Southwestern Coll, KS	B
Southwestern Oklahoma State U, OK	B
Southwest Minnesota State U, MN	B
Spring Arbor U, MI	B
Tabor Coll, KS	A,B
Taylor U, IN	B
Transylvania U, KY	B
Trinity Christian Coll, IL	B
Trinity International U, IL	B
Tri-State U, IN	B
Truman State U, MO	B
Turtle Mountain Comm Coll, ND	A
Union Coll, NE	B
The U of Akron, OH	B
U of Central Oklahoma, OK	B
U of Chicago, IL	B
U of Cincinnati, OH	B
U of Dayton, OH	B
The U of Findlay, OH	A,B
U of Illinois at Springfield, IL	B
U of Illinois at Urbana–Champaign, IL	B
U of Indianapolis, IN	B
The U of Iowa, IA	B
U of Michigan, MI	B
U of Michigan–Flint, MI	B
U of Minnesota, Duluth, MN	B
U of Minnesota, Morris, MN	B
U of Minnesota, Twin Cities Campus, MN	B
U of Missouri–Columbia, MO	B
U of Missouri–Kansas City, MO	B
U of Missouri–Rolla, MO	B
U of Missouri–St. Louis, MO	B
U of Nebraska at Omaha, NE	B
U of New Orleans, LA	B
U of North Dakota, ND	B
U of Northern Iowa, IA	B
U of Rio Grande, OH	A,B
U of St. Francis, IL	B
U of Sioux Falls, SD	B
The U of Toledo, OH	B
U of Tulsa, OK	B
U of Wisconsin–Green Bay, WI	B
U of Wisconsin–Madison, WI	B
U of Wisconsin–Milwaukee, WI	B
U of Wisconsin–Oshkosh, WI	B
U of Wisconsin–Parkside, WI	B
U of Wisconsin–Platteville, WI	B
U of Wisconsin–River Falls, WI	B
U of Wisconsin–Superior, WI	B
Valparaiso U, IN	B
Walsh U, OH	B
Wartburg Coll, IA	B
Washington U in St. Louis, MO	B
Webster U, MO	B
Western Michigan U, MI	B
Westminster Coll, MO	B
Wheaton Coll, IL	B
William Jewell Coll, MO	B
William Penn U, IA	B
Wilmington Coll, OH	B
Winona State U, MN	B
Wittenberg U, OH	B
Wright State U, OH	B
Xavier U, OH	B
Youngstown State U, OH	B

Computer Software and Media Applications Related
AIB Coll of Business, IA	A
Dakota Wesleyan U, SD	B
Indiana U–Purdue U Fort Wayne, IN	A,B
Kaplan Coll–Indianapolis, IN	A
Kilian Comm Coll, SD	A

Computer Software Engineering
Carroll Coll, WI	B
Clarkson U, NY	B
Grantham U, MO	A,B
ITT Tech Inst, Indianapolis, IN	B
ITT Tech Inst, Newburgh, IN	A
ITT Tech Inst, MN	B
ITT Tech Inst, Arnold, MO	B
ITT Tech Inst, NE	B
ITT Tech Inst, Green Bay, WI	B
Michigan Technological U, MI	B
Milwaukee School of Engineering, WI	B
Rose-Hulman Inst of Technology, IN	B
South Dakota State U, SD	B
U of Phoenix–Cincinnati Campus, OH	B
U of Phoenix–Cleveland Campus, OH	B
U of Phoenix–Columbus Ohio Campus, OH	B
U of Phoenix–Indianapolis Campus, IN	B
U of Phoenix–Metro Detroit Campus, MI	B
U of Phoenix–St. Louis Campus, MO	B
U of Phoenix–Springfield Campus, MO	B
U of Wisconsin–Platteville, WI	B

Computer Software Technology
ITT Tech Inst, Burr Ridge, IL	A
ITT Tech Inst, Fort Wayne, IN	B
ITT Tech Inst, Indianapolis, IN	B
ITT Tech Inst, Newburgh, IN	B
ITT Tech Inst, MN	B
ITT Tech Inst, Arnold, MO	B
ITT Tech Inst, NE	B
ITT Tech Inst, Green Bay, WI	B
ITT Tech Inst, Greenfield, WI	A

Computer Systems Analysis
Baker Coll of Flint, MI	A,B
Baldwin-Wallace Coll, OH	B
Davenport U, Dearborn, MI	A,B
DeVry U, Tinley Park, IL	B
Kent State U, OH	B
Metropolitan State U, MN	B
Miami U, OH	B
Miami U Hamilton, OH	B
St. Ambrose U, IA	B
The U of Akron, OH	A
The U of Toledo, OH	A

Computer Systems Networking and Telecommunications
Aakers Coll, Fargo, ND	A
Academy Coll, MN	A
AIB Coll of Business, IA	A
Aurora U, IL	B

Baker Coll of Allen Park, MI	A
Baker Coll of Flint, MI	A
Baldwin-Wallace Coll, OH	B
Bowling Green State U–Firelands Coll, OH	A
Capella U, MN	B
DePaul U, IL	B
DeVry U, Addison, IL	A
DeVry U, Chicago, IL	A,B
DeVry U, Tinley Park, IL	A,B
DeVry U, Indianapolis, IN	A
DeVry U, MN	A
DeVry U, Kansas City, MO	B
DeVry U, Columbus, OH	A,B
DeVry U, OK	A
Herzing Coll, MN	A
Herzing Coll, WI	A
ITT Tech Inst, Orland Park, IL	A
ITT Tech Inst, Fort Wayne, IN	A
ITT Tech Inst, Indianapolis, IN	A
ITT Tech Inst, Newburgh, IN	A
ITT Tech Inst, MN	A
ITT Tech Inst, Arnold, MO	B
ITT Tech Inst, Earth City, MO	A
ITT Tech Inst, Kansas City, MO	A
ITT Tech Inst, NE	B
ITT Tech Inst, Oklahoma City, OK	A
ITT Tech Inst, Tulsa, OK	A
ITT Tech Inst, Green Bay, WI	A
ITT Tech Inst, Greenfield, WI	A
Michigan Technological U, MI	B
Minnesota School of Business, MN	A
Minnesota School of Business–Brooklyn Center, MN	A
Minnesota School of Business–Plymouth, MN	A
Minnesota School of Business–Richfield, MN	A
Minnesota School of Business–St. Cloud, MN	A
Minnesota School of Business–Shakopee, MN	A
Northern Michigan U, MI	B
Northwestern Oklahoma State U, OK	B
Robert Morris Coll, IL	A
Roosevelt U, IL	B
St. Ambrose U, IA	B
The U of Findlay, OH	B
U of Phoenix–St. Louis Campus, MO	A
U of Wisconsin–Stout, WI	B

Computer Teacher Education
Alma Coll, MI	B
Baker Coll of Flint, MI	A
Buena Vista U, IA	B
Capital U, OH	B
Central Christian Coll of Kansas, KS	A
Central Michigan U, MI	B
Concordia U, IL	B
Concordia U, NE	B
Dakota State U, SD	B
Dordt Coll, IA	B
Eastern Michigan U, MI	B
Michigan Technological U, MI	B
South Dakota State U, SD	B
Union Coll, NE	B
The U of Akron, OH	B
U of Nebraska–Lincoln, NE	B

U of Wisconsin–River Falls, WI	B
Viterbo U, WI	B
Wright State U, OH	B

Computer/Technical Support
Bowling Green State U–Firelands Coll, OH	A
Davenport U, Dearborn, MI	A

Computer Technology/Computer Systems Technology
DeVry U, Addison, IL	B
DeVry U, Chicago, IL	B
DeVry U, Kansas City, MO	A
Miami U Hamilton, OH	B
Southeast Missouri State U, MO	A
Southwestern Coll, KS	B

Computer Typography and Composition Equipment Operation
Baker Coll of Auburn Hills, MI	A
Baker Coll of Cadillac, MI	A
Baker Coll of Clinton Township, MI	A
Baker Coll of Flint, MI	A
Baker Coll of Jackson, MI	A
Calumet Coll of Saint Joseph, IN	A
The U of Toledo, OH	A

Conducting
Calvin Coll, MI	B
Ohio U, OH	B

Conservation Biology
St. Gregory's U, Shawnee, OK	B

Construction Engineering
Andrews U, MI	B
Bradley U, IL	B
Clarkson U, NY	B
Michigan Technological U, MI	B
North Dakota State U, ND	B
Purdue U, IN	B
U of Cincinnati, OH	B
Western Michigan U, MI	B

Construction Engineering Technology
Baker Coll of Owosso, MI	A
Bemidji State U, MN	B
Bowling Green State U, OH	B
Central Michigan U, MI	B
Eastern Michigan U, MI	B
Ferris State U, MI	A
Fort Berthold Comm Coll, ND	A
Indiana U–Purdue U Fort Wayne, IN	B
Lake Superior State U, MI	A
Lawrence Technological U, MI	B
Morrison Inst of Technology, IL	A
Pittsburg State U, KS	B
Purdue U Calumet, IN	A,B
Purdue U North Central, IN	A
South Dakota State U, SD	B
Southeast Missouri State U, MO	B
Southern Illinois U Carbondale, IL	B
Southern Illinois U Edwardsville, IL	B
The U of Akron, OH	A
U of Cincinnati, OH	A,B

U of Nebraska at Omaha, NE	B
U of Nebraska–Lincoln, NE	B
The U of Toledo, OH	A,B
U of Wisconsin–Stout, WI	B
Western Michigan U, MI	B
Wright State U, OH	A

Construction Management
Baker Coll of Flint, MI	A
Eastern Michigan U, MI	B
Ferris State U, MI	B
ITT Tech Inst, Indianapolis, IN	B
ITT Tech Inst, Arnold, MO	B
ITT Tech Inst, Earth City, MO	B
ITT Tech Inst, Oklahoma City, OK	B
ITT Tech Inst, Tulsa, OK	B
Lawrence Technological U, MI	B
Michigan State U, MI	B
Milwaukee School of Engineering, WI	B
Minnesota State U Mankato, MN	B
North Carolina Ag and Tech State U, NC	B
North Dakota State U, ND	B
Northern Michigan U, MI	B
Oklahoma State U, OK	B
Pittsburg State U, KS	B
U of Cincinnati, OH	B
U of Minnesota, Twin Cities Campus, MN	B
U of Northern Iowa, IA	B
U of Wisconsin–Madison, WI	B
U of Wisconsin–Platteville, WI	B
Western Michigan U, MI	B

Construction Trades
Northern Michigan U, MI	A

Construction Trades Related
Hope Coll, MI	B

Consumer Merchandising/Retailing Management
Baker Coll of Owosso, MI	A
East Central U, OK	B
Ferris State U, MI	B
Fontbonne U, MO	B
Indiana U Bloomington, IN	B
International Business Coll, Fort Wayne, IN	A,B
Lindenwood U, MO	B
Madonna U, MI	A,B
Northwest Missouri State U, MO	B
U of Central Oklahoma, OK	B
The U of Toledo, OH	A
Winona State U, MN	B

Consumer Services and Advocacy
Coll of the Ozarks, MO	B
South Dakota State U, SD	B
U of Wisconsin–Madison, WI	B

Cooking and Related Culinary Arts
Kendall Coll, IL	A,B
Lexington Coll, IL	A,B

Corrections
Baker Coll of Muskegon, MI	A
Coll of the Ozarks, MO	B
East Central U, OK	B
Lake Superior State U, MI	A,B
Langston U, OK	B

A—associate degree; B—bachelor's degree

Marygrove Coll, MI A
Minnesota State U Mankato, MN B
Northern Michigan U, MI A
Oklahoma City U, OK B
Saint Louis U, MO B
Saint Mary's U of Minnesota, MN B
Southeast Missouri State U, MO B
Tiffin U, OH B
The U of Akron, OH B
U of Indianapolis, IN A,B
The U of Toledo, OH A
Washburn U, KS A,B
Winona State U, MN B
Xavier U, OH A

Corrections and Criminal Justice Related
Hastings Coll, NE B
Mount Mary Coll, WI B
North Dakota State U, ND B
U of Michigan–Flint, MI B
U of Phoenix–St. Louis Campus, MO B
U of Phoenix–West Michigan Campus, MI B

Counseling Psychology
Crossroads Coll, MN B
Grace Coll, IN B
Jamestown Coll, ND B
Kilian Comm Coll, SD A
Morningside Coll, IA B
Newman U, KS B
Northwestern U, IL B
Oak Hills Christian Coll, MN B
Rochester Coll, MI B
Saint Xavier U, IL B
Taylor U Fort Wayne, IN B
Wayne State Coll, NE B

Counselor Education/School Counseling and Guidance
Buena Vista U, IA B
DePaul U, IL B
East Central U, OK B
Northwest Missouri State U, MO B
Oglala Lakota Coll, SD A,B
St. Cloud State U, MN B
U of Central Oklahoma, OK B
Wright State U, OH B

Court Reporting
AIB Coll of Business, IA A
Kaplan U, IA A
U of Cincinnati, OH B

Crafts, Folk Art and Artisanry
Bowling Green State U, OH B
The Cleveland Inst of Art, OH B
Indiana U–Purdue U Fort Wayne, IN B
Kent State U, OH B
School of the Art Inst of Chicago, IL B
The U of Akron, OH B
U of Illinois at Urbana–Champaign, IL B

Creative Writing
Antioch Coll, OH B
Ashland U, OH B
Augustana Coll, IL B
Beloit Coll, WI B
Bluffton U, OH B
Bowling Green State U, OH B

Briar Cliff U, IA B
Capital U, OH B
Cardinal Stritch U, WI B
Carroll Coll, WI B
Central Michigan U, MI B
Coe Coll, IA B
Coll of St. Catherine, MN B
Columbia Coll Chicago, IL B
Concordia Coll, MN B
Cornerstone U, MI B
Denison U, OH B
DePaul U, IL B
Drury U, MO B
Eastern Michigan U, MI B
Grand Valley State U, MI B
Hastings Coll, NE B
Indiana U–Purdue U Fort Wayne, IN B
Indiana Wesleyan U, IN B
Kansas City Art Inst, MO B
Kenyon Coll, OH B
Knox Coll, IL B
Loras Coll, IA B
Manchester Coll, IN A
Marquette U, WI B
Miami U, OH B
Miami U Hamilton, OH B
Millikin U, IL B
Minnesota State U Mankato, MN B
North Central Coll, IL B
Northern Michigan U, MI B
Northland Coll, WI B
Northwestern Coll, MN B
Oberlin Coll, OH B
Ohio Northern U, OH B
The Ohio State U, OH B
Ohio U, OH B
Ohio Wesleyan U, OH B
Oklahoma Christian U, OK B
Rockhurst U, MO B
St. Cloud State U, MN B
Saint Joseph's Coll, IN B
Saint Mary's Coll, IN B
School of the Art Inst of Chicago, IL B
Southwest Minnesota State U, MN B
Stephens Coll, MO B
Taylor U, IN B
U of Chicago, IL B
U of Evansville, IN B
The U of Findlay, OH B
U of Michigan, MI B
U of Nebraska at Omaha, NE B
U of St. Thomas, MN B
U of Wisconsin–Parkside, WI B
Waldorf Coll, IA B
Washington U in St. Louis, MO B
Wayne State Coll, NE B
Western Michigan U, MI B

Criminal Justice/Law Enforcement Administration
Aakers Coll, Fargo, ND A
Adrian Coll, MI A,B
Anderson U, IN A,B
Ashland U, OH A,B
Aurora U, IL B
Baldwin-Wallace Coll, OH B
Ball State U, IN A,B
Bellevue U, NE B
Bemidji State U, MN A,B
Blackburn Coll, IL B
Bradley U, IL B
Briar Cliff U, IA B

Bryant and Stratton Coll, Cleveland, OH A
Calumet Coll of Saint Joseph, IN A,B
Carroll Coll, WI B
Cedarville U, OH B
Central Christian Coll of Kansas, KS A
Chicago State U, IL B
Coll of the Ozarks, MO B
Columbia Coll, MO A,B
Concordia U, MI B
Concordia U Wisconsin, WI B
Culver-Stockton Coll, MO B
Dakota Wesleyan U, SD A,B
Dana Coll, NE B
Dordt Coll, IA B
East Central U, OK B
Edgewood Coll, WI B
Evangel U, MO B
Finlandia U, MI A
Grace Coll, IN B
Graceland U, IA B
Grand Valley State U, MI B
Grand View Coll, IA B
Grantham U, MO A,B
Greenville Coll, IL B
Gustavus Adolphus Coll, MN B
Hamline U, MN B
Hannibal-LaGrange Coll, MO A,B
Harris-Stowe State U, MO B
Indiana Tech, IN A,B
Indiana U Northwest, IN A,B
Indiana U South Bend, IN A,B
Iowa Wesleyan Coll, IA B
ITT Tech Inst, Fort Wayne, IN B
ITT Tech Inst, Indianapolis, IN B
ITT Tech Inst, Newburgh, IN B
ITT Tech Inst, Arnold, MO B
ITT Tech Inst, Earth City, MO B
ITT Tech Inst, Kansas City, MO B
ITT Tech Inst, NE A
ITT Tech Inst, Oklahoma City, OK B
ITT Tech Inst, Tulsa, OK B
ITT Tech Inst, Green Bay, WI B
ITT Tech Inst, Greenfield, WI B
Kent State U, Trumbull Campus, OH A,B
Kilian Comm Coll, SD A
Lake Superior State U, MI A,B
Langston U, OK B
Lewis U, IL B
Lincoln U, MO A,B
Lindenwood U, MO B
Lourdes Coll, OH A,B
MacMurray Coll, IL A,B
Marian Coll of Fond du Lac, WI B
McKendree Coll, IL B
Metropolitan State U, MN B
Michigan State U, MI B
Missouri Southern State U, MO B
Missouri Valley Coll, MO B
Mount Vernon Nazarene U, OH B
Newman U, KS B
Northeastern State U, OK B
Northern Michigan U, MI A,B
Oglala Lakota Coll, SD A,B
Ohio Dominican U, OH B
Ohio Northern U, OH B
Ohio U, OH B

Ohio U–Zanesville, OH B
Oklahoma City U, OK B
Park U, MO A,B
Peru State Coll, NE B
Purdue U Calumet, IN B
Rogers State U, OK A
St. Cloud State U, MN B
Saint Louis U, MO B
Saint Mary's U of Minnesota, MN B
Simpson Coll, IA B
Southern Illinois U Carbondale, IL B
Southwestern Coll, KS B
Southwestern Oklahoma State U, OK B
Taylor U Fort Wayne, IN B
Tiffin U, OH B
Tri-State U, IN A,B
Truman State U, MO B
The U of Akron, OH B
U of Central Missouri, MO B
U of Central Oklahoma, OK B
U of Cincinnati, OH A,B
U of Dayton, OH B
The U of Findlay, OH A,B
U of Indianapolis, IN A,B
U of Missouri–Kansas City, MO B
U of Phoenix–Chicago Campus, IL B
U of Phoenix–Cincinnati Campus, OH B
U of Phoenix–Cleveland Campus, OH B
U of Phoenix–Columbus Ohio Campus, OH A,B
U of Phoenix–Indianapolis Campus, IN A,B
U of Phoenix–Kansas City Campus, MO B
U of Phoenix–Metro Detroit Campus, MI B
U of Phoenix–Oklahoma City Campus, OK B
U of Phoenix–St. Louis Campus, MO A
U of Phoenix–Springfield Campus, MO A,B
U of Phoenix–Tulsa Campus, OK B
U of Phoenix–West Michigan Campus, MI B
U of Phoenix–Wichita Campus, KS B
U of Phoenix–Wisconsin Campus, WI B
The U of South Dakota, SD B
U of Wisconsin–Milwaukee, WI B
U of Wisconsin–Oshkosh, WI B
U of Wisconsin–Parkside, WI B
U of Wisconsin–Platteville, WI B
Washburn U, KS A,B
Wayne State Coll, NE B
Western Illinois U, IL B
Wilmington Coll, OH B
Winona State U, MN B
Youngstown State U, OH B

Criminal Justice/Police Science
Bemidji State U, MN B
Cameron U, OK A,B
Chicago State U, IL B
Coll of the Ozarks, MO B
East Central U, OK B

Ferris State U, MI — B
Grand Valley State U, MI — B
Grantham U, MO — A,B
Kent State U, Ashtabula Campus, OH — A
Kent State U, Tuscarawas Campus, OH — A,B
Lake Superior State U, MI — A,B
Langston U, OK — B
MacMurray Coll, IL — A,B
Metropolitan State U, MN — B
Minnesota State U Mankato, MN — B
Missouri Southern State U, MO — A
Northeastern State U, OK — B
Northern Michigan U, MI — A,B
Northern State U, SD — B
Northwestern Oklahoma State U, OK — B
Ohio Northern U, OH — B
Ohio U, OH — A
Oklahoma City U, OK — B
Purdue U Calumet, IN — B
Rogers State U, OK — A
St. Gregory's U, Shawnee, OK — B
Saint Louis U, MO — B
Saint Mary's U of Minnesota, MN — B
Tiffin U, OH — A,B
Truman State U, MO — B
The U of Akron, OH — A
U of Cincinnati, OH — A,B
U of Mary, ND — B
The U of Toledo, OH — A
U of Wisconsin–Milwaukee, WI — B
Washburn U, KS — A,B
Wayne State Coll, NE — B
Winona State U, MN — B
Wright State U, OH — B

Criminal Justice/Safety
Ashford U, IA — B
Augsburg Coll, MN — B
Aurora U, IL — B
Bethany Coll, KS — B
Bluffton U, OH — B
Bowling Green State U, OH — B
Bowling Green State U–Firelands Coll, OH — A,B
Buena Vista U, IA — B
Butler U, IN — B
Capital U, OH — B
Central Christian Coll of Kansas, KS — A
Central Methodist U, MO — B
Concordia U, St. Paul, MN — B
Fort Hays State U, KS — B
Gannon U, PA — A,B
Grantham U, MO — A,B
Illinois State U, IL — B
Indiana U Bloomington, IN — B
Indiana U East, IN — A
Indiana U Kokomo, IN — A,B
Indiana U–Purdue U Fort Wayne, IN — A,B
Indiana U–Purdue U Indianapolis, IN — A,B
Indiana Wesleyan U, IN — A,B
Jamestown Coll, ND — B
Judson Coll, IL — B
Kaplan U, IA — A,B
Lakeland Coll, WI — B
Loras Coll, IA — B

Loyola U Chicago, IL — B
Madonna U, MI — A,B
Manchester Coll, IN — A
Metropolitan State U, MN — B
Michigan State U, MI — B
Minot State U, ND — B
Missouri Baptist U, MO — B
Missouri State U, MO — B
Missouri Western State U, MO — A,B
Mount Marty Coll, SD — B
Northeastern Illinois U, IL — B
Northwestern Coll, MN — B
Ohio Northern U, OH — B
The Ohio State U, OH — B
Ohio U, OH — B
Quincy U, IL — B
Saginaw Valley State U, MI — B
St. Ambrose U, IA — B
St. Gregory's U, Shawnee, OK — A
Saint Joseph's Coll, IN — B
Saint Xavier U, IL — B
Southeastern Oklahoma State U, OK — B
Southern Illinois U Edwardsville, IL — B
Southwest Minnesota State U, MN — B
Tiffin U, OH — B
The U of Akron, OH — B
U of Central Oklahoma, OK — B
U of Illinois at Chicago, IL — B
U of Michigan–Dearborn, MI — B
U of Nebraska at Kearney, NE — B
U of Nebraska at Omaha, NE — B
U of North Dakota, ND — B
The U of Toledo, OH — B
U of West Florida, FL — B
U of Wisconsin–Eau Claire, WI — B
U of Wisconsin–Superior, WI — B
Viterbo U, WI — B
Wayne State Coll, NE — B
Western Michigan U, MI — B
Wichita State U, KS — B
Xavier U, OH — A,B
Youngstown State U, OH — A,B

Criminology
Ball State U, IN — A,B
Bethel Coll, KS — B
Capital U, OH — B
Central Michigan U, MI — B
Coll of Mount St. Joseph, OH — B
Coll of the Ozarks, MO — B
Dominican U, IL — B
Drury U, MO — B
Eastern Michigan U, MI — B
Indiana State U, IN — A,B
Lindenwood U, MO — B
Marquette U, WI — A,B
Maryville U of Saint Louis, MO — B
The Ohio State U, OH — B
Ohio U, OH — B
St. Cloud State U, MN — B
U of Minnesota, Duluth, MN — B
U of Missouri–Kansas City, MO — B
U of Missouri–St. Louis, MO — B
U of Northern Iowa, IA — B
U of Oklahoma, OK — B
U of St. Thomas, MN — B
Upper Iowa U, IA — B
Valparaiso U, IN — B
Western Michigan U, MI — B

William Penn U, IA — B
Wright State U, OH — B

Crop Production
North Dakota State U, ND — B

Culinary Arts
The Art Insts International Minnesota, MN — A,B
Baker Coll of Muskegon, MI — A
The Illinois Inst of Art–Chicago, IL — A
Kendall Coll, IL — A,B
Lexington Coll, IL — A,B
Metropolitan State U, MN — B
Purdue U Calumet, IN — A
Robert Morris Coll, IL — A
St. Augustine Coll, IL — A
The U of Akron, OH — A

Culinary Arts Related
Lexington Coll, IL — A,B

Cultural Studies
Cornell Coll, IA — B
Indiana Wesleyan U, IN — A,B
Kent State U, OH — B
Minnesota State U Mankato, MN — B
The Ohio State U, OH — B
Ohio Wesleyan U, OH — B
Saint Mary-of-the-Woods Coll, IN — B
St. Olaf Coll, MN — B
U of Wisconsin–Milwaukee, WI — B
Washington U in St. Louis, MO — B

Curriculum and Instruction
Ohio U, OH — B
U of Saint Mary, KS — B
The U of South Dakota, SD — B
Washburn U, KS — B
Wright State U, OH — B

Customer Service Management
U of Wisconsin–Stout, WI — B

Cytogenetics/Genetics/Clinical Genetics Technology
Saint Mary's U of Minnesota, MN — B

Cytotechnology
Ashford U, IA — B
Barnes-Jewish Coll of Nursing and Allied Health, MO — B
Edgewood Coll, WI — B
Elmhurst Coll, IL — B
Illinois Coll, IL — B
Indiana U–Purdue U Indianapolis, IN — A,B
Indiana U Southeast, IN — A,B
Marian Coll of Fond du Lac, WI — B
Michigan Technological U, MI — B
Northern Michigan U, MI — B
Saint Mary's Coll, IN — B
Saint Mary's U of Minnesota, MN — B
U of Kansas, KS — B
U of North Dakota, ND — B
Winona State U, MN — B

Dairy Science
Iowa State U of Science and Technology, IA — B

South Dakota State U, SD — B
U of Wisconsin–Madison, WI — B
U of Wisconsin–River Falls, WI — B

Dance
Alma Coll, MI — B
Antioch Coll, OH — B
Ball State U, IN — B
Bowling Green State U, OH — B
Butler U, IN — B
Cleveland State U, OH — B
Columbia Coll Chicago, IL — B
Denison U, OH — B
Eastern Michigan U, MI — B
Gustavus Adolphus Coll, MN — B
Hope Coll, MI — B
Indiana U Bloomington, IN — B
Kent State U, OH — B
Kenyon Coll, OH — B
Lindenwood U, MO — B
Luther Coll, IA — B
Marygrove Coll, MI — B
Missouri State U, MO — B
Northwestern U, IL — B
Oakland U, MI — B
Oberlin Coll, OH — B
The Ohio State U, OH — B
Ohio U, OH — B
Oklahoma City U, OK — B
St. Gregory's U, Shawnee, OK — B
St. Olaf Coll, MN — B
Southern Methodist U, TX — B
Stephens Coll, MO — B
The U of Akron, OH — B
U of Central Oklahoma, OK — B
U of Cincinnati, OH — B
U of Illinois at Urbana–Champaign, IL — B
The U of Iowa, IA — B
U of Kansas, KS — B
U of Michigan, MI — B
U of Minnesota, Twin Cities Campus, MN — B
U of Missouri–Kansas City, MO — B
U of Nebraska–Lincoln, NE — B
U of Oklahoma, OK — B
U of Wisconsin–Milwaukee, WI — B
U of Wisconsin–Stevens Point, WI — B
Washington U in St. Louis, MO — B
Webster U, MO — B
Western Michigan U, MI — B
Wittenberg U, OH — B
Wright State U, OH — B

Dance Therapy
Columbia Coll Chicago, IL — B

Data Entry/Microcomputer Applications
Baker Coll of Allen Park, MI — A

Data Entry/Microcomputer Applications Related
AIB Coll of Business, IA — A
Baker Coll of Allen Park, MI — A

Data Modeling/Warehousing and Database Administration
Davenport U, Dearborn, MI — B

A—associate degree; B—bachelor's degree

Data Processing and Data Processing Technology

Academy Coll, MN	A
Baker Coll of Auburn Hills, MI	A
Baker Coll of Cadillac, MI	A
Baker Coll of Clinton Township, MI	A
Baker Coll of Flint, MI	A
Baker Coll of Jackson, MI	A
Baker Coll of Muskegon, MI	A
Baker Coll of Owosso, MI	A
Baker Coll of Port Huron, MI	A
Bemidji State U, MN	B
Dordt Coll, IA	A
Indiana U Kokomo, IN	B
Indiana U Northwest, IN	B
Lewis Coll of Business, MI	A
Minnesota State U Mankato, MN	B
Missouri Southern State U, MO	A
Mount Vernon Nazarene U, OH	B
Northern State U, SD	A
Northwest Missouri State U, MO	B
The U of Akron, OH	A
U of Cincinnati, OH	A
U of Southern Indiana, IN	B
The U of Toledo, OH	A
Wright State U, OH	A
Youngstown State U, OH	A

Dental Assisting

Herzing Coll, MN	A
Robert Morris Coll, IL	A
U of Southern Indiana, IN	A

Dental Hygiene

Argosy U, Twin Cities, Eagan, MN	A
Baker Coll of Port Huron, MI	A
Ferris State U, MI	A
Herzing Coll, MN	A
Indiana U Northwest, IN	A
Indiana U–Purdue U Fort Wayne, IN	A
Indiana U–Purdue U Indianapolis, IN	A,B
Indiana U South Bend, IN	A
Marquette U, WI	B
Minnesota State U Mankato, MN	A,B
Missouri Southern State U, MO	A
The Ohio State U, OH	B
Shawnee State U, OH	A
Southern Illinois U Carbondale, IL	B
U of Michigan, MI	B
U of Minnesota, Twin Cities Campus, MN	B
U of Missouri–Kansas City, MO	B
U of Nebraska Medical Center, NE	B
U of Oklahoma Health Sciences Center, OK	B
The U of South Dakota, SD	A,B
U of Southern Indiana, IN	A,B
Wichita State U, KS	A,B
Youngstown State U, OH	A

Dental Laboratory Technology

Indiana U–Purdue U Fort Wayne, IN	A

Southern Illinois U Carbondale, IL	A

Design and Applied Arts Related

The Illinois Inst of Art–Chicago, IL	B
Ohio U, OH	B
Robert Morris Coll, IL	B
St. Cloud State U, MN	B
School of the Art Inst of Chicago, IL	B
The U of Akron, OH	B
U of Saint Francis, IN	B
U of Wisconsin–Stout, WI	B

Design and Visual Communications

Academy Coll, MN	A
Alma Coll, MI	B
Bowling Green State U, OH	B
Bowling Green State U–Firelands Coll, OH	B
Columbia Coll Chicago, IL	B
Drury U, MO	B
The Illinois Inst of Art–Chicago, IL	B
The Illinois Inst of Art–Schaumburg, IL	B
Illinois Inst of Technology, IL	B
International Academy of Design & Technology, IL	B
Iowa State U of Science and Technology, IA	B
Missouri State U, MO	B
Mount Union Coll, OH	B
Ohio Northern U, OH	B
The Ohio State U, OH	B
Ohio U, OH	B
Purdue U, IN	B
Saginaw Valley State U, MI	B
St. Ambrose U, IA	B
Saint Mary-of-the-Woods Coll, IN	B
School of the Art Inst of Chicago, IL	B
Southern Illinois U Carbondale, IL	B
Truman State U, MO	B
U of Evansville, IN	B
U of Kansas, KS	B
U of Michigan, MI	B
U of Notre Dame, IN	B
U of Oklahoma, OK	B
Viterbo U, WI	B
Washington U in St. Louis, MO	B
William Woods U, MO	B

Desktop Publishing and Digital Imaging Design

Davenport U, Dearborn, MI	A
Ferris State U, MI	B

Developmental and Child Psychology

Edgewood Coll, WI	B
Langston U, OK	B
Metropolitan State U, MN	B
Minnesota State U Mankato, MN	B
Northern Michigan U, MI	B
Northwest Missouri State U, MO	B
The U of Akron, OH	B
U of Minnesota, Twin Cities Campus, MN	B
U of Sioux Falls, SD	A

The U of Toledo, OH	B
U of Wisconsin–Green Bay, WI	B
U of Wisconsin–Madison, WI	B

Development Economics and International Development

Calvin Coll, MI	B
The Ohio State U, OH	B

Diagnostic Medical Sonography and Ultrasound Technology

Argosy U, Twin Cities, Eagan, MN	A
Baker Coll of Auburn Hills, MI	A
Baker Coll of Owosso, MI	A
Baker Coll of Port Huron, MI	A
Coll of St. Catherine, MN	A
Ferris State U, MI	A
Nebraska Methodist Coll, NE	A,B
U of Missouri–Columbia, MO	B
U of Nebraska Medical Center, NE	B

Dietetics

Andrews U, MI	B
Ashland U, OH	B
Ball State U, IN	A,B
Bowling Green State U, OH	B
Case Western Reserve U, OH	B
Central Michigan U, MI	B
Coll of Saint Benedict, MN	B
Coll of St. Catherine, MN	B
Coll of the Ozarks, MO	B
Concordia Coll, MN	B
Dominican U, IL	B
Eastern Michigan U, MI	B
Fontbonne U, MO	B
Gannon U, PA	B
Indiana U Bloomington, IN	B
Iowa State U of Science and Technology, IA	B
Kansas State U, KS	B
Langston U, OK	B
Miami U, OH	B
Miami U Hamilton, OH	B
Michigan State U, MI	B
Minnesota State U Mankato, MN	B
Missouri State U, MO	B
Mount Mary Coll, WI	B
North Carolina Ag and Tech State U, NC	B
North Dakota State U, ND	B
Northwest Missouri State U, MO	B
The Ohio State U, OH	B
Saint John's U, MN	B
South Dakota State U, SD	B
The U of Akron, OH	B
U of Central Missouri, MO	B
U of Central Oklahoma, OK	B
U of Dayton, OH	B
U of Illinois at Chicago, IL	B
U of Illinois at Urbana–Champaign, IL	B
U of Minnesota, Crookston, MN	A
U of Missouri–Columbia, MO	B
U of Nebraska at Kearney, NE	B
U of North Dakota, ND	B
U of Oklahoma Health Sciences Center, OK	B
U of Wisconsin–Madison, WI	B
U of Wisconsin–Stevens Point, WI	B

U of Wisconsin–Stout, WI	B
Viterbo U, WI	B
Western Michigan U, MI	B
Youngstown State U, OH	A,B

Dietetics and Clinical Nutrition Services Related

Madonna U, MI	B

Dietitian Assistant

Youngstown State U, OH	A

Digital Communication and Media/Multimedia

The Art Insts International Minnesota, MN	A,B
Calvin Coll, MI	B
Cameron U, OK	A
Clarkson U, NY	B
Grace Bible Coll, MI	B
Huntington U, IN	B
The Illinois Inst of Art–Schaumburg, IL	B
Kent State U, OH	B
Lindenwood U, MO	B
Michigan Technological U, MI	B
Minot State U, ND	B
Northwestern Coll, MN	B
School of the Art Inst of Chicago, IL	B
U of Northern Iowa, IA	B
U of Phoenix–Kansas City Campus, MO	B
U of Phoenix–Metro Detroit Campus, MI	B
U of Phoenix–St. Louis Campus, MO	B
U of Phoenix–Springfield Campus, MO	B

Directing and Theatrical Production

Coe Coll, IA	B
Drake U, IA	B
Oakland U, MI	B
Ohio U, OH	B
Western Michigan U, MI	B

Divinity/Ministry

Baptist Bible Coll, MO	B
Barclay Coll, KS	B
Cardinal Stritch U, WI	B
Central Christian Coll of Kansas, KS	B
Cincinnati Christian U, OH	B
Faith Baptist Bible Coll and Theological Seminary, IA	A,B
Global U of the Assemblies of God, MO	B
Grace Coll, IN	B
Great Lakes Christian Coll, MI	B
Huntington U, IN	B
Kuyper Coll, MI	B
Messenger Coll, MO	B
Oak Hills Christian Coll, MN	B
Oklahoma Wesleyan U, OK	B
Tabor Coll, KS	B
U of Mary, ND	B
Viterbo U, WI	B

Drafting and Design Technology

Baker Coll of Auburn Hills, MI	A
Baker Coll of Cadillac, MI	A
Baker Coll of Clinton Township, MI	A

Majors and Degrees
Drafting and Design Technology

Baker Coll of Flint, MI	A,B	Augsburg Coll, MN	B	Hiram Coll, OH	B	Rockford Coll, IL	B

Baker Coll of Flint, MI — A,B
Baker Coll of Muskegon, MI — A
Baker Coll of Owosso, MI — A,B
Baker Coll of Port Huron, MI — A
Black Hills State U, SD — A
Cameron U, OK — B
East Central U, OK — B
Ferris State U, MI — B
Herzing Coll, WI — A,B
Hillsdale Coll, MI — B
Langston U, OK — A
Lincoln U, MO — A
Missouri Southern State U, MO — A
Morrison Inst of Technology, IL — A
Northern Michigan U, MI — A,B
Robert Morris Coll, IL — A
Tri-State U, IN — A,B
The U of Akron, OH — A
U of Central Missouri, MO — A,B
U of Cincinnati, OH — A
U of Rio Grande, OH — A,B
The U of Toledo, OH — A
Washburn U, KS — A
Wright State U, OH — A
Youngstown State U, OH — A

Drafting/Design Engineering Technologies Related
The U of Akron, OH — A

Drafting/Design Technology
ITT Tech Inst, Oklahoma City, OK — A

Drama and Dance Teacher Education
Bowling Green State U, OH — B
Capital U, OH — B
Central Christian Coll of Kansas, KS — A
Coll of St. Catherine, MN — B
Concordia U, NE — B
Dana Coll, NE — B
Dordt Coll, IA — B
Hastings Coll, NE — B
Hope Coll, MI — B
Huntington U, IN — B
Indiana U–Purdue U Fort Wayne, IN — B
The Ohio State U, OH — B
Ohio Wesleyan U, OH — B
Southwest Minnesota State U, MN — B
The U of Akron, OH — B
U of Evansville, IN — B
The U of Iowa, IA — B
U of St. Thomas, MN — B
The U of South Dakota, SD — B
Valparaiso U, IN — B
Viterbo U, WI — B
Waldorf Coll, IA — B
Washington U in St. Louis, MO — B
Wayne State Coll, NE — B
William Jewell Coll, MO — B
Youngstown State U, OH — B

Dramatic/Theater Arts
Adrian Coll, MI — A,B
Albion Coll, MI — B
Alma Coll, MI — B
Anderson U, IN — B
Antioch Coll, OH — B
Aquinas Coll, MI — B
Ashland U, OH — B

Augsburg Coll, MN — B
Augustana Coll, IL — B
Augustana Coll, SD — B
Avila U, MO — B
Baker U, KS — B
Ball State U, IN — B
Beloit Coll, WI — B
Bemidji State U, MN — B
Benedictine Coll, KS — B
Bethany Lutheran Coll, MN — B
Bethel Coll, KS — B
Bethel U, MN — B
Bowling Green State U, OH — B
Bradley U, IL — B
Briar Cliff U, IA — B
Butler U, IN — B
Calvin Coll, MI — B
Capital U, OH — B
Cardinal Stritch U, WI — B
Carroll Coll, WI — B
Case Western Reserve U, OH — B
Cedarville U, OH — B
Central Coll, IA — B
Central Methodist U, MO — B
Central Michigan U, MI — B
Clarke Coll, IA — B
Cleveland State U, OH — B
Coe Coll, IA — B
Coll of Saint Benedict, MN — B
Coll of St. Catherine, MN — B
Coll of the Ozarks, MO — B
The Coll of Wooster, OH — B
Columbia Coll Chicago, IL — B
Concordia Coll, MN — B
Concordia U, IL — B
Concordia U, MI — B
Concordia U, NE — B
Concordia U, St. Paul, MN — B
Cornell Coll, IA — B
Creighton U, NE — B
Culver-Stockton Coll, MO — B
Dakota Wesleyan U, SD — B
Denison U, OH — B
DePaul U, IL — B
DePauw U, IN — B
Dickinson State U, ND — B
Doane Coll, NE — B
Dominican U, IL — B
Dordt Coll, IA — B
Drake U, IA — B
Drury U, MO — B
Earlham Coll, IN — B
Eastern Illinois U, IL — B
Eastern Michigan U, MI — B
Edgewood Coll, WI — B
Elmhurst Coll, IL — B
Emporia State U, KS — B
Fontbonne U, MO — B
Franciscan U of Steubenville, OH — B
Franklin Coll, IN — B
Gannon U, PA — B
Goshen Coll, IN — B
Graceland U, IA — B
Grand Valley State U, MI — B
Grand View Coll, IA — B
Greenville Coll, IL — B
Grinnell Coll, IA — B
Gustavus Adolphus Coll, MN — B
Hamline U, MN — B
Hannibal-LaGrange Coll, MO — B
Hanover Coll, IN — B
Hastings Coll, NE — B
Heidelberg Coll, OH — B
Hillsdale Coll, MI — B

Hiram Coll, OH — B
Hope Coll, MI — B
Huntington U, IN — B
Illinois Coll, IL — B
Illinois State U, IL — B
Illinois Wesleyan U, IL — B
Indiana State U, IN — B
Indiana U Bloomington, IN — A,B
Indiana U Northwest, IN — B
Indiana U–Purdue U Fort Wayne, IN — B
Indiana U South Bend, IN — B
Iowa State U of Science and Technology, IA — B
Jamestown Coll, ND — B
Judson Coll, IL — B
Kalamazoo Coll, MI — B
Kansas State U, KS — B
Kent State U, OH — B
Kenyon Coll, OH — B
Knox Coll, IL — B
Langston U, OK — B
Lawrence U, WI — B
Lewis U, IL — B
Lindenwood U, MO — B
Loyola U Chicago, IL — B
Luther Coll, IA — B
Macalester Coll, MN — B
MacMurray Coll, IL — B
Manchester Coll, IN — B
Marietta Coll, OH — B
Marquette U, WI — B
Metropolitan State U, MN — B
Miami U, OH — B
Michigan State U, MI — B
Millikin U, IL — B
Minnesota State U Mankato, MN — B
Missouri Southern State U, MO — B
Missouri State U, MO — B
Missouri Valley Coll, MO — B
Morningside Coll, IA — B
Mount Mercy Coll, IA — B
Mount Union Coll, OH — B
Mount Vernon Nazarene U, OH — B
Nebraska Wesleyan U, NE — B
North Carolina Ag and Tech State U, NC — B
North Central Coll, IL — B
North Dakota State U, ND — B
Northeastern State U, OK — B
Northern Illinois U, IL — B
Northern Michigan U, MI — B
Northern State U, SD — B
Northwestern Coll, IA — B
Northwestern Coll, MN — B
Northwestern U, IL — B
Northwest Missouri State U, MO — B
Oberlin Coll, OH — B
Ohio Northern U, OH — B
The Ohio State U, OH — B
Ohio U, OH — B
Ohio Wesleyan U, OH — B
Oklahoma Christian U, OK — B
Oklahoma City U, OK — B
Oklahoma State U, OK — B
Oral Roberts U, OK — B
Ottawa U, KS — B
Otterbein Coll, OH — B
Park U, MO — B
Purdue U, IN — B
Ripon Coll, WI — B

Rockford Coll, IL — B
Roosevelt U, IL — B
Saginaw Valley State U, MI — B
St. Ambrose U, IA — B
St. Cloud State U, MN — B
Saint John's U, MN — B
Saint Joseph's Coll, IN — B
Saint Louis U, MO — B
Saint Mary-of-the-Woods Coll, IN — B
Saint Mary's Coll, IN — B
Saint Mary's U of Minnesota, MN — B
St. Olaf Coll, MN — B
Shawnee State U, OH — B
Simpson Coll, IA — B
South Dakota State U, SD — B
Southeastern Oklahoma State U, OK — B
Southeast Missouri State U, MO — B
Southern Illinois U Carbondale, IL — B
Southern Illinois U Edwardsville, IL — B
Southern Methodist U, TX — B
Southwest Baptist U, MO — B
Southwest Minnesota State U, MN — B
Stephens Coll, MO — B
Sterling Coll, KS — B
Taylor U, IN — B
Transylvania U, KY — B
Truman State U, MO — B
The U of Akron, OH — B
U of Central Missouri, MO — B
U of Central Oklahoma, OK — B
U of Cincinnati, OH — B
U of Dallas, TX — B
U of Dayton, OH — B
U of Evansville, IN — B
The U of Findlay, OH — B
U of Illinois at Chicago, IL — B
U of Illinois at Urbana–Champaign, IL — B
U of Indianapolis, IN — B
The U of Iowa, IA — B
U of Kansas, KS — B
U of Michigan, MI — B
U of Michigan–Flint, MI — B
U of Minnesota, Duluth, MN — B
U of Minnesota, Morris, MN — B
U of Minnesota, Twin Cities Campus, MN — B
U of Missouri–Columbia, MO — B
U of Missouri–Kansas City, MO — B
U of Nebraska at Kearney, NE — B
U of Nebraska at Omaha, NE — B
U of Nebraska–Lincoln, NE — B
U of North Dakota, ND — B
U of Northern Iowa, IA — B
U of Notre Dame, IN — B
U of Oklahoma, OK — B
U of Saint Mary, KS — B
U of St. Thomas, MN — B
U of Science and Arts of Oklahoma, OK — B
U of Sioux Falls, SD — A,B
The U of South Dakota, SD — B
U of Southern Indiana, IN — B
The U of Toledo, OH — B
U of Tulsa, OK — B
U of West Florida, FL — B

A—associate degree; B—bachelor's degree

U of Wisconsin–Eau Claire, WI	B
U of Wisconsin–Green Bay, WI	A,B
U of Wisconsin–La Crosse, WI	B
U of Wisconsin–Madison, WI	B
U of Wisconsin–Milwaukee, WI	
U of Wisconsin–Oshkosh, WI	B
U of Wisconsin–Parkside, WI	B
U of Wisconsin–River Falls, WI	
U of Wisconsin–Stevens Point, WI	B
U of Wisconsin–Superior, WI	B
U of Wisconsin–Whitewater, WI	B
Valparaiso U, IN	B
Viterbo U, WI	B
Wabash Coll, IN	B
Waldorf Coll, IA	B
Washburn U, KS	B
Washington U in St. Louis, MO	B
Wayne State Coll, NE	B
Webster U, MO	B
Western Illinois U, IL	B
Western Michigan U, MI	B
Wichita State U, KS	B
William Jewell Coll, MO	B
William Woods U, MO	B
Wilmington Coll, OH	B
Winona State U, MN	B
Wisconsin Lutheran Coll, WI	B
Wittenberg U, OH	B
Wright State U, OH	B

Dramatic/Theater Arts and Stagecraft Related

Baldwin-Wallace Coll, OH	B
Bowling Green State U, OH	B
DePaul U, IL	B
Drake U, IA	B
Nebraska Wesleyan U, NE	B
Ohio U, OH	B
St. Cloud State U, MN	B
The U of Akron, OH	B

Drawing

Antioch Coll, OH	B
Aquinas Coll, MI	B
Art Academy of Cincinnati, OH	B
Ball State U, IN	B
Bethany Coll, KS	B
The Cleveland Inst of Art, OH	B
Coll of Visual Arts, MN	B
Columbia Coll, MO	B
DePaul U, IL	B
Drake U, IA	B
Grace Coll, IN	B
Grand Valley State U, MI	B
Indiana U Bloomington, IN	B
Indiana U–Purdue U Fort Wayne, IN	B
Judson Coll, IL	B
Lewis U, IL	B
Lindenwood U, MO	B
Minneapolis Coll of Art and Design, MN	
Minnesota State U Mankato, MN	
Northwest Missouri State U, MO	
The Ohio State U, OH	B
Ohio U, OH	B
St. Cloud State U, MN	B

School of the Art Inst of Chicago, IL	B
Shawnee State U, OH	B
Trinity Christian Coll, IL	B
The U of Akron, OH	B
The U of Iowa, IA	B
U of Michigan, MI	B
U of Missouri–St. Louis, MO	B
The U of Toledo, OH	B
Washington U in St. Louis, MO	B
Winona State U, MN	B
Wright State U, OH	B

Driver and Safety Teacher Education

U of Northern Iowa, IA	B
William Penn U, IA	B

Early Childhood Education

Alma Coll, MI	B
Baker Coll of Allen Park, MI	A
Baker Coll of Jackson, MI	A
Baldwin-Wallace Coll, OH	B
Bethel U, MN	B
Capital U, OH	B
Carroll Coll, WI	B
Cedarville U, OH	B
Central Methodist U, MO	B
Chicago State U, IL	B
Cleveland State U, OH	B
Coll of Saint Mary, NE	A,B
Columbia Coll Chicago, IL	B
Concordia U, MI	B
Concordia U, NE	B
Concordia U, St. Paul, MN	B
Cornerstone U, MI	B
Crown Coll, MN	A,B
East Central U, OK	B
Evangel U, MO	B
Gannon U, PA	A,B
Grace Bible Coll, MI	B
Greenville Coll, IL	B
Hannibal-LaGrange Coll, MO	B
Harris-Stowe State U, MO	B
Hastings Coll, NE	B
Hillsdale Coll, MI	B
Illinois Coll, IL	B
Illinois State U, IL	B
Indiana State U, IN	B
Indiana U–Purdue U Fort Wayne, IN	A
Iowa State U of Science and Technology, IA	B
Kendall Coll, IL	B
Kent State U, Tuscarawas Campus, OH	A
Lake Superior State U, MI	A,B
Leech Lake Tribal Coll, MN	A
Lincoln U, MO	A,B
Loras Coll, IA	B
Malone Coll, OH	B
Miami U, OH	B
Miami U Hamilton, OH	B
Millikin U, IL	B
Missouri State U, MO	B
Mount Union Coll, OH	B
Mount Vernon Nazarene U, OH	B
Northeastern Illinois U, IL	B
Northern Michigan U, MI	B
Northwestern Coll, MN	B
Notre Dame Coll, OH	B
Ohio Dominican U, OH	B
Ohio Northern U, OH	B
The Ohio State U–Mansfield Campus, OH	B

Ohio U, OH	B
Ohio Wesleyan U, OH	B
Oklahoma Christian U, OK	B
Oral Roberts U, OK	B
Park U, MO	B
Purdue U, IN	B
Ripon Coll, WI	B
Rochester Coll, MI	B
St. Ambrose U, IA	B
St. Augustine Coll, IL	A
Shawnee State U, OH	B
Southern Illinois U Carbondale, IL	B
Southern Illinois U Edwardsville, IL	B
Southwestern Coll, KS	B
Stephens Coll, MO	B
Taylor U Fort Wayne, IN	A
U of Mary, ND	B
U of Michigan–Dearborn, MI	B
U of Michigan–Flint, MI	B
U of Minnesota, Crookston, MN	B
U of Missouri–Columbia, MO	B
U of Missouri–Kansas City, MO	B
U of Missouri–St. Louis, MO	B
U of New Orleans, LA	B
U of North Dakota, ND	B
U of Oklahoma, OK	B
U of Science and Arts of Oklahoma, OK	B
U of West Florida, FL	B
U of Wisconsin–Stout, WI	B
U of Wisconsin–Whitewater, WI	B
Ursuline Coll, OH	B
Waldorf Coll, IA	B
Washburn U, KS	A,B
Wayne State Coll, NE	B
Youngstown State U, OH	B

East Asian Languages

U of Kansas, KS	B

East Asian Languages Related

Michigan State U, MI	B
Northwestern U, IL	B
Washington U in St. Louis, MO	B

Ecology

Ball State U, IN	B
Bemidji State U, MN	B
Bradley U, IL	B
Clarkson U, NY	B
East Central U, OK	B
Iowa State U of Science and Technology, IA	B
Kent State U, OH	B
Lawrence U, WI	B
Manchester Coll, IN	B
Michigan Technological U, MI	B
Minnesota State U Mankato, MN	B
Missouri Southern State U, MO	B
Northern Michigan U, MI	B
Northland Coll, WI	B
Northwestern U, IL	B
Northwest Missouri State U, MO	B
Oberlin Coll, OH	B
St. Cloud State U, MN	B
The U of Akron, OH	B
U of Illinois at Urbana–Champaign, IL	B
U of Michigan–Flint, MI	B

U of Minnesota, Twin Cities Campus, MN	B
U of Northern Iowa, IA	B
U of Rio Grande, OH	B
U of Wisconsin–Milwaukee, WI	B
Winona State U, MN	B

E-Commerce

Clarkson U, NY	B
Davenport U, Dearborn, MI	B
ITT Tech Inst, Orland Park, IL	B
Maryville U of Saint Louis, MO	B
U of Phoenix–Chicago Campus, IL	B
U of Phoenix–Cincinnati Campus, OH	B
U of Phoenix–Cleveland Campus, OH	B
U of Phoenix–Columbus Ohio Campus, OH	B
U of Phoenix–Indianapolis Campus, IN	B
U of Phoenix–Kansas City Campus, MO	B
U of Phoenix–Metro Detroit Campus, MI	B
U of Phoenix–St. Louis Campus, MO	B
U of Phoenix–Springfield Campus, MO	B
U of Phoenix–West Michigan Campus, MI	B
U of Phoenix–Wisconsin Campus, WI	B
U of Southern Indiana, IN	B
Western Michigan U, MI	B

Econometrics and Quantitative Economics

Baldwin-Wallace Coll, OH	B
Miami U Hamilton, OH	B
Southern Methodist U, TX	B
U of St. Thomas, MN	B

Economics

Adrian Coll, MI	A,B
Albion Coll, MI	B
Alma Coll, MI	B
Andrews U, MI	B
Antioch Coll, OH	B
Aquinas Coll, MI	B
Ashland U, OH	B
Augsburg Coll, MN	B
Augustana Coll, IL	B
Augustana Coll, SD	B
Aurora U, IL	B
Baker U, KS	B
Baldwin-Wallace Coll, OH	B
Ball State U, IN	B
Beloit Coll, WI	B
Bemidji State U, MN	B
Benedictine Coll, KS	B
Benedictine U, IL	B
Bethel U, MN	B
Bluffton U, OH	B
Bowling Green State U, OH	B
Bradley U, IL	B
Butler U, IN	B
Calvin Coll, MI	B
Capital U, OH	B
Carleton Coll, MN	B
Case Western Reserve U, OH	B
Central Christian Coll of Kansas, KS	A
Central Coll, IA	B
Central Methodist U, MO	B

Central Michigan U, MI	B	Miami U, OH	B	The U of Findlay, OH	B	Southern Methodist U, TX	B
Central State U, OH	B	Miami U Hamilton, OH	B	U of Illinois at Chicago, IL	B	Truman State U, MO	B
Chicago State U, IL	B	Miami U–Middletown Campus,		U of Illinois at Springfield, IL	B	The U of Akron, OH	B
Clarke Coll, IA	B	OH	A	U of Illinois at Urbana–		U of Dallas, TX	B
Cleveland State U, OH	B	Michigan State U, MI	A	Champaign, IL	B	U of Illinois at Urbana–	
Coe Coll, IA	B	Michigan Technological U, MI	B	The U of Iowa, IA	B	Champaign, IL	B
Coll of Saint Benedict, MN	B	Minnesota State U Mankato,		U of Kansas, KS	B	Valparaiso U, IN	B
Coll of St. Catherine, MN	B	MN	B	U of Michigan, MI	B	Wright State U, OH	B
The Coll of Wooster, OH	B	Minot State U, ND	B	U of Michigan–Dearborn, MI	B		
Concordia Coll, MN	B	Missouri State U, MO	B	U of Michigan–Flint, MI	B	**Education**	
Concordia U Wisconsin, WI	B	Missouri Valley Coll, MO	B	U of Minnesota, Duluth, MN	B	Adrian Coll, MI	B
Cornell Coll, IA	B	Missouri Western State U, MO	B	U of Minnesota, Morris, MN	B	Albion Coll, MI	B
Creighton U, NE	B	Mount Union Coll, OH	B	U of Minnesota, Twin Cities		Alma Coll, MI	B
Denison U, OH	B	Nebraska Wesleyan U, NE	B	Campus, MN	B	Alverno Coll, WI	B
DePaul U, IL	B	North Carolina Ag and Tech		U of Missouri–Columbia, MO	B	Anderson U, IN	B
DePauw U, IN	B	State U, NC	B	U of Missouri–Kansas City,		Andrews U, MI	B
Doane Coll, NE	B	North Central Coll, IL	B	MO	B	Antioch Coll, OH	B
Dominican U, IL	B	Northeastern Illinois U, IL	B	U of Missouri–Rolla, MO	B	Aquinas Coll, MI	B
Drury U, MO	B	Northern Illinois U, IL	B	U of Missouri–St. Louis, MO	B	Ashford U, IA	B
Earlham Coll, IN	B	Northern Michigan U, MI	B	U of Nebraska at Kearney, NE	B	Ashland U, OH	B
Eastern Illinois U, IL	B	Northern State U, SD	B	U of Nebraska–Lincoln, NE	B	Augsburg Coll, MN	B
Eastern Michigan U, MI	B	Northland Coll, WI	B	U of New Orleans, LA	B	Augustana Coll, IL	B
Edgewood Coll, WI	B	Northwestern Coll, IA	B	U of North Dakota, ND	B	Baker Coll of Auburn Hills, MI	A
Elmhurst Coll, IL	B	Northwestern U, IL	B	U of Northern Iowa, IA	B	Baker Coll of Cadillac, MI	A
Emporia State U, KS	B	Northwest Missouri State U,		U of Notre Dame, IN	B	Ball State U, IN	B
Fort Hays State U, KS	B	MO	B	U of Oklahoma, OK	B	Beloit Coll, WI	B
Franciscan U of Steubenville,		Oakland U, MI	B	U of Rio Grande, OH	B	Bemidji State U, MN	B
OH	B	Oberlin Coll, OH	B	U of St. Thomas, MN	B	Benedictine U, IL	B
Franklin Coll, IN	B	Ohio Dominican U, OH	B	U of Science and Arts of		Bethany Coll, KS	B
Goshen Coll, IN	B	The Ohio State U, OH	B	Oklahoma, OK	B	Bowling Green State U, OH	B
Graceland U, IA	B	Ohio U, OH	B	U of Sioux Falls, SD	A,B	Bowling Green State U–	
Grand Valley State U, MI	B	Ohio Wesleyan U, OH	B	The U of South Dakota, SD	B	Firelands Coll, OH	A
Gustavus Adolphus Coll, MN	B	Oklahoma State U, OK	B	U of Southern Indiana, IN	B	Briar Cliff U, IA	B
Hamline U, MN	B	Otterbein Coll, OH	B	The U of Toledo, OH	B	Cameron U, OK	B
Hanover Coll, IN	B	Park U, MO	B	U of Tulsa, OK	B	Capital U, OH	B
Hastings Coll, NE	B	Pittsburg State U, KS	B	U of West Florida, FL	B	Cardinal Stritch U, WI	B
Heidelberg Coll, OH	B	Purdue U, IN	B	U of Wisconsin–Eau Claire,		Carroll Coll, WI	B
Hillsdale Coll, MI	B	Purdue U Calumet, IN	B	WI	B	Central Methodist U, MO	B
Hiram Coll, OH	B	Ripon Coll, WI	B	U of Wisconsin–Green Bay,		Chicago State U, IL	B
Hope Coll, MI	B	Rockford Coll, IL	B	WI	A,B	Cincinnati Christian U, OH	A,B
Huntington U, IN	B	Rockhurst U, MO	B	U of Wisconsin–La Crosse, WI	B	Clarke Coll, IA	B
Illinois Coll, IL	B	Roosevelt U, IL	B	U of Wisconsin–Milwaukee,		Cleveland State U, OH	B
Illinois State U, IL	B	Rose-Hulman Inst of		WI	B	Coe Coll, IA	B
Illinois Wesleyan U, IL	B	Technology, IN	B	U of Wisconsin–Oshkosh, WI	B	Coll of Menominee Nation,	
Indiana State U, IN	B	Saginaw Valley State U, MI	B	U of Wisconsin–Parkside, WI	B	WI	A
Indiana U Bloomington, IN	B	St. Ambrose U, IA	B	U of Wisconsin–Platteville, WI	B	Coll of Saint Benedict, MN	B
Indiana U Northwest, IN	B	St. Cloud State U, MN	B	U of Wisconsin–River Falls,		Coll of St. Catherine, MN	B
Indiana U–Purdue U Fort		Saint John's U, MN	B	WI	B	Coll of Saint Mary, NE	B
Wayne, IN	B	Saint Joseph's Coll, IN	B	U of Wisconsin–Stevens Point,		Coll of the Ozarks, MO	B
Indiana U–Purdue U		Saint Louis U, MO	B	WI	B	Columbia Coll, MO	B
Indianapolis, IN	B	Saint Mary's Coll, IN	B	U of Wisconsin–Superior, WI	B	Concordia Coll, MN	B
Indiana U South Bend, IN	B	St. Norbert Coll, WI	B	U of Wisconsin–Whitewater,		Concordia U, IL	B
Indiana U Southeast, IN	B	St. Olaf Coll, MN	B	WI	B	Concordia U, NE	B
Indiana Wesleyan U, IN	B	Simpson Coll, IA	B	Valparaiso U, IN	B	Concordia U, St. Paul, MN	B
Iowa State U of Science and		South Dakota State U, SD	B	Wabash Coll, IN	B	Concordia U Wisconsin, WI	B
Technology, IA	B	Southeastern Oklahoma State		Wartburg Coll, IA	B	Concord U, WV	B
Kansas State U, KS	B	U, OK	B	Washburn U, KS	B	Cornerstone U, MI	B
Kent State U, OH	B	Southeast Missouri State U,		Washington U in St. Louis,		Dakota Wesleyan U, SD	B
Kenyon Coll, OH	B	MO	B	MO	B	Dana Coll, NE	B
Knox Coll, IL	B	Southern Illinois U		Webster U, MO	B	DePaul U, IL	B
Lake Forest Coll, IL	B	Carbondale, IL	B	Western Illinois U, IL	B	Dickinson State U, ND	B
Langston U, OK	B	Southern Illinois U		Western Michigan U, MI	B	Dordt Coll, IA	B
Lawrence U, WI	B	Edwardsville, IL	B	Westminster Coll, MO	B	Drury U, MO	B
Lewis U, IL	B	Southern Methodist U, TX	B	Wheaton Coll, IL	B	East Central U, OK	B
Lincoln U, MO	B	Taylor U, IN	B	Wichita State U, KS	B	Edgewood Coll, WI	B
Lindenwood U, MO	B	Transylvania U, KY	B	William Jewell Coll, MO	B	Elmhurst Coll, IL	B
Loras Coll, IA	B	Truman State U, MO	B	Wilmington Coll, OH	B	Evangel U, MO	A,B
Loyola U Chicago, IL	B	The U of Akron, OH	B	Winona State U, MN	B	Finlandia U, MI	B
Luther Coll, IA	B	U of Central Missouri, MO	B	Wittenberg U, OH	B	Fontbonne U, MO	B
Macalester Coll, MN	B	U of Central Oklahoma, OK	B	Wright State U, OH	B	Goshen Coll, IN	B
Manchester Coll, IN	B	U of Chicago, IL	B	Xavier U, OH	B	Graceland U, IA	B
Marietta Coll, OH	B	U of Cincinnati, OH	B	Youngstown State U, OH	B	Grand Valley State U, MI	B
Marquette U, WI	B	U of Dallas, TX	B			Great Lakes Christian Coll, MI	B
McKendree Coll, IL	B	U of Dayton, OH	B	**Economics Related**		Gustavus Adolphus Coll, MN	B
Metropolitan State U, MN	B	U of Evansville, IN	B	Eastern Michigan U, MI	B	Hamline U, MN	B

A—associate degree; B—bachelor's degree

Hannibal-LaGrange Coll, MO	B
Hastings Coll, NE	B
Heidelberg Coll, OH	B
Hillsdale Coll, MI	B
Huntington U, IN	B
Illinois Coll, IL	B
Illinois Wesleyan U, IL	B
Indiana U Bloomington, IN	B
Indiana U East, IN	B
Indiana U Northwest, IN	B
Indiana U–Purdue U Fort Wayne, IN	B
Indiana U–Purdue U Indianapolis, IN	B
Indiana U South Bend, IN	B
Indiana U Southeast, IN	B
Indiana Wesleyan U, IN	B
Iowa State U of Science and Technology, IA	B
Iowa Wesleyan Coll, IA	B
Judson Coll, IL	B
Kendall Coll, IL	B
Kent State U, OH	A,B
Knox Coll, IL	B
Lake Forest Coll, IL	B
Lake Superior State U, MI	B
Langston U, OK	B
Lewis U, IL	B
Lindenwood U, MO	B
Loras Coll, IA	B
Madonna U, MI	B
Manchester Coll, IN	B
Maranatha Baptist Bible Coll, WI	B
Marian Coll, IN	B
Marian Coll of Fond du Lac, WI	B
Marietta Coll, OH	B
Marquette U, WI	B
Marygrove Coll, MI	B
Mayville State U, ND	B
Miami U–Middletown Campus, OH	A
Michigan State U, MI	B
Minnesota State U Mankato, MN	B
Missouri Southern State U, MO	B
Missouri Valley Coll, MO	B
Morningside Coll, IA	B
Mount Marty Coll, SD	B
Mount Mary Coll, WI	B
Mount Mercy Coll, IA	B
Mount Vernon Nazarene U, OH	B
Newman U, KS	B
North Carolina Ag and Tech State U, NC	B
North Central Coll, IL	B
Northeastern State U, OK	B
Northern Illinois U, IL	B
Northern Michigan U, MI	B
Northern State U, SD	B
Northland Coll, WI	B
Northwestern U, IL	B
Northwest Missouri State U, MO	B
Ohio Northern U, OH	B
Ohio U, OH	B
Ohio Wesleyan U, OH	B
Oklahoma City U, OK	B
Oklahoma State U, OK	B
Oklahoma Wesleyan U, OK	B
Oral Roberts U, OK	B
Otterbein Coll, OH	B
Peru State Coll, NE	B

Purdue U, IN	B
Purdue U Calumet, IN	B
Ripon Coll, WI	B
Rockford Coll, IL	B
Rockhurst U, MO	B
Roosevelt U, IL	B
St. Ambrose U, IA	B
St. Cloud State U, MN	B
Saint John's U, MN	B
Saint Louis U, MO	B
Saint Mary-of-the-Woods Coll, IN	B
Saint Mary's Coll, IN	B
Shawnee State U, OH	B
Simpson Coll, IA	B
Sitting Bull Coll, ND	A
South Dakota State U, SD	B
Southeastern Oklahoma State U, OK	B
Southwestern Oklahoma State U, OK	B
Southwest Minnesota State U, MN	B
Tabor Coll, KS	B
Taylor U, IN	B
Taylor U Fort Wayne, IN	B
Trinity Christian Coll, IL	B
Trinity International U, IL	B
Tri-State U, IN	B
Union Coll, NE	B
The U of Akron, OH	B
U of Central Missouri, MO	B
U of Charleston, WV	B
U of Cincinnati, OH	B
U of Dallas, TX	B
U of Dayton, OH	B
U of Evansville, IN	B
The U of Findlay, OH	B
U of Indianapolis, IN	B
U of Michigan, MI	B
U of Michigan–Dearborn, MI	B
U of Michigan–Flint, MI	B
U of Minnesota, Duluth, MN	B
U of Minnesota, Morris, MN	B
U of Minnesota, Twin Cities Campus, MN	B
U of Missouri–Columbia, MO	B
U of Missouri–St. Louis, MO	B
U of Rio Grande, OH	B
U of Saint Francis, IN	B
U of Saint Mary, KS	B
U of Sioux Falls, SD	B
The U of South Dakota, SD	B
U of Southern Indiana, IN	A
The U of Toledo, OH	B
U of Tulsa, OK	B
U of Wisconsin–Milwaukee, WI	B
U of Wisconsin–Oshkosh, WI	B
U of Wisconsin–Platteville, WI	B
U of Wisconsin–River Falls, WI	B
U of Wisconsin–Stevens Point, WI	B
U of Wisconsin–Superior, WI	B
U of Wisconsin–Whitewater, WI	B
Upper Iowa U, IA	B
Valley City State U, ND	B
Waldorf Coll, IA	B
Walsh U, OH	B
Washburn U, KS	B
Washington U in St. Louis, MO	B
Wayne State Coll, NE	B
Webster U, MO	B

William Jewell Coll, MO	B
William Penn U, IA	B
William Woods U, MO	B
Wilmington Coll, OH	B
Winona State U, MN	B
Wittenberg U, OH	B
Wright State U, OH	B
Xavier U, OH	B
York Coll, NE	B
Youngstown State U, OH	B

Educational Administration and Supervision Related
Kendall Coll, IL	B

Educational, Instructional, and Curriculum Supervision
Wright State U, OH	B

Educational/Instructional Media Design
Ball State U, IN	B
Capital U, OH	B
Indiana State U, IN	B
Lindenwood U, MO	B
St. Cloud State U, MN	B
U of Central Oklahoma, OK	B
The U of Toledo, OH	B
Western Illinois U, IL	B

Educational Leadership and Administration
Baldwin-Wallace Coll, OH	B
Cleveland State U, OH	B
Jamestown Coll, ND	B
Kendall Coll, IL	B
Lindenwood U, MO	B
Northwest Missouri State U, MO	B
Ohio U, OH	B
Oral Roberts U, OK	B
St. Cloud State U, MN	B
U of Central Oklahoma, OK	B
U of Wisconsin–Superior, WI	B
Wright State U, OH	B

Educational System Administration and Superintendency
Dordt Coll, IA	B

Education (K–12)
Adrian Coll, MI	B
Augustana Coll, SD	B
Coll of Saint Mary, NE	B
The Coll of St. Scholastica, MN	B
Dickinson State U, ND	B
Dominican U, IL	B
Dordt Coll, IA	B
Finlandia U, MI	B
Graceland U, IA	B
Hamline U, MN	B
Hillsdale Coll, MI	B
Illinois Coll, IL	B
Indiana Wesleyan U, IN	B
Jamestown Coll, ND	B
Lewis U, IL	B
Lindenwood U, MO	B
McKendree Coll, IL	B
Northwestern Coll, IA	B
Ohio Dominican U, OH	B
Ohio Wesleyan U, OH	B
St. Ambrose U, IA	B
Saint Mary-of-the-Woods Coll, IN	B
Tabor Coll, KS	B
Trinity International U, IL	B
U of Minnesota, Morris, MN	B

U of St. Thomas, MN	B
Washington U in St. Louis, MO	B

Education (Multiple Levels)
Concordia U Wisconsin, WI	B
Dakota Wesleyan U, SD	B
Gannon U, PA	B
Lake Superior State U, MI	B
Martin Luther Coll, MN	B
Miami U Hamilton, OH	B
Ohio Northern U, OH	B
Ohio Wesleyan U, OH	B
Oral Roberts U, OK	B
Saint Louis U, MO	B
Shawnee State U, OH	B
The U of Akron, OH	B
U of Nebraska–Lincoln, NE	B
U of Rio Grande, OH	B
Waldorf Coll, IA	B
Wright State U, OH	B
York Coll, NE	B

Education Related
Bowling Green State U, OH	B
Cleveland State U, OH	B
Concordia U, St. Paul, MN	B
Kendall Coll, IL	B
Madonna U, MI	B
Messenger Coll, MO	B
Ohio Northern U, OH	B
Park U, MO	B
Roosevelt U, IL	B
The U of Akron, OH	A
U of Missouri–Columbia, MO	B
Wright State U, OH	B

Education (Specific Levels and Methods) Related
Columbia Coll Chicago, IL	B
Kendall Coll, IL	B
St. Cloud State U, MN	B
The U of Akron, OH	B
The U of Toledo, OH	B
Washington U in St. Louis, MO	B
Wright State U, OH	B
Xavier U, OH	B

Education (Specific Subject Areas) Related
Avila U, MO	B
Baker U, KS	B
Bowling Green State U, OH	B
Bradley U, IL	B
Cameron U, OK	B
Central Michigan U, MI	B
Columbia Coll Chicago, IL	B
Hope Coll, MI	B
Madonna U, MI	B
Marquette U, WI	B
Minot State U, ND	B
Missouri State U, MO	B
Ohio U, OH	B
The U of Akron, OH	B
U of Central Oklahoma, OK	B
U of Michigan–Flint, MI	B
U of Nebraska–Lincoln, NE	B
U of Oklahoma, OK	B
U of St. Thomas, MN	B
The U of Toledo, OH	B
U of Wisconsin–Eau Claire, WI	B
Wright State U, OH	B

Electrical and Electronic Engineering Technologies Related

Lawrence Technological U, MI	A
Miami U Hamilton, OH	A
Southern Illinois U Carbondale, IL	B

Electrical, Electronic and Communications Engineering Technology

Andrews U, MI	A,B
Baker Coll of Cadillac, MI	A
Baker Coll of Muskegon, MI	A,B
Baker Coll of Owosso, MI	A,B
Bowling Green State U, OH	B
Bowling Green State U–Firelands Coll, OH	A
Bradley U, IL	B
Bryant and Stratton Coll, Cleveland, OH	A,B
Cameron U, OK	A,B
Central Michigan U, MI	B
Cleveland State U, OH	B
Davenport U, Dearborn, MI	A
DeVry U, Addison, IL	A,B
DeVry U, Chicago, IL	A,B
DeVry U, Tinley Park, IL	A,B
DeVry U, Indianapolis, IN	A
DeVry U, MN	A
DeVry U, Kansas City, MO	A,B
DeVry U, Columbus, OH	A,B
East Central U, OK	B
Eastern Michigan U, MI	B
East-West U, IL	B
Ferris State U, MI	B
Grantham U, MO	A,B
Herzing Coll, WI	A,B
Indiana State U, IN	A,B
Indiana U–Purdue U Fort Wayne, IN	A,B
Indiana U–Purdue U Indianapolis, IN	A,B
ITT Tech Inst, Mount Prospect, IL	A,B
ITT Tech Inst, Orland Park, IL	A
ITT Tech Inst, Fort Wayne, IN	B
ITT Tech Inst, Indianapolis, IN	B
ITT Tech Inst, Newburgh, IN	B
ITT Tech Inst, MN	B
ITT Tech Inst, Arnold, MO	B
ITT Tech Inst, Earth City, MO	B
ITT Tech Inst, NE	A,B
ITT Tech Inst, Oklahoma City, OK	B
ITT Tech Inst, Tulsa, OK	B
ITT Tech Inst, Green Bay, WI	B
ITT Tech Inst, Greenfield, WI	A,B
Kent State U, Ashtabula Campus, OH	A
Kent State U, Trumbull Campus, OH	A
Kent State U, Tuscarawas Campus, OH	A
Lake Superior State U, MI	A,B
Langston U, OK	A
Lawrence Technological U, MI	A
Miami U–Middletown Campus, OH	A
Michigan Technological U, MI	A,B
Minnesota State U Mankato, MN	B
Missouri Western State U, MO	A,B
Northeastern State U, OK	B
Northern Michigan U, MI	A,B
Northern State U, SD	A,B
Oglala Lakota Coll, SD	A
Ohio U, OH	A
Oklahoma State U, OK	B
Pittsburg State U, KS	A,B
Purdue U, IN	A,B
Purdue U Calumet, IN	A,B
Purdue U North Central, IN	A
Roosevelt U, IL	B
St. Cloud State U, MN	B
South Dakota State U, SD	B
The U of Akron, OH	A,B
U of Central Missouri, MO	B
U of Cincinnati, OH	A,B
U of Dayton, OH	B
U of Nebraska–Lincoln, NE	B
The U of Toledo, OH	A,B
Wright State U, OH	A
Youngstown State U, OH	A,B

Electrical, Electronics and Communications Engineering

Bradley U, IL	B
Calvin Coll, MI	B
Case Western Reserve U, OH	B
Cedarville U, OH	B
Clarkson U, NY	B
Cleveland State U, OH	B
Dominican U, IL	B
Dordt Coll, IA	B
East-West U, IL	B
Gannon U, PA	B
Grand Valley State U, MI	B
Illinois Inst of Technology, IL	B
Indiana Tech, IN	B
Indiana U–Purdue U Fort Wayne, IN	B
Indiana U–Purdue U Indianapolis, IN	B
Iowa State U of Science and Technology, IA	B
Kansas State U, KS	B
Kettering U, MI	B
Lake Superior State U, MI	B
Lawrence Technological U, MI	B
Marquette U, WI	B
Miami U, OH	B
Michigan State U, MI	B
Michigan Technological U, MI	B
Milwaukee School of Engineering, WI	B
Minnesota State U Mankato, MN	B
North Carolina Ag and Tech State U, NC	B
North Dakota State U, ND	B
Northern Illinois U, IL	B
Northwestern U, IL	B
Oakland U, MI	B
Ohio Northern U, OH	B
The Ohio State U, OH	B
Ohio U, OH	B
Oklahoma Christian U, OK	B
Oklahoma State U, OK	B
Oral Roberts U, OK	B
Purdue U, IN	B
Purdue U Calumet, IN	B
Rose-Hulman Inst of Technology, IN	B
Saginaw Valley State U, MI	B
St. Cloud State U, MN	B
Saint Louis U, MO	B
South Dakota School of Mines and Technology, SD	B
South Dakota State U, SD	B
Southern Illinois U Carbondale, IL	B
Southern Illinois U Edwardsville, IL	B
Southern Methodist U, TX	B
Tri-State U, IN	B
The U of Akron, OH	B
U of Cincinnati, OH	B
U of Dayton, OH	B
U of Evansville, IN	B
U of Illinois at Chicago, IL	B
U of Illinois at Urbana–Champaign, IL	B
The U of Iowa, IA	B
U of Kansas, KS	B
U of Michigan, MI	B
U of Michigan–Dearborn, MI	B
U of Minnesota, Duluth, MN	B
U of Minnesota, Twin Cities Campus, MN	B
U of Missouri–Columbia, MO	B
U of Missouri–Kansas City, MO	B
U of Missouri–Rolla, MO	B
U of Missouri–St. Louis, MO	B
U of Nebraska at Omaha, NE	B
U of Nebraska–Lincoln, NE	B
U of New Orleans, LA	B
U of North Dakota, ND	B
U of Notre Dame, IN	B
U of Oklahoma, OK	B
U of St. Thomas, MN	B
The U of Toledo, OH	B
U of Tulsa, OK	B
U of West Florida, FL	B
U of Wisconsin–Madison, WI	B
U of Wisconsin–Milwaukee, WI	B
U of Wisconsin–Platteville, WI	B
Valparaiso U, IN	B
Washington U in St. Louis, MO	B
Western Michigan U, MI	B
Wichita State U, KS	B
Wright State U, OH	B
Youngstown State U, OH	B

Electromechanical Technology

Miami U Hamilton, OH	B
Miami U–Middletown Campus, OH	A
Michigan Technological U, MI	A
Northern Michigan U, MI	A
Shawnee State U, OH	A
The U of Akron, OH	A
U of Northern Iowa, IA	B
The U of Toledo, OH	B
Wright State U, OH	A

Elementary and Middle School Administration/Principalship

Ohio U, OH	B

Elementary Education

Adrian Coll, MI	B
Albion Coll, MI	B
Alma Coll, MI	B
Alverno Coll, WI	B
Anderson U, IN	B
Andrews U, MI	B
Aquinas Coll, MI	B
Ashford U, IA	B
Ashland U, OH	B
Augsburg Coll, MN	B
Augustana Coll, IL	B
Augustana Coll, SD	B
Aurora U, IL	B
Avila U, MO	B
Baker U, KS	B
Baldwin-Wallace Coll, OH	B
Ball State U, IN	B
Baptist Bible Coll, MO	B
Barclay Coll, KS	B
Beloit Coll, WI	B
Bemidji State U, MN	B
Benedictine Coll, KS	B
Benedictine U, IL	B
Bethany Coll, KS	B
Bethany Lutheran Coll, MN	B
Bethel Coll, KS	B
Bethel U, MN	B
Blackburn Coll, IL	B
Black Hills State U, SD	B
Bluffton U, OH	B
Bowling Green State U, OH	B
Bradley U, IL	B
Briar Cliff U, IA	B
Buena Vista U, IA	B
Butler U, IN	B
Calumet Coll of Saint Joseph, IN	B
Calvary Bible Coll and Theological Seminary, MO	B
Calvin Coll, MI	B
Cameron U, OK	B
Capital U, OH	B
Cardinal Stritch U, WI	B
Carroll Coll, WI	B
Central Christian Coll of Kansas, KS	A
Central Coll, IA	B
Central Methodist U, MO	B
Central Michigan U, MI	B
Chicago State U, IL	B
Clarke Coll, IA	B
Cleveland State U, OH	B
Coe Coll, IA	B
Coll of Saint Benedict, MN	B
Coll of St. Catherine, MN	B
Coll of Saint Mary, NE	B
The Coll of St. Scholastica, MN	B
Coll of the Ozarks, MO	B
Concordia Coll, MN	B
Concordia U, IL	B
Concordia U, MI	B
Concordia U, NE	B
Concordia U, St. Paul, MN	B
Concordia U Wisconsin, WI	B
Concord U, WV	B
Cornell Coll, IA	B
Cornerstone U, MI	B
Creighton U, NE	B
Crown Coll, MN	B
Culver-Stockton Coll, MO	B
Dakota State U, SD	B
Dakota Wesleyan U, SD	B
Dana Coll, NE	B
DePaul U, IL	B
DePauw U, IN	B
Dickinson State U, ND	B
Doane Coll, NE	B
Dominican U, IL	B
Dordt Coll, IA	B
Drake U, IA	B
Drury U, MO	B
East Central U, OK	B
Eastern Illinois U, IL	B
Eastern Michigan U, MI	B
Edgewood Coll, WI	B

A—associate degree; B—bachelor's degree

Elmhurst Coll, IL	B	Marietta Coll, OH	B	Quincy U, IL	B	U of Nebraska at Kearney, NE	B
Emporia State U, KS	B	Marquette U, WI	B	Ripon Coll, WI	B	U of Nebraska at Omaha, NE	B
Evangel U, MO	B	Martin Luther Coll, MN	B	Rochester Coll, MI	B	U of Nebraska–Lincoln, NE	B
Faith Baptist Bible Coll and Theological Seminary, IA	B	Maryville U of Saint Louis, MO	B	Rockford Coll, IL	B	U of New Orleans, LA	B
Ferris State U, MI	B	Mayville State U, ND	B	Rockhurst U, MO	B	U of North Dakota, ND	B
Fontbonne U, MO	B	McKendree Coll, IL	B	Rogers State U, OK	A	U of Northern Iowa, IA	B
Fort Hays State U, KS	B	Miami U, OH	B	Roosevelt U, IL	B	U of Oklahoma, OK	B
Franciscan U of Steubenville, OH	B	Miami U–Middletown Campus, OH	A	Saginaw Valley State U, MI	B	U of Rio Grande, OH	B
Franklin Coll, IN	B	Michigan State U, MI	B	St. Ambrose U, IA	B	U of St. Francis, IL	B
Gannon U, PA	B	Millikin U, IL	B	St. Cloud State U, MN	B	U of Saint Francis, IN	B
God's Bible School and Coll, OH	A,B	Minnesota State U Mankato, MN	B	Saint John's U, MN	B	U of Saint Mary, KS	B
Goshen Coll, IN	B	Minot State U, ND	B	Saint Joseph's Coll, IN	B	U of St. Thomas, MN	B
Grace Bible Coll, MI	B	Missouri Baptist U, MO	B	Saint Mary-of-the-Woods Coll, IN	B	U of Science and Arts of Oklahoma, OK	B
Grace Coll, IN	B	Missouri Southern State U, MO	B	Saint Mary's Coll, IN	B	U of Sioux Falls, SD	B
Graceland U, IA	B	Missouri State U, MO	B	Saint Mary's U of Minnesota, MN	B	The U of South Dakota, SD	B
Grand Valley State U, MI	B	Missouri Valley Coll, MO	B	St. Norbert Coll, WI	B	U of Southern Indiana, IN	B
Grand View Coll, IA	B	Missouri Western State U, MO	B	Saint Xavier U, IL	B	The U of Toledo, OH	B
Greenville Coll, IL	B	Morningside Coll, IA	B	Shawnee State U, OH	B	U of Tulsa, OK	B
Gustavus Adolphus Coll, MN	B	Mount Marty Coll, SD	B	Silver Lake Coll, WI	B	U of West Florida, FL	B
Hamline U, MN	B	Mount Mary Coll, WI	B	Simpson Coll, IA	B	U of Wisconsin–Eau Claire, WI	B
Hannibal-LaGrange Coll, MO	B	Mount Mercy Coll, IA	B	Southeastern Oklahoma State U, OK	B	U of Wisconsin–Green Bay, WI	B
Harris-Stowe State U, MO	B	Mount Vernon Nazarene U, OH	B	Southeast Missouri State U, MO	B	U of Wisconsin–La Crosse, WI	B
Hastings Coll, NE	B	Nebraska Wesleyan U, NE	B	Southern Illinois U Carbondale, IL	B	U of Wisconsin–Madison, WI	B
Heidelberg Coll, OH	B	Newman U, KS	B	Southern Illinois U Edwardsville, IL	B	U of Wisconsin–Milwaukee, WI	B
Hillsdale Coll, MI	B	North Carolina Ag and Tech State U, NC	B	Southern Methodist U, TX	B	U of Wisconsin–Oshkosh, WI	B
Hillsdale Free Will Baptist Coll, OK	A	North Central Coll, IL	B	Southwest Baptist U, MO	B	U of Wisconsin–Platteville, WI	B
Hiram Coll, OH	B	North Dakota State U, ND	B	Southwestern Coll, KS	B	U of Wisconsin–River Falls, WI	B
Hope Coll, MI	B	Northeastern Illinois U, IL	B	Southwestern Oklahoma State U, OK	B	U of Wisconsin–Stevens Point, WI	B
Huntington U, IN	B	Northeastern State U, OK	B	Southwest Minnesota State U, MN	B	U of Wisconsin–Superior, WI	B
Illinois Coll, IL	B	Northern Illinois U, IL	B	Spring Arbor U, MI	B	U of Wisconsin–Whitewater, WI	B
Illinois State U, IL	B	Northern Michigan U, MI	B	Stephens Coll, MO	B	Upper Iowa U, IA	B
Illinois Wesleyan U, IL	B	Northern State U, SD	B	Sterling Coll, KS	B	Valley City State U, ND	B
Indiana State U, IN	B	Northland Coll, WI	B	Tabor Coll, KS	B	Valparaiso U, IN	B
Indiana U Bloomington, IN	B	Northwestern Coll, IA	B	Taylor U, IN	B	Vennard Coll, IA	A,B
Indiana U East, IN	B	Northwestern Coll, MN	B	Transylvania U, KY	B	Viterbo U, WI	B
Indiana U Kokomo, IN	B	Northwestern Oklahoma State U, OK	B	Trinity Christian Coll, IL	B	Waldorf Coll, IA	B
Indiana U Northwest, IN	B	Northwest Missouri State U, MO	B	Trinity International U, IL	B	Walsh U, OH	B
Indiana U–Purdue U Fort Wayne, IN	B	Notre Dame Coll, OH	B	Tri-State U, IN	B	Wartburg Coll, IA	B
Indiana U–Purdue U Indianapolis, IN	B	Oakland U, MI	B	Turtle Mountain Comm Coll, ND	A	Washburn U, KS	B
Indiana U South Bend, IN	B	Oglala Lakota Coll, SD	A,B	Union Coll, NE	B	Washington U in St. Louis, MO	B
Indiana U Southeast, IN	B	Ohio Northern U, OH	B	The U of Akron, OH	B	Wayne State Coll, NE	B
Indiana Wesleyan U, IN	B	The Ohio State U at Lima, OH	B	U of Central Missouri, MO	B	Webster U, MO	B
Iowa State U of Science and Technology, IA	B	The Ohio State U at Marion, OH	B	U of Central Oklahoma, OK	B	Western Illinois U, IL	B
Iowa Wesleyan Coll, IA	B	The Ohio State U–Mansfield Campus, OH	B	U of Charleston, WV	B	Western Michigan U, MI	B
Jamestown Coll, ND	B	The Ohio State U–Newark Campus, OH	B	U of Cincinnati, OH	B	Westminster Coll, MO	B
Judson Coll, IL	B	Ohio U, OH	B	U of Dallas, TX	B	Wheaton Coll, IL	B
Kansas State U, KS	B	Ohio U–Zanesville, OH	B	U of Dayton, OH	B	Wichita State U, KS	B
Kendall Coll, IL	B	Ohio Wesleyan U, OH	B	U of Evansville, IN	B	William Jewell Coll, MO	B
Kuyper Coll, MI	B	Oklahoma Christian U, OK	B	The U of Findlay, OH	B	William Penn U, IA	B
Lake Forest Coll, IL	B	Oklahoma City U, OK	B	U of Illinois at Chicago, IL	B	William Woods U, MO	B
Lakeland Coll, WI	B	Oklahoma Panhandle State U, OK	B	U of Illinois at Urbana–Champaign, IL	B	Wilmington Coll, OH	B
Lake Superior State U, MI	B	Oklahoma State U, OK	B	U of Indianapolis, IN	B	Winona State U, MN	B
Langston U, OK	B	Oklahoma Wesleyan U, OK	B	The U of Iowa, IA	B	Wisconsin Lutheran Coll, WI	B
Lewis U, IL	B	Oral Roberts U, OK	B	U of Kansas, KS	B	Wright State U, OH	B
Lincoln U, MO	B	Ottawa U, KS	B	U of Mary, ND	B	Xavier U, OH	B
Lindenwood U, MO	B	Otterbein Coll, OH	B	U of Michigan, MI	B	York Coll, NE	B
Loras Coll, IA	B	Ozark Christian Coll, MO	A	U of Michigan–Dearborn, MI	B	Youngstown State U, OH	B
Loyola U Chicago, IL	B	Park U, MO	B	U of Michigan–Flint, MI	B		
Luther Coll, IA	B	Peru State Coll, NE	B	U of Minnesota, Duluth, MN	B	**Emergency Care Attendant (EMT Ambulance)**	
MacMurray Coll, IL	B	Pittsburg State U, KS	B	U of Minnesota, Morris, MN	B	Trinity Coll of Nursing and Health Sciences, IL	A
Madonna U, MI	B	Purdue U, IN	B	U of Minnesota, Twin Cities Campus, MN	B		
Maharishi U of Management, IA	B	Purdue U Calumet, IN	B	U of Missouri–Columbia, MO	B	**Emergency Medical Technology (EMT Paramedic)**	
Manchester Coll, IN	B	Purdue U North Central, IN	B	U of Missouri–Kansas City, MO	B	Baker Coll of Cadillac, MI	A
Maranatha Baptist Bible Coll, WI	B			U of Missouri–St. Louis, MO	B	Baker Coll of Clinton Township, MI	A
Marian Coll, IN	B					Baker Coll of Muskegon, MI	A
Marian Coll of Fond du Lac, WI	B						

Ball State U, IN	A
Creighton U, NE	A,B
Hannibal-LaGrange Coll, MO	A
Indiana U–Purdue U Indianapolis, IN	A
Kent State U, Geauga Campus, OH	A
Missouri Western State U, MO	A
Nebraska Methodist Coll, NE	A,B
Rogers State U, OK	A
Shawnee State U, OH	A
Southwest Baptist U, MO	A
Turtle Mountain Comm Coll, ND	A
U of Minnesota, Twin Cities Campus, MN	B
U of Saint Francis, IN	A
The U of Toledo, OH	A
Youngstown State U, OH	A

Energy Management and Systems Technology

Baker Coll of Flint, MI	A
U of Cincinnati, OH	A
U of Rio Grande, OH	A

Engineering

Beloit Coll, WI	B
Bethany Lutheran Coll, MN	B
Calvin Coll, MI	B
Case Western Reserve U, OH	B
Central Christian Coll of Kansas, KS	A
Clarkson U, NY	B
Cleveland State U, OH	B
Coll of the Ozarks, MO	B
Dordt Coll, IA	B
Drury U, MO	B
Fontbonne U, MO	B
Grand Valley State U, MI	B
Hope Coll, MI	B
Indiana U–Purdue U Indianapolis, IN	B
Iowa State U of Science and Technology, IA	B
Lake Superior State U, MI	A
Marquette U, WI	B
Miami U–Middletown Campus, OH	A
Michigan State U, MI	B
Michigan Technological U, MI	B
North Dakota State U, ND	B
Northwestern U, IL	B
Oakland U, MI	B
Ohio Northern U, OH	B
Ohio U, OH	B
Oklahoma Christian U, OK	B
Oklahoma State U, OK	B
Purdue U Calumet, IN	B
St. Cloud State U, MN	B
Union Coll, NE	A
The U of Akron, OH	B
U of Cincinnati, OH	B
U of Illinois at Urbana–Champaign, IL	B
The U of Iowa, IA	B
U of Michigan, MI	B
U of Oklahoma, OK	B
U of Southern Indiana, IN	B
The U of Toledo, OH	B
U of Wisconsin–Madison, WI	B
U of Wisconsin–Milwaukee, WI	B
Wartburg Coll, IA	B
Washington U in St. Louis, MO	B
Western Michigan U, MI	B
Winona State U, MN	B
Wright State U, OH	B
Youngstown State U, OH	B

Engineering/Industrial Management

Grand Valley State U, MI	B
Grantham U, MO	A,B
Illinois Inst of Technology, IL	B
International Business Coll, Fort Wayne, IN	A,B
Kettering U, MI	B
Lake Superior State U, MI	B
Lawrence Technological U, MI	B
Miami U, OH	B
Miami U Hamilton, OH	B
Saginaw Valley State U, MI	B
Saint Louis U, MO	B
South Dakota State U, SD	B
Tri-State U, IN	B
U of Evansville, IN	B
U of Illinois at Chicago, IL	B
U of Missouri–Rolla, MO	B
U of Wisconsin–Stout, WI	B
Western Michigan U, MI	B

Engineering Mechanics

Cleveland State U, OH	B
Dordt Coll, IA	B
Michigan Technological U, MI	B
Oral Roberts U, OK	B
U of Cincinnati, OH	B
U of Illinois at Urbana–Champaign, IL	B
U of Wisconsin–Madison, WI	B

Engineering Physics

Augustana Coll, IL	B
Augustana Coll, SD	B
Aurora U, IL	B
Bemidji State U, MN	B
Bradley U, IL	B
Case Western Reserve U, OH	B
Hope Coll, MI	B
Loras Coll, IA	B
Miami U, OH	B
Miami U Hamilton, OH	B
Michigan Technological U, MI	B
Missouri State U, MO	B
Morningside Coll, IA	B
North Carolina Ag and Tech State U, NC	B
Northeastern State U, OK	B
The Ohio State U, OH	B
Rose-Hulman Inst of Technology, IN	B
St. Ambrose U, IA	B
Saint Mary's U of Minnesota, MN	B
South Dakota State U, SD	B
Southeast Missouri State U, MO	B
Southwestern Coll, KS	B
Southwestern Oklahoma State U, OK	B
Taylor U, IN	B
The U of Akron, OH	B
U of Illinois at Chicago, IL	B
U of Illinois at Urbana–Champaign, IL	B
U of Kansas, KS	B
U of Michigan, MI	B
U of Nebraska at Omaha, NE	B
U of Northern Iowa, IA	B
U of Oklahoma, OK	B

The U of Toledo, OH	B
U of Tulsa, OK	B
U of Wisconsin–Madison, WI	B
Washington U in St. Louis, MO	B
Wright State U, OH	B

Engineering Related

Augustana Coll, IL	B
Cleveland State U, OH	B
Eastern Illinois U, IL	B
Iowa State U of Science and Technology, IA	B
Loras Coll, IA	B
Madonna U, MI	B
Marquette U, WI	B
Northwestern U, IL	B
Ohio Northern U, OH	B
Ohio U, OH	B
Ohio Wesleyan U, OH	B
Park U, MO	B
Purdue U, IN	B
Rose-Hulman Inst of Technology, IN	B
U of Michigan–Dearborn, MI	B
U of Nebraska–Lincoln, NE	B
Wheaton Coll, IL	B
Wright State U, OH	B

Engineering Science

Benedictine U, IL	B
Bethel U, MN	B
Case Western Reserve U, OH	B
Cleveland State U, OH	B
Iowa State U of Science and Technology, IA	B
Manchester Coll, IN	B
Northwestern U, IL	B
Ohio Wesleyan U, OH	B
U of Cincinnati, OH	A,B
U of Mary, ND	B
U of Michigan, MI	B
U of Michigan–Flint, MI	B
U of New Orleans, LA	B
Washington U in St. Louis, MO	B
Wright State U, OH	B

Engineering Technologies Related

Bowling Green State U, OH	B
Bowling Green State U–Firelands Coll, OH	A
Cameron U, OK	A,B
McNally Smith Coll of Music, MN	A
Ohio U, OH	B
Rogers State U, OK	A,B
The U of Akron, OH	A
U of Southern Indiana, IN	B
Western Michigan U, MI	B

Engineering Technology

Andrews U, MI	A,B
Cleveland State U, OH	B
Dordt Coll, IA	B
Eastern Michigan U, MI	B
Kent State U, Ashtabula Campus, OH	A
Kent State U, Tuscarawas Campus, OH	A
Lake Superior State U, MI	A
Lawrence Technological U, MI	B
Miami U, OH	B
Miami U Hamilton, OH	B
Miami U–Middletown Campus, OH	A,B

Michigan Technological U, MI	A
Morrison Inst of Technology, IL	A
Northern Illinois U, IL	B
Oklahoma State U, OK	B
Pittsburg State U, KS	B
Purdue U Calumet, IN	B
Southern Illinois U Carbondale, IL	B
Southwestern Oklahoma State U, OK	B
Tri-State U, IN	A
The U of Akron, OH	B
U of West Florida, FL	B
U of Wisconsin–River Falls, WI	B
U of Wisconsin–Stout, WI	B
William Penn U, IA	B
Youngstown State U, OH	A,B

English

Adrian Coll, MI	A,B
Albion Coll, MI	B
Alma Coll, MI	B
Alverno Coll, WI	B
Anderson U, IN	B
Andrews U, MI	B
Antioch Coll, OH	B
Aquinas Coll, MI	B
Ashford U, IA	B
Ashland U, OH	B
Augsburg Coll, MN	B
Augustana Coll, IL	B
Augustana Coll, SD	B
Aurora U, IL	B
Avila U, MO	B
Baker U, KS	B
Baldwin-Wallace Coll, OH	B
Ball State U, IN	B
Beloit Coll, WI	B
Bemidji State U, MN	B
Benedictine Coll, KS	B
Benedictine U, IL	B
Bethany Coll, KS	B
Bethany Lutheran Coll, MN	B
Bethel Coll, KS	B
Bethel U, MN	B
Blackburn Coll, IL	B
Black Hills State U, SD	B
Bluffton U, OH	B
Bowling Green State U, OH	B
Bradley U, IL	B
Briar Cliff U, IA	B
Buena Vista U, IA	B
Butler U, IN	B
Calumet Coll of Saint Joseph, IN	A,B
Calvin Coll, MI	B
Cameron U, OK	B
Capital U, OH	B
Cardinal Stritch U, WI	B
Carleton Coll, MN	B
Carroll Coll, WI	B
Case Western Reserve U, OH	B
Cedarville U, OH	B
Central Coll, IA	B
Central Methodist U, MO	A,B
Central Michigan U, MI	B
Central State U, OH	B
Chicago State U, IL	B
Clarke Coll, IA	B
Cleveland State U, OH	B
Coe Coll, IA	B
Coll of Mount St. Joseph, OH	B
Coll of Saint Benedict, MN	B

A—associate degree; B—bachelor's degree

College	Degree
Coll of St. Catherine, MN	B
Coll of Saint Mary, NE	B
The Coll of St. Scholastica, MN	B
Coll of the Ozarks, MO	B
The Coll of Wooster, OH	B
Columbia Coll, MO	B
Concordia Coll, MN	B
Concordia U, IL	B
Concordia U, MI	B
Concordia U, NE	B
Concordia U, St. Paul, MN	B
Concordia U Wisconsin, WI	B
Concord U, WV	B
Cornell Coll, IA	B
Cornerstone U, MI	B
Creighton U, NE	B
Crown Coll, MN	B
Culver-Stockton Coll, MO	B
Dakota Wesleyan U, SD	B
Dana Coll, NE	B
Denison U, OH	B
DePaul U, IL	B
DePauw U, IN	B
Dickinson State U, ND	B
Doane Coll, NE	B
Dominican U, IL	B
Dordt Coll, IA	B
Drake U, IA	B
Drury U, MO	B
Earlham Coll, IN	B
East Central U, OK	B
Eastern Illinois U, IL	B
Eastern Michigan U, MI	B
East-West U, IL	B
Edgewood Coll, WI	B
Elmhurst Coll, IL	B
Emporia State U, KS	B
Evangel U, MO	B
Fontbonne U, MO	B
Fort Hays State U, KS	B
Franciscan U of Steubenville, OH	B
Franklin Coll, IN	B
Goshen Coll, IN	B
Grace Coll, IN	B
Graceland U, IA	B
Grand Valley State U, MI	B
Grand View Coll, IA	B
Greenville Coll, IL	B
Grinnell Coll, IA	B
Gustavus Adolphus Coll, MN	B
Hamline U, MN	B
Hannibal-LaGrange Coll, MO	A,B
Hanover Coll, IN	B
Hastings Coll, NE	B
Heidelberg Coll, OH	B
Hillsdale Coll, MI	B
Hillsdale Free Will Baptist Coll, OK	A
Hiram Coll, OH	B
Hope Coll, MI	B
Huntington U, IN	B
Illinois Coll, IL	B
Illinois State U, IL	B
Illinois Wesleyan U, IL	B
Indiana State U, IN	B
Indiana U Bloomington, IN	B
Indiana U East, IN	B
Indiana U Kokomo, IN	B
Indiana U Northwest, IN	B
Indiana U–Purdue U Fort Wayne, IN	A,B
Indiana U–Purdue U Indianapolis, IN	B
Indiana U South Bend, IN	B
Indiana U Southeast, IN	B
Indiana Wesleyan U, IN	A,B
Iowa State U of Science and Technology, IA	B
Iowa Wesleyan Coll, IA	B
Jamestown Coll, ND	B
Judson Coll, IL	B
Kalamazoo Coll, MI	B
Kansas State U, KS	B
Kent State U, OH	B
Kent State U, Trumbull Campus, OH	B
Kenyon Coll, OH	B
Knox Coll, IL	B
Lake Forest Coll, IL	B
Lakeland Coll, WI	B
Lake Superior State U, MI	B
Langston U, OK	B
Lawrence U, WI	B
Lewis U, IL	B
Lincoln U, MO	B
Lindenwood U, MO	B
Loras Coll, IA	B
Lourdes Coll, OH	A,B
Loyola U Chicago, IL	B
Luther Coll, IA	B
Macalester Coll, MN	B
MacMurray Coll, IL	B
Madonna U, MI	A,B
Maharishi U of Management, IA	B
Malone Coll, OH	B
Manchester Coll, IN	A,B
Marian Coll, IN	B
Marian Coll of Fond du Lac, WI	B
Marietta Coll, OH	B
Marquette U, WI	B
Marygrove Coll, MI	B
Maryville U of Saint Louis, MO	B
Mayville State U, ND	B
McKendree Coll, IL	B
Metropolitan State U, MN	B
Miami U, OH	B
Miami U Hamilton, OH	B
Miami U–Middletown Campus, OH	A
Michigan State U, MI	B
Michigan Technological U, MI	B
Millikin U, IL	B
Minnesota State U Mankato, MN	B
Minot State U, ND	B
Missouri Baptist U, MO	B
Missouri Southern State U, MO	B
Missouri State U, MO	B
Missouri Valley Coll, MO	B
Missouri Western State U, MO	B
Morningside Coll, IA	B
Mount Marty Coll, SD	B
Mount Mary Coll, WI	B
Mount Mercy Coll, IA	B
Mount Union Coll, OH	B
Mount Vernon Nazarene U, OH	B
Nebraska Wesleyan U, NE	B
Newman U, KS	B
North Carolina Ag and Tech State U, NC	B
North Central Coll, IL	B
North Dakota State U, ND	B
Northeastern Illinois U, IL	B
Northeastern State U, OK	B
Northern Illinois U, IL	B
Northern Michigan U, MI	B
Northern State U, SD	B
Northland Coll, WI	B
Northwestern Coll, IA	B
Northwestern Coll, MN	B
Northwestern Oklahoma State U, OK	B
Northwestern U, IL	B
Northwest Missouri State U, MO	B
Notre Dame Coll, OH	B
Oakland U, MI	B
Oberlin Coll, OH	B
Ohio Dominican U, OH	B
Ohio Northern U, OH	B
The Ohio State U, OH	B
The Ohio State U at Lima, OH	B
The Ohio State U at Marion, OH	B
The Ohio State U–Mansfield Campus, OH	B
The Ohio State U–Newark Campus, OH	B
Ohio U, OH	B
Ohio Wesleyan U, OH	B
Oklahoma Christian U, OK	B
Oklahoma City U, OK	B
Oklahoma Panhandle State U, OK	B
Oklahoma State U, OK	B
Oklahoma Wesleyan U, OK	B
Oral Roberts U, OK	B
Ottawa U, KS	B
Otterbein Coll, OH	B
Park U, MO	B
Peru State Coll, NE	B
Pittsburg State U, KS	B
Pontifical Coll Josephinum, OH	B
Presentation Coll, SD	A
Purdue U, IN	B
Purdue U Calumet, IN	B
Purdue U North Central, IN	B
Quincy U, IL	B
Ripon Coll, WI	B
Rochester Coll, MI	B
Rockford Coll, IL	B
Rockhurst U, MO	B
Roosevelt U, IL	B
Saginaw Valley State U, MI	B
St. Ambrose U, IA	B
St. Cloud State U, MN	B
St. Gregory's U, Shawnee, OK	B
Saint John's U, MN	B
Saint Joseph's Coll, IN	B
Saint Louis U, MO	B
Saint Mary-of-the-Woods Coll, IN	B
Saint Mary's U of Minnesota, MN	B
St. Norbert Coll, WI	B
St. Olaf Coll, MN	B
Saint Xavier U, IL	B
Shawnee State U, OH	B
Silver Lake Coll, WI	B
Simpson Coll, IA	B
South Dakota State U, SD	B
Southeastern Oklahoma State U, OK	B
Southeast Missouri State U, MO	B
Southern Illinois U Carbondale, IL	B
Southern Illinois U Edwardsville, IL	B
Southern Methodist U, TX	B
Southwest Baptist U, MO	B
Southwestern Coll, KS	B
Southwestern Oklahoma State U, OK	B
Southwest Minnesota State U, MN	B
Spring Arbor U, MI	B
Stephens Coll, MO	B
Sterling Coll, KS	B
Tabor Coll, KS	B
Taylor U, IN	B
Taylor U Fort Wayne, IN	B
Tiffin U, OH	B
Transylvania U, KY	B
Trinity Christian Coll, IL	B
Trinity International U, IL	B
Tri-State U, IN	B
Truman State U, MO	B
Turtle Mountain Comm Coll, ND	A
Union Coll, NE	B
The U of Akron, OH	B
U of Central Missouri, MO	B
U of Central Oklahoma, OK	B
U of Chicago, IL	B
U of Cincinnati, OH	B
U of Dallas, TX	B
U of Dayton, OH	B
U of Evansville, IN	B
The U of Findlay, OH	B
U of Illinois at Chicago, IL	B
U of Illinois at Springfield, IL	B
U of Illinois at Urbana–Champaign, IL	B
U of Indianapolis, IN	B
The U of Iowa, IA	B
U of Kansas, KS	B
U of Mary, ND	B
U of Michigan, MI	B
U of Michigan–Dearborn, MI	B
U of Michigan–Flint, MI	B
U of Minnesota, Duluth, MN	B
U of Minnesota, Morris, MN	B
U of Minnesota, Twin Cities Campus, MN	B
U of Missouri–Columbia, MO	B
U of Missouri–Kansas City, MO	B
U of Missouri–Rolla, MO	B
U of Missouri–St. Louis, MO	B
U of Nebraska at Kearney, NE	B
U of Nebraska at Omaha, NE	B
U of Nebraska–Lincoln, NE	B
U of New Orleans, LA	B
U of North Dakota, ND	B
U of Northern Iowa, IA	B
U of Notre Dame, IN	B
U of Oklahoma, OK	B
U of Rio Grande, OH	A,B
U of St. Francis, IL	B
U of Saint Francis, IN	B
U of Saint Mary, KS	B
U of St. Thomas, MN	B
U of Science and Arts of Oklahoma, OK	B
U of Sioux Falls, SD	B
The U of South Dakota, SD	B
U of Southern Indiana, IN	B
The U of Toledo, OH	B
U of Tulsa, OK	B
U of West Florida, FL	B
U of Wisconsin–Eau Claire, WI	B
U of Wisconsin–Green Bay, WI	A,B

Majors and Degrees
English

U of Wisconsin–La Crosse, WI	B
U of Wisconsin–Madison, WI	B
U of Wisconsin–Milwaukee, WI	B
U of Wisconsin–Oshkosh, WI	B
U of Wisconsin–Parkside, WI	B
U of Wisconsin–Platteville, WI	B
U of Wisconsin–River Falls, WI	B
U of Wisconsin–Stevens Point, WI	B
U of Wisconsin–Superior, WI	B
U of Wisconsin–Whitewater, WI	B
Upper Iowa U, IA	B
Ursuline Coll, OH	B
Valley City State U, ND	B
Valparaiso U, IN	B
Viterbo U, WI	B
Wabash Coll, IN	B
Waldorf Coll, IA	B
Walsh U, OH	B
Wartburg Coll, IA	B
Washburn U, KS	B
Washington U in St. Louis, MO	B
Wayne State Coll, NE	B
Webster U, MO	B
Western Illinois U, IL	B
Western Michigan U, MI	B
Westminster Coll, MO	B
Wheaton Coll, IL	B
Wichita State U, KS	B
William Jewell Coll, MO	B
William Woods U, MO	B
Wilmington Coll, OH	B
Winona State U, MN	B
Wisconsin Lutheran Coll, WI	B
Wittenberg U, OH	B
Wright State U, OH	B
Xavier U, OH	A,B
York Coll, NE	B
Youngstown State U, OH	B

English as a Second/Foreign Language (Teaching)

Aquinas Coll, MI	B
Bethel U, MN	B
Calvin Coll, MI	B
Concordia U, NE	B
Concordia U, St. Paul, MN	B
Concordia U Wisconsin, WI	B
Doane Coll, NE	B
Goshen Coll, IN	B
Langston U, OK	B
Northwestern Coll, MN	B
Ohio Dominican U, OH	B
Ohio U, OH	B
Oklahoma Christian U, OK	B
Oklahoma Wesleyan U, OK	B
Oral Roberts U, OK	B
The U of Findlay, OH	B
The U of Iowa, IA	B
U of Nebraska–Lincoln, NE	B
U of Northern Iowa, IA	B
U of Wisconsin–Oshkosh, WI	B
U of Wisconsin–River Falls, WI	B
William Penn U, IA	B
Wright State U, OH	B

English Composition

Aurora U, IL	B
Bethel U, MN	B
DePauw U, IN	B
Eastern Michigan U, MI	B

Graceland U, IA	B
Jamestown Coll, ND	B
Lakeland Coll, WI	B
Metropolitan State U, MN	B
Miami U Hamilton, OH	B
Mount Union Coll, OH	B
U of Evansville, IN	B
U of Illinois at Urbana–Champaign, IL	B
U of Michigan–Flint, MI	B
Wartburg Coll, IA	B
Western Michigan U, MI	B
William Woods U, MO	B

English/French as a Second/Foreign Language (Teaching) Related

Western Michigan U, MI	B

English Language and Literature Related

Dakota State U, SD	B
Hastings Coll, NE	B
St. Gregory's U, Shawnee, OK	B
Saint Mary-of-the-Woods Coll, IN	B
U of Chicago, IL	B
The U of Iowa, IA	B
U of Oklahoma, OK	B
Viterbo U, WI	B
Washington U in St. Louis, MO	B
Webster U, MO	B

English/Language Arts Teacher Education

Alma Coll, MI	B
Alverno Coll, WI	B
Anderson U, IN	B
Aquinas Coll, MI	B
Bethany Coll, KS	B
Bethel U, MN	B
Bowling Green State U, OH	B
Buena Vista U, IA	B
Calumet Coll of Saint Joseph, IN	B
Capital U, OH	B
Carroll Coll, WI	B
Cedarville U, OH	B
Central Michigan U, MI	B
Central State U, OH	B
Chicago State U, IL	B
Coll of St. Catherine, MN	B
Coll of the Ozarks, MO	B
Concordia Coll, MN	B
Concordia U, IL	B
Concordia U, MI	B
Concordia U, NE	B
Cornerstone U, MI	B
Crown Coll, MN	B
Culver-Stockton Coll, MO	B
Dakota State U, SD	B
Dakota Wesleyan U, SD	B
Dana Coll, NE	B
East Central U, OK	B
Eastern Michigan U, MI	B
Elmhurst Coll, IL	B
Faith Baptist Bible Coll and Theological Seminary, IA	B
Franklin Coll, IN	B
Grace Coll, IN	B
Greenville Coll, IL	B
Hannibal-LaGrange Coll, MO	B
Hastings Coll, NE	B
Hope Coll, MI	B
Illinois Wesleyan U, IL	B

Indiana U Bloomington, IN	B
Indiana U Northwest, IN	B
Indiana U–Purdue U Fort Wayne, IN	B
Indiana U–Purdue U Indianapolis, IN	B
Indiana U South Bend, IN	B
Indiana U Southeast, IN	B
Indiana Wesleyan U, IN	B
Jamestown Coll, ND	B
Kent State U, OH	B
Lincoln U, MO	B
Malone Coll, OH	B
Marian Coll of Fond du Lac, WI	B
Marquette U, WI	B
Maryville U of Saint Louis, MO	B
Mayville State U, ND	B
McKendree Coll, IL	B
Miami U, OH	B
Miami U Hamilton, OH	B
Michigan Technological U, MI	B
Minot State U, ND	B
Missouri State U, MO	B
Missouri Western State U, MO	B
Mount Marty Coll, SD	B
Mount Mary Coll, WI	B
Mount Vernon Nazarene U, OH	B
Nebraska Wesleyan U, NE	B
North Dakota State U, ND	B
Northern Michigan U, MI	B
Northwestern Coll, MN	B
Ohio Northern U, OH	B
Oklahoma Christian U, OK	B
Oral Roberts U, OK	B
Pittsburg State U, KS	B
Rochester Coll, MI	B
Saginaw Valley State U, MI	B
St. Ambrose U, IA	B
St. Gregory's U, Shawnee, OK	B
Saint Mary's U of Minnesota, MN	B
Saint Xavier U, IL	B
Shawnee State U, OH	B
Southeastern Oklahoma State U, OK	B
Southeast Missouri State U, MO	B
Southwest Baptist U, MO	B
Southwestern Oklahoma State U, OK	B
Southwest Minnesota State U, MN	B
Trinity Christian Coll, IL	B
Tri-State U, IN	B
Union Coll, NE	B
The U of Akron, OH	B
U of Central Oklahoma, OK	B
U of Evansville, IN	B
U of Illinois at Chicago, IL	B
U of Illinois at Urbana–Champaign, IL	B
U of Indianapolis, IN	B
U of Mary, ND	B
U of Minnesota, Twin Cities Campus, MN	B
U of Missouri–St. Louis, MO	B
U of Nebraska–Lincoln, NE	B
U of New Orleans, LA	B
U of Oklahoma, OK	B
U of Rio Grande, OH	B
U of St. Francis, IL	B
U of Saint Francis, IN	B

U of St. Thomas, MN	B
The U of South Dakota, SD	B
The U of Toledo, OH	B
U of West Florida, FL	B
U of Wisconsin–River Falls, WI	B
U of Wisconsin–Superior, WI	B
Ursuline Coll, OH	B
Valley City State U, ND	B
Valparaiso U, IN	B
Viterbo U, WI	B
Waldorf Coll, IA	B
Washington U in St. Louis, MO	B
Wayne State Coll, NE	B
Western Michigan U, MI	B
William Penn U, IA	B
William Woods U, MO	B
Wright State U, OH	B
York Coll, NE	B
Youngstown State U, OH	B

English Literature (British and Commonwealth)

Gannon U, PA	B
Indiana U–Purdue U Fort Wayne, IN	B
Oral Roberts U, OK	B
Saint Mary's Coll, IN	B
Washington U in St. Louis, MO	B

Entomology

Iowa State U of Science and Technology, IA	B
Michigan State U, MI	B
The Ohio State U, OH	B
Oklahoma State U, OK	B
Purdue U, IN	B
U of Illinois at Urbana–Champaign, IL	B
U of Wisconsin–Madison, WI	B

Entrepreneurial and Small Business Related

Kendall Coll, IL	B

Entrepreneurship

Baker Coll of Flint, MI	A
Bradley U, IL	B
Buena Vista U, IA	B
Davenport U, Dearborn, MI	A,B
East Central U, OK	B
Eastern Michigan U, MI	B
Iowa State U of Science and Technology, IA	B
Kendall Coll, IL	B
Millikin U, IL	B
Newman U, KS	B
Northern Michigan U, MI	B
Northwood U, MI	A,B
Union Coll, NE	B
The U of Akron, OH	A
U of Illinois at Chicago, IL	B
U of Illinois at Urbana–Champaign, IL	B
U of Indianapolis, IN	B
The U of Iowa, IA	B
U of North Dakota, ND	B
U of Oklahoma, OK	B
U of Phoenix–Kansas City Campus, MO	B
U of Phoenix–Metro Detroit Campus, MI	B
U of St. Thomas, MN	B
U of Southern Indiana, IN	B
The U of Toledo, OH	B

A—associate degree; B—bachelor's degree

Washington U in St. Louis, MO — B
Wichita State U, KS — B
Xavier U, OH — B

Environmental Biology
Antioch Coll, OH — B
Beloit Coll, WI — B
Cedarville U, OH — B
Central Methodist U, MO — B
Chicago State U, IL — B
Cornerstone U, MI — B
Greenville Coll, IL — B
Heidelberg Coll, OH — B
Iowa Wesleyan Coll, IA — B
Marygrove Coll, MI — B
Michigan State U, MI — B
Minnesota State U Mankato, MN — B
Mount Union Coll, OH — B
Northland Coll, WI — B
Ohio U, OH — B
Otterbein Coll, OH — B
St. Cloud State U, MN — B
Saint Mary's U of Minnesota, MN — B
Simpson Coll, IA — B
Tabor Coll, KS — B
Taylor U, IN — B
U of Charleston, WV — B
U of Dayton, OH — B
Ursuline Coll, OH — B
William Penn U, IA — B
Winona State U, MN — B

Environmental Design/ Architecture
Ball State U, IN — B
Bowling Green State U, OH — B
Kent State U, OH — B
Lawrence Technological U, MI — B
Miami U, OH — B
North Dakota State U, ND — B
U of Oklahoma, OK — B

Environmental Education
Northland Coll, WI — B
The Ohio State U, OH — B

Environmental Engineering Technology
Baker Coll of Flint, MI — A
Baker Coll of Owosso, MI — A
Baker Coll of Port Huron, MI — A
Kent State U, Trumbull Campus, OH — A
Lake Superior State U, MI — B
Ohio U, OH — A
Shawnee State U, OH — B
U of Cincinnati, OH — A
The U of Toledo, OH — A
U of Wisconsin–Whitewater, WI — B
Wright State U, OH — B

Environmental/Environmental Health Engineering
Bradley U, IL — B
Clarkson U, NY — B
Gannon U, PA — B
Illinois Inst of Technology, IL — B
Marquette U, WI — B
Michigan Technological U, MI — B
Northwestern U, IL — B
Ohio U, OH — A
South Dakota School of Mines and Technology, SD — B
South Dakota State U, SD — B

Southern Methodist U, TX — B
U of Michigan, MI — B
U of Missouri–Rolla, MO — B
U of North Dakota, ND — B
U of Notre Dame, IN — B
U of Oklahoma, OK — B
U of Wisconsin–Madison, WI — B
U of Wisconsin–Platteville, WI — B

Environmental Health
Bowling Green State U, OH — B
Clarkson U, NY — B
East Central U, OK — B
Ferris State U, MI — B
Illinois State U, IL — B
Indiana State U, IN — B
Iowa Wesleyan Coll, IA — B
Missouri Southern State U, MO — B
Oakland U, MI — B
The U of Akron, OH — A
U of Michigan–Flint, MI — B
U of Wisconsin–Eau Claire, WI — B
Wright State U, OH — B

Environmental Science
Aquinas Coll, MI — B
Bethel U, MN — B
Blackburn Coll, IL — B
Briar Cliff U, IA — B
Capital U, OH — B
Carroll Coll, WI — B
Central Methodist U, MO — B
Concordia U, St. Paul, MN — B
Drake U, IA — B
East Central U, OK — B
Gannon U, PA — B
Heidelberg Coll, OH — B
Iowa State U of Science and Technology, IA — B
Lindenwood U, MO — B
Marietta Coll, OH — B
Maryville U of Saint Louis, MO — B
Miami U Hamilton, OH — B
Michigan State U, MI — B
Michigan Technological U, MI — B
Northwestern Coll, IA — B
Northwestern U, IL — B
Notre Dame Coll, OH — B
Otterbein Coll, OH — B
Saint Louis U, MO — B
St. Norbert Coll, WI — B
Southeastern Oklahoma State U, OK — B
U of Charleston, WV — B
U of Evansville, IN — B
U of Illinois at Urbana–Champaign, IL — B
The U of Iowa, IA — B
U of Michigan–Dearborn, MI — B
U of Northern Iowa, IA — B
U of Oklahoma, OK — B
U of St. Francis, IL — B
U of Wisconsin–Green Bay, WI — A,B
Upper Iowa U, IA — B
Valparaiso U, IN — B
Western Michigan U, MI — B
Westminster Coll, MO — B
Wright State U, OH — B

Environmental Studies
Adrian Coll, MI — B
Albion Coll, MI — B
Alverno Coll, WI — B
Antioch Coll, OH — B

Aquinas Coll, MI — B
Ashland U, OH — B
Augustana Coll, IL — B
Aurora U, IL — B
Ball State U, IN — B
Beloit Coll, WI — B
Bemidji State U, MN — B
Benedictine U, IL — B
Black Hills State U, SD — B
Calvin Coll, MI — B
Case Western Reserve U, OH — B
Central Christian Coll of Kansas, KS — A
Central Coll, IA — B
Central Michigan U, MI — B
Clarkson U, NY — B
Cleveland State U, OH — B
Coe Coll, IA — B
Coll of Saint Benedict, MN — B
Columbia Coll, MO — B
Concordia Coll, MN — B
Concordia U, IL — B
Cornell Coll, IA — B
Creighton U, NE — B
Dana Coll, NE — B
Denison U, OH — B
DePaul U, IL — B
DePauw U, IN — B
Dickinson State U, ND — A,B
Doane Coll, NE — B
Dominican U, IL — B
Dordt Coll, IA — B
Drake U, IA — B
Drury U, MO — B
Earlham Coll, IN — B
East Central U, OK — B
Elmhurst Coll, IL — B
Fort Berthold Comm Coll, ND — A
Goshen Coll, IN — B
Gustavus Adolphus Coll, MN — B
Hamline U, MN — B
Heidelberg Coll, OH — B
Hiram Coll, OH — B
Hope Coll, MI — B
Illinois Coll, IL — B
Illinois Wesleyan U, IL — B
Indiana U Bloomington, IN — B
Iowa State U of Science and Technology, IA — B
Kent State U, Ashtabula Campus, OH — A
Kent State U, Tuscarawas Campus, OH — A
Kenyon Coll, OH — B
Knox Coll, IL — B
Lake Forest Coll, IL — B
Lake Superior State U, MI — B
Lawrence U, WI — B
Lewis U, IL — B
Loyola U Chicago, IL — B
Macalester Coll, MN — B
Maharishi U of Management, IA — B
Manchester Coll, IN — B
Marietta Coll, OH — B
Marygrove Coll, MI — B
Maryville U of Saint Louis, MO — B
Miami U Hamilton, OH — B
Michigan State U, MI — B
Minnesota State U Mankato, MN — B
Northeastern Illinois U, IL — B
Northern Michigan U, MI — B
Northern State U, SD — B
Northland Coll, WI — B

Northwestern U, IL — B
Oberlin Coll, OH — B
Ohio Northern U, OH — B
The Ohio State U, OH — B
Ohio Wesleyan U, OH — B
Oklahoma State U, OK — B
Pittsburg State U, KS — B
Ripon Coll, WI — B
Saint John's U, MN — B
St. Norbert Coll, WI — B
St. Olaf Coll, MN — B
Sitting Bull Coll, ND — A
Southern Methodist U, TX — B
Southwest Minnesota State U, MN — B
Stephens Coll, MO — B
Taylor U, IN — B
Tri-State U, IN — B
Turtle Mountain Comm Coll, ND — A
U of Chicago, IL — B
U of Cincinnati, OH — A
U of Dayton, OH — B
U of Evansville, IN — B
The U of Findlay, OH — A,B
U of Indianapolis, IN — B
The U of Iowa, IA — B
U of Kansas, KS — B
U of Michigan, MI — B
U of Michigan–Dearborn, MI — B
U of Minnesota, Crookston, MN — B
U of Minnesota, Duluth, MN — B
U of Minnesota, Twin Cities Campus, MN — B
U of Missouri–Columbia, MO — B
U of Nebraska at Omaha, NE — B
U of Nebraska–Lincoln, NE — B
U of New Orleans, LA — B
U of Saint Francis, IN — B
The U of Toledo, OH — A,B
U of Tulsa, OK — B
U of West Florida, FL — B
U of Wisconsin–Green Bay, WI — A,B
U of Wisconsin–River Falls, WI — B
Washington U in St. Louis, MO — B
Webster U, MO — B
Western Michigan U, MI — B
Westminster Coll, MO — B
Wheaton Coll, IL — B
Wittenberg U, OH — B

Equestrian Studies
National American U, Rapid City, SD — A,B
North Dakota State U, ND — B
Ohio U, OH — A
Otterbein Coll, OH — B
Rogers State U, OK — A
Saint Mary-of-the-Woods Coll, IN — A,B
Stephens Coll, MO — B
Truman State U, MO — B
The U of Findlay, OH — A,B
U of Minnesota, Crookston, MN — A,B
U of Wisconsin–River Falls, WI — B
William Woods U, MO — B

Ethics
Drake U, IA — B
U of Michigan–Flint, MI — B

Ethnic, Cultural Minority, and Gender Studies Related

Bowling Green State U, OH	B
Cornell Coll, IA	B
Kenyon Coll, OH	B
Lawrence U, WI	B
Metropolitan State U, MN	B
Miami U Hamilton, OH	B
St. Olaf Coll, MN	B
Washington U in St. Louis, MO	B

European Studies

Antioch Coll, OH	B
Beloit Coll, WI	B
Central Michigan U, MI	B
Hamline U, MN	B
Hillsdale Coll, MI	B
Ohio U, OH	B
Southern Methodist U, TX	B
U of Kansas, KS	B
U of Michigan, MI	B
U of Minnesota, Morris, MN	B
U of Minnesota, Twin Cities Campus, MN	B
U of Missouri–Columbia, MO	B
U of Northern Iowa, IA	B
The U of Toledo, OH	B
Washington U in St. Louis, MO	B

European Studies (Central and Eastern)

Hamline U, MN	B
Indiana U Bloomington, IN	B
Kent State U, OH	B
U of Chicago, IL	B
U of Missouri–Columbia, MO	B

European Studies (Western)

Illinois Wesleyan U, IL	B
The Ohio State U, OH	B
U of Nebraska–Lincoln, NE	B

Evolutionary Biology

Case Western Reserve U, OH	B
The U of Akron, OH	B

Executive Assistant/Executive Secretary

Baker Coll of Allen Park, MI	A
Baker Coll of Flint, MI	A
Robert Morris Coll, IL	A
Rockford Business Coll, IL	A
The U of Akron, OH	A

Exercise Physiology

The Coll of St. Scholastica, MN	B
Concordia U Wisconsin, WI	B
Miami U Hamilton, OH	B

Experimental Psychology

Blackburn Coll, IL	B
The U of Toledo, OH	B
U of Wisconsin–Madison, WI	B

Facilities Planning and Management

Eastern Michigan U, MI	B
North Dakota State U, ND	B

Family and Community Services

Andrews U, MI	B
Baker Coll of Flint, MI	A
Bowling Green State U–Firelands Coll, OH	A
Central Christian Coll of Kansas, KS	A
God's Bible School and Coll, OH	B
Goshen Coll, IN	B
Iowa State U of Science and Technology, IA	B
Michigan State U, MI	B
Oklahoma Christian U, OK	B
U of Minnesota, Twin Cities Campus, MN	B
U of Northern Iowa, IA	B
Youngstown State U, OH	B

Family and Consumer Economics Related

Andrews U, MI	B
Ashland U, OH	B
Ball State U, IN	B
Indiana U Bloomington, IN	B
Iowa State U of Science and Technology, IA	B
Miami U, OH	B
Minnesota State U Mankato, MN	B
Northwest Missouri State U, MO	B
The U of Akron, OH	B
U of Missouri–Columbia, MO	B
U of Nebraska at Kearney, NE	B
U of Nebraska–Lincoln, NE	B
U of Northern Iowa, IA	B
U of Wisconsin–Madison, WI	B
U of Wisconsin–Stevens Point, WI	B

Family and Consumer Sciences/Home Economics Teacher Education

Ashland U, OH	B
Ball State U, IN	B
Bluffton U, OH	B
Coll of St. Catherine, MN	B
Coll of the Ozarks, MO	B
Concordia U, NE	B
East Central U, OK	B
Ferris State U, MI	B
Fontbonne U, MO	B
Iowa State U of Science and Technology, IA	B
Kent State U, OH	B
Langston U, OK	B
Madonna U, MI	B
Miami U, OH	B
Michigan State U, MI	B
Minnesota State U Mankato, MN	B
Missouri State U, MO	B
Mount Vernon Nazarene U, OH	B
North Carolina Ag and Tech State U, NC	B
North Dakota State U, ND	B
Northeastern State U, OK	B
Northern Illinois U, IL	B
Northwest Missouri State U, MO	B
Pittsburg State U, KS	B
South Dakota State U, SD	B
Southeast Missouri State U, MO	B
The U of Akron, OH	B
U of Central Oklahoma, OK	B
U of Minnesota, Twin Cities Campus, MN	B
U of Wisconsin–Madison, WI	B
U of Wisconsin–Stevens Point, WI	B
U of Wisconsin–Stout, WI	B
Wayne State Coll, NE	B
Western Michigan U, MI	B
Youngstown State U, OH	B

Family and Consumer Sciences/Human Sciences

Ashland U, OH	B
Ball State U, IN	B
Bluffton U, OH	B
Cameron U, OK	B
Coll of St. Catherine, MN	B
Coll of the Ozarks, MO	B
East Central U, OK	B
Eastern Illinois U, IL	B
Fontbonne U, MO	B
Hope Coll, MI	B
Illinois State U, IL	B
Indiana State U, IN	B
Iowa State U of Science and Technology, IA	B
Kent State U, OH	B
Langston U, OK	B
Madonna U, MI	B
Miami U, OH	B
Michigan State U, MI	B
Minnesota State U Mankato, MN	B
Mount Vernon Nazarene U, OH	A,B
North Carolina Ag and Tech State U, NC	B
Northeastern State U, OK	B
Northwest Missouri State U, MO	B
Oglala Lakota Coll, SD	A
Ohio U, OH	B
Pittsburg State U, KS	B
Purdue U, IN	B
Southeast Missouri State U, MO	B
The U of Akron, OH	B
U of Central Missouri, MO	B
U of Central Oklahoma, OK	B
U of Nebraska at Omaha, NE	B
U of Wisconsin–Madison, WI	B
Wayne State Coll, NE	B
Western Illinois U, IL	B
Youngstown State U, OH	B

Family and Consumer Sciences/Human Sciences Communication

U of Nebraska at Omaha, NE	B

Family/Community Studies

Coll of the Ozarks, MO	B
St. Olaf Coll, MN	B

Family Resource Management

Bradley U, IL	B
Iowa State U of Science and Technology, IA	B
The Ohio State U, OH	B
Ohio U, OH	B
U of Nebraska at Omaha, NE	B

Family Systems

Anderson U, IN	B
Central Michigan U, MI	B
Spring Arbor U, MI	B
The U of Akron, OH	B
Western Michigan U, MI	B

Farm and Ranch Management

Fort Berthold Comm Coll, ND	A
Iowa State U of Science and Technology, IA	B
Northwest Missouri State U, MO	B
Oklahoma Panhandle State U, OK	A
Rogers State U, OK	A
Sitting Bull Coll, ND	A
The U of Findlay, OH	B
U of Minnesota, Crookston, MN	B
U of Wisconsin–Madison, WI	B

Fashion/Apparel Design

Coll of St. Catherine, MN	B
Columbia Coll Chicago, IL	B
Columbus Coll of Art & Design, OH	B
Dominican U, IL	B
The Illinois Inst of Art–Chicago, IL	B
Indiana U Bloomington, IN	A,B
International Academy of Design & Technology, IL	A,B
Iowa State U of Science and Technology, IA	B
Kent State U, OH	B
Lindenwood U, MO	B
Michigan State U, MI	B
Minnesota State U Mankato, MN	B
Mount Mary Coll, WI	B
Northwest Missouri State U, MO	B
School of the Art Inst of Chicago, IL	B
Stephens Coll, MO	B
U of Cincinnati, OH	B
Ursuline Coll, OH	B
Washington U in St. Louis, MO	B

Fashion Merchandising

Ashland U, OH	B
Ball State U, IN	B
Bowling Green State U, OH	B
Central Michigan U, MI	B
Coll of St. Catherine, MN	B
Dominican U, IL	B
East Central U, OK	B
Eastern Michigan U, MI	B
Fontbonne U, MO	B
The Illinois Inst of Art–Chicago, IL	B
Indiana U Bloomington, IN	B
International Academy of Design & Technology, IL	A,B
Kent State U, OH	B
Lindenwood U, MO	B
Mount Mary Coll, WI	B
Northeastern State U, OK	B
Northwest Missouri State U, MO	B
Northwood U, MI	A,B
South Dakota State U, SD	B
Stephens Coll, MO	B
The U of Akron, OH	A,B
U of Central Oklahoma, OK	B
U of Illinois at Urbana–Champaign, IL	B
U of Wisconsin–Madison, WI	B
Ursuline Coll, OH	B
Wayne State Coll, NE	B
Youngstown State U, OH	B

A—associate degree; B—bachelor's degree

Fiber, Textile and Weaving Arts

The Cleveland Inst of Art, OH	B
Finlandia U, MI	B
Kansas City Art Inst, MO	B
Northwest Missouri State U, MO	B
School of the Art Inst of Chicago, IL	B
U of Kansas, KS	B
U of Michigan, MI	B
U of Wisconsin–Milwaukee, WI	B

Film/Cinema Studies

Baldwin-Wallace Coll, OH	B
Bowling Green State U, OH	B
Calvin Coll, MI	B
Columbia Coll Chicago, IL	B
Denison U, OH	B
Eastern Michigan U, MI	B
Grand Valley State U, MI	B
Huntington U, IN	B
Indiana U South Bend, IN	A
Northern Michigan U, MI	B
Northwestern U, IL	B
Ohio U, OH	B
Oral Roberts U, OK	B
St. Cloud State U, MN	B
School of the Art Inst of Chicago, IL	B
Southern Methodist U, TX	B
U of Chicago, IL	B
The U of Iowa, IA	B
U of Michigan, MI	B
U of Minnesota, Twin Cities Campus, MN	B
U of Nebraska–Lincoln, NE	B
The U of Toledo, OH	B
U of Tulsa, OK	B
U of Wisconsin–Milwaukee, WI	B
Washington U in St. Louis, MO	B
Webster U, MO	B
Wright State U, OH	B

Film/Video and Photographic Arts Related

The Illinois Inst of Art–Chicago, IL	B
School of the Art Inst of Chicago, IL	B
Southern Methodist U, TX	B
The U of Iowa, IA	B

Finance

Academy Coll, MN	A
AIB Coll of Business, IA	A
Anderson U, IN	B
Ashland U, OH	B
Augsburg Coll, MN	B
Augustana Coll, IL	B
Aurora U, IL	B
Avila U, MO	B
Baldwin-Wallace Coll, OH	B
Ball State U, IN	B
Benedictine U, IL	B
Bowling Green State U, OH	B
Bradley U, IL	B
Butler U, IN	B
Capital U, OH	B
Carroll Coll, WI	B
Cedarville U, OH	B
Central Christian Coll of Kansas, KS	A
Central Michigan U, MI	B

Central State U, OH	B
Chicago State U, IL	B
Clarkson U, NY	B
Cleary U, MI	B
Cleveland State U, OH	B
Columbia Coll, MO	B
Concordia U, St. Paul, MN	B
Creighton U, NE	B
Culver-Stockton Coll, MO	B
Dakota State U, SD	B
Dakota Wesleyan U, SD	B
Davenport U, Dearborn, MI	A,B
DePaul U, IL	B
Dickinson State U, ND	B
Drake U, IA	B
Drury U, MO	B
East Central U, OK	B
Eastern Illinois U, IL	B
Eastern Michigan U, MI	B
East-West U, IL	B
Elmhurst Coll, IL	B
Ferris State U, MI	B
Fontbonne U, MO	B
Fort Hays State U, KS	B
Gannon U, PA	B
Grand Valley State U, MI	B
Hillsdale Coll, MI	B
Illinois Coll, IL	B
Illinois State U, IL	B
Indiana State U, IN	B
Indiana U Bloomington, IN	B
Indiana U–Purdue U Fort Wayne, IN	B
Indiana U South Bend, IN	A
Indiana Wesleyan U, IN	A,B
International Business Coll, Fort Wayne, IN	A,B
Iowa State U of Science and Technology, IA	B
Kansas State U, KS	B
Kent State U, OH	B
Kent State U, Ashtabula Campus, OH	A
Kettering U, MI	B
Lake Superior State U, MI	B
Lewis U, IL	B
Lindenwood U, MO	B
Loras Coll, IA	B
Loyola U Chicago, IL	B
MacMurray Coll, IL	B
Manchester Coll, IN	B
Marian Coll, IN	A,B
Marian Coll of Fond du Lac, WI	B
Marquette U, WI	B
McKendree Coll, IL	B
Metropolitan State U, MN	B
Miami U, OH	B
Miami U Hamilton, OH	B
Michigan State U, MI	B
Michigan Technological U, MI	B
Millikin U, IL	B
Minnesota State U Mankato, MN	B
Minot State U, ND	B
Missouri Southern State U, MO	B
Missouri State U, MO	B
Missouri Western State U, MO	B
National American U, Rapid City, SD	B
Newman U, KS	B
North Central Coll, IL	B
Northeastern Illinois U, IL	B
Northeastern State U, OK	B
Northern Illinois U, IL	B

Northern Michigan U, MI	B
Northern State U, SD	B
Northwestern Coll, MN	B
Northwest Missouri State U, MO	B
Oakland U, MI	B
Ohio Dominican U, OH	B
The Ohio State U, OH	B
Oklahoma City U, OK	B
Oklahoma State U, OK	B
Oral Roberts U, OK	B
Otterbein Coll, OH	B
Pittsburg State U, KS	B
Quincy U, IL	B
Rockford Coll, IL	B
Roosevelt U, IL	B
Saginaw Valley State U, MI	B
St. Ambrose U, IA	B
St. Cloud State U, MN	B
Saint Mary's Coll, IN	B
Southeastern Oklahoma State U, OK	B
Southeast Missouri State U, MO	B
Southern Illinois U Carbondale, IL	B
Southern Methodist U, TX	B
Southwestern Oklahoma State U, OK	B
Taylor U, IN	B
Tiffin U, OH	B
Truman State U, MO	B
The U of Akron, OH	B
U of Central Missouri, MO	B
U of Central Oklahoma, OK	B
U of Charleston, WV	B
U of Cincinnati, OH	A,B
U of Dayton, OH	B
U of Evansville, IN	B
U of Illinois at Chicago, IL	B
U of Illinois at Urbana–Champaign, IL	B
The U of Iowa, IA	B
U of Kansas, KS	B
U of Michigan–Dearborn, MI	B
U of Michigan–Flint, MI	B
U of Minnesota, Duluth, MN	B
U of Minnesota, Twin Cities Campus, MN	B
U of Missouri–Columbia, MO	B
U of Missouri–St. Louis, MO	B
U of Nebraska at Omaha, NE	B
U of Nebraska–Lincoln, NE	B
U of New Orleans, LA	B
U of North Dakota, ND	B
U of Northern Iowa, IA	B
U of Notre Dame, IN	B
U of Oklahoma, OK	B
U of Phoenix–Cincinnati Campus, OH	B
U of Phoenix–Cleveland Campus, OH	A,B
U of Phoenix–Columbus Ohio Campus, OH	B
U of Phoenix–Indianapolis Campus, IN	B
U of Phoenix–Kansas City Campus, MO	B
U of Phoenix–Metro Detroit Campus, MI	B
U of Phoenix–Oklahoma City Campus, OK	B
U of Phoenix–St. Louis Campus, MO	B
U of Phoenix–Springfield Campus, MO	B

U of Phoenix–Tulsa Campus, OK	B
U of Phoenix–Wisconsin Campus, WI	B
U of St. Francis, IL	B
U of St. Thomas, MN	B
The U of South Dakota, SD	B
U of Southern Indiana, IN	B
The U of Toledo, OH	B
U of Tulsa, OK	B
U of West Florida, FL	B
U of Wisconsin–Eau Claire, WI	B
U of Wisconsin–La Crosse, WI	B
U of Wisconsin–Madison, WI	B
U of Wisconsin–Milwaukee, WI	B
U of Wisconsin–Oshkosh, WI	B
U of Wisconsin–Parkside, WI	B
U of Wisconsin–River Falls, WI	B
U of Wisconsin–Superior, WI	B
U of Wisconsin–Whitewater, WI	B
Valparaiso U, IN	B
Waldorf Coll, IA	B
Walsh U, OH	A,B
Wartburg Coll, IA	B
Washburn U, KS	B
Washington U in St. Louis, MO	B
Wayne State Coll, NE	B
Western Illinois U, IL	B
Western Michigan U, MI	B
Wichita State U, KS	B
Winona State U, MN	B
Wright State U, OH	B
Xavier U, OH	B
Youngstown State U, OH	A,B

Finance and Financial Management Services Related

Grace Bible Coll, MI	B
Park U, MO	B
The U of Akron, OH	B

Financial Planning and Services

Bethany Coll, KS	B
Central Michigan U, MI	B
Cleary U, MI	B
Jamestown Coll, ND	B
Northern Michigan U, MI	B
The Ohio State U at Lima, OH	B
Southern Methodist U, TX	B
Trinity Christian Coll, IL	B
Western Michigan U, MI	B

Fine Arts Related

Bowling Green State U, OH	B
Indiana State U, IN	B
Loyola U Chicago, IL	B
Madonna U, MI	B
Mount Vernon Nazarene U, OH	B
School of the Art Inst of Chicago, IL	B
The U of Akron, OH	B
U of Saint Francis, IN	B

Fine/Studio Arts

Alma Coll, MI	B
Anderson U, IN	B
Aquinas Coll, MI	B
Art Academy of Cincinnati, OH	B
Ashland U, OH	B

Augsburg Coll, MN	B	Marygrove Coll, MI	B	U of Tulsa, OK	B
Augustana Coll, IL	B	Maryville U of Saint Louis,		U of West Florida, FL	B
Baker U, KS	B	MO	B	U of Wisconsin–Milwaukee,	
Baldwin-Wallace Coll, OH	B	Miami U, OH	B	WI	B
Ball State U, IN	B	Millikin U, IL	B	U of Wisconsin–Oshkosh, WI	B
Beloit Coll, WI	B	Minneapolis Coll of Art and		U of Wisconsin–Stevens Point,	
Bemidji State U, MN	B	Design, MN	B	WI	B
Benedictine U, IL	B	Minnesota State U Mankato,		U of Wisconsin–Superior, WI	B
Bethel Coll, KS	B	MN	B	Ursuline Coll, OH	B
Bowling Green State U, OH	B	Missouri State U, MO	B	Valparaiso U, IN	B
Bradley U, IL	B	Morningside Coll, IA	B	Viterbo U, WI	B
Calvin Coll, MI	B	Northeastern State U, OK	B	Washington U in St. Louis,	
Capital U, OH	B	Northern Illinois U, IL	B	MO	B
Cardinal Stritch U, WI	B	Northland Coll, WI	B	Webster U, MO	B
Carleton Coll, MN	B	Northwestern Coll, MN	B	Western Illinois U, IL	B
Carroll Coll, WI	B	Northwest Missouri State U,		William Woods U, MO	B
Cedarville U, OH	B	MO	B	Winona State U, MN	B
Chicago State U, IL	B	Notre Dame Coll, OH	B	Xavier U, OH	B
Clarke Coll, IA	B	Oberlin Coll, OH	B	Youngstown State U, OH	B
Coe Coll, IA	B	Ohio Dominican U, OH	B		
Coll of Mount St. Joseph, OH	B	Ohio Northern U, OH	B	**Fire Protection and Safety**	
Coll of Saint Benedict, MN	B	The Ohio State U, OH	B	**Technology**	
Coll of St. Catherine, MN	B	Ohio U, OH	B	Oklahoma State U, OK	B
Coll of the Ozarks, MO	B	Ohio Wesleyan U, OH	B	The U of Akron, OH	A
Coll of Visual Arts, MN	B	Oklahoma City U, OK	B	U of Cincinnati, OH	A,B
The Coll of Wooster, OH	B	Oral Roberts U, OK	B	U of Nebraska–Lincoln, NE	A
Columbia Coll Chicago, IL	B	Park U, MO	B	The U of Toledo, OH	A
Columbus Coll of Art &		Saginaw Valley State U, MI	B		
Design, OH	B	St. Ambrose U, IA	B	**Fire Protection Related**	
Concordia Coll, MN	B	St. Cloud State U, MN	B	The U of Akron, OH	B
Concordia U, NE	B	St. Gregory's U, Shawnee, OK	A,B		
Concordia U, St. Paul, MN	B	Saint John's U, MN	B	**Fire Science**	
Denison U, OH	B	Saint Joseph's Coll, IN	B	Lake Superior State U, MI	A,B
DePaul U, IL	B	Saint Louis U, MO	B	Madonna U, MI	A,B
DePauw U, IN	B	Saint Mary-of-the-Woods Coll,		U of Cincinnati, OH	A
Drake U, IA	B	IN	B		
Drury U, MO	B	Saint Mary's U of Minnesota,		**Fire Services Administration**	
Ferris State U, MI	B	MN	B	Concordia U, MI	B
Finlandia U, MI	B	School of the Art Inst of		Southern Illinois U	
Fontbonne U, MO	B	Chicago, IL	B	Carbondale, IL	B
Graceland U, IA	B	Shawnee State U, OH	B		
Grand Valley State U, MI	B	Southern Illinois U		**Fish/Game Management**	
Grand View Coll, IA	B	Carbondale, IL	B	Iowa State U of Science and	
Hamline U, MN	B	Southern Illinois U		Technology, IA	B
Hiram Coll, OH	B	Edwardsville, IL	B	Lake Superior State U, MI	B
Hope Coll, MI	B	Southern Methodist U, TX	B	Northland Coll, WI	B
Illinois State U, IL	B	Southwest Minnesota State U,		Pittsburg State U, KS	B
Indiana U Bloomington, IN	B	MN	B	South Dakota State U, SD	B
Indiana U–Purdue U Fort		Transylvania U, KY	B	Southeastern Oklahoma State	
Wayne, IN	B	Truman State U, MO	B	U, OK	B
Indiana U–Purdue U		Union Coll, NE	B	Turtle Mountain Comm Coll,	
Indianapolis, IN	B	The U of Akron, OH	B	ND	A
Indiana U South Bend, IN	B	U of Central Missouri, MO	B	U of Minnesota, Duluth, MN	B
Indiana U Southeast, IN	B	U of Chicago, IL	B	U of Minnesota, Twin Cities	
Iowa Wesleyan Coll, IA	B	U of Dallas, TX	B	Campus, MN	B
Jamestown Coll, ND	B	U of Dayton, OH	B	U of Missouri–Columbia, MO	B
Judson Coll, IL	B	U of Illinois at Chicago, IL	B		
Kent State U, OH	B	U of Indianapolis, IN	B	**Fishing and Fisheries**	
Kenyon Coll, OH	B	The U of Iowa, IA	B	**Sciences and Management**	
Lake Forest Coll, IL	B	U of Kansas, KS	B	The Ohio State U, OH	B
Lawrence U, WI	B	U of Michigan–Flint, MI	B	U of Missouri–Columbia, MO	B
Lewis U, IL	B	U of Minnesota, Duluth, MN	B		
Lincoln U, MO	B	U of Minnesota, Morris, MN	B	**Folklore**	
Lindenwood U, MO	B	U of Missouri–Kansas City,		Indiana U Bloomington, IN	B
Loras Coll, IA	B	MO	B	The Ohio State U, OH	B
Macalester Coll, MN	B	U of Missouri–St. Louis, MO	B		
MacMurray Coll, IL	B	U of Nebraska at Omaha, NE	B	**Food/Nutrition**	
Maharishi U of Management,		U of Nebraska–Lincoln, NE	B	Southern Illinois U	
IA	B	U of New Orleans, LA	B	Carbondale, IL	B
Malone Coll, OH	B	U of Northern Iowa, IA	B		
Manchester Coll, IN	A,B	U of Notre Dame, IN	B	**Food Preparation**	
Marian Coll, IN	B	U of Oklahoma, OK	B	Lexington Coll, IL	A,B
Marian Coll of Fond du Lac,		U of Science and Arts of			
WI	B	Oklahoma, OK	B	**Foods and Nutrition Related**	
Marietta Coll, OH	B	The U of Toledo, OH	B	Kent State U, OH	B
				U of Wisconsin–Stout, WI	B
				Food Science	
				Dominican U, IL	B
				Kansas State U, KS	B

Michigan State U, MI	B
North Carolina Ag and Tech	
State U, NC	B
North Dakota State U, ND	B
Northwest Missouri State U,	
MO	B
The Ohio State U, OH	B
Purdue U, IN	B
South Dakota State U, SD	B
The U of Akron, OH	B
U of Illinois at Urbana–	
Champaign, IL	B
U of Missouri–Columbia, MO	B
U of Nebraska–Lincoln, NE	B
U of Wisconsin–Madison, WI	B
U of Wisconsin–River Falls,	
WI	B

Food Sciences

U of Illinois at Urbana–	
Champaign, IL	B

Food Service and Dining Room Management

Lexington Coll, IL	A,B

Food Services Technology

Iowa State U of Science and	
Technology, IA	B
Madonna U, MI	B
Purdue U Calumet, IN	A
Washburn U, KS	B

Foodservice Systems Administration

Central Michigan U, MI	B
Dominican U, IL	B
U of Wisconsin–Stout, WI	B
Western Michigan U, MI	B

Foods, Nutrition, and Wellness

Andrews U, MI	B
Ashland U, OH	B
Bluffton U, OH	B
Bowling Green State U, OH	B
Coll of Saint Benedict, MN	B
Coll of St. Catherine, MN	B
Coll of the Ozarks, MO	B
Concordia Coll, MN	B
Dominican U, IL	B
Indiana State U, IN	B
Indiana U Bloomington, IN	B
Iowa State U of Science and	
Technology, IA	B
Kansas State U, KS	B
Kent State U, OH	B
Langston U, OK	B
Leech Lake Tribal Coll, MN	A
Loyola U Chicago, IL	B
Madonna U, MI	A,B
Minnesota State U Mankato,	
MN	B
Mount Marty Coll, SD	B
North Carolina Ag and Tech	
State U, NC	B
Northeastern State U, OK	B
Northern Illinois U, IL	B
Northwest Missouri State U,	
MO	B
The Ohio State U, OH	B
Ohio U, OH	B
Purdue U, IN	B
Saint John's U, MN	B
Saint Louis U, MO	B
South Dakota State U, SD	B
Southern Illinois U	
Carbondale, IL	B

A—associate degree; B—bachelor's degree

The U of Akron, OH — B
U of Central Oklahoma, OK — B
U of Cincinnati, OH — B
U of Dayton, OH — B
U of Minnesota, Twin Cities Campus, MN — B
U of Missouri–Columbia, MO — B
U of Nebraska–Lincoln, NE — B
U of Northern Iowa, IA — B
U of Wisconsin–Madison, WI — B
Youngstown State U, OH — B

Foreign Languages and Literatures
Augustana Coll, SD — B
Central Methodist U, MO — B
Eastern Illinois U, IL — B
Emporia State U, KS — B
Gannon U, PA — B
Graceland U, IA — B
Hastings Coll, NE — B
Indiana State U, IN — B
Kansas State U, KS — B
Kenyon Coll, OH — B
Knox Coll, IL — B
Marian Coll of Fond du Lac, WI — B
Millikin U, IL — B
Purdue U, IN — B
Roosevelt U, IL — B
Saint Louis U, MO — B
Southern Illinois U Edwardsville, IL — B
Southern Methodist U, TX — B
U of North Dakota, ND — B
U of Northern Iowa, IA — B
Wright State U, OH — B
Youngstown State U, OH — B

Foreign Languages Related
Marquette U, WI — B
Southern Illinois U Carbondale, IL — B
U of Michigan–Flint, MI — B
U of Northern Iowa, IA — B
U of St. Thomas, MN — B

Foreign Language Teacher Education
Bowling Green State U, OH — B
Carroll Coll, WI — B
Central Methodist U, MO — B
Dana Coll, NE — B
Eastern Michigan U, MI — B
Gannon U, PA — B
Hastings Coll, NE — B
Kent State U, OH — B
Marquette U, WI — B
Ohio Dominican U, OH — B
Ohio Northern U, OH — B
Ohio Wesleyan U, OH — B
Oral Roberts U, OK — B
Southeast Missouri State U, MO — B
The U of Akron, OH — B
U of Illinois at Chicago, IL — B
U of Illinois at Urbana–Champaign, IL — B
U of Minnesota, Twin Cities Campus, MN — B
U of Nebraska–Lincoln, NE — B
U of New Orleans, LA — B
U of Northern Iowa, IA — B
U of Oklahoma, OK — B
U of St. Thomas, MN — B
The U of South Dakota, SD — B
U of West Florida, FL — B

Valparaiso U, IN — B
Wayne State Coll, NE — B
Western Michigan U, MI — B
Wright State U, OH — B
Youngstown State U, OH — B

Forensic Psychology
St. Ambrose U, IA — B
Tiffin U, OH — B

Forensic Science and Technology
Carroll Coll, WI — B
Coll of the Ozarks, MO — B
Columbia Coll, MO — B
Indiana U Bloomington, IN — B
Northern Michigan U, MI — B
Tiffin U, OH — B
Tri-State U, IN — B
U of Central Oklahoma, OK — B
U of North Dakota, ND — B
Washburn U, KS — B
Youngstown State U, OH — B

Forest/Forest Resources Management
U of Minnesota, Twin Cities Campus, MN — B

Forest Products Technology
Pittsburg State U, KS — A

Forestry
Coll of Saint Benedict, MN — B
Iowa State U of Science and Technology, IA — B
Michigan State U, MI — B
Michigan Technological U, MI — B
Northland Coll, WI — B
Northwest Missouri State U, MO — B
The Ohio State U, OH — B
Oklahoma State U, OK — B
Purdue U, IN — B
Saint John's U, MN — B
Southern Illinois U Carbondale, IL — B
U of Illinois at Urbana–Champaign, IL — B
U of Minnesota, Twin Cities Campus, MN — B
U of Missouri–Columbia, MO — B
U of Wisconsin–Madison, WI — B
U of Wisconsin–Milwaukee, WI — B
U of Wisconsin–Stevens Point, WI — B

Forestry Technology
Michigan Technological U, MI — A

Forest Sciences and Biology
U of Illinois at Urbana–Champaign, IL — B

French
Adrian Coll, MI — A,B
Albion Coll, MI — B
Alma Coll, MI — B
Anderson U, IN — B
Andrews U, MI — B
Antioch Coll, OH — B
Aquinas Coll, MI — B
Ashland U, OH — B
Augsburg Coll, MN — B
Augustana Coll, IL — B
Augustana Coll, SD — B
Baker U, KS — B
Baldwin-Wallace Coll, OH — B
Ball State U, IN — B

Beloit Coll, WI — B
Benedictine Coll, KS — B
Bethel U, MN — B
Bowling Green State U, OH — B
Bradley U, IL — B
Butler U, IN — B
Calvin Coll, MI — B
Capital U, OH — B
Cardinal Stritch U, WI — B
Carleton Coll, MN — B
Case Western Reserve U, OH — B
Central Coll, IA — B
Central Methodist U, MO — B
Central Michigan U, MI — B
Clarke Coll, IA — B
Cleveland State U, OH — B
Coe Coll, IA — B
Coll of Saint Benedict, MN — B
Coll of St. Catherine, MN — B
Coll of the Ozarks, MO — B
The Coll of Wooster, OH — B
Concordia Coll, MN — B
Cornell Coll, IA — B
Creighton U, NE — B
Denison U, OH — B
DePaul U, IL — B
DePauw U, IN — B
Doane Coll, NE — B
Dominican U, IL — B
Drury U, MO — B
Earlham Coll, IN — B
Eastern Michigan U, MI — B
Edgewood Coll, WI — B
Elmhurst Coll, IL — B
Fort Hays State U, KS — B
Franciscan U of Steubenville, OH — B
Franklin Coll, IN — B
Grace Coll, IN — B
Grand Valley State U, MI — B
Grinnell Coll, IA — B
Gustavus Adolphus Coll, MN — B
Hamline U, MN — B
Hanover Coll, IN — B
Hillsdale Coll, MI — B
Hiram Coll, OH — B
Hope Coll, MI — B
Illinois Coll, IL — B
Illinois State U, IL — B
Illinois Wesleyan U, IL — B
Indiana State U, IN — B
Indiana U Bloomington, IN — B
Indiana U Northwest, IN — B
Indiana U–Purdue U Fort Wayne, IN — A,B
Indiana U–Purdue U Indianapolis, IN — B
Indiana U South Bend, IN — B
Indiana U Southeast, IN — B
Iowa State U of Science and Technology, IA — B
Kalamazoo Coll, MI — B
Kent State U, OH — B
Kenyon Coll, OH — B
Knox Coll, IL — B
Lake Forest Coll, IL — B
Lawrence U, WI — B
Lindenwood U, MO — B
Loras Coll, IA — B
Loyola U Chicago, IL — B
Luther Coll, IA — B
Macalester Coll, MN — B
Madonna U, MI — B
Manchester Coll, IN — B
Marian Coll, IN — B
Marquette U, WI — B

Miami U, OH — B
Miami U Hamilton, OH — B
Michigan State U, MI — B
Millikin U, IL — B
Minnesota State U Mankato, MN — B
Minot State U, ND — B
Missouri Southern State U, MO — B
Missouri State U, MO — B
Missouri Western State U, MO — B
Mount Mary Coll, WI — B
Mount Union Coll, OH — B
Nebraska Wesleyan U, NE — B
North Carolina Ag and Tech State U, NC — B
North Central Coll, IL — B
North Dakota State U, ND — B
Northeastern Illinois U, IL — B
Northern Illinois U, IL — B
Northern Michigan U, MI — B
Northern State U, SD — B
Northwestern U, IL — B
Northwest Missouri State U, MO — B
Oakland U, MI — B
Oberlin Coll, OH — B
Ohio Northern U, OH — B
The Ohio State U, OH — B
Ohio U, OH — B
Ohio Wesleyan U, OH — B
Oklahoma City U, OK — B
Oklahoma State U, OK — B
Oral Roberts U, OK — B
Otterbein Coll, OH — B
Pittsburg State U, KS — B
Purdue U Calumet, IN — B
Ripon Coll, WI — B
Rockford Coll, IL — B
Rockhurst U, MO — B
Saginaw Valley State U, MI — B
St. Ambrose U, IA — B
St. Cloud State U, MN — B
Saint John's U, MN — B
Saint Louis U, MO — B
Saint Mary-of-the-Woods Coll, IN — B
Saint Mary's Coll, IN — B
Saint Mary's U of Minnesota, MN — B
St. Norbert Coll, WI — B
St. Olaf Coll, MN — B
Simpson Coll, IA — B
South Dakota State U, SD — B
Southeast Missouri State U, MO — B
Southern Illinois U Carbondale, IL — B
Southern Methodist U, TX — B
Taylor U, IN — B
Transylvania U, KY — B
Truman State U, MO — B
Union Coll, NE — B
The U of Akron, OH — B
U of Central Missouri, MO — B
U of Central Oklahoma, OK — B
U of Chicago, IL — B
U of Cincinnati, OH — B
U of Dallas, TX — B
U of Dayton, OH — B
U of Evansville, IN — B
U of Illinois at Chicago, IL — B
U of Illinois at Urbana–Champaign, IL — B
U of Indianapolis, IN — B
The U of Iowa, IA — B

U of Kansas, KS	B
U of Michigan, MI	B
U of Michigan–Dearborn, MI	B
U of Michigan–Flint, MI	B
U of Minnesota, Morris, MN	B
U of Minnesota, Twin Cities Campus, MN	B
U of Missouri–Columbia, MO	B
U of Missouri–Kansas City, MO	B
U of Missouri–St. Louis, MO	B
U of Nebraska at Kearney, NE	B
U of Nebraska at Omaha, NE	B
U of Nebraska–Lincoln, NE	B
U of New Orleans, LA	B
U of North Dakota, ND	B
U of Northern Iowa, IA	B
U of Notre Dame, IN	B
U of Oklahoma, OK	B
U of St. Thomas, MN	B
The U of South Dakota, SD	B
U of Southern Indiana, IN	B
The U of Toledo, OH	B
U of Tulsa, OK	B
U of Wisconsin–Eau Claire, WI	B
U of Wisconsin–Green Bay, WI	A,B
U of Wisconsin–La Crosse, WI	B
U of Wisconsin–Madison, WI	B
U of Wisconsin–Milwaukee, WI	B
U of Wisconsin–Oshkosh, WI	B
U of Wisconsin–Parkside, WI	B
U of Wisconsin–River Falls, WI	B
U of Wisconsin–Stevens Point, WI	B
U of Wisconsin–Whitewater, WI	B
Valparaiso U, IN	B
Wabash Coll, IN	B
Walsh U, OH	B
Wartburg Coll, IA	B
Washburn U, KS	B
Washington U in St. Louis, MO	B
Wayne State Coll, NE	B
Webster U, MO	B
Western Illinois U, IL	B
Western Michigan U, MI	B
Westminster Coll, MO	B
Wheaton Coll, IL	B
Wichita State U, KS	B
William Jewell Coll, MO	B
Winona State U, MN	B
Wittenberg U, OH	B
Wright State U, OH	B
Xavier U, OH	A,B
Youngstown State U, OH	B

French as a Second/Foreign Language (Teaching)

Western Michigan U, MI	B

French Language Teacher Education

Alma Coll, MI	B
Anderson U, IN	B
Bethel U, MN	B
Carroll Coll, WI	B
Central Michigan U, MI	B
Coll of St. Catherine, MN	B
Coll of the Ozarks, MO	B
Concordia Coll, MN	B
Eastern Michigan U, MI	B

Elmhurst Coll, IL	B
Franklin Coll, IN	B
Grace Coll, IN	B
Hope Coll, MI	B
Illinois Wesleyan U, IL	B
Indiana U Bloomington, IN	B
Indiana U Northwest, IN	B
Indiana U–Purdue U Fort Wayne, IN	B
Indiana U–Purdue U Indianapolis, IN	B
Indiana U South Bend, IN	B
Kent State U, OH	B
Lindenwood U, MO	B
Miami U Hamilton, OH	B
Minot State U, ND	B
Missouri State U, MO	B
Missouri Western State U, MO	B
Mount Mary Coll, WI	B
North Dakota State U, ND	B
Northern Michigan U, MI	B
Ohio Northern U, OH	B
Ohio U, OH	B
Ohio Wesleyan U, OH	B
Oral Roberts U, OK	B
Pittsburg State U, KS	B
St. Ambrose U, IA	B
Saint Mary's U of Minnesota, MN	B
The U of Akron, OH	B
U of Evansville, IN	B
U of Illinois at Chicago, IL	B
U of Illinois at Urbana–Champaign, IL	B
U of Indianapolis, IN	B
The U of Iowa, IA	B
U of Michigan–Flint, MI	B
U of Minnesota, Duluth, MN	B
U of Missouri–St. Louis, MO	B
U of Nebraska–Lincoln, NE	B
The U of South Dakota, SD	B
The U of Toledo, OH	B
U of Wisconsin–River Falls, WI	B
Valparaiso U, IN	B
Washington U in St. Louis, MO	B
Western Michigan U, MI	B
William Woods U, MO	B
Youngstown State U, OH	B

French Studies

Carleton Coll, MN	B
Case Western Reserve U, OH	B
Coe Coll, IA	B
Lake Superior State U, MI	B

Funeral Service and Mortuary Science

Gannon U, PA	B
Lindenwood U, MO	B
Mid-America Coll of Funeral Service, IN	A
Southern Illinois U Carbondale, IL	B
U of Central Oklahoma, OK	B
U of Minnesota, Twin Cities Campus, MN	B

Furniture Design and Manufacturing

Ferris State U, MI	B

General Studies

Alverno Coll, WI	B
Anderson U, IN	A
Aquinas Coll, MI	B

Ashford U, IA	B
Avila U, MO	A,B
Barclay Coll, KS	A
Black Hills State U, SD	A
Calumet Coll of Saint Joseph, IN	A,B
Central Coll, IA	B
Chicago State U, IL	B
Cleveland State U, OH	B
Coll of Saint Mary, NE	A,B
Concordia U, MI	A
Concordia U, St. Paul, MN	A,B
Concordia U Wisconsin, WI	B
Crown Coll, MN	A,B
Dakota State U, SD	A
DePaul U, IL	B
Dordt Coll, IA	B
East Central U, OK	B
Emporia State U, KS	B
Finlandia U, MI	A
Franciscan U of Steubenville, OH	A
God's Bible School and Coll, OH	B
Grantham U, MO	A,B
Hillsdale Free Will Baptist Coll, OK	A
Hope Coll, MI	B
Indiana U Bloomington, IN	A,B
Indiana U East, IN	A,B
Indiana U Kokomo, IN	A,B
Indiana U Northwest, IN	A,B
Indiana U–Purdue U Fort Wayne, IN	A,B
Indiana U–Purdue U Indianapolis, IN	A,B
Indiana U South Bend, IN	A,B
Indiana U Southeast, IN	A,B
Indiana Wesleyan U, IN	A,B
Kent State U, OH	B
Kent State U, Trumbull Campus, OH	B
Kettering Coll of Medical Arts, OH	A
Lawrence Technological U, MI	A
Loyola U Chicago, IL	B
Madonna U, MI	B
Marygrove Coll, MI	B
Mayville State U, ND	B
Mercy Coll of Northwest Ohio, OH	A
Messenger Coll, MO	A
Metropolitan State U, MN	B
Miami U Hamilton, OH	A
Michigan Technological U, MI	B
Minot State U, ND	B
Mount Marty Coll, SD	A,B
Mount Vernon Nazarene U, OH	A
Northern Michigan U, MI	A
Northwestern U, IL	A
Oak Hills Christian Coll, MN	A
Ohio Dominican U, OH	A,B
Ohio Northern U, OH	B
Ohio U, OH	B
Ohio Wesleyan U, OH	B
Oklahoma Panhandle State U, OK	A
Pittsburg State U, KS	B
Presentation Coll, SD	A
Saginaw Valley State U, MI	B
St. Augustine Coll, IL	A
Shawnee State U, OH	A,B
Shimer Coll, IL	A
Silver Lake Coll, WI	A

South Dakota School of Mines and Technology, SD	A
Southeastern Oklahoma State U, OK	B
Southeast Missouri State U, MO	B
Southwest Baptist U, MO	A
Southwestern Coll, KS	B
Taylor U Fort Wayne, IN	A
U of Charleston, WV	B
U of Dayton, OH	B
U of Illinois at Urbana–Champaign, IL	B
U of Mary, ND	B
U of Michigan, MI	B
U of Michigan–Dearborn, MI	B
U of Missouri–Columbia, MO	B
U of Missouri–St. Louis, MO	B
U of Nebraska at Kearney, NE	B
U of Nebraska at Omaha, NE	B
U of New Orleans, LA	B
U of North Dakota, ND	B
U of Phoenix–Cincinnati Campus, OH	B
U of Phoenix–Cleveland Campus, OH	A
U of Phoenix–Columbus Ohio Campus, OH	A
U of Phoenix–Indianapolis Campus, IN	A
U of Phoenix–St. Louis Campus, MO	A
U of Phoenix–Springfield Campus, MO	A
U of Rio Grande, OH	A
The U of South Dakota, SD	A
The U of Toledo, OH	A,B
U of Wisconsin–Green Bay, WI	B
U of Wisconsin–La Crosse, WI	B
U of Wisconsin–Stevens Point, WI	B
U of Wisconsin–Superior, WI	A
Vennard Coll, IA	A
Western Michigan U, MI	B
York Coll, NE	B
Youngstown State U, OH	B

Genetics

Iowa State U of Science and Technology, IA	B
Ohio Wesleyan U, OH	B

Geochemistry

Western Michigan U, MI	B

Geography

Aquinas Coll, MI	B
Augustana Coll, IL	B
Ball State U, IN	B
Bemidji State U, MN	B
Bowling Green State U, OH	B
Calvin Coll, MI	B
Central Michigan U, MI	B
Chicago State U, IL	B
Concordia U, IL	B
Concordia U, NE	B
Concord U, WV	B
DePaul U, IL	B
Dickinson State U, ND	B
Eastern Illinois U, IL	B
Eastern Michigan U, MI	B
Elmhurst Coll, IL	B
Gustavus Adolphus Coll, MN	B
Illinois State U, IL	B
Indiana State U, IN	B

A—associate degree; B—bachelor's degree

Indiana U Bloomington, IN	B
Indiana U–Purdue U Indianapolis, IN	B
Indiana U Southeast, IN	B
Kansas State U, KS	B
Kent State U, OH	B
Macalester Coll, MN	B
Miami U, OH	B
Miami U Hamilton, OH	B
Miami U–Middletown Campus, OH	A
Michigan State U, MI	B
Minnesota State U Mankato, MN	B
Missouri State U, MO	B
Northeastern Illinois U, IL	B
Northeastern State U, OK	B
Northern Illinois U, IL	B
Northern Michigan U, MI	B
Northwestern U, IL	B
Northwest Missouri State U, MO	B
The Ohio State U, OH	B
Ohio U, OH	B
Ohio Wesleyan U, OH	B
Oklahoma State U, OK	B
Park U, MO	B
Pittsburg State U, KS	B
Roosevelt U, IL	B
St. Cloud State U, MN	B
South Dakota State U, SD	B
Southeast Missouri State U, MO	B
Southern Illinois U Carbondale, IL	B
Southern Illinois U Edwardsville, IL	B
The U of Akron, OH	B
U of Central Missouri, MO	B
U of Central Oklahoma, OK	B
U of Chicago, IL	B
U of Cincinnati, OH	B
U of Illinois at Urbana–Champaign, IL	B
The U of Iowa, IA	B
U of Kansas, KS	B
U of Minnesota, Duluth, MN	B
U of Minnesota, Twin Cities Campus, MN	B
U of Missouri–Columbia, MO	B
U of Missouri–Kansas City, MO	B
U of Nebraska at Kearney, NE	B
U of Nebraska at Omaha, NE	B
U of Nebraska–Lincoln, NE	B
U of New Orleans, LA	B
U of North Dakota, ND	B
U of Northern Iowa, IA	B
U of Oklahoma, OK	B
U of St. Thomas, MN	B
The U of Toledo, OH	B
U of Wisconsin–Eau Claire, WI	B
U of Wisconsin–La Crosse, WI	B
U of Wisconsin–Madison, WI	B
U of Wisconsin–Milwaukee, WI	B
U of Wisconsin–Oshkosh, WI	B
U of Wisconsin–Parkside, WI	B
U of Wisconsin–River Falls, WI	B
U of Wisconsin–Stevens Point, WI	B
U of Wisconsin–Whitewater, WI	B
Valparaiso U, IN	B

Wayne State Coll, NE	B
Western Illinois U, IL	B
Western Michigan U, MI	B
Wittenberg U, OH	B
Wright State U, OH	A,B
Youngstown State U, OH	B

Geography Teacher Education

Chicago State U, IL	B
Concordia U, NE	B
Mayville State U, ND	B
Northern Michigan U, MI	B
Shawnee State U, OH	B
U of Evansville, IN	B
The U of Iowa, IA	B
Valparaiso U, IN	B
Wayne State Coll, NE	B
Western Michigan U, MI	B

Geological and Earth Sciences/Geosciences Related

Ohio U, OH	B
Southeast Missouri State U, MO	B
The U of Akron, OH	B
U of Illinois at Urbana–Champaign, IL	B
U of Northern Iowa, IA	B
U of Oklahoma, OK	B
Western Michigan U, MI	B

Geological Engineering

U of North Dakota, ND	B

Geological/Geophysical Engineering

Michigan Technological U, MI	B
South Dakota School of Mines and Technology, SD	B
The U of Akron, OH	B
U of Minnesota, Twin Cities Campus, MN	B
U of Missouri–Rolla, MO	B

Geology/Earth Science

Adrian Coll, MI	A,B
Albion Coll, MI	B
Antioch Coll, OH	B
Ashland U, OH	B
Augustana Coll, IL	B
Ball State U, IN	B
Beloit Coll, WI	B
Bemidji State U, MN	B
Bowling Green State U, OH	B
Bradley U, IL	B
Calvin Coll, MI	B
Carleton Coll, MN	B
Case Western Reserve U, OH	B
Central Michigan U, MI	B
Cleveland State U, OH	B
The Coll of Wooster, OH	B
Cornell Coll, IA	B
Denison U, OH	B
DePauw U, IN	B
Dickinson State U, ND	B
Earlham Coll, IN	B
Eastern Illinois U, IL	B
Eastern Michigan U, MI	B
Emporia State U, KS	B
Fort Hays State U, KS	B
Grand Valley State U, MI	B
Gustavus Adolphus Coll, MN	B
Hanover Coll, IN	B
Hope Coll, MI	B
Illinois State U, IL	B
Indiana State U, IN	B
Indiana U Bloomington, IN	B
Indiana U East, IN	A

Indiana U Northwest, IN	B
Indiana U–Purdue U Fort Wayne, IN	B
Indiana U–Purdue U Indianapolis, IN	B
Iowa State U of Science and Technology, IA	B
Kansas State U, KS	B
Kent State U, OH	B
Lake Superior State U, MI	B
Lawrence U, WI	B
Macalester Coll, MN	B
Marietta Coll, OH	B
Miami U, OH	B
Miami U Hamilton, OH	B
Michigan State U, MI	B
Michigan Technological U, MI	B
Minnesota State U Mankato, MN	B
Minot State U, ND	B
Missouri State U, MO	B
Mount Union Coll, OH	B
North Dakota State U, ND	B
Northeastern Illinois U, IL	B
Northern Illinois U, IL	B
Northern Michigan U, MI	B
Northland Coll, WI	B
Northwestern U, IL	B
Northwest Missouri State U, MO	B
Oberlin Coll, OH	B
The Ohio State U, OH	B
Ohio U, OH	B
Ohio Wesleyan U, OH	B
Oklahoma State U, OK	B
Purdue U, IN	B
St. Cloud State U, MN	B
Saint Louis U, MO	B
St. Norbert Coll, WI	B
South Dakota School of Mines and Technology, SD	B
Southern Illinois U Carbondale, IL	B
Southern Methodist U, TX	B
The U of Akron, OH	B
U of Central Missouri, MO	B
U of Cincinnati, OH	B
U of Dayton, OH	B
U of Illinois at Chicago, IL	B
U of Illinois at Urbana–Champaign, IL	B
U of Indianapolis, IN	B
The U of Iowa, IA	B
U of Kansas, KS	B
U of Michigan, MI	B
U of Michigan–Dearborn, MI	B
U of Minnesota, Duluth, MN	B
U of Minnesota, Morris, MN	B
U of Minnesota, Twin Cities Campus, MN	B
U of Missouri–Columbia, MO	B
U of Missouri–Kansas City, MO	B
U of Missouri–Rolla, MO	B
U of Nebraska at Omaha, NE	B
U of Nebraska–Lincoln, NE	B
U of New Orleans, LA	B
U of North Dakota, ND	B
U of Northern Iowa, IA	B
U of Notre Dame, IN	B
U of Oklahoma, OK	B
U of St. Thomas, MN	B
The U of South Dakota, SD	B
U of Southern Indiana, IN	B
The U of Toledo, OH	B
U of Tulsa, OK	B

U of Wisconsin–Eau Claire, WI	B
U of Wisconsin–Green Bay, WI	A,B
U of Wisconsin–Madison, WI	B
U of Wisconsin–Milwaukee, WI	B
U of Wisconsin–Oshkosh, WI	B
U of Wisconsin–Parkside, WI	B
U of Wisconsin–Platteville, WI	B
U of Wisconsin–River Falls, WI	B
Valparaiso U, IN	B
Washington U in St. Louis, MO	B
Western Illinois U, IL	B
Western Michigan U, MI	B
Wheaton Coll, IL	B
Wichita State U, KS	B
Winona State U, MN	B
Wittenberg U, OH	B
Wright State U, OH	B
Youngstown State U, OH	B

Geophysics and Seismology

Eastern Michigan U, MI	B
Hope Coll, MI	B
Michigan State U, MI	B
Michigan Technological U, MI	B
Saint Louis U, MO	B
Southern Methodist U, TX	B
The U of Akron, OH	B
U of Chicago, IL	B
U of Minnesota, Twin Cities Campus, MN	B
U of Missouri–Rolla, MO	B
U of New Orleans, LA	B
U of Oklahoma, OK	B
U of Tulsa, OK	B
U of Wisconsin–Madison, WI	B
Western Michigan U, MI	B
Wright State U, OH	B

German

Adrian Coll, MI	A,B
Albion Coll, MI	B
Alma Coll, MI	B
Antioch Coll, OH	B
Aquinas Coll, MI	B
Augsburg Coll, MN	B
Augustana Coll, IL	B
Augustana Coll, SD	B
Baker U, KS	B
Baldwin-Wallace Coll, OH	B
Ball State U, IN	B
Beloit Coll, WI	B
Bemidji State U, MN	B
Bowling Green State U, OH	B
Bradley U, IL	B
Butler U, IN	B
Calvin Coll, MI	B
Carleton Coll, MN	B
Case Western Reserve U, OH	B
Central Michigan U, MI	B
Coe Coll, IA	B
Coll of Saint Benedict, MN	B
Coll of the Ozarks, MO	B
The Coll of Wooster, OH	B
Concordia Coll, MN	B
Concordia U Wisconsin, WI	B
Cornell Coll, IA	B
Creighton U, NE	B
Dana Coll, NE	B
Denison U, OH	B
DePaul U, IL	B
DePauw U, IN	B
Doane Coll, NE	B

German

Dordt Coll, IA	B
Drury U, MO	B
Earlham Coll, IN	B
Eastern Michigan U, MI	B
Elmhurst Coll, IL	B
Fort Hays State U, KS	B
Franciscan U of Steubenville, OH	B
Grace Coll, IN	B
Graceland U, IA	B
Grand Valley State U, MI	B
Grinnell Coll, IA	B
Gustavus Adolphus Coll, MN	B
Hamline U, MN	B
Hanover Coll, IN	B
Hastings Coll, NE	B
Heidelberg Coll, OH	B
Hillsdale Coll, MI	B
Hiram Coll, OH	B
Hope Coll, MI	B
Illinois Coll, IL	B
Illinois State U, IL	B
Illinois Wesleyan U, IL	B
Indiana State U, IN	B
Indiana U Bloomington, IN	B
Indiana U–Purdue U Fort Wayne, IN	A,B
Indiana U–Purdue U Indianapolis, IN	B
Indiana U South Bend, IN	B
Indiana U Southeast, IN	B
Iowa State U of Science and Technology, IA	B
Kalamazoo Coll, MI	B
Kent State U, OH	B
Kenyon Coll, OH	B
Knox Coll, IL	B
Lakeland Coll, WI	B
Lawrence U, WI	B
Loyola U Chicago, IL	B
Luther Coll, IA	B
Manchester Coll, IN	B
Marquette U, WI	B
Miami U, OH	B
Miami U Hamilton, OH	B
Michigan State U, MI	B
Millikin U, IL	B
Minnesota State U Mankato, MN	B
Minot State U, ND	B
Missouri Southern State U, MO	B
Missouri State U, MO	B
Mount Union Coll, OH	B
Nebraska Wesleyan U, NE	B
North Central Coll, IL	B
Northern Illinois U, IL	B
Northern State U, SD	B
Northwestern U, IL	B
Oakland U, MI	B
Oberlin Coll, OH	B
The Ohio State U, OH	B
Ohio U, OH	B
Ohio Wesleyan U, OH	B
Oklahoma City U, OK	B
Oklahoma State U, OK	B
Oral Roberts U, OK	B
Purdue U Calumet, IN	B
Ripon Coll, WI	B
St. Ambrose U, IA	B
St. Cloud State U, MN	B
Saint John's U, MN	B
Saint Louis U, MO	B
St. Norbert Coll, WI	B
St. Olaf Coll, MN	B

Simpson Coll, IA	B
South Dakota State U, SD	B
Southeast Missouri State U, MO	B
Southern Illinois U Carbondale, IL	B
Southern Methodist U, TX	B
Truman State U, MO	B
Union Coll, NE	B
The U of Akron, OH	B
U of Central Missouri, MO	B
U of Central Oklahoma, OK	B
U of Chicago, IL	B
U of Cincinnati, OH	B
U of Dallas, TX	B
U of Dayton, OH	B
U of Evansville, IN	B
U of Illinois at Chicago, IL	B
U of Illinois at Urbana–Champaign, IL	B
U of Indianapolis, IN	B
The U of Iowa, IA	B
U of Michigan, MI	B
U of Minnesota, Morris, MN	B
U of Minnesota, Twin Cities Campus, MN	B
U of Missouri–Columbia, MO	B
U of Missouri–Kansas City, MO	B
U of Missouri–St. Louis, MO	B
U of Nebraska at Kearney, NE	B
U of Nebraska at Omaha, NE	B
U of Nebraska–Lincoln, NE	B
U of North Dakota, ND	B
U of Northern Iowa, IA	B
U of Notre Dame, IN	B
U of Oklahoma, OK	B
U of St. Thomas, MN	B
The U of South Dakota, SD	B
U of Southern Indiana, IN	B
The U of Toledo, OH	B
U of Tulsa, OK	B
U of Wisconsin–La Crosse, WI	B
U of Wisconsin–Madison, WI	B
U of Wisconsin–Milwaukee, WI	B
U of Wisconsin–Oshkosh, WI	B
U of Wisconsin–Parkside, WI	B
U of Wisconsin–Platteville, WI	B
U of Wisconsin–River Falls, WI	B
U of Wisconsin–Stevens Point, WI	B
U of Wisconsin–Whitewater, WI	B
Valparaiso U, IN	B
Wabash Coll, IN	B
Wartburg Coll, IA	B
Washburn U, KS	B
Washington U in St. Louis, MO	B
Wayne State Coll, NE	B
Webster U, MO	B
Western Michigan U, MI	B
Wheaton Coll, IL	B
Winona State U, MN	B
Wittenberg U, OH	B
Wright State U, OH	B
Xavier U, OH	A,B

Germanic Languages

Bethel Coll, KS	B
Cleveland State U, OH	B
Eastern Michigan U, MI	B
U of Kansas, KS	B

U of Wisconsin–Eau Claire, WI	B
U of Wisconsin–Green Bay, WI	A,B
Washington U in St. Louis, MO	B

Germanic Languages Related

Calvin Coll, MI	B
Ohio Northern U, OH	B

German Language Teacher Education

Alma Coll, MI	B
Carroll Coll, WI	B
Central Michigan U, MI	B
Concordia Coll, MN	B
Concordia U Wisconsin, WI	B
Eastern Michigan U, MI	B
Elmhurst Coll, IL	B
Grace Coll, IN	B
Hastings Coll, NE	B
Hope Coll, MI	B
Indiana U Bloomington, IN	B
Indiana U–Purdue U Fort Wayne, IN	B
Indiana U–Purdue U Indianapolis, IN	B
Indiana U South Bend, IN	B
Miami U Hamilton, OH	B
Minot State U, ND	B
Missouri State U, MO	B
Ohio Northern U, OH	B
Ohio U, OH	B
Ohio Wesleyan U, OH	B
Oral Roberts U, OK	B
St. Ambrose U, IA	B
The U of Akron, OH	B
U of Evansville, IN	B
U of Illinois at Chicago, IL	B
U of Illinois at Urbana–Champaign, IL	B
The U of Iowa, IA	B
U of Minnesota, Duluth, MN	B
U of Missouri–St. Louis, MO	B
U of Nebraska–Lincoln, NE	B
The U of South Dakota, SD	B
The U of Toledo, OH	B
U of Wisconsin–River Falls, WI	B
Valparaiso U, IN	B
Washington U in St. Louis, MO	B
Western Michigan U, MI	B

German Studies

Case Western Reserve U, OH	B
Central Coll, IA	B
Coe Coll, IA	B
The Coll of Wooster, OH	B
Southern Methodist U, TX	B

Gerontological Services

Coll of Mount St. Joseph, OH	B

Gerontology

Alma Coll, MI	B
Bowling Green State U, OH	B
Case Western Reserve U, OH	B
Cleveland State U, OH	B
Coll of the Ozarks, MO	B
Dominican U, IL	B
Langston U, OK	B
Lindenwood U, MO	B
Madonna U, MI	A,B
Manchester Coll, IN	A
Miami U Hamilton, OH	B

Missouri State U, MO	B
Ohio Dominican U, OH	A
Roosevelt U, IL	B
St. Cloud State U, MN	B
Saint Mary-of-the-Woods Coll, IN	B
The U of Akron, OH	B
U of Nebraska at Omaha, NE	B
U of Northern Iowa, IA	B
The U of Toledo, OH	A
Washburn U, KS	A,B
Wichita State U, KS	B

Graphic and Printing Equipment Operation/Production

Ball State U, IN	A
Pittsburg State U, KS	B
Western Illinois U, IL	B

Graphic Communications

Carroll Coll, WI	B
Drury U, MO	B
Grand View Coll, IA	B
Indiana Tech, IN	A
Notre Dame Coll, OH	B
Pittsburg State U, KS	B
Robert Morris Coll, IL	A
School of the Art Inst of Chicago, IL	B
U of Northern Iowa, IA	B
U of Phoenix–Cleveland Campus, OH	A,B
U of Phoenix–Columbus Ohio Campus, OH	A
U of Phoenix–Indianapolis Campus, IN	A
U of Phoenix–St. Louis Campus, MO	A
U of Phoenix–Springfield Campus, MO	A

Graphic Communications Related

The Art Insts International Minnesota, MN	A,B

Graphic Design

Academy Coll, MN	A
Alma Coll, MI	B
Art Academy of Cincinnati, OH	A,B
The Art Insts International Minnesota, MN	A,B
Briar Cliff U, IA	B
Cedarville U, OH	B
The Cleveland Inst of Art, OH	B
Coll of Mount St. Joseph, OH	A,B
Coll of Visual Arts, MN	B
Columbia Coll, MO	B
Columbus Coll of Art & Design, OH	B
Concordia U Wisconsin, WI	B
Creighton U, NE	B
Dordt Coll, IA	B
Drake U, IA	B
Drury U, MO	B
Grand View Coll, IA	B
Huntington U, IN	B
Indiana U–Purdue U Fort Wayne, IN	B
Iowa State U of Science and Technology, IA	B
Iowa Wesleyan Coll, IA	B
Kansas City Art Inst, MO	B
Marietta Coll, OH	B

A—associate degree; B—bachelor's degree

Maryville U of Saint Louis, MO	B
Miami U, OH	B
Miami U Hamilton, OH	B
Missouri Western State U, MO	B
Mount Mary Coll, WI	B
Mount Vernon Nazarene U, OH	B
North Central Coll, IL	B
Northwestern Coll, MN	B
Ohio Dominican U, OH	B
Ohio Northern U, OH	B
Park U, MO	B
Quincy U, IL	B
St. Ambrose U, IA	B
Saint Mary's U of Minnesota, MN	B
School of the Art Inst of Chicago, IL	B
Shawnee State U, OH	B
Union Coll, NE	A,B
U of Evansville, IN	B
U of Illinois at Chicago, IL	B
U of Illinois at Urbana–Champaign, IL	B
U of Kansas, KS	B
U of Michigan–Flint, MI	B
U of Missouri–St. Louis, MO	B
U of North Dakota, ND	B
U of Rio Grande, OH	B
Ursuline Coll, OH	B
Viterbo U, WI	B
Washington U in St. Louis, MO	B
Wayne State Coll, NE	B
Youngstown State U, OH	B

Graphic/Printing Equipment

Coll of the Ozarks, MO	B

Hazardous Materials Information Systems Technology

Ohio U, OH	A

Hazardous Materials Management and Waste Technology

Ohio U, OH	A

Health and Medical Administrative Services Related

Kent State U, OH	A,B
The U of Akron, OH	A
U of Michigan–Flint, MI	B
Ursuline Coll, OH	B

Health and Physical Education

Anderson U, IN	B
Baker U, KS	B
Bethel Coll, KS	B
Bethel U, MN	B
Black Hills State U, SD	B
Bluffton U, OH	B
Cameron U, OK	B
Capital U, OH	B
Carroll Coll, WI	B
Cedarville U, OH	B
Central Christian Coll of Kansas, KS	A
Coll of St. Catherine, MN	B
Coll of the Ozarks, MO	B
Concordia Coll, MN	B
Concordia U, MI	B
Concordia U, NE	B
Concordia U Wisconsin, WI	B
Dana Coll, NE	B
Doane Coll, NE	B
Dordt Coll, IA	B
Eastern Michigan U, MI	B
Elmhurst Coll, IL	B
Evangel U, MO	B
Hamline U, MN	B
Hastings Coll, NE	B
Iowa State U of Science and Technology, IA	B
Lindenwood U, MO	B
Loras Coll, IA	B
Luther Coll, IA	B
Malone Coll, OH	B
Mayville State U, ND	B
Miami U, OH	B
Missouri Western State U, MO	B
Mount Vernon Nazarene U, OH	A
Nebraska Wesleyan U, NE	B
Northwestern Coll, MN	B
Ohio Northern U, OH	B
Ohio U, OH	B
Pittsburg State U, KS	B
Robert Morris Coll, IL	A
St. Ambrose U, IA	B
South Dakota State U, SD	B
Southeast Missouri State U, MO	B
Southern Illinois U Edwardsville, IL	B
Southwestern Coll, KS	B
Southwest Minnesota State U, MN	B
Sterling Coll, KS	B
U of Evansville, IN	B
U of Kansas, KS	B
U of Mary, ND	B
U of Nebraska at Omaha, NE	B
U of Northern Iowa, IA	B
U of Oklahoma, OK	B
U of Rio Grande, OH	B
U of St. Thomas, MN	B
U of Science and Arts of Oklahoma, OK	B
U of West Florida, FL	B
U of Wisconsin–Stevens Point, WI	B
U of Wisconsin–Superior, WI	B
Valparaiso U, IN	B
William Penn U, IA	B
Youngstown State U, OH	B

Health and Physical Education Related

Avila U, MO	B
Bowling Green State U, OH	B
Capital U, OH	B
Coe Coll, IA	B
Concordia U Wisconsin, WI	B
Cornell Coll, IA	B
Gustavus Adolphus Coll, MN	B
Mayville State U, ND	B
Ohio Northern U, OH	B
The U of Akron, OH	B
U of Central Oklahoma, OK	B
U of Minnesota, Twin Cities Campus, MN	B
U of Wisconsin–Superior, WI	B

Health/Health Care Administration

Ashford U, IA	B
Augustana Coll, SD	B
Baker Coll of Auburn Hills, MI	A,B
Baker Coll of Flint, MI	A,B
Baker Coll of Muskegon, MI	A,B
Baker Coll of Owosso, MI	B
Baker Coll of Port Huron, MI	B
Bellevue U, NE	B
Benedictine U, IL	B
Black Hills State U, SD	B
Bowling Green State U, OH	B
Calumet Coll of Saint Joseph, IN	B
Concordia Coll, MN	B
Concordia U Wisconsin, WI	B
Creighton U, NE	B
Davenport U, Dearborn, MI	B
Eastern Michigan U, MI	B
Ferris State U, MI	B
Harris-Stowe State U, MO	B
Hastings Coll, NE	B
Heidelberg Coll, OH	B
Indiana U Northwest, IN	B
Indiana U–Purdue U Indianapolis, IN	B
Indiana U South Bend, IN	B
Langston U, OK	B
Lewis U, IL	B
Lindenwood U, MO	B
Madonna U, MI	A,B
Mercy Coll of Health Sciences, IA	B
Mercy Coll of Northwest Ohio, OH	B
Northeastern State U, OK	B
Roosevelt U, IL	B
Saint Louis U, MO	B
Southern Illinois U Carbondale, IL	B
Southwestern Oklahoma State U, OK	B
Spring Arbor U, MI	B
U of Cincinnati, OH	B
U of Evansville, IN	B
U of Michigan–Dearborn, MI	B
U of Michigan–Flint, MI	B
U of Minnesota, Crookston, MN	B
U of Phoenix–Cleveland Campus, OH	B
U of Phoenix–Indianapolis Campus, IN	B
U of Phoenix–Kansas City Campus, MO	B
U of Phoenix–Metro Detroit Campus, MI	B
U of Phoenix–Oklahoma City Campus, OK	B
U of Phoenix–Tulsa Campus, OK	B
U of Phoenix–West Michigan Campus, MI	B
U of St. Francis, IL	B
U of Wisconsin–Eau Claire, WI	B
U of Wisconsin–Milwaukee, WI	B
Upper Iowa U, IA	B
Ursuline Coll, OH	B
Western Illinois U, IL	B
Western Michigan U, MI	B
Wichita State U, KS	B
Winona State U, MN	B
Wright State U, OH	B

Health Information/Medical Records Administration

Baker Coll of Auburn Hills, MI	A,B
Baker Coll of Cadillac, MI	A
Baker Coll of Clinton Township, MI	A
Baker Coll of Flint, MI	A,B
Baker Coll of Jackson, MI	A
Baker Coll of Port Huron, MI	A
Bowling Green State U–Firelands Coll, OH	A
Chicago State U, IL	B
Coll of Saint Mary, NE	A,B
The Coll of St. Scholastica, MN	B
Dakota State U, SD	B
East Central U, OK	B
Ferris State U, MI	A,B
Fort Berthold Comm Coll, ND	A
Illinois State U, IL	B
Indiana U Northwest, IN	A,B
Indiana U–Purdue U Indianapolis, IN	B
Northern Michigan U, MI	A
The Ohio State U, OH	B
Park U, MO	A
Saint Louis U, MO	B
Southwestern Oklahoma State U, OK	B
Turtle Mountain Comm Coll, ND	A
U of Illinois at Chicago, IL	B
U of Kansas, KS	B
The U of Toledo, OH	B
U of Wisconsin–Milwaukee, WI	B

Health Information/Medical Records Technology

Baker Coll of Flint, MI	A
Baker Coll of Jackson, MI	A
Coll of St. Catherine, MN	A
Dakota State U, SD	A
Davenport U, Dearborn, MI	A
DeVry U, Chicago, IL	A
DeVry U, MN	A
DeVry U, Columbus, OH	A
ITT Tech Inst, Fort Wayne, IN	B
ITT Tech Inst, Indianapolis, IN	A
ITT Tech Inst, Newburgh, IN	A
ITT Tech Inst, Earth City, MO	A
ITT Tech Inst, Kansas City, MO	B
ITT Tech Inst, Green Bay, WI	A
Mercy Coll of Northwest Ohio, OH	A
Missouri Western State U, MO	A
Robert Morris Coll, IL	A
Washburn U, KS	A

Health/Medical Preparatory Programs Related

Aurora U, IL	B
Avila U, MO	B
Coll of the Ozarks, MO	B
Concordia U, NE	B
Gannon U, PA	B
Madonna U, MI	B
Maryville U of Saint Louis, MO	B
Roosevelt U, IL	B
St. Cloud State U, MN	B
Union Coll, NE	A
U of Evansville, IN	B
U of Missouri–Columbia, MO	B
Wheaton Coll, IL	B
Wright State U, OH	B

Health Occupations Teacher Education

U of Central Oklahoma, OK	B

Health Professions Related

Bowling Green State U, OH	B

Health Professions Related (continued)

Bowling Green State U–
Firelands Coll, OH — A
Bradley U, IL — B
Cleveland State U, OH — B
Gannon U, PA — B
The Ohio State U, OH — B
Purdue U, IN — B
U of Northern Iowa, IA — B
U of Saint Francis, IN — B
U of Southern Indiana, IN — B
Washington U in St. Louis,
MO — B

Health Science
Alma Coll, MI — B
Ball State U, IN — B
Benedictine U, IL — B
Bradley U, IL — B
Chicago State U, IL — B
Coll of the Ozarks, MO — B
Drury U, MO — B
Gannon U, PA — B
Graceland U, IA — B
Grand Valley State U, MI — B
Hiram Coll, OH — B
Kalamazoo Coll, MI — B
Kansas State U, KS — B
Kettering Coll of Medical Arts,
OH — B
Manchester Coll, IN — B
Maryville U of Saint Louis,
MO — B
Minnesota State U Mankato,
MN — B
Newman U, KS — A,B
Northern Illinois U, IL — B
Northwest Missouri State U,
MO — B
Oakland U, MI — B
Oklahoma State U, OK — B
Oral Roberts U, OK — B
Roosevelt U, IL — B
Truman State U, MO — B
Union Coll, NE — A
U of Saint Francis, IN — B
U of St. Thomas, MN — B
U of Wisconsin–Milwaukee,
WI — B
Waldorf Coll, IA — B
Winona State U, MN — B
Youngstown State U, OH — B

Health Services Administration
Indiana U–Purdue U Fort
Wayne, IN — B
U of Phoenix–Cincinnati
Campus, OH — B
U of Phoenix–Cleveland
Campus, OH — A
U of Phoenix–Columbus Ohio
Campus, OH — A,B
U of Phoenix–Indianapolis
Campus, IN — A,B
U of Phoenix–Kansas City
Campus, MO — B
U of Phoenix–Metro Detroit
Campus, MI — B
U of Phoenix–Oklahoma City
Campus, OK — B
U of Phoenix–St. Louis
Campus, MO — A
U of Phoenix–Springfield
Campus, MO — A,B
U of Phoenix–Tulsa Campus,
OK — B

U of Phoenix–West Michigan
Campus, MI — B
U of Phoenix–Wichita Campus,
KS — B
Ursuline Coll, OH — B
Washburn U, KS — B

Health Services/Allied Health/Health Sciences
Aakers Coll, Fargo, ND — A
The Coll of St. Scholastica,
MN — B
Kent State U, OH — B
Missouri Southern State U,
MO — B
The Ohio State U at Lima,
OH — B
St. Cloud State U, MN — B
U of Minnesota, Crookston,
MN — B
Ursuline Coll, OH — B

Health Teacher Education
Alma Coll, MI — B
Aquinas Coll, MI — B
Ashland U, OH — B
Augsburg Coll, MN — B
Baldwin-Wallace Coll, OH — B
Ball State U, IN — B
Bemidji State U, MN — B
Bethel U, MN — B
Bowling Green State U, OH — B
Capital U, OH — B
Carroll Coll, WI — B
Cedarville U, OH — B
Central Christian Coll of
Kansas, KS — A
Central Michigan U, MI — B
Central State U, OH — B
Chicago State U, IL — B
Concordia Coll, MN — B
Concordia U, NE — B
Concordia U, St. Paul, MN — B
Concord U, WV — B
DePaul U, IL — B
East Central U, OK — B
Eastern Illinois U, IL — B
Graceland U, IA — B
Gustavus Adolphus Coll, MN — B
Hamline U, MN — B
Heidelberg Coll, OH — B
Illinois State U, IL — B
Indiana State U, IN — B
Indiana U–Purdue U
Indianapolis, IN — B
Iowa State U of Science and
Technology, IA — B
Kent State U, OH — B
Malone Coll, OH — B
Manchester Coll, IN — B
Mayville State U, ND — B
Miami U, OH — B
Miami U Hamilton, OH — B
Minnesota State U Mankato,
MN — B
Missouri Baptist U, MO — B
Missouri Valley Coll, MO — B
Mount Vernon Nazarene U,
OH — B
North Carolina Ag and Tech
State U, NC — B
North Dakota State U, ND — B
Northeastern State U, OK — B
Northern Illinois U, IL — B
Northern Michigan U, MI — B
Northern State U, SD — B

Northwestern Oklahoma State
U, OK — B
Northwest Missouri State U,
MO — B
Ohio Northern U, OH — B
Ohio Wesleyan U, OH — B
Otterbein Coll, OH — B
Peru State Coll, NE — B
Pittsburg State U, KS — B
St. Ambrose U, IA — B
St. Cloud State U, MN — B
Southeastern Oklahoma State
U, OK — B
Southern Illinois U
Carbondale, IL — B
Southern Illinois U
Edwardsville, IL — B
Southwest Minnesota State U,
MN — B
Tabor Coll, KS — B
The U of Akron, OH — B
U of Charleston, WV — B
U of Cincinnati, OH — B
U of Dayton, OH — B
U of Minnesota, Duluth, MN — B
U of Nebraska–Lincoln, NE — B
U of Northern Iowa, IA — B
U of Rio Grande, OH — B
U of Saint Francis, IN — B
U of St. Thomas, MN — B
U of Sioux Falls, SD — B
The U of South Dakota, SD — B
The U of Toledo, OH — B
U of Wisconsin–La Crosse, WI — B
Valley City State U, ND — B
Waldorf Coll, IA — B
Western Illinois U, IL — B
Western Michigan U, MI — B
William Penn U, IA — B
Wilmington Coll, OH — B
Winona State U, MN — B
Wright State U, OH — B
Youngstown State U, OH — B

Heating, Air Conditioning, Ventilation and Refrigeration Maintenance Technology
Ferris State U, MI — A,B
Northern Michigan U, MI — A
U of Cincinnati, OH — A

Heavy Equipment Maintenance Technology
Ferris State U, MI — A,B

Hebrew
Concordia U Wisconsin, WI — B
The Ohio State U, OH — B
U of Illinois at Urbana–
Champaign, IL — B
U of Michigan, MI — B
U of Minnesota, Twin Cities
Campus, MN — B
U of Wisconsin–Madison, WI — B
U of Wisconsin–Milwaukee,
WI — B
Washington U in St. Louis,
MO — B

Higher Education/Higher Education Administration
Wright State U, OH — B

Hindi
U of Chicago, IL — B

Hispanic-American, Puerto Rican, and Mexican-American/Chicano Studies
St. Olaf Coll, MN — B
U of Minnesota, Twin Cities
Campus, MN — B
U of Wisconsin–Madison, WI — B

Histologic Technology/Histotechnologist
Argosy U, Twin Cities, Eagan,
MN — A
Michigan Technological U, MI — B
Northern Michigan U, MI — B

Historic Preservation and Conservation
Ursuline Coll, OH — B

History
Adrian Coll, MI — A,B
Albion Coll, MI — B
Alma Coll, MI — B
Alverno Coll, WI — B
Anderson U, IN — B
Andrews U, MI — B
Antioch Coll, OH — B
Aquinas Coll, MI — B
Ashland U, OH — B
Augsburg Coll, MN — B
Augustana Coll, IL — B
Augustana Coll, SD — B
Aurora U, IL — B
Avila U, MO — B
Baker U, KS — B
Baldwin-Wallace Coll, OH — B
Ball State U, IN — B
Beloit Coll, WI — B
Bemidji State U, MN — B
Benedictine Coll, KS — B
Benedictine U, IL — B
Bethany Coll, KS — B
Bethany Lutheran Coll, MN — B
Bethel Coll, KS — B
Bethel U, MN — B
Blackburn Coll, IL — B
Black Hills State U, SD — B
Bluffton U, OH — B
Bowling Green State U, OH — B
Bradley U, IL — B
Briar Cliff U, IA — B
Buena Vista U, IA — B
Butler U, IN — B
Calvin Coll, MI — B
Cameron U, OK — B
Capital U, OH — B
Cardinal Stritch U, WI — B
Carleton Coll, MN — B
Carroll Coll, WI — B
Case Western Reserve U, OH — B
Cedarville U, OH — B
Central Christian Coll of
Kansas, KS — A
Central Coll, IA — B
Central Methodist U, MO — B
Central Michigan U, MI — B
Central State U, OH — B
Chicago State U, IL — B
Clarke Coll, IA — B
Clarkson U, NY — B
Coe Coll, IA — B
Coll of Mount St. Joseph, OH — B
Coll of Saint Benedict, MN — B
Coll of St. Catherine, MN — B
The Coll of St. Scholastica,
MN — B

A—associate degree; B—bachelor's degree

College	Degree
Coll of the Ozarks, MO	B
The Coll of Wooster, OH	B
Columbia Coll, MO	B
Concordia Coll, MN	B
Concordia U, IL	B
Concordia U, MI	B
Concordia U, NE	B
Concordia U, St. Paul, MN	B
Concordia U Wisconsin, WI	B
Concord U, WV	B
Cornell Coll, IA	B
Cornerstone U, MI	B
Creighton U, NE	B
Crown Coll, MN	B
Culver-Stockton Coll, MO	B
Dakota Wesleyan U, SD	B
Dana Coll, NE	B
Denison U, OH	B
DePaul U, IL	B
DePauw U, IN	B
Dickinson State U, ND	B
Doane Coll, NE	B
Dominican U, IL	B
Dordt Coll, IA	B
Drake U, IA	B
Drury U, MO	B
Earlham Coll, IN	B
East Central U, OK	B
Eastern Illinois U, IL	B
Eastern Michigan U, MI	B
Edgewood Coll, WI	B
Elmhurst Coll, IL	B
Emporia State U, KS	B
Evangel U, MO	B
Fontbonne U, MO	B
Fort Hays State U, KS	B
Franciscan U of Steubenville, OH	B
Franklin Coll, IN	B
Gannon U, PA	B
Goshen Coll, IN	B
Graceland U, IA	B
Grand Valley State U, MI	B
Grand View Coll, IA	B
Grinnell Coll, IA	B
Gustavus Adolphus Coll, MN	B
Hamline U, MN	B
Hannibal-LaGrange Coll, MO	B
Hanover Coll, IN	B
Hastings Coll, NE	B
Heidelberg Coll, OH	B
Hillsdale Coll, MI	B
Hiram Coll, OH	B
Hope Coll, MI	B
Huntington U, IN	B
Illinois Coll, IL	B
Illinois State U, IL	B
Illinois Wesleyan U, IL	B
Indiana State U, IN	B
Indiana U Bloomington, IN	B
Indiana U East, IN	A
Indiana U Northwest, IN	B
Indiana U–Purdue U Fort Wayne, IN	A,B
Indiana U–Purdue U Indianapolis, IN	B
Indiana U South Bend, IN	B
Indiana U Southeast, IN	B
Indiana Wesleyan U, IN	A,B
Iowa State U of Science and Technology, IA	B
Iowa Wesleyan Coll, IA	B
Jamestown Coll, ND	B
Judson Coll, IL	B
Kalamazoo Coll, MI	B
Kansas State U, KS	B
Kent State U, OH	B
Kenyon Coll, OH	B
Knox Coll, IL	B
Lake Forest Coll, IL	B
Lakeland Coll, WI	B
Lake Superior State U, MI	B
Langston U, OK	B
Lawrence U, WI	B
Lewis U, IL	B
Lincoln U, MO	B
Lindenwood U, MO	B
Loras Coll, IA	B
Lourdes Coll, OH	A,B
Loyola U Chicago, IL	B
Luther Coll, IA	B
Macalester Coll, MN	B
MacMurray Coll, IL	B
Madonna U, MI	B
Malone Coll, OH	B
Manchester Coll, IN	B
Marian Coll, IN	A,B
Marian Coll of Fond du Lac, WI	B
Marietta Coll, OH	B
Marquette U, WI	B
Marygrove Coll, MI	B
Maryville U of Saint Louis, MO	B
McKendree Coll, IL	B
Metropolitan State U, MN	B
Miami U, OH	B
Miami U Hamilton, OH	B
Miami U–Middletown Campus, OH	A
Michigan State U, MI	B
Michigan Technological U, MI	B
Millikin U, IL	B
Minnesota State U Mankato, MN	B
Minot State U, ND	B
Missouri Baptist U, MO	B
Missouri Southern State U, MO	B
Missouri State U, MO	B
Missouri Valley Coll, MO	B
Missouri Western State U, MO	B
Morningside Coll, IA	B
Mount Marty Coll, SD	B
Mount Mary Coll, WI	B
Mount Mercy Coll, IA	B
Mount Union Coll, OH	B
Mount Vernon Nazarene U, OH	B
Nebraska Wesleyan U, NE	B
Newman U, KS	B
North Carolina Ag and Tech State U, NC	B
North Central Coll, IL	B
North Dakota State U, ND	B
Northeastern Illinois U, IL	B
Northeastern State U, OK	B
Northern Illinois U, IL	B
Northern Michigan U, MI	B
Northern State U, SD	B
Northland Coll, WI	B
Northwestern Coll, IA	B
Northwestern Coll, MN	B
Northwestern Oklahoma State U, OK	B
Northwestern U, IL	B
Northwest Missouri State U, MO	B
Notre Dame Coll, OH	B
Oakland U, MI	B
Oberlin Coll, OH	B
Oglala Lakota Coll, SD	B
Ohio Dominican U, OH	B
Ohio Northern U, OH	B
The Ohio State U, OH	B
The Ohio State U at Lima, OH	B
The Ohio State U at Marion, OH	B
The Ohio State U–Mansfield Campus, OH	B
The Ohio State U–Newark Campus, OH	B
Ohio Wesleyan U, OH	B
Oklahoma Christian U, OK	B
Oklahoma City U, OK	B
Oklahoma Panhandle State U, OK	B
Oklahoma State U, OK	B
Oklahoma Wesleyan U, OK	B
Oral Roberts U, OK	B
Ottawa U, KS	B
Otterbein Coll, OH	B
Park U, MO	B
Peru State Coll, NE	B
Pittsburg State U, KS	B
Pontifical Coll Josephinum, OH	B
Purdue U, IN	B
Purdue U Calumet, IN	B
Quincy U, IL	B
Ripon Coll, WI	B
Rochester Coll, MI	B
Rockford Coll, IL	B
Rockhurst U, MO	B
Rogers State U, OK	A
Roosevelt U, IL	B
Saginaw Valley State U, MI	B
St. Ambrose U, IA	B
St. Cloud State U, MN	B
St. Gregory's U, Shawnee, OK	B
Saint John's U, MN	B
Saint Joseph's Coll, IN	B
Saint Louis U, MO	B
Saint Mary-of-the-Woods Coll, IN	B
Saint Mary's Coll, IN	B
Saint Mary's U of Minnesota, MN	B
St. Norbert Coll, WI	B
St. Olaf Coll, MN	B
Saint Xavier U, IL	B
Shawnee State U, OH	B
Silver Lake Coll, WI	B
Simpson Coll, IA	B
South Dakota State U, SD	B
Southeastern Oklahoma State U, OK	B
Southeast Missouri State U, MO	B
Southern Illinois U Carbondale, IL	B
Southern Illinois U Edwardsville, IL	B
Southern Methodist U, TX	B
Southwest Baptist U, MO	B
Southwestern Coll, KS	B
Southwestern Oklahoma State U, OK	B
Southwest Minnesota State U, MN	B
Spring Arbor U, MI	B
Sterling Coll, KS	B
Tabor Coll, KS	B
Taylor U, IN	B
Tiffin U, OH	B
Transylvania U, KY	B
Trinity Christian Coll, IL	B
Trinity International U, IL	B
Truman State U, MO	B
Turtle Mountain Comm Coll, ND	A
Union Coll, NE	B
The U of Akron, OH	B
U of Central Missouri, MO	B
U of Central Oklahoma, OK	B
U of Charleston, WV	B
U of Chicago, IL	B
U of Cincinnati, OH	B
U of Dallas, TX	B
U of Dayton, OH	B
U of Evansville, IN	B
The U of Findlay, OH	B
U of Illinois at Chicago, IL	B
U of Illinois at Springfield, IL	B
U of Illinois at Urbana–Champaign, IL	B
U of Indianapolis, IN	B
The U of Iowa, IA	B
U of Kansas, KS	B
U of Michigan, MI	B
U of Michigan–Dearborn, MI	B
U of Michigan–Flint, MI	B
U of Minnesota, Duluth, MN	B
U of Minnesota, Morris, MN	B
U of Minnesota, Twin Cities Campus, MN	B
U of Missouri–Columbia, MO	B
U of Missouri–Kansas City, MO	B
U of Missouri–Rolla, MO	B
U of Missouri–St. Louis, MO	B
U of Nebraska at Kearney, NE	B
U of Nebraska at Omaha, NE	B
U of Nebraska–Lincoln, NE	B
U of New Orleans, LA	B
U of North Dakota, ND	B
U of Northern Iowa, IA	B
U of Notre Dame, IN	B
U of Oklahoma, OK	B
U of Rio Grande, OH	A,B
U of St. Francis, IL	B
U of Saint Francis, IN	B
U of Saint Mary, KS	B
U of St. Thomas, MN	B
U of Science and Arts of Oklahoma, OK	
U of Sioux Falls, SD	
The U of South Dakota, SD	B
U of Southern Indiana, IN	B
The U of Toledo, OH	B
U of Tulsa, OK	B
U of West Florida, FL	B
U of Wisconsin–Eau Claire, WI	B
U of Wisconsin–Green Bay, WI	A,B
U of Wisconsin–La Crosse, WI	B
U of Wisconsin–Madison, WI	B
U of Wisconsin–Milwaukee, WI	B
U of Wisconsin–Oshkosh, WI	B
U of Wisconsin–Parkside, WI	B
U of Wisconsin–Platteville, WI	B
U of Wisconsin–River Falls, WI	B
U of Wisconsin–Stevens Point, WI	B
U of Wisconsin–Superior, WI	B
U of Wisconsin–Whitewater, WI	B
Ursuline Coll, OH	B
Valley City State U, ND	B
Valparaiso U, IN	B

Wabash Coll, IN	B
Waldorf Coll, IA	B
Walsh U, OH	B
Wartburg Coll, IA	B
Washburn U, KS	B
Washington U in St. Louis, MO	B
Wayne State Coll, NE	B
Webster U, MO	B
Western Illinois U, IL	B
Western Michigan U, MI	B
Westminster Coll, MO	B
Wheaton Coll, IL	B
Wichita State U, KS	B
William Jewell Coll, MO	B
William Penn U, IA	B
William Woods U, MO	B
Wilmington Coll, OH	B
Winona State U, MN	B
Wisconsin Lutheran Coll, WI	B
Wittenberg U, OH	B
Wright State U, OH	A,B
Xavier U, OH	A,B
York Coll, NE	B
Youngstown State U, OH	B

History and Philosophy of Science and Technology
Case Western Reserve U, OH	B
U of Wisconsin–Madison, WI	B

History of Philosophy
Marquette U, WI	B

History Related
Ashford U, IA	B
Coll of the Ozarks, MO	B
Marquette U, WI	B
The Ohio State U, OH	B
Saint Mary's U of Minnesota, MN	B
Washburn U, KS	B

History Teacher Education
Alma Coll, MI	B
Buena Vista U, IA	B
Carroll Coll, WI	B
Central Christian Coll of Kansas, KS	A
Central Michigan U, MI	B
Coll of the Ozarks, MO	B
Concordia U, IL	B
Concordia U, MI	B
Concordia U, NE	B
Concordia U Wisconsin, WI	B
Cornerstone U, MI	B
Crown Coll, MN	B
Culver-Stockton Coll, MO	B
Dakota Wesleyan U, SD	B
Dana Coll, NE	B
Dordt Coll, IA	B
East Central U, OK	B
Eastern Michigan U, MI	B
Elmhurst Coll, IL	B
Evangel U, MO	B
Greenville Coll, IL	B
Hannibal-LaGrange Coll, MO	B
Hastings Coll, NE	B
Hope Coll, MI	B
Illinois Wesleyan U, IL	B
Jamestown Coll, ND	B
Lindenwood U, MO	B
Marian Coll of Fond du Lac, WI	B
Maryville U of Saint Louis, MO	B
Mayville State U, ND	B
McKendree Coll, IL	B
Minot State U, ND	B
Missouri State U, MO	B
Mount Marty Coll, SD	B
Mount Mary Coll, WI	B
North Dakota State U, ND	B
Northern Michigan U, MI	B
Ohio Northern U, OH	B
Ohio Wesleyan U, OH	B
Pittsburg State U, KS	B
Rochester Coll, MI	B
St. Ambrose U, IA	B
Saint Xavier U, IL	B
Shawnee State U, OH	B
Southwestern Oklahoma State U, OK	B
Taylor U, IN	B
Trinity Christian Coll, IL	B
Union Coll, NE	B
The U of Akron, OH	B
U of Central Oklahoma, OK	B
U of Illinois at Chicago, IL	B
The U of Iowa, IA	B
U of Mary, ND	B
U of Michigan–Flint, MI	B
U of Nebraska–Lincoln, NE	B
U of Rio Grande, OH	B
The U of South Dakota, SD	B
U of Wisconsin–River Falls, WI	B
U of Wisconsin–Superior, WI	B
Valley City State U, ND	B
Valparaiso U, IN	B
Wartburg Coll, IA	B
Washington U in St. Louis, MO	B
Wayne State Coll, NE	B
Western Michigan U, MI	B
York Coll, NE	B

Horse Husbandry/Equine Science and Management
Stephens Coll, MO	B

Horticultural Science
Andrews U, MI	A
Coll of the Ozarks, MO	B
Iowa State U of Science and Technology, IA	B
Kansas State U, KS	B
Michigan State U, MI	B
Missouri State U, MO	B
North Dakota State U, ND	B
Northwest Missouri State U, MO	B
The Ohio State U, OH	B
Oklahoma State U, OK	B
Purdue U, IN	B
Truman State U, MO	B
U of Illinois at Urbana–Champaign, IL	B
U of Minnesota, Crookston, MN	A,B
U of Nebraska–Lincoln, NE	B
U of Wisconsin–Madison, WI	B
U of Wisconsin–River Falls, WI	B

Hospital and Health Care Facilities Administration
Avila U, MO	B
Black Hills State U, SD	B
Central Michigan U, MI	B
The U of South Dakota, SD	B
The U of Toledo, OH	B
Ursuline Coll, OH	B
Youngstown State U, OH	B

Hospitality Administration
Baker Coll of Flint, MI	A
Baker Coll of Owosso, MI	A
Bowling Green State U, OH	B
Central Michigan U, MI	B
Concordia U, MI	B
Concord U, WV	B
Eastern Michigan U, MI	B
Ferris State U, MI	B
Indiana U–Purdue U Fort Wayne, IN	A,B
International Business Coll, Fort Wayne, IN	A,B
Kendall Coll, IL	A,B
Lexington Coll, IL	A,B
Madonna U, MI	B
Metropolitan State U, MN	B
Michigan State U, MI	B
Missouri State U, MO	B
North Dakota State U, ND	B
Northern Michigan U, MI	B
The Ohio State U, OH	B
The Ohio State U at Lima, OH	B
Roosevelt U, IL	B
The U of Akron, OH	A
U of Illinois at Urbana–Champaign, IL	B
U of Minnesota, Crookston, MN	A
U of New Orleans, LA	B
U of Phoenix–Cincinnati Campus, OH	B
U of Phoenix–Cleveland Campus, OH	B
U of Phoenix–Columbus Ohio Campus, OH	B
U of Phoenix–Indianapolis Campus, IN	B
U of Phoenix–St. Louis Campus, MO	B
U of Phoenix–Springfield Campus, MO	B
U of West Florida, FL	B
U of Wisconsin–Stout, WI	B
Youngstown State U, OH	A,B

Hospitality Administration Related
Indiana U–Purdue U Indianapolis, IN	B
Kendall Coll, IL	B
Kent State U, OH	B
Lexington Coll, IL	A,B
Purdue U, IN	A

Hospitality and Recreation Marketing
AIB Coll of Business, IA	A
Kendall Coll, IL	B
Northern Michigan U, MI	B
Northwest Missouri State U, MO	B
The U of Akron, OH	A

Hotel and Restaurant Management
Coll of the Ozarks, MO	B

Hotel/Motel Administration
Ashland U, OH	B
Baker Coll of Muskegon, MI	A
Baker Coll of Owosso, MI	A
Baker Coll of Port Huron, MI	A
Central State U, OH	B
Concord U, WV	B
Grand Valley State U, MI	B
Indiana U–Purdue U Indianapolis, IN	A
Iowa State U of Science and Technology, IA	B
Kansas State U, KS	B
Kendall Coll, IL	A,B
Langston U, OK	B
Lexington Coll, IL	A,B
Michigan State U, MI	B
Northwood U, MI	A,B
Oklahoma State U, OK	B
Purdue U, IN	B
Purdue U Calumet, IN	A,B
South Dakota State U, SD	B
The U of Akron, OH	A
U of Central Missouri, MO	B
U of Central Oklahoma, OK	B
The U of Findlay, OH	B
U of Minnesota, Crookston, MN	A,B
U of Missouri–Columbia, MO	B

Housing and Human Environments
Missouri State U, MO	B
Ohio U, OH	B
The U of Akron, OH	B
U of Missouri–Columbia, MO	B
U of Nebraska–Lincoln, NE	B
U of Northern Iowa, IA	B

Human Development and Family Studies
Antioch Coll, OH	B
Antioch U McGregor, OH	B
Ashland U, OH	B
Concordia U, MI	B
Indiana State U, IN	B
Indiana U Bloomington, IN	B
Kansas State U, KS	B
Kent State U, OH	B
Miami U, OH	B
Missouri State U, MO	B
North Dakota State U, ND	B
Northern Illinois U, IL	B
The Ohio State U, OH	B
Ohio U, OH	B
Oklahoma State U, OK	B
Purdue U, IN	B
St. Olaf Coll, MN	B
South Dakota State U, SD	B
U of Chicago, IL	B
U of Illinois at Urbana–Champaign, IL	B
U of Missouri–Columbia, MO	B
U of Wisconsin–Stout, WI	B
Youngstown State U, OH	B

Human Development and Family Studies Related
Kent State U, OH	B
Park U, MO	B
The U of Toledo, OH	A

Human Ecology
Kansas State U, KS	B

Humanities
Alma Coll, MI	B
Antioch Coll, OH	B
Antioch U McGregor, OH	B
Ashford U, IA	B
Augsburg Coll, MN	B
Aurora U, IL	B

A—associate degree; B—bachelor's degree

Bemidji State U, MN	B
Bowling Green State U–Firelands Coll, OH	A
Clarkson U, NY	B
Coll of Saint Benedict, MN	B
Coll of Saint Mary, NE	B
The Coll of St. Scholastica, MN	B
Concordia Coll, MN	B
Concordia U Wisconsin, WI	B
Franciscan U of Steubenville, OH	B
Grand Valley State U, MI	B
Hope Coll, MI	B
Indiana U Kokomo, IN	B
Kansas State U, KS	B
Kenyon Coll, OH	B
Lawrence Technological U, MI	B
Macalester Coll, MN	B
Maranatha Baptist Bible Coll, WI	B
Michigan State U, MI	B
Michigan Technological U, MI	A
Minnesota State U Mankato, MN	B
North Central Coll, IL	B
North Dakota State U, ND	B
Northwestern Coll, IA	B
Northwestern U, IL	B
Northwest Missouri State U, MO	B
The Ohio State U, OH	B
Ohio U, OH	A
Ohio Wesleyan U, OH	B
Oklahoma City U, OK	B
Oklahoma Panhandle State U, OK	B
Pontifical Coll Josephinum, OH	B
Purdue U, IN	B
Quincy U, IL	B
Rockford Coll, IL	B
St. Gregory's U, Shawnee, OK	A,B
Saint John's U, MN	B
Saint Louis U, MO	B
Saint Mary-of-the-Woods Coll, IN	B
Saint Mary's Coll, IN	B
St. Norbert Coll, WI	B
Shawnee State U, OH	A
Shimer Coll, IL	B
Southeast Missouri State U, MO	B
Southern Methodist U, TX	B
Tabor Coll, KS	B
Taylor U Fort Wayne, IN	A
Trinity International U, IL	B
The U of Akron, OH	B
U of Chicago, IL	B
U of Cincinnati, OH	A,B
The U of Findlay, OH	A
U of Illinois at Urbana–Champaign, IL	B
U of Kansas, KS	B
U of Michigan, MI	B
U of Michigan–Dearborn, MI	B
U of Northern Iowa, IA	B
U of Rio Grande, OH	B
U of Sioux Falls, SD	A
The U of Toledo, OH	B
U of West Florida, FL	B
U of Wisconsin–Green Bay, WI	A,B
U of Wisconsin–Parkside, WI	B
Ursuline Coll, OH	B
Valparaiso U, IN	B

Waldorf Coll, IA	B
Washburn U, KS	A
Washington U in St. Louis, MO	B
Wright State U, OH	B

Human/Medical Genetics
Northern Michigan U, MI	B

Human Nutrition
Case Western Reserve U, OH	B
Kent State U, OH	B
U of Missouri–Columbia, MO	B

Human Resources Development
Trinity International U, IL	B

Human Resources Management
Antioch U McGregor, OH	B
Baker Coll of Owosso, MI	A,B
Baldwin-Wallace Coll, OH	B
Ball State U, IN	B
Black Hills State U, SD	B
Bowling Green State U, OH	B
Briar Cliff U, IA	B
Buena Vista U, IA	B
Capital U, OH	B
Central Christian Coll of Kansas, KS	A
Central Michigan U, MI	B
Clarkson U, NY	B
Cleary U, MI	B
DePaul U, IL	B
East Central U, OK	B
Grand Valley State U, MI	B
Hastings Coll, NE	B
Indiana State U, IN	B
Indiana Tech, IN	B
Judson Coll, IL	B
Lewis U, IL	B
Lindenwood U, MO	B
Loras Coll, IA	B
Loyola U Chicago, IL	B
Madonna U, MI	B
Marietta Coll, OH	B
Marquette U, WI	B
Metropolitan State U, MN	B
Miami U, OH	B
Michigan State U, MI	B
Millikin U, IL	B
North Central Coll, IL	B
Northeastern Illinois U, IL	B
Northeastern State U, OK	B
Notre Dame Coll, OH	B
Oakland U, MI	B
The Ohio State U, OH	B
Purdue U Calumet, IN	B
Roosevelt U, IL	B
St. Cloud State U, MN	B
Saint Louis U, MO	B
Saint Mary-of-the-Woods Coll, IN	B
Saint Mary's U of Minnesota, MN	B
Silver Lake Coll, WI	B
Southwestern Coll, KS	B
Spring Arbor U, MI	B
Taylor U, IN	B
Trinity Christian Coll, IL	B
Trinity International U, IL	B
The U of Akron, OH	B
U of Central Missouri, MO	B
U of Central Oklahoma, OK	B
The U of Findlay, OH	A,B
U of Illinois at Urbana–Champaign, IL	B

The U of Iowa, IA	B
U of Michigan–Dearborn, MI	B
U of Michigan–Flint, MI	B
U of Minnesota, Duluth, MN	B
U of Nebraska at Omaha, NE	B
U of St. Francis, IL	B
U of Saint Francis, IN	A,B
U of St. Thomas, MN	B
The U of Toledo, OH	B
U of Wisconsin–Milwaukee, WI	B
U of Wisconsin–Whitewater, WI	B
Ursuline Coll, OH	B
Valley City State U, ND	B
Washington U in St. Louis, MO	B
Webster U, MO	B
Western Illinois U, IL	B
Western Michigan U, MI	B
Wichita State U, KS	B
Winona State U, MN	B
Wright State U, OH	B
Xavier U, OH	B
York Coll, NE	B

Human Resources Management and Services Related
Aakers Coll, Fargo, ND	A
Bryant and Stratton Coll, Cleveland, OH	A
Capella U, MN	B
Miami U Hamilton, OH	B
Park U, MO	B
U of Oklahoma, OK	B

Human Services
Adrian Coll, MI	A,B
Albion Coll, MI	B
Antioch U McGregor, OH	B
Ashford U, IA	B
Baker Coll of Clinton Township, MI	A
Baker Coll of Flint, MI	A
Baker Coll of Muskegon, MI	A
Black Hills State U, SD	B
Bowling Green State U–Firelands Coll, OH	A
Calumet Coll of Saint Joseph, IN	B
Concordia U, St. Paul, MN	B
Dakota Wesleyan U, SD	B
Doane Coll, NE	B
East Central U, OK	B
Finlandia U, MI	B
Fontbonne U, MO	B
Fort Berthold Comm Coll, ND	A
Grace Bible Coll, MI	B
Graceland U, IA	B
Grand View Coll, IA	B
Hannibal-LaGrange Coll, MO	B
Hastings Coll, NE	B
Indiana Tech, IN	B
Indiana U East, IN	A
Indiana U–Purdue U Fort Wayne, IN	A,B
Judson Coll, IL	B
Kendall Coll, IL	A,B
Kent State U, Ashtabula Campus, OH	A
Lake Superior State U, MI	B
Lindenwood U, MO	B
Metropolitan State U, MN	B
Missouri Baptist U, MO	B
Missouri Valley Coll, MO	B
Mount Marty Coll, SD	B

Mount Vernon Nazarene U, OH	A
Oglala Lakota Coll, SD	A,B
Ohio U, OH	A
Ottawa U, KS	B
Park U, MO	B
Roosevelt U, IL	B
Saint Mary-of-the-Woods Coll, IN	B
Saint Mary's U of Minnesota, MN	B
Sitting Bull Coll, ND	A
Southwest Baptist U, MO	B
Tiffin U, OH	B
Turtle Mountain Comm Coll, ND	A
U of Cincinnati, OH	A
U of Minnesota, Morris, MN	B
U of Phoenix–Chicago Campus, IL	B
U of Phoenix–Indianapolis Campus, IN	B
U of Phoenix–Kansas City Campus, MO	B
U of Phoenix–Metro Detroit Campus, MI	B
U of Phoenix–Oklahoma City Campus, OK	B
U of Phoenix–St. Louis Campus, MO	B
U of Phoenix–Springfield Campus, MO	B
U of Phoenix–Tulsa Campus, OK	B
U of Phoenix–West Michigan Campus, MI	B
U of Phoenix–Wisconsin Campus, WI	B
U of Saint Francis, IN	A
U of Wisconsin–Oshkosh, WI	B
Upper Iowa U, IA	B
Walsh U, OH	A,B
Washburn U, KS	A,B
William Penn U, IA	B

Hydrology and Water Resources Science
East Central U, OK	B
Grand Valley State U, MI	B
Heidelberg Coll, OH	B
Lake Superior State U, MI	A
Northern Michigan U, MI	B
Northland Coll, WI	B
U of Wisconsin–Madison, WI	B
U of Wisconsin–Stevens Point, WI	B
Western Michigan U, MI	B
Wright State U, OH	B

Illustration
Art Academy of Cincinnati, OH	B
The Cleveland Inst of Art, OH	B
Columbia Coll, MO	B
Columbus Coll of Art & Design, OH	B
Kansas City Art Inst, MO	B
Lawrence Technological U, MI	B
School of the Art Inst of Chicago, IL	B
U of Kansas, KS	B
Washington U in St. Louis, MO	B

Industrial and Organizational Psychology
Clarkson U, NY	B

Madonna U, MI	B
Maryville U of Saint Louis, MO	B
Nebraska Wesleyan U, NE	B
Saint Xavier U, IL	B
U of Illinois at Urbana–Champaign, IL	B
Washington U in St. Louis, MO	B
Wright State U, OH	B

Industrial Arts

Andrews U, MI	B
Ball State U, IN	B
Bemidji State U, MN	B
Chicago State U, IL	B
Coll of the Ozarks, MO	B
Fort Hays State U, KS	B
Langston U, OK	B
Minnesota State U Mankato, MN	B
North Carolina Ag and Tech State U, NC	B
Northeastern State U, OK	B
Northern State U, SD	B
Ohio Northern U, OH	B
Oklahoma Panhandle State U, OK	B
Pittsburg State U, KS	B
St. Cloud State U, MN	B
Southwestern Oklahoma State U, OK	B
U of Cincinnati, OH	A
U of Wisconsin–Platteville, WI	B
William Penn U, IA	B

Industrial Design

The Cleveland Inst of Art, OH	B
Columbia Coll Chicago, IL	B
Columbus Coll of Art & Design, OH	B
Ferris State U, MI	A
Finlandia U, MI	B
The Ohio State U, OH	B
U of Cincinnati, OH	B
U of Illinois at Chicago, IL	B
U of Illinois at Urbana–Champaign, IL	B
U of Kansas, KS	B
U of Michigan, MI	B
U of Wisconsin–Platteville, WI	B
Western Michigan U, MI	B

Industrial Engineering

Bradley U, IL	B
Central Michigan U, MI	B
Central State U, OH	B
Cleveland State U, OH	B
Ferris State U, MI	B
Gannon U, PA	B
Grand Valley State U, MI	B
Iowa State U of Science and Technology, IA	B
Kansas State U, KS	B
Kent State U, OH	B
Kettering U, MI	B
Marquette U, WI	B
Miami U, OH	B
Michigan Technological U, MI	B
Milwaukee School of Engineering, WI	B
North Carolina Ag and Tech State U, NC	B
North Dakota State U, ND	B
Northern Illinois U, IL	B
Northwestern U, IL	B

The Ohio State U, OH	B
Ohio U, OH	B
Oklahoma State U, OK	B
Purdue U, IN	B
St. Ambrose U, IA	B
St. Cloud State U, MN	B
South Dakota School of Mines and Technology, SD	B
Southern Illinois U Edwardsville, IL	B
U of Cincinnati, OH	B
U of Illinois at Chicago, IL	B
U of Illinois at Urbana–Champaign, IL	B
The U of Iowa, IA	B
U of Michigan, MI	B
U of Michigan–Dearborn, MI	B
U of Minnesota, Duluth, MN	B
U of Minnesota, Twin Cities Campus, MN	B
U of Missouri–Columbia, MO	B
U of Missouri–Rolla, MO	B
U of Nebraska–Lincoln, NE	B
U of Oklahoma, OK	B
The U of Toledo, OH	A,B
U of Wisconsin–Madison, WI	B
U of Wisconsin–Milwaukee, WI	B
U of Wisconsin–Platteville, WI	B
Western Michigan U, MI	B
Wichita State U, KS	B
Youngstown State U, OH	B

Industrial/Manufacturing Engineering

Indiana Tech, IN	B

Industrial Production Technologies Related

Central Michigan U, MI	B
Ferris State U, MI	A
Southwestern Coll, KS	B
The U of Akron, OH	B
U of Nebraska–Lincoln, NE	A,B
U of Wisconsin–Stout, WI	B
Wayne State Coll, NE	B

Industrial Radiologic Technology

Baker Coll of Owosso, MI	A,B
Ball State U, IN	A
Briar Cliff U, IA	B
Concordia U Wisconsin, WI	B
Ferris State U, MI	A
Fort Hays State U, KS	A
Jamestown Coll, ND	B
Madonna U, MI	B
U of Cincinnati, OH	A
U of Sioux Falls, SD	B

Industrial Safety Technology

South Dakota State U, SD	B

Industrial Technology

Baker Coll of Flint, MI	B
Baker Coll of Muskegon, MI	A
Ball State U, IN	A,B
Bemidji State U, MN	B
Black Hills State U, SD	B
Bowling Green State U, OH	B
Bowling Green State U–Firelands Coll, OH	A,B
Bradley U, IL	B
Cameron U, OK	A
Central State U, OH	B
Cleveland State U, OH	B
Eastern Illinois U, IL	B

Eastern Michigan U, MI	B
Ferris State U, MI	A,B
Illinois Inst of Technology, IL	B
Illinois State U, IL	B
Indiana State U, IN	B
Indiana U–Purdue U Fort Wayne, IN	A,B
ITT Tech Inst, Fort Wayne, IN	B
ITT Tech Inst, Indianapolis, IN	B
ITT Tech Inst, Newburgh, IN	B
Kent State U, OH	A,B
Kent State U, Ashtabula Campus, OH	A
Kent State U, Geauga Campus, OH	A
Kent State U, Trumbull Campus, OH	A,B
Kent State U, Tuscarawas Campus, OH	A,B
Lake Superior State U, MI	B
Langston U, OK	B
Lawrence Technological U, MI	B
Miami U–Middletown Campus, OH	A
Minnesota State U Mankato, MN	B
Missouri Southern State U, MO	B
North Carolina Ag and Tech State U, NC	B
Northeastern State U, OK	B
Northern Illinois U, IL	B
Ohio Northern U, OH	B
Ohio U, OH	B
Oklahoma Panhandle State U, OK	A,B
Pittsburg State U, KS	B
Purdue U Calumet, IN	A,B
Purdue U North Central, IN	A
Saint Mary's U of Minnesota, MN	B
South Dakota State U, SD	B
Southeastern Oklahoma State U, OK	B
Southeast Missouri State U, MO	B
Southern Illinois U Carbondale, IL	B
Southwestern Oklahoma State U, OK	B
Tri-State U, IN	A
The U of Akron, OH	A,B
U of Central Missouri, MO	A,B
U of Cincinnati, OH	A
U of Dayton, OH	B
U of Nebraska at Omaha, NE	B
U of Nebraska–Lincoln, NE	B
U of North Dakota, ND	B
U of Northern Iowa, IA	B
U of Rio Grande, OH	A,B
The U of Toledo, OH	A,B
U of Wisconsin–Platteville, WI	B
Washburn U, KS	A
Western Illinois U, IL	B
William Penn U, IA	B
Wright State U, OH	B

Information Resources Management

Clarkson U, NY	B
U of Wisconsin–Eau Claire, WI	B

Information Science/Studies

Anderson U, IN	B

Andrews U, MI	B
Ashland U, OH	B
Baker Coll of Cadillac, MI	A,B
Baker Coll of Clinton Township, MI	A
Baker Coll of Flint, MI	A,B
Baker Coll of Jackson, MI	A,B
Baker Coll of Muskegon, MI	A,B
Baker Coll of Owosso, MI	A,B
Baker Coll of Port Huron, MI	A,B
Baker U, KS	B
Baldwin-Wallace Coll, OH	B
Ball State U, IN	A,B
Bellevue U, NE	B
Bemidji State U, MN	B
Benedictine U, IL	B
Bluffton U, OH	B
Bradley U, IL	B
Butler U, IN	B
Calumet Coll of Saint Joseph, IN	A,B
Carroll Coll, WI	B
Cedarville U, OH	B
Central Coll, IA	B
Chicago State U, IL	B
Clarke Coll, IA	B
Cleary U, MI	B
Cleveland State U, OH	B
Concordia U, IL	B
Concord U, WV	B
Cornerstone U, MI	B
Culver-Stockton Coll, MO	B
Dakota State U, SD	A,B
DePaul U, IL	B
DeVry U, Tinley Park, IL	B
Dominican U, IL	B
Eastern Michigan U, MI	B
Edgewood Coll, WI	B
Emporia State U, KS	B
Ferris State U, MI	B
Fort Berthold Comm Coll, ND	A
Fort Hays State U, KS	B
Goshen Coll, IN	B
Grand Valley State U, MI	B
Grand View Coll, IA	B
Harris-Stowe State U, MO	B
Heidelberg Coll, OH	B
Illinois Coll, IL	B
Illinois Inst of Technology, IL	B
Illinois State U, IL	B
Indiana Tech, IN	A,B
Iowa Wesleyan Coll, IA	B
Judson Coll, IL	B
Kansas State U, KS	B
Kettering U, MI	B
Lewis Coll of Business, MI	A
Lincoln U, MO	B
MacMurray Coll, IL	B
Madonna U, MI	B
Marietta Coll, OH	B
Marquette U, WI	B
McKendree Coll, IL	B
Metropolitan State U, MN	B
Miami U–Middletown Campus, OH	A
Michigan Technological U, MI	B
Minnesota State U Mankato, MN	B
Missouri Southern State U, MO	A,B
Missouri Western State U, MO	B
Mount Union Coll, OH	B
National American U, Rapid City, SD	A,B
Nebraska Wesleyan U, NE	B

A—associate degree; B—bachelor's degree

Newman U, KS	A,B
Northern Michigan U, MI	B
Northland Coll, WI	B
Northwestern Oklahoma State U, OK	B
Northwestern U, IL	B
Northwest Missouri State U, MO	B
Notre Dame Coll, OH	B
Ohio Dominican U, OH	B
The Ohio State U, OH	B
Oklahoma Christian U, OK	B
Oklahoma Panhandle State U, OK	A,B
Oklahoma Wesleyan U, OK	A,B
Ottawa U, KS	B
Purdue U Calumet, IN	B
Purdue U North Central, IN	A
Quincy U, IL	B
Rogers State U, OK	A
St. Ambrose U, IA	B
St. Cloud State U, MN	B
Saint Mary-of-the-Woods Coll, IN	B
Saint Mary's U of Minnesota, MN	B
Silver Lake Coll, WI	B
Simpson Coll, IA	B
South Dakota State U, SD	B
Southeastern Oklahoma State U, OK	B
Southern Illinois U Carbondale, IL	B
Taylor U, IN	B
Tiffin U, OH	B
Trinity Christian Coll, IL	B
Union Coll, NE	A,B
U of Charleston, WV	B
U of Cincinnati, OH	A,B
U of Dayton, OH	B
U of Michigan–Flint, MI	B
U of Minnesota, Crookston, MN	A,B
U of Missouri–Rolla, MO	B
U of North Dakota, ND	B
U of Saint Mary, KS	B
U of Sioux Falls, SD	B
The U of Toledo, OH	A,B
U of Tulsa, OK	B
U of Wisconsin–Green Bay, WI	A,B
U of Wisconsin–River Falls, WI	B
U of Wisconsin–Superior, WI	B
Waldorf Coll, IA	B
Wartburg Coll, IA	B
Washington U in St. Louis, MO	B
Wayne State Coll, NE	B
Webster U, MO	B
William Jewell Coll, MO	B
Winona State U, MN	B
Wright State U, OH	B

Information Technology

Bellevue U, NE	B
Bluffton U, OH	B
Bryant and Stratton Coll, Cleveland, OH	A
Capella U, MN	B
Coll of the Ozarks, MO	B
Dakota State U, SD	B
Davenport U, Dearborn, MI	A,B
DeVry U, Addison, IL	B
DeVry U, Kansas City, MO	B
DeVry U, Columbus, OH	B
Grantham U, MO	A,B

Illinois Inst of Technology, IL	B
Illinois State U, IL	B
Indiana Tech, IN	A
International Academy of Design & Technology, IL	A
ITT Tech Inst, Indianapolis, IN	A
Kaplan U, IA	A,B
Kent State U, Geauga Campus, OH	A
Kilian Comm Coll, SD	A
Lawrence Technological U, MI	B
Lewis U, IL	B
Marian Coll of Fond du Lac, WI	B
Minnesota School of Business, MN	A,B
Minnesota School of Business–Brooklyn Center, MN	A,B
Minnesota School of Business–Plymouth, MN	A,B
Minnesota School of Business–Richfield, MN	A,B
Minnesota School of Business–St. Cloud, MN	A,B
Minnesota School of Business–Shakopee, MN	A,B
Mount Marty Coll, SD	B
National American U, KS	A
Robert Morris Coll, IL	B
U of Michigan–Flint, MI	B
U of Missouri–Kansas City, MO	B
U of Phoenix–Chicago Campus, IL	B
U of Phoenix–Cincinnati Campus, OH	A,B
U of Phoenix–Cleveland Campus, OH	B
U of Phoenix–Columbus Ohio Campus, OH	A,B
U of Phoenix–Indianapolis Campus, IN	A,B
U of Phoenix–Kansas City Campus, MO	B
U of Phoenix–Metro Detroit Campus, MI	B
U of Phoenix–Oklahoma City Campus, OK	B
U of Phoenix–St. Louis Campus, MO	A,B
U of Phoenix–Springfield Campus, MO	A,B
U of Phoenix–Tulsa Campus, OK	B
U of Phoenix–West Michigan Campus, MI	B
U of Phoenix–Wichita Campus, KS	B
U of Phoenix–Wisconsin Campus, WI	B
U of Rio Grande, OH	B
U of St. Francis, IL	B
U of Wisconsin–Whitewater, WI	B

Institutional Food Workers

Kendall Coll, IL	A,B
Lexington Coll, IL	A,B

Insurance

Ball State U, IN	B
Bradley U, IL	B
Ferris State U, MI	B
Gannon U, PA	B
Illinois State U, IL	B
Illinois Wesleyan U, IL	B

Indiana State U, IN	B
Minnesota State U Mankato, MN	B
Missouri State U, MO	B
The Ohio State U, OH	B
Roosevelt U, IL	B
St. Cloud State U, MN	B
U of Cincinnati, OH	A,B
U of Minnesota, Twin Cities Campus, MN	B
U of Wisconsin–Madison, WI	B

Intercultural/Multicultural and Diversity Studies

Coll of St. Catherine, MN	B
Evangel U, MO	B
Marquette U, WI	B
St. Olaf Coll, MN	B
Taylor U Fort Wayne, IN	B

Interdisciplinary Studies

Antioch Coll, OH	B
Augsburg Coll, MN	B
Beloit Coll, WI	B
Blackburn Coll, IL	B
Bowling Green State U–Firelands Coll, OH	A
Calvin Coll, MI	B
Capital U, OH	B
Cardinal Stritch U, WI	A
Carleton Coll, MN	B
Cedarville U, OH	B
Central Coll, IA	B
Central Methodist U, MO	A,B
Clarkson U, NY	B
Cleveland State U, OH	B
Coe Coll, IA	B
Coll of the Ozarks, MO	B
The Coll of Wooster, OH	B
Columbia Coll Chicago, IL	B
Cornell Coll, IA	B
Cornerstone U, MI	B
Dana Coll, NE	B
DePaul U, IL	B
DePauw U, IN	B
Earlham Coll, IN	B
Elmhurst Coll, IL	B
Grand Valley State U, MI	B
Grantham U, MO	A,B
Grinnell Coll, IA	B
Gustavus Adolphus Coll, MN	B
Harris-Stowe State U, MO	B
Hillsdale Coll, MI	B
Hillsdale Free Will Baptist Coll, OK	A,B
Hiram Coll, OH	B
Hope Coll, MI	B
Illinois Coll, IL	B
Illinois State U, IL	B
Illinois Wesleyan U, IL	B
Iowa State U of Science and Technology, IA	B
Kalamazoo Coll, MI	B
Kansas State U, KS	A
Kenyon Coll, OH	B
Lake Superior State U, MI	B
Luther Coll, IA	B
Macalester Coll, MN	B
Manchester Coll, IN	B
Marquette U, WI	B
Martin Luther Coll, MN	B
Maryville U of Saint Louis, MO	B
Miami U, OH	B
Miami U–Middletown Campus, OH	A
Millikin U, IL	B

Minneapolis Coll of Art and Design, MN	B
Morningside Coll, IA	B
Mount Union Coll, OH	B
Nebraska Wesleyan U, NE	B
Northland Coll, WI	B
Northwestern U, IL	B
Oberlin Coll, OH	B
Ohio Dominican U, OH	A,B
Ohio U, OH	B
Purdue U, IN	B
Ripon Coll, WI	B
Rochester Coll, MI	B
St. Cloud State U, MN	B
Saint Mary's Coll, IN	B
Silver Lake Coll, WI	B
South Dakota School of Mines and Technology, SD	B
Southeast Missouri State U, MO	B
Southwest Minnesota State U, MN	B
Stephens Coll, MO	B
Sterling Coll, KS	B
Tabor Coll, KS	A,B
The U of Akron, OH	A,B
U of Chicago, IL	B
The U of Iowa, IA	B
U of Michigan, MI	B
U of Minnesota, Crookston, MN	B
U of Minnesota, Duluth, MN	B
U of Missouri–Columbia, MO	B
U of Missouri–Kansas City, MO	B
U of North Dakota, ND	B
U of Saint Mary, KS	B
U of St. Thomas, MN	B
U of Sioux Falls, SD	A,B
U of Wisconsin–Green Bay, WI	A,B
U of Wisconsin–Milwaukee, WI	B
U of Wisconsin–Parkside, WI	B
Washington U in St. Louis, MO	B
Wayne State Coll, NE	B
Webster U, MO	B
William Jewell Coll, MO	B
William Woods U, MO	B
Wisconsin Lutheran Coll, WI	B

Interior Architecture

Bowling Green State U, OH	B
Central Michigan U, MI	B
Indiana State U, IN	B
Kansas State U, KS	B
Lawrence Technological U, MI	B
School of the Art Inst of Chicago, IL	B
U of Central Missouri, MO	B
U of Missouri–Columbia, MO	B
U of Nebraska–Lincoln, NE	B

Interior Design

Adrian Coll, MI	B
The Art Insts International Minnesota, MN	A,B
Baker Coll of Allen Park, MI	A
Baker Coll of Auburn Hills, MI	A
Baker Coll of Clinton Township, MI	A
Baker Coll of Flint, MI	A,B
Baker Coll of Muskegon, MI	A
Baker Coll of Owosso, MI	A
Baker Coll of Port Huron, MI	A
The Cleveland Inst of Art, OH	B

Interior Design

Coll of Mount St. Joseph, OH — A,B
Columbia Coll Chicago, IL — B
Columbus Coll of Art & Design, OH — B
Concordia U Wisconsin, WI — B
Eastern Michigan U, MI — B
Ferris State U, MI — B
Harrington Coll of Design, IL — A,B
The Illinois Inst of Art–Chicago, IL — A,B
The Illinois Inst of Art–Schaumburg, IL — B
Indiana U Bloomington, IN — B
Indiana U–Purdue U Fort Wayne, IN — A
Indiana U–Purdue U Indianapolis, IN — B
International Academy of Design & Technology, IL — A,B
Iowa State U of Science and Technology, IA — B
Kansas State U, KS — B
Kent State U, OH — B
Marian Coll, IN — A
Maryville U of Saint Louis, MO — B
Miami U, OH — B
Miami U Hamilton, OH — B
Michigan State U, MI — B
Minnesota State U Mankato, MN — B
Mount Mary Coll, WI — B
North Dakota State U, ND — B
Northwest Missouri State U, MO — B
The Ohio State U, OH — B
Oklahoma Christian U, OK — B
Park U, MO — B
Robert Morris Coll, IL — A
School of the Art Inst of Chicago, IL — B
South Dakota State U, SD — B
Southern Illinois U Carbondale, IL — B
The U of Akron, OH — B
U of Central Missouri, MO — B
U of Central Oklahoma, OK — B
U of Cincinnati, OH — B
U of Kansas, KS — B
U of Minnesota, Twin Cities Campus, MN — B
U of Northern Iowa, IA — B
U of Oklahoma, OK — B
U of Wisconsin–Madison, WI — B
U of Wisconsin–Stevens Point, WI — B
Ursuline Coll, OH — B
Wayne State Coll, NE — B
Western Michigan U, MI — B
William Woods U, MO — B

Intermedia/Multimedia

Academy Coll, MN — A
Art Academy of Cincinnati, OH — B
The Art Insts International Minnesota, MN — A,B
Calumet Coll of Saint Joseph, IN — B
The Cleveland Inst of Art, OH — B
Columbia Coll Chicago, IL — B
International Academy of Design & Technology, IL — A
Kansas City Art Inst, MO — B
Lewis U, IL — B

Minneapolis Coll of Art and Design, MN — B
Minnesota School of Business, MN — A
Minnesota School of Business–Brooklyn Center, MN — A
Minnesota School of Business–Plymouth, MN — A
Minnesota School of Business–Richfield, MN — A
Minnesota School of Business–St. Cloud, MN — A
Minnesota School of Business–Shakopee, MN — A
Northern Michigan U, MI — B
Robert Morris Coll, IL — A
School of the Art Inst of Chicago, IL — B
U of Michigan, MI — B

International Agriculture

Iowa State U of Science and Technology, IA — B
U of Missouri–Columbia, MO — B

International Business/Trade/Commerce

Adrian Coll, MI — B
Alma Coll, MI — B
Alverno Coll, WI — B
Aquinas Coll, MI — B
Augsburg Coll, MN — B
Avila U, MO — B
Baker U, KS — B
Benedictine U, IL — B
Bethany Coll, KS — B
Bowling Green State U, OH — B
Bradley U, IL — B
Buena Vista U, IA — B
Butler U, IN — B
Cardinal Stritch U, WI — B
Cedarville U, OH — B
Central Coll, IA — B
Central Michigan U, MI — B
Clarke Coll, IA — B
Clarkson U, NY — B
Coll of St. Catherine, MN — B
The Coll of St. Scholastica, MN — B
Coll of the Ozarks, MO — B
Columbia Coll, MO — B
Concordia Coll, MN — B
Cornell Coll, IA — B
Creighton U, NE — B
Davenport U, Dearborn, MI — B
DePaul U, IL — B
Dickinson State U, ND — B
Dominican U, IL — B
Drake U, IA — B
Drury U, MO — B
Eastern Michigan U, MI — B
Elmhurst Coll, IL — B
Ferris State U, MI — B
Finlandia U, MI — B
Gannon U, PA — B
Grace Coll, IN — B
Graceland U, IA — B
Grand Valley State U, MI — B
Gustavus Adolphus Coll, MN — B
Hamline U, MN — B
Hiram Coll, OH — B
Illinois State U, IL — B
Illinois Wesleyan U, IL — B
Iowa State U of Science and Technology, IA — B
Jamestown Coll, ND — B

Judson Coll, IL — B
Lakeland Coll, WI — B
Lewis U, IL — B
Loras Coll, IA — B
Madonna U, MI — B
Marietta Coll, OH — B
Marquette U, WI — B
Marygrove Coll, MI — B
Metropolitan State U, MN — B
Millikin U, IL — B
Milwaukee School of Engineering, WI — B
Minnesota State U Mankato, MN — B
Minot State U, ND — B
Missouri Southern State U, MO — B
Mount Union Coll, OH — B
National American U, Rapid City, SD — B
Nebraska Wesleyan U, NE — B
North Central Coll, IL — B
Northern State U, SD — B
Northwestern Coll, MN — B
Northwest Missouri State U, MO — B
Northwood U, MI — A,B
Ohio Dominican U, OH — B
Ohio Northern U, OH — B
The Ohio State U, OH — B
Ohio Wesleyan U, OH — B
Oklahoma City U, OK — B
Oral Roberts U, OK — B
Otterbein Coll, OH — B
Pittsburg State U, KS — B
Roosevelt U, IL — B
Saginaw Valley State U, MI — B
St. Ambrose U, IA — B
St. Cloud State U, MN — B
Saint Louis U, MO — B
Saint Mary's Coll, IN — B
Saint Mary's U of Minnesota, MN — B
St. Norbert Coll, WI — B
Saint Xavier U, IL — B
Simpson Coll, IA — B
Taylor U, IN — B
Trinity International U, IL — B
The U of Akron, OH — B
U of Dayton, OH — B
U of Evansville, IN — B
The U of Findlay, OH — B
U of Indianapolis, IN — B
U of Minnesota, Twin Cities Campus, MN — B
U of Missouri–Columbia, MO — B
U of Missouri–St. Louis, MO — B
U of Nebraska–Lincoln, NE — B
U of Oklahoma, OK — B
U of Phoenix–Cincinnati Campus, OH — B
U of Phoenix–Cleveland Campus, OH — B
U of Phoenix–Columbus Ohio Campus, OH — B
U of Phoenix–Indianapolis Campus, IN — B
U of Phoenix–Kansas City Campus, MO — B
U of Phoenix–Metro Detroit Campus, MI — B
U of Phoenix–Oklahoma City Campus, OK — B
U of Phoenix–St. Louis Campus, MO — B

U of Phoenix–Springfield Campus, MO — B
U of Phoenix–Tulsa Campus, OK — B
U of Phoenix–Wisconsin Campus, WI — B
U of Rio Grande, OH — B
U of St. Thomas, MN — B
The U of Toledo, OH — B
U of Tulsa, OK — B
U of Wisconsin–La Crosse, WI — B
Valparaiso U, IN — B
Wartburg Coll, IA — B
Washington U in St. Louis, MO — B
Webster U, MO — B
Westminster Coll, MO — B
Wichita State U, KS — B
William Jewell Coll, MO — B
William Woods U, MO — B
Xavier U, OH — B

International Economics

Coll of St. Catherine, MN — B
Eastern Michigan U, MI — B
Hamline U, MN — B
Hiram Coll, OH — B
Lawrence U, WI — B
Ohio U, OH — B
Rockford Coll, IL — B
Taylor U, IN — B
U of Missouri–Columbia, MO — B
U of St. Thomas, MN — B
Valparaiso U, IN — B
Washington U in St. Louis, MO — B

International Finance

The U of Akron, OH — B
Washington U in St. Louis, MO — B

International/Global Studies

Alverno Coll, WI — B
Baker U, KS — B
Baldwin-Wallace Coll, OH — B
Case Western Reserve U, OH — B
Central Coll, IA — B
The Coll of St. Scholastica, MN — B
Concordia Coll, MN — B
Hanover Coll, IN — B
Hope Coll, MI — B
Illinois Wesleyan U, IL — B
Kenyon Coll, OH — B
Lewis U, IL — B
Marquette U, WI — B
Miami U Hamilton, OH — B
Michigan State U, MI — B
Nebraska Wesleyan U, NE — B
North Dakota State U, ND — B
Northern Michigan U, MI — B
Oral Roberts U, OK — B
Pittsburg State U, KS — B
Rockford Coll, IL — B
Saint Mary's U of Minnesota, MN — B
Southern Methodist U, TX — B
U of Chicago, IL — B
The U of Iowa, IA — B
U of Nebraska at Omaha, NE — B
U of New Orleans, LA — B
U of North Dakota, ND — B
U of Wisconsin–Whitewater, WI — B
Western Michigan U, MI — B

A—associate degree; B—bachelor's degree

International Marketing

The U of Akron, OH — B

International Relations and Affairs

Adrian Coll, MI — B
Albion Coll, MI — B
Alverno Coll, WI — B
Antioch Coll, OH — B
Aquinas Coll, MI — B
Ashland U, OH — B
Augsburg Coll, MN — B
Augustana Coll, SD — B
Beloit Coll, WI — B
Benedictine U, IL — B
Bethel U, MN — B
Bowling Green State U, OH — B
Bradley U, IL — B
Butler U, IN — B
Calvin Coll, MI — B
Capital U, OH — B
Carleton Coll, MN — B
Carroll Coll, WI — B
Case Western Reserve U, OH — B
Cedarville U, OH — B
Central Michigan U, MI — B
Cleveland State U, OH — B
Coll of St. Catherine, MN — B
The Coll of Wooster, OH — B
Cornell Coll, IA — B
Creighton U, NE — B
Denison U, OH — B
DePaul U, IL — B
Doane Coll, NE — B
Drake U, IA — B
Earlham Coll, IN — B
Edgewood Coll, WI — B
Graceland U, IA — B
Grand Valley State U, MI — B
Hamline U, MN — B
Hastings Coll, NE — B
Heidelberg Coll, OH — B
Hillsdale Coll, MI — B
Illinois Coll, IL — B
Iowa State U of Science and Technology, IA — B
Kent State U, OH — B
Kenyon Coll, OH — B
Knox Coll, IL — B
Lake Forest Coll, IL — B
Lawrence U, WI — B
Lindenwood U, MO — B
Loras Coll, IA — B
Loyola U Chicago, IL — B
Luther Coll, IA — B
Macalester Coll, MN — B
Marian Coll of Fond du Lac, WI — B
Marquette U, WI — B
McKendree Coll, IL — B
Miami U, OH — B
Michigan State U, MI — B
Millikin U, IL — B
Minnesota State U Mankato, MN — B
Missouri Southern State U, MO — B
Mount Mary Coll, WI — B
Mount Mercy Coll, IA — B
North Central Coll, IL — B
Northwestern U, IL — B
Ohio Northern U, OH — B
The Ohio State U, OH — B
Ohio U, OH — B
Ohio Wesleyan U, OH — B
Oral Roberts U, OK — B
Otterbein Coll, OH — B

Rockhurst U, MO — B
Roosevelt U, IL — B
Saginaw Valley State U, MI — B
St. Cloud State U, MN — B
Saint Joseph's Coll, IN — B
Saint Louis U, MO — B
St. Norbert Coll, WI — B
Saint Xavier U, IL — B
Shawnee State U, OH — B
Simpson Coll, IA — B
Southern Methodist U, TX — B
Stephens Coll, MO — B
Tabor Coll, KS — B
Taylor U, IN — B
Tiffin U, OH — B
Union Coll, NE — B
U of Cincinnati, OH — B
U of Dayton, OH — B
U of Evansville, IN — B
U of Indianapolis, IN — B
U of Kansas, KS — B
U of Michigan, MI — B
U of Minnesota, Duluth, MN — B
U of Minnesota, Twin Cities Campus, MN — B
U of Nebraska at Kearney, NE — B
U of Nebraska–Lincoln, NE — B
U of St. Thomas, MN — B
U of Southern Indiana, IN — B
The U of Toledo, OH — B
U of West Florida, FL — B
U of Wisconsin–Madison, WI — B
U of Wisconsin–Milwaukee, WI — B
U of Wisconsin–Oshkosh, WI — B
U of Wisconsin–Parkside, WI — B
U of Wisconsin–Platteville, WI — B
U of Wisconsin–Stevens Point, WI — B
U of Wisconsin–Superior, WI — B
U of Wisconsin–Whitewater, WI — B
Valparaiso U, IN — B
Wartburg Coll, IA — B
Washington U in St. Louis, MO — B
Webster U, MO — B
Westminster Coll, MO — B
Wheaton Coll, IL — B
William Jewell Coll, MO — B
William Woods U, MO — B
Winona State U, MN — B
Wright State U, OH — B
Xavier U, OH — B

Islamic Studies

East-West U, IL — B
The Ohio State U, OH — B
U of Michigan, MI — B
Washington U in St. Louis, MO — B

Italian

DePaul U, IL — B
Dominican U, IL — B
Indiana U Bloomington, IN — B
Loyola U Chicago, IL — B
Northwestern U, IL — B
Oakland U, MI — B
The Ohio State U, OH — B
U of Chicago, IL — B
U of Illinois at Chicago, IL — B
U of Illinois at Urbana–Champaign, IL — B
The U of Iowa, IA — B
U of Michigan, MI — B

U of Minnesota, Twin Cities Campus, MN — B
U of Notre Dame, IN — B
U of Wisconsin–Madison, WI — B
U of Wisconsin–Milwaukee, WI — B
Washington U in St. Louis, MO — B
Youngstown State U, OH — B

Italian Studies

Miami U, OH — B
Southern Methodist U, TX — B

Japanese

Antioch Coll, OH — B
Aquinas Coll, MI — B
Augustana Coll, IL — B
Ball State U, IN — B
DePaul U, IL — B
Eastern Michigan U, MI — B
Gustavus Adolphus Coll, MN — B
Hope Coll, MI — B
Indiana U Bloomington, IN — B
Lawrence U, WI — B
Mount Union Coll, OH — B
North Central Coll, IL — B
The Ohio State U, OH — B
U of Chicago, IL — B
The U of Findlay, OH — B
The U of Iowa, IA — B
U of Michigan, MI — B
U of Minnesota, Twin Cities Campus, MN — B
U of Notre Dame, IN — B
U of St. Thomas, MN — B
U of Wisconsin–Madison, WI — B
Washington U in St. Louis, MO — B

Japanese Studies

Case Western Reserve U, OH — B
Earlham Coll, IN — B
Gustavus Adolphus Coll, MN — B

Jazz

Hope Coll, MI — B
The U of Akron, OH — B

Jazz/Jazz Studies

Augustana Coll, IL — B
Bowling Green State U, OH — B
Capital U, OH — B
Central State U, OH — B
DePaul U, IL — B
Drake U, IA — B
Hope Coll, MI — B
Indiana U Bloomington, IN — B
Indiana U South Bend, IN — A
Michigan State U, MI — B
North Central Coll, IL — B
Northwestern U, IL — B
Oberlin Coll, OH — B
The Ohio State U, OH — B
Roosevelt U, IL — B
St. Cloud State U, MN — B
U of Cincinnati, OH — B
The U of Iowa, IA — B
U of Michigan, MI — B
U of Minnesota, Duluth, MN — B

Jewish/Judaic Studies

DePaul U, IL — B
Hamline U, MN — B
Indiana U Bloomington, IN — B
Oberlin Coll, OH — B
The Ohio State U, OH — B
U of Chicago, IL — B
U of Cincinnati, OH — B

U of Michigan, MI — B
U of Minnesota, Twin Cities Campus, MN — B
Washington U in St. Louis, MO — B

Journalism

Andrews U, MI — B
Ashford U, IA — B
Ashland U, OH — B
Augustana Coll, SD — B
Ball State U, IN — A,B
Bemidji State U, MN — B
Bowling Green State U, OH — B
Bradley U, IL — B
Butler U, IN — B
Carroll Coll, WI — B
Central Michigan U, MI — B
Cincinnati Christian U, OH — B
Coll of St. Catherine, MN — B
Coll of the Ozarks, MO — B
Columbia Coll Chicago, IL — B
Concordia Coll, MN — B
Concordia U, MI — B
Creighton U, NE — B
Dordt Coll, IA — B
Drake U, IA — B
Drury U, MO — B
Eastern Illinois U, IL — B
Eastern Michigan U, MI — B
Evangel U, MO — A,B
Fort Hays State U, KS — B
Franklin Coll, IN — B
Goshen Coll, IN — B
Grace Coll, IN — B
Grand Valley State U, MI — B
Grand View Coll, IA — B
Hastings Coll, NE — B
Huntington U, IN — B
Illinois State U, IL — B
Indiana State U, IN — B
Indiana U Bloomington, IN — B
Indiana U–Purdue U Indianapolis, IN — B
Indiana U Southeast, IN — A
Iowa State U of Science and Technology, IA — B
Judson Coll, IL — B
Kansas State U, KS — B
Kent State U, OH — B
Langston U, OK — B
Lewis U, IL — B
Lincoln U, MO — B
Lindenwood U, MO — B
Loras Coll, IA — B
Loyola U Chicago, IL — B
Madonna U, MI — A,B
Manchester Coll, IN — A
Marietta Coll, OH — B
Marquette U, WI — B
Miami U, OH — B
Miami U Hamilton, OH — B
Michigan State U, MI — B
Minnesota State U Mankato, MN — B
Missouri State U, MO — B
Mount Vernon Nazarene U, OH — B
North Central Coll, IL — B
Northeastern State U, OK — B
Northern Illinois U, IL — B
Northwestern Coll, MN — B
Northwestern U, IL — B
Northwest Missouri State U, MO — B
Oakland U, MI — B
Ohio Northern U, OH — B

The Ohio State U, OH — B
Ohio U, OH — B
Ohio Wesleyan U, OH — B
Oklahoma Christian U, OK — B
Oklahoma City U, OK — B
Oklahoma State U, OK — B
Oral Roberts U, OK — B
Otterbein Coll, OH — B
Purdue U Calumet, IN — B
Quincy U, IL — B
Roosevelt U, IL — B
St. Ambrose U, IA — B
St. Cloud State U, MN — B
St. Gregory's U, Shawnee, OK — B
Saint Mary-of-the-Woods Coll, IN — B
South Dakota State U, SD — B
Southern Illinois U Carbondale, IL — B
Southern Methodist U, TX — B
Tabor Coll, KS — B
Truman State U, MO — B
Turtle Mountain Comm Coll, ND — A
Union Coll, NE — B
U of Central Missouri, MO — B
U of Central Oklahoma, OK — B
U of Dayton, OH — B
The U of Findlay, OH — B
U of Illinois at Urbana–Champaign, IL — B
The U of Iowa, IA — B
U of Kansas, KS — B
U of Minnesota, Twin Cities Campus, MN — B
U of Missouri–Columbia, MO — B
U of Nebraska at Kearney, NE — B
U of Nebraska at Omaha, NE — B
U of Oklahoma, OK — B
U of St. Thomas, MN — B
U of Southern Indiana, IN — B
The U of Toledo, OH — B
U of Wisconsin–Eau Claire, WI — B
U of Wisconsin–Madison, WI — B
U of Wisconsin–Milwaukee, WI — B
U of Wisconsin–Oshkosh, WI — B
U of Wisconsin–River Falls, WI — B
U of Wisconsin–Superior, WI — B
U of Wisconsin–Whitewater, WI — B
Valparaiso U, IN — B
Waldorf Coll, IA — B
Wartburg Coll, IA — B
Wayne State Coll, NE — B
Webster U, MO — B
Western Illinois U, IL — B
Western Michigan U, MI — B
William Penn U, IA — B
Winona State U, MN — B
Youngstown State U, OH — B

Journalism Related

Central State U, OH — B
Grace Coll, IN — B
Kent State U, OH — B
Ohio U, OH — B
Roosevelt U, IL — B
U of Nebraska–Lincoln, NE — B
U of St. Thomas, MN — B

Juvenile Corrections

East Central U, OK — B
Harris-Stowe State U, MO — B

Kindergarten/Preschool Education

Alma Coll, MI — B
Ashford U, IA — B
Ashland U, OH — B
Augsburg Coll, MN — B
Baker Coll of Clinton Township, MI — A
Baker Coll of Muskegon, MI — A
Baker Coll of Owosso, MI — A
Ball State U, IN — B
Black Hills State U, SD — B
Bluffton U, OH — B
Bowling Green State U, OH — B
Bowling Green State U–Firelands Coll, OH — B
Bradley U, IL — B
Cardinal Stritch U, WI — B
Carroll Coll, WI — B
Central Christian Coll of Kansas, KS — A
Central Methodist U, MO — B
Central State U, OH — B
Chicago State U, IL — B
Cincinnati Christian U, OH — B
Clarke Coll, IA — B
Coll of Mount St. Joseph, OH — A,B
Coll of St. Catherine, MN — B
Columbia Coll Chicago, IL — B
Concordia Coll, MN — B
Concordia U, IL — B
Concordia U, NE — B
Concordia U, St. Paul, MN — B
Concordia U Wisconsin, WI — B
Concord U, WV — B
Crown Coll, MN — A,B
DePaul U, IL — B
East Central U, OK — B
Eastern Illinois U, IL — B
Edgewood Coll, WI — B
Elmhurst Coll, IL — B
Evangel U, MO — B
Fontbonne U, MO — B
Fort Berthold Comm Coll, ND — A
Fort Hays State U, KS — B
Goshen Coll, IN — B
Hannibal-LaGrange Coll, MO — B
Harris-Stowe State U, MO — B
Hesston Coll, KS — A
Hillsdale Coll, MI — B
Indiana U Bloomington, IN — B
Indiana U–Purdue U Indianapolis, IN — A
Indiana U South Bend, IN — A
Iowa Wesleyan Coll, IA — B
Judson Coll, IL — B
Kendall Coll, IL — A,B
Kent State U, OH — B
Kent State U, Ashtabula Campus, OH — A
Lakeland Coll, WI — B
Langston U, OK — B
Lindenwood U, MO — B
Loras Coll, IA — B
Lourdes Coll, OH — A,B
Manchester Coll, IN — A
Maranatha Baptist Bible Coll, WI — A,B
Marian Coll, IN — A,B
Marian Coll of Fond du Lac, WI — B
Martin Luther Coll, MN — B
Marygrove Coll, MI — A,B
Maryville U of Saint Louis, MO — B

Metropolitan State U, MN — B
Miami U, OH — B
Miami U–Middletown Campus, OH — A
Minnesota State U Mankato, MN — B
Missouri Baptist U, MO — B
Missouri Southern State U, MO — B
Mount Mary Coll, WI — B
Mount Vernon Nazarene U, OH — B
North Carolina Ag and Tech State U, NC — B
Northeastern Illinois U, IL — B
Northeastern State U, OK — B
Northern Illinois U, IL — B
Northwestern Oklahoma State U, OK — B
Northwest Missouri State U, MO — B
Notre Dame Coll, OH — B
Oglala Lakota Coll, SD — A,B
Ohio Dominican U, OH — B
Ohio Northern U, OH — B
The Ohio State U–Mansfield Campus, OH — B
Ohio U, OH — B
Ohio Wesleyan U, OH — B
Oklahoma Christian U, OK — B
Oklahoma City U, OK — B
Oral Roberts U, OK — B
Peru State Coll, NE — B
Purdue U, IN — B
Purdue U Calumet, IN — A
Roosevelt U, IL — B
St. Cloud State U, MN — B
Saint Mary-of-the-Woods Coll, IN — B
Saint Xavier U, IL — B
Shawnee State U, OH — B
Silver Lake Coll, WI — B
Simpson Coll, IA — B
South Dakota State U, SD — B
Southeastern Oklahoma State U, OK — B
Southeast Missouri State U, MO — B
Southwest Minnesota State U, MN — B
Stephens Coll, MO — B
Tabor Coll, KS — B
Taylor U, IN — A,B
Turtle Mountain Comm Coll, ND — A
The U of Akron, OH — B
U of Central Oklahoma, OK — B
U of Cincinnati, OH — B
U of Dayton, OH — B
U of Illinois at Urbana–Champaign, IL — B
U of Michigan–Flint, MI — B
U of Minnesota, Duluth, MN — B
U of Minnesota, Twin Cities Campus, MN — B
U of Missouri–Columbia, MO — B
U of Northern Iowa, IA — B
U of Rio Grande, OH — A
U of Sioux Falls, SD — A
The U of Toledo, OH — B
U of Wisconsin–Madison, WI — B
U of Wisconsin–Milwaukee, WI — B
U of Wisconsin–Oshkosh, WI — B
U of Wisconsin–Platteville, WI — B

U of Wisconsin–Stevens Point, WI — B
Waldorf Coll, IA — B
Walsh U, OH — B
Wartburg Coll, IA — B
Winona State U, MN — B
Wright State U, OH — B

Kinesiology and Exercise Science

Adrian Coll, MI — B
Alma Coll, MI — B
Augustana Coll, SD — B
Baker U, KS — B
Baldwin-Wallace Coll, OH — B
Ball State U, IN — B
Bethel U, MN — B
Calvin Coll, MI — B
Capital U, OH — B
Carroll Coll, WI — B
Cedarville U, OH — B
Central Christian Coll of Kansas, KS — B
Central Coll, IA — B
Cleveland State U, OH — B
Concordia Coll, MN — B
Concordia U, IL — B
Concordia U, NE — B
Concordia U, St. Paul, MN — B
Cornerstone U, MI — B
Creighton U, NE — B
Dakota State U, SD — B
DePauw U, IN — B
Dordt Coll, IA — B
Drury U, MO — B
Elmhurst Coll, IL — B
Greenville Coll, IL — B
Hamline U, MN — B
Hastings Coll, NE — B
Hope Coll, MI — B
Huntington U, IN — B
Illinois State U, IL — B
Indiana Wesleyan U, IN — B
Iowa Wesleyan Coll, IA — B
Kansas State U, KS — B
Kent State U, OH — B
Lake Superior State U, MI — B
Loras Coll, IA — B
Malone Coll, OH — B
Manchester Coll, IN — A
Marquette U, WI — B
Mayville State U, ND — B
Miami U, OH — B
Michigan State U, MI — B
Missouri Southern State U, MO — B
Mount Union Coll, OH — B
Mount Vernon Nazarene U, OH — B
Nebraska Wesleyan U, NE — B
North Central Coll, IL — B
Northwestern Coll, IA — B
Northwestern Coll, MN — B
Ohio Northern U, OH — B
The Ohio State U, OH — B
Ohio U, OH — B
Oklahoma City U, OK — B
Oklahoma Wesleyan U, OK — B
Oral Roberts U, OK — B
Saginaw Valley State U, MI — B
St. Cloud State U, MN — B
Saint Louis U, MO — B
St. Olaf Coll, MN — B
Spring Arbor U, MI — B
Transylvania U, KY — B

A—associate degree; B—bachelor's degree

Truman State U, MO — B
Union Coll, NE — B
U of Dayton, OH — B
U of Evansville, IN — B
U of Illinois at Chicago, IL — B
U of Illinois at Urbana–Champaign, IL — B
U of Indianapolis, IN — B
The U of Iowa, IA — B
U of Mary, ND — B
U of Michigan, MI — B
U of Minnesota, Duluth, MN — B
U of Nebraska–Lincoln, NE — B
U of North Dakota, ND — B
U of Sioux Falls, SD — B
U of Southern Indiana, IN — B
The U of Toledo, OH — B
U of Tulsa, OK — B
U of Wisconsin–Eau Claire, WI — B
U of Wisconsin–La Crosse, WI — B
U of Wisconsin–Superior, WI — B
Upper Iowa U, IA — B
Valparaiso U, IN — B
Wayne State Coll, NE — B
Western Michigan U, MI — B
Winona State U, MN — B
Youngstown State U, OH — B

Labor and Industrial Relations

Cleveland State U, OH — B
Ferris State U, MI — B
Grand Valley State U, MI — B
Indiana U Bloomington, IN — A,B
Indiana U Kokomo, IN — A,B
Indiana U Northwest, IN — A,B
Indiana U–Purdue U Indianapolis, IN — A,B
Indiana U South Bend, IN — A,B
Indiana U Southeast, IN — A,B
Roosevelt U, IL — B
The U of Akron, OH — A
The U of Iowa, IA — B
U of Wisconsin–Madison, WI — B
U of Wisconsin–Milwaukee, WI — B
Winona State U, MN — B
Youngstown State U, OH — A

Labor Studies

Eastern Michigan U, MI — B
Indiana U–Purdue U Fort Wayne, IN — A,B

Landscape Architecture

Ball State U, IN — B
Iowa State U of Science and Technology, IA — B
Kansas State U, KS — B
Michigan State U, MI — B
North Carolina Ag and Tech State U, NC — B
North Dakota State U, ND — B
Northwest Missouri State U, MO — B
The Ohio State U, OH — B
Oklahoma State U, OK — B
Purdue U, IN — B
U of Illinois at Urbana–Champaign, IL — B
U of Michigan, MI — B
U of Minnesota, Twin Cities Campus, MN — B
U of Wisconsin–Madison, WI — B

Landscaping and Groundskeeping

Andrews U, MI — B

South Dakota State U, SD — B
U of Nebraska–Lincoln, NE — B

Land Use Planning and Management

Grand Valley State U, MI — B
Northland Coll, WI — B
U of Wisconsin–Platteville, WI — B
U of Wisconsin–River Falls, WI — B

Laser and Optical Technology

Indiana U Bloomington, IN — A

Latin

Augustana Coll, IL — B
Ball State U, IN — B
Butler U, IN — B
Calvin Coll, MI — B
Carleton Coll, MN — B
The Coll of Wooster, OH — B
Concordia Coll, MN — B
Cornell Coll, IA — B
Creighton U, NE — B
DePauw U, IN — B
Hope Coll, MI — B
Indiana U Bloomington, IN — B
Kent State U, OH — B
Kenyon Coll, OH — B
Lawrence U, WI — B
Loyola U Chicago, IL — B
Luther Coll, IA — B
Macalester Coll, MN — B
Miami U, OH — B
Miami U Hamilton, OH — B
Missouri State U, MO — B
Oberlin Coll, OH — B
Ohio U, OH — B
Rockford Coll, IL — B
Saint Louis U, MO — B
St. Olaf Coll, MN — B
U of Chicago, IL — B
The U of Iowa, IA — B
U of Michigan, MI — B
U of Minnesota, Twin Cities Campus, MN — B
U of Missouri–Columbia, MO — B
U of Nebraska–Lincoln, NE — B
U of Notre Dame, IN — B
U of St. Thomas, MN — B
U of Wisconsin–Madison, WI — B
U of Wisconsin–Milwaukee, WI — B
Wabash Coll, IN — B
Washington U in St. Louis, MO — B
Western Michigan U, MI — B
Wichita State U, KS — B

Latin American Studies

Ball State U, IN — B
Beloit Coll, WI — B
Carleton Coll, MN — B
Cornell Coll, IA — B
Denison U, OH — B
DePaul U, IL — B
Earlham Coll, IN — B
Gustavus Adolphus Coll, MN — B
Hamline U, MN — B
Hanover Coll, IN — B
Illinois Wesleyan U, IL — B
Indiana U Bloomington, IN — B
Kent State U, OH — B
Lake Forest Coll, IL — B
Macalester Coll, MN — B
Oakland U, MI — B
Oberlin Coll, OH — B
The Ohio State U, OH — B

Ohio U, OH — B
Ohio Wesleyan U, OH — B
Pontifical Coll Josephinum, OH — B
Ripon Coll, WI — B
St. Cloud State U, MN — B
St. Olaf Coll, MN — B
Southern Methodist U, TX — B
U of Chicago, IL — B
U of Cincinnati, OH — B
U of Illinois at Chicago, IL — B
U of Illinois at Urbana–Champaign, IL — B
The U of Iowa, IA — B
U of Kansas, KS — B
U of Michigan, MI — B
U of Minnesota, Morris, MN — B
U of Minnesota, Twin Cities Campus, MN — B
U of Missouri–Columbia, MO — B
U of Nebraska at Omaha, NE — B
U of Nebraska–Lincoln, NE — B
U of Northern Iowa, IA — B
The U of Toledo, OH — B
U of Wisconsin–Eau Claire, WI — B
U of Wisconsin–Madison, WI — B
U of Wisconsin–Milwaukee, WI — B
Washington U in St. Louis, MO — B

Latin Teacher Education

Bowling Green State U, OH — B
Hope Coll, MI — B
Kent State U, OH — B
Miami U Hamilton, OH — B
Ohio Wesleyan U, OH — B
U of Illinois at Urbana–Champaign, IL — B
The U of Iowa, IA — B
Western Michigan U, MI — B

Law and Legal Studies Related

U of Nebraska–Lincoln, NE — B

Legal Administrative Assistant

Bryant and Stratton Coll, Cleveland, OH — A

Legal Administrative Assistant/Secretary

AIB Coll of Business, IA — A
Baker Coll of Auburn Hills, MI — A
Baker Coll of Clinton Township, MI — A
Baker Coll of Flint, MI — A
Baker Coll of Jackson, MI — A
Baker Coll of Muskegon, MI — A
Baker Coll of Owosso, MI — A
Baker Coll of Port Huron, MI — A
Ball State U, IN — A,B
Dordt Coll, IA — A
Ferris State U, MI — A
International Business Coll, Fort Wayne, IN — A,B
Kent State U, Ashtabula Campus, OH — A
Lewis Coll of Business, MI — A
Miami U–Middletown Campus, OH — A
Minnesota School of Business, MN — A
Minnesota School of Business–Brooklyn Center, MN — A
Northwest Missouri State U, MO — B
Robert Morris Coll, IL — A

Rockford Business Coll, IL — A
Rogers State U, OK — A
Shawnee State U, OH — A
Tabor Coll, KS — B
The U of Akron, OH — A
U of Cincinnati, OH — A
U of Rio Grande, OH — A
The U of Toledo, OH — A
Washburn U, KS — A
Wright State U, OH — A
Youngstown State U, OH — A

Legal Assistant/Paralegal

Avila U, MO — B
Ball State U, IN — A,B
Calumet Coll of Saint Joseph, IN — B
Coll of Mount St. Joseph, OH — A,B
Coll of Saint Mary, NE — A,B
Concordia U Wisconsin, WI — B
Eastern Michigan U, MI — B
Everest Coll, Springfield, MO — B
Ferris State U, MI — A
Gannon U, PA — A,B
Grand Valley State U, MI — B
Hamline U, MN — B
Indiana U South Bend, IN — A
International Business Coll, Fort Wayne, IN — A,B
Kaplan U, IA — A,B
Lake Superior State U, MI — A,B
Madonna U, MI — A,B
Maryville U of Saint Louis, MO — B
Minnesota School of Business–Richfield, MN — A,B
Missouri Western State U, MO — A
National American U, KS — A
National American U, Rapid City, SD — A
Oglala Lakota Coll, SD — A,B
Robert Morris Coll, IL — A
Rockford Business Coll, IL — A
Rogers State U, OK — A
Roosevelt U, IL — B
Saint Mary-of-the-Woods Coll, IN — A,B
Shawnee State U, OH — A
Southern Illinois U Carbondale, IL — B
The U of Akron, OH — A
U of Cincinnati, OH — A
The U of Toledo, OH — A
Ursuline Coll, OH — B
William Woods U, MO — A,B
Winona State U, MN — B

Legal Professions and Studies Related

Bethany Coll, KS — B
U of Evansville, IN — B
U of Nebraska–Lincoln, NE — B
U of Tulsa, OK — B

Legal Studies

Aakers Coll, Fargo, ND — A
Central Christian Coll of Kansas, KS — A
Concordia U, IL — B
East Central U, OK — B
Franciscan U of Steubenville, OH — B
Gannon U, PA — B
Grand Valley State U, MI — B
Hamline U, MN — B
Hope Coll, MI — B
Indiana U–Purdue U Fort Wayne, IN — B

Kenyon Coll, OH	B
Lake Superior State U, MI	A,B
Northwestern U, IL	B
Oberlin Coll, OH	B
Ohio Dominican U, OH	A
Park U, MO	B
Pittsburg State U, KS	B
Roosevelt U, IL	B
U of Illinois at Springfield, IL	B
U of Wisconsin–Superior, WI	B
Washburn U, KS	B
Webster U, MO	B
Winona State U, MN	B

Liberal Arts and Sciences and Humanities Related

Central Christian Coll of Kansas, KS	B
Ferris State U, MI	B
Malone Coll, OH	B
Ohio U, OH	B
Shimer Coll, IL	B
Southwestern Coll, KS	B
The U of Akron, OH	A,B
U of Nebraska–Lincoln, NE	B
U of North Dakota, ND	B
U of Wisconsin–Whitewater, WI	B
Wright State U, OH	B

Liberal Arts and Sciences/ Liberal Studies

Alma Coll, MI	B
Alverno Coll, WI	A,B
Andrews U, MI	B
Antioch U McGregor, OH	B
Aquinas Coll, MI	B
Ashford U, IA	A,B
Ashland U, OH	A,B
Augsburg Coll, MN	B
Augustana Coll, IL	B
Augustana Coll, SD	B
Ball State U, IN	A,B
Bemidji State U, MN	A,B
Benedictine Coll, KS	B
Bethany Lutheran Coll, MN	A,B
Bethel U, MN	A
Blackburn Coll, IL	B
Bowling Green State U, OH	B
Bowling Green State U–Firelands Coll, OH	A
Bradley U, IL	B
Briar Cliff U, IA	A
Butler U, IN	A
Calumet Coll of Saint Joseph, IN	A,B
Capital U, OH	B
Cardinal Stritch U, WI	A,B
Central Christian Coll of Kansas, KS	B
Chicago State U, IL	B
Clarke Coll, IA	A
Clarkson U, NY	B
Cleveland State U, OH	B
Coe Coll, IA	B
Coll of Menominee Nation, WI	A
Coll of Mount St. Joseph, OH	B
Coll of Saint Benedict, MN	B
Coll of St. Catherine, MN	A
The Coll of St. Scholastica, MN	B
Columbia Coll, MO	A,B
Columbia Coll Chicago, IL	B
Conception Seminary Coll, MO	B

Concordia U Wisconsin, WI	B
Cornell Coll, IA	B
Cottey Coll, MO	A
Crossroads Coll, MN	A,B
Crown Coll, MN	A,B
Dakota Wesleyan U, SD	A
Dickinson State U, ND	A,B
Eastern Illinois U, IL	B
East-West U, IL	A
Edgewood Coll, WI	A,B
Ferris State U, MI	A
Finlandia U, MI	B
Fontbonne U, MO	B
Fort Berthold Comm Coll, ND	A
Fort Hays State U, KS	B
Gannon U, PA	A,B
Goshen Coll, IN	B
Grace Bible Coll, MI	A
Graceland U, IA	B
Grand Valley State U, MI	B
Grand View Coll, IA	A,B
Greenville Coll, IL	B
Hannibal-LaGrange Coll, MO	B
Hastings Coll, NE	B
Hesston Coll, KS	A
Hillsdale Free Will Baptist Coll, OK	A
Holy Cross Coll, IN	A,B
Hope Coll, MI	B
Illinois Coll, IL	B
Indiana State U, IN	A,B
Iowa State U of Science and Technology, IA	B
Iowa Wesleyan Coll, IA	B
Kent State U, OH	A,B
Kent State U, Ashtabula Campus, OH	A
Kent State U, Geauga Campus, OH	A
Kent State U, Trumbull Campus, OH	A
Kent State U, Tuscarawas Campus, OH	A,B
Kilian Comm Coll, SD	A
Kuyper Coll, MI	A
Lake Superior State U, MI	A
Langston U, OK	B
Leech Lake Tribal Coll, MN	A
Lewis Coll of Business, MI	A
Lewis U, IL	B
Lindenwood U, MO	B
Loras Coll, IA	A,B
Lourdes Coll, OH	A,B
MacMurray Coll, IL	B
Maranatha Baptist Bible Coll, WI	B
Marian Coll, IN	A
Marian Coll of Fond du Lac, WI	B
Marietta Coll, OH	A,B
Marygrove Coll, MI	A
Maryville U of Saint Louis, MO	B
Metropolitan State U, MN	B
Miami U–Middletown Campus, OH	A
Michigan Technological U, MI	B
Minnesota State U Mankato, MN	A,B
Missouri Valley Coll, MO	A,B
Mount Marty Coll, SD	A,B
Mount Mary Coll, WI	B
National American U, Rapid City, SD	A
Newman U, KS	A,B

North Central Coll, IL	B
Northeastern Illinois U, IL	B
Northern Illinois U, IL	B
Northern Michigan U, MI	A
Northern State U, SD	A
Northwestern Coll, MN	A
Northwestern U, IL	B
Oglala Lakota Coll, SD	A
Ohio Dominican U, OH	B
The Ohio State U at Lima, OH	A
The Ohio State U at Marion, OH	A
The Ohio State U–Mansfield Campus, OH	A
The Ohio State U–Newark Campus, OH	A
Ohio U, OH	A,B
Ohio U–Zanesville, OH	A,B
Oklahoma Christian U, OK	B
Oklahoma City U, OK	B
Oklahoma State U, OK	B
Oklahoma Wesleyan U, OK	A
Oral Roberts U, OK	B
Park U, MO	A,B
Purdue U North Central, IN	B
Rochester Coll, MI	A
Rogers State U, OK	A,B
Roosevelt U, IL	B
Sacred Heart Major Seminary, MI	B
Saginaw Chippewa Tribal Coll, MI	A
St. Augustine Coll, IL	A
St. Cloud State U, MN	A,B
St. Gregory's U, Shawnee, OK	A,B
Saint Mary-of-the-Woods Coll, IN	A,B
St. Olaf Coll, MN	B
Saint Xavier U, IL	B
Shimer Coll, IL	B
Sitting Bull Coll, ND	A
Southern Illinois U Carbondale, IL	B
Southern Illinois U Edwardsville, IL	B
Southwestern Coll, KS	B
Spring Arbor U, MI	A
Stephens Coll, MO	A,B
Taylor U Fort Wayne, IN	A
Trinity International U, IL	B
Tri-State U, IN	A
Turtle Mountain Comm Coll, ND	A
The U of Akron, OH	A,B
U of Central Oklahoma, OK	B
U of Chicago, IL	B
U of Cincinnati, OH	A,B
U of Evansville, IN	B
U of Illinois at Springfield, IL	B
U of Illinois at Urbana–Champaign, IL	B
U of Indianapolis, IN	A,B
The U of Iowa, IA	B
U of Kansas, KS	B
U of Michigan–Dearborn, MI	B
U of Michigan–Flint, MI	B
U of Minnesota, Morris, MN	B
U of Missouri–Kansas City, MO	B
U of Missouri–St. Louis, MO	B
U of Nebraska–Lincoln, NE	B
U of Northern Iowa, IA	B
U of Notre Dame, IN	B
U of Oklahoma, OK	B

U of St. Francis, IL	B
U of Saint Francis, IN	A,B
U of Saint Mary, KS	A,B
U of Sioux Falls, SD	B
The U of South Dakota, SD	B
U of Southern Indiana, IN	B
The U of Toledo, OH	A,B
U of Tulsa, OK	B
U of West Florida, FL	A
U of Wisconsin–Eau Claire, WI	A
U of Wisconsin–Oshkosh, WI	A,B
U of Wisconsin–Platteville, WI	A,B
U of Wisconsin–River Falls, WI	B
U of Wisconsin–Stevens Point, WI	A
U of Wisconsin–Whitewater, WI	A,B
Upper Iowa U, IA	A
Viterbo U, WI	B
Walsh U, OH	A,B
Washburn U, KS	A,B
Washington U in St. Louis, MO	B
Webster U, MO	B
Western Illinois U, IL	B
Wichita State U, KS	B
Wilmington Coll, OH	B
Winona State U, MN	B
Wittenberg U, OH	B
Wright State U, OH	B
Xavier U, OH	A,B
York Coll, NE	A,B
Youngstown State U, OH	A,B

Library Assistant

Ohio Dominican U, OH	A

Library Science

Concord U, WV	B
Hope Coll, MI	B
Northeastern State U, OK	B
St. Cloud State U, MN	B
U of Nebraska at Omaha, NE	B
U of Oklahoma, OK	B

Library Science Related

Bethel U, MN	B

Linguistics

Central Coll, IA	B
Cleveland State U, OH	B
Crown Coll, MN	B
Eastern Michigan U, MI	B
Indiana U Bloomington, IN	B
Iowa State U of Science and Technology, IA	B
Judson Coll, IL	B
Lawrence U, WI	B
Macalester Coll, MN	B
Miami U, OH	B
Miami U Hamilton, OH	B
Northeastern Illinois U, IL	B
Northwestern U, IL	B
Oakland U, MI	B
The Ohio State U, OH	B
Ohio U, OH	B
Oklahoma Wesleyan U, OK	A,B
St. Cloud State U, MN	B
Southern Illinois U Carbondale, IL	B
U of Chicago, IL	B
U of Cincinnati, OH	B
U of Illinois at Urbana–Champaign, IL	B
The U of Iowa, IA	B

A—associate degree; B—bachelor's degree

U of Kansas, KS	B
U of Michigan, MI	B
U of Minnesota, Twin Cities Campus, MN	B
U of Missouri–Columbia, MO	B
U of Oklahoma, OK	B
The U of Toledo, OH	B
U of Wisconsin–Madison, WI	B
U of Wisconsin–Milwaukee, WI	B
Wright State U, OH	B

Linguistics of ASL and Other Sign Languages

Kent State U, OH	B

Literature

Antioch Coll, OH	B
Augustana Coll, IL	B
Beloit Coll, WI	B
Blackburn Coll, IL	B
Capital U, OH	B
Chicago State U, IL	B
Coe Coll, IA	B
Coll of St. Catherine, MN	B
DePaul U, IL	B
East Central U, OK	B
Graceland U, IA	B
Grand Valley State U, MI	B
Hastings Coll, NE	B
Judson Coll, IL	B
Kenyon Coll, OH	B
Lake Superior State U, MI	B
Manchester Coll, IN	A
Minnesota State U Mankato, MN	B
Morningside Coll, IA	B
Northwest Missouri State U, MO	B
Ohio Wesleyan U, OH	B
Otterbein Coll, OH	B
Purdue U Calumet, IN	B
Rochester Coll, MI	B
Rockford Coll, IL	B
Roosevelt U, IL	B
Shimer Coll, IL	B
Southwest Minnesota State U, MN	B
Taylor U, IN	B
The U of Akron, OH	B
U of Cincinnati, OH	B
The U of Iowa, IA	B
U of Missouri–St. Louis, MO	B
The U of Toledo, OH	B
U of Wisconsin–Milwaukee, WI	B
Washington U in St. Louis, MO	B
Wayne State Coll, NE	B
Webster U, MO	B

Logistics and Materials Management

Bowling Green State U, OH	B
Central Michigan U, MI	B
Clarkson U, NY	B
Elmhurst Coll, IL	B
Iowa State U of Science and Technology, IA	B
Michigan State U, MI	B
The Ohio State U, OH	B
Park U, MO	A,B
The U of Akron, OH	A
The U of Findlay, OH	B
The U of Toledo, OH	A,B
Western Michigan U, MI	B
Wright State U, OH	B

Machine Tool Technology

Ferris State U, MI	A
Missouri Southern State U, MO	A

Management Information Systems

Academy Coll, MN	A
Augsburg Coll, MN	B
Augustana Coll, SD	B
Aurora U, IL	B
Baker Coll of Flint, MI	B
Baldwin-Wallace Coll, OH	B
Ball State U, IN	B
Bellevue U, NE	B
Bethel Coll, KS	B
Bowling Green State U, OH	B
Bradley U, IL	B
Briar Cliff U, IA	B
Buena Vista U, IA	B
Calvin Coll, MI	B
Cameron U, OK	A
Central Michigan U, MI	B
Central State U, OH	B
Chicago State U, IL	B
Clarke Coll, IA	B
Clarkson U, NY	B
Cleary U, MI	B
Coll of St. Catherine, MN	B
Concordia U, NE	B
Concordia U, St. Paul, MN	B
Cornerstone U, MI	B
Creighton U, NE	B
Dana Coll, NE	B
Davenport U, Dearborn, MI	A,B
DePaul U, IL	B
Dordt Coll, IA	B
East Central U, OK	B
Eastern Michigan U, MI	B
Elmhurst Coll, IL	B
Ferris State U, MI	B
Fontbonne U, MO	B
Gannon U, PA	B
Grace Coll, IN	B
Graceland U, IA	B
Grand Valley State U, MI	B
Grand View Coll, IA	B
Greenville Coll, IL	B
Herzing Coll, MN	B
Illinois Coll, IL	B
Indiana State U, IN	B
Indiana U Bloomington, IN	B
Iowa State U of Science and Technology, IA	B
Jamestown Coll, ND	B
Judson Coll, IL	B
Kaplan U, IA	B
Kettering U, MI	B
Lake Superior State U, MI	A
Lewis U, IL	B
Lindenwood U, MO	B
Loras Coll, IA	B
Loyola U Chicago, IL	B
Luther Coll, IA	B
MacMurray Coll, IL	B
Madonna U, MI	B
Marquette U, WI	B
Maryville U of Saint Louis, MO	B
Metropolitan State U, MN	B
Miami U, OH	B
Miami U Hamilton, OH	A
Miami U–Middletown Campus, OH	A
Michigan Technological U, MI	B
Millikin U, IL	B

Milwaukee School of Engineering, WI	B
Minot State U, ND	B
Missouri State U, MO	B
Morningside Coll, IA	B
National American U, Rapid City, SD	B
Newman U, KS	B
North Central Coll, IL	B
Northern Illinois U, IL	B
Northern Michigan U, MI	A,B
Northern State U, SD	B
Northwestern Coll, MN	B
Northwest Missouri State U, MO	B
Northwood U, MI	A,B
Oakland U, MI	B
The Ohio State U, OH	B
Oklahoma City U, OK	B
Oklahoma State U, OK	B
Oral Roberts U, OK	B
Park U, MO	B
Peru State Coll, NE	B
Robert Morris Coll, IL	A
Rockford Coll, IL	B
St. Augustine Coll, IL	A
St. Gregory's U, Shawnee, OK	B
Saint Joseph's Coll, IN	A,B
Saint Louis U, MO	B
Saint Mary's Coll, IN	B
Shawnee State U, OH	A,B
Southern Illinois U Edwardsville, IL	B
Southwestern Coll, KS	B
Spring Arbor U, MI	B
Taylor U, IN	A
Trinity Christian Coll, IL	B
Tri-State U, IN	B
The U of Akron, OH	B
U of Central Missouri, MO	B
U of Cincinnati, OH	B
U of Dayton, OH	B
U of Illinois at Chicago, IL	B
The U of Iowa, IA	B
U of Mary, ND	B
U of Michigan–Dearborn, MI	B
U of Minnesota, Twin Cities Campus, MN	B
U of Missouri–Columbia, MO	B
U of Missouri–St. Louis, MO	B
U of Nebraska at Omaha, NE	B
U of New Orleans, LA	B
U of Northern Iowa, IA	B
U of Notre Dame, IN	B
U of Oklahoma, OK	B
U of Phoenix–Chicago Campus, IL	B
U of Phoenix–Cincinnati Campus, OH	B
U of Phoenix–Cleveland Campus, OH	B
U of Phoenix–Columbus Ohio Campus, OH	B
U of Phoenix–Indianapolis Campus, IN	B
U of Phoenix–Metro Detroit Campus, MI	B
U of Phoenix–Oklahoma City Campus, OK	B
U of Phoenix–St. Louis Campus, MO	B
U of Phoenix–Springfield Campus, MO	B
U of Phoenix–Tulsa Campus, OK	B

U of Phoenix–West Michigan Campus, MI	B
U of Phoenix–Wisconsin Campus, WI	B
U of Sioux Falls, SD	B
The U of Toledo, OH	B
U of Tulsa, OK	B
U of West Florida, FL	B
U of Wisconsin–La Crosse, WI	B
U of Wisconsin–Milwaukee, WI	B
U of Wisconsin–Oshkosh, WI	B
U of Wisconsin–River Falls, WI	B
U of Wisconsin–Whitewater, WI	B
Upper Iowa U, IA	B
Ursuline Coll, OH	B
Viterbo U, WI	B
Webster U, MO	B
Western Illinois U, IL	B
Westminster Coll, MO	B
Wichita State U, KS	B
William Woods U, MO	B
Winona State U, MN	B
Wright State U, OH	A,B
Xavier U, OH	B
Youngstown State U, OH	B

Management Information Systems and Services Related

Bowling Green State U, OH	B
Buena Vista U, IA	B
Carroll Coll, WI	B
Coll of Mount St. Joseph, OH	A,B
Lewis U, IL	B
Purdue U, IN	A,B
Rogers State U, OK	B
Southeastern Oklahoma State U, OK	B
U of Southern Indiana, IN	A

Management Science

Capella U, MN	B
Central Methodist U, MO	B
Columbia Coll, MO	B
Grace Bible Coll, MI	B
Lourdes Coll, OH	B
Madonna U, MI	B
Miami U, OH	B
Minnesota State U Mankato, MN	B
Ohio Northern U, OH	B
Oklahoma State U, OK	B
Oral Roberts U, OK	B
Roosevelt U, IL	B
St. Ambrose U, IA	B
St. Gregory's U, Shawnee, OK	B
Southeastern Oklahoma State U, OK	B
Southern Illinois U Carbondale, IL	B
Southern Methodist U, TX	B
Southwestern Coll, KS	B
Trinity International U, IL	B
The U of Iowa, IA	B
U of Mary, ND	B
U of Minnesota, Morris, MN	B
U of Missouri–St. Louis, MO	B
U of Nebraska–Lincoln, NE	B
U of Phoenix–Chicago Campus, IL	B
U of Phoenix–Cincinnati Campus, OH	B
U of Phoenix–Cleveland Campus, OH	B

U of Phoenix–Columbus Ohio
Campus, OH — B
U of Phoenix–Kansas City
Campus, MO — B
U of Phoenix–Metro Detroit
Campus, MI — B
U of Phoenix–Oklahoma City
Campus, OK — B
U of Phoenix–St. Louis
Campus, MO — B
U of Phoenix–Springfield
Campus, MO — B
U of Phoenix–Tulsa Campus,
OK — B
U of Phoenix–West Michigan
Campus, MI — B
U of Phoenix–Wisconsin
Campus, WI — B
Valparaiso U, IN — B
Wright State U, OH — B

Management Sciences and Quantitative Methods Related
Indiana State U, IN — B
Ohio Northern U, OH — B
The U of Iowa, IA — B
The U of Toledo, OH — B
Valparaiso U, IN — B

Manufacturing Engineering
Clarkson U, NY — B
North Dakota State U, ND — B
Northwestern U, IL — B
Southern Illinois U
Edwardsville, IL — B
U of Michigan–Dearborn, MI — B
U of Missouri–Rolla, MO — B
U of Wisconsin–Stout, WI — B
Western Michigan U, MI — B
Wichita State U, KS — B

Manufacturing Technology
Eastern Michigan U, MI — B
Illinois Inst of Technology, IL — B
Lawrence Technological U, MI — A
Missouri Western State U, MO — A
Northern Michigan U, MI — B
Southwestern Coll, KS — B
U of Nebraska at Omaha, NE — B
U of Northern Iowa, IA — B
Western Illinois U, IL — B

Marine Biology
Michigan Technological U, MI — B

Marine Biology and Biological Oceanography
Ball State U, IN — B
Bemidji State U, MN — B
Missouri Southern State U,
MO — B
Southwestern Coll, KS — B
U of West Florida, FL — B

Marketing/Marketing Management
AIB Coll of Business, IA — A
Alma Coll, MI — B
Alverno Coll, WI — B
Anderson U, IN — B
Andrews U, MI — B
Ashland U, OH — B
Augsburg Coll, MN — B
Augustana Coll, IL — B
Aurora U, IL — B
Avila U, MO — B
Baker Coll of Allen Park, MI — A

Baker Coll of Auburn Hills, MI — A,B
Baker Coll of Cadillac, MI — A
Baker Coll of Clinton
Township, MI — A
Baker Coll of Flint, MI — A,B
Baker Coll of Jackson, MI — A,B
Baker Coll of Muskegon, MI — A,B
Baker Coll of Owosso, MI — A,B
Baker Coll of Port Huron, MI — A,B
Baldwin-Wallace Coll, OH — B
Ball State U, IN — A,B
Bellevue U, NE — B
Benedictine U, IL — B
Blackburn Coll, IL — B
Black Hills State U, SD — B
Bradley U, IL — B
Buena Vista U, IA — B
Butler U, IN — B
Capital U, OH — B
Carroll Coll, WI — B
Cedarville U, OH — B
Central Christian Coll of
Kansas, KS — A
Central Michigan U, MI — B
Central State U, OH — B
Chicago State U, IL — B
Clarke Coll, IA — B
Clarkson U, NY — B
Cleary U, MI — B
Cleveland State U, OH — B
Coll of St. Catherine, MN — B
The Coll of St. Scholastica,
MN — B
Coll of the Ozarks, MO — B
Columbia Coll, MO — B
Columbia Coll Chicago, IL — B
Concordia U Wisconsin, WI — B
Cornerstone U, MI — B
Creighton U, NE — B
Dakota State U, SD — B
Dakota Wesleyan U, SD — B
Davenport U, Dearborn, MI — A,B
DePaul U, IL — B
Dickinson State U, ND — B
Drake U, IA — B
Drury U, MO — B
East Central U, OK — B
Eastern Illinois U, IL — B
Eastern Michigan U, MI — B
Elmhurst Coll, IL — B
Emporia State U, KS — B
Evangel U, MO — B
Ferris State U, MI — B
Fontbonne U, MO — B
Fort Berthold Comm Coll, ND — A
Fort Hays State U, KS — B
Gannon U, PA — B
Grace Bible Coll, MI — B
Grand Valley State U, MI — B
Greenville Coll, IL — B
Hannibal-LaGrange Coll, MO — B
Harris-Stowe State U, MO — B
Hastings Coll, NE — B
Hillsdale Coll, MI — B
Illinois State U, IL — B
Indiana State U, IN — B
Indiana Tech, IN — B
Indiana U Bloomington, IN — B
Indiana U–Purdue U Fort
Wayne, IN — B
Indiana U South Bend, IN — B
Indiana Wesleyan U, IN — B
Iowa State U of Science and
Technology, IA — B
Jamestown Coll, ND — B

Kansas State U, KS — B
Kendall Coll, IL — B
Kent State U, OH — B
Kent State U, Ashtabula
Campus, OH — A
Kettering U, MI — B
Lakeland Coll, WI — B
Lewis U, IL — B
Lincoln U, MO — B
Lindenwood U, MO — B
Loras Coll, IA — B
Loyola U Chicago, IL — B
MacMurray Coll, IL — B
Madonna U, MI — B
Manchester Coll, IN — B
Marian Coll of Fond du Lac,
WI — B
Marietta Coll, OH — B
Marquette U, WI — B
Marygrove Coll, MI — B
Maryville U of Saint Louis,
MO — B
McKendree Coll, IL — B
Metropolitan State U, MN — B
Miami U, OH — B
Miami U Hamilton, OH — A
Miami U–Middletown Campus,
OH — A
Michigan State U, MI — B
Michigan Technological U, MI — B
Millikin U, IL — B
Minnesota State U Mankato,
MN — B
Minot State U, ND — B
Missouri Baptist U, MO — B
Missouri Southern State U,
MO — B
Missouri State U, MO — B
Missouri Valley Coll, MO — B
Missouri Western State U, MO — B
Morningside Coll, IA — B
Mount Mary Coll, WI — B
Mount Mercy Coll, IA — B
Mount Vernon Nazarene U,
OH — B
National American U, Rapid
City, SD — B
Newman U, KS — B
North Central Coll, IL — B
Northeastern Illinois U, IL — B
Northeastern State U, OK — B
Northern Illinois U, IL — B
Northern Michigan U, MI — B
Northern State U, SD — B
Northwestern Coll, MN — B
Northwest Missouri State U,
MO — B
Northwood U, MI — B
Notre Dame Coll, OH — B
Oakland U, MI — B
The Ohio State U, OH — B
Oklahoma Christian U, OK — B
Oklahoma City U, OK — B
Oklahoma State U, OK — B
Oral Roberts U, OK — B
Otterbein Coll, OH — B
Park U, MO — B
Peru State Coll, NE — B
Pittsburg State U, KS — B
Purdue U Calumet, IN — B
Purdue U North Central, IN — A
Quincy U, IL — B
Rochester Coll, MI — B
Rockford Business Coll, IL — A
Rockford Coll, IL — B

Roosevelt U, IL — B
St. Ambrose U, IA — B
St. Cloud State U, MN — B
St. Gregory's U, Shawnee, OK — B
Saint Louis U, MO — B
Saint Mary-of-the-Woods Coll,
IN — B
Saint Mary's Coll, IN — B
Saint Mary's U of Minnesota,
MN — B
Sitting Bull Coll, ND — A
Southeastern Oklahoma State
U, OK — B
Southeast Missouri State U,
MO — B
Southern Illinois U
Carbondale, IL — B
Southern Methodist U, TX — B
Southwestern Oklahoma State
U, OK — B
Southwest Minnesota State U,
MN — A,B
Stephens Coll, MO — B
Tabor Coll, KS — B
Taylor U, IN — B
Tiffin U, OH — B
Trinity Christian Coll, IL — B
Trinity International U, IL — B
Tri-State U, IN — B
Turtle Mountain Comm Coll,
ND — A
The U of Akron, OH — B
U of Central Missouri, MO — B
U of Central Oklahoma, OK — B
U of Charleston, WV — B
U of Cincinnati, OH — A,B
U of Dayton, OH — B
U of Evansville, IN — B
The U of Findlay, OH — B
U of Illinois at Chicago, IL — B
U of Indianapolis, IN — B
The U of Iowa, IA — B
U of Michigan–Dearborn, MI — B
U of Michigan–Flint, MI — B
U of Minnesota, Duluth, MN — B
U of Minnesota, Twin Cities
Campus, MN — B
U of Missouri–Columbia, MO — B
U of Missouri–St. Louis, MO — B
U of Nebraska at Omaha, NE — B
U of Nebraska–Lincoln, NE — B
U of New Orleans, LA — B
U of North Dakota, ND — B
U of Northern Iowa, IA — B
U of Notre Dame, IN — B
U of Oklahoma, OK — B
U of Phoenix–Chicago
Campus, IL — B
U of Phoenix–Cincinnati
Campus, OH — B
U of Phoenix–Cleveland
Campus, OH — B
U of Phoenix–Columbus Ohio
Campus, OH — B
U of Phoenix–Indianapolis
Campus, IN — B
U of Phoenix–Kansas City
Campus, MO — B
U of Phoenix–Metro Detroit
Campus, MI — B
U of Phoenix–Oklahoma City
Campus, OK — B
U of Phoenix–St. Louis
Campus, MO — B

A—associate degree; B—bachelor's degree

U of Phoenix–Springfield Campus, MO — B
U of Phoenix–Tulsa Campus, OK — B
U of Phoenix–West Michigan Campus, MI — B
U of Phoenix–Wisconsin Campus, WI — B
U of Rio Grande, OH — B
U of St. Francis, IL — B
U of Saint Francis, IN — B
U of St. Thomas, MN — B
U of Sioux Falls, SD — A,B
The U of South Dakota, SD — B
U of Southern Indiana, IN — B
The U of Toledo, OH — B
U of Tulsa, OK — B
U of West Florida, FL — B
U of Wisconsin–Eau Claire, WI — B
U of Wisconsin–La Crosse, WI — B
U of Wisconsin–Milwaukee, WI — B
U of Wisconsin–Oshkosh, WI — B
U of Wisconsin–River Falls, WI — B
U of Wisconsin–Superior, WI — B
U of Wisconsin–Whitewater, WI — B
Upper Iowa U, IA — B
Ursuline Coll, OH — B
Valparaiso U, IN — B
Viterbo U, WI — B
Waldorf Coll, IA — B
Walsh U, OH — A,B
Wartburg Coll, IA — B
Washburn U, KS — B
Washington U in St. Louis, MO — B
Webster U, MO — B
Western Illinois U, IL — B
Western Michigan U, MI — B
Wichita State U, KS — B
Wilmington Coll, OH — B
Winona State U, MN — B
Wright State U, OH — A,B
Xavier U, OH — B
Youngstown State U, OH — A,B

Marketing Related
Bowling Green State U, OH — B
Capella U, MN — B
Central Michigan U, MI — B
Miami U Hamilton, OH — B
The U of Akron, OH — B
U of Illinois at Urbana–Champaign, IL — B
The U of Iowa, IA — B
Washington U in St. Louis, MO — B
Western Michigan U, MI — B

Marketing Research
Ashland U, OH — B
Baker Coll of Jackson, MI — B
Saginaw Valley State U, MI — B
The U of Toledo, OH — B

Massage Therapy
Herzing Coll, MN — A
Mercy Coll of Northwest Ohio, OH — A
Minnesota School of Business, MN — A
Minnesota School of Business–Brooklyn Center, MN — A
Minnesota School of Business–Plymouth, MN — A

Minnesota School of Business–Richfield, MN — A
Minnesota School of Business–St. Cloud, MN — A
Minnesota School of Business–Shakopee, MN — A
Ohio Coll of Massotherapy, OH — A

Mass Communication/Media
Adrian Coll, MI — A,B
Albion Coll, MI — B
Anderson U, IN — B
Andrews U, MI — B
Antioch Coll, OH — B
Ashland U, OH — B
Augsburg Coll, MN — B
Augustana Coll, IL — B
Baker U, KS — B
Baldwin-Wallace Coll, OH — B
Beloit Coll, WI — B
Bemidji State U, MN — B
Benedictine Coll, KS — B
Bethel Coll, KS — B
Bethel U, MN — B
Black Hills State U, SD — A,B
Briar Cliff U, IA — B
Buena Vista U, IA — B
Calvary Bible Coll and Theological Seminary, MO — B
Calvin Coll, MI — B
Clarke Coll, IA — B
Coll of St. Catherine, MN — B
Coll of the Ozarks, MO — B
The Coll of Wooster, OH — B
Concordia Coll, MN — B
Concordia U, NE — B
Concordia U, St. Paul, MN — B
Concordia U Wisconsin, WI — B
Concord U, WV — B
Cornerstone U, MI — A,B
Culver-Stockton Coll, MO — B
Denison U, OH — B
DePaul U, IL — B
DePauw U, IN — B
Doane Coll, NE — B
Dominican U, IL — B
Dordt Coll, IA — B
Drake U, IA — B
Drury U, MO — B
East Central U, OK — B
Edgewood Coll, WI — B
Evangel U, MO — A,B
Ferris State U, MI — B
Fort Hays State U, KS — B
Goshen Coll, IN — B
Grace Coll, IN — B
Grand Valley State U, MI — B
Grand View Coll, IA — B
Greenville Coll, IL — B
Gustavus Adolphus Coll, MN — B
Hamline U, MN — B
Hanover Coll, IN — B
Hastings Coll, NE — B
Heidelberg Coll, OH — B
Hiram Coll, OH — B
Huntington U, IN — B
Illinois Coll, IL — B
Illinois State U, IL — B
Indiana U Bloomington, IN — B
Indiana U Northwest, IN — B
Indiana U South Bend, IN — B
Iowa State U of Science and Technology, IA — B
Iowa Wesleyan Coll, IA — B
Judson Coll, IL — B
Kent State U, OH — B

Langston U, OK — B
Lewis U, IL — B
Lindenwood U, MO — B
Loras Coll, IA — B
Madonna U, MI — A,B
Manchester Coll, IN — B
Marian Coll, IN — B
Marquette U, WI — B
Maryville U of Saint Louis, MO — B
McKendree Coll, IL — B
Miami U, OH — B
Miami U Hamilton, OH — B
Miami U–Middletown Campus, OH — A
Michigan State U, MI — B
Minnesota State U Mankato, MN — B
Missouri Southern State U, MO — B
Missouri State U, MO — B
Missouri Valley Coll, MO — B
Morningside Coll, IA — B
Mount Union Coll, OH — B
Newman U, KS — B
North Carolina Ag and Tech State U, NC — B
North Dakota State U, ND — B
Northern Michigan U, MI — B
Northwestern Coll, IA — B
Northwestern Oklahoma State U, OK — B
Northwest Missouri State U, MO — B
Oglala Lakota Coll, SD — A
Ohio Northern U, OH — B
Oklahoma Christian U, OK — B
Oklahoma City U, OK — B
Oklahoma Wesleyan U, OK — B
Ottawa U, KS — B
Purdue U Calumet, IN — B
St. Ambrose U, IA — B
St. Cloud State U, MN — B
Saint Joseph's Coll, IN — B
Saint Mary-of-the-Woods Coll, IN — B
Simpson Coll, IA — B
South Dakota State U, SD — B
Southern Illinois U Edwardsville, IL — B
Southwestern Oklahoma State U, OK — B
Stephens Coll, MO — B
Tabor Coll, KS — B
Taylor U, IN — B
Truman State U, MO — B
The U of Akron, OH — B
U of Cincinnati, OH — B
U of Dayton, OH — B
U of Evansville, IN — B
U of Illinois at Urbana–Champaign, IL — B
The U of Iowa, IA — B
U of Mary, ND — B
U of Michigan–Flint, MI — B
U of Minnesota, Twin Cities Campus, MN — B
U of Missouri–Columbia, MO — B
U of Missouri–Kansas City, MO — B
U of Missouri–St. Louis, MO — B
U of Nebraska at Kearney, NE — B
U of Rio Grande, OH — A,B
U of St. Francis, IL — B
U of Saint Francis, IN — B
U of Saint Mary, KS — B

U of Sioux Falls, SD — B
The U of South Dakota, SD — B
The U of Toledo, OH — B
U of Wisconsin–Eau Claire, WI — B
U of Wisconsin–Madison, WI — B
U of Wisconsin–Milwaukee, WI — B
U of Wisconsin–Oshkosh, WI — B
U of Wisconsin–Platteville, WI — B
U of Wisconsin–Superior, WI — B
Upper Iowa U, IA — B
Valley City State U, ND — B
Valparaiso U, IN — B
Waldorf Coll, IA — B
Wartburg Coll, IA — B
Washburn U, KS — B
Wayne State Coll, NE — B
William Penn U, IA — B
Wilmington Coll, OH — B
Winona State U, MN — B
Wright State U, OH — B

Mass Communications
East Central U, OK — B
Rochester Coll, MI — B
Southern Methodist U, TX — B

Materials Engineering
Case Western Reserve U, OH — B
Clarkson U, NY — B
Illinois Inst of Technology, IL — B
Iowa State U of Science and Technology, IA — B
Michigan Technological U, MI — B
Northwestern U, IL — B
The Ohio State U, OH — B
Purdue U, IN — B
U of Michigan, MI — B
U of Minnesota, Twin Cities Campus, MN — B
U of Missouri–Rolla, MO — B
U of Wisconsin–Milwaukee, WI — B
Winona State U, MN — B
Wright State U, OH — B

Materials Science
Case Western Reserve U, OH — B
Clarkson U, NY — B
Kent State U, Ashtabula Campus, OH — A
Michigan State U, MI — B
Northwestern U, IL — B
The Ohio State U, OH — B
U of Illinois at Urbana–Champaign, IL — B
U of Michigan, MI — B
U of Minnesota, Twin Cities Campus, MN — B

Mathematical Statistics and Probability
Northern Illinois U, IL — B

Mathematics
Adrian Coll, MI — B
Albion Coll, MI — B
Alma Coll, MI — B
Alverno Coll, WI — B
Anderson U, IN — B
Andrews U, MI — B
Antioch Coll, OH — B
Aquinas Coll, MI — B
Ashland U, OH — B
Augsburg Coll, MN — B
Augustana Coll, IL — B
Augustana Coll, SD — B

Majors and Degrees
Mathematics

Aurora U, IL	B	Edgewood Coll, WI	B	Marian Coll of Fond du Lac, WI	B	Purdue U North Central, IN	B

Aurora U, IL — B
Avila U, MO — B
Baker U, KS — B
Baldwin-Wallace Coll, OH — B
Ball State U, IN — B
Beloit Coll, WI — B
Bemidji State U, MN — B
Benedictine Coll, KS — B
Benedictine U, IL — B
Bethany Coll, KS — B
Bethel Coll, KS — B
Bethel U, MN — B
Blackburn Coll, IL — B
Black Hills State U, SD — B
Bluffton U, OH — B
Bowling Green State U, OH — B
Bradley U, IL — B
Briar Cliff U, IA — B
Buena Vista U, IA — B
Butler U, IN — B
Calvin Coll, MI — B
Cameron U, OK — B
Capital U, OH — B
Cardinal Stritch U, WI — B
Carleton Coll, MN — B
Carroll Coll, WI — B
Case Western Reserve U, OH — B
Cedarville U, OH — B
Central Christian Coll of Kansas, KS — A
Central Coll, IA — B
Central Methodist U, MO — B
Central Michigan U, MI — B
Central State U, OH — B
Chicago State U, IL — B
Clarke Coll, IA — B
Clarkson U, NY — B
Cleveland State U, OH — B
Coe Coll, IA — B
Coll of Mount St. Joseph, OH — B
Coll of Saint Benedict, MN — B
Coll of St. Catherine, MN — B
Coll of Saint Mary, NE — B
The Coll of St. Scholastica, MN — B
Coll of the Ozarks, MO — B
The Coll of Wooster, OH — B
Columbia Coll, MO — B
Concordia Coll, MN — B
Concordia U, IL — B
Concordia U, MI — B
Concordia U, NE — B
Concordia U, St. Paul, MN — B
Concordia U Wisconsin, WI — B
Concord U, WV — B
Cornell Coll, IA — B
Cornerstone U, MI — B
Creighton U, NE — A,B
Culver-Stockton Coll, MO — B
Dakota Wesleyan U, SD — B
Dana Coll, NE — B
Denison U, OH — B
DePaul U, IL — B
DePauw U, IN — B
Dickinson State U, ND — B
Doane Coll, NE — B
Dominican U, IL — B
Dordt Coll, IA — B
Drake U, IA — B
Drury U, MO — B
Earlham Coll, IN — B
East Central U, OK — B
Eastern Illinois U, IL — B
Eastern Michigan U, MI — B
East-West U, IL — B

Edgewood Coll, WI — B
Elmhurst Coll, IL — B
Emporia State U, KS — B
Evangel U, MO — B
Ferris State U, MI — B
Fontbonne U, MO — B
Fort Berthold Comm Coll, ND — A
Fort Hays State U, KS — B
Franciscan U of Steubenville, OH — B
Franklin Coll, IN — B
Gannon U, PA — B
Goshen Coll, IN — B
Grace Coll, IN — B
Graceland U, IA — B
Grand Valley State U, MI — B
Greenville Coll, IL — B
Grinnell Coll, IA — B
Gustavus Adolphus Coll, MN — B
Hamline U, MN — B
Hannibal-LaGrange Coll, MO — B
Hanover Coll, IN — B
Hastings Coll, NE — B
Heidelberg Coll, OH — B
Hillsdale Coll, MI — B
Hillsdale Free Will Baptist Coll, OK — A
Hiram Coll, OH — B
Hope Coll, MI — B
Huntington U, IN — B
Illinois Coll, IL — B
Illinois State U, IL — B
Illinois Wesleyan U, IL — B
Indiana State U, IN — B
Indiana U Bloomington, IN — B
Indiana U East, IN — A
Indiana U Kokomo, IN — B
Indiana U Northwest, IN — B
Indiana U–Purdue U Fort Wayne, IN — A,B
Indiana U–Purdue U Indianapolis, IN — B
Indiana U South Bend, IN — B
Indiana U Southeast, IN — B
Indiana Wesleyan U, IN — A,B
Iowa State U of Science and Technology, IA — B
Iowa Wesleyan Coll, IA — B
Jamestown Coll, ND — B
Judson Coll, IL — B
Kalamazoo Coll, MI — B
Kansas State U, KS — B
Kent State U, OH — B
Kenyon Coll, OH — B
Knox Coll, IL — B
Lake Forest Coll, IL — B
Lakeland Coll, WI — B
Lake Superior State U, MI — B
Langston U, OK — B
Lawrence Technological U, MI — B
Lawrence U, WI — B
Lewis U, IL — B
Lincoln U, MO — B
Lindenwood U, MO — B
Loras Coll, IA — B
Loyola U Chicago, IL — B
Luther Coll, IA — B
Macalester Coll, MN — B
MacMurray Coll, IL — B
Madonna U, MI — B
Maharishi U of Management, IA — B
Malone Coll, OH — B
Manchester Coll, IN — B
Marian Coll, IN — B

Marian Coll of Fond du Lac, WI — B
Marietta Coll, OH — B
Marquette U, WI — B
Marygrove Coll, MI — B
Maryville U of Saint Louis, MO — B
Mayville State U, ND — B
McKendree Coll, IL — B
Miami U, OH — B
Miami U Hamilton, OH — B
Miami U–Middletown Campus, OH — A
Michigan State U, MI — B
Michigan Technological U, MI — B
Millikin U, IL — B
Minnesota State U Mankato, MN — B
Minot State U, ND — B
Missouri Baptist U, MO — B
Missouri Southern State U, MO — B
Missouri State U, MO — B
Missouri Valley Coll, MO — B
Missouri Western State U, MO — B
Morningside Coll, IA — B
Mount Marty Coll, SD — B
Mount Mary Coll, WI — B
Mount Mercy Coll, IA — B
Mount Union Coll, OH — B
Mount Vernon Nazarene U, OH — B
Nebraska Wesleyan U, NE — B
Newman U, KS — B
North Carolina Ag and Tech State U, NC — B
North Central Coll, IL — B
North Dakota State U, ND — B
Northeastern Illinois U, IL — B
Northeastern State U, OK — B
Northern Illinois U, IL — B
Northern Michigan U, MI — B
Northern State U, SD — B
Northland Coll, WI — B
Northwestern Coll, IA — B
Northwestern Coll, MN — B
Northwestern Oklahoma State U, OK — B
Northwestern U, IL — B
Northwest Missouri State U, MO — B
Notre Dame Coll, OH — B
Oakland U, MI — B
Oberlin Coll, OH — B
Ohio Dominican U, OH — B
Ohio Northern U, OH — B
The Ohio State U, OH — B
The Ohio State U at Lima, OH — B
Ohio U, OH — B
Ohio Wesleyan U, OH — B
Oklahoma Christian U, OK — B
Oklahoma City U, OK — B
Oklahoma Panhandle State U, OK — B
Oklahoma State U, OK — B
Oklahoma Wesleyan U, OK — B
Oral Roberts U, OK — B
Ottawa U, KS — B
Otterbein Coll, OH — B
Park U, MO — B
Peru State Coll, NE — B
Pittsburg State U, KS — B
Purdue U, IN — B
Purdue U Calumet, IN — B

Purdue U North Central, IN — B
Ripon Coll, WI — B
Rockford Coll, IL — B
Rockhurst U, MO — B
Rogers State U, OK — A
Roosevelt U, IL — B
Rose-Hulman Inst of Technology, IN — B
Saginaw Valley State U, MI — B
St. Ambrose U, IA — B
St. Cloud State U, MN — B
St. Gregory's U, Shawnee, OK — B
Saint John's U, MN — B
Saint Joseph's Coll, IN — B
Saint Louis U, MO — B
Saint Mary-of-the-Woods Coll, IN — B
Saint Mary's Coll, IN — B
Saint Mary's U of Minnesota, MN — B
St. Norbert Coll, WI — B
St. Olaf Coll, MN — B
Saint Xavier U, IL — B
Shawnee State U, OH — B
Silver Lake Coll, WI — B
Simpson Coll, IA — B
South Dakota School of Mines and Technology, SD — B
South Dakota State U, SD — B
Southeastern Oklahoma State U, OK — B
Southeast Missouri State U, MO — B
Southern Illinois U Carbondale, IL — B
Southern Illinois U Edwardsville, IL — B
Southern Methodist U, TX — B
Southwest Baptist U, MO — B
Southwestern Coll, KS — B
Southwestern Oklahoma State U, OK — B
Southwest Minnesota State U, MN — B
Spring Arbor U, MI — B
Sterling Coll, KS — B
Tabor Coll, KS — B
Taylor U, IN — B
Transylvania U, KY — B
Trinity Christian Coll, IL — B
Trinity International U, IL — B
Tri-State U, IN — A,B
Truman State U, MO — B
Turtle Mountain Comm Coll, ND — A
Union Coll, NE — B
The U of Akron, OH — B
U of Central Missouri, MO — B
U of Central Oklahoma, OK — B
U of Chicago, IL — B
U of Cincinnati, OH — B
U of Dallas, TX — B
U of Dayton, OH — B
U of Evansville, IN — B
The U of Findlay, OH — B
U of Illinois at Chicago, IL — B
U of Illinois at Springfield, IL — B
U of Illinois at Urbana–Champaign, IL — B
U of Indianapolis, IN — B
The U of Iowa, IA — B
U of Kansas, KS — B
U of Mary, ND — B
U of Michigan, MI — B
U of Michigan–Dearborn, MI — B

A—associate degree; B—bachelor's degree

U of Michigan–Flint, MI	B
U of Minnesota, Duluth, MN	B
U of Minnesota, Morris, MN	B
U of Minnesota, Twin Cities Campus, MN	B
U of Missouri–Columbia, MO	B
U of Missouri–Kansas City, MO	B
U of Missouri–St. Louis, MO	B
U of Nebraska at Kearney, NE	B
U of Nebraska at Omaha, NE	B
U of Nebraska–Lincoln, NE	B
U of New Orleans, LA	B
U of North Dakota, ND	B
U of Northern Iowa, IA	B
U of Notre Dame, IN	B
U of Oklahoma, OK	B
U of Rio Grande, OH	A,B
U of St. Francis, IL	B
U of Saint Francis, IN	B
U of Saint Mary, KS	B
U of St. Thomas, MN	B
U of Science and Arts of Oklahoma, OK	B
U of Sioux Falls, SD	B
The U of South Dakota, SD	B
U of Southern Indiana, IN	B
The U of Toledo, OH	B
U of Tulsa, OK	B
U of West Florida, FL	B
U of Wisconsin–Eau Claire, WI	B
U of Wisconsin–Green Bay, WI	A,B
U of Wisconsin–La Crosse, WI	B
U of Wisconsin–Madison, WI	B
U of Wisconsin–Milwaukee, WI	B
U of Wisconsin–Oshkosh, WI	B
U of Wisconsin–Parkside, WI	B
U of Wisconsin–Platteville, WI	B
U of Wisconsin–River Falls, WI	B
U of Wisconsin–Stevens Point, WI	B
U of Wisconsin–Superior, WI	B
U of Wisconsin–Whitewater, WI	B
Upper Iowa U, IA	B
Ursuline Coll, OH	B
Valley City State U, ND	B
Valparaiso U, IN	B
Viterbo U, WI	B
Wabash Coll, IN	B
Walsh U, OH	B
Wartburg Coll, IA	B
Washburn U, KS	B
Washington U in St. Louis, MO	B
Wayne State Coll, NE	B
Webster U, MO	B
Western Illinois U, IL	B
Western Michigan U, MI	B
Westminster Coll, MO	B
Wheaton Coll, IL	B
Wichita State U, KS	B
William Jewell Coll, MO	B
William Woods U, MO	B
Wilmington Coll, OH	B
Winona State U, MN	B
Wisconsin Lutheran Coll, WI	B
Wittenberg U, OH	B
Wright State U, OH	B
Xavier U, OH	B
Youngstown State U, OH	B

Mathematics and Computer Science

Anderson U, IN	B
Augustana Coll, IL	B
Cardinal Stritch U, WI	B
Central Coll, IA	B
Eastern Illinois U, IL	B
Lake Superior State U, MI	B
Lawrence Technological U, MI	B
Lawrence U, WI	B
Loyola U Chicago, IL	B
St. Gregory's U, Shawnee, OK	B
Saint John's U, MN	B
Saint Joseph's Coll, IN	B
Saint Mary's Coll, IN	B
Saint Mary's U of Minnesota, MN	B
The U of Akron, OH	B
U of Illinois at Chicago, IL	B
U of Illinois at Urbana–Champaign, IL	
U of St. Francis, IL	B
Washington U in St. Louis, MO	B

Mathematics and Statistics Related

Anderson U, IN	B
Bradley U, IL	B
Dakota State U, SD	B
Ferris State U, MI	B
Miami U Hamilton, OH	B
The Ohio State U, OH	B
The U of Akron, OH	B

Mathematics Related

Hillsdale Coll, MI	B
Ohio Northern U, OH	B

Mathematics Teacher Education

Alma Coll, MI	B
Alverno Coll, WI	B
Anderson U, IN	B
Bethany Coll, KS	B
Bethel U, MN	B
Black Hills State U, SD	B
Bowling Green State U, OH	B
Buena Vista U, IA	B
Capital U, OH	B
Carroll Coll, WI	B
Cedarville U, OH	B
Central Christian Coll of Kansas, KS	A
Central Michigan U, MI	B
Central State U, OH	B
Chicago State U, IL	B
Coll of St. Catherine, MN	B
Coll of the Ozarks, MO	B
Concordia Coll, MN	B
Concordia U, IL	B
Concordia U, MI	B
Concordia U, NE	B
Concordia U, St. Paul, MN	B
Cornerstone U, MI	B
Culver-Stockton Coll, MO	B
Dakota State U, SD	B
Dakota Wesleyan U, SD	B
Dana Coll, NE	B
East Central U, OK	B
Eastern Michigan U, MI	B
Elmhurst Coll, IL	B
Ferris State U, MI	B
Franklin Coll, IN	B
Grace Coll, IN	B
Greenville Coll, IL	B
Gustavus Adolphus Coll, MN	B

Hannibal-LaGrange Coll, MO	B
Hastings Coll, NE	B
Hope Coll, MI	B
Illinois Wesleyan U, IL	B
Indiana U Bloomington, IN	B
Indiana U Northwest, IN	B
Indiana U–Purdue U Fort Wayne, IN	B
Indiana U South Bend, IN	B
Indiana U Southeast, IN	B
Indiana Wesleyan U, IN	B
Jamestown Coll, ND	B
Lincoln U, MO	B
Lindenwood U, MO	B
Madonna U, MI	B
Marian Coll of Fond du Lac, WI	B
Marquette U, WI	B
Maryville U of Saint Louis, MO	B
Mayville State U, ND	B
McKendree Coll, IL	B
Miami U Hamilton, OH	B
Michigan Technological U, MI	B
Minot State U, ND	B
Missouri State U, MO	B
Mount Marty Coll, SD	B
Mount Mary Coll, WI	B
Mount Vernon Nazarene U, OH	B
North Dakota State U, ND	B
Northern Michigan U, MI	B
Northwestern Coll, MN	B
Northwestern U, IL	B
Oakland U, MI	B
Ohio Dominican U, OH	B
Ohio Northern U, OH	B
Ohio U, OH	B
Ohio Wesleyan U, OH	B
Oklahoma Christian U, OK	B
Oral Roberts U, OK	B
Pittsburg State U, KS	B
Rochester Coll, MI	B
St. Ambrose U, IA	B
St. Gregory's U, Shawnee, OK	B
Saint Mary's U of Minnesota, MN	B
Saint Xavier U, IL	B
Shawnee State U, OH	B
Southeastern Oklahoma State U, OK	B
Southeast Missouri State U, MO	B
Southwest Baptist U, MO	B
Southwest Minnesota State U, MN	B
Trinity Christian Coll, IL	B
Tri-State U, IN	B
Union Coll, NE	B
The U of Akron, OH	B
U of Central Oklahoma, OK	B
U of Evansville, IN	B
U of Illinois at Chicago, IL	B
U of Indianapolis, IN	B
The U of Iowa, IA	B
U of Mary, ND	B
U of Michigan–Dearborn, MI	B
U of Minnesota, Duluth, MN	B
U of Minnesota, Twin Cities Campus, MN	B
U of Missouri–Columbia, MO	B
U of Missouri–St. Louis, MO	B
U of Nebraska–Lincoln, NE	B
U of New Orleans, LA	B
U of North Dakota, ND	B
U of Northern Iowa, IA	B

U of Oklahoma, OK	B
U of Rio Grande, OH	B
U of St. Francis, IL	B
U of St. Thomas, MN	B
The U of South Dakota, SD	B
The U of Toledo, OH	B
U of West Florida, FL	B
U of Wisconsin–River Falls, WI	B
U of Wisconsin–Superior, WI	B
Ursuline Coll, OH	B
Valley City State U, ND	B
Valparaiso U, IN	B
Viterbo U, WI	B
Wartburg Coll, IA	B
Washington U in St. Louis, MO	B
Wayne State Coll, NE	B
Western Michigan U, MI	B
William Penn U, IA	B
William Woods U, MO	B
Wright State U, OH	B
York Coll, NE	B
Youngstown State U, OH	B

Mechanical Design Technology

Bowling Green State U, OH	B
Bowling Green State U–Firelands Coll, OH	A
Ferris State U, MI	A
Lincoln U, MO	B

Mechanical Drafting

Cameron U, OK	A

Mechanical Drafting and CAD/CADD

Baker Coll of Flint, MI	A
Cameron U, OK	A
Eastern Michigan U, MI	B
Indiana U–Purdue U Indianapolis, IN	A
Morrison Inst of Technology, IL	A
Purdue U, IN	A,B

Mechanical Engineering

Andrews U, MI	B
Baker Coll of Flint, MI	B
Bradley U, IL	B
Calvin Coll, MI	B
Case Western Reserve U, OH	B
Cedarville U, OH	B
Clarkson U, NY	B
Cleveland State U, OH	B
Dordt Coll, IA	B
Gannon U, PA	B
Grand Valley State U, MI	B
Illinois Inst of Technology, IL	B
Indiana Tech, IN	B
Indiana U–Purdue U Fort Wayne, IN	B
Indiana U–Purdue U Indianapolis, IN	B
Iowa State U of Science and Technology, IA	B
Kansas State U, KS	B
Kettering U, MI	B
Lake Superior State U, MI	B
Lawrence Technological U, MI	B
Marquette U, WI	B
Miami U, OH	B
Michigan State U, MI	B
Michigan Technological U, MI	B
Milwaukee School of Engineering, WI	B

Minnesota State U Mankato, MN	B
North Carolina Ag and Tech State U, NC	B
North Dakota State U, ND	B
Northern Illinois U, IL	B
Northwestern U, IL	B
Oakland U, MI	B
Ohio Northern U, OH	B
The Ohio State U, OH	B
Ohio U, OH	B
Oklahoma Christian U, OK	B
Oklahoma State U, OK	B
Oral Roberts U, OK	B
Purdue U, IN	B
Purdue U Calumet, IN	B
Rose-Hulman Inst of Technology, IN	B
Saginaw Valley State U, MI	B
St. Cloud State U, MN	B
Saint Louis U, MO	B
South Dakota School of Mines and Technology, SD	B
South Dakota State U, SD	B
Southern Illinois U Carbondale, IL	B
Southern Illinois U Edwardsville, IL	B
Southern Methodist U, TX	B
Tri-State U, IN	B
The U of Akron, OH	B
U of Cincinnati, OH	B
U of Dayton, OH	B
U of Evansville, IN	B
U of Illinois at Chicago, IL	B
U of Illinois at Urbana–Champaign, IL	B
U of Indianapolis, IN	B
The U of Iowa, IA	B
U of Kansas, KS	B
U of Michigan, MI	B
U of Michigan–Dearborn, MI	B
U of Minnesota, Twin Cities Campus, MN	B
U of Missouri–Columbia, MO	B
U of Missouri–Kansas City, MO	B
U of Missouri–Rolla, MO	B
U of Missouri–St. Louis, MO	B
U of Nebraska–Lincoln, NE	B
U of New Orleans, LA	B
U of North Dakota, ND	B
U of Notre Dame, IN	B
U of Oklahoma, OK	B
U of St. Thomas, MN	B
The U of Toledo, OH	B
U of Tulsa, OK	B
U of Wisconsin–Madison, WI	B
U of Wisconsin–Milwaukee, WI	B
U of Wisconsin–Platteville, WI	B
Valparaiso U, IN	B
Washington U in St. Louis, MO	B
Western Michigan U, MI	B
Wichita State U, KS	B
William Penn U, IA	B
Winona State U, MN	B
Wright State U, OH	B
Youngstown State U, OH	B

Mechanical Engineering/Mechanical Technology

Andrews U, MI	A,B
Baker Coll of Flint, MI	A

Bowling Green State U, OH	B
Central Michigan U, MI	B
Eastern Michigan U, MI	B
Ferris State U, MI	A
Indiana U–Purdue U Fort Wayne, IN	A,B
Indiana U–Purdue U Indianapolis, IN	A,B
Kent State U, Ashtabula Campus, OH	A
Kent State U, Trumbull Campus, OH	A
Kent State U, Tuscarawas Campus, OH	A
Lake Superior State U, MI	A,B
Lawrence Technological U, MI	A
Miami U Hamilton, OH	A,B
Miami U–Middletown Campus, OH	A
Michigan Technological U, MI	A,B
Northern Michigan U, MI	B
Ohio U, OH	B
Oklahoma State U, OK	B
Pittsburg State U, KS	B
Purdue U Calumet, IN	A,B
Purdue U North Central, IN	A,B
The U of Akron, OH	A,B
U of Cincinnati, OH	A,B
U of Dayton, OH	B
U of Rio Grande, OH	A,B
The U of Toledo, OH	A,B
Western Michigan U, MI	B
Youngstown State U, OH	A,B

Mechanical Engineering Technologies Related

Cleveland State U, OH	B
Indiana State U, IN	B
Purdue U, IN	A,B

Mechanic and Repair Technologies Related

Hope Coll, MI	B

Medical Administrative Assistant

Minnesota School of Business, MN	A
Minnesota School of Business–Brooklyn Center, MN	A
Minnesota School of Business–Plymouth, MN	A
Minnesota School of Business–St. Cloud, MN	A

Medical Administrative Assistant and Medical Secretary

AIB Coll of Business, IA	A
Baker Coll of Auburn Hills, MI	A,B
Baker Coll of Cadillac, MI	A
Baker Coll of Clinton Township, MI	A
Baker Coll of Flint, MI	A
Baker Coll of Jackson, MI	A
Baker Coll of Muskegon, MI	A
Baker Coll of Owosso, MI	A
Baker Coll of Port Huron, MI	A
Dickinson State U, ND	A
Hannibal-LaGrange Coll, MO	A
Lewis Coll of Business, MI	A
Miami U–Middletown Campus, OH	A
Tabor Coll, KS	B
The U of Akron, OH	A
U of Cincinnati, OH	A

U of Rio Grande, OH	A
Wright State U, OH	A

Medical/Clinical Assistant

Argosy U, Twin Cities, Eagan, MN	A
Baker Coll of Allen Park, MI	A
Baker Coll of Auburn Hills, MI	A
Baker Coll of Cadillac, MI	A
Baker Coll of Clinton Township, MI	A
Baker Coll of Flint, MI	A
Baker Coll of Jackson, MI	A
Baker Coll of Muskegon, MI	A
Baker Coll of Owosso, MI	A
Baker Coll of Port Huron, MI	A
Davenport U, Dearborn, MI	A
Herzing Coll, MN	A
International Business Coll, Fort Wayne, IN	A,B
Kaplan U, IA	A
Minnesota School of Business–Richfield, MN	A
Ohio U, OH	A
Palmer Coll of Chiropractic, IA	A
Presentation Coll, SD	A
Robert Morris Coll, IL	A
Rockford Business Coll, IL	A
The U of Akron, OH	A
The U of Toledo, OH	A
Youngstown State U, OH	A

Medical Illustration

Alma Coll, MI	B
The Cleveland Inst of Art, OH	B
Iowa State U of Science and Technology, IA	B

Medical Informatics

DeVry U, Addison, IL	B
DeVry U, Chicago, IL	B
DeVry U, Columbus, OH	B

Medical Insurance Coding

Baker Coll of Allen Park, MI	A
Herzing Coll, MN	A
Kilian Comm Coll, SD	A

Medical Insurance/Medical Billing

Baker Coll of Allen Park, MI	A

Medical Laboratory Technology

Argosy U, Twin Cities, Eagan, MN	A
Evangel U, MO	A
ITT Tech Inst, Arnold, MO	A
ITT Tech Inst, Greenfield, WI	A
Oakland U, MI	B
Rockhurst U, MO	B
Roosevelt U, IL	B
Southeastern Oklahoma State U, OK	B
U of Cincinnati, OH	B
U of Oklahoma, OK	B

Medical Microbiology and Bacteriology

Ball State U, IN	B
Bowling Green State U, OH	B
Central Michigan U, MI	B
Indiana U Bloomington, IN	B
Miami U, OH	B
Michigan Technological U, MI	B
Minnesota State U Mankato, MN	B

Missouri Southern State U, MO	B
Northeastern State U, OK	B
Northern Michigan U, MI	B
The Ohio State U, OH	B
Ohio U, OH	B
Ohio Wesleyan U, OH	B
St. Cloud State U, MN	B
South Dakota State U, SD	B
The U of Akron, OH	B
U of Cincinnati, OH	B
U of Minnesota, Twin Cities Campus, MN	B
U of Wisconsin–Madison, WI	B
U of Wisconsin–Oshkosh, WI	B

Medical Office Assistant

Concordia U Wisconsin, WI	B
Mercy Coll of Health Sciences, IA	A

Medical Office Computer Specialist

Baker Coll of Allen Park, MI	A

Medical Office Management

Kilian Comm Coll, SD	A
Minnesota School of Business–Richfield, MN	A
The U of Akron, OH	A

Medical Radiologic Technology

Argosy U, Twin Cities, Eagan, MN	A
Avila U, MO	B
Coll of St. Catherine, MN	A
Gannon U, PA	A,B
Indiana U Northwest, IN	A,B
Indiana U–Purdue U Indianapolis, IN	A,B
Indiana U South Bend, IN	A
Marian Coll of Fond du Lac, WI	B
Mercy Coll of Health Sciences, IA	A
Mercy Coll of Northwest Ohio, OH	A
Minot State U, ND	B
Missouri Southern State U, MO	A
Missouri State U, MO	B
Mount Marty Coll, SD	B
North Central Coll, IL	B
The Ohio State U, OH	B
Presentation Coll, SD	A,B
Roosevelt U, IL	B
Shawnee State U, OH	B
Southeast Missouri Hospital Coll of Nursing and Health Sciences, MO	A
Southern Illinois U Carbondale, IL	B
Trinity Coll of Nursing and Health Sciences, IL	A
The U of Akron, OH	B
U of Michigan–Flint, MI	B
U of Missouri–Columbia, MO	B
U of Nebraska Medical Center, NE	B
U of St. Francis, IL	A
U of Saint Francis, IN	A
U of Southern Indiana, IN	A
Washburn U, KS	B

A—associate degree; B—bachelor's degree

Medical Staff Services Technology
East Central U, OK — B

Medical Transcription
Baker Coll of Flint, MI — A
Baker Coll of Jackson, MI — A
Kaplan U, IA — A
Kilian Comm Coll, SD — A
Presentation Coll, SD — A
Rockford Business Coll, IL — A

Medicinal and Pharmaceutical Chemistry
Butler U, IN — B
Ohio Northern U, OH — B

Medicinal/Pharmaceutical Chemistry
Michigan Technological U, MI — B

Medieval and Renaissance Studies
Cornell Coll, IA — B
Hanover Coll, IN — B
Ohio Wesleyan U, OH — B
Southern Methodist U, TX — B
U of Chicago, IL — B
The U of Iowa, IA — B
U of Michigan, MI — B
U of Nebraska–Lincoln, NE — B
U of Notre Dame, IN — B
The U of Toledo, OH — B
Washington U in St. Louis, MO — B

Mental and Social Health Services and Allied Professions Related
The U of Toledo, OH — B
Wright State U, OH — B

Mental Health Counseling
Washburn U, KS — A,B

Mental Health/Rehabilitation
Evangel U, MO — A,B
Lake Superior State U, MI — A
Newman U, KS — B
St. Augustine Coll, IL — A
St. Cloud State U, MN — B
The U of Toledo, OH — A

Merchandising
Michigan State U, MI — B
The U of Akron, OH — A

Merchandising, Sales, and Marketing Operations Related (General)
Eastern Michigan U, MI — B
The U of Akron, OH — B
Washington U in St. Louis, MO — B

Merchandising, Sales, and Marketing Operations Related (Specialized)
Eastern Michigan U, MI — B
Gannon U, PA — B
The U of Akron, OH — B

Metal and Jewelry Arts
The Cleveland Inst of Art, OH — B
Ferris State U, MI — B
Grand Valley State U, MI — B
Indiana U Bloomington, IN — B
Kent State U, OH — B
Northwest Missouri State U, MO — B

School of the Art Inst of Chicago, IL — B
The U of Akron, OH — B
The U of Iowa, IA — B
U of Kansas, KS — B
U of Michigan, MI — B
U of Wisconsin–Milwaukee, WI — B

Metallurgical Engineering
Cleveland State U, OH — B
Illinois Inst of Technology, IL — B
Michigan Technological U, MI — B
The Ohio State U, OH — B
South Dakota School of Mines and Technology, SD — B
U of Cincinnati, OH — B
U of Michigan, MI — B
U of Missouri–Rolla, MO — B
U of Wisconsin–Madison, WI — B

Metallurgical Technology
Purdue U Calumet, IN — A
U of Cincinnati, OH — B

Meteorology
Saint Louis U, MO — B
Western Illinois U, IL — B

Mexican-American Studies
Southern Methodist U, TX — B

Microbiological Sciences and Immunology Related
Wright State U, OH — B

Microbiology
Iowa State U of Science and Technology, IA — B
Miami U Hamilton, OH — B
Michigan State U, MI — B
Michigan Technological U, MI — B
North Dakota State U, ND — B
Northern Michigan U, MI — B
Southern Illinois U Carbondale, IL — B
U of Illinois at Urbana–Champaign, IL — B
The U of Iowa, IA — B
U of Kansas, KS — B
U of Michigan–Dearborn, MI — B
U of Missouri–Columbia, MO — B
U of Northern Iowa, IA — B
U of Oklahoma, OK — B
U of Wisconsin–La Crosse, WI — B

Middle School Education
Alverno Coll, WI — B
Antioch Coll, OH — B
Ashford U, IA — B
Ashland U, OH — B
Avila U, MO — B
Baldwin-Wallace Coll, OH — B
Black Hills State U, SD — B
Bluffton U, OH — B
Bowling Green State U, OH — B
Capital U, OH — B
Carroll Coll, WI — B
Central Methodist U, MO — B
Central State U, OH — B
Chicago State U, IL — B
Clarke Coll, IA — B
Cleveland State U, OH — B
Coll of Mount St. Joseph, OH — B
Coll of the Ozarks, MO — B
Concordia U, NE — B
Concordia U, St. Paul, MN — B
Concordia U Wisconsin, WI — B
Dakota Wesleyan U, SD — B

Eastern Illinois U, IL — B
Evangel U, MO — B
Fontbonne U, MO — B
Harris-Stowe State U, MO — B
Huntington U, IN — B
Indiana Wesleyan U, IN — B
Kent State U, OH — B
Lakeland Coll, WI — B
Lake Superior State U, MI — B
Lincoln U, MO — B
Lindenwood U, MO — B
Lourdes Coll, OH — B
Malone Coll, OH — B
Marian Coll of Fond du Lac, WI — B
Marquette U, WI — B
Maryville U of Saint Louis, MO — B
McKendree Coll, IL — B
Miami U, OH — B
Missouri Baptist U, MO — B
Missouri Southern State U, MO — B
Missouri State U, MO — B
Mount Mercy Coll, IA — B
Mount Union Coll, OH — B
Mount Vernon Nazarene U, OH — B
Nebraska Wesleyan U, NE — B
Northland Coll, WI — B
Northwest Missouri State U, MO — B
Notre Dame Coll, OH — B
Ohio Dominican U, OH — B
Ohio Northern U, OH — B
Ohio U, OH — B
Ohio Wesleyan U, OH — B
Otterbein Coll, OH — B
Peru State Coll, NE — B
St. Cloud State U, MN — B
Shawnee State U, OH — B
Southeast Missouri State U, MO — B
Southwest Baptist U, MO — B
Taylor U, IN — B
Transylvania U, KY — B
Trinity Christian Coll, IL — B
The U of Akron, OH — B
U of Central Missouri, MO — B
U of Kansas, KS — B
U of Minnesota, Duluth, MN — B
U of Missouri–Columbia, MO — B
U of Missouri–Kansas City, MO — B
U of Nebraska–Lincoln, NE — B
U of New Orleans, LA — B
U of North Dakota, ND — B
U of Northern Iowa, IA — B
U of St. Thomas, MN — B
U of Sioux Falls, SD — B
The U of South Dakota, SD — B
U of West Florida, FL — B
U of Wisconsin–Platteville, WI — B
Ursuline Coll, OH — B
Valparaiso U, IN — B
Waldorf Coll, IA — B
Washington U in St. Louis, MO — B
Wayne State Coll, NE — B
Westminster Coll, MO — B
William Woods U, MO — B
Winona State U, MN — B
Wright State U, OH — B
Xavier U, OH — B
York Coll, NE — B
Youngstown State U, OH — B

Military Technologies
Wright State U, OH — B

Mining and Mineral Engineering
South Dakota School of Mines and Technology, SD — B
Southern Illinois U Carbondale, IL — B
U of Missouri–Rolla, MO — B
U of Wisconsin–Madison, WI — B

Missionary Studies and Missiology
Calvary Bible Coll and Theological Seminary, MO — B
Cedarville U, OH — B
Central Christian Coll of Kansas, KS — A,B
Concordia U, St. Paul, MN — B
Concordia U Wisconsin, WI — B
Crossroads Coll, MN — B
Crown Coll, MN — B
Dordt Coll, IA — B
Faith Baptist Bible Coll and Theological Seminary, IA — A,B
Global U of the Assemblies of God, MO — B
God's Bible School and Coll, OH — A,B
Grace Bible Coll, MI — B
Hillsdale Free Will Baptist Coll, OK — A,B
Huntington U, IN — B
Kuyper Coll, MI — B
Messenger Coll, MO — B
Northwestern Coll, MN — B
Oklahoma Christian U, OK — B
Oral Roberts U, OK — B
Rochester Coll, MI — B
Vennard Coll, IA — B

Modern Greek
Ball State U, IN — B
Butler U, IN — B
Calvin Coll, MI — B
Concordia U, MI — B
Concordia U Wisconsin, WI — B
Cornell Coll, IA — B
Kenyon Coll, OH — B
Macalester Coll, MN — B
Miami U, OH — B
Oberlin Coll, OH — B
The Ohio State U, OH — B
Saint Louis U, MO — B
The U of Iowa, IA — B
U of Michigan, MI — B
U of Minnesota, Twin Cities Campus, MN — B
U of Missouri–Columbia, MO — B
U of Wisconsin–Madison, WI — B
U of Wisconsin–Milwaukee, WI — B
Wabash Coll, IN — B
Wright State U, OH — B

Modern Languages
Albion Coll, MI — B
Alma Coll, MI — B
Ball State U, IN — B
Beloit Coll, WI — B
Bemidji State U, MN — B
Cornell Coll, IA — B
DePaul U, IL — B
Greenville Coll, IL — B
Kenyon Coll, OH — B
Minnesota State U Mankato, MN — B

Stephens Coll, MO — B
U of Chicago, IL — B
Walsh U, OH — B
Washington U in St. Louis, MO — B
Wayne State Coll, NE — B
Wilmington Coll, OH — B
Wright State U, OH — B

Molecular Biochemistry
Michigan Technological U, MI — B

Molecular Biology
Alverno Coll, WI — B
Baker U, KS — B
Ball State U, IN — B
Beloit Coll, WI — B
Benedictine U, IL — B
Bethel U, MN — B
Blackburn Coll, IL — B
Bradley U, IL — B
Chicago State U, IL — B
Clarkson U, NY — B
Coe Coll, IA — B
The Coll of Wooster, OH — B
Kenyon Coll, OH — B
Marquette U, WI — B
Missouri State U, MO — B
Northwestern U, IL — B
Ohio Northern U, OH — B
Otterbein Coll, OH — B
U of Kansas, KS — B
U of Michigan, MI — B
U of Minnesota, Duluth, MN — B
U of Wisconsin–Eau Claire, WI — B
U of Wisconsin–Madison, WI — B
U of Wisconsin–Parkside, WI — B
William Jewell Coll, MO — B

Montessori Teacher Education
Oklahoma City U, OK — B
Xavier U, OH — B

Mortuary Science and Embalming
Ferris State U, MI — A

Multi-/Interdisciplinary Studies Related
Ashford U, IA — B
Bethel U, MN — B
Bluffton U, OH — B
Bowling Green State U, OH — B
Buena Vista U, IA — B
Capital U, OH — B
Cleveland State U, OH — B
Coll of the Ozarks, MO — B
The Coll of Wooster, OH — B
Columbia Coll, MO — B
Columbia Coll Chicago, IL — B
Cornell Coll, IA — B
Cornerstone U, MI — B
DePauw U, IN — B
Eastern Illinois U, IL — B
Emporia State U, KS — B
Gannon U, PA — B
Grace Bible Coll, MI — B
Greenville Coll, IL — B
Hope Coll, MI — B
Illinois Inst of Technology, IL — B
Iowa State U of Science and Technology, IA — B
Kaplan U, IA — A
Kent State U, OH — B
Kenyon Coll, OH — B
Knox Coll, IL — B

Marquette U, WI — B
Miami U, OH — B
Miami U Hamilton, OH — B
Missouri Baptist U, MO — B
Missouri Western State U, MO — B
North Central Coll, IL — B
North Dakota State U, ND — B
Northwestern U, IL — B
Notre Dame Coll, OH — B
Ohio U, OH — A
Ohio Wesleyan U, OH — B
Otterbein Coll, OH — B
Park U, MO — B
Purdue U, IN — B
Rochester Coll, MI — B
St. Ambrose U, IA — B
St. Cloud State U, MN — B
St. Olaf Coll, MN — B
Southeast Missouri State U, MO — B
Southern Illinois U Carbondale, IL — B
The U of Akron, OH — A
U of Evansville, IN — B
U of Michigan–Dearborn, MI — B
U of Nebraska at Omaha, NE — B
U of North Dakota, ND — B
U of Oklahoma, OK — B
U of St. Francis, IL — B
U of Saint Mary, KS — B
U of St. Thomas, MN — B
The U of Toledo, OH — A,B
U of Wisconsin–Superior, WI — B
Ursuline Coll, OH — B
Valparaiso U, IN — B
Vennard Coll, IA — B
Viterbo U, WI — B
Washington U in St. Louis, MO — B
Wheaton Coll, IL — B
Wisconsin Lutheran Coll, WI — B
Wright State U, OH — B

Museum Studies
Beloit Coll, WI — B
The U of Iowa, IA — B

Music
Adrian Coll, MI — B
Albion Coll, MI — B
Alma Coll, MI — B
Alverno Coll, WI — A,B
Andrews U, MI — B
Antioch Coll, OH — B
Aquinas Coll, MI — B
Ashford U, IA — B
Ashland U, OH — B
Augsburg Coll, MN — B
Augustana Coll, IL — B
Augustana Coll, SD — B
Baker U, KS — B
Ball State U, IN — B
Baptist Bible Coll, MO — B
Beloit Coll, WI — B
Bemidji State U, MN — B
Benedictine Coll, KS — B
Benedictine U, IL — B
Bethany Coll, KS — B
Bethany Lutheran Coll, MN — B
Bethel U, MN — B
Blackburn Coll, IL — B
Black Hills State U, SD — B
Bluffton U, OH — B
Bowling Green State U, OH — B
Bradley U, IL — B
Briar Cliff U, IA — B

Butler U, IN — B
Calvin Coll, MI — B
Cameron U, OK — B
Capital U, OH — B
Cardinal Stritch U, WI — B
Carleton Coll, MN — B
Carroll Coll, WI — B
Case Western Reserve U, OH — B
Cedarville U, OH — B
Central Christian Coll of Kansas, KS — B
Central Coll, IA — B
Central Methodist U, MO — B
Central Michigan U, MI — B
Central State U, OH — B
Chicago State U, IL — B
Clarke Coll, IA — B
Cleveland Inst of Music, OH — B
Cleveland State U, OH — B
Coe Coll, IA — B
Coll of Mount St. Joseph, OH — B
Coll of Saint Benedict, MN — B
Coll of St. Catherine, MN — B
Coll of the Ozarks, MO — B
The Coll of Wooster, OH — B
Columbia Coll Chicago, IL — B
Concordia Coll, MN — B
Concordia U, IL — B
Concordia U, MI — B
Concordia U, NE — B
Concordia U, St. Paul, MN — B
Concordia U Wisconsin, WI — B
Cornell Coll, IA — B
Cornerstone U, MI — B
Creighton U, NE — B
Crown Coll, MN — A,B
Culver-Stockton Coll, MO — B
Dakota Wesleyan U, SD — B
Dana Coll, NE — B
Denison U, OH — B
DePaul U, IL — B
DePauw U, IN — B
Dickinson State U, ND — B
Doane Coll, NE — B
Dordt Coll, IA — B
Drake U, IA — B
Drury U, MO — B
Earlham Coll, IN — B
East Central U, OK — B
Eastern Illinois U, IL — B
Eastern Michigan U, MI — B
Edgewood Coll, WI — B
Elmhurst Coll, IL — B
Emporia State U, KS — B
Evangel U, MO — B
Fort Hays State U, KS — B
Goshen Coll, IN — B
Grace Bible Coll, MI — B
Graceland U, IA — B
Grand Valley State U, MI — B
Grand View Coll, IA — B
Great Lakes Christian Coll, MI — B
Greenville Coll, IL — B
Grinnell Coll, IA — B
Gustavus Adolphus Coll, MN — B
Hamline U, MN — B
Hannibal-LaGrange Coll, MO — B
Hanover Coll, IN — B
Hastings Coll, NE — B
Heidelberg Coll, OH — B
Hillsdale Coll, MI — B
Hillsdale Free Will Baptist Coll, OK — A
Hiram Coll, OH — B
Hope Coll, MI — B

Huntington U, IN — B
Illinois Coll, IL — B
Illinois State U, IL — B
Illinois Wesleyan U, IL — B
Indiana State U, IN — B
Indiana U Bloomington, IN — B
Indiana U–Purdue U Fort Wayne, IN — B
Indiana U Southeast, IN — B
Indiana Wesleyan U, IN — A,B
Iowa State U of Science and Technology, IA — B
Iowa Wesleyan Coll, IA — B
Jamestown Coll, ND — B
Judson Coll, IL — B
Kalamazoo Coll, MI — B
Kansas State U, KS — B
Kent State U, OH — B
Kenyon Coll, OH — B
Knox Coll, IL — B
Lake Forest Coll, IL — B
Lakeland Coll, WI — B
Langston U, OK — B
Lawrence U, WI — B
Lewis U, IL — B
Lindenwood U, MO — B
Loras Coll, IA — B
Lourdes Coll, OH — A
Loyola U Chicago, IL — B
Luther Coll, IA — B
Macalester Coll, MN — B
MacMurray Coll, IL — B
Madonna U, MI — B
Malone Coll, OH — B
Manchester Coll, IN — B
Maranatha Baptist Bible Coll, WI — B
Marian Coll, IN — A,B
Marian Coll of Fond du Lac, WI — B
Marietta Coll, OH — B
Marygrove Coll, MI — B
McKendree Coll, IL — B
McNally Smith Coll of Music, MN — A
Messenger Coll, MO — B
Miami U, OH — B
Miami U Hamilton, OH — B
Michigan State U, MI — B
Millikin U, IL — B
Minnesota State U Mankato, MN — B
Minot State U, ND — B
Missouri Southern State U, MO — B
Missouri State U, MO — B
Missouri Valley Coll, MO — B
Missouri Western State U, MO — B
Morningside Coll, IA — B
Mount Marty Coll, SD — B
Mount Mary Coll, WI — B
Mount Mercy Coll, IA — B
Mount Union Coll, OH — B
Mount Vernon Nazarene U, OH — A,B
Nebraska Wesleyan U, NE — B
North Central Coll, IL — B
North Dakota State U, ND — B
Northeastern Illinois U, IL — B
Northeastern State U, OK — B
Northern Illinois U, IL — B
Northern Michigan U, MI — B
Northern State U, SD — B
Northland Coll, WI — B
Northwestern Coll, IA — B

A—associate degree; B—bachelor's degree

Northwestern Coll, MN	B
Northwestern Oklahoma State U, OK	B
Northwestern U, IL	B
Northwest Missouri State U, MO	B
Oakland U, MI	B
Oberlin Coll, OH	B
Ohio Northern U, OH	B
The Ohio State U, OH	B
Ohio U, OH	B
Ohio Wesleyan U, OH	B
Oklahoma Christian U, OK	B
Oklahoma City U, OK	B
Oklahoma State U, OK	B
Oklahoma Wesleyan U, OK	B
Oral Roberts U, OK	B
Ottawa U, KS	B
Otterbein Coll, OH	B
Park U, MO	B
Peru State Coll, NE	B
Pittsburg State U, KS	B
Quincy U, IL	B
Ripon Coll, WI	B
Rochester Coll, MI	B
Rockford Coll, IL	B
Roosevelt U, IL	B
Saginaw Valley State U, MI	B
St. Ambrose U, IA	B
St. Cloud State U, MN	B
Saint John's U, MN	B
Saint Louis U, MO	B
Saint Mary-of-the-Woods Coll, IN	B
Saint Mary's Coll, IN	B
Saint Mary's U of Minnesota, MN	B
St. Norbert Coll, WI	B
St. Olaf Coll, MN	B
Saint Xavier U, IL	B
Shawnee State U, OH	A
Silver Lake Coll, WI	B
Simpson Coll, IA	B
South Dakota State U, SD	B
Southeastern Oklahoma State U, OK	B
Southeast Missouri State U, MO	B
Southern Illinois U Carbondale, IL	B
Southern Illinois U Edwardsville, IL	B
Southern Methodist U, TX	B
Southwest Baptist U, MO	B
Southwestern Coll, KS	B
Southwestern Oklahoma State U, OK	B
Southwest Minnesota State U, MN	B
Spring Arbor U, MI	B
Sterling Coll, KS	B
Tabor Coll, KS	B
Taylor U, IN	B
Trinity Christian Coll, IL	B
Trinity International U, IL	B
Truman State U, MO	B
Union Coll, NE	B
The U of Akron, OH	B
U of Central Missouri, MO	B
U of Central Oklahoma, OK	B
U of Chicago, IL	B
U of Cincinnati, OH	B
U of Dayton, OH	B
U of Evansville, IN	B
U of Illinois at Chicago, IL	B
U of Illinois at Urbana–Champaign, IL	B
U of Indianapolis, IN	B
The U of Iowa, IA	B
U of Kansas, KS	B
U of Michigan, MI	B
U of Michigan–Flint, MI	B
U of Minnesota, Duluth, MN	B
U of Minnesota, Morris, MN	B
U of Minnesota, Twin Cities Campus, MN	B
U of Missouri–Columbia, MO	B
U of Missouri–Kansas City, MO	B
U of Missouri–St. Louis, MO	B
U of Nebraska at Kearney, NE	B
U of Nebraska at Omaha, NE	B
U of Nebraska–Lincoln, NE	B
U of New Orleans, LA	B
U of North Dakota, ND	B
U of Northern Iowa, IA	B
U of Notre Dame, IN	B
U of Oklahoma, OK	B
U of Rio Grande, OH	A,B
U of St. Francis, IL	B
U of St. Thomas, MN	B
U of Science and Arts of Oklahoma, OK	B
The U of South Dakota, SD	B
The U of Toledo, OH	B
U of Tulsa, OK	B
U of Wisconsin–Eau Claire, WI	B
U of Wisconsin–Green Bay, WI	B
U of Wisconsin–La Crosse, WI	B
U of Wisconsin–Madison, WI	B
U of Wisconsin–Milwaukee, WI	B
U of Wisconsin–Oshkosh, WI	B
U of Wisconsin–Parkside, WI	B
U of Wisconsin–Platteville, WI	B
U of Wisconsin–River Falls, WI	B
U of Wisconsin–Stevens Point, WI	B
U of Wisconsin–Superior, WI	B
U of Wisconsin–Whitewater, WI	B
Valley City State U, ND	B
Valparaiso U, IN	B
Viterbo U, WI	B
Wabash Coll, IN	B
Wartburg Coll, IA	B
Washburn U, KS	B
Washington U in St. Louis, MO	B
Wayne State Coll, NE	B
Webster U, MO	B
Western Illinois U, IL	B
Western Michigan U, MI	B
Wheaton Coll, IL	B
Wichita State U, KS	B
William Jewell Coll, MO	B
Winona State U, MN	B
Wisconsin Lutheran Coll, WI	B
Wittenberg U, OH	B
Wright State U, OH	B
Xavier U, OH	B
York Coll, NE	B
Youngstown State U, OH	B

Musical Instrument Fabrication and Repair

Ball State U, IN	B
Indiana U Bloomington, IN	A

Music History, Literature, and Theory

Baldwin-Wallace Coll, OH	B
Butler U, IN	B
Calvin Coll, MI	B
Central Christian Coll of Kansas, KS	A
Central Michigan U, MI	B
The Coll of Wooster, OH	B
Hastings Coll, NE	B
Indiana U Bloomington, IN	B
Northwestern U, IL	B
Oberlin Coll, OH	B
The Ohio State U, OH	B
Ohio U, OH	B
Otterbein Coll, OH	B
Roosevelt U, IL	B
St. Cloud State U, MN	B
Saint Joseph's Coll, IN	B
Trinity International U, IL	B
The U of Akron, OH	B
U of Chicago, IL	B
U of Cincinnati, OH	B
U of Illinois at Urbana–Champaign, IL	B
U of Michigan, MI	B
U of Wisconsin–Milwaukee, WI	B
Washington U in St. Louis, MO	B
Western Michigan U, MI	B
Wheaton Coll, IL	B
Wright State U, OH	B
Youngstown State U, OH	B

Music Management and Merchandising

Anderson U, IN	B
Butler U, IN	B
Capital U, OH	B
Coll of the Ozarks, MO	B
Columbia Coll Chicago, IL	B
DePaul U, IL	B
DePauw U, IN	B
Drake U, IA	B
Elmhurst Coll, IL	B
Ferris State U, MI	B
Greenville Coll, IL	B
Heidelberg Coll, OH	B
Huntington U, IN	B
Lewis U, IL	B
Madonna U, MI	B
Marian Coll of Fond du Lac, WI	B
McNally Smith Coll of Music, MN	A,B
Millikin U, IL	B
Minnesota State U Mankato, MN	B
Northwest Missouri State U, MO	B
Ohio Northern U, OH	B
Ohio U, OH	B
Oklahoma City U, OK	B
Otterbein Coll, OH	B
Peru State Coll, NE	B
Saint Joseph's Coll, IN	B
Saint Mary's U of Minnesota, MN	B
South Dakota State U, SD	B
Southwestern Oklahoma State U, OK	B
Tabor Coll, KS	B
Taylor U, IN	B
U of Evansville, IN	B
The U of Iowa, IA	B

U of Sioux Falls, SD	B
Valparaiso U, IN	B
Waldorf Coll, IA	B
Winona State U, MN	B

Musicology and Ethnomusicology

Bowling Green State U, OH	B
Northwestern U, IL	B
The U of Akron, OH	B
U of Kansas, KS	B

Music Pedagogy

Cedarville U, OH	B
Hastings Coll, NE	B
Lawrence U, WI	B
Michigan State U, MI	B
Roosevelt U, IL	B
St. Cloud State U, MN	B
Trinity International U, IL	B
Viterbo U, WI	B

Music Performance

Alma Coll, MI	B
Anderson U, IN	B
Aquinas Coll, MI	B
Augustana Coll, IL	B
Avila U, MO	B
Baldwin-Wallace Coll, OH	B
Bethel U, MN	B
Black Hills State U, SD	B
Bowling Green State U, OH	B
Bradley U, IL	B
Buena Vista U, IA	B
Calvin Coll, MI	B
Capital U, OH	B
Cedarville U, OH	B
Central Christian Coll of Kansas, KS	A
Central Methodist U, MO	B
Coe Coll, IA	B
The Coll of St. Scholastica, MN	B
The Coll of Wooster, OH	B
Columbia Coll Chicago, IL	B
Concordia Coll, MN	B
Cornerstone U, MI	B
DePaul U, IL	B
DePauw U, IN	B
Dordt Coll, IA	B
Drake U, IA	B
Drury U, MO	B
Eastern Michigan U, MI	B
Hastings Coll, NE	B
Hope Coll, MI	B
Illinois State U, IL	B
Indiana U South Bend, IN	B
Jamestown Coll, ND	B
Kent State U, OH	B
Lawrence U, WI	B
Marygrove Coll, MI	B
McNally Smith Coll of Music, MN	A,B
Miami U, OH	B
Michigan State U, MI	B
Millikin U, IL	B
Missouri Baptist U, MO	B
Missouri State U, MO	B
Mount Union Coll, OH	B
Nebraska Wesleyan U, NE	B
Northwestern Coll, MN	A,B
Northwestern U, IL	B
Oakland U, MI	B
Ohio Northern U, OH	B
The Ohio State U, OH	B
Ohio U, OH	B
Ohio Wesleyan U, OH	B
Oklahoma Wesleyan U, OK	B

Oral Roberts U, OK	B	St. Olaf Coll, MN	B
Otterbein Coll, OH	B	School of the Art Inst of	
Rockford Coll, IL	B	Chicago, IL	B
Roosevelt U, IL	B	Transylvania U, KY	B
St. Cloud State U, MN	B	U of Tulsa, OK	B
Saint Mary-of-the-Woods Coll, IN	B	U of Wisconsin–Green Bay, WI	B
Saint Mary's U of Minnesota, MN	B	Western Illinois U, IL	B
St. Olaf Coll, MN	B	Wheaton Coll, IL	B
Saint Xavier U, IL	B		
Simpson Coll, IA	B	**Music Teacher Education**	
Southeastern Oklahoma State U, OK	B	Adrian Coll, MI	B
Taylor U, IN	B	Alma Coll, MI	B
Transylvania U, KY	B	Alverno Coll, WI	B
Trinity Christian Coll, IL	B	Anderson U, IN	B
Truman State U, MO	B	Andrews U, MI	B
Union Coll, NE	B	Aquinas Coll, MI	B
The U of Akron, OH	B	Ashford U, IA	B
U of Evansville, IN	B	Ashland U, OH	B
U of Illinois at Urbana– Champaign, IL	B	Augsburg Coll, MN	B
U of Indianapolis, IN	B	Augustana Coll, IL	B
U of Kansas, KS	B	Augustana Coll, SD	B
U of Mary, ND	B	Baker U, KS	B
U of Missouri–Kansas City, MO	B	Baldwin-Wallace Coll, OH	B
U of Missouri–St. Louis, MO	B	Ball State U, IN	B
U of Nebraska at Omaha, NE	B	Baptist Bible Coll, MO	B
U of North Dakota, ND	B	Beloit Coll, WI	B
U of Northern Iowa, IA	B	Bemidji State U, MN	B
U of Oklahoma, OK	B	Benedictine Coll, KS	B
U of St. Francis, IL	B	Benedictine U, IL	B
U of West Florida, FL	B	Bethany Coll, KS	B
U of Wisconsin–Superior, WI	B	Bethel U, MN	B
Valparaiso U, IN	B	Bluffton U, OH	B
Viterbo U, WI	B	Bowling Green State U, OH	B
Waldorf Coll, IA	B	Bradley U, IL	B
Wartburg Coll, IA	B	Buena Vista U, IA	B
Webster U, MO	B	Butler U, IN	B
Western Michigan U, MI	B	Calvary Bible Coll and Theological Seminary, MO	B
Wheaton Coll, IL	B	Calvin Coll, MI	B
William Jewell Coll, MO	B	Capital U, OH	B
Wittenberg U, OH	B	Carroll Coll, WI	B
Wright State U, OH	B	Case Western Reserve U, OH	B
Youngstown State U, OH	B	Cedarville U, OH	B
		Central Christian Coll of Kansas, KS	A
Music Related		Central Coll, IA	B
Bethel Coll, KS	B	Central Methodist U, MO	B
Bowling Green State U, OH	B	Central Michigan U, MI	B
Calvary Bible Coll and Theological Seminary, MO	B	Central State U, OH	B
Capital U, OH	B	Chicago State U, IL	B
Central Michigan U, MI	B	Clarke Coll, IA	B
Coll of the Ozarks, MO	B	Coe Coll, IA	B
Greenville Coll, IL	B	Coll of St. Catherine, MN	B
Indiana State U, IN	B	Coll of the Ozarks, MO	B
Minnesota School of Business, MN	A	The Coll of Wooster, OH	B
Minnesota School of Business– Brooklyn Center, MN	A	Concordia Coll, MN	B
		Concordia U, IL	B
Minnesota School of Business– Plymouth, MN	A	Concordia U, MI	B
		Concordia U, NE	B
Minnesota School of Business– Richfield, MN	A	Concordia U, St. Paul, MN	B
		Concordia U Wisconsin, WI	B
Minnesota School of Business– St. Cloud, MN	A	Concord U, WV	B
		Cornell Coll, IA	B
Minnesota School of Business– Shakopee, MN	A	Cornerstone U, MI	B
		Crown Coll, MN	B
Northwestern U, IL	B	Culver-Stockton Coll, MO	B
Ohio Northern U, OH	B	Dakota Wesleyan U, SD	B
Roosevelt U, IL	B	Dana Coll, NE	B
Saint Mary's U of Minnesota, MN	B	DePaul U, IL	B
		DePauw U, IN	B
		Dickinson State U, ND	B
		Dordt Coll, IA	B
		Drake U, IA	B
		Drury U, MO	B

East Central U, OK	B	Northern Illinois U, IL	B
Eastern Michigan U, MI	B	Northern Michigan U, MI	B
Elmhurst Coll, IL	B	Northern State U, SD	B
Emporia State U, KS	B	Northland Coll, WI	B
Evangel U, MO	B	Northwestern Coll, IA	B
Faith Baptist Bible Coll and Theological Seminary, IA	B	Northwestern Coll, MN	B
Fort Hays State U, KS	B	Northwestern Oklahoma State U, OK	B
God's Bible School and Coll, OH	B	Northwestern U, IL	B
Goshen Coll, IN	B	Northwest Missouri State U, MO	B
Grace Bible Coll, MI	B	Oakland U, MI	B
Grace Coll, IN	B	Oberlin Coll, OH	B
Graceland U, IA	B	Ohio Northern U, OH	B
Grand Valley State U, MI	B	The Ohio State U, OH	B
Greenville Coll, IL	B	Ohio U, OH	B
Gustavus Adolphus Coll, MN	B	Ohio Wesleyan U, OH	B
Hamline U, MN	B	Oklahoma Christian U, OK	B
Hannibal-LaGrange Coll, MO	B	Oklahoma City U, OK	B
Hastings Coll, NE	B	Oklahoma State U, OK	B
Heidelberg Coll, OH	B	Oral Roberts U, OK	B
Hope Coll, MI	B	Ottawa U, KS	B
Huntington U, IN	B	Otterbein Coll, OH	B
Illinois State U, IL	B	Peru State Coll, NE	B
Illinois Wesleyan U, IL	B	Pittsburg State U, KS	B
Indiana U Bloomington, IN	B	Quincy U, IL	B
Indiana U–Purdue U Fort Wayne, IN	B	Ripon Coll, WI	B
Indiana U South Bend, IN	B	Roosevelt U, IL	B
Indiana Wesleyan U, IN	B	Saginaw Valley State U, MI	B
Iowa State U of Science and Technology, IA	B	St. Ambrose U, IA	B
Iowa Wesleyan Coll, IA	B	St. Cloud State U, MN	B
Jamestown Coll, ND	B	Saint Mary-of-the-Woods Coll, IN	B
Judson Coll, IL	B	Saint Mary's Coll, IN	B
Kansas State U, KS	B	Saint Mary's U of Minnesota, MN	B
Kent State U, OH	B	St. Norbert Coll, WI	B
Lakeland Coll, WI	B	St. Olaf Coll, MN	B
Langston U, OK	B	Saint Xavier U, IL	B
Lawrence U, WI	B	Silver Lake Coll, WI	B
Lincoln U, MO	B	Simpson Coll, IA	B
Lindenwood U, MO	B	South Dakota State U, SD	B
MacMurray Coll, IL	B	Southeastern Oklahoma State U, OK	B
Madonna U, MI	B	Southeast Missouri State U, MO	B
Malone Coll, OH	B	Southwest Baptist U, MO	B
Manchester Coll, IN	B	Southwestern Coll, KS	B
Maranatha Baptist Bible Coll, WI	B	Southwestern Oklahoma State U, OK	B
Marian Coll, IN	B	Southwest Minnesota State U, MN	B
Marian Coll of Fond du Lac, WI	B	Spring Arbor U, MI	B
McKendree Coll, IL	B	Sterling Coll, KS	B
Miami U, OH	B	Tabor Coll, KS	B
Miami U Hamilton, OH	B	Taylor U, IN	B
Michigan State U, MI	B	Transylvania U, KY	B
Millikin U, IL	B	Trinity Christian Coll, IL	B
Minnesota State U Mankato, MN	B	Trinity International U, IL	B
Minot State U, ND	B	Union Coll, NE	A,B
Missouri Baptist U, MO	B	The U of Akron, OH	B
Missouri State U, MO	B	U of Central Missouri, MO	B
Missouri Western State U, MO	B	U of Central Oklahoma, OK	B
Morningside Coll, IA	B	U of Charleston, WV	B
Mount Marty Coll, SD	B	U of Cincinnati, OH	B
Mount Mary Coll, WI	B	U of Dayton, OH	B
Mount Mercy Coll, IA	B	U of Evansville, IN	B
Mount Union Coll, OH	B	U of Illinois at Urbana– Champaign, IL	B
Mount Vernon Nazarene U, OH	B	U of Indianapolis, IN	B
Nebraska Wesleyan U, NE	B	The U of Iowa, IA	B
North Carolina Ag and Tech State U, NC	B	U of Kansas, KS	B
North Central Coll, IL	B	U of Mary, ND	B
North Dakota State U, ND	B	U of Michigan, MI	B
Northeastern State U, OK	B	U of Michigan–Flint, MI	B

A—associate degree; B—bachelor's degree

U of Minnesota, Duluth, MN	B
U of Minnesota, Twin Cities Campus, MN	B
U of Missouri–Columbia, MO	B
U of Missouri–Kansas City, MO	B
U of Missouri–St. Louis, MO	B
U of Nebraska at Omaha, NE	B
U of Nebraska–Lincoln, NE	B
U of New Orleans, LA	B
U of North Dakota, ND	B
U of Northern Iowa, IA	B
U of Rio Grande, OH	B
U of St. Francis, IL	B
U of St. Thomas, MN	B
U of Sioux Falls, SD	B
The U of South Dakota, SD	B
The U of Toledo, OH	B
U of Tulsa, OK	B
U of West Florida, FL	B
U of Wisconsin–Madison, WI	B
U of Wisconsin–Milwaukee, WI	B
U of Wisconsin–Oshkosh, WI	B
U of Wisconsin–River Falls, WI	B
U of Wisconsin–Stevens Point, WI	B
U of Wisconsin–Superior, WI	B
U of Wisconsin–Whitewater, WI	B
Valley City State U, ND	B
Valparaiso U, IN	B
Viterbo U, WI	B
Waldorf Coll, IA	B
Wartburg Coll, IA	B
Washburn U, KS	B
Wayne State Coll, NE	B
Webster U, MO	B
Western Michigan U, MI	B
Wheaton Coll, IL	B
Wichita State U, KS	B
William Jewell Coll, MO	B
Wilmington Coll, OH	B
Winona State U, MN	B
Wittenberg U, OH	B
Wright State U, OH	B
Xavier U, OH	B
York Coll, NE	B
Youngstown State U, OH	B

Music Theory and Composition

Baldwin-Wallace Coll, OH	B
Bowling Green State U, OH	B
Bradley U, IL	B
Calvin Coll, MI	B
Capital U, OH	B
Cedarville U, OH	B
Central Michigan U, MI	B
Coe Coll, IA	B
The Coll of Wooster, OH	B
Concordia Coll, MN	B
Cornerstone U, MI	B
DePaul U, IL	B
DePauw U, IN	B
Drury U, MO	B
Hope Coll, MI	B
Huntington U, IN	B
Indiana Wesleyan U, IN	B
Lawrence U, WI	B
Michigan State U, MI	B
Missouri State U, MO	B
Northwestern Coll, MN	B
Northwestern U, IL	B
Oakland U, MI	B
Oberlin Coll, OH	B

The Ohio State U, OH	B
Ohio U, OH	B
Oklahoma City U, OK	B
Oral Roberts U, OK	B
Roosevelt U, IL	B
St. Cloud State U, MN	B
St. Olaf Coll, MN	B
Southern Methodist U, TX	B
Trinity International U, IL	B
The U of Akron, OH	B
U of Central Missouri, MO	B
U of Illinois at Urbana–Champaign, IL	B
The U of Iowa, IA	B
U of Kansas, KS	B
U of Michigan, MI	B
U of Missouri–Kansas City, MO	B
U of Nebraska at Omaha, NE	B
U of Northern Iowa, IA	B
U of Oklahoma, OK	B
Valparaiso U, IN	B
Wartburg Coll, IA	B
Washington U in St. Louis, MO	B
Webster U, MO	B
Western Michigan U, MI	B
Wheaton Coll, IL	B
William Jewell Coll, MO	B
Wittenberg U, OH	B
Wright State U, OH	B
Youngstown State U, OH	B

Music Therapy

Alverno Coll, WI	B
Augsburg Coll, MN	B
Baldwin-Wallace Coll, OH	B
The Coll of Wooster, OH	B
Eastern Michigan U, MI	B
Indiana U–Purdue U Fort Wayne, IN	B
Maryville U of Saint Louis, MO	B
Michigan State U, MI	B
Saint Mary-of-the-Woods Coll, IN	B
Southern Methodist U, TX	B
Southwestern Oklahoma State U, OK	B
U of Dayton, OH	B
U of Evansville, IN	B
The U of Iowa, IA	B
U of Kansas, KS	B
U of Minnesota, Twin Cities Campus, MN	B
U of North Dakota, ND	B
U of Wisconsin–Eau Claire, WI	B
U of Wisconsin–Milwaukee, WI	B
U of Wisconsin–Oshkosh, WI	B
Wartburg Coll, IA	B
Western Michigan U, MI	B

Natural Resource Economics

Michigan State U, MI	B

Natural Resources and Conservation Related

St. Gregory's U, Shawnee, OK	B
U of Michigan–Flint, MI	B

Natural Resources/ Conservation

Carroll Coll, WI	B
Central Michigan U, MI	B
Coll of Menominee Nation, WI	A

Kent State U, OH	B
Mount Vernon Nazarene U, OH	B
Northern Michigan U, MI	B
Northland Coll, WI	B
Northwest Missouri State U, MO	B
Peru State Coll, NE	B
Purdue U, IN	B
Southeastern Oklahoma State U, OK	B
U of Illinois at Urbana–Champaign, IL	B
U of Michigan–Flint, MI	B
U of Minnesota, Crookston, MN	A
U of Missouri–Columbia, MO	B
U of Nebraska–Lincoln, NE	B
U of Wisconsin–Milwaukee, WI	B
U of Wisconsin–River Falls, WI	B
U of Wisconsin–Stevens Point, WI	B
Upper Iowa U, IA	B
Washington U in St. Louis, MO	B
Winona State U, MN	B

Natural Resources/ Conservation Related

U of Illinois at Urbana–Champaign, IL	B

Natural Resources Management

The Ohio State U, OH	B

Natural Resources Management and Policy

Ball State U, IN	B
Bowling Green State U, OH	B
Fort Hays State U, KS	B
Grand Valley State U, MI	B
Huntington U, IN	B
Iowa State U of Science and Technology, IA	B
Lake Superior State U, MI	A
North Dakota State U, ND	B
Northland Coll, WI	B
Oglala Lakota Coll, SD	A
The Ohio State U, OH	B
Turtle Mountain Comm Coll, ND	A
U of Michigan, MI	B
U of Minnesota, Crookston, MN	A,B
U of Minnesota, Twin Cities Campus, MN	B
U of Nebraska–Lincoln, NE	B
U of Wisconsin–Madison, WI	B
U of Wisconsin–Stevens Point, WI	B

Natural Sciences

Antioch Coll, OH	B
Augsburg Coll, MN	B
Avila U, MO	B
Bemidji State U, MN	B
Benedictine Coll, KS	B
Bethel Coll, KS	B
Calvin Coll, MI	B
Cameron U, OK	B
Case Western Reserve U, OH	B
Central Christian Coll of Kansas, KS	B
Central Coll, IA	B
Coll of Mount St. Joseph, OH	B

Coll of Saint Benedict, MN	B
Coll of Saint Mary, NE	B
The Coll of St. Scholastica, MN	B
Concordia U, IL	B
Concordia U, NE	B
Concordia U, St. Paul, MN	B
Doane Coll, NE	B
Dordt Coll, IA	B
Edgewood Coll, WI	B
Goshen Coll, IN	B
Grand Valley State U, MI	B
Iowa Wesleyan Coll, IA	B
Kenyon Coll, OH	B
Lourdes Coll, OH	A
Madonna U, MI	A,B
Minnesota State U Mankato, MN	B
Missouri Western State U, MO	B
Northland Coll, WI	B
Oklahoma Panhandle State U, OK	B
Oklahoma Wesleyan U, OK	B
Park U, MO	B
Peru State Coll, NE	B
St. Cloud State U, MN	B
St. Gregory's U, Shawnee, OK	B
Saint John's U, MN	B
Shawnee State U, OH	A,B
Shimer Coll, IL	B
Stephens Coll, MO	B
Tabor Coll, KS	B
Taylor U, IN	B
The U of Akron, OH	B
U of Cincinnati, OH	A,B
U of Nebraska at Omaha, NE	B
U of Science and Arts of Oklahoma, OK	B
The U of Toledo, OH	A,B
U of Wisconsin–River Falls, WI	B
U of Wisconsin–Stevens Point, WI	B
Washburn U, KS	A
Washington U in St. Louis, MO	B
Wayne State Coll, NE	B
Winona State U, MN	B
Xavier U, OH	B
York Coll, NE	B

Naval Architecture and Marine Engineering

U of Michigan, MI	B
U of New Orleans, LA	B

Near and Middle Eastern Studies

Indiana U Bloomington, IN	B
Oberlin Coll, OH	B
The Ohio State U, OH	B
U of Chicago, IL	B
U of Michigan, MI	B
U of Minnesota, Twin Cities Campus, MN	B
The U of Toledo, OH	B
Washington U in St. Louis, MO	B

Neurobiology and Neurophysiology

Andrews U, MI	B

Neuroscience

Baldwin-Wallace Coll, OH	B
Bowling Green State U, OH	B
Central Michigan U, MI	B
Drake U, IA	B

Neuroscience

Kenyon Coll, OH	B
Lawrence U, WI	B
Macalester Coll, MN	B
Northwestern U, IL	B
Oberlin Coll, OH	B
Ohio Wesleyan U, OH	B
U of Minnesota, Twin Cities Campus, MN	B
Washington U in St. Louis, MO	B

Nonprofit Management

Clarkson U, NY	B
Lakeland Coll, WI	B
Manchester Coll, IN	B
Saint Mary-of-the-Woods Coll, IN	B
Trinity International U, IL	B
Washburn U, KS	B

Nuclear Engineering

Kansas State U, KS	B
Purdue U, IN	B
U of Cincinnati, OH	B
U of Illinois at Urbana–Champaign, IL	B
U of Michigan, MI	B
U of Missouri–Rolla, MO	B
U of Wisconsin–Madison, WI	B

Nuclear Medical Technology

Ball State U, IN	A
Benedictine U, IL	B
Ferris State U, MI	A,B
Indiana U–Purdue U Indianapolis, IN	B
Kettering Coll of Medical Arts, OH	A
Loras Coll, IA	B
North Central Coll, IL	B
Peru State Coll, NE	B
Roosevelt U, IL	B
St. Cloud State U, MN	B
Saint Louis U, MO	B
Saint Mary's U of Minnesota, MN	B
U of Cincinnati, OH	B
The U of Findlay, OH	A,B
The U of Iowa, IA	B
U of Missouri–Columbia, MO	B
U of Nebraska Medical Center, NE	B
U of Oklahoma Health Sciences Center, OK	B
U of St. Francis, IL	B
U of Wisconsin–La Crosse, WI	B

Nurse Anesthetist

Webster U, MO	B

Nursing Administration

Central Methodist U, MO	B
Nebraska Wesleyan U, NE	B
U of Phoenix–Indianapolis Campus, IN	B

Nursing Assistant/Aide and Patient Care Assistant

Central Christian Coll of Kansas, KS	A

Nursing (Licensed Practical/Vocational Nurse Training)

Central Christian Coll of Kansas, KS	A
Coll of Menominee Nation, WI	A

Dickinson State U, ND	A
Fort Berthold Comm Coll, ND	A

Nursing (Registered Nurse Training)

Allen Coll, IA	B
Alverno Coll, WI	B
Anderson U, IN	B
Andrews U, MI	B
Augsburg Coll, MN	B
Augustana Coll, SD	B
Aurora U, IL	B
Baker Coll of Clinton Township, MI	A
Baker Coll of Flint, MI	A
Baker Coll of Muskegon, MI	A
Baker Coll of Owosso, MI	A
Baker U, KS	B
Ball State U, IN	A,B
Barnes-Jewish Coll of Nursing and Allied Health, MO	A,B
Bemidji State U, MN	B
Bethel Coll, KS	B
Bethel U, MN	B
Blessing-Rieman Coll of Nursing, IL	B
Bowling Green State U, OH	B
Bowling Green State U–Firelands Coll, OH	A
Bradley U, IL	B
Briar Cliff U, IA	B
Calvin Coll, MI	B
Capital U, OH	B
Cardinal Stritch U, WI	A,B
Carroll Coll, WI	B
Case Western Reserve U, OH	B
Cedarville U, OH	B
Central Christian Coll of Kansas, KS	A
Central Methodist U, MO	B
Chicago State U, IL	B
Cleveland State U, OH	B
Coe Coll, IA	B
Coll of Mount St. Joseph, OH	B
Coll of Saint Benedict, MN	B
Coll of St. Catherine, MN	B
Coll of Saint Mary, NE	A,B
The Coll of St. Scholastica, MN	B
Columbia Coll, MO	A
Concordia Coll, MN	B
Concordia U, IL	B
Concordia U Wisconsin, WI	B
Creighton U, NE	B
Crown Coll, MN	B
Culver-Stockton Coll, MO	B
Dakota Wesleyan U, SD	A
Davenport U, Dearborn, MI	A,B
DePaul U, IL	B
Dickinson State U, ND	B
Dordt Coll, IA	B
East Central U, OK	B
Eastern Michigan U, MI	B
Edgewood Coll, WI	B
Elmhurst Coll, IL	B
Emporia State U, KS	B
Ferris State U, MI	A,B
Finlandia U, MI	B
Fort Hays State U, KS	B
Franciscan U of Steubenville, OH	B
Gannon U, PA	B
Goshen Coll, IN	B
Graceland U, IA	B
Grand Valley State U, MI	B

Grand View Coll, IA	B
Gustavus Adolphus Coll, MN	B
Hannibal-LaGrange Coll, MO	A,B
Hesston Coll, KS	A
Hillsdale Free Will Baptist Coll, OK	A
Hope Coll, MI	B
Illinois State U, IL	B
Illinois Wesleyan U, IL	B
Indiana State U, IN	B
Indiana U East, IN	A,B
Indiana U Kokomo, IN	A,B
Indiana U Northwest, IN	A,B
Indiana U–Purdue U Fort Wayne, IN	A,B
Indiana U–Purdue U Indianapolis, IN	A,B
Indiana U South Bend, IN	A,B
Indiana U Southeast, IN	B
Indiana Wesleyan U, IN	B
Iowa Wesleyan Coll, IA	B
Jamestown Coll, ND	B
Judson Coll, IL	B
Kent State U, OH	A,B
Kent State U, Ashtabula Campus, OH	A
Kent State U, Tuscarawas Campus, OH	A,B
Kettering Coll of Medical Arts, OH	A
Kuyper Coll, MI	B
Lake Superior State U, MI	B
Langston U, OK	B
Lewis U, IL	B
Lincoln U, MO	A,B
Lourdes Coll, OH	B
Loyola U Chicago, IL	B
Luther Coll, IA	B
MacMurray Coll, IL	B
Madonna U, MI	B
Malone Coll, OH	B
Maranatha Baptist Bible Coll, WI	B
Marian Coll, IN	B
Marian Coll of Fond du Lac, WI	B
Marquette U, WI	B
Maryville U of Saint Louis, MO	B
McKendree Coll, IL	B
Medcenter One Coll of Nursing, ND	B
Mercy Coll of Health Sciences, IA	A
Mercy Coll of Northwest Ohio, OH	A,B
Metropolitan State U, MN	B
Miami U, OH	B
Miami U–Middletown Campus, OH	A,B
Michigan State U, MI	B
Millikin U, IL	B
Milwaukee School of Engineering, WI	B
Minnesota School of Business, MN	B
Minnesota State U Mankato, MN	B
Minot State U, ND	B
Missouri Southern State U, MO	B
Missouri State U, MO	B
Missouri Western State U, MO	B
Morningside Coll, IA	B
Mount Marty Coll, SD	B

Mount Mary Coll, WI	B
Mount Mercy Coll, IA	B
Nebraska Methodist Coll, NE	A,B
Newman U, KS	B
North Carolina Ag and Tech State U, NC	B
North Dakota State U, ND	B
Northeastern State U, OK	B
Northern Illinois U, IL	B
Northern Michigan U, MI	B
Northwestern Oklahoma State U, OK	B
Oakland U, MI	B
Oglala Lakota Coll, SD	A
The Ohio State U, OH	B
Ohio U–Zanesville, OH	A,B
Oklahoma City U, OK	B
Oklahoma Panhandle State U, OK	A,B
Oklahoma Wesleyan U, OK	B
Oral Roberts U, OK	B
Otterbein Coll, OH	B
Park U, MO	A
Pittsburg State U, KS	B
Presentation Coll, SD	A,B
Purdue U, IN	B
Purdue U Calumet, IN	A,B
Purdue U North Central, IN	A,B
Quincy U, IL	B
Research Coll of Nursing, MO	B
Rockford Coll, IL	B
Rockhurst U, MO	B
Rogers State U, OK	A
Saginaw Valley State U, MI	B
St. Ambrose U, IA	B
Saint Anthony Coll of Nursing, IL	B
St. Cloud State U, MN	B
Saint Francis Medical Center Coll of Nursing, IL	B
Saint John's U, MN	B
Saint Joseph's Coll, IN	B
Saint Louis U, MO	B
St. Luke's Coll, IA	A
Saint Luke's Coll, MO	B
Saint Mary's Coll, IN	B
St. Olaf Coll, MN	B
Saint Xavier U, IL	B
Shawnee State U, OH	A,B
South Dakota State U, SD	B
Southeast Missouri Hospital Coll of Nursing and Health Sciences, MO	A
Southeast Missouri State U, MO	B
Southern Illinois U Edwardsville, IL	B
Southwest Baptist U, MO	A
Southwestern Coll, KS	B
Southwestern Oklahoma State U, OK	B
Trinity Christian Coll, IL	B
Trinity Coll of Nursing and Health Sciences, IL	A,B
Truman State U, MO	B
Turtle Mountain Comm Coll, ND	A
Union Coll, NE	B
The U of Akron, OH	B
U of Central Missouri, MO	B
U of Central Oklahoma, OK	B
U of Charleston, WV	A,B
U of Cincinnati, OH	A,B
U of Evansville, IN	B
U of Illinois at Chicago, IL	B

A—associate degree; B—bachelor's degree

U of Indianapolis, IN A,B
The U of Iowa, IA B
U of Mary, ND B
U of Michigan, MI B
U of Michigan–Flint, MI B
U of Minnesota, Twin Cities Campus, MN B
U of Missouri–Columbia, MO B
U of Missouri–Kansas City, MO
U of Missouri–St. Louis, MO B
U of Nebraska Medical Center, NE B
U of North Dakota, ND B
U of Oklahoma Health Sciences Center, OK B
U of Phoenix–Cincinnati Campus, OH B
U of Phoenix–Cleveland Campus, OH B
U of Phoenix–Columbus Ohio Campus, OH B
U of Phoenix–Indianapolis Campus, IN B
U of Phoenix–Kansas City Campus, MO B
U of Phoenix–Metro Detroit Campus, MI B
U of Phoenix–Oklahoma City Campus, OK B
U of Phoenix–St. Louis Campus, MO B
U of Phoenix–Springfield Campus, MO B
U of Phoenix–Tulsa Campus, OK B
U of Phoenix–West Michigan Campus, MI B
U of Rio Grande, OH A
U of St. Francis, IL B
U of Saint Francis, IN A,B
The U of South Dakota, SD A
U of Southern Indiana, IN A,B
The U of Toledo, OH A,B
U of Tulsa, OK B
U of West Florida, FL B
U of Wisconsin–Eau Claire, WI B
U of Wisconsin–Madison, WI B
U of Wisconsin–Milwaukee, WI B
U of Wisconsin–Oshkosh, WI B
U of Wisconsin–Parkside, WI B
Ursuline Coll, OH B
Valparaiso U, IN B
Viterbo U, WI B
Walsh U, OH A,B
Washburn U, KS B
Webster U, MO B
Western Michigan U, MI B
William Jewell Coll, MO B
Winona State U, MN B
Wright State U, OH B
Youngstown State U, OH B

Nursing Related
Alverno Coll, WI B
Avila U, MO B
Capital U, OH B
Madonna U, MI A,B
Minot State U, ND B
Rogers State U, OK A
The U of Akron, OH B
U of Saint Francis, IN B
The U of Toledo, OH B
Wright State U, OH B

Nursing Science
Benedictine U, IL B
Clarke Coll, IA B
Coll of Mount St. Joseph, OH B
Davenport U, Dearborn, MI A
Kent State U, Geauga Campus, OH B
Kent State U, Trumbull Campus, OH B
Mercy Coll of Health Sciences, IA B
Minnesota School of Business–Brooklyn Center, MN B
Minnesota School of Business–Plymouth, MN B
Minnesota School of Business–Richfield, MN B
Minnesota School of Business–St. Cloud, MN B
Minnesota School of Business–Shakopee, MN B
Missouri Baptist U, MO B
The Ohio State U, OH B
Trinity Coll of Nursing and Health Sciences, IL A,B
The U of Akron, OH B
U of Kansas, KS B
U of Phoenix–Metro Detroit Campus, MI B
U of Wisconsin–Green Bay, WI B
Wichita State U, KS B
Xavier U, OH B

Nutrition Sciences
Benedictine U, IL B
Case Western Reserve U, OH B
Elmhurst Coll, IL B
Michigan State U, MI B
U of Missouri–Columbia, MO B
U of Wisconsin–Green Bay, WI B

Occupational Health and Industrial Hygiene
Clarkson U, NY B

Occupational Safety and Health Technology
Ball State U, IN B
Ferris State U, MI A,B
Grand Valley State U, MI B
Indiana State U, IN B
Indiana U Bloomington, IN A
North Carolina Ag and Tech State U, NC B
Oakland U, MI B
Southeastern Oklahoma State U, OK B
Southwest Baptist U, MO A,B
U of Central Missouri, MO B
U of Central Oklahoma, OK B
U of Cincinnati, OH A
U of North Dakota, ND B
U of Wisconsin–Whitewater, WI B
Wright State U, OH A

Occupational Therapist Assistant
Baker Coll of Muskegon, MI A
Coll of St. Catherine, MN A
Grand Valley State U, MI B
U of Saint Francis, IN A
U of Southern Indiana, IN A

Occupational Therapy
Augustana Coll, IL B

Baker Coll of Flint, MI B
Calvin Coll, MI B
Cleveland State U, OH B
Coll of Saint Benedict, MN B
Coll of St. Catherine, MN B
Concordia Coll, MN B
Concordia U Wisconsin, WI B
Drury U, MO B
Eastern Michigan U, MI B
Elmhurst Coll, IL B
Hamline U, MN B
Illinois Coll, IL B
Indiana U–Purdue U Indianapolis, IN B
McKendree Coll, IL B
Mount Mary Coll, WI B
The Ohio State U, OH B
Saint John's U, MN B
Saint Louis U, MO B
Shawnee State U, OH A,B
Stephens Coll, MO B
The U of Findlay, OH B
U of Kansas, KS B
U of Minnesota, Twin Cities Campus, MN B
U of Missouri–Columbia, MO B
U of Southern Indiana, IN B
U of Wisconsin–Madison, WI B
U of Wisconsin–Milwaukee, WI B
Wartburg Coll, IA B
Western Michigan U, MI B
Xavier U, OH B

Oceanography (Chemical and Physical)
Central Michigan U, MI B
U of Michigan, MI B

Office Management
Academy Coll, MN A
Baker Coll of Flint, MI A,B
Baker Coll of Jackson, MI A
Central Michigan U, MI B
Dakota State U, SD A
Eastern Michigan U, MI B
God's Bible School and Coll, OH A
Indiana State U, IN B
Lake Superior State U, MI A
Mayville State U, ND B
Metropolitan State U, MN B
Miami U Hamilton, OH B
Miami U–Middletown Campus, OH A
Park U, MO A
Shawnee State U, OH A
Southeastern Oklahoma State U, OK B
Southeast Missouri State U, MO B
U of Central Missouri, MO B
U of Nebraska–Lincoln, NE B
U of Southern Indiana, IN B
Valley City State U, ND B
Washburn U, KS A
Wright State U, OH B

Office Occupations and Clerical Services
Sitting Bull Coll, ND A
Wright State U, OH A

Operations Management
Aurora U, IL B
Baker Coll of Flint, MI A,B
Bowling Green State U, OH B

Bowling Green State U–Firelands Coll, OH A
Central Michigan U, MI B
Clarkson U, NY B
DeVry U, Tinley Park, IL B
Indiana U–Purdue U Fort Wayne, IN A,B
Indiana U–Purdue U Indianapolis, IN A,B
Iowa State U of Science and Technology, IA B
Kent State U, OH B
Kettering U, MI B
Loyola U Chicago, IL B
Metropolitan State U, MN B
Miami U, OH B
Michigan State U, MI B
Michigan Technological U, MI B
Missouri Baptist U, MO B
National American U, Rapid City, SD B
Northern Illinois U, IL B
The Ohio State U, OH B
Pittsburg State U, KS B
Purdue U, IN A,B
Saginaw Valley State U, MI B
Tri-State U, IN B
U of Illinois at Urbana–Champaign, IL B
U of Indianapolis, IN B
U of Michigan–Flint, MI B
U of Nebraska at Kearney, NE B
U of Phoenix–Cincinnati Campus, OH B
U of Phoenix–Columbus Ohio Campus, OH B
U of Phoenix–Indianapolis Campus, IN B
U of Phoenix–St. Louis Campus, MO B
U of Phoenix–Springfield Campus, MO B
U of St. Thomas, MN B
The U of Toledo, OH B
U of Wisconsin–Stout, WI B
U of Wisconsin–Whitewater, WI B
Washington U in St. Louis, MO B
Wright State U, OH B
Youngstown State U, OH B

Operations Research
DePaul U, IL B
Miami U, OH B
U of Cincinnati, OH B

Ophthalmic and Optometric Support Services and Allied Professions Related
Concordia Coll, MN B

Ophthalmic Laboratory Technology
Indiana U Bloomington, IN A

Ophthalmic/Optometric Services
Gannon U, PA B
Indiana U Bloomington, IN B
Northeastern State U, OK B

Optical Sciences
Saginaw Valley State U, MI B

Opticianry
Ferris State U, MI A
The U of Akron, OH A

Optometric Technician

Indiana U Bloomington, IN   A

Organizational Behavior

Anderson U, IN	B
Baldwin-Wallace Coll, OH	B
Benedictine U, IL	B
Bluffton U, OH	B
Calvary Bible Coll and Theological Seminary, MO	B
Carroll Coll, WI	B
The Coll of St. Scholastica, MN	B
Concordia U, St. Paul, MN	B
Denison U, OH	B
Greenville Coll, IL	B
Loyola U Chicago, IL	B
Miami U, OH	B
Northwestern U, IL	B
St. Ambrose U, IA	B
Saint Louis U, MO	B
Southern Methodist U, TX	B
U of Illinois at Urbana–Champaign, IL	B
U of Michigan–Flint, MI	B
U of Phoenix–Cincinnati Campus, OH	B
U of Phoenix–Cleveland Campus, OH	B
U of Phoenix–Columbus Ohio Campus, OH	B
U of Phoenix–Indianapolis Campus, IN	B
U of St. Francis, IL	B
The U of Toledo, OH	B

Organizational Communication

Aquinas Coll, MI	B
Buena Vista U, IA	B
Capital U, OH	B
Carroll Coll, WI	B
Creighton U, NE	A
Dana Coll, NE	B
Indiana U–Purdue U Fort Wayne, IN	B
McKendree Coll, IL	B
North Central Coll, IL	B
Ohio Northern U, OH	B
U of Michigan–Flint, MI	B
U of Northern Iowa, IA	B
Valparaiso U, IN	B
Western Michigan U, MI	B
Wright State U, OH	B

Ornamental Horticulture

Ferris State U, MI	A
Iowa State U of Science and Technology, IA	B
U of Illinois at Urbana–Champaign, IL	B
U of Wisconsin–Platteville, WI	B

Orthotics/Prosthetics

Baker Coll of Flint, MI   A

Painting

Aquinas Coll, MI	B
Art Academy of Cincinnati, OH	B
Bethany Coll, KS	B
The Cleveland Inst of Art, OH	B
Coe Coll, IA	B
Columbia Coll, MO	B
Drake U, IA	B
Grace Coll, IN	B
Indiana U–Purdue U Fort Wayne, IN	

Indiana Wesleyan U, IN	B
Kansas City Art Inst, MO	B
Lewis U, IL	B
Minneapolis Coll of Art and Design, MN	B
Ohio Northern U, OH	B
The Ohio State U, OH	B
Ohio U, OH	B
St. Cloud State U, MN	B
School of the Art Inst of Chicago, IL	B
Shawnee State U, OH	B
Trinity Christian Coll, IL	B
The U of Akron, OH	B
U of Dallas, TX	B
U of Illinois at Urbana–Champaign, IL	B
The U of Iowa, IA	B
U of Kansas, KS	B
U of Michigan, MI	B
U of Michigan–Flint, MI	B
U of Missouri–St. Louis, MO	B
Washington U in St. Louis, MO	B
Youngstown State U, OH	B

Paralegal/Legal Assistant

Bryant and Stratton Coll, Cleveland, OH	A
Davenport U, Dearborn, MI	A,B
Minnesota School of Business, MN	A,B
Minnesota School of Business–Brooklyn Center, MN	A,B
Minnesota School of Business–Plymouth, MN	A,B
Minnesota School of Business–St. Cloud, MN	A,B
Minnesota School of Business–Shakopee, MN	A,B
Newman U, KS	A

Parks, Recreation and Leisure

Ashland U, OH	B
Bemidji State U, MN	B
Bethany Coll, KS	B
Black Hills State U, SD	B
Bluffton U, OH	B
Bowling Green State U, OH	B
Calvin Coll, MI	B
Central Christian Coll of Kansas, KS	A,B
Central Michigan U, MI	B
Central State U, OH	B
Chicago State U, IL	B
Dordt Coll, IA	B
Emporia State U, KS	B
Evangel U, MO	B
Ferris State U, MI	B
Graceland U, IA	B
Greenville Coll, IL	B
Huntington U, IN	B
Indiana U Bloomington, IN	B
Lake Superior State U, MI	B
Minnesota State U Mankato, MN	B
Missouri State U, MO	B
Missouri Valley Coll, MO	B
North Carolina Ag and Tech State U, NC	B
North Dakota State U, ND	B
Northland Coll, WI	B
Northwest Missouri State U, MO	B
Ohio U, OH	B

Oklahoma Panhandle State U, OK	A,B
South Dakota State U, SD	B
Southeastern Oklahoma State U, OK	B
Southeast Missouri State U, MO	B
Southern Illinois U Carbondale, IL	B
Southwest Baptist U, MO	B
Southwestern Oklahoma State U, OK	B
U of Central Missouri, MO	B
U of Illinois at Urbana–Champaign, IL	B
The U of Iowa, IA	B
U of Minnesota, Duluth, MN	B
U of Missouri–Columbia, MO	B
U of Nebraska at Kearney, NE	B
U of Nebraska at Omaha, NE	B
U of North Dakota, ND	B
U of Northern Iowa, IA	B
The U of South Dakota, SD	B
The U of Toledo, OH	B
U of Wisconsin–Madison, WI	B
U of Wisconsin–Milwaukee, WI	B
Upper Iowa U, IA	B
Western Michigan U, MI	B
William Penn U, IA	B
Winona State U, MN	B

Parks, Recreation and Leisure Facilities Management

Ball State U, IN	B
Central Michigan U, MI	B
Coll of the Ozarks, MO	B
Concord U, WV	B
Eastern Illinois U, IL	B
Eastern Michigan U, MI	B
Grand Valley State U, MI	B
Hannibal-LaGrange Coll, MO	B
Hastings Coll, NE	B
Illinois State U, IL	B
Indiana State U, IN	B
Indiana Tech, IN	A,B
Indiana U Bloomington, IN	B
Indiana U Southeast, IN	B
Indiana Wesleyan U, IN	B
Kansas State U, KS	B
Kent State U, OH	B
Lake Superior State U, MI	B
Michigan State U, MI	B
Minnesota State U Mankato, MN	B
Missouri Valley Coll, MO	B
Missouri Western State U, MO	B
Mount Marty Coll, SD	B
Northern Michigan U, MI	B
Northland Coll, WI	B
Ohio U, OH	B
South Dakota State U, SD	B
Tri-State U, IN	B
U of Minnesota, Twin Cities Campus, MN	B
U of North Dakota, ND	B
U of St. Francis, IL	B
U of Wisconsin–La Crosse, WI	B
Western Illinois U, IL	B
Winona State U, MN	B

Parks, Recreation, and Leisure Related

Culver-Stockton Coll, MO	B
Franklin Coll, IN	B
Madonna U, MI	B

Malone Coll, OH	B
The U of Toledo, OH	B

Pastoral Counseling and Specialized Ministries Related

Calvary Bible Coll and Theological Seminary, MO	B
Cedarville U, OH	B
Coll of Mount St. Joseph, OH	B
Greenville Coll, IL	B
Malone Coll, OH	B
Oak Hills Christian Coll, MN	B
Trinity International U, IL	B
Vennard Coll, IA	B

Pastoral Studies/Counseling

Baptist Bible Coll, MO	B
Barclay Coll, KS	B
Calvary Bible Coll and Theological Seminary, MO	B
Cedarville U, OH	B
Central Christian Coll of Kansas, KS	B
Concordia U, IL	B
Concordia U, NE	B
Concordia U Wisconsin, WI	B
Cornerstone U, MI	B
Crown Coll, MN	B
Dordt Coll, IA	B
Faith Baptist Bible Coll and Theological Seminary, IA	B
Global U of the Assemblies of God, MO	B
God's Bible School and Coll, OH	B
Grace Bible Coll, MI	B
Grace Coll, IN	B
Greenville Coll, IL	B
Hesston Coll, KS	A
Indiana Wesleyan U, IN	A,B
Kuyper Coll, MI	B
Lindenwood U, MO	B
Madonna U, MI	B
Messenger Coll, MO	B
Newman U, KS	B
Notre Dame Coll, OH	A,B
Oak Hills Christian Coll, MN	B
Oral Roberts U, OK	B
St. Gregory's U, Shawnee, OK	B
Saint Joseph's Coll, IN	B
Saint Mary-of-the-Woods Coll, IN	B
Southwest Baptist U, MO	B
Southwestern Coll, KS	B
Tabor Coll, KS	B
Union Coll, NE	B
U of Saint Mary, KS	B
U of Sioux Falls, SD	B
Vennard Coll, IA	B
Walsh U, OH	B

Peace Studies and Conflict Resolution

Antioch Coll, OH	B
Bethel Coll, KS	B
Coll of Saint Benedict, MN	B
DePauw U, IN	B
Earlham Coll, IN	B
Goshen Coll, IN	B
Hamline U, MN	B
Kent State U, OH	B
Manchester Coll, IN	B
Northland Coll, WI	B
Ohio Dominican U, OH	B
The Ohio State U, OH	B
Saint John's U, MN	B

A—associate degree; B—bachelor's degree

U of Missouri–Columbia, MO   B
U of St. Thomas, MN   B
U of Wisconsin–Milwaukee, WI   B
U of Wisconsin–Superior, WI   B

Pediatric Nursing
Youngstown State U, OH   B

Personal and Culinary Services Related
Lexington Coll, IL   A,B

Petroleum Engineering
Marietta Coll, OH   B
U of Kansas, KS   B
U of Missouri–Rolla, MO   B
U of Oklahoma, OK   B
U of Tulsa, OK   B

Pharmacology
U of Cincinnati, OH   B
U of Wisconsin–Madison, WI   B

Pharmacology and Toxicology
Wright State U, OH   B

Pharmacy
Butler U, IN   B
Drake U, IA   B
North Dakota State U, ND   B
Ohio Northern U, OH   B
The Ohio State U, OH   B
Purdue U, IN   B
St. Louis Coll of Pharmacy, MO   B
South Dakota State U, SD   B
Southwestern Oklahoma State U, OK   B
Turtle Mountain Comm Coll, ND   A
U of Cincinnati, OH   B
The U of Iowa, IA   B
U of Kansas, KS   B
U of Michigan, MI   B
U of Missouri–Kansas City, MO   B
The U of Toledo, OH   B
U of Wisconsin–Madison, WI   B

Pharmacy Administration/ Pharmaceutics
Drake U, IA   B

Pharmacy, Pharmaceutical Sciences, and Administration Related
Ferris State U, MI   B
Ohio Northern U, OH   B
The U of Toledo, OH   B

Pharmacy Technician
Baker Coll of Flint, MI   A
Baker Coll of Jackson, MI   A
Baker Coll of Muskegon, MI   A

Philosophy
Adrian Coll, MI   B
Albion Coll, MI   B
Alma Coll, MI   B
Alverno Coll, WI   B
Anderson U, IN   B
Antioch Coll, OH   B
Aquinas Coll, MI   B
Ashland U, OH   B
Augsburg Coll, MN   B
Augustana Coll, IL   B
Augustana Coll, SD   B
Aurora U, IL   B
Baker U, KS   B
Baldwin-Wallace Coll, OH   B

Ball State U, IN   B
Beloit Coll, WI   B
Bemidji State U, MN   B
Benedictine Coll, KS   B
Benedictine U, IL   B
Bethany Coll, KS   B
Bethel U, MN   B
Bowling Green State U, OH   B
Bradley U, IL   B
Butler U, IN   B
Calvin Coll, MI   B
Capital U, OH   B
Carleton Coll, MN   B
Case Western Reserve U, OH   B
Cedarville U, OH   B
Central Coll, IA   B
Central Methodist U, MO   B
Central Michigan U, MI   B
Clarke Coll, IA   B
Cleveland State U, OH   B
Coe Coll, IA   B
Coll of Saint Benedict, MN   B
Coll of St. Catherine, MN   B
Coll of the Ozarks, MO   B
The Coll of Wooster, OH   B
Concordia Coll, MN   B
Concordia U, IL   B
Concordia U, MI   B
Cornell Coll, IA   B
Cornerstone U, MI   B
Creighton U, NE   B
Dakota Wesleyan U, SD   B
Denison U, OH   B
DePaul U, IL   B
DePauw U, IN   B
Doane Coll, NE   B
Dominican U, IL   B
Dordt Coll, IA   B
Drake U, IA   B
Drury U, MO   B
Earlham Coll, IN   B
Eastern Illinois U, IL   B
Eastern Michigan U, MI   B
Elmhurst Coll, IL   B
Fort Hays State U, KS   B
Franciscan U of Steubenville, OH   B
Franklin Coll, IN   B
Gannon U, PA   B
Grand Valley State U, MI   B
Greenville Coll, IL   B
Grinnell Coll, IA   B
Gustavus Adolphus Coll, MN   B
Hamline U, MN   B
Hanover Coll, IN   B
Hastings Coll, NE   B
Heidelberg Coll, OH   B
Hillsdale Coll, MI   B
Hiram Coll, OH   B
Hope Coll, MI   B
Huntington U, IN   B
Illinois Coll, IL   B
Illinois State U, IL   B
Illinois Wesleyan U, IL   B
Indiana State U, IN   B
Indiana U Bloomington, IN   B
Indiana U Northwest, IN   B
Indiana U–Purdue U Fort Wayne, IN   B
Indiana U–Purdue U Indianapolis, IN   B
Indiana U South Bend, IN   B
Indiana U Southeast, IN   B
Indiana Wesleyan U, IN   B
Iowa State U of Science and Technology, IA   B

Jamestown Coll, ND   B
Judson Coll, IL   B
Kalamazoo Coll, MI   B
Kansas State U, KS   B
Kent State U, OH   B
Kenyon Coll, OH   B
Knox Coll, IL   B
Lake Forest Coll, IL   B
Lawrence U, WI   B
Lewis U, IL   B
Loras Coll, IA   B
Loyola U Chicago, IL   B
Luther Coll, IA   B
Macalester Coll, MN   B
MacMurray Coll, IL   B
Madonna U, MI   B
Manchester Coll, IN   B
Marian Coll, IN   B
Marietta Coll, OH   B
Marquette U, WI   B
McKendree Coll, IL   B
Metropolitan State U, MN   B
Miami U, OH   B
Miami U Hamilton, OH   B
Miami U–Middletown Campus, OH   A
Michigan State U, MI   B
Millikin U, IL   B
Minnesota State U Mankato, MN   B
Missouri State U, MO   B
Missouri Valley Coll, MO   B
Morningside Coll, IA   B
Mount Mary Coll, WI   B
Mount Union Coll, OH   B
Mount Vernon Nazarene U, OH   B
Nebraska Wesleyan U, NE   B
North Central Coll, IL   B
North Dakota State U, ND   B
Northeastern Illinois U, IL   B
Northern Illinois U, IL   B
Northern Michigan U, MI   B
Northland Coll, WI   B
Northwestern Coll, IA   B
Northwestern U, IL   B
Northwest Missouri State U, MO   B
Oakland U, MI   B
Oberlin Coll, OH   B
Ohio Dominican U, OH   B
Ohio Northern U, OH   B
The Ohio State U, OH   B
Ohio U, OH   B
Ohio Wesleyan U, OH   B
Oklahoma City U, OK   B
Oklahoma State U, OK   B
Oral Roberts U, OK   B
Otterbein Coll, OH   B
Pontifical Coll Josephinum, OH   B
Purdue U, IN   B
Purdue U Calumet, IN   B
Quincy U, IL   B
Ripon Coll, WI   B
Rockford Coll, IL   B
Rockhurst U, MO   B
Roosevelt U, IL   B
Sacred Heart Major Seminary, MI   B
St. Ambrose U, IA   B
St. Cloud State U, MN   B
St. Gregory's U, Shawnee, OK   B
Saint John's U, MN   B
Saint Joseph's Coll, IN   B
Saint Louis U, MO   B

Saint Mary's Coll, IN   B
Saint Mary's U of Minnesota, MN   B
St. Norbert Coll, WI   B
St. Olaf Coll, MN   B
Saint Xavier U, IL   B
Simpson Coll, IA   B
Southeast Missouri State U, MO   B
Southern Illinois U Carbondale, IL   B
Southern Illinois U Edwardsville, IL   B
Southern Methodist U, TX   B
Southwest Minnesota State U, MN   B
Spring Arbor U, MI   B
Stephens Coll, MO   B
Tabor Coll, KS   B
Taylor U, IN   B
Transylvania U, KY   B
Trinity Christian Coll, IL   B
Trinity International U, IL   B
Truman State U, MO   B
The U of Akron, OH   B
U of Central Oklahoma, OK   B
U of Chicago, IL   B
U of Cincinnati, OH   B
U of Dallas, TX   B
U of Dayton, OH   B
U of Evansville, IN   B
The U of Findlay, OH   B
U of Illinois at Chicago, IL   B
U of Illinois at Springfield, IL   B
U of Illinois at Urbana–Champaign, IL   B
U of Indianapolis, IN   B
The U of Iowa, IA   B
U of Kansas, KS   B
U of Michigan, MI   B
U of Michigan–Dearborn, MI   B
U of Michigan–Flint, MI   B
U of Minnesota, Duluth, MN   B
U of Minnesota, Morris, MN   B
U of Minnesota, Twin Cities Campus, MN   B
U of Missouri–Columbia, MO   B
U of Missouri–Kansas City, MO   B
U of Missouri–Rolla, MO   B
U of Missouri–St. Louis, MO   B
U of Nebraska at Omaha, NE   B
U of Nebraska–Lincoln, NE   B
U of New Orleans, LA   B
U of North Dakota, ND   B
U of Northern Iowa, IA   B
U of Notre Dame, IN   B
U of Oklahoma, OK   B
U of St. Thomas, MN   B
U of Sioux Falls, SD   B
The U of South Dakota, SD   B
U of Southern Indiana, IN   B
The U of Toledo, OH   B
U of Tulsa, OK   B
U of West Florida, FL   B
U of Wisconsin–Eau Claire, WI   B
U of Wisconsin–Green Bay, WI   A,B
U of Wisconsin–La Crosse, WI   B
U of Wisconsin–Madison, WI   B
U of Wisconsin–Milwaukee, WI   B
U of Wisconsin–Oshkosh, WI   B
U of Wisconsin–Parkside, WI   B
U of Wisconsin–Platteville, WI   B

U of Wisconsin–Stevens Point, WI — B
Ursuline Coll, OH — B
Valparaiso U, IN — B
Wabash Coll, IN — B
Walsh U, OH — B
Wartburg Coll, IA — B
Washburn U, KS — B
Washington U in St. Louis, MO — B
Webster U, MO — B
Western Illinois U, IL — B
Western Michigan U, MI — B
Westminster Coll, MO — B
Wheaton Coll, IL — B
Wichita State U, KS — B
William Jewell Coll, MO — B
Wilmington Coll, OH — B
Wittenberg U, OH — B
Wright State U, OH — B
Xavier U, OH — B
Youngstown State U, OH — B

Philosophy and Religious Studies Related
Buena Vista U, IA — B
Capital U, OH — B
Coll of the Ozarks, MO — B
Columbia Coll, MO — B
Graceland U, IA — B
Iowa Wesleyan Coll, IA — B
Saint Joseph's Coll, IN — B
Southwestern Coll, KS — B
Sterling Coll, KS — B
U of Notre Dame, IN — B
Viterbo U, WI — B
Washington U in St. Louis, MO — B

Philosophy Related
Ohio Northern U, OH — B

Photographic and Film/Video Technology
Kent State U, OH — B
Ohio U, OH — B

Photography
Andrews U, MI — A,B
Aquinas Coll, MI — B
Art Academy of Cincinnati, OH —
Ball State U, IN — B
Bowling Green State U, OH — B
Carroll Coll, WI — B
Central Christian Coll of Kansas, KS — A
The Cleveland Inst of Art, OH — B
Coe Coll, IA — B
Coll of Visual Arts, MN — B
Columbia Coll, MO — B
Columbia Coll Chicago, IL — B
Columbus Coll of Art & Design, OH — B
Dominican U, IL — B
Grand Valley State U, MI — B
Indiana U Bloomington, IN — B
Indiana U–Purdue U Fort Wayne, IN — B
Indiana Wesleyan U, IN — B
Kansas City Art Inst, MO — B
Minneapolis Coll of Art and Design, MN — B
Morningside Coll, IA — B
Saint Mary-of-the-Woods Coll, IN — B

School of the Art Inst of Chicago, IL — B
Shawnee State U, OH — B
Trinity Christian Coll, IL — B
The U of Akron, OH — B
U of Central Missouri, MO — B
U of Central Oklahoma, OK —
U of Dayton, OH — B
U of Illinois at Chicago, IL — B
U of Illinois at Urbana–Champaign, IL —
The U of Iowa, IA — B
U of Michigan, MI — B
U of Michigan–Flint, MI —
U of Missouri–St. Louis, MO — B
U of Oklahoma, OK —
Washington U in St. Louis, MO — B
Webster U, MO — B
Wright State U, OH — B
Youngstown State U, OH — B

Photojournalism
St. Gregory's U, Shawnee, OK — B
U of Missouri–Columbia, MO — B

Physical and Theoretical Chemistry
Michigan State U, MI — B

Physical Education Teaching and Coaching
Adrian Coll, MI — A,B
Albion Coll, MI — B
Alma Coll, MI — B
Anderson U, IN — B
Aquinas Coll, MI — B
Ashland U, OH — B
Augsburg Coll, MN — B
Augustana Coll, IL — B
Augustana Coll, SD — B
Aurora U, IL — B
Baldwin-Wallace Coll, OH — B
Ball State U, IN — B
Bellevue U, NE — B
Bemidji State U, MN — B
Benedictine Coll, KS — B
Bethany Coll, KS — B
Bethel U, MN — B
Blackburn Coll, IL — B
Bowling Green State U, OH — B
Briar Cliff U, IA — B
Buena Vista U, IA — B
Calvin Coll, MI — B
Capital U, OH — B
Carroll Coll, WI — B
Cedarville U, OH — B
Central Christian Coll of Kansas, KS — A
Central Methodist U, MO — B
Central Michigan U, MI — B
Central State U, OH — B
Chicago State U, IL — B
Clarke Coll, IA — B
Cleveland State U, OH — B
Coe Coll, IA — B
Coll of St. Catherine, MN — B
Coll of the Ozarks, MO — B
Concordia Coll, MN — B
Concordia U, IL — B
Concordia U, MI — B
Concordia U, NE — B
Concordia U, St. Paul, MN — B
Concordia U Wisconsin, WI — B
Concord U, WV — B
Cornell Coll, IA — B

Cornerstone U, MI — B
Crown Coll, MN — B
Culver-Stockton Coll, MO — B
Dakota State U, SD — B
Dakota Wesleyan U, SD — B
Dana Coll, NE — B
Denison U, OH — B
DePaul U, IL — B
DePauw U, IN — B
Dickinson State U, ND — B
Doane Coll, NE — B
Dordt Coll, IA — B
East Central U, OK — B
Eastern Illinois U, IL — B
Eastern Michigan U, MI — B
Elmhurst Coll, IL — B
Evangel U, MO — B
Fort Hays State U, KS — B
Franklin Coll, IN — B
Goshen Coll, IN — B
Grace Coll, IN — B
Graceland U, IA — B
Grand Valley State U, MI — B
Greenville Coll, IL — B
Gustavus Adolphus Coll, MN — B
Hamline U, MN — B
Hannibal-LaGrange Coll, MO — B
Hanover Coll, IN — B
Hastings Coll, NE — B
Heidelberg Coll, OH — B
Hillsdale Coll, MI — B
Hillsdale Free Will Baptist Coll, OK — A
Hope Coll, MI — B
Huntington U, IN — B
Illinois Coll, IL — B
Illinois State U, IL — B
Indiana State U, IN — B
Indiana U Bloomington, IN — B
Indiana U–Purdue U Indianapolis, IN — B
Indiana Wesleyan U, IN — B
Iowa Wesleyan Coll, IA — B
Jamestown Coll, ND — B
Judson Coll, IL — B
Kent State U, OH — B
Langston U, OK — B
Lewis U, IL — B
Lincoln U, MO — B
Lindenwood U, MO — B
Loras Coll, IA — B
Luther Coll, IA — B
MacMurray Coll, IL — B
Malone Coll, OH — B
Manchester Coll, IN — B
Maranatha Baptist Bible Coll, WI — B
Marian Coll, IN — B
Mayville State U, ND — B
McKendree Coll, IL — B
Miami U, OH — B
Miami U Hamilton, OH — B
Michigan State U, MI — B
Millikin U, IL — B
Minnesota State U Mankato, MN — B
Minot State U, ND — B
Missouri Baptist U, MO — B
Missouri State U, MO — B
Missouri Valley Coll, MO — B
Mount Marty Coll, SD — B
Mount Union Coll, OH — B
Mount Vernon Nazarene U, OH — B
Nebraska Wesleyan U, NE — B

North Carolina Ag and Tech State U, NC — B
North Central Coll, IL — B
North Dakota State U, ND — B
Northeastern Illinois U, IL — B
Northeastern State U, OK — B
Northern Illinois U, IL — B
Northern Michigan U, MI — B
Northern State U, SD — B
Northwestern Coll, IA — B
Northwestern Coll, MN — B
Northwestern Oklahoma State U, OK — B
Northwest Missouri State U, MO — B
Ohio Northern U, OH — B
The Ohio State U, OH — B
Ohio U, OH — B
Ohio Wesleyan U, OH — B
Oklahoma Christian U, OK — B
Oklahoma City U, OK — B
Oklahoma Panhandle State U, OK — B
Oklahoma State U, OK — B
Oklahoma Wesleyan U, OK — B
Oral Roberts U, OK — B
Ottawa U, KS — B
Otterbein Coll, OH — B
Peru State Coll, NE — B
Pittsburg State U, KS — B
Purdue U, IN — B
Quincy U, IL — B
Ripon Coll, WI — B
Rockford Coll, IL — B
Saginaw Valley State U, MI — B
St. Ambrose U, IA — B
St. Cloud State U, MN — B
Saint Joseph's Coll, IN — B
Simpson Coll, IA — B
South Dakota State U, SD — B
Southeastern Oklahoma State U, OK — B
Southeast Missouri State U, MO — B
Southern Illinois U Carbondale, IL — B
Southwest Baptist U, MO — B
Southwestern Oklahoma State U, OK — B
Southwest Minnesota State U, MN — B
Spring Arbor U, MI — B
Sterling Coll, KS — B
Tabor Coll, KS — B
Taylor U, IN — B
Transylvania U, KY — B
Trinity Christian Coll, IL — B
Trinity International U, IL — B
Tri-State U, IN — B
Union Coll, NE — B
The U of Akron, OH — B
U of Central Missouri, MO — B
U of Central Oklahoma, OK — B
U of Cincinnati, OH — B
U of Dayton, OH — B
U of Evansville, IN — B
The U of Findlay, OH — B
U of Indianapolis, IN — B
U of Kansas, KS — B
U of Mary, ND — B
U of Michigan, MI — B
U of Minnesota, Duluth, MN — B
U of Minnesota, Twin Cities Campus, MN — B
U of Missouri–St. Louis, MO — B

A—associate degree; B—bachelor's degree

U of Nebraska at Kearney, NE B
U of Nebraska at Omaha, NE B
U of Nebraska–Lincoln, NE B
U of New Orleans, LA B
U of North Dakota, ND B
U of Northern Iowa, IA B
U of Rio Grande, OH A,B
U of St. Thomas, MN B
U of Sioux Falls, SD B
The U of South Dakota, SD B
U of Southern Indiana, IN B
The U of Toledo, OH B
U of Wisconsin–Madison, WI B
U of Wisconsin–Oshkosh, WI B
U of Wisconsin–River Falls, WI B
U of Wisconsin–Stevens Point, WI B
U of Wisconsin–Superior, WI B
U of Wisconsin–Whitewater, WI B
Upper Iowa U, IA B
Valley City State U, ND B
Valparaiso U, IN B
Waldorf Coll, IA B
Walsh U, OH B
Wartburg Coll, IA B
Washburn U, KS B
Wayne State Coll, NE B
Western Illinois U, IL B
Western Michigan U, MI B
Westminster Coll, MO B
Wichita State U, KS B
William Penn U, IA B
William Woods U, MO B
Wilmington Coll, OH B
Winona State U, MN B
Wright State U, OH B
York Coll, NE B
Youngstown State U, OH B

Physical Sciences

Antioch Coll, OH B
Bemidji State U, MN B
Black Hills State U, SD B
Calvin Coll, MI B
Central Michigan U, MI B
Coe Coll, IA B
Concordia U, IL B
Concordia U, NE B
Dakota State U, SD B
Doane Coll, NE B
Emporia State U, KS B
Fort Hays State U, KS B
Goshen Coll, IN B
Graceland U, IA B
Grand Valley State U, MI B
Grand View Coll, IA B
Judson Coll, IL B
Kansas State U, KS B
Loras Coll, IA B
Mayville State U, ND B
Michigan State U, MI B
Michigan Technological U, MI B
Minnesota State U Mankato, MN B
Minot State U, ND B
Northwest Missouri State U, MO B
Otterbein Coll, OH B
Ripon Coll, WI B
Rogers State U, OK A
St. Cloud State U, MN B
Shawnee State U, OH B
Southwest Minnesota State U, MN B
Taylor U, IN B

Tri-State U, IN B
U of Dayton, OH B
U of Rio Grande, OH B
The U of Toledo, OH B
U of Wisconsin–River Falls, WI B
U of Wisconsin–Superior, WI B
Wayne State Coll, NE B
Winona State U, MN B
Wittenberg U, OH B

Physical Sciences Related

The Coll of St. Scholastica, MN B
Eastern Michigan U, MI B
Ohio U, OH B

Physical Science Technologies Related

Missouri State U, MO B
The U of Akron, OH A

Physical Therapist Assistant

Baker Coll of Flint, MI A
Baker Coll of Muskegon, MI A
Coll of St. Catherine, MN A
Finlandia U, MI A
Missouri Western State U, MO A
Southern Illinois U Carbondale, IL A
U of Evansville, IN A
U of Indianapolis, IN A
U of Saint Francis, IN A
Washburn U, KS A

Physical Therapy

Andrews U, MI B
Bowling Green State U, OH B
Bradley U, IL B
Clarke Coll, IA B
Cleveland State U, OH B
Coll of Saint Benedict, MN B
Concordia Coll, MN B
Concordia U Wisconsin, WI B
Elmhurst Coll, IL B
Grand Valley State U, MI B
Gustavus Adolphus Coll, MN B
Hamline U, MN B
Indiana U–Purdue U Indianapolis, IN B
Kent State U, Ashtabula Campus, OH A
Langston U, OK B
Marquette U, WI B
Mount Vernon Nazarene U, OH B
Northern Illinois U, IL B
The Ohio State U, OH B
Oklahoma Wesleyan U, OK B
St. Cloud State U, MN B
Saint John's U, MN B
Saint Louis U, MO B
Saint Mary's U of Minnesota, MN B
Shawnee State U, OH A
Simpson Coll, IA B
Turtle Mountain Comm Coll, ND A
U of Cincinnati, OH A
The U of Findlay, OH B
U of Minnesota, Morris, MN B
U of Minnesota, Twin Cities Campus, MN B
U of North Dakota, ND B
The U of Toledo, OH B
U of Wisconsin–La Crosse, WI B

U of Wisconsin–Milwaukee, WI B
Winona State U, MN B

Physician Assistant

Augsburg Coll, MN B
Butler U, IN B
Central Christian Coll of Kansas, KS A
Elmhurst Coll, IL B
Gannon U, PA B
Grand Valley State U, MI B
Kettering Coll of Medical Arts, OH A,B
Marquette U, WI B
Minnesota School of Business, MN A
Minnesota School of Business–Brooklyn Center, MN A
Minnesota School of Business–Plymouth, MN A
Minnesota School of Business–St. Cloud, MN A
Minnesota School of Business–Shakopee, MN A
Peru State Coll, NE B
Saint Louis U, MO B
Southern Illinois U Carbondale, IL B
Union Coll, NE B
The U of Findlay, OH B
U of Saint Francis, IN B
U of Wisconsin–La Crosse, WI B
U of Wisconsin–Madison, WI B
Wichita State U, KS B

Physics

Adrian Coll, MI A,B
Albion Coll, MI B
Alma Coll, MI B
Anderson U, IN B
Andrews U, MI B
Antioch Coll, OH B
Aquinas Coll, MI B
Ashland U, OH B
Augsburg Coll, MN B
Augustana Coll, IL B
Augustana Coll, SD B
Baker U, KS B
Baldwin-Wallace Coll, OH B
Ball State U, IN B
Beloit Coll, WI B
Bemidji State U, MN B
Benedictine Coll, KS B
Benedictine U, IL B
Bethel Coll, KS B
Bethel U, MN B
Bluffton U, OH B
Bowling Green State U, OH B
Bradley U, IL B
Buena Vista U, IA B
Butler U, IN B
Calvin Coll, MI B
Cameron U, OK B
Carleton Coll, MN B
Cedarville U, OH B
Central Coll, IA B
Central Methodist U, MO B
Central Michigan U, MI B
Chicago State U, IL B
Clarkson U, NY B
Cleveland State U, OH B
Coe Coll, IA B
Coll of Saint Benedict, MN B
Coll of St. Catherine, MN B
The Coll of Wooster, OH B
Concordia Coll, MN B

Concordia U, MI B
Cornell Coll, IA B
Creighton U, NE B
Denison U, OH B
DePaul U, IL B
DePauw U, IN B
Doane Coll, NE B
Dordt Coll, IA B
Drake U, IA B
Drury U, MO B
Earlham Coll, IN B
East Central U, OK B
Eastern Illinois U, IL B
Eastern Michigan U, MI B
Elmhurst Coll, IL B
Emporia State U, KS B
Fort Hays State U, KS B
Goshen Coll, IN B
Grand Valley State U, MI B
Greenville Coll, IL B
Grinnell Coll, IA B
Gustavus Adolphus Coll, MN B
Hamline U, MN B
Hanover Coll, IN B
Hastings Coll, NE B
Heidelberg Coll, OH B
Hillsdale Coll, MI B
Hiram Coll, OH B
Hope Coll, MI B
Illinois Coll, IL B
Illinois Inst of Technology, IL B
Illinois State U, IL B
Illinois Wesleyan U, IL B
Indiana State U, IN B
Indiana U Bloomington, IN B
Indiana U–Purdue U Fort Wayne, IN B
Indiana U–Purdue U Indianapolis, IN B
Indiana U South Bend, IN B
Iowa State U of Science and Technology, IA B
Kalamazoo Coll, MI B
Kansas State U, KS B
Kent State U, OH B
Kenyon Coll, OH B
Kettering U, MI B
Knox Coll, IL B
Lake Forest Coll, IL B
Lawrence Technological U, MI B
Lawrence U, WI B
Lewis U, IL B
Lincoln U, MO B
Loras Coll, IA B
Loyola U Chicago, IL B
Luther Coll, IA B
Macalester Coll, MN B
MacMurray Coll, IL B
Manchester Coll, IN B
Marietta Coll, OH B
Marquette U, WI B
Miami U, OH B
Miami U Hamilton, OH B
Miami U–Middletown Campus, OH A
Michigan State U, MI B
Michigan Technological U, MI B
Millikin U, IL B
Minnesota State U Mankato, MN B
Minot State U, ND B
Missouri Southern State U, MO B
Missouri State U, MO B
Morningside Coll, IA B
Mount Union Coll, OH B

College	Degree
Nebraska Wesleyan U, NE	B
North Carolina Ag and Tech State U, NC	B
North Central Coll, IL	B
North Dakota State U, ND	B
Northeastern Illinois U, IL	B
Northeastern State U, OK	B
Northern Illinois U, IL	B
Northwestern Oklahoma State U, OK	B
Northwestern U, IL	B
Northwest Missouri State U, MO	B
Oakland U, MI	B
Oberlin Coll, OH	B
Ohio Northern U, OH	B
The Ohio State U, OH	B
Ohio U, OH	B
Ohio Wesleyan U, OH	B
Oklahoma City U, OK	B
Oklahoma State U, OK	B
Oral Roberts U, OK	B
Otterbein Coll, OH	B
Pittsburg State U, KS	B
Purdue U, IN	B
Purdue U Calumet, IN	B
Purdue U North Central, IN	B
Rockhurst U, MO	B
Rose-Hulman Inst of Technology, IN	B
Saginaw Valley State U, MI	B
St. Ambrose U, IA	B
St. Cloud State U, MN	B
Saint John's U, MN	B
Saint Louis U, MO	B
St. Norbert Coll, WI	B
St. Olaf Coll, MN	B
South Dakota School of Mines and Technology, SD	B
South Dakota State U, SD	B
Southeast Missouri State U, MO	B
Southern Illinois U Carbondale, IL	B
Southern Illinois U Edwardsville, IL	B
Southern Methodist U, TX	B
Southwestern Coll, KS	B
Southwestern Oklahoma State U, OK	B
Taylor U, IN	B
Transylvania U, KY	B
Truman State U, MO	B
Union Coll, NE	B
The U of Akron, OH	B
U of Central Missouri, MO	B
U of Central Oklahoma, OK	B
U of Chicago, IL	B
U of Cincinnati, OH	B
U of Dallas, TX	B
U of Dayton, OH	B
U of Evansville, IN	B
U of Illinois at Chicago, IL	B
U of Illinois at Urbana–Champaign, IL	B
U of Indianapolis, IN	B
The U of Iowa, IA	B
U of Kansas, KS	B
U of Michigan–Dearborn, MI	B
U of Michigan–Flint, MI	B
U of Minnesota, Duluth, MN	B
U of Minnesota, Morris, MN	B
U of Minnesota, Twin Cities Campus, MN	B
U of Missouri–Columbia, MO	B
U of Missouri–Kansas City, MO	B
U of Missouri–Rolla, MO	B
U of Missouri–St. Louis, MO	B
U of Nebraska at Kearney, NE	B
U of Nebraska at Omaha, NE	B
U of Nebraska–Lincoln, NE	B
U of New Orleans, LA	B
U of North Dakota, ND	B
U of Notre Dame, IN	B
U of Oklahoma, OK	B
U of St. Thomas, MN	B
U of Science and Arts of Oklahoma, OK	B
The U of South Dakota, SD	B
The U of Toledo, OH	B
U of Tulsa, OK	B
U of West Florida, FL	B
U of Wisconsin–Eau Claire, WI	B
U of Wisconsin–La Crosse, WI	B
U of Wisconsin–Milwaukee, WI	B
U of Wisconsin–Oshkosh, WI	B
U of Wisconsin–Parkside, WI	B
U of Wisconsin–River Falls, WI	B
U of Wisconsin–Stevens Point, WI	B
U of Wisconsin–Whitewater, WI	B
Valparaiso U, IN	B
Wabash Coll, IN	B
Wartburg Coll, IA	B
Washburn U, KS	B
Washington U in St. Louis, MO	B
Western Illinois U, IL	B
Western Michigan U, MI	B
Westminster Coll, MO	B
Wheaton Coll, IL	B
Wichita State U, KS	B
William Jewell Coll, MO	B
Winona State U, MN	B
Wittenberg U, OH	B
Xavier U, OH	B
Youngstown State U, OH	B

Physics Related

College	Degree
The Coll of Wooster, OH	B
Lawrence Technological U, MI	B
Ohio Northern U, OH	B
Ohio U, OH	B
The U of Akron, OH	B
U of Northern Iowa, IA	B
U of Notre Dame, IN	B
Wright State U, OH	B

Physics Teacher Education

College	Degree
Alma Coll, MI	B
Baldwin-Wallace Coll, OH	B
Bethel U, MN	B
Buena Vista U, IA	B
Carroll Coll, WI	B
Cedarville U, OH	B
Central Methodist U, MO	B
Central Michigan U, MI	B
Chicago State U, IL	B
Concordia Coll, MN	B
Concordia U, NE	B
East Central U, OK	B
Eastern Michigan U, MI	B
Elmhurst Coll, IL	B
Greenville Coll, IL	B
Gustavus Adolphus Coll, MN	B
Hastings Coll, NE	B
Hope Coll, MI	B
Illinois Wesleyan U, IL	B
Indiana U Bloomington, IN	B
Indiana U–Purdue U Fort Wayne, IN	B
Indiana U South Bend, IN	B
Lincoln U, MO	B
Mayville State U, ND	B
Miami U Hamilton, OH	B
Minot State U, ND	B
Missouri State U, MO	B
North Dakota State U, ND	B
Ohio Dominican U, OH	B
Ohio Northern U, OH	B
Ohio Wesleyan U, OH	B
Pittsburg State U, KS	B
St. Ambrose U, IA	B
Saint Mary's U of Minnesota, MN	B
Shawnee State U, OH	B
Union Coll, NE	B
The U of Akron, OH	B
U of Central Missouri, MO	B
U of Evansville, IN	B
U of Illinois at Chicago, IL	B
The U of Iowa, IA	B
U of Michigan–Flint, MI	B
U of Missouri–Columbia, MO	B
U of Missouri–St. Louis, MO	B
U of Nebraska–Lincoln, NE	B
U of Rio Grande, OH	B
U of St. Thomas, MN	B
The U of South Dakota, SD	B
U of Wisconsin–River Falls, WI	B
Valparaiso U, IN	B
Washington U in St. Louis, MO	B
Western Michigan U, MI	B
Xavier U, OH	B

Physiological Psychology/ Psychobiology

College	Degree
Grand Valley State U, MI	B
Hiram Coll, OH	B
Oberlin Coll, OH	B
Ripon Coll, WI	B
U of Evansville, IN	B
York Coll, NE	B

Physiology

College	Degree
Michigan State U, MI	B
Oklahoma State U, OK	B
Southern Illinois U Carbondale, IL	B
U of Illinois at Urbana–Champaign, IL	B

Piano and Organ

College	Degree
Andrews U, MI	B
Augustana Coll, IL	B
Baldwin-Wallace Coll, OH	B
Ball State U, IN	B
Bowling Green State U, OH	B
Butler U, IN	B
Calvary Bible Coll and Theological Seminary, MO	B
Calvin Coll, MI	B
Capital U, OH	B
Cedarville U, OH	B
Cincinnati Christian U, OH	B
Cleveland Inst of Music, OH	B
Concordia Coll, MN	B
Concordia U, IL	B
Concordia U, NE	B
DePaul U, IL	B
Dordt Coll, IA	B
Drake U, IA	B
East Central U, OK	B
Grace Coll, IN	B
Grand Valley State U, MI	B
Hannibal-LaGrange Coll, MO	B
Hastings Coll, NE	B
Heidelberg Coll, OH	B
Hope Coll, MI	B
Huntington U, IN	B
Illinois Wesleyan U, IL	B
Indiana U Bloomington, IN	B
Indiana U–Purdue U Fort Wayne, IN	B
Kent State U, OH	B
Lawrence U, WI	B
Millikin U, IL	B
Minnesota State U Mankato, MN	B
Northeastern State U, OK	B
Northwestern Coll, MN	B
Northwestern U, IL	B
Northwest Missouri State U, MO	B
Oberlin Coll, OH	B
The Ohio State U, OH	B
Ohio U, OH	B
Oklahoma City U, OK	B
Otterbein Coll, OH	B
Roosevelt U, IL	B
St. Cloud State U, MN	B
Southern Methodist U, TX	B
Southwestern Oklahoma State U, OK	B
Spring Arbor U, MI	B
Tabor Coll, KS	B
Taylor U, IN	B
Trinity Christian Coll, IL	B
Truman State U, MO	B
The U of Akron, OH	B
U of Central Oklahoma, OK	B
U of Cincinnati, OH	B
The U of Iowa, IA	B
U of Kansas, KS	B
U of Michigan, MI	B
U of Minnesota, Duluth, MN	B
U of Oklahoma, OK	B
U of Sioux Falls, SD	B
U of Tulsa, OK	B
Valparaiso U, IN	B

Plant Pathology/ Phytopathology

College	Degree
Michigan State U, MI	B
The Ohio State U, OH	B

Plant Protection and Integrated Pest Management

College	Degree
Iowa State U of Science and Technology, IA	B
North Dakota State U, ND	B
U of Nebraska–Lincoln, NE	B

Plant Sciences

College	Degree
The Ohio State U, OH	B
Oklahoma State U, OK	B
Southern Illinois U Carbondale, IL	B
U of Minnesota, Twin Cities Campus, MN	B
U of Missouri–Columbia, MO	B

Plastics Engineering Technology

College	Degree
Ball State U, IN	B
Eastern Michigan U, MI	B

A—associate degree; B—bachelor's degree

Ferris State U, MI   A,B
Kent State U, Tuscarawas
   Campus, OH   A
Pittsburg State U, KS
Shawnee State U, OH   A,B
Western Michigan U, MI   B

Platemaking/Imaging
Western Michigan U, MI   B

Playwriting and Screenwriting
Columbia Coll Chicago, IL   B
DePaul U, IL   B
Metropolitan State U, MN   B
Ohio U, OH   B

Polish
Madonna U, MI   B
U of Illinois at Chicago, IL   B

Political Communication
Nebraska Wesleyan U, NE   B

Political Science and Government
Adrian Coll, MI   A,B
Albion Coll, MI   B
Alma Coll, MI   B
Alverno Coll, WI   B
Anderson U, IN   B
Andrews U, MI   B
Antioch Coll, OH   B
Aquinas Coll, MI   B
Ashland U, OH   B
Augsburg Coll, MN   B
Augustana Coll, IL   B
Augustana Coll, SD   B
Aurora U, IL   B
Avila U, MO   B
Baker U, KS   B
Baldwin-Wallace Coll, OH   B
Ball State U, IN   B
Beloit Coll, WI   B
Bemidji State U, MN   B
Benedictine Coll, KS   B
Benedictine U, IL   B
Bethany Coll, KS   B
Bethel U, MN   B
Blackburn Coll, IL   B
Black Hills State U, SD   B
Bowling Green State U, OH   B
Bradley U, IL   B
Briar Cliff U, IA   B
Buena Vista U, IA   B
Butler U, IN   B
Calumet Coll of Saint Joseph,
   IN   B
Calvin Coll, MI   B
Cameron U, OK   B
Capital U, OH   B
Cardinal Stritch U, WI   B
Carleton Coll, MN   B
Carroll Coll, WI   B
Case Western Reserve U, OH   B
Cedarville U, OH   B
Central Coll, IA   B
Central Methodist U, MO   B
Central Michigan U, MI   B
Central State U, OH   B
Chicago State U, IL   B
Clarkson U, NY   B
Cleveland State U, OH   B
Coe Coll, IA   B
Coll of Menominee Nation,
   WI   A
Coll of Saint Benedict, MN   B
Coll of St. Catherine, MN   B
Coll of the Ozarks, MO   B

The Coll of Wooster, OH   B
Columbia Coll, MO   B
Concordia Coll, MN   B
Concordia U, IL   B
Concord U, WV   B
Cornell Coll, IA   B
Cornerstone U, MI   B
Creighton U, NE   B
Denison U, OH   B
DePaul U, IL   B
DePauw U, IN   B
Dickinson State U, ND   B
Doane Coll, NE   B
Dominican U, IL   B
Dordt Coll, IA   B
Drake U, IA   B
Drury U, MO   B
Earlham Coll, IN   B
East Central U, OK   B
Eastern Illinois U, IL   B
Eastern Michigan U, MI   B
Edgewood Coll, WI   B
Elmhurst Coll, IL   B
Emporia State U, KS   B
Evangel U, MO   B
Fort Hays State U, KS   B
Franciscan U of Steubenville,
   OH   B
Franklin Coll, IN   B
Gannon U, PA   B
Grand Valley State U, MI   B
Grand View Coll, IA   B
Grinnell Coll, IA   B
Gustavus Adolphus Coll, MN   B
Hamline U, MN   B
Hanover Coll, IN   B
Hastings Coll, NE   B
Heidelberg Coll, OH   B
Hillsdale Coll, MI   B
Hiram Coll, OH   B
Hope Coll, MI   B
Huntington U, IN   B
Illinois Coll, IL   B
Illinois Inst of Technology, IL   B
Illinois State U, IL   B
Illinois Wesleyan U, IL   B
Indiana State U, IN   B
Indiana U Bloomington, IN   B
Indiana U Northwest, IN   B
Indiana U–Purdue U Fort
   Wayne, IN   A,B
Indiana U–Purdue U
   Indianapolis, IN   B
Indiana U South Bend, IN   B
Indiana U Southeast, IN   B
Indiana Wesleyan U, IN   A,B
Iowa State U of Science and
   Technology, IA   B
Jamestown Coll, ND   B
Kalamazoo Coll, MI   B
Kansas State U, KS   B
Kent State U, OH   B
Kenyon Coll, OH   B
Knox Coll, IL   B
Lake Forest Coll, IL   B
Lake Superior State U, MI   B
Lawrence U, WI   B
Lewis U, IL   B
Lincoln U, MO   B
Lindenwood U, MO   B
Loras Coll, IA   B
Loyola U Chicago, IL   B
Luther Coll, IA   B
Macalester Coll, MN   B
MacMurray Coll, IL   B
Malone Coll, OH   B

Manchester Coll, IN   B
Marian Coll of Fond du Lac,
   WI   B
Marietta Coll, OH   B
Marquette U, WI   B
Marygrove Coll, MI   B
McKendree Coll, IL   B
Miami U, OH   B
Miami U Hamilton, OH   B
Miami U–Middletown Campus,
   OH   A
Michigan State U, MI   B
Millikin U, IL   B
Minnesota State U Mankato,
   MN   B
Missouri Southern State U,
   MO   B
Missouri State U, MO   B
Missouri Valley Coll, MO   B
Missouri Western State U, MO   B
Morningside Coll, IA   B
Mount Mercy Coll, IA   B
Mount Union Coll, OH   B
Nebraska Wesleyan U, NE   B
North Carolina Ag and Tech
   State U, NC   B
North Central Coll, IL   B
North Dakota State U, ND   B
Northeastern Illinois U, IL   B
Northeastern State U, OK   B
Northern Illinois U, IL   B
Northern Michigan U, MI   B
Northern State U, SD   B
Northwestern Coll, IA   B
Northwestern Oklahoma State
   U, OK   B
Northwestern U, IL   B
Northwest Missouri State U,
   MO   B
Notre Dame Coll, OH   B
Oakland U, MI   B
Oberlin Coll, OH   B
Ohio Dominican U, OH   B
Ohio Northern U, OH   B
The Ohio State U, OH   B
Ohio U, OH   B
Ohio Wesleyan U, OH   B
Oklahoma City U, OK   B
Oklahoma State U, OK   B
Oklahoma Wesleyan U, OK   B
Oral Roberts U, OK   B
Ottawa U, KS   B
Otterbein Coll, OH   B
Park U, MO   B
Pittsburg State U, KS   B
Purdue U, IN   B
Purdue U Calumet, IN   B
Quincy U, IL   B
Ripon Coll, WI   B
Rockford Coll, IL   B
Rockhurst U, MO   B
Rogers State U, OK   A
Roosevelt U, IL   B
Saginaw Valley State U, MI   B
St. Ambrose U, IA   B
St. Cloud State U, MN   B
St. Gregory's U, Shawnee, OK   B
Saint John's U, MN   B
Saint Joseph's Coll, IN   B
Saint Louis U, MO   B
Saint Mary's Coll, IN   B
St. Norbert Coll, WI   B
St. Olaf Coll, MN   B
Saint Xavier U, IL   B
Simpson Coll, IA   B
South Dakota State U, SD   B

Southeastern Oklahoma State
   U, OK   B
Southeast Missouri State U,
   MO   B
Southern Illinois U
   Carbondale, IL   B
Southern Illinois U
   Edwardsville, IL   B
Southern Methodist U, TX   B
Southwest Baptist U, MO   B
Southwestern Oklahoma State
   U, OK   B
Southwest Minnesota State U,
   MN   B
Stephens Coll, MO   B
Taylor U, IN   B
Transylvania U, KY   B
Truman State U, MO   B
The U of Akron, OH   B
U of Central Missouri, MO   B
U of Central Oklahoma, OK   B
U of Chicago, IL   B
U of Cincinnati, OH   B
U of Dayton, OH   B
U of Evansville, IN   B
The U of Findlay, OH   B
U of Illinois at Chicago, IL   B
U of Illinois at Springfield, IL   B
U of Illinois at Urbana–
   Champaign, IL   B
U of Indianapolis, IN   B
The U of Iowa, IA   B
U of Kansas, KS   B
U of Michigan, MI   B
U of Michigan–Dearborn, MI   B
U of Michigan–Flint, MI   B
U of Minnesota, Duluth, MN   B
U of Minnesota, Morris, MN   B
U of Minnesota, Twin Cities
   Campus, MN   B
U of Missouri–Columbia, MO   B
U of Missouri–Kansas City,
   MO   B
U of Missouri–St. Louis, MO   B
U of Nebraska at Kearney, NE   B
U of Nebraska at Omaha, NE   B
U of Nebraska–Lincoln, NE   B
U of New Orleans, LA   B
U of North Dakota, ND   B
U of Northern Iowa, IA   B
U of Notre Dame, IN   B
U of Oklahoma, OK   B
U of Rio Grande, OH   B
U of St. Francis, IL   B
U of Saint Mary, KS   B
U of St. Thomas, MN   B
U of Science and Arts of
   Oklahoma, OK   B
U of Sioux Falls, SD   B
The U of South Dakota, SD   B
U of Southern Indiana, IN   B
The U of Toledo, OH   A,B
U of Tulsa, OK   B
U of West Florida, FL   B
U of Wisconsin–Eau Claire,
   WI   B
U of Wisconsin–Green Bay,
   WI   A,B
U of Wisconsin–La Crosse, WI   B
U of Wisconsin–Madison, WI   B
U of Wisconsin–Milwaukee,
   WI   B
U of Wisconsin–Oshkosh, WI   B
U of Wisconsin–Parkside, WI   B
U of Wisconsin–Platteville, WI   B

U of Wisconsin–River Falls, WI	B
U of Wisconsin–Stevens Point, WI	B
U of Wisconsin–Superior, WI	B
U of Wisconsin–Whitewater, WI	B
Valparaiso U, IN	B
Wabash Coll, IN	B
Walsh U, OH	B
Wartburg Coll, IA	B
Washburn U, KS	B
Washington U in St. Louis, MO	B
Wayne State Coll, NE	B
Webster U, MO	B
Western Illinois U, IL	B
Western Michigan U, MI	B
Westminster Coll, MO	B
Wheaton Coll, IL	B
Wichita State U, KS	B
William Jewell Coll, MO	B
William Penn U, IA	B
William Woods U, MO	B
Wilmington Coll, OH	B
Winona State U, MN	B
Wisconsin Lutheran Coll, WI	B
Wittenberg U, OH	B
Wright State U, OH	B
Xavier U, OH	A,B
Youngstown State U, OH	B

Political Science and Government Related

Buena Vista U, IA	B
Capital U, OH	B
Saint Mary's U of Minnesota, MN	B
The U of Akron, OH	B
U of Northern Iowa, IA	B

Polymer Chemistry

The U of Akron, OH	B
U of Wisconsin–Stevens Point, WI	B
Winona State U, MN	B

Polymer/Plastics Engineering

Ball State U, IN	B
Case Western Reserve U, OH	B
Ferris State U, MI	B
Kettering U, MI	B
North Dakota State U, ND	B
The U of Akron, OH	B
Winona State U, MN	B

Portuguese

Indiana U Bloomington, IN	B
The Ohio State U, OH	B
U of Illinois at Urbana–Champaign, IL	B
The U of Iowa, IA	B
U of Minnesota, Twin Cities Campus, MN	B
U of Wisconsin–Madison, WI	B

Poultry Science

U of Wisconsin–Madison, WI	B

Precision Production Trades

Hope Coll, MI	B

Pre-Dentistry Studies

Alma Coll, MI	B
Anderson U, IN	B
Ashland U, OH	B
Augsburg Coll, MN	B
Augustana Coll, IL	B

Augustana Coll, SD	B
Ball State U, IN	B
Beloit Coll, WI	B
Benedictine U, IL	B
Blackburn Coll, IL	B
Calvin Coll, MI	B
Capital U, OH	B
Cardinal Stritch U, WI	B
Carroll Coll, WI	B
Cedarville U, OH	B
Central Christian Coll of Kansas, KS	
Chicago State U, IL	B
Clarkson U, NY	B
Coe Coll, IA	B
Coll of Saint Benedict, MN	B
Coll of St. Catherine, MN	B
Coll of Saint Mary, NE	B
Columbia Coll, MO	B
Concordia Coll, MN	B
Concordia U, IL	B
Concordia U, NE	B
Concordia U Wisconsin, WI	A
Cornerstone U, MI	B
Dickinson State U, ND	B
Dominican U, IL	B
Dordt Coll, IA	B
Drake U, IA	B
Drury U, MO	B
East Central U, OK	B
Edgewood Coll, WI	B
Elmhurst Coll, IL	B
Evangel U, MO	B
Gannon U, PA	B
Goshen Coll, IN	B
Graceland U, IA	B
Grand Valley State U, MI	B
Gustavus Adolphus Coll, MN	B
Hamline U, MN	B
Hastings Coll, NE	B
Heidelberg Coll, OH	B
Hillsdale Coll, MI	B
Hiram Coll, OH	B
Huntington U, IN	B
Illinois Coll, IL	B
Indiana U Bloomington, IN	B
Indiana U–Purdue U Fort Wayne, IN	B
Indiana U–Purdue U Indianapolis, IN	B
Indiana Wesleyan U, IN	B
Iowa State U of Science and Technology, IA	B
Iowa Wesleyan Coll, IA	B
Kansas State U, KS	B
Kent State U, OH	B
Kenyon Coll, OH	B
Lake Forest Coll, IL	B
Lake Superior State U, MI	B
Langston U, OK	B
Lawrence U, WI	B
Lewis U, IL	B
Lindenwood U, MO	B
MacMurray Coll, IL	B
Madonna U, MI	B
Manchester Coll, IN	B
Marian Coll, IN	B
Marian Coll of Fond du Lac, WI	B
Marquette U, WI	B
Mayville State U, ND	B
McKendree Coll, IL	B
Miami U, OH	B
Michigan Technological U, MI	B
Millikin U, IL	B

Minnesota State U Mankato, MN	B
Missouri Southern State U, MO	B
Missouri Valley Coll, MO	B
Morningside Coll, IA	B
Mount Mary Coll, WI	B
Mount Mercy Coll, IA	B
Mount Vernon Nazarene U, OH	B
Newman U, KS	B
North Central Coll, IL	B
Northeastern State U, OK	B
Northern Michigan U, MI	B
Northern State U, SD	B
Northland Coll, WI	B
Northwestern Oklahoma State U, OK	B
Northwest Missouri State U, MO	B
Ohio Northern U, OH	B
Ohio Wesleyan U, OH	B
Oklahoma City U, OK	B
Oklahoma Wesleyan U, OK	B
Oral Roberts U, OK	B
Otterbein Coll, OH	B
Peru State Coll, NE	B
Purdue U Calumet, IN	B
Quincy U, IL	B
Ripon Coll, WI	B
Rockford Coll, IL	B
Roosevelt U, IL	B
St. Cloud State U, MN	B
St. Gregory's U, Shawnee, OK	B
Saint John's U, MN	B
Saint Mary-of-the-Woods Coll, IN	B
Simpson Coll, IA	B
South Dakota State U, SD	B
Southwestern Oklahoma State U, OK	B
Southwest Minnesota State U, MN	B
Tabor Coll, KS	B
Taylor U, IN	B
Trinity Christian Coll, IL	B
Truman State U, MO	B
U of Central Missouri, MO	B
U of Dallas, TX	B
U of Dayton, OH	B
U of Evansville, IN	B
U of Illinois at Chicago, IL	B
U of Indianapolis, IN	B
The U of Iowa, IA	B
U of Minnesota, Duluth, MN	B
U of Minnesota, Morris, MN	B
U of Minnesota, Twin Cities Campus, MN	B
U of Missouri–Rolla, MO	B
U of Missouri–St. Louis, MO	B
U of Nebraska–Lincoln, NE	B
U of Rio Grande, OH	B
U of St. Francis, IL	B
U of Saint Francis, IN	B
U of Sioux Falls, SD	B
The U of Toledo, OH	B
U of Wisconsin–Green Bay, WI	B
U of Wisconsin–Milwaukee, WI	B
U of Wisconsin–Oshkosh, WI	B
U of Wisconsin–Parkside, WI	B
U of Wisconsin–River Falls, WI	B
Upper Iowa U, IA	B

Valley City State U, ND	B
Walsh U, OH	B
Washburn U, KS	B
Washington U in St. Louis, MO	B
Western Michigan U, MI	B
William Jewell Coll, MO	B
William Penn U, IA	B
Wilmington Coll, OH	B
Winona State U, MN	B
Wright State U, OH	B
Youngstown State U, OH	B

Pre-Engineering

Anderson U, IN	A
Baldwin-Wallace Coll, OH	B
Bowling Green State U–Firelands Coll, OH	A
Columbia Coll, MO	B
Drake U, IA	B
Edgewood Coll, WI	A
Ferris State U, MI	A
Hannibal-LaGrange Coll, MO	A
Lincoln U, MO	A
Marian Coll, IN	A
Miami U–Middletown Campus, OH	A
Minnesota State U Mankato, MN	A
Missouri Southern State U, MO	A
Newman U, KS	A,B
Northern State U, SD	
Oral Roberts U, OK	B
Purdue U North Central, IN	A
St. Gregory's U, Shawnee, OK	A
Shawnee State U, OH	A
Turtle Mountain Comm Coll, ND	A
U of Sioux Falls, SD	A
Valley City State U, ND	B

Pre-Law Studies

Albion Coll, MI	B
Alma Coll, MI	B
Anderson U, IN	B
Andrews U, MI	B
Antioch Coll, OH	B
Aquinas Coll, MI	B
Ashford U, IA	B
Ashland U, OH	B
Augsburg Coll, MN	B
Augustana Coll, IL	B
Augustana Coll, SD	B
Ball State U, IN	B
Beloit Coll, WI	B
Bemidji State U, MN	B
Benedictine U, IL	B
Blackburn Coll, IL	
Bowling Green State U, OH	B
Calumet Coll of Saint Joseph, IN	A,B
Calvin Coll, MI	B
Cardinal Stritch U, WI	B
Cedarville U, OH	B
Central Christian Coll of Kansas, KS	B
Chicago State U, IL	B
Clarkson U, NY	B
Coe Coll, IA	B
Coll of Saint Benedict, MN	B
Coll of St. Catherine, MN	B
Coll of Saint Mary, NE	B
Coll of the Ozarks, MO	B
Columbia Coll, MO	B
Concordia Coll, MN	B

A—associate degree; B—bachelor's degree

Concordia U, IL	B
Concordia U, MI	B
Concordia U, NE	B
Concordia U Wisconsin, WI	B
Cornerstone U, MI	B
Creighton U, NE	B
Crown Coll, MN	B
DePaul U, IL	B
Dickinson State U, ND	B
Dominican U, IL	B
Dordt Coll, IA	B
Drake U, IA	B
Drury U, MO	B
Earlham Coll, IN	B
East Central U, OK	B
Edgewood Coll, WI	B
Elmhurst Coll, IL	B
Evangel U, MO	B
Ferris State U, MI	A
Fontbonne U, MO	B
Fort Hays State U, KS	B
Gannon U, PA	B
Goshen Coll, IN	B
Graceland U, IA	B
Grand Valley State U, MI	B
Grand View Coll, IA	B
Gustavus Adolphus Coll, MN	B
Hamline U, MN	B
Hannibal-LaGrange Coll, MO	B
Hastings Coll, NE	B
Heidelberg Coll, OH	B
Hiram Coll, OH	B
Huntington U, IN	B
Illinois Coll, IL	B
Indiana U Bloomington, IN	B
Indiana U–Purdue U Indianapolis, IN	B
Indiana Wesleyan U, IN	B
Iowa State U of Science and Technology, IA	B
Iowa Wesleyan Coll, IA	B
Judson Coll, IL	B
Kenyon Coll, OH	B
Lake Forest Coll, IL	B
Lake Superior State U, MI	B
Langston U, OK	B
Lawrence U, WI	B
Lewis U, IL	B
Lindenwood U, MO	B
MacMurray Coll, IL	B
Madonna U, MI	B
Manchester Coll, IN	B
Marian Coll, IN	B
Marian Coll of Fond du Lac, WI	B
Marquette U, WI	B
Mayville State U, ND	B
McKendree Coll, IL	B
Miami U, OH	B
Michigan State U, MI	B
Michigan Technological U, MI	B
Millikin U, IL	B
Minnesota State U Mankato, MN	B
Missouri Valley Coll, MO	B
Morningside Coll, IA	B
Mount Mary Coll, WI	B
Mount Mercy Coll, IA	B
Mount Vernon Nazarene U, OH	B
National American U, Rapid City, SD	B
Newman U, KS	B
North Central Coll, IL	B
Northeastern State U, OK	B
Northern Michigan U, MI	B
Northern State U, SD	B
Northland Coll, WI	B
Northwestern Oklahoma State U, OK	B
Northwest Missouri State U, MO	B
Notre Dame Coll, OH	B
Ohio Northern U, OH	B
Ohio U, OH	B
Ohio Wesleyan U, OH	B
Oklahoma Christian U, OK	B
Oklahoma City U, OK	B
Oklahoma Wesleyan U, OK	B
Oral Roberts U, OK	B
Otterbein Coll, OH	B
Peru State Coll, NE	B
Purdue U Calumet, IN	B
Ripon Coll, WI	B
Rockford Coll, IL	B
Roosevelt U, IL	B
St. Cloud State U, MN	B
St. Gregory's U, Shawnee, OK	B
Saint John's U, MN	B
Saint Mary-of-the-Woods Coll, IN	B
Shawnee State U, OH	B
Simpson Coll, IA	B
South Dakota State U, SD	B
Southwestern Oklahoma State U, OK	B
Southwest Minnesota State U, MN	B
Stephens Coll, MO	B
Taylor U, IN	B
Taylor U Fort Wayne, IN	B
Tiffin U, OH	B
Tri-State U, IN	B
Truman State U, MO	B
The U of Akron, OH	B
U of Cincinnati, OH	B
U of Dallas, TX	B
U of Dayton, OH	B
The U of Findlay, OH	B
U of Illinois at Chicago, IL	B
U of Illinois at Urbana–Champaign, IL	B
U of Indianapolis, IN	B
The U of Iowa, IA	B
U of Minnesota, Duluth, MN	B
U of Minnesota, Morris, MN	B
U of Minnesota, Twin Cities Campus, MN	B
U of Missouri–Rolla, MO	B
U of Missouri–St. Louis, MO	B
U of Rio Grande, OH	B
U of Saint Francis, IN	B
U of Sioux Falls, SD	B
The U of Toledo, OH	B
U of Wisconsin–Milwaukee, WI	B
U of Wisconsin–Oshkosh, WI	B
U of Wisconsin–Parkside, WI	B
U of Wisconsin–River Falls, WI	B
U of Wisconsin–Superior, WI	B
Valley City State U, ND	B
Wabash Coll, IN	B
Washburn U, KS	B
Western Michigan U, MI	B
Westminster Coll, MO	B
William Jewell Coll, MO	B
William Penn U, IA	B
Wilmington Coll, OH	B
Winona State U, MN	B
Wright State U, OH	B
Youngstown State U, OH	B

Pre-Medical Studies

Adrian Coll, MI	B
Albion Coll, MI	B
Alma Coll, MI	B
Anderson U, IN	B
Andrews U, MI	B
Antioch Coll, OH	B
Ashford U, IA	B
Ashland U, OH	B
Augsburg Coll, MN	B
Augustana Coll, IL	B
Augustana Coll, SD	B
Ball State U, IN	B
Beloit Coll, WI	B
Bemidji State U, MN	B
Benedictine U, IL	B
Blackburn Coll, IL	B
Bluffton U, OH	B
Calvin Coll, MI	B
Capital U, OH	B
Cardinal Stritch U, WI	B
Carroll Coll, WI	B
Cedarville U, OH	B
Central Christian Coll of Kansas, KS	B
Chicago State U, IL	B
Clarkson U, NY	B
Coe Coll, IA	B
Coll of Saint Benedict, MN	B
Coll of St. Catherine, MN	B
Coll of Saint Mary, NE	B
Coll of the Ozarks, MO	B
Columbia Coll, MO	B
Concordia Coll, MN	B
Concordia U, IL	B
Concordia U, MI	B
Concordia U, NE	B
Concordia U Wisconsin, WI	A
Concord U, WV	B
Cornerstone U, MI	B
Dickinson State U, ND	B
Dordt Coll, IA	B
Drake U, IA	B
Drury U, MO	B
Earlham Coll, IN	B
East Central U, OK	B
Edgewood Coll, WI	B
Elmhurst Coll, IL	B
Evangel U, MO	B
Fontbonne U, MO	B
Gannon U, PA	B
Goshen Coll, IN	B
Graceland U, IA	B
Grand Valley State U, MI	B
Gustavus Adolphus Coll, MN	B
Hamline U, MN	B
Hastings Coll, NE	B
Heidelberg Coll, OH	B
Hillsdale Coll, MI	B
Hiram Coll, OH	B
Huntington U, IN	B
Illinois Coll, IL	B
Indiana U Bloomington, IN	B
Indiana U–Purdue U Fort Wayne, IN	B
Indiana U–Purdue U Indianapolis, IN	B
Indiana Wesleyan U, IN	B
Iowa State U of Science and Technology, IA	B
Iowa Wesleyan Coll, IA	B
Judson Coll, IL	B
Kansas State U, KS	B
Kent State U, OH	B
Kenyon Coll, OH	B
Lake Forest Coll, IL	B
Langston U, OK	B
Lawrence U, WI	B
Lewis U, IL	B
Lindenwood U, MO	B
Lourdes Coll, OH	B
MacMurray Coll, IL	B
Madonna U, MI	B
Manchester Coll, IN	B
Marian Coll, IN	B
Marian Coll of Fond du Lac, WI	B
Marquette U, WI	B
Mayville State U, ND	B
McKendree Coll, IL	B
Miami U, OH	B
Michigan State U, MI	B
Michigan Technological U, MI	B
Millikin U, IL	B
Minnesota State U Mankato, MN	B
Missouri Southern State U, MO	B
Missouri Valley Coll, MO	B
Morningside Coll, IA	B
Mount Mary Coll, WI	B
Mount Mercy Coll, IA	B
Mount Vernon Nazarene U, OH	B
Newman U, KS	B
North Central Coll, IL	B
Northeastern State U, OK	B
Northern Michigan U, MI	B
Northern State U, SD	B
Northland Coll, WI	B
Northwestern Oklahoma State U, OK	B
Northwestern U, IL	B
Northwest Missouri State U, MO	B
Notre Dame Coll, OH	B
Ohio Northern U, OH	B
Ohio Wesleyan U, OH	B
Oklahoma City U, OK	B
Oklahoma Wesleyan U, OK	B
Oral Roberts U, OK	B
Otterbein Coll, OH	B
Peru State Coll, NE	B
Purdue U Calumet, IN	B
Quincy U, IL	B
Ripon Coll, WI	B
Rockford Coll, IL	B
Roosevelt U, IL	B
St. Cloud State U, MN	B
St. Gregory's U, Shawnee, OK	B
Saint John's U, MN	B
Saint Mary-of-the-Woods Coll, IN	B
Shawnee State U, OH	B
Simpson Coll, IA	B
South Dakota State U, SD	B
Southwestern Oklahoma State U, OK	B
Southwest Minnesota State U, MN	B
Stephens Coll, MO	B
Tabor Coll, KS	B
Taylor U, IN	B
Trinity Christian Coll, IL	B
Trinity International U, IL	B
Tri-State U, IN	B
Truman State U, MO	B
U of Central Missouri, MO	B
U of Cincinnati, OH	B
U of Dallas, TX	B
U of Dayton, OH	B

U of Evansville, IN	B
The U of Findlay, OH	B
U of Indianapolis, IN	B
The U of Iowa, IA	B
U of Minnesota, Duluth, MN	B
U of Minnesota, Morris, MN	B
U of Minnesota, Twin Cities Campus, MN	B
U of Missouri–Rolla, MO	B
U of Missouri–St. Louis, MO	B
U of Nebraska–Lincoln, NE	B
U of Notre Dame, IN	B
U of Rio Grande, OH	B
U of St. Francis, IL	B
U of Saint Francis, IN	B
U of Sioux Falls, SD	B
The U of Toledo, OH	B
U of Wisconsin–Milwaukee, WI	B
U of Wisconsin–Oshkosh, WI	B
U of Wisconsin–Parkside, WI	B
U of Wisconsin–River Falls, WI	B
Upper Iowa U, IA	B
Valley City State U, ND	B
Wabash Coll, IN	B
Walsh U, OH	B
Washburn U, KS	B
Washington U in St. Louis, MO	B
Wayne State Coll, NE	B
Western Michigan U, MI	B
William Jewell Coll, MO	B
William Penn U, IA	B
Wilmington Coll, OH	B
Winona State U, MN	B
Wright State U, OH	B
Youngstown State U, OH	B

Pre-Nursing Studies

Cleveland State U, OH	B
Concordia U, NE	B
Concordia U Wisconsin, WI	A
Dordt Coll, IA	B
Lindenwood U, MO	B
Missouri Valley Coll, MO	B
Oklahoma City U, OK	B
St. Gregory's U, Shawnee, OK	B
Trinity International U, IL	A

Pre-Pharmacy Studies

Ashland U, OH	B
Carroll Coll, WI	B
Central Christian Coll of Kansas, KS	B
Coll of Saint Benedict, MN	B
Coll of the Ozarks, MO	B
Concordia U, NE	B
Dordt Coll, IA	B
Drury U, MO	B
East Central U, OK	B
Elmhurst Coll, IL	B
Ferris State U, MI	A
Iowa Wesleyan Coll, IA	B
Madonna U, MI	B
Mayville State U, ND	B
Michigan Technological U, MI	B
Missouri Southern State U, MO	B
Missouri Valley Coll, MO	B
Mount Vernon Nazarene U, OH	B
Oklahoma City U, OK	B
Roosevelt U, IL	B
St. Cloud State U, MN	B
St. Gregory's U, Shawnee, OK	B

Saint John's U, MN	B
Saint Mary-of-the-Woods Coll, IN	B
Truman State U, MO	B
U of Central Missouri, MO	B
U of Charleston, WV	B
U of Evansville, IN	B
The U of Iowa, IA	B
U of Minnesota, Duluth, MN	B
U of Minnesota, Morris, MN	B
U of Missouri–St. Louis, MO	B
U of Nebraska–Lincoln, NE	B
U of Saint Francis, IN	B
U of Wisconsin–Parkside, WI	B
U of Wisconsin–River Falls, WI	B
Valley City State U, ND	B
Washburn U, KS	B
Washington U in St. Louis, MO	B
Wright State U, OH	B
Youngstown State U, OH	B

Pre-Theology/Pre-Ministerial Studies

Alma Coll, MI	B
Ashland U, OH	B
Central Christian Coll of Kansas, KS	B
Coll of Saint Benedict, MN	B
Concordia Coll, MN	B
Concordia U, IL	B
Concordia U, MI	B
Concordia U, NE	B
Cornerstone U, MI	B
Kuyper Coll, MI	B
Loras Coll, IA	B
Loyola U Chicago, IL	B
Manchester Coll, IN	A
Martin Luther Coll, MN	B
Minnesota State U Mankato, MN	B
Northwestern Coll, MN	B
Ohio Northern U, OH	B
Ohio Wesleyan U, OH	B
St. Gregory's U, Shawnee, OK	A
Saint John's U, MN	B
Trinity Christian Coll, IL	B
Trinity International U, IL	B
U of Dallas, TX	B
U of Indianapolis, IN	B
U of Rio Grande, OH	B
Viterbo U, WI	B
Washburn U, KS	B

Pre-Veterinary Studies

Adrian Coll, MI	B
Albion Coll, MI	B
Alma Coll, MI	B
Anderson U, IN	B
Andrews U, MI	B
Antioch Coll, OH	B
Ashland U, OH	B
Augsburg Coll, MN	B
Augustana Coll, IL	B
Augustana Coll, SD	B
Bemidji State U, MN	B
Benedictine U, IL	B
Blackburn Coll, IL	B
Calvin Coll, MI	B
Capital U, OH	B
Cardinal Stritch U, WI	B
Carroll Coll, WI	B
Cedarville U, OH	B
Central Christian Coll of Kansas, KS	B

Chicago State U, IL	B
Clarkson U, NY	B
Coe Coll, IA	B
Coll of Saint Benedict, MN	B
Coll of St. Catherine, MN	B
Coll of Saint Mary, NE	B
Coll of the Ozarks, MO	B
Columbia Coll, MO	B
Concordia Coll, MN	B
Concordia U, NE	B
Concord U, WV	B
Cornerstone U, MI	B
Dickinson State U, ND	B
Dominican U, IL	B
Dordt Coll, IA	B
Drake U, IA	B
Drury U, MO	B
East Central U, OK	B
Edgewood Coll, WI	B
Elmhurst Coll, IL	B
Evangel U, MO	B
Gannon U, PA	B
Goshen Coll, IN	B
Grand Valley State U, MI	B
Gustavus Adolphus Coll, MN	B
Hamline U, MN	B
Hastings Coll, NE	B
Heidelberg Coll, OH	B
Hillsdale Coll, MI	B
Hiram Coll, OH	B
Huntington U, IN	B
Illinois Coll, IL	B
Indiana U–Purdue U Indianapolis, IN	B
Indiana Wesleyan U, IN	B
Iowa State U of Science and Technology, IA	B
Iowa Wesleyan Coll, IA	B
Kansas State U, KS	B
Kenyon Coll, OH	B
Lake Forest Coll, IL	B
Langston U, OK	B
Lawrence U, WI	B
Lewis U, IL	B
Lindenwood U, MO	B
MacMurray Coll, IL	B
Madonna U, MI	B
Manchester Coll, IN	B
Marian Coll, IN	B
Marian Coll of Fond du Lac, WI	B
Mayville State U, ND	B
McKendree Coll, IL	B
Miami U, OH	B
Michigan State U, MI	B
Michigan Technological U, MI	B
Millikin U, IL	B
Minnesota State U Mankato, MN	B
Missouri Southern State U, MO	B
Missouri Valley Coll, MO	B
Morningside Coll, IA	B
Mount Mary Coll, WI	B
Mount Mercy Coll, IA	B
Mount Vernon Nazarene U, OH	B
Newman U, KS	B
North Central Coll, IL	B
Northeastern State U, OK	B
Northern Michigan U, MI	B
Northland Coll, WI	B
Northwest Missouri State U, MO	B
Ohio Northern U, OH	B

Ohio Wesleyan U, OH	B
Oklahoma City U, OK	B
Oklahoma State U, OK	B
Oklahoma Wesleyan U, OK	B
Otterbein Coll, OH	B
Peru State Coll, NE	B
Purdue U Calumet, IN	B
Quincy U, IL	B
Ripon Coll, WI	B
Rockford Coll, IL	B
St. Cloud State U, MN	B
Saint John's U, MN	B
Saint Mary-of-the-Woods Coll, IN	B
Shawnee State U, OH	A
Simpson Coll, IA	B
South Dakota State U, SD	B
Southwestern Oklahoma State U, OK	B
Southwest Minnesota State U, MN	B
Stephens Coll, MO	B
Taylor U, IN	B
Trinity Christian Coll, IL	B
Tri-State U, IN	B
Truman State U, MO	B
U of Central Missouri, MO	B
U of Cincinnati, OH	B
U of Evansville, IN	B
The U of Findlay, OH	B
U of Illinois at Urbana–Champaign, IL	B
U of Indianapolis, IN	B
The U of Iowa, IA	B
U of Minnesota, Duluth, MN	B
U of Minnesota, Morris, MN	B
U of Minnesota, Twin Cities Campus, MN	B
U of Missouri–St. Louis, MO	B
U of Nebraska–Lincoln, NE	B
U of Rio Grande, OH	B
U of St. Francis, IL	B
U of Saint Francis, IN	B
U of Sioux Falls, SD	B
The U of Toledo, OH	B
U of Wisconsin–Oshkosh, WI	B
U of Wisconsin–Parkside, WI	B
U of Wisconsin–River Falls, WI	B
Upper Iowa U, IA	B
Valley City State U, ND	B
Wabash Coll, IN	B
Walsh U, OH	B
Washburn U, KS	B
Washington U in St. Louis, MO	B
Wayne State Coll, NE	B
William Jewell Coll, MO	B
Wilmington Coll, OH	B
Winona State U, MN	B
Wright State U, OH	B
Youngstown State U, OH	B

Printing Management

Carroll Coll, WI	B
U of Central Missouri, MO	B
U of Wisconsin–Stout, WI	B

Printmaking

Aquinas Coll, MI	B
Art Academy of Cincinnati, OH	B
Ball State U, IN	B
The Cleveland Inst of Art, OH	B
Coll of Visual Arts, MN	B
Columbia Coll, MO	B

A—associate degree; B—bachelor's degree

Drake U, IA — B
Grand Valley State U, MI — B
Indiana U–Purdue U Fort Wayne, IN — B
Indiana Wesleyan U, IN — B
Kansas City Art Inst, MO — B
Kent State U, OH — B
Minneapolis Coll of Art and Design, MN — B
Ohio Northern U, OH — B
The Ohio State U, OH — B
Ohio U, OH — B
St. Cloud State U, MN — B
School of the Art Inst of Chicago, IL — B
Trinity Christian Coll, IL — B
The U of Akron, OH — B
U of Dallas, TX — B
The U of Iowa, IA — B
U of Kansas, KS — B
U of Michigan, MI — B
U of Michigan–Flint, MI — B
U of Missouri–St. Louis, MO — B
Washington U in St. Louis, MO — B
Youngstown State U, OH — B

Professional Studies
Bemidji State U, MN — B
Briar Cliff U, IA — B
Kent State U, OH — B
Missouri Southern State U, MO — B
Saint Mary-of-the-Woods Coll, IN — B
U of Oklahoma, OK — B
Western Michigan U, MI — B

Psychiatric/Mental Health Services Technology
Franciscan U of Steubenville, OH — B
Lake Superior State U, MI — A
The U of Toledo, OH — A

Psychology
Adrian Coll, MI — A,B
Albion Coll, MI — B
Alma Coll, MI — B
Alverno Coll, WI — B
Anderson U, IN — B
Andrews U, MI — B
Antioch Coll, OH — B
Aquinas Coll, MI — B
Argosy U, Twin Cities, Eagan, MN — B
Ashford U, IA — B
Ashland U, OH — B
Augsburg Coll, MN — B
Augustana Coll, IL — B
Augustana Coll, SD — B
Aurora U, IL — B
Avila U, MO — B
Baker U, KS — B
Baldwin-Wallace Coll, OH — B
Ball State U, IN — B
Barclay Coll, KS — B
Beloit Coll, WI — B
Bemidji State U, MN — B
Benedictine Coll, KS — B
Benedictine U, IL — B
Bethany Coll, KS — B
Bethany Lutheran Coll, MN — B
Bethel Coll, KS — B
Bethel U, MN — B
Blackburn Coll, IL — B
Black Hills State U, SD — B
Bluffton U, OH — B

Bowling Green State U, OH — B
Bradley U, IL — B
Briar Cliff U, IA — B
Buena Vista U, IA — B
Butler U, IN — B
Calumet Coll of Saint Joseph, IN — B
Calvin Coll, MI — B
Cameron U, OK — B
Capital U, OH — B
Cardinal Stritch U, WI — B
Carleton Coll, MN — B
Carroll Coll, WI — B
Case Western Reserve U, OH — B
Cedarville U, OH — B
Central Christian Coll of Kansas, KS — B
Central Coll, IA — B
Central Methodist U, MO — A,B
Central Michigan U, MI — B
Central State U, OH — B
Chicago State U, IL — B
Cincinnati Christian U, OH — B
Clarke Coll, IA — B
Clarkson U, NY — B
Cleveland State U, OH — B
Coe Coll, IA — B
Coll of Mount St. Joseph, OH — B
Coll of Saint Benedict, MN — B
Coll of St. Catherine, MN — B
Coll of Saint Mary, NE — B
The Coll of St. Scholastica, MN — B
Coll of the Ozarks, MO — B
The Coll of Wooster, OH — B
Columbia Coll, MO — B
Concordia Coll, MN — B
Concordia U, IL — B
Concordia U, MI — B
Concordia U, NE — B
Concordia U, St. Paul, MN — B
Concordia U Wisconsin, WI — B
Concord U, WV — B
Cornell Coll, IA — B
Cornerstone U, MI — B
Creighton U, NE — B
Crown Coll, MN — A,B
Culver-Stockton Coll, MO — B
Dakota Wesleyan U, SD — B
Dana Coll, NE — B
Denison U, OH — B
DePaul U, IL — B
DePauw U, IN — B
Dickinson State U, ND — B
Doane Coll, NE — B
Dominican U, IL — B
Dordt Coll, IA — B
Drake U, IA — B
Drury U, MO — B
Earlham Coll, IN — B
East Central U, OK — B
Eastern Illinois U, IL — B
Eastern Michigan U, MI — B
Edgewood Coll, WI — B
Elmhurst Coll, IL — B
Emporia State U, KS — B
Evangel U, MO — B
Fontbonne U, MO — B
Fort Hays State U, KS — B
Franciscan U of Steubenville, OH — B
Franklin Coll, IN — B
Gannon U, PA — B
Goshen Coll, IN — B
Grace Coll, IN — B
Graceland U, IA — B

Grand Valley State U, MI — B
Grand View Coll, IA — B
Greenville Coll, IL — B
Grinnell Coll, IA — B
Gustavus Adolphus Coll, MN — B
Hamline U, MN — B
Hannibal-LaGrange Coll, MO — B
Hanover Coll, IN — B
Hastings Coll, NE — B
Heidelberg Coll, OH — B
Hillsdale Coll, MI — B
Hillsdale Free Will Baptist Coll, OK — A
Hiram Coll, OH — B
Hope Coll, MI — B
Huntington U, IN — B
Illinois Coll, IL — B
Illinois Inst of Technology, IL — B
Illinois State U, IL — B
Illinois Wesleyan U, IL — B
Indiana State U, IN — B
Indiana Tech, IN — B
Indiana U Bloomington, IN — B
Indiana U East, IN — B
Indiana U Kokomo, IN — B
Indiana U Northwest, IN — B
Indiana U–Purdue U Fort Wayne, IN — A,B
Indiana U–Purdue U Indianapolis, IN — B
Indiana U South Bend, IN — B
Indiana U Southeast, IN — B
Indiana Wesleyan U, IN — B
Iowa State U of Science and Technology, IA — B
Iowa Wesleyan Coll, IA — B
Jamestown Coll, ND — B
Judson Coll, IL — B
Kalamazoo Coll, MI — B
Kansas State U, KS — B
Kent State U, OH — B
Kenyon Coll, OH — B
Knox Coll, IL — B
Lake Forest Coll, IL — B
Lakeland Coll, WI — B
Lake Superior State U, MI — B
Langston U, OK — B
Lawrence Technological U, MI — B
Lawrence U, WI — B
Lewis U, IL — B
Lincoln U, MO — B
Lindenwood U, MO — B
Loras Coll, IA — B
Lourdes Coll, OH — A,B
Loyola U Chicago, IL — B
Luther Coll, IA — B
Macalester Coll, MN — B
MacMurray Coll, IL — B
Madonna U, MI — B
Malone Coll, OH — B
Manchester Coll, IN — B
Marian Coll, IN — A,B
Marian Coll of Fond du Lac, WI — B
Marietta Coll, OH — B
Marquette U, WI — B
Marygrove Coll, MI — B
Maryville U of Saint Louis, MO — B
McKendree Coll, IL — B
Metropolitan State U, MN — B
Miami U, OH — B
Miami U Hamilton, OH — B
Miami U–Middletown Campus, OH — A
Michigan State U, MI — B

Michigan Technological U, MI — B
Millikin U, IL — B
Minnesota State U Mankato, MN — B
Minot State U, ND — B
Missouri Baptist U, MO — B
Missouri Southern State U, MO — B
Missouri State U, MO — B
Missouri Valley Coll, MO — B
Missouri Western State U, MO — B
Morningside Coll, IA — B
Mount Marty Coll, SD — B
Mount Mary Coll, WI — B
Mount Mercy Coll, IA — B
Mount Union Coll, OH — B
Mount Vernon Nazarene U, OH — B
Nebraska Wesleyan U, NE — B
Newman U, KS — B
North Carolina Ag and Tech State U, NC — B
North Central Coll, IL — B
North Dakota State U, ND — B
Northeastern Illinois U, IL — B
Northeastern State U, OK — B
Northern Illinois U, IL — B
Northern Michigan U, MI — B
Northern State U, SD — B
Northland Coll, WI — B
Northwestern Coll, IA — B
Northwestern Coll, MN — B
Northwestern Oklahoma State U, OK — B
Northwestern U, IL — B
Northwest Missouri State U, MO — B
Notre Dame Coll, OH — B
Oakland U, MI — B
Oberlin Coll, OH — B
Ohio Dominican U, OH — B
Ohio Northern U, OH — B
The Ohio State U, OH — B
The Ohio State U at Lima, OH — B
The Ohio State U at Marion, OH — B
The Ohio State U–Mansfield Campus, OH — B
The Ohio State U–Newark Campus, OH — B
Ohio U, OH — B
Ohio Wesleyan U, OH — B
Oklahoma Christian U, OK — B
Oklahoma City U, OK — B
Oklahoma Panhandle State U, OK — B
Oklahoma State U, OK — B
Oral Roberts U, OK — B
Ottawa U, KS — B
Otterbein Coll, OH — B
Park U, MO — B
Peru State Coll, NE — B
Pittsburg State U, KS — B
Purdue U, IN — B
Purdue U Calumet, IN — B
Quincy U, IL — B
Ripon Coll, WI — B
Rochester Coll, MI — B
Rockford Coll, IL — B
Rockhurst U, MO — B
Roosevelt U, IL — B
Saginaw Valley State U, MI — B
St. Ambrose U, IA — B
St. Cloud State U, MN — B
St. Gregory's U, Shawnee, OK — B

Saint John's U, MN	B
Saint Joseph's Coll, IN	B
Saint Louis U, MO	B
Saint Mary-of-the-Woods Coll, IN	B
Saint Mary's Coll, IN	B
Saint Mary's U of Minnesota, MN	B
St. Norbert Coll, WI	B
St. Olaf Coll, MN	B
Saint Xavier U, IL	B
Shawnee State U, OH	B
Silver Lake Coll, WI	B
Simpson Coll, IA	B
South Dakota State U, SD	B
Southeastern Oklahoma State U, OK	B
Southeast Missouri State U, MO	B
Southern Illinois U Carbondale, IL	B
Southern Illinois U Edwardsville, IL	B
Southern Methodist U, TX	B
Southwest Baptist U, MO	B
Southwestern Coll, KS	B
Southwestern Oklahoma State U, OK	B
Southwest Minnesota State U, MN	B
Spring Arbor U, MI	B
Stephens Coll, MO	B
Tabor Coll, KS	B
Taylor U, IN	B
Tiffin U, OH	B
Transylvania U, KY	B
Trinity Christian Coll, IL	B
Trinity International U, IL	B
Tri-State U, IN	B
Truman State U, MO	B
Union Coll, NE	B
The U of Akron, OH	B
U of Central Missouri, MO	B
U of Central Oklahoma, OK	B
U of Charleston, WV	B
U of Chicago, IL	B
U of Cincinnati, OH	B
U of Dallas, TX	B
U of Dayton, OH	B
U of Evansville, IN	B
The U of Findlay, OH	B
U of Illinois at Chicago, IL	B
U of Illinois at Springfield, IL	B
U of Illinois at Urbana–Champaign, IL	B
U of Indianapolis, IN	B
The U of Iowa, IA	B
U of Kansas, KS	B
U of Mary, ND	B
U of Michigan, MI	B
U of Michigan–Dearborn, MI	B
U of Michigan–Flint, MI	B
U of Minnesota, Duluth, MN	B
U of Minnesota, Morris, MN	B
U of Minnesota, Twin Cities Campus, MN	B
U of Missouri–Columbia, MO	B
U of Missouri–Kansas City, MO	B
U of Missouri–Rolla, MO	B
U of Missouri–St. Louis, MO	B
U of Nebraska at Kearney, NE	B
U of Nebraska at Omaha, NE	B
U of Nebraska–Lincoln, NE	B
U of New Orleans, LA	B

U of North Dakota, ND	B
U of Northern Iowa, IA	B
U of Notre Dame, IN	B
U of Oklahoma, OK	B
U of Phoenix–Cincinnati Campus, OH	B
U of Phoenix–Cleveland Campus, OH	B
U of Phoenix–Columbus Ohio Campus, OH	B
U of Phoenix–Indianapolis Campus, IN	B
U of Phoenix–Oklahoma City Campus, OK	B
U of Phoenix–St. Louis Campus, MO	B
U of Phoenix–Springfield Campus, MO	B
U of Phoenix–Tulsa Campus, OK	B
U of Rio Grande, OH	A
U of St. Francis, IL	B
U of Saint Francis, IN	B
U of Saint Mary, KS	B
U of St. Thomas, MN	B
U of Science and Arts of Oklahoma, OK	B
U of Sioux Falls, SD	B
The U of South Dakota, SD	B
U of Southern Indiana, IN	B
The U of Toledo, OH	B
U of Tulsa, OK	B
U of West Florida, FL	B
U of Wisconsin–Eau Claire, WI	B
U of Wisconsin–Green Bay, WI	A,B
U of Wisconsin–La Crosse, WI	B
U of Wisconsin–Madison, WI	B
U of Wisconsin–Milwaukee, WI	B
U of Wisconsin–Oshkosh, WI	B
U of Wisconsin–Parkside, WI	B
U of Wisconsin–Platteville, WI	B
U of Wisconsin–River Falls, WI	B
U of Wisconsin–Stevens Point, WI	B
U of Wisconsin–Stout, WI	B
U of Wisconsin–Superior, WI	B
U of Wisconsin–Whitewater, WI	B
Upper Iowa U, IA	B
Ursuline Coll, OH	B
Valley City State U, ND	B
Valparaiso U, IN	B
Vennard Coll, IA	B
Viterbo U, WI	B
Wabash Coll, IN	B
Waldorf Coll, IA	B
Walsh U, OH	B
Wartburg Coll, IA	B
Washburn U, KS	B
Washington U in St. Louis, MO	B
Wayne State Coll, NE	B
Webster U, MO	B
Western Illinois U, IL	B
Western Michigan U, MI	B
Westminster Coll, MO	B
Wheaton Coll, IL	B
Wichita State U, KS	B
William Jewell Coll, MO	B
William Penn U, IA	B
William Woods U, MO	B

Wilmington Coll, OH	B
Winona State U, MN	B
Wisconsin Lutheran Coll, WI	B
Wittenberg U, OH	B
Wright State U, OH	A,B
Xavier U, OH	A,B
York Coll, NE	B
Youngstown State U, OH	B

Psychology Related

Buena Vista U, IA	B
Loyola U Chicago, IL	B
Madonna U, MI	B
Mayville State U, ND	B
Ohio Northern U, OH	B
U of Michigan–Flint, MI	B
U of St. Thomas, MN	B
The U of Toledo, OH	B

Psychology Teacher Education

Alma Coll, MI	B
Carroll Coll, WI	B
Central Christian Coll of Kansas, KS	A
Ohio Wesleyan U, OH	B
Pittsburg State U, KS	B
St. Ambrose U, IA	B
Shawnee State U, OH	B
U of Evansville, IN	B
U of Michigan–Flint, MI	B
U of Missouri–St. Louis, MO	B
Valparaiso U, IN	B
Wayne State Coll, NE	B
York Coll, NE	B

Psychometrics and Quantitative Psychology

North Dakota State U, ND	B

Public Administration

Augustana Coll, IL	B
Blackburn Coll, IL	B
Bowling Green State U, OH	B
Buena Vista U, IA	B
Calvin Coll, MI	B
Capital U, OH	B
Cedarville U, OH	B
Central Methodist U, MO	A,B
Cleveland State U, OH	B
Doane Coll, NE	B
Eastern Michigan U, MI	B
Edgewood Coll, WI	B
Evangel U, MO	B
Ferris State U, MI	B
Fort Berthold Comm Coll, ND	A
Grand Valley State U, MI	B
Hamline U, MN	B
Harris-Stowe State U, MO	B
Hastings Coll, NE	B
Heidelberg Coll, OH	B
Indiana U Bloomington, IN	A,B
Indiana U Northwest, IN	A,B
Indiana U–Purdue U Fort Wayne, IN	A,B
Indiana U–Purdue U Indianapolis, IN	A,B
Indiana U South Bend, IN	A,B
Iowa State U of Science and Technology, IA	B
Lewis U, IL	B
Lincoln U, MO	B
Lindenwood U, MO	B
Metropolitan State U, MN	B
Miami U, OH	B
Miami U Hamilton, OH	B
Michigan State U, MI	B

Minnesota State U Mankato, MN	B
Missouri State U, MO	B
Missouri Valley Coll, MO	B
Northern Michigan U, MI	B
Northern State U, SD	B
Northwest Missouri State U, MO	B
Notre Dame Coll, OH	B
Oakland U, MI	B
Ohio Wesleyan U, OH	B
Park U, MO	B
Roosevelt U, IL	B
Saginaw Valley State U, MI	B
St. Ambrose U, IA	B
St. Cloud State U, MN	B
Southwest Minnesota State U, MN	B
U of Kansas, KS	B
U of Michigan–Flint, MI	B
U of Missouri–St. Louis, MO	B
U of Northern Iowa, IA	B
U of Oklahoma, OK	B
U of Phoenix–Cincinnati Campus, OH	B
U of Phoenix–Cleveland Campus, OH	B
U of Phoenix–Columbus Ohio Campus, OH	B
U of Phoenix–Indianapolis Campus, IN	B
U of Phoenix–Kansas City Campus, MO	B
U of Phoenix–Metro Detroit Campus, MI	B
U of Phoenix–St. Louis Campus, MO	B
U of Phoenix–Springfield Campus, MO	B
U of St. Thomas, MN	B
U of Wisconsin–Stevens Point, WI	B
U of Wisconsin–Whitewater, WI	B
Upper Iowa U, IA	B
Washburn U, KS	B
Wayne State Coll, NE	B
Western Michigan U, MI	B
Winona State U, MN	B
Wright State U, OH	B

Public Administration and Social Service Professions Related

Eastern Michigan U, MI	B
Indiana U–Purdue U Fort Wayne, IN	A
Northeastern Illinois U, IL	B
Ohio U, OH	B
Quincy U, IL	B
Roosevelt U, IL	B
Taylor U Fort Wayne, IN	B
The U of Akron, OH	A
U of Phoenix–Kansas City Campus, MO	B
U of Phoenix–West Michigan Campus, MI	B
U of Saint Francis, IN	A,B

Public Health

Alma Coll, MI	B
Central Michigan U, MI	B
Grand Valley State U, MI	B
Indiana U Bloomington, IN	B
Indiana U–Purdue U Indianapolis, IN	B

A—associate degree; B—bachelor's degree

Maryville U of Saint Louis, MO — B
Minnesota State U Mankato, MN — B
Truman State U, MO — B
U of Cincinnati, OH — B
U of Minnesota, Twin Cities Campus, MN — B
Winona State U, MN — B

Public Health/Community Nursing
Capital U, OH — B
Northern Illinois U, IL — B
Wright State U, OH — B

Public Health Education and Promotion
Baldwin-Wallace Coll, OH — B
Malone Coll, OH — B
Oakland U, MI — B
U of Michigan–Flint, MI — B
U of St. Thomas, MN — B
The U of Toledo, OH — B

Public Health Related
Malone Coll, OH — B
U of Illinois at Urbana–Champaign, IL — B

Public Policy Analysis
Albion Coll, MI — B
DePaul U, IL — B
Edgewood Coll, WI — B
Grand Valley State U, MI — B
Indiana U Bloomington, IN — A,B
Indiana U–Purdue U Fort Wayne, IN — B
Kenyon Coll, OH — B
Northwestern U, IL — B
St. Cloud State U, MN — B
Southern Methodist U, TX — B
U of Charleston, WV — B
U of Chicago, IL — B
U of Cincinnati, OH — B
The U of Toledo, OH — B
U of Wisconsin–Whitewater, WI — B

Public Relations
Southern Methodist U, TX — B

Public Relations, Advertising, and Applied Communication Related
Buena Vista U, IA — B
Carroll Coll, WI — B
The Coll of St. Scholastica, MN — B
East Central U, OK — B
Madonna U, MI — A,B
Marietta Coll, OH — B
Notre Dame Coll, OH — B
Saint Mary's U of Minnesota, MN — B
The U of Akron, OH — B
Western Michigan U, MI — B

Public Relations/Image Management
Andrews U, MI — B
Baldwin-Wallace Coll, OH — B
Ball State U, IN — B
Bowling Green State U, OH — B
Bradley U, IL — B
Butler U, IN — B
Capital U, OH — B
Cardinal Stritch U, WI — B
Central Michigan U, MI — B

Clarke Coll, IA — B
Cleveland State U, OH — B
Coe Coll, IA — B
Coll of the Ozarks, MO — B
Columbia Coll Chicago, IL — B
Concordia Coll, MN — B
Doane Coll, NE — B
Drake U, IA — B
Drury U, MO — B
East Central U, OK — B
Eastern Michigan U, MI — B
Ferris State U, MI — B
Fort Hays State U, KS — B
Grand Valley State U, MI — B
Greenville Coll, IL — B
Hastings Coll, NE — B
Heidelberg Coll, OH — B
Huntington U, IN — B
Illinois State U, IL — B
Indiana U Northwest, IN — B
Kent State U, OH — B
Lewis U, IL — B
Lindenwood U, MO — B
Loras Coll, IA — B
Madonna U, MI — A,B
Marquette U, WI — B
McKendree Coll, IL — B
Minnesota State U Mankato, MN — B
Mount Mary Coll, WI — B
Northern Michigan U, MI — B
Northwestern Coll, MN — B
Northwest Missouri State U, MO — B
Ohio Dominican U, OH — B
Ohio Northern U, OH — B
Ohio U, OH — B
Ohio U–Zanesville, OH — B
Oklahoma Christian U, OK — B
Oklahoma City U, OK — B
Oral Roberts U, OK — B
Otterbein Coll, OH — B
Purdue U Calumet, IN — B
Quincy U, IL — B
Roosevelt U, IL — B
St. Ambrose U, IA — B
St. Cloud State U, MN — B
Saint Mary-of-the-Woods Coll, IN — B
Southern Methodist U, TX — B
Stephens Coll, MO — B
Tabor Coll, KS — B
Trinity Christian Coll, IL — B
Union Coll, NE — B
U of Central Missouri, MO — B
U of Central Oklahoma, OK — B
U of Dayton, OH — B
The U of Findlay, OH — B
U of Northern Iowa, IA — B
U of Oklahoma, OK — B
U of Rio Grande, OH — B
U of Sioux Falls, SD — B
U of Southern Indiana, IN — B
U of Wisconsin–Madison, WI — B
U of Wisconsin–River Falls, WI — B
Ursuline Coll, OH — B
Valparaiso U, IN — B
Wartburg Coll, IA — B
Webster U, MO — B
William Penn U, IA — B
William Woods U, MO — B
Winona State U, MN — B
Xavier U, OH — A,B

Publishing
Benedictine U, IL — B

Graceland U, IA — B
Saint Mary's U of Minnesota, MN — B
U of Missouri–Columbia, MO — B

Purchasing, Procurement/Acquisitions and Contracts Management
Miami U, OH — B
Miami U Hamilton, OH — A
Southwestern Coll, KS — B
Washburn U, KS — A
Wright State U, OH — B

Quality Control and Safety Technologies Related
Madonna U, MI — A,B

Quality Control Technology
Baker Coll of Cadillac, MI — A
Baker Coll of Flint, MI — A
Baker Coll of Muskegon, MI — A
Bowling Green State U, OH — B
Ferris State U, MI — B
U of Cincinnati, OH — A
Winona State U, MN — B

Radiation Biology
Grand Valley State U, MI — B

Radio and Television
Ashland U, OH — A,B
Bemidji State U, MN — B
Bradley U, IL — B
Cedarville U, OH — B
Central Michigan U, MI — B
Central State U, OH — B
Columbia Coll Chicago, IL — B
Concordia Coll, MN — B
Drake U, IA — B
East Central U, OK — B
Evangel U, MO — B
Fort Hays State U, KS — B
Gannon U, PA — B
Grand Valley State U, MI — B
Grand View Coll, IA — B
Hastings Coll, NE — B
Indiana State U, IN — B
Indiana U Bloomington, IN — B
Kent State U, OH — B
Langston U, OK — B
Lawrence Technological U, MI — A
Lindenwood U, MO — B
Marietta Coll, OH — B
Michigan State U, MI — B
Minot State U, ND — B
North Central Coll, IL — B
Northwestern Coll, MN — A,B
Northwestern U, IL — B
Northwest Missouri State U, MO — B
Ohio Northern U, OH — B
Ohio U, OH — A,B
Ohio U–Zanesville, OH — A
Oklahoma Christian U, OK — B
Oklahoma City U, OK — B
Oral Roberts U, OK — B
Otterbein Coll, OH — B
Purdue U Calumet, IN — B
Quincy U, IL — B
Rogers State U, OK — A
Roosevelt U, IL — B
St. Ambrose U, IA — B
St. Cloud State U, MN — B
Southern Illinois U Carbondale, IL — B
Southern Methodist U, TX — B

Southwest Minnesota State U, MN — B
Stephens Coll, MO — B
U of Central Missouri, MO — B
U of Central Oklahoma, OK — B
U of Cincinnati, OH — B
U of Dayton, OH — B
U of Missouri–Columbia, MO — B
U of Northern Iowa, IA — B
U of Sioux Falls, SD — B
U of Southern Indiana, IN — B
U of Wisconsin–Madison, WI — B
U of Wisconsin–Oshkosh, WI — B
U of Wisconsin–River Falls, WI — B
U of Wisconsin–Superior, WI — B
Valparaiso U, IN — B
Washburn U, KS — B
Webster U, MO — B
Western Illinois U, IL — B
Western Michigan U, MI — B
William Woods U, MO — B
Winona State U, MN — B
Xavier U, OH — A,B
Youngstown State U, OH — B

Radio and Television Broadcasting Technology
Eastern Michigan U, MI — B
Lewis U, IL — B
Ohio U, OH — B

Radiologic Technology/Science
Allen Coll, IA — A
Baker Coll of Clinton Township, MI — A
Baker Coll of Muskegon, MI — A
Indiana U Northwest, IN — A,B
Indiana U–Purdue U Fort Wayne, IN — A
Jamestown Coll, ND — B
Kent State U, OH — B
Kettering Coll of Medical Arts, OH — A,B
Missouri State U, MO — B
Nebraska Methodist Coll, NE — A
Newman U, KS — A
North Dakota State U, ND — B
The Ohio State U, OH — B
St. Luke's Coll, IA — A
U of Charleston, WV — B
The U of Iowa, IA — B
U of Mary, ND — B
U of Michigan, MI — B
U of Missouri–Columbia, MO — B
U of Nebraska Medical Center, NE — B
U of Oklahoma Health Sciences Center, OK — B
U of Rio Grande, OH — A
U of St. Francis, IL — B
Washburn U, KS — A

Radio, Television, and Digital Communication Related
Capital U, OH — B
Drake U, IA — B
Madonna U, MI — B

Range Science and Management
Fort Hays State U, KS — B
South Dakota State U, SD — B
U of Nebraska–Lincoln, NE — B

Reading Teacher Education
Aquinas Coll, MI — B

Dordt Coll, IA	B
Eastern Michigan U, MI	B
Grand Valley State U, MI	B
Northeastern State U, OK	B
Northwest Missouri State U, MO	B
Oakland U, MI	B
Ohio U, OH	B
St. Cloud State U, MN	B
U of Central Missouri, MO	B
U of Central Oklahoma, OK	B
U of Nebraska–Lincoln, NE	B
U of Northern Iowa, IA	B
U of Wisconsin–Superior, WI	B
Upper Iowa U, IA	B
William Penn U, IA	B
Winona State U, MN	B
Wright State U, OH	B
York Coll, NE	B

Real Estate

Ball State U, IN	B
Ferris State U, MI	A
Indiana U Bloomington, IN	B
Kent State U, Ashtabula Campus, OH	A
Miami U Hamilton, OH	A
Miami U–Middletown Campus, OH	A
Minnesota State U Mankato, MN	B
The Ohio State U, OH	B
St. Cloud State U, MN	B
Southern Methodist U, TX	B
U of Central Oklahoma, OK	B
U of Cincinnati, OH	A,B
U of Illinois at Urbana–Champaign, IL	B
U of Missouri–Columbia, MO	B
U of Nebraska at Omaha, NE	B
U of Northern Iowa, IA	B
U of St. Thomas, MN	B
U of Wisconsin–Madison, WI	B
U of Wisconsin–Milwaukee, WI	B

Receptionist

Baker Coll of Allen Park, MI	A

Recording Arts Technology

Columbia Coll Chicago, IL	B
Malone Coll, OH	B

Recreation Products/Services Marketing Operations

Oral Roberts U, OK	B

Rehabilitation and Therapeutic Professions Related

Central Michigan U, MI	B
Southern Illinois U Carbondale, IL	B
U of Wisconsin–La Crosse, WI	B

Rehabilitation Therapy

Baker Coll of Muskegon, MI	B

Religious Education

Andrews U, MI	B
Aquinas Coll, MI	B
Ashland U, OH	B
Baptist Bible Coll, MO	B
Barclay Coll, KS	B
Calvary Bible Coll and Theological Seminary, MO	A,B
Capital U, OH	B
Cardinal Stritch U, WI	B
Cedarville U, OH	B

Cincinnati Christian U, OH	A,B
Coll of Mount St. Joseph, OH	B
Coll of Saint Benedict, MN	B
Concordia U, IL	B
Concordia U, MI	B
Concordia U, NE	B
Concordia U, St. Paul, MN	B
Cornerstone U, MI	A,B
Crossroads Coll, MN	B
Crown Coll, MN	B
Faith Baptist Bible Coll and Theological Seminary, IA	B
Franciscan U of Steubenville, OH	B
Global U of the Assemblies of God, MO	B
Great Lakes Christian Coll, MI	A
Hannibal-LaGrange Coll, MO	B
Hillsdale Free Will Baptist Coll, OK	A,B
Indiana Wesleyan U, IN	A,B
Kuyper Coll, MI	A,B
Malone Coll, OH	B
Maranatha Baptist Bible Coll, WI	B
Marian Coll, IN	B
Messenger Coll, MO	B
Missouri Baptist U, MO	B
Mount Mary Coll, WI	B
Mount Vernon Nazarene U, OH	B
Northwestern Coll, IA	B
Northwestern Coll, MN	B
Oak Hills Christian Coll, MN	B
Oklahoma Christian U, OK	B
Oklahoma City U, OK	B
Ozark Christian Coll, MO	B
Saint John's U, MN	B
Saint Mary's U of Minnesota, MN	B
Sterling Coll, KS	B
Taylor U, IN	B
Trinity Christian Coll, IL	B
Union Coll, NE	B
U of Dayton, OH	B
Vennard Coll, IA	B
Viterbo U, WI	B
Wheaton Coll, IL	B
York Coll, NE	B

Religious/Sacred Music

Anderson U, IN	B
Aquinas Coll, MI	A,B
Augustana Coll, IL	B
Barclay Coll, KS	B
Bethany Lutheran Coll, MN	B
Bethel U, MN	B
Calvary Bible Coll and Theological Seminary, MO	B
Calvin Coll, MI	B
Cedarville U, OH	B
Cincinnati Christian U, OH	A,B
Coll of the Ozarks, MO	B
Concordia U, IL	B
Concordia U, MI	B
Concordia U, NE	B
Concordia U, St. Paul, MN	B
Crossroads Coll, MN	B
Drake U, IA	B
Evangel U, MO	B
Faith Baptist Bible Coll and Theological Seminary, IA	B
God's Bible School and Coll, OH	B
Gustavus Adolphus Coll, MN	B

Hannibal-LaGrange Coll, MO	B
Hillsdale Free Will Baptist Coll, OK	A,B
Huntington U, IN	B
Indiana Wesleyan U, IN	A,B
Kuyper Coll, MI	B
Malone Coll, OH	B
Maranatha Baptist Bible Coll, WI	B
Messenger Coll, MO	B
Millikin U, IL	B
Missouri Baptist U, MO	B
Mount Vernon Nazarene U, OH	A,B
Oklahoma City U, OK	B
Oral Roberts U, OK	B
Ozark Christian Coll, MO	B
Southwestern Oklahoma State U, OK	B
Taylor U, IN	B
Trinity International U, IL	B
Valparaiso U, IN	B
Vennard Coll, IA	A
Wartburg Coll, IA	B
William Jewell Coll, MO	B
Wittenberg U, OH	B

Religious Studies

Adrian Coll, MI	A,B
Albion Coll, MI	B
Alma Coll, MI	B
Alverno Coll, WI	B
Anderson U, IN	B
Andrews U, MI	B
Antioch Coll, OH	B
Aquinas Coll, MI	B
Ashford U, IA	B
Ashland U, OH	B
Augsburg Coll, MN	B
Augustana Coll, IL	B
Augustana Coll, SD	B
Avila U, MO	B
Baker U, KS	B
Baldwin-Wallace Coll, OH	B
Ball State U, IN	B
Beloit Coll, WI	B
Bemidji State U, MN	B
Benedictine Coll, KS	B
Bethany Coll, KS	B
Bethel Coll, KS	B
Bluffton U, OH	B
Bradley U, IL	B
Butler U, IN	B
Calumet Coll of Saint Joseph, IN	A,B
Calvin Coll, MI	B
Capital U, OH	B
Cardinal Stritch U, WI	B
Carleton Coll, MN	B
Carroll Coll, WI	B
Case Western Reserve U, OH	B
Cedarville U, OH	B
Central Christian Coll of Kansas, KS	A,B
Central Coll, IA	B
Central Methodist U, MO	B
Central Michigan U, MI	B
Clarke Coll, IA	B
Cleveland State U, OH	B
Coe Coll, IA	B
Coll of Mount St. Joseph, OH	B
The Coll of St. Scholastica, MN	B
The Coll of Wooster, OH	B
Concordia Coll, MN	B

Concordia U, MI	B
Concordia U Wisconsin, WI	B
Cornell Coll, IA	B
Cornerstone U, MI	B
Culver-Stockton Coll, MO	B
Dakota Wesleyan U, SD	B
Dana Coll, NE	B
Denison U, OH	B
DePaul U, IL	B
DePauw U, IN	B
Doane Coll, NE	B
Dominican U, IL	B
Dordt Coll, IA	B
Drake U, IA	B
Drury U, MO	B
Earlham Coll, IN	B
Edgewood Coll, WI	B
Fontbonne U, MO	B
Franklin Coll, IN	B
Global U of the Assemblies of God, MO	A
Goshen Coll, IN	B
Grace Bible Coll, MI	A
Graceland U, IA	B
Grand View Coll, IA	B
Greenville Coll, IL	B
Grinnell Coll, IA	B
Gustavus Adolphus Coll, MN	B
Hamline U, MN	B
Hastings Coll, NE	B
Heidelberg Coll, OH	B
Hillsdale Coll, MI	B
Hiram Coll, OH	B
Hope Coll, MI	B
Huntington U, IN	B
Illinois Coll, IL	B
Illinois Wesleyan U, IL	B
Indiana U Bloomington, IN	B
Indiana U–Purdue U Indianapolis, IN	B
Iowa State U of Science and Technology, IA	B
Jamestown Coll, ND	B
Judson Coll, IL	B
Kalamazoo Coll, MI	B
Kenyon Coll, OH	B
Lakeland Coll, WI	B
Lawrence U, WI	B
Lewis U, IL	B
Lindenwood U, MO	B
Loras Coll, IA	B
Lourdes Coll, OH	A,B
Luther Coll, IA	B
Macalester Coll, MN	B
MacMurray Coll, IL	B
Madonna U, MI	A,B
Manchester Coll, IN	A,B
Maranatha Baptist Bible Coll, WI	A,B
Marquette U, WI	B
Marygrove Coll, MI	B
McKendree Coll, IL	B
Messenger Coll, MO	B
Miami U, OH	B
Michigan State U, MI	B
Missouri Baptist U, MO	A,B
Missouri State U, MO	B
Missouri Valley Coll, MO	B
Morningside Coll, IA	B
Mount Marty Coll, SD	A,B
Mount Mary Coll, WI	B
Mount Mercy Coll, IA	B
Mount Union Coll, OH	B
Nebraska Wesleyan U, NE	B
North Central Coll, IL	B

A—associate degree; B—bachelor's degree

Northland Coll, WI	B
Northwestern Coll, IA	B
Northwestern U, IL	B
Oberlin Coll, OH	B
Ohio Northern U, OH	B
The Ohio State U, OH	B
Ohio Wesleyan U, OH	B
Oklahoma Christian U, OK	B
Oklahoma City U, OK	B
Oklahoma Wesleyan U, OK	B
Oral Roberts U, OK	B
Ottawa U, KS	B
Otterbein Coll, OH	B
Presentation Coll, SD	A
Ripon Coll, WI	B
Saint Mary-of-the-Woods Coll, IN	B
Saint Mary's Coll, IN	B
St. Norbert Coll, WI	B
St. Olaf Coll, MN	B
Saint Xavier U, IL	B
Simpson Coll, IA	B
Southern Methodist U, TX	B
Southwest Baptist U, MO	B
Spring Arbor U, MI	B
Tabor Coll, KS	A,B
Taylor U, IN	B
Transylvania U, KY	B
Trinity Christian Coll, IL	B
Truman State U, MO	B
Union Coll, NE	B
U of Chicago, IL	B
U of Dayton, OH	B
U of Evansville, IN	B
The U of Findlay, OH	A,B
U of Illinois at Urbana–Champaign, IL	B
U of Indianapolis, IN	B
The U of Iowa, IA	B
U of Kansas, KS	B
U of Michigan, MI	B
U of Minnesota, Twin Cities Campus, MN	B
U of Missouri–Columbia, MO	B
U of Nebraska at Omaha, NE	B
U of North Dakota, ND	B
U of Northern Iowa, IA	B
U of Oklahoma, OK	B
U of Saint Francis, IN	B
U of St. Thomas, MN	B
U of Sioux Falls, SD	A,B
The U of Toledo, OH	B
U of Tulsa, OK	B
U of West Florida, FL	B
U of Wisconsin–Eau Claire, WI	B
U of Wisconsin–Milwaukee, WI	B
U of Wisconsin–Oshkosh, WI	B
Vennard Coll, IA	A,B
Viterbo U, WI	B
Wabash Coll, IN	B
Walsh U, OH	B
Wartburg Coll, IA	B
Washburn U, KS	B
Washington U in St. Louis, MO	B
Webster U, MO	B
Western Michigan U, MI	B
Westminster Coll, MO	B
Wheaton Coll, IL	B
William Jewell Coll, MO	B
Wilmington Coll, OH	B
Wittenberg U, OH	B
Wright State U, OH	B

York Coll, NE	B
Youngstown State U, OH	B

Religious Studies Related

Ohio Northern U, OH	B
Ursuline Coll, OH	B

Resort Management

Lakeland Coll, WI	B

Respiratory Care Therapy

Ball State U, IN	A
Bowling Green State U–Firelands Coll, OH	A
Cameron U, OK	A
Coll of St. Catherine, MN	B
Dakota State U, SD	A,B
Ferris State U, MI	A
Gannon U, PA	A,B
Indiana U Northwest, IN	A
Indiana U–Purdue U Indianapolis, IN	A,B
Kettering Coll of Medical Arts, OH	A,B
Missouri Southern State U, MO	A
Missouri State U, MO	B
Nebraska Methodist Coll, NE	A,B
Newman U, KS	A
North Dakota State U, ND	B
The Ohio State U, OH	B
St. Augustine Coll, IL	A
St. Luke's Coll, IA	A
Shawnee State U, OH	A
Southern Illinois U Carbondale, IL	A
The U of Akron, OH	A
U of Indianapolis, IN	B
U of Kansas, KS	B
U of Mary, ND	B
U of Missouri–Columbia, MO	B
U of Southern Indiana, IN	A
The U of Toledo, OH	A
Washburn U, KS	A
Youngstown State U, OH	B

Restaurant, Culinary, and Catering Management

The Art Insts International Minnesota, MN	B
Ferris State U, MI	A
Kendall Coll, IL	B
Lexington Coll, IL	A,B
Lindenwood U, MO	B
The U of Akron, OH	A
U of Illinois at Urbana–Champaign, IL	B

Restaurant/Food Services Management

Ferris State U, MI	A
Kendall Coll, IL	B
Lexington Coll, IL	A,B
U of Missouri–Columbia, MO	B

Retail Management

U of Phoenix–Cincinnati Campus, OH	B
U of Phoenix–Columbus Ohio Campus, OH	B
U of Phoenix–Indianapolis Campus, IN	B
U of Phoenix–Kansas City Campus, MO	B
U of Phoenix–Metro Detroit Campus, MI	B
U of Phoenix–Oklahoma City Campus, OK	B

U of Phoenix–St. Louis Campus, MO	B
U of Phoenix–Springfield Campus, MO	B
U of Phoenix–Tulsa Campus, OK	B

Robotics Technology

Indiana State U, IN	B
Indiana U–Purdue U Indianapolis, IN	A,B
Lake Superior State U, MI	B
Purdue U, IN	A,B
U of Rio Grande, OH	A,B

Romance Languages

Beloit Coll, WI	B
Cameron U, OK	B
Carleton Coll, MN	B
DePauw U, IN	B
Kenyon Coll, OH	B
Northwest Missouri State U, MO	B
Oberlin Coll, OH	B
Ripon Coll, WI	B
Rockford Coll, IL	B
U of Chicago, IL	B
U of Cincinnati, OH	B
U of Michigan, MI	B
Washington U in St. Louis, MO	B

Russian

Beloit Coll, WI	B
Bowling Green State U, OH	B
Carleton Coll, MN	B
Cornell Coll, IA	B
Grinnell Coll, IA	B
Gustavus Adolphus Coll, MN	B
Indiana U Bloomington, IN	B
Kent State U, OH	B
Knox Coll, IL	B
Lawrence U, WI	B
Macalester Coll, MN	B
Miami U, OH	B
Miami U Hamilton, OH	B
Michigan State U, MI	B
Northern Illinois U, IL	B
Oberlin Coll, OH	B
The Ohio State U, OH	B
Ohio U, OH	B
Oklahoma State U, OK	B
Saint Louis U, MO	B
St. Olaf Coll, MN	B
Southern Illinois U Carbondale, IL	B
Southern Methodist U, TX	B
Truman State U, MO	B
U of Chicago, IL	B
U of Illinois at Chicago, IL	B
U of Illinois at Urbana–Champaign, IL	B
The U of Iowa, IA	B
U of Michigan, MI	B
U of Minnesota, Twin Cities Campus, MN	B
U of Missouri–Columbia, MO	B
U of Nebraska–Lincoln, NE	B
U of Northern Iowa, IA	B
U of Notre Dame, IN	B
U of Oklahoma, OK	B
U of St. Thomas, MN	B
U of Wisconsin–Madison, WI	B
U of Wisconsin–Milwaukee, WI	B
Washington U in St. Louis, MO	B

Russian Studies

Beloit Coll, WI	B
Carleton Coll, MN	B
The Coll of Wooster, OH	B
Concordia Coll, MN	B
DePauw U, IN	B
Grand Valley State U, MI	B
Gustavus Adolphus Coll, MN	B
Hamline U, MN	B
Indiana U Bloomington, IN	B
Iowa State U of Science and Technology, IA	B
Kent State U, OH	B
Knox Coll, IL	B
Lawrence U, WI	B
Macalester Coll, MN	B
Oberlin Coll, OH	B
The Ohio State U, OH	B
St. Olaf Coll, MN	B
Southern Methodist U, TX	B
U of Chicago, IL	B
U of Illinois at Urbana–Champaign, IL	B
The U of Iowa, IA	B
U of Kansas, KS	B
U of Michigan, MI	B
U of Minnesota, Twin Cities Campus, MN	B
U of Missouri–Columbia, MO	B
U of Northern Iowa, IA	B
U of St. Thomas, MN	B
U of Wisconsin–Milwaukee, WI	B
Washington U in St. Louis, MO	B
Western Michigan U, MI	B
Wittenberg U, OH	B

Safety/Security Technology

Madonna U, MI	A,B
Ohio U, OH	A
U of Central Oklahoma, OK	B
U of Cincinnati, OH	A

Sales and Marketing/Marketing and Distribution Teacher Education

Bowling Green State U, OH	B
Central Christian Coll of Kansas, KS	A
Central Michigan U, MI	B
Eastern Michigan U, MI	B
Kent State U, OH	B
U of Nebraska–Lincoln, NE	B
U of North Dakota, ND	B
U of Wisconsin–Stout, WI	B
Wright State U, OH	B

Sales, Distribution and Marketing

Academy Coll, MN	A
Baker Coll of Flint, MI	A
Baker Coll of Jackson, MI	A
Black Hills State U, SD	B
Central Michigan U, MI	B
McKendree Coll, IL	B
Metropolitan State U, MN	B
Purdue U North Central, IN	A,B
Saint Mary's U of Minnesota, MN	B
Trinity Christian Coll, IL	B
The U of Findlay, OH	A,B
U of Illinois at Urbana–Champaign, IL	B
U of Wisconsin–Stout, WI	B
U of Wisconsin–Superior, WI	B
Wichita State U, KS	B

Sanitation Technology
Grand Valley State U, MI — B

Sanskrit and Classical Indian Languages
U of Chicago, IL — B

Scandinavian Languages
Augsburg Coll, MN — B
Augustana Coll, IL — B
Concordia Coll, MN — B
Gustavus Adolphus Coll, MN — B
St. Olaf Coll, MN — B
U of Minnesota, Twin Cities Campus, MN — B
U of North Dakota, ND — B
U of Wisconsin–Madison, WI — B

Scandinavian Studies
Gustavus Adolphus Coll, MN — B
Luther Coll, IA — B
U of Michigan, MI — B

School Librarian/School Library Media
The Coll of St. Scholastica, MN — B
Ohio Dominican U, OH — B

School Psychology
Fort Hays State U, KS — B

Science Teacher Education
Adrian Coll, MI — B
Alma Coll, MI — B
Alverno Coll, WI — B
Anderson U, IN — B
Andrews U, MI — B
Antioch Coll, OH — B
Aquinas Coll, MI — B
Ashford U, IA — B
Ashland U, OH — B
Augustana Coll, IL — B
Baldwin-Wallace Coll, OH — B
Ball State U, IN — B
Beloit Coll, WI — B
Bemidji State U, MN — B
Benedictine U, IL — B
Bethel U, MN — B
Black Hills State U, SD — B
Bowling Green State U, OH — B
Buena Vista U, IA — B
Calumet Coll of Saint Joseph, IN — B
Calvin Coll, MI — B
Capital U, OH — B
Cardinal Stritch U, WI — B
Carroll Coll, WI — B
Cedarville U, OH — B
Central Christian Coll of Kansas, KS — A
Central Methodist U, MO — B
Central Michigan U, MI — B
Central State U, OH — B
Chicago State U, IL — B
Coe Coll, IA — B
Coll of Saint Mary, NE — B
Coll of the Ozarks, MO — B
Concordia Coll, MN — B
Concordia U, IL — B
Concordia U, MI — B
Concordia U, NE — B
Concordia U, St. Paul, MN — B
Concordia U Wisconsin, WI — B
Cornerstone U, MI — B
Culver-Stockton Coll, MO — B
Dakota Wesleyan U, SD — B

Dana Coll, NE — B
Dickinson State U, ND — B
Dordt Coll, IA — B
East Central U, OK — B
Eastern Michigan U, MI — B
Evangel U, MO — B
Ferris State U, MI — B
Fort Hays State U, KS — B
Goshen Coll, IN — B
Grace Coll, IN — B
Graceland U, IA — B
Grand Valley State U, MI — B
Hamline U, MN — B
Hannibal-LaGrange Coll, MO — B
Hastings Coll, NE — B
Heidelberg Coll, OH — B
Hope Coll, MI — B
Huntington U, IN — B
Indiana State U, IN — B
Indiana U Bloomington, IN — B
Indiana U–Purdue U Fort Wayne, IN — B
Indiana U South Bend, IN — B
Indiana U Southeast, IN — B
Indiana Wesleyan U, IN — B
Judson Coll, IL — B
Kent State U, OH — B
Lakeland Coll, WI — B
Lindenwood U, MO — B
Madonna U, MI — B
Malone Coll, OH — B
Manchester Coll, IN — B
Maranatha Baptist Bible Coll, WI — B
Marian Coll of Fond du Lac, WI — B
Marquette U, WI — B
Miami U, OH — B
Miami U Hamilton, OH — B
Michigan Technological U, MI — B
Minnesota State U Mankato, MN — B
Minot State U, ND — B
Missouri Baptist U, MO — B
Missouri State U, MO — B
Missouri Valley Coll, MO — B
Morningside Coll, IA — B
Mount Mercy Coll, IA — B
Mount Vernon Nazarene U, OH — B
Nebraska Wesleyan U, NE — B
North Dakota State U, ND — B
Northern Michigan U, MI — B
Northland Coll, WI — B
Northwestern Oklahoma State U, OK — B
Northwest Missouri State U, MO — B
Oakland U, MI — B
Ohio Dominican U, OH — B
Ohio Northern U, OH — B
Ohio U, OH — B
Oklahoma Christian U, OK — B
Oklahoma City U, OK — B
Oklahoma Panhandle State U, OK — B
Oklahoma Wesleyan U, OK — B
Oral Roberts U, OK — B
Otterbein Coll, OH — B
Peru State Coll, NE — B
Purdue U Calumet, IN — B
Rochester Coll, MI — B
Saginaw Valley State U, MI — B
St. Ambrose U, IA — B
St. Cloud State U, MN — B

Shawnee State U, OH — B
Southeastern Oklahoma State U, OK — B
Southeast Missouri State U, MO — B
Southern Illinois U Edwardsville, IL — B
Southwest Baptist U, MO — B
Southwestern Oklahoma State U, OK — B
Tabor Coll, KS — B
Taylor U, IN — B
Trinity Christian Coll, IL — B
Tri-State U, IN — B
The U of Akron, OH — B
U of Central Oklahoma, OK — B
U of Charleston, WV — B
U of Cincinnati, OH — A
U of Dayton, OH — B
U of Evansville, IN — B
The U of Findlay, OH — B
U of Illinois at Chicago, IL — B
U of Illinois at Urbana–Champaign, IL — B
U of Indianapolis, IN — B
The U of Iowa, IA — B
U of Michigan–Dearborn, MI — B
U of Minnesota, Duluth, MN — B
U of Minnesota, Twin Cities Campus, MN — B
U of Missouri–Columbia, MO — B
U of Nebraska–Lincoln, NE — B
U of New Orleans, LA — B
U of North Dakota, ND — B
U of Northern Iowa, IA — B
U of Notre Dame, IN — B
U of Oklahoma, OK — B
U of Rio Grande, OH — B
U of St. Francis, IL — B
U of Saint Francis, IN — B
U of St. Thomas, MN — B
U of Sioux Falls, SD — B
The U of South Dakota, SD — B
The U of Toledo, OH — B
U of West Florida, FL — B
U of Wisconsin–Eau Claire, WI — B
U of Wisconsin–La Crosse, WI — B
U of Wisconsin–Madison, WI — B
U of Wisconsin–Platteville, WI — B
U of Wisconsin–River Falls, WI — B
U of Wisconsin–Superior, WI — B
U of Wisconsin–Whitewater, WI — B
Upper Iowa U, IA — B
Ursuline Coll, OH — B
Valley City State U, ND — B
Valparaiso U, IN — B
Viterbo U, WI — B
Walsh U, OH — B
Washington U in St. Louis, MO — B
Wayne State Coll, NE — B
Western Michigan U, MI — B
Wheaton Coll, IL — B
Wichita State U, KS — B
William Penn U, IA — B
William Woods U, MO — B
Wilmington Coll, OH — B
Winona State U, MN — B
Wright State U, OH — B
Xavier U, OH — B
York Coll, NE — B
Youngstown State U, OH — B

Science Technologies Related
Hope Coll, MI — B
Madonna U, MI — A,B
U of Wisconsin–Stout, WI — B

Science, Technology and Society
Butler U, IN — B
Cleveland State U, OH — B
Coll of the Ozarks, MO — B
Michigan State U, MI — B
Northwestern U, IL — B
Washington U in St. Louis, MO — B

Sculpture
Antioch Coll, OH — B
Aquinas Coll, MI — B
Art Academy of Cincinnati, OH — B
Ball State U, IN — B
Bethany Coll, KS — B
The Cleveland Inst of Art, OH — B
Coll of Visual Arts, MN — B
DePaul U, IL — B
Drake U, IA — B
Grand Valley State U, MI — B
Indiana U Bloomington, IN — B
Indiana U–Purdue U Fort Wayne, IN — B
Kansas City Art Inst, MO — B
Kent State U, OH — B
Minneapolis Coll of Art and Design, MN — B
Minnesota State U Mankato, MN — B
Northwest Missouri State U, MO — B
Ohio Northern U, OH — B
The Ohio State U, OH — B
Ohio U, OH — B
St. Cloud State U, MN — B
School of the Art Inst of Chicago, IL — B
Trinity Christian Coll, IL — B
The U of Akron, OH — B
U of Dallas, TX — B
U of Illinois at Urbana–Champaign, IL — B
The U of Iowa, IA — B
U of Kansas, KS — B
U of Michigan, MI — B
U of Michigan–Flint, MI — B
U of Wisconsin–Milwaukee, WI — B
Washington U in St. Louis, MO — B
Western Michigan U, MI — B

Secondary Education
Adrian Coll, MI — B
Albion Coll, MI — B
Alma Coll, MI — B
Andrews U, MI — B
Antioch Coll, OH — B
Aquinas Coll, MI — B
Ashford U, IA — B
Ashland U, OH — B
Augsburg Coll, MN — B
Augustana Coll, IL — B
Augustana Coll, SD — B
Baker U, KS — B
Ball State U, IN — B
Beloit Coll, WI — B
Bemidji State U, MN — B
Benedictine Coll, KS — B

A—associate degree; B—bachelor's degree

Benedictine U, IL	B
Blackburn Coll, IL	B
Black Hills State U, SD	B
Briar Cliff U, IA	B
Butler U, IN	B
Calumet Coll of Saint Joseph, IN	B
Calvary Bible Coll and Theological Seminary, MO	B
Calvin Coll, MI	B
Capital U, OH	B
Cardinal Stritch U, WI	B
Carroll Coll, WI	B
Cedarville U, OH	B
Central Christian Coll of Kansas, KS	A
Central Methodist U, MO	B
Chicago State U, IL	B
Clarke Coll, IA	B
Coe Coll, IA	B
Coll of Saint Benedict, MN	B
Coll of St. Catherine, MN	B
Coll of Saint Mary, NE	B
Coll of the Ozarks, MO	B
Concordia Coll, MN	B
Concordia U, IL	B
Concordia U, MI	B
Concordia U, NE	B
Concordia U, St. Paul, MN	B
Concordia U Wisconsin, WI	B
Concord U, WV	B
Cornell Coll, IA	B
Cornerstone U, MI	B
Dakota Wesleyan U, SD	B
Dana Coll, NE	B
DePaul U, IL	B
Dickinson State U, ND	B
Doane Coll, NE	B
Dordt Coll, IA	B
Drake U, IA	B
Drury U, MO	B
East Central U, OK	B
Elmhurst Coll, IL	B
Emporia State U, KS	B
Evangel U, MO	B
Ferris State U, MI	B
Fontbonne U, MO	B
Gannon U, PA	B
Goshen Coll, IN	B
Grace Bible Coll, MI	B
Graceland U, IA	B
Grand Valley State U, MI	B
Gustavus Adolphus Coll, MN	B
Hamline U, MN	B
Hannibal-LaGrange Coll, MO	B
Harris-Stowe State U, MO	B
Hastings Coll, NE	B
Heidelberg Coll, OH	B
Hillsdale Coll, MI	B
Hiram Coll, OH	B
Hope Coll, MI	B
Huntington U, IN	B
Illinois Coll, IL	B
Illinois Wesleyan U, IL	B
Indiana U Bloomington, IN	B
Indiana U East, IN	B
Indiana U Northwest, IN	B
Indiana U–Purdue U Fort Wayne, IN	B
Indiana U–Purdue U Indianapolis, IN	B
Indiana U South Bend, IN	B
Indiana U Southeast, IN	B
Indiana Wesleyan U, IN	B
Iowa State U of Science and Technology, IA	B
Iowa Wesleyan Coll, IA	B
Jamestown Coll, ND	B
Judson Coll, IL	B
Kansas State U, KS	B
Kuyper Coll, MI	B
Lake Forest Coll, IL	B
Lakeland Coll, WI	B
Lake Superior State U, MI	B
Langston U, OK	B
Lawrence U, WI	B
Lewis U, IL	B
Lindenwood U, MO	B
Loras Coll, IA	B
MacMurray Coll, IL	B
Madonna U, MI	B
Maharishi U of Management, IA	B
Manchester Coll, IN	B
Maranatha Baptist Bible Coll, WI	B
Marian Coll, IN	B
Marian Coll of Fond du Lac, WI	B
Marietta Coll, OH	B
Marquette U, WI	B
Maryville U of Saint Louis, MO	B
McKendree Coll, IL	B
Miami U, OH	B
Michigan Technological U, MI	B
Minnesota State U Mankato, MN	B
Missouri Southern State U, MO	B
Missouri Valley Coll, MO	B
Morningside Coll, IA	B
Mount Marty Coll, SD	B
Mount Mary Coll, WI	B
Mount Mercy Coll, IA	B
Mount Vernon Nazarene U, OH	B
Newman U, KS	B
North Central Coll, IL	B
Northeastern State U, OK	B
Northern Michigan U, MI	B
Northern State U, SD	B
Northland Coll, WI	B
Northwestern Coll, IA	B
Northwestern Oklahoma State U, OK	B
Northwestern U, IL	B
Northwest Missouri State U, MO	B
Ohio Dominican U, OH	B
Ohio Northern U, OH	B
Ohio U, OH	B
Ohio Wesleyan U, OH	B
Oklahoma Christian U, OK	B
Oklahoma City U, OK	B
Oklahoma Panhandle State U, OK	B
Oklahoma State U, OK	B
Oklahoma Wesleyan U, OK	B
Otterbein Coll, OH	B
Peru State Coll, NE	B
Purdue U Calumet, IN	B
Ripon Coll, WI	B
Rochester Coll, MI	B
Rockford Coll, IL	B
Rockhurst U, MO	B
Rogers State U, OK	A
Roosevelt U, IL	B
St. Ambrose U, IA	B
St. Cloud State U, MN	B
Saint John's U, MN	B
Saint Joseph's Coll, IN	B
Saint Mary-of-the-Woods Coll, IN	B
Shawnee State U, OH	B
Simpson Coll, IA	B
South Dakota State U, SD	B
Southeastern Oklahoma State U, OK	B
Southwestern Oklahoma State U, OK	B
Southwest Minnesota State U, MN	B
Spring Arbor U, MI	B
Tabor Coll, KS	B
Taylor U, IN	B
Trinity Christian Coll, IL	B
Trinity International U, IL	B
Tri-State U, IN	B
Union Coll, NE	B
The U of Akron, OH	B
U of Central Missouri, MO	B
U of Central Oklahoma, OK	B
U of Cincinnati, OH	B
U of Dallas, TX	B
U of Dayton, OH	B
The U of Findlay, OH	B
U of Illinois at Chicago, IL	B
U of Illinois at Urbana–Champaign, IL	B
U of Indianapolis, IN	B
The U of Iowa, IA	B
U of Kansas, KS	B
U of Michigan, MI	B
U of Michigan–Dearborn, MI	B
U of Minnesota, Morris, MN	B
U of Missouri–Columbia, MO	B
U of Missouri–Kansas City, MO	B
U of Missouri–Rolla, MO	B
U of Missouri–St. Louis, MO	B
U of Nebraska at Omaha, NE	B
U of Rio Grande, OH	B
U of Saint Francis, IN	B
U of Sioux Falls, SD	B
The U of South Dakota, SD	B
The U of Toledo, OH	B
U of Wisconsin–Madison, WI	B
U of Wisconsin–Milwaukee, WI	B
U of Wisconsin–Oshkosh, WI	B
U of Wisconsin–Platteville, WI	B
U of Wisconsin–River Falls, WI	B
U of Wisconsin–Stevens Point, WI	B
U of Wisconsin–Whitewater, WI	B
Valley City State U, ND	B
Valparaiso U, IN	B
Vennard Coll, IA	A,B
Walsh U, OH	B
Wartburg Coll, IA	B
Washburn U, KS	B
Washington U in St. Louis, MO	B
Western Michigan U, MI	B
Westminster Coll, MO	B
Wichita State U, KS	B
William Jewell Coll, MO	B
William Penn U, IA	B
William Woods U, MO	B
Wilmington Coll, OH	B
Winona State U, MN	B
Wright State U, OH	B
York Coll, NE	B
Youngstown State U, OH	B

Securities Services Administration
Southwestern Coll, KS	B

Security and Protective Services Related
Eastern Michigan U, MI	B
Lewis U, IL	B
North Dakota State U, ND	B
Ohio U, OH	A
St. Ambrose U, IA	B
Taylor U Fort Wayne, IN	B
U of Phoenix–Cincinnati Campus, OH	B
U of Phoenix–Cleveland Campus, OH	B
U of Phoenix–Columbus Ohio Campus, OH	B
U of Phoenix–Indianapolis Campus, IN	B
U of Phoenix–Kansas City Campus, MO	B
U of Phoenix–Metro Detroit Campus, MI	B
U of Phoenix–St. Louis Campus, MO	B
U of Phoenix–Springfield Campus, MO	B
Washburn U, KS	B

Selling Skills and Sales
The U of Akron, OH	A

Sign Language Interpretation and Translation
Cincinnati Christian U, OH	A
Coll of St. Catherine, MN	A
Columbia Coll Chicago, IL	B
Goshen Coll, IN	B
Indiana U–Purdue U Indianapolis, IN	B
MacMurray Coll, IL	B
Ozark Christian Coll, MO	B
William Woods U, MO	B

Slavic Languages
Indiana U Bloomington, IN	B
Northwestern U, IL	B
U of Chicago, IL	B
U of Illinois at Chicago, IL	B
U of Kansas, KS	B
U of Wisconsin–Madison, WI	B
U of Wisconsin–Milwaukee, WI	B

Slavic Studies
Lawrence U, WI	B
Northwestern U, IL	B
Oakland U, MI	B

Small Business Administration
Central Christian Coll of Kansas, KS	A,B
Kendall Coll, IL	B
North Central Coll, IL	B
Northern Michigan U, MI	B

Social and Philosophical Foundations of Education
Northwestern U, IL	B
Washington U in St. Louis, MO	B

Social Psychology
Central Christian Coll of Kansas, KS	A
Lawrence U, WI	B
Maryville U of Saint Louis, MO	B

Park U, MO — A,B
U of Wisconsin–Superior, WI — B

Social Sciences
Adrian Coll, MI — A,B
Alma Coll, MI — B
Alverno Coll, WI — B
Andrews U, MI — B
Antioch Coll, OH — B
Aquinas Coll, MI — B
Ashford U, IA — B
Ashland U, OH — B
Augsburg Coll, MN — B
Ball State U, IN — B
Bemidji State U, MN — B
Benedictine Coll, KS — B
Benedictine U, IL — B
Bethany Lutheran Coll, MN — B
Bethel U, MN — B
Black Hills State U, SD — B
Bluffton U, OH — B
Bowling Green State U–Firelands Coll, OH — A
Buena Vista U, IA — B
Calvin Coll, MI — B
Cardinal Stritch U, WI — B
Central Christian Coll of Kansas, KS — B
Central Coll, IA — B
Central Michigan U, MI — B
Clarkson U, NY — B
Cleveland State U, OH — B
Coll of Saint Benedict, MN — B
Coll of St. Catherine, MN — B
Coll of Saint Mary, NE — B
The Coll of St. Scholastica, MN — B
Concordia U, MI — B
Concordia U, NE — B
Crown Coll, MN — A
DePaul U, IL — B
Dickinson State U, ND — B
Doane Coll, NE — B
Dominican U, IL — B
Dordt Coll, IA — B
Eastern Michigan U, MI — B
East-West U, IL — B
Edgewood Coll, WI — B
Emporia State U, KS — B
Evangel U, MO — A,B
Fontbonne U, MO — B
Graceland U, IA — B
Grand Valley State U, MI — B
Gustavus Adolphus Coll, MN — B
Hamline U, MN — B
Hope Coll, MI — B
Indiana Wesleyan U, IN — A,B
Judson Coll, IL — B
Kansas State U, KS — B
Kent State U, OH — B
Lake Superior State U, MI — B
Marian Coll of Fond du Lac, WI — B
Marygrove Coll, MI — B
Mayville State U, ND — B
McKendree Coll, IL — B
Metropolitan State U, MN — B
Miami U–Middletown Campus, OH — A
Michigan State U, MI — B
Michigan Technological U, MI — B
Minnesota State U Mankato, MN — B
Minot State U, ND — B
Missouri Baptist U, MO — B

Mount Vernon Nazarene U, OH — B
North Carolina Ag and Tech State U, NC — B
North Central Coll, IL — B
North Dakota State U, ND — B
Northern Michigan U, MI — B
Northland Coll, WI — B
Northwestern Coll, MN — B
Northwestern Oklahoma State U, OK — B
Northwest Missouri State U, MO — B
The Ohio State U, OH — B
Ohio U, OH — A,B
Ohio U–Zanesville, OH — A
Oklahoma Panhandle State U, OK — B
Oklahoma Wesleyan U, OK — B
Peru State Coll, NE — B
Purdue U, IN — B
Rockford Coll, IL — B
Rockhurst U, MO — B
Rogers State U, OK — A,B
Roosevelt U, IL — B
St. Cloud State U, MN — B
St. Gregory's U, Shawnee, OK — B
Saint John's U, MN — B
Saint Louis U, MO — B
Saint Mary-of-the-Woods Coll, IN — B
Saint Mary's U of Minnesota, MN — B
Saint Xavier U, IL — B
Shawnee State U, OH — A,B
Shimer Coll, IL — B
Silver Lake Coll, WI — B
Simpson Coll, IA — B
Southern Illinois U Carbondale, IL — B
Southern Methodist U, TX — B
Spring Arbor U, MI — B
Tabor Coll, KS — B
Taylor U, IN — B
Trinity International U, IL — B
Tri-State U, IN — A,B
Turtle Mountain Comm Coll, ND — A
Union Coll, NE — B
The U of Akron, OH — B
U of Chicago, IL — B
U of Cincinnati, OH — A,B
The U of Findlay, OH — A,B
U of Mary, ND — B
U of Michigan, MI — B
U of Michigan–Dearborn, MI — B
U of Michigan–Flint, MI — B
U of Minnesota, Morris, MN — B
U of North Dakota, ND — B
U of Rio Grande, OH — B
U of St. Thomas, MN — B
U of Sioux Falls, SD — A,B
U of Southern Indiana, IN — A,B
The U of Toledo, OH — A
U of West Florida, FL — B
U of Wisconsin–Madison, WI — B
U of Wisconsin–Platteville, WI — B
U of Wisconsin–River Falls, WI — B
U of Wisconsin–Stevens Point, WI — B
U of Wisconsin–Superior, WI — B
U of Wisconsin–Whitewater, WI — B
Upper Iowa U, IA — B

Valley City State U, ND — B
Valparaiso U, IN — A
Viterbo U, WI — B
Washington U in St. Louis, MO — B
Wayne State Coll, NE — B
Webster U, MO — B
Western Michigan U, MI — B
Wilmington Coll, OH — B
Winona State U, MN — B
Wisconsin Lutheran Coll, WI — B
Youngstown State U, OH — B

Social Sciences Related
Bethel Coll, KS — B
Central Michigan U, MI — B
Cleveland State U, OH — B
Eastern Michigan U, MI — B
Greenville Coll, IL — B
Northwestern U, IL — B
Roosevelt U, IL — B
Transylvania U, KY — B
The U of Akron, OH — B
U of West Florida, FL — B
Washington U in St. Louis, MO — B

Social Science Teacher Education
Alma Coll, MI — B
Alverno Coll, WI — B
Buena Vista U, IA — B
Carroll Coll, WI — B
Central Christian Coll of Kansas, KS — A
Central Methodist U, MO — B
Central Michigan U, MI — B
Concordia U, IL — B
Concordia U, NE — B
Cornerstone U, MI — B
Dana Coll, NE — B
Dordt Coll, IA — B
Eastern Illinois U, IL — B
Eastern Michigan U, MI — B
Emporia State U, KS — B
Hastings Coll, NE — B
Lindenwood U, MO — B
Marquette U, WI — B
Mayville State U, ND — B
McKendree Coll, IL — B
Michigan State U, MI — B
Millikin U, IL — B
Minot State U, ND — B
Nebraska Wesleyan U, NE — B
North Dakota State U, ND — B
Northern Michigan U, MI — B
St. Ambrose U, IA — B
Saint Mary's U of Minnesota, MN — B
Southwest Baptist U, MO — B
Southwestern Oklahoma State U, OK — B
Taylor U, IN — B
Union Coll, NE — B
The U of Akron, OH — B
U of Evansville, IN — B
U of Illinois at Chicago, IL — B
U of Mary, ND — B
U of Minnesota, Twin Cities Campus, MN — B
U of Nebraska–Lincoln, NE — B
U of Northern Iowa, IA — B
U of Rio Grande, OH — B
The U of South Dakota, SD — B
U of West Florida, FL — B

U of Wisconsin–River Falls, WI — B
U of Wisconsin–Superior, WI — B
Upper Iowa U, IA — B
Valley City State U, ND — B
Valparaiso U, IN — B
Wartburg Coll, IA — B
Washington U in St. Louis, MO — B
Wayne State Coll, NE — B
Western Michigan U, MI — B
William Penn U, IA — B
York Coll, NE — B
Youngstown State U, OH — B

Social Studies Teacher Education
Alma Coll, MI — B
Alverno Coll, WI — B
Anderson U, IN — B
Aquinas Coll, MI — B
Augustana Coll, SD — B
Bethany Coll, KS — B
Bethel U, MN — B
Bowling Green State U, OH — B
Calumet Coll of Saint Joseph, IN — B
Capital U, OH — B
Carroll Coll, WI — B
Cedarville U, OH — B
Central Christian Coll of Kansas, KS — A
Central Michigan U, MI — B
Central State U, OH — B
Coll of St. Catherine, MN — B
Concordia Coll, MN — B
Concordia U, MI — B
Concordia U, St. Paul, MN — B
Cornerstone U, MI — B
Crown Coll, MN — B
Dakota Wesleyan U, SD — B
Dordt Coll, IA — B
Eastern Michigan U, MI — B
Franklin Coll, IN — B
Gannon U, PA — B
Grand Valley State U, MI — B
Gustavus Adolphus Coll, MN — B
Hastings Coll, NE — B
Hope Coll, MI — B
Illinois State U, IL — B
Indiana State U, IN — B
Indiana U Bloomington, IN — B
Indiana U Northwest, IN — B
Indiana U–Purdue U Fort Wayne, IN — B
Indiana U–Purdue U Indianapolis, IN — B
Indiana U South Bend, IN — B
Indiana U Southeast, IN — B
Indiana Wesleyan U, IN — B
Kent State U, OH — B
Madonna U, MI — B
Malone Coll, OH — B
Marquette U, WI — B
Miami U, OH — B
Miami U Hamilton, OH — B
Minnesota State U Mankato, MN — B
Mount Vernon Nazarene U, OH — B
Northwestern Coll, MN — B
Ohio Dominican U, OH — B
Ohio Northern U, OH — B
Ohio U, OH — B
Ohio Wesleyan U, OH — B

A—associate degree; B—bachelor's degree

Oklahoma Christian U, OK	B
Oral Roberts U, OK	B
Pittsburg State U, KS	B
Rochester Coll, MI	B
St. Gregory's U, Shawnee, OK	B
St. Olaf Coll, MN	B
Shawnee State U, OH	B
Southeastern Oklahoma State U, OK	B
Southeast Missouri State U, MO	B
Tri-State U, IN	B
The U of Akron, OH	B
U of Central Oklahoma, OK	B
U of Charleston, WV	B
U of Evansville, IN	B
U of Illinois at Urbana–Champaign, IL	B
U of Indianapolis, IN	B
The U of Iowa, IA	B
U of Michigan–Dearborn, MI	B
U of Minnesota, Duluth, MN	B
U of Missouri–Columbia, MO	B
U of Missouri–St. Louis, MO	B
U of New Orleans, LA	B
U of Northern Iowa, IA	B
U of Oklahoma, OK	B
U of St. Francis, IL	B
U of Saint Francis, IN	B
U of St. Thomas, MN	B
The U of Toledo, OH	B
U of Wisconsin–Eau Claire, WI	B
U of Wisconsin–La Crosse, WI	B
U of Wisconsin–River Falls, WI	B
U of Wisconsin–Superior, WI	B
Ursuline Coll, OH	B
Viterbo U, WI	B
Waldorf Coll, IA	B
Washington U in St. Louis, MO	B
Wheaton Coll, IL	B
Wright State U, OH	B
York Coll, NE	B
Youngstown State U, OH	B

Social Work

Adrian Coll, MI	B
Anderson U, IN	B
Andrews U, MI	B
Ashland U, OH	B
Augsburg Coll, MN	B
Augustana Coll, SD	B
Aurora U, IL	B
Avila U, MO	B
Ball State U, IN	B
Bemidji State U, MN	B
Bethany Coll, KS	B
Bethel Coll, KS	B
Bethel U, MN	B
Bluffton U, OH	B
Bowling Green State U, OH	B
Bradley U, IL	B
Briar Cliff U, IA	B
Buena Vista U, IA	B
Calvin Coll, MI	B
Capital U, OH	B
Cedarville U, OH	B
Central Christian Coll of Kansas, KS	A
Central Michigan U, MI	B
Central State U, OH	B
Clarke Coll, IA	B
Cleveland State U, OH	B
Coll of Menominee Nation, WI	A

Coll of Mount St. Joseph, OH	B
Coll of Saint Benedict, MN	B
Coll of St. Catherine, MN	B
The Coll of St. Scholastica, MN	B
Coll of the Ozarks, MO	B
Columbia Coll, MO	B
Concordia Coll, MN	B
Concordia U, IL	B
Concordia U Wisconsin, WI	B
Concord U, WV	B
Cornerstone U, MI	B
Creighton U, NE	B
Dana Coll, NE	B
Dickinson State U, ND	B
Dordt Coll, IA	B
East Central U, OK	B
Eastern Michigan U, MI	B
Evangel U, MO	B
Ferris State U, MI	B
Fort Hays State U, KS	B
Franciscan U of Steubenville, OH	B
Gannon U, PA	B
Goshen Coll, IN	B
Grace Coll, IN	B
Graceland U, IA	B
Grand Valley State U, MI	B
Greenville Coll, IL	B
Hope Coll, MI	B
Huntington U, IN	B
Illinois State U, IL	B
Indiana State U, IN	B
Indiana U Bloomington, IN	B
Indiana U East, IN	A,B
Indiana U–Purdue U Indianapolis, IN	B
Indiana Wesleyan U, IN	B
Kansas State U, KS	B
Kent State U, OH	B
Kilian Comm Coll, SD	A
Kuyper Coll, MI	B
Lewis U, IL	B
Lindenwood U, MO	B
Loras Coll, IA	B
Lourdes Coll, OH	B
Loyola U Chicago, IL	B
Luther Coll, IA	B
MacMurray Coll, IL	B
Madonna U, MI	B
Malone Coll, OH	B
Manchester Coll, IN	B
Marian Coll of Fond du Lac, WI	B
Marquette U, WI	B
Marygrove Coll, MI	B
McKendree Coll, IL	B
Metropolitan State U, MN	B
Miami U, OH	B
Miami U–Middletown Campus, OH	A
Michigan State U, MI	B
Minnesota State U Mankato, MN	B
Minot State U, ND	B
Missouri State U, MO	B
Missouri Western State U, MO	B
Mount Mary Coll, WI	B
Mount Mercy Coll, IA	B
Mount Vernon Nazarene U, OH	B
Nebraska Wesleyan U, NE	B
North Carolina Ag and Tech State U, NC	B
Northeastern Illinois U, IL	B
Northeastern State U, OK	B

Northern Michigan U, MI	B
Northern State U, SD	A
Northwestern Coll, IA	B
Northwestern Oklahoma State U, OK	B
Oglala Lakota Coll, SD	A,B
Ohio Dominican U, OH	B
The Ohio State U, OH	B
Ohio U, OH	B
Oral Roberts U, OK	B
Pittsburg State U, KS	B
Presentation Coll, SD	B
Quincy U, IL	B
Rockford Coll, IL	B
Saginaw Valley State U, MI	B
St. Augustine Coll, IL	B
St. Cloud State U, MN	B
Saint John's U, MN	B
Saint Joseph's Coll, IN	B
Saint Louis U, MO	B
Saint Mary's Coll, IN	B
St. Olaf Coll, MN	B
Sitting Bull Coll, ND	A
Southeast Missouri State U, MO	B
Southern Illinois U Carbondale, IL	B
Southern Illinois U Edwardsville, IL	B
Southwestern Oklahoma State U, OK	B
Southwest Minnesota State U, MN	B
Spring Arbor U, MI	B
Taylor U, IN	B
Taylor U Fort Wayne, IN	B
Trinity Christian Coll, IL	B
Turtle Mountain Comm Coll, ND	A
Union Coll, NE	B
The U of Akron, OH	B
U of Central Missouri, MO	B
U of Cincinnati, OH	A,B
The U of Findlay, OH	B
U of Illinois at Chicago, IL	B
U of Illinois at Springfield, IL	B
U of Indianapolis, IN	B
The U of Iowa, IA	B
U of Kansas, KS	B
U of Mary, ND	B
U of Michigan–Flint, MI	B
U of Missouri–Columbia, MO	B
U of Missouri–St. Louis, MO	B
U of Nebraska at Kearney, NE	B
U of Nebraska at Omaha, NE	B
U of North Dakota, ND	B
U of Northern Iowa, IA	B
U of Oklahoma, OK	B
U of Rio Grande, OH	A,B
U of St. Francis, IL	B
U of Saint Francis, IN	B
U of St. Thomas, MN	B
U of Sioux Falls, SD	B
The U of South Dakota, SD	B
U of Southern Indiana, IN	B
The U of Toledo, OH	A,B
U of West Florida, FL	B
U of Wisconsin–Eau Claire, WI	B
U of Wisconsin–Green Bay, WI	A,B
U of Wisconsin–Madison, WI	B
U of Wisconsin–Milwaukee, WI	B
U of Wisconsin–Oshkosh, WI	B

U of Wisconsin–River Falls, WI	B
U of Wisconsin–Superior, WI	B
U of Wisconsin–Whitewater, WI	B
Ursuline Coll, OH	B
Valparaiso U, IN	B
Viterbo U, WI	B
Wartburg Coll, IA	B
Washburn U, KS	B
Western Illinois U, IL	B
Western Michigan U, MI	B
Wichita State U, KS	B
William Woods U, MO	B
Wilmington Coll, OH	B
Winona State U, MN	B
Wright State U, OH	A,B
Xavier U, OH	B
Youngstown State U, OH	B

Social Work Related
Miami U Hamilton, OH	B

Sociobiology
Beloit Coll, WI	B

Sociology
Adrian Coll, MI	A,B
Albion Coll, MI	B
Alma Coll, MI	B
Anderson U, IN	B
Andrews U, MI	B
Antioch Coll, OH	B
Aquinas Coll, MI	B
Ashland U, OH	B
Augsburg Coll, MN	B
Augustana Coll, IL	B
Augustana Coll, SD	B
Aurora U, IL	B
Avila U, MO	B
Baker U, KS	B
Baldwin-Wallace Coll, OH	B
Ball State U, IN	B
Beloit Coll, WI	B
Bemidji State U, MN	B
Benedictine Coll, KS	B
Benedictine U, IL	B
Bethany Coll, KS	B
Bethany Lutheran Coll, MN	B
Black Hills State U, SD	B
Bluffton U, OH	B
Bowling Green State U, OH	B
Bradley U, IL	B
Buena Vista U, IA	B
Butler U, IN	B
Calvin Coll, MI	B
Cameron U, OK	B
Capital U, OH	B
Cardinal Stritch U, WI	B
Carleton Coll, MN	B
Carroll Coll, WI	B
Case Western Reserve U, OH	B
Cedarville U, OH	B
Central Christian Coll of Kansas, KS	A
Central Coll, IA	B
Central Methodist U, MO	B
Central Michigan U, MI	B
Central State U, OH	B
Chicago State U, IL	B
Clarke Coll, IA	B
Clarkson U, NY	B
Cleveland State U, OH	B
Coe Coll, IA	B
Coll of Mount St. Joseph, OH	B
Coll of Saint Benedict, MN	B
Coll of St. Catherine, MN	B
Coll of the Ozarks, MO	B

The Coll of Wooster, OH	B	Lake Superior State U, MI	B	St. Cloud State U, MN	B	U of Wisconsin–Eau Claire, WI	B
Columbia Coll, MO	B	Langston U, OK	B	St. Gregory's U, Shawnee, OK	B	U of Wisconsin–La Crosse, WI	B
Concordia Coll, MN	B	Lewis U, IL	B	Saint John's U, MN	B	U of Wisconsin–Madison, WI	B
Concordia U, IL	B	Lincoln U, MO	B	Saint Joseph's Coll, IN	B	U of Wisconsin–Milwaukee, WI	B
Concordia U, MI	B	Lindenwood U, MO	B	Saint Louis U, MO	B	U of Wisconsin–Oshkosh, WI	B
Concordia U, NE	B	Loras Coll, IA	B	Saint Mary's Coll, IN	B	U of Wisconsin–Parkside, WI	B
Concordia U, St. Paul, MN	B	Lourdes Coll, OH	A,B	St. Norbert Coll, WI	B	U of Wisconsin–River Falls, WI	B
Concord U, WV	B	Loyola U Chicago, IL	B	St. Olaf Coll, MN	B	U of Wisconsin–Stevens Point, WI	B
Cornell Coll, IA	B	Luther Coll, IA	B	Saint Xavier U, IL	B	U of Wisconsin–Superior, WI	B
Cornerstone U, MI	B	Macalester Coll, MN	B	Shawnee State U, OH	B	U of Wisconsin–Whitewater, WI	B
Creighton U, NE	B	Madonna U, MI	B	Simpson Coll, IA	B	Upper Iowa U, IA	B
Dakota Wesleyan U, SD	B	Manchester Coll, IN	B	South Dakota State U, SD	B	Ursuline Coll, OH	B
Dana Coll, NE	B	Marian Coll, IN	B	Southeastern Oklahoma State U, OK	B	Valparaiso U, IN	B
Denison U, OH	B	Marian Coll of Fond du Lac, WI	B	Southeast Missouri State U, MO	B	Viterbo U, WI	B
DePaul U, IL	B	Marquette U, WI	B	Southern Illinois U Carbondale, IL	B	Walsh U, OH	B
DePauw U, IN	B	Maryville U of Saint Louis, MO	B	Southern Illinois U Edwardsville, IL	B	Wartburg Coll, IA	B
Doane Coll, NE	B	McKendree Coll, IL	B	Southern Methodist U, TX	B	Washburn U, KS	B
Dominican U, IL	B	Miami U, OH	B	Southwest Baptist U, MO	B	Wayne State Coll, NE	B
Dordt Coll, IA	B	Miami U Hamilton, OH	B	Southwest Minnesota State U, MN	B	Western Illinois U, IL	B
Drake U, IA	B	Miami U–Middletown Campus, OH	A	Spring Arbor U, MI	B	Western Michigan U, MI	B
Drury U, MO	B	Michigan State U, MI	B	Tabor Coll, KS	B	Westminster Coll, MO	B
Earlham Coll, IN	B	Millikin U, IL	B	Taylor U, IN	B	Wheaton Coll, IL	B
East Central U, OK	B	Minnesota State U Mankato, MN	B	Transylvania U, KY	B	Wichita State U, KS	B
Eastern Illinois U, IL	B	Minot State U, ND	B	Trinity Christian Coll, IL	B	William Penn U, IA	B
Eastern Michigan U, MI	B	Missouri Southern State U, MO	B	Truman State U, MO	B	Winona State U, MN	B
East-West U, IL	B	Missouri State U, MO	B	The U of Akron, OH	B	Wittenberg U, OH	B
Edgewood Coll, WI	B	Missouri Valley Coll, MO	B	U of Central Missouri, MO	B	Wright State U, OH	A,B
Elmhurst Coll, IL	B	Mount Mercy Coll, IA	B	U of Central Oklahoma, OK	B	Xavier U, OH	A,B
Emporia State U, KS	B	Mount Union Coll, OH	B	U of Chicago, IL	B	Youngstown State U, OH	B
Evangel U, MO	B	Mount Vernon Nazarene U, OH	B	U of Cincinnati, OH	B		
Fort Hays State U, KS	B	Nebraska Wesleyan U, NE	B	U of Dayton, OH	B	**Soil Conservation**	
Franciscan U of Steubenville, OH	B	Newman U, KS	B	U of Evansville, IN	B	Ball State U, IN	B
Franklin Coll, IN	B	North Carolina Ag and Tech State U, NC	B	The U of Findlay, OH	B	The Ohio State U, OH	B
Goshen Coll, IN	B	North Central Coll, IL	B	U of Illinois at Chicago, IL	B	U of Minnesota, Crookston, MN	A
Grace Coll, IN	B	North Dakota State U, ND	B	U of Illinois at Springfield, IL	B	U of Wisconsin–Stevens Point, WI	B
Graceland U, IA	B	Northeastern Illinois U, IL	B	U of Illinois at Urbana–Champaign, IL	B		
Grand Valley State U, MI	B	Northeastern State U, OK	B	U of Indianapolis, IN	B	**Soil Science and Agronomy**	
Grand View Coll, IA	A	Northern Illinois U, IL	B	The U of Iowa, IA	B	Michigan State U, MI	B
Greenville Coll, IL	B	Northern Michigan U, MI	B	U of Kansas, KS	B	North Dakota State U, ND	B
Grinnell Coll, IA	B	Northern State U, SD	B	U of Michigan, MI	B	U of Minnesota, Twin Cities Campus, MN	B
Gustavus Adolphus Coll, MN	B	Northland Coll, WI	B	U of Michigan–Dearborn, MI	B	U of Nebraska–Lincoln, NE	B
Hamline U, MN	B	Northwestern Coll, IA	B	U of Michigan–Flint, MI	B	U of Wisconsin–River Falls, WI	B
Hannibal-LaGrange Coll, MO	B	Northwestern Oklahoma State U, OK	B	U of Minnesota, Duluth, MN	B		
Hanover Coll, IN	B	Northwestern U, IL	B	U of Minnesota, Morris, MN	B	**South Asian Languages**	
Hastings Coll, NE	B	Northwest Missouri State U, MO	B	U of Minnesota, Twin Cities Campus, MN		Northwestern U, IL	B
Hillsdale Coll, MI	B	Oakland U, MI	B	U of Missouri–Columbia, MO	B	Oakland U, MI	B
Hiram Coll, OH	B	Oberlin Coll, OH	B	U of Missouri–Kansas City, MO	B	U of Chicago, IL	B
Hope Coll, MI	B	Ohio Dominican U, OH	B	U of Missouri–St. Louis, MO	B		
Huntington U, IN	B	Ohio Northern U, OH	B	U of Nebraska at Kearney, NE	B	**Spanish**	
Illinois Coll, IL	B	The Ohio State U, OH	B	U of Nebraska at Omaha, NE	B	Adrian Coll, MI	A,B
Illinois State U, IL	B	Ohio U, OH	B	U of Nebraska–Lincoln, NE	B	Albion Coll, MI	B
Illinois Wesleyan U, IL	B	Ohio Wesleyan U, OH	B	U of New Orleans, LA	B	Alma Coll, MI	B
Indiana State U, IN	B	Oklahoma City U, OK	B	U of North Dakota, ND	B	Anderson U, IN	B
Indiana U Bloomington, IN	B	Oklahoma State U, OK	B	U of Northern Iowa, IA	B	Andrews U, MI	B
Indiana U East, IN	B	Ottawa U, KS	B	U of Notre Dame, IN	B	Antioch Coll, OH	B
Indiana U Kokomo, IN	B	Otterbein Coll, OH	B	U of Oklahoma, OK	B	Aquinas Coll, MI	B
Indiana U Northwest, IN	B	Park U, MO	B	U of Rio Grande, OH	A,B	Ashland U, OH	B
Indiana U–Purdue U Fort Wayne, IN	B	Pittsburg State U, KS	B	U of Saint Mary, KS	B	Augsburg Coll, MN	B
Indiana U–Purdue U Indianapolis, IN	B	Purdue U, IN	B	U of St. Thomas, MN	B	Augustana Coll, IL	B
Indiana U South Bend, IN	B	Purdue U Calumet, IN	B	U of Science and Arts of Oklahoma, OK	B	Augustana Coll, SD	B
Indiana U Southeast, IN	B	Ripon Coll, WI	B	U of Sioux Falls, SD	B	Baker U, KS	B
Indiana Wesleyan U, IN	B	Rockford Coll, IL	B	The U of South Dakota, SD	B	Baldwin-Wallace Coll, OH	B
Iowa State U of Science and Technology, IA	B	Rockhurst U, MO	B	U of Southern Indiana, IN	B	Ball State U, IN	B
Judson Coll, IL	B	Roosevelt U, IL	B	The U of Toledo, OH	B	Beloit Coll, WI	B
Kalamazoo Coll, MI	B	Saginaw Valley State U, MI	B	U of Tulsa, OK	B	Bemidji State U, MN	B
Kansas State U, KS	B	St. Ambrose U, IA	B	U of West Florida, FL	B	Benedictine Coll, KS	B
Kent State U, OH	B					Benedictine U, IL	B
Kenyon Coll, OH	B					Bethel Coll, KS	B
Knox Coll, IL	B						
Lake Forest Coll, IL	B						
Lakeland Coll, WI	B						

A—associate degree; B—bachelor's degree

Bethel U, MN	B
Blackburn Coll, IL	B
Black Hills State U, SD	B
Bluffton U, OH	B
Bowling Green State U, OH	B
Bradley U, IL	B
Briar Cliff U, IA	B
Buena Vista U, IA	B
Butler U, IN	B
Calvin Coll, MI	B
Capital U, OH	B
Cardinal Stritch U, WI	B
Carleton Coll, MN	B
Carroll Coll, WI	B
Case Western Reserve U, OH	B
Cedarville U, OH	B
Central Coll, IA	B
Central Methodist U, MO	B
Central Michigan U, MI	B
Chicago State U, IL	B
Clarke Coll, IA	B
Cleveland State U, OH	B
Coe Coll, IA	B
Coll of Saint Benedict, MN	B
Coll of St. Catherine, MN	B
Coll of the Ozarks, MO	B
The Coll of Wooster, OH	B
Concordia Coll, MN	B
Concordia U, MI	B
Concordia U, NE	B
Concordia U Wisconsin, WI	B
Cornell Coll, IA	B
Cornerstone U, MI	B
Creighton U, NE	B
Dakota Wesleyan U, SD	B
Dana Coll, NE	B
Denison U, OH	B
DePaul U, IL	B
DePauw U, IN	B
Dickinson State U, ND	B
Doane Coll, NE	B
Dominican U, IL	B
Dordt Coll, IA	B
Drury U, MO	B
Earlham Coll, IN	B
Eastern Michigan U, MI	B
Edgewood Coll, WI	B
Elmhurst Coll, IL	B
Evangel U, MO	B
Fort Hays State U, KS	B
Franciscan U of Steubenville, OH	B
Franklin Coll, IN	B
Goshen Coll, IN	B
Grace Coll, IN	B
Graceland U, IA	B
Grand Valley State U, MI	B
Greenville Coll, IL	B
Grinnell Coll, IA	B
Gustavus Adolphus Coll, MN	B
Hamline U, MN	B
Hanover Coll, IN	B
Hastings Coll, NE	B
Heidelberg Coll, OH	B
Hillsdale Coll, MI	B
Hiram Coll, OH	B
Hope Coll, MI	B
Illinois Coll, IL	B
Illinois State U, IL	B
Illinois Wesleyan U, IL	B
Indiana State U, IN	B
Indiana U Bloomington, IN	B
Indiana U Northwest, IN	B
Indiana U–Purdue U Fort Wayne, IN	A,B

Indiana U–Purdue U Indianapolis, IN	B
Indiana U South Bend, IN	B
Indiana U Southeast, IN	B
Indiana Wesleyan U, IN	B
Iowa State U of Science and Technology, IA	B
Kalamazoo Coll, MI	B
Kent State U, OH	B
Kenyon Coll, OH	B
Knox Coll, IL	B
Lake Forest Coll, IL	B
Lakeland Coll, WI	B
Lawrence U, WI	B
Lincoln U, MO	B
Lindenwood U, MO	B
Loras Coll, IA	B
Loyola U Chicago, IL	B
Luther Coll, IA	B
Macalester Coll, MN	B
MacMurray Coll, IL	B
Madonna U, MI	B
Malone Coll, OH	B
Manchester Coll, IN	B
Marian Coll, IN	B
Marian Coll of Fond du Lac, WI	B
Marietta Coll, OH	B
Marquette U, WI	B
Miami U, OH	B
Miami U Hamilton, OH	B
Miami U–Middletown Campus, OH	A
Michigan State U, MI	B
Millikin U, IL	B
Minnesota State U Mankato, MN	B
Minot State U, ND	B
Missouri Southern State U, MO	B
Missouri State U, MO	B
Missouri Western State U, MO	B
Morningside Coll, IA	B
Mount Mary Coll, WI	B
Mount Union Coll, OH	B
Mount Vernon Nazarene U, OH	B
Nebraska Wesleyan U, NE	B
North Central Coll, IL	B
North Dakota State U, ND	B
Northeastern Illinois U, IL	B
Northeastern State U, OK	B
Northern Illinois U, IL	B
Northern Michigan U, MI	B
Northern State U, SD	B
Northwestern Coll, IA	B
Northwestern Oklahoma State U, OK	B
Northwestern U, IL	B
Northwest Missouri State U, MO	B
Oakland U, MI	B
Oberlin Coll, OH	B
Ohio Northern U, OH	B
The Ohio State U, OH	B
Ohio U, OH	B
Ohio Wesleyan U, OH	B
Oklahoma Christian U, OK	B
Oklahoma City U, OK	B
Oklahoma State U, OK	B
Oral Roberts U, OK	B
Otterbein Coll, OH	B
Park U, MO	B
Pittsburg State U, KS	B
Purdue U Calumet, IN	B
Ripon Coll, WI	B

Rockford Coll, IL	B
Rockhurst U, MO	B
Roosevelt U, IL	B
Saginaw Valley State U, MI	B
St. Ambrose U, IA	B
St. Cloud State U, MN	B
Saint John's U, MN	B
Saint Louis U, MO	B
Saint Mary-of-the-Woods Coll, IN	B
Saint Mary's Coll, IN	B
Saint Mary's U of Minnesota, MN	B
St. Norbert Coll, WI	B
St. Olaf Coll, MN	B
Saint Xavier U, IL	B
Simpson Coll, IA	B
South Dakota State U, SD	B
Southeastern Oklahoma State U, OK	B
Southeast Missouri State U, MO	B
Southern Illinois U Carbondale, IL	B
Southern Methodist U, TX	B
Southwest Baptist U, MO	B
Southwest Minnesota State U, MN	B
Spring Arbor U, MI	B
Taylor U, IN	B
Transylvania U, KY	B
Trinity Christian Coll, IL	B
Truman State U, MO	B
Union Coll, NE	B
The U of Akron, OH	B
U of Central Missouri, MO	B
U of Central Oklahoma, OK	B
U of Chicago, IL	B
U of Cincinnati, OH	B
U of Dallas, TX	B
U of Dayton, OH	B
U of Evansville, IN	B
The U of Findlay, OH	B
U of Illinois at Chicago, IL	B
U of Illinois at Urbana–Champaign, IL	B
U of Indianapolis, IN	B
The U of Iowa, IA	B
U of Kansas, KS	B
U of Michigan, MI	B
U of Michigan–Dearborn, MI	B
U of Michigan–Flint, MI	B
U of Minnesota, Duluth, MN	B
U of Minnesota, Morris, MN	B
U of Minnesota, Twin Cities Campus, MN	B
U of Missouri–Columbia, MO	B
U of Missouri–Kansas City, MO	B
U of Missouri–St. Louis, MO	B
U of Nebraska at Kearney, NE	B
U of Nebraska at Omaha, NE	B
U of Nebraska–Lincoln, NE	B
U of New Orleans, LA	B
U of North Dakota, ND	B
U of Northern Iowa, IA	B
U of Notre Dame, IN	B
U of Oklahoma, OK	B
U of St. Thomas, MN	B
The U of South Dakota, SD	B
U of Southern Indiana, IN	B
The U of Toledo, OH	B
U of Tulsa, OK	B
U of Wisconsin–Eau Claire, WI	B

U of Wisconsin–Green Bay, WI	A,B
U of Wisconsin–La Crosse, WI	B
U of Wisconsin–Madison, WI	B
U of Wisconsin–Milwaukee, WI	B
U of Wisconsin–Oshkosh, WI	B
U of Wisconsin–Parkside, WI	B
U of Wisconsin–Platteville, WI	B
U of Wisconsin–River Falls, WI	B
U of Wisconsin–Stevens Point, WI	B
U of Wisconsin–Whitewater, WI	B
Valley City State U, ND	B
Valparaiso U, IN	B
Viterbo U, WI	B
Wabash Coll, IN	B
Walsh U, OH	B
Wartburg Coll, IA	B
Washburn U, KS	B
Washington U in St. Louis, MO	B
Wayne State Coll, NE	B
Webster U, MO	B
Western Illinois U, IL	B
Western Michigan U, MI	B
Westminster Coll, MO	B
Wheaton Coll, IL	B
Wichita State U, KS	B
William Jewell Coll, MO	B
William Woods U, MO	B
Wilmington Coll, OH	B
Winona State U, MN	B
Wisconsin Lutheran Coll, WI	B
Wittenberg U, OH	B
Wright State U, OH	B
Xavier U, OH	A,B
Youngstown State U, OH	B

Spanish and Iberian Studies

Coe Coll, IA	B
Southern Methodist U, TX	B

Spanish Language Teacher Education

Alma Coll, MI	B
Anderson U, IN	B
Bethel U, MN	B
Buena Vista U, IA	B
Carroll Coll, WI	B
Cedarville U, OH	B
Central Michigan U, MI	B
Chicago State U, IL	B
Coll of St. Catherine, MN	B
Concordia Coll, MN	B
Concordia U, NE	B
Concordia U Wisconsin, WI	B
Dordt Coll, IA	B
Eastern Michigan U, MI	B
Elmhurst Coll, IL	B
Evangel U, MO	B
Franklin Coll, IN	B
Grace Coll, IN	B
Greenville Coll, IL	B
Hastings Coll, NE	B
Hope Coll, MI	B
Illinois Wesleyan U, IL	B
Indiana U Bloomington, IN	B
Indiana U Northwest, IN	B
Indiana U–Purdue U Fort Wayne, IN	B
Indiana U–Purdue U Indianapolis, IN	B
Indiana U South Bend, IN	B
Kent State U, OH	B

Spanish Language Teacher Education

Lindenwood U, MO	B
Malone Coll, OH	B
Marian Coll of Fond du Lac, WI	B
Miami U Hamilton, OH	B
Minot State U, ND	B
Missouri State U, MO	B
Missouri Western State U, MO	B
Mount Mary Coll, WI	B
Mount Vernon Nazarene U, OH	B
North Dakota State U, ND	B
Northern Michigan U, MI	B
Notre Dame Coll, OH	B
Ohio Northern U, OH	B
Ohio U, OH	B
Ohio Wesleyan U, OH	B
Oral Roberts U, OK	B
Pittsburg State U, KS	B
St. Ambrose U, IA	B
Saint Mary's U of Minnesota, MN	B
Saint Xavier U, IL	B
Southeastern Oklahoma State U, OK	B
Taylor U, IN	B
The U of Akron, OH	B
U of Evansville, IN	B
U of Illinois at Chicago, IL	B
U of Illinois at Urbana–Champaign, IL	B
U of Indianapolis, IN	B
The U of Iowa, IA	B
U of Michigan–Flint, MI	B
U of Minnesota, Duluth, MN	B
U of Missouri–St. Louis, MO	B
U of Nebraska–Lincoln, NE	B
The U of South Dakota, SD	B
The U of Toledo, OH	B
U of Wisconsin–River Falls, WI	B
Valley City State U, ND	B
Valparaiso U, IN	B
Viterbo U, WI	B
Washington U in St. Louis, MO	B
Western Michigan U, MI	B
Youngstown State U, OH	B

Special Education

Ashland U, OH	B
Augustana Coll, SD	B
Avila U, MO	B
Ball State U, IN	B
Benedictine Coll, KS	B
Benedictine U, IL	B
Black Hills State U, SD	B
Bowling Green State U, OH	B
Buena Vista U, IA	B
Calvin Coll, MI	B
Capital U, OH	B
Cardinal Stritch U, WI	B
Cedarville U, OH	B
Central State U, OH	B
Chicago State U, IL	B
Clarke Coll, IA	B
Cleveland State U, OH	B
Coll of Mount St. Joseph, OH	B
Coll of Saint Mary, NE	B
Concordia U, NE	B
Concord U, WV	B
Culver-Stockton Coll, MO	B
Dakota State U, SD	B
Dakota Wesleyan U, SD	B
Dana Coll, NE	B

Doane Coll, NE	B
East Central U, OK	B
Eastern Illinois U, IL	B
Eastern Michigan U, MI	B
Elmhurst Coll, IL	B
Evangel U, MO	B
Fontbonne U, MO	B
Gannon U, PA	B
Grace Coll, IN	B
Grand Valley State U, MI	B
Greenville Coll, IL	B
Hastings Coll, NE	B
Heidelberg Coll, OH	B
Huntington U, IN	B
Illinois State U, IL	B
Indiana State U, IN	B
Indiana U Bloomington, IN	B
Indiana U South Bend, IN	B
Indiana U Southeast, IN	B
Indiana Wesleyan U, IN	B
Iowa Wesleyan Coll, IA	B
Kent State U, OH	B
Langston U, OK	B
Lewis U, IL	B
Lincoln U, MO	B
Lindenwood U, MO	B
Loyola U Chicago, IL	B
MacMurray Coll, IL	B
Madonna U, MI	B
Manchester Coll, IN	B
Marian Coll, IN	B
Miami U, OH	B
Miami U Hamilton, OH	B
Michigan State U, MI	B
Missouri Southern State U, MO	B
Missouri State U, MO	B
Missouri Valley Coll, MO	B
Morningside Coll, IA	B
Mount Marty Coll, SD	B
Mount Vernon Nazarene U, OH	B
Nebraska Wesleyan U, NE	B
North Carolina Ag and Tech State U, NC	B
Northeastern Illinois U, IL	B
Northeastern State U, OK	B
Northern Illinois U, IL	B
Northern Michigan U, MI	B
Northern State U, SD	B
Northwestern Oklahoma State U, OK	B
Northwest Missouri State U, MO	B
Oakland U, MI	B
Oglala Lakota Coll, SD	B
Ohio Dominican U, OH	B
The Ohio State U, OH	B
Ohio U, OH	B
Oral Roberts U, OK	B
Peru State Coll, NE	B
Purdue U Calumet, IN	B
Quincy U, IL	B
Rockford Coll, IL	B
Roosevelt U, IL	B
Saginaw Valley State U, MI	B
St. Augustine Coll, IL	A
St. Cloud State U, MN	B
Saint Mary-of-the-Woods Coll, IN	B
Shawnee State U, OH	B
Southeast Missouri State U, MO	B
Southern Illinois U Carbondale, IL	B

Southern Illinois U Edwardsville, IL	B
Southwestern Oklahoma State U, OK	B
Tabor Coll, KS	B
Trinity Christian Coll, IL	B
U of Central Missouri, MO	B
U of Central Oklahoma, OK	B
U of Cincinnati, OH	B
U of Dayton, OH	B
U of Evansville, IN	B
The U of Findlay, OH	B
U of Illinois at Urbana–Champaign, IL	B
U of Minnesota, Duluth, MN	B
U of Missouri–St. Louis, MO	B
U of Nebraska at Kearney, NE	B
U of Northern Iowa, IA	B
U of Oklahoma, OK	B
U of St. Francis, IL	B
U of Saint Francis, IN	B
The U of South Dakota, SD	B
The U of Toledo, OH	B
U of West Florida, FL	B
U of Wisconsin–Eau Claire, WI	B
U of Wisconsin–Madison, WI	B
U of Wisconsin–Milwaukee, WI	B
U of Wisconsin–Oshkosh, WI	B
U of Wisconsin–Superior, WI	B
U of Wisconsin–Whitewater, WI	B
Ursuline Coll, OH	B
Walsh U, OH	B
Wayne State Coll, NE	B
Western Illinois U, IL	B
William Penn U, IA	B
William Woods U, MO	B
Winona State U, MN	B
Xavier U, OH	B
York Coll, NE	B
Youngstown State U, OH	B

Special Education (Administration)

Wright State U, OH	B

Special Education (Early Childhood)

U of Northern Iowa, IA	B

Special Education (Emotionally Disturbed)

Augsburg Coll, MN	B
Bradley U, IL	B
Central Michigan U, MI	B
Eastern Michigan U, MI	B
Hope Coll, MI	B
Loras Coll, IA	B
Marygrove Coll, MI	B
Trinity Christian Coll, IL	B
The U of Toledo, OH	B
Wright State U, OH	B

Special Education (Gifted and Talented)

Wright State U, OH	B

Special Education (Hearing Impaired)

Augustana Coll, SD	B
Bowling Green State U, OH	B
Eastern Michigan U, MI	B
MacMurray Coll, IL	B
Michigan State U, MI	B
Minot State U, ND	B

U of Nebraska–Lincoln, NE	B
U of Science and Arts of Oklahoma, OK	B
The U of Toledo, OH	B

Special Education (Mentally Retarded)

Bradley U, IL	B
Central Michigan U, MI	B
Eastern Michigan U, MI	B
Loras Coll, IA	B
Minot State U, ND	B
Northern Michigan U, MI	B
Silver Lake Coll, WI	B
Trinity Christian Coll, IL	B
The U of Akron, OH	B
U of Mary, ND	B
U of Northern Iowa, IA	B
U of Rio Grande, OH	B
U of West Florida, FL	B
Western Michigan U, MI	B
Wright State U, OH	B

Special Education (Multiply Disabled)

Ohio U, OH	B
The U of Akron, OH	B
U of Northern Iowa, IA	B
The U of Toledo, OH	B
Wright State U, OH	B

Special Education (Orthopedic and Other Physical Health Impairments)

Eastern Michigan U, MI	B
Wright State U, OH	B

Special Education Related

Minot State U, ND	A,B
Southeastern Oklahoma State U, OK	B
The U of Akron, OH	B
U of Missouri–Columbia, MO	B
U of Nebraska–Lincoln, NE	B
U of Southern Indiana, IN	B
The U of Toledo, OH	B
Wright State U, OH	B

Special Education (Specific Learning Disabilities)

Aquinas Coll, MI	B
Baldwin-Wallace Coll, OH	B
Bradley U, IL	B
Eastern Michigan U, MI	B
Hope Coll, MI	B
Malone Coll, OH	B
Michigan State U, MI	B
Northwestern U, IL	B
Notre Dame Coll, OH	B
Silver Lake Coll, WI	B
Trinity Christian Coll, IL	B
The U of Akron, OH	B
U of Rio Grande, OH	B
The U of Toledo, OH	B
Wright State U, OH	B

Special Education (Speech or Language Impaired)

Eastern Michigan U, MI	B
Minot State U, ND	B
The U of Akron, OH	B
U of Nebraska at Omaha, NE	A
The U of Toledo, OH	B

Special Education (Vision Impaired)

Eastern Michigan U, MI	B

A—associate degree; B—bachelor's degree

The U of Toledo, OH — B
Western Michigan U, MI — B

Special Products Marketing
Ball State U, IN — A,B
Concord U, WV — B
Dominican U, IL — B
Ferris State U, MI — A
Iowa State U of Science and Technology, IA — B
Lindenwood U, MO — B
Madonna U, MI — B
U of Minnesota, Crookston, MN — A
Wayne State Coll, NE — B

Speech and Rhetoric
Ashland U, OH — B
Augsburg Coll, MN — B
Augustana Coll, IL — B
Ball State U, IN — B
Bemidji State U, MN — B
Blackburn Coll, IL — B
Black Hills State U, SD — B
Bowling Green State U, OH — B
Bradley U, IL — B
Butler U, IN — B
Calvin Coll, MI — B
Capital U, OH — B
Cedarville U, OH — B
Central Michigan U, MI — B
Chicago State U, IL — B
Coe Coll, IA — B
Coll of Saint Benedict, MN — B
Coll of St. Catherine, MN — B
Coll of the Ozarks, MO — B
Concordia Coll, MN — B
Concordia U, NE — B
Cornell Coll, IA — B
Cornerstone U, MI — B
Creighton U, NE — B
Denison U, OH — B
Dickinson State U, ND — B
Doane Coll, NE — B
Drake U, IA — B
East Central U, OK — B
Evangel U, MO — B
Ferris State U, MI — A
Graceland U, IA — B
Greenville Coll, IL — B
Gustavus Adolphus Coll, MN — B
Hannibal-LaGrange Coll, MO — B
Hastings Coll, NE — B
Hillsdale Coll, MI — B
Illinois Coll, IL — B
Illinois State U, IL — B
Indiana U Bloomington, IN — B
Indiana U South Bend, IN — B
Iowa State U of Science and Technology, IA — B
Judson Coll, IL — B
Kent State U, OH — B
Lewis U, IL — B
Madonna U, MI — A,B
Manchester Coll, IN — B
Maranatha Baptist Bible Coll, WI — B
Marietta Coll, OH — B
Marquette U, WI — B
McKendree Coll, IL — B
Miami U, OH — B
Minnesota State U Mankato, MN — B
Minot State U, ND — B
Missouri Valley Coll, MO — B
Mount Mercy Coll, IA — B
Nebraska Wesleyan U, NE — B

North Carolina Ag and Tech State U, NC — B
North Central Coll, IL — B
North Dakota State U, ND — B
Northeastern Illinois U, IL — B
Northern Michigan U, MI — B
Northern State U, SD — B
Northwestern Coll, IA — B
Northwestern Oklahoma State U, OK — B
Northwestern U, IL — B
Northwest Missouri State U, MO — B
Ohio U, OH — B
Oklahoma Christian U, OK — B
Oklahoma City U, OK — B
Oklahoma State U, OK — B
Oral Roberts U, OK — B
St. Cloud State U, MN — B
Saint John's U, MN — B
Simpson Coll, IA — B
South Dakota State U, SD — B
Southeast Missouri State U, MO — B
Southern Illinois U Carbondale, IL — B
Southern Illinois U Edwardsville, IL — B
Truman State U, MO — B
The U of Akron, OH — B
U of Central Missouri, MO — B
U of Illinois at Chicago, IL — B
U of Illinois at Urbana–Champaign, IL — B
The U of Iowa, IA — B
U of Kansas, KS — B
U of Michigan, MI — B
U of Minnesota, Morris, MN — B
U of Nebraska at Kearney, NE — B
U of Nebraska at Omaha, NE — B
U of Northern Iowa, IA — B
U of Sioux Falls, SD — B
U of Wisconsin–Platteville, WI — B
U of Wisconsin–River Falls, WI — B
U of Wisconsin–Superior, WI — B
U of Wisconsin–Whitewater, WI — B
Wabash Coll, IN — B
Wayne State Coll, NE — B
William Jewell Coll, MO — B
Winona State U, MN — B
Youngstown State U, OH — B

Speech-Language Pathology
Augustana Coll, IL — B
Baker Coll of Muskegon, MI — A
Eastern Michigan U, MI — B
Miami U, OH — B
Miami U Hamilton, OH — B
Northern Michigan U, MI — B
Northwestern U, IL — B
Rockhurst U, MO — B
St. Cloud State U, MN — B
Saint Xavier U, IL — B
Southern Methodist U, TX — B
The U of Akron, OH — B
U of Central Missouri, MO — B
U of Nebraska–Lincoln, NE — B
U of Northern Iowa, IA — B
U of Oklahoma Health Sciences Center, OK — B
U of Science and Arts of Oklahoma, OK — B
The U of Toledo, OH — B
U of Wisconsin–Whitewater, WI — B

Speech Teacher Education
Anderson U, IN — B
Buena Vista U, IA — B
Capital U, OH — B
Central Christian Coll of Kansas, KS — A
Central Michigan U, MI — B
Coll of St. Catherine, MN — B
Concordia U, IL — B
Concordia U, MI — B
Concordia U, NE — B
Dana Coll, NE — B
Dordt Coll, IA — B
East Central U, OK — B
Evangel U, MO — B
Hastings Coll, NE — B
Indiana U Bloomington, IN — B
Indiana U–Purdue U Fort Wayne, IN — B
Indiana U–Purdue U Indianapolis, IN — B
North Dakota State U, ND — B
Northwestern Oklahoma State U, OK — B
Pittsburg State U, KS — B
St. Ambrose U, IA — B
Southeast Missouri State U, MO — B
Southwest Baptist U, MO — B
Southwest Minnesota State U, MN — B
Taylor U, IN — B
The U of Akron, OH — B
U of Indianapolis, IN — B
The U of Iowa, IA — B
U of Michigan–Flint, MI — B
U of Northern Iowa, IA — B
U of Rio Grande, OH — B
The U of South Dakota, SD — B
Wayne State Coll, NE — B
William Jewell Coll, MO — B
York Coll, NE — B

Speech/Theater Education
Augustana Coll, SD — B
Bemidji State U, MN — B
Culver-Stockton Coll, MO — B
Dickinson State U, ND — B
Graceland U, IA — B
Hamline U, MN — B
Lewis U, IL — B
McKendree Coll, IL — B
Missouri Western State U, MO — B
Northwestern Coll, IA — B
Oklahoma City U, OK — B
Saginaw Valley State U, MI — B
St. Ambrose U, IA — B
Southwest Minnesota State U, MN — B
U of Minnesota, Morris, MN — B
U of St. Thomas, MN — B
Viterbo U, WI — B
Wartburg Coll, IA — B
William Woods U, MO — B
York Coll, NE — B

Speech Therapy
Augustana Coll, IL — B
Fontbonne U, MO — B
Indiana U Bloomington, IN — B
Northeastern State U, OK — B
Northwestern U, IL — B
St. Cloud State U, MN — B
U of Oklahoma Health Sciences Center, OK — B
The U of Toledo, OH — B

U of Wisconsin–Madison, WI — B
U of Wisconsin–River Falls, WI — B

Sport and Fitness Administration/Management
Augustana Coll, SD — B
Baldwin-Wallace Coll, OH — B
Ball State U, IN — B
Bemidji State U, MN — B
Bethany Coll, KS — B
Black Hills State U, SD — B
Bluffton U, OH — B
Bowling Green State U, OH — B
Buena Vista U, IA — B
Calvin Coll, MI — B
Cedarville U, OH — B
Central Christian Coll of Kansas, KS — B
Central Methodist U, MO — B
Central Michigan U, MI — B
Cleveland State U, OH — B
Concordia U, NE — B
Concordia U Wisconsin, WI — B
Cornerstone U, MI — B
Crown Coll, MN — B
Drury U, MO — B
Elmhurst Coll, IL — B
Graceland U, IA — B
Greenville Coll, IL — B
Hastings Coll, NE — B
Indiana U Bloomington, IN — B
Indiana Wesleyan U, IN — B
Iowa Wesleyan Coll, IA — B
Judson Coll, IL — B
Lake Superior State U, MI — A
Lindenwood U, MO — B
Loras Coll, IA — B
Luther Coll, IA — B
MacMurray Coll, IL — B
Malone Coll, OH — B
Marian Coll of Fond du Lac, WI — B
Miami U, OH — B
Minnesota State U Mankato, MN — B
Minot State U, ND — B
Missouri Baptist U, MO — B
Missouri Valley Coll, MO — B
Mount Union Coll, OH — B
Mount Vernon Nazarene U, OH — B
Nebraska Wesleyan U, NE — B
North Central Coll, IL — B
North Dakota State U, ND — B
Northern Michigan U, MI — B
Northwest Missouri State U, MO — B
Northwood U, MI — A,B
Notre Dame Coll, OH — B
Ohio Dominican U, OH — B
Ohio Northern U, OH — B
Ohio U, OH — B
Otterbein Coll, OH — B
Quincy U, IL — B
Rochester Coll, MI — B
St. Ambrose U, IA — B
Shawnee State U, OH — B
Simpson Coll, IA — B
Southeast Missouri State U, MO — B
Southwest Baptist U, MO — B
Southwestern Coll, KS — B
Spring Arbor U, MI — B
Taylor U, IN — B
Tri-State U, IN — B
Union Coll, NE — B

U of Dayton, OH	B
U of Indianapolis, IN	B
The U of Iowa, IA	B
U of Michigan, MI	B
U of Minnesota, Crookston, MN	B
U of Nebraska at Kearney, NE	B
U of Saint Mary, KS	B
U of Tulsa, OK	B
U of Wisconsin–Parkside, WI	B
Valparaiso U, IN	B
Wartburg Coll, IA	B
Wayne State Coll, NE	B
William Penn U, IA	B
Wilmington Coll, OH	B
Winona State U, MN	B
Xavier U, OH	B

Statistics

Bowling Green State U, OH	B
Case Western Reserve U, OH	B
Central Michigan U, MI	B
Clarkson U, NY	B
DePaul U, IL	B
Eastern Michigan U, MI	B
Ferris State U, MI	B
Grand Valley State U, MI	B
Indiana U–Purdue U Fort Wayne, IN	B
Iowa State U of Science and Technology, IA	B
Kansas State U, KS	B
Kenyon Coll, OH	B
Kettering U, MI	B
Loyola U Chicago, IL	B
Luther Coll, IA	B
Marquette U, WI	B
Miami U, OH	B
Miami U Hamilton, OH	B
Michigan State U, MI	B
Michigan Technological U, MI	B
North Dakota State U, ND	B
Northwestern U, IL	B
Oakland U, MI	B
Ohio Northern U, OH	B
Ohio Wesleyan U, OH	B
Oklahoma State U, OK	B
Purdue U, IN	B
Purdue U North Central, IN	B
Roosevelt U, IL	B
St. Cloud State U, MN	B
Southern Methodist U, TX	B
The U of Akron, OH	B
U of Chicago, IL	B
U of Illinois at Chicago, IL	B
U of Illinois at Urbana–Champaign, IL	B
The U of Iowa, IA	B
U of Michigan, MI	B
U of Minnesota, Duluth, MN	B
U of Minnesota, Morris, MN	B
U of Missouri–Columbia, MO	B
U of Missouri–Kansas City, MO	B
U of Nebraska at Kearney, NE	B
U of Wisconsin–Madison, WI	B
U of Wisconsin–Milwaukee, WI	B
Washington U in St. Louis, MO	B
Western Michigan U, MI	B
Winona State U, MN	B
Wright State U, OH	B

Statistics Related

Ohio Northern U, OH	B

Stringed Instruments

U of Kansas, KS	B

Structural Engineering

Clarkson U, NY	B
U of Illinois at Urbana–Champaign, IL	B
The U of Toledo, OH	B
Western Michigan U, MI	B

Substance Abuse/Addiction Counseling

Calumet Coll of Saint Joseph, IN	B
Coll of St. Catherine, MN	B
Graceland U, IA	B
Indiana U–Purdue U Fort Wayne, IN	B
Indiana Wesleyan U, IN	A,B
Metropolitan State U, MN	B
Minot State U, ND	B
Newman U, KS	A,B
Rogers State U, OK	A
St. Augustine Coll, IL	B
St. Cloud State U, MN	B
The U of Akron, OH	A
U of Mary, ND	B
The U of South Dakota, SD	B
The U of Toledo, OH	A
Washburn U, KS	A,B

Surgical Technology

Baker Coll of Clinton Township, MI	A
Baker Coll of Flint, MI	A
Baker Coll of Jackson, MI	A
Baker Coll of Muskegon, MI	A
Mercy Coll of Health Sciences, IA	A
Presentation Coll, SD	A
Robert Morris Coll, IL	A
Trinity Coll of Nursing and Health Sciences, IL	A
The U of Akron, OH	A
U of Saint Francis, IN	A

Survey Technology

Ferris State U, MI	A,B
Michigan Technological U, MI	B
Morrison Inst of Technology, IL	A
The Ohio State U, OH	B
Purdue U, IN	B
The U of Akron, OH	A,B
U of Wisconsin–Madison, WI	B

Swedish

Augustana Coll, IL	B

System Administration

Academy Coll, MN	A
AIB Coll of Business, IA	A
Dordt Coll, IA	B
Michigan Technological U, MI	B
U of Minnesota, Crookston, MN	B
U of St. Francis, IL	B

System, Networking, and LAN/WAN Management

Academy Coll, MN	A
Baker Coll of Auburn Hills, MI	A
Carroll Coll, WI	B
Davenport U, Dearborn, MI	B
DeVry U, Chicago, IL	B
DeVry U, Tinley Park, IL	A
DeVry U, Kansas City, MO	A
DeVry U, Columbus, OH	A

ITT Tech Inst, Burr Ridge, IL	A
ITT Tech Inst, Mount Prospect, IL	A
ITT Tech Inst, Orland Park, IL	A
ITT Tech Inst, MN	A
National American U, Rapid City, SD	B
U of Minnesota, Crookston, MN	B
U of Northern Iowa, IA	B
U of Phoenix–Cincinnati Campus, OH	B
U of Phoenix–Cleveland Campus, OH	A
U of Phoenix–Columbus Ohio Campus, OH	A
U of Phoenix–Indianapolis Campus, IN	A
U of Phoenix–Springfield Campus, MO	A

Systems Engineering

Case Western Reserve U, OH	B
Oakland U, MI	B
The Ohio State U, OH	B
Ohio U, OH	B
Rose-Hulman Inst of Technology, IN	B
U of Missouri–Rolla, MO	B
Washington U in St. Louis, MO	B
Wright State U, OH	B

Systems Science and Theory

Indiana U Bloomington, IN	B
Miami U, OH	B
Miami U–Middletown Campus, OH	A
Washington U in St. Louis, MO	B
Wright State U, OH	B

Tamil

U of Chicago, IL	B

Taxation

Capital U, OH	B
Minnesota School of Business, MN	A
Minnesota School of Business–Brooklyn Center, MN	A
Minnesota School of Business–Plymouth, MN	A
Minnesota School of Business–Richfield, MN	A
Minnesota School of Business–St. Cloud, MN	A

Teacher Assistant/Aide

Alverno Coll, WI	A
Dordt Coll, IA	A
Sitting Bull Coll, ND	A
The U of Akron, OH	A
U of Phoenix–Cincinnati Campus, OH	B
U of Phoenix–Cleveland Campus, OH	A
U of Phoenix–Columbus Ohio Campus, OH	A
U of Phoenix–Indianapolis Campus, IN	A
U of Phoenix–St. Louis Campus, MO	A

Technical and Business Writing

Bowling Green State U, OH	B
Cedarville U, OH	B

Chicago State U, IL	B
Clarkson U, NY	B
Eastern Michigan U, MI	B
Ferris State U, MI	A,B
Grand Valley State U, MI	B
Illinois Inst of Technology, IL	B
Iowa State U of Science and Technology, IA	B
Madonna U, MI	B
Metropolitan State U, MN	B
Miami U, OH	B
Miami U Hamilton, OH	B
Michigan State U, MI	B
Michigan Technological U, MI	B
Missouri State U, MO	B
Mount Mary Coll, WI	B
Northern Michigan U, MI	B
Northwestern Coll, MN	B
Ohio Northern U, OH	B
U of Michigan–Flint, MI	B
U of Wisconsin–Stout, WI	B
Webster U, MO	B
Youngstown State U, OH	B

Technical Teacher Education

Bowling Green State U, OH	B
Eastern Illinois U, IL	B
The Ohio State U, OH	B
The U of Akron, OH	B
U of Missouri–Columbia, MO	B
U of Nebraska at Kearney, NE	B
U of Wisconsin–Stout, WI	B
Valley City State U, ND	B
Wright State U, OH	B

Technology/Industrial Arts Teacher Education

Bemidji State U, MN	B
Central Michigan U, MI	B
Chicago State U, IL	B
Coll of the Ozarks, MO	B
Concordia U, NE	B
Eastern Michigan U, MI	B
Illinois State U, IL	B
Kent State U, OH	B
Lindenwood U, MO	B
Michigan Technological U, MI	B
Missouri Southern State U, MO	B
Northern Michigan U, MI	B
The Ohio State U, OH	B
Oklahoma Panhandle State U, OK	B
Pittsburg State U, KS	B
Purdue U, IN	B
St. Cloud State U, MN	B
Southeast Missouri State U, MO	B
Southwestern Oklahoma State U, OK	B
U of Nebraska–Lincoln, NE	B
U of Northern Iowa, IA	B
U of Wisconsin–Stout, WI	B
Valley City State U, ND	B
Viterbo U, WI	B
Western Michigan U, MI	B

Telecommunications

Ball State U, IN	B
Bowling Green State U, OH	B
Butler U, IN	B
Grand Valley State U, MI	B
Indiana U Bloomington, IN	B
Michigan State U, MI	B
Ohio U, OH	B
Roosevelt U, IL	B

A—associate degree; B—bachelor's degree

Southern Methodist U, TX — B
U of Wisconsin–Platteville, WI — B
Western Michigan U, MI — B
Winona State U, MN — B

Theater Design and Technology

Bowling Green State U, OH — B
Coe Coll, IA — B
Columbia Coll Chicago, IL — B
DePaul U, IL — B
Huntington U, IN — B
Indiana U Bloomington, IN — A
Michigan Technological U, MI — B
Ohio U, OH — B
Oklahoma City U, OK — B
The U of Akron, OH — B
U of Kansas, KS — B
U of Michigan, MI — B
U of Northern Iowa, IA — B
U of Rio Grande, OH — A
Webster U, MO — B
Western Michigan U, MI — B
William Woods U, MO — B
Wright State U, OH — B

Theater Literature, History and Criticism

Buena Vista U, IA — B
DePaul U, IL — B
Northwestern U, IL — B
Ohio U, OH — B
U of Northern Iowa, IA — B
Washington U in St. Louis, MO — B

Theater/Theater Arts Management

East Central U, OK — B
Eastern Michigan U, MI — B
Miami U Hamilton, OH — B
Ohio Northern U, OH — B
Ohio U, OH — B
St. Cloud State U, MN — B
U of Evansville, IN — B
The U of Iowa, IA — B
Western Michigan U, MI — B

Theological and Ministerial Studies Related

God's Bible School and Coll, OH — B
Huntington U, IN — B
Messenger Coll, MO — B
Quincy U, IL — B
U of Saint Francis, IN — A,B

Theology

Anderson U, IN — B
Andrews U, MI — B
Augsburg Coll, MN — B
Briar Cliff U, IA — A,B
Calumet Coll of Saint Joseph, IN — B
Calvin Coll, MI — B
Cedarville U, OH — B
Central Christian Coll of Kansas, KS — A
Coll of Saint Benedict, MN — B
Coll of St. Catherine, MN — B
Concordia U, IL — B
Concordia U, NE — B
Concordia U, St. Paul, MN — B
Concordia U Wisconsin, WI — B
Creighton U, NE — A,B
Crossroads Coll, MN — B
Crown Coll, MN — B
Dakota Wesleyan U, SD — B

Dordt Coll, IA — B
Elmhurst Coll, IL — B
Franciscan U of Steubenville, OH — A,B
Gannon U, PA — B
Global U of the Assemblies of God, MO — B
Grace Bible Coll, MI — B
Great Lakes Christian Coll, MI — B
Hanover Coll, IN — B
Hillsdale Free Will Baptist Coll, OK — B
Huntington U, IN — B
Indiana Wesleyan U, IN — B
Kuyper Coll, MI — B
Loyola U Chicago, IL — B
Marian Coll, IN — A,B
Martin Luther Coll, MN — B
Mount Vernon Nazarene U, OH — B
Newman U, KS — B
Notre Dame Coll, OH — B
Ohio Dominican U, OH — A,B
Oklahoma Wesleyan U, OK — B
Oral Roberts U, OK — B
Ozark Christian Coll, MO — A,B
Quincy U, IL — B
Rockhurst U, MO — B
Sacred Heart Major Seminary, MI — A
St. Ambrose U, IA — B
St. Gregory's U, Shawnee, OK — B
Saint John's U, MN — B
Saint Louis U, MO — B
Saint Mary-of-the-Woods Coll, IN — B
Saint Mary's U of Minnesota, MN — B
Silver Lake Coll, WI — B
Southwest Baptist U, MO — B
Taylor U, IN — B
Trinity Christian Coll, IL — B
Union Coll, NE — B
U of Dallas, TX — B
U of Mary, ND — B
U of Notre Dame, IN — B
U of St. Francis, IL — B
U of Saint Mary, KS — B
Valparaiso U, IN — B
Vennard Coll, IA — B
Walsh U, OH — B
Wisconsin Lutheran Coll, WI — B
Xavier U, OH — A,B

Theology and Religious Vocations Related

Crossroads Coll, MN — B
Hope Coll, MI — B
Missouri Baptist U, MO — B
Taylor U Fort Wayne, IN — B

Therapeutic Recreation

Ashland U, OH — B
Calvin Coll, MI — B
Central Michigan U, MI — B
Coll of Mount St. Joseph, OH — B
Eastern Michigan U, MI — B
Grand Valley State U, MI — B
Indiana Tech, IN — A,B
Indiana U Bloomington, IN — B
Indiana U–Purdue U Fort Wayne, IN — B
Minnesota State U Mankato, MN — B
Northland Coll, WI — B
Northwest Missouri State U, MO — B

St. Cloud State U, MN — B
Southwestern Oklahoma State U, OK — B
The U of Iowa, IA — B
U of Nebraska at Kearney, NE — B
U of Wisconsin–La Crosse, WI — B
U of Wisconsin–Milwaukee, WI — B
Winona State U, MN — B

Tibetan

U of Chicago, IL — B

Tourism and Travel Services Management

AIB Coll of Business, IA — A
Baker Coll of Flint, MI — A
Baker Coll of Muskegon, MI — A
Ball State U, IN — B
Black Hills State U, SD — A,B
Concord U, WV — B
Grand Valley State U, MI — B
International Business Coll, Fort Wayne, IN — A,B
Kaplan U, IA — A
Northeastern State U, OK — B
Ohio U, OH — A
Robert Morris Coll, IL — A
St. Cloud State U, MN — B
The U of Akron, OH — A
Western Michigan U, MI — B

Tourism and Travel Services Marketing

AIB Coll of Business, IA — A
Ohio U, OH — A
U of Central Missouri, MO — B
U of Missouri–Columbia, MO — B
Western Michigan U, MI — B

Tourism Promotion

AIB Coll of Business, IA — A
Bowling Green State U, OH — B

Toxicology

Ashland U, OH — B
Clarkson U, NY — B
Eastern Michigan U, MI — B
Minnesota State U Mankato, MN — B
U of Wisconsin–Madison, WI — B

Trade and Industrial Teacher Education

Ball State U, IN — B
Bemidji State U, MN — B
Cincinnati Christian U, OH — A
Concordia U, NE — B
Indiana State U, IN — A,B
Iowa State U of Science and Technology, IA — B
Kent State U, OH — B
Madonna U, MI — B
North Carolina Ag and Tech State U, NC — B
Northeastern State U, OK — B
Pittsburg State U, KS — B
Purdue U, IN — A
Southern Illinois U Carbondale, IL — B
Turtle Mountain Comm Coll, ND — A
U of Central Oklahoma, OK — B
U of Nebraska–Lincoln, NE — B
The U of Toledo, OH — B
U of West Florida, FL — B
Upper Iowa U, IA — B
Wayne State Coll, NE — B

Western Illinois U, IL — B
Wright State U, OH — B

Transportation and Materials Moving Related

Hope Coll, MI — B

Transportation Management

U of Wisconsin–Superior, WI — B

Transportation Technology

Baker Coll of Flint, MI — A
North Carolina Ag and Tech State U, NC — B
U of Cincinnati, OH — A,B
The U of Toledo, OH — A

Turf and Turfgrass Management

North Dakota State U, ND — B
The Ohio State U, OH — B
U of Minnesota, Crookston, MN — B

Turkish

U of Chicago, IL — B

Urban Education and Leadership

Harris-Stowe State U, MO — B
U of Missouri–Kansas City, MO — B

Urban Studies/Affairs

Aquinas Coll, MI — B
Augsburg Coll, MN — B
Calvary Bible Coll and Theological Seminary, MO — B
Cleveland State U, OH — B
The Coll of Wooster, OH — B
DePaul U, IL — B
Elmhurst Coll, IL — B
Hamline U, MN — B
Harris-Stowe State U, MO — B
Indiana U Bloomington, IN — B
Langston U, OK — B
Macalester Coll, MN — B
Minnesota State U Mankato, MN — B
Mount Mercy Coll, IA — B
Northeastern Illinois U, IL — B
Northwestern U, IL — B
Ohio Wesleyan U, OH — B
Roosevelt U, IL — B
St. Cloud State U, MN — B
Saint Louis U, MO — B
U of Cincinnati, OH — B
U of Minnesota, Duluth, MN — B
U of Minnesota, Twin Cities Campus, MN — B
U of Missouri–Kansas City, MO — B
U of New Orleans, LA — B
The U of Toledo, OH — B
U of Wisconsin–Green Bay, WI — A,B
U of Wisconsin–Madison, WI — B
U of Wisconsin–Milwaukee, WI — B
U of Wisconsin–Oshkosh, WI — B
Washington U in St. Louis, MO — B
Wittenberg U, OH — B
Wright State U, OH — B

Urdu

U of Chicago, IL — B

Majors and Degrees

Vehicle and Vehicle Parts and Accessories Marketing

Vehicle and Vehicle Parts and Accessories Marketing
Northwood U, MI — A,B

Vehicle/Equipment Operation
Baker Coll of Flint, MI — A

Veterinary/Animal Health Technology
Baker Coll of Cadillac, MI — A
Baker Coll of Jackson, MI — A
Baker Coll of Muskegon, MI — A
Michigan State U, MI — B
North Dakota State U, ND — B
Purdue U, IN — A,B
U of Nebraska–Lincoln, NE — B

Veterinary Sciences
Northland Coll, WI — B

Veterinary Technology
Argosy U, Twin Cities, Eagan, MN — A
Michigan State U, MI — B
Minnesota School of Business, MN — A
Minnesota School of Business–Brooklyn Center, MN — A
Minnesota School of Business–Plymouth, MN — A
Minnesota School of Business–Richfield, MN — A
Minnesota School of Business–St. Cloud, MN — A
Minnesota School of Business–Shakopee, MN — A
National American U, Rapid City, SD — A
Turtle Mountain Comm Coll, ND — A

Violin, Viola, Guitar and Other Stringed Instruments
Augustana Coll, IL — B
Ball State U, IN — B
Butler U, IN — B
Capital U, OH — B
Cleveland Inst of Music, OH — B
DePaul U, IL — B
Grand Valley State U, MI — B
Hastings Coll, NE — B
Heidelberg Coll, OH — B
Hope Coll, MI — B
Illinois Wesleyan U, IL — B
Lawrence U, WI — B
Northwestern U, IL — B
Northwest Missouri State U, MO — B
Oberlin Coll, OH — B
Oklahoma City U, OK — B
Otterbein Coll, OH — B
Roosevelt U, IL — B
St. Cloud State U, MN — B
The U of Akron, OH — B
U of Central Oklahoma, OK — B
U of Cincinnati, OH — B
The U of Iowa, IA — B
U of Kansas, KS — B
U of Michigan, MI — B
U of Oklahoma, OK — B
U of Wisconsin–Milwaukee, WI — B

Visual and Performing Arts
Antioch Coll, OH — B
Ashford U, IA — B
Bethel Coll, KS — B

Cameron U, OK — B
Gannon U, PA — B
Indiana U East, IN — A
Iowa State U of Science and Technology, IA — B
Loras Coll, IA — B
Missouri State U, MO — B
Northwestern U, IL — B
Ohio Northern U, OH — B
Ohio U, OH — B
Quincy U, IL — B
St. Gregory's U, Shawnee, OK — B
St. Olaf Coll, MN — B
School of the Art Inst of Chicago, IL — B
South Dakota State U, SD — B
Southeast Missouri State U, MO — B
U of Michigan, MI — B
U of Michigan–Flint, MI — B
U of Rio Grande, OH — B
U of St. Francis, IL — B
U of Saint Mary, KS — B
U of Wisconsin–Superior, WI — B
Viterbo U, WI — B
Wichita State U, KS — B

Visual and Performing Arts Related
Coll of Visual Arts, MN — B
Illinois State U, IL — B
Illinois Wesleyan U, IL — B
Ohio Northern U, OH — B
St. Cloud State U, MN — B
School of the Art Inst of Chicago, IL — B
The U of Akron, OH — B
U of Oklahoma, OK — B

Vocational Rehabilitation Counseling
Emporia State U, KS — B
Maryville U of Saint Louis, MO — B
U of Illinois at Urbana–Champaign, IL — B
U of Wisconsin–Stout, WI — B
Wright State U, OH — B

Voice and Opera
Andrews U, MI — B
Augustana Coll, IL — B
Ball State U, IN — B
Black Hills State U, SD — B
Bowling Green State U, OH — B
Butler U, IN — B
Calvary Bible Coll and Theological Seminary, MO — B
Calvin Coll, MI — B
Capital U, OH — B
Cedarville U, OH — B
Cincinnati Christian U, OH — B
Clarke Coll, IA — B
Cleveland Inst of Music, OH — B
Concordia Coll, MN — B
Concordia U, IL — B
Concordia U, NE — B
DePaul U, IL — B
Dordt Coll, IA — B
Drake U, IA — B
East Central U, OK — B
Grand Valley State U, MI — B
Hannibal-LaGrange Coll, MO — B
Hastings Coll, NE — B
Heidelberg Coll, OH — B
Hope Coll, MI — B

Huntington U, IN — B
Illinois Wesleyan U, IL — B
Indiana U Bloomington, IN — B
Indiana U–Purdue U Fort Wayne, IN — B
Judson Coll, IL — B
Langston U, OK — B
Lawrence U, WI — B
Lindenwood U, MO — B
Millikin U, IL — B
Minnesota State U Mankato, MN — B
Mount Mercy Coll, IA — B
Northeastern State U, OK — B
Northern State U, SD — B
Northwestern Coll, MN — B
Northwestern U, IL — B
Northwest Missouri State U, MO — B
Oberlin Coll, OH — B
The Ohio State U, OH — B
Ohio U, OH — B
Oklahoma Christian U, OK — B
Oklahoma City U, OK — B
Otterbein Coll, OH — B
Peru State Coll, NE — B
Roosevelt U, IL — B
St. Cloud State U, MN — B
Southwestern Oklahoma State U, OK — B
Tabor Coll, KS — B
Taylor U, IN — B
Trinity Christian Coll, IL — B
Truman State U, MO — B
The U of Akron, OH — B
U of Central Oklahoma, OK — B
U of Cincinnati, OH — B
U of Illinois at Urbana–Champaign, IL — B
The U of Iowa, IA — B
U of Kansas, KS — B
U of Michigan, MI — B
U of Nebraska at Omaha, NE — B
U of Oklahoma, OK — B
U of Sioux Falls, SD — B
U of Tulsa, OK — B
U of Wisconsin–Milwaukee, WI — B
Valparaiso U, IN — B
Washington U in St. Louis, MO — B
Winona State U, MN — B

Water Quality and Wastewater Treatment Management and Recycling Technology
Lake Superior State U, MI — A
Wright State U, OH — A

Water Resources Engineering
Central State U, OH — B

Water, Wetlands, and Marine Resources Management
U of Minnesota, Crookston, MN — B

Web/Multimedia Management and Webmaster
Academy Coll, MN — A
Dana Coll, NE — B
ITT Tech Inst, Burr Ridge, IL — A
ITT Tech Inst, Orland Park, IL — A
ITT Tech Inst, Indianapolis, IN — A
ITT Tech Inst, Newburgh, IN — A

ITT Tech Inst, Arnold, MO — A
ITT Tech Inst, Earth City, MO — A
ITT Tech Inst, NE — A
ITT Tech Inst, Green Bay, WI — A
U of St. Francis, IL — B

Web Page, Digital/Multimedia and Information Resources Design
Academy Coll, MN — A
The Art Insts International Minnesota, MN — A,B
Baker Coll of Allen Park, MI — A
Baldwin-Wallace Coll, OH — B
Bellevue U, NE — B
Capella U, MN — B
The Cleveland Inst of Art, OH — B
Columbia Coll Chicago, IL — B
Dakota State U, SD — B
Dana Coll, NE — B
DePaul U, IL — B
The Illinois Inst of Art–Chicago, IL — B
The Illinois Inst of Art–Schaumburg, IL — B
Indiana Tech, IN — A
ITT Tech Inst, Burr Ridge, IL — A
ITT Tech Inst, Mount Prospect, IL — A
ITT Tech Inst, Orland Park, IL — A
ITT Tech Inst, Fort Wayne, IN — A
ITT Tech Inst, Indianapolis, IN — A
ITT Tech Inst, Newburgh, IN — A
ITT Tech Inst, MN — A
ITT Tech Inst, Arnold, MO — A
ITT Tech Inst, Earth City, MO — A
ITT Tech Inst, NE — A
ITT Tech Inst, Tulsa, OK — A
ITT Tech Inst, Green Bay, WI — A
ITT Tech Inst, Greenfield, WI — A
Minnesota School of Business, MN — A
Minnesota School of Business–Brooklyn Center, MN — A
Minnesota School of Business–Plymouth, MN — A
Minnesota School of Business–Richfield, MN — A
Minnesota School of Business–St. Cloud, MN — A
Minnesota School of Business–Shakopee, MN — A
Robert Morris Coll, IL — A
School of the Art Inst of Chicago, IL — B
Silver Lake Coll, WI — B
U of Wisconsin–Stevens Point, WI — B
Viterbo U, WI — B

Welding Technology
Ferris State U, MI — A,B
The U of Toledo, OH — A

Western Civilization
Grand Valley State U, MI — B

Wildlife and Wildlands Science and Management
Coll of the Ozarks, MO — B
Dakota Wesleyan U, SD — B
Fort Hays State U, KS — B
Grand Valley State U, MI — B
Lake Superior State U, MI — B
Michigan Technological U, MI — B

A—associate degree; B—bachelor's degree

Missouri State U, MO — B
Northland Coll, WI — B
Northwest Missouri State U, MO — B
The Ohio State U, OH — B
Peru State Coll, NE — B
Purdue U, IN — B
South Dakota State U, SD — B
Southeastern Oklahoma State U, OK — B
Turtle Mountain Comm Coll, ND — A
U of Illinois at Urbana–Champaign, IL — B
U of Minnesota, Crookston, MN — A,B
U of Missouri–Columbia, MO — B
U of Wisconsin–Madison, WI — B
U of Wisconsin–Stevens Point, WI — B
Winona State U, MN — A,B

Wildlife Biology
Baker U, KS — B
Ball State U, IN — B
Central Christian Coll of Kansas, KS — A
Grand Valley State U, MI — B
Kansas State U, KS — B
Northeastern State U, OK — B
Northland Coll, WI — B
Northwest Missouri State U, MO — B
Ohio U, OH — B
St. Cloud State U, MN — B
U of Michigan, MI — B
U of Michigan–Flint, MI — B
U of North Dakota, ND — B
Winona State U, MN — B

Wind/Percussion Instruments
Augustana Coll, IL — B
Ball State U, IN — B
Butler U, IN — B
Capital U, OH — B
Cleveland Inst of Music, OH — B
Concordia U, IL — B
DePaul U, IL — B
Grand Valley State U, MI — B
Illinois Wesleyan U, IL — B
Indiana U Bloomington, IN — B
Lawrence U, WI — B
Minnesota State U Mankato, MN — B
Northwestern U, IL — B
Northwest Missouri State U, MO — B
Oberlin Coll, OH — B
Oklahoma Christian U, OK — B

Oklahoma City U, OK — B
Otterbein Coll, OH — B
Peru State Coll, NE — B
Roosevelt U, IL — B
Southwestern Oklahoma State U, OK — B
The U of Akron, OH — B
U of Central Oklahoma, OK — B
U of Cincinnati, OH — B
The U of Iowa, IA — B
U of Kansas, KS — B
U of Michigan, MI — B
U of Oklahoma, OK — B
U of Sioux Falls, SD — B
U of Wisconsin–Milwaukee, WI — B

Women's Studies
Albion Coll, MI — B
Antioch Coll, OH — B
Augsburg Coll, MN — B
Augustana Coll, IL — B
Beloit Coll, WI — B
Bowling Green State U, OH — B
Carleton Coll, MN — B
Case Western Reserve U, OH — B
Central Michigan U, MI — B
Coll of St. Catherine, MN — B
The Coll of Wooster, OH — B
Cornell Coll, IA — B
Denison U, OH — B
DePaul U, IL — B
DePauw U, IN — B
Earlham Coll, IN — B
Eastern Michigan U, MI — B
Grand Valley State U, MI — B
Hamline U, MN — B
Illinois Wesleyan U, IL — B
Indiana U Bloomington, IN — B
Indiana U–Purdue U Fort Wayne, IN — A,B
Indiana U South Bend, IN — B
Iowa State U of Science and Technology, IA — B
Kansas State U, KS — B
Kenyon Coll, OH — B
Knox Coll, IL — B
Loyola U Chicago, IL — B
Macalester Coll, MN — B
Marquette U, WI — B
Metropolitan State U, MN — B
Miami U, OH — B
Minnesota State U Mankato, MN — B
Nebraska Wesleyan U, NE — B
Northeastern Illinois U, IL — B
Northwestern U, IL — B
Oakland U, MI — B
Oberlin Coll, OH — B

The Ohio State U, OH — B
Ohio Wesleyan U, OH — B
Roosevelt U, IL — B
Saint Louis U, MO — B
St. Olaf Coll, MN — B
U of Illinois at Urbana–Champaign, IL — B
The U of Iowa, IA — B
U of Kansas, KS — B
U of Michigan, MI — B
U of Michigan–Dearborn, MI — B
U of Minnesota, Duluth, MN — B
U of Minnesota, Morris, MN — B
U of Minnesota, Twin Cities Campus, MN — B
U of Nebraska at Omaha, NE — B
U of Nebraska–Lincoln, NE — B
U of New Orleans, LA — B
U of Oklahoma, OK — B
U of St. Thomas, MN — B
The U of Toledo, OH — B
U of Wisconsin–Madison, WI — B
U of Wisconsin–Milwaukee, WI — B
U of Wisconsin–Whitewater, WI — B
Washington U in St. Louis, MO — B
Western Illinois U, IL — B
Western Michigan U, MI — B
Wichita State U, KS — B
Wright State U, OH — B

Wood Science and Wood Products/Pulp and Paper Technology
Miami U, OH — B
U of Minnesota, Twin Cities Campus, MN — B
U of Wisconsin–Stevens Point, WI — B
Western Michigan U, MI — B

Word Processing
Baker Coll of Allen Park, MI — A

Work and Family Studies
Miami U Hamilton, OH — B
Ursuline Coll, OH — B

Youth Ministry
Andrews U, MI — B
Benedictine Coll, KS — B
Bethel U, MN — B
Bluffton U, OH — B
Calvary Bible Coll and Theological Seminary, MO — B
Cedarville U, OH — B
Central Christian Coll of Kansas, KS — B

Concordia U Wisconsin, WI — B
Crossroads Coll, MN — B
Dordt Coll, IA — B
Grace Bible Coll, MI — B
Greenville Coll, IL — B
Kuyper Coll, MI — B
Lindenwood U, MO — B
Malone Coll, OH — B
Messenger Coll, MO — B
Mount Vernon Nazarene U, OH — B
Northwestern Coll, MN — B
Oak Hills Christian Coll, MN — B
Rochester Coll, MI — B
Saint Mary's U of Minnesota, MN — B
Spring Arbor U, MI — B
Trinity International U, IL — B
U of Indianapolis, IN — B
Vennard Coll, IA — B

Youth Services
Indiana U–Purdue U Fort Wayne, IN — B

Zoology/Animal Biology
Andrews U, MI — B
Ball State U, IN — B
Central Christian Coll of Kansas, KS — A
Kent State U, OH — B
Malone Coll, OH — B
Miami U, OH — B
Miami U Hamilton, OH — B
Miami U–Middletown Campus, OH — A
Michigan State U, MI — B
North Dakota State U, ND — B
Northeastern State U, OK — B
Northern Michigan U, MI — B
Northland Coll, WI — B
Northwest Missouri State U, MO — B
The Ohio State U, OH — B
Ohio U, OH — B
Ohio Wesleyan U, OH — B
Oklahoma State U, OK — B
Southeastern Oklahoma State U, OK — B
Southern Illinois U Carbondale, IL — B
The U of Akron, OH — B
U of Michigan, MI — B
U of Oklahoma, OK — B
U of Wisconsin–Madison, WI — B
U of Wisconsin–Milwaukee, WI — B
Winona State U, MN — B

Athletic Programs and Scholarships

Archery
Case Western Reserve U, OH	M, W
Miami U, OH	M, W
North Dakota State U, ND	M, W

Badminton
Carleton Coll, MN	M, W
The Coll of Wooster, OH	M, W
Dickinson State U, ND	M, W

Baseball
Adrian Coll, MI	M
Albion Coll, MI	M
Alma Coll, MI	M
Anderson U, IN	M
Aquinas Coll, MI	M(s)
Ashford U, IA	M(s)
Ashland U, OH	M(s)
Augsburg Coll, MN	M
Augustana Coll, IL	M
Augustana Coll, SD	M(s)
Aurora U, IL	M
Avila U, MO	M(s)
Baker U, KS	M(s)
Baldwin-Wallace Coll, OH	M
Ball State U, IN	M(s)
Barclay Coll, KS	M
Bellevue U, NE	M(s)
Beloit Coll, WI	M
Bemidji State U, MN	M(s)
Benedictine Coll, KS	M(s)
Benedictine U, IL	M
Bethany Coll, KS	M(s)
Bethany Lutheran Coll, MN	M
Bethel U, MN	M
Blackburn Coll, IL	M
Blessing-Rieman Coll of Nursing, IL	M(s), W(s)
Bluffton U, OH	M
Bowling Green State U, OH	M(s)
Bradley U, IL	M(s)
Briar Cliff U, IA	M(s)
Buena Vista U, IA	M
Butler U, IN	M(s)
Calumet Coll of Saint Joseph, IN	M
Calvin Coll, MI	M
Cameron U, OK	M(s)
Capital U, OH	M
Cardinal Stritch U, WI	M
Carleton Coll, MN	M
Carroll Coll, WI	M
Case Western Reserve U, OH	M
Cedarville U, OH	M(s)
Central Christian Coll of Kansas, KS	M(s)
Central Coll, IA	M
Central Methodist U, MO	M(s)
Central Michigan U, MI	M(s)
Chicago State U, IL	M(s)
Clarke Coll, IA	M
Clarkson U, NY	M
Cleveland State U, OH	M(s)
Coe Coll, IA	M
Coll of Mount St. Joseph, OH	M

The Coll of St. Scholastica, MN	M
Coll of the Ozarks, MO	M(s)
The Coll of Wooster, OH	M
Concordia Coll, MN	M
Concordia U, IL	M
Concordia U, MI	M(s)
Concordia U, NE	M(s)
Concordia U, St. Paul, MN	M(s)
Concordia U Wisconsin, WI	M
Concord U, WV	M(s)
Cornell Coll, IA	M
Creighton U, NE	M(s)
Crossroads Coll, MN	M
Crown Coll, MN	M
Culver-Stockton Coll, MO	M(s)
Dakota State U, SD	M
Dakota Wesleyan U, SD	M(s)
Dana Coll, NE	M(s)
Denison U, OH	M
DePauw U, IN	M
Dickinson State U, ND	M(s)
Doane Coll, NE	M(s)
Dominican U, IL	M
Dordt Coll, IA	M(s)
Drury U, MO	M(s)
Earlham Coll, IN	M
East Central U, OK	M(s)
Eastern Illinois U, IL	M(s)
Eastern Michigan U, MI	M(s)
Edgewood Coll, WI	M
Elmhurst Coll, IL	M
Emporia State U, KS	M(s)
Evangel U, MO	M(s)
Finlandia U, MI	M
Fontbonne U, MO	M
Fort Hays State U, KS	M(s)
Franklin Coll, IN	M
Gannon U, PA	M(s)
Goshen Coll, IN	M(s)
Grace Coll, IN	M(s)
Graceland U, IA	M(s)
Grand Valley State U, MI	M(s)
Grand View Coll, IA	M(s)
Greenville Coll, IL	M
Grinnell Coll, IA	M
Gustavus Adolphus Coll, MN	M
Hamline U, MN	M
Hannibal-LaGrange Coll, MO	M(s)
Hanover Coll, IN	M
Harris-Stowe State U, MO	M(s)
Hastings Coll, NE	M(s)
Heidelberg Coll, OH	M
Hesston Coll, KS	M(s)
Hillsdale Coll, MI	M
Hillsdale Free Will Baptist Coll, OK	M
Hiram Coll, OH	M
Hope Coll, MI	M
Huntington U, IN	M(s)
Illinois Coll, IL	M
Illinois Inst of Technology, IL	M(s)
Illinois State U, IL	M(s)

Illinois Wesleyan U, IL	M
Indiana State U, IN	M(s)
Indiana Tech, IN	M(s)
Indiana U Bloomington, IN	M(s)
Indiana U Northwest, IN	M
Indiana U–Purdue U Fort Wayne, IN	M(s)
Indiana U Southeast, IN	M
Indiana Wesleyan U, IN	M(s)
Iowa Wesleyan Coll, IA	M(s)
Jamestown Coll, ND	M(s)
Judson Coll, IL	M(s)
Kalamazoo Coll, MI	M
Kansas State U, KS	M(s)
Kent State U, OH	M(s)
Kenyon Coll, OH	M
Knox Coll, IL	M
Lakeland Coll, WI	M
Lawrence U, WI	M
Lewis U, IL	M(s)
Lincoln U, MO	M(s)
Lindenwood U, MO	M(s)
Loras Coll, IA	M
Luther Coll, IA	M
Macalester Coll, MN	M
MacMurray Coll, IL	M
Madonna U, MI	M(s)
Malone Coll, OH	M(s)
Manchester Coll, IN	M
Maranatha Baptist Bible Coll, WI	M
Marian Coll, IN	M(s)
Marian Coll of Fond du Lac, WI	M
Marietta Coll, OH	M
Marquette U, WI	M
Martin Luther Coll, MN	M
Maryville U of Saint Louis, MO	M
Mayville State U, ND	M(s)
McKendree Coll, IL	M(s)
Miami U, OH	M(s)
Miami U Hamilton, OH	M
Miami U–Middletown Campus, OH	M
Michigan State U, MI	M
Millikin U, IL	M
Milwaukee School of Engineering, WI	M
Minnesota State U Mankato, MN	M(s)
Minot State U, ND	M(s)
Missouri Baptist U, MO	M(s)
Missouri Southern State U, MO	M(s)
Missouri State U, MO	M(s)
Missouri Valley Coll, MO	M(s)
Missouri Western State U, MO	M(s)
Morningside Coll, IA	M(s)
Mount Marty Coll, SD	M(s)
Mount Mercy Coll, IA	M
Mount Union Coll, OH	M
Mount Vernon Nazarene U, OH	M(s)
Nebraska Wesleyan U, NE	M
Newman U, KS	M(s)
North Carolina Ag and Tech State U, NC	M(s)
North Central Coll, IL	M
North Dakota State U, ND	M(s)

M—for men; W—for women; (s)—scholarship offered

Northeastern State U, OK	M(s)	U of Cincinnati, OH	M	York Coll, NE	M(s)
Northern Illinois U, IL	M(s)	U of Dallas, TX	M	Youngstown State U, OH	M(s)
Northern State U, SD	M	U of Dayton, OH	M(s)	**Basketball**	
Northland Coll, WI	M	U of Evansville, IN	M(s)	Adrian Coll, MI	M, W
Northwestern Coll, IA	M(s)	The U of Findlay, OH	M(s)	Albion Coll, MI	M, W
Northwestern Coll, MN	M	U of Illinois at Chicago, IL	M(s)	Alma Coll, MI	M, W
Northwestern Oklahoma State U, OK	M(s)	U of Illinois at Urbana–Champaign, IL	M(s)	Alverno Coll, WI	W
Northwestern U, IL	M(s)	U of Indianapolis, IN	M(s)	Anderson U, IN	M, W
Northwest Missouri State U, MO	M(s)	The U of Iowa, IA	M(s)	Aquinas Coll, MI	M(s), W(s)
Northwood U, MI	M(s)	U of Kansas, KS	M(s)	Ashford U, IA	M(s), W(s)
Notre Dame Coll, OH	M(s)	U of Mary, ND	M(s)	Ashland U, OH	M(s), W(s)
Oakland U, MI	M(s)	U of Michigan, MI	M(s)	Augsburg Coll, MN	M, W
Oberlin Coll, OH	M	U of Minnesota, Crookston, MN	M(s)	Augustana Coll, IL	M, W
Ohio Dominican U, OH	M(s)	U of Minnesota, Duluth, MN	M(s)	Augustana Coll, SD	M(s), W(s)
Ohio Northern U, OH	M	U of Minnesota, Morris, MN	M	Aurora U, IL	M, W
The Ohio State U, OH	M	U of Minnesota, Twin Cities Campus,		Avila U, MO	M(s), W(s)
Ohio U, OH	M(s)	MN	M(s)	Baker U, KS	M(s), W(s)
Ohio U–Zanesville, OH	M	U of Missouri–Columbia, MO	M(s)	Baldwin-Wallace Coll, OH	M, W
Ohio Wesleyan U, OH	M	U of Missouri–Rolla, MO	M(s)	Ball State U, IN	M(s), W(s)
Oklahoma City U, OK	M(s)	U of Missouri–St. Louis, MO	M(s)	Baptist Bible Coll, MO	M, W
Oklahoma Panhandle State U, OK	M(s)	U of Nebraska at Kearney, NE	M(s)	Barclay Coll, KS	M, W
Oklahoma State U, OK	M(s)	U of Nebraska at Omaha, NE	M(s)	Bellevue U, NE	M(s)
Oklahoma Wesleyan U, OK	M(s)	U of Nebraska–Lincoln, NE	M(s)	Beloit Coll, WI	M, W
Oral Roberts U, OK	M(s)	U of New Orleans, LA	M(s)	Bemidji State U, MN	M(s), W(s)
Ottawa U, KS	M(s)	U of North Dakota, ND	M(s)	Benedictine Coll, KS	M(s), W(s)
Otterbein Coll, OH	M	U of Northern Iowa, IA	M(s)	Benedictine U, IL	M, W
Park U, MO	M(s)	U of Notre Dame, IN	M(s)	Bethany Coll, KS	M(s), W(s)
Peru State Coll, NE	M(s)	U of Oklahoma, OK	M(s)	Bethany Lutheran Coll, MN	M, W
Pittsburg State U, KS	M(s)	U of Rio Grande, OH	M(s)	Bethel Coll, KS	M(s), W(s)
Presentation Coll, SD	M	U of St. Francis, IL	M(s)	Bethel U, MN	M, W
Purdue U, IN	M(s)	U of Saint Francis, IN	M(s)	Blackburn Coll, IL	M, W
Quincy U, IL	M(s)	U of Saint Mary, KS	M(s)	Black Hills State U, SD	M(s), W(s)
Research Coll of Nursing, MO	M(s)	U of St. Thomas, MN	M	Blessing-Rieman Coll of Nursing, IL	M(s), W(s)
Ripon Coll, WI	M	U of Science and Arts of Oklahoma,		Bluffton U, OH	M, W
Robert Morris Coll, IL	M(s)	OK	M(s)	Bowling Green State U, OH	M(s), W(s)
Rochester Coll, MI	M(s)	U of Sioux Falls, SD	M(s)	Bradley U, IL	M(s), W(s)
Rockford Coll, IL	M	The U of South Dakota, SD	M(s)	Briar Cliff U, IA	M(s), W(s)
Rockhurst U, MO	M(s)	U of Southern Indiana, IN	M(s)	Buena Vista U, IA	M, W
Rose-Hulman Inst of Technology, IN	M	The U of Toledo, OH	M(s)	Butler U, IN	M(s), W(s)
Saginaw Valley State U, MI	M(s)	U of West Florida, FL	M(s)	Calumet Coll of Saint Joseph, IN	M, W
St. Ambrose U, IA	M(s)	U of Wisconsin–La Crosse, WI	M	Calvary Bible Coll and Theological	
St. Cloud State U, MN	M(s)	U of Wisconsin–Milwaukee, WI	M	Seminary, MO	M, W
St. Gregory's U, Shawnee, OK	M(s)	U of Wisconsin–Oshkosh, WI	M	Calvin Coll, MI	M, W
Saint John's U, MN	M	U of Wisconsin–Parkside, WI	M(s)	Cameron U, OK	M(s), W(s)
Saint Joseph's Coll, IN	M(s)	U of Wisconsin–Platteville, WI	M	Capital U, OH	M, W
Saint Louis U, MO	M(s)	U of Wisconsin–Stevens Point, WI	M	Cardinal Stritch U, WI	M, W
Saint Mary's U of Minnesota, MN	M	U of Wisconsin–Stout, WI	M	Carleton Coll, MN	M, W
St. Norbert Coll, WI	M	U of Wisconsin–Superior, WI	M	Carroll Coll, WI	M, W
St. Olaf Coll, MN	M	U of Wisconsin–Whitewater, WI	M	Case Western Reserve U, OH	M, W
Saint Xavier U, IL	M(s)	Upper Iowa U, IA	M	Cedarville U, OH	M(s), W(s)
Shawnee State U, OH	M	Valley City State U, ND	M(s)	Central Christian Coll of Kansas, KS	M(s), W(s)
Simpson Coll, IA	M	Valparaiso U, IN	M(s)	Central Coll, IA	M, W
South Dakota State U, SD	M(s)	Viterbo U, WI	M(s)	Central Methodist U, MO	M(s), W(s)
Southeastern Oklahoma State U, OK	M(s)	Wabash Coll, IN	M	Central Michigan U, MI	M(s), W(s)
Southeast Missouri State U, MO	M(s)	Waldorf Coll, IA	M(s)	Central State U, OH	M(s), W(s)
Southern Illinois U Carbondale, IL	M(s)	Walsh U, OH	M(s)	Chicago State U, IL	M(s), W(s)
Southern Illinois U Edwardsville, IL	M(s)	Wartburg Coll, IA	M	Cincinnati Christian U, OH	M, W
Southern Methodist U, TX	M	Washburn U, KS	M(s)	Clarke Coll, IA	M, W
Southwest Baptist U, MO	M(s)	Washington U in St. Louis, MO	M	Clarkson U, NY	M, W
Southwestern Oklahoma State U, OK	M(s)	Wayne State Coll, NE	M(s)	Cleveland State U, OH	M(s), W(s)
Southwest Minnesota State U, MN	M(s)	Webster U, MO	M	Coe Coll, IA	M, W
Spring Arbor U, MI	M(s)	Western Illinois U, IL	M(s)	Coll of Mount St. Joseph, OH	M, W
Sterling Coll, KS	M(s)	Western Michigan U, MI	M(s)	Coll of Saint Benedict, MN	W
Tabor Coll, KS	M(s)	Westminster Coll, MO	M	Coll of St. Catherine, MN	W
Taylor U, IN	M(s)	Wheaton Coll, IL	M	Coll of Saint Mary, NE	W(s)
Tiffin U, OH	M(s)	Wichita State U, KS	M(s)	The Coll of St. Scholastica, MN	M, W
Transylvania U, KY	M	William Jewell Coll, MO	M(s)	Coll of the Ozarks, MO	M(s), W(s)
Trinity Christian Coll, IL	M(s)	William Penn U, IA	M(s)	The Coll of Wooster, OH	M, W
Trinity International U, IL	M(s)	William Woods U, MO	M(s)	Columbia Coll, MO	M(s), W(s)
Tri-State U, IN	M	Wilmington Coll, OH	M	Concordia Coll, MN	M, W
Truman State U, MO	M(s)	Winona State U, MN	M(s)	Concordia U, IL	M, W
The U of Akron, OH	M(s)	Wisconsin Lutheran Coll, WI	M	Concordia U, MI	M(s), W(s)
U of Central Missouri, MO	M(s)	Wittenberg U, OH	M	Concordia U, NE	M(s), W(s)
U of Central Oklahoma, OK	M(s)	Wright State U, OH	M(s)	Concordia U, St. Paul, MN	M(s), W(s)
U of Charleston, WV	M(s)	Xavier U, OH	M(s)	Concordia U Wisconsin, WI	M, W
U of Chicago, IL	M			Concord U, WV	M(s), W(s)

Athletic Programs and Scholarships
Basketball

Cornell Coll, IA	M, W	Jamestown Coll, ND	M(s), W(s)	Oberlin Coll, OH	M, W
Cornerstone U, MI	M(s), W(s)	Judson Coll, IL	M(s), W(s)	Ohio Dominican U, OH	M(s), W(s)
Cottey Coll, MO	W	Kalamazoo Coll, MI	M, W	Ohio Northern·U, OH	M, W
Creighton U, NE	M(s), W(s)	Kansas State U, KS	M(s), W(s)	The Ohio State U, OH	M(s), W(s)
Crossroads Coll, MN	M, W	Kent State U, OH	M(s), W(s)	The Ohio State U at Lima, OH	M, W
Crown Coll, MN	M, W	Kenyon Coll, OH	M, W	Ohio U, OH	M(s), W(s)
Culver-Stockton Coll, MO	M(s), W(s)	Knox Coll, IL	M, W	Ohio U–Zanesville, OH	M, W
Dakota State U, SD	M(s), W(s)	Lake Forest Coll, IL	M, W	Ohio Wesleyan U, OH	M, W
Dakota Wesleyan U, SD	M(s), W(s)	Lakeland Coll, WI	M, W	Oklahoma Christian U, OK	M(s), W(s)
Dana Coll, NE	M(s), W(s)	Lake Superior State U, MI	M(s), W(s)	Oklahoma City U, OK	M(s), W(s)
Denison U, OH	M, W	Langston U, OK	M(s), W(s)	Oklahoma Panhandle State U, OK	M(s), W(s)
DePaul U, IL	M(s), W(s)	Lawrence U, WI	M, W	Oklahoma State U, OK	M(s), W(s)
DePauw U, IN	M, W	Lewis Coll of Business, MI	M	Oklahoma Wesleyan U, OK	M(s), W(s)
Dickinson State U, ND	M(s), W(s)	Lewis U, IL	M(s), W(s)	Oral Roberts U, OK	M(s), W(s)
Doane Coll, NE	M(s), W(s)	Lincoln U, MO	M(s), W(s)	Ottawa U, KS	M(s), W(s)
Dominican U, IL	M, W	Lindenwood U, MO	M(s), W(s)	Otterbein Coll, OH	M, W
Dordt Coll, IA	M(s), W(s)	Loras Coll, IA	M, W	Ozark Christian Coll, MO	M, W
Drake U, IA	M(s), W(s)	Loyola U Chicago, IL	M(s), W(s)	Park U, MO	M(s), W(s)
Drury U, MO	M(s)	Luther Coll, IA	M, W	Peru State Coll, NE	M(s), W(s)
Earlham Coll, IN	M, W	Macalester Coll, MN	M, W	Pittsburg State U, KS	M(s), W(s)
East Central U, OK	M(s), W(s)	MacMurray Coll, IL	M, W	Presentation Coll, SD	M, W
Eastern Illinois U, IL	M(s), W(s)	Madonna U, MI	M(s), W(s)	Purdue U, IN	M(s), W(s)
Eastern Michigan U, MI	M(s), W(s)	Malone Coll, OH	M(s), W(s)	Purdue U Calumet, IN	M(s), W(s)
East-West U, IL	M	Manchester Coll, IN	M, W	Quincy U, IL	M(s), W(s)
Edgewood Coll, WI	M, W	Maranatha Baptist Bible Coll, WI	M, W	Research Coll of Nursing, MO	M(s), W(s)
Elmhurst Coll, IL	M, W	Marian Coll, IN	M(s), W(s)	Ripon Coll, WI	M, W
Emporia State U, KS	M(s), W(s)	Marian Coll of Fond du Lac, WI	M, W	Robert Morris Coll, IL	M(s), W(s)
Evangel U, MO	M(s), W(s)	Marietta Coll, OH	M, W	Rochester Coll, MI	M(s), W(s)
Faith Baptist Bible Coll and		Marquette U, WI	M(s), W(s)	Rockford Coll, IL	M, W
Theological Seminary, IA	M, W	Martin Luther Coll, MN	M, W	Rockhurst U, MO	M(s), W(s)
Ferris State U, MI	M(s), W(s)	Marygrove Coll, MI	M, W	Rose-Hulman Inst of Technology, IN	M, W
Finlandia U, MI	M, W	Maryville U of Saint Louis, MO	M, W	Saginaw Valley State U, MI	M(s), W(s)
Fontbonne U, MO	M, W	Mayville State U, ND	M(s), W(s)	St. Ambrose U, IA	M(s), W(s)
Fort Berthold Comm Coll, ND	M, W	McKendree Coll, IL	M(s), W(s)	St. Cloud State U, MN	M(s), W(s)
Fort Hays State U, KS	M(s), W(s)	Messenger Coll, MO	M, W	St. Gregory's U, Shawnee, OK	M(s), W(s)
Franklin Coll, IN	M, W	Miami U, OH	M(s), W(s)	Saint John's U, MN	M
Gannon U, PA	M(s), W(s)	Miami U Hamilton, OH	M, W	Saint Joseph's Coll, IN	M(s), W(s)
Goshen Coll, IN	M(s), W(s)	Miami U–Middletown Campus, OH	M, W	St. Louis Coll of Pharmacy, MO	M, W
Grace Bible Coll, MI·	M, W	Michigan State U, MI	M(s), W(s)	Saint Louis U, MO	M(s), W(s)
Grace Coll, IN	M(s), W(s)	Michigan Technological U, MI	M(s), W(s)	Saint Mary-of-the-Woods Coll, IN	W(s)
Graceland U, IA	M(s), W(s)	Millikin U, IL	M, W	Saint Mary's Coll, IN	W
Grand Valley State U, MI	M(s), W(s)	Milwaukee School of Engineering, WI	M, W	Saint Mary's U of Minnesota, MN	M, W
Grand View Coll, IA	M(s), W(s)	Minnesota State U Mankato, MN	M(s), W(s)	St. Norbert Coll, WI	M, W
Great Lakes Christian Coll, MI	M, W	Minot State U, ND	M(s), W(s)	St. Olaf Coll, MN	M, W
Greenville Coll, IL	M, W	Missouri Baptist U, MO	M(s), W(s)	Saint Xavier U, IL	M(s)
Grinnell Coll, IA	M, W	Missouri Southern State U, MO	M(s), W(s)	Shawnee State U, OH	M, W
Gustavus Adolphus Coll, MN	M, W	Missouri State U, MO	M(s), W(s)	Silver Lake Coll, WI	W
Hamline U, MN	M, W	Missouri Valley Coll, MO	M(s), W(s)	Simpson Coll, IA	M, W
Hannibal-LaGrange Coll, MO	M(s), W(s)	Missouri Western State U, MO	M(s), W(s)	Sitting Bull Coll, ND	M, W
Hanover Coll, IN	M, W	Morningside Coll, IA	M(s), W(s)	South Dakota School of Mines and	
Harris-Stowe State U, MO	M(s), W(s)	Mount Marty Coll, SD	M(s), W(s)	Technology, SD	M(s), W(s)
Hastings Coll, NE	M(s), W(s)	Mount Mary Coll, WI	W	South Dakota State U, SD	M(s), W(s)
Heidelberg Coll, OH	M, W	Mount Mercy Coll, IA	M, W	Southeastern Oklahoma State U, OK	M(s), W(s)
Hesston Coll, KS	M(s), W(s)	Mount Union Coll, OH	M, W	Southeast Missouri State U, MO	M(s), W(s)
Hillsdale Coll, MI	M, W	Mount Vernon Nazarene U, OH	M(s), W(s)	Southern Illinois U Carbondale, IL	M(s), W(s)
Hillsdale Free Will Baptist Coll, OK	M, W	Nebraska Wesleyan U, NE	M, W	Southern Illinois U Edwardsville, IL	M(s), W(s)
Hiram Coll, OH	M, W	Newman U, KS	M(s), W(s)	Southern Methodist U, TX	M(s), W(s)
Holy Cross Coll, IN	M	North Carolina Ag and Tech State U,		Southwest Baptist U, MO	M(s), W(s)
Hope Coll, MI	M, W	NC	M(s), W(s)	Southwestern Coll, KS	M(s), W(s)
Huntington U, IN	M(s), W(s)	North Central Coll, IL	M, W	Southwestern Oklahoma State U, OK	M(s), W(s)
Illinois Inst of Technology, IL	M(s), W(s)	North Dakota State U, ND	M(s), W(s)	Southwest Minnesota State U, MN	M(s), W(s)
Illinois State U, IL	M(s), W(s)	Northeastern State U, OK	M(s), W(s)	Spring Arbor U, MI	M(s), W(s)
Illinois Wesleyan U, IL	M, W	Northern Illinois U, IL	M(s), W(s)	Stephens Coll, MO	W
Indiana State U, IN	M(s), W(s)	Northern Michigan U, MI	M, W	Sterling Coll, KS	M(s), W(s)
Indiana Tech, IN	M(s), W(s)	Northern State U, SD	M(s), W(s)	Tabor Coll, KS	M(s), W(s)
Indiana U Bloomington, IN	M(s), W(s)	Northland Coll, WI	M, W	Taylor U, IN	M(s), W(s)
Indiana U Northwest, IN	M	Northwestern Coll, IA	M(s), W(s)	Taylor U Fort Wayne, IN	M, W
Indiana U–Purdue U Fort Wayne, IN	M(s), W(s)	Northwestern Coll, MN	M, W	Tiffin U, OH	M(s), W(s)
Indiana U–Purdue U Indianapolis, IN	M(s), W(s)	Northwestern Oklahoma State U, OK	M(s), W(s)	Transylvania U, KY	M, W
Indiana U South Bend, IN	M(s), W(s)	Northwestern U, IL	M(s), W(s)	Trinity Christian Coll, IL	M(s), W(s)
Indiana U Southeast, IN	M(s), W(s)	Northwest Missouri State U, MO	M(s), W(s)	Trinity International U, IL	M(s), W(s)
Indiana Wesleyan U, IN	M(s), W(s)	Northwood U, MI	M(s), W(s)	Tri-State U, IN	M, W
Iowa State U of Science and		Notre Dame Coll, OH	M(s), W(s)	Truman State U, MO	M(s), W(s)
Technology, IA	M(s), W(s)	Oak Hills Christian Coll, MN	M, W	Union Coll, NE	M, W
Iowa Wesleyan Coll, IA	M(s), W(s)	Oakland U, MI	M(s), W(s)	The U of Akron, OH	M(s), W(s)

M—for men; W—for women; (s)—scholarship offered

U of Central Missouri, MO	M(s), W(s)
U of Central Oklahoma, OK	M(s), W(s)
U of Charleston, WV	M(s), W(s)
U of Chicago, IL	M, W
U of Cincinnati, OH	M(s), W(s)
U of Dallas, TX	M, W
U of Dayton, OH	M(s), W(s)
U of Evansville, IN	M(s), W(s)
The U of Findlay, OH	M(s), W(s)
U of Illinois at Chicago, IL	M(s), W(s)
U of Illinois at Springfield, IL	M(s), W(s)
U of Illinois at Urbana–Champaign, IL	M(s), W(s)
U of Indianapolis, IN	M(s), W(s)
The U of Iowa, IA	M(s), W(s)
U of Kansas, KS	M(s), W(s)
U of Mary, ND	M(s), W(s)
U of Michigan, MI	M(s), W(s)
U of Michigan–Dearborn, MI	M(s), W(s)
U of Minnesota, Crookston, MN	M(s), W(s)
U of Minnesota, Duluth, MN	M(s), W(s)
U of Minnesota, Morris, MN	M, W
U of Minnesota, Twin Cities Campus, MN	M(s), W(s)
U of Missouri–Columbia, MO	M(s), W(s)
U of Missouri–Kansas City, MO	M(s), W(s)
U of Missouri–Rolla, MO	M(s), W(s)
U of Missouri–St. Louis, MO	M(s), W(s)
U of Nebraska at Kearney, NE	M(s), W(s)
U of Nebraska at Omaha, NE	M(s), W(s)
U of Nebraska–Lincoln, NE	M(s), W(s)
U of New Orleans, LA	M(s), W(s)
U of North Dakota, ND	M(s), W(s)
U of Northern Iowa, IA	M(s), W(s)
U of Notre Dame, IN	M(s), W(s)
U of Oklahoma, OK	M(s), W(s)
U of Rio Grande, OH	M(s), W(s)
U of St. Francis, IL	M(s), W(s)
U of Saint Francis, IN	M(s), W(s)
U of Saint Mary, KS	M(s), W(s)
U of St. Thomas, MN	M, W
U of Science and Arts of Oklahoma, OK	M(s), W(s)
U of Sioux Falls, SD	M(s), W(s)
The U of South Dakota, SD	M(s), W(s)
U of Southern Indiana, IN	M(s), W(s)
The U of Toledo, OH	M(s), W(s)
U of Tulsa, OK	M(s), W(s)
U of West Florida, FL	M(s), W(s)
U of Wisconsin–Eau Claire, WI	M, W
U of Wisconsin–Green Bay, WI	M(s), W(s)
U of Wisconsin–La Crosse, WI	M, W
U of Wisconsin–Madison, WI	M(s), W(s)
U of Wisconsin–Milwaukee, WI	M(s), W(s)
U of Wisconsin–Oshkosh, WI	M, W
U of Wisconsin–Parkside, WI	M(s), W(s)
U of Wisconsin–Platteville, WI	M, W
U of Wisconsin–River Falls, WI	M, W
U of Wisconsin–Stevens Point, WI	M, W
U of Wisconsin–Stout, WI	M, W
U of Wisconsin–Superior, WI	M, W
U of Wisconsin–Whitewater, WI	M, W
Upper Iowa U, IA	M, W
Ursuline Coll, OH	W(s)
Valley City State U, ND	M(s), W(s)
Valparaiso U, IN	M(s), W(s)
Vennard Coll, IA	M, W
Viterbo U, WI	M(s), W(s)
Wabash Coll, IN	M
Waldorf Coll, IA	M(s), W(s)
Walsh U, OH	M(s), W(s)
Wartburg Coll, IA	M, W
Washburn U, KS	M(s), W(s)
Washington U in St. Louis, MO	M, W
Wayne State Coll, NE	M(s), W(s)
Webster U, MO	M, W
Western Illinois U, IL	M(s), W(s)

Western Michigan U, MI	M(s), W(s)
Westminster Coll, MO	M, W
Wheaton Coll, IL	M, W
Wichita State U, KS	M(s), W(s)
William Jewell Coll, MO	M(s), W(s)
William Penn U, IA	M(s), W(s)
William Woods U, MO	W(s)
Wilmington Coll, OH	M, W
Winona State U, MN	M(s), W(s)
Wisconsin Lutheran Coll, WI	M, W
Wittenberg U, OH	M, W
Wright State U, OH	M(s), W(s)
Xavier U, OH	M(s), W(s)
York Coll, NE	M(s), W(s)
Youngstown State U, OH	M(s), W(s)

Bowling

Clarkson U, NY	M, W
Fontbonne U, MO	W
Lindenwood U, MO	M(s), W(s)
McKendree Coll, IL	M(s), W(s)
Missouri Baptist U, MO	M, W
Missouri State U, MO	M, W
Newman U, KS	M(s), W(s)
North Dakota State U, ND	M, W
Robert Morris Coll, IL	M(s)
Saginaw Valley State U, MI	M(s)
St. Cloud State U, MN	M, W
U of Central Missouri, MO	M, W
U of Minnesota, Duluth, MN	M, W
U of Nebraska–Lincoln, NE	M
U of Wisconsin–Platteville, WI	M, W
U of Wisconsin–Whitewater, WI	M, W
Wichita State U, KS	M, W
Winona State U, MN	M, W

Cheerleading

Albion Coll, MI	M, W
Augustana Coll, IL	M, W
Augustana Coll, SD	W
Avila U, MO	W(s)
Baker U, KS	M(s), W(s)
Barclay Coll, KS	M, W
Benedictine Coll, KS	M(s), W(s)
Bethel U, MN	W
Blackburn Coll, IL	M, W
Bradley U, IL	M, W
Calumet Coll of Saint Joseph, IN	W
Calvary Bible Coll and Theological Seminary, MO	W
Case Western Reserve U, OH	M, W
Central Christian Coll of Kansas, KS	M(s), W(s)
Central State U, OH	M(s), W(s)
Coe Coll, IA	W
Coll of Mount St. Joseph, OH	W
Coll of the Ozarks, MO	M, W
The Coll of Wooster, OH	W
Columbia Coll, MO	W
Concordia Coll, MN	W
Concordia U, IL	W
Concord U, WV	M, W
Culver-Stockton Coll, MO	M(s), W(s)
Dakota State U, SD	M, W
Dakota Wesleyan U, SD	M(s), W(s)
DePauw U, IN	M, W
Dickinson State U, ND	M, W
Drake U, IA	M(s), W(s)
Earlham Coll, IN	M, W
East Central U, OK	M, W
Emporia State U, KS	M(s), W(s)
Ferris State U, MI	M, W
Fontbonne U, MO	W
Grace Coll, IN	M(s), W(s)
Grand Valley State U, MI	M, W
Hannibal-LaGrange Coll, MO	M(s), W(s)
Harris-Stowe State U, MO	M(s), W(s)
Hope Coll, MI	M, W

Illinois Coll, IL	W
Illinois Wesleyan U, IL	M, W
Indiana Tech, IN	M(s), W(s)
Indiana Wesleyan U, IN	M(s), W(s)
Lake Forest Coll, IL	M, W
Lewis U, IL	M, W
Lindenwood U, MO	M(s), W(s)
MacMurray Coll, IL	M, W
Malone Coll, OH	M, W
Manchester Coll, IN	M, W
Marian Coll, IN	M(s), W(s)
Marietta Coll, OH	W
Marquette U, WI	M, W
McKendree Coll, IL	M(s), W(s)
Miami U Hamilton, OH	W
Michigan State U, MI	M, W
Milwaukee School of Engineering, WI	M, W
Minnesota State U Mankato, MN	M, W
Minot State U, ND	W
Missouri Valley Coll, MO	W
Mount Mercy Coll, IA	W
Mount Union Coll, OH	W
Newman U, KS	M(s), W(s)
North Central Coll, IL	W
North Dakota State U, ND	M, W
Northeastern State U, OK	M, W
Northern Michigan U, MI	M, W
Northwestern Coll, MN	W
Northwestern Oklahoma State U, OK	M(s), W(s)
Northwestern U, IL	M, W
Northwest Missouri State U, MO	M(s), W(s)
Northwood U, MI	M(s), W(s)
Oberlin Coll, OH	W
Ohio Dominican U, OH	M, W
The Ohio State U, OH	M, W
Ohio U, OH	M, W
Oklahoma City U, OK	M(s), W(s)
Oklahoma Wesleyan U, OK	W
Otterbein Coll, OH	M, W
Ozark Christian Coll, MO	M, W
Purdue U North Central, IN	M, W
Ripon Coll, WI	W
Rose-Hulman Inst of Technology, IN	M, W
Saginaw Valley State U, MI	M, W
St. Ambrose U, IA	W(s)
St. Cloud State U, MN	M, W
Saint Joseph's Coll, IN	M, W
Simpson Coll, IA	M, W
Southeast Missouri State U, MO	M(s), W(s)
Southern Illinois U Carbondale, IL	M(s), W(s)
Southwest Baptist U, MO	M, W
Southwestern Coll, KS	M(s), W(s)
Southwestern Oklahoma State U, OK	M, W
Sterling Coll, KS	W(s)
Tabor Coll, KS	M, W(s)
Taylor U Fort Wayne, IN	M, W
Tiffin U, OH	M(s), W(s)
Transylvania U, KY	M, W
Truman State U, MO	M, W
The U of Akron, OH	M, W
U of Charleston, WV	W(s)
U of Cincinnati, OH	M, W
U of Illinois at Urbana–Champaign, IL	M, W
U of Minnesota, Duluth, MN	W
U of Missouri–Kansas City, MO	W
U of St. Francis, IL	W
U of Saint Francis, IN	M(s), W(s)
U of Science and Arts of Oklahoma, OK	M(s), W(s)
U of Sioux Falls, SD	W(s)
U of Southern Indiana, IN	M, W
U of Wisconsin–Madison, WI	M, W
U of Wisconsin–Platteville, WI	M, W
U of Wisconsin–Superior, WI	M, W
U of Wisconsin–Whitewater, WI	M, W
Walsh U, OH	W

Athletic Programs and Scholarships

Cheerleading

Wartburg Coll, IA	W
Washburn U, KS	M(s), W(s)
Wheaton Coll, IL	W
Wichita State U, KS	M, W
William Jewell Coll, MO	M(s), W(s)
William Penn U, IA	M(s), W(s)
Wittenberg U, OH	M, W

Crew

Beloit Coll, WI	M, W
Bowling Green State U, OH	M
Butler U, IN	M, W
Carleton Coll, MN	M, W
Case Western Reserve U, OH	M, W
Coll of Saint Benedict, MN	W
Creighton U, NE	W(s)
Denison U, OH	M
DePauw U, IN	M, W
Drake U, IA	W
Eastern Michigan U, MI	W(s)
Grand Valley State U, MI	M, W
Holy Cross Coll, IN	M, W
Indiana U Bloomington, IN	W(s)
Kansas State U, KS	W(s)
Lawrence U, WI	M, W
Macalester Coll, MN	M, W
Marietta Coll, OH	M, W
Marquette U, WI	M, W
Michigan State U, MI	W(s)
Northern Michigan U, MI	M, W
Oklahoma City U, OK	M, W
St. Cloud State U, MN	M, W
Saint John's U, MN	M
Saint Louis U, MO	M, W
Saint Mary's Coll, IN	W
Southern Methodist U, TX	M, W(s)
U of Charleston, WV	M(s), W(s)
U of Cincinnati, OH	M, W
U of Dayton, OH	W
The U of Iowa, IA	M, W(s)
U of Kansas, KS	M, W(s)
U of Michigan, MI	W
U of Nebraska–Lincoln, NE	M, W
U of Notre Dame, IN	W(s)
U of St. Thomas, MN	M, W
U of Tulsa, OK	W(s)
Wabash Coll, IN	M
Washburn U, KS	M, W
Washington U in St. Louis, MO	M, W
Wheaton Coll, IL	M, W
Wichita State U, KS	M, W
Wittenberg U, OH	M, W
Xavier U, OH	M, W

Cross-Country Running

Adrian Coll, MI	M, W
Albion Coll, MI	M, W
Alma Coll, MI	M, W
Alverno Coll, WI	W
Anderson U, IN	M, W
Aquinas Coll, MI	M(s), W(s)
Ashford U, IA	M(s), W(s)
Ashland U, OH	M(s), W(s)
Augsburg Coll, MN	M, W
Augustana Coll, IL	M, W
Augustana Coll, SD	M(s), W(s)
Baker U, KS	M(s), W(s)
Baldwin-Wallace Coll, OH	M, W
Ball State U, IN	M(s), W(s)
Beloit Coll, WI	M, W
Bemidji State U, MN	W
Benedictine Coll, KS	M(s), W(s)
Benedictine U, IL	M, W
Bethany Coll, KS	M(s), W(s)
Bethel Coll, KS	M(s), W(s)
Bethel U, MN	M, W

Blackburn Coll, IL	M, W
Black Hills State U, SD	M(s), W(s)
Bluffton U, OH	M, W
Bowling Green State U, OH	M(s), W(s)
Bradley U, IL	M(s), W(s)
Briar Cliff U, IA	M(s), W(s)
Buena Vista U, IA	M, W
Butler U, IN	M(s), W(s)
Calumet Coll of Saint Joseph, IN	M, W
Calvin Coll, MI	M, W
Cameron U, OK	M(s)
Capital U, OH	M, W
Cardinal Stritch U, WI	M, W
Carleton Coll, MN	M, W
Carroll Coll, WI	M, W
Case Western Reserve U, OH	M, W
Cedarville U, OH	M(s), W(s)
Central Christian Coll of Kansas, KS	M(s), W(s)
Central Coll, IA	M, W
Central Methodist U, MO	M(s), W(s)
Central Michigan U, MI	M(s), W(s)
Central State U, OH	M(s), W(s)
Chicago State U, IL	M(s), W(s)
Clarke Coll, IA	M, W
Clarkson U, NY	M, W
Cleveland State U, OH	W(s)
Coe Coll, IA	M, W
Coll of Mount St. Joseph, OH	M, W
Coll of Saint Benedict, MN	W
Coll of St. Catherine, MN	W
Coll of Saint Mary, NE	W(s)
The Coll of St. Scholastica, MN	M, W
The Coll of Wooster, OH	M, W
Concordia Coll, MN	M, W
Concordia U, IL	M, W
Concordia U, MI	M(s), W(s)
Concordia U, NE	M(s), W(s)
Concordia U, St. Paul, MN	M(s), W(s)
Concordia U Wisconsin, WI	M, W
Concord U, WV	M(s), W(s)
Cornell Coll, IA	M, W
Cornerstone U, MI	M(s), W(s)
Creighton U, NE	M(s), W(s)
Crown Coll, MN	M, W
Dakota State U, SD	M(s), W(s)
Dakota Wesleyan U, SD	M(s), W(s)
Dana Coll, NE	M(s), W(s)
Denison U, OH	M, W
DePaul U, IL	M(s), W(s)
DePauw U, IN	M, W
Dickinson State U, ND	M(s), W(s)
Doane Coll, NE	M(s), W(s)
Dominican U, IL	M, W
Dordt Coll, IA	M(s), W(s)
Drake U, IA	M(s), W(s)
Drury U, MO	M(s), W(s)
Earlham Coll, IN	M, W
East Central U, OK	M(s), W(s)
Eastern Illinois U, IL	M(s), W(s)
Eastern Michigan U, MI	M(s), W(s)
Edgewood Coll, WI	M, W
Elmhurst Coll, IL	M, W
Emporia State U, KS	M(s), W(s)
Evangel U, MO	M(s), W(s)
Ferris State U, MI	M(s), W(s)
Finlandia U, MI	M, W
Fontbonne U, MO	M, W
Fort Berthold Comm Coll, ND	M, W
Fort Hays State U, KS	M(s), W(s)
Franklin Coll, IN	M, W
Gannon U, PA	M(s), W(s)
Goshen Coll, IN	M(s), W(s)
Grace Coll, IN	M(s), W(s)
Graceland U, IA	M(s), W(s)
Grand Valley State U, MI	M(s), W(s)

Grand View Coll, IA	M(s), W(s)
Greenville Coll, IL	M, W
Grinnell Coll, IA	M, W
Gustavus Adolphus Coll, MN	M, W
Hamline U, MN	M, W
Hannibal-LaGrange Coll, MO	M(s), W(s)
Hanover Coll, IN	M, W
Hastings Coll, NE	M(s), W(s)
Heidelberg Coll, OH	M, W
Hiram Coll, OH	M, W
Holy Cross Coll, IN	M, W
Hope Coll, MI	M, W
Huntington U, IN	M(s), W(s)
Illinois Coll, IL	M, W
Illinois Inst of Technology, IL	M(s), W(s)
Illinois State U, IL	M(s), W(s)
Illinois Wesleyan U, IL	M, W
Indiana State U, IN	M(s), W(s)
Indiana U Bloomington, IN	M(s), W(s)
Indiana U–Purdue U Fort Wayne, IN	M(s), W(s)
Indiana U–Purdue U Indianapolis, IN	M(s), W(s)
Indiana Wesleyan U, IN	M(s), W(s)
Iowa State U of Science and Technology, IA	M(s), W(s)
Jamestown Coll, ND	M(s), W(s)
Judson Coll, IL	M(s), W(s)
Kalamazoo Coll, MI	M, W
Kansas State U, KS	M(s), W(s)
Kent State U, OH	M(s), W(s)
Kenyon Coll, OH	M, W
Knox Coll, IL	M, W
Lake Forest Coll, IL	M, W
Lakeland Coll, WI	M, W
Lake Superior State U, MI	M(s), W(s)
Lawrence U, WI	M, W
Lewis U, IL	M(s), W(s)
Lincoln U, MO	W(s)
Lindenwood U, MO	M(s), W(s)
Loras Coll, IA	M, W
Loyola U Chicago, IL	M(s), W(s)
Luther Coll, IA	M, W
Macalester Coll, MN	M, W
MacMurray Coll, IL	M, W
Madonna U, MI	M, W
Malone Coll, OH	M(s), W(s)
Manchester Coll, IN	M, W
Maranatha Baptist Bible Coll, WI	M, W
Marian Coll, IN	M(s), W(s)
Marietta Coll, OH	M, W
Marquette U, WI	M(s), W(s)
Martin Luther Coll, MN	M, W
Maryville U of Saint Louis, MO	M, W
McKendree Coll, IL	M(s), W(s)
Miami U, OH	M(s), W(s)
Michigan State U, MI	M(s), W(s)
Michigan Technological U, MI	M, W
Millikin U, IL	M, W
Milwaukee School of Engineering, WI	M, W
Minnesota State U Mankato, MN	M(s), W(s)
Minot State U, ND	M(s), W(s)
Missouri Baptist U, MO	M(s), W(s)
Missouri Southern State U, MO	M(s), W(s)
Missouri State U, MO	M(s), W(s)
Missouri Valley Coll, MO	M(s), W(s)
Morningside Coll, IA	M(s), W(s)
Mount Marty Coll, SD	M(s), W(s)
Mount Mercy Coll, IA	M, W
Mount Union Coll, OH	M, W
Mount Vernon Nazarene U, OH	M, W
Nebraska Wesleyan U, NE	M, W
Newman U, KS	M(s), W(s)
North Carolina Ag and Tech State U, NC	M(s), W(s)
North Central Coll, IL	M, W
North Dakota State U, ND	M(s), W(s)

M—for men; W—for women; (s)—scholarship offered

Northern Illinois U, IL	W
Northern Michigan U, MI	W
Northern State U, SD	M(s), W(s)
Northland Coll, WI	M, W
Northwestern Coll, IA	M(s), W(s)
Northwestern Coll, MN	M, W
Northwestern Oklahoma State U, OK	M(s), W(s)
Northwestern U, IL	W(s)
Northwest Missouri State U, MO	M(s), W(s)
Northwood U, MI	M(s), W(s)
Notre Dame Coll, OH	M(s), W(s)
Oakland U, MI	M(s), W(s)
Oberlin Coll, OH	M, W
Ohio Dominican U, OH	M, W
Ohio Northern U, OH	M, W
The Ohio State U, OH	M(s), W(s)
Ohio U, OH	M(s), W(s)
Ohio Wesleyan U, OH	M, W
Oklahoma Christian U, OK	M(s), W(s)
Oklahoma Panhandle State U, OK	M(s), W(s)
Oklahoma State U, OK	M(s), W(s)
Oral Roberts U, OK	M(s), W(s)
Ottawa U, KS	M(s), W(s)
Otterbein Coll, OH	M, W
Park U, MO	M(s), W(s)
Peru State Coll, NE	W(s)
Pittsburg State U, KS	M(s), W(s)
Presentation Coll, SD	M, W
Purdue U, IN	M(s), W(s)
Ripon Coll, WI	M, W
Robert Morris Coll, IL	M(s), W(s)
Rose-Hulman Inst of Technology, IN	M, W
Saginaw Valley State U, MI	M(s), W(s)
St. Ambrose U, IA	M(s), W(s)
St. Cloud State U, MN	M(s), W(s)
St. Gregory's U, Shawnee, OK	M(s), W(s)
Saint John's U, MN	M
Saint Joseph's Coll, IN	M(s), W(s)
St. Louis Coll of Pharmacy, MO	M, W
Saint Louis U, MO	M(s), W(s)
Saint Mary's Coll, IN	W
Saint Mary's U of Minnesota, MN	M, W
St. Norbert Coll, WI	M, W
St. Olaf Coll, MN	M, W
Saint Xavier U, IL	W(s)
Shawnee State U, OH	M, W
Silver Lake Coll, WI	M, W
Simpson Coll, IA	M, W
South Dakota School of Mines and Technology, SD	M(s), W(s)
South Dakota State U, SD	M(s), W(s)
Southeastern Oklahoma State U, OK	W(s)
Southeast Missouri State U, MO	M(s), W(s)
Southern Illinois U Carbondale, IL	M(s), W(s)
Southern Illinois U Edwardsville, IL	M(s), W(s)
Southern Methodist U, TX	M(s), W(s)
Southwest Baptist U, MO	M(s), W(s)
Southwestern Coll, KS	M(s), W(s)
Southwestern Oklahoma State U, OK	W(s)
Spring Arbor U, MI	M(s), W(s)
Sterling Coll, KS	M(s), W(s)
Tabor Coll, KS	M(s), W(s)
Taylor U, IN	M(s), W(s)
Tiffin U, OH	M(s), W(s)
Transylvania U, KY	M, W
Trinity Christian Coll, IL	M(s), W(s)
Tri-State U, IN	M, W
Truman State U, MO	M(s), W(s)
The U of Akron, OH	M(s), W(s)
U of Central Missouri, MO	M(s), W(s)
U of Central Oklahoma, OK	M(s), W(s)
U of Charleston, WV	M(s), W(s)
U of Chicago, IL	M, W
U of Cincinnati, OH	M(s), W(s)
U of Dallas, TX	M, W
U of Dayton, OH	M(s), W(s)

U of Evansville, IN	M(s), W(s)
The U of Findlay, OH	M(s), W(s)
U of Illinois at Chicago, IL	M(s), W(s)
U of Illinois at Urbana–Champaign, IL	M(s), W(s)
U of Indianapolis, IN	M(s), W(s)
The U of Iowa, IA	M(s), W(s)
U of Kansas, KS	M(s), W(s)
U of Mary, ND	M(s), W(s)
U of Michigan, MI	M(s), W(s)
U of Minnesota, Crookston, MN	W
U of Minnesota, Duluth, MN	M(s), W(s)
U of Minnesota, Morris, MN	W
U of Minnesota, Twin Cities Campus, MN	M(s), W(s)
U of Missouri–Columbia, MO	M(s), W(s)
U of Missouri–Kansas City, MO	M(s), W(s)
U of Missouri–Rolla, MO	M(s), W(s)
U of Nebraska at Kearney, NE	M(s), W(s)
U of Nebraska at Omaha, NE	W(s)
U of Nebraska–Lincoln, NE	M(s), W(s)
U of New Orleans, LA	M(s), W(s)
U of North Dakota, ND	M, W
U of Northern Iowa, IA	M(s), W(s)
U of Notre Dame, IN	M(s), W(s)
U of Oklahoma, OK	M(s), W(s)
U of Rio Grande, OH	M(s), W(s)
U of St. Francis, IL	W(s)
U of Saint Francis, IN	M(s), W(s)
U of St. Thomas, MN	M, W
U of Sioux Falls, SD	M(s), W(s)
The U of South Dakota, SD	M(s), W(s)
U of Southern Indiana, IN	M(s), W(s)
The U of Toledo, OH	M(s), W(s)
U of Tulsa, OK	M(s), W(s)
U of West Florida, FL	M(s), W(s)
U of Wisconsin–Eau Claire, WI	M, W
U of Wisconsin–Green Bay, WI	M(s), W(s)
U of Wisconsin–La Crosse, WI	M, W
U of Wisconsin–Madison, WI	M(s), W(s)
U of Wisconsin–Milwaukee, WI	M(s), W(s)
U of Wisconsin–Oshkosh, WI	M, W
U of Wisconsin–Parkside, WI	M(s), W(s)
U of Wisconsin–Platteville, WI	M, W
U of Wisconsin–River Falls, WI	M, W
U of Wisconsin–Stevens Point, WI	M, W
U of Wisconsin–Stout, WI	M, W
U of Wisconsin–Superior, WI	M, W
U of Wisconsin–Whitewater, WI	M, W
Ursuline Coll, OH	W(s)
Valparaiso U, IN	M(s), W(s)
Wabash Coll, IN	M
Walsh U, OH	M(s), W(s)
Wartburg Coll, IA	M, W
Washington U in St. Louis, MO	M, W
Wayne State Coll, NE	M(s), W(s)
Webster U, MO	W
Western Illinois U, IL	M(s), W(s)
Western Michigan U, MI	W(s)
Wheaton Coll, IL	M, W
Wichita State U, KS	M(s), W(s)
William Jewell Coll, MO	M(s), W(s)
William Penn U, IA	M(s), W(s)
William Woods U, MO	M(s), W(s)
Wilmington Coll, OH	M, W
Winona State U, MN	M, W(s)
Wisconsin Lutheran Coll, WI	M, W
Wittenberg U, OH	M, W
Wright State U, OH	M(s), W(s)
Xavier U, OH	M(s), W(s)
York Coll, NE	M(s), W(s)
Youngstown State U, OH	M(s), W(s)

Equestrian Sports

Ball State U, IN	M, W
Carleton Coll, MN	M, W
Denison U, OH	M, W
Earlham Coll, IN	M, W

Hillsdale Coll, MI	W
Hiram Coll, OH	M, W
Kenyon Coll, OH	M, W
Miami U, OH	M, W
Michigan State U, MI	M, W
Missouri State U, MO	M, W
National American U, Rapid City, SD	M(s), W(s)
Northern Michigan U, MI	M, W
Oberlin Coll, OH	M, W
Ohio U, OH	M, W
Ohio Wesleyan U, OH	M, W
Oklahoma Panhandle State U, OK	W
Oklahoma State U, OK	W(s)
Otterbein Coll, OH	M, W
St. Cloud State U, MN	M, W
Saint Mary-of-the-Woods Coll, IN	W(s)
Saint Mary's Coll, IN	W
South Dakota State U, SD	W
Southwestern Oklahoma State U, OK	M(s), W(s)
Taylor U, IN	M, W
Truman State U, MO	M, W
U of Wisconsin–River Falls, WI	M, W
Washington U in St. Louis, MO	M, W
William Woods U, MO	M, W
Wittenberg U, OH	W

Fencing

Beloit Coll, WI	M, W
Bradley U, IL	M, W
Carleton Coll, MN	M, W
Case Western Reserve U, OH	M, W
Cleveland State U, OH	M(s), W(s)
Lake Forest Coll, IL	M, W
Lawrence U, WI	M, W
Macalester Coll, MN	M, W
Marquette U, WI	M, W
Miami U, OH	M, W
Michigan Technological U, MI	M, W
Northwestern U, IL	W(s)
Oberlin Coll, OH	M, W
The Ohio State U, OH	M(s), W(s)
St. Cloud State U, MN	M, W
Saint Louis U, MO	M, W
Southern Methodist U, TX	M, W
U of Kansas, KS	M, W
U of Nebraska–Lincoln, NE	M, W
U of Notre Dame, IN	M(s), W(s)
Washington U in St. Louis, MO	M, W
Winona State U, MN	M, W
Xavier U, OH	M, W

Field Hockey

Adrian Coll, MI	M, W
Ball State U, IN	W(s)
Carleton Coll, MN	W
Central Michigan U, MI	W(s)
The Coll of Wooster, OH	W
Denison U, OH	W
DePauw U, IN	W
Earlham Coll, IN	W
Indiana U Bloomington, IN	W
Kent State U, OH	W(s)
Kenyon Coll, OH	W
Lindenwood U, MO	W(s)
Miami U, OH	W(s)
Michigan State U, MI	W(s)
Missouri State U, MO	W(s)
Northwestern U, IL	W(s)
Notre Dame Coll, OH	W(s)
Oberlin Coll, OH	W
The Ohio State U, OH	W(s)
Ohio U, OH	W(s)
Ohio Wesleyan U, OH	W
Saint Louis U, MO	W(s)
Saint Mary's Coll, IN	W
Transylvania U, KY	W
The U of Iowa, IA	W(s)

Athletic Programs and Scholarships

Field Hockey

U of Michigan, MI	W(s)
Washington U in St. Louis, MO	W
Wittenberg U, OH	W

Football

Adrian Coll, MI	M
Albion Coll, MI	M
Alma Coll, MI	M
Anderson U, IN	M
Ashland U, OH	M(s)
Augsburg Coll, MN	M
Augustana Coll, IL	M
Augustana Coll, SD	M(s)
Aurora U, IL	M
Avila U, MO	M(s)
Baker U, KS	M(s)
Baldwin-Wallace Coll, OH	M
Ball State U, IN	M(s)
Beloit Coll, WI	M
Bemidji State U, MN	M(s)
Benedictine Coll, KS	M(s)
Benedictine U, IL	M
Bethany Coll, KS	M(s)
Bethel Coll, KS	M(s)
Bethel U, MN	M
Blackburn Coll, IL	M
Black Hills State U, SD	M(s)
Blessing-Rieman Coll of Nursing, IL	M(s)
Bluffton U, OH	M
Bowling Green State U, OH	M(s)
Briar Cliff U, IA	M(s)
Buena Vista U, IA	M
Butler U, IN	M
Capital U, OH	M
Carleton Coll, MN	M
Carroll Coll, WI	M
Case Western Reserve U, OH	M
Central Coll, IA	M
Central Methodist U, MO	M(s)
Central Michigan U, MI	M(s)
Coe Coll, IA	M
Coll of Mount St. Joseph, OH	M
The Coll of Wooster, OH	M
Concordia Coll, MN	M
Concordia U, IL	M
Concordia U, NE	M(s)
Concordia U, St. Paul, MN	M(s)
Concordia U Wisconsin, WI	M
Concord U, WV	M(s)
Cornell Coll, IA	M
Crown Coll, MN	M
Culver-Stockton Coll, MO	M(s)
Dakota State U, SD	M(s)
Dakota Wesleyan U, SD	M(s)
Dana Coll, NE	M(s)
Denison U, OH	M
DePauw U, IN	M
Dickinson State U, ND	M(s)
Doane Coll, NE	M(s)
Drake U, IA	M
Earlham Coll, IN	M
East Central U, OK	M(s)
Eastern Illinois U, IL	M(s)
Eastern Michigan U, MI	M(s)
Elmhurst Coll, IL	M
Emporia State U, KS	M(s)
Evangel U, MO	M(s)
Ferris State U, MI	M(s)
Fort Hays State U, KS	M(s)
Franklin Coll, IN	M
Gannon U, PA	M
Graceland U, IA	M(s)
Grand Valley State U, MI	M(s)
Greenville Coll, IL	M
Grinnell Coll, IA	M

Gustavus Adolphus Coll, MN	M
Hamline U, MN	M
Hanover Coll, IN	M
Hastings Coll, NE	M(s)
Heidelberg Coll, OH	M
Hillsdale Coll, MI	M(s)
Hiram Coll, OH	M
Hope Coll, MI	M
Illinois Coll, IL	M
Illinois State U, IL	M(s)
Illinois Wesleyan U, IL	M
Indiana State U, IN	M(s)
Indiana U Bloomington, IN	M(s)
Iowa State U of Science and Technology, IA	M(s)
Iowa Wesleyan Coll, IA	M(s)
Jamestown Coll, ND	M(s)
Kalamazoo Coll, MI	M
Kansas State U, KS	M(s)
Kent State U, OH	M(s)
Kenyon Coll, OH	M
Knox Coll, IL	M
Lake Forest Coll, IL	M
Lakeland Coll, WI	M
Langston U, OK	M(s)
Lawrence U, WI	M
Lincoln U, MO	M(s)
Lindenwood U, MO	M(s)
Loras Coll, IA	M
Luther Coll, IA	M
Macalester Coll, MN	M
MacMurray Coll, IL	M
Malone Coll, OH	M(s)
Manchester Coll, IN	M
Maranatha Baptist Bible Coll, WI	M
Marietta Coll, OH	M
Marquette U, WI	M
Martin Luther Coll, MN	M
Mayville State U, ND	M(s)
McKendree Coll, IL	M(s)
Miami U, OH	M(s)
Michigan State U, MI	M(s)
Michigan Technological U, MI	M(s)
Millikin U, IL	M
Minnesota State U Mankato, MN	M(s)
Minot State U, ND	M(s)
Missouri Southern State U, MO	M(s)
Missouri State U, MO	M(s)
Missouri Valley Coll, MO	M(s)
Missouri Western State U, MO	M(s)
Morningside Coll, IA	M(s)
Mount Union Coll, OH	M
Nebraska Wesleyan U, NE	M
North Carolina Ag and Tech State U, NC	M(s)
North Central Coll, IL	M
North Dakota State U, ND	M(s)
Northeastern State U, OK	M(s)
Northern Illinois U, IL	M(s)
Northern Michigan U, MI	M
Northern State U, SD	M(s)
Northwestern Coll, IA	M(s)
Northwestern Coll, MN	M
Northwestern Oklahoma State U, OK	M(s)
Northwestern U, IL	M(s)
Northwest Missouri State U, MO	M(s)
Northwood U, MI	M(s)
Oberlin Coll, OH	M
Ohio Dominican U, OH	M(s)
Ohio Northern U, OH	M
The Ohio State U, OH	M(s)
Ohio U, OH	M(s)
Ohio Wesleyan U, OH	M
Oklahoma Panhandle State U, OK	M(s)
Oklahoma State U, OK	M(s)

Ottawa U, KS	M(s)
Otterbein Coll, OH	M
Peru State Coll, NE	M(s)
Pittsburg State U, KS	M(s)
Purdue U, IN	M(s)
Quincy U, IL	M(s)
Ripon Coll, WI	M
Rockford Coll, IL	M
Rose-Hulman Inst of Technology, IN	M
Saginaw Valley State U, MI	M(s)
St. Ambrose U, IA	M(s)
St. Cloud State U, MN	M(s)
Saint John's U, MN	M
Saint Joseph's Coll, IN	M(s)
St. Norbert Coll, WI	M
St. Olaf Coll, MN	M
Saint Xavier U, IL	M(s)
Simpson Coll, IA	M
South Dakota School of Mines and Technology, SD	M(s)
South Dakota State U, SD	M(s)
Southeastern Oklahoma State U, OK	M(s)
Southeast Missouri State U, MO	M(s)
Southern Illinois U Carbondale, IL	M(s)
Southern Methodist U, TX	M(s)
Southwest Baptist U, MO	M(s)
Southwestern Coll, KS	M(s)
Southwestern Oklahoma State U, OK	M(s)
Southwest Minnesota State U, MN	M(s)
Sterling Coll, KS	M(s)
Tabor Coll, KS	M(s)
Taylor U, IN	M(s)
Tiffin U, OH	M(s)
Trinity International U, IL	M(s)
Tri-State U, IN	M
Truman State U, MO	M(s)
The U of Akron, OH	M(s)
U of Central Missouri, MO	M(s)
U of Central Oklahoma, OK	M(s)
U of Charleston, WV	M(s)
U of Chicago, IL	M
U of Cincinnati, OH	M(s)
U of Dayton, OH	M
The U of Findlay, OH	M(s)
U of Illinois at Urbana–Champaign, IL	M(s)
U of Indianapolis, IN	M(s)
The U of Iowa, IA	M(s)
U of Kansas, KS	M(s)
U of Mary, ND	M(s)
U of Michigan, MI	M(s)
U of Minnesota, Crookston, MN	M(s)
U of Minnesota, Duluth, MN	M(s)
U of Minnesota, Morris, MN	M
U of Minnesota, Twin Cities Campus, MN	M(s)
U of Missouri–Columbia, MO	M(s)
U of Missouri–Rolla, MO	M(s)
U of Nebraska at Kearney, NE	M(s)
U of Nebraska at Omaha, NE	M(s)
U of Nebraska–Lincoln, NE	M(s)
U of North Dakota, ND	M(s)
U of Northern Iowa, IA	M(s)
U of Notre Dame, IN	M(s)
U of Oklahoma, OK	M(s)
U of St. Francis, IL	M(s)
U of Saint Francis, IN	M(s)
U of Saint Mary, KS	M(s)
U of St. Thomas, MN	M
U of Sioux Falls, SD	M(s)
The U of South Dakota, SD	M(s)
The U of Toledo, OH	M(s)
U of Tulsa, OK	M(s)
U of Wisconsin–Eau Claire, WI	M
U of Wisconsin–La Crosse, WI	M
U of Wisconsin–Madison, WI	M(s)

M—for men; W—for women; (s)—scholarship offered

U of Wisconsin–Oshkosh, WI	M
U of Wisconsin–Platteville, WI	M
U of Wisconsin–River Falls, WI	M
U of Wisconsin–Stevens Point, WI	M
U of Wisconsin–Stout, WI	M
U of Wisconsin–Whitewater, WI	M
Upper Iowa U, IA	M
Valley City State U, ND	M(s)
Valparaiso U, IN	M
Wabash Coll, IN	M
Waldorf Coll, IA	M(s)
Walsh U, OH	M(s)
Wartburg Coll, IA	M
Washburn U, KS	M(s)
Washington U in St. Louis, MO	M
Wayne State Coll, NE	M(s)
Western Illinois U, IL	M(s)
Western Michigan U, MI	M(s)
Westminster Coll, MO	M
Wheaton Coll, IL	M
William Jewell Coll, MO	M(s)
William Penn U, IA	M(s)
Wilmington Coll, OH	M
Winona State U, MN	M(s)
Wisconsin Lutheran Coll, WI	M
Wittenberg U, OH	M
Youngstown State U, OH	M(s)

Golf

Adrian Coll, MI	M, W
Albion Coll, MI	M, W
Alma Coll, MI	M, W
Anderson U, IN	M, W
Aquinas Coll, MI	M(s), W(s)
Ashford U, IA	M(s), W(s)
Ashland U, OH	M(s), W(s)
Augsburg Coll, MN	M, W
Augustana Coll, IL	M, W
Augustana Coll, SD	M, W
Aurora U, IL	M
Avila U, MO	W(s)
Baker U, KS	M(s), W(s)
Baldwin-Wallace Coll, OH	M, W
Ball State U, IN	M(s)
Beloit Coll, WI	M, W
Bemidji State U, MN	M, W
Benedictine Coll, KS	M(s), W(s)
Benedictine U, IL	M
Bethany Coll, KS	M(s)
Bethany Lutheran Coll, MN	M
Bethel Coll, KS	M(s), W(s)
Bethel U, MN	M
Blackburn Coll, IL	M, W
Black Hills State U, SD	W
Bowling Green State U, OH	M(s), W(s)
Bradley U, IL	M(s), W(s)
Briar Cliff U, IA	M(s), W(s)
Buena Vista U, IA	M, W
Butler U, IN	M(s), W(s)
Calumet Coll of Saint Joseph, IN	M, W
Calvin Coll, MI	M, W
Cameron U, OK	M(s), W(s)
Capital U, OH	M, W
Carleton Coll, MN	M, W
Carroll Coll, WI	M, W
Cedarville U, OH	M(s)
Central Christian Coll of Kansas, KS	M(s), W(s)
Central Coll, IA	M, W
Central State U, OH	M(s), W(s)
Chicago State U, IL	M(s), W(s)
Cincinnati Christian U, OH	M
Clarke Coll, IA	M, W
Clarkson U, NY	M
Cleveland State U, OH	M(s)
Coe Coll, IA	M, W
Coll of Mount St. Joseph, OH	M, W
Coll of Saint Benedict, MN	W

The Coll of Wooster, OH	M
Concordia Coll, MN	M, W
Concordia U, IL	M
Concordia U, MI	M(s), W(s)
Concordia U, NE	M(s), W(s)
Concordia U, St. Paul, MN	W(s)
Concordia U Wisconsin, WI	M, W
Concord U, WV	M(s)
Cornell Coll, IA	M, W
Cornerstone U, MI	M(s)
Creighton U, NE	M(s), W(s)
Crossroads Coll, MN	M, W
Crown Coll, MN	M, W
Culver-Stockton Coll, MO	M(s), W(s)
Dakota Wesleyan U, SD	M(s), W(s)
Dana Coll, NE	W(s)
Denison U, OH	M
DePaul U, IL	M(s), W
DePauw U, IN	M, W
Dickinson State U, ND	M(s), W(s)
Doane Coll, NE	M(s), W(s)
Dominican U, IL	M, W
Dordt Coll, IA	M(s)
Drake U, IA	M(s), W
Drury U, MO	M(s), W(s)
East Central U, OK	M(s), W
Eastern Illinois U, IL	M(s), W(s)
Eastern Michigan U, MI	M(s), W(s)
Edgewood Coll, WI	M, W
Elmhurst Coll, IL	M, W
Evangel U, MO	M(s), W(s)
Ferris State U, MI	M(s), W(s)
Fontbonne U, MO	M, W
Fort Hays State U, KS	M(s)
Franklin Coll, IN	M, W
Gannon U, PA	M(s), W(s)
Goshen Coll, IN	M(s)
Grace Coll, IN	M(s)
Graceland U, IA	M(s), W(s)
Grand Valley State U, MI	M(s), W(s)
Grand View Coll, IA	M(s), W(s)
Grinnell Coll, IA	M, W
Gustavus Adolphus Coll, MN	M, W
Hannibal-LaGrange Coll, MO	M(s)
Hanover Coll, IN	M, W
Hastings Coll, NE	M(s), W(s)
Heidelberg Coll, OH	M, W
Hiram Coll, OH	M, W
Hope Coll, MI	M, W
Huntington U, IN	M(s)
Illinois Coll, IL	M, W
Illinois State U, IL	M(s), W(s)
Illinois Wesleyan U, IL	M, W
Indiana U Bloomington, IN	M(s), W(s)
Indiana U Northwest, IN	M, W
Indiana U–Purdue U Indianapolis, IN	M(s), W
Indiana Wesleyan U, IN	M(s)
Iowa State U of Science and Technology, IA	M(s), W(s)
Iowa Wesleyan Coll, IA	M(s), W(s)
Jamestown Coll, ND	M(s), W(s)
Kalamazoo Coll, MI	M, W
Kansas State U, KS	M(s), W(s)
Kent State U, OH	M(s), W(s)
Kenyon Coll, OH	M
Knox Coll, IL	M, W
Lake Forest Coll, IL	M, W
Lakeland Coll, WI	M, W
Lake Superior State U, MI	M
Lawrence U, WI	M
Lewis U, IL	M(s), W(s)
Lincoln U, MO	M(s)
Lindenwood U, MO	M(s), W(s)
Loras Coll, IA	M, W
Loyola U Chicago, IL	M(s), W(s)
Luther Coll, IA	M, W

Macalester Coll, MN	M, W
MacMurray Coll, IL	M, W
Madonna U, MI	M(s), W(s)
Maharishi U of Management, IA	M, W
Malone Coll, OH	M(s), W(s)
Manchester Coll, IN	M, W
Marian Coll, IN	M(s), W(s)
Marian Coll of Fond du Lac, WI	M, W
Marquette U, WI	M(s)
Martin Luther Coll, MN	M
Maryville U of Saint Louis, MO	M, W
McKendree Coll, IL	M(s), W(s)
Miami U, OH	M(s)
Miami U Hamilton, OH	M
Miami U–Middletown Campus, OH	M, W
Michigan State U, MI	M(s), W(s)
Millikin U, IL	M, W
Milwaukee School of Engineering, WI	M, W
Minnesota State U Mankato, MN	M(s), W(s)
Minot State U, ND	M, W
Missouri Baptist U, MO	M(s), W
Missouri Southern State U, MO	M(s)
Missouri State U, MO	M(s), W(s)
Missouri Valley Coll, MO	M(s), W(s)
Missouri Western State U, MO	M(s), W
Morningside Coll, IA	M(s), W(s)
Mount Mercy Coll, IA	M, W
Mount Union Coll, OH	M, W
Mount Vernon Nazarene U, OH	M(s)
Nebraska Wesleyan U, NE	M, W
Newman U, KS	M(s), W(s)
North Central Coll, IL	M, W
North Dakota State U, ND	M, W
Northeastern State U, OK	M(s), W(s)
Northern Illinois U, IL	M(s), W(s)
Northern Michigan U, MI	M
Northern State U, SD	M, W(s)
Northwestern Coll, IA	M(s), W(s)
Northwestern Coll, MN	M
Northwestern Oklahoma State U, OK	M(s), W(s)
Northwestern U, IL	M(s), W(s)
Northwest Missouri State U, MO	M(s)
Northwood U, MI	M(s), W(s)
Notre Dame Coll, OH	M(s), W(s)
Oakland U, MI	M(s), W(s)
Oberlin Coll, OH	M, W
Ohio Dominican U, OH	M, W
Ohio Northern U, OH	M, W
The Ohio State U, OH	M(s), W(s)
The Ohio State U at Lima, OH	M
Ohio U, OH	M(s), W(s)
Ohio U–Zanesville, OH	M, W
Ohio Wesleyan U, OH	M
Oklahoma Christian U, OK	M(s)
Oklahoma City U, OK	M(s), W(s)
Oklahoma Panhandle State U, OK	M(s), W(s)
Oklahoma State U, OK	M(s), W(s)
Oklahoma Wesleyan U, OK	M(s)
Oral Roberts U, OK	M(s), W(s)
Ottawa U, KS	M(s)
Otterbein Coll, OH	M, W
Park U, MO	W
Peru State Coll, NE	W(s)
Pittsburg State U, KS	M(s)
Presentation Coll, SD	M, W
Purdue U, IN	M(s), W(s)
Quincy U, IL	M(s), W(s)
Research Coll of Nursing, MO	M, W
Ripon Coll, WI	M, W
Robert Morris Coll, IL	M(s), W(s)
Rockford Coll, IL	M
Rockhurst U, MO	M(s), W(s)
Rose-Hulman Inst of Technology, IN	M, W
Saginaw Valley State U, MI	M(s)
St. Ambrose U, IA	M(s), W(s)
St. Cloud State U, MN	M, W(s)

St. Gregory's U, Shawnee, OK	M(s), W(s)
Saint John's U, MN	M
Saint Joseph's Coll, IN	M(s), W(s)
Saint Louis U, MO	M(s)
Saint Mary's U of Minnesota, MN	M, W
St. Norbert Coll, WI	M, W
St. Olaf Coll, MN	M, W
Saint Xavier U, IL	M(s)
Shawnee State U, OH	M
Simpson Coll, IA	M, W
South Dakota School of Mines and Technology, SD	M, W
South Dakota State U, SD	M(s), W(s)
Southeast Missouri State U, MO	M(s)
Southern Illinois U Carbondale, IL	M(s), W(s)
Southern Illinois U Edwardsville, IL	M(s), W(s)
Southern Methodist U, TX	M(s), W(s)
Southwest Baptist U, MO	M(s)
Southwestern Coll, KS	M(s), W(s)
Southwestern Oklahoma State U, OK	M(s), W(s)
Southwest Minnesota State U, MN	W(s)
Spring Arbor U, MI	M(s)
Tabor Coll, KS	M(s), W(s)
Taylor U, IN	M(s)
Tiffin U, OH	M(s), W(s)
Transylvania U, KY	M, W
Tri-State U, IN	M, W
Truman State U, MO	M(s), W(s)
The U of Akron, OH	M(s)
U of Central Missouri, MO	M(s)
U of Central Oklahoma, OK	M(s), W(s)
U of Charleston, WV	M(s)
U of Cincinnati, OH	M(s)
U of Dallas, TX	M
U of Dayton, OH	M(s), W(s)
U of Evansville, IN	M(s)
The U of Findlay, OH	M(s), W(s)
U of Illinois at Urbana–Champaign, IL	M(s), W(s)
U of Indianapolis, IN	M(s), W(s)
The U of Iowa, IA	M(s), W(s)
U of Kansas, KS	M(s), W(s)
U of Mary, ND	M(s), W(s)
U of Michigan, MI	M(s), W(s)
U of Minnesota, Crookston, MN	M, W
U of Minnesota, Morris, MN	M, W
U of Minnesota, Twin Cities Campus, MN	M(s), W(s)
U of Missouri–Columbia, MO	M(s), W(s)
U of Missouri–Kansas City, MO	M(s), W(s)
U of Missouri–St. Louis, MO	M(s), W(s)
U of Nebraska at Kearney, NE	M(s), W(s)
U of Nebraska at Omaha, NE	W
U of Nebraska–Lincoln, NE	M(s), W(s)
U of New Orleans, LA	M(s), W(s)
U of North Dakota, ND	M, W
U of Northern Iowa, IA	M(s), W(s)
U of Notre Dame, IN	M(s), W(s)
U of Oklahoma, OK	M(s), W(s)
U of St. Francis, IL	M(s), W(s)
U of Saint Francis, IN	M(s), W
U of St. Thomas, MN	M, W
U of Sioux Falls, SD	M(s), W(s)
U of Southern Indiana, IN	M(s), W(s)
The U of Toledo, OH	M(s), W(s)
U of Tulsa, OK	M(s), W(s)
U of West Florida, FL	M(s)
U of Wisconsin–Eau Claire, WI	M, W
U of Wisconsin–Madison, WI	M(s), W(s)
U of Wisconsin–Oshkosh, WI	W
U of Wisconsin–Parkside, WI	M(s)
U of Wisconsin–Platteville, WI	W
U of Wisconsin–Stevens Point, WI	W
U of Wisconsin–Superior, WI	W
U of Wisconsin–Whitewater, WI	W
Upper Iowa U, IA	M, W
Ursuline Coll, OH	W(s)
Wabash Coll, IN	M
Waldorf Coll, IA	M(s), W(s)
Walsh U, OH	M(s), W(s)
Wartburg Coll, IA	M, W
Washburn U, KS	M(s)
Washington U in St. Louis, MO	M, W
Wayne State Coll, NE	M(s), W(s)
Webster U, MO	M
Western Illinois U, IL	M(s), W
Western Michigan U, MI	W(s)
Westminster Coll, MO	M, W
Wheaton Coll, IL	M, W
Wichita State U, KS	M(s), W(s)
William Jewell Coll, MO	M(s), W(s)
William Penn U, IA	M(s)
William Woods U, MO	M(s), W(s)
Wilmington Coll, OH	M, W
Winona State U, MN	M(s), W(s)
Wisconsin Lutheran Coll, WI	M, W
Wittenberg U, OH	M, W
Wright State U, OH	M(s)
Xavier U, OH	M(s), W(s)
York Coll, NE	M(s), W(s)
Youngstown State U, OH	M(s), W

Gymnastics

Ball State U, IN	W(s)
Bowling Green State U, OH	W(s)
Carleton Coll, MN	W
Central Michigan U, MI	W(s)
Eastern Michigan U, MI	W(s)
Gustavus Adolphus Coll, MN	W
Hamline U, MN	W
Illinois State U, IL	W(s)
Iowa State U of Science and Technology, IA	W(s)
Kent State U, OH	W(s)
Miami U, OH	M, W
Michigan State U, MI	M, W(s)
Northern Illinois U, IL	W(s)
The Ohio State U, OH	M(s), W(s)
Saint Mary's Coll, IN	W
Southeast Missouri State U, MO	W(s)
U of Illinois at Chicago, IL	M(s), W(s)
U of Illinois at Urbana–Champaign, IL	M(s), W(s)
The U of Iowa, IA	M(s), W(s)
U of Michigan, MI	M(s), W(s)
U of Minnesota, Twin Cities Campus, MN	M(s), W(s)
U of Missouri–Columbia, MO	W(s)
U of Nebraska–Lincoln, NE	M(s), W(s)
U of Oklahoma, OK	M(s), W(s)
U of Wisconsin–Eau Claire, WI	W
U of Wisconsin–La Crosse, WI	W
U of Wisconsin–Oshkosh, WI	W
U of Wisconsin–Stout, WI	W
U of Wisconsin–Whitewater, WI	W
Washington U in St. Louis, MO	M, W
Western Michigan U, MI	W(s)
Winona State U, MN	W(s)

Ice Hockey

Augsburg Coll, MN	M, W
Ball State U, IN	M
Beloit Coll, WI	M, W
Bemidji State U, MN	M(s), W(s)
Bethel U, MN	M, W
Bowling Green State U, OH	M(s)
Bradley U, IL	M
Butler U, IN	M
Calvin Coll, MI	M
Carleton Coll, MN	M, W
Case Western Reserve U, OH	M, W
Clarkson U, NY	M(s), W(s)
Coll of Saint Benedict, MN	W
Coll of St. Catherine, MN	W
The Coll of St. Scholastica, MN	M
Concordia Coll, MN	M, W
Denison U, OH	M
Dordt Coll, IA	M(s)
Ferris State U, MI	M(s)
Finlandia U, MI	M, W
Grand Valley State U, MI	M
Gustavus Adolphus Coll, MN	M, W
Hamline U, MN	M, W
Hillsdale Coll, MI	M
Hope Coll, MI	M
Kettering U, MI	M
Lake Forest Coll, IL	M, W
Lake Superior State U, MI	M(s)
Lawrence U, WI	M, W
Lindenwood U, MO	M(s), W(s)
Loras Coll, IA	M
Macalester Coll, MN	M, W
Marian Coll of Fond du Lac, WI	M
McKendree Coll, IL	M
Miami U, OH	M(s)
Michigan State U, MI	M(s), W
Michigan Technological U, MI	M(s), W
Milwaukee School of Engineering, WI	M
Minnesota State U Mankato, MN	M(s), W(s)
Minot State U, ND	M
Missouri State U, MO	M
North Dakota State U, ND	M
Northern Michigan U, MI	M, W
Northland Coll, WI	M
Northwestern Coll, MN	M
Oak Hills Christian Coll, MN	M
Oakland U, MI	M, W
Oberlin Coll, OH	M, W
The Ohio State U, OH	M(s), W(s)
Ohio U, OH	M
Ohio Wesleyan U, OH	M, W
Ripon Coll, WI	M, W
St. Cloud State U, MN	M(s), W(s)
Saint John's U, MN	M
Saint Louis U, MO	M
Saint Mary's U of Minnesota, MN	M, W
St. Norbert Coll, WI	M
St. Olaf Coll, MN	M, W
South Dakota State U, SD	M, W
Southern Methodist U, TX	M
The U of Findlay, OH	M, W
The U of Iowa, IA	M
U of Michigan, MI	M(s)
U of Michigan–Dearborn, MI	M
U of Minnesota, Crookston, MN	M
U of Minnesota, Duluth, MN	M(s), W
U of Minnesota, Twin Cities Campus, MN	M(s), W(s)
U of Missouri–St. Louis, MO	M
U of Nebraska at Omaha, NE	M(s)
U of North Dakota, ND	M(s), W(s)
U of Notre Dame, IN	M(s)
U of St. Thomas, MN	M, W
U of Southern Indiana, IN	M
The U of Toledo, OH	M(s), W(s)
U of Wisconsin–Eau Claire, WI	M, W
U of Wisconsin–Madison, WI	M(s), W(s)
U of Wisconsin–Platteville, WI	M, W
U of Wisconsin–River Falls, WI	M, W
U of Wisconsin–Stevens Point, WI	M, W
U of Wisconsin–Stout, WI	M, W
U of Wisconsin–Superior, WI	M, W
U of Wisconsin–Whitewater, WI	M, W
Washington U in St. Louis, MO	M
Western Michigan U, MI	M(s)
Wheaton Coll, IL	M
Wichita State U, KS	M, W

M—for men; W—for women; (s)—scholarship offered

Winona State U, MN	M
Wittenberg U, OH	M

Lacrosse

Adrian Coll, MI	M, W
Augustana Coll, IL	M
Beloit Coll, WI	M, W
Butler U, IN	M(s)
Calvin Coll, MI	M, W
Carleton Coll, MN	M, W
Clarkson U, NY	M, W
Coll of Saint Benedict, MN	W
The Coll of Wooster, OH	M, W
Denison U, OH	M, W
Dordt Coll, IA	M
Earlham Coll, IN	M, W
Gannon U, PA	W(s)
Gustavus Adolphus Coll, MN	M
Hillsdale Coll, MI	M
Holy Cross Coll, IN	M
Hope Coll, MI	M
Illinois Wesleyan U, IL	M
Kenyon Coll, OH	M, W
Kettering U, MI	M
Lake Forest Coll, IL	M, W
Lindenwood U, MO	M(s), W(s)
Marietta Coll, OH	M
Marquette U, WI	M
Miami U, OH	M
Michigan State U, MI	M
Missouri Baptist U, MO	W
Missouri State U, MO	M
Newman U, KS	M
Northern Michigan U, MI	M
Northwestern U, IL	W(s)
Oberlin Coll, OH	M, W
The Ohio State U, OH	M(s), W(s)
Ohio U, OH	M, W
Ohio Wesleyan U, OH	M, W
Saginaw Valley State U, MI	W
Saint John's U, MN	M
Saint Louis U, MO	M, W
Southern Methodist U, TX	M
Taylor U, IN	M, W
Truman State U, MO	M, W
U of Dallas, TX	W
The U of Iowa, IA	M, W
U of Minnesota, Duluth, MN	M, W
U of Notre Dame, IN	M(s), W(s)
U of St. Thomas, MN	M, W
The U of Toledo, OH	M(s), W(s)
U of Wisconsin–Platteville, WI	M, W
U of Wisconsin–Whitewater, WI	M
Wabash Coll, IN	M
Washington U in St. Louis, MO	M, W
Wheaton Coll, IL	M, W
Wittenberg U, OH	M, W
Xavier U, OH	M, W

Racquetball

Miami U, OH	M, W
Michigan Technological U, MI	M, W
Missouri State U, MO	M, W
Wichita State U, KS	M, W

Riflery

Coll of Saint Benedict, MN	W
Denison U, OH	M, W
Hillsdale Coll, MI	M, W
Lindenwood U, MO	M(s), W(s)
Michigan Technological U, MI	M, W
Missouri State U, MO	M, W
North Dakota State U, ND	M, W
The Ohio State U, OH	M, W
Rose-Hulman Inst of Technology, IN	M, W
Saint John's U, MN	M
The U of Akron, OH	M, W
U of Missouri–Kansas City, MO	M(s), W(s)

U of Nebraska–Lincoln, NE	W(s)
U of Wisconsin–Oshkosh, WI	M, W
Xavier U, OH	M(s), W(s)

Rugby

Ball State U, IN	M, W
Butler U, IN	M
Carleton Coll, MN	M, W
Coll of Saint Benedict, MN	W
The Coll of Wooster, OH	M, W
Denison U, OH	M, W
DePauw U, IN	M
Earlham Coll, IN	M, W
Eastern Illinois U, IL	M, W(s)
Grand Valley State U, MI	M, W
Gustavus Adolphus Coll, MN	M, W
Hiram Coll, OH	M, W
Kenyon Coll, OH	M, W
Lake Forest Coll, IL	M, W
Loras Coll, IA	M
Macalester Coll, MN	M, W
Marquette U, WI	M, W
Miami U, OH	M
Michigan State U, MI	M, W
North Dakota State U, ND	M, W
Northern Michigan U, MI	M, W
Oberlin Coll, OH	M, W
Ohio U, OH	M, W
Ohio Wesleyan U, OH	M, W
Ripon Coll, WI	M
St. Cloud State U, MN	M, W
Saint John's U, MN	M
Saint Louis U, MO	M
South Dakota State U, SD	M, W
Southern Methodist U, TX	M
Tabor Coll, KS	M
Truman State U, MO	M, W
U of Central Missouri, MO	M, W
U of Cincinnati, OH	M
The U of Iowa, IA	M, W
U of Kansas, KS	M, W
U of Minnesota, Duluth, MN	M, W
U of Southern Indiana, IN	M
U of Wisconsin–Platteville, WI	M, W
U of Wisconsin–River Falls, WI	M, W
U of Wisconsin–Whitewater, WI	M, W
Wabash Coll, IN	M
Washington U in St. Louis, MO	M, W
Wayne State Coll, NE	M, W
Wichita State U, KS	M
Winona State U, MN	M, W
Wittenberg U, OH	M, W
Xavier U, OH	M, W

Sailing

Ball State U, IN	M, W
Carleton Coll, MN	M, W
Denison U, OH	M, W
Grand Valley State U, MI	M, W
Hiram Coll, OH	M, W
Lake Forest Coll, IL	M, W
Miami U, OH	M, W
Michigan State U, MI	M, W
Ohio Wesleyan U, OH	M, W
Saint Mary's Coll, IN	W
Southern Methodist U, TX	M, W
The U of Iowa, IA	M, W
U of Wisconsin–Madison, WI	M, W
Wabash Coll, IN	M
Washington U in St. Louis, MO	M, W

Skiing (Cross-Country)

Carleton Coll, MN	M, W
Clarkson U, NY	M, W
Coll of Saint Benedict, MN	W
Concordia Coll, MN	M, W
Finlandia U, MI	M, W
Gustavus Adolphus Coll, MN	M, W

Macalester Coll, MN	M, W
Michigan State U, MI	M, W
Michigan Technological U, MI	M, W
Northern Michigan U, MI	M, W
St. Cloud State U, MN	M, W(s)
Saint John's U, MN	M
St. Olaf Coll, MN	M, W
U of Wisconsin–Green Bay, WI	M(s), W(s)

Skiing (Downhill)

Carleton Coll, MN	M, W
Clarkson U, NY	M, W
Denison U, OH	M, W
Grand Valley State U, MI	M, W
Loras Coll, IA	M
Marquette U, WI	M
Michigan State U, MI	M
Michigan Technological U, MI	M, W
Northern Michigan U, MI	M, W
St. Cloud State U, MN	M, W
Saint Mary's Coll, IN	W
St. Olaf Coll, MN	W
U of Minnesota, Duluth, MN	M, W
U of St. Thomas, MN	M, W
Winona State U, MN	M, W

Soccer

Adrian Coll, MI	M, W
Albion Coll, MI	M, W
Alma Coll, MI	M, W
Alverno Coll, WI	W
Anderson U, IN	M, W
Aquinas Coll, MI	M(s), W(s)
Ashford U, IA	M(s), W(s)
Ashland U, OH	M(s), W(s)
Augsburg Coll, MN	M, W
Augustana Coll, IL	M, W
Augustana Coll, SD	W(s)
Aurora U, IL	M, W
Avila U, MO	M(s), W(s)
Baker U, KS	M(s), W(s)
Baldwin-Wallace Coll, OH	M, W
Ball State U, IN	M, W
Baptist Bible Coll, MO	M
Barclay Coll, KS	M
Bellevue U, NE	M(s), W
Beloit Coll, WI	M, W
Bemidji State U, MN	W(s)
Benedictine Coll, KS	M(s), W(s)
Benedictine U, IL	M, W
Bethany Coll, KS	M(s), W(s)
Bethany Lutheran Coll, MN	M, W
Bethel Coll, KS	M(s), W(s)
Bethel U, MN	M, W
Blackburn Coll, IL	M, W
Blessing-Rieman Coll of Nursing, IL	M(s), W(s)
Bluffton U, OH	M, W
Bowling Green State U, OH	M(s)
Bradley U, IL	M(s), W
Briar Cliff U, IA	M(s), W(s)
Buena Vista U, IA	M, W
Butler U, IN	M(s), W(s)
Calumet Coll of Saint Joseph, IN	M, W
Calvary Bible Coll and Theological Seminary, MO	M
Calvin Coll, MI	M, W
Capital U, OH	M, W
Cardinal Stritch U, WI	M, W
Carleton Coll, MN	M, W
Carroll Coll, WI	M, W
Case Western Reserve U, OH	M, W
Cedarville U, OH	M(s), W(s)
Central Christian Coll of Kansas, KS	M(s), W(s)
Central Coll, IA	M, W
Central Methodist U, MO	M(s), W(s)
Central Michigan U, MI	W(s)
Cincinnati Christian U, OH	M, W

Clarke Coll, IA	M, W	Indiana U–Purdue U Indianapolis, IN	M(s), W(s)	Oklahoma Christian U, OK	M(s), W(s)
Clarkson U, NY	M, W	Indiana Wesleyan U, IN	M(s), W(s)	Oklahoma City U, OK	M(s), W(s)
Cleveland State U, OH	M(s)	Iowa State U of Science and		Oklahoma State U, OK	W(s)
Coe Coll, IA	M, W	Technology, IA	W(s)	Oklahoma Wesleyan U, OK	M(s), W(s)
Coll of Mount St. Joseph, OH	M, W	Iowa Wesleyan Coll, IA	M(s), W(s)	Oral Roberts U, OK	M(s), W(s)
Coll of Saint Benedict, MN	W	Jamestown Coll, ND	W(s)	Ottawa U, KS	M(s), W(s)
Coll of St. Catherine, MN	W	Judson Coll, IL	M(s), W(s)	Otterbein Coll, OH	M, W
Coll of Saint Mary, NE	W(s)	Kalamazoo Coll, MI	M, W	Ozark Christian Coll, MO	M
The Coll of St. Scholastica, MN	M, W	Kent State U, OH	W(s)	Park U, MO	M(s), W(s)
The Coll of Wooster, OH	M, W	Kenyon Coll, OH	M, W	Presentation Coll, SD	M, W
Columbia Coll, MO	M(s)	Kettering U, MI	M	Purdue U, IN	W(s)
Concordia Coll, MN	M, W	Knox Coll, IL	M, W	Quincy U, IL	M(s), W(s)
Concordia U, IL	M, W	Lake Forest Coll, IL	M, W	Research Coll of Nursing, MO	M(s), W(s)
Concordia U, MI	M(s), W(s)	Lakeland Coll, WI	M, W	Ripon Coll, WI	M, W
Concordia U, NE	M(s), W(s)	Lawrence U, WI	M, W	Robert Morris Coll, IL	M(s), W(s)
Concordia U, St. Paul, MN	M, W(s)	Lewis U, IL	M(s), W(s)	Rochester Coll, MI	M(s), W(s)
Concordia U Wisconsin, WI	M, W	Lindenwood U, MO	M(s), W(s)	Rockford Coll, IL	M, W
Concord U, WV	W(s)	Loras Coll, IA	M, W	Rockhurst U, MO	M(s), W(s)
Cornell Coll, IA	M, W	Loyola U Chicago, IL	M(s), W(s)	Rose-Hulman Inst of Technology, IN	M, W
Cornerstone U, MI	M(s), W(s)	Luther Coll, IA	M, W	Saginaw Valley State U, MI	M(s), W(s)
Creighton U, NE	M(s), W(s)	Macalester Coll, MN	M, W	St. Ambrose U, IA	M(s), W(s)
Crown Coll, MN	M, W	MacMurray Coll, IL	M, W	St. Cloud State U, MN	M, W(s)
Culver-Stockton Coll, MO	M(s), W(s)	Madonna U, MI	M(s), W(s)	St. Gregory's U, Shawnee, OK	M(s), W(s)
Dana Coll, NE	M(s), W(s)	Maharishi U of Management, IA	M, W	Saint John's U, MN	M
Denison U, OH	M, W	Malone Coll, OH	M(s), W(s)	Saint Joseph's Coll, IN	M(s), W(s)
DePaul U, IL	M(s), W(s)	Manchester Coll, IN	M, W	Saint Louis U, MO	M(s), W(s)
DePauw U, IN	M, W	Maranatha Baptist Bible Coll, WI	M, W	Saint Mary-of-the-Woods Coll, IN	W(s)
Doane Coll, NE	M(s), W(s)	Marian Coll, IN	M(s), W(s)	Saint Mary's Coll, IN	W
Dominican U, IL	M, W	Marian Coll of Fond du Lac, WI	M, W	Saint Mary's U of Minnesota, MN	M, W
Dordt Coll, IA	M(s), W(s)	Marietta Coll, OH	M, W	St. Norbert Coll, WI	M, W
Drake U, IA	M(s), W(s)	Marquette U, WI	M(s), W(s)	St. Olaf Coll, MN	M, W
Drury U, MO	M(s), W(s)	Martin Luther Coll, MN	M, W	Saint Xavier U, IL	M(s), W(s)
Earlham Coll, IN	M, W	Maryville U of Saint Louis, MO	M, W	Shawnee State U, OH	M, W
East Central U, OK	W(s)	Mayville State U, ND	M(s), W(s)	Simpson Coll, IA	M, W
Eastern Illinois U, IL	M(s), W(s)	McKendree Coll, IL	M(s), W(s)	South Dakota State U, SD	M, W(s)
Eastern Michigan U, MI	W(s)	Miami U, OH	M, W	Southeast Missouri State U, MO	W(s)
Edgewood Coll, WI	M, W	Michigan State U, MI	M(s), W	Southern Illinois U Edwardsville, IL	M(s), W(s)
Elmhurst Coll, IL	W	Michigan Technological U, MI	M, W	Southern Methodist U, TX	M(s), W(s)
Emporia State U, KS	W(s)	Millikin U, IL	M, W	Southwest Baptist U, MO	M, W(s)
Faith Baptist Bible Coll and		Milwaukee School of Engineering, WI	M, W	Southwestern Coll, KS	M(s), W(s)
Theological Seminary, IA	M, W	Minnesota State U Mankato, MN	W(s)	Southwestern Oklahoma State U, OK	W(s)
Finlandia U, MI	M, W	Missouri Baptist U, MO	M(s), W(s)	Southwest Minnesota State U, MN	W(s)
Fontbonne U, MO	M, W	Missouri Southern State U, MO	M(s), W(s)	Spring Arbor U, MI	M(s), W(s)
Franklin Coll, IN	M, W	Missouri State U, MO	M(s), W(s)	Stephens Coll, MO	W
Gannon U, PA	M(s), W(s)	Missouri Valley Coll, MO	M(s), W(s)	Sterling Coll, KS	M(s), W(s)
Goshen Coll, IN	M(s), W(s)	Missouri Western State U, MO	W	Tabor Coll, KS	M(s), W(s)
Grace Bible Coll, MI	M	Morningside Coll, IA	M(s), W(s)	Taylor U, IN	M(s), W(s)
Grace Coll, IN	M(s), W(s)	Mount Marty Coll, SD	M(s), W(s)	Taylor U Fort Wayne, IN	M
Graceland U, IA	M(s), W(s)	Mount Mary Coll, WI	W	Tiffin U, OH	M(s), W(s)
Grand Valley State U, MI	M, W(s)	Mount Mercy Coll, IA	M, W	Transylvania U, KY	M, W
Grand View Coll, IA	M(s), W(s)	Mount Union Coll, OH	M, W	Trinity Christian Coll, IL	M, W
Great Lakes Christian Coll, MI	M, W	Mount Vernon Nazarene U, OH	M(s), W(s)	Trinity International U, IL	M(s), W(s)
Greenville Coll, IL	M, W	Nebraska Wesleyan U, NE	M, W	Tri-State U, IN	M, W
Grinnell Coll, IA	M, W	Newman U, KS	M(s), W(s)	Truman State U, MO	M(s), W(s)
Gustavus Adolphus Coll, MN	M, W	North Central Coll, IL	M, W	The U of Akron, OH	M(s), W
Hamline U, MN	M, W	North Dakota State U, ND	M, W(s)	U of Central Missouri, MO	M, W
Hannibal-LaGrange Coll, MO	M(s), W(s)	Northeastern State U, OK	M(s), W(s)	U of Central Oklahoma, OK	W(s)
Hanover Coll, IN	M, W	Northern Illinois U, IL	M(s), W(s)	U of Charleston, WV	M(s), W(s)
Harris-Stowe State U, MO	M(s), W(s)	Northern Michigan U, MI	W	U of Chicago, IL	M, W
Hastings Coll, NE	M(s), W(s)	Northern State U, SD	W(s)	U of Cincinnati, OH	M(s), W(s)
Heidelberg Coll, OH	M, W	Northland Coll, WI	M, W	U of Dallas, TX	M, W
Hesston Coll, KS	M(s)	Northwestern Coll, IA	M(s), W(s)	U of Dayton, OH	M(s), W(s)
Hillsdale Coll, MI	W	Northwestern Coll, MN	M, W	U of Evansville, IN	M(s), W(s)
Hiram Coll, OH	M, W	Northwestern Oklahoma State U, OK	W(s)	The U of Findlay, OH	M(s), W(s)
Holy Cross Coll, IN	M, W	Northwestern U, IL	M(s), W(s)	U of Illinois at Chicago, IL	M(s)
Hope Coll, MI	M, W	Northwest Missouri State U, MO	W(s)	U of Illinois at Springfield, IL	M(s)
Huntington U, IN	M(s), W(s)	Northwood U, MI	M(s), W(s)	U of Illinois at Urbana–Champaign, IL	W(s)
Illinois Coll, IL	M, W	Notre Dame Coll, OH	M(s), W(s)	U of Indianapolis, IN	M(s), W(s)
Illinois Inst of Technology, IL	M(s), W(s)	Oakland U, MI	M(s), W(s)	The U of Iowa, IA	M, W(s)
Illinois State U, IL	W(s)	Oberlin Coll, OH	M, W	U of Kansas, KS	W(s)
Illinois Wesleyan U, IL	M, W	Ohio Dominican U, OH	M(s), W(s)	U of Mary, ND	M(s), W(s)
Indiana State U, IN	W(s)	Ohio Northern U, OH	M, W	U of Michigan, MI	M, W(s)
Indiana Tech, IN	M(s), W(s)	The Ohio State U, OH	M(s), W(s)	U of Minnesota, Crookston, MN	W(s)
Indiana U Bloomington, IN	M(s), W(s)	Ohio U, OH	M, W(s)	U of Minnesota, Duluth, MN	M, W(s)
Indiana U–Purdue U Fort Wayne, IN	M(s), W(s)	Ohio Wesleyan U, OH	M, W	U of Minnesota, Morris, MN	W

M—for men; W—for women; (s)—scholarship offered

U of Minnesota, Twin Cities Campus, MN	W(s)
U of Missouri–Columbia, MO	W(s)
U of Missouri–Kansas City, MO	M(s)
U of Missouri–Rolla, MO	M(s), W(s)
U of Missouri–St. Louis, MO	M(s), W(s)
U of Nebraska at Omaha, NE	W
U of Nebraska–Lincoln, NE	W(s)
U of North Dakota, ND	W
U of Northern Iowa, IA	W(s)
U of Notre Dame, IN	M(s), W(s)
U of Oklahoma, OK	W(s)
U of Rio Grande, OH	M(s), W
U of St. Francis, IL	M(s), W(s)
U of Saint Francis, IN	M(s), W(s)
U of Saint Mary, KS	M(s), W(s)
U of St. Thomas, MN	M, W
U of Science and Arts of Oklahoma, OK	M(s), W(s)
U of Sioux Falls, SD	M(s), W(s)
U of Southern Indiana, IN	M(s), W(s)
The U of Toledo, OH	W(s)
U of Tulsa, OK	M(s), W(s)
U of West Florida, FL	M(s), W(s)
U of Wisconsin–Eau Claire, WI	W
U of Wisconsin–Green Bay, WI	M(s), W(s)
U of Wisconsin–La Crosse, WI	W
U of Wisconsin–Madison, WI	M(s), W(s)
U of Wisconsin–Milwaukee, WI	M(s), W(s)
U of Wisconsin–Oshkosh, WI	M, W
U of Wisconsin–Parkside, WI	M(s), W(s)
U of Wisconsin–Platteville, WI	M, W
U of Wisconsin–River Falls, WI	M, W
U of Wisconsin–Stevens Point, WI	W
U of Wisconsin–Stout, WI	M, W
U of Wisconsin–Superior, WI	M, W
U of Wisconsin–Whitewater, WI	M, W
Upper Iowa U, IA	M, W
Ursuline Coll, OH	W(s)
Valparaiso U, IN	M(s), W(s)
Vennard Coll, IA	M
Viterbo U, WI	M(s), W(s)
Wabash Coll, IN	M
Waldorf Coll, IA	M(s), W(s)
Walsh U, OH	M(s), W(s)
Wartburg Coll, IA	M, W
Washburn U, KS	W(s)
Washington U in St. Louis, MO	M, W
Wayne State Coll, NE	M, W(s)
Webster U, MO	M, W
Western Illinois U, IL	M(s), W(s)
Western Michigan U, MI	M(s), W(s)
Westminster Coll, MO	M, W
Wheaton Coll, IL	M, W
Wichita State U, KS	M, W
William Jewell Coll, MO	M(s), W(s)
William Penn U, IA	M(s), W(s)
William Woods U, MO	M(s), W(s)
Wilmington Coll, OH	M, W
Winona State U, MN	M, W(s)
Wisconsin Lutheran Coll, WI	M, W
Wittenberg U, OH	M, W
Wright State U, OH	M(s), W(s)
Xavier U, OH	M(s), W(s)
York Coll, NE	M(s), W(s)
Youngstown State U, OH	W

Softball

Adrian Coll, MI	W
Albion Coll, MI	W
Alma Coll, MI	W
Alverno Coll, WI	W
Anderson U, IN	W
Aquinas Coll, MI	W(s)
Ashford U, IA	W(s)
Ashland U, OH	M, W(s)
Augsburg Coll, MN	W
Augustana Coll, IL	W
Augustana Coll, SD	W(s)
Aurora U, IL	W
Avila U, MO	W(s)
Baker U, KS	W(s)
Baldwin-Wallace Coll, OH	W
Ball State U, IN	W
Bellevue U, NE	W(s)
Beloit Coll, WI	W
Bemidji State U, MN	W(s)
Benedictine Coll, KS	W(s)
Benedictine U, IL	W
Bethany Coll, KS	W(s)
Bethany Lutheran Coll, MN	W
Bethel U, MN	W
Blackburn Coll, IL	W
Bluffton U, OH	W
Bowling Green State U, OH	W(s)
Bradley U, IL	W(s)
Briar Cliff U, IA	W(s)
Buena Vista U, IA	W
Butler U, IN	W(s)
Calumet Coll of Saint Joseph, IN	W
Calvin Coll, MI	W
Cameron U, OK	W(s)
Capital U, OH	W
Cardinal Stritch U, WI	W
Carleton Coll, MN	W
Carroll Coll, WI	W
Case Western Reserve U, OH	W
Cedarville U, OH	W(s)
Central Christian Coll of Kansas, KS	W(s)
Central Coll, IA	W
Central Methodist U, MO	W(s)
Central Michigan U, MI	W(s)
Clarke Coll, IA	W
Cleveland State U, OH	W(s)
Coe Coll, IA	W
Coll of Mount St. Joseph, OH	W
Coll of Saint Benedict, MN	W
Coll of St. Catherine, MN	W
Coll of Saint Mary, NE	W(s)
The Coll of St. Scholastica, MN	W
The Coll of Wooster, OH	W
Columbia Coll, MO	W(s)
Concordia Coll, MN	W
Concordia U, IL	W
Concordia U, MI	W(s)
Concordia U, NE	W(s)
Concordia U, St. Paul, MN	W(s)
Concordia U Wisconsin, WI	W
Cornell Coll, IA	W
Cornerstone U, MI	W(s)
Creighton U, NE	W(s)
Crossroads Coll, MN	W
Crown Coll, MN	W
Culver-Stockton Coll, MO	W(s)
Dakota State U, SD	W
Dakota Wesleyan U, SD	W(s)
Dana Coll, NE	W(s)
Denison U, OH	W
DePaul U, IL	W(s)
DePauw U, IN	W
Dickinson State U, ND	W(s)
Doane Coll, NE	W(s)
Dominican U, IL	W
Dordt Coll, IA	W(s)
Drake U, IA	W(s)
East Central U, OK	W(s)
Eastern Illinois U, IL	W(s)
Eastern Michigan U, MI	W(s)
Edgewood Coll, WI	W
Elmhurst Coll, IL	W
Emporia State U, KS	W(s)
Evangel U, MO	W(s)
Ferris State U, MI	W(s)
Finlandia U, MI	W
Fontbonne U, MO	W
Fort Hays State U, KS	W
Franklin Coll, IN	W
Gannon U, PA	W(s)
Goshen Coll, IN	W(s)
Grace Coll, IN	W(s)
Graceland U, IA	W(s)
Grand Valley State U, MI	W(s)
Grand View Coll, IA	W(s)
Greenville Coll, IL	W
Grinnell Coll, IA	W
Gustavus Adolphus Coll, MN	W
Hamline U, MN	W
Hannibal-LaGrange Coll, MO	W(s)
Hanover Coll, IN	W
Harris-Stowe State U, MO	W(s)
Hastings Coll, NE	W(s)
Heidelberg Coll, OH	W
Hesston Coll, KS	W(s)
Hillsdale Coll, MI	W(s)
Hillsdale Free Will Baptist Coll, OK	W
Hiram Coll, OH	W
Hope Coll, MI	W
Huntington U, IN	W(s)
Illinois Coll, IL	W
Illinois State U, IL	W(s)
Illinois Wesleyan U, IL	W
Indiana State U, IN	W
Indiana Tech, IN	W(s)
Indiana U Bloomington, IN	W(s)
Indiana U Northwest, IN	W
Indiana U–Purdue U Fort Wayne, IN	W(s)
Indiana U–Purdue U Indianapolis, IN	W(s)
Indiana Wesleyan U, IN	W(s)
Iowa State U of Science and Technology, IA	W(s)
Iowa Wesleyan Coll, IA	W(s)
Jamestown Coll, ND	W(s)
Judson Coll, IL	W(s)
Kalamazoo Coll, MI	W
Kent State U, OH	W(s)
Kenyon Coll, OH	W
Knox Coll, IL	W
Lake Forest Coll, IL	W
Lakeland Coll, WI	W
Lake Superior State U, MI	W
Lawrence U, WI	W
Lewis U, IL	W(s)
Lincoln U, MO	W(s)
Lindenwood U, MO	W(s)
Loras Coll, IA	W
Loyola U Chicago, IL	W(s)
Luther Coll, IA	W
Macalester Coll, MN	W
MacMurray Coll, IL	W
Madonna U, MI	W(s)
Malone Coll, OH	W(s)
Manchester Coll, IN	W
Maranatha Baptist Bible Coll, WI	W
Marian Coll, IN	W(s)
Marian Coll of Fond du Lac, WI	W
Marietta Coll, OH	W
Marquette U, WI	W
Martin Luther Coll, MN	W
Maryville U of Saint Louis, MO	W
Mayville State U, ND	W(s)
McKendree Coll, IL	W(s)
Miami U, OH	W(s)
Miami U Hamilton, OH	W
Miami U–Middletown Campus, OH	W
Michigan State U, MI	W
Mid-America Coll of Funeral Service, IN	M, W
Millikin U, IL	W
Milwaukee School of Engineering, WI	W

Minnesota State U Mankato, MN	W(s)	Southeast Missouri State U, MO	W(s)	Upper Iowa U, IA	W
Minot State U, ND	W(s)	Southern Illinois U Carbondale, IL	W(s)	Ursuline Coll, OH	W(s)
Missouri Baptist U, MO	W(s)	Southern Illinois U Edwardsville, IL	W(s)	Valley City State U, ND	W(s)
Missouri Southern State U, MO	W(s)	Southwest Baptist U, MO	W(s)	Valparaiso U, IN	W(s)
Missouri State U, MO	W(s)	Southwestern Coll, KS	W(s)	Viterbo U, WI	W(s)
Missouri Valley Coll, MO	W(s)	Southwestern Oklahoma State U, OK	W(s)	Waldorf Coll, IA	W(s)
Missouri Western State U, MO	W(s)	Southwest Minnesota State U, MN	W(s)	Walsh U, OH	W(s)
Morningside Coll, IA	W(s)	Spring Arbor U, MI	W(s)	Wartburg Coll, IA	W
Mount Marty Coll, SD	W(s)	Sterling Coll, KS	W(s)	Washburn U, KS	W(s)
Mount Mary Coll, WI	W	Tabor Coll, KS	W(s)	Washington U in St. Louis, MO	W
Mount Mercy Coll, IA	W	Taylor U, IN	W(s)	Wayne State Coll, NE	W(s)
Mount Union Coll, OH	W	Taylor U Fort Wayne, IN	W	Webster U, MO	W
Mount Vernon Nazarene U, OH	W(s)	Tiffin U, OH	W(s)	Western Illinois U, IL	W(s)
Nebraska Wesleyan U, NE	W	Transylvania U, KY	W	Western Michigan U, MI	W(s)
Newman U, KS	W(s)	Trinity Christian Coll, IL	W(s)	Westminster Coll, MO	W
North Carolina Ag and Tech State U, NC	W	Trinity International U, IL	W(s)	Wheaton Coll, IL	W
North Central Coll, IL	W	Tri-State U, IN	W	Wichita State U, KS	W(s)
North Dakota State U, ND	W(s)	Truman State U, MO	W(s)	William Jewell Coll, MO	W(s)
Northeastern State U, OK	W(s)	The U of Akron, OH	W(s)	William Penn U, IA	W(s)
Northern Illinois U, IL	W(s)	U of Central Missouri, MO	W(s)	William Woods U, MO	W(s)
Northern Michigan U, MI	W	U of Central Oklahoma, OK	W(s)	Wilmington Coll, OH	W
Northern State U, SD	W(s)	U of Charleston, WV	W(s)	Winona State U, MN	W(s)
Northland Coll, WI	W	U of Chicago, IL	W	Wisconsin Lutheran Coll, WI	W
Northwestern Coll, IA	W(s)	U of Dallas, TX	W	Wittenberg U, OH	W
Northwestern Coll, MN	W	U of Dayton, OH	W(s)	Wright State U, OH	W(s)
Northwestern Oklahoma State U, OK	W(s)	U of Evansville, IN	W(s)	Xavier U, OH	W
Northwestern U, IL	W(s)	The U of Findlay, OH	W(s)	York Coll, NE	W(s)
Northwest Missouri State U, MO	W(s)	U of Illinois at Chicago, IL	W(s)	Youngstown State U, OH	W(s)
Northwood U, MI	W(s)	U of Illinois at Springfield, IL	W(s)		
Notre Dame Coll, OH	W(s)	U of Indianapolis, IN	W(s)	**Squash**	
Oakland U, MI	W(s)	The U of Iowa, IA	W(s)	Denison U, OH	M, W
Oberlin Coll, OH	W	U of Kansas, KS	W(s)	Kenyon Coll, OH	M, W
Ohio Dominican U, OH	W(s)	U of Mary, ND	W(s)	Michigan Technological U, MI	M, W
Ohio Northern U, OH	W	U of Michigan, MI	W(s)		
The Ohio State U, OH	W(s)	U of Minnesota, Crookston, MN	W(s)	**Swimming and Diving**	
Ohio U, OH	W(s)	U of Minnesota, Duluth, MN	W(s)	Albion Coll, MI	M, W
Ohio U–Zanesville, OH	W	U of Minnesota, Morris, MN	W	Alma Coll, MI	M, W
Ohio Wesleyan U, OH	W	U of Minnesota, Twin Cities Campus, MN	W(s)	Ashland U, OH	M(s), W(s)
Oklahoma Christian U, OK	W(s)			Augustana Coll, IL	M, W
Oklahoma City U, OK	W(s)	U of Missouri–Columbia, MO	W(s)	Baldwin-Wallace Coll, OH	M, W
Oklahoma Panhandle State U, OK	W(s)	U of Missouri–Kansas City, MO	W(s)	Ball State U, IN	M(s), W(s)
Oklahoma State U, OK	W(s)	U of Missouri–Rolla, MO	W(s)	Beloit Coll, WI	M, W
Oklahoma Wesleyan U, OK	W(s)	U of Missouri–St. Louis, MO	W(s)	Benedictine U, IL	M, W
Ottawa U, KS	W(s)	U of Nebraska at Kearney, NE	W(s)	Bowling Green State U, OH	M(s), W(s)
Otterbein Coll, OH	W	U of Nebraska at Omaha, NE	W(s)	Butler U, IN	M, W
Park U, MO	W(s)	U of Nebraska–Lincoln, NE	W(s)	Calvin Coll, MI	M, W
Peru State Coll, NE	W(s)	U of North Dakota, ND	W(s)	Carleton Coll, MN	M, W
Pittsburg State U, KS	W(s)	U of Northern Iowa, IA	W(s)	Carroll Coll, WI	M, W
Presentation Coll, SD	W	U of Notre Dame, IN	W(s)	Case Western Reserve U, OH	M, W
Purdue U, IN	W(s)	U of Oklahoma, OK	W(s)	Clarkson U, NY	M, W
Purdue U North Central, IN	W	U of Rio Grande, OH	W(s)	Cleveland State U, OH	M(s), W(s)
Quincy U, IL	W(s)	U of St. Francis, IL	W(s)	Coe Coll, IA	M, W
Ripon Coll, WI	W	U of Saint Francis, IN	W(s)	Coll of Saint Benedict, MN	W
Robert Morris Coll, IL	W(s)	U of Saint Mary, KS	W(s)	Coll of St. Catherine, MN	W
Rochester Coll, MI	W(s)	U of St. Thomas, MN	W	The Coll of Wooster, OH	M, W
Rockford Coll, IL	W	U of Science and Arts of Oklahoma, OK	W(s)	Concordia Coll, MN	W
Rockhurst U, MO	W(s)			Denison U, OH	M, W
Rose-Hulman Inst of Technology, IN	W	U of Sioux Falls, SD	W(s)	DePauw U, IN	M, W
Saginaw Valley State U, MI	W(s)	The U of South Dakota, SD	W(s)	Drury U, MO	M(s), W(s)
St. Ambrose U, IA	W(s)	U of Southern Indiana, IN	W(s)	Eastern Illinois U, IL	M(s), W(s)
St. Cloud State U, MN	W(s)	The U of Toledo, OH	W(s)	Eastern Michigan U, MI	M(s), W(s)
St. Gregory's U, Shawnee, OK	W(s)	U of Tulsa, OK	W(s)	Gannon U, PA	M(s), W(s)
Saint Joseph's Coll, IN	W(s)	U of West Florida, FL	W(s)	Grand Valley State U, MI	M(s), W(s)
Saint Louis U, MO	W(s)	U of Wisconsin–Eau Claire, WI	W	Grinnell Coll, IA	M, W
Saint Mary-of-the-Woods Coll, IN	W(s)	U of Wisconsin–Green Bay, WI	W(s)	Gustavus Adolphus Coll, MN	M, W
Saint Mary's Coll, IN	W	U of Wisconsin–La Crosse, WI	W	Hamline U, MN	M, W
Saint Mary's U of Minnesota, MN	W	U of Wisconsin–Madison, WI	W	Hillsdale Coll, MI	W(s)
St. Norbert Coll, WI	W	U of Wisconsin–Oshkosh, WI	W	Hiram Coll, OH	M, W
St. Olaf Coll, MN	W	U of Wisconsin–Parkside, WI	W(s)	Hope Coll, MI	M, W
Saint Xavier U, IL	W(s)	U of Wisconsin–Platteville, WI	W	Illinois Inst of Technology, IL	M(s), W(s)
Shawnee State U, OH	W	U of Wisconsin–River Falls, WI	W	Illinois State U, IL	W(s)
Simpson Coll, IA	W	U of Wisconsin–Stevens Point, WI	W	Illinois Wesleyan U, IL	M, W
South Dakota State U, SD	W(s)	U of Wisconsin–Stout, WI	W	Indiana U Bloomington, IN	M(s), W(s)
Southeastern Oklahoma State U, OK	W(s)	U of Wisconsin–Superior, WI	W	Indiana U–Purdue U Indianapolis, IN	M(s), W(s)
		U of Wisconsin–Whitewater, WI	W	Iowa State U of Science and Technology, IA	M(s), W(s)

M—for men; W—for women; (s)—scholarship offered

Kalamazoo Coll, MI	M, W
Kenyon Coll, OH	M, W
Knox Coll, IL	M, W
Lake Forest Coll, IL	M, W
Lawrence U, WI	M, W
Lewis U, IL	M(s), W(s)
Lindenwood U, MO	M(s), W(s)
Loras Coll, IA	M, W
Luther Coll, IA	M, W
Macalester Coll, MN	M, W
MacMurray Coll, IL	M, W
Marquette U, WI	M, W
Miami U, OH	M(s), W(s)
Michigan State U, MI	M(s), W(s)
Michigan Technological U, MI	M, W
Millikin U, IL	M, W
Minnesota State U Mankato, MN	M(s), W(s)
Missouri State U, MO	M(s), W(s)
Morningside Coll, IA	M(s), W(s)
Mount Union Coll, OH	M, W
North Carolina Ag and Tech State U, NC	W(s)
North Central Coll, IL	M, W
Northern Illinois U, IL	M(s), W(s)
Northern Michigan U, MI	W
Northwestern U, IL	M(s), W(s)
Oakland U, MI	M(s), W(s)
Oberlin Coll, OH	M, W
Ohio Northern U, OH	M, W
The Ohio State U, OH	M(s), W(s)
Ohio U, OH	M(s), W(s)
Ohio Wesleyan U, OH	M, W
Purdue U, IN	M(s), W(s)
Ripon Coll, WI	M, W
Rose-Hulman Inst of Technology, IN	M, W
St. Cloud State U, MN	M(s), W(s)
Saint John's U, MN	M
Saint Louis U, MO	M(s), W(s)
Saint Mary's Coll, IN	W
Saint Mary's U of Minnesota, MN	M, W
St. Norbert Coll, WI	W
St. Olaf Coll, MN	M, W
Simpson Coll, IA	M, W
South Dakota State U, SD	M(s), W(s)
Southern Illinois U Carbondale, IL	M(s), W(s)
Southern Methodist U, TX	M(s), W(s)
Stephens Coll, MO	W
Transylvania U, KY	M, W
Truman State U, MO	M(s), W(s)
The U of Akron, OH	W
U of Charleston, WV	M(s), W(s)
U of Chicago, IL	M, W
U of Cincinnati, OH	M(s), W(s)
U of Evansville, IN	M(s), W(s)
The U of Findlay, OH	M(s), W(s)
U of Illinois at Chicago, IL	M(s), W(s)
U of Illinois at Urbana–Champaign, IL	W(s)
U of Indianapolis, IN	M(s), W(s)
The U of Iowa, IA	M(s), W(s)
U of Kansas, KS	W(s)
U of Michigan, MI	M(s), W(s)
U of Minnesota, Morris, MN	W
U of Minnesota, Twin Cities Campus, MN	M(s), W(s)
U of Missouri–Columbia, MO	M(s), W(s)
U of Missouri–Rolla, MO	M(s)
U of Nebraska at Kearney, NE	W(s)
U of Nebraska at Omaha, NE	W
U of Nebraska–Lincoln, NE	W(s)
U of North Dakota, ND	M, W
U of Northern Iowa, IA	W(s)
U of Notre Dame, IN	M(s), W(s)
U of St. Thomas, MN	M, W
The U of South Dakota, SD	M(s), W
The U of Toledo, OH	M(s), W(s)
U of Wisconsin–Eau Claire, WI	M, W

U of Wisconsin–Green Bay, WI	M(s), W(s)
U of Wisconsin–La Crosse, WI	M, W
U of Wisconsin–Madison, WI	M(s), W(s)
U of Wisconsin–Milwaukee, WI	M(s), W(s)
U of Wisconsin–Oshkosh, WI	M, W
U of Wisconsin–River Falls, WI	M, W
U of Wisconsin–Stevens Point, WI	M, W
U of Wisconsin–Whitewater, WI	M, W
Valparaiso U, IN	M(s), W(s)
Wabash Coll, IN	M
Washington U in St. Louis, MO	M, W
Webster U, MO	M, W
Western Illinois U, IL	M(s), W(s)
Wheaton Coll, IL	M, W
Wichita State U, KS	M, W
Wilmington Coll, OH	M, W
Wittenberg U, OH	M, W
Wright State U, OH	M(s), W(s)
Xavier U, OH	M(s), W(s)
Youngstown State U, OH	W

Table Tennis

Bradley U, IL	M, W
Hiram Coll, OH	M, W
Michigan Technological U, MI	M, W
The U of Iowa, IA	M, W
Washington U in St. Louis, MO	M, W

Tennis

Adrian Coll, MI	M, W
Albion Coll, MI	M, W
Alma Coll, MI	M, W
Anderson U, IN	M, W
Aquinas Coll, MI	M(s), W(s)
Ashland U, OH	M, W
Augustana Coll, IL	M, W
Augustana Coll, SD	M, W
Aurora U, IL	M, W
Baker U, KS	M(s), W(s)
Baldwin-Wallace Coll, OH	M, W
Ball State U, IN	M(s), W(s)
Barclay Coll, KS	M, W
Beloit Coll, WI	M, W
Bemidji State U, MN	W(s)
Benedictine Coll, KS	M(s), W(s)
Benedictine U, IL	W
Bethany Coll, KS	M(s), W(s)
Bethany Lutheran Coll, MN	M, W
Bethel Coll, KS	M(s), W(s)
Bethel U, MN	M, W
Blackburn Coll, IL	W
Bluffton U, OH	M, W
Bowling Green State U, OH	M(s), W(s)
Bradley U, IL	M(s), W(s)
Briar Cliff U, IA	W
Buena Vista U, IA	M, W
Butler U, IN	M(s), W(s)
Calvin Coll, MI	M, W
Cameron U, OK	M(s), W(s)
Capital U, OH	M, W
Carleton Coll, MN	M, W
Carroll Coll, WI	M, W
Case Western Reserve U, OH	M, W
Cedarville U, OH	M(s), W(s)
Central Christian Coll of Kansas, KS	M(s), W(s)
Central Coll, IA	M, W
Central State U, OH	M(s), W(s)
Chicago State U, IL	M(s), W(s)
Clarke Coll, IA	M, W
Clarkson U, NY	M, W
Cleveland State U, OH	W(s)
Coe Coll, IA	M, W
Coll of Mount St. Joseph, OH	M, W
Coll of Saint Benedict, MN	W
Coll of St. Catherine, MN	W
The Coll of St. Scholastica, MN	M, W
The Coll of Wooster, OH	M, W

Concordia Coll, MN	M, W
Concordia U, IL	M, W
Concordia U, NE	M(s), W(s)
Concordia U Wisconsin, WI	M, W
Concord U, WV	M(s), W(s)
Cornell Coll, IA	M, W
Creighton U, NE	M(s), W(s)
Crossroads Coll, MN	M, W
Denison U, OH	M, W
DePaul U, IL	M(s), W(s)
DePauw U, IN	M, W
Doane Coll, NE	M, W
Dominican U, IL	M, W
Dordt Coll, IA	M(s), W(s)
Drake U, IA	M(s), W(s)
Drury U, MO	M(s), W(s)
Earlham Coll, IN	M, W
East Central U, OK	M(s), W(s)
Eastern Illinois U, IL	M(s), W(s)
Eastern Michigan U, MI	W(s)
Edgewood Coll, WI	M, W
Elmhurst Coll, IL	M, W
Emporia State U, KS	M(s), W(s)
Evangel U, MO	M(s), W(s)
Ferris State U, MI	M(s), W(s)
Fontbonne U, MO	M, W
Fort Hays State U, KS	W(s)
Franklin Coll, IN	M, W
Goshen Coll, IN	M(s), W(s)
Grace Coll, IN	M(s), W(s)
Graceland U, IA	M(s), W(s)
Grand Valley State U, MI	M(s), W(s)
Greenville Coll, IL	M, W
Grinnell Coll, IA	M, W
Gustavus Adolphus Coll, MN	M, W
Hamline U, MN	M, W
Hanover Coll, IN	M, W
Harris-Stowe State U, MO	M(s), W(s)
Hastings Coll, NE	M(s), W(s)
Heidelberg Coll, OH	M, W
Hesston Coll, KS	M(s), W(s)
Hiram Coll, OH	M, W
Hope Coll, MI	M, W
Huntington U, IN	M(s), W(s)
Illinois Coll, IL	M, W
Illinois State U, IL	M(s), W(s)
Illinois Wesleyan U, IL	M, W
Indiana State U, IN	M(s), W(s)
Indiana U Bloomington, IN	M(s), W(s)
Indiana U–Purdue U Fort Wayne, IN	M(s), W(s)
Indiana U–Purdue U Indianapolis, IN	M(s), W(s)
Indiana U Southeast, IN	M, W
Indiana Wesleyan U, IN	M(s), W(s)
Iowa State U of Science and Technology, IA	W(s)
Judson Coll, IL	M(s), W(s)
Kalamazoo Coll, MI	M, W
Kansas State U, KS	W(s)
Kenyon Coll, OH	M, W
Knox Coll, IL	M, W
Lake Forest Coll, IL	M, W
Lakeland Coll, WI	M, W
Lake Superior State U, MI	M(s), W(s)
Lawrence U, WI	M, W
Lewis U, IL	M(s), W(s)
Lincoln U, MO	W(s)
Lindenwood U, MO	M(s), W(s)
Loras Coll, IA	M, W
Luther Coll, IA	M, W
Macalester Coll, MN	M, W
MacMurray Coll, IL	M, W
Malone Coll, OH	M(s), W(s)
Manchester Coll, IN	M, W
Marian Coll, IN	M(s), W(s)
Marian Coll of Fond du Lac, WI	M, W
Marietta Coll, OH	M, W

Marquette U, WI	M(s), W(s)	Southwest Minnesota State U, MN	W(s)	William Jewell Coll, MO	M(s), W(s)
Martin Luther Coll, MN	M, W	Spring Arbor U, MI	M(s), W(s)	Wilmington Coll, OH	M, W
Maryville U of Saint Louis, MO	M, W	Stephens Coll, MO	W	Winona State U, MN	M(s), W(s)
McKendree Coll, IL	M(s), W(s)	Tabor Coll, KS	M(s), W(s)	Wisconsin Lutheran Coll, WI	W
Miami U, OH	M, W(s)	Taylor U, IN	M(s), W(s)	Wittenberg U, OH	M, W
Miami U Hamilton, OH	M, W	Tiffin U, OH	M(s), W(s)	Wright State U, OH	M(s), W(s)
Miami U–Middletown Campus, OH	M, W	Transylvania U, KY	M, W	Xavier U, OH	M(s), W(s)
Michigan State U, MI	M(s), W(s)	Tri-State U, IN	M, W	Youngstown State U, OH	M(s), W(s)
Michigan Technological U, MI	M, W(s)	Truman State U, MO	M(s), W(s)		
Millikin U, IL	W	The U of Akron, OH	M(s), W(s)	**Track and Field**	
Milwaukee School of Engineering, WI	M, W	U of Central Oklahoma, OK	M(s), W(s)	Adrian Coll, MI	M, W
Minnesota State U Mankato, MN	M(s), W(s)	U of Charleston, WV	M(s), W(s)	Albion Coll, MI	M, W
Missouri Baptist U, MO	W	U of Chicago, IL	M, W	Alma Coll, MI	M, W
Missouri Southern State U, MO	W(s)	U of Cincinnati, OH	M, W	Anderson U, IN	M, W
Missouri State U, MO	M(s), W(s)	U of Dallas, TX	M, W	Aquinas Coll, MI	M(s), W(s)
Missouri Valley Coll, MO	M(s), W(s)	U of Dayton, OH	M(s), W(s)	Ashford U, IA	M(s), W(s)
Missouri Western State U, MO	W(s)	U of Evansville, IN	W(s)	Ashland U, OH	M(s), W(s)
Morningside Coll, IA	M(s), W(s)	The U of Findlay, OH	M(s), W(s)	Augsburg Coll, MN	M, W
Mount Mary Coll, WI	W	U of Illinois at Chicago, IL	M(s), W(s)	Augustana Coll, IL	M, W
Mount Union Coll, OH	M, W	U of Illinois at Springfield, IL	M(s), W(s)	Augustana Coll, SD	M(s), W(s)
Nebraska Wesleyan U, NE	M, W	U of Illinois at Urbana–Champaign, IL	M(s), W(s)	Baker U, KS	M(s), W(s)
Newman U, KS	M(s), W(s)	U of Indianapolis, IN	M(s), W(s)	Baldwin-Wallace Coll, OH	M, W
North Carolina Ag and Tech State U, NC	M(s), W(s)	The U of Iowa, IA	M(s), W(s)	Ball State U, IN	M(s), W(s)
North Central Coll, IL	M, W	U of Kansas, KS	W(s)	Beloit Coll, WI	M, W
Northeastern State U, OK	W(s)	U of Mary, ND	M(s), W(s)	Bemidji State U, MN	M(s), W(s)
Northern Illinois U, IL	M(s), W(s)	U of Michigan, MI	M(s), W(s)	Benedictine Coll, KS	M(s), W(s)
Northern State U, SD	M, W(s)	U of Minnesota, Crookston, MN	W	Benedictine U, IL	M, W
Northwestern Coll, MN	M, W	U of Minnesota, Duluth, MN	M(s), W(s)	Bethany Coll, KS	M(s), W(s)
Northwestern U, IL	M(s), W(s)	U of Minnesota, Morris, MN	M, W	Bethel Coll, KS	M(s), W(s)
Northwest Missouri State U, MO	M(s), W(s)	U of Minnesota, Twin Cities Campus, MN	M(s), W(s)	Bethel U, MN	M, W
Northwood U, MI	M(s), W(s)	U of Missouri–Columbia, MO	W(s)	Black Hills State U, SD	M(s), W(s)
Notre Dame Coll, OH	M(s)	U of Missouri–Kansas City, MO	M(s), W(s)	Bluffton U, OH	M, W
Oakland U, MI	W(s)	U of Missouri–St. Louis, MO	M(s), W(s)	Bowling Green State U, OH	M(s), W(s)
Oberlin Coll, OH	M, W	U of Nebraska at Kearney, NE	M(s), W(s)	Bradley U, IL	W(s)
Ohio Dominican U, OH	M(s), W(s)	U of Nebraska at Omaha, NE	W	Briar Cliff U, IA	M(s), W(s)
Ohio Northern U, OH	M, W	U of Nebraska–Lincoln, NE	M(s), W(s)	Buena Vista U, IA	M, W
The Ohio State U, OH	M(s), W(s)	U of New Orleans, LA	M(s), W(s)	Butler U, IN	M, W
Ohio U–Zanesville, OH	M, W	U of North Dakota, ND	W	Calvin Coll, MI	M, W
Ohio Wesleyan U, OH	M, W	U of Northern Iowa, IA	M, W(s)	Capital U, OH	M, W
Oklahoma Christian U, OK	M(s), W(s)	U of Notre Dame, IN	M(s), W(s)	Carleton Coll, MN	M, W
Oklahoma State U, OK	M(s), W(s)	U of Oklahoma, OK	M(s), W(s)	Carroll Coll, WI	M, W
Oklahoma Wesleyan U, OK	M(s), W(s)	U of St. Francis, IL	M(s), W(s)	Case Western Reserve U, OH	M, W
Oral Roberts U, OK	M(s), W(s)	U of Saint Francis, IN	M(s), W(s)	Cedarville U, OH	M(s), W(s)
Otterbein Coll, OH	M, W	U of St. Thomas, MN	M, W	Central Coll, IA	M, W
Purdue U, IN	M(s), W(s)	U of Sioux Falls, SD	M(s), W(s)	Central Methodist U, MO	M(s), W(s)
Quincy U, IL	M(s), W(s)	The U of South Dakota, SD	M(s), W(s)	Central Michigan U, MI	M(s), W(s)
Research Coll of Nursing, MO	M(s), W(s)	U of Southern Indiana, IN	M(s), W(s)	Central State U, OH	M(s), W(s)
Ripon Coll, WI	M, W	The U of Toledo, OH	M(s), W(s)	Chicago State U, IL	M(s), W(s)
Robert Morris Coll, IL	W(s)	U of Tulsa, OK	M(s), W(s)	Cleveland State U, OH	W(s)
Rockford Coll, IL	M, W	U of West Florida, FL	M(s), W(s)	Coe Coll, IA	M, W
Rockhurst U, MO	M(s), W(s)	U of Wisconsin–Eau Claire, WI	M, W	Coll of Mount St. Joseph, OH	M, W
Rose-Hulman Inst of Technology, IN	M(s), W(s)	U of Wisconsin–Green Bay, WI	M(s), W(s)	Coll of Saint Benedict, MN	W
Saginaw Valley State U, MI	W(s)	U of Wisconsin–La Crosse, WI	M, W	Coll of St. Catherine, MN	W
St. Ambrose U, IA	M(s), W(s)	U of Wisconsin–Madison, WI	M(s), W(s)	The Coll of St. Scholastica, MN	M, W
St. Cloud State U, MN	M(s), W(s)	U of Wisconsin–Milwaukee, WI	M(s), W(s)	The Coll of Wooster, OH	M, W
Saint John's U, MN	M	U of Wisconsin–Oshkosh, WI	M, W	Concordia Coll, MN	M, W
Saint Joseph's Coll, IN	M(s), W(s)	U of Wisconsin–River Falls, WI	W	Concordia U, IL	M, W
Saint Louis U, MO	M(s), W(s)	U of Wisconsin–Stevens Point, WI	W	Concordia U, NE	M(s), W(s)
Saint Mary's Coll, IN	W	U of Wisconsin–Stout, WI	W	Concordia U, St. Paul, MN	M(s), W(s)
Saint Mary's U of Minnesota, MN	M, W	U of Wisconsin–Whitewater, WI	M, W	Concordia U Wisconsin, WI	M, W
St. Norbert Coll, WI	M, W	Upper Iowa U, IA	M, W	Concord U, WV	M(s), W(s)
St. Olaf Coll, MN	M, W	Ursuline Coll, OH	W(s)	Cornell Coll, IA	M, W
Shawnee State U, OH	W	Valparaiso U, IN	M(s), W(s)	Cornerstone U, MI	M(s), W(s)
Simpson Coll, IA	M, W	Wabash Coll, IN	M	Dakota State U, SD	M(s), W(s)
South Dakota School of Mines and Technology, SD	M	Walsh U, OH	M(s), W(s)	Dakota Wesleyan U, SD	M(s), W(s)
South Dakota State U, SD	M(s), W(s)	Wartburg Coll, IA	M, W	Dana Coll, NE	M(s), W(s)
Southeastern Oklahoma State U, OK	M(s), W(s)	Washburn U, KS	M(s), W(s)	Denison U, OH	M, W
Southeast Missouri State U, MO	W(s)	Washington U in St. Louis, MO	M, W	DePaul U, IL	M(s), W(s)
Southern Illinois U Carbondale, IL	M(s), W(s)	Webster U, MO	M, W	DePauw U, IN	M, W
Southern Illinois U Edwardsville, IL	M(s), W(s)	Western Illinois U, IL	M(s), W(s)	Dickinson State U, ND	M(s), W(s)
Southern Methodist U, TX	M(s), W(s)	Western Michigan U, MI	M(s), W(s)	Doane Coll, NE	M(s), W(s)
Southwest Baptist U, MO	M(s), W(s)	Westminster Coll, MO	M, W	Dordt Coll, IA	M(s), W(s)
Southwestern Coll, KS	M(s), W(s)	Wheaton Coll, IL	M, W	Drake U, IA	M(s), W(s)
		Wichita State U, KS	M(s), W(s)	Earlham Coll, IN	M, W
				East Central U, OK	M, W

M—for men; W—for women; (s)—scholarship offered

Eastern Illinois U, IL	M(s), W(s)
Eastern Michigan U, MI	M(s), W(s)
Elmhurst Coll, IL	M, W
Emporia State U, KS	M(s), W(s)
Evangel U, MO	M(s), W(s)
Ferris State U, MI	M(s), W(s)
Fort Hays State U, KS	M(s), W(s)
Franklin Coll, IN	M, W
Goshen Coll, IN	M(s), W(s)
Grace Coll, IN	M(s), W(s)
Graceland U, IA	M(s), W(s)
Grand Valley State U, MI	M(s), W(s)
Grand View Coll, IA	M(s), W(s)
Greenville Coll, IL	M, W
Grinnell Coll, IA	M, W
Gustavus Adolphus Coll, MN	M, W
Hamline U, MN	M, W
Hanover Coll, IN	M, W
Harris-Stowe State U, MO	W(s)
Hastings Coll, NE	M(s), W(s)
Heidelberg Coll, OH	M, W
Hillsdale Coll, MI	M(s), W(s)
Hiram Coll, OH	M, W
Hope Coll, MI	M, W
Huntington U, IN	M(s), W(s)
Illinois Coll, IL	M, W
Illinois State U, IL	M(s), W(s)
Illinois Wesleyan U, IL	M, W
Indiana State U, IN	M(s), W(s)
Indiana U Bloomington, IN	M(s), W(s)
Indiana U–Purdue U Fort Wayne, IN	W(s)
Indiana Wesleyan U, IN	M(s), W(s)
Iowa State U of Science and Technology, IA	M(s), W(s)
Iowa Wesleyan Coll, IA	M(s), W(s)
Jamestown Coll, ND	M(s), W(s)
Kansas State U, KS	M(s), W(s)
Kent State U, OH	M(s), W(s)
Kenyon Coll, OH	M, W
Knox Coll, IL	M, W
Lake Forest Coll, IL	M, W
Lake Superior State U, MI	M(s), W(s)
Langston U, OK	M(s), W(s)
Lawrence U, WI	M, W
Lewis U, IL	M(s), W(s)
Lincoln U, MO	M(s), W(s)
Lindenwood U, MO	M(s), W(s)
Loras Coll, IA	M, W
Loyola U Chicago, IL	M(s), W(s)
Luther Coll, IA	M, W
Macalester Coll, MN	M, W
Malone Coll, OH	M(s), W(s)
Manchester Coll, IN	M, W
Marietta Coll, OH	M, W
Marquette U, WI	M(s), W(s)
Martin Luther Coll, MN	M, W
Maryville U of Saint Louis, MO	M, W
McKendree Coll, IL	M(s), W(s)
Miami U, OH	M(s), W(s)
Michigan State U, MI	M(s), W(s)
Michigan Technological U, MI	M, W
Millikin U, IL	M, W
Milwaukee School of Engineering, WI	M, W
Minnesota State U Mankato, MN	M(s), W(s)
Minot State U, ND	M(s), W(s)
Missouri Baptist U, MO	M, W
Missouri Southern State U, MO	M(s), W(s)
Missouri State U, MO	M(s), W(s)
Missouri Valley Coll, MO	M(s), W(s)
Morningside Coll, IA	M(s), W(s)
Mount Marty Coll, SD	M(s), W(s)
Mount Mercy Coll, IA	M, W
Mount Union Coll, OH	M, W
Nebraska Wesleyan U, NE	M, W

North Carolina Ag and Tech State U, NC	M(s), W(s)
North Central Coll, IL	M, W
North Dakota State U, ND	M(s), W(s)
Northern Michigan U, MI	W
Northern State U, SD	M(s), W(s)
Northwestern Coll, IA	M(s), W(s)
Northwestern Coll, MN	M, W
Northwest Missouri State U, MO	M(s), W(s)
Northwood U, MI	M(s), W(s)
Notre Dame Coll, OH	M, W
Oakland U, MI	M, W
Oberlin Coll, OH	M, W
Ohio Northern U, OH	M, W
The Ohio State U, OH	M(s), W(s)
Ohio U, OH	M(s), W(s)
Ohio Wesleyan U, OH	M, W
Oklahoma Christian U, OK	M(s), W(s)
Oklahoma State U, OK	M(s), W(s)
Oral Roberts U, OK	M(s), W(s)
Ottawa U, KS	M(s), W(s)
Otterbein Coll, OH	M, W
Park U, MO	M(s), W(s)
Pittsburg State U, KS	M(s), W(s)
Purdue U, IN	M(s), W(s)
Ripon Coll, WI	M, W
Rose-Hulman Inst of Technology, IN	M, W
Saginaw Valley State U, MI	M(s), W(s)
St. Ambrose U, IA	M(s), W(s)
St. Cloud State U, MN	M(s), W(s)
St. Gregory's U, Shawnee, OK	M(s), W(s)
Saint John's U, MN	M
Saint Joseph's Coll, IN	M(s), W(s)
Saint Mary's U of Minnesota, MN	M, W
St. Norbert Coll, WI	M, W
St. Olaf Coll, MN	M, W
Simpson Coll, IA	M, W
South Dakota School of Mines and Technology, SD	M(s), W(s)
South Dakota State U, SD	M(s), W(s)
Southeast Missouri State U, MO	M(s), W(s)
Southern Illinois U Carbondale, IL	M(s), W(s)
Southern Illinois U Edwardsville, IL	M(s), W(s)
Southern Methodist U, TX	M(s), W(s)
Southwest Baptist U, MO	M, W
Southwestern Coll, KS	M(s), W(s)
Spring Arbor U, MI	M(s), W(s)
Sterling Coll, KS	M(s), W(s)
Tabor Coll, KS	M(s), W(s)
Taylor U, IN	M(s), W(s)
Tiffin U, OH	M(s), W(s)
Trinity Christian Coll, IL	M(s), W(s)
Trinity International U, IL	M, W
Tri-State U, IN	M, W
Truman State U, MO	M(s), W(s)
The U of Akron, OH	M(s), W(s)
U of Central Missouri, MO	M(s), W(s)
U of Charleston, WV	M(s), W(s)
U of Chicago, IL	M, W
U of Cincinnati, OH	M(s), W(s)
U of Dallas, TX	M, W
U of Dayton, OH	W(s)
The U of Findlay, OH	M(s), W(s)
U of Illinois at Chicago, IL	M(s), W(s)
U of Illinois at Urbana–Champaign, IL	M(s), W(s)
U of Indianapolis, IN	M(s), W(s)
The U of Iowa, IA	M(s), W(s)
U of Kansas, KS	M(s), W(s)
U of Mary, ND	M(s), W(s)
U of Michigan, MI	M(s), W(s)
U of Minnesota, Duluth, MN	M(s), W(s)
U of Minnesota, Morris, MN	M, W
U of Minnesota, Twin Cities Campus, MN	M(s), W(s)
U of Missouri–Columbia, MO	M(s), W(s)
U of Missouri–Kansas City, MO	M(s), W(s)

U of Missouri–Rolla, MO	M(s), W(s)
U of Nebraska at Kearney, NE	M(s), W(s)
U of Nebraska–Lincoln, NE	M(s), W(s)
U of New Orleans, LA	M(s), W(s)
U of North Dakota, ND	M(s), W(s)
U of Northern Iowa, IA	M(s), W(s)
U of Notre Dame, IN	M(s), W(s)
U of Oklahoma, OK	M(s), W(s)
U of Rio Grande, OH	M(s), W(s)
U of St. Francis, IL	W(s)
U of Saint Francis, IN	M(s), W(s)
U of St. Thomas, MN	M, W
U of Sioux Falls, SD	M(s), W(s)
The U of South Dakota, SD	M(s), W(s)
The U of Toledo, OH	M(s), W(s)
U of Tulsa, OK	M(s), W(s)
U of West Florida, FL	W
U of Wisconsin–Eau Claire, WI	M, W
U of Wisconsin–La Crosse, WI	M, W
U of Wisconsin–Madison, WI	M(s), W(s)
U of Wisconsin–Milwaukee, WI	M(s), W(s)
U of Wisconsin–Oshkosh, WI	M, W
U of Wisconsin–Parkside, WI	M(s), W(s)
U of Wisconsin–Platteville, WI	M, W
U of Wisconsin–River Falls, WI	M, W
U of Wisconsin–Stevens Point, WI	M, W
U of Wisconsin–Stout, WI	M, W
U of Wisconsin–Superior, WI	M, W
U of Wisconsin–Whitewater, WI	M, W
Upper Iowa U, IA	M, W
Valparaiso U, IN	M, W
Wabash Coll, IN	M
Walsh U, OH	M(s), W(s)
Wartburg Coll, IA	M, W
Washington U in St. Louis, MO	M, W
Wayne State Coll, NE	M(s), W(s)
Western Illinois U, IL	M(s), W(s)
Western Michigan U, MI	W(s)
Wheaton Coll, IL	M, W
Wichita State U, KS	M(s), W(s)
William Jewell Coll, MO	M(s), W(s)
William Penn U, IA	M(s), W(s)
William Woods U, MO	M, W
Wilmington Coll, OH	M, W
Winona State U, MN	W(s)
Wisconsin Lutheran Coll, WI	M, W
Wittenberg U, OH	M, W
Wright State U, OH	W(s)
York Coll, NE	M(s), W(s)
Youngstown State U, OH	M(s), W(s)

Ultimate Frisbee

Augustana Coll, IL	M, W
Carleton Coll, MN	M, W
Case Western Reserve U, OH	M, W
Coll of Saint Benedict, MN	W
Earlham Coll, IN	M, W
Gustavus Adolphus Coll, MN	M, W
Illinois Wesleyan U, IL	M, W
Kenyon Coll, OH	M, W
Lake Forest Coll, IL	M, W
Lawrence U, WI	M, W
Macalester Coll, MN	W
Missouri Baptist U, MO	M, W
Missouri State U, MO	M, W
Oberlin Coll, OH	M, W
Ohio Wesleyan U, OH	M, W
St. Cloud State U, MN	M, W
Saint John's U, MN	M
Saint Louis U, MO	M, W
Saint Mary's Coll, IN	W
The U of Iowa, IA	M, W
U of Southern Indiana, IN	M, W
U of Wisconsin–Madison, WI	M, W
U of Wisconsin–Platteville, WI	M, W
Washington U in St. Louis, MO	M, W

Volleyball

Adrian Coll, MI	W
Albion Coll, MI	M, W
Alma Coll, MI	W
Alverno Coll, WI	W
Anderson U, IN	W
Aquinas Coll, MI	W(s)
Ashford U, IA	W(s)
Ashland U, OH	W(s)
Augsburg Coll, MN	W
Augustana Coll, IL	M, W
Augustana Coll, SD	W(s)
Aurora U, IL	W
Avila U, MO	W(s)
Baker U, KS	W(s)
Baldwin-Wallace Coll, OH	W
Ball State U, IN	M(s), W(s)
Baptist Bible Coll, MO	W
Barclay Coll, KS	W
Bellevue U, NE	W(s)
Beloit Coll, WI	W
Bemidji State U, MN	W(s)
Benedictine Coll, KS	W(s)
Benedictine U, IL	W
Bethany Coll, KS	W(s)
Bethany Lutheran Coll, MN	
Bethel Coll, KS	W(s)
Bethel U, MN	M, W
Blackburn Coll, IL	W
Black Hills State U, SD	W(s)
Blessing-Rieman Coll of Nursing, IL	M(s), W(s)
Bluffton U, OH	W
Bowling Green State U, OH	M, W(s)
Bradley U, IL	W(s)
Briar Cliff U, IA	W(s)
Buena Vista U, IA	W
Butler U, IN	W(s)
Calumet Coll of Saint Joseph, IN	M, W
Calvary Bible Coll and Theological Seminary, MO	W
Calvin Coll, MI	W
Cameron U, OK	W(s)
Capital U, OH	W
Cardinal Stritch U, WI	M, W
Carleton Coll, MN	M, W
Carroll Coll, WI	W
Case Western Reserve U, OH	M, W
Cedarville U, OH	W(s)
Central Christian Coll of Kansas, KS	W(s)
Central Coll, IA	W
Central Methodist U, MO	W(s)
Central Michigan U, MI	W(s)
Central State U, OH	W(s)
Chicago State U, IL	W(s)
Cincinnati Christian U, OH	W
Clarke Coll, IA	M, W
Clarkson U, NY	M, W
Cleveland State U, OH	W(s)
Coe Coll, IA	W
Coll of Mount St. Joseph, OH	W
Coll of Saint Benedict, MN	W
Coll of St. Catherine, MN	W
Coll of Saint Mary, NE	W(s)
The Coll of St. Scholastica, MN	W
Coll of the Ozarks, MO	W(s)
The Coll of Wooster, OH	M, W
Columbia Coll, MO	W(s)
Concordia Coll, MN	M, W
Concordia U, IL	W
Concordia U, MI	W(s)
Concordia U, NE	W(s)
Concordia U, St. Paul, MN	W(s)
Concordia U Wisconsin, WI	W
Concord U, WV	W(s)
Cornell Coll, IA	M, W
Cornerstone U, MI	W(s)
Cottey Coll, MO	W
Creighton U, NE	W(s)
Crossroads Coll, MN	M, W
Crown Coll, MN	W
Culver-Stockton Coll, MO	W(s)
Dakota State U, SD	W(s)
Dakota Wesleyan U, SD	W(s)
Dana Coll, NE	W(s)
Denison U, OH	W
DePaul U, IL	W(s)
DePauw U, IN	W
Dickinson State U, ND	W(s)
Doane Coll, NE	W(s)
Dominican U, IL	W
Dordt Coll, IA	W(s)
Drake U, IA	W(s)
Drury U, MO	W(s)
Earlham Coll, IN	M, W
Eastern Illinois U, IL	W(s)
Eastern Michigan U, MI	W(s)
Edgewood Coll, WI	W
Elmhurst Coll, IL	W
Emporia State U, KS	W(s)
Evangel U, MO	W(s)
Faith Baptist Bible Coll and Theological Seminary, IA	W
Ferris State U, MI	W(s)
Finlandia U, MI	W
Fontbonne U, MO	W
Fort Hays State U, KS	W(s)
Franklin Coll, IN	W
Gannon U, PA	W(s)
Goshen Coll, IN	W(s)
Grace Bible Coll, MI	W
Grace Coll, IN	W
Graceland U, IA	M(s), W(s)
Grand Valley State U, MI	M, W(s)
Grand View Coll, IA	W(s)
Great Lakes Christian Coll, MI	W
Greenville Coll, IL	W
Grinnell Coll, IA	W
Gustavus Adolphus Coll, MN	M, W
Hamline U, MN	W
Hannibal-LaGrange Coll, MO	W(s)
Hanover Coll, IN	W
Harris-Stowe State U, MO	W(s)
Hastings Coll, NE	W(s)
Heidelberg Coll, OH	M, W
Hesston Coll, KS	W
Hillsdale Coll, MI	W(s)
Hiram Coll, OH	W
Hope Coll, MI	W
Huntington U, IN	W(s)
Illinois Coll, IL	W
Illinois Inst of Technology, IL	W(s)
Illinois State U, IL	W(s)
Illinois Wesleyan U, IL	M, W
Indiana State U, IN	W(s)
Indiana Tech, IN	W
Indiana U Bloomington, IN	W(s)
Indiana U Northwest, IN	W
Indiana U–Purdue U Fort Wayne, IN	M(s), W(s)
Indiana U–Purdue U Indianapolis, IN	W(s)
Indiana U Southeast, IN	W(s)
Indiana Wesleyan U, IN	W(s)
Iowa State U of Science and Technology, IA	W(s)
Iowa Wesleyan Coll, IA	W(s)
Jamestown Coll, ND	W(s)
Judson Coll, IL	W(s)
Kalamazoo Coll, MI	W
Kansas State U, KS	W(s)
Kent State U, OH	W(s)
Kenyon Coll, OH	W
Kettering U, MI	M
Knox Coll, IL	W
Lake Forest Coll, IL	M, W
Lakeland Coll, WI	M, W
Lake Superior State U, MI	W(s)
Lawrence U, WI	M, W
Lewis U, IL	M(s), W(s)
Lindenwood U, MO	M(s), W(s)
Loras Coll, IA	M, W
Loyola U Chicago, IL	M(s), W(s)
Luther Coll, IA	W
Macalester Coll, MN	M, W
MacMurray Coll, IL	W
Madonna U, MI	W(s)
Malone Coll, OH	W(s)
Manchester Coll, IN	W
Maranatha Baptist Bible Coll, WI	W
Marian Coll, IN	W(s)
Marian Coll of Fond du Lac, WI	W
Marietta Coll, OH	W
Marquette U, WI	M, W(s)
Martin Luther Coll, MN	W
Maryville U of Saint Louis, MO	W
Mayville State U, ND	W(s)
McKendree Coll, IL	W(s)
Messenger Coll, MO	W
Miami U, OH	M, W(s)
Miami U Hamilton, OH	W
Miami U–Middletown Campus, OH	W
Michigan State U, MI	M, W(s)
Michigan Technological U, MI	W(s)
Millikin U, IL	W
Milwaukee School of Engineering, WI	M, W
Minnesota State U Mankato, MN	W(s)
Minot State U, ND	W(s)
Missouri Baptist U, MO	M(s), W(s)
Missouri Southern State U, MO	W(s)
Missouri State U, MO	M, W(s)
Missouri Valley Coll, MO	M(s), W(s)
Missouri Western State U, MO	W(s)
Morningside Coll, IA	W(s)
Mount Marty Coll, SD	W(s)
Mount Mary Coll, WI	W
Mount Mercy Coll, IA	W
Mount Union Coll, OH	W
Mount Vernon Nazarene U, OH	W(s)
National American U, Rapid City, SD	W(s)
Nebraska Wesleyan U, NE	W
Newman U, KS	M(s), W(s)
North Carolina Ag and Tech State U, NC	W(s)
North Central Coll, IL	W
North Dakota State U, ND	M, W(s)
Northern Illinois U, IL	W(s)
Northern Michigan U, MI	W
Northern State U, SD	W
Northland Coll, WI	W
Northwestern Coll, IA	W(s)
Northwestern Coll, MN	W
Northwestern U, IL	W(s)
Northwest Missouri State U, MO	W(s)
Northwood U, MI	W(s)
Notre Dame Coll, OH	W(s)
Oak Hills Christian Coll, MN	W
Oakland U, MI	W(s)
Oberlin Coll, OH	M, W
Ohio Dominican U, OH	W(s)
Ohio Northern U, OH	W
The Ohio State U, OH	M(s), W(s)
Ohio U, OH	M, W(s)
Ohio U–Zanesville, OH	W
Ohio Wesleyan U, OH	M, W
Oklahoma Panhandle State U, OK	W(s)
Oklahoma Wesleyan U, OK	W(s)
Oral Roberts U, OK	W(s)

M—for men; W—for women; (s)—scholarship offered

Ottawa U, KS	W(s)
Otterbein Coll, OH	W
Ozark Christian Coll, MO	W
Park U, MO	M(s), W(s)
Peru State Coll, NE	W(s)
Pittsburg State U, KS	W(s)
Presentation Coll, SD	W
Purdue U, IN	W(s)
Quincy U, IL	M(s), W(s)
Research Coll of Nursing, MO	W(s)
Ripon Coll, WI	W
Robert Morris Coll, IL	W(s)
Rochester Coll, MI	W
Rockford Coll, IL	M, W
Rockhurst U, MO	W(s)
Rose-Hulman Inst of Technology, IN	W
Saginaw Valley State U, MI	W(s)
St. Ambrose U, IA	M(s), W(s)
St. Cloud State U, MN	M, W(s)
St. Gregory's U, Shawnee, OK	W
Saint John's U, MN	M
Saint Joseph's Coll, IN	W(s)
St. Louis Coll of Pharmacy, MO	W
Saint Louis U, MO	M, W(s)
Saint Mary's Coll, IN	W
Saint Mary's U of Minnesota, MN	W
St. Norbert Coll, WI	W
St. Olaf Coll, MN	W
Saint Xavier U, IL	W(s)
Shawnee State U, OH	W
Simpson Coll, IA	W
South Dakota School of Mines and Technology, SD	W(s)
South Dakota State U, SD	W(s)
Southeastern Oklahoma State U, OK	W(s)
Southeast Missouri State U, MO	W(s)
Southern Illinois U Carbondale, IL	W(s)
Southern Illinois U Edwardsville, IL	W(s)
Southern Methodist U, TX	W(s)
Southwest Baptist U, MO	W(s)
Southwestern Coll, KS	W(s)
Southwest Minnesota State U, MN	W(s)
Spring Arbor U, MI	W(s)
Stephens Coll, MO	W
Sterling Coll, KS	W(s)
Tabor Coll, KS	W(s)
Taylor U, IN	M, W(s)
Taylor U Fort Wayne, IN	W
Tiffin U, OH	W(s)
Transylvania U, KY	W
Trinity Christian Coll, IL	W(s)
Trinity International U, IL	W(s)
Tri-State U, IN	W
Truman State U, MO	M, W(s)
Union Coll, NE	W
The U of Akron, OH	W(s)
U of Central Missouri, MO	W(s)
U of Central Oklahoma, OK	W(s)
U of Charleston, WV	W(s)
U of Chicago, IL	W
U of Cincinnati, OH	W(s)
U of Dallas, TX	W
U of Dayton, OH	W(s)
U of Evansville, IN	W(s)
The U of Findlay, OH	W(s)
U of Illinois at Chicago, IL	W(s)
U of Illinois at Springfield, IL	W(s)
U of Illinois at Urbana–Champaign, IL	W(s)
U of Indianapolis, IN	W(s)
The U of Iowa, IA	M, W(s)
U of Kansas, KS	W(s)
U of Mary, ND	W(s)
U of Michigan, MI	W(s)
U of Michigan–Dearborn, MI	W(s)
U of Minnesota, Crookston, MN	W(s)
U of Minnesota, Duluth, MN	M, W(s)

U of Minnesota, Morris, MN	W
U of Minnesota, Twin Cities Campus, MN	W(s)
U of Missouri–Columbia, MO	W(s)
U of Missouri–Kansas City, MO	W(s)
U of Missouri–St. Louis, MO	W(s)
U of Nebraska at Kearney, NE	W(s)
U of Nebraska at Omaha, NE	W(s)
U of Nebraska–Lincoln, NE	W(s)
U of New Orleans, LA	W(s)
U of North Dakota, ND	W(s)
U of Northern Iowa, IA	W(s)
U of Notre Dame, IN	W(s)
U of Oklahoma, OK	W(s)
U of Rio Grande, OH	W(s)
U of St. Francis, IL	W(s)
U of Saint Francis, IN	W(s)
U of Saint Mary, KS	W(s)
U of St. Thomas, MN	W
U of Sioux Falls, SD	W(s)
The U of South Dakota, SD	W(s)
U of Southern Indiana, IN	W(s)
The U of Toledo, OH	W(s)
U of Tulsa, OK	W(s)
U of West Florida, FL	W
U of Wisconsin–Eau Claire, WI	W
U of Wisconsin–Green Bay, WI	W(s)
U of Wisconsin–La Crosse, WI	W
U of Wisconsin–Madison, WI	W(s)
U of Wisconsin–Milwaukee, WI	M, W(s)
U of Wisconsin–Oshkosh, WI	W
U of Wisconsin–Parkside, WI	W(s)
U of Wisconsin–Platteville, WI	M, W
U of Wisconsin–River Falls, WI	M, W
U of Wisconsin–Stevens Point, WI	W
U of Wisconsin–Stout, WI	M, W
U of Wisconsin–Superior, WI	W
U of Wisconsin–Whitewater, WI	M, W
Upper Iowa U, IA	M, W
Ursuline Coll, OH	W(s)
Valley City State U, ND	W(s)
Valparaiso U, IN	W(s)
Vennard Coll, IA	W
Viterbo U, WI	W(s)
Waldorf Coll, IA	W(s)
Walsh U, OH	W(s)
Wartburg Coll, IA	W
Washburn U, KS	W(s)
Washington U in St. Louis, MO	M, W
Wayne State Coll, NE	W(s)
Webster U, MO	W
Western Illinois U, IL	W(s)
Western Michigan U, MI	W(s)
Westminster Coll, MO	W
Wheaton Coll, IL	M, W
Wichita State U, KS	M, W(s)
William Jewell Coll, MO	W(s)
William Penn U, IA	W(s)
William Woods U, MO	M(s), W(s)
Wilmington Coll, OH	W
Winona State U, MN	M, W
Wisconsin Lutheran Coll, WI	M, W
Wittenberg U, OH	M, W
Wright State U, OH	W(s)
Xavier U, OH	M, W(s)
York Coll, NE	W
Youngstown State U, OH	W(s)

Water Polo

Ball State U, IN	M
Bowling Green State U, OH	M, W
Carleton Coll, MN	M, W
Gannon U, PA	M, W
Grand Valley State U, MI	M, W
Illinois Wesleyan U, IL	M
Indiana U Bloomington, IN	W(s)
Lake Forest Coll, IL	M, W

Lindenwood U, MO	M(s), W(s)
Macalester Coll, MN	M, W
Michigan State U, MI	M, W
Michigan Technological U, MI	M, W
Oberlin Coll, OH	M, W
Ohio U, OH	M, W
Saint John's U, MN	M
Saint Mary's Coll, IN	W
The U of Findlay, OH	M, W
U of Michigan, MI	W
U of Wisconsin–Madison, WI	M, W
Wabash Coll, IN	M
Washington U in St. Louis, MO	M, W
Wheaton Coll, IL	W

Weight Lifting

Bowling Green State U, OH	M, W
Ohio U, OH	M
U of Minnesota, Duluth, MN	M, W
U of Wisconsin–River Falls, WI	M, W
U of Wisconsin–Whitewater, WI	M

Wrestling

Ashland U, OH	M(s)
Augsburg Coll, MN	M
Augustana Coll, IL	M
Augustana Coll, SD	M(s)
Baldwin-Wallace Coll, OH	M
Ball State U, IN	M
Briar Cliff U, IA	M(s)
Buena Vista U, IA	M
Case Western Reserve U, OH	M
Central Coll, IA	M
Central Michigan U, MI	M(s)
Cleveland State U, OH	M(s)
Coe Coll, IA	M
Coll of Mount St. Joseph, OH	M
Concordia Coll, MN	M
Concordia U Wisconsin, WI	M
Cornell Coll, IA	M
Dakota Wesleyan U, SD	M(s)
Dana Coll, NE	M(s)
Dickinson State U, ND	M(s)
Eastern Illinois U, IL	M(s)
Eastern Michigan U, MI	M(s)
Elmhurst Coll, IL	M
Fort Hays State U, KS	M(s)
Gannon U, PA	M(s)
Grand Valley State U, MI	M
Heidelberg Coll, OH	M
Illinois Coll, IL	M
Indiana U Bloomington, IN	M(s)
Iowa State U of Science and Technology, IA	M(s)
Jamestown Coll, ND	M(s)
Kent State U, OH	M(s)
Knox Coll, IL	M
Lake Forest Coll, IL	M, W
Lakeland Coll, WI	M
Lawrence U, WI	M
Lindenwood U, MO	M(s)
Loras Coll, IA	M
Luther Coll, IA	M
MacMurray Coll, IL	M, W
Manchester Coll, IN	M
Maranatha Baptist Bible Coll, WI	M
McKendree Coll, IL	M(s)
Miami U, OH	M
Michigan State U, MI	M(s)
Millikin U, IL	M
Milwaukee School of Engineering, WI	M
Minnesota State U Mankato, MN	M(s)
Missouri Baptist U, MO	M(s)
Missouri State U, MO	M
Missouri Valley Coll, MO	M(s), W(s)
Morningside Coll, IA	M(s)
Mount Union Coll, OH	M

Newman U, KS	M(s)	Southern Methodist U, TX	M	U of Oklahoma, OK	M(s)
North Central Coll, IL	M	Southwest Minnesota State U, MN	M(s)	U of Wisconsin–Eau Claire, WI	M
North Dakota State U, ND	M(s)	Tri-State U, IN	M	U of Wisconsin–La Crosse, WI	M
Northern Illinois U, IL	M(s)	Truman State U, MO	M(s)	U of Wisconsin–Madison, WI	M(s)
Northern State U, SD	M(s)	U of Central Missouri, MO	M(s)	U of Wisconsin–Oshkosh, WI	M
Northwestern Coll, IA	M(s)	U of Central Oklahoma, OK	M(s)	U of Wisconsin–Parkside, WI	M(s)
Northwestern U, IL	M(s)	U of Chicago, IL	M	U of Wisconsin–Platteville, WI	M
Ohio Northern U, OH	M	The U of Findlay, OH	M(s)	U of Wisconsin–Stevens Point, WI	M
The Ohio State U, OH	M(s)	U of Illinois at Urbana–Champaign, IL	M(s)	U of Wisconsin–Whitewater, WI	M
Ohio U, OH	M(s)	U of Indianapolis, IN	M(s)	Upper Iowa U, IA	M
Oklahoma State U, OK	M(s)	The U of Iowa, IA	M(s)	Wabash Coll, IN	M
Purdue U, IN	M(s)	U of Mary, ND	M(s)	Waldorf Coll, IA	M(s)
Ripon Coll, WI	M, W	U of Michigan, MI	M(s)	Wartburg Coll, IA	M
Rose-Hulman Inst of Technology, IN	M	U of Minnesota, Twin Cities Campus,		Wheaton Coll, IL	M
St. Cloud State U, MN	M(s)	MN	M(s)	Wichita State U, KS	M
Saint John's U, MN	M	U of Missouri–Columbia, MO	M(s)	William Penn U, IA	M(s)
St. Olaf Coll, MN	M	U of Nebraska at Kearney, NE	M(s)	Wilmington Coll, OH	M
Simpson Coll, IA	M	U of Nebraska at Omaha, NE	M(s)	Winona State U, MN	M
South Dakota State U, SD	M(s)	U of Nebraska–Lincoln, NE	M(s)	York Coll, NE	M
Southern Illinois U Edwardsville, IL	M(s)	U of Northern Iowa, IA	M(s)		

M—for men; W—for women; (s)—scholarship offered

ROTC Programs

Allen Coll, IA	A(c)
Alma Coll, MI	A(c)
Alverno Coll, WI	A(c), AF(c)
Augsburg Coll, MN	A(c), N(c), AF(c)
Aurora U, IL	A(c)
Avila U, MO	A(c)
Baker U, KS	A(c), AF(c)
Baldwin-Wallace Coll, OH	AF(c)
Ball State U, IN	A
Baptist Bible Coll, MO	A(c)
Bellevue U, NE	A(c), AF(c)
Benedictine Coll, KS	A
Benedictine U, IL	A(c)
Bethany Lutheran Coll, MN	A(c)
Bethel U, MN	A(c), AF(c)
Black Hills State U, SD	A(c)
Bowling Green State U, OH	A, AF
Bowling Green State U–Firelands Coll, OH	A(c), AF(c)
Bradley U, IL	A(c)
Butler U, IN	A, AF(c)
Calvary Bible Coll and Theological Seminary, MO	A(c)
Calvin Coll, MI	A(c)
Cameron U, OK	A
Capital U, OH	A, AF(c)
Carroll Coll, WI	A(c), AF(c)
Case Western Reserve U, OH	A(c), AF(c)
Cedarville U, OH	A(c), AF(c)
Central Methodist U, MO	A(c), AF(c)
Central Michigan U, MI	A
Central State U, OH	A
Chicago State U, IL	A, N(c), AF(c)
Clarke Coll, IA	A(c)
Clarkson U, NY	A, AF
Cleveland Inst of Music, OH	A(c), AF(c)
Cleveland State U, OH	A(c), N(c), AF(c)
Coe Coll, IA	A(c), AF(c)
Coll of Mount St. Joseph, OH	A(c), AF(c)
Coll of Saint Benedict, MN	A(c)
Coll of St. Catherine, MN	A(c), AF(c)
Coll of Saint Mary, NE	A(c), AF(c)
The Coll of St. Scholastica, MN	AF(c)
Coll of the Ozarks, MO	A
Columbia Coll, MO	A(c), N(c), AF(c)
Concordia Coll, MN	A(c), AF(c)
Concordia U, MI	A(c), AF(c)
Concordia U, NE	A(c), AF(c)
Concordia U, St. Paul, MN	A(c), N(c), AF(c)
Cornerstone U, MI	A(c)
Creighton U, NE	A, AF(c)
Dakota State U, SD	A, AF(c)
Dana Coll, NE	A(c), AF(c)
Denison U, OH	A(c)
DePaul U, IL	A(c)
DePauw U, IN	A(c), AF(c)
DeVry U, Columbus, OH	A(c)
Doane Coll, NE	A(c), AF(c)
Drake U, IA	A, AF(c)
Drury U, MO	A(c)
Eastern Illinois U, IL	A
Eastern Michigan U, MI	A, N(c), AF(c)
Elmhurst Coll, IL	A(c), AF(c)
Evangel U, MO	A
Ferris State U, MI	A(c)
Finlandia U, MI	A(c), AF(c)
Fontbonne U, MO	A(c), AF(c)
Franciscan U of Steubenville, OH	A(c)
Franklin Coll, IN	A(c)
Gannon U, PA	A
Grace Bible Coll, MI	A(c)
Grand View Coll, IA	A(c), AF(c)
Gustavus Adolphus Coll, MN	A(c)
Hamline U, MN	AF(c)
Harris-Stowe State U, MO	AF(c)
Heidelberg Coll, OH	A(c), AF(c)
Holy Cross Coll, IN	A(c), AF(c)
Hope Coll, MI	A(c)
Illinois Inst of Technology, IL	A, N, AF
Illinois State U, IL	A
Illinois Wesleyan U, IL	A(c)
Indiana State U, IN	A, AF
Indiana U Bloomington, IN	A, AF
Indiana U Kokomo, IN	A(c)
Indiana U Northwest, IN	A
Indiana U–Purdue U Indianapolis, IN	A, N(c), AF(c)
Indiana U South Bend, IN	A(c), N(c), AF(c)
Indiana U Southeast, IN	A, N
Indiana Wesleyan U, IN	A(c)
Iowa State U of Science and Technology, IA	A, N, AF
Judson Coll, IL	A(c)
Kalamazoo Coll, MI	A(c)
Kansas State U, KS	A, AF
Kent State U, OH	A, AF
Kent State U, Ashtabula Campus, OH	A(c)
Kent State U, Geauga Campus, OH	A(c), AF(c)
Kent State U, Trumbull Campus, OH	A(c), AF(c)
Kent State U, Tuscarawas Campus, OH	A(c), AF(c)
Langston U, OK	A(c)
Lawrence Technological U, MI	A(c), N(c), AF(c)
Lewis U, IL	A(c), AF(c)
Lincoln U, MO	A, N(c), AF(c)
Lindenwood U, MO	A, AF(c)
Loras Coll, IA	A(c)
Lourdes Coll, OH	A(c), AF(c)
Loyola U Chicago, IL	A(c), N(c), AF(c)
Macalester Coll, MN	N(c), AF(c)
Malone Coll, OH	A(c), AF(c)
Maranatha Baptist Bible Coll, WI	A
Marian Coll, IN	A(c)
Marian Coll of Fond du Lac, WI	A
Marquette U, WI	A, N, AF
Maryville U of Saint Louis, MO	A(c)
Mayville State U, ND	A(c), AF(c)
McKendree Coll, IL	A(c), AF(c)
Miami U, OH	A(c), N, AF
Miami U Hamilton, OH	N(c), AF(c)
Miami U–Middletown Campus, OH	AF(c)
Michigan State U, MI	A, AF
Michigan Technological U, MI	A, AF
Milwaukee School of Engineering, WI	A(c), N(c), AF(c)
Minnesota State U Mankato, MN	A
Missouri Baptist U, MO	A(c)
Missouri State U, MO	A
Missouri Valley Coll, MO	A
Missouri Western State U, MO	A
Morningside Coll, IA	A(c)
Mount Marty Coll, SD	A(c)
Mount Mary Coll, WI	A(c)
Mount Union Coll, OH	A(c), AF(c)
National American U, Rapid City, SD	A(c)
Nebraska Methodist Coll, NE	A(c), AF(c)
Nebraska Wesleyan U, NE	A(c), AF(c)
North Carolina Ag and Tech State U, NC	A, AF
North Central Coll, IL	A(c), AF(c)
North Dakota State U, ND	A, AF
Northeastern Illinois U, IL	A(c), AF(c)
Northeastern State U, OK	A
Northern Illinois U, IL	A, AF(c)
Northern Michigan U, MI	A
Northwestern Coll, MN	A(c), AF(c)
Northwestern U, IL	A(c), N, AF(c)
Northwest Missouri State U, MO	A
Oakland U, MI	AF(c)
Ohio Dominican U, OH	A(c)
Ohio Northern U, OH	A(c), AF(c)
The Ohio State U, OH	A, N, AF
The Ohio State U at Lima, OH	A(c), N(c), AF(c)
The Ohio State U at Marion, OH	A(c), N(c), AF(c)
The Ohio State U–Mansfield Campus, OH	A(c), N(c), AF(c)
The Ohio State U–Newark Campus, OH	A(c), N(c), AF(c)
Ohio U, OH	A, AF
Ohio Wesleyan U, OH	A(c), AF(c)
Oklahoma Christian U, OK	A(c), AF(c)
Oklahoma City U, OK	A(c), AF(c)
Oklahoma State U, OK	A, AF
Oral Roberts U, OK	AF(c)
Otterbein Coll, OH	A(c), AF(c)
Park U, MO	A
Peru State Coll, NE	A(c), AF(c)
Pittsburg State U, KS	A
Purdue U, IN	A, N, AF
Research Coll of Nursing, MO	A(c)
Ripon Coll, WI	A
Robert Morris Coll, IL	A(c)
Rockford Coll, IL	A(c)
Rockhurst U, MO	A(c)
Rogers State U, OK	AF(c)
Rose-Hulman Inst of Technology, IN	A, AF
St. Cloud State U, MN	A
St. Gregory's U, Shawnee, OK	AF(c)
Saint John's U, MN	A
St. Louis Coll of Pharmacy, MO	A(c), AF(c)
Saint Louis U, MO	A(c), AF
Saint Mary-of-the-Woods Coll, IN	A(c), AF(c)
Saint Mary's Coll, IN	A(c), N(c), AF(c)
Saint Mary's U of Minnesota, MN	A(c)
St. Norbert Coll, WI	A
Saint Xavier U, IL	AF(c)
South Dakota School of Mines and Technology, SD	A
South Dakota State U, SD	A, AF
Southeast Missouri State U, MO	AF
Southern Illinois U Carbondale, IL	A, AF
Southern Illinois U Edwardsville, IL	A, AF
Southern Methodist U, TX	A, AF(c)

A—Army; N—Navy; AF—Air Force; (c)—available through a cooperating host institution

ROTC Programs

Southwest Baptist U, MO	A(c)	U of Missouri–Kansas City, MO	A, AF(c)	U of Wisconsin–Oshkosh, WI	A
Spring Arbor U, MI	A, AF(c)	U of Missouri–Rolla, MO	A, N(c), AF	U of Wisconsin–Parkside, WI	A(c)
Stephens Coll, MO	A(c), AF(c)	U of Missouri–St. Louis, MO	A(c), AF(c)	U of Wisconsin–Platteville, WI	A(c)
Tiffin U, OH	A(c), AF(c)	U of Nebraska at Omaha, NE	A(c), AF	U of Wisconsin–Stevens Point, WI	A
Transylvania U, KY	A(c), AF(c)	U of Nebraska–Lincoln, NE	A, N, AF	U of Wisconsin–Superior, WI	AF(c)
Truman State U, MO	A	U of Nebraska Medical Center, NE	A(c), AF(c)	U of Wisconsin–Whitewater, WI	A, AF
The U of Akron, OH	A, AF(c)	U of New Orleans, LA	A(c), N(c), AF(c)	Ursuline Coll, OH	A(c)
U of Central Missouri, MO	A, AF(c)	U of North Dakota, ND	A, AF	Valparaiso U, IN	AF(c)
U of Central Oklahoma, OK	A	U of Northern Iowa, IA	A	Viterbo U, WI	A(c)
U of Charleston, WV	A	U of Notre Dame, IN	A, N, AF	Washburn U, KS	A, N(c), AF(c)
U of Chicago, IL	A(c), AF(c)	U of Oklahoma, OK	A, N, AF	Washington U in St. Louis, MO	A, AF(c)
U of Cincinnati, OH	A, AF	U of Oklahoma Health Sciences Center, OK	A(c), AF(c)	Wayne State Coll, NE	A
U of Dallas, TX	A(c), AF(c)	U of Rio Grande, OH	A(c)	Webster U, MO	A(c), AF(c)
U of Dayton, OH	A, AF(c)	U of Saint Mary, KS	A(c), AF(c)	Western Illinois U, IL	A
The U of Findlay, OH	A(c), AF(c)	U of St. Thomas, MN	A(c), N(c), AF	Western Michigan U, MI	A
U of Illinois at Chicago, IL	A, N(c), AF(c)	The U of South Dakota, SD	A	Westminster Coll, MO	A(c), AF(c)
U of Illinois at Urbana–Champaign, IL	A, N, AF	U of Southern Indiana, IN	A	Wheaton Coll, IL	A
U of Indianapolis, IN	A(c)	The U of Toledo, OH	A, AF(c)	William Woods U, MO	A(c), N(c), AF(c)
The U of Iowa, IA	A, AF	U of Tulsa, OK	AF(c)	Winona State U, MN	A(c)
U of Kansas, KS	A, N, AF	U of West Florida, FL	A, AF	Wisconsin Lutheran Coll, WI	A(c), N(c), AF(c)
U of Michigan, MI	A, AF	U of Wisconsin–Green Bay, WI	A(c)	Wittenberg U, OH	A(c), AF(c)
U of Michigan–Dearborn, MI	A(c), N(c), AF(c)	U of Wisconsin–La Crosse, WI	A	Wright State U, OH	A, AF
U of Minnesota, Crookston, MN	AF(c)	U of Wisconsin–Madison, WI	A, N, AF	Xavier U, OH	A, AF(c)
U of Minnesota, Duluth, MN	AF	U of Wisconsin–Milwaukee, WI	A(c), AF(c)	York Coll, NE	A(c), N(c), AF(c)
U of Minnesota, Twin Cities Campus, MN	A, N, AF			Youngstown State U, OH	A, AF(c)
U of Missouri–Columbia, MO	A, N, AF				

A—Army; N—Navy; AF—Air Force; (c)—available through a cooperating host institution

Alphabetical Listing of Colleges and Universities

In this index, the page locations of the **Profiles** are printed in regular type, **Profiles** with **Special Messages** in *italics*, and **Close-Ups** in **bold type**.

Aakers College, Fargo, ND ... 169
Academy College, MN ... 126
Adrian College, MI ... 108
AIB College of Business, IA ... 87
Albion College, MI ... 108, **230**
Allegheny Wesleyan College, OH ... 173
Allen College, IA ... 87
Alma College, MI ... 108
Alverno College, WI ... 214, **232**
American Academy of Art, IL ... 45
American InterContinental University Online, IL ... 45
Ancilla College, IN ... 69
Anderson University, IN ... 69
Andrews University, MI ... 109
Antioch College, OH ... 173
Antioch University McGregor, OH ... 173
Aquinas College, MI ... *109*
Argosy University, Chicago, IL ... 45
Argosy University, Schaumburg, IL ... 45
Argosy University, Twin Cities, Eagan, MN ... 126
Art Academy of Cincinnati, OH ... 173
The Art Institute of Indianapolis, IN ... 70
The Art Institutes International Minnesota, MN ... 126
Ashford University, IA ... 87
Ashland University, OH ... 174
Augsburg College, MN ... 127
Augustana College, IL ... 45
Augustana College, SD ... 209
Aurora University, IL ... *45*, **234**
Ave Maria College, MI ... 110
Avila University, MO ... 142
Bacone College, OK ... 201
Baker College of Allen Park, MI ... 110
Baker College of Auburn Hills, MI ... 110
Baker College of Cadillac, MI ... 110
Baker College of Clinton Township, MI ... 110
Baker College of Flint, MI ... 111
Baker College of Jackson, MI ... 111
Baker College of Muskegon, MI ... 111
Baker College of Owosso, MI ... 111
Baker College of Port Huron, MI ... 112
Baker University, KS ... 100
Baldwin-Wallace College, OH ... 174, **236**
Ball State University, IN ... *70*, **238**
Baptist Bible College, MO ... 142
Barclay College, KS ... 100
Barnes-Jewish College of Nursing and Allied Health, MO ... 143
Bellevue University, NE ... 162
Bellin College of Nursing, WI ... 214
Beloit College, WI ... 214
Bemidji State University, MN ... 127
Benedictine College, KS ... 101
Benedictine University, IL ... 46, **240**
Bethany College, KS ... 101
Bethany Lutheran College, MN ... 127
Bethel College, IN ... 71

Bethel College, KS ... 101
Bethel University, MN ... *128*
Blackburn College, IL ... 46
Black Hills State University, SD ... 210
Blessing-Rieman College of Nursing, IL ... 46
Bluffton University, OH ... 174
Bohecker's Business College, OH ... 175
Bowling Green State University, OH ... 175
Bowling Green State University–Firelands College, OH ... 175
Bradley University, IL ... 47
Briar Cliff University, IA ... 88
Brown College, MN ... 128
Bryant and Stratton College, Cleveland, OH ... 175
Bryant and Stratton College, Parma, OH ... 176
Bryant and Stratton College, WI ... 215
Bryant and Stratton College, Wauwatosa Campus, WI ... 215
Buena Vista University, IA ... 88
Butler University, IN ... 71
Calumet College of Saint Joseph, IN ... 71
Calvary Bible College and Theological Seminary, MO ... 143
Calvin College, MI ... 112
Cameron University, OK ... 201
Capella University, MN ... 128
Capital University, OH ... 176
Cardinal Stritch University, WI ... 215
Carleton College, MN ... 129
Carroll College, WI ... 215
Carthage College, WI ... 216
Case Western Reserve University, OH ... 176
Cedarville University, OH ... 177
Central Bible College, MO ... 143
Central Christian College of Kansas, KS ... 102
Central Christian College of the Bible, MO ... 143
Central College, IA ... 88
Central Methodist University, MO ... 143
Central Michigan University, MI ... 112
Central State University, OH ... 177
Chadron State College, NE ... 162
Chamberlain College of Nursing, MO ... 144
Chatfield College, OH ... 177
Chicago State University, IL ... 47
Christian Life College, IL ... 47
Cincinnati Christian University, OH ... 177
Cincinnati College of Mortuary Science, OH ... 178
Clarke College, IA ... 89
Clarkson College, NE ... 163
Clarkson University, NY ... *310*, **314**
Cleary University, MI ... 113
Cleveland Chiropractic College-Kansas City Campus, MO ... 144
The Cleveland Institute of Art, OH ... 178
Cleveland Institute of Music, OH ... 178

Cleveland State University, OH ... 179
Coe College, IA ... 89
College for Creative Studies, MI ... 113
College of Menominee Nation, WI ... 216
College of Mount St. Joseph, OH ... 179
College of Saint Benedict, MN ... 129
College of St. Catherine, MN ... 129
College of St. Catherine–Minneapolis, MN ... 130
College of Saint Mary, NE ... 163
The College of St. Scholastica, MN ... 130
College of the Ozarks, MO ... 144
College of Visual Arts, MN ... 130
The College of Wooster, OH ... 179, **242**
Colorado Technical University Sioux Falls Campus, SD ... 210
Columbia College, MO ... *144*
Columbia College Chicago, IL ... *48*, **244**
Columbia College of Nursing, WI ... 216
Columbus College of Art & Design, OH ... 180
Conception Seminary College, MO ... 145
Concordia College, MN ... 130
Concordia University, IL ... 48
Concordia University, MI ... 113
Concordia University, NE ... 163
Concordia University, St. Paul, MN ... 131
Concordia University Wisconsin, WI ... 216
Concord University, WV ... *313*, **316**
Cornell College, IA ... 89
Cornerstone University, MI ... 114
Cottey College, MO ... 145
Cox College of Nursing and Health Sciences, MO ... 146
Creighton University, NE ... 163
Crossroads Bible College, IN ... 72
Crossroads College, MN ... 131
Crown College, MN ... *131*
Culver-Stockton College, MO ... 146, **246**
Dakota State University, SD ... 210
Dakota Wesleyan University, SD ... 210
Dana College, NE ... 164
Davenport University, Granger, IN ... 72
Davenport University, Hammond, IN ... 72
Davenport University, Merrillville, IN ... 72
Davenport University, Alma, MI ... 114
Davenport University, Bad Axe, MI ... 114
Davenport University, Bay City, MI ... 114
Davenport University, Caro, MI ... 114
Davenport University, Dearborn, MI ... 114
Davenport University, Midland, MI ... 114
Davenport University, Saginaw, MI ... 114
Defiance College, OH ... 180
Denison University, OH ... 180
DePaul University, IL ... 48
DePauw University, IN ... 72
DeVry University, Addison, IL ... 49
DeVry University, Chicago, IL ... 49
DeVry University, Elgin, IL ... 49
DeVry University, Gurnee, IL ... 49
DeVry University, Naperville, IL ... 49

Alphabetical Listing of Colleges and Universities

DeVry University, Oakbrook Terrace, IL ... 49
DeVry University, Tinley Park, IL ... 50
DeVry University, Indianapolis, IN ... 72
DeVry University, Merrillville, IN ... 72
DeVry University, MN ... 132
DeVry University, Kansas City, MO ... 146
DeVry University, Kansas City, MO ... 146
DeVry University, St. Louis, MO ... 146
DeVry University, Cleveland, OH ... 180
DeVry University, Columbus, OH ... 181
DeVry University, Seven Hills, OH ... 181
DeVry University, OK ... 201
DeVry University, Milwaukee, WI ... 216
DeVry University, Waukesha, WI ... 217
DeVry University Online, IL ... 50
Dickinson State University, ND ... 169, 248
Divine Word College, IA ... 90
Doane College, NE ... 164
Dominican University, IL ... 50
Donnelly College, KS ... 102
Dordt College, IA ... 90
Drake University, IA ... 90
Drury University, MO ... 147
Dunwoody College of Technology, MN ... 132
Earlham College, IN ... 72
East Central University, OK ... 201
Eastern Illinois University, IL ... 50
Eastern Michigan University, MI ... 114
East-West University, IL ... 51
Edgewood College, WI ... 217
Elmhurst College, IL ... 51
Emmaus Bible College, IA ... 90
Emporia State University, KS ... 102
Eureka College, IL ... 51
Evangel University, MO ... 147
Everest College, Springfield, MO ... 147
Faith Baptist Bible College and Theological Seminary, IA ... 91
Ferris State University, MI ... 115
Finlandia University, MI ... 115
Fontbonne University, MO ... 147
Fort Berthold Community College, ND ... 169
Fort Hays State University, KS ... 102
Franciscan University of Steubenville, OH ... 181
Franklin College, IN ... 73
Franklin University, OH ... 181
Friends University, KS ... 103
Gallipolis Career College, OH ... 181
Gannon University, PA ... 311, 318
Global University of the Assemblies of God, MO ... 148
Globe College, MN ... 132
God's Bible School and College, OH ... 181
Goshen College, IN ... 73
Governors State University, IL ... 51
Grace Bible College, MI ... 116
Grace College, IN ... 73
Graceland University, IA ... 91, 250
Grace University, NE ... 164
Grand Valley State University, MI ... 116
Grand View College, IA ... 91
Grantham University, MO ... 148
Great Lakes Christian College, MI ... 116
Greenville College, IL ... 51
Grinnell College, IA ... 92
Gustavus Adolphus College, MN ... 132
Hamilton College, Cedar Falls, IA ... 92
Hamilton College, Cedar Rapids, IA ... 92
Hamilton College-Omaha, NE ... 164
Hamilton Technical College, IA ... 92
Hamline University, MN ... 133
Hannibal-LaGrange College, MO ... 148
Hanover College, IN ... 74
Harrington College of Design, IL ... 52

Harris-Stowe State University, MO ... 148
Haskell Indian Nations University, KS ... 103
Hastings College, NE ... 164
Hebrew Theological College, IL ... 52
Heidelberg College, OH ... 182, 252
Herzing College, MN ... 133
Herzing College, WI ... 217
Hesston College, KS ... 103
Hickey College, MO ... 149
Hillsdale College, MI ... 116
Hillsdale Free Will Baptist College, OK ... 202
Hiram College, OH ... 182
Holy Cross College, IN ... 74
Hope College, MI ... 117
Huntington University, IN ... 74
IHM Health Studies Center, MO ... 149
Illinois College, IL ... 52
The Illinois Institute of Art–Chicago, IL ... 52, 254
The Illinois Institute of Art–Schaumburg, IL ... 53
Illinois Institute of Technology, IL ... 53, 256
Illinois State University, IL ... 53
Illinois Wesleyan University, IL ... 54
Indiana State University, IN ... 75
Indiana Tech, IN ... 75
Indiana University Bloomington, IN ... 75
Indiana University East, IN ... 76
Indiana University Kokomo, IN ... 76
Indiana University Northwest, IN ... 76
Indiana University–Purdue University Fort Wayne, IN ... 77
Indiana University–Purdue University Indianapolis, IN ... 77
Indiana University South Bend, IN ... 77
Indiana University Southeast, IN ... 78
Indiana Wesleyan University, IN ... 78
International Academy of Design & Technology, IL ... 54, 258
International Business College, Fort Wayne, IN ... 78
Iowa State University of Science and Technology, IA ... 92
Iowa Wesleyan College, IA ... 93
ITT Technical Institute, Burr Ridge, IL ... 54
ITT Technical Institute, Mount Prospect, IL ... 54
ITT Technical Institute, Orland Park, IL ... 55
ITT Technical Institute, Fort Wayne, IN ... 79
ITT Technical Institute, Indianapolis, IN ... 79
ITT Technical Institute, Newburgh, IN ... 79
ITT Technical Institute, MN ... 133
ITT Technical Institute, Arnold, MO ... 149
ITT Technical Institute, Earth City, MO ... 149
ITT Technical Institute, Kansas City, MO ... 149
ITT Technical Institute, NE ... 165
ITT Technical Institute, Oklahoma City, OK ... 202
ITT Technical Institute, Tulsa, OK ... 202
ITT Technical Institute, Green Bay, WI ... 217
ITT Technical Institute, Greenfield, WI ... 217
Ivy Tech Community College–Northwest, IN ... 79
Jamestown College, ND ... 169
John Carroll University, OH ... 182
Judson College, IL ... 55
Kalamazoo College, MI ... 117
Kansas City Art Institute, MO ... 149

Kansas State University, KS ... 103
Kansas Wesleyan University, KS ... 103
Kaplan College–Indianapolis, IN ... 79
Kaplan University, IA ... 93
Kendall College, IL ... 55
Kent State University, OH ... 182, 260
Kent State University, Ashtabula Campus, OH ... 183
Kent State University, Geauga Campus, OH ... 183
Kent State University, Salem Campus, OH ... 183
Kent State University, Stark Campus, OH ... 183
Kent State University, Trumbull Campus, OH ... 183
Kent State University, Tuscarawas Campus, OH ... 184
Kenyon College, OH ... 184
Kettering College of Medical Arts, OH ... 184
Kettering University, MI ... 117, 262
Kilian Community College, SD ... 211
Knox College, IL ... 55
Kuyper College, MI ... 118
Lake Erie College, OH ... 185
Lake Forest College, IL ... 56
Lakeland College, WI ... 218
Lake Superior State University, MI ... 118
Lakeview College of Nursing, IL ... 56
Langston University, OK ... 202
Laura and Alvin Siegal College of Judaic Studies, OH ... 185
Lawrence Technological University, MI ... 118
Lawrence University, WI ... 218
Leech Lake Tribal College, MN ... 133
Lewis College of Business, MI ... 119
Lewis University, IL ... 56
Lexington College, IL ... 56
Lincoln Christian College, IL ... 57
Lincoln College, IL ... 57
Lincoln College–Normal, IL ... 57
Lincoln University, MO ... 150
Lindenwood University, MO ... 150
Little Priest Tribal College, NE ... 165
Logan University-College of Chiropractic, MO ... 150
Loras College, IA ... 93
Lourdes College, OH ... 185
Loyola University Chicago, IL ... 57, 264
Luther College, IA ... 93
Macalester College, MN ... 134
MacCormac College, IL ... 57
MacMurray College, IL ... 58
Madonna University, MI ... 119
Maharishi University of Management, IA ... 94
Malone College, OH ... 185
Manchester College, IN ... 80, 266
Manhattan Christian College, KS ... 103
Maranatha Baptist Bible College, WI ... 218
Marian College, IN ... 80
Marian College of Fond du Lac, WI ... 219
Marietta College, OH ... 186
Marquette University, WI ... 219
Martin Luther College, MN ... 134
Martin University, IN ... 80
Marygrove College, MI ... 119
Maryville University of Saint Louis, MO ... 151
Mayville State University, ND ... 170
McKendree College, IL ... 58
McNally Smith College of Music, MN ... 134
McPherson College, KS ... 103
Medcenter One College of Nursing, ND ... 170
MedCentral College of Nursing, OH ... 186
Mercy College of Health Sciences, IA ... 94

Mercy College of Northwest Ohio, OH 186
Messenger College, MO 151
Metro Business College, Cape Girardeau, MO 151
Metropolitan State University, MN 135
Miami University, OH 186
Miami University Hamilton, OH 187
Miami University–Middletown Campus, OH 187
Michigan Jewish Institute, MI 120
Michigan State University, MI 120
Michigan Technological University, MI 120
Mid-America Christian University, OK 203
Mid-America College of Funeral Service, IN 80
MidAmerica Nazarene University, KS 104
Midland Lutheran College, NE 165
Midstate College, IL 58
Midwest University, MO 151
Millikin University, IL 58
Milwaukee Institute of Art and Design, WI 219
Milwaukee School of Engineering, WI 219, 268
Minneapolis College of Art and Design, MN 135
Minnesota School of Business, MN 135
Minnesota School of Business–Brooklyn Center, MN 135
Minnesota School of Business–Plymouth, MN 136
Minnesota School of Business–Richfield, MN 136
Minnesota School of Business–St. Cloud, MN 136
Minnesota School of Business–Shakopee, MN 136
Minnesota State University Mankato, MN 137
Minnesota State University Moorhead, MN 137
Minot State University, ND 170
Missouri Baptist University, MO 151
Missouri Southern State University, MO 152
Missouri State University, MO 152
Missouri Tech, MO 152
Missouri Valley College, MO 152
Missouri Western State University, MO 153
Monmouth College, IL 59
Moody Bible Institute, IL 59
Morningside College, IA 94, 270
Morrison Institute of Technology, IL 59
Mount Carmel College of Nursing, OH 187
Mount Marty College, SD 211
Mount Mary College, WI 220, 272
Mount Mercy College, IA 95, 274
Mount Union College, OH 187
Mount Vernon Nazarene University, OH 188
Muskingum College, OH 188
Myers University, OH 188
National American University, KS 104
National American University, Roseville, MN 137
National American University, MO 153
National American University, Rapid City, SD 211
National American University–Sioux Falls Branch, SD 212
National-Louis University, IL 59
Nebraska Christian College, NE 165
Nebraska Methodist College, NE 165
Nebraska Wesleyan University, NE 165
Newman University, KS 104

North Carolina Agricultural and Technical State University, NC 311, 320
North Central College, IL 59, 276
North Central University, MN 137
North Dakota State University, ND 171
Northeastern Illinois University, IL 60
Northeastern State University, OK 203
Northern Illinois University, IL 60
Northern Michigan University, MI 121
Northern State University, SD 212
Northland College, WI 220
North Park University, IL 60
Northwestern College, IA 95
Northwestern College, MN 137
Northwestern Oklahoma State University, OK 203
Northwestern University, IL 60
Northwest Missouri State University, MO 153
Northwood University, MI 121
Notre Dame College, OH 188
Oak Hills Christian College, MN 138
Oakland City University, IN 80
Oakland University, MI 121
Oberlin College, OH 188
Oglala Lakota College, SD 212
Ohio Christian University, OH 189
Ohio College of Massotherapy, OH 189
Ohio Dominican University, OH 189
Ohio Northern University, OH 189
The Ohio State University, OH 190
The Ohio State University at Lima, OH 190
The Ohio State University at Marion, OH 191
The Ohio State University–Mansfield Campus, OH 191
The Ohio State University–Newark Campus, OH 191
Ohio University, OH 191
Ohio University–Chillicothe, OH 192
Ohio University–Eastern, OH 192
Ohio University–Lancaster, OH 192
Ohio University–Southern Campus, OH 192
Ohio University–Zanesville, OH 192
Ohio Wesleyan University, OH 192, 278
Oklahoma Baptist University, OK 203
Oklahoma Christian University, OK 203
Oklahoma City University, OK 204
Oklahoma Panhandle State University, OK 204
Oklahoma State University, OK 204
Oklahoma Wesleyan University, OK 205
Olivet College, MI 122
Olivet Nazarene University, IL 61, 280
Oral Roberts University, OK 205
Ottawa University, KS 104
Otterbein College, OH 193
Ozark Christian College, MO 153
Palmer College of Chiropractic, IA 96
Park University, MO 154
Peru State College, NE 166
Pillsbury Baptist Bible College, MN 138
Pittsburg State University, KS 104
Pontifical College Josephinum, OH 193
Presentation College, SD 212
Principia College, IL 61
Purdue University, IN 81
Purdue University Calumet, IN 81
Purdue University North Central, IN 81
Quincy University, IL 61, 282
Rabbinical College of Telshe, OH 194
Ranken Technical College, MO 154
Research College of Nursing, MO 154
Ripon College, WI 220
Robert Morris College, IL 61, 284
Rochester College, MI 122

Rochester Community and Technical College, MN 138
Rockford Business College, IL 61
Rockford College, IL 62
Rockhurst University, MO 154
Rogers State University, OK 205
Roosevelt University, IL 62
Rosedale Bible College, OH 194
Rose-Hulman Institute of Technology, IN 82
Rush University, IL 62
Sacred Heart Major Seminary, MI 122
Saginaw Chippewa Tribal College, MI 122
Saginaw Valley State University, MI 123
St. Ambrose University, IA 96
Saint Anthony College of Nursing, IL 62
St. Augustine College, IL 63
St. Cloud State University, MN 138
Saint Francis Medical Center College of Nursing, IL 63
St. Gregory's University, Shawnee, OK 206
St. John's College, IL 63
Saint John's University, MN 138
Saint Joseph's College, IN 82
St. Louis Christian College, MO 155
St. Louis College of Pharmacy, MO 155
Saint Louis University, MO 155
St. Luke's College, IA 96
Saint Luke's College, MO 156
Saint Mary-of-the-Woods College, IN 82
Saint Mary's College, IN 83, 286
Saint Mary's University of Minnesota, MN 139
St. Norbert College, WI 221
St. Olaf College, MN 139
Saint Xavier University, IL 63
Sanford-Brown College, Fenton, MO 156
School of the Art Institute of Chicago, IL 64
Shawnee State University, OH 194
Shimer College, IL 64
Siena Heights University, MI 123
Silver Lake College, WI 221
Simpson College, IA 97, 288
Sinte Gleska University, SD 212
Sitting Bull College, ND 171
South Dakota School of Mines and Technology, SD 212
South Dakota State University, SD 213
Southeastern Oklahoma State University, OK 206
Southeast Missouri Hospital College of Nursing and Health Sciences, MO 156
Southeast Missouri State University, MO 156
Southern Illinois University Carbondale, IL 64, 290
Southern Illinois University Edwardsville, IL 65
Southern Methodist University, TX 312, 322
Southern Nazarene University, OK 206
Southwest Baptist University, MO 156
Southwestern Christian University, OK 206
Southwestern College, KS 105
Southwestern Oklahoma State University, OK 207
Southwest Minnesota State University, MN 139
Spartan College of Aeronautics and Technology, OK 207
Spring Arbor University, MI 123
Springfield College in Illinois, IL 65
Stephens College, MO 157, 292
Sterling College, KS 105
Tabor College, KS 105
Taylor University, IN 83
Taylor University Fort Wayne, IN 83
Telshe Yeshiva–Chicago, IL 65

Alphabetical Listing of Colleges and Universities

Temple Baptist College, OH ... 194
Tiffin University, OH ... 194
Transylvania University, KY ... 309, **324**
Trinity Bible College, ND ... 171
Trinity Christian College, IL ... 65
Trinity College of Nursing and Health
  Sciences, IL ... 65
Trinity International University, IL ... 66
Tri-State Bible College, OH ... 194
Tri-State University, IN ... 84, **294**
Truman State University, MO ... 157, **296**
Turtle Mountain Community College,
  ND ... 171
Union College, NE ... 166
Union Institute & University, OH ... 194
The University of Akron, OH ... 195
University of Central Missouri, MO ... 157
University of Central Oklahoma, OK ... 207
University of Charleston, WV ... 313, **326**
University of Chicago, IL ... 66
University of Cincinnati, OH ... 195
University of Dallas, TX ... 312, **328**
University of Dayton, OH ... *195*
University of Detroit Mercy, MI ... 123
University of Dubuque, IA ... 97
University of Evansville, IN ... 84
The University of Findlay, OH ... 196, **298**
University of Illinois at Chicago, IL ... 66
University of Illinois at Springfield, IL ... 67
University of Illinois at Urbana–
  Champaign, IL ... 67
University of Indianapolis, IN ... 85
The University of Iowa, IA ... 98
University of Kansas, KS ... 106
University of Mary, ND ... 172
University of Michigan, MI ... 123
University of Michigan–Dearborn, MI ... 124
University of Michigan–Flint, MI ... 124
University of Minnesota, Crookston,
  MN ... 140
University of Minnesota, Duluth, MN ... 140
University of Minnesota, Morris, MN ... 140
University of Minnesota, Twin Cities
  Campus, MN ... 141
University of Missouri–Columbia, MO ... 158
University of Missouri–Kansas City,
  MO ... 158
University of Missouri–Rolla, MO ... 159
University of Missouri–St. Louis, MO ... 159
University of Nebraska at Kearney, NE ... 166
University of Nebraska at Omaha, NE ... 167
University of Nebraska–Lincoln, NE ... 167
University of Nebraska Medical
  Center, NE ... 168
University of New Orleans, LA ... 309, **330**
University of North Dakota, ND ... 172
University of Northern Iowa, IA ... 98
University of Northwestern Ohio, OH ... 196
University of Notre Dame, IN ... 85
University of Oklahoma, OK ... 207

University of Oklahoma Health
  Sciences Center, OK ... 208
University of Phoenix–Chicago
  Campus, IL ... 68
University of Phoenix–Cincinnati
  Campus, OH ... 197
University of Phoenix–Cleveland
  Campus, OH ... 197
University of Phoenix–Columbus Ohio
  Campus, OH ... 197
University of Phoenix–Indianapolis
  Campus, IN ... 85
University of Phoenix–Kansas City
  Campus, MO ... 159
University of Phoenix–Metro Detroit
  Campus, MI ... 124
University of Phoenix–Oklahoma City
  Campus, OK ... 208
University of Phoenix–St. Louis
  Campus, MO ... 160
University of Phoenix–Springfield
  Campus, MO ... 160
University of Phoenix–Tulsa Campus,
  OK ... 208
University of Phoenix–West Michigan
  Campus, MI ... 125
University of Phoenix–Wichita
  Campus, KS ... 106
University of Phoenix–Wisconsin
  Campus, WI ... 221
University of Rio Grande, OH ... 197
University of St. Francis, IL ... 68, **300**
University of Saint Francis, IN ... 85
University of Saint Mary, KS ... 106
University of St. Thomas, MN ... 141
University of Science and Arts of
  Oklahoma, OK ... 208
University of Sioux Falls, SD ... 213
The University of South Dakota, SD ... 214
University of Southern Indiana, IN ... 86
The University of Toledo, OH ... 198
University of Tulsa, OK ... 209
University of West Florida, FL ... 309, **332**
University of Wisconsin–Eau Claire,
  WI ... 222
University of Wisconsin–Green Bay,
  WI ... 222
University of Wisconsin–La Crosse,
  WI ... 222
University of Wisconsin–Madison, WI ... 223
University of Wisconsin–Milwaukee,
  WI ... 223
University of Wisconsin–Oshkosh, WI ... 223
University of Wisconsin–Parkside, WI ... 224
University of Wisconsin–Platteville,
  WI ... 224
University of Wisconsin–River Falls,
  WI ... 225
University of Wisconsin–Stevens Point,
  WI ... 225

University of Wisconsin–Stout, WI ... 225
University of Wisconsin–Superior, WI ... 226
University of Wisconsin–Whitewater,
  WI ... 226
Upper Iowa University, IA ... 98
Urbana University, OH ... 198
Ursuline College, OH ... 198
Valley City State University, ND ... 172
Valparaiso University, IN ... 86, **302**
VanderCook College of Music, IL ... 68
Vatterott College, IA ... 99
Vatterott College, St. Ann, MO ... 160
Vatterott College, Sunset Hills, MO ... 160
Vennard College, IA ... 99
Viterbo University, WI ... 226
Wabash College, IN ... 87
Walden University, MN ... 142
Waldorf College, IA ... 99
Walsh College of Accountancy and
  Business Administration, MI ... 125
Walsh University, OH ... 199
Wartburg College, IA ... 99
Washburn University, KS ... 107
Washington University in St. Louis,
  MO ... 160
Wayne State College, NE ... 168
Wayne State University, MI ... 125
Webster University, MO ... 161
Wentworth Military Academy and
  Junior College, MO ... 161
Western Illinois University, IL ... 68
Western Michigan University, MI ... 125, **304**
Westminster College, MO ... 161
West Suburban College of Nursing, IL ... 69
Westwood College–Chicago Du Page,
  IL ... 69
Westwood College–Chicago Loop
  Campus, IL ... 69
Westwood College–Chicago O'Hare
  Airport, IL ... 69
Westwood College–Chicago River
  Oaks, IL ... 69
Wheaton College, IL ... 69
Wichita State University, KS ... 107
Wilberforce University, OH ... 199
William Jewell College, MO ... 161
William Penn University, IA ... 100
William Woods University, MO ... 162
Wilmington College, OH ... 199
Winona State University, MN ... 142
Wisconsin Lutheran College, WI ... 227
Wittenberg University, OH ... 199
Worsham College of Mortuary
  Science, IL ... 69
Wright State University, OH ... 200
Xavier University, OH ... 200
Yeshiva Geddolah of Greater Detroit
  Rabbinical College, MI ... 126
York College, NE ... 168
Youngstown State University, OH ... 200

Peterson's
Book Satisfaction Survey

Give Us Your Feedback

Thank you for choosing Peterson's as your source for personalized solutions for your education and career achievement. Please take a few minutes to answer the following questions. Your answers will go a long way in helping us to produce the most user-friendly and comprehensive resources to meet your individual needs.

When completed, please tear out this page and mail it to us at:

Publishing Department
Peterson's, a Nelnet company
2000 Lenox Drive
Lawrenceville, NJ 08648

You can also complete this survey online at **www.petersons.com/booksurvey**.

1. **What is the ISBN of the book you have purchased? (The ISBN can be found on the book's back cover in the lower right-hand corner.)** _____

2. **Where did you purchase this book?**
   - ❏ Retailer, such as Barnes & Noble
   - ❏ Online reseller, such as Amazon.com
   - ❏ Petersons.com
   - ❏ Other (please specify) _____

3. **If you purchased this book on Petersons.com, please rate the following aspects of your online purchasing experience on a scale of 4 to 1 (4 = Excellent and 1 = Poor).**

	4	3	2	1
Comprehensiveness of Peterson's Online Bookstore page	❏	❏	❏	❏
Overall online customer experience	❏	❏	❏	❏

4. **Which category best describes you?**
   - ❏ High school student
   - ❏ Parent of high school student
   - ❏ College student
   - ❏ Graduate/professional student
   - ❏ Returning adult student
   - ❏ Teacher
   - ❏ Counselor
   - ❏ Working professional/military
   - ❏ Other (please specify) _____

5. **Rate your overall satisfaction with this book.**

Extremely Satisfied	Satisfied	Not Satisfied
❏	❏	❏

6. **Rate each of the following aspects of this book on a scale of 4 to 1 (4 = Excellent and 1 = Poor).**

	4	3	2	1
Comprehensiveness of the information	❑	❑	❑	❑
Accuracy of the information	❑	❑	❑	❑
Usability	❑	❑	❑	❑
Cover design	❑	❑	❑	❑
Book layout	❑	❑	❑	❑
Special features (e.g., CD, flashcards, charts, etc.)	❑	❑	❑	❑
Value for the money	❑	❑	❑	❑

7. **This book was recommended by:**
   - ❑ Guidance counselor
   - ❑ Parent/guardian
   - ❑ Family member/relative
   - ❑ Friend
   - ❑ Teacher
   - ❑ Not recommended by anyone—I found the book on my own
   - ❑ Other (please specify) _____

8. **Would you recommend this book to others?**

Yes	Not Sure	No
❑	❑	❑

9. **Please provide any additional comments.**

   _____

   _____

   _____

   _____

   _____

Remember, you can tear out this page and mail it to us at:

    Publishing Department
    Peterson's, a Nelnet company
    2000 Lenox Drive
    Lawrenceville, NJ 08648

or you can complete the survey online at **www.petersons.com/booksurvey.**

Your feedback is important to us at Peterson's, and we thank you for your time!

If you would like us to keep in touch with you about new products and services, please include your e-mail address here: _____